The Unicode Standard

Worldwide Character Encoding

Version 1.0, Volume 1

The Unicode Consortium

Addison-Wesley Publishing Company, Inc.

Reading, Massachusetts · Menlo Park, California · New York
Don Mills, Ontario · Wokingham, England · Amsterdam
Bonn · Sydney · Singapore · Tokyo · Madrid · San Juan
Paris · Seoul · Milan · Mexico City · Taipei

Many of the designations used by manufacturers and sellers to distinguish their products are claimed as trademarks. Where those designations appear in this book and Addison-Wesley was aware of a trademark claim, the designations have been printed in initial capital letters.

The authors and publishers have taken care in preparation of this book, but make no expressed or implied warranty of any kind and assume no responsibility for errors or omissions. No liability is assumed for incidental or consequential damages in connection with or arising out of the use of the information or programs contained herein.

ISBN 0–201–56788–1

Printed in the United States of America.
Published simultaneously in Canada.

This book was designed and typeset by Burwell Davis.
It is set in Minion, designed by Rob Slimbach at Adobe Systems, Inc.
It was set on an Apple Macintosh computer using Microsoft Word and QuarkXPress.
The character charts, names list, and index were created on a Xerox ViewPoint document creation system using Xerox corporate fonts. The Unicode mappings to other character encodings were maintained in a Fourth Dimension database.

Adobe®, PostScript® and Minion™ are registered trademarks and trademark of Adobe Systems, Inc.

Apple® and Macintosh® are registered trademarks of Apple Computer, Inc.

CJK® is a registered trademark and servicemark of the Research Libraries Group, Inc.

Fourth Dimension® is a registered trademark of ACI/ACIUS, Inc.

Intel® is a registered trademark of the Intel Corporation.

ITC Zapf Dingbats® is a registered trademark of the International Typeface Corporation.

Microsoft®, Microsoft Word® and Microsoft Windows™ are registered trademarks and trademarks of the Microsoft Corporation.

Motorola® is a registered trademark of Motorola, Inc.

QuarkXPress® is a registered trademark of Quark, Inc.

Xerox®, ViewPoint™ and Star™ are registered trademark and trademarks of the Xerox Corporation.

All other company and product names are trademarks or registered trademarks of the company or manufacturer respectively.

1 2 3 4 5 6 7 8 9 AL 9594939291
First printing, October 1991

Acknowledgments

The design and content of *The Unicode Standard: Worldwide Character Encoding, Version 1.0*, are the responsibility of the Unicode Technical Committee, composed of representatives from many different companies. These representatives include: Joan Aliprand (Research Libraries Group), Lloyd Anderson (Ecological Linguistics), Joe Becker (Xerox), John Bennett (Go), F. Avery Bishop (DEC), Joe Bosurgi (Go), Juan Bulnes (Novell), Jim Caldwell (Pacific Rim Connections), Layne Cannon (WordPerfect), Lee Collins (Apple), Mark Davis (Apple), Wayne Davison (Research Libraries Group), Bill English (Sun Microsystems), Asmus Freytag (Microsoft), Anas Jarrah (Aldus), Phil Karren (Novell), Mike Kernaghan (Metaphor), Rick McGowan (NeXT), Pamela Ottaviano (Microsoft), Isai Scheinberg (IBM), Stuart Smith (WordPerfect), Michel Suignard (Microsoft), Karen Smith-Yoshimura (Research Libraries Group), Bill Tuthill (Sun Microsystems), J. G. Van Stee (IBM), Ken Whistler (Metaphor), Eric Wilson (Lotus), and Glenn Wright (Sun Microsystems).

The production of this standard has required the dedication of many individuals over considerable time. The contributions of the following people were central to the design and authorship of this book: Joan Aliprand, Joe Becker, Lee Collins, Mark Davis, Asmus Freytag, Rick McGowan, and Ken Whistler. The development and maintainence of the Unicode character standard databases and character mappings are principally due to the efforts of Joe Becker, Lee Collins, Ken Whistler, Cora Lee, Pamela Ottaviano, Michel Suignard, and Isai Scheinberg.

The Han databases also benefitted from major contributions as the result of collaboration with the Unicode CJK Unification Verification Project (University of Toronto, Department of East Asian Studies): Professor Kazuko Nakajima (team leader), Dr. Xiao-jie Yang (principal investigator), Mr. Charles Chan, Mr. Jian Zhao, Mrs. Hye-young Im, and project consultants Prof. Wayne Schlepp (University of Toronto, East Asian Studies), Mr. Jack Cain (Utlas International), and Mr. Jae Chong (Hahn Computer Institute); and with the Center for Computer and Information Research and Development (CCID): Mr. Zhang Zhoucai, Ms. Huang Weimin, and with Mr. Zhu Yan (National Library of China).

Significant contributions of time and energy to the creation or review of *The Unicode Standard: Worldwide Character Encoding, Version 1.0* have also been made by the following people: Mati Allouche (IBM), David J. Birnbaum (University of Pittsburgh), Robin Cover (University of Texas, Arlington), Cuong T. Nguyen (Stanford), Burwell Davis (Adobe), James Do (SCS), Madjid Dormiani (Apogee), Peter Fenwick, Lars Erik Fredriksson (Far Eastern Library, Stockholm), Adiva Gera (IBM), Alaa Ghoneim (IBM), Wassef Haroun (Microsoft), Maha Hassan, Masami Hasegawa (DEC), John Jenkins (Apple), Yasuo Kida (Apple), Haesung Kim (Apple), Kyongsok Kim

(University of North Dakota), Takao Kitano (Microsoft), Mike Ksar (HP), Huan Mei Liao (Apple), Sten Lindberg (IBM), Doug Merritt, Sherif El-Rafei (IBM), Jony Rosenne (IBM), Hugh MacGregor Ross, Mohamad Saba (Apple), Gidi Shalom-Bendor (Apple), Thanh Van Nguyen (Sun), Tuoc V. Luong (Pyramid), Dimitri Vulis (City University of New York), Joan Winters (SHARE), Tom Yap (Sun), and hundreds of other people who have supplied additional feedback on successive drafts of *The Unicode Standard: Worldwide Character Encoding, Version 1.0*. These people are not responsible for errors or omissions in this work.

Editorial work is due principally to the efforts of Erica Liederman. The book was designed and typeset by Burwell Davis (Adobe). Thanks also go to Madeline Weisey for her work in mailing draft standards worldwide.

The support given to creation of *The Unicode Standard: Worldwide Character Encoding, Version 1.0* by the member corporations has been crucial to its development, especially the considerable backing in facilities, equipment, and resources supplied by Apple, IBM, Metaphor, Microsoft, The Research Libraries Group, Sun Microsystems and Xerox. Finally, the members of the board of directors of Unicode, Inc. must be acknowledged for their support and promotion of the Unicode standard: Robert M. Carr, John Gage, Richard J. Holleman, Charles Irby, Jay E. Israel, Paul Maritz, David Richards, Lawrence Tesler, and Bud Tribble.

Contents

About This Book

This book is the authoritative source of information on the Unicode character encoding standard (henceforth referred to simply as "the Unicode standard"), an international character code for information processing. The aim of the creators of the Unicode standard is to encode all characters used for written communication, both modern and historic, in a simple and consistent manner. Version 1.0 of the Unicode standard includes all major scripts used in the world; future editions will add less commonly used scripts and those of primarily historical interest.

The Unicode standard had its genesis in early 1988 when a group of information professionals with extensive experience in multilingual computing agreed that no encoding methodology used in their field possessed the elegance and simplicity of ASCII. The Unicode character encoding was established as a fixed-width encoding of 16 bits, which would provide a sufficient number of unique codes for the world's scripts and technical symbols in common use, and at the same time promote efficient and flexible system design.

In January 1991, The Unicode Consortium was incorporated as *Unicode, Inc.*, a non-profit organization whose charter is to maintain and promote the Unicode standard worldwide. Founding members of the Consortium include major companies and institutions involved in international computing. Membership is open to any organization interested in contributing to the design, implementation, and maintenance of the Unicode standard.

How to Use This Book

The Unicode Standard: Worldwide Character Encoding, Version 1.0 is divided into two volumes. Volume One contains introductory material, coding architecture, and conformance requirements, as well as code charts and names lists for all non-ideographic characters and a large number of supplementary mapping tables for the non-ideographic characters.

Volume Two is devoted to the East Asian (Han) ideographic characters. It contains code charts and cross-tabulations with equivalent characters from existing national and corporate standards. It also contains a radical/stroke index to the ideographic characters.

The essential component of Volume One is the coding charts. The complete Unicode character repertoire is laid out in successive panels of 256 code points. For the convenience of users of the Unicode character encoding standard, codes have been grouped by linguistic and functional categories into character blocks. Section 3.1, General Scripts, describes the scope of each block and the origin of its characters. In the section following the code charts (Section 3.8), all non-ideographic characters, with the exception of Korean Hangul syllables, are named.

The principles and architecture of the Unicode standard are covered in the initial chapters that precede the coding charts. A complete explanation of the design and structure of the Unicode standard is provided in Section 2.2 of this book. This chapter also includes information on significant implementation issues, such as directionality, which affect conformance of an implementation. A separate appendix, Implementation Guidelines, addresses common questions.

The coding charts alone are not sufficient to implement the Unicode character encoding scheme. Characters must be categorized according to specific properties, such as case mapping, or directional properties which can be found in Chapter 4, Character Properties.

Additional tables are provided in Chapter 5 to promote uniform mapping in specific circumstances. Tables for composed characters show how text elements may be made up of sequences of Unicode characters.

To facilitate the introduction and widespread adoption of the Unicode standard, mapping tables are provided in Chapter 6 to link characters from the Unicode standard to characters in other standards; specifically, ISO standards 8859, 8879 (SGML), and DIS 6862.2, JIS, and some vendor encodings. Additional mapping tables will be included in future editions as needed.

There are two indexes at the back of the book: an index to non-ideographic character names and a general index. The index to character names includes alternative names (aliases) in addition to the formal Unicode standard designation for each character. The general index covers broader topics, and gives the page where information on the topic appears. A quick guide to all the character blocks included in version 1.0 of the Unicode standard and the code range for each can be found at the end of the book (pp. 681–82).

Please contact The Unicode Consortium if information is missing or you have difficulty using this book. The Appendix includes instructions on how to propose a new character for inclusion in the Unicode standard. You do not have to belong to The Unicode Consortium to suggest improvements to the Unicode standard.

Notations and Conventions

Codes

An individual Unicode value is expressed as U+nnnn, where nnnn is a four digit number in hexadecimal notation, using the digits 0–9 and the letters A–F (for 10 through 15 respectively).

U+0416 is the Unicode value for the character named CYRILLIC CAPITAL LETTER ZHE

A range of Unicode values is expressed as U+xxxx→U+yyyy, where xxxx and yyyy are the first and last Unicode values in the range.

U+0900 → U+097F

In charts and tables the U+ is omitted.

A sequence of Unicode values or names is expressed using a special plus sign between successive items.

U+0259 ✛ U+02DE and SCHWA ✛ RHOTIC HOOK

The codespace is presented as successive panels of 256 code values. The upper left and right hand corners of each chart page show the beginning and ending Unicode values.

Images

The image shown in a grid cell of a panel should not be considered to be the prescriptive form of a character, but is merely intended as a typical representation of the character encoded by the value.

U+0061 LATIN SMALL LETTER A can be represented by a or *a*.

Where a character is commonly represented in more than one way, alternate images are separated by a vertical line.

U+0024 DOLLAR SIGN $ | $ | $

A character that is shown with a dashed circle must be rendered in relation to the previous characters in the data stream.

U+0308 NON-SPACING DIAERESIS and U+093F DEVANAGARI VOWEL SIGN I

A character that is shown as text surrounded by a dashed box has no visible manifestation on its own.

U+200A HAIR SPACE

The *geta* ▬ (a missing glyph symbol) has been placed at code points in the Han character block (U+4000→) when the appropriate glyph was unavailable. (These missing glyphs will be added in a future version of the Unicode Standard.)

Names

All characters included in the Unicode standard, except for Han ideographs, have unique names. The Unicode standard names follow the character naming conventions of the International Organization for Standardization; that is, names are written only in uppercase letters of the English alphabet plus the hyphen.

Wherever possible, names are taken from published standards, or, in the absence of a published standard, follow the recommendation of an authoritative organization. Where a systematic list of names does not exist, names in the Unicode standard describe the glyphs that depict the characters.

In running text, a formal Unicode name is shown in small capitals.

GREEK SMALL LETTER MU

Alternative names for Unicode characters (aliases) appear in italics in running text,

umlaut

in italics, preceded by an equals sign, in the character lists by block,

= *stress mark*

and in lower case (no capitalization) in the Unicode index to character names.

st. andrews cross

Italics are also used in running text to refer to characters collectively,

. . . variant forms of *cedilla* . . .

to refer to a text element that is not explicitly encoded,

. . . *pasekh alef* can be composed from other characters

or to set off a foreign word.

the Welsh word *ynghyd*

Names List Annotations

The following symbols are used in the Character Names List of each character block:

=　　　　Identifies alternative names by which the character is known, that is, the names that are synonyms or aliases for the Unicode name

```
0023 # NUMBER SIGN
     = pound sign
```

x　　　　Indicates a cross-reference to another Unicode character, which is *not* synonymous.

→　　　　Within a cross-reference, points to the Unicode value of the character referenced.

The cross-references fall into the following classes:

Explicit inequality, in which the two characters do not have the same semantic meaning although the glyphs that depict them are identical or very close.

```
003A : COLON
     x (ratio → 2236)
```

Case form mapping, in which the other case form is encoded in another character block.

```
00FF ÿ LATIN SMALL LETTER Y DIAERESIS
     x (latin capital letter y diaeresis→ 0178)
```

Other linguistic relationship

```
01C9 lj LATIN SMALL LETTER L J
     x (cyrillic small letter lje → 0459)
     The Serbo-Croatian language may be written as Croatian using Latin
     script or as Serbian using Cyrillic script.
```

The character at this position in the source standard was not included in the Unicode standard at the corresponding position; the Unicode value given in the cross-reference should be used instead.

```
0373    x (pound sign → 00A3)
```

In the Character Names List, the language(s) using a given character are noted in cases where this information may be helpful. (Such annotation is given only after the lowercase form of case pairs, to avoid needless repetition.) An ellipsis "…" indicates that the listed languages cited are merely the principal ones among many. If the annotation *does not* end with an ellipsis, then the cited list is thought to be complete.

Notice

The Unicode Standard Version 1.0 is intended to be a complete, implementable character encoding which reflects the final decisions made by the Unicode Technical Committee. However, recent developments in the international standards community have raised the possibility that by allowing some flexibility in the content of Unicode 1.0, it will be possible to reach the goal of a single, universal, international character encoding standard.

The International Standards Organization committee responsible for multibyte character encoding (ISO JTC1/SC2/WG2) has been developing a 32-bit character encoding standard known as ISO DIS 10646. During the first half of 1991, ISO member countries had voted on whether to approve 10646 as an international standard; it failed by a significant margin. A majority of the negative votes reflected a strong desire to merge 10646 and the Unicode standard into a single international standard. Recently, members of the Unicode Consortium and the ISO committee have been making considerable progress towards a merger of the two encoding standards; the Unicode Technical Committee and the officers of the Unicode Consortium also strongly support these efforts.

At the August 1991 meeting of WG2 in Geneva resolutions constituting a merger were approved. The proposed framework for the actual encoding provides for the Unicode standard as a two-byte subset of a canonical 4-byte international standard character encoding.

The international standard resulting from this cooperation between the two groups may differ in some respects from version 1.0 of the Unicode standard. Insofar as minor changes to the Unicode standard may be necessary in order to produce the merged standard, the last article of section 2.3 ("Existing characters will not be reassigned or removed") is amended to read: "Except as required for merger with ISO 10646, future versions of the Unicode standard will not reassign, rename or remove Unicode 1.0 characters."

Specifically, the following changes were agreed upon at the August WG2 meeting (too late to be reflected in this volume):

- Expanded Compatibility Zone. U+F800 → U+FDFF will be removed from the Private Use Area and be encoded as additional characters in the Compatibility Zone, in order to accomodate additional repertoire merged in from ISO DIS 10646. Implementations of Unicode 1.0 should treat this range as reserved, unassigned characters.

- The Corporate Use Zone of the Private Use Area should start at U+F7FF and utilize descending code values, rather than starting at U+FDFF.

- The unified Han ideographic characters may not start at U+4000, but at some higher value. Software should not rely on 0x4000 as a valid indicator of the edge of that zone.

- Pending reconfirmation of the encoding of ISO 10646 APL characters, use of U+2300 APL COMPOSE OPERATOR and U+2301 APL OUT is discouraged, as those characters may be withdrawn to reach merger with 10646.

- The official IS 10646 may have character names which differ from Unicode 1.0 character names in some respects.

The nature of the international standards process does not permit the schedule for the merger to be determined with precision; however, if all goes well, a new Draft International Standard should be issued by the end of 1991, and that should become a final International Standard by mid-1992. The Unicode Consortium is aware of the time pressures facing current implementers of the Unicode standard, but due to the overall benefit of merging the two encodings, it is felt necessary to maintain some flexibility in allowing the reassignment of code points for the purposes of the merger.

In the event that minor changes are made to Unicode 1.0 to accommodate merger with ISO 10646, the Unicode Consortium will designate the modified Unicode standard as the Unicode Standard, Version 1.1. (This is different than the expanded edition that has been referred to as "Version 1.1" in previous contexts.)

August 30, 1991

The officers of the Unicode Consortium:

Mark Davis, President
Mike Kernaghan, Vice President
Joe Becker, Technical Vice President
Bill English, Treasurer
Ken Whistler, Secretary
Lee Collins, Technical Director
Asmus Freytag, Technical Director

1.0 Introduction

The Unicode character encoding standard is a fixed-width, uniform text and character encoding scheme. It includes characters from the world's scripts, as well as technical symbols in common use. The Unicode standard is modeled on the ASCII character set. Since ASCII's 7-bit character size is inadequate to handle multilingual text, the Unicode Consortium adopted a 16-bit architecture which extends the benefits of ASCII to multilingual text. Unicode characters are consistently 16 bits wide, regardless of language, so no escape sequence or control code is required to specify any character in any language. Unicode character encoding treats symbols, alphabetic characters, and ideographic characters identically, so that they can be used simultaneously and with equal facility. Computer programs that use Unicode character encoding to represent characters but do not display or print text can (for the most part) remain unaltered when new scripts or characters are introduced.

1.1 Background

The primary goal of the Unicode project was to remedy serious problems common to most multilingual computer programs: overloading of the font mechanism when encoding characters, and use of multiple, inconsistent character codes caused by conflicting national character standards. Few national standards allowed for special purpose characters, such as proprietary or typographical characters. The ASCII character set and its extensions, although widely used and accepted as standard in most computing systems, are limited to 256 characters. ASCII is therefore inadequate in an increasingly complex global computing environment.

The groups most affected by the lack of a consistent international character standard are the publishers of scientific and mathematical software, newspaper and book publishers, bibliographic information services, and academic researchers.

Designers of the Unicode standard envisioned a uniform method of character identification that would be more efficient and flexible than current encoding systems. Their system would be complete enough to satisfy the needs of technical and multilingual computing, as well as text publishing. Their main goals were to eliminate the special case systems and complex application codes currently in use in many character encoding standards, and to make a larger range of characters available in order to meet the requirements of professional quality typesetting and desktop publishing internationally.

Research and analysis revealed that an efficient character code standard would meet the following requirements:

• *Completeness.* The coded character set would be large enough to encompass all characters that were likely to be used in general text interchange.

• *Efficiency.* Plain text, composed of a sequence of fixed-width characters, provided an extremely useful model because it was simple to parse: software would not have to maintain state, look for special escape sequences, or search forward or backward through text to identify characters.

• *Uniformity.* For efficient sorting, searching, display, and editing of text, a fixed character code size would be preferable to the more complex run-length encoding schemes in current use. Although a wide character code is not always necessary, particularly in the case of scripts that contain a limited number of characters, the many benefits of a uniform character width outweigh the argument in favor of codespace economy. Text compression should not be defined by the character code standard; rather, it should be independent of the character code standard.

1.2 Conformance

There is a set of unambiguous criteria to which a Unicode-conformant implementation must adhere, to ensure that it can interoperate with other conformant implementations.

An application may be considered to conform to the Unicode standard if it makes use of independent fixed-width 16-bit characters and uses Unicode code points to represent Unicode-defined characters. Code conversion from other standards to the Unicode standard will be considered conformant if the matching table produces accurate conversions in both directions. Explicit rules for conformance are found in Section 2.6 of this volume. Information on handling missing characters is found in Appendix C.

1.3 Coverage

This first edition of The Unicode Standard contains over 28,000 characters from the world's scripts. These characters are more than sufficient for modern communication, as well as classical forms of languages such as Greek, Hebrew, Latin, Pali, Sanskrit and literary Chinese. Over 20,000 unique characters defined by national and industry standards of China, Japan, Korea, and Taiwan are included. The Unicode standard also includes math operators and technical symbols, geometric shapes and dingbats. Figure 1-1 shows the scripts included in version 1.0 of the Unicode standard and the code range for each.

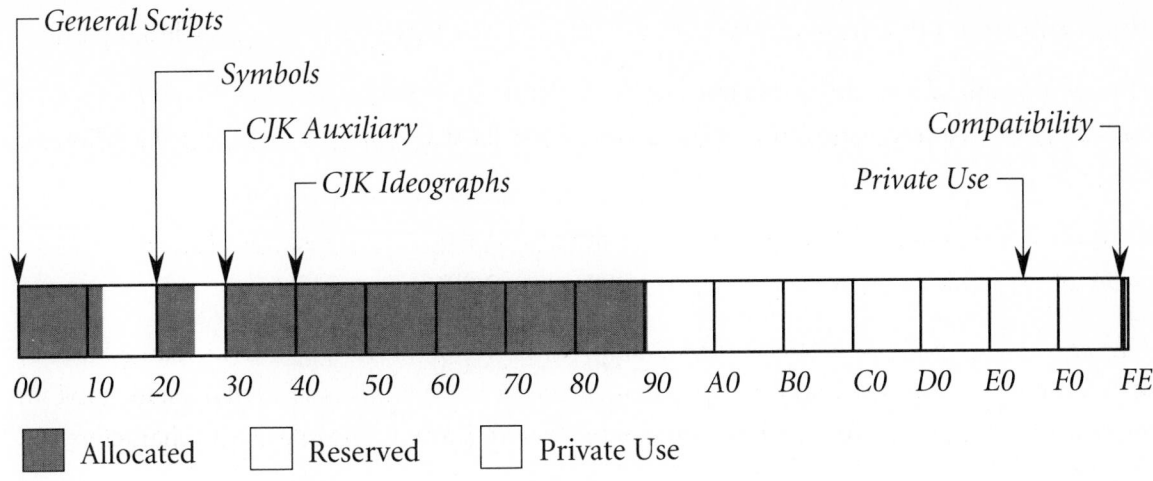

Figure 1-1. Table of Zones and Code Ranges

To define the content of the Unicode standard, the Unicode Technical Committee relied primarily on existing standards. Many characters have been included solely because they are part of an existing standard in widespread use, despite the fact that they violate the general principles of the Unicode standard in some instances.

The Unicode standard includes the character content of all major International Standards approved and published before December 31, 1990, in particular, the ISO *International Register of Character Sets*, and the ISO 6937 and ISO 8859 families of standards, as well as ISO 8879 (SGML). Characters from other standards have also been included, specifically, from bibliographic standards used in libraries (ANSI Z39.47-1985 [Roman], and ANSI Z39.64-1990 [East Asian]), and from important national standards (ISCII 1988 [India], GB 2312-1980 [China], JIS X 0208-1990 and JIS X 0212-1990 [Japan], and CNS 11643-1986 [Taiwan]). Also included are characters from certain draft standards (such as ISO DIS 6861.2, Glagolitic, Old Cyrillic and Romanian Cyrillic for bibliographic information interchange), and from various industry standards in common use (such as code pages and character sets from Adobe, Apple, IBM, Lotus, Microsoft, WordPerfect, Xerox and others).

Another source of characters is from numerous papers and national bodies' contributions to the ISO SC2/WG2 committee on character encoding.

The Unicode standard version 1.0 does not encode rare, obsolete, idiosyncratic, personal, novel, rarely exchanged or private-use characters, nor does it encode logos or graphics. Artificial entities, whose sole function is to serve transiently in the input of text, are also excluded from the Unicode standard. Graphologies unrelated to text, for example, musical and dance notations, are outside the scope of the Unicode standard. Braille symbols were not encoded, since Braille is an alternative way to present text (it can be considered a font variant).

Statistics of Version 1.0

The following table shows the proportions of the Unicode codespace which have been allocated to various types of scripts in version 1.0 of the Unicode standard:

	Allocated	Unassigned	% Assigned	
General	2,336	5,856	29%	
Symbols	1,290	2,806	31%	
CJK symbols	763	261	75%	
Hangul	2,350	450	84%	
Han Compatibility	268	4	99%	(Volume 2)
Ideographic & other	20,733	22,275	48%	(Volume 2)
User Space	5,632	N/A	N/A	
Compatibility Zone	362	133	73%	
Special	1	13		
FEFF	1	0		
FFFE, FFFF	N/A	2		
Totals	28,706	(assigned)		
	+ 5,632	(private use)		
	= 34,338	(allocated) 52%		

With over 30,000 unallocated character positions, the Unicode character encoding provides sufficient space for forseeable future expansion.

Future Plans

Less common and archaic scripts will be added to future versions of the Unicode Standard. Scripts of this type were not included in the initial release because of the difficulty of evaluating their content. For many of these scripts, extensive research will be necessary to produce an agreed-upon encoding. The five scripts that are included here in draft form (Ethiopian, Burmese, Khmer, Sinhala, and Mongolian) will be added to the Unicode standard when reliable information has been obtained. (See Appendix E.) Other scripts that are being considered for possible addition to the Unicode standard are:

- *Inuktitut/Cree Syllabary.* The Department of Communications, Canada, is pursuing standardization of the several variant syllabaries and computer encodings now in use for Cree and/or Inuktitut.

- *Egyptian Hieroglyphics.* A uniform standard for computer encoding exists and is being investigated.

- *Korean Hangul Syllables.* There may also be a number of additional Korean Hangul syllables added.

Interest has also been expressed in including Cuneiform, the Cherokee syllabary, the Maldivian and Syriac scripts, and Glagolitic.

The Unicode Consortium welcomes the submission of new characters for possible inclusion in the Unicode standard. For instructions on how to submit characters to the Unicode Consortium, see Appendix D.

1.4 The Unicode Consortium

The Unicode Consortium was formalized in January 1991 to promote the Unicode standard as an international encoding system for information interchange, to aid in its implementation, and to maintain quality control over future revisions. The Unicode Consortium was incorporated as a non-profit organization under the name *Unicode, Inc.*, to provide a central focus and contact point for conducting these activities. Membership is open to organizations anywhere in the world that support the Unicode standard in principle and that would like to assist in its widespread implementation. The consortium is supported through the volunteer efforts of its members (and their companies), and financially through the membership dues.

The Consortium's board of directors and officers come from a variety of organizations and represent a wide spectrum of text-encoding and computing applications. The Consortium's activities are conducted by the Unicode Technical Committee.

The Unicode Technical Committee

The Unicode Technical Committee (UTC) is the working group within the Consortium responsible for the creation, maintenance, and quality of the Unicode standard. The UTC controls all input to the standard and makes associated content decisions. Voting members of the UTC are representatives from Consortium members. However, visitors are welcome to participate in the discussions, since the intent of the UTC is to act as an open forum for free exchange of technical ideas.

The predecessor of the UTC was the less formal Unicode Working Group. Engineering teams from Apple and Xerox, who had been very active in the area of multilingual operating systems, realized their own character encoding methods could be improved. Together they produced the original Unicode design. They were joined by representatives of other companies who were experiencing similar problems. The participants worked for companies and institutions whose businesses required multilingual information systems, including Go, IBM, Metaphor, Claris, Microsoft, NeXT, Sun Microsystems, and The Research Libraries Group. The potential for mutual benefit encouraged them to share the results of past efforts and to explore the opportunities for collaboration.

The *Unicode Standard, Draft 1*, issued in September 1989, contained a preliminary repertoire of characters. A second draft, the *Unicode Preview*, issued in October 1990, contained a much more extensive repertoire of characters, as well as the framework for Han character unification. The

Unicode 1.0 Draft Standard Final Review Document, issued in December 1990, was sent out for worldwide review. Feedback on the final review document was incorporated into the standard during the first part of 1991. This book, *The Unicode Standard: Worldwide Character Encoding, Version 1.0*, finalizes the character repertoire, and provides an implementable standard on which vendors and software developers may base their applications.

2.0 General Principles of the Unicode Standard

This chapter discusses the fundamental principles governing design of the Unicode standard. It includes discussion of text processes, unification principles, allocation of codespace, character properties, and a detailed definition and description of non-spacing marks and how they are employed in Unicode character encoding. This chapter also details the formal requirements for creating a text processing system that conforms to the Unicode standard.

2.1 Architectural Context of a Character Encoding

Character codes are like nuts and bolts—they are minor components that hold together a host of different useful systems.

A character code standard such as the Unicode standard enables the implementation of useful processes operating on textual data. The interesting end products are not the character codes but the text processes, since these directly serve the needs of system users.

Text Elements, Code Elements, and Text Processes

One of the more profound challenges in designing a worldwide character encoding stems from the fact that languages differ in what they consider a fundamental unit of text, or *text element.*

For example, in Spanish, the combination "ll" is a text element for the process of sorting but not for the process of rendering; in Croatian, the objects "lj" and "l-followed by-j" are distinct text elements for transliteration, but not for the process of rendering; and in English, the objects "A" and "a" are distinct text elements for the process of rendering but generally not for the process of spell-checking. Notice that the text elements in a given language depend upon the specific text process.

A character encoding standard has fundamental units of encoding, *code elements* or characters, which must exist in a unique relationship to the assigned *code points.*

The design of the character encoding scheme must provide precisely that set of code elements which allows programmers to design applications that can perform text processes in the languages they intend to support.

Most computer systems provide low-level functionality for a small number of basic text processes, out of which more sophisticated text-processing capabilities are built. The following is a list of text processes used by most computer systems:

- Rendering characters visible (including ligatures, contextual forms and so on)

- Breaking lines while rendering (including hyphenation)

- Computing directionality

- Modifying appearance, such as kerning, underlining, slant, and boldface

- Determining units such as "word," and "sentence"

- Interacting with users in processes such as resolving mouse selection and highlighting text

- Modifying keyboard input, and editing stored text through insertion and deletion

- Comparing text in operations such as determining sort order of two strings, or filtering or matching strings

- Analyzing text content in operations such as spell-checking, hyphenation, and parsing morphology

- Treating text as bulk data for operations such as compressing and decompressing, truncating, and transmitting and receiving

In the case of an English encoding such as ASCII, the relationships between the encoding and the basic text processes built on it are seemingly straightforward: Characters are rendered visible one by one in defined rectangles from left to right in a linear order. Thus one character code inside the computer corresponds to one logical character in a process such as simple English rendering.

When designing an international and multilingual text encoding system such as the Unicode standard, the relationship between the encoding scheme and implementation of basic text processes must be considered explicitly, for several reasons:

- Some or all of the assumptions about character rendering that hold true for English fail for other writing systems. Outside of English, characters are not necessarily rendered visible one by one in rectangles from left to right. In many cases, character positioning is quite complex and does not proceed in a linear fashion.

- The set of text characters appropriate for encoding a language is often debatable. For example, there is disagreement about the encoding of commonly used characters in French and German: ISO 8859 defines letters such as "â" and "ü" as individual characters, whereas ISO 6937 represents them by composition instead. While this reflects the difference in the identity of these characters between German and French, neither encoding is ideally suited to handle both.

- No encoding can include all basic text processes equally well. As a result, some trade-off is necessary. For example, ASCII defines separate codes for upper- and lowercase letters. This causes some text processes, such as rendering, to be carried out more easily, and some processes, such as comparison, to be more difficult. A different encoding design for English, such as case-shift control codes would have made the opposite true. In designing a new encoding for complex scripts, such tradeoffs must be evaluated, and decisions made explicitly, rather than unwittingly.

The design of the Unicode encoding scheme is independent of the design of basic text processing algorithms, with the exception of directionality (see Appendix A). Unicode implementations are assumed to contain suitable text processing and/or rendering algorithms, which may be more or less complex. In particular, sorting and string comparison algorithms cannot assume that the assignment of Unicode character code numbers provides an alphabetical ordering for lexicographic string comparison. In general, the culturally expected sorting orders require arbitrarily complex sorting algorithms. The expected sort sequence for the same characters differs across languages, so in general no single linear ordering exists. The Unicode standard does not assume any particular string comparison process, but its design does assume the capability to implement sufficiently powerful algorithms.

There is no reason to expect text processes in general to be as simple as they are for English. Nevertheless, a computer system that can offer its users highly sophisticated operating and graphical windowing environments can also be sophisticated enough to transmit and render text in a user's own script and language.

Plain and Fancy Text

Plain text is a pure sequence of character codes; plain Unicode text is a sequence of Unicode character codes. *Fancy text* is any text representation consisting of plain text plus added information such as font size, color, and so on. For example, a multifont text as formatted by a desktop publishing system is fancy text.

The kinds of data structures that can be built into fancy text are of many possible types. To give but one example, in fancy text containing ideographs, it would be possible to store the phonetic reading of each ideograph somewhere in the text structure. On the other hand, the simplicity of plain text gives it a natural role as a major structural element.

Both plain and fancy text are already familiar constructs in ASCII-based systems and their relative functional roles are well known:

- Plain text is public, standardized, and universally readable.

- Fancy text is often intended to be private, implementation-specific, and is often proprietary.

- Plain text is the underlying *content* stream to which formatting can be *applied*.

The details of any particular fancy text design can be made public or standardized, but the fact remains that most fancy text designs are vehicles for particular implementations, and are not readable by other implementations. Since fancy text equals plain text plus added information, the extra information in fancy text can always be stripped away to reveal the "pure" text underneath. This operation is familiar, for example, in word processing systems that deal with both their own private fancy format and with the universal plain ASCII text file format. Thus by default, plain text represents *the basic, interchangeable content of text.*

Since plain text represents character content, plain text as such has no appearance at all. It requires a rendering process to make it visible.

If the same plain text sequence is given to disparate rendering processes, there is no expectation that rendered text in each instance should have the same appearance; all that is required from disparate rendering processes is to make the text legible according to the intended reading. Therefore, the relationship between appearance and content of plain text may be stated as follows: *Plain text must contain enough information to permit the text to be rendered legibly, nothing more.*

2.2 The Basic Design of the Unicode Character Encoding

This section presents the basic principles which have served to guide the overall design of the Unicode standard. It also clarifies the distinction between encoding characters and glyphs.

Unicode Principles

Design of the Unicode standard reflects the following principles. Not all principles can be satisfied simultaneously. While every effort has been made to maintain consistency for the sake of simplicity and efficiency, there were many cases where exceptions were made to maintain compatibility with existing standards.

1. All Unicode characters have a uniform width of 16 bits. Plain Unicode text consists of pure 16-bit Unicode character streams (in files or strings).

2. The full codespace (over 65,000 characters) is available to represent characters. ISO 646 and 8859 control code positions have been retained for compatiblity, and a number of codes have been reserved for use as signals in the text stream.

3. Characters are made visible through a rendering process which (at its lowest level) requires that characters be mapped to glyphs. The default rendering order of Unicode text characters is logical (keystroke) order.

4. The Unicode standard allows dynamic composition of accented forms or static composed forms. Common static-form single character codes such as LATIN CAPITAL U WITH DIAERESIS "Ü" are included for compatibility with current international standards. However, because the

process of character composition is open-ended, additional letters with modifying non-spacing marks can be created from a combination of base letters and non-spacing marks.

Unicode non-spacing marks (accents and so on) used to create composite forms are *productive*. This means that they are *in practice* combined with a large number of base form characters. For example, the diaeresis, "¨", can be combined with all vowels and a number of consonants in languages using the Latin script or others. The stroke used in the Polish LATIN CAPITAL LETTER L SLASH, however, is of limited use, hence LATIN CAPITAL LETTER L SLASH is always treated as a single unit and not composed of two distinct characters. This productivity extends to non-Roman languages as well.

5. The Unicode standard encodes characters in scripts which can be used for a number of different natural languages. Punctuation and symbols which are common across scripts are given a single code.

6. The Unicode standard avoids duplication of characters by unifying them across languages: characters that are equivalent in form, usage, and essential properties are given a single code. Common letters, punctuation marks, symbols, and diacritics are given one code each, regardless of language, as are common Chinese/Japanese/Korean (CJK) ideographs. Letters, symbols, and CJK ideographs with common shapes but different functions are given separate codes. Other than what is required to preserve plain text distinctions, the Unicode standard does not attempt to encode features such as language, font, size, positioning, glyphs, and so forth. For example, it does not preserve language as a part of character encoding: Chinese "zi" (字), Japanese "ji" (字) and Korean "ja" (字) are all represented as the same character code, as are French "i grecque" (Y), German "ypsilon" (Y), and English "wye" (Y).

7. The distinction between the Unicode standard and other forms of data (ASCII, pictures, and so on) is the function of a higher-level protocol (text classes and layout) and not specified by the Unicode standard itself. The 64 control code positions of ISO 646 and 8859 are retained only for compatibility.

8. Character identity is preserved over a number of different combined national standards. Where variant forms are given separate codes within one included standard, they are also kept separate within the Unicode standard. This guarantees that there will always be a mapping between the Unicode standard and included national standards.

9. In determining whether or not to unify ideographic variant forms across standards, the Unicode standard follows the guidelines published by JIS. These guidelines are found in the Japan Industrial Standard *Jouhou koukan you kanji fugoukei* (Code of the Japanese Graphic Character Set for Information Interchange). C 6226-1983 §3.4 *Kanji no itaiji no toriatsukai* (The handling of variant Han characters.) Though written with Japanese usage in mind, they are general enough to be applied to Chinese and Korean as well. Where these guidelines suggest that two

forms constitute a trivial (*wazukana*) difference, the Unicode standard assigns a single code. Otherwise, separate codes are assigned.

Conversion between Unicode text and text in other character codes must be done by explicit table-matching processes. There is no guaranteed bit-for-bit compatibility with other codes, even though accurate convertability is guaranteed between Unicode and other widely accepted international standards as of December 1, 1990. Unicode text may be compressed for storage or transmission like any other binary data, but the Unicode standard specifies no preferred compression algorithm and guarantees no bit-for-bit identity in compressed format.

Glyphs

The Unicode standard was designed to encode characters. There are various relationships between character and glyph: a single glyph may correspond to a single character, or to a number of characters, or multiple glyphs may result from a single character.

"Glyphs" may be considered as discrete components of writing. The distinction between characters and glyphs is illustrated in the following table:

Glyph	Unicode Character(s)
A	U+0041 LATIN CAPITAL LETTER A
fi, fi	U+0066 + U+0069 LATIN SMALL LETTER F followed by LATIN SMALL LETTER I
a, a, *a*	U+0061 LATIN SMALL LETTER A
٥ ﻪ ﻔ ﻬ	U+0647 ARABIC LETTER HEH (positional forms)

Unicode characters represent primarily, but not exclusively, the letters, punctuation, and other signs that comprise natural language text and scientific and technical documentation. Characters reside only in the machine, as strings in memory or on disk, in the backing store. The Unicode standard deals only with character codes. In contrast to characters, glyphs appear on the screen or paper as particular representations of one or more backing store characters. A repertoire of glyphs comprises a font.

Glyph shape and glyph identifier assignments are the responsibility of individual font vendors and of the glyph identifier standards.

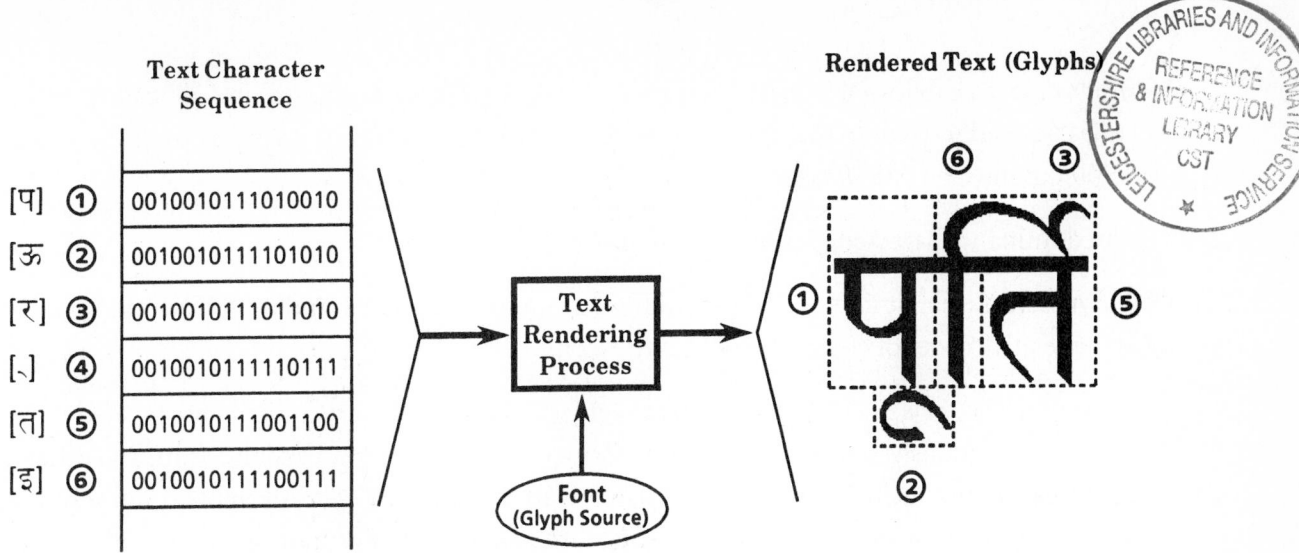

Figure 2-1. Unicode Character Code to Rendered Text Glyph

The process of mapping from characters in the backing store to glyphs is one aspect of text rendering. The final appearance of rendered text is dependent on context (neighboring characters in the backing store), variations in typographic design of the fonts used, and formatting information (point size, superscript, subscript, and so on). The results on screen or paper can differ considerably from the expected or prototypical shape of a letter or character. The glyph "A" displayed on the screen must not be confused with the character "A" in the backing store.

2.3 Codespace Allocation

All codes in the Unicode standard are equally accessible electronically; the exact arrangement of codes is of minor consequence for information processing. But, for the convenience of people who will use them, the codes are grouped by linguistic and functional categories.

Codespace in the Unicode standard is divided into six zones: General Scripts (alphabetic and other scripts that have relatively small character sets), Symbols, CJK (Chinese, Japanese, and Korean) Auxiliary, CJK Ideographs, Private Use, and Compatibility.

The General Script zone covers alphabetic or syllabic scripts such as Latin, Cyrillic, Greek, Hebrew, Arabic, Devanagari and Thai. The Symbol zone includes a large variety of characters for punctuation, mathematics, chemistry, dingbats, and so on. The CJK Auxiliary zone includes punctuation, symbols, Kana, Bopomofo, and single and composite Hangul. The CJK Ideographic zone currently provides space for over 20,000 ideographic characters or characters from other scripts. The Private Use zone (5,632 code points) is used for defining user- or vendor-specific graphic characters. The Compatibility Zone contains characters from widely used corporate and national standards that have other canonical representations in Unicode encoding. (See figure 1-1 for an overview of Unicode codespace allocation.)

Methods that were followed in earlier international standards for arranging and allocating character codes were adhered to in the Unicode standard whenever they did not seriously compromise principles of the Unicode standard.

The predominant characteristics of Unicode codespace assignment are:

- Where there is a single accepted standard for a script, the Unicode standard follows that standard for the relative order of characters within the script.

- Commonly used sets of characters or characters with common characteristics are located together contiguously. For example, Arabic script characters used in Persian, Urdu, and other languages, but not included in ASMO 449, follow the basic ASMO set. All right-to-left scripts are grouped together, including reserved space for future addition of right to left scripts. Codes that represent letters, punctuation, symbols, and diacritics that are shared by multiple languages are grouped together.

- The Unicode standard makes no pretense to correlate character encoding with collation or case. Even in ASCII, raw character codes alone are not sufficient for collating. Upper- and lowercase correlation is language dependent.

- The first 256 codes follow precisely the arrangement of ISO 646 (ASCII) and ISO 8859-1 (Latin 1).

- Chinese, Japanese and Korean phonetic symbols are grouped together by language in standard order.

- Only sixty-five codes (U+0000→U+001F and U+007F→U+009F) are reserved specifically as control codes. U+FFFF and U+FFFE are reserved and should not be transmitted or stored. All other code points are reserved for graphic characters. Null (U+0000) can be used as a string terminator as in the C language.

- 5.5K of user space has been allocated in the range U+E800→U+FDFF. There is no escape mechanism for extension into a larger codespace, so it is not necessary to test every character for escape sequences.

- Code points unassigned in the Unicode standard, version 1.0 are available for assignment in later versions of the Unicode standard to characters of any script. Existing characters will not be reassigned or removed.

2.4 Character Properties, Controls, and Sequences

This section provides an overview of character properties, control characters, and bidirectional character ordering.

Properties

Character properties tables are provided for use in parsing, sorting, and other algorithms requiring semantic knowledge about the code points. The properties identified by the Unicode standard include: digits, numbers, space characters, non-spacing marks, and direction. Tables of character properties are located in Chapter 4.

Control Characters

The Unicode standard provides ranges of codespace for the representation of control characters, which are not to be used for graphic characters. These ranges are U+0000→U+001F and U+007F→U+009F, which correspond to the 8-bit controls 00 to 1F (C0 controls) and 7F to 9F (*delete* and C1 controls); the Unicode values are simply zero-extended from the 8-bit values. For example, the 8-bit version of HT (horizontal tab) is at 09: the Unicode standard 16-bit version of HT is at U+0009.

Some systems may use a sequence of characters beginning with a control code to encode additional information about text, such as formatting attributes or structure. These sequences can be represented in a Unicode encoding, but must be represented in terms of 16-bit characters. For example, suppose that an application allows embedded font information to be transmitted by means of the 8-bit sequence

$$\wedge ATimes \wedge B = 01,54,69,6D,65,73,02.$$

Then the corresponding sequence of Unicode character codes would be

$$\wedge ATimes \wedge B = 0001,0054,0069,006D,0065,0073,0002$$

where the embedded text is viewed as Unicode text, or

$$\wedge ATimes \wedge B = 0001,5469,6D65,7300,0002$$

where the embedded data is interpreted by some other protocol. It cannot be

$$\wedge ATimes \wedge B = 0154,696D,6573,0200$$

because, in a Unicode character encoding, this sequence represents three characters—U+0154 LATIN CAPITAL LETTER R ACUTE, and the two Han characters U+696D and U+6573—and a fourth value, U+0200, is currently unassigned. None of these is a control character. If a control sequence contains embedded binary data, then that data does not need to be zero-extended because the control sequence constitutes a higher protocol.

If a system does use control code sequences to embed additional information, then such sequences form a higher-level protocol. Such higher-level protocols are not specified by the Unicode standard; their existence cannot be assumed without a separate agreement.

For example, use of the ISO control sequences (extended to 16 bits) for controlling bidirectional formatting is a legitimate higher-level protocol layered on top of the plain text of the Unicode encoding.

Paragraph/Line Separators

Implementers may follow existing practices in the use of control characters for these designators. The Unicode standard provides unambiguous characters, U+2028 LINE SEPARATOR, and U+2029 PARAGRAPH SEPARATOR, for general use. This is the canonical form of paragraph and line separation in the Unicode encoding.

Ordering of Character Sequences

In a Unicode encoding, text is stored in sequential order in the backing store. Logical or backing store order corresponds to the order in which text is typed on the keyboard after corrections such as insertions, deletions, and overtyping have taken place. Conversion of Unicode text in the backing store to readable text is handled by higher-level text rendering processes.

The distinction between logical order and display order for reading is shown in the following figure:

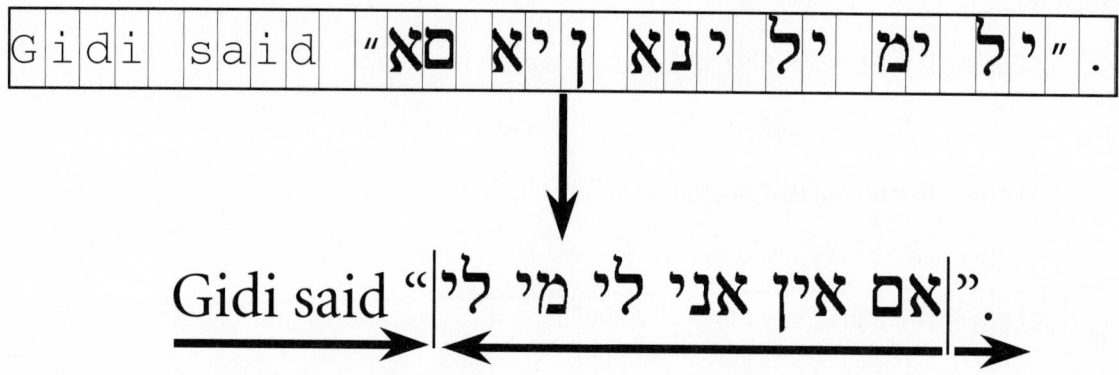

Figure 2-2. Bidirectional Ordering

In the examples, the first character of each backing store string is at position 0, but in the displayed text, logical order is independent of display order. When text is ordered for display, the glyph that represents the character at position 0 of the English text is at the left. The logical start character of the Hebrew text, however, is represented by the glyph closest to the right margin. The succeeding Hebrew glyphs are laid out to the left.

In a Unicode encoding, all scripts are stored in logical order. This applies even when characters of different dominant direction are mixed: left-to-right (Greek, Roman, Thai) with right-to-left (Arabic, Hebrew), or with vertical (Mongolian) script. Properties of directionality inherent in most characters determine the correct display order of text. But an author will sometimes override the inherent directionality for literary reasons. Moreover, some characters do not have inherent directionality (such as spaces and punctuation). Therefore, the Unicode encoding scheme includes characters to specify changes in direction. Appendix A provides rules for the correct presentation of text containing left-to-right and right-to-left scripts. Characters such as the medial form of the *short i* in Devanagari are displayed before the characters that they logically follow in the backing store. (See the Devanagari character block description for further explanation.)

Non-spacing marks (accent marks in the Greek and Roman scripts, vowel marks in Arabic and Devanagari, and so on) do not appear linearly in the final rendered text. In a Unicode character code sequence, all such characters follow the base character which they modify, or the character after which they would be articulated in phonetic order (for example, Roman "ã" is stored as "a~" when not stored in a precomposed form).

Alternate Spellings

In many cases, the same graphic appearance can be produced by several different sequences of Unicode values. These cases can result where there is a precomposed character that is the same as a composed character sequence, when there are two non-spacing marks whose order does not determine a different placement, or when there are alternate characters with different reordering semantics. For example:

LATIN SMALL LETTER A + NON-SPACING DOT ABOVE

LATIN SMALL LETTER A TILDE
LATIN SMALL LETTER A + NON-SPACING TILDE

LATIN SMALL LETTER A + NON-SPACING DOT BELOW + NON-SPACING DOT ABOVE
LATIN SMALL LETTER A + NON-SPACING DOT ABOVE + NON-SPACING DOT BELOW

LATIN SMALL LETTER A TILDE + NON-SPACING DOT BELOW
LATIN SMALL LETTER A + NON-SPACING TILDE + NON-SPACING DOT BELOW
LATIN SMALL LETTER A + NON-SPACING DOT BELOW + NON-SPACING TILDE

Similarly, the appearance is the same for the sequences THAI VOWEL SIGN SARA E + THAI LETTER KO KAI and THAI LETTER KO KAI + THAI PHONETIC ORDER VOWEL SIGN SARA E.

In such cases, the Unicode standard does not prescribe one particular sequence; all of the sequences are equivalent. Systems may choose to normalize Unicode text to one particular sequence, such as normalizing composed character sequences into precomposed characters or vice versa. Only a relatively small number of precomposed base-character-plus-diacritics have independent Unicode character values, namely those which have existed in dominant standards.

2.5 Non-spacing Marks

Characters intended to be positioned relative to an associated base character are depicted in the character code charts above, below, or through a dotted circle. They are also annotated in the names list or in the character properties list as "non-spacing." When rendered, these characters are intended to be positioned relative to the preceding base character in some manner, and not to occupy a spacing position by themselves. This is the motivation for the term "non-spacing." Diacritics are the principal class of non-spacing marks used in European alphabets. (In the charts for Indian scripts, some vowels are depicted to the left of dotted circles. This is a special case to be carefully distinguished from that of general non-spacing characters. Such vowel signs are rendered to the left of a consonant letter or consonant cluster, even though their logical order in the Unicode encoding is following the consonant letter. The decision to code these in pronunciation order and not in visual order was made by the developers of the ISCII standard.)

There is a separate block for generic diacritics, intended to be used with any script. There is an additional block for symbol diacritics, intended to be used with symbol base characters. There are additional non-spacing marks in the blocks for particular scripts when they are primarily used with these scripts. However, the allocation of a non-spacing mark to one block or another identifies only its primary usage; it is not intended to define or limit the range of characters to which it may be applied. In the Unicode standard, all sequences of character codes are permitted.

Some scripts, such as Hebrew, Arabic, and the scripts of India and Southeast Asia, also have non-spacing marks indicated in the charts in relation to dotted circles to show their position relative to the base character. Many of these non-spacing marks encode vowel letters; as such they are not generally referred to as "diacritics."

Typical diacritics have a very strong interaction with the base character to which they are applied, in the sense that the combination is a semantically indivisible unit. However, in the Unicode standard, the term "diacritic" is interpreted more broadly, to include accents as well.

Sequence of Base Letters and Non-Spacing Marks

In the Unicode standard, all non-spacing marks are encoded following the base characters. The Unicode sequence U+0061 LATIN SMALL LETTER A "a" + U+0308 NON-SPACING DIAERESIS " ¨ " + U+0075 LATIN SMALL LETTER U "u" unambiguously encodes as "äu" not "aü."

This convention is different from the convention in ISO 6937, and the bibliographic standard ISO 5926. The reasons for the old convention were conformity with "dead keys" on mechanical typewriters (no longer a consideration for computers), and considerations of efficiency in serial parsing of character streams which included diacritics.

The convention used by the Unicode standard is consistent with the logical order of other non-spacing marks in Semitic and Indic scripts, the great majority of which follow the base characters with respect to which they are positioned. To avoid the complication of defining and implementing non-spacing marks on both sides of base characters, the Unicode standard specifies that all non-spacing marks must follow their base characters. This convention conforms to the way modern font technology handles the rendering of non-spacing graphical forms, so that mapping from character store to font rendering is simplified.

Spacing Clones of European Diacritical Marks

By convention, diacritical marks used by the Unicode encoding scheme may be exhibited in (apparent) isolation by applying them to U+0020 SPACE or to U+00A0 NON-BREAKING SPACE. This might be done, for example, when talking about the diacritical mark itself as a mark, rather than using it in its normal way in text. The Unicode standard separately encodes clones of many common European diacritical marks that are spacing characters, largely to provide compatibility with existing character sets. These related characters are cross-referenced.

Multiple Non-spacing Marks

There are instances where more than one diacritical mark is applied to a single base character. The Unicode standard does not restrict the number of non-spacing marks that can follow a baseform character. The following rules apply:

1. If the non-spacing marks can interact typographically—for example, a non-spacing macron and a non-spacing diaeresis—then the order of graphic display is determined by the order of coded characters. The diacritics or other non-spacing marks are positioned from the base character outward. Non-spacing marks placed above a base character will be stacked vertically, starting with the first encountered in the logical store and continuing for as many marks above as are required by the character codes following the base character. For non-spacing marks placed below a base character, the situation is inverted, with the non-spacing marks starting from the base character and stacking downward.

An example of multiple non-spacing characters above the base character is found in Thai, where a consonant letter can have above it one of the vowels U+0E34 through U+0E37 and, above that, one of four tone marks U+0E48 through U+0E4B. The order of character codes which produces this graphic display is base consonant character code, plus vowel character code, plus one tone character code.

2. Some specific non-spacing marks override the default stacking behavior by being positioned horizontally rather than stacking, or by ligaturing with an adjacent non-spacing mark. When positioned horizontally, the order of codes is reflected by positioning in the dominant order of the script with which they are used. For example, horizontal accents, in a left-to-right script would be coded left-to-right.

Prominent characters that show such override behavior are associated with specific scripts or alphabets. The Greek "breathing marks" U+0371 and U+0372 require that they together with a following acute or grave accent be rendered side-by-side above a letter, rather than the accent marks being stacked above the breathing marks. The order of codes here is base character code plus breathing mark code plus accent mark code.

GREEK SMALL LETTER ALPHA ✚ GREEK NON-SPACING PSILI PNEUMATA ✚ NON-SPACING ACUTE

GREEK SMALL LETTER ALPHA ✚ NON-SPACING ACUTE ✚ GREEK NON-SPACING PSILI PNEUMATA

Two Vietnamese tone marks which have the same graphic appearance as the Latin acute and grave accent marks do not stack above the three Vietnamese vowel letters which already contain the circumflex diacritic (â ê ô). Instead, they form ligatures with the circumflex component of the base vowel characters.

LATIN SMALL LETTER A CIRCUMFLEX ✚ NON-SPACING ACUTE TONE MARK

LATIN SMALL LETTER A CIRCUMFLEX + NON-SPACING ACUTE
LATIN SMALL LETTER A + NON-SPACING CIRCUMFLEX + NON-SPACING ACUTE

LATIN SMALL LETTER A ACUTE + NON-SPACING CIRCUMFLEX
LATIN SMALL LETTER A + NON-SPACING ACUTE + NON-SPACING CIRCUMFLEX

3. If the non-spacing marks cannot interact typographically—for example, when one nonspacing mark is above a baseform and another is below—then the Unicode standard does not specify that a distinct graphic form will be rendered if the codes are in different orders. In such cases it is up to the user and application to decide on a consistent and useful order of codes. (This may often reflect the fact that one non-spacing character is more tightly bound structurally to the base letter than the other.) No distinction of graphic form will generally result from such alternative orderings of codes.

2.6 Formal Requirements for Unicode Conformance

A computing system (a hardware device or a software application) may perform various processes on text character sequences. This clause specifies in general terms when a text process conforms to the Unicode standard. The purpose of this clause is to state clearly the intentions of the Unicode design in order to provide implementors a method of producing systems that conform to the Unicode standard and that will work consistently and cooperatively with each other. This clause is not intended to prescribe a procedure for evaluating systems as conforming or non-conforming.

IN SUMMARY: For each 16-bit character code in a text sequence, a process that conforms to the Unicode standard must either interpret the code value according to its Unicode semantics as specified in this standard, or not interpret it at all. An interchange process may not change a code that it cannot interpret; other than that, the behavior of processes relative to codes it cannot interpret is unspecified.

1. *Public Interchange of bit sequences as character codes*

"Interchange" refers to processes which transmit and receive (including store and retrieve) sequence of bits that are to be treated as sequences of coded text characters. "Public Interchange" refers to processes that exchange or record bits in such a way that the bits might ever be accessed by other processes that conform to the Unicode encoding scheme, and which are not under their control or coordination (for example, transmission in e-mail or storage to a file). "Private Interchange" refers to processes which exchange or record bits in such a way that access to those bits is available only to other processes (not necessarily Unicode-conformant) under their control or coordination (for example, encrypted transmission or storage in a temporary data structure).

The terms "Unicode" and "Unicode text" refer exclusively to the unique representation of character code sequences specified above. This design is not intended to preclude encrypted, compressed, or byte-swapped text from being used in Private Interchange settings, but it does separate such usage from the question of public conformance to the Unicode standard.

The basic conformance requirements for Public Interchange of character codes are:

A conformant process must treat textual information in 16-bit units, and must obey the rules specified elsewhere in this standard regarding each sub-range of Unicode values:

U+0000 → U+001F	Control codes
U+0020 → U+007E	Graphic character codes
U+007F → U+009F	Control codes
U+00A0 → U+E7FF	Graphic character codes
U+E800 → U+FDFF	Private Use Area
U+FE00 → U+FEFE	Compatibility Zone
U+FEFF	Byte order mark
U+FF00 → U+FFEF	Compatibility Zone
U+FFF0 → U+FFFD	Graphic character codes
U+FFFE → U+FFFF	Not character codes
Bidirectional text	Appendix A

A Unicode-conformant process must not assign any semantic or character identity to any code point left unassigned in this version of the standard, with the exception of the codes in the Private Use Area.

NOTE: This does not preclude the assignment of certain generic semantics (for example, left-to-right or right-to-left directionality) which allow graceful behavior of algorithms in the presence of codes which are outside the adopted subset.

Unicode code points are 16-bit quantities. Machine architectures differ in the ordering of whether the most significant byte or the least significant byte comes first. These are known as "big-endian" and "little-endian" orders, respectively.

The Unicode standard does not specify any order of bytes or bits inside the 16-bit sequence of a Unicode code point. However, in Public Interchange and in the absence of any information to the contrary provided by a higher protocol, a conformant process may assume that Unicode character sequences it receives are in the order of the most significant byte first.

NOTE: The majority of all Interchange occurs with processes running on the same or a similar configuration. This makes intra-domain Interchange of Unicode text in the domain-specific byte order fully conformant, and limits the role of the canonical byte order to Interchange of Unicode text across domain, or where the nature of the originating domain is unknown. Processes may prefix data with U+FEFF BYTE ORDER MARK, and a receiving process may interpret that character as verification that the text arrived with the byte order expected by the receiving process. Alternatively, on receiving U+FFFE, the receiving process may recover text data by attempting to re-read it in byte-swapped order.

2. Interpretation

"Interpretation" refers to processes which take 16-bit values as input and produce results based on the assumption that these values represent codes for specific text characters with known identities (semantics). The conformance requirement with regard to Interpretation is:

> *If a conformant process is able to Interpret a given character code, then the Interpretation must be consistent with the Unicode character semantics.*

One important usage of Interpretation merits particular mention. "Rendering" (or "Presentation") refers to processes having access to fonts and other resources, which take 16-bit values as input, interpret their character identities, and draw a visible graphic depiction of the text. As a corollary of the preceding, the conformance requirement with regard to Rendering is:

> *If a conformant Rendering process is able to Interpret and draw a given character code, then the graphic depiction must be consistent with the Unicode character semantics.*

3. Modification

"Modification" refers to processes which make any change at all to a sequence of bits that are to be treated as sequences of text characters. The conformance requirement with regard to Modification is:

> *A conformant (Public) Interchange process which in any way receives and retransmits encoded text must not change the 16-bit value of any character code that it cannot interpret. It must transmit such a code unchanged from the value that was received.*

In other words, any change that a conformant system makes in a given sequence of bits treated as text characters must be made intentionally by processes that have knowingly interpreted the codes.

4. Interpretable subsets of characters

In conforming to the Unicode standard, no conditions are set regarding the subset of 16-bit values that any process may or may not be able to Interpret. As a corollary of all the foregoing, the conformance requirement with regard to interpretable subsets is:

> *A conformant process may or may not be able to Interpret (including Render) any particular set of 16-bit values. In general, the behavior of a conformant process with respect to code values that it cannot Interpret is intentionally left unspecified. However, if a process cannot Interpret a character code and is required to Interchange it, it must transmit the code unchanged.*

This design is not intended to preclude enumerations or specifications of the characters that a process or system is able to Interpret, but it does separate supported subset enumerations from the question of conformance. In real life, any system may occasionally receive an unfamiliar character code which it is unable to Interpret; all that really matters is that it be able to retransmit the code undamaged.

Examples of Conformant and Non-Conformant Processing

The following are examples of text processes that conform to the Unicode standard:

- A system receives any text sequence and retransmits it unchanged. Whether or not it could have performed any other process on the text (display it, spell-check it, and so on) is immaterial.

- A system receives a sequence of English text and retransmits it all converted to uppercase (presumably an intentional change consistent with the text's semantics).

- A system is capable of rendering only characters in the "8859-1" range (Unicode values 0000-00FF), although it treats those code numbers in full 16-bit form. Such a system may be unable to render other character codes or sequences legibly (for example, if it is given a sequence of Bengali characters). It might render a black box or ring a bell or do nothing. Behavior in such cases is not specified or restricted.

- A system renders a given sequence of English text in any Latin font style, line length, page layout and so on of its choice, such that the text is conventionally readable with the intended interpretation.

The following are examples of text processes that do not conform to the Unicode standard:

- A system receives a sequence of English text and retransmits it all converted to random Bengali characters, or vice versa (presumably an unintentional change inconsistent with the text's semantics).

- A system takes in a sequence of Unicode characters and treats it as though it were a sequence of ASCII bytes.

- A system produces results constituting an Interpretation of an unassigned Unicode value (excluding User Space).

- A system interprets non-spacing marks as preceding base characters. For example, the sequence "a", "¨", "u" as "aü" and not "äu."

3.0 *Character Blocks*

The character codes in these charts are the core of the Unicode standard. The characters cover modern communication and computer usage in the major scripts of the world and consist of approximately 2,300 general (alphabetic or syllabic) letters, 1,200 textual symbols, and 3,300 CJK phonetics, punctuation, symbols, and Korean Hangul syllables. Over 20,000 Han (East Asian ideographic) characters are covered, beginning with U+4000.

The following block descriptions are written so that they can be read alone, but by themselves are not sufficient to implement the Unicode character encoding. It is also vital to understand the general architecture of the Unicode standard (covered in Chapter 2).

The block introductions and character blocks are ordered by their code range location. Thus, the character blocks are ordered in the following sequence: General Scripts, Symbols, CJK Symbols, CJK Ideographs, and User and Compatibility Zones. (See Figure 1-1 for an overview of scripts included in version 1.0 of the Unicode standard.)

3.1 General Scripts

The General Script area of the Unicode standard includes the encoding of all Latin and non-ideographic script characters.

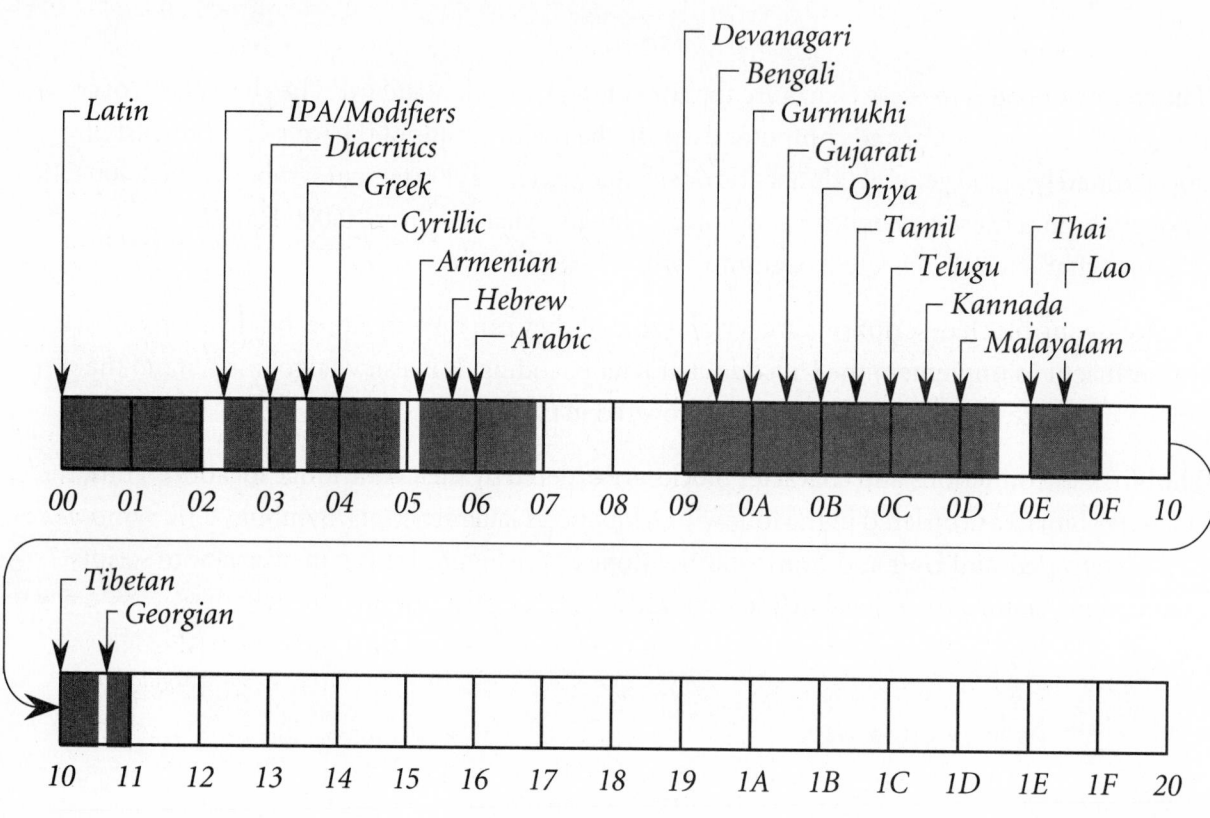

Figure 3-1. General Scripts

ASCII U+0000 → U+007F

Standards. The Unicode standard adapts the ISO 7-bit standard for character encoding by retaining the semantics and numeric values of these codes, merely supplying enough leading zeros to convert them into 16-bit values. The content and arrangement of these standards is far from optimal in the context of a 16-bit space, but the Unicode standard retains them without change because of their prevalence in existing usage.

ISO 646   The ISO character encoding standards are founded on ISO 646, *ISO 7-bit Coded Character Set for Information Interchange.* This standard provides an international set of interpretations for code values 00 to 7F, which are intended to be localized into national standard codes.

ANSI X3.4   This is ASCII: *American National Standard Code for Information Interchange.* ASCII is the version of ISO 646 localized into the national standard code for the USA. In the few places where ISO 646 and ASCII differ, the Unicode standard gives priority to the specific interpretations of ASCII rather than to the generic interpretations of ISO 646. (For example, at code point 24, ISO 646 has the generic *international currency symbol,* whereas in ASCII and for the Unicode value U+0024 this is localized to the *dollar sign.*) The Unicode principle is to designate unambiguous character codes. U+0024 is interpreted as DOLLAR SIGN because code point 24 is the *dollar sign* in ASCII. Other currency symbols are likewise given their own code points within the appropriate blocks, principally U+20A0 → U+20CF, Currency Symbols. The graphic used at code point 24 in ISO 646 is assigned to U+00A4, CURRENCY SIGN.

ASCII C0 Control Codes. The Unicode standard makes no particular use of these control codes, but provides for the passage of the numeric code values intact, neither adding to nor subtracting from their semantics. For more information on control codes, see Section 2.4.

There is a simple one-to-one mapping between 8-bit control codes and Unicode control codes: every 8-bit control code is simply zero-extended to a 16-bit code. For example, if line feed (0A) is to be used for terminal control, then "AB<LF>CD" would be transmitted in plain Unicode text as the following 16-bit values: "0041 0042 000A 0043 0044." Any interpretation of these control codes is outside the scope of the Unicode standard; programmers should refer to the relevant standard (for example, ISO 6429) which specifies control code interpretations.

ASCII Graphic Characters. (U+007F DELETE is a control code, and the remaining 95 codes in this range are graphic characters.) Some of the non-letter characters in this range suffer from overburdened usage as a result of the limited number of codes in a 7-bit space. Some coding consequences of this are discussed below under "Simple Semantic Encoding versus Encoding Characters with Multiple Semantic Value" and "Loose vs. Precise Semantics." The rather haphazard ASCII collection of punctuation and mathematical signs are isolated from the larger body of Unicode punctuation, signs, and symbols (which are encoded in ranges starting at U+2000) only because the relative locations within ASCII are so widely used in standards and software.

Simple Semantic Encoding vs. Encoding Characters with Multiple Semantic Values. Code values in the ASCII range are well-established and used in widely various implementations. The Unicode standard therefore provides only minimal specifications on the typographic appearance of corresponding glyphs. For example, the value U+0024 ($) (derived from ASCII 24) has the semantic *dollar sign*, leaving open the question of whether the dollar sign is to be rendered with one vertical stroke or two. The Unicode value U+0024 refers to the *dollar sign semantic*, not to its precise appearance. Likewise, for other characters in this range that have alternative glyphs, the Unicode character is displayed with the basic or most common glyph, and rendering software may present any other graphical form of that character.

Loose vs. Precise Semantics. Some ASCII characters have multiple uses, either through ambiguity in the original standards or through accumulated reinterpretations of a limited codeset. For example, 27 hex is defined in ANSI X3.4 as *apostrophe (closing single quotation mark; acute accent)*, and 2D hex as *hyphen minus*. In general, the Unicode standard provides the same interpretation for the equivalent code values, without adding to or subtracting from their semantics. The Unicode standard supplies *unambiguous* codes elsewhere for the most useful particular interpretations of these ASCII values; the corresponding unambiguous characters are cross-referenced in the character names list for this block. In a few cases, the Unicode standard indicates the generic interpretation of an ASCII code in the name of the corresponding Unicode character, for example U+0027 is APOSTROPHE-QUOTE '.

Diacritics. ASCII contains four codes which are ambiguous: they may be treated either as spacing or as non-spacing marks. The equivalents in the Unicode encoding are: U+005E CIRCUMFLEX ^; U+005F SPACING UNDERSCORE _ ; U+0060 GRAVE `; U+007E TILDE ~. In the Unicode encoding, these code points are restricted to use as spacing characters. The Unicode standard provides unambiguous non-spacing marks in other blocks which can be used to represent accented Latin letters as composed character sequences.

Semantics of Paired Punctuation. Paired punctuation marks such as parentheses (U+0028, U+0029), square brackets (U+005B, U+005D), and braces (U+007B, U+007D) are defined in the Unicode standard as "Opening" and "Closing" rather than "Left" and "Right" so that the semantic will not change in such languages as Arabic, Hebrew or Chinese, where text may flow from right to left or top to bottom. *These characters therefore have consistant semantics but alternative glyphs depending upon the directional flow rendered by a given software program.* The software must ensure that the rendered glyph is the correct one.

Encoding Structure. The Unicode character block for the ASCII character set is divided into the following ranges:

U+0000	→ U+001F	ASCII C0 control codes
U+0020	→ U+007F	ASCII graphic characters

Latin1 Characters   U+0080 → U+00FF

Standards. ISO 8859-1, *Latin1*, is intended to extend ISO 646 by providing additional letters for major languages of Europe (listed below). Like ASCII, the Latin1 set also includes a miscellaneous set of punctuation and mathematical signs. Punctuation, signs, and symbols not included in ASCII and Latin1 are encoded in the range starting at U+2000.

Languages. The languages targeted for coverage by Latin1, ISO 8859-1 are Danish, Dutch, Faroese, Finnish, French, German, Icelandic, Irish, Italian, Norwegian, Portuguese, Spanish, and Swedish. Many other languages can be written with this set of letters, including Hawaiian, Indonesian/ Malay, and Swahili.

C1 Control Codes. Control codes in the C1 range are assigned interpretations in various ISO standards, but do not have the force of long established usage as do those in the ASCII C0 range. Whatever the eventual assignments in the C1 range may be, the Unicode standard makes no particular use of them; their definition is left to other standards.

Diacritics. Latin1 contains five codes which are ambiguous; they may be treated either as spacing or as non-spacing marks. The equivalents in the Unicode encoding are U+00A8, U+00AF, U+00B0, U+00B4, U+00B8. In the Unicode standard, these code points are restricted to use as spacing characters. The Unicode standard provides unambiguous non-spacing marks in other blocks which can be used to represent accented Latin letters as composed character sequences.

U+00AD SOFT HYPHEN indicates a hyphenation point, where a line-break is preferred when a word is to be hyphenated. Depending on the script, the visible rendering of this character when a line break occurs may differ (for example, in some scripts it is rendered as a *hyphen* -, while in others it may be invisible). See also U+2027 HYPHENATION POINT.

U+00A0 NON-BREAKING SPACE is included for compatibility with existing standards. The appearance (width) is the same as the standard space (U+0020), but the NON-BREAKING SPACE generally disallows line breaks on either side.

Quotation Marks. The *guillemets*, U+00AB « and U+00BB », have heterogeneous semantics. They may represent open or close quotation marks, depending on which language they are used with: «in quotes» or »in quotes«.

Encoding Structure. The Unicode Latin1 block is divided into the following ranges:

U+0080	→ U+009F	C1 control codes
U+00A0	→ U+00FF	Latin1 graphic characters

European Latin U+0100 → U+017F

The European Latin block contains a collection of letters which, when added to the letters contained in the ASCII and Latin1 blocks, allow the representation of most European languages using the Latin script. Many other languages can also be written with this set of letters. Most of these letters are precomposed characters, which can also be represented as composed character sequences. See Section 2.5, Non-spacing Marks.

Standards. This block includes characters contained in the International Standard *Information Processing—8-bit Single-byte Coded Graphic Character Sets*—ISO 8859 Part 2, Part 3, Part 4, and Part 9, also known as Latin2, Latin3, Latin4 and Latin5. This block also includes the repertoire specified for ISO 6937. Many of the other graphic characters contained in these standards such as punctuation, signs, symbols, and diacritical marks are already encoded in the Latin1 block.

Languages. Most languages covered by this block also require characters contained in the ASCII and Latin1 blocks. When combined with these two blocks, the European Latin block covers Afrikaans, Breton, Basque, Catalan, Croatian, Czech, Danish, Dutch, Esperanto, Estonian, Faroese, Finnish, Flemish, Frisian, Greenlandic, Hungarian, Icelandic, Italian, Latin, Latvian, Lithuanian, Malay, Maltese, Norwegian, Polish, Portuguese, Provençal, Rhaeto-Romanic, Romanian, Romany, Slovak, Slovenian, Serbian, Spanish, Swedish, Turkish, Welsh.

Alternative Graphics. Some characters have alternative representations, although they have a common semantic. When Czech is printed in books, letter/apostrophe forms are frequently used. In typewritten or handwritten documents, letter/hacek forms are preferred.

Exceptional Case Pairs. The letters U+0130 LATIN CAPITAL LETTER I DOT and U+0131 LATIN SMALL LETTER DOTLESS I (used primarily in Turkish) are assumed to take ASCII "i" and "I" as their case alternates. This mapping makes the corresponding back mapping ambiguous, but the Unicode standard follows industry practice in this regard.

Encoding Structure. The letters are laid out in alphabetic order, the small letters following the capital letters.

Extended Latin U+0180 → U+01FF

The Extended Latin block contains letterforms used to extend Latin scripts to represent non-European languages. It also contains phonetic symbols not in the International Phonetic Alphabet (the Standard Phonetic block, U+0250 → U+02AF).

Standards. This block covers, among other things, ISO 6438, graphic characters of African languages, *Pinyin* Latin transcription characters from the People's Republic of China national standard GB 2312 and from the Japanese national standard JIS X 0212, and Lapp characters from ECMA Registry #144 under ISO 2375.

Arrangement. The characters are arranged in approximate Latin alphabetical order, followed by a small collection of Latinate forms. Upper- and lowercase pairs are placed together where possible, but in many instances the other case form is encoded at some rather distant location, and so is cross-referenced. Variations on the same base letter are arranged in the following order: turned, inverted, hook attachment, stroke extension or modification, different style (script), small cap, modified basic form, ligature, Greek-derived.

Croatian Digraphs Matching Serbian Cyrillic Letters. The Unicode standard generally avoids encoding digraphs and other multiple letterforms. An exception is made for Serbo-Croatian, which is a single language with paired alphabets: a Latin script (Croatian) and a Cyrillic script (Serbian). A set of digraph codes is provided to enable direct one-to-one character transliteration between Serbian and Croatian. There are two potential uppercase forms, depending on whether only the initial letter is to be capitalized, or both (for the case of all uppercase). The Unicode standard offers both forms so that software can convert one form to the other without changing font sets. The appropriate cross-references are given for the lowercase letters.

Pinyin Diacritic-Vowel Combinations. The PRC standard GB 2312, as well as JIS X 0212, includes a set of codes for *Pinyin*, the Latin transcription of Mandarin Chinese. Most of the letters used in Pinyin romanization (even those with non-spacing marks) are already covered in the preceding Latin blocks. The group of sixteen codes here complete the Pinyin character set specified in GB 2312 and in JIS X 0212.

Case Pairs. A number of characters in this block are uppercase forms of characters whose lowercase form is part of some other grouping. Many of these came from the International Phonetic Alphabet; they acquired novel uppercase forms when they were adopted into the Latin-based scripts of real languages. Occasionally *alternative* uppercase forms arose by this process. If research has found that alternative uppercase forms are merely variants of the same character they are assigned a single Unicode value, as is the case of U+01B7 LATIN CAPITAL LETTER YOGH. When research has found that two uppercase forms are actually used in different ways, then they are given different codes; such is the case for U+018E LATIN CAPITAL LETTER TURNED-E and U+018F LATIN CAPITAL LETTER SCHWA . In this case, the shared lowercase form is cloned: U+01D5 LATIN SMALL LETTER TURNED E is a clone of U+0259 LATIN SMALL LETTER SCHWA to enable unique case-pair mappings if desired.

Languages. Some indication of language or other usage is given for most characters.

Encoding Structure. The Unicode block for Extended Latin is divided into the following ranges:

U+0180 → U+01C3	Extended Latin
U+01C4 → U+01CC	Croatian digraphs matching Serbian Cyrillic letters
U+01CD → U+01DC	Pinyin diacritic-vowel combinations
U+01DD → U+01F0	Additional characters
U+01F1 → U+01FF	Currently unassigned

Standard Phonetic U+0250 → U+02AF

The Standard Phonetic block contains primarily the unique symbols of the International Phonetic Alphabet (IPA), which is a standard system for indicating specific sounds. The IPA was first introduced in 1886, and has undergone occasional revisions of content and usage since that time. The Unicode standard covers all single symbols and all diacritics in the last published IPA revision (1989), as well as a few symbols in former IPA usage which are no longer currently sanctioned. The use of non-spacing diacritical marks for close phonetic transcription is an integral part of IPA, as is the use of modifier letters. The IPA diacritics and modifiers are encoded in the two blocks following this one. A few symbols have been added to this block that are part of the transcriptional practices of Sinologists, Americanists and other linguists. Some of these practices have usages independent of the IPA and may use extended Latin letters rather than IPA forms. Note also that a few non-standard or obsolete phonetic symbols are encoded in the block preceding this one (Extended Latin).

Standards. The characters in this block are taken from the 1989 revision of the International Phonetic Alphabet, published by the International Phonetic Association. This standard considers IPA forms to be a separate alphabet, so it includes the Latin alphabet a-z and other symbols as separate and distinct characters. In contrast, the Unicode standard does not duplicate the Latin alphabet a-z in encoding IPA.

The alphabetic run of characters from U+0299 → U+02A8 represents additions to the Unicode standard reflecting IPA (1989). Some obsolete characters from earlier versions of IPA have also been included.

Unifications. IPA includes the entire lowercase Latin alphabet a-z, a number of extended Latin letters such as U+0153 LATIN SMALL LETTER OE œ , and a few Greek letters. The question of whether these characters are identical when used in an IPA context, or whether all IPA forms should be considered unique characters of a separate alphabet, has many reasonable arguments on both sides. Unicode principles prescribe unification whenever practical and consistent with other principles. Therefore, the IPA symbols are unified as much as possible with other letters (though not with non-letter symbols such as U+222B INTEGRAL SIGN ∫ .) A primary reason, aside from reduced duplication, is that the IPA symbols have been adopted into Latin scripts for many languages (such as in Africa). It is futile to attempt to distinguish a transcription from an actual script in such cases. Therefore, many IPA symbols are found outside the IPA block. The Latin alphabet is, of course, coded in the first block. Other IPA characters that are not found in the IPA block are listed as cross-references at the beginning of the character names list for this block.

IPA Alternates. In a few cases IPA practice has evolved alternate forms, such as U+0269 LATIN SMALL LETTER IOTA "ɩ" versus U+026A LATIN LETTER SMALL CAPITAL I "ɪ," the Unicode standard provides separate encodings for the two alternates.

Case Pairs. IPA does not sanction case distinctions, so in effect its phonetic symbols are all lowercase. When IPA symbols are adopted into the actual script of a language, as for example has occurred in Africa, they acquire uppercase forms. Since these uppercase forms are not themselves IPA symbols, they are encoded in the block preceding this one (Extended Latin), and are cross-referenced with the IPA names list.

Typographic Variants. IPA includes typographic variants of certain Latin letters which would ordinarily be considered variations of font style rather than of character identity, such as *small capital* letter forms. These forms are encoded as separate characters in the Unicode standard because they have distinct semantics in plain text. The Unicode standard also separately encodes the unique IPA typographic variant of the Greek letter *phi* ɸ as well as the borrowed letter Greek *iota* ι which has a unique Latin uppercase form.

Non-spacing Marks. The Unicode character encoding scheme presumes the necessity of dynamically-applied marks. This principle is an essential element of IPA orthography. Therefore IPA diacritical mark characters are coded in the Generic Diacritical Marks block, U+0300 → U+036F. In IPA, diacritical marks can be freely applied to baseform letters to indicate fine degrees of phonetic differentiation required for precise recording of different languages. In the Unicode standard, all diacritical marks are encoded in sequence *after the base characters* to which they apply. For more details, see the block description for Generic Diacritical Marks, and Section 2.5, Non-spacing Marks.

Affricate Ligatures. IPA officially sanctions six ligatures used in transcription of coronal affricates. These are encoded at U+02A3 → U+02A8. The Unicode standard does not normally encode typographical ligatures, but the IPA ligatures differ in being explicitly defined in IPA and also in having semantic values which make them not simply rendering forms. Thus, for example, while U+02A6 LATIN SMALL LETTER T S is a transcription for the sounds which could also be transcribed in IPA as U+0074 U+0073, "ts," the choice of the ligature may be the result of a deliberate distinction made by the transcriber regarding the systematic phonetic status of the affricate. It certainly should not be a choice left up to rendering software whether to ligate or not based on the font available.

Encoding Structure. The Standard Phonetic block is arranged in approximate alphabetical order according to the Latin letter that is graphically most similar to each symbol. This has nothing to do with a phonetic arrangement of the IPA letters.

Modifier Letters U+02B0 → U+02FF

Modifier Letters are an assorted collection of small signs that are generally used to indicate modifications of the preceding letter. A few may modify the following letter, and some may serve as independent letters. These signs are distinguished from diacritical marks in that modifier letters are treated as free-standing, spacing characters. They are distinguished from similar—or identical—appearing punctuation or symbols by the fact that the members of this block are considered to be letter characters that do not break up a word. They should be interpreted as having the "alphabetic" character property. The majority of these signs are phonetic modifiers, including the characters required for coverage of the International Phonetic Alphabet (IPA).

Phonetic Usage. In phonetic usage, the modifier letters are sometimes called "diacritics," which is correct in the logical sense that they are modifiers of the preceding letter. However, in the Unicode standard, the term "diacritical marks" refers specifically to non-spacing marks, whereas the codes in the current block specify *spacing characters.* For this reason, many of the modifier letters in this block correspond to separate diacritical mark codes which are cross-referenced in the character names list. Modifier letters have relatively well-defined phonetic interpretations. Their usage is generally to indicate a specific articulatory modification of a sound represented by another letter, or to convey a particular level of stress or tone.

Standards. The modifier letters in the Unicode standard are collated from a variety of sources, the most important of which is the IPA.

Encoding Principles. In this set, there are different characters for the same semantic values, and there are also different semantic values attributed to the same character in different contexts. For example, the letters U+02BC, U+02BE, and U+02C0 have all been used in various publications as a Latin transliteration of the glottal stop (Arabic *hamza*), while U+02BC, at least, has numerous other usages as well. There are also instances where an IPA modifier letter is explicitly equated in semantic value to an IPA non-spacing diacritic form. The intention of the Unicode encoding is not to resolve the variations in usage, but merely to supply implementers with a set of useful forms to choose from. The list of usages given for each modifier letter should not be considered exhaustive.

Latin Superscripts. Graphically, some of the phonetic modifier signs are raised or superscripted, some are lowered or subscripted, and some are vertically centered. The raised signs that derive from Latin letters might suggest the superscripting of the entire Latin alphabet, but the intention here is to encode only those few forms that have specific usage in IPA or other major phonetic systems. The Unicode standard does not in general provide separate codes for superscripted or subscripted characters (although an exception is also made for a limited set of numeric forms to preserve one-to-one mapping with existing standards).

Spacing Clones of Diacritics. Some corporate standards distinguish spacing and non-spacing forms of diacritical marks, and the Unicode standard provides matching codes for these interpretations when practical. The majority of the spacing forms are covered in the Unicode Latin1 block (derived from ISO 8859-1). The six common European diacritics which do not have encodings in ISO 8859-1 are added as spacing characters in the current block. Since the characters frame multiple semantics, these forms may be used with any suitable semantic interpretation (such as U+02D9 SPACING DOT ABOVE ˙ as an indicator of Mandarin Chinese fifth tone).

Rhotic Hook. U+02DE RHOTIC HOOK is defined in IPA as a free-standing modifier letter. However, in common usage it is treated as a ligated hook on a baseform letter. Hence, U+0259 SCHWA + U+02DE RHOTIC HOOK can be treated as equivalent to U+025A SCHWA HOOK.

Tone Letters. U+02E5 → U+02E9 comprise a set of basic tone letters, defined in IPA and commonly used in detailed tone transcription of African and other languages. Each tone letter refers to one of five distinguishable tone levels. In order to represent contour tones, the tone letters may be used in combinations, and their rendering is handled by a regular set of ligation rules which result in a graphic image of the contour:

$$\rceil + \rfloor = \diagdown$$

Encoding Structure. The block for Modifier Letters is divided into the following ranges:

U+02B0	→ U+02B8	Phonetic modifiers derived from Latin letters
U+02B9	→ U+02D7	Miscellaneous phonetic modifiers
U+02D8	→ U+02DD	Spacing clones of non-spacing diacritic marks
U+02DE		Miscellaneous phonetic modifier
U+02DF		Currently unassigned
U+02E0	→ U+02E4	Phonetic modifiers derived from Latin letters
U+02E5	→ U+02E9	IPA tone letters
U+02EA	→ U+02FF	Currently unassigned

Generic Diacritical Marks U+0300 → U+036F

The diacritical marks in this block are intended for generic use with any scripts. Diacritical marks which are specific to some particular script are encoded along with the alphabet for that script. Diacritical marks which are primarily used with symbols are defined in code range U+20D0 → U+20FF, Diacritical Marks for Symbols.

Standards. The generic diacritical marks are derived from a variety of sources, including ISO 6937, ISO 5426, and IPA.

Sequence of Base Letters and Diacritics. In the Unicode character encoding, all non-spacing marks, including diacritics, are encoded *after* the base character. For example, the Unicode sequence U+0061 "a", U+0308 " ¨ ", U+0075 "u" unambiguously encodes äu, not aü.

The Unicode convention is consistent with the logical order of other non-spacing marks in Semitic and Indic scripts, the great majority of which follow the base characters with respect to which they are positioned. This convention is also in line with the way modern font technology handles the rendering of non-spacing glyphic forms, so that mapping from character store to font rendering is simplified.

Details concerning the use of diacritics are included in the general introduction in Section 2.5.

Diacritics Positioned Over Two or More Base Characters. IPA and a few languages such as Tagalog use diacritics which are applied to two Latin baseform characters. These diacritics will be included in a future version of the Unicode standard.

Marks as Spacing Characters. By convention, Unicode non-spacing marks may be exhibited in (apparent) isolation by applying them to the SPACE character U+0020 or to the NON-BREAKING SPACE U+00A0. This might be done, for example, when talking about the diacritical mark itself as a mark, rather than using it in its normal way in text. Also, the Unicode standard separately encodes clones of many common European diacritical marks that are spacing characters, largely to provide compatibility with existing character sets. These related characters are cross-referenced in the character names list.

Encoding Principles. Because non-spacing marks have such a wide variety of applications, the characters in this block may have multiple semantic values. For example, U+0308 = *diaeresis* = *umlaut* = *double derivative*. There are also cases of several different Unicode characters for equivalent semantic values; variants of CEDILLA include at least U+0312, U+0326, and U+0327.

Encoding Structure. The Unicode block for generic diacritical marks is divided into the following ranges:

U+0300	→ U+0333	Ordinary diacritics
U+0334	→ U+0338	Overstruck diacritics
U+0339	→ U+033F	Ordinary diacritics
U+0340	→ U+0341	Vietnamese tone mark diacritics
U+0342	→ U+036F	Currently unassigned

Greek U+0370 → U+03FF

The Greek script is used for writing the Greek language, and (in an extended variant) for the Coptic language. Greek is ancestral to the family of scripts including Latin and Cyrillic.

The Greek script is written in linear sequence from left to right with the occasional use of non-spacing marks. Greek letters come in upper- and lowercase pairs.

Standards. The ECMA registry under ISO 2375 for use with ISO 2022 contains many Greek subsets. Unicode is based on the latest and most prominent of these: ISO 8859-7, which equals the Greek national standard ELOT 928, and also ECMA-118.

ISO 8859-7 The Unicode standard encodes Greek characters in the same relative positions as in 8859-7. Generic punctuation characters (17 of them) are unified with characters in other Unicode ranges; cross-references to such codes are given in the character names list.

ISO 5428 A number of variant and archaic characters are taken into the Unicode standard from this bibliographic standard.

Polytonic Greek. Polytonic Greek, used for ancient Greek (classical and Byzantine) is coded in the Unicode encoding scheme with composed character sequences, rather than as single precomposed characters.

Non-spacing Marks. Several non-spacing marks may be used with Greek. These are found in the Generic Diacritical Marks range:

U+0300	NON-SPACING GRAVE
U+0301	NON-SPACING ACUTE
U+0302	NON-SPACING CIRCUMFLEX
U+0303	NON-SPACING TILDE
U+0304	NON-SPACING MACRON
U+0306	NON-SPACING BREVE
U+0308	NON-SPACING DIAERESIS
U+0313	NON-SPACING COMMA ABOVE
U+0314	NON-SPACING REVERSED COMMA ABOVE

Since the marks in this range are encoded by shape, not by meaning, they are appropriate for use in Greek where applicable. Multiple non-spacing marks applied onto the same baseform character are to be spelled as the baseform character followed by the several non-spacing mark characters in sequence. The order of non-spacing marks is from the base form outward. See the general rules for applying non-spacing marks in Section 2.5.

Variant Letterforms. Variant forms of Greek letters (sigma and beta) are encoded as separate characters in ISO 8859-7 and ISO 5428, therefore this approach is taken in the Unicode character set.

Greek Letters as Symbols. A few of the Greek variants that are used primarily as technical symbols are placed in this range since they are clearly forms of Greek letters. In some cases, however, Greek letters borrowed into symbol usage may be said to have acquired separate identities, such as U+2126 OHM SIGN Ω vs. U+03A9 GREEK CAPITAL LETTER OMEGA Ω, or U+00B5 MICRO SIGN μ vs. U+03BC GREEK SMALL LETTER MU μ. Despite identical glyphs, the semantic distinctions are so great that these characters are assigned separate codes which are cross-referenced to distinguish them.

Punctuation-like Characters. The question of which punctuation-like characters are uniquely Greek and which ones can be unified with generic Western punctuation has no definitive answer. The Greek question mark U+03D7 ";" was retained for use by systems which treat it as a sentence-final punctuation distinct from the semicolon.

Historic Letters. Historic letters have been retained from ISO 5428. The Unicode standard also includes their lower-case forms.

Coptic-Unique Letters. The Coptic script is regarded as a font/style variant of the Greek alphabet. The letters unique to Coptic have been added, including their lower-case forms. A complete Coptic set would be obtained by rendering the whole Greek alphabet in that same style.

Encoding Structure. The Unicode block for the Greek script is divided into the following ranges:

U+0370	→ U+03CF	Letters, punctuation, and diacritical marks from ISO 8859-7
U+03D0	→ U+03D6	Variant letterforms
U+03D7	→ U+03D9	Punctuation-like characters
U+03DA	→ U+03E1	Historic letters
U+03E2	→ U+03EF	Coptic-unique letters
U+03F0	→ U+03F2	Variant letter forms
U+03F3	→ U+03F5	Spacing clones of diacritical marks
U+03F6	→ U+03FF	Currently unassigned

Cyrillic U+0400 → U+ 04FF

The Cyrillic script is a member of the family of scripts derived from ancient Greek. Cyrillic has traditionally been used for writing various Slavic languages, among which Russian is now predominant. In the 19th and early 20th Centuries Cyrillic was extended to write the non-Slavic minority languages of the Soviet Union.

The Cyrillic script is written in linear sequence from left to right with the occasional use of nonspacing marks. Cyrillic letters come in upper- and lowercase pairs.

Standards. The ECMA registry under ISO 2375 for use with ISO 2022 contains several Cyrillic subsets. The Cyrillic block of the Unicode standard is based on the latest and most prominent of these: ISO 8859-5.The Unicode standard encodes Cyrillic characters in the same relative positions as in 8859-5. Four generic punctuation characters are unified with characters in other Unicode character ranges; cross-references to these characters appear in the character names list for this block.

Accented Characters. Some letter forms that might be considered decomposable are not so considered by the Unicode standard when the mark appears integral to the body of the letter. Such letters are encoded as independent characters in order to avoid dispute over whether they have marks or protrusions. For example, many extended Cyrillic characters contain a protrusion at the lower right corner which is subject to wide typographic variability. Also, a few combinations used in archaic Cyrillic are encoded whole because their attachments are not productive.

Unifications. The recently-created alphabets including Extended Cyrillic characters for Soviet minority languages are not well-established. Latin characters included in those alphabets (such as q and w for Kurdish, or U+0292 LATIN SMALL LETTER YOGH for Abkhasian) are not given unique Cyrillic encodings.

Historic Letters. The early form of the Cyrillic alphabet is regarded as a *font change* from modern Cyrillic, because the early Cyrillic forms are relatively close to the modern appearance and because some of them are still in modern use in languages other than Russian (such as U+0406 CYRILLIC CAPITAL LETTER I "I" used in modern Ukrainian and Belorussian). Since the early Cyrillic letters outside of ISO 8859-5, that is, those in the range U+0460 → U+0486, rarely occur in modern form, those letters are shown in the charts in an archaic font.

Extended Cyrillic. These are the letters used in alphabets for minority languages of the Soviet Union. Note that the scripts of some Soviet minority languages have often been revised in the past; the Unicode standard includes only the alphabets in current use, not the rejected old letterforms.

The Unicode Standard • Version 1.0

If, at some future date, the old letterforms are adequately documented and the need for them demonstrated, then they can be added to this block.

Glagolitic. The history of the creation of the Cyrillic and Glagolitic scripts and their relationship has been lost. The Unicode standard regards Glagolitic as a *separate* script from Cyrillic, *not* as a font change from Cyrillic. This is primarily because Glagolitic appears unrecognizably different from Cyrillic, and secondarily because Glagolitic has not grown to match the expansion of Cyrillic. Since Glagolitic is essentially extinct, it is not encoded in the Unicode standard version 1.0.

Encoding Structure. The Unicode block for the Cyrillic script is divided into the following ranges:

U+0400		Currently unassigned
U+0401	→ U+040C	Cyrillic characters from ISO 8859-5
U+040D		Currently unassigned
U+040E	→ U+044F	Cyrillic characters from ISO 8859-5
U+0450		Currently unassigned
U+0451	→ U+045C	Cyrillic characters from ISO 8859-5
U+045D		Currently unassigned
U+045E	→ U+045F	Cyrillic characters from ISO 8859-5
U+0460	→ U+0481	Historic letters
U+0482	→ U+0486	Historic miscellaneous
U+0487	→ U+048F	Currently unassigned
U+0490	→ U+04CC	Extended Cyrillic
U+04CD	→ U+04FF	Currently unassigned

Armenian U+0530 → U+058F

The Armenian script is used primarily for writing the Armenian language. The script is simple, without diacritics. It does have upper- and lower-case pairs.

Modifier Letters. The small marks in the group called Armenian modifier letters are sometimes said to be placed above the alphabetic letters of the words to which they apply, but in modern Armenian typography they are quite uniformly placed *above and to the right,* so that they actually occupy a letter position of their own. Therefore, in the Unicode standard these objects are treated as spacing letters rather than as non-spacing marks.

Encoding Structure. The block for the Armenian script is divided into the following ranges:

U+0530		Currently unassigned
U+0531	→ U+0556	Uppercase letters
U+0557	→ U+0558	Currently unassigned
U+0559	→ U+055F	Modifier letters
U+0560		Currently unassigned
U+0561	→ U+0586	Lowercase letters
U+0587	→ U+0588	Currently unassigned
U+0589		Punctuation
U+058A	→ U+058F	Currently unassigned

Hebrew U+0590 → U+05FF

The Hebrew script is used for writing the Hebrew language as well as other languages, primarily Yiddish and Judezmo (Ladino). Vowels and various other marks are written as *points* applied to consonantal base letters; these points are usually omitted in Hebrew. Five Hebrew letters assume a different graphic form when last in a word.

The Hebrew script is written from right to left (the only other right-to-left script currently encoded in Unicode is Arabic). For a general discussion of character ordering including right-to-left scripts, see Appendix A, Directionality.

Standards. The Unicode standard encodes the Hebrew alphabetic characters in the same relative positions as in ISO 8859-8; however, there are no points or Hebrew punctuation characters in ISO 8859-8.

Vowels and Other Marks of Pronunciation. These non-spacing marks, generically called *points,* indicate vowels or other modifications of consonantal letters. The occurrence of a character in the points and punctuation range, depicted with relation to a dashed circle, constitutes an assertion that this character is intended to be applied via some process *to the consonantal character that precedes it* in the text stream. General rules for applying non-spacing marks are given in Section 2.5.

Shin *and* Sin. Separate characters for the dotted letters *shin* and *sin* are not included in the Unicode standard. When it is necessary to distinguish between the two forms, they should be encoded as U+05E9 HEBREW LETTER SHIN followed by the appropriate dot (U+05C1 or U+05C2). This is consistent with Israeli standard encoding.

Cantillation Accents. Cantillation accents have not been included in this edition of the Unicode standard because the Standards Institution of Israel is currently working on a definitive standard for these.

Punctuation. Most punctuation marks used with the Hebrew script are not given independent codes (that is, they are unified with Latin punctuation), except for the few cases where the mark has a unique form in Hebrew: namely *maqaf* (U+05BE), *paseq* (U+05C0), *sof pasuq* (U+05C3), *geresh* (U+05F3), and *gershayim* (U+05F4).

Final (Contextual Variant) Letterforms. Variant forms of five Hebrew letters are encoded as separate characters in all Hebrew standards; therefore this practice is followed in the Unicode standard.

Yiddish Digraphs. These are considered to be independent characters in Yiddish. The Unicode standard has included them as separate characters in order to distinguish certain letter combinations in Yiddish text; for example, to distinguish the digraph *double vav* from an occurrence of a consonantal *vav* followed by a vocalic *vav*. The use of digraphs is consistent with standard Yiddish orthography. Other letters of the Yiddish alphabet, such as *pasekh alef* can be composed from other characters and therefore do not have independent Unicode values.

Encoding Structure.   The Unicode character block for the Hebrew script is divided into the following ranges:

U+0590 → U+05AF	Currently unassigned
U+05B0 → U+05C3	Points and punctuation
U+05C4 → U+05CF	Unassigned
U+05D0 → U+05EA	Hebrew letters
U+05EB → U+05EF	Currently unassigned
U+05F0 → U+05F2	Yiddish digraphs
U+05F3 → U+05F4	Additional punctuation
U+05F5	Additional point
U+05F6 → U+05FF	Currently unassigned

Arabic   U+0600 → U+ 06FF

The Arabic script is used for writing the Arabic language, and has been extended for representing a number of other languages both major and minor: Persian, Urdu, Pashto, Sindhi and Kurdish among others. Some languages which formerly used the Arabic script now employ the Latin or Cyrillic scripts: Indonesian/Malay, Turkish, Ingush and so on.

The Arabic script is cursive, even in its printed form. As a result, in the handwritten tradition the same letter may be written in different forms depending on how it joins with its neighbors. Vowels and various other marks may be written as *harakat* applied to consonantal base letters; in normal writing, however, these *harakat* are omitted. The script is written from right to left. Arabic and Hebrew are the only scripts currently encoded in the Unicode standard that are written right to left. (See Appendix A, Directionality.)

Standards.   The Unicode standard encodes the basic Arabic characters in the same relative positions as in ISO 8859-6 (= ECMA-114 = ASMO 449).

Encoding Principles.   The alphabet of the Arabic language is well-defined. Each letter receives only one Unicode character value, no matter how many different contextual appearances it may exhibit in text. Each Unicode character value may be said to represent the inherent semantic identity of the letter. A word is spelled as a sequence of these letters. The graphic form (glyph) shown in the Unicode character chart for an Arabic letter (usually the form of the letter when standing by itself) is *not* the identity of that character. The process of converting electronic or abstract code to visual text form and the graphic elements used to compose visual forms are beyond the scope of the Unicode standard. (See also Compatibility Zone.)

Punctuation.   Most punctuation marks used with the Arabic script are *not* given independent codes (that is, are unified with Latin punctuation), *except* for the few cases where the mark has a significantly different appearance in Arabic, namely: U+060C COMMA, U+061B SEMICOLON, U+061F QUESTION MARK, and U+066A PERCENT SIGN. Note that for paired punctuation such as parentheses, the Unicode standard follows a semantic encoding scheme, so that the glyph chosen to represent U+0028 OPENING PARENTHESIS, will depend upon the direction of the rendered text.

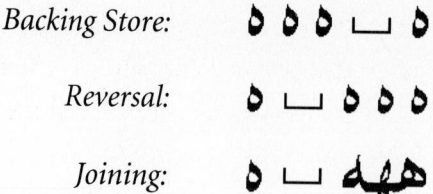

Backing Store:

Reversal:

Joining:

Figure 3-2. Reversal and Cursive Connection

The Non-joiner and the Joiner. The Unicode standard provides two user-selectable zero-width formatting codes: U+200C ᴢᴇʀᴏ ᴡɪᴅᴛʜ ɴᴏɴ-ᴊᴏɪɴᴇʀ and U+200D ᴢᴇʀᴏ ᴡɪᴅᴛʜ ᴊᴏɪɴᴇʀ. The use of a non-joiner between two letters prevents them from attaching to each other when rendered. Each letter assumes the correct form, while the context analysis algorithm stays perfectly regular. Examples include the Persian plural suffix, some Persian proper names, and Ottoman Turkish vowels. For further discussion of joiners and non-joiners, see the General Punctuation block description.

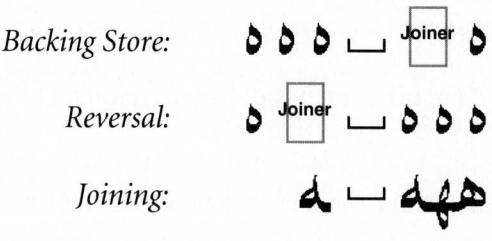

Backing Store:

Reversal:

Joining:

Figure 3-3. Using Joiner

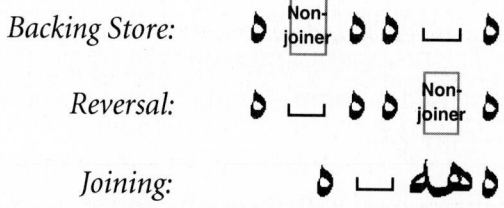

Backing Store:

Reversal:

Joining:

Figure 3-4. Using Non-Joiner

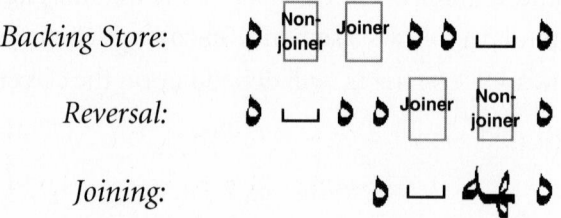

Backing Store:

Reversal:

Joining:

Figure 3-5. Using Joiner & Non-Joiner

Harakat (Vowel) Non-spacing Marks. *Harakat* are marks that indicate vowels or other modifications of consonant letters. The occurrence of a character in the *harakat* range, and its depiction in relation to a dashed circle, constitute an assertion that this character is intended to be applied via some process *to the consonantal character that precedes it* in the text stream, the base character. General rules for applying non-spacing marks are given in the Generic Diacritical Mark block description section. The Unicode standard does not specify a sequence order in case of multiple marks applied to the same Arabic base character, since there is no possible ambiguity of interpretation.

Arabic-Indic Digits. The names for the forms of decimal digits vary widely across different languages. The decimal numbering system originated in India (for example, Devanagari ०१२३ . . .) and was subsequently adopted in the Arabic world with a different appearance (for example, Arabic ٠١٢٣ . . .). The Europeans adopted decimal numbers from the Arabic world, although once again the forms of the digits changed greatly (European 0 1 2 3 . . .). The European forms were later adopted widely around the world, and are used even in many Arabic-speaking countries in North Africa. In each case, the interpretation of decimal numbers remained the same. However, the forms of the digits changed to a degree that they are no longer recognizably the same characters. Because of the origin of these characters, the European decimal numbers are widely known as "Arabic numerals" or "Hindi-Arabic numerals," while the decimal numbers in use in the Arabic world are widely known there as "Hindi numbers."

The Unicode standard includes both Indic digits (including forms used with different Indic scripts), Arabic digits (with forms used in most of the Arabic world), and European digits (now used internationally). Because of this, the traditional names could not be retained without confusion. In addition, there are two main variants of the Arabic-Indic digits, those used in Eastern countries for languages such as Persian and Urdu, and those used in other parts of the Arabic world. The Eastern variant digits are given separate codes in the Unicode standard to account for the differences in appearance and directional treatment when rendering them. (For a complete discussion of directional formatting in the Unicode standard, see Appendix A.)

In summary, the following names will be used in the running text of the Unicode standard:

Name	Code Points	Forms
European	U+0030 → U+0039	0 1 2 3 . . .
Arabic-Indic	U+0660 → U+0669	٠١٢٣ . . .
Eastern Arabic-Indic	U+06F0 → U+06F9	٠١٢٣ . . .
Indic	U+0966 → U+096F	Devanagari ०१२३ . . .
	U+09E6 → U+09EF	Bengali

and so on.

These names have been chosen so as to reduce the confusion involved in the use of the decimal number forms. They do not have any normative content; as with the choice of any other names, they are meant to be unique distinguishing labels, and should not be viewed as favoring one culture over another.

Extended Arabic Letters. Arabic script is used to write major languages, such as Persian and Urdu, but it has also been used to transcribe some relatively obscure languages, such as Baluchi and Lahnda, which have little tradition in printed typography. As a result, the set of characters encoded in this section unavoidably contains spurious forms. The Unicode standard encodes multiple forms of the Extended Arabic letters, because for a number of languages, the character forms and usages are not well documented. This approach was felt to be the most practical in the interest of minimizing the risk of omitting valid characters.

Languages. The languages using a given character are indicated, even though this information is incomplete. When such an annotation ends with an ellipsis (...) then the languages cited are merely the principal ones among many.

Reserved Range. The characters in the range U+0700 → U+08FF are unassigned and reserved for use in future right-to-left scripts. See Appendix B, Implementation Guidelines for a discussion of the implications of this.

Encoding Structure. The Arabic block is divided into the following ranges:

U+0600 → U+064A	Arabic letters and punctuation from ISO 8859-6
U+064B → U+0652	Non-spacing characters from 8859-6
U+0653 → U+065F	Currently unassigned
U+0660 → U+0669	Arabic-Indic digits
U+066A → U+066C	Arabic punctuation
U+066D → U+066F	Currently unassigned
U+0670	Additional non-spacing character
U+0671 → U+06D5	Extended Arabic letters
U+06D6 → U+06EF	Currently unassigned
U+06F0 → U+06F9	Eastern Arabic-Indic digits
U+06FA → U+06FF	Currently unassigned

Devanagari U+0900 → U+097F

The Devanagari script is used for writing classical Sanskrit and its modern derivative, Hindi. Extensions to Devanagari are used to write other related languages of northern India (such as Marathi) and of Nepal (Nepali). In addition to the languages mentioned above, the Devanagari script is also used to write the following languages: Awadhi, Bagheli, Bhatneri, Bhili, Bihari, Braj Bhasha, Chhattisgarhi, Garhwali, Gondi (Betul, Chhindwara, Mandla dialects), Harauti, Ho, Jaipuri, Kachchhi, Kanauji, Konkani, Kului, Kumaoni, Kurku, Kurukh, Marwari, Mundari, Newari, Palpa, and Santali.

All other Indian scripts, as well as the Sinhala script of Sri Lanka and the Southeast Asian scripts (Thai, Lao, Khmer, and Burmese) are historically connected with the Devanagari script as descendants of the ancient Brahmi script, and the entire family of scripts shares a large number of structural features.

The Unicode standard follows the ISCII (Indian Standard Code for Information Interchange) code standard in treating all nine of the official Indian scripts (Devanagari, Bengali, Gurmukhi, Gujarati, Oriya, Tamil, Telugu, Kannada, and Malayalam) in a parallel way. This emphasizes the structural similarities of the scripts and follows the stated intention of the Indian coding standards to enable one-to-one mappings between analogous coding positions in different scripts in the family. Sinhala, Thai, Lao, Khmer, and Burmese depart to a greater extent from the Devanagari structural pattern. The Unicode standard does not attempt to provide any direct mappings for Thai or Lao to the Devanagari order, and future versions of the Unicode standard will not provide direct mappings for Sinhala, Khmer, or Burmese to the Devanagari order.

The principles of the Indian scripts are covered in some detail in this introduction to the Devanagari scripts. The remaining introductions to the Indian scripts are abbreviated, so as to highlight the differences from Devanagari, where appropriate.

General Principles of Indian Scripts. Devanagari and other Indian scripts constitute a cross between syllabic writing systems and alphabets. The effective unit for understanding how the system works is a graphemic syllable, consisting of a CV core and any number of preceding consonants. The canonical structure is ((C)C)CV. The graphemic syllable need not correspond exactly with a phonological syllable, especially when a consonant cluster is involved, but the writing system is built on phonological principles and tends to correspond quite closely to pronunciation.

The graphemic syllable is built up of alphabetic pieces, the actual letters of the Devanagari script. These consist of three major types: consonants, dependent vowels, and independent vowels.

Consonants. The consonant letters each represent a single consonantal sound, but also have the peculiarity of having an inherent vowel, generally *a*. Thus U+0915 DEVANAGARI LETTER KA represents not just *k* but *ka*. In the presence of a dependent vowel, the inherent vowel in a consonant letter is overridden by the dependent vowel.

Consonant letters also occur in half-forms, which are presentational forms used as the initial consonant in CCV consonant clusters. These half-consonants do not have an inherent vowel. Their rendered forms in Devanagari often resemble the full consonant, but are missing the vertical stem which marks a syllabic core. (The stem glyph is graphically and historically related to the *a* vowel.)

Some Devanagari consonant letters have multiple glyphic forms which are contextually dependent on neighboring consonants. This is especially true of U+0930 DEVANAGARI LETTER RA, which has numerous different forms, both as the initial and as the final element of a consonant cluster.

The traditional Sanskrit/Devanagari alphabetic order for consonants follows articulatory phonetic principles, starting with velar consonants and moving forward to bilabial consonants, followed by liquids and then fricatives. ISCII and the Unicode standard both observe this traditional order.

Independent Vowels. The independent vowels in Devanagari are consonant letters which can stand on their own. The writing system treats independent vowels as CV syllables in which the consonant is a *zero*. (This means there is no actual consonant articulation involved, but there is a phonological placeholder treated as if a consonant were present.) The independent vowel letters are used to write syllables which start with a vowel.

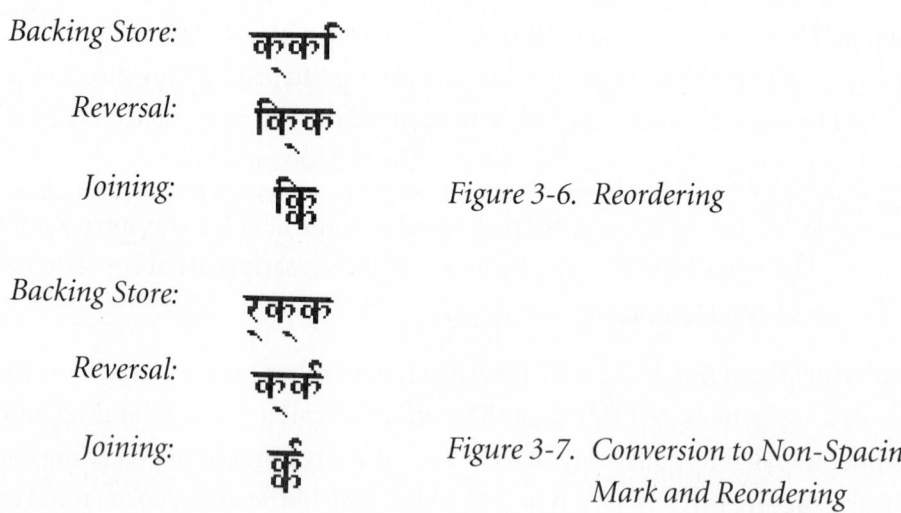

Backing Store:

Reversal:

Joining: Figure 3-6. Reordering

Backing Store:

Reversal:

Joining: Figure 3-7. Conversion to Non-Spacing
Mark and Reordering

Consonant Conjuncts. The Indian scripts are also noted for a large number of consonant conjunct letters. The default behavior for some classes of consonants when combined in clusters is to stack the two consonants vertically. Such forms often involve modification of the glyph forms, or complete substitution of distinct forms for the combination. Glyph modification for combinations of half-consonants with consonant letters is also noted. Such combinations are called conjuncts in

Indian scripts. Well-designed Indian script fonts may contain hundreds of conjuncts, but since they are the result of ligation of distinct consonant letters, those conjuncts are not encoded as Unicode characters. Indian script rendering software must be able to map appropriate combinations of characters in context to the available conjuncts in fonts.

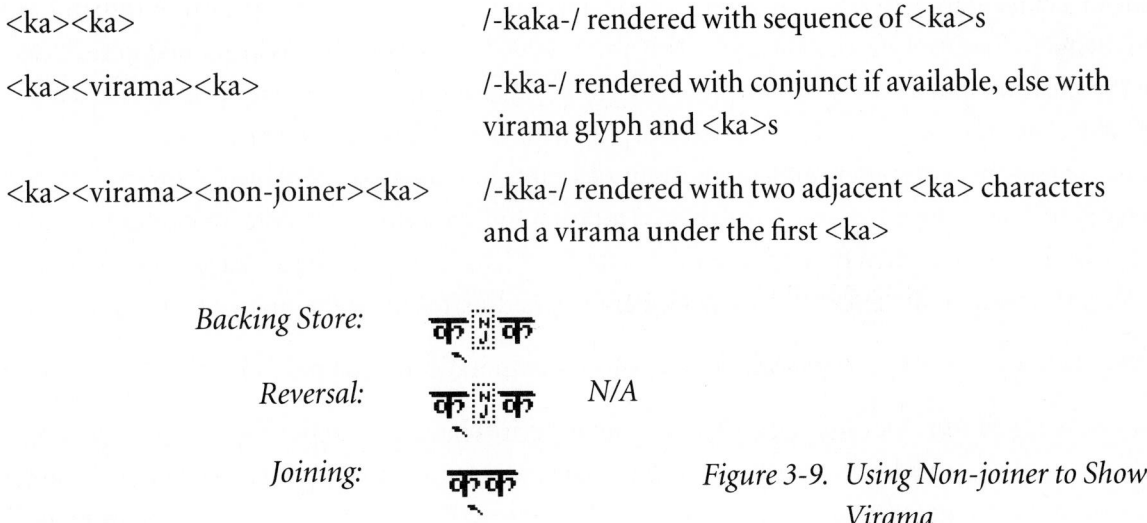

Backing Store:

Reversal: *N/A*

Joining: *Figure 3-8. Conjunct Characters*

Virama. Devanagari and other Indian scripts contain a special character known as the *virama*, or *halant*. The virama combines two successive consonant letters into a cluster, while cancelling the inherent vowel of the first consonant. In Devanagari, the *virama* (U+094D) is a non-spacing subscript character, but its shape may vary from script to script. It is written (in Devanagari) underneath the first of the sequence of consonant letters to be conjoined.

In the Unicode standard, explicit coding of a virama is taken as an indication that the text should be rendered with a conjunct if possible in the font. If the conjunct cannot be formed, then the virama is rendered in relation to the previous character. The ZERO WIDTH NON-JOINER can be used to prevent the formation of conjuncts, if desired. For this purpose, the non-joiner must be placed after the virama in the code stream:

<ka><ka>   /-kaka-/ rendered with sequence of <ka>s

<ka><virama><ka>   /-kka-/ rendered with conjunct if available, else with
                                  virama glyph and <ka>s

<ka><virama><non-joiner><ka>   /-kka-/ rendered with two adjacent <ka> characters
                                  and a virama under the first <ka>

Backing Store:

Reversal: *N/A*

Joining: *Figure 3-9. Using Non-joiner to Show
                                                    Virama*

Dependent Vowels (Matras). The dependent vowels are the usual vowel letters, generally referred to as *vowel signs* or as *matra*s in Sanskrit. The dependent vowels do not stand alone; they depend on a consonant letter for their presentation. A single consonant, or a consonant cluster, has the dependent vowel applied to it to indicate the vowel quality of the syllable. Explicit appearance of a dependent vowel in a syllable effectively cancels the inherent vowel of a single consonant letter.

The greatest variation between different Indian scripts is found in the way that the dependent vowels are applied to the consonant letters. Devanagari has a collection of non-spacing dependent vowel signs which may appear above or below a consonant letter, as well as spacing dependent vowel signs which may occur to the right or to the left of a consonant letter (or cluster of consonant letters). Other Indian scripts generally have one or more of these forms, but what is non-spacing in one script may be a spacing letter in another. Also, some of the Indian scripts have one or more instances of a single dependent vowel indicated by two glyphic pieces—and those glyphic pieces may *surround* a consonant letter both to the left and right or may occur both above and below it.

The logical order for storage of text in Devanagari and all other Indian scripts follows the phonetic order: that is, a CV syllable with a dependent vowel is always encoded as C plus the dependent vowel V in the backing store. Since Devanagari and other Indian scripts have some dependent vowels that are rendered to the left of their consonant letter, the software that renders the Indian scripts must be able to reorder in mapping from the logical (character) store to the presentational (glyph) rendering. In Devanagari, the single vowel sign which is reordered in rendering (but not in the backing store) is U+093F DEVANAGARI VOWEL SIGN I. (Some other Indian scripts have more than one such vowel sign.) Therefore, in the Indic script charts, the dotted circle stands for the base character that precedes it in the backing store.

Devanagari does not have two-part vowel signs—vowels in which half of the vowel is placed on one side of a consonant letter, and the other on the opposite side—but some of the other Indian scripts do. Bengali, for example, has two: U+09CB and U+09CC. The vowel signs are coded in each case in the position in the charts isomorphic with the corresponding vowel in Devanagari. Hence U+09CC BENGALI VOWEL SIGN AU is isomorphic with U+094C DEVANAGARI VOWEL SIGN AU. In order to simplify computer implementations of scripts that use two-part vowel signs, the Unicode starndard uses three positions in the charts (for each Indian script) to encode one or more of the parts of the vowels, when they are not otherwise encodable as two separate characters. Thus U+09D7 BENGALI AU LENGTH MARK is a separate encoding for the right portion of U+09CC.

Other Letters. U+0903 DEVANAGARI SIGN VISARGA is an indicator of final aspiration on a syllable.

Non-spacing Marks. Devanagari and other Indian scripts have a number of non-spacing marks which could be considered diacritic. One class of these is represented by U+0901 DEVANAGARI SIGN CANDRABINDU and U+0902 DEVANAGARI SIGN ANUSVARA. These indicate nasalization or final nasal closure of a syllable.

U+093C DEVANAGARI SIGN NUKTA is a true diacritic. It is used to extend the basic set of consonant letters by modifying them (with a subscript dot in Devanagari) to create new letters.

U+0951 → U+0954 are a set of non-spacing marks used in transcription of Sanskrit texts.

Digits. Each Indian script has a distinct set of digits appropriate to that script. These may or may not be used in ordinary text in that script. European digits have displaced the Indian script forms in modern usage in many of the scripts. Some Indian scripts—notably Tamil—lack a distinct digit for zero.

Punctuation and Symbols. U+0964 DEVANAGARI DANDA is a functional period. Corresponding forms occur in many other Indian scripts. U+0965 DEVANAGARI DOUBLE DANDA marks the end of a verse in traditional texts.

Many modern languages written in the Devanagari script can intersperse punctuation derived from the Latin script. Thus U+002C COMMA and U+002E PERIOD are freely used in writing Hindi, and the *danda* is usually restricted to more traditional texts.

Standards. The Devanagari block of the Unicode standard is based on the ISCII Code as issued by the Department of Electronics of the Government of India, dated 5 July 1988, and as adopted by the Department of Official Language of the Ministry of Home Affairs, Government of India in their publication "Mechanical Facilities in Devanagari." The ISCII standard of 1988 (ISCII-1988) differs from and is an update of earlier ISCII standards issued in 1983 and in 1986. The Unicode standard encodes Devanagari characters in the same relative position as those coded in positions A0 - F4 in the ISCII-1988 standard. The same layout of character encoding points is followed for the other eight Indian scripts in the Unicode standard.

Unifications. ISCII-SPACE (A4) is unified with U+0020 SPACE.

ISCII-INV (DB) is an invisible consonant, used for presentation of dependent vowels in isolation. This character is unified with U+200C ZERO WIDTH NON-JOINER.

Encoding Structure. The Unicode standard lays out the nine Indian scripts in blocks of 128 encoding points, organized in eight columns of sixteen characters each.

The first six columns in each script (0 to 5 or 8 to D) are isomorphic with the ISCII-1988 encoding, except that the last eleven positions (U+0955 → U+095F in Devanagari, for example), which are unassigned or undefined in ISCII-1988, are in fact used in the Unicode encoding.

The seventh column in each script (6 or E), along with the last eleven positions in the sixth column, represent additional character assignments in the Unicode standard which are isomorphic across all nine scripts. For example, positions U+xx66 → U+xx6F or U+xxE6 → U+xxEF code the Indic script digits for each script.

The eighth column in each script (7 or F) is reserved for script-specific additions which do not correspond from one Indian script to the next.

The Unicode block for the Devanagari script is divided into the following specific ranges:

U+0900	Unassigned
U+0901 → U+0903	Various signs
U+0904	Unassigned
U+0905 → U+0914	Independent vowels
U+0915 → U+0939	Consonants
U+093A → U+093B	Unassigned
U+093C → U+093D	Various signs
U+093E → U+094C	Dependent vowel signs
U+094D	Devanagari *Virama*
U+094E → U+094F	Unassigned
U+0950 → U+0954	Various signs
U+0955 → U+0957	Unassigned
U+0958 → U+095F	Additional consonants composed with Nukta
U+0960 → U+0961	Additional independent vowels
U+0962 → U+0963	Additional dependent vowel signs
U+0964 → U+0965	Additional punctuation
U+0966 → U+096F	Devanagari digits
U+0970	Devanagari-specific addition: abbreviation sign
U+0971 → U+097F	Unassigned

The numerous gaps in the Unicode encoding of the Devanagari script result from the following considerations:

U+0900	Reflects undefined position in ISCII-1988.
U+0904	Results from unification of ISCII-SPACE with Unicode SPACE.
U+0934	ISCII-1988 leaves an unassigned position at D4, with the inferred intention of leaving a collation position for Tamil l. The Unicode standard assigns the corresponding Devanagari character (not used in Hindi) to the U+0934 position.
U+093A	ISCII-1988 leaves an unassigned position at DA, with the inferred intention of leaving a position for a marker to aid in the collation of Malayalam. The Unicode standard leaves this position unassigned.
U+093B	Results from unification of ISCII-INV with Unicode ZERO WIDTH NON-JOINER.
U+094E	Reflects unassigned position in ISCII-1988.

U+094F	Reflects undefined position in ISCII-1988.
U+0955 → U+0957	Reflect unassigned positions in ISCII-1988 which are used in the Unicode standard to encode various length marks in Indian scripts other than Devanagari.
U+0958 → U+095E	Reflect unassigned positions in ISCII-1988 which are used in the Unicode standard to encode composite consonant letters formed with U+093C DEVANAGARI SIGN NUKTA (or its correspondent form in other Indian scripts). In Devanagari these represent extended-Hindi letters used, for example, in the transcription of Arabic or Persian loanwords in Urdu.
U+095F	Reflects undefined position in ISCII-1988 which is used in the Unicode standard analogously to the range U+0958 → U+095E.
U+0971 → U+097F	Do not correspond to any position in ISCII-1988, so are simply unassigned positions in the Unicode standard.

Bengali U+0980 → U+09FF

The Bengali script is a North Indian script closely related to Devanagari. It is used to write the Bengali language in West Bengal state (India) and in the nation of Bangladesh. It is also used to write Assamese in Assam (India) and a number of other minority languages (Daphla, Garo, Hallam, Khasi, Manipuri, Mizo, Naga, Munda, Rian, and Santali) in northeastern India.

Special Characters. U+09D7 BENGALI AU LENGTH MARK is provided as an encoding for the right side of the two-part vowel U+09CC BENGALI VOWEL SIGN AU.

U+09F2 → U+09F9 are a series of Bengali additions for writing currency and fractions.

Encoding Structure. The Unicode character block for the Bengali script is divided into the following ranges:

U+0980	→ U+09EF	Follow the Devanagari prototype
U+09F0	→ U+09F9	Bengali-specific additions: currency symbols and so on
U+09FA	→ U+09FF	Unassigned

Gurmukhi U+0A00 → U+0A7F

The Gurmukhi script is a North Indian script historically derived from an older script called Lahnda. It is quite closely related to Devanagari structurally. Gurmukhi is used to write the Punjabi language in the Punjab in India.

Encoding Structure. The Unicode character block for the Gurmukhi script is divided into the following ranges:

U+0A00 → U+0A6F	Follow the Devanagari prototype
U+0A70 → U+0A75	Gurmukhi-specific additions: letters, diacritics
U+0A76 → U+0A7F	Unassigned

Gujarati U+0A80 → U+0AFF

The Gujarati script is a North Indian script closely related to Devanagari. It is most obviously distinguished from Devanagari by not having a horizontal bar for its letter forms, a characteristic of the older Kaithi script which Gujarati is related to. The Gujarati script is used to write the Gujarati language, of Gujarat state, India.

Encoding Structure. The Unicode block for the Gujarati script is divided into the following ranges:

U+0A80	→ U+0AEF	Follow the Devanagari prototype
U+0AF0	→ U+0AFF	Unassigned

Oriya U+0B00 → U+0B7F

The Oriya script is a North Indian script structurally similar to Devanagari, but with semicircular lines at the top of most letters, instead of the straight horizontal bars of Devanagari. The actual shapes of the letters, particularly for vowel signs, show similarities to Tamil. The Oriya script is used to write the Oriya language, of Orissa state, India, as well as minority languages such as Khondi and Santali.

Special Characters. U+0B57 ORIYA AU LENGTH MARK is provided as an encoding for the right side of the two-part vowel U+0B4C ORIYA VOWEL SIGN AU.

Encoding Structure. The Unicode block for the Oriya script is divided into the following ranges:

U+0B00 → U+0B6F	Follow the Devanagari prototype
U+0B70	Oriya-specific addition
U+0B71 → U+0B7F	Unassigned

Tamil U+0B80 → U+0BFF

The Tamil script is a South Indian script. South Indian scripts are structurally related to the North Indian scripts, but they are used to write Dravidian languages of southern India and of Sri Lanka, which are genetically unrelated to the North Indian languages such as Hindi, Bengali, and Gujarati. The shapes of letters in the South Indian scripts are generally quite distinct from the shapes of letters in Devanagari and its related scripts. This is partly a result of the fact that the South Indian scripts were originally carved with needles on palm leaves, a technology which apparently favored rounded letter shapes rather than square, blocky shapes.

The Tamil script is used to write the Tamil language, of Tamil Nadu state in India as well as minority languages such as Badaga. Tamil is also used in Sri Lanka, Singapore, and parts of Malaysia.

The Tamil script has fewer consonants than the other Indian scripts. It also lacks conjunct consonant forms. Instead of conjunct consonant forms, the *virama* (U+0BCD) is widely used in Tamil text. A form of Tamil known as Tamil Granta adds the consonant letters needed to transcribe Sanskrit and Pali consonants.

Naming Conventions for Mid Vowels. The Unicode character encoding for Tamil uses a distinct set of naming conventions for mid vowels in the South Indian (Dravidian) scripts. These conventions are illustrated by U+0B8E TAMIL LETTER E and U+0B8F TAMIL LETTER EE, to be contrasted with the isomorphic positions in Devanagari: U+090E DEVANAGARI LETTER SHORT E and U+090F DEVANAGARI LETTER E. The Dravidian languages have a regular length distinction in the mid vowels which is not reflected in normal Devanagari. U+090E DEVANAGARI LETTER SHORT E is an addition to Devanagari to enable transcription of the Dravidian short vowel forms. The naming conventions are chosen to best reflect the actual character of the vowels in question in the Dravidian scripts, as well as in Devanagari and the other North Indian scripts.

Special Characters. U+0BD7 TAMIL AU LENGTH MARK is provided as an encoding for the right side of the two-part vowel U+0BCC TAMIL VOWEL SIGN AU.

Encoding Structure. The Unicode block for the Tamil script is divided into the following ranges:

U+0B80 → U+0BEF	Follow the Devanagari prototype
U+0BF0 → U+0BF2	Tamil-specific additions
U+0BF3 → U+0BFF	Unassigned

Telugu U+0C00 → U+0C7F

The Telugu script is a South Indian script used to write the Telugu language of Andhra Pradesh state in India, as well as minority languages such as Gondi (Adilabad and Koi dialects) and Lambadi.

Unlike Tamil, the Telugu script writes conjunct consonants with subscripted letters. There are also numerous consonant letters with contextual shape changes when used in conjuncts. Some vowel signs also change their shape in specified combinations.

Special Characters. U+0C55 TELUGU LENGTH MARK is provided as an encoding for the second element of the vowel U+0C47 TELUGU VOWEL SIGN EE. U+0C56 TELUGU AI LENGTH MARK is provided as an encoding for the second element of the two-part vowel U+0C48 TELUGU VOWEL SIGN AI. The length marks are both non-spacing characters.

Encoding Structure. The Unicode block for the Telugu script is divided into the following ranges:

U+0C00 → U+0C6F	Follow the Devanagari prototype
U+0C70 → U+0C7F	Unassigned

Kannada U+0C80 → U+0CFF

The Kannada script is a South Indian script used to write the Kannada (or Kanarese) language of Karnataka state, as well as minority languages such as Tulu.

The Kannada script is very closely related to the Telugu script both with regard to the shapes of the letters and in the way conjunct consonants behave.

Special Characters. U+0CD5 KANNADA LENGTH MARK is provided as an encoding for the right side of the two-part vowel U+0CC7 KANNADA VOWEL SIGN EE. U+0CD6 KANNADA AI LENGTH MARK is provided as an encoding for the right side of the two-part vowel U+0CC8 KANNADA VOWEL SIGN AI. The Kannada two-part vowels actually consist of a non-spacing element above the consonant letter and one or more spacing letters to the right of the consonant letter.

Encoding Structure. The Unicode block for the Kannada script is divided into the following ranges:

U+0C80 → U+0CEF	Follow the Devanagari prototype
U+0CF0 → U+0CFF	Unassigned

Malayalam U+0D00 → U+0D7F

The Malayalam script is a South Indian script used to write the Malayalam language of Kerala state.

The shapes of Malayalam letters closely resemble those of Tamil. However, Malayalam has a very full and complex set of conjunct consonant forms.

Special Characters. U+0D57 MALAYALAM AU LENGTH MARK is provided as an encoding for the right side of the two-part vowel U+0D4C MALAYALAM VOWEL SIGN AU.

Encoding Structure. The Unicode block for the Malayalam script is divided into the following ranges:

U+0D00 → U+0D6F	Follow the Devanagari prototype
U+0D70 → U+0D7F	Unassigned

Thai U+0E00 → U+0E7F

The Thai script is used to write Thai and other Southeast Asian languages, such as Kuy, Lavna, and Pali. It is a member of the Indic family of scripts descended from Brahmi. Thai modifies the original Brahmi letter shapes and extends the number of letters to accommodate features unique to the Thai language, including tone marks derived from superscript digits.

Standards. Thai layout in the Unicode standard is based on the Thai Industrial Standard 620-2529.

General Principles of the Thai Script. In common with the Indic scripts, each Thai letter is a consonant possessing an inherent vowel sound. Thai letters further feature inherent tones. The inherent vowel and tone can be modified by means of letters attached to the base consonant letter. These modifier letters consist of floating vowel signs, floating tone marks, and independent vowel letters. The floating and independent modifier letters are treated somewhat differently in implementations. The floating letters follow the modified consonant in the text stream. The independent vowels are treated as other independent letters and precede or follow the consonant depending on their visual position. The encoding for Thai differs from other Indic alphabets because TIS and ISCII standards made different choices.

Thai Punctuation. Common Thai punctuation includes U+0E46 THAI MAY YAMOK to mark repetition of preceding letters and U+0E5A THAI ANGKHANKHU for ellipsis. U+0E5B THAI KOMUT marks the beginning of religious texts. Thai also uses punctuation marks such as U+002E PERIOD and U+002C COMMA, encoded in the ASCII and Latin1 block.

Thai Transcription of Pali and Sanskrit. Thai is frequently used to write Pali and Sanskrit. When so used, consonant clusters are represented by the explicit use of U+0E3A THAI VOWEL SIGN PHINTHU (*virama*), to mark the removal of the inherent vowel. There is no conjoining behavior, unlike other Indic scripts. U+0E4D THAI VOWEL SIGH NIKKIHIT is the Pali *nigghahita* and Sanskrit *anusvara*. U+0E30 THAI VOWEL SIGN SARA A is the Sanskrit *visarga*. U+0E24 THAI LETTER RY and U+0E26 THAI LETTER LY are vocalic *r* and *l*, with U+0E45 THAI LAAK KANG used to indicate their lengthening.

Alternate Ordering. Alternate Thai vowel signs have been added to permit systems to handle Indic and Thai reordering in a consistent fashion. The phonetic order vowel signs behave as the DEVANAGARI VOWEL SIGN I: they reorder before the preceding consonant. In addition, the *virama* can be used to link consonants into a cluster, so that the phonetic order vowel signs appear before the whole cluster. As with Devanagari, the non-joiner can be used to make the *virama* visible for use in Pali; the non-joiner has no effect on the reordering of the phonetic order vowel signs.

The Unicode Standard · Version 1.0

Encoding Structure. The Unicode block for the Thai script is divided into the following ranges:

U+0E01	Currently unassigned
U+0E01 → U+0E2E	Consonant letters
U+0E2F	Punctuation
U+0E30 → U+0E3A	Vowel signs
U+0E3B → U+0E3E	Currently unassigned
U+0E3F	Currency symbol (*baht*)
U+0E40 → U+0E44	Vowel signs (written to the left of a consonant)
U+0E45 → U+0E46	Punctuation
U+0E47	Vowel sign
U+0E48 → U+0E4B	Tone marks (diacritics)
U+0E4C → U+0E4D	Vowel signs
U+0E4E → U+0E4F	Misc. signs
U+0E50 → U+0E59	Thai digits
U+0E5A → U+0E5B	Misc. signs
U+0E5C → U+0E7F	Currently unassigned

Lao U+0E80 → U+0EFF

The Lao language and script are closely related to Thai. The Unicode standard encodes the Lao script in the same relative order as Thai.

There are a few additional letters in Lao that have no match in Thai. These are U+0EBB LAO VOWEL SIGH MAI KON, U+0EBC LAO SEMIVOWEL SIGN LO, and U+0EBD LAO SEMIVOWEL SIGN NYO.

The preceding two semivowel signs are the last remnants "yl" of the system of subscript medials which in Burmese also includes original "rw." (In Burmese and Khmer, and in Indian scripts, there is in addition a full set of subscript consonant forms used for conjuncts. Thai no longer uses any of these. Lao has just the two.)

There are also two ligatures in the Unicode character encoding for Lao: U+0EDC LAO HO NO and U+0EDD LAO HO MO. These correspond to Thai sequences of [h] plus [n] or [h] plus [m] without ligaturing. Their function in Lao is to provide versions of the [n] and [m] consonants with a different inherent tonal implication. They are regarded as distinct letters.

Tibetan U+1000 → U+105F

The Tibetan script is used for writing Tibetan in Tibet proper and for Tibetan and related languages, such as Ladakhi and Lahuli, spoken elsewhere in the Himalayan region, including Bhutan, India, and Nepal. The Tibetan script is a member of the Indic family of scripts descended from Brahmi. The original Brahmi letter shapes can still be clearly discerned in Tibetan, but Tibetan removes the Brahmi voiced aspirates and adds letters for Tibetan sounds not found in Brahmi.

General Principles of the Tibetan Script. As in all Indic scripts, each Tibetan letter is a consonant containing an inherent vowel sound. Tibetan letters each also contain an inherent tone related to the voicing or non-voicing of the original Brahmi letters. This is not marked in the script. The inherent vowels are modified by means of floating non-spacing characters attached to the base letter. Removal of the inherent vowel is not always marked in native Tibetan words and must be determined from context. Consonant clusters are rendered as conjuncts formed by stacking letters along a vertical axis. Conjuncts are represented in the text stream by placing a Tibetan conjunct marker (virama) between letters to be conjoined.

Tibetan Punctuation. Common Tibetan punctuation includes U+1034 SHEY to mark phrases. *Shey* is doubled to mark full stops. U+1039 TIBETAN RINCHENPUNGSHEY is a decorative variant. U+1035 TSEK is a syllable delimiter. Automatic line wrapping processes can generally wrap after occurrences of *tsek* (there are no interword spaces in Tibetan). U+103A TIBETAN DRUISHEY is sometimes used at the beginning (and less frequently the end) of a text. The character U+1033 TIBETAN GOYIK is an honorific flourish, double (*swasti*) and triple forms of which are used at the beginnings of texts. It normally joins with one or two more occurrences of the same character to form ligatures, and is almost never used alone; it is often followed by *shey* in a decorative form. The *Wheel of Dharma*, which occurs sometimes in Tibetan texts, is encoded in the Miscellaneous Dingbats block at U+2638.

Tibetan Transcription of Sanskrit. Tibetan is also used to write Sanskrit. The Sanskrit retroflex letters are retained; the voiced aspirates are represented by conjuncts formed of consonants placed above the letter U+1021 HA. U+102C NAMCHEY is the *visarga* (see Devanagari), and U+102E NGARO is the *anusvara*.

When the Tibetan script is used to write Sanskrit, consonants are frequently stacked vertically in ways that do not occur in native Tibetan words; this usually indicates deletion of one or more vowel sounds. This stacking behavior is indicated by insertion of a U+104B VIRAMA between the consonants to be stacked. In native Tibetan, the letter U+101A AA sometimes appears as a subscript below another consonant to mark vowel lengthening, with or without another vowel sign. This stacking is also indicated by inserting a *virama* between the consonant and letter AA.

The Unicode standard does not encode superscript and subscript forms for the letters WA (U+1017), RA, (U+101C) and YA, (U+101B), as these shape changes can be determined from context and by the typographical rules for Tibetan. Examples of these modified forms are *ra-ta* (*ra* subjoined) and *ra-go* (*ra* head). In some rare cases, conjoining occurs in written Tibetan without the normal shape changes (non-morphological conjunction); such cases may be encoded in plain text by using a ZERO WIDTH JOINER (U+200D) instead of the *virama* between the letters to be conjoined. The normal rules for form changes in written Tibetan are contained in various grammatical treatises on the Tibetan language.

Encoding Structure. The Unicode block for the Tibetan script is divided into the following ranges:

U+1000	→ U+1022	Consonant letters
U+1023	→ U+1025	Currently unassigned
U+1026	→ U+102A	Non-spacing Vowel Signs
U+102B	→ U+103C	Symbols
U+103D	→ U+103E	Double vowel signs
U+103F		Currently unassigned
U+1040	→ U+1049	Digits
U+104A	→ U+104C	Symbols
U+104D	→ U+105F	Currently unassigned

Georgian U+10A0 → U+10FF

The Georgian script is used primarily for writing the Georgian language. Upper- and lowercase pairs exist only in archaic forms of the script.

Archaic Script Form. The modern Georgian script is a style called *mkhedruli* (soldier's), which originated as the secular derivative of a form called *khutsuri* (ecclesiastical) that had uppercase/lowercase pairs. While *khutsuri* is essentially extinct, it is occasionally seen; the Unicode standard encodes the uppercase form of *khutsuri* as well as the lowercase letters of modern Georgian. The archaic Georgian paragraph separator has a distinct representation, so has been separately encoded at U+10FB instead of being unified with the PARAGRAPH SEPARATOR of the General Punctuation block.

For the Georgian full stop, use U+0589.

Encoding Structure. The Unicode block for the Georgian script is divided into the following ranges:

U+10A0	→ U+10C5	Historic (uppercase) letters
U+10C6	→ U+10CF	Currently unassigned
U+10D0	→ U+10F0	Modern letters
U+10F1	→ U+10F6	Archaic (lowercase) letters
U+10F7	→ U+10FA	Currently unassigned
U+10FB		Punctuation
U+10FC	→ U+10FF	Currently unassigned

3.2 Symbols

The Symbols area of the Unicode standard includes the encoding of symbolic characters, including punctuation, numbers, pictures for control codes, and dingbats.

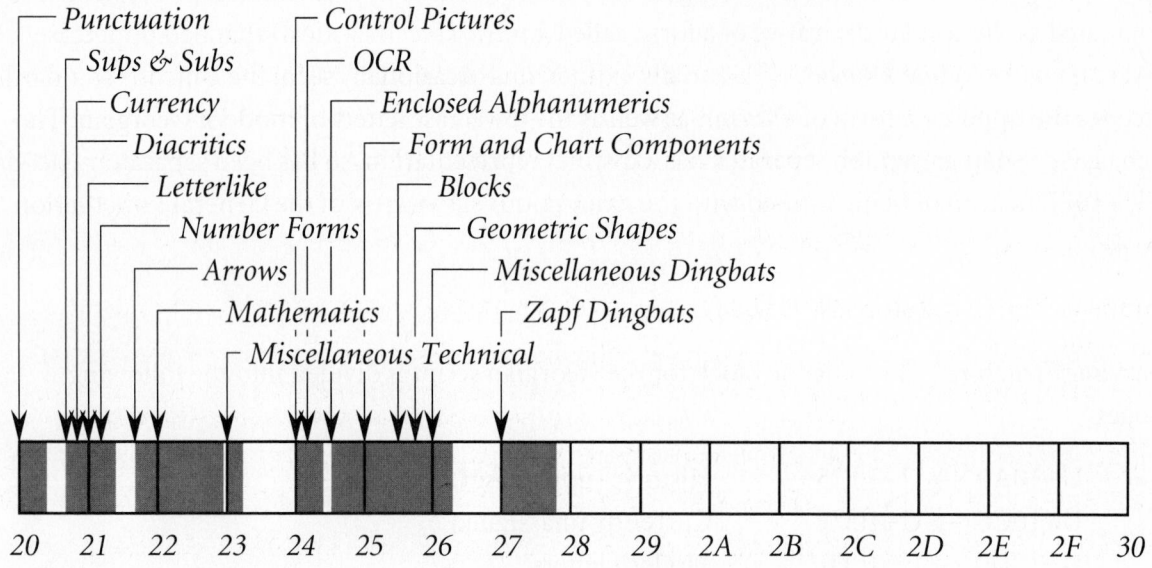

Figure 3-10. Symbols

General Punctuation U+2000 → U+206F

General Punctuation combines punctuation characters and character-like elements used to achieve certain text layout effects. Some punctuation characters can be used with many different scripts. Many general punctuation characters can also be found in the Unicode standard ASCII and Latin1 blocks.

In many cases, current standards include generic characters for punctuation instead of the more precisely specified characters used in printing. Examples include the single and double quotes, period, dash, and space. The Unicode standard includes these generic characters, but also encodes the unambiguous characters independently: various forms of quotation mark, decimal period, em-dash, en-dash, minus, hyphen, em-space, en-space, hair-space, zero-width space and so on.

Punctuation that is considered to belong to a specific script is found in the block corresponding to that script, such as U+03D7 GREEK QUESTION MARK ";" or the punctuation used with ideographs in the CJK Symbols block. Characters drawn with a dotted box are invisible in normal rendering.

Typographical Space Characters. Spaces all have the semantics of being word-break characters. Other than that, the main difference is in the width of the characters. U+2000 → U+2006 are standard quad widths used in typography. The figure space is provided for use in some languages as a thousands separator. The punctuation space is a space defined to be the same width as a period. The thin space and hair space are successively smaller-width spaces used for narrow word gaps and for justification of type. All of the fixed-width space characters are derived from conventional (hot lead) typography. Their functions are mostly replaced by algorithmic kerning and justification in computerized typography.

The *zero-width space* can be used in languages that have no visible word spacing in order to represent word-breaks, such as in Thai or Japanese. There are several varieties of zero-width spaces; the standard one is the *word-break space*, used to add soft word breaks in languages without word spaces. Additionally, there are two spaces which can be used in controlling cursive forms of characters, the *zero-width joiner* and *zero-width non-joiner*. There are also zero-width directional spaces, the *right-to-left zero-width space* and the *left-to-right zero-width space*. All of these properties are orthogonal: the *word-break space* does not affect joining or direction; the joiners neither cause a word-break nor have a direction; the directional spaces neither cause word-breaks nor affect joining.

Having a zero width makes the *zero-width space* similar in some respects to the zero-width layout characters; however, since it is used to delimit word breaks, it may be significant for searching or sorting operations. See also U+0020 SPACE, U+00A0 NON-BREAKING SPACE, and U+3000 IDEO-GRAPHIC SPACE.

Dashes. U+2010 HYPHEN is a unique character (unlike U+002D) that represents the hyphen as found in words such as "left-to-right." U+2011 NON-BREAKING HYPHEN and the U+2012 FIGURE DASH are present for compatibility with existing standards. The NON-BREAKING HYPHEN has the same semantic as U+2010 HYPHEN but should not be broken across lines. FIGURE DASH has the same (ambiguous) semantic as the U+002D HYPHEN-MINUS, but has the same width as digits (if they are monospaced). The EN DASH is used to indicate a range of values, such as 1973–1984. It should be distinguished from the U+2122 MINUS, which is an arithmetic operator. The U+2014 EM DASH is used to make a break—like this—in the flow of a sentence. It is commonly represented with a typewriter as a double-hyphen. In older mathematical typography, the EM DASH is also used to indicate a binary minus sign. A QUOTATION DASH is used to indicate the source of quotations. For general compatibility in interpreting formulas, the U+002D HYPHEN-MINUS, and FIGURE DASH should all be taken as indicating a minus sign, as in "x = a−b."

Quotation Marks. U+201A LOW SINGLE COMMA QUOTATION MARK, U+201E LOW DOUBLE COMMA QUOTATION MARK, U+2039 LEFT POINTING SINGLE GUILLEMET, and U+203A RIGHT POINTING SINGLE GUILLEMET have heterogeneous semantics. They may represent opening or closing quotation marks depending on which language they are used with.

Hyphenation Point. U+2027 HYPHENATION POINT is a raised dot used to indicate correct word breaking as in dic·tion·ar·ies. This is a punctuation mark, to be distinguished from U+00B7 MIDDLE DOT , which has multiple semantics.

Fraction Slash. U+2013 FRACTION SLASH is used between digits to represent rational values: 2/3, 3/9, and so on. Implementations may choose to change the size, shape and positioning of the digits and slash to reflect typographic concerns: such as representing 2/3 as a fraction similar in appearance to U+2154 FRACTION TWO THIRDS. When implementations choose to change the presentation of FRACTION SLASH and surrounding digits, NON-JOINER or a space (including thin spaces) can be used to separate digits that should not be included in the fraction.

Spacing Overscore. U+204E SPACING OVERSCORE corresponds to U+005F SPACING UNDERSCORE. It is a spacing character, not to be confused with U+0305 NON-SPACING OVERSCORE or U+0304 NON-SPACING MACRON. As with all over- or underscores, a sequence of these characters should connect in an unbroken line.

Zero-Width Layout Characters. In some circumstances, it is necessary for text formatting software to be able to specify whether or not adjacent characters may be grouped together. In the case of mixed left-to-right/right-to-left nested text runs, the formatting software must be able to specify the direction of characters that do not have an intrinsic directionality. For this purpose, the Unicode standard provides zero-width layout characters.

These characters are also significant in the Unicode bidirectional formatting algorithm (see Appendix A).

The Non-Joiner. U+200C ZERO WIDTH NON-JOINER is used to request that characters be rendered separately, when they would otherwise normally combine in some manner. For example, a ZERO WIDTH NON-JOINER between an "f" and an "i" will prevent an "fi" ligature from being displayed; a ZERO WIDTH NON-JOINER between an Arabic NOON and MEEM will prevent the normal cursive connection from being rendered, and a ZERO WIDTH NON-JOINER between an "a" and a NON-SPACING ACUTE will cause the NON-SPACING ACUTE to be displayed as a spacing character, and keep it from being superimposed on the "a" (that is, "a′" instead of "á"). The ZERO WIDTH NON-JOINER is also used in script-dependent ways; in Indic scripts, for example, to show the *virama* explicitly. (See the Devanagari block introduction.)

The Joiner. U+200D ZERO WIDTH JOINER is used to request that a character be rendered with a cursive connection when it otherwise would not. For example, to display the presentation form GLYPH FOR INITIAL ARABIC BAA (U+FE90), the Arabic letter *baa* can be followed by a ZERO WIDTH JOINER. The ZERO WIDTH JOINER does not have the semantic value of backspacing, and should not be used for overstriking characters. For example, *a-acute* is not correctly represented by *a-joiner-spacing acute*. The ZERO WIDTH JOINER can be used to indicate a tighter cursive connection between characters or to form a ligature (if available) when the default would be not to form one. On the other hand, the ZERO WIDTH JOINER can be placed between already cursively-connected text with no effect: thus Arabic *baa-joiner-meem* will have the same appearance as *baa meem*. The ZERO WIDTH JOINER also has other uses in some scripts, such as Tibetan. (See the Tibetan block description.)

Left-to-Right and Right-to-Left Marks. U+200E LEFT-TO-RIGHT MARK and U+200F RIGHT-TO-LEFT MARK are treated by directional layout algorithms as though they were normal left-to-right or right-to-left characters, but can be used to achieve many special effects because they are invisible in rendering. (See Appendix A on bidirectional character encoding.)

Layout Characters. Except for their effect on the layout of the text in which they are contained, the zero-width layout characters can be treated just as any other character by the processing software; in particular they do not introduce a mode or state into the character sequence. For any non-layout text processing, such as sorting, searching, and so on, the zero-width layout characters can simply be filtered out.

Bidirectional Ordering Codes. These codes are used in the Bidirectional Formatting Algorithm, described in Appendix A. Systems that handle bidirectional scripts (Arabic and Hebrew) should be sensitive to these codes. The codes include:

U+202A	Left-to-Right Embedding	(LRE)
U+202B	Right-to-Left Embedding	(RLE)
U+202C	Pop Directional Formatting	(PDF)
U+202D	Left-to-Right Override	(RLO)
U+202E	Right-to-Left Override	(LRO)

As with the other zero-width character codes, except for their effect on the layout of the text in which they are contained, the bidirectional ordering characters can be treated just as any other character by the processing software. For non-layout text processing, such as sorting, searching and so on, the zero-width layout characters can simply be filtered out. However, when modifying text, care should be taken to maintain these correctly, since the matching pairs of zero-width formatting characters must be coördinated. (See Appendix A.)

Line and Paragraph Separator. For historical reasons, carriage-return and line-feed are not used consistently across different systems. The Unicode standard provides (and encourages use of) the *line* and *paragraph separator* characters to provide clear information about where line and paragraph boundaries occur. A paragraph separator indicates where a new paragraph should start. This could cause, for example, the line to be broken, the inter-paragraph line spacing to be applied, and indentation of the first line. A line separator indicates that a line-break should occur at this point; although the text continues on the next line, it does not start a new paragraph: no inter-paragraph line spacing nor paragraphic indentation is applied. Since these are separator codes, it is not necessary to start the first line or paragraph, or end the last line or paragraph with them.

Encoding Structure. The Unicode block for General Punctuation is divided into the following ranges:

U+2000 → U+200A	Typographical space characters
U+200B	Zero-width space
U+200C → U+200F	Zero-width layout characters
U+2010 → U+2027	Printing punctuation characters
U+2028 → U+2029	Line and paragraph separators
U+202A → U+202E	Bidirectional ordering codes
U+202F	Currently unassigned
U+2030 → U+2044	Printing punctuation characters
U+2045 → U+206F	Currently unassigned

Superscripts and Subscripts U+2070 → U+209F

Superscripts and subscripts have been included in the Unicode standard solely to provide compatibility with existing character sets. In general, the Unicode character encoding does not attempt to describe the positioning of a character above or below the baseline in typographical layout. The superscript digits one, two, and three are coded in the Latin1 block.

Standards. The characters in this block are from sets registered with ECMA under ISO 2375 for use with ISO 2022.

Encoding Structure. The Unicode block for Superscripts and Subscripts is divided into the following ranges:

U+2070	Superscript zero
U+2071 → U+2073	Currently unassigned
U+2074 → U+2079	Superscript numbers
U+207A → U+207F	Superscript mathematical operators
U+2080 → U+2089	Subscript numbers
U+208A → U+208E	Subscript mathematical operators
U+208F → U+209F	Currently unassigned

Currency Symbols U+20A0 → U+20CF

This block contains currency symbols not encoded in other blocks. Where the Unicode standard follows the layout of an existing standard, such as for the ASCII, Latin1 and Thai blocks, the currency symbols are encoded in those blocks, rather than here.

Unification. The Unicode standard does not duplicate encodings where more than one currency is expressed with the same symbol. Many currency symbols are overstruck letters. There are therefore many minor variants, such as the U+0024 DOLLAR SIGN $, ₫, or $, with one or two vertical bars, or other graphical variation. The Unicode standard considers these variants to be typographical and provides a single encoding.

Claims that glyph variants of a certain currency symbol are used consistently to indicate a particular currency could not be substantiated upon further research. Please refer to ISO DIS 10367, Annex B (informative) for an example of multiple renderings for U+00A3 POUND SIGN.

Encoding Structure. The Unicode block for Currency Symbols is divided into the following ranges:

U+20A0 → U+20AA	Currency symbols
U+20AB → U+20CF	Currently unassigned

The following table lists common currency symbols encoded in other blocks.

Dollar, milreis, escudo	U+0024	DOLLAR SIGN
Cent	U+00A2	CENT SIGN
Pound	U+00A3	POUND SIGN
General currency	U+00A4	CURRENCY SIGN
Yen or yuan	U+00A5	YEN SIGN
Dutch florin	U+0192	LATIN SMALL LETTER SCRIPT F
Baht	U+0E3F	THAI BAHT SIGN

Diacritical Marks for Symbols U+20D0 → U+20FF

Diacritical marks for symbols are generally applied to mathematical or technical symbols. These can be used to extend the range of the symbol set. For example, U+20D3 NON-SPACING SHORT VERTICAL BAR can be used to express negation. Its presentation may change in those circumstances, changing length or slant. That is, U+2261 IDENTICAL TO, followed by U+20D3 is equivalent to U+2262 NOT IDENTICAL TO. In this case, there was a precomposed form for the negated symbol. However, this is not always true, and U+20D3 can be used with other symbols to form the negation. For example, U+2258 CORRESPONDS TO followed by U+20D3 can be used to express *does not correspond to*, without requiring that a precomposed form be part of the Unicode standard.

Other non-spacing characters can also be used in mathematical expressions, of course. For example, a U+0304 NON-SPACING MACRON is commonly used in propostional logic to indicate logical negation.

Enclosing Diacritics. These non-spacing characters are supplied for compatibility with existing standards, allowing individual base characters to be enclosed in several ways. For example, U+2460 CIRCLED DIGIT ONE ① can be expressed as U+0030 DIGIT ONE "1" + U+20DD ENCLOSING CIRCLE O. As with other non-spacing characters, this one can also be applied productively; *circled letter alef* can be produced by the sequence: U+05D0 HEBREW LETTER ALEPH א + U+20DD ENCLOSING CIRCLE O. The non-spacing enclosing diacritics cannot be used to enclose a sequence of base characters. For example, there is no way to represent U+246A CIRCLED NUMBER ELEVEN with the ENCLOSING CIRCLE, since there is no single character NUMBER ELEVEN.

Encoding Structure. The Unicode block for Diacritical Marks for Symbols is divided into the following ranges:

U+20D0 → U+20E1	Symbol diacritics
U+20E2 → U+20FF	Currently unassigned

Letterlike Symbols U+2100 → U+214F

Letterlike symbols are symbols which are derived in some way from ordinary letters of an alphabetic script. The Unicode standard includes symbols here based on Latin, Greek, and Hebrew letters. They are distinct from ordinary letters in that they do not have the alphabetic character property and do not normally collate in alphabetic sequence. They may also have different directional properties from normal letters; for example, the four transfinite cardinal symbols (U+2135 → U+2138) are used in ordinary mathematical text and do not share the strong right-to-left directionality of the Hebrew letters they are derived from.

Styles. The letterlike symbols constitute one of the few instances in which the Unicode standard encodes stylistic variants of letters as distinct characters. For example, there are instances of black letter, double-struck, and script styles for certain Latin letters used as mathematical symbols. The choice of these stylistic variants for encoding reflects their common use as distinct symbols. It is recognized that a particular style can be applied to any Latin letter with a resulting semantic distinction in mathematical or logical text; applications which require such systematic stylistic semantics should achieve them by using styles directly, rather than by seeking to extend the character-by-character encoding of such variants in the Unicode standard.

The black-letter style is often referred to as *Fraktur* or *Gothic* in various sources. Technically, Fraktur and Gothic typefaces are distinct designs from black letter, but no encoding distinctions are implied in the various symbol sources. The Unicode standard simply uses black letter forms as the archetypes.

A similar consideration applies to the double-struck style. This style is not literally double-struck, but is instead an open outline design which gives the visual appearance of being struck twice with a horizontal shift. For encoding purposes this style can be considered equivalent to letterlike symbols rendered in outlined or shadowed typefaces to carry conventional semantic distinctions.

The Unicode standard does not encode serif versus sans-serif styles distinctly among letterlike symbols. This style is always of typographical significance only, and never carries a semantic distinction.

Standards. The Unicode standard encodes letterlike symbols from many different national standards and corporate collections.

Encoding Structure. The Unicode block for Letterlike Symbols is divided into the following ranges:

U+2100	→ U+2138	Letterlike symbols
U+2139	→ U+214F	Currently unassigned

The Unicode Standard · Version 1.0

Number Forms U+2150 → U+218F

Number Form characters are presented solely for compatibility with existing standards. The fractions can be equivalently represented with the U+2044 FRACTION SLASH. The Roman numerals can be composed of sequences of the appropriate Latin letters. U+2180 ROMAN NUMERAL ONE THOUSAND C D and U+216F ROMAN NUMERAL ONE THOUSAND are actually variants of the same glyph, but are distinguished because of existing standards; similarly, the upper- and lowercase variants of Roman numerals have been separately encoded. U+2181 ROMAN NUMERAL FIVE THOUSAND, and U+2182 ROMAN NUMERAL TEN THOUSAND are useful characters, since they represent characters used in Roman numerals that do not have good substitutes elsewhere in the Unicode standard.

Encoding Structure. The Unicode block for Number Forms is divided into the following ranges:

U+2150	→ U+2152	Currently unassigned
U+2153	→ U+215F	Vulgar fractions
U+2160	→ U+2182	Roman numerals and small roman numerals
U+2183	→ U+218F	Currently unassigned

Arrows U+2190 → U+21FF

Arrows are used for a variety of purposes: to imply directional relation, logical derivation or implication, or to represent the cursor control keys.

The Unicode standard attempts to provide fairly complete encodings for generic arrow shapes, especially where there are established usages with well defined semantics; the Unicode standard does not attempt to encode separately every possible stylistic variant of arrows, especially where their use is mainly decorative. For most arrow variants, the Unicode standard provides encodings in the two horizontal directions, often in the four cardinal directions. For the single and double arrows the Unicode standard provides encodings in eight directions.

Standards. The Unicode standard encodes arrows from many different national standards and corporate collections.

Unifications. Arrows expressing mathematical relations have been encoded in the arrows block. For example, U+21D2 RIGHT DOUBLE ARROW ⇒ may be the equivalent of *implies*.

Long and short arrow forms encoded in glyph standards or typesetting systems such as T$_E$X are not represented by separate Unicode values.

Encoding Principles. Because the arrows have such a wide variety of applications, there may be several semantic values for the same Unicode character value: for example, U+21B5 DOWNWARD ARROW WITH CORNER LEFT ↵ may be the equivalent of *carriage return*; U+2191 UP ARROW ↑ may be the equivalent of *increases* or *exponent*.

Encoding Structure. The Unicode block for arrows is divided into the following ranges:

U+2190	→ U+21EA	Arrows
U+21EB	→ U+21FF	Currently unassigned

Mathematical Operators U+2200 → U+22FF

The Mathematical Operators block includes character encodings for operators, relations, geometric symbols, and a few other symbols with special usages confined largely to mathematical contexts.

In addition to the characters in this block, mathematical operators are also found in the ASCII and Latin1 blocks. A few of the symbols from the Miscellaneous Technical block, and characters from General Punctuation are also used in mathematical notation.

Latin letters in special font styles and used as mathematical operators, such as U+2118 SCRIPT P ℘, as well as the Hebrew letter *alef* used as the operator U+2135 FIRST TRANSFINITE CARDINAL ℵ, are encoded in the block for letterlike symbols.

Standards. Many national standards' mathematical operators are covered by the characters encoded in this block. These standards include such special collections as ANSI Y10.20, ISO DIS 6862.2, ISO 8879, and the collection of the American Mathematical Society, as well as the original repertoire of T$_E$X.

Encoding Principles. Mathematical operators often have more than one meaning. Therefore the encoding of this block is intentionally shape-based, with numerous instances in which several semantic values can be attributed to the same Unicode value. For example, U+2218 ∘ RING OPERATOR may be the equivalent of *white small circle* or *composite function* or *apl jot*. The Unicode standard does not attempt to distinguish all the possible semantic values which may be applied to these symbols.

On the other hand, mathematical operators, and especially relation symbols, may appear in various standards, handbooks, and fonts with a large number of purely graphical variants. Where variants were recognizable as such from the sources, they were not encoded separately.

Unifications. Mathematical operators such as U+21D2 IMPLIES ⇒ and U+2194 IF AND ONLY IF ↔ have been unified with the corresponding arrows in the Arrows block.

The operator U+2208 ELEMENT OF is occasionally rendered with a taller shape than shown here. Mathematical handbooks and standards consulted treat these as variants of the same glyph. U+220A SMALL ELEMENT OF is separately encoded, because some existing standards distinguish it from U+2208.

The operators U+226B MUCH GREATER THAN and U+226A MUCH LESS THAN are sometimes rendered in a nested shape. Since no semantic distinction applies, the Unicode standard provides a single encoding for each of these operators.

A large class of unifications applies to variants of relation symbols involving equality, similarity, and/or negation. Variants involving one- or two-barred *equal signs*, one- or two-*tilde similarity signs*, and vertical or slanted *negation slashes* and *negation slashes* of different lengths are not separately encoded. Thus, for example, U+2288 NEITHER A SUBSET OF NOR EQUAL TO, is the prototype for at least six different glyph variants noted in various collections.

There are two instances in which essentially stylistic variants are separately encoded: U+2265 GREATER THAN OR EQUAL TO ≥ is distinguished from U+2267 GREATER THAN OVER EQUAL TO ≧ ; the same distinction applies to LESS THAN OR EQUAL TO. This exception to the general rule regarding variation results from character mapping requirements to some Asian standards which distinguish the two forms.

Greek-Derived Symbols. Several mathematical operators derived from Greek characters have been given separate encodings to match usage in existing standards. These operators may occasionally occur in context with variables using the same characters, or are used typographically quite distinct from normal Greek letters. These operators include U+2206 INCREMENT Δ, U+220F N-ARY PRODUCT ∏ , and U+2211 N-ARY SUMMATION ∑.

Other duplicated Greek characters are those for U+00B5 MICRO SIGN μ in the Latin1 block and U+2126 OHM Ω in Letterlike symbols. All other Greek characters with special mathematical semantics have been unified with the Greek characters in the Greek block since their mathematical semantics do not distinguish them substantially from Greek letters.

Miscellaneous Symbols. U+2212 MINUS SIGN – is a mathematical operator, to be distinguished from the ASCII-derived U+002D HYPHEN-MINUS -, which may look the same as minus sign, or may be shorter in length. U+22EE → U+22F1 are a set of ellipses used in matrix notation.

Encoding structure. The Unicode block for Mathematical Operators is divided into the following ranges:

U+2200	→ U+22F1	Mathematical operators
U+22F2	→ U+22FF	Currently unassigned

Miscellaneous Technical U+2300 → U+23FF

This block encodes technical symbols including keytop labels such as U+232B DELETE TO THE LEFT KEY. Excluded from consideration were symbols that are not normally used in one-dimensional text, but are intended for two-dimensional diagrammatic use, such as symbols for electronic circuits. An unusually large expansion space is provided since it is anticipated that there are a large number of technical symbols that were not considered in the first version of the Unicode standard.

Encoding Structure. The Unicode block for Miscellaneous Technical symbols is divided into the following ranges:

U+2300 → U+2301	APL symbols
U+2302 → U+2307	Miscellaneous symbols
U+2308 → U+230B	Ceilings and floors
U+230C → U+230F	Crops
U+2310 → U+2317	Miscellaneous symbols
U+2318	Keyboard symbol
U+2319 → U+231B	Miscellaneous symbols
U+231C → U+231F	Quine corners
U+2320 → U+2321	Partial math symbols for compatibility
U+2322 → U+2323	Miscellaneous symbols
U+2324 → U+2328	Keyboard symbols
U+2329 → U+232A	Bra and Ket
U+232B	Keyboard symbol
U+232C	Benzene ring
U+232D → U+23FF	Currently unassigned

The usage of crops and quine corners is as indicated in this diagram:

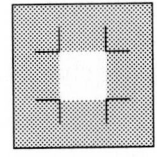

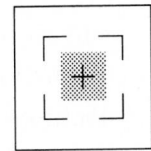

Use of crops　　*Use of quine corners*

Pictures for Control Codes   U+2400 → U+243F

The need to show the presence of the C0 control codes and the SPACE unequivocally when data is displayed has led to conventional representations for these non-graphic characters.

By definition, control codes themselves are manifested only by their action. However, it is sometimes necessary to show the position of a control code within a data stream. Conventional illustrations for the ASCII C0 control codes have been developed.

By definition, the SPACE is a blank graphic. Conventions have also been established for the explicit representation of the SPACE.

Standards. The CNS 11643 standard encodes characters for pictures of control codes. Standard representations for control characters have been defined, for example, in ANSI X3.32 and ISO 2047, but for the control code graphics U+2400 → U+241F only the semantic is encoded in the Unicode standard. This allows a particular application to use the graphic representation it prefers.

Pictures for ASCII Space. Two specific glyphs are provided that may be used to represent the ASCII space character (U+2420 and U+2422).

Code Points for Pictures for Control Codes. The remaining code points in this block are not associated with specific glyphs, but rather are available to encode *any* desired pictorial representation of the given control code. The assumption is that the particular pictures used to represent control codes are often specific to different systems, and are not often the subject of text interchange between systems.

Encoding Structure. The Unicode block for Pictures for Control Codes is divided into the following ranges:

U+2400 → U+241F	Code points for pictures for control codes U+0000 → U+001F
U+2420	Picture for the ASCII space character
U+2421	Picture for *delete*
U+2422 → U+2423	Pictures for the ASCII space character
U+2424	Picture for *new line*
U+2425 → U+243F	Currently unassigned

Optical Character Recognition U+2440 → U+245F

This block includes the symbolic characters of the OCR-A character set that do not correspond to ASCII characters, and magnetic ink character recognition (MICR) symbols used in check processing.

Standards. Both sets of symbols are specified in ISO 2033.

Encoding Structure. The Unicode block for Optical Character Recognitions is divided into the following ranges:

U+2440	→ U+2445	OCR-A symbols
U+2446	→ U+244A	MICR symbols
U+244B	→ U+245F	Currently unassigned

Enclosed Alphanumerics U+2460 → U+24FF

The enclosed numbers and Latin letters of this block come from several sources, chiefly East Asian standards, and are provided for compatibility with them.

Standards. Enclosed letters and numbers occur in the Korean National Standard, KS C 5601, and in the Chinese national standard, GB 2312, as well as in various East Asian industry standards.

The Zapf Dingbats character set contains four sets of encircled numbers (including encircled zero). The black on white set that has numbers with serifs is encoded here (U+2460 → U+2468, and U+24EA). The other three sets are encoded in the range U+2776 → U+2793 in the Zapf Dingbats block.

Decompositions. The parenthesized letters or numbers may be decomposed to a sequence of opening parenthesis, letter or digit(s), closing parenthesis. The numbers with period may be decomposed to digit(s), followed by a period. The encircled letters and single digit numbers may be decomposed to letter or digit followed by U+20DD ENCLOSING CIRCLE. The encircled numbers 10 though 20 may not be decomposed.

Encoding Structure. The Unicode block for Enclosed Alphanumerics is divided into the following ranges:

U+2460 → U+2473	Encircled numbers 1–20
U+2474 → U+2487	Parenthesized numbers 1–20
U+2488 → U+249B	Numbers with period 1–20
U+249C → U+24B5	Parenthesized small Latin a–z
U+24B6 → U+24CF	Encircled capital Latin A–Z
U+24D0 → U+24E9	Encircled small Latin a–z
U+24EA	Encircled number 0
U+24EB → U+24FF	Currently unassigned

Form and Chart Components U+2500 → U+257F

The characters in the Form and Chart Components block are encoded solely for compatibility with existing standards.

Standards. GB 2312, KS C 5601 and industry standards.

Encoding structure. The Unicode block for Form and Chart Components is divided into the following ranges:

U+2500	→ U+254F	Single line box and line drawing elements
U+2550	→ U+256C	Line box drawing elements with double line segments
U+256D	→ U+2570	Curved corner segments
U+2571	→ U+2573	Diagonal line segments and miscellaneous
U+2574	→ U+257F	Line end pieces and connectors

Blocks U+2580 → U+259F

The Blocks represent a graphic compatibility zone in the Unicode standard. A number of existing national and vendor standards, including IBM PC Code Page 437, contain a number of characters intended to enable a simple kind of character cell graphic by filling some fraction of each cell, or by filling each character cell by some degree of shading. The Unicode standard does not encourage this kind of character-based graphics model, but includes a minimal set of such characters encoded for backwards compatibility with the existing standards.

Half-block fill characters are included for each half of a character cell, plus a graduated series of vertical and horizontal fractional fills based on one-eighth parts. Also included are a series of shades based on one-quarter shadings. The fractional fills do not form a logically complete set, but are only intended for backwards compatibility; future versions of the Unicode standard should not extend this set.

Encoding Structure. The Unicode block for Blocks is divided into the following ranges:

U+2580	→ U+2590	Character cell fractional fill characters
U+2591	→ U+2593	Percent shade characters
U+2594	→ U+2595	More character cell fractional fill characters
U+2596	→ U+259F	Currently unassigned

Geometric Shapes U+25A0 → U+25FF

The Geometric Shapes are a collection of characters intended to encode prototypes for various commonly used geometrical shapes—mostly squares, triangles, and circles. The collection is somewhat arbitrary in scope; it is a compendium of shapes from various character and glyph standards. The typical distinctions more systematically encoded include black versus white, large versus small, basic shape (square versus triangle versus circle), orientation, and top versus bottom or left versus right part.

The hatched and cross-hatched squares at U+25A4 → U+25A9 derive from the Korean national standard (KS C 5601), in which they were probably intended as representations of fill patterns; however, since the semantics of those characters are insufficiently defined in that standard, the Unicode character encoding simply carries the glyphs themselves as geometric shapes to provide a mapping for that standard.

U+25CA LOZENGE ◊ is a typographical symbol seen in PostScript and in the Macintosh character set. It should be distinguished both from the generic U+25C7 WHITE DIAMOND and the U+2662 WHITE DIAMOND SUIT, as well as from another character sometimes called a lozenge: U+2311 SQUARE LOZENGE.

The squares and triangles at U+25E7 → U+25EE are derived from the Linotype font collection.

Standards. The Geometric Shapes are derived from a large range of national and vendor character standards.

Encoding Structure. The Unicode block for Geometric Shapes is divided into the following ranges:

U+25A0 → U+25AB	Geometric shapes based on squares
U+25AC → U+25AF	Geometric shapes based on rectangles
U+25B0 → U+25B1	Geometric shapes based on parallelograms
U+25B2 → U+25C5	Geometric shapes based on triangles
U+25C6 → U+25C8	Geometric shapes based on diamonds
U+25C9 → U+25CA	Geometric shapes (miscellaneous)
U+25CB → U+25E1	Geometric shapes based on circles and arcs
U+25E2 → U+25E5	Geometric shapes based on right triangles
U+25E6	Geometric shape based on bullet
U+25E7 → U+25EB	Geometric shapes based on squares
U+25EC → U+25EE	Geometric shapes based on triangles
U+25EF → U+25FF	Currently unassigned

Miscellaneous Dingbats U+2600 → U+26FF

The Miscellaneous Dingbats block consists of a very heterogenous collection of symbols which do not fit in any other Unicode block, and which tend to be rather pictographic in nature. The term "dingbat" is borrowed from the Zapf Dingbats (see the block starting at U+2700), and has come to mean any of a large number of non-alphabetic picture-like symbols which fall outside the more conventional sets of mathematical and technical symbols. The usage of dingbats is typically text-decorative, but they may also be seen treated as normal text characters in such textual applications as typesetting of chess books, card game manuals, horoscopes and so on.

Characters in the Miscellaneous Dingbats set can be rendered in more than one way, unlike characters in the Zapf Dingbats block, in which characters correspond to an explicit glyph. U+2641 EARTH, and U+2645 URANUS, which belong to the Miscellaneous Dingbats set, both have alternative glyphs.

The order of the Miscellaneous Dingbats is completely arbitrary, but an attempt has been made to keep like symbols together and to group subsets of them into meaningful orders. Some of these subsets include weather and astronomical symbols, pointing hands, religious and ideological symbols, the I Ching trigrams; planet and zodiacal symbols, chess pieces, card suits, and musical dingbats. For other moon phases, see Geometric Shapes.

Corporate logos and collections of pictures of animals, vehicles, foods, and so on are not included since they tend either to be very specific in usage (logos, political party symbols) or nonconventional in appearance and semantic interpretation (pictures of cows or cats; fizzing champagne bottles), and hence are inappropriate for encoding as characters. The Unicode standard recommends that such items be incorporated in text via higher protocols which allow intermixing of graphic images with text, rather than by indefinite extension of the number of Miscellaneous Dingbats encoded as characters. However, a large unassigned space has been set aside in the Miscellaneous Dingbats block with the expectation that other conventional sets of such symbols will be found appropriate for character encoding in the future.

Note in particular that the musical dingbats are just that—dingbats—a small set of text decorative characters. No attempt is made to provide a complete character encoding for musical notation. The Unicode standard considers musical notation to be a higher-order text format which requires two-dimensional layout control and complex structures.

Standards. The Miscellaneous Dingbats are derived from a large range of national and vendor character standards.

Encoding Structure. The Unicode block for Miscellaneous Dingbats is divided into the following ranges:

U+2600	→ U+2603	Weather symbols
U+2604	→ U+2613	Miscellaneous dingbats
U+2614	→ U+2619	Currently unassigned
U+261A	→ U+262F	Miscellaneous dingbats
U+2630	→ U+2637	I-Ching symbols
U+2638	→ U+263C	Miscellaneous dingbats
U+263D	→ U+2644	Moon phases and planets
U+2645	→ U+2647	Miscellaneous dingbats
U+2648	→ U+2653	Signs of the zodiac
U+2654	→ U+265F	Chess pieces
U+2660	→ U+2667	Card suits
U+2668		Miscellaneous dingbat
U+2669	→ U+266F	Musical symbols
U+2670	→ U+26FF	Currently unassigned

Zapf Dingbats   U+2700 → U+27BF

The Zapf Dingbats are a well-established set of symbols comprising the industry standard "Zapf Dingbat" font—currently available in most laser printers. Other series of Zapf Dingbats also exist, but are not encoded in the Unicode standard because they are not widely implemented in existing hardware and software as character-encoded fonts. Dingbats that are part of other standards have been encoded in the context of Geometrical Forms and Shapes, Encircled Alphanumerics, and Miscellaneous Dingbats. The order of the remaining dingbats follows the PostScript encoding.

The Zapf Dingbats differ in their treatment in the Unicode standard from all other characters. They are encoded as absolutely specific glyph shapes, rather than as glyphic archetypes for abstract characters which can be represented in different faces and styles. Thus it would be incorrect to arbitrarily replace U+279D TRIANGLE-HEADED RIGHT ARROW → with any other right arrow dingbat or with any of the generic arrows from the Unicode Arrows block (U+2190 → U+21FF). In other words, since the Zapf Dingbats refer to glyphs from a specific typeface, their semantic value *is* their shape.

Unifications. A number of the Zapf Dingbats represent shapes which overlap with regular Unicode symbol characters. Instead of coding both a Zapf Dingbat glyph shape and a separate character whose glyphic representation is normally indistinguishable from that shape, the Unicode standard unifies the two. The characters in question include: card suits, BLACK STAR, BLACK TELEPHONE, and BLACK RIGHT-POINTING INDEX (see Miscellaneous Dingbats); BLACK CIRCLE and BLACK SQUARE (see Geometric Shapes); white encircled numbers 1 to 10 (see Enclosed Alphanumerics); and several generic arrows (see Arrows).

The positions of these unified characters are left unassigned in the Zapf Dingbats block and are cross-referenced to the assigned positions in the other blocks. Applications are free to choose alternative glyphs for representing those characters (as for any normal Unicode characters), including, of course, the exact shapes required for rendering them in the Zapf Dingbat font on an imaging device.

To illustrate this distinction, an application encoding an encircled digit one with U+2460 ① CIRCLED DIGIT ONE may allow for the rendition of that encircled digit in any appropriate typeface — serif or sans serif, roman or italic, and with the circle rendered in different thicknesses. On the other hand, an application encoding an encircled digit one with the Zapf Dingbat U+2780 SANS-SERIF CIRCLED DIGIT ONE ① requires an explicit sans serif glyph from the Zapf Dingbat font for rendering.

Encoding Structure. The Unicode block for Zapf Dingbats is divided into the following ranges:

U+2700	Currently unassigned
U+2701 → U+27BE	ITC Zapf Dingbats, series 100
U+27BF	Currently unassigned

3.3 CJK Phonetics and Symbols

The CJK Phonetics and Symbols area of the Unicode standard includes the encoding of punctuation marks and symbols used in the CJK (Chinese, Japanese, Korean) phonetic alphabets.

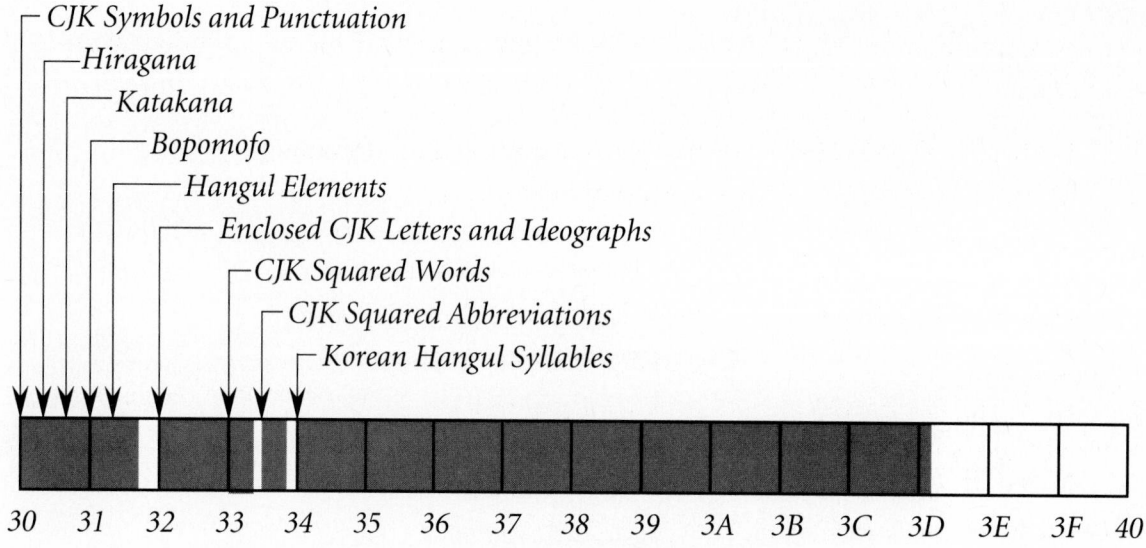

Figure 3-11. CJK Phonetics and Symbols

CJK Symbols and Punctuation U+3000 → U+303F

This block encodes punctuation marks and symbols in use with Han ideographs and Asian phonetic alphabets.

Most of these characters are found in East Asian standards.

Encoding Structure. The Unicode block for CJK Punctuation and Symbols is divided into the following ranges:

U+3000 → U+3006	Ideographic space and punctuation
U+3007	Ideographic zero
U+3008 → U+3011	CJK quotation marks and brackets
U+3012 → U+3013	CJK symbols
U+3014 → U+301F	More CJK symbols and brackets
U+3020	Postal mark face
U+3021 → U+3029	Hangzhou numerals
U+302A → U+302F	Tone marks
U+3030 → U+3036	Other CJK symbols
U+3037 → U+303E	Currently unassigned
U+303F	Ideographic half-fill character

Hiragana   U+3040 → U+309F

Hiragana is the cursive syllabary used to write Japanese words phonetically and also to write sentence particles and inflectional endings. Hiragana is commonly used as well to indicate the pronunciation of Japanese words. Hiragana syllables are phonetically equivalent to corresponding Katakana syllables.

Standards. The Unicode Hiragana block is based on the JIS X 0208-1990 standard, extended by the non-standard syllable U+3094 VU, which is included in some Japanese corporate standards.

Non-spacing Marks. Hiragana and the related script Katakana use the two non-spacing characters encoded in this block to generate voiced and semi-voiced syllables from the base syllables. All normal composites using these marks are already encoded as characters, and use of these composite forms is the predominant JIS usage. In the Unicode design, these non-spacing marks follow the base character. As most implementations and the JIS standard treat these as spacing characters, the Unicode standard also contains two corresponding spacing marks at U+309B and U+309C.

Punctuation-like Characters. These are the Hiragana specific iteration and voiced iteration marks.

Encoding Structure. The Unicode block for the Hiragana script is divided into the following ranges:

U+3040 → U+3093	Mapping of the JIS X 0208 standard
U+3094	Variant form
U+3095 → U+3098	Currently unassigned
U+3099 → U+309A	Non-spacing diacritical marks
U+309B → U+309C	Spacing diacritical marks
U+309D → U+309E	Punctuation-like characters
U+309F	Currently unassigned

Katakana U+30A0 → U+30FF

Katakana is the syllabary used to write Japanese words of Western origin. Katakana is commonly used as well to write Japanese words in order to create visual emphasis. Katakana syllables are phonetically equivalent to corresponding Hiragana syllables.

Standards. The Unicode Katakana block is based on the JIS X 0208-1990 standard.

Punctuation-like Characters. These are the Katakana *conjunctive dot*, the Hiragana/Katakana *prolonged-syllable mark*, the *specific iteration* and the *voiced iteration marks*.

Encoding Structure. The Unicode block for the Katakana script is divided into the following ranges:

U+30A0 → U+30F6	Mapping of the JIS X 0208 standard
U+30F7 → U+30FA	Currently unassigned
U+30FB → U+30FE	Punctuation-like characters
U+30FF	Currently unassigned

Bopomofo U+3100 → U+312F

Bopomofo are a set of letters used to annotate or teach the phonetics of Chinese, primarily the standard Mandarin language. They are used in dictionaries and teaching materials, not in the actual writing of Chinese text. Proper Chinese names for this alphabet would be *Zhuyin-Zimu* ("phonetic alphabet") or *Zhuyin-Fuhao* ("phonetic symbols"), but the informal term "Bopomofo" (analogous to "ABCs") provides a more serviceable English name. The Bopomofo were developed as part of a populist literacy campaign following the 1911 revolution; thus they are acceptable to all branches of modern Chinese culture, although in the People's Republic of China their function has been largely taken over by the Pinyin romanization.

Standards. The standard Mandarin set of Bopomofo are included in the People's Republic of China standard GB 2312-80 and in the Republic of China standard CNS 11643-86.

Mandarin Tone Marks. Small modifier letters used to indicate the five Mandarin tones are part of the Bopomofo system, but in the Unicode standard they have been unified into the Modifier Letter range, as follows:

first tone	U+02C9	MODIFIER LETTER MACRON
second tone	U+02CA	MODIFIER LETTER ACUTE
third tone	U+02C7	MODIFIER LETTER HACEK
fourth tone	U+2CB0	MODIFIER LETTER GRAVE
light tone	U+0209	SPACING DOT ABOVE

Standard Mandarin Bopomofo. The order of Bopomofo letters is standard worldwide. The code offset of the first letter U+3105 BOPOMOFO LETTER B from a multiple of 16 is included to match the offset in the ISO-registered standard GB 2312-80. The character U+3127 BOPOMOFO LETTER I is usually written as a horizontal stroke when the Bopomofo text is set vertically; in the Unicode standard this is considered to be a rendering variation and not a separate character code.

Non-Mandarin Letters. These are very rarely used, but are included for completeness. There are no standard Bopomofo letters for the phonetics of Cantonese or other dialects.

Encoding Structure. The Unicode block for Bopomofo is divided into the following ranges:

elsewhere	Mandarin tone marks
U+3105 → U+3129	Standard Mandarin Bopomofo
U+312A → U+312C	Dialect (non-Mandarin) letters

Hangul Elements   U+3130 → U+318F

Standards. The Unicode standard follows KS C 5601 for Hangul elements.

Encoding Structure. The Unicode block for Hangul Elements is divided into the following ranges:

U+3130	Currently unassigned
U+3131 → U+3163	Modern Jamo elements
U+3164 → U+318E	Archaic Jamo elements
U+318F	Currently unassigned

NOTE: The Jamos encoded in the first version of the Unicode standard are non-combining and are provided for use with data from current Korean standards which contain non-combining Jamos.

CJK Miscellaneous U+3190 → U+31FF

This block currently contains only a set of Kanbun marks used in Japanese texts to indicate the Japanese reading order of classical Chinese texts. They are not encoded in any current character encoding standards, but are widely used in literature.

Encoding structure. The Unicode block for CJK Miscellaneous is divided into the following ranges:

U+3190 → U+319F	Kanbun marks
U+31A0 → U+31FF	Currently unassigned

Enclosed CJK Letters and Ideographs U+3200 → U+32FF

Standards. The CJK Enclosed block provides mapping for all the enclosed Hangul elements from Korean standard KS C 5601 as well as parenthesized ideographic characters from JIS 0208-1990 standard, CNS 11643, and several corporate registries.

Encoding Structure. The Unicode block for CJK parenthesized letters and ideographs is divided into the following ranges:

U+3200 → U+320D	Parenthesized Hangul elements
U+320E → U+321C	Parenthesized Hangul syllables
U+321D → U+321F	Currently unassigned
U+3220 → U+3243	Parenthesized ideographs
U+3244 → U+325F	Currently unassigned
U+3260 → U+326D	Circled Hangul elements
U+326E → U+327B	Circled Hangul syllables
U+327C → U+327E	Currently unassigned
U+327F	Korean standard symbol
U+3280 → U+32B0	Circled ideographs
U+32B1 → U+32CF	Currently unassigned
U+32D0 → U+32FE	Circled Katakana
U+32FF	Japanese Industrial Standard symbol

CJK Squared Words U+3300 → U+337F

CJK squared Katakana words are Katakana-spelled words that fill a single character position if intermixed with ideographic Han (Kanji) characters. Likewise, squared Latin abbreviation symbols are designed to fill a single character position when mixed with Han characters.

Standards. Squared Katakana words are derived from various corporate registries.

Encoding Structure. The Unicode block for CJK Squared Words is divided into the following ranges:

U+3300 → U+3357	Squared symbolic Katakana words
U+3358 → U+337A	Currently unassigned
U+337B → U+337E	Japanese era names

The Japanese era names refer to the following dates:

U+337B	Heisei era	1989/1/7 to present day
U+337C	Showa era	1926/12/24 to 1989/1/6
U+337D	Taishou era	1912/7/29 to 1926/12/23
U+337E	Meiji era	1867 to 1912/7/28

CJK Squared Abbreviations U+3380 → U+33FF

CJK squared abbreviations are encoded solely for compatibility with existing standards.

Standards. Squared Latin abbreviation symbols are derived from the KS C 5601 and CNS 11643 standards.

Encoding Structure. The Unicode block for CJK Squared Abbreviations is divided into the following ranges:

U+3380 → U+33DD	Squared Latin abbreviation symbols
U+33DE → U+33FF	Currently unassigned

Korean Hangul Syllables U+3400 → U+3D2F

Standards. The Hangul Syllables are taken from KS C 5601 and are encoded in the same order as that standard. This means that the Unicode and KS code values can be computed from each other via a simple formula, rather than requiring table lookup.

Encoding Structure. The Unicode block for Hangul syllables is divided into the following ranges:

U+3400 → U+3D2D	KS C 5601 Hangul syllables
U+3D2E → U+3D2F	Currently unassigned

This page intentionally left blank. The material is undergoing review. The revised version will appear in Volume 2.

3.4 CJK Ideographs

This area of the Unicode standard encodes the ideographic Han characters.

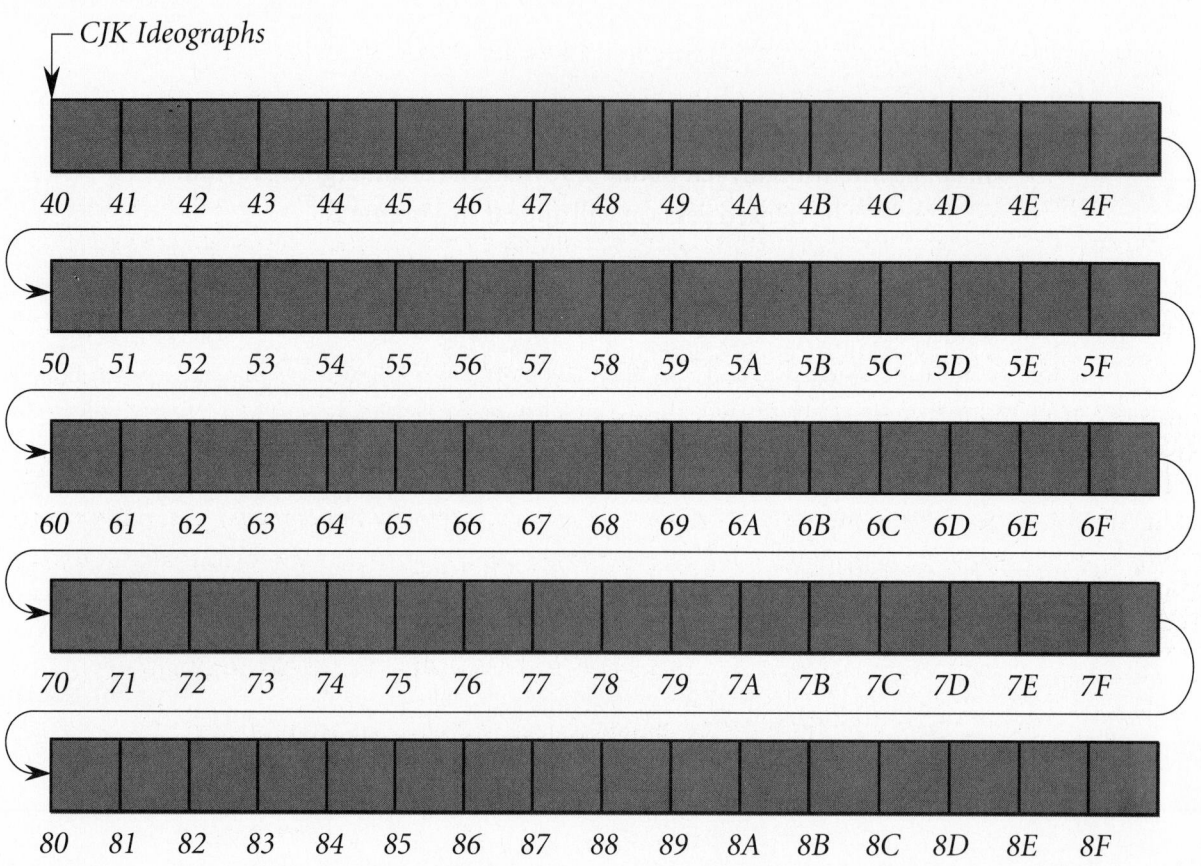

Figure 3-12. CJK Ideographs

Chinese/Japanese/Korean Ideographs U+4000 → U+8BFF

The Unicode standard encodes in this block a set of international Han ideographic characters used in the Chinese, Japanese, and Korean languages.

The authoritative Japanese dictionary *Kouzien*, defines Han characters to be

> characters that originated among the Chinese to write the Chinese language. They are now used in China, Japan, and Korea. They are logographic (each character represents a word, not just a sound) characters that developed from pictographic and ideographic principles. They are also used phonetically. In Japan they are generally called *kanzi* (Han, that is, Chinese, characters) including the "national characters"(*kokuzi*) such as *touge* (mountain pass), which have been created using the same principles. They are also called *mana* (true names, as opposed to *kana*, false or borrowed names).[1]

Until its recent replacement by the English alphabet, written Chinese was the accepted written standard of East Asia. The impact on the writing of the modern Chinese, Japanese, and Korean languages is similar to the impact of Latin on the vocabulary and syntax of languages in the West. This is immediately visible in the mixture of Han characters and native phonetic scripts (*kana* in Japan, *hangul* in Korea) now used in the orthographies of Japan and Korea.

Han Character	Chinese	Japanese	Korean	English translation
天	tian^1*	ten, ame	chen	heaven, sky
地	di^4	ti, tuti	ci	earth, ground
人	ren^2	zin, hito	in	man, person
山	shan^1	san, yama	san	mountain
水	shui^3	sui, mizu	swu	water
上	shang^4	zyou, ue	sang	above
下	xia^4	ka, sita	ha	below

*The superscripted numbers in this table represent Chinese tone marks.

The evolution of character shapes and semantic drift over the centuries have sometimes resulted in changes to the original forms and meanings. For example, the Chinese character 湯 *tang* (Japanese *tou* or *yu*, Korean *thang*) which originally meant "hot water" has come to mean "soup"

---

1. Lee Collins' translation from the Japanese, *Kouzien*, Izuru, Shinmura, ed. (Tokyo: Iwanami Syoten, 1983).

in Chinese. "Hot water" remains the primary meaning in Japanese and Korean, while "soup" appears in more recent borrowings from Chinese, such as "soup noodles" (Japanese *tanmen*; Korean *thangmyen*.) Still, the similarities in appearance and meaning are dramatic and more than justify the Unicode concept of a generic Han script that transcends language.

The "nationality" of the Han characters only became an issue when each country began to create coded character sets (for example, China's GB 2312-80, Japan's JIS X0208-1978, and Korea's KS C 5601-86) based on purely local needs. This problem appears to have arisen more from the priority placed on local requirements, different levels of computerization in the respective countries, and lack of coordination with other countries, rather than out of conscious design.

Efforts to create an international Han character encoding are at least as venerable as the existing national standards. The Chinese Character Code for Information Interchange (CCCII) developed in Taiwan has been in use since 1980. It contains characters for use in China, Taiwan, and Japan. In somewhat modified form, it has been adopted for use in the United states as ANSI Z39.64-1989, also known as the East Asian Character Code (EACC) for bibliographic use. In 1981, Takahashi Tokutaro of Japan's National Diet Library proposed standardization of a character set for common use among East Asian countries.[2]

Of particular relevance to the Unicode standard is China's GB 13000, a universal Han character set that contains all of the characters from the CNS, GB, JIS, and KS C standards. The designers of GB 13000 and of the Unicode Han character set consulted closely for several years on the development of both standards. Because of overlap in their goals and design criteria, in April, 1991, both groups decided to merge their efforts so that the repertoire and ordering of GB 13000 was aligned with that of the Unicode Han character set.

These efforts are all based on the intuitive notion of those literate in the Han script that the identity of the Han characters is independent of language. The existence of an enormous body of cognate characters can be backed by objective evidence including dictionary definitions and vocabulary lists. Statistics assembled by China and the Unicode consortium further show that the overlap among characters encoded in each of the local standards is significant enough for this effort to be worth undertaking.

Distinguishing Han Character Usage between Languages. There is some concern that unifying the Han characters can lead to confusion because they are sometimes used differently in the three languages. Computationally, Han character unification presents no more problems than having a single character set for the Roman alphabet that is used to write languages as different as English and Vietnamese. Programmers do not expect the characters *c h a* and *t* alone to tell us whether *chat* is a French word for "cat" or an English word meaning "informal talk." Likewise, we depend on context to identify the American hood (of a car) with the British bonnet. Few computer users are con-

2. Cited in John Clews, *Language Automation Worldwide: The Development of Character Set Standards*, (Harrowgate, England: Sesame Computer Projects, 1988).

fused by the fact that ASCII can also be used to represent such words as the Welsh word *ynghyd*, which are strange looking to English eyes. Although it would be convenient to identify words by language for programs such as spell-checkers, it is neither practical nor productive to encode a separate Latin character set for every language which uses it.

Similarly, the Han characters are often combined to "spell" words whose meaning may not be evident from the constituent characters. For example, the two characters "to cut" and "hand" mean "postal stamp" in Japanese, but may be nonsense to a speaker of Chinese or Korean. Chinese and Korean use the word 郵票 (Chinese: *youpiao*, Korean: *wuphyo*). However, as a result of Japan's colonial occupation of Korea, many older Koreans probably recognize "cut hand" (*celswu* in Korean) as the Japanese word for "stamp."

$$\underset{\text{to cut}}{切} \; + \; \underset{\text{hand}}{手} \quad = \quad \begin{array}{l} \text{1. Japanese "stamp"} \\ \text{2. Chinese "cut hand"} \end{array}$$

Even within one language, for a computer to distinguish the meanings of words represented by coded characters requires context. The word *tyhuugoku* in Japanese, for example, may refer to China or to a district in central, west Honshuu:

$$\underset{\text{middle}}{中} \; + \; \underset{\text{country}}{国} \quad = \quad \begin{array}{l} \text{1. China} \\ \text{2. Chuugoku district of Honshuu} \end{array}$$

Coding these two characters as four so as to capture this distinction would probably cause more confusion and still not provide a general solution. The Unicode standard leaves the general solution up to a higher level of software and does not attempt to encode the language of the Han characters.

Standards. The Unicode standard draws its Han character repertoire from the following Han character standards:

Standard	Number of Characters
ANSI Z39.64-1989 (EACC)	13,481
Big Five	13,053
CCCII, level 1	4,808
CNS 11643-1986	13,051
CNS 11643-1986 User Characters	3,418
GB 2312-1980 (GB_0)	6,763
GB 12345-90 (GB_1)*	2,176
GB 7589-87 (GB_3)	7,327
GB 7590-87 (GB_5)	7,039
General Use Characters for Modern Chinese (GB_7)†	41
GB 8565-89 (GB_8)‡	287

Standard	Number of Characters
GB 12052-89 (Korean)	94
Han Character Shapes Permitted for Personal Names§	103
IBM Selected Japanese	360
IBM Selected Korean	6
JEF (Fujitsu)	3,149
JIS X 0208-1990	6,355
JIS X 0212-1990	5,801
KS C 5601-1987	4,888
PRC Telegraph Code	~8,000
Taiwan Telegraph Code	9,040
Xerox Chinese	9,776
Total characters covered	~119,016
Total unique characters	21,001

* Characters not already included in GB_0.

† Characters not already included in GB_0, GB_1, GB_3, GB_5, or GB_8.

‡ Characters not already included in GB_0, GB_1, GB_3, or GB_5.

§ The Japanese title of "Han characters Shapes Permitted for Personal Names (Japan)" is
   "Jinmei-you kanzi kyoyou zitai-hyou," from "Zyouyou kanzi-hyou gendai kanazukai"
   (Ministry of Finance Printing Department; Tokyo, 1991).

Selection of Han Characters. The Unicode standard preserves the identity of characters across the combined source standards. This allows the Unicode standard to maintain any distinctions in character shape and usage defined as significant in each standard and guarantees a unique mapping to and from the source standards. Thus, where variant forms are given separate codes within one standard, they are also kept separate within the Unicode standard.

For example, the Unicode standard preserves all six variants of the character "sword" found in JIS X 0208-1990:

劍 劍 剱 劔 劒 釼

sword

Note, though, that 劍 and 劒 from KS C 5601-1987 are "unified" with the corresponding characters from JIS X 0208-1990.

Also, the Unicode standard separately codes the approximately 2,000 modern Chinese simplified characters which have corresponding traditional variants in extensions to the GB standards.

The process of merging Han characters from the different source character sets is as follows:

1. Group each character from one of the source character sets with cognate characters from the other sets.

2. Encode cognates that are separate in any one of the source national standards as separate characters in the unified set. This permits a simple round-trip mapping between the unified set and each source set.

3. Encode cognates whose appearance is sufficiently dissimilar and unique to a single source set as separate characters in the unified set.

This algorithm is the method used in creating the Unicode standard and GB 13000. The validity of this approach was verified in 1991 by an independent team of East Asian experts at the University of Toronto. (See the *Unicode CJK Unification Verification Project Final Report*. Kazuko Nakajima, Project Leader, Associate Professor, Department of East Asian Studies, University of Toronto.)

The most interesting question in unifying the Han characters is how to handle variations in character shape across the standards. In unification, the Unicode standard attempts to preserve the same tolerance for variation allowed within any single standard. The Unicode standard relies primarily on the guidelines published by JIS, the Chinese proposal for a common Han character encoding, ISO/JTC1/WG2/N480, and recommendations from the University of Toronto. Where these guidelines suggest that two forms constitute a minor difference, the Unicode standard assigns a single code. Otherwise, separate codes are assigned.

JIS X 0208-1990, §3.4 漢字の異体字の取扱 "The handling of variant Han characters" gives the following six examples of minor differences:

1. Differences in the direction, length, or curve of a stroke:

    羽 ≈ 羽 ， 說 ≈ 説

2. Whether strokes touch or intersect each other:

    包 ≈ 包 ， 雪 ≈ 雪

3. Fusion of strokes:

    研 ≈ 研 ， 每 ≈ 毎

4. The addition or subtraction of a stroke:

    者 ≈ 者 ， 近 ≈ 近

5. Differences in stroke type:

    靑 ≈ 青 ， 喝 ≈ 喝

6. Stroke simplification:

    卽 ≈ 即 ， 社 ≈ 社

These rules are applied after filtering out characters with distinct semantics such as

$$土 \quad ≠ \quad 士$$

earth   warrior, scholar

where a superficial application of rule 1, for example, would result in a false unification.

The small number of national characters invented outside of China such as Korean 乭 (*mal*, phonetic used in place names), Japanese 辻 (*tsuji*, cross roads) and 峠 (*touge*, mountain pass) are of course coded separately. Note, however, that 峠 (Korean reading *sang*) is also found in KS C 5601-1987, and therefore unified with the JIS character in the Unicode standard.

Han Character Ordering. The ordering of the Unicode Han characters follows GB 13000. The GB 13000 ordering is based on the position of characters as they are listed in four major Han character dictionaries. In order of priority, these are: the *Kang Xi Zidian* (general East Asia), the *Dai Kanwa Ziten* (Japan), *Hanyu Da Zidian* (China), and the *Dae Jaweon* (Korea). The *Kang Xi Zidian* was chosen as primary because it contains most of the source characters and because the dictionary itself and the principles of character ordering it employs are commonly used throughout East Asia.

Characters are first assigned a *Kang Xi* ordering if they have one. This becomes the basis for the ordering of the main character list. Characters not found in *Kang Xi* are then ordered according to their position in the *Dai Kanwa Ziten*. These characters are then merged into the main list by placing each of them after the closest preceding *Dai Kanwa Ziten* character that also has a position in the main list. Where there are conflicts, the *Dai Kanwa Ziten* ordering is followed in placing characters after the common character from the main list. The process is then repeated for characters that appear only in the *Hanyu Da Zidian* and the *Dae Jaweon*.

GB characters with simplified *Kang Xi* radicals are placed in a group following the traditional *Kang Xi* radical from which the simplified radical is derived. For example, characters with the simplified radical 讠 corresponding to *Kang Xi* radical 言 follow the last non-simplified character having 言 as a radical. The sub-ordering for these simplified characters is that of the *Hanyu Da Zidian*.

The few characters which are not found in any of the four dictionaries are placed following characters with the same *Kang Xi* radical and stroke count.

Selection of Glyphs for the Charts. Since the Unicode standard is not a glyph standard, the selection of font for any particular character should not be considered normative. Rather, the intent is to suggest an acceptable range of appearance based on JIS X 0208-1990, §3.4 and on the Chinese principles for recognition of common Han characters, ISO/JTC1/WG2/N480.

The selection of a particular glyph is based on the availability of that glyph in a font. Where several glyphs are available, the preferred order reflects the legibility of the glyphs in the available font. This ordering from clearest to least clear is: Morisawa Ryumin Light, Song, Macintosh Myongjo,

Macintosh Simplified Chinese Screen font, and CCCII bitmap. Many glyphs have been drawn just for the Unicode standard.

Geta in Code Cells. Space within the Unicode Han block has been left for a small number of characters defined in GB 13000 and included in the Unicode standard, but for which glyphs were not available for printing. The proper glyphs will be added in a subsequent version of the Unicode standard.

3.5 Private Use Area

The Private Use area of the Unicode standard encodes area reserved for private use.

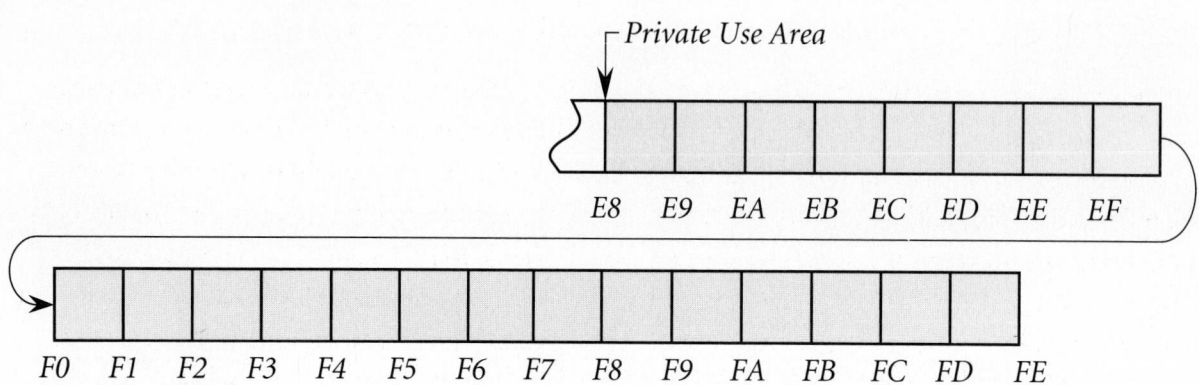

Figure 3-13. Private Use Area

Private Use Area U+E800 → U+FDFF

The Private Use Area is reserved for use by software developers and end users who need a special set of characters for their application programs. The code points in this area are reserved for private use and do not have defined, interpretable semantics except by private agreement.

Corporate Use Zone. Systems vendors and/or software developers may need to reserve some private use characters for internal use by their software. The Corporate Use Zone is the preferred area for such reservations. Assignments of character semantics in this zone could be completely internal, hidden from the end users, and used only for vendor-specific application support, or could be published as vendor-specific character assignments available to applications and end users. An example of the former case would be assignment of a character code to a system support operation such as <MOVE> or <COPY>; an example of the latter case would be assignment of a character code to a vendor-specific logo character such as Apple's *apple* character.

End User Zone. The End User Zone is intended for private use character definition by end users, or for scratch allocations of character space by end user applications.

Allocation of Zones. Vendors may choose to reserve private use codes in the Corporate Use Zone and make some defined portion of the End User Zone available for completely free end user definition. This convention is for the convenience of system vendors and software developers. No firm dividing line between the two zones is defined, as different users may have different requirements. No provision is made in the Unicode standard for avoiding a "stack-heap collision" between the two zones in the Private Use Area.

Promotion of Private Use Characters. In future versions of the Unicode standard, some characters which have been defined by one vendor or another in the Corporate Use Zone may be defined as regular Unicode characters, if their usage is widespread enough that they become candidates for general use. Likewise, some well-defined set of characters (such as an ancient script) may be used by private agreement in the End User Zone and later be proposed for formal inclusion as a defined block in normal Unicode character code space.

These possibilities are to be distinguished from the treatment of characters defined in the Compatibility Zone.

Encoding Structure. The Private Use Area is divided into the following ranges:

> U+E800 → U+FDFF   Reserved for private use

By convention, the Private Use Area is divided into a Corporate Use Zone, starting at U+FDFF and extending downward in values, and an End User Zone, starting at U+E800 and extending upward in values.

3.6 Compatibility Zone

The Compatibility Zone of the Unicode standard contains characters that can be mapped to other areas.

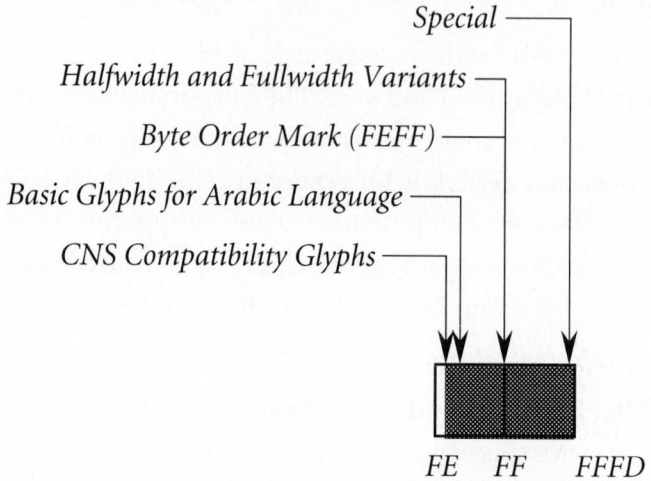

Figure 3-14. Compatibility Zone

The Unicode Standard · Version 1.0

Compatibility Zone U+FE00 → U+FFEF

Description. The Compatibility Zone is so named because it contains miscellaneous glyphs, contextual or orientational variants, and width variants that can legitimately be mapped to other characters in the Unicode standard, but which require specific Unicode values for compatibility with pre-existing character standards. Receivers of Compatibility Zone characters, if they so desire, are free to replace those characters by corresponding regular Unicode characters under any circumstances without being considered non-conformant. Tables for canonical mappings between Compatibility Zone characters and characters in the Unicode character encoding are located in Chapter 5.

Compatibility Zone characters are provided solely for backwards compatibility to existing standards. The content of the Compatibility Zone includes characters which are in widespread use in existing implementations, but whose semantics or usage (such as vertical forms, contextual shapes, small, half width or full width variants) is fundamentally at odds with the way in which the Unicode character encoding generally handles characters. Compatibility Zone characters are publicly defined for Unicode code interchange, but are *not* candidates for inclusion in the Unicode standard.

Standards. The Compatibility Zone includes basic contextual forms of Arabic glyphs that are encoded on some corporate code pages, as well as spacing forms of Arabic accents. The Compatibility Zone also contains characters for compatibility with CNS 11643, JIS X 0208, and KS C 5601, and their implementation in "shift" forms in corporate standards and other coded implementations of the CJK standards.

CNS 11643 Compatibility Glyphs. U+FE30 → U+FE4F contain vertical rendering forms for a number of glyphs, as well as other glyphs included for compatibility with CNS 11643. The vertical rendering forms should be mapped to their non-vertical prototypes, as Unicode-conformant software should adjust horizontal and vertical rendering forms by rendering context, rather than encoding them as distinct characters.

Small Glyph Variants. U+FE50 → U+FE6F contain small glyph variants for compatibility with CNS 11643. The semantic of these small variants is unclear, although they may be intended for superscript rendering. They should be mapped to corresponding characters in the Unicode standard.

Contextual Shape Forms for Arabic Glyphs. U+FE70 → U+FEFE contain contextual shape forms for initial, medial, final, and isolated forms of Arabic glyphs, for compatibility with pre-existing standards and implementations which use these forms as characters. They can be replaced by letters from the Arabic block (U+0600 → U+06FF). Implementations can handle contextual glyph shaping by rendering rules when accessing glyphs from fonts, rather than by encoding contextual shapes as characters.

Halfwidth and Fullwidth Variants. The Unicode standard includes the basic halfwidth Katakana and Hangul as well as fullwidth ASCII characters for compatibility with the various CJK coding standards. The term "halfwidth" refers to characters which are, in East Asian computer implementations, rendered at half the standard width of a normal ideographic character. "Fullwidth" refers to the normal width of a Hangul or Chinese character. In many Japanese systems, for instance, ASCII characters print as halfwidth, but are cloned in a fullwidth version in the JIS character set; the fullwidth version of ASCII characters are encoded in the Compatibility Zone to distinguish them from the halfwidth version when necessary for backwards compatibility with preexisting data. In the Unicode standard, the preferred way to distinguish between full- and halfwidth characters is through font changes.

Encoding structure. The Unicode block for the Compatibility Zone is divided into the following ranges:

U+FE00	→ U+FE2F	Currently unassigned
U+FE30	→ U+FE44	Vertical glyph variants
U+FE45	→ U+FE48	Currently unassigned
U+FE49	→ U+FE4F	Overscores and underscores
U+FE50	→ U+FE6B	Small glyph variants
U+FE6C	→ U+FE6F	Currently unassigned
U+FE70	→ U+FEFC	Glyphs for basic Arabic
U+FEFD	→ U+FEFE	Currently unassigned
U+FEFF		Byte order mark
U+FF00		Currently unassigned
U+FF01	→ U+FF5E	Fullwidth ASCII
U+FF5F		Currently unassigned
U+FF60	→ U+FF9F	Halfwidth Katakana
U+FFA0	→ U+FFDF	Halfwidth Hangul
U+FFE0	→ U+FFE6	Fullwidth symbols
U+FFE7	→ U+FFEF	Currently unassigned

Special U+FFF0 → U+FFFD

The fourteen Unicode values from U+FFF0 → U+FFFD are reserved for special character definition. The only special character currently defined is U+FFFD REPLACEMENT CHARACTER, which is the general substitute character in the Unicode standard. That character can be substituted for any "unknown" character in another encoding which cannot be mapped in terms of known Unicode values (see Appendix C).

In addition, there are two 16-bit unsigned hexadecimal values which are defined NOT to be Unicode character values, and one value which may be used to flag and test for correct byte order polarity. U+FEFF BYTE ORDER MARK and U+FFFE are the (byte-swapped) mirror image of each other. They are not control characters that select the byte order of text; rather, their function is to assure recipients that they are looking at a correctly byte-ordered file.

U+FEFF. This Unicode special character is defined to be a signal of correct byte-order polarity. An application may use this signal character to explicitly enable the "big-endian" or "little-endian" byte order to be determined in Unicode text which may exist in either byte order (for example in networks which mix Intel and Motorola or RISC CPU architectures for data storage). U+FEFF is the "correct" or legal order; finding a value U+FFFE is a signal that text of the "incorrect" byte order for an interpreting process has been encountered.

U+FFFE. The 16-bit unsigned hexadecimal value U+FFFE is *not* a Unicode character value, and should be taken as a signal that Unicode characters should be byte-swapped before interpretation. U+FFFE should only be interpreted as an incorrectly byte-swapped version of U+FEFF.

U+FFFF. The 16-bit unsigned hexadecimal value U+FFFF is *not* a Unicode character value, and can be used by an application as a error code or other non-character value. The specific interpretation of U+FFFF is not defined by the Unicode standard, so it can be viewed as a kind of private-use non-character.

Encoding Structure. The Unicode block for Special characters is divided into the following ranges:

U+FFF0 → U+FFFC	Currently unassigned
U+FFFD	Replacement character
U+FEFF	Byte order mark
U+FFFE	Not a character; signal value
U+FFFF	Not a character

3.7 Code Charts

This section contains the Unicode code charts. These charts are laid out in blocks of 256 characters each to assist in the identification of hexadecimal Unicode values. The charts are in column order; the code values increase sequentially down in each column.

The individual character blocks are divided by heavy vertical lines. Each character block is associated with a general block description earlier in this chapter. Character block boundaries are not indicative of formal subsets, conformance requirements, or code structure except insofar as they coincide with major zones (for example, the Compatibility Zone) or directional properties referenced by the bidirectional algorithm (for example, Hebrew and Arabic character blocks).

The code charts for all East Asian ideographic characters are located in the Unicode Standard, Volume Two.

	Control		ASCII							Control		Latin1					
	000	001	002	003	004	005	006	007	008	009	00A	00B	00C	00D	00E	00F
0	NUL	DLE	SPACE	0	@	P	`	p	CTRL	CTRL	NB SP	°	À	Ð	à	ð
1	SOH	DC1	!	1	A	Q	a	q	CTRL	CTRL	¡	±	Á	Ñ	á	ñ
2	STX	DC2	"	2	B	R	b	r	CTRL	CTRL	¢	²	Â	Ò	â	ò
3	ETX	DC3	#	3	C	S	c	s	CTRL	CTRL	£	³	Ã	Ó	ã	ó
4	EOT	DC4	$\|$	4	D	T	d	t	CTRL	CTRL	¤	´	Ä	Ô	ä	ô
5	ENQ	NAK	%	5	E	U	e	u	CTRL	CTRL	¥|¥	µ	Å	Õ	å	õ
6	ACK	SYN	&	6	F	V	f	v	CTRL	CTRL	¦	¶	Æ	Ö	æ	ö
7	BEL	ETB	'	7	G	W	g	w	CTRL	CTRL	§	·	Ç	×	ç	÷
8	BS	CAN	(	8	H	X	h	x	CTRL	CTRL	¨	¸	È	Ø	è	ø
9	HT	EM	)	9	I	Y	i	y	CTRL	CTRL	©	¹	É	Ù	é	ù
A	LF	SUB	*	:	J	Z	j	z	CTRL	CTRL	ª	º	Ê	Ú	ê	ú
B	VT	ESC	+	;	K	[	k	{	CTRL	CTRL	«	»	Ë	Û	ë	û
C	FF	FS	,	<	L	\	l	|	CTRL	CTRL	¬	¼|¼	Ì	Ü	ì	ü
D	CR	GS	—	=	M	]	m	}	CTRL	CTRL		½|½	Í	Ý	í	ý
E	SO	RS	.	>	N	^	n	~|˜	CTRL	CTRL	®	¾|¾	Î	Þ	î	þ
F	SI	US	/	?	O	_	o	DEL	CTRL	CTRL	¯	¿	Ï	ß	ï	ÿ

European Latin / Extended Latin

	010	011	012	013	014	015	016	017	018	019	01A	01B	01C	01D	01E	01F
0	Ā	Đ	Ġ	İ	l·	Ő	Š	Ű	ђ	Ɛ	Ɔ	ư	||/	ǐ	Ǟ	ǰ
1	ā	đ	ġ	ı	Ł	ő	š	ű	Ɓ	Ƒ	σ	Ʊ	‖//	Ǒ	ǟ	
2	Ă	Ē	Ģ	Ĳ	ł	Œ	Ţ|Ť	Ų	Ƃ	ƒ	Ɵ	Ʋ	⧺⧸	ǒ	Ǣ	
3	ă	ē	ǧ|ǵ	ĳ	Ń	œ	ţ|ť	ų	ƃ	Ɠ	ƪ	Ƴ	!	Ǔ	ǣ	
4	Ą	Ĕ	Ĥ	Ĵ	ń	Ŕ	Ŧ|Ŧ	Ŵ	Ƅ	Ɣ	Ƥ	ƴ	DŽ	ǔ	Ǥ	
5	ą	ĕ	ĥ	ĵ	Ņ	ŕ	ŧ|ť	ŵ	ƅ	ƕ	ƥ|ƥ	Z	Dž	Ǖ	ǥ	
6	Ć	Ė	Ħ	Ķ	ņ	Ŗ	Ŧ	Ŷ	Ɔ	ɩ	Ř	ƶ	dž	Ǘ	Ǧ	
7	ć	ė	ħ	ķ	Ň	ŗ	ŧ	ŷ	Ƈ	Ɨ	ƨ	Ȝ|Ȝ	LJ	Ǘ	ǧ	
8	Ĉ	Ę	Ĩ	ĸ	ň	Ř	Ũ	Ÿ	ƈ	Ƙ	ə	Ʒ	Lj	ǘ	Ǩ	
9	ĉ	ę	ĩ	Ĺ	ʼn	ř	ũ	Ź	Đ	ƙ	Ɯ	ƹ	lj	Ǚ	ǩ	
A	Ċ	Ě	Ī	ĺ	ŊN	Ś	Ū	ź	Ɗ	ƚ	ɩ	ƺ	NJ	ǚ	Ǫ	
B	ċ	ě	ī	Ļ	ŋ	ś	ū	Ż	Ƌ	ƛ	ƫ	ƻ	Nj	Ǜ	ǫ	
C	Č	Ĝ	Ĭ	ļ	Ō	Ŝ	ŭ	ż	ƌ	ɯ	Ƭ	Ƽ	nj	ǜ	Ǭ	
D	č	ĝ	ĭ	Ľ|Ľ	ō	ŝ	ŭ	Ž	ƍ	Ɲ	ƫ	ƽ	Ǎ	ǝ	ǭ	
E	Ď|Ď	Ğ	Į	ĭ|ľ	Ŏ	Ş|Ş	Ů	ž	Ǝ	ƞ	Ʈ	ƾ	ǎ	Ǟ	ǯ	
F	ď|ď	ğ	į	Ŀ	ŏ	ş|ş	ů		ǝ	Ɵ|Ɵ	Ʊ	ƿ	ǐ	ǟ	ǯ	

	Unassigned					Standard Phonetic						Modifier Letters				
	020	021	022	023	024	025	026	027	028	029	02A	02B	02C	02D	02E	02F
0						ʁ	ɠ	ɰ	ʀ	ʑ	ʤ	ʰ	ˀ	˸	ˠ	
1						ɑ	ɡ	ɱ	ʁ	ʐ	ʡ	ʱ	ˁ	˙	ˡ	
2						ɒ	ɢ	ɲ	ʂ	ʒ	ʢ	ʲ	˂	˒	ˢ	
3						ɓ	ɣ	ŋ	ʃ	ʓ	ʣ	ʳ	˃	˓	ˣ	
4						ɔ	ɤ	ɴ	ʄ	ʔ	ʥ	ʴ	˄	˔	ˤ	
5						ɕ	ɥ	ɵ	ʅ	ʕ	ʤ	ʵ	˅	˕	˥	
6						ɖ	ɦ	œ	ʆ	ʖ	ʦ	ʶ	ˆ	˖	˦	
7						ɗ	ɧ	ɷ	ʇ	ʗ	ʧ	ʷ	ˇ	˗	˧	
8						ə	ɨ	ɸ	ʈ	ʘ	ʨ	ʸ	ˈ	˘	˨	
9						ə	ɩ	ɹ	ʉ	ʙ		ʹ	ˉ	˙	˩	
A						ɚ	ɪ	ɺ	ʊ	ʚ		ʺ	ˊ	˚		
B						ɛ	ɫ	ɻ	ʋ	ɢ		ʻ	ˋ	˛		
C						ɜ	ɬ	ɼ	ʌ	ʜ		ʼ	ˌ	˜		
D						ɝ	ɭ	ɽ	ʍ	ʝ		ʽ	ˍ	˝		
E						ɞ	ɮ	ɾ	ʎ	ʞ		ʾ	ˎ	˞		
F						ʄ	ɯ	ɿ	ʏ	ʟ		ʿ	ˏ			

Generic Diacritical Marks　　　Greek

	030	031	032	033	034	035	036	037	038	039	03A	03B	03C	03D	03E	03F
0	◌̀	◌̇	◌̠	◌̃	◌ VIET			◌		ΐ	Π	ϋ	π	ϐ	♌	ϰ
1	◌́	◌̂	◌̡	◌̣	◌ VIET			◌		Α	Ρ	α	ρ	ϑ	♉	ϱ
2	◌̂	◌̆	◌̢	◌̲				◌		Β		β	ς	ϒ	Ш	ϲ
3	◌̃	◌̇	◌̣	◌̳						Γ	Σ	γ	σ	ʹΥ	щ	ʼ
4	◌̄	◌̈	◌̤	◌̴				◌	΄	Δ	Τ	δ	τ	Ϋ	ϥ	¨
5	◌̅	◌̉	◌̥	◌̵				◌	΅	Ε	Υ	ε	υ	φ	ϙ	ˌ
6	◌̆	◌̊	◌̦	↔					Ά	Ζ	Φ	ζ	φ	ϖ	ђ	
7	◌̇	◌̋	◌̧	◌̷						Η	ʼΧ	η	χ	;	ꙅϩ	
8	◌̈	◌̌	◌̨	◌̸					Έ	Θ	Ψ	θ	ψ	ʹ	ꙃ	
9	◌̉	◌̍	◌̩	◌̹					Ή	Ι	Ω	ι	ω	،	ꙉ	
A	◌̊	◌̎	◌̪	◌̺					Ί	Κ	Ϊ	κ	ϊ	Ϛ	ꙍ	
B	◌̋	◌̏	◌̫	◌̻						Λ	Ϋ	λ	ϋ	ϛ	ꙋ	
C	◌̌	◌̧	◌̬	◌̼					Ό	Μ	ά	μ	ό	Ϝ	ϭ	
D	◌̍	◌̦	◌̭	◌̽						Ν	έ	ν	ύ	ϝ	ϭ	
E	◌̎	◌̞	◌̮	◌̾					Ύ	Ξ	ή	ξ	ώ	4Ϙ	ϯ	
F	◌̏	◌̟	◌̯	◌̿					Ώ	Ο	ί	ο	ο	4ϙ	✝	

Cyrillic

	040	041	042	043	044	045	046	047	048	049	04A	04B	04C	04D	04E	04F
0		А	Р	а	р		ꙩ	Ѱ	Ç	Ґ	Ӄ	Ӱ	І			
1	Ё	Б	С	б	с	ё	ѡ	ѱ	ç	ґ	ӄ	ӱ	Ӂ			
2	Ђ	В	Т	в	т	ђ	ѣ	Ѳ	⚹	Ғ‖Ғ	Ӈ	Х	ӂ			
3	Ѓ	Г	У	г	у	ѓ	ѣ	ѳ	̒	Ғ‖Ғ	ӈ	х	Ӄ			
4	Є	Д	Ф	д	ф	є	Ѥ	Ѵ	̂	Ҕ	Ӊ	Ц	ҕ			
5	Ѕ	Е	Х	е	х	ѕ	ѥ	ѵ	ꙓ	ҕ	ӊ	ц	Ӄ			
6	І	Ж	Ц	ж	ц	і	Ѧ	ѷ	ꙓ	Җ	Ӎ	Ч	ӄ			
7	Ї	З	Ч	з	ч	ї	ѧ	ѷ		җ	ӎ	ч	Ӈ			
8	Ј	И	Ш	и	ш	ј	Ѩ	Оү		З|З	Ѽ	Ҷ	ӈ			
9	Љ	Й	Щ	й	щ	љ	ѩ	оү		з|з	ѽ	ҷ	Ӽ			
A	Њ	К	Ъ	к	ъ	њ	Ж	Ѡ		Қ	Ҫ|Ҫ	Һ	ӽ			
B	Ћ	Л	Ы	л	ы	ћ	ж	ꙩ		қ	ҫ|ҫ	һ	Ч			
C	Ќ	М	Ь	м	ь	ќ	Ꙗ	ꙭ		Ҝ	Т	Ҿ	ч			
D		Н	Э	н	э		ꙗ	ꙭ		ҝ	т	ҿ				
E	ў	О	Ю	о	ю	ў	Ꙃ	ꙮ		Ҟ	Ү	Ҽ|Ҽ				
F	Џ	П	Я	п	я	џ	ꙃ	ѿ		ҟ	ү	ҽ|ҽ				

	Unassigned			Armenian						Hebrew						
	050	051	052	053	054	055	056	057	058	059	05A	05B	05C	05D	05E	05F
0					Հ	Ր		հ	ր			◌ְ	׀	א	נ	װ
1				Ա	Ձ	Ց	ա	ձ	ց			◌ֱ	◌ׁ	ב	ס	ױ
2				Բ	Ղ	Ւ	բ	ղ	ւ			◌ֲ	◌ׂ	ג	ע	ײ
3				Գ	Ճ	Փ	գ	ճ	փ			◌ֳ	׃	ד	ף	׳
4				Դ	Մ	Ք	դ	մ	ք			◌ִ		ה	פ	״
5				Ե	Յ	Օ	ե	յ	օ			◌ֵ		ו	ץ	◌̆
6				Զ	Ն	Ֆ	զ	ն	ֆ			◌ֶ		ז	צ	
7				Է	Շ		է	շ				◌ַ		ח	ק	
8				Ը	Ո		ը	ո				◌ָ		ט	ר	
9				Թ	Չ	ՙ	թ	չ	։			◌ֹ		י	ש	
A				Ժ	Պ	՚	ժ	պ						ך	ת	
B				Ի	Ջ	՛	ի	ջ				◌ֻ		כ		
C				Լ	Ռ	՜	լ	ռ				◌ּ		ל		
D				Խ	Ս	՝	խ	ս				◌ֽ		ם		
E				Ծ	Վ	՞	ծ	վ				־		מ		
F				Կ	Տ	՟	կ	տ				◌ֿ		ן		

Arabic

	060	061	062	063	064	065	066	067	068	069	06A	06B	06C	06D	06E	06F
0				ذ	ـ	◌ِ	٠	◌ٰ	ڀ	ڐ	ڠ	ڰ	ۀ	ې		۰
1			ء	ر	ف	◌ّ	١	ٱ	ځ	ڑ	ڡ	ڱ	ہ	ۑ		۱
2			آ	ز	ق	◌ْ	٢	ٲ	ڂ	ڒ	ڢ	ڲ	ۂ	ے		۲
3			أ	س	ك		٣	ٳ	ڃ	ړ	ڣ	ڳ	ۃ	ۓ		۳
4			ؤ	ش	ل		٤	ٴ	ڄ	ڔ	ڤ	ڴ	ۄ	۔		۴
5			إ	ص	م		٥	ٵ	څ	ڕ	ڥ	ڵ	ۅ	ە		۵
6			ئ	ض	ن		٦	ٶ	چ	ږ	ڦ	ڶ	ۆ			۶
7			ا	ط	ه		٧	ٷ	ڇ	ڗ	ڧ	ڷ	ۇ			۷
8			ب	ظ	و		٨	ٸ	ڈ	ژ	ڨ		ۈ			۸
9			ة	ع	ى		٩	ٹ	ډ	ڙ	ک		ۉ			۹
A			ت	غ	ي		٪	ٺ	ڊ	ښ	ڪ	ں	ۊ			
B		؛	ث		◌ً		٫	ٻ	ڋ	ڛ	ګ	ڻ	ۋ			
C	،		ج		◌ٌ		٬	ټ	ڌ	ڜ	ڬ	ڼ	ی			
D			ح		◌ٍ			ٽ	ڍ	ڝ	ڭ	ڽ	ۍ			
E			خ		◌َ			پ	ڎ	ڞ	ڮ	ھ	ێ			
F		؟	د		◌ُ			ٿ	ڏ	ڟ	گ					

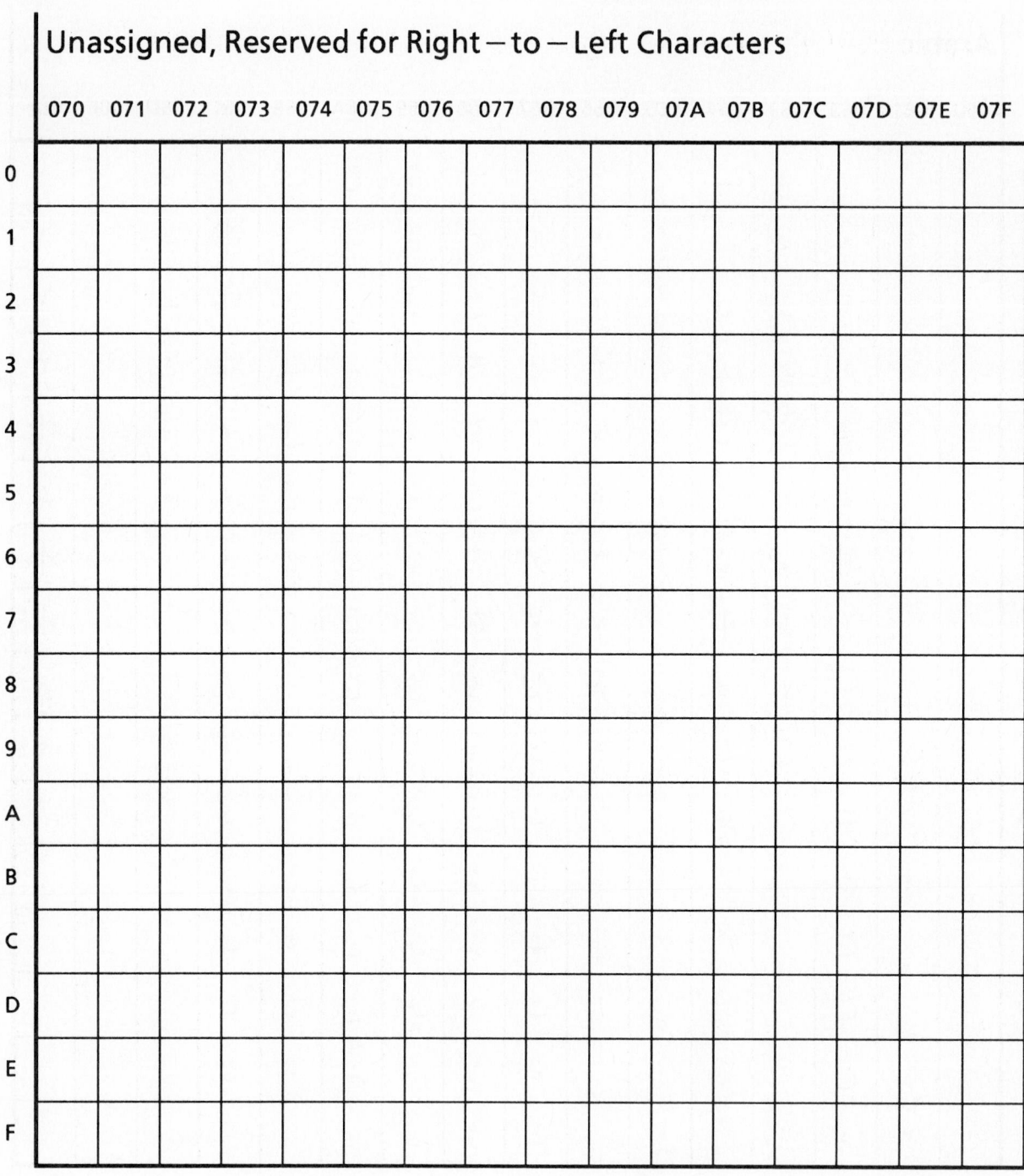

Unassigned, Reserved for Right – to – Left Characters (cont.)

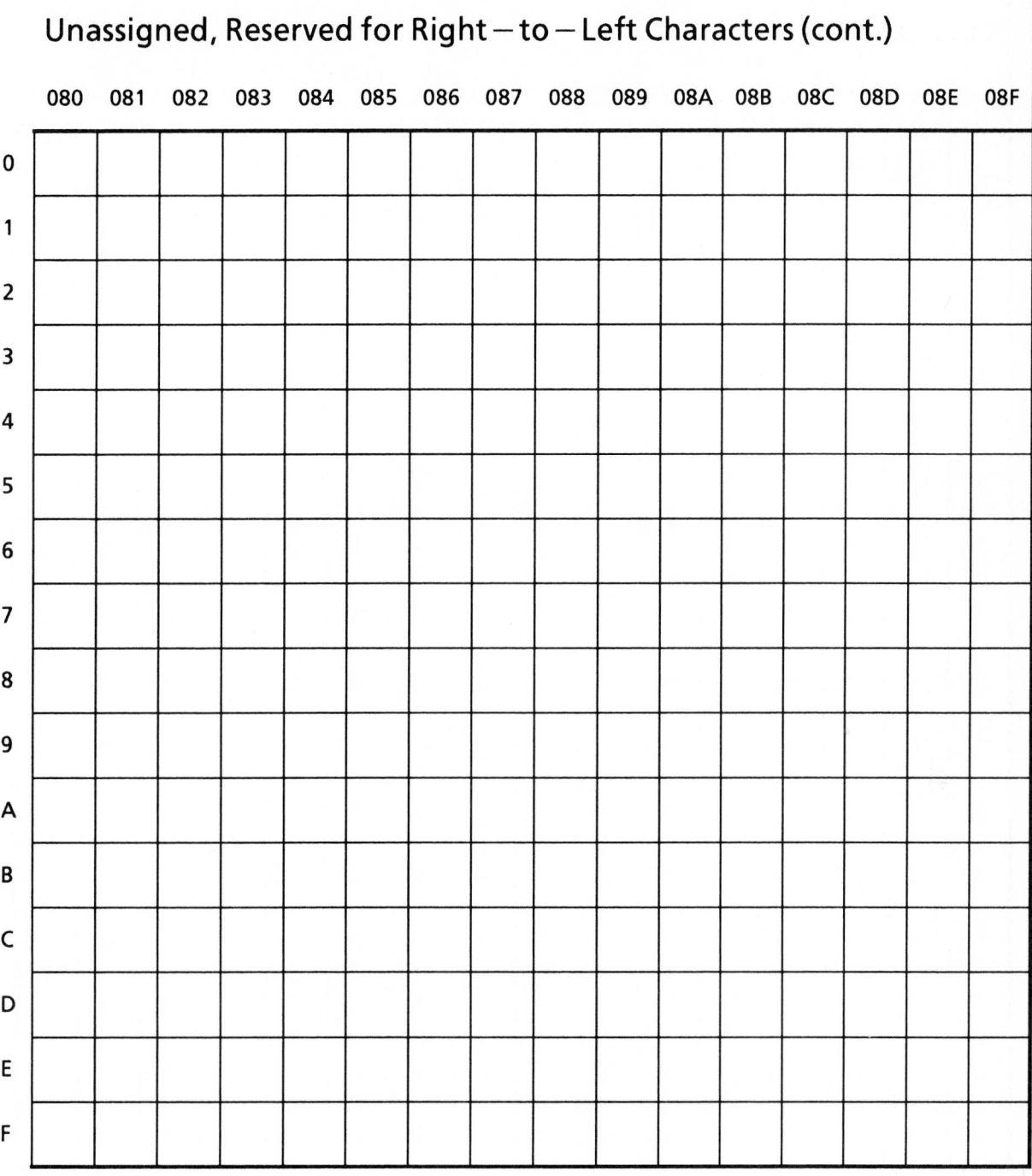

	080	081	082	083	084	085	086	087	088	089	08A	08B	08C	08D	08E	08F
0																
1																
2																
3																
4																
5																
6																
7																
8																
9																
A																
B																
C																
D																
E																
F																

Devanagari | Bengali

	090	091	092	093	094	095	096	097	098	099	09A	09B	09C	09D	09E	09F
0		ऐ	ठ	र	ी	ॐ	ॠ	०		ঐ	ঠ	র	ী		ক্ষ	ব
1	ँ	ऑ	ड	ऱ	ि	़	ॡ		ঁ		ড		ু		ৡ	ৱ
2	ं	ऒ	ढ	ल	ु	॒	ॢ		২		ঢ	ল	ূ		ৢ	৲
3	ः	ओ	णग	ळ	ृ	॑	ॣ		ঃ	ও	ণ		ৃ		ৣ	ট
4		औ	त	ऴ	ॄ	॔	।			ঔ	ত		ৄ			৴
5	अग्र	क	थ	व	ॅ		॥		অ	ক	থ					৵
6	आ	ख	द	श	ॆ		०		আ	খ	দ	শ			০	৶
7	इ	ग	ध	ष	े		१		ই	গ	ধ	ষ	ে	ৗ	১	৷
8	ई	घ	न	स	ै	क़	२		ঈ	ঘ	ন	স	ৈ		২	৸
9	उ	ङ	ऩ	ह	ॉ	ख़	३		উ	ঙ		হ			৩	৹
A	ऊ	च	प		ॊ	ग़	४		ঊ	চ	প				৪	৺
B	ऋ	छ	फ		ो	ज़	५५		ঋ	ছ	ফ		ো		৫	
C	ऌ	ज	ब	ॕ	ौ	ड़	६		ৌ	জ	ব	ঃ	ৌ	ড়	৬	
D	ऍ	झभ	भ	ऽ	ॗ	ढ़	७			ঝ	ভ		ৗ	ঢ়	৭	
E	ऎ	ञ	म	ा		फ़	८८			ঞ	ম	া			৮	
F	ए	ट	य	ि		य़	९ह		এ	ট	য	ি		য়	৯	

Gurmukhi

Gujarati

	0A0	0A1	0A2	0A3	0A4	0A5	0A6	0A7	0A8	0A9	0AA	0AB	0AC	0AD	0AE	0AF
0		ਐ	ਠ	ਰ	ੀ			ਁ		ઐ	ઠ	ર	ા	ૐ	ૠ	
1			ਡ		ੁ			ਂ	ઁ		ડ		િ			
2	ਂ		ਢ	ਲ	ੂ			ੲ	ં		ઢ	લ	ી			
3		ੳ	ਣ	ਲ਼				ੳ	ઃ	ઓ	ણ	ળ	ુ			
4		ਅਁ	ਤ					ੴ		ઔ	ત		ૂ			
5	ਅ	ਕ	ਥ	ਵ					ચ	ક	થ	વ	ૃ			
6	ਆ	ਖ	ਦ	ਸ਼			੦		ચા	ખ	દ	શ			૦	
7	ਇ	ਗ	ਧ		ੇ		੧		ઇ	ગ	ધ	ષ	ે		૧	
8	ਈ	ਘ	ਨ	ਸ	ੈ		੨		ઈ	ઘ	ન	સ	ૈ		૨	
9	ਉ	ਙ		ਹ		ਖ਼	੩		ઉ	ઙ		હ			૩	
A	ਊ	ਚ	ਪ			ਗ਼	੪		ઊ	ચ	પ				૪	
B		ਛ	ਫ	ੋ	ਜ਼	੫			ઋ	છ	ફ		ો		૫	
C		ਜ	ਬ	ੌ	ੜ	੬				જ	બ	ઃ	ૌ		૬	
D		ਝ	ਭ			੭				ઝ	ભ	૨	્		૭	
E		ਞ	ਮ	ੇ	ੜ੍ਹ	੮				ઞ	મ	ૉ			૮	
F	ਏ	ਟ	ਯ	ਿ		੯			એ	ટ	ય	િ			૯	

	Oriya								Tamil							
	0B0	0B1	0B2	0B3	0B4	0B5	0B6	0B7	0B8	0B9	0BA	0BB	0BC	0BD	0BE	0BF
0		ଐ	ଠ	ର	ୀ		ୠ	୰		ஐ		ர	ீ			௰
1	ଁ		ଡ		ୁ		ୡ					ற	ு			௱
2	ଂ		ଢ	ଲ	ୂ				ஂ	ஒ		ல	ூ			௲
3	ଃ	ଓ	ଣ	ଳ	ୃ				ஃ	ஓ	ண	ள				
4		ଔ	ତ							ஔ	த	ழ				
5	ଅ	କ	ଥ						அ	க		வ				
6	ଆ	ଖ	ଦ	ଶ			୦		ஆ				ெ			
7	ଇ	ଗ	ଧ	ଷ	େ	ୗ	୧		இ			ஷ	ே	ௗ	௧	
8	ଈ	ଘ	ନ	ସ	ୈ		୨		ஈ		ந	ஸ	ை		௨	
9	ଉ	ଙ		ହ			୩		உ	ங	ன	ஹ			௩	
A	ଊ	ଚ	ପ				୪		ஊ	ச	ப		ொ		௪	
B	ଋ	ଛ	ଫ		ୋ		୫						ோ		௫	
C	ଌ	ଜ	ବ	଼	ୌ	ଡ଼	୬			ஜ			ௌ		௬	
D		ଝ	ଭ	ଽ	୍	ଢ଼	୭						்		௭	
E		ଞ	ମ	ା			୮		எ	ஞ	ம	ா			௮	
F	ଏ	ଟ	ଯ	ି		ୟ	୯		ஏ	ட	ய	ி			௯	

Telugu

Kannada

	0C0	0C1	0C2	0C3	0C4	0C5	0C6	0C7	0C8	0C9	0CA	0CB	0CC	0CD	0CE	0CF
0		ఐ	ఠ	ర	ీ		ౠ			ಐ	ಠ	ರ	ೀ		ೠ	
1	ఁ		డ	ఱ	ు		ౡ				ಡ	ಱ	ು		ೡ	
2	ం	ఒ	ఢ	ల	ూ				ಂ	ಒ	ಢ	ಲ	ೂ			
3	ః	ఓ	ణ	ళ	ృ				ಃ	ಓ	ಣ	ಳ	ೃ			
4		ఔ	త		ౄ					ಔ	ತ		ೄ			
5	అ	క	థ	వ		ౕ			ಅ	ಕ	ಥ	ವ		ೕ		
6	ఆ	ఖ	ద	శ	ె	ౖ	౦		ಆ	ಖ	ದ	ಶ	ೆ	ೖ	೦	
7	ఇ	గ	ధ	ష	ే		౧		ಇ	ಗ	ಧ	ಷ	ೇ		೧	
8	ఈ	ఘ	న	స	ై		౨		ಈ	ಘ	ನ	ಸ	ೈ		೨	
9	ఉ	ఙ		హ			౩		ಉ	ಙ		ಹ			೩	
A	ఊ	చ	ప		ొ		౪		ಊ	ಚ	ಪ		ೊ		೪	
B	ఋ	ఛ	ఫ		ో		౫		ಋ	ಛ	ಫ		ೋ		೫	
C	ఌ	జ	బ		ౌ		౬		ಌ	ಜ	ಬ		ೌ		೬	
D		ఝ	భ		్		౭			ಝ	ಭ		್		೭	
E	ఎ	ఞ	మ	ా			౮		ಎ	ಞ	ಮ	ಾ		ೞ	೮	
F	ఏ	ట	య	ి			౯		ಏ	ಟ	ಯ	ಿ			೯	

Malayalam   Unassigned

	0D0	0D1	0D2	0D3	0D4	0D5	0D6	0D7	0D8	0D9	0DA	0DB	0DC	0DD	0DE	0DF
0		ഐ	ഠ	ര	ീ		ൠ									
1			ഡ	റ	ു		ൡ									
2	ം	ഒ	ഢ	ല	ൂ											
3	ഃ	ഓ	ണ	ള	ൃ											
4		ഔ	ത	ഴ												
5	അ	ക	ഥ	വ												
6	ആ	ഖ	ദ	ശ	െ		൦									
7	ഇ	ഗ	ധ	ഷ	േ	ൗ	൧									
8	ഈ	ഘ	ന	സ	ൈ		൨									
9	ഉ	ങ		ഹ			൩									
A	ഊ	ച	പ		ൊ		൪									
B	ഋ	ഛ	ഫ		ോ		൫									
C	ഌ	ജ	ബ		ൌ		൬									
D		ഝ	ഭ		്		൭									
E	എ	ഞ	മ	ാ			൮									
F	ഏ	ട	യ	ി			൯									

Thai | Lao

	OE0	OE1	OE2	OE3	OE4	OE5	OE6	OE7	OE8	OE9	OEA	OEB	OEC	OED	OEE	OEF
0		ฐ	ภ	ะ	เ	๐		เ◌				◌ั	ເ	໐		ເ◌
1	ก	ฑ	ม	◌ั	แ	๑		แ◌	ກ		ມ	◌ั	ແ	໑		ແ◌
2	ข	ฒ	ย	า	โ	๒		โ◌	ຂ		ຢ	າ	ໂ	໖		ໂ◌
3	ฃ	ณ	ร	◌ำ	ใ	๓		ใ◌			ຣ	◌ຳ	ໃ	ມ		ໃ◌
4	ค	ด	ฤ	◌ิ	ไ	๔		ไ◌	ຄ	ດ		◌ິ	ໄ	໔		ໄ◌
5	ฅ	ต	ล	◌ี	ๅ	๕				ຕ	ລ	◌ີ		໕		
6	ฆ	ถ	ฦ	◌ึ	ๆ	๖				ຖ		◌ຶ	ໆ	ຝ		
7	ง	ท	ว	◌ื	◌ู	๗			ງ	ທ	ວ	◌ື		໗		
8	จ	ธ	ศ	◌ุ	◌ู	๘			ຈ			◌ຸ	◌ຸ	ຘ		
9	ฉ	น	ษ	◌ู	◌ู	๙				ມ		◌ູ	◌ຶ	໙		
A	ช	บ	ส	◌ฺ	◌ํ	๚			ຊ	ບ	ສ		◌ໍ			
B	ซ	ป	ห		◌ํ	ฯ				ປ	ທ	◌ີ	◌ໍ			
C	ฌ	ผ	ฬ		◌ี					ຜ		◌ຸ	◌ໍ	ທນ		
D	ญ	ฝ	อ		◌ํ				ຍ	ຝ	ອ	◌ໄ	◌ໍ	ຫນ		
E	ฎ	พ	ฮ		◌ะ					ພ	ຣ					
F	ฏ	ฟ	๏	฿	◎					ຟ	ຯ					

Unassigned

	0F0	0F1	0F2	0F3	0F4	0F5	0F6	0F7	0F8	0F9	0FA	0FB	0FC	0FD	0FE	0FF
0																
1																
2																
3																
4																
5																
6																
7																
8																
9																
A																
B																
C																
D																
E																
F																

	Tibetan						Unassigned				Georgian					
	100	101	102	103	104	105	106	107	108	109	10A	10B	10C	10D	10E	10F
0	ཀ	ཐ	ཥ	◌	ༀ						ⴀ	ⴋ	ⴜ	ა	ნ	ვ
1	ཁ	ད	ཧ	✕	༁						ⴁ	ⴌ	ⴝ	ბ	ჟ	ჱ
2	ག	ད	ཨ		༂						ⴂ	ⴍ	ⴞ	გ	ჩ	ჲ
3	ང	ན	◌	༃						ⴃ	ⴎ	ⴟ	ᒪ	ᒣ	ჳ
4	ཅ	ན		།	◌						ⴄ	ⴏ	ⴠ	ჯ	ჰ	ჴ
5	ཆ	ཕ		◌	◌						ⴅ	ⴐ	ⴡ	ჵ	ჶ	ჷ
6	ᒪ	ᒫ	◌	◌	◌						ⴆ	ⴑ		ჶ	ᒬ	ჸ
7	ᒣ	ᒪ	◌	◌	◌						ⴇ	ⴒ		თ	ᯧ	
8	ᒪ	ᒫ	◌	◌	◌						ⴈ	ⴓ		ი	ᒫ	
9	ᒪ	ᒣ	◌	◌	◌						ⴉ	ⴔ		კ	ᒬ	
A	ᒪ	ᒫ	◌	◌	◌						ⴊ	ⴕ		ᯥ	ᒮ	
B	ᒫ	ᒬ	◌	◌	◌						ᒪ	ᒫ		მ	ᒬ	∴
C	ᒪ	ᒫ	◌	◌	◌						ᒪ	ᒫ		ნ	ᯮ	
D	ᒪ	ᒪ		◌							ᒪ	ᒮ		ᯯ	ᒯ	
E	ᒫ	ᒫ	◌	◌							ᒯ	ᒫ		ᒬ	ᒮ	
F	ᒯ	ᒯ	ᒬ								ᒫ	ᒯ		ᒭ	ᒮ	

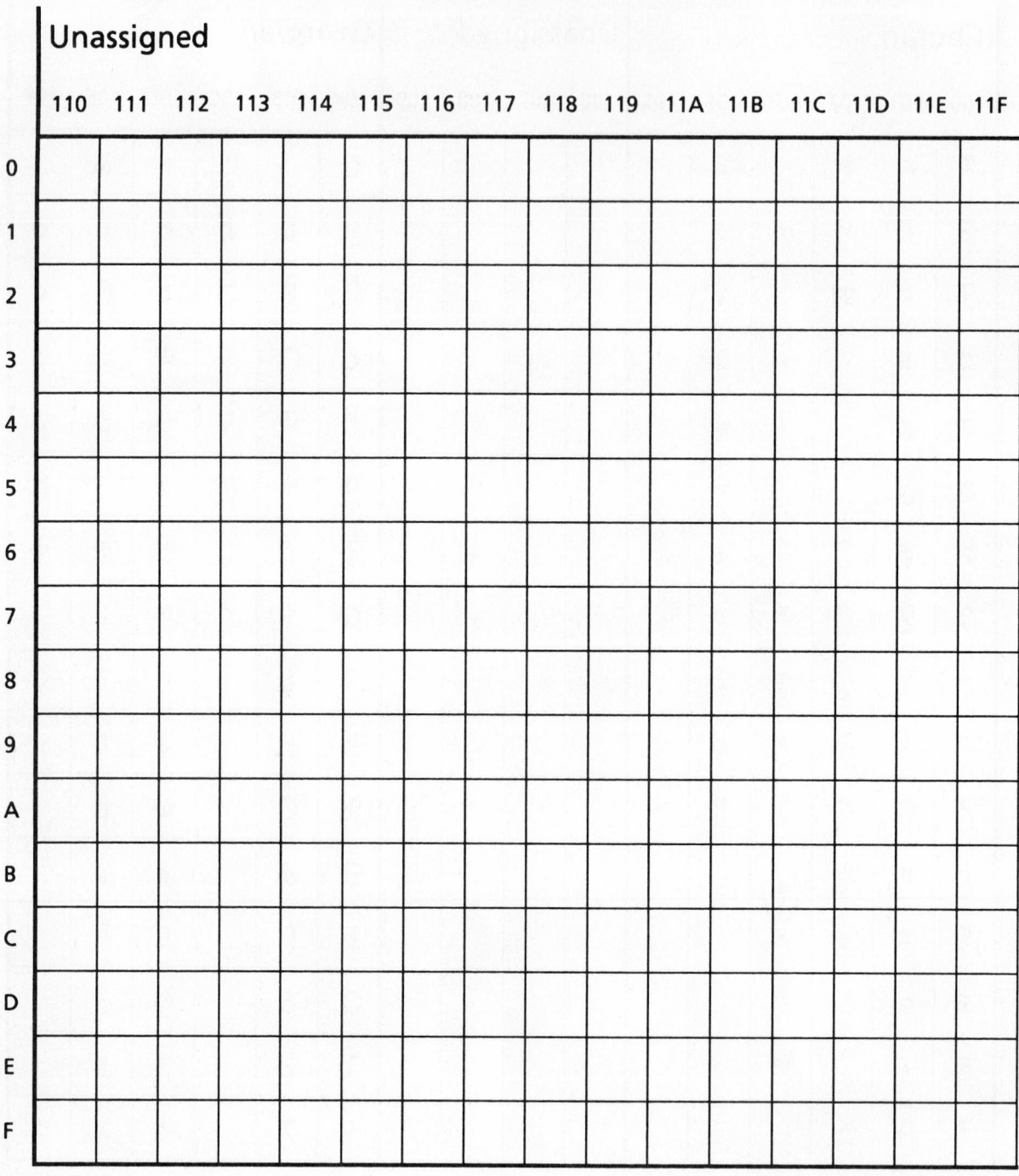

General Punctuation　　Sups & Subs　　Currency　　Diacritics

	200	201	202	203	204	205	206	207	208	209	20A	20B	20C	20D	20E	20F
0	En Quad	Hyphen	†	‰	⌢			0	0		₠			◌̃	⃝	
1	Em Quad	NB	‡	‱	⋌				1		₡			◌̑	↔	
2	En SP	Figure	•	′	**				2		₢			⃒		
3	Em SP	—	▶	″	▬				3		₣			⃓		
4	3 Em SP	—	·	‴	∕			4	4		£			◌↺		
5	4 Em SP	—	··	‵				5	5		₥			◌↻		
6	6 Em SP	‖	···	‶				6	6		₦			◌←		
7	Fig SP	═	HyphenPt	‷				7	7		₧			◌→		
8	Punct SP	'	Line Sepr	∧				8	8		Rs			◌⊙		
9	Thin SP	'	Para Sepr	‹				9	9		₩			◌⊙		
A	Hair SP	'	LRE	›				+	+		₪			◌⊙		
B	ZW SP	'	RLE	※				−	−					◌⋯		
C	Non-Joiner	"	PDF	‼				=	=					◌⋯		
D	Joiner	"	LRO	⸮				(	(					◯		
E	L-R Mark	"	RLO	―				)	)					▢		
F	R-L Mark	"						n						◇		

Letterlike Symbols   Number Forms   Arrows

	210	211	212	213	214	215	216	217	218	219	21A	21B	21C	21D	21E	21F
0	a/c	ℐ	SM	ℰ			I	i	ℂ	←	↠	↰	→	⇐	⇠	
1	a/s	ℑ	TEL	ℱ			II	ii	ⅅ	↑	↡	↱	⇁	⇑	⇡	
2	ℂ	ℒ	™	Ⅎ			III	iii	⅏	→	↢	↲	↓	⇒	⇢	
3	℃	ℓ	ℕ	ℳ		⅓	IV	iv		↓	↣	↳	↧	⇓	⇣	
4	℄	℔	ℤ	ℴ		⅔	V	v		↔	↤	↴	⇄	⇔	↞	
5	℅	N	ℨ	ℵ		⅕	VI	vi		↕	↥	↵	⇅	⇕	↠	
6	℆	№	Ω	ℶ		⅖	VII	vii		↖	↦	↶	⇆	⇖	⇐	
7	ℇ	℗	℧	ℷ		⅗	VIII	viii		↗	↧	↷	⇇	⇗	⇑	
8	℈	℘	ℨ	ℸ		⅘	IX	ix		↘	↨	↸	⇈	⇘	⇨	
9	℉	ℙ	℩			⅙	X	x		↙	↩	↹	⇉	⇙	⇓	
A	ℊ	ℚ	K			⅚	XI	xi		↚	↪	↺	⇊	⇚	⇧	
B	ℋ	ℛ	Å			⅛	XII	xii		↛	↫	↻	⇋	⇛	
C	ℌ	ℜ	ℬ			⅜	L	l		↜	↬	↼	⇌	⇜	
D	ℍ	ℝ	ℭ			⅝	C	c		↝	↭	↽	⇍	⇝	
E	ℎ	℞	℮			⅞	D	d		↞	↮	↾	⇎	↕	
F	ℏ\ℏ	℟	ℯ			⅟	M	m		↟	↯	↿	⇏	↨	

Mathematical Operators

	220	221	222	223	224	225	226	227	228	229	22A	22B	22C	22D	22E	22F
0	∀	∐	∠	∰	≀	≐	≠	≰	⊀	⊐	⊠	⊰	⋀	⋐	⋠	⋰
1	∁	∑	∡	∱	≁	÷	≡	≱	⊁	⊑	⊡	⊱	⋁	⋑	⋡	⋱
2	∂	−	∢	∲	≂	≒	≢	≲	⊂	⊒	⊢	⊲	⋂	⋒	⋢	
3	∃	∓	∣	∳	≃	≓	≣	≳	⊃	⊓	⊣	⊳	⋃	⋓	⋣	
4	∄	∔	∤	∴	≄	≔	≤	≴	⊄	⊔	⊤	⊴	⋄	⋔	⋤	
5	∅	∕	∥	∵	≅	≕	≥	≵	⊅	⊕	⊥	⊵	⋅	⋕	⋥	
6	∆	∖	∦	∶	≆	≖	≦	≶	⊆	⊖	⊦	⊶	⋆	⋖	⋦	
7	∇	∗	∧	∷	≇	≗	≧	≷	⊇	⊗	⊧	⊷	⋇	⋗	⋧	
8	∈	∘	∨	∸	≈	≘	≨	≸	⊈	⊘	⊨	⊸	⋈	⋘	⋨	
9	∉	∙	∩	∹	≉	≙	≩	≹	⊉	⊙	⊩	⊹	⋉	⋙	⋩	
A	∊	√	∪	∺	≊	≚	≪	≺	⊊	⊚	⊪	⊺	⋊	⋚	⋪	
B	∋	∛	∫	∻	≋	≛	≫	≻	⊋	⊛	⊫	⊻	⋋	⋛	⋫	
C	∌	∜	∬	∼	≌	≜	≬	≼	⊌	⊜	⊬	⊼	⋌	⋜	⋬	
D	∍	∝	∭	∽	≍	≝	≭	≽	⊍	⊝	⊭	⊽	⋍	⋝	⋭	
E	∎	∞	∮	∾	≎	≞	≮	≾	⊎	⊞	⊮	⊾	⋎	⋞	⋮	
F	∏	∟	∯	∿	≏	≟	≯	≿	⊏	⊟	⊯	⊿	⋏	⋟	⋯	

Miscellaneous Technical

	230	231	232	233	234	235	236	237	238	239	23A	23B	23C	23D	23E	23F
0	APL COMPOSE	⌐	⌠													
1	⍊	⌑	⌡													
2	⌂	⌒	⌢													
3	⌃	⌓	⌣													
4	⌄	⌔	⌤													
5	⌅	⌕	⌥													
6	⌆	⌖	⌦													
7	⌇	⌗	⌧													
8	⌈	⌘	⌨													
9	⌉	⌙	〈													
A	⌊	⌚	〉													
B	⌋	⌛	⌫													
C	⌌	⌜	⬡													
D	⌍	⌝														
E	⌎	⌞														
F	⌏	⌟														

The Unicode Standard • Version 1.0

Control Pictures | OCR | Enclosed Alphanumerics

	240	241	242	243	244	245	246	247	248	249	24A	24B	24C	24D	24E	24F
0	NUL	DLE	SP		⌐		①	⑰	(13)	9.	(e)	(u)	Ⓚ	ⓐ	ⓠ	
1	SOH	DC1	DEL		ꓕ		②	⑱	(14)	10.	(f)	(v)	Ⓛ	ⓑ	ⓡ	
2	STX	DC2	ƀ		Ꝑ		③	⑲	(15)	11.	(g)	(w)	Ⓜ	ⓒ	ⓢ	
3	ETX	DC3	␣		ꓕ		④	⑳	(16)	12.	(h)	(x)	Ⓝ	ⓓ	ⓣ	
4	EOT	DC4	NL		Ⲓ		⑤	(1)	(17)	13.	(i)	(y)	Ⓞ	ⓔ	ⓤ	
5	ENQ	NAK			⋈		⑥	(2)	(18)	14.	(j)	(z)	Ⓟ	ⓕ	ⓥ	
6	ACK	SYN			⁝		⑦	(3)	(19)	15.	(k)	Ⓐ	Ⓠ	ⓖ	ⓦ	
7	BEL	ETB			꜌		⑧	(4)	(20)	16.	(l)	Ⓑ	Ⓡ	ⓗ	ⓧ	
8	BS	CAN			꜌		⑨	(5)	1.	17.	(m)	Ⓒ	Ⓢ	ⓘ	ⓨ	
9	HT	EM			⫶		⑩	(6)	2.	18.	(n)	Ⓓ	Ⓣ	ⓙ	ⓩ	
A	LF	SUB			⫽		⑪	(7)	3.	19.	(o)	Ⓔ	Ⓤ	ⓚ	ⓞ	
B	VT	ESC					⑫	(8)	4.	20.	(p)	Ⓕ	Ⓥ	ⓛ		
C	FF	FS					⑬	(9)	5.	(a)	(q)	Ⓖ	Ⓦ	ⓜ		
D	CR	GS					⑭	(10)	6.	(b)	(r)	Ⓗ	Ⓧ	ⓝ		
E	SO	RS					⑮	(11)	7.	(c)	(s)	Ⓘ	Ⓨ	ⓞ		
F	SI	US					⑯	(12)	8.	(d)	(t)	Ⓙ	Ⓩ	ⓟ		

Form and Chart Components

Blocks

Geometric Shapes

	250	251	252	253	254	255	256	257	258	259	25A	25B	25C	25D	25E	25F
0	─	┐	├	┬	┼	═	╊	╰	▀	▐	■	◢	◀	◐	⌒	
1	━	┑	┝	┭	┿	║	╉	╱	▁	░	□	▱	◁	◑	◡	
2	│	┒	┞	┮	╁	╒	╄	╲	▂	▒	▢	▲	◂	◒	◣	
3	┃	┓	┟	┯	╀	╓	╃	╳	▃	▓	▣	△	◃	◓	◤	
4	┄	└	┠	┴	┽	╔	╤	╴	▄	▔	▤	▴	◄	◔	◥	
5	┅	┕	┡	┵	┾	╕	╥	╵	▅	▕	▥	▵	◅	◕	◢	
6	┆	┖	┢	┶	╆	╖	╦	╶	▆		▦	▶	◆	◖	◦	
7	┇	┗	┣	┷	╅	╗	╧	╷	▇		▧	▷	◇	◗	◧	
8	┈	┘	┥	┸	╇	╘	╨	╸	█		▨	▸	◈	◘	◨	
9	┉	┙	┦	┹	╈	╙	╩	╹	█		▩	▹	◉	◙	◩	
A	┊	┚	┧	┺	┼	╚	╪	╺	█		▪	►	◊	◚	◪	
B	┋	┛	┨	┻	╉	╛	╫	╻	█		▫	▻	○	◛	◫	
C	┌	┝	┰	┼	╌	╜	╬	╼	█		▬	▼	◌	◜	◬	
D	┍	┞	┱	┽	╍	╝	╭	╽	█		▭	▽	◍	◝	◭	
E	┎	┟	┲	┾	┊	╞	╮	╾	▌		▮	▾	◎	◞	◮	
F	┏	┠	┳	┿	╏	╟	╯	╿	▍		▯	▿	●	◟		

The Unicode Standard · Version 1.0

Miscellaneous Dingbats

	260	261	262	263	264	265	266	267	268	269	26A	26B	26C	26D	26E	26F
0	☀	☐	☠	☰	♀	⚁	♠									
1	♣	☑	⚡	☱	♁	♑	♡									
2	☂	☒	☢	☲	♂	♒	♢									
3	☃	☓	☣	☳	♃	♓	♣									
4	☄		☤	☴	♄	♔	♤									
5	★		☥	☵	♅	♕	♥									
6	☆		☦	☶	♆	♖	♦									
7	☇		☧	☷	♇	♗	♧									
8	☈		☨	☸	♈	♘	♨									
9	☉		☩	☹	♉	♙	♩									
A	☊	☚	☪	☺	♊	♚	♪									
B	☋	☛	☫	☻	♋	♛	♫									
C	☌	☜	☬	☼	♌	♜	♬									
D	☍	☝	☭	☽	♍	♝	♭									
E	☎	☞	☮	☾	♎	♞	♮									
F	☏	☟	☯	☿	♏	♟	♯									

Zapf Dingbats

Unassigned

	270	271	272	273	274	275	276	277	278	279	27A	27B	27C	27D	27E	27F
0		✏	✲	✰	✾	❏			①	❼	➠	➰				
1	✁	✑	✡	✱	❁	❐	❡		②	❽	➡	➱				
2	✂	✒	✢	✲	❂	❑	❢		③	❾	➢	➲				
3	✃	✓	✣	✳	❃		❣		④	❿	➣	➳				
4	✄	✔	✤	✴	❄		❤		⑤	➔	➤	➴				
5		✕	✥	✵	❅		❥		⑥		➥	➵				
6	✆	✖	✦	✶	❆	❖	❦	❶	⑦		➦	➶				
7	✇	✗	✧	✷	❇		❧	❷	⑧		➧	➷				
8	✈	✘		✸	❈	❘		❸	⑨	➘	➨	➸				
9	✉	✙	✩	✹	❉	❙		❹	⑩	➙	➩	➹				
A		✚	✪	✺	❊	❚		❺	❶	➚	➪	➺				
B		✛	✫	✻	❋	❛		❻	❷	➛	➫	➻				
C	✌	✜	✬	✼		❜		❼	❸	➜	➬	➼				
D	✍	✝	✭	✽	❍	❝		❽	❹	➝	➭	➽				
E	✎	✞	✮	✾		❞		❾	❺	➞	➮	➾				
F	✏	✟	✯	✿	❏			❿	❻	➟	➯					

CJK Symbols   Hiragana   Katakana

	300	301	302	303	304	305	306	307	308	309	30A	30B	30C	30D	30E	30F
0	ideo SP	【	☗	〰		ぐ	だ	ば	む	ゐ		グ	ダ	バ	ム	ヰ
1	、	】	∣	く	ぁ	け	ち	ぱ	め	ゑ	ァ	ケ	チ	パ	メ	ヱ
2	。	〒	‖	ぐ	あ	げ	ぢ	ひ	も	を	ア	ゲ	ヂ	ヒ	モ	ヲ
3	〃	〓	⫴	／	い	こ	っ	び	ゃ	ん	イ	コ	ッ	ビ	ャ	ン
4	仝	〔	ㄨ	⟋	ぃ	ご	つ	ぴ	や	ゔ	イ	ゴ	ツ	ピ	ヤ	ヴ
5	々	〕	ㄐ	＼	う	さ	づ	ふ	ゅ		ゥ	サ	ヅ	フ	ユ	ヵ
6	〆	〖	⊥	㊢	う	ざ	て	ぶ	ゆ		ウ	ザ	テ	ブ	ユ	ヶ
7	〇	〗	⊤		ぇ	し	で	ぷ	よ		エ	シ	デ	プ	ヨ	
8	〈	〘	⊜		え	じ	と	へ	よ		エ	ジ	ト	ヘ	ヨ	
9	〉	〙	夕		ぉ	す	ど	べ	ら	゙	オ	ス	ド	ベ	ラ	
A	《	〚	◌		お	ず	な	ぺ	り	゚	オ	ズ	ナ	ペ	リ	
B	》	〛	◌		か	せ	に	ほ	る	゛	カ	セ	ニ	ホ	ル	・
C	「	〜	◌		が	ぜ	ぬ	ぼ	れ	゜	ガ	ゼ	ヌ	ボ	レ	ー
D	」	〝	◌		き	そ	ね	ぽ	ろ	ヽ	キ	ソ	ネ	ポ	ロ	ヽ
E	『	〞	◌		ぎ	ぞ	の	ま	わ	ゞ	ギ	ゾ	ノ	マ	ワ	ヾ
F	』	〟	◌	〿	く	た	は	み	わ			ク	タ	ハ	ミ	ワ

Bopomofo   Hangul Elements   CJK Miscellaneous

	310	311	312	313	314	315	316	317	318	319	31A	31B	31C	31D	31E	31F
0		ㄐ	ㄠ		퉗	ㅐ	ㅠ	ㅁㅿ	ㅇㅇ	㆐						
1		ㄑ	ㄡ	ㄱ	ㅁ	ㅑ	ㅡ	ㅱ	ㆁ	㆑						
2		ㄒ	ㄢ	ㄲ	ㅂ	ㅒ	ㅢ	ㅲ	ㅄ	㆒						
3		ㄓ	ㄣ	ㄳ	ㅃ	ㅓ	ㅣ	ㅳ	ㆆㅿ	㆓						
4		ㄔ	ㄤ	ㄴ	ㅄ	ㅔ	(채움)	ㅄㄱ	ㆄ	㆔						
5	ㄅ	ㄕ	ㄥ	ㄵ	ㅅ	ㅕ	ㅗ	ㅄㄷ	ㆅ	㆕						
6	ㄆ	ㄖ	ㄦ	ㄶ	ㅆ	ㅖ	ㅘ	ㅄㅂ	ㆆ	㆖						
7	ㄇ	ㄗ	ㄧ	ㄷ	ㅇ	ㅗ	ㅙ	ㅮ	ㅑ	㆗						
8	ㄈ	ㄘ	ㄨ	ㄸ	ㅈ	ㅘ	ㄴㅿ	ㅸ	ㅒ	㆘						
9	ㄉ	ㄙ	ㄩ	ㄹ	ㅉ	ㅙ	ㄽ	ㅹ	ㅢ	㆙						
A	ㄊ	ㄚ	ㄪ	ㄺ	ㅊ	ㅚ	ㄾ	ㅅㄱ	ㅕ	㆚						
B	ㄋ	ㄛ	ㄫ	ㄻ	ㅋ	ㅛ	ㅩ	ㅅ	ㅖ	㆛						
C	ㄌ	ㄜ	ㄬ	ㄼ	ㅌ	ㅜ	ㄿ	ㅺ	ㅟ	㆜						
D	ㄍ	ㄝ		ㄽ	ㅍ	ㅝ	ㄹㆆ	ㅻ	·	㆝						
E	ㄎ	ㄞ		ㄾ	ㅎ	ㅞ	ㅁㆁ	ㅆ	ㆍ	㆞						
F	ㄏ	ㄟ		ㄿ	ㅏ	ㅟ	ㅁㅅ	ㅿ		㆟						

The Unicode Standard • Version 1.0

Enclosed CJK Letters and Ideographs

	320	321	322	323	324	325	326	327	328	329	32A	32B	32C	32D	32E	32F
0	(ㄱ)	(다)	(一)	(日)	祭		ㄱ	다	一	日	頂	夜		イ	レ	コ
1	(ㄴ)	(라)	(二)	(株)	(休)		ㄴ	라	二	株	休			ロ	ソ	ヱ
2	(ㄷ)	(마)	(三)	(有)	(自)		ㄷ	마	三	有	写			ハ	ツ	テ
3	(ㄹ)	(바)	(四)	(社)	(至)		ㄹ	바	四	社	正			ニ	ネ	ア
4	(ㅁ)	(사)	(五)	(名)			ㅁ	사	五	名	上			ホ	ナ	サ
5	(ㅂ)	(아)	(六)	(特)			ㅂ	아	六	特	中			ヘ	ラ	キ
6	(ㅅ)	(자)	(七)	(財)			ㅅ	자	七	財	下			ト	ム	ユ
7	(ㅇ)	(차)	(八)	(祝)			ㅇ	차	八	祝	左			チ	ウ	メ
8	(ㅈ)	(카)	(九)	(労)			ㅈ	카	九	労	右			リ	ヰ	ミ
9	(ㅊ)	(타)	(十)	(代)			ㅊ	타	十	秘	医			ヌ	ノ	シ
A	(ㅋ)	(파)	(月)	(呼)			ㅋ	파	月	男	宗			ル	オ	エ
B	(ㅌ)	(하)	(火)	(学)			ㅌ	하	火	女	学			ヲ	ク	ヒ
C	(ㅍ)	(주)	(水)	(監)			ㅍ		水	適	監			ワ	ヤ	モ
D	(ㅎ)		(木)	(企)			ㅎ		木	優	企			カ	マ	セ
E	(가)		(金)	(資)			가		金	印	資			ヨ	ケ	ス
F	(나)		(土)	(協)			나	K	土	注	協			タ	フ	♪

CJK Squared Words / CJK Squared Abbreviations

	330	331	332	333	334	335	336	337	338	339	33A	33B	33C	33D	33E	33F
0	アパート	ギガ	サンチーム	ピコ	ポンド	ユアン			pA	Hz	cm²	ps	kΩ	lm		
1	アルファ	ギニー	シリング	ビル	ホール	リットル			nA	kHz	m²	ns	MΩ	ln		
2	アンペア	キュリー	センチ	ファラッド	ホーン	リラ			μA	MHz	km²	μs	a.m.	log		
3	アール	ギルダー	セント	フィート	マイクロ	ルピー			mA	GHz	mm³	ms	Bq	lx		
4	イニング	キロ	ダース	ブッシェル	マイル	ルーブル			kA	THz	cm³	pV	cc	mb		
5	インチ	キログラム	デシ	フラン	マッハ	レム			KB	μl	m³	nV	cd	mil		
6	ウオン	キロメートル	ドル	ヘクタール	マルク	レントゲン			MB	ml	km³	μV	C/kg	mol		
7	エスクード	キロワット	トン	ペソ	マンション	ワット			GB	dl	m/s	mV	Ca.	PH		
8	エーカー	グラム	ナノ	ペニヒ	ミクロン				cal	kl	m/s²	kV	dB	p.m.		
9	オンス	グラムトン	ノット	ヘルツ	ミリ				kcal	fm	Pa	MV	Gy	PPM		
A	オーム	クルゼイロ	ハイツ	ペンス	ミリバール				pF	nm	kPa	pW	ha	PR		
B	カイリ	クローネ	パーセント	ページ	メガ			平成	nF	μm	MPa	nW	HP	sr		
C	カラット	ケース	バーツ	ベータ	メガトン			昭和	μF	mm	GPa	μW	in	Sv		
D	カロリー	コルナ	バーレル	ポイント	メートル			大正	μg	cm	rad	mW	KK	Wb		
E	ガロン	ユーボ	ピアストル	ボルト	ヤード			明治	mg	km	rad/s	kW	KM			
F	ガンマ	サイクル	ピクル	ホン	ヤール			株式会社	kg	mm²	rad/s²	MW	kt			

Korean Hangul Syllables

	340	341	342	343	344	345	346	347	348	349	34A	34B	34C	34D	34E	34F
0	가	갚	걍	곁	곌	골	괏	교	궁	귓	긱	깖	꺄	껨	꼽	꿸
1	각	갛	걔	겂	겸	곪	광	곤	궂	규	긴	깜	꺅	껫	꼿	꿉
2	간	개	걘	겅	겹	곬	괘	곯	궈	균	긷	깝	꺌	껭	꽁	꿍
3	갇	객	걜	게	겻	곯	괜	곱	궉	굴	길	깟	꺼	껴	꽂	꾜
4	갈	갠	거	겐	겼	곰	괠	곳	권	그	깂	깠	꺽	껸	꽃	꾸
5	갉	갤	걱	겔	경	곱	괩	구	궐	극	김	깡	꺾	껼	꽈	꾹
6	갊	갬	건	겜	곁	곳	괬	국	궓	근	깁	깥	껀	꼇	꽉	꾼
7	감	갭	걷	겝	계	공	괭	군	궝	귿	깃	깨	껄	꼈	꽐	꿀
8	갑	갯	걸	겟	곈	곶	괴	굳	궤	글	깅	깩	껌	꼉	꽜	꿇
9	값	갰	걺	겠	곌	과	괵	굴	궷	긁	깆	깬	껍	꼐	꽝	꿈
A	갓	갱	검	겡	곕	곽	괸	굵	귀	금	깊	깭	껏	꼬	꽤	꿉
B	갔	갸	겁	겨	곗	관	괼	굶	귁	급	까	깸	껐	꼭	꽥	꿋
C	강	갹	것	격	고	괄	굄	굻	귄	긋	깍	깹	껑	꼰	꽹	꿍
D	갖	갼	겄	겪	곡	곪	굅	굼	귈	긍	깎	깻	께	꼱	꾀	꿎
E	갗	걀	겅	견	곤	곰	굇	굽	귐	긔	깐	깼	껙	꼲	꾄	꿔
F	갘	걋	겆	겯	곧	곱	굉	굿	귑	기	깔	깽	껜	꼽	꾈	꿜

Korean Hangul Syllables (cont.)

	350	351	352	353	354	355	356	357	358	359	35A	35B	35C	35D	35E	35F
0	꿨	끅	낍	낯	냘	네	녕	놴	누	뉩	능	다	닷	덛	뎃	돎
1	꿩	끈	낏	낮	냙	넥	녁	놝	눅	뉴	늑	닥	당	덜	뎄	돔
2	꿰	끊	낑	낱	냥	넨	녜	놨	눈	뉵	늒	닦	대	덞	뎅	돕
3	꿱	끌	나	낳	너	넬	녠	뇌	눋	뉼	늬	단	댁	덟	뎌	돗
4	꿴	끎	낙	내	넉	넴	노	뇐	눌	늎	닌	닫	댄	덤	뎐	동
5	꿸	끏	낚	낵	넋	넵	녹	뇔	눔	늚	닐	달	댈	덥	뎔	돚
6	꿺	끔	난	낸	넌	넷	논	뇜	눕	늜	니	닭	댐	덧	뎠	돛
7	꿻	끕	낟	낼	널	넸	놀	뇝	눗	느	닉	닮	댑	덩	뎡	돠
8	꿽	끗	날	냄	넓	넹	놂	뇟	눙	늑	닌	닯	댓	덫	뎨	돤
9	뀌	끙	낡	냅	넙	녀	놈	뇨	눠	는	닐	닳	댔	덮	뎬	돨
A	뀐	끝	낢	냇	넘	녁	놉	뇼	눴	늘	닒	담	댕	데	도	돼
B	뀔	끼	남	냈	넙	년	놋	논	눼	늙	님	답	댜	덱	독	됐
C	뀜	끽	납	냉	넛	녈	농	놀	뉘	늡	닙	닷	더	덴	돈	되
D	뀝	낀	낫	냐	넜	념	높	놉	뇐	늠	닛	닸	덕	델	돌	된
E	뀨	낄	났	냑	넝	녑	놓	놋	뇔	늡	닝	당	덖	뎀	돌	될
F	끄	낌	낭	냥	넣	녔	놔	농	뇜	늣	닢	닺	던	뎁	돎	됨

Korean Hangul Syllables (cont.)

	360	361	362	363	364	365	366	367	368	369	36A	36B	36C	36D	36E	36F
0	됩	된	듬	따	땟	떽	딸	띕	띤	랗	러	렛	록	룃	뤄	룡
1	뒷	딀	듭	딱	땠	뗀	뫠	띵	띨	랑	럭	렝	론	룅	뤘	륭
2	됴	됩	듯	딴	땡	뗄	뫼	뜨	띰	래	런	려	롤	툐	뭬	르
3	두	뒷	등	딸	떠	뗌	뛴	뜩	띱	랙	럴	력	롬	론	뤼	륵
4	둑	뒹	듸	땀	떡	떱	뚜	뜬	띳	랜	럼	련	롭	롤	뤽	른
5	둔	듀	디	땁	떤	뗏	뚝	뜯	띵	랠	럽	렬	롯	룝	뤤	를
6	둘	둰	딕	땃	떨	뗐	뚠	뜰	라	램	럿	렴	롱	룃	뤱	름
7	둠	듈	딘	땄	떫	뗑	뚤	뜸	락	랩	렀	렵	롸	룡	뤔	릅
8	둡	듐	딛	땅	떪	떠	뚱	뜹	란	랫	렁	렷	롼	루	뤗	릇
9	둣	듕	딜	땋	떱	뗘	뚬	뜻	랄	랬	렁	렸	뢍	룩	뤙	릉
A	둥	드	딤	때	떱	또	뚱	띄	람	랭	레	령	뢨	류	류	릉
B	둬	득	딥	땍	떳	똑	뛔	뛴	랍	랴	렉	례	뢰	룩	륙	릍
C	뒀	든	딧	땐	떴	똔	뛰	띨	랏	략	렌	롄	뢴	룬	륜	릎
D	뒈	듦	딨	땔	떵	똘	뛴	띔	랐	랸	렐	렙	뢸	룸	률	리
E	뒝	들	딩	땜	떻	똥	뙬	띕	랑	럇	렘	렛	룀	룽	륨	릭
F	뒤	듧	딪	땝	떼	똬	똬	띠	랗	량	렙	로	룁	룽	륩	린

Korean Hangul Syllables (cont.)

	370	371	372	373	374	375	376	377	378	379	37A	37B	37C	37D	37E	37F
0	릴	망	먈	멜	목	뫱	뭄	문	밉	밤	박	벤	볍	뵀	붐	뷴
1	림	맞	먕	멤	몫	묏	뭅	뮬	밋	밥	뱐	벨	볘	뵈	붑	뷸
2	립	맡	머	멥	몬	묑	뭇	뮴	밌	밧	뱝	벩	볜	복	붓	뷺
3	릿	맣	먹	멧	몰	묘	뭉	뮷	밍	방	버	벰	보	뵌	붕	붗
4	링	매	먼	멨	몲	푠	뭍	므	및	밭	벅	벱	복	뵐	붙	붛
5	마	맥	멀	멩	몸	폴	뭉	믄	밑	배	번	벳	볶	뵙	붛	브
6	막	맨	멺	며	몹	폽	뭐	믈	바	백	벋	벴	본	뵜	붜	북
7	만	맬	멈	멱	못	묫	뭔	믐	박	밴	벌	벵	볼	묘	뷜	븐
8	많	맴	멉	면	몽	무	뭘	믓	밖	밸	벎	벼	봄	묜	뷌	블
9	맏	맵	멋	멸	꽈	묵	뭡	미	밪	뱀	범	벽	봅	부	붸	븜
A	말	맷	멍	몃	꽌	뮤	뭣	믹	반	뱁	법	변	봇	북	뷔	븝
B	맑	맸	멎	몄	꽜	문	뭬	민	받	뱃	벗	별	봉	분	뷕	붓
C	맒	맹	멓	명	꽝	묻	뮈	믿	발	뱄	벙	볍	봐	붇	뷘	비
D	맘	맺	메	몇	뫼	물	뮌	밀	밝	뱅	벚	볏	봔	불	뷜	빅
E	맙	먀	멕	몌	묀	묽	뮐	밂	밟	뱊	베	볐	봤	붉	뷩	빈
F	맛	먁	멘	모	묄	묾	뮤	밈	밞	뱌	벡	병	봬	붊	뷰	빌

Korean Hangul Syllables (cont.)

	380	381	382	383	384	385	386	387	388	389	38A	38B	38C	38D	38E	38F
0	븱	빵	쁜	뽀	뿅	사	샌	셴	섰	셤	솝	쉰	숟	솅	슥	싯
1	빔	빻	쁟	뽁	뷰	삭	샐	셜	성	셥	솟	쉴	술	쉬	슨	싱
2	빕	빼	쁠	뽄	뿡	삯	샘	셈	섶	셧	송	쉼	숨	쉭	슬	싶
3	빗	빽	쁨	뽈	쁘	산	샙	생	세	셨	솥	쉽	숩	쉰	슭	싸
4	빙	뺀	쁫	뽐	쁜	삳	샛	서	섹	셩	솨	쉿	숫	쉴	슴	싹
5	빚	뺄	쁬	뽑	쁠	살	샜	석	센	셰	솩	쇼	숭	쉼	습	쌌
6	빛	뺌	쁭	뽕	쁨	삵	생	섞	셀	셴	솬	속	숯	쉽	숫	싼
7	빠	뺍	쁮	뾔	쁩	삶	샤	섰	셈	셸	솰	손	숱	쉿	승	쌀
8	빡	뺏	쁯	뾰	쁴	삼	샥	선	셉	셍	상	솔	숲	싱	시	쌈
9	빤	뺐	뼈	뾩	쁵	삽	샨	섣	셋	소	쇄	솜	숴	슈	식	쌉
A	빨	뺑	뼉	뿌	쁸	삿	샬	설	셌	속	쇈	솝	슀	숙	신	쌌
B	빪	빠	뼊	뿍	쁷	샀	샴	섧	셍	솈	솟	쉐	술	싣	쌍
C	빰	뺙	뼌	뿐	쁺	상	샵	섭	셔	손	솀	솧	쉭	숩	실	쌓
D	빱	뺨	뼛	뿔	쁻	삳	샷	섬	셕	솔	솟	수	쉔	숫	싫	쌔
E	빳	뼈	뼜	뿜	쁵	새	샹	섧	션	솜	솼	숙	쉘	숭	심	쌕
F	빴	뼉	뼝	뿟	삥	색	섀	섯	셜	솝	쇠	순	쉠	숫	십	쌘

Korean Hangul Syllables (cont.)

	390	391	392	393	394	395	396	397	398	399	39A	39B	39C	39D	39E	39F
0	썔	쎈	쫴	쒔	씜	앎	앳	얠	억	엷	옛	완	윌	율	웩	윤
1	쌤	쎌	쬈	쒜	씨	앏	앵	어	엎	염	오	왈	윔	윪	웬	윩
2	쌉	쎤	쬐	쒸	씩	암	야	억	에	엽	옥	왐	윕	윫	웰	윰
3	쌨	쏘	쬔	쒼	씬	압	약	언	엑	없	온	왑	윗	윬	웸	윱
4	쌩	쏙	쬘	쓩	씰	앗	얀	얹	엔	엿	올	왓	윙	윭	웹	윳
5	썅	쏜	쬠	쓰	씱	았	얄	언	엘	엾	욹	왔	요	윮	웽	융
6	써	쏟	쬡	쓱	씹	앙	얇	얼	엠	영	옶	왕	욕	융	위	윶
7	썩	쏠	쑈	쓴	씻	앝	얌	얽	엡	옅	욻	왜	욘	워	윅	으
8	썬	쏢	쑤	쓸	씽	앞	얍	엃	엣	엽	욼	왝	욜	웍	윈	윽
9	썰	쏨	쑥	쓻	아	애	얏	엄	엥	옇	옴	왞	욤	원	윌	은
A	썲	쏩	쑨	쓼	악	액	양	업	여	예	옵	왬	욥	월	윔	을
B	썸	쏭	쑬	씀	안	앤	얕	없	역	옌	옷	왯	욧	웝	윕	읊
C	썹	쐇	쑴	씁	앉	앨	얖	엇	엮	옐	옹	왱	용	웞	윗	음
D	썼	쏴	쑵	씌	않	앰	얘	었	연	옘	옺	외	우	웠	윙	읍
E	썽	쫜	쑹	씐	알	앱	얜	엉	열	옙	와	왹	욱	웡	유	읏
F	쎄	쫬	쒀	씔	앍	앳	얠	엊	엶	옛	왁	왼	운	웨	육	응

Korean Hangul Syllables (cont.)

	3A0	3A1	3A2	3A3	3A4	3A5	3A6	3A7	3A8	3A9	3AA	3AB	3AC	3AD	3AE	3AF
0	읏	읾	잠	쟉	젓	졌	좍	죽	쥐	즙	짜	쨉	쩨	짰	쭤	찟
1	웇	잃	잡	쟌	정	졍	좔	존	쥑	줏	짝	쨋	쩽	쫴	찟	찡
2	읓	임	잣	쟎	젖	졔	좝	종	쥔	중	짠	쨌	쩌	쨁	찟	차
3	읕	입	잤	쟐	제	조	좟	주	쥘	지	짢	쨍	쩠	쬐	쮜	착
4	읖	잇	장	쟘	젝	족	좡	죽	쥠	직	짤	쨔	쪼	쬔	쮸	찬
5	읗	있	잦	쟝	젠	존	좨	준	집	진	짧	쨘	쪽	쬘	쯔	찭
6	의	잉	재	쟤	젤	졸	좼	줄	쥣	질	짬	쟝	쫀	쬠	쯤	찰
7	읜	잊	잭	쟨	젬	좀	좽	줅	쥬	질	짭	쩌	쫄	쬡	쯧	참
8	읠	잎	잰	쟬	젭	좀	죄	줆	준	짋	짰	쩍	쫌	쫑	쯩	찹
9	읨	자	잴	저	젯	좁	죈	줌	줄	짐	짰	쩐	쫍	쭈	찌	찻
A	윗	작	잼	적	젱	좃	죌	줍	줌	집	짱	쩔	쫏	쭉	찍	찼
B	이	잔	잽	전	져	종	죕	줏	즈	짓	째	쩜	쫑	쭌	찐	창
C	익	잖	잿	절	견	좇	죗	줐	즉	징	쩩	쩝	쫓	쭐	찔	찿
D	인	잗	쟀	젊	결	좋	죘	줘	즌	짖	쩐	쩟	좌	쭒	찜	채
E	일	잘	쟁	점	졉	좋	죙	줬	즐	짗	쩰	쩠	좍	쭙	찝	책
F	읽	젊	쟈	접	졉	좌	죠	줴	즘	짚	쩸	쩡	좔	쭝	찡	챈

Korean Hangul Syllables (cont.)

	3B0	3B1	3B2	3B3	3B4	3B5	3B6	3B7	3B8	3B9	3BA	3BB	3BC	3BD	3BE	3BF
0	챌	첨	체	췬	춰	츠	칫	캣	케	쳬	쾡	쿼	큰	탈	탸	템
1	챔	첩	쳔	칠	쳤	측	칭	캤	켁	코	쾨	쾽	클	탉	탕	텝
2	챕	첫	쳥	침	췌	츤	카	캥	켄	콕	쾩	퀴	큼	탐	터	텟
3	챗	첯	초	칩	쳰	츨	칵	캬	켈	콘	쿄	퀵	큽	탑	턱	텡
4	챘	청	촉	칫	취	츰	칸	캭	켐	콜	쿠	퀸	쿵	탓	턴	터
5	챙	쳬	촌	칭	췬	츱	칼	캥	켑	콤	쿡	퀼	키	탔	털	텬
6	챠	첵	촐	쵸	칠	춧	캄	커	켓	콥	쿤	큄	킥	탕	텶	텼
7	챤	첸	촘	촘	침	층	캅	컥	켕	콧	쿨	큅	킨	태	텀	톄
8	챹	쳴	촙	추	칩	치	캇	컨	켜	콩	쿰	큇	킬	택	텁	톈
9	챨	쳄	촛	축	칯	칙	캉	컫	켠	콰	쿱	큉	킴	탠	텃	토
A	참	첩	총	춘	칳	친	캐	컬	켤	콱	쿳	큐	킵	탤	텄	톡
B	챵	쳇	촤	출	츄	칖	캑	컴	켬	콴	쿵	쿤	킷	탬	텅	톤
C	처	쳉	촨	춤	춘	칠	캔	컵	켭	콸	쿼	큘	킹	탭	테	톨
D	척	쳐	촬	춥	출	칮	캘	컷	켯	쾀	쿤	큠	타	탯	텍	톰
E	천	쳔	촹	춧	츕	칚	캠	컸	켰	쾅	퀄	크	탁	탰	텐	톱
F	철	쳣	최	충	춤	칩	캡	컹	켱	쾌	쿵	큭	탄	탱	텔	톳

The Unicode Standard • Version 1.0

Korean Hangul Syllables (cont.)

	3C0	3C1	3C2	3C3	3C4	3C5	3C6	3C7	3C8	3C9	3CA	3CB	3CC	3CD	3CE	3CF
0	퉁	툿	튱	틱	퐀	펀	편	퐷	퓸	픙	하	햏	헳	혈	홧	홀
1	툫	퉁	트	틴	퐁	펄	펼	퐁	픔	픙	학	행	헴	협	황	홉
2	퇘	퉈	특	틸	팥	펌	폄	퐈	픕	프	한	햐	헵	호	홰	훗
3	퇀	퉸	튼	팀	패	펍	폅	퐝	풋	픈	할	향	헷	혹	홱	후
4	퇘	퉤	튿	팁	팩	펏	폈	픠	퐁	플	핥	허	헹	혼	홴	훅
5	퇴	튀	틀	팃	팬	펐	평	핀	풔	픔	함	헉	혀	홀	홵	훈
6	퇸	퉥	틂	팅	팰	펑	폐	표	핑	픕	합	헌	혁	홂	행	홅
7	퇷	퉨	틈	파	팸	페	폘	폰	퓌	풋	핫	헐	현	홈	회	홇
8	퇺	틜	틉	팍	팹	펙	폡	폴	퓐	피	항	헒	혈	홉	획	훔
9	툐	틤	틋	퐈	팻	펜	폣	폼	퓔	픽	해	험	협	홋	횐	훗
A	투	팁	틔	판	팼	펠	포	퐁	퓜	핀	핵	헙	협	홍	횔	홍
B	툭	퉁	틴	팔	팽	펨	폭	푸	퓟	필	핸	헛	혓	홀	횝	훠
C	툰	튜	틸	팞	갸	펩	폰	푹	퓨	핌	핼	형	혔	화	횟	훤
D	툴	튠	팀	팜	퍅	펫	폴	푼	퓬	핍	햄	헤	형	확	횡	훵
E	툼	튤	팁	팝	퍼	펭	폼	푿	퓰	핏	햅	헥	혜	환	효	훰
F	툽	튬	티	팟	퍽	펴	폽	풀	퓹	핑	햇	헨	현	활	혼	횡

Hangul (c.)   Unassigned

	3D0	3D1	3D2	3D3	3D4	3D5	3D6	3D7	3D8	3D9	3DA	3DB	3DC	3DD	3DE	3DF
0	훼	훌	희													
1	휔	훔	흰													
2	휀	훗	힐													
3	휄	훙	힘													
4	휑	흐	힙													
5	휘	흑	횅													
6	휙	흔	히													
7	휜	흚	힉													
8	휠	흘	힌													
9	휨	흜	힐													
A	휩	흝	힘													
B	횟	흠	힙													
C	횡	흡	힛													
D	휴	훗	힝													
E	흌	흥														
F	훈	흩														

This page intentionally left blank. The material is undergoing review. The revised version will appear in Volume 2.

This page intentionally left blank. The material is undergoing review. The revised version will appear in Volume 2.

	Unassigned			CNS		Small		Basic Glyphs for Arabic Language								
	FE0	FE1	FE2	FE3	FE4	FE5	FE6	FE7	FE8	FE9	FEA	FEB	FEC	FED	FEE	FEF
0				：	⌣	，	&	ء	ء	بـ	جـ	زـ	ضـ	غـ	لل	ى
1				۱	⌐	،	*	ء	آ	بـ	حـ	سـ	طـ	فـ	مـ	ي
2				۱	⌐	．	+	ء	آ	بـ	حـ	سـ	طـ	فـ	مـ	؛
3				۱	⌐		–		أ	ةـ	حـ	سـ	طـ	فـ	مـ	ة
4				﴾	⌐	；	<	ء	أ	ةـ	حـ	سـ	طـ	فـ	مـ	ي
5				⌣		：	>		ؤ	تـ	خـ	شـ	ظـ	قـ	نـ	آ
6				⌣		？	=	ء	ؤ	تـ	خـ	شـ	ظـ	قـ	نـ	آ
7				⌢		！	¯	ء	إ	ةـ	خـ	شـ	ظـ	قـ	نـ	أ
8				⌣		─	١	ء	إ	تـ	خـ	شـ	ظـ	قـ	نـ	لا
9				⌣	⠶	(	$	ء	ئـ	ثـ	دـ	صـ	عـ	كـ	هـ	لإ
A				⌣	⠶	)	%	ء	ؤـ	ثـ	دـ	صـ	عـ	كـ	هـ	لإ
B				⌐	⌢	{	@	ء	ة	ذـ	دـ	صـ	عـ	كـ	هـ	لا
C				⌣	⌢	}		ء	ئـ	ثـ	ذـ	صـ	عـ	كـ	هـ	لا
D				⩘	⠶	(		ء	ا	جـ	رـ	ضـ	غـ	لـ	وـ	
E				⩘	⠶	)		ء	ا	جـ	رـ	ضـ	غـ	لـ	وـ	
F				⌢	⌣	#		ء	بـ	جـ	زـ	ضـ	غـ	لـ	ى	[Byte Order Mark]

Halfwidth and Fullwidth Variants · Sp.

	FF0	FF1	FF2	FF3	FF4	FF5	FF6	FF7	FF8	FF9	FFA	FFB	FFC	FFD	FFE	FFF
0		０	＠	Ｐ	｀	ｐ		ｰ	ﾀ	ﾐ	ﾠ	ﾰ			￠	
1	！	１	Ａ	Ｑ	ａ	ｑ	｡	ｱ	ﾁ	ﾑ	ﾡ	ﾱ			￡	
2	＂	２	Ｂ	Ｒ	ｂ	ｒ	｢	ｲ	ﾂ	ﾒ	ﾢ	ﾲ	ﾂ	ﾒ	￢	
3	＃	３	Ｃ	Ｓ	ｃ	ｓ	｣	ｳ	ﾃ	ﾓ	ﾣ	ﾳ	ﾃ	ﾓ	￣	
4	＄	４	Ｄ	Ｔ	ｄ	ｔ	､	ｴ	ﾄ	ﾔ	ﾤ	ﾴ	ﾄ	ﾔ	￤	
5	％	５	Ｅ	Ｕ	ｅ	ｕ	･	ｵ	ﾅ	ﾕ	ﾥ	ﾵ	ﾅ	ﾕ	￥	
6	＆	６	Ｆ	Ｖ	ｆ	ｖ	ｦ	ｶ	ﾆ	ﾖ	ﾦ	ﾶ	ﾆ	ﾖ	￦	
7	＇	７	Ｇ	Ｗ	ｇ	ｗ	ｧ	ｷ	ﾇ	ﾗ	ﾧ	ﾷ	ﾇ	ﾗ		
8	（	８	Ｈ	Ｘ	ｈ	ｘ	ｨ	ｸ	ﾈ	ﾘ	ﾨ	ﾸ				
9	）	９	Ｉ	Ｙ	ｉ	ｙ	ｩ	ｹ	ﾉ	ﾙ	ﾩ	ﾹ				
A	＊	：	Ｊ	Ｚ	ｊ	ｚ	ｪ	ｺ	ﾊ	ﾚ	ﾪ	ﾺ	ﾊ	ﾚ		
B	＋	；	Ｋ	［	ｋ	｛	ｫ	ｻ	ﾋ	ﾛ	ﾫ	ﾻ	ﾋ	ﾛ		
C	，	＜	Ｌ	＼	ｌ	｜	ｬ	ｼ	ﾌ	ﾜ	ﾬ	ﾼ	ﾌ	ﾜ		
D	－	＝	Ｍ	］	ｍ	｝	ｭ	ｽ	ﾍ	ﾝ	ﾭ	ﾽ	ﾍ			�
E	．	＞	Ｎ	＾	ｎ	～	ｮ	ｾ	ﾎ	ﾞ	ﾮ	ﾾ	ﾎ			
F	／	？	Ｏ	＿	ｏ		ｯ	ｿ	ﾏ	ﾟ	ﾯ		ﾏ			

The Unicode Standard · Version 1.0

3.8 Block-by-Block Charts

The block-by-block charts contain the listing of the Unicode character names. Each Unicode character, except for the East Asian ideographic characters and Hangul syllables, is given a unique name. The character names contain only upper-case Latin letters A through z, SPACE, and HYPHEN-MINUS; this convention makes it easy to generate computer language identifiers automatically from the Unicode character names.

The code chart for each character block is repeated with the names listing for convenience of reference. Each chart is enlarged to show the appearance of small characters more clearly.

The names listing also contains clarificatory comments, as well as common character aliases and cross-references to other characters which could be confused with the character in question. For a detailed description of the conventions used in this section, see the "Notations and Conventions" section in the front matter of this volume.

	000	001	002	003	004	005	006	007
0	NUL	DLE	SPACE	0	@	P	`	p
1	SOH	DC1	!	1	A	Q	a	q
2	STX	DC2	"	2	B	R	b	r
3	ETX	DC3	#	3	C	S	c	s
4	EOT	DC4	$\|$	4	D	T	d	t
5	ENQ	NAK	%	5	E	U	e	u
6	ACK	SYN	&	6	F	V	f	v
7	BEL	ETB	'	7	G	W	g	w
8	BS	CAN	(	8	H	X	h	x
9	HT	EM	)	9	I	Y	i	y
A	LF	SUB	*	:	J	Z	j	z
B	VT	ESC	+	;	K	[	k	{
C	FF	FS	,	<	L	\	l	|
D	CR	GS	—	=	M	]	m	}
E	SO	RS	.	>	N	^	n	~|~
F	SI	US	/	?	O	_	o	DEL

C0 ASCII control codes

0000	NUL	NULL
0001	SOH	START OF HEADING
0002	STX	START OF TEXT
0003	ETX	END OF TEXT
0004	EOT	END OF TRANSMISSION
0005	ENQ	ENQUIRY
0006	ACK	ACKNOWLEDGE
0007	BEL	BELL
0008	BS	BACKSPACE
0009	HT	HORIZONTAL TABULATION
000A	LF	LINE FEED
000B	VT	VERTICAL TABULATION
000C	FF	FORM FEED
000D	CR	CARRIAGE RETURN
000E	SO	SHIFT OUT
000F	SI	SHIFT IN
0010	DLE	DATA LINK ESCAPE
0011	DC1	DEVICE CONTROL ONE
0012	DC2	DEVICE CONTROL TWO
0013	DC3	DEVICE CONTROL THREE
0014	DC4	DEVICE CONTROL FOUR
0015	NAK	NEGATIVE ACKNOWLEDGE
0016	SYN	SYNCHRONOUS IDLE
0017	ETB	END OF TRANSMISSION BLOCK
0018	CAN	CANCEL
0019	EM	END OF MEDIUM
001A	SUB	SUBSTITUTE

× (replacement character → FFFD)

001B	ESC	ESCAPE
001C	FS	FILE SEPARATOR
001D	GS	GROUP SEPARATOR
001E	RS	RECORD SEPARATOR
001F	US	UNIT SEPARATOR

ASCII

0020 ␣ SPACE
sometimes considered a control code
other space characters: 2000-200B
× *(non-breaking space → 00A0)*
× *(ideographic space → 3000)*

0021 ! EXCLAMATION MARK
= *factorial*
× *(inverted exclamation mark → 00A1)*
× *(latin letter exclamation mark → 01C3)*
× *(double exclamation mark → 203C)*
× *(heavy exclamation mark ornament → 2762)*

0022 " QUOTATION MARK
= *APL quote*
neutral (vertical), used as opening or closing quotation mark
preferred characters for paired quotation marks are 201C & 201D
× *(modifier letter double prime → 02BA)*
× *(non-spacing double acute → 030B)*
× *(non-spacing double vertical line above → 030E)*
× *(double turned comma quotation mark → 201C)*
× *(double comma quotation mark → 201D)*
× *(double prime → 2033)*

0023 # NUMBER SIGN
= *pound sign*

0024 $|$ DOLLAR SIGN
= *milreis*
= *escudo*
either glyph is acceptable
this code is unambiguously dollar sign, not "currency sign" or any other currency symbol
× *(currency sign → 00A4)*

0025 % PERCENT SIGN
× *(arabic percent sign → 066A)*
× *(per mille sign → 2030)*
× *(per ten thousand sign → 2031)*

0026 & AMPERSAND

0027 ' APOSTROPHE-QUOTE
= *ISO APOSTROPHE*
neutral (vertical) glyph having mixed usage
preferred character for apostrophe is 02BC
preferred character for opening single quotation mark is 2018
preferred character for closing single quotation mark is 2019
× *(modifier letter prime → 02B9)*
× *(modifier letter apostrophe → 02BC)*
× *(modifier letter vertical line → 02C8)*
× *(non-spacing acute → 0301)*
× *(single turned comma quotation mark → 2018)*
× *(single comma quotation mark → 2019)*
× *(prime → 2032)*

0028 (OPENING PARENTHESIS
= *ISO LEFT PARENTHESIS*

0029) CLOSING PARENTHESIS
= *ISO RIGHT PARENTHESIS*
see discussion on semantics of paired bracketing characters

002A * ASTERISK
× *(asterisk operator → 2217)*
× *(heavy asterisk → 2731)*

002B + PLUS SIGN

002C	,	COMMA
		× *(arabic comma → 060C)*
		× *(ideographic comma → 3001)*
002D	—	HYPHEN-MINUS
		= *hyphen or minus sign*
		= *hyphus*
		used for either hyphen or minus sign
		other hyphen and dash characters:
		2010-2015
		× *(hyphen → 2010)*
		× *(non-breaking hyphen → 2011)*
		× *(minus sign → 2212)*
002E	.	PERIOD
		= *ISO FULL STOP*
		× *(ideographic period → 3002)*
002F	/	SLASH
		= *ISO SOLIDUS*
		= *virgule*
		= *shilling (British)*
		× *(latin letter pipe → 01C0)*
		× *(fraction slash → 2044)*
		× *(division slash → 2215)*
0030	0	DIGIT ZERO
0031	1	DIGIT ONE
0032	2	DIGIT TWO
0033	3	DIGIT THREE
0034	4	DIGIT FOUR
0035	5	DIGIT FIVE
0036	6	DIGIT SIX
0037	7	DIGIT SEVEN
0038	8	DIGIT EIGHT
0039	9	DIGIT NINE
003A	:	COLON
		× *(armenian period → 0589)*
		× *(ratio → 2236)*
003B	;	SEMICOLON
		× *(greek question mark → 03D7)*
		× *(arabic semicolon → 061B)*
003C	<	LESS-THAN SIGN
		× *(left pointing single guillemet → 2039)*
		× *(bra → 2329)*
		× *(opening angle bracket → 3008)*
003D	=	EQUALS SIGN
		× *(not equal to → 2260)*
003E	>	GREATER-THAN SIGN
		× *(right pointing single guillemet → 203A)*
		× *(ket → 232A)*
		× *(closing angle bracket → 3009)*
003F	?	QUESTION MARK
		× *(inverted question mark → 00BF)*
		× *(greek question mark → 03D7)*
		× *(arabic question mark → 061F)*
		× *(interrobang → 203D)*
0040	@	COMMERCIAL AT

0041	A	LATIN CAPITAL LETTER A
0042	B	LATIN CAPITAL LETTER B
		× *(script b → 212C)*
0043	C	LATIN CAPITAL LETTER C
		× *(double-struck c → 2102)*
		× *(black-letter c → 212D)*
0044	D	LATIN CAPITAL LETTER D
0045	E	LATIN CAPITAL LETTER E
		× *(eulers → 2107)*
		× *(script e → 2130)*
0046	F	LATIN CAPITAL LETTER F
		× *(script f → 2131)*
		× *(turned f → 2132)*
0047	G	LATIN CAPITAL LETTER G
0048	H	LATIN CAPITAL LETTER H
		× *(script h → 210B)*
		× *(black-letter h → 210C)*
		× *(double-struck h → 210D)*
0049	I	LATIN CAPITAL LETTER I
		× *(latin capital letter i dot → 0130)*
		× *(latin small letter dotless i → 0131)*
		× *(script i → 2110)*
		× *(black-letter i → 2111)*
004A	J	LATIN CAPITAL LETTER J
004B	K	LATIN CAPITAL LETTER K
		× *(degrees kelvin → 212A)*
004C	L	LATIN CAPITAL LETTER L
		× *(script l → 2112)*
004D	M	LATIN CAPITAL LETTER M
		× *(script m → 2133)*
004E	N	LATIN CAPITAL LETTER N
		× *(double-struck n → 2115)*
004F	O	LATIN CAPITAL LETTER O
0050	P	LATIN CAPITAL LETTER P
		× *(script p → 2118)*
		× *(double-struck p → 2119)*
0051	Q	LATIN CAPITAL LETTER Q
		× *(double-struck q → 211A)*
0052	R	LATIN CAPITAL LETTER R
		× *(script r → 211B)*
		× *(black-letter r → 211C)*
		× *(double-struck r → 211D)*
0053	S	LATIN CAPITAL LETTER S
0054	T	LATIN CAPITAL LETTER T
0055	U	LATIN CAPITAL LETTER U
0056	V	LATIN CAPITAL LETTER V
0057	W	LATIN CAPITAL LETTER W
0058	X	LATIN CAPITAL LETTER X
0059	Y	LATIN CAPITAL LETTER Y
005A	Z	LATIN CAPITAL LETTER Z
		× *(double-struck z → 2124)*
		× *(black-letter z → 2128)*

005B	[	OPENING SQUARE BRACKET = *ISO LEFT SQUARE BRACKET* *other bracket characters: 3008-301B*
005C	\	BACKSLASH = *ISO REVERSE SOLIDUS* ✕ *(set minus → 2216)*
005D	]	CLOSING SQUARE BRACKET = *ISO RIGHT SQUARE BRACKET*
005E	^	SPACING CIRCUMFLEX = *ISO CIRCUMFLEX ACCENT* *this is a spacing character* ✕ *(modifier letter up arrowhead → 02C4)* ✕ *(modifier letter circumflex → 02C6)* ✕ *(non-spacing circumflex → 0302)* ✕ *(up arrowhead → 2303)*
005F	__	SPACING UNDERSCORE = *ISO LOW LINE* *this is a spacing character* ✕ *(modifier letter low macron → 02CD)* ✕ *(non-spacing macron below → 0331)* ✕ *(non-spacing underscore → 0332)* ✕ *(spacing double underscore → 2017)*
0060	`	SPACING GRAVE = *ISO GRAVE ACCENT* *this is a spacing character* ✕ *(modifier letter grave → 02CB)* ✕ *(non-spacing grave → 0300)* ✕ *(reversed prime → 2035)*
0061	a	LATIN SMALL LETTER A
0062	b	LATIN SMALL LETTER B
0063	c	LATIN SMALL LETTER C
0064	d	LATIN SMALL LETTER D
0065	e	LATIN SMALL LETTER E ✕ *(estimated symbol → 212E)* ✕ *(script small e → 212F)*
0066	f	LATIN SMALL LETTER F
0067	g	LATIN SMALL LETTER G ✕ *(latin small letter script g → 0261)* ✕ *(script small g → 210A)*
0068	h	LATIN SMALL LETTER H ✕ *(cyrillic small letter h → 04BB)* ✕ *(planck constant → 210E)*
0069	i	LATIN SMALL LETTER I ✕ *(latin capital letter i dot → 0130)* ✕ *(latin small letter dotless i → 0131)*
006A	j	LATIN SMALL LETTER J
006B	k	LATIN SMALL LETTER K
006C	l	LATIN SMALL LETTER L ✕ *(script small l → 2113)*
006D	m	LATIN SMALL LETTER M
006E	n	LATIN SMALL LETTER N
006F	o	LATIN SMALL LETTER O ✕ *(script small o → 2134)*
0070	p	LATIN SMALL LETTER P
0071	q	LATIN SMALL LETTER Q
0072	r	LATIN SMALL LETTER R
0073	s	LATIN SMALL LETTER S
0074	t	LATIN SMALL LETTER T
0075	u	LATIN SMALL LETTER U
0076	v	LATIN SMALL LETTER V
0077	w	LATIN SMALL LETTER W
0078	x	LATIN SMALL LETTER X
0079	y	LATIN SMALL LETTER Y
007A	z	LATIN SMALL LETTER Z ✕ *(latin small letter z bar → 01B6)*
007B	{	OPENING CURLY BRACKET = *ISO LEFT CURLY BRACKET* = *opening brace*
007C	|	VERTICAL BAR = *ISO VERTICAL LINE* ✕ *(latin letter pipe → 01C0)* ✕ *(divides → 2223)* ✕ *(light vertical bar → 2758)*
007D	}	CLOSING CURLY BRACKET = *ISO RIGHT CURLY BRACKET* = *closing brace*
007E	~	TILDE *this is a spacing character* ✕ *(spacing tilde → 02DC)* ✕ *(non-spacing tilde → 0303)* ✕ *(tilde operator → 223C)*
007F	DEL	DELETE *control code*

	008	009	00A	00B	00C	00D	00E	00F
0	CTRL	CTRL	NB SP	°	À	Ð	à	ð
1	CTRL	CTRL	¡	±	Á	Ñ	á	ñ
2	CTRL	CTRL	¢	²	Â	Ò	â	ò
3	CTRL	CTRL	£	³	Ã	Ó	ã	ó
4	CTRL	CTRL	¤	´	Ä	Ô	ä	ô
5	CTRL	CTRL	¥	µ	Å	Õ	å	õ
6	CTRL	CTRL	¦	¶	Æ	Ö	æ	ö
7	CTRL	CTRL	§	·	Ç	×	ç	÷
8	CTRL	CTRL	¨	¸	È	Ø	è	ø
9	CTRL	CTRL	©	¹	É	Ù	é	ù
A	CTRL	CTRL	ª	º	Ê	Ú	ê	ú
B	CTRL	CTRL	«	»	Ë	Û	ë	û
C	CTRL	CTRL	¬	¼	Ì	Ü	ì	ü
D	CTRL	CTRL	—	½	Í	Ý	í	ý
E	CTRL	CTRL	®	¾	Î	Þ	î	þ
F	CTRL	CTRL	¯	¿	Ï	ß	ï	ÿ

         The Unicode Standard • Version 1.0

C1 control codes

Codes 0080 - 009F reserved for control codes

ISO 8859-1 (aka Latin1)

00A0   NON-BREAKING SPACE
= ISO NO-BREAK SPACE
× (space → 0020)

00A1 ¡ INVERTED EXCLAMATION MARK
Spanish
× (exclamation mark → 0021)

00A2 ¢ CENT SIGN

00A3 £ POUND SIGN
= pound sterling
× (lira sign → 20A4)

00A4 ¤ CURRENCY SIGN
other currency symbol characters: 20A0-20CF
× (dollar sign → 0024)

00A5 ¥|¥ YEN SIGN
= yuan sign
either glyph is acceptable

00A6 ¦ BROKEN VERTICAL BAR
= ISO BROKEN BAR

00A7 § SECTION SIGN
linked s's
paragraph sign in some European usage

00A8 ¨ SPACING DIAERESIS
= ISO DIAERESIS
this is a spacing character
× (non-spacing diaeresis → 0308)

00A9 © COPYRIGHT SIGN
× (sound recording copyright → 2117)

00AA ª FEMININE ORDINAL INDICATOR
Spanish

00AB « LEFT POINTING GUILLEMET
= ISO LEFT-POINTING DOUBLE ANGLE QUOTATION MARK
usually opening, sometimes closing
× (much less than → 226A)
× (opening double angle bracket → 300A)

00AC ¬ NOT SIGN
× (reversed not sign → 2310)

00AD — SOFT HYPHEN
= discretionary hyphen

00AE ® REGISTERED TRADE MARK SIGN
= ISO REGISTERED SIGN

00AF ¯ SPACING MACRON
= ISO MACRON
= overline
= APL overbar
this is a spacing character
× (modifier letter macron → 02C9)
× (non-spacing macron → 0304)
× (non-spacing overscore → 0305)

00B0 ° DEGREE SIGN
this is a spacing character
× (spacing ring above → 02DA)
× (non-spacing ring above → 030A)
× (ring operator → 2218)

00B1 ± PLUS-OR-MINUS SIGN
= ISO PLUS-MINUS SIGN
× (minus-or-plus sign → 2213)

00B2 ² SUPERSCRIPT DIGIT TWO
= ISO SUPERSCRIPT TWO
= squared
× (superscript digit one → 00B9)

00B3 ³ SUPERSCRIPT DIGIT THREE
= ISO SUPERSCRIPT THREE
= cubed
× (superscript digit one → 00B9)

00B4 ´ SPACING ACUTE
= ISO ACUTE ACCENT
this is a spacing character
× (modifier letter prime → 02B9)
× (modifier letter acute → 02CA)
× (non-spacing acute → 0301)
× (prime → 2032)

00B5 µ MICRO SIGN
× (greek small letter mu → 03BC)

00B6 ¶ PARAGRAPH SIGN
= ISO PILCROW SIGN
reversed PH ligature
section sign in some European usage
× (curved stem paragraph sign ornament → 2761)

00B7 · MIDDLE DOT
= Georgian comma
= Greek middle dot
× (bullet → 2022)
× (one dot leader → 2024)
× (bullet operator → 2219)
× (dot operator → 22C5)
× (katakana middle dot → 30FB)

00B8 ¸ SPACING CEDILLA
= ISO CEDILLA
this is a spacing character
other spacing accent characters: 02D8-02DB
× (non-spacing cedilla → 0327)

00B9 ¹ SUPERSCRIPT DIGIT ONE
= ISO SUPERSCRIPT ONE
other superscript digit characters: 2070-2079
× (superscript digit two → 00B2)
× (superscript digit three → 00B3)

00BA º MASCULINE ORDINAL INDICATOR
Spanish

00BB	»	RIGHT POINTING GUILLEMET = *ISO RIGHT-POINTING DOUBLE ANGLE* *QUOTATION MARK* *usually closing, sometimes opening* × *(much greater than → 226B)* × *(closing double angle bracket →* *300B)*
00BC	¼	FRACTION ONE QUARTER = *ISO VULGAR FRACTION ONE* *QUARTER* *either glyph is acceptable*
00BD	½	FRACTION ONE HALF = *ISO VULGAR FRACTION ONE HALF* *either glyph is acceptable*
00BE	¾	FRACTION THREE QUARTERS = *ISO VULGAR FRACTION THREE* *QUARTERS* *either glyph is acceptable* *other fraction characters: 2153-215E*
00BF	¿	INVERTED QUESTION MARK = *turned question mark* *Spanish* × *(question mark → 003F)*
00C0	À	LATIN CAPITAL LETTER A GRAVE = *ISO LATIN CAPITAL LETTER A WITH* *GRAVE* *(many of the following have similar* *name transformations)*
00C1	Á	LATIN CAPITAL LETTER A ACUTE
00C2	Â	LATIN CAPITAL LETTER A CIRCUMFLEX
00C3	Ã	LATIN CAPITAL LETTER A TILDE
00C4	Ä	LATIN CAPITAL LETTER A DIAERESIS
00C5	Å	LATIN CAPITAL LETTER A RING = *ISO LATIN CAPITAL LETTER A WITH* *RING ABOVE* × *(angstrom unit → 212B)*
00C6	Æ	LATIN CAPITAL LETTER A E = *ISO LATIN CAPITAL LETTER AE*
00C7	Ç	LATIN CAPITAL LETTER C CEDILLA
00C8	È	LATIN CAPITAL LETTER E GRAVE
00C9	É	LATIN CAPITAL LETTER E ACUTE
00CA	Ê	LATIN CAPITAL LETTER E CIRCUMFLEX
00CB	Ë	LATIN CAPITAL LETTER E DIAERESIS
00CC	Ì	LATIN CAPITAL LETTER I GRAVE
00CD	Í	LATIN CAPITAL LETTER I ACUTE
00CE	Î	LATIN CAPITAL LETTER I CIRCUMFLEX
00CF	Ï	LATIN CAPITAL LETTER I DIAERESIS
00D0	Đ	LATIN CAPITAL LETTER ETH × *(latin small letter eth → 00F0)* × *(latin capital letter d bar → 0110)* × *(latin capital letter african d → 0189)*
00D1	Ñ	LATIN CAPITAL LETTER N TILDE
00D2	Ò	LATIN CAPITAL LETTER O GRAVE
00D3	Ó	LATIN CAPITAL LETTER O ACUTE

00D4	Ô	LATIN CAPITAL LETTER O CIRCUMFLEX
00D5	Õ	LATIN CAPITAL LETTER O TILDE
00D6	Ö	LATIN CAPITAL LETTER O DIAERESIS
00D7	×	MULTIPLICATION SIGN
00D8	Ø	LATIN CAPITAL LETTER O SLASH = *ISO LATIN CAPITAL LETTER O WITH* *STROKE* × *(empty set → 2205)*
00D9	Ù	LATIN CAPITAL LETTER U GRAVE
00DA	Ú	LATIN CAPITAL LETTER U ACUTE
00DB	Û	LATIN CAPITAL LETTER U CIRCUMFLEX
00DC	Ü	LATIN CAPITAL LETTER U DIAERESIS
00DD	Ý	LATIN CAPITAL LETTER Y ACUTE
00DE	Þ	LATIN CAPITAL LETTER THORN
00DF	ß	LATIN SMALL LETTER SHARP S = *ess-zed* *German* *uppercase is "SS"* × *(greek small letter beta → 03B2)*
00E0	à	LATIN SMALL LETTER A GRAVE = *ISO LATIN SMALL LETTER A WITH* *GRAVE* *(many of the following have similar* *name transformations)*
00E1	á	LATIN SMALL LETTER A ACUTE
00E2	â	LATIN SMALL LETTER A CIRCUMFLEX
00E3	ã	LATIN SMALL LETTER A TILDE *Portuguese*
00E4	ä	LATIN SMALL LETTER A DIAERESIS
00E5	å	LATIN SMALL LETTER A RING = *ISO LATIN SMALL LETTER A WITH* *RING ABOVE* *Danish, Norwegian, Swedish*
00E6	æ	LATIN SMALL LETTER A E = *ISO LATIN SMALL LETTER AE* *IPA* × *(latin small letter o e → 0153)*
00E7	ç	LATIN SMALL LETTER C CEDILLA
00E8	è	LATIN SMALL LETTER E GRAVE
00E9	é	LATIN SMALL LETTER E ACUTE
00EA	ê	LATIN SMALL LETTER E CIRCUMFLEX
00EB	ë	LATIN SMALL LETTER E DIAERESIS
00EC	ì	LATIN SMALL LETTER I GRAVE *Italian, Malagash*
00ED	í	LATIN SMALL LETTER I ACUTE
00EE	î	LATIN SMALL LETTER I CIRCUMFLEX
00EF	ï	LATIN SMALL LETTER I DIAERESIS
00F0	ð	LATIN SMALL LETTER ETH *Icelandic, Faroese, old English, IPA* × *(latin capital letter eth → 00D0)*
00F1	ñ	LATIN SMALL LETTER N TILDE
00F2	ò	LATIN SMALL LETTER O GRAVE

00F3	ó	LATIN SMALL LETTER O ACUTE
00F4	ô	LATIN SMALL LETTER O CIRCUMFLEX
00F5	õ	LATIN SMALL LETTER O TILDE
		Portuguese, Estonian
00F6	ö	LATIN SMALL LETTER O DIAERESIS
00F7	÷	DIVISION SIGN
00F8	ø	LATIN SMALL LETTER O SLASH
		= ISO LATIN SMALL LETTER O WITH STROKE
		Danish, Norwegian, Faroese, IPA
00F9	ù	LATIN SMALL LETTER U GRAVE
		French, Italian
00FA	ú	LATIN SMALL LETTER U ACUTE
00FB	û	LATIN SMALL LETTER U CIRCUMFLEX
00FC	ü	LATIN SMALL LETTER U DIAERESIS
00FD	ý	LATIN SMALL LETTER Y ACUTE
		Czech, Slovak, Icelandic, Faroese, Malagash
00FE	þ	LATIN SMALL LETTER THORN
		Icelandic, old English, IPA
		Runic letter borrowed into Latin script
00FF	ÿ	LATIN SMALL LETTER Y DIAERESIS
		French
		✕ *(latin capital letter y diaeresis →* *0178)*

	010	011	012	013	014	015	016	017
0	Ā	Đ	Ġ	İ	l·	Ő	Š	Ű
1	ā	đ	ġ	ı	Ł	ő	š	ű
2	Ă	Ē	Ģ	Ĳ	ł	Œ	Ţ|Ț	Ų
3	ă	ē	ǧ|ǵ	ĳ	Ń	œ	ţ|ț	ų
4	Ą	Ĕ	Ĥ	Ĵ	ń	Ŕ	Ť|Ť'	Ŵ
5	ą	ĕ	ĥ	ĵ	Ņ	ŕ	ť|ť'	ŵ
6	Ć	Ė	Ħ	Ķ	ņ	Ŗ	Ŧ	Ŷ
7	ć	ė	ħ	ķ	Ň	ŗ	ŧ	ŷ
8	Ĉ	Ę	Ĩ	ĸ	ň	Ř	Ũ	Ÿ
9	ĉ	ę	ĩ	Ĺ	ŉ	ř	ũ	Ź
A	Ċ	Ě	Ī	Í	ŋ|Ŋ	Ś	Ū	ź
B	ċ	ě	ī	Ļ	ŋ	ś	ū	Ż
C	Č	Ĝ	Ĭ	ļ	Ō	Ŝ	Ŭ	ż
D	č	ĝ	ĭ	Ľ|Ľ	ō	ŝ	ŭ	Ž
E	Ď|Ď'	Ğ	Į	ľ|ľ	Ŏ	Ş|Ș	ů	ž
F	ď|ď'	ğ	į	Ŀ	ŏ	ş|ș	ů	

European Latin

0100	Ā	LATIN CAPITAL LETTER A MACRON
0101	ā	LATIN SMALL LETTER A MACRON *= ISO LATIN ... LETTER A WITH MACRON* *Latvian, ...*
0102	Ă	LATIN CAPITAL LETTER A BREVE
0103	ă	LATIN SMALL LETTER A BREVE *Romanian, Vietnamese, ...*
0104	Ą	LATIN CAPITAL LETTER A OGONEK
0105	ą	LATIN SMALL LETTER A OGONEK *Polish, Lithuanian, ...*
0106	Ć	LATIN CAPITAL LETTER C ACUTE
0107	ć	LATIN SMALL LETTER C ACUTE *Polish, Croatian, ...* × *(cyrillic small letter tshe → 045B)*
0108	Ĉ	LATIN CAPITAL LETTER C CIRCUMFLEX
0109	ĉ	LATIN SMALL LETTER C CIRCUMFLEX *Esperanto*
010A	Ċ	LATIN CAPITAL LETTER C DOT
010B	ċ	LATIN SMALL LETTER C DOT *= ISO LATIN ... LETTER C WITH DOT ABOVE* *Maltese*
010C	Č	LATIN CAPITAL LETTER C HACEK
010D	č	LATIN SMALL LETTER C HACEK *= ISO LATIN ... LETTER C WITH CARON* *(many)*
010E	ĎĎ'	LATIN CAPITAL LETTER D HACEK *the form using hacek is preferred in all contexts*
010F	ďď'	LATIN SMALL LETTER D HACEK *Czech, Slovak* *the form using apostrophe is preferred in typesetting*
0110	Đ	LATIN CAPITAL LETTER D BAR × *(latin capital letter eth → 00D0)* × *(latin small letter d bar → 0111)* × *(latin capital letter african d → 0189)*
0111	đ	LATIN SMALL LETTER D BAR *= ISO LATIN ... LETTER D WITH STROKE* *Croatian, Vietnamese, Lappish* × *(latin capital letter d bar → 0110)* × *(cyrillic small letter dje → 0452)*
0112	Ē	LATIN CAPITAL LETTER E MACRON
0113	ē	LATIN SMALL LETTER E MACRON *Latvian, ...*
0114	Ĕ	LATIN CAPITAL LETTER E BREVE
0115	ĕ	LATIN SMALL LETTER E BREVE *Malay, ...*
0116	Ė	LATIN CAPITAL LETTER E DOT
0117	ė	LATIN SMALL LETTER E DOT *Lithuanian*
0118	Ę	LATIN CAPITAL LETTER E OGONEK
0119	ę	LATIN SMALL LETTER E OGONEK *Polish, Lithuanian, ...*
011A	Ě	LATIN CAPITAL LETTER E HACEK
011B	ě	LATIN SMALL LETTER E HACEK *Czech, ...*
011C	Ĝ	LATIN CAPITAL LETTER G CIRCUMFLEX
011D	ĝ	LATIN SMALL LETTER G CIRCUMFLEX *Esperanto*
011E	Ğ	LATIN CAPITAL LETTER G BREVE
011F	ğ	LATIN SMALL LETTER G BREVE *Turkish* × *(latin small letter g hacek → 01E7)*
0120	Ġ	LATIN CAPITAL LETTER G DOT
0121	ġ	LATIN SMALL LETTER G DOT *Maltese, ...*
0122	Ģ	LATIN CAPITAL LETTER G CEDILLA
0123	ģ	LATIN SMALL LETTER G CEDILLA *Latvian, Lappish* *there are three glyph variants*
0124	Ĥ	LATIN CAPITAL LETTER H CIRCUMFLEX
0125	ĥ	LATIN SMALL LETTER H CIRCUMFLEX *Esperanto*
0126	Ħ	LATIN CAPITAL LETTER H BAR
0127	ħ	LATIN SMALL LETTER H BAR *Maltese, IPA, ...* × *(cyrillic small letter tshe → 045B)* × *(planck constant over 2 pi → 210F)*
0128	Ĩ	LATIN CAPITAL LETTER I TILDE
0129	ĩ	LATIN SMALL LETTER I TILDE *Greenlandic*
012A	Ī	LATIN CAPITAL LETTER I MACRON
012B	ī	LATIN SMALL LETTER I MACRON *Latvian, ...*
012C	Ĭ	LATIN CAPITAL LETTER I BREVE
012D	ĭ	LATIN SMALL LETTER I BREVE *Latin, ...*
012E	Į	LATIN SMALL LETTER I OGONEK
012F	į	LATIN SMALL LETTER I OGONEK *Lithuanian, ...*
0130	İ	LATIN CAPITAL LETTER I DOT *= ISO LATIN CAPITAL LETTER I WITH DOT ABOVE* *Turkish* *has same lowercase as does 0049 LATIN CAPITAL LETTER I* *providing a unique caseform clone for this letter would seem contrary to current practice* × *(latin capital letter i → 0049)* × *(latin small letter i → 0069)*

0131	ı	LATIN SMALL LETTER DOTLESS I = *ISO LATIN SMALL LETTER I WITH NO DOT* *Turkish* *has same uppercase as does 0069 LATIN SMALL LETTER I* *providing a unique caseform clone for this letter would seem contrary to current practice* ✕ *(latin capital letter i → 0049)* ✕ *(latin small letter i → 0069)*
0132	IJ	LATIN CAPITAL LETTER I J
0133	ij	LATIN SMALL LETTER I J = *ISO LATIN … LIGATURE IJ* *Dutch*
0134	Ĵ	LATIN CAPITAL LETTER J CIRCUMFLEX
0135	ĵ	LATIN SMALL LETTER J CIRCUMFLEX *Esperanto*
0136	Ķ	LATIN CAPITAL LETTER K CEDILLA
0137	ķ	LATIN SMALL LETTER K CEDILLA *Latvian, …*
0138	ĸ	LATIN SMALL LETTER KRA *old Greenlandic*
0139	Ĺ	LATIN CAPITAL LETTER L ACUTE
013A	ĺ	LATIN SMALL LETTER L ACUTE *Slovak*
013B	Ļ	LATIN CAPITAL LETTER L CEDILLA
013C	ļ	LATIN SMALL LETTER L CEDILLA *Latvian*
013D	Ľ|Ľ	LATIN CAPITAL LETTER L HACEK
013E	ľ|ľ	LATIN SMALL LETTER L HACEK *Slovak* *the form using apostrophe is preferred in typesetting*
013F	Ŀ	LATIN CAPITAL LETTER L WITH MIDDLE DOT
0140	ŀ	LATIN SMALL LETTER L WITH MIDDLE DOT *Catalan*
0141	Ł	LATIN CAPITAL LETTER L SLASH
0142	ł	LATIN SMALL LETTER L SLASH *Polish, …* ✕ *(latin small letter barred l → 019A)*
0143	Ń	LATIN CAPITAL LETTER N ACUTE
0144	ń	LATIN SMALL LETTER N ACUTE *Polish, …*
0145	Ņ	LATIN CAPITAL LETTER N CEDILLA
0146	ņ	LATIN SMALL LETTER N CEDILLA *Latvian*
0147	Ň	LATIN CAPITAL LETTER N HACEK
0148	ň	LATIN SMALL LETTER N HACEK *Czech, Slovak*
0149	ŉ	LATIN SMALL LETTER APOSTROPHE N = *ISO LATIN SMALL LETTER N PRECEDED BY APOSTROPHE* *Afrikaans* *this is not actually a single letter*
014A	Ŋ|Ŋ	LATIN CAPITAL LETTER ENG
014B	ŋ	LATIN SMALL LETTER ENG *Lappish, IPA, …*
014C	Ō	LATIN CAPITAL LETTER O MACRON
014D	ō	LATIN SMALL LETTER O MACRON *Latvian, …*
014E	Ŏ	LATIN CAPITAL LETTER O BREVE
014F	ŏ	LATIN SMALL LETTER O BREVE *Latin*
0150	Ő	LATIN CAPITAL LETTER O DOUBLE ACUTE
0151	ő	LATIN SMALL LETTER O DOUBLE ACUTE *Hungarian*
0152	Œ	LATIN CAPITAL LETTER O E
0153	œ	LATIN SMALL LETTER O E = *ISO LATIN … LIGATURE OE* *French, IPA, …* ✕ *(latin small letter a e → 00E6)* ✕ *(latin letter small capital o e → 0276)*
0154	Ŕ	LATIN CAPITAL LETTER R ACUTE
0155	ŕ	LATIN SMALL LETTER R ACUTE *Slovak, …*
0156	Ŗ	LATIN CAPITAL LETTER R CEDILLA
0157	ŗ	LATIN SMALL LETTER R CEDILLA *Latvian*
0158	Ř	LATIN CAPITAL LETTER R HACEK
0159	ř	LATIN SMALL LETTER R HACEK *Czech, …*
015A	Ś	LATIN CAPITAL LETTER S ACUTE
015B	ś	LATIN SMALL LETTER S ACUTE *Polish, …*
015C	Ŝ	LATIN CAPITAL LETTER S CIRCUMFLEX
015D	ŝ	LATIN SMALL LETTER S CIRCUMFLEX *Esperanto*
015E	Ş|Ş	LATIN CAPITAL LETTER S CEDILLA
015F	ş|ş	LATIN SMALL LETTER S CEDILLA *Turkish, Romanian, …* *the form using under-comma is taken to be a glyph variant*
0160	Š	LATIN CAPITAL LETTER S HACEK
0161	š	LATIN SMALL LETTER S HACEK *(many)*
0162	Ţ|Ţ	LATIN CAPITAL LETTER T CEDILLA
0163	ţ|ţ	LATIN SMALL LETTER T CEDILLA *Romanian, …* *the form using under-comma is taken to be a glyph variant*

0164	Ť|Ť'	LATIN CAPITAL LETTER T HACEK

the form using hacek is preferred in all
contexts

0165	ť|ť'	LATIN SMALL LETTER T HACEK

Czech, Slovak
the form using apostrophe is preferred
in typesetting

0166	Ŧ	LATIN CAPITAL LETTER T BAR
0167	ŧ	LATIN SMALL LETTER T BAR

Lappish

0168	Ũ	LATIN CAPITAL LETTER U TILDE
0169	ũ	LATIN SMALL LETTER U TILDE

Greenlandic

016A	Ū	LATIN CAPITAL LETTER U MACRON
016B	ū	LATIN SMALL LETTER U MACRON

Latvian, Lithuanian, …

016C	Ŭ	LATIN CAPITAL LETTER U BREVE
016D	ŭ	LATIN SMALL LETTER U BREVE

Latin, Esperanto, …

016E	Ů	LATIN CAPITAL LETTER U RING
016F	ů	LATIN SMALL LETTER U RING

Czech, …

0170	Ű	LATIN CAPITAL LETTER U DOUBLE ACUTE
0171	ű	LATIN SMALL LETTER U DOUBLE ACUTE

Hungarian

0172	Ų	LATIN CAPITAL LETTER U OGONEK
0173	ų	LATIN SMALL LETTER U OGONEK

Lithuanian

0174	Ŵ	LATIN CAPITAL LETTER W CIRCUMFLEX
0175	ŵ	LATIN SMALL LETTER W CIRCUMFLEX

Welsh

0176	Ŷ	LATIN CAPITAL LETTER Y CIRCUMFLEX
0177	ŷ	LATIN SMALL LETTER Y CIRCUMFLEX

Welsh

0178	Ÿ	LATIN CAPITAL LETTER Y DIAERESIS

French
× *(latin small letter y diaeresis → 00FF)*

0179	Ź	LATIN CAPITAL LETTER Z ACUTE
017A	ź	LATIN SMALL LETTER Z ACUTE

Polish, …

017B	Ż	LATIN CAPITAL LETTER Z DOT
017C	ż	LATIN SMALL LETTER Z DOT

Polish, …

017D	Ž	LATIN CAPITAL LETTER Z HACEK
017E	ž	LATIN SMALL LETTER Z HACEK

(many)

	018	019	01A	01B	01C	01D	01E	01F
0	ƀ	Ɛ	Ơ	ư	ǀ	ǐ	Ǡ	ǰ
1	Ɓ	Ƒ	ơ	Ʊ	ǁ	Ǒ	ǡ	
2	Ƃ	ƒ	Ƣ	Ʋ	ǂ	ǒ	Ǣ	
3	ƃ	Ɠ	ƣ	Ƴ	ǃ	Ǔ	ǣ	
4	Ƅ	Ɣ	Ƥ	ƴ	Ǆ	ǔ	Ǥ	
5	ƅ	ƕ	ƥ	Ƶ	ǅ	Ǖ	ǥ	
6	Ɔ	Ɩ	Ʀ	ƶ	ǆ	ǖ	Ǧ	
7	Ƈ	Ɨ	Ƨ	Ʒ	Ǉ	Ǘ	ǧ	
8	ƈ	Ƙ	ƨ	Ƹ	ǈ	ǘ	Ǩ	
9	Ɖ	ƙ	Ʃ	ƹ	ǉ	Ǚ	ǩ	
A	Ɗ	ƚ	ƪ	ƺ	Ǌ	ǚ	Ǫ	
B	Ƌ	ƛ	ƫ	ƻ	ǋ	Ǜ	ǫ	
C	ƌ	Ɯ	Ƭ	Ƽ	ǌ	ǜ	Ǭ	
D	ƍ	Ɲ	ƭ	ƽ	Ǎ	ǝ	ǭ	
E	Ǝ	ƞ	Ʈ	ƾ	ǎ	Ǟ	Ǯ	
F	Ə	Ɵ	ƿ	Ǐ	ǟ	ǯ		

The Unicode Standard • Version 1.0

Extended Latin

0180	ƀ	**LATIN SMALL LETTER B BAR**
		Americanist usage for phonetic beta
		× *(greek small letter beta → 03B2)*
		× *(blank → 2422)*
0181	Ɓ	**LATIN CAPITAL LETTER B HOOK**
		× *(latin small letter b hook → 0253)*
0182	Ƃ	**LATIN CAPITAL LETTER B TOPBAR**
0183	ƃ	**LATIN SMALL LETTER B TOPBAR**
		Soviet minority language scripts
		× *(cyrillic capital letter be → 0411)*
0184	Ƅ	**LATIN CAPITAL LETTER TONE SIX**
0185	ƅ	**LATIN SMALL LETTER TONE SIX**
		Zhuang
		Zhuang tone three is Cyrillic ze
		Zhuang tone four is Cyrillic che
		× *(latin small letter tone two → 01A8)*
		× *(latin small letter tone five → 01BD)*
		× *(cyrillic small letter ze → 0437)*
		× *(cyrillic small letter che → 0447)*
		× *(cyrillic small letter soft sign → 044C)*
0186	Ɔ	**LATIN CAPITAL LETTER OPEN O**
		typographically a turned C
		× *(latin small letter open o → 0254)*
0187	Ƈ	**LATIN CAPITAL LETTER C HOOK**
0188	ƈ	**LATIN SMALL LETTER C HOOK**
		African
0189	Ɖ	**LATIN CAPITAL LETTER AFRICAN D**
		× *(latin capital letter eth → 00D0)*
		× *(latin capital letter d bar → 0110)*
		× *(latin small letter d retroflex hook →*
		0256)
018A	Ɗ	**LATIN CAPITAL LETTER D HOOK**
		African
		× *(latin small letter d hook → 0257)*
018B	Ƌ	**LATIN CAPITAL LETTER D TOPBAR**
018C	ƌ	**LATIN SMALL LETTER D TOPBAR**
		Soviet minority language scripts
018D	ƍ	**LATIN SMALL LETTER TURNED DELTA**
		archaic phonetic for labialized dental
		fricative
		recommended spellings 007A 02B7 or
		007A 032B
018E	Ǝ	**LATIN CAPITAL LETTER TURNED E**
		Nigerian
		alternate uppercase usage to the
		following
		× *(latin small letter turned e → 01DD)*
018F	Ə	**LATIN CAPITAL LETTER SCHWA**
		Azerbaijani, ...
		× *(latin small letter schwa → 0259)*
0190	Ɛ	**LATIN CAPITAL LETTER EPSILON**
		African
		× *(latin small letter epsilon → 025B)*
		× *(eulers → 2107)*

0191	Ƒ	**LATIN CAPITAL LETTER F HOOK**
		African
		× *(latin small letter script f → 0192)*
0192	ƒ	**LATIN SMALL LETTER SCRIPT F**
		= *ISO SMALL LETTER F WITH HOOK*
		= *Florin currency symbol (Dutch)*
		= *function symbol*
		× *(latin capital letter f hook → 0191)*
0193	Ɠ	**LATIN CAPITAL LETTER G HOOK**
		African
		× *(latin small letter g hook → 0260)*
0194	Ɣ	**LATIN CAPITAL LETTER GAMMA**
		African
		× *(latin small letter gamma → 0263)*
0195	ƕ	**LATIN SMALL LETTER H V**
		Gothic
0196	Ɩ	**LATIN CAPITAL LETTER IOTA**
		African
		× *(latin small letter iota → 0269)*
0197	Ɨ	**LATIN CAPITAL LETTER BARRED I**
		= *i bar*
		African
		ISO 6438 gives lowercase as 026A, not
		0268
		× *(latin letter small capital i → 026A)*
0198	Ƙ	**LATIN CAPITAL LETTER K HOOK**
0199	ƙ	**LATIN SMALL LETTER K HOOK**
		African
019A	ƚ	**LATIN SMALL LETTER BARRED L**
		= *l bar*
		Americanist phonetic usage
		× *(latin small letter l slash → 0142)*
019B	ƛ	**LATIN SMALL LETTER BARRED LAMBDA**
		= *lambda bar*
		Americanist phonetic usage
019C	Ɯ	**LATIN CAPITAL LETTER TURNED M**
		Zhuang
		× *(latin small letter turned m → 026F)*
019D	Ɲ	**LATIN CAPITAL LETTER N HOOK**
		African
		× *(latin small letter n hook → 0272)*
019E	ƞ	**LATIN SMALL LETTER N WITH LONG RIGHT LEG**
		archaic phonetic for Japanese syllabic
		"n"
		recommended spelling 006E 0329
019F	Ɵ	**LATIN CAPITAL LETTER BARRED O**
		= *o bar*
		African, Soviet minority language scripts
		× *(latin small letter barred o → 0275)*
01A0	Ơ	**LATIN CAPITAL LETTER O HORN**
01A1	ơ	**LATIN SMALL LETTER O HORN**
		Vietnamese
01A2	Ƣ	**LATIN CAPITAL LETTER O I**
01A3	ƣ	**LATIN SMALL LETTER O I**
		old Azerbaijani

01A4   ℙ   LATIN CAPITAL LETTER P HOOK

01A5   ƥ|ƥ   LATIN SMALL LETTER P HOOK
     African

01A6   Ʀ   LATIN LETTER Y R
     old Norse
     from German Standard DIN 31624

01A7   Ƨ   LATIN CAPITAL LETTER TONE TWO

01A8   ƨ   LATIN SMALL LETTER TONE TWO
     Zhuang
     typographically a reversed S
     ✕ *(latin small letter tone six → 0185)*

01A9   Ʃ   LATIN CAPITAL LETTER ESH
     African
     ✕ *(latin small letter esh → 0283)*
     ✕ *(greek capital letter sigma → 03A3)*

01AA   ƪ   LATIN LETTER REVERSED ESH LOOP
     archaic phonetic for labialized palato-alveolar or palatal fricative
     Twi
     recommended spellings 0283 02B7, 00E7 02B7, 0068 0265, etc.

01AB   ƫ   LATIN SMALL LETTER T PALATAL HOOK
     archaic phonetic for palatalized alveolar or dental stop
     recommended spelling 0074 02B2

01AC   Ƭ   LATIN CAPITAL LETTER T HOOK

01AD   ƭ   LATIN SMALL LETTER T HOOK
     African

01AE   Ʈ   LATIN CAPITAL LETTER T RETROFLEX HOOK
     African
     ✕ *(latin small letter t retroflex hook → 0288)*

01AF   Ư   LATIN CAPITAL LETTER U HORN

01B0   ư   LATIN SMALL LETTER U HORN
     Vietnamese

01B1   Ʊ   LATIN CAPITAL LETTER UPSILON
     African
     typographically based on turned capital Greek omega
     ✕ *(latin small letter upsilon → 028A)*
     ✕ *(mho → 2127)*

01B2   Ʋ   LATIN CAPITAL LETTER SCRIPT V
     = *ISO LATIN CAPITAL LETTER V WITH HOOK*
     African
     ✕ *(latin small letter script v → 028B)*

01B3   Ƴ   LATIN CAPITAL LETTER Y HOOK

01B4   ƴ   LATIN SMALL LETTER Y HOOK
     African

01B5   Ƶ   LATIN CAPITAL LETTER Z BAR

01B6   ƶ   LATIN SMALL LETTER Z BAR
     variant of Latin "z"
     ✕ *(latin small letter z → 007A)*

01B7   Ʒ|Ʒ   LATIN CAPITAL LETTER YOGH
     African
     ✕ *(latin small letter yogh → 0292)*

01B8   Ƹ   LATIN CAPITAL LETTER REVERSED YOGH

01B9   ƹ   LATIN SMALL LETTER REVERSED YOGH
     archaic phonetic for voiced pharyngeal fricative
     sometimes typographically rendered with a turned digit 3
     recommended spelling 0295
     ✕ *(latin letter reversed glottal stop → 0295)*
     ✕ *(arabic letter ain → 0639)*

01BA   ƺ   LATIN SMALL LETTER YOGH WITH TAIL
     archaic phonetic for labialized voiced palato-alveolar or palatal fricative
     Twi
     recommended spellings 0292 02B7 or 006A 02B7

01BB   ƻ   LATIN LETTER TWO BAR
     archaic phonetic for [dz] affricate
     recommended spellings 0292 or 0064 007A

01BC   Ƽ   LATIN CAPITAL LETTER TONE FIVE

01BD   ƽ   LATIN SMALL LETTER TONE FIVE
     Zhuang
     ✕ *(latin small letter tone six → 0185)*

01BE   ƾ   LATIN LETTER INVERTED GLOTTAL STOP BAR
     archaic phonetic for [ts] affricate
     recommended spelling 0074 0073

01BF   ƿ   LATIN LETTER WYNN
     Runic letter borrowed into Latin script
     replaced by "w" in modern transcriptions of Old English

01C0   ǀ|ǀ   LATIN LETTER PIPE
     = *dental click*
     Khoisan tradition
     "c" in Zulu orthography
     ✕ *(slash → 002F)*
     ✕ *(vertical bar → 007C)*
     ✕ *(latin small letter turned t → 0287)*
     ✕ *(divides → 2223)*

01C1   ǁ|ǁ   LATIN LETTER DOUBLE PIPE
     = *lateral click*
     Khoisan tradition
     "x" in Zulu orthography
     ✕ *(latin letter inverted glottal stop → 0296)*
     ✕ *(parallel to → 2225)*

01C2   ǂ|ǂ   LATIN LETTER PIPE DOUBLE BAR
     = *alveolar (or palatal) click*
     Khoisan tradition
     no IPA equivalent
     ✕ *(not equal to → 2260)*

01C3   !   LATIN LETTER EXCLAMATION MARK
       = palatal (or alveolar) click
       Khoisan tradition
       "q" in Zulu orthography
       ✕ (exclamation mark → 0021)
       ✕ (latin letter stretched c → 0297)

Croatian digraphs matching Serbian Cyrillic letters

01C4   DŽ   LATIN CAPITAL LETTER D Z HACEK
01C5   Dž   LATIN LETTER CAPITAL D SMALL Z HACEK
01C6   dž   LATIN SMALL LETTER D Z HACEK
       ✕ (cyrillic small letter dzhe → 045F)

01C7   LJ   LATIN CAPITAL LETTER L J
01C8   Lj   LATIN LETTER CAPITAL L SMALL J
01C9   lj   LATIN SMALL LETTER L J
       ✕ (cyrillic small letter lje → 0459)

01CA   NJ   LATIN CAPITAL LETTER N J
01CB   Nj   LATIN LETTER CAPITAL N SMALL J
01CC   nj   LATIN SMALL LETTER N J
       ✕ (cyrillic small letter nje → 045A)

Pinyin diacritic-vowel combinations

01CD   Ǎ   LATIN CAPITAL LETTER A HACEK
01CE   ǎ   LATIN SMALL LETTER A HACEK
       Pinyin third tone
01CF   Ǐ   LATIN CAPITAL LETTER I HACEK
01D0   ǐ   LATIN SMALL LETTER I HACEK
       Pinyin third tone
01D1   Ǒ   LATIN CAPITAL LETTER O HACEK
01D2   ǒ   LATIN SMALL LETTER O HACEK
       Pinyin third tone
01D3   Ǔ   LATIN CAPITAL LETTER U HACEK
01D4   ǔ   LATIN SMALL LETTER U HACEK
       Pinyin third tone
01D5   Ǖ   LATIN CAPITAL LETTER U DIAERESIS MACRON
01D6   ǖ   LATIN SMALL LETTER U DIAERESIS MACRON
       Pinyin first tone
01D7   Ǘ   LATIN CAPITAL LETTER U DIAERESIS ACUTE
01D8   ǘ   LATIN SMALL LETTER U DIAERESIS ACUTE
       Pinyin second tone
01D9   Ǚ   LATIN CAPITAL LETTER U DIAERESIS HACEK
01DA   ǚ   LATIN SMALL LETTER U DIAERESIS HACEK
       Pinyin third tone
01DB   Ǜ   LATIN CAPITAL LETTER U DIAERESIS GRAVE
01DC   ǜ   LATIN SMALL LETTER U DIAERESIS GRAVE
       Pinyin fourth tone

Additions

01DD   ə   LATIN SMALL LETTER TURNED E
       Nigerian
       all other usages of schwa are 0259
       ✕ (latin capital letter turned e → 018E)
       ✕ (latin small letter schwa → 0259)

01DE   Ǟ   LATIN CAPITAL LETTER A DIAERESIS MACRON
01DF   ǟ   LATIN SMALL LETTER A DIAERESIS MACRON
       Lappish
01E0   Ǡ   LATIN CAPITAL LETTER A DOT MACRON
01E1   ǡ   LATIN SMALL LETTER A DOT MACRON
       Lappish
01E2   Ǣ   LATIN CAPITAL LETTER A E MACRON
01E3   ǣ   LATIN SMALL LETTER A E MACRON
       Lappish, Old English
01E4   Ǥ   LATIN CAPITAL LETTER G BAR
01E5   ǥ   LATIN SMALL LETTER G BAR
       Lappish
01E6   Ǧ   LATIN CAPITAL LETTER G HACEK
01E7   ǧ   LATIN SMALL LETTER G HACEK
       Lappish; sometimes used in writing Turkish
       ✕ (latin small letter g breve → 011F)
01E8   Ǩ   LATIN CAPITAL LETTER K HACEK
01E9   ǩ   LATIN SMALL LETTER K HACEK
       Lappish
01EA   Ǫ   LATIN CAPITAL LETTER O OGONEK
01EB   ǫ   LATIN SMALL LETTER O OGONEK
       Lappish, Iroquoian
01EC   Ǭ   LATIN CAPITAL LETTER O OGONEK MACRON
01ED   ǭ   LATIN SMALL LETTER O OGONEK MACRON
       Lappish
01EE   Ǯ   LATIN CAPITAL LETTER YOGH HACEK
01EF   ǯ   LATIN SMALL LETTER YOGH HACEK
       Lappish
01F0   ǰ   LATIN SMALL LETTER J HACEK
       IPA

	025	026	027	028	029	02A
0	ɐ	ɠ	barred ɰ	ʀ	ʐ	ɟ
1	ɑ	ɡ	ɱ	ʁ	ʑ	ʄ
2	ɒ	ɢ	ɲ	ʂ	ʒ	ƛ
3	ɓ	ɣ	ɳ	ʃ	ʓ	ʣ
4	ɔ	ɤ	ɴ	ʄ	ʔ	ʤ
5	ɕ	ɥ	θ	ʅ	ʕ	ʥ
6	ɖ	ɦ	Œ	ʆ	ʖ	ʦ
7	ɗ	ɧ	ɷ	ʇ	ʗ	ʧ
8	ə	ɨ	ɸ	ʈ	ʘ	ʨ
9	ɘ	ɩ	ɹ	ʉ	ʙ	
A	ɚ	ɪ	ɺ	ʊ	ɵ	
B	ɛ	ɫ	ɻ	ʋ	ʛ	
C	ɜ	ɬ	ɼ	ʌ	ʜ	
D	ɝ	ɭ	ɽ	ʍ	ʝ	
E	ɞ	ɮ	ɾ	ʎ	ʞ	
F	ɟ	ɯ	ɿ	ʏ	ʟ	

Standard phonetic

✕ *(latin small letter a e → 00E6)*
✕ *(latin small letter c cedilla → 00E7)*
✕ *(latin small letter eth → 00F0)*
✕ *(latin small letter o slash → 00F8)*
✕ *(latin small letter h bar → 0127)*
✕ *(latin small letter eng → 014B)*
✕ *(latin small letter o e → 0153)*
✕ *(greek small letter beta → 03B2)*
✕ *(greek small letter theta → 03B8)*
✕ *(greek small letter lambda → 03BB)*
✕ *(greek small letter chi → 03C7)*

0250   ɐ   LATIN SMALL LETTER TURNED A
low central unrounded vowel

0251   ɑ   LATIN SMALL LETTER SCRIPT A
low back unrounded vowel
✕ *(greek small letter alpha → 03B1)*

0252   ɒ   LATIN SMALL LETTER TURNED SCRIPT A
low back rounded vowel

0253   ɓ   LATIN SMALL LETTER B HOOK
implosive bilabial stop
✕ *(latin capital letter b hook → 0181)*

0254   ɔ   LATIN SMALL LETTER OPEN O
typographically a turned c
lower-mid back rounded vowel
✕ *(latin capital letter open o → 0186)*

0255   ɕ   LATIN SMALL LETTER C CURL
voiceless alveolo-palatal laminal fricative
used in transcription of Mandarin Chinese
sound spelled with 015B in Polish

0256   ɖ   LATIN SMALL LETTER D RETROFLEX HOOK
voiced retroflex stop
✕ *(latin capital letter african d → 0189)*

0257   ɗ   LATIN SMALL LETTER D HOOK
implosive dental or alveolar stop
✕ *(latin capital letter d hook → 018A)*

0258   ɘ   LATIN SMALL LETTER REVERSED E
upper-mid central unrounded vowel

0259   ə   LATIN SMALL LETTER SCHWA
mid-central unrounded vowel
variant uppercase form 018E is associated with clone 01DD
✕ *(latin capital letter schwa → 018F)*
✕ *(latin small letter turned e → 01DD)*

025A   ɚ   LATIN SMALL LETTER SCHWA HOOK
rhotacized schwa

025B   ɛ   LATIN SMALL LETTER EPSILON
lower-mid front unrounded vowel
✕ *(latin capital letter epsilon → 0190)*
✕ *(greek small letter epsilon → 03B5)*

025C   ɜ   LATIN SMALL LETTER REVERSED EPSILON
lower-mid central unrounded vowel

025D   ɝ   LATIN SMALL LETTER REVERSED EPSILON HOOK
rhotacized lower-mid central vowel

025E   ɞ   LATIN SMALL LETTER CLOSED REVERSED EPSILON
lower-mid central rounded vowel

025F   ɟ   LATIN SMALL LETTER DOTLESS J BAR
voiced palatal stop
typographically a turned f
"gy" in Hungarian orthography

0260   ɠ   LATIN SMALL LETTER G HOOK
implosive velar stop
✕ *(latin capital letter g hook → 0193)*

0261   ɡ   LATIN SMALL LETTER SCRIPT G
voiced velar stop
✕ *(latin small letter g → 0067)*

0262   ɢ   LATIN LETTER SMALL CAPITAL G
voiced uvular stop

0263   ɣ   LATIN SMALL LETTER GAMMA
voiced velar fricative
✕ *(latin capital letter gamma → 0194)*
✕ *(greek small letter gamma → 03B3)*

0264   ɤ   LATIN SMALL LETTER BABY GAMMA
upper-mid back unrounded vowel

0265   ɥ   LATIN SMALL LETTER TURNED H
voiced rounded palatal approximant

0266   ɦ   LATIN SMALL LETTER H HOOK
breathy-voiced glottal fricative
✕ *(modifier letter small h hook → 02B1)*

0267   ɧ   LATIN SMALL LETTER HENG HOOK
voiceless coarticulated velar and palato-alveolar fricative
"tj" or "kj" in some Swedish dialects

0268   ɨ   LATIN SMALL LETTER BARRED I
= i bar
high central unrounded vowel
ISO 6438 gives lowercase of 0197 as 026A, not 0268

0269   ɩ   LATIN SMALL LETTER IOTA
semi-high front unrounded vowel
obsoleted by IPA in 1989
preferred use is 026A LATIN LETTER SMALL CAPITAL I
✕ *(latin capital letter iota → 0196)*
✕ *(greek small letter iota → 03B9)*

026A   ɪ   LATIN LETTER SMALL CAPITAL I
semi-high front unrounded vowel
preferred IPA alternate
✕ *(latin capital letter barred i → 0197)*

026B   ɫ   LATIN SMALL LETTER L WITH MIDDLE TILDE
velarized voiced alveolar lateral approximant

026C   ɬ   LATIN SMALL LETTER L BELT
voiceless alveolar lateral fricative

026D   ɭ   LATIN SMALL LETTER L RETROFLEX HOOK
voiced retroflex lateral

026E   ɮ   LATIN SMALL LETTER L YOGH
voiced lateral fricative
"dhl" in Zulu orthography

026F   ɯ   LATIN SMALL LETTER TURNED M
high back unrounded vowel
× *(latin capital letter turned m → 019C)*

0270   ɰ   LATIN SMALL LETTER TURNED M WITH LONG LEG
voiced velar approximant

0271   ɱ   LATIN SMALL LETTER M HOOK
voiced labiodental nasal

0272   ɲ   LATIN SMALL LETTER N HOOK
voiced palatal nasal
× *(latin capital letter n hook → 019D)*

0273   ɳ   LATIN SMALL LETTER N RETROFLEX HOOK
voiced retroflex nasal

0274   ɴ   LATIN LETTER SMALL CAPITAL N
voiced uvular nasal

0275   ɵ   LATIN SMALL LETTER BARRED O
= *o bar*
rounded mid-central vowel, i.e. rounded schwa
× *(latin capital letter barred o → 019F)*
× *(greek small letter theta → 03B8)*
× *(cyrillic small letter fita → 0473)*

0276   Œ   LATIN LETTER SMALL CAPITAL O E
low front rounded vowel
× *(latin small letter o e → 0153)*

0277   ω   LATIN SMALL LETTER CLOSED OMEGA
semi-high back rounded vowel
obsoleted by IPA in 1989
preferred use is 028A LATIN LETTER SMALL UPSILON

0278   ɸ   LATIN SMALL LETTER PHI
voiceless bilabial fricative
× *(greek small letter phi → 03C6)*

0279   ɹ   LATIN SMALL LETTER TURNED R
voiced alveolar approximant
× *(modifier letter small turned r → 02B4)*

027A   ɺ   LATIN SMALL LETTER TURNED R WITH LONG LEG
voiced lateral flap

027B   ɻ   LATIN SMALL LETTER TURNED R HOOK
voiced retroflex approximant
× *(modifier letter small turned r hook → 02B5)*

027C   ɼ   LATIN SMALL LETTER R WITH LONG LEG
voiced strident apico-alveolar trill
sound spelled with 0159 in Czech

027D   ɽ   LATIN SMALL LETTER R HOOK
voiced retroflex flap

027E   ɾ   LATIN SMALL LETTER FISHHOOK R
voiced alveolar flap or tap

027F   ɿ   LATIN SMALL LETTER REVERSED FISHHOOK R
apical dental vowel
used in Sinological tradition
IPA spelling → 007A 0329

0280   ʀ   LATIN LETTER SMALL CAPITAL R
voiced uvular trill

0281   ʁ   LATIN LETTER SMALL CAPITAL INVERTED R
voiced uvular fricative or approximant
× *(modifier letter small capital inverted r → 02B6)*

0282   ʂ   LATIN SMALL LETTER S HOOK
voiceless retroflex fricative

0283   ʃ   LATIN SMALL LETTER ESH
voiceless postalveolar fricative
× *(latin capital letter esh → 01A9)*
× *(integral → 222B)*

0284   ʄ   LATIN SMALL LETTER DOTLESS J BAR HOOK
implosive palatal stop
typographically based on 025F, not on 0283

0285   ʅ   LATIN SMALL LETTER SQUAT REVERSED ESH
apical retroflex vowel
used in Sinological tradition
IPA spelling → 0290 0329

0286   ʆ   LATIN SMALL LETTER ESH CURL
palatalized voiceless postalveolar fricative
suggested spelling → 0283 02B2

0287   ʇ   LATIN SMALL LETTER TURNED T
dental click (sound of "tsk tsk")
× *(latin letter pipe → 01C0)*

0288   ʈ   LATIN SMALL LETTER T RETROFLEX HOOK
voiceless retroflex stop
× *(latin capital letter t retroflex hook → 01AE)*

0289   ʉ   LATIN SMALL LETTER U BAR
high central rounded vowel

028A   ʊ   LATIN SMALL LETTER UPSILON
semi-high back rounded vowel
preferred IPA alternate
× *(latin capital letter upsilon → 01B1)*
× *(greek small letter upsilon → 03C5)*

028B   ʋ   LATIN SMALL LETTER SCRIPT V
voiced labiodental approximant
× *(latin capital letter script v → 01B2)*
× *(greek small letter upsilon → 03C5)*

028C   ʌ   LATIN SMALL LETTER TURNED V
= *caret*
= *wedge*
lower-mid back unrounded vowel

028D   ʍ   LATIN SMALL LETTER TURNED W
voiceless rounded labiovelar approximant

028E   ʎ   LATIN SMALL LETTER TURNED Y
voiced lateral approximant

028F   ʏ   LATIN LETTER SMALL CAPITAL Y
semi-high front rounded vowel

0290   ʐ   LATIN SMALL LETTER Z RETROFLEX HOOK
voiced retroflex fricative

0291   ʑ   LATIN SMALL LETTER Z CURL
           voiced alveolo-palatal laminal fricative
           sound spelled with 017A in Polish

0292   ʒ   LATIN SMALL LETTER YOGH
           = dram
           old Irish, old English
           voiced postalveolar fricative
           × *(latin capital letter yogh → 01B7)*
           × *(ounce → 2125)*

0293   ʓ   LATIN SMALL LETTER YOGH CURL
           palatalized voiced postalveolar fricative

0294   ʔ   LATIN LETTER GLOTTAL STOP
           × *(modifier letter glottal stop → 02C0)*

0295   ʕ   LATIN LETTER REVERSED GLOTTAL STOP
           voiced pharyngeal fricative
           ain
           × *(latin small letter reversed yogh →
           01B9)*
           × *(modifier letter reversed glottal stop
           → 02C1)*

0296   ʖ   LATIN LETTER INVERTED GLOTTAL STOP
           lateral click
           × *(latin letter double pipe → 01C1)*

0297   ʗ   LATIN LETTER STRETCHED C
           palatal (or alveolar) click
           × *(latin letter exclamation mark →
           01C3)*
           × *(complement → 2201)*

0298   ʘ   LATIN LETTER BULLSEYE
           bilabial click
           × *(circled dot operator → 2299)*

0299   ʙ   LATIN LETTER SMALL CAPITAL B
           bilabial trill

029A   ɚ   LATIN SMALL LETTER CLOSED EPSILON
           lower-mid front rounded vowel
           *non-IPA alternate for the preferred
           0153*

029B   ɢ   LATIN LETTER SMALL CAPITAL G HOOK
           voiced uvular implosive

029C   ʜ   LATIN LETTER SMALL CAPITAL H
           voiceless epiglotto-pharyngeal fricative

029D   ʝ   LATIN SMALL LETTER CROSSED-TAIL J
           voiced palatal fricative

029E   ʞ   LATIN SMALL LETTER TURNED K
           proposed for velar click
           withdrawn by IPA in 1970

029F   ʟ   LATIN LETTER SMALL CAPITAL L
           velar lateral approximant

02A0   ʠ   LATIN SMALL LETTER Q HOOK
           voiceless uvular implosive

02A1   ʡ   LATIN LETTER GLOTTAL STOP BAR
           voiced epiglottal-pharyngeal stop

02A2   ʢ   LATIN LETTER REVERSED GLOTTAL STOP
           BAR
           voiced epiglottal-pharyngeal fricative

02A3   ʣ   LATIN SMALL LETTER D Z
           voiced dental affricate

02A4   ʤ   LATIN SMALL LETTER D YOGH
           voiced postalveolar affricate

02A5   ʥ   LATIN SMALL LETTER D Z CURL
           voiced alveolo-palatal affricate

02A6   ʦ   LATIN SMALL LETTER T S
           voiceless dental affricate

02A7   ʧ   LATIN SMALL LETTER T ESH
           voiceless postalveolar affricate

02A8   ʨ   LATIN SMALL LETTER T C CURL
           voiceless alveolo-palatal affricate

	02B	02C	02D	02E	02F
0	h	ʔ	(marks)	ɣ	
1	ɦ	ʕ	ˎ	l	
2	j	<	）	s	
3	r	>	ｃ	x	
4	ɹ	∧	⊥	ʕ	
5	ɻ	∨	⊤	⌐	
6	ʙ	^	+	⊣	
7	w	ˇ	⊢	⊣	
8	y	ˈ	˘	⊢	
9	ˊ	—	˙	⌐	
A	˝	ˏ	°		
B	ˋ	ˎ	ˌ		
C	ˏ	ˌ	~		
D	˞	—	˶		
E	ˠ	ˏ	˷		
F	ˤ	ˏ			

The Unicode Standard • Version 1.0

Phonetic modifiers derived from Latin letters

02B0   h   MODIFIER LETTER SMALL H
    aspiration

02B1   ɦ   MODIFIER LETTER SMALL H HOOK
    breathy voiced, murmured
    ✕ *(latin small letter h hook → 0266)*
    ✕ *(non-spacing double dot below → 0324)*

02B2   j   MODIFIER LETTER SMALL J
    palatalization
    ✕ *(non-spacing palatalized hook below → 0321)*

02B3   r   MODIFIER LETTER SMALL R

02B4   ɹ   MODIFIER LETTER SMALL TURNED R
    ✕ *(latin small letter turned r → 0279)*

02B5   ɻ   MODIFIER LETTER SMALL TURNED R HOOK
    ✕ *(latin small letter turned r hook → 027B)*

02B6   ʁ   MODIFIER LETTER SMALL CAPITAL INVERTED R
    preceding four used for r-coloring or r-offglides
    ✕ *(latin letter small capital inverted r → 0281)*

02B7   w   MODIFIER LETTER SMALL W
    labialization
    ✕ *(non-spacing inverted double arch below → 032B)*

02B8   y   MODIFIER LETTER SMALL Y
    palatalization
    common Americanist substitution for 02B2

Miscellaneous phonetic modifiers

02B9   ′   MODIFIER LETTER PRIME
    primary stress, emphasis
    transliteration of mjagkij znak (Cyrillic soft sign: palatalization)
    ✕ *(apostrophe-quote → 0027)*
    ✕ *(spacing acute → 00B4)*
    ✕ *(modifier letter acute → 02CA)*
    ✕ *(non-spacing acute → 0301)*
    ✕ *(greek upper numeral sign → 03D8)*
    ✕ *(prime → 2032)*

02BA   ″   MODIFIER LETTER DOUBLE PRIME
    exaggerated stress, contrastive stress
    transliteration of tverdyj znak (Cyrillic hard sign: no palatalization)
    ✕ *(quotation mark → 0022)*
    ✕ *(non-spacing double acute → 030B)*
    ✕ *(double prime → 2033)*

02BB   ʻ   MODIFIER LETTER TURNED COMMA
    typographical alternate for 02BD or 02BF
    ✕ *(non-spacing turned comma above → 0312)*
    ✕ *(single turned comma quotation mark → 2018)*

02BC   ʼ   MODIFIER LETTER APOSTROPHE
    = apostrophe
    glottal stop, glottalization, ejective; elision
    spacing clone of Greek smooth breathing mark
    this is the preferred character for apostrophe
    ✕ *(apostrophe-quote → 0027)*
    ✕ *(non-spacing comma above → 0313)*
    ✕ *(non-spacing comma above right → 0315)*
    ✕ *(greek non-spacing psili pneumata → 0372)*
    ✕ *(armenian modifier letter right half ring → 055A)*
    ✕ *(single comma quotation mark → 2019)*

02BD   ʽ   MODIFIER LETTER REVERSED COMMA
    weak aspiration
    spacing clone of Greek rough breathing mark
    ✕ *(non-spacing reversed comma above → 0314)*
    ✕ *(greek non-spacing dasia pneumata → 0371)*
    ✕ *(armenian modifier letter left half ring → 0559)*
    ✕ *(single reversed comma quotation mark → 201B)*

02BE   ʾ   MODIFIER LETTER RIGHT HALF RING
    transliteration of Arabic hamzah (glottal stop)
    ✕ *(armenian modifier letter right half ring → 055A)*
    ✕ *(arabic letter hamzah → 0621)*

02BF   ʿ   MODIFIER LETTER LEFT HALF RING
    transliteration of Arabic ain (voiced pharyngeal fricative)
    ✕ *(armenian modifier letter left half ring → 0559)*
    ✕ *(arabic letter ain → 0639)*

02C0   ʔ   MODIFIER LETTER GLOTTAL STOP
    ejective or glottalized
    typographical alternate for 02BC or 02BE
    ✕ *(latin letter glottal stop → 0294)*
    ✕ *(non-spacing hook above → 0309)*

02C1   ʕ   MODIFIER LETTER REVERSED GLOTTAL STOP
    typographical alternate for 02BF
    ✕ *(latin letter reversed glottal stop → 0295)*

02C2   <   MODIFIER LETTER LEFT ARROWHEAD
fronted articulation

02C3   >   MODIFIER LETTER RIGHT ARROWHEAD
backed articulation

02C4   ^   MODIFIER LETTER UP ARROWHEAD
raised articulation
× *(spacing circumflex → 005E)*
× *(up arrowhead → 2303)*

02C5   ˅   MODIFIER LETTER DOWN ARROWHEAD
lowered articulation

02C6   ^   MODIFIER LETTER CIRCUMFLEX
*rising-falling tone, falling tone,
secondary stress, etc.*
× *(spacing circumflex → 005E)*
× *(non-spacing circumflex → 0302)*

02C7   ˇ   MODIFIER LETTER HACEK
falling-rising tone
Mandarin Chinese third tone
× *(non-spacing hacek → 030C)*

02C8   '   MODIFIER LETTER VERTICAL LINE
primary stress, downstep
precedes letter or syllable modified
× *(apostrophe-quote → 0027)*
× *(non-spacing vertical line above →
030D)*

02C9   ‾   MODIFIER LETTER MACRON
high level tone
*precedes or follows letter or syllable
modified*
Mandarin Chinese first tone
× *(spacing macron → 00AF)*
× *(non-spacing macron → 0304)*

02CA   ´   MODIFIER LETTER ACUTE
*high-rising tone (IPA), high tone,
primary stress*
Mandarin Chinese second tone
× *(spacing acute → 00B4)*
× *(modifier letter prime → 02B9)*
× *(non-spacing acute → 0301)*
× *(greek upper numeral sign → 03D8)*
× *(armenian emphasis mark → 055B)*

02CB   `   MODIFIER LETTER GRAVE
*high-falling tone (IPA), low tone,
secondary or tertiary stress*
Mandarin Chinese fourth tone
× *(spacing grave → 0060)*
× *(non-spacing grave → 0300)*
× *(armenian comma → 055D)*

02CC   ˌ   MODIFIER LETTER LOW VERTICAL LINE
secondary stress
precedes letter or syllable modified
× *(non-spacing vertical line below →
0329)*

02CD   _   MODIFIER LETTER LOW MACRON
low level tone
× *(spacing underscore → 005F)*
× *(non-spacing macron below → 0331)*

02CE   ˎ   MODIFIER LETTER LOW GRAVE
low-falling tone

02CF   ˏ   MODIFIER LETTER LOW ACUTE
low-rising tone
× *(greek lower numeral sign → 03D9)*

02D0   :   MODIFIER LETTER TRIANGULAR COLON
length mark

02D1   ·   MODIFIER LETTER HALF TRIANGULAR
COLON
half-length mark

02D2   ˒   MODIFIER LETTER CENTERED RIGHT HALF
RING
more rounded articulation

02D3   ˓   MODIFIER LETTER CENTERED LEFT HALF
RING
less rounded articulation

02D4   ˔   MODIFIER LETTER UP TACK
vowel raising or closing
× *(non-spacing up tack below → 031D)*
× *(non-spacing dot below → 0323)*

02D5   ˕   MODIFIER LETTER DOWN TACK
vowel lowering or opening
× *(non-spacing left half ring below →
031C)*
× *(non-spacing down tack below →
031E)*

02D6   +   MODIFIER LETTER PLUS SIGN
advanced or fronted articulation
× *(non-spacing plus sign below → 031F)*

02D7   −   MODIFIER LETTER MINUS SIGN
retracted or backed articulation
glyph may have small end-serifs
× *(non-spacing minus sign below →
0320)*

Spacing clones of diacritics

02D8   ˘   SPACING BREVE
× *(non-spacing breve → 0306)*

02D9   ˙   SPACING DOT ABOVE
Mandarin Chinese fifth (neutral) tone
× *(non-spacing dot above → 0307)*

02DA   °   SPACING RING ABOVE
× *(degree sign → 00B0)*
× *(non-spacing ring above → 030A)*

02DB   ˛   SPACING OGONEK
× *(non-spacing ogonek → 0328)*

02DC   ~   SPACING TILDE
× *(tilde → 007E)*
× *(non-spacing tilde → 0303)*
× *(tilde operator → 223C)*

02DD   ˝   SPACING DOUBLE ACUTE
× *(non-spacing double acute → 030B)*

Additions based on 1989 IPA

02DE   ˞   MODIFIER LETTER RHOTIC HOOK
rhotacization in vowel
*often ligated: 025A = 0259 + 02DE;
025D = 025C + 02DE*

02DF

02E0   ɣ   MODIFIER LETTER SMALL GAMMA
      these modifier letters are occasionally
      used in transcription of affricates

02E1   ˡ   MODIFIER LETTER SMALL L

02E2   ˢ   MODIFIER LETTER SMALL S

02E3   ˣ   MODIFIER LETTER SMALL X

02E4   ˤ   MODIFIER LETTER SMALL REVERSED
GLOTTAL STOP

Tone letters

02E5   ˥   MODIFIER LETTER EXTRA-HIGH TONE BAR

02E6   ˦   MODIFIER LETTER HIGH TONE BAR

02E7   ˧   MODIFIER LETTER MID TONE BAR

02E8   ˨   MODIFIER LETTER LOW TONE BAR

02E9   ˩   MODIFIER LETTER EXTRA-LOW TONE BAR

	030	031	032	033	034	035	036
0	̀	̐	̠	̰	VIET		
1	́	̑	̡	̱	VIET		
2	̂	̒	̢	̲			
3	̃	̓	̣	̳			
4	̄	̔	̤	̴			
5	̅	̕	̥	̵			
6	̆	̖	̦	̶			
7	̇	̗	̧	̷			
8	̈	̘	̨	̸			
9	̉	̙	̩	̹			
A	̊	̚	̪	̺			
B	̋	̛	̫	̻			
C	̌	̜	̬	̼			
D	̍	̝	̭	̽			
E	̎	̞	̮	̾			
F	̏	̟	̯	̿			

Ordinary diacritics

0300   NON-SPACING GRAVE
     × (spacing grave → 0060)
     × (modifier letter grave → 02CB)

0301   NON-SPACING ACUTE
     = stress mark
     × (apostrophe -quote→ 0027)
     × (spacing acute → 00B4)
     × (modifier letter prime → 02B9)
     × (modifier letter acute → 02CA)

0302   NON-SPACING CIRCUMFLEX
     = hat
     × (spacing circumflex → 005E)
     × (modifier letter circumflex → 02C6)

0303   NON-SPACING TILDE
     IPA: nasalization
     Vietnamese tone mark
     × (tilde → 007E)
     × (spacing tilde → 02DC)

0304   NON-SPACING MACRON
     = ISO HORIZONTAL INDICATOR OF NEGATION
     = long
     distinguish from the following
     × (spacing macron → 00AF)
     × (modifier letter macron → 02C9)

0305   NON-SPACING OVERSCORE
     = overline
     connects on left and right
     × (spacing macron → 00AF)

0306   NON-SPACING BREVE
     = short
     × (spacing breve → 02D8)

0307   NON-SPACING DOT ABOVE
     = derivative
     IPA (unofficial): palatalization
     × (spacing dot above → 02D9)

0308   NON-SPACING DIAERESIS
     = double dot above
     = umlaut
     = double derivative
     × (spacing diaeresis → 00A8)

0309   NON-SPACING HOOK ABOVE
     kerns left or right of circumflex over vowels
     Vietnamese tone mark
     × (modifier letter glottal stop → 02C0)

030A   NON-SPACING RING ABOVE
     × (degree sign → 00B0)
     × (spacing ring above → 02DA)

030B   NON-SPACING DOUBLE ACUTE
     Hungarian, Chuvash
     × (quotation mark → 0022)
     × (modifier letter double prime → 02BA)
     × (spacing double acute → 02DD)

030C   NON-SPACING HACEK
     = caron
     = V ABOVE
     × (modifier letter hacek → 02C7)

030D   NON-SPACING VERTICAL LINE ABOVE
     Marshallese
     × (modifier letter vertical line → 02C8)
     × (greek capital letter alpha tonos → 0386)

030E   NON-SPACING DOUBLE VERTICAL LINE ABOVE
     Marshallese
     × (quotation mark → 0022)

030F   NON-SPACING DOUBLE GRAVE
     Serbocroatian

0310   NON-SPACING CANDRABINDU
     × (devanagari sign candrabindu → 0901)

0311   NON-SPACING INVERTED BREVE

0312   NON-SPACING TURNED COMMA ABOVE
     = cedilla above
     Latvian
     × (modifier letter turned comma → 02BB)

0313   NON-SPACING COMMA ABOVE
     × (modifier letter apostrophe → 02BC)

0314   NON-SPACING REVERSED COMMA ABOVE
     × (modifier letter reversed comma → 02BD)

0315   NON-SPACING COMMA ABOVE RIGHT
     × (modifier letter apostrophe → 02BC)

0316   NON-SPACING GRAVE BELOW

0317   NON-SPACING ACUTE BELOW

0318   NON-SPACING LEFT TACK BELOW

0319   NON-SPACING TACK BELOW

031A   NON-SPACING LEFT ANGLE ABOVE
     IPA: unreleased stop

031B   NON-SPACING HORN
     Vietnamese

031C   NON-SPACING LEFT HALF RING BELOW
     IPA: open variety of vowel
     × (modifier letter down tack → 02D5)
     × (non-spacing down tack below → 031E)

031D   NON-SPACING UP TACK BELOW
     IPA: vowel raising or closing
     × (modifier letter up tack → 02D4)
     × (non-spacing dot below → 0323)

031E   NON-SPACING DOWN TACK BELOW
     IPA: vowel lowering or opening
     × (modifier letter down tack → 02D5)
     × (non-spacing left half ring below → 031C)

031F   NON-SPACING PLUS SIGN BELOW
     IPA: advanced or fronted articulation
     × (modifier letter plus sign → 02D6)

0320 NON-SPACING MINUS SIGN BELOW
IPA: retracted or backed articulation
glyph may have small end-serifs
× (modifier letter minus sign → 02D7)

0321 NON-SPACING PALATALIZED HOOK BELOW
IPA: palatalization
× (modifier letter small j → 02B2)

0322 NON-SPACING RETROFLEX HOOK BELOW
IPA: retroflexion
× (non-spacing dot below → 0323)

0323 NON-SPACING DOT BELOW
IPA: closer variety of vowel
Americanist: retraction or retroflexion
Semiticist: velarization or pharyngealization
Vietnamese tone mark
× (modifier letter up tack → 02D4)
× (non-spacing up tack below → 031D)
× (non-spacing retroflex hook below → 0322)
× (non-spacing double underscore → 0333)

0324 NON-SPACING DOUBLE DOT BELOW
IPA: breathy-voice or murmur
× (modifier letter small h hook → 02B1)

0325 NON-SPACING RING BELOW
IPA: voiceless
Madurese

0326 NON-SPACING COMMA BELOW
variant of the following

0327 NON-SPACING CEDILLA
× (spacing cedilla → 00B8)

0328 NON-SPACING OGONEK
Americanist: nasalization
× (spacing ogonek → 02DB)

0329 NON-SPACING VERTICAL LINE BELOW
IPA: syllabic
Yoruba
× (modifier letter low vertical line → 02CC)

032A NON-SPACING BRIDGE BELOW
IPA: dental
× (non-spacing circumflex below → 032D)

032B NON-SPACING INVERTED DOUBLE ARCH BELOW
IPA: labialization
× (modifier letter small w → 02B7)

032C NON-SPACING HACEK BELOW
IPA: voiced
Hittite

032D NON-SPACING CIRCUMFLEX BELOW
Americanist: fronted articulation
× (non-spacing bridge below → 032A)

032E NON-SPACING BREVE BELOW

032F NON-SPACING INVERTED BREVE BELOW
Americanist: fronted articulation (variant of 032D)
Indo-European: semivowel

0330 NON-SPACING TILDE BELOW
IPA: creaky voice

0331 NON-SPACING MACRON BELOW
× (spacing underscore → 005F)
× (modifier letter low macron → 02CD)

0332 NON-SPACING UNDERSCORE
= underline
connects on left and right
× (spacing underscore → 005F)

0333 NON-SPACING DOUBLE UNDERSCORE
= double underline
connects on left and right
× (non-spacing dot below → 0323)
× (spacing double underscore → 2017)

Overstruck diacritics

0334 NON-SPACING TILDE OVERLAY
IPA: velarization or pharyngealization

0335 NON-SPACING SHORT BAR OVERLAY

0336 NON-SPACING LONG BAR OVERLAY

0337 NON-SPACING SHORT SLASH OVERLAY
= short slash overlay

0338 NON-SPACING LONG SLASH OVERLAY
= ISO OBLIQUE INDICATOR OF NEGATION
= long slash overlay

Additions

0339 NON-SPACING RIGHT HALF RING BELOW

033A NON-SPACING INVERTED BRIDGE BELOW

033B NON-SPACING SQUARE BELOW

033C NON-SPACING SEAGULL BELOW

033D NON-SPACING X ABOVE

033E NON-SPACING VERTICAL TILDE
Cyrillic palatalization
× (cyrillic non-spacing palatalization → 0484)

033F NON-SPACING DOUBLE OVERSCORE

Vietnamese tone marks

0340 NON-SPACING GRAVE TONE MARK
kerns left of circumflex over vowels

0341 NON-SPACING ACUTE TONE MARK
kerns right of circumflex over vowels

	037	038	039	03A	03B	03C	03D	03E	03F
0	◌ͅ		ΐ	Π	ϋ	π	ϐ	ϰ	ϰ
1	◌ͱ		Α	Ρ	α	ρ	ϑ	ϱ	ϱ
2	◌͂		Β		β	ς	Υ	ɰ	ϲ
3			Γ	Σ	γ	σ	ϓ	ɰ	'
4		◌ͤ	Δ	Τ	δ	τ	ϔ	ϙ	˙
5		◌ͥ	Ε	Υ	ε	υ	φ	ϙ	ͺ
6	Ά		Ζ	Φ	ζ	φ	ϖ	ħ	
7			Η	Χ	η	χ	;	ҫ	
8	Έ	Θ	Ψ	θ	ψ	΄	ϟ	
9	Ή	Ι	Ω	ι	ω	,	ϟ	
A	Ί	Κ	Ϊ	κ	ϊ	Ϛ	ϰ	
B		Λ	Ϋ	λ	ϋ	ϛ	ϰ	
C	Ό	Μ	ά	μ	ό	Ϝ	ϭ	
D		Ν	έ	ν	ύ	ϝ	ϭ	
E	Ύ	Ξ	ή	ξ	ώ	ϞϘ	ϯ	
F	Ώ	Ο	ί	ο		ϞϘ	ϯ	

Based on ISO 8859-7

0370	◌	GREEK NON-SPACING IOTA BELOW
		= iota subscript
		✕ (greek spacing iota below → 03F5)
0371	◌	GREEK NON-SPACING DASIA PNEUMATA
		= rough breathing
		✕ (modifier letter reversed comma → 02BD)
		✕ (cyrillic non-spacing dasia pneumata → 0485)
		✕ (armenian modifier letter left half ring → 0559)
0372	◌	GREEK NON-SPACING PSILI PNEUMATA
		= smooth breathing
		✕ (modifier letter apostrophe → 02BC)
		✕ (cyrillic non-spacing psili pneumata → 0486)
		✕ (armenian modifier letter right half ring → 055A)
0373		✕ (pound sign → 00A3)
0374		
0375		
0376		✕ (broken vertical bar → 00A6)
0377		✕ (paragraph sign → 00B6)
0378		✕ (non-spacing diaeresis → 0308)
0379		✕ (copyright sign → 00A9)
037A		
037B		✕ (left pointing guillemet → 00AB)
037C		✕ (not sign → 00AC)
037D		✕ (soft hyphen → 00AD)
037E		
037F		✕ (quotation dash → 2015)
0380		✕ (degree sign → 00B0)
0381		✕ (plus-or-minus sign → 00B1)
0382		✕ (superscript digit two → 00B2)
0383		✕ (superscript digit three → 00B3)
0384	◌	GREEK NON-SPACING TONOS
		✕ (greek spacing tonos → 03F3)
0385	◌	GREEK NON-SPACING DIAERESIS TONOS
		= ISO ACUTE ACCENT AND DIAERESIS
		✕ (greek spacing diaeresis tonos → 03F4)
0386	Ά	GREEK CAPITAL LETTER ALPHA TONOS
		✕ (non-spacing vertical line above → 030D)
0387		✕ (middle dot → 00B7)
0388	Έ	GREEK CAPITAL LETTER EPSILON TONOS
0389	Ή	GREEK CAPITAL LETTER ETA TONOS
038A	Ί	GREEK CAPITAL LETTER IOTA TONOS
038B		✕ (right pointing guillemet → 00BB)
038C	Ό	GREEK CAPITAL LETTER OMICRON TONOS
038D		✕ (fraction one half → 00BD)
038E	Ύ	GREEK CAPITAL LETTER UPSILON TONOS
038F	Ώ	GREEK CAPITAL LETTER OMEGA TONOS
0390	ΐ	GREEK SMALL LETTER IOTA DIAERESIS TONOS
0391	A	GREEK CAPITAL LETTER ALPHA
0392	B	GREEK CAPITAL LETTER BETA
0393	Γ	GREEK CAPITAL LETTER GAMMA
		= GAMMA FUNCTION
0394	Δ	GREEK CAPITAL LETTER DELTA
		✕ (increment → 2206)
0395	E	GREEK CAPITAL LETTER EPSILON
0396	Z	GREEK CAPITAL LETTER ZETA
0397	H	GREEK CAPITAL LETTER ETA
0398	Θ	GREEK CAPITAL LETTER THETA
0399	I	GREEK CAPITAL LETTER IOTA
039A	K	GREEK CAPITAL LETTER KAPPA
039B	Λ	GREEK CAPITAL LETTER LAMBDA
039C	M	GREEK CAPITAL LETTER MU
039D	N	GREEK CAPITAL LETTER NU
039E	Ξ	GREEK CAPITAL LETTER XI
039F	O	GREEK CAPITAL LETTER OMICRON
03A0	Π	GREEK CAPITAL LETTER PI
		✕ (n-ary product → 220F)
03A1	P	GREEK CAPITAL LETTER RHO
03A2		
03A3	Σ	GREEK CAPITAL LETTER SIGMA
		✕ (latin capital letter esh → 01A9)
		✕ (n-ary summation → 2211)
03A4	T	GREEK CAPITAL LETTER TAU
03A5	Υ	GREEK CAPITAL LETTER UPSILON
03A6	Φ	GREEK CAPITAL LETTER PHI
03A7	X	GREEK CAPITAL LETTER CHI
03A8	Ψ	GREEK CAPITAL LETTER PSI
03A9	Ω	GREEK CAPITAL LETTER OMEGA
		✕ (ohm → 2126)
		✕ (mho → 2127)
03AA	Ϊ	GREEK CAPITAL LETTER IOTA DIAERESIS
03AB	Ϋ	GREEK CAPITAL LETTER UPSILON DIAERESIS
03AC	ά	GREEK SMALL LETTER ALPHA TONOS
03AD	έ	GREEK SMALL LETTER EPSILON TONOS
03AE	ή	GREEK SMALL LETTER ETA TONOS
03AF	ί	GREEK SMALL LETTER IOTA TONOS
03B0	ΰ	GREEK SMALL LETTER UPSILON DIAERESIS TONOS

03B1	α	GREEK SMALL LETTER ALPHA
		× *(latin small letter script a → 0251)*
		× *(proportional to → 221D)*
03B2	β	GREEK SMALL LETTER BETA
		× *(latin small letter sharp s → 00DF)*
		× *(latin small letter b bar → 0180)*
03B3	γ	GREEK SMALL LETTER GAMMA
		× *(latin small letter gamma → 0263)*
03B4	δ	GREEK SMALL LETTER DELTA
03B5	ε	GREEK SMALL LETTER EPSILON
		× *(latin small letter epsilon → 025B)*
03B6	ζ	GREEK SMALL LETTER ZETA
03B7	η	GREEK SMALL LETTER ETA
03B8	θ	GREEK SMALL LETTER THETA
		× *(latin small letter barred o → 0275)*
		× *(cyrillic small letter fita → 0473)*
03B9	ι	GREEK SMALL LETTER IOTA
		× *(latin small letter iota → 0269)*
		× *(turned greek small letter iota → 2129)*
03BA	κ	GREEK SMALL LETTER KAPPA
03BB	λ	GREEK SMALL LETTER LAMBDA
03BC	μ	GREEK SMALL LETTER MU
		× *(micro sign → 00B5)*
03BD	ν	GREEK SMALL LETTER NU
03BE	ξ	GREEK SMALL LETTER XI
03BF	ο	GREEK SMALL LETTER OMICRON
03C0	π	GREEK SMALL LETTER PI
		math constant 3.141592...
03C1	ρ	GREEK SMALL LETTER RHO
03C2	ς	GREEK SMALL LETTER FINAL SIGMA
03C3	σ	GREEK SMALL LETTER SIGMA
03C4	τ	GREEK SMALL LETTER TAU
03C5	υ	GREEK SMALL LETTER UPSILON
		× *(latin small letter upsilon → 028A)*
		× *(latin small letter script v → 028B)*
03C6	φ	GREEK SMALL LETTER PHI
		× *(latin small letter phi → 0278)*
03C7	χ	GREEK SMALL LETTER CHI
03C8	ψ	GREEK SMALL LETTER PSI
03C9	ω	GREEK SMALL LETTER OMEGA
03CA	ϊ	GREEK SMALL LETTER IOTA DIAERESIS
03CB	ϋ	GREEK SMALL LETTER UPSILON DIAERESIS
03CC	ό	GREEK SMALL LETTER OMICRON TONOS
03CD	ύ	GREEK SMALL LETTER UPSILON TONOS
03CE	ώ	GREEK SMALL LETTER OMEGA TONOS
03CF		

Variant letterforms

03D0	β	GREEK SMALL LETTER CURLED BETA

03D1	ϑ	GREEK SMALL LETTER SCRIPT THETA
		used as technical symbol
03D2	ϒ	GREEK CAPITAL LETTER UPSILON HOOK
03D3	'ϒ	GREEK CAPITAL LETTER UPSILON HOOK TONOS
03D4	ϔ	GREEK CAPITAL LETTER UPSILON HOOK DIAERESIS
03D5	φ	GREEK SMALL LETTER SCRIPT PHI
		used as technical symbol
03D6	ϖ	GREEK SMALL LETTER OMEGA PI
		used as technical symbol
		a variant of pi, looking like omega

Punctuation-like characters

03D7	;	GREEK QUESTION MARK
		sentence-final punctuation
		× *(semicolon → 003B)*
		× *(question mark → 003F)*
03D8	'	GREEK UPPER NUMERAL SIGN
		for numeric use of letters
		× *(modifier letter prime → 02B9)*
		× *(modifier letter acute → 02CA)*
03D9	,	GREEK LOWER NUMERAL SIGN
		for numeric use of letters
		× *(modifier letter low acute → 02CF)*

Archaic letters

03DA	Ϛ	GREEK CAPITAL LETTER STIGMA
03DB	ϛ	GREEK SMALL LETTER STIGMA
03DC	Ϝ	GREEK CAPITAL LETTER DIGAMMA
03DD	ϝ	GREEK SMALL LETTER DIGAMMA
03DE	Ϟ	GREEK CAPITAL LETTER KOPPA
03DF	ϟ	GREEK SMALL LETTER KOPPA
03E0	Ϡ	GREEK CAPITAL LETTER SAMPI
03E1	ϡ	GREEK SMALL LETTER SAMPI

Coptic-unique letters

03E2	Ш	GREEK CAPITAL LETTER SHEI
03E3	ш	GREEK SMALL LETTER SHEI
03E4	Ч	GREEK CAPITAL LETTER FEI
03E5	ч	GREEK SMALL LETTER FEI
03E6	Ⳇ	GREEK CAPITAL LETTER KHEI
03E7	ⳇ	GREEK SMALL LETTER KHEI
03E8	Ⳋ	GREEK CAPITAL LETTER HORI
03E9	ⳋ	GREEK SMALL LETTER HORI
03EA	Ⳝ	GREEK CAPITAL LETTER GANGIA
03EB	ⳝ	GREEK SMALL LETTER GANGIA
03EC	Ϭ	GREEK CAPITAL LETTER SHIMA
03ED	ϭ	GREEK SMALL LETTER SHIMA
03EE	Ϯ	GREEK CAPITAL LETTER DEI

03EF   ✝   GREEK SMALL LETTER DEI

Additions

03F0   ϰ   GREEK SMALL LETTER SCRIPT KAPPA
                   used as technical symbol

03F1   ϱ   GREEK SMALL LETTER TAILED RHO
                   used as technical symbol

03F2   ϲ   GREEK SMALL LETTER LUNATE SIGMA

Spacing clones of Greek diacritics

03F3   ʹ   GREEK SPACING TONOS
                   ✕ *(greek non-spacing tonos → 0384)*

03F4   ¨ʹ   GREEK SPACING DIAERESIS TONOS
                   ✕ *(greek non-spacing diaeresis tonos →*
                   0385)

03F5   ͺ   GREEK SPACING IOTA BELOW
                   ✕ *(greek non-spacing iota below →*
                   0370)

	040	041	042	043	044	045	046	047
0		А	Р	а	р		Ѡ	Ѱ
1	Ё	Б	С	б	с	ё	ѡ	ѱ
2	Ђ	В	Т	в	т	ђ	Ѣ	Ѳ
3	Ѓ	Г	У	г	у	ѓ	ѣ	ѳ
4	Є	Д	Ф	д	ф	є	Ѥ	Ѵ
5	Ѕ	Е	Х	е	х	ѕ	ѥ	ѵ
6	І	Ж	Ц	ж	ц	і	Ѧ	Ѷ
7	Ї	З	Ч	з	ч	ї	ѧ	ѷ
8	Ј	И	Ш	и	ш	ј	Ѩ	Оу
9	Љ	Й	Щ	й	щ	љ	ѩ	оу
A	Њ	К	Ъ	к	ъ	њ	Ѫ	Ѻ
B	Ћ	Л	Ы	л	ы	ћ	ѫ	ѻ
C	Ќ	М	Ь	м	ь	ќ	Ѭ	ѽ
D		Н	Э	н	э		ѭ	ѽ
E	Ў	О	Ю	о	ю	ў	Ѯ	ѽ
F	Џ	П	Я	п	я	џ	ѯ	ѿ

	048	049	04A	04B	04C	04D	04E	04F
0	Ҁ	Ґ	Ҡ	Ұ	Ӏ			
1	ҁ	ґ	ҡ	ұ	Ӂ			
2	҂	Ғ|Ғ	Ң	Х	ӂ			
3	҃	Ғ|Ғ	ң	х	Ӄ			
4	҄	Ҕ	Ҥ	Ҵ	ӄ			
5	҅|҆	ҕ	ҥ	ҵ	Ӆ			
6	҆|҆	Җ	Ҧ	Ҷ	ӆ			
7		җ	ҧ	ҷ	Ӈ			
8		Ҙ|Ҙ	Ҩ	Ҹ	ӈ			
9		ҙ|ҙ	ҩ	ҹ	Ӊ			
A		Қ	Ҫ|Ҫ	Һ	ӊ			
B		қ	ҫ|ҫ	һ	Ӌ			
C		Ҝ	Ҭ	Ҽ	ӌ			
D		ҝ	ҭ	ҽ				
E		Ҟ	Ү	Ҿ|Ҿ				
F		ҟ	ү	ҿ|ҿ				

Based on ISO 8859-5

0400		× (non-breaking space → 00A0)
0401	Ё	CYRILLIC CAPITAL LETTER IO
0402	Ђ	CYRILLIC CAPITAL LETTER DJE
0403	Ѓ	CYRILLIC CAPITAL LETTER GJE
0404	Є	CYRILLIC CAPITAL LETTER E
0405	Ѕ	CYRILLIC CAPITAL LETTER DZE
0406	І	CYRILLIC CAPITAL LETTER I
		× (cyrillic letter i → 04C0)
0407	Ї	CYRILLIC CAPITAL LETTER YI
0408	Ј	CYRILLIC CAPITAL LETTER JE
0409	Љ	CYRILLIC CAPITAL LETTER LJE
040A	Њ	CYRILLIC CAPITAL LETTER NJE
040B	Ћ	CYRILLIC CAPITAL LETTER TSHE
		× (cyrillic small letter tshe → 045B)
040C	Ќ	CYRILLIC CAPITAL LETTER KJE
040D		× (soft hyphen → 00AD)
040E	Ў	CYRILLIC CAPITAL LETTER SHORT U
040F	Џ	CYRILLIC CAPITAL LETTER DZHE

Basic Russian alphabet

0410	А	CYRILLIC CAPITAL LETTER A
0411	Б	CYRILLIC CAPITAL LETTER BE
		× (latin small letter b topbar → 0183)
0412	В	CYRILLIC CAPITAL LETTER VE
0413	Г	CYRILLIC CAPITAL LETTER GE
0414	Д	CYRILLIC CAPITAL LETTER DE
0415	Е	CYRILLIC CAPITAL LETTER IE
0416	Ж	CYRILLIC CAPITAL LETTER ZHE
0417	З	CYRILLIC CAPITAL LETTER ZE
0418	И	CYRILLIC CAPITAL LETTER II
0419	Й	CYRILLIC CAPITAL LETTER SHORT II
041A	К	CYRILLIC CAPITAL LETTER KA
041B	Л	CYRILLIC CAPITAL LETTER EL
041C	М	CYRILLIC CAPITAL LETTER EM
041D	Н	CYRILLIC CAPITAL LETTER EN
041E	О	CYRILLIC CAPITAL LETTER O
041F	П	CYRILLIC CAPITAL LETTER PE
0420	Р	CYRILLIC CAPITAL LETTER ER
0421	С	CYRILLIC CAPITAL LETTER ES
0422	Т	CYRILLIC CAPITAL LETTER TE
0423	У	CYRILLIC CAPITAL LETTER U
		× (cyrillic capital letter uk digraph → 0478)
		× (cyrillic small letter straight u → 04AF)
0424	Ф	CYRILLIC CAPITAL LETTER EF
0425	Х	CYRILLIC CAPITAL LETTER KHA

0426	Ц	CYRILLIC CAPITAL LETTER TSE
0427	Ч	CYRILLIC CAPITAL LETTER CHE
0428	Ш	CYRILLIC CAPITAL LETTER SHA
0429	Щ	CYRILLIC CAPITAL LETTER SHCHA
042A	Ъ	CYRILLIC CAPITAL LETTER HARD SIGN
042B	Ы	CYRILLIC CAPITAL LETTER YERI
042C	Ь	CYRILLIC CAPITAL LETTER SOFT SIGN
042D	Э	CYRILLIC CAPITAL LETTER REVERSED E
042E	Ю	CYRILLIC CAPITAL LETTER IU
042F	Я	CYRILLIC CAPITAL LETTER IA
0430	а	CYRILLIC SMALL LETTER A
0431	б	CYRILLIC SMALL LETTER BE
0432	в	CYRILLIC SMALL LETTER VE
0433	г	CYRILLIC SMALL LETTER GE
0434	д	CYRILLIC SMALL LETTER DE
0435	е	CYRILLIC SMALL LETTER IE
0436	ж	CYRILLIC SMALL LETTER ZHE
0437	з	CYRILLIC SMALL LETTER ZE
		× (latin small letter tone six → 0185)
0438	и	CYRILLIC SMALL LETTER II
0439	й	CYRILLIC SMALL LETTER SHORT II
043A	к	CYRILLIC SMALL LETTER KA
043B	л	CYRILLIC SMALL LETTER EL
043C	м	CYRILLIC SMALL LETTER EM
043D	н	CYRILLIC SMALL LETTER EN
043E	о	CYRILLIC SMALL LETTER O
043F	п	CYRILLIC SMALL LETTER PE
0440	р	CYRILLIC SMALL LETTER ER
0441	с	CYRILLIC SMALL LETTER ES
0442	т	CYRILLIC SMALL LETTER TE
0443	у	CYRILLIC SMALL LETTER U
0444	ф	CYRILLIC SMALL LETTER EF
0445	х	CYRILLIC SMALL LETTER KHA
0446	ц	CYRILLIC SMALL LETTER TSE
0447	ч	CYRILLIC SMALL LETTER CHE
		× (latin small letter tone six → 0185)
0448	ш	CYRILLIC SMALL LETTER SHA
0449	щ	CYRILLIC SMALL LETTER SHCHA
044A	ъ	CYRILLIC SMALL LETTER HARD SIGN
044B	ы	CYRILLIC SMALL LETTER YERI
044C	ь	CYRILLIC SMALL LETTER SOFT SIGN
		× (latin small letter tone six → 0185)
044D	э	CYRILLIC SMALL LETTER REVERSED E
044E	ю	CYRILLIC SMALL LETTER IU
044F	я	CYRILLIC SMALL LETTER IA

0450	✕	(numero → 2116)
0451	ё	CYRILLIC SMALL LETTER IO *Russian, ...*
0452	ђ	CYRILLIC SMALL LETTER DJE *Serbian* ✕ (latin small letter d bar → 0111)
0453	ѓ	CYRILLIC SMALL LETTER GJE *Macedonian*
0454	є	CYRILLIC SMALL LETTER E = Old Cyrillic yest *Ukrainian, ...*
0455	ѕ	CYRILLIC SMALL LETTER DZE = Old Cyrillic zelo *Macedonian*
0456	і	CYRILLIC SMALL LETTER I = Old Cyrillic i *Ukrainian, Byelorussian, ...*
0457	ї	CYRILLIC SMALL LETTER YI *Ukrainian*
0458	ј	CYRILLIC SMALL LETTER JE *Serbian, Azerbaijan, Altaic*
0459	љ	CYRILLIC SMALL LETTER LJE *Serbian, Macedonian* ✕ (latin small letter l j → 01C9)
045A	њ	CYRILLIC SMALL LETTER NJE *Serbian, Macedonian* ✕ (latin small letter n j → 01CC)
045B	ћ	CYRILLIC SMALL LETTER TSHE = Old Cyrillic derv *Serbian* ✕ (latin small letter c acute → 0107) ✕ (latin small letter h bar → 0127) ✕ (cyrillic capital letter tshe → 040B) ✕ (planck constant over 2 pi → 210F)
045C	ќ	CYRILLIC SMALL LETTER KJE *Macedonian*
045D		✕ (section sign → 00A7)
045E	ў	CYRILLIC SMALL LETTER SHORT U *Byelorussian, Uzbek, ...*
045F	џ	CYRILLIC SMALL LETTER DZHE *Serbian, Macedonian, Abkhasian* ✕ (latin small letter d z hacek → 01C6)

Historic letters

0460	Ѡ	CYRILLIC CAPITAL LETTER OMEGA
0461	ѡ	CYRILLIC SMALL LETTER OMEGA
0462	ѣ	CYRILLIC CAPITAL LETTER YAT
0463	ѣ	CYRILLIC SMALL LETTER YAT
0464	Ѥ	CYRILLIC CAPITAL LETTER IOTIFIED E
0465	ѥ	CYRILLIC SMALL LETTER IOTIFIED E
0466	Ѧ	CYRILLIC CAPITAL LETTER LITTLE YUS
0467	ѧ	CYRILLIC SMALL LETTER LITTLE YUS

0468	Ѩ	CYRILLIC CAPITAL LETTER IOTIFIED LITTLE YUS
0469	ѩ	CYRILLIC SMALL LETTER IOTIFIED LITTLE YUS
046A	Ѫ	CYRILLIC CAPITAL LETTER BIG YUS
046B	ѫ	CYRILLIC SMALL LETTER BIG YUS
046C	Ѭ	CYRILLIC CAPITAL LETTER IOTIFIED BIG YUS
046D	ѭ	CYRILLIC SMALL LETTER IOTIFIED BIG YUS
046E	Ѯ	CYRILLIC CAPITAL LETTER KSI
046F	ѯ	CYRILLIC SMALL LETTER KSI
0470	Ѱ	CYRILLIC CAPITAL LETTER PSI
0471	ѱ	CYRILLIC SMALL LETTER PSI
0472	Ѳ	CYRILLIC CAPITAL LETTER FITA
0473	ѳ	CYRILLIC SMALL LETTER FITA ✕ (latin small letter barred o → 0275) ✕ (greek small letter theta → 03B8)
0474	Ѵ	CYRILLIC CAPITAL LETTER IZHITSA
0475	ѵ	CYRILLIC SMALL LETTER IZHITSA
0476	Ѷ	CYRILLIC CAPITAL LETTER IZHITSA DOUBLE GRAVE
0477	ѷ	CYRILLIC SMALL LETTER IZHITSA DOUBLE GRAVE
0478	Оу	CYRILLIC CAPITAL LETTER UK DIGRAPH *basic Old Cyrillic uk is unified with* *CYRILLIC LETTER U* ✕ (cyrillic capital letter u → 0423)
0479	оу	CYRILLIC SMALL LETTER UK DIGRAPH
047A	Ѻ	CYRILLIC CAPITAL LETTER ROUND OMEGA
047B	ѻ	CYRILLIC SMALL LETTER ROUND OMEGA
047C	Ѽ	CYRILLIC CAPITAL LETTER OMEGA TITLO
047D	ѽ	CYRILLIC SMALL LETTER OMEGA TITLO
047E	Ѿ	CYRILLIC CAPITAL LETTER OT
047F	ѿ	CYRILLIC SMALL LETTER OT
0480	Ҁ	CYRILLIC CAPITAL LETTER KOPPA
0481	ҁ	CYRILLIC SMALL LETTER KOPPA

Historic miscellaneous

0482	҂	CYRILLIC THOUSANDS SIGN
0483	҃	CYRILLIC NON-SPACING TITLO
0484	҄	CYRILLIC NON-SPACING PALATALIZATION ✕ (non-spacing vertical tilde → 033E)
0485	҅	CYRILLIC NON-SPACING DASIA PNEUMATA ✕ (greek non-spacing *dasia pneumata* → 0371)
0486	҆	CYRILLIC NON-SPACING PSILI PNEUMATA ✕ (greek non-spacing *psili pneumata* → 0372)
0487		
0488		
0489		

048A		
048B		
048C		
048D		
048E		
048F		

Extended Cyrillic

0490	Ґ	CYRILLIC CAPITAL LETTER GE WITH UPTURN
0491	ґ	CYRILLIC SMALL LETTER GE WITH UPTURN *Old Ukrainian*
0492	Ғ|Ғ	CYRILLIC CAPITAL LETTER GE BAR
0493	ғ|ғ	CYRILLIC SMALL LETTER GE BAR *Azerbaijani, Bashkir, ...* *full bar form preferred*
0494	Ҕ	CYRILLIC CAPITAL LETTER GE HOOK
0495	ҕ	CYRILLIC SMALL LETTER GE HOOK *Abkhasian, Yakut*
0496	Җ	CYRILLIC CAPITAL LETTER ZHE WITH RIGHT DESCENDER
0497	җ	CYRILLIC SMALL LETTER ZHE WITH RIGHT DESCENDER *Tatar, ...*
0498	Ҙ|Ҙ	CYRILLIC CAPITAL LETTER ZE CEDILLA
0499	ҙ|ҙ	CYRILLIC SMALL LETTER ZE CEDILLA *Bashkir* *cedilla form preferred*
049A	Қ	CYRILLIC CAPITAL LETTER KA WITH RIGHT DESCENDER
049B	қ	CYRILLIC SMALL LETTER KA WITH RIGHT DESCENDER *Abkhasian, Tajik, ...*
049C	Ҝ	CYRILLIC CAPITAL LETTER KA VERTICAL BAR
049D	ҝ	CYRILLIC SMALL LETTER KA VERTICAL BAR *Azerbaijan*
049E	Ҟ	CYRILLIC CAPITAL LETTER KA BAR
049F	ҟ	CYRILLIC SMALL LETTER KA BAR *Abkhasian*
04A0	Ҡ	CYRILLIC CAPITAL LETTER REVERSED GE KA
04A1	ҡ	CYRILLIC SMALL LETTER REVERSED GE KA *Bashkir*
04A2	Ң	CYRILLIC CAPITAL LETTER EN WITH RIGHT DESCENDER
04A3	ң	CYRILLIC SMALL LETTER EN WITH RIGHT DESCENDER *Bashkir, ...*
04A4	Ҥ	CYRILLIC CAPITAL LETTER EN GE
04A5	ҥ	CYRILLIC SMALL LETTER EN GE *Altaic, Mari, Yakut*

04A6	Ҧ	CYRILLIC CAPITAL LETTER PE HOOK
04A7	ҧ	CYRILLIC SMALL LETTER PE HOOK *Abkhasian*
04A8	Ҩ	CYRILLIC CAPITAL LETTER O HOOK
04A9	ҩ	CYRILLIC SMALL LETTER O HOOK *Abkhasian*
04AA	Ҫ|Ҫ	CYRILLIC CAPITAL LETTER ES CEDILLA
04AB	ҫ|ҫ	CYRILLIC SMALL LETTER ES CEDILLA *Bashkir, Chuvash* *cedilla form preferred*
04AC	Ҭ	CYRILLIC CAPITAL LETTER TE WITH RIGHT DESCENDER
04AD	ҭ	CYRILLIC SMALL LETTER TE WITH RIGHT DESCENDER *Abkhasian*
04AE	Ү	CYRILLIC CAPITAL LETTER STRAIGHT U
04AF	ү	CYRILLIC SMALL LETTER STRAIGHT U *stem is straight, unlike LETTER U* *Azerbaijan, Bashkir, ...* ✕ (cyrillic capital letter u → 0423)
04B0	Ұ	CYRILLIC CAPITAL LETTER STRAIGHT U BAR
04B1	ұ	CYRILLIC SMALL LETTER STRAIGHT U BAR *Kazakh*
04B2	Х	CYRILLIC CAPITAL LETTER KHA WITH RIGHT DESCENDER
04B3	х	CYRILLIC SMALL LETTER KHA WITH RIGHT DESCENDER *Abkhasian, Tajik, ...*
04B4	Ҵ	CYRILLIC CAPITAL LETTER TE TSE
04B5	ҵ	CYRILLIC SMALL LETTER TE TSE *Abkhasian*
04B6	Ҷ	CYRILLIC CAPITAL LETTER CHE WITH RIGHT DESCENDER
04B7	ҷ	CYRILLIC SMALL LETTER CHE WITH RIGHT DESCENDER *Abkhasian, Tajik*
04B8	Ҹ	CYRILLIC CAPITAL LETTER CHE VERTICAL BAR
04B9	ҹ	CYRILLIC SMALL LETTER CHE VERTICAL BAR *Azerbaijan*
04BA	Һ	CYRILLIC CAPITAL LETTER H
04BB	һ	CYRILLIC SMALL LETTER H *basically just a Latin "h", but uppercase form 04BA is closer to an inverted che (0427)* *Azerbaijan, Bashkir, ...* ✕ (latin small letter h → 0068)
04BC	Ҽ	CYRILLIC CAPITAL LETTER IE HOOK
04BD	ҽ	CYRILLIC SMALL LETTER IE HOOK *Abkhasian* *represents a "che"*

04BE	ҿ҇ҿ	CYRILLIC CAPITAL LETTER IE HOOK OGONEK
04BF	ҿ҇ҿ	CYRILLIC SMALL LETTER IE HOOK OGONEK

      Abkhasian
      ogonek form preferred

04C0	I	CYRILLIC LETTER I

      aspiration sign in many Caucasian
      languages
      has no "lowercase form", i.e. is case-
      invariant
      × *(cyrillic capital letter i → 0406)*

04C1	Ӂ	CYRILLIC CAPITAL LETTER SHORT ZHE
04C2	ӂ	CYRILLIC SMALL LETTER SHORT ZHE

      Moldavian

04C3	Ӄ	CYRILLIC CAPITAL LETTER KA HOOK
04C4	ӄ	CYRILLIC SMALL LETTER KA HOOK

      Khanty, Chukchi

04C5	Ӄ	CYRILLIC CAPITAL LETTER KA OGONEK
04C6	ӄ	CYRILLIC SMALL LETTER KA OGONEK

      Uzbek

04C7	Ӈ	CYRILLIC CAPITAL LETTER EN HOOK
04C8	ӈ	CYRILLIC SMALL LETTER EN HOOK

      Khanty, Chukchi

04C9	Ӽ	CYRILLIC CAPITAL LETTER KHA OGONEK
04CA	ӽ	CYRILLIC SMALL LETTER KHA OGONEK

      Uzbek

04CB	Ч	CYRILLIC CAPITAL LETTER CHE WITH LEFT DESCENDER
04CC	ч	CYRILLIC SMALL LETTER CHE WITH LEFT DESCENDER

      Khakassian

	053	054	055	056	057	058
0		Հ	Ր		հ	Ր
1	Ա	Ձ	Յ	ա	ձ	ց
2	Բ	Ղ	Ի	բ	ղ	ւ
3	Գ	Ճ	Փ	գ	ճ	փ
4	Դ	Մ	Ք	դ	մ	ֆ
5	Ե	Յ	Օ	ե	յ	օ
6	Զ	Ն	Ֆ	զ	ն	ֆ
7	Է	Շ		է	շ	
8	Ը	Ո		ը	ո	
9	Թ	Չ	ՙ	թ	չ	։
A	Ժ	Պ	՚	ժ	պ	
B	Ի	Ջ	՛	ի	ջ	
C	Լ	Ռ	՜	լ	ռ	
D	Խ	Ս	՝	խ	ս	
E	Ծ	Վ	՞	ծ	վ	
F	Կ	Տ	՟	կ	տ	

Uppercase letters

0530		
0531	Ա	ARMENIAN CAPITAL LETTER AYB
0532	Բ	ARMENIAN CAPITAL LETTER BEN
0533	Գ	ARMENIAN CAPITAL LETTER GIM
0534	Դ	ARMENIAN CAPITAL LETTER DA
0535	Ե	ARMENIAN CAPITAL LETTER ECH
0536	Զ	ARMENIAN CAPITAL LETTER ZA
0537	Է	ARMENIAN CAPITAL LETTER EH
0538	Ը	ARMENIAN CAPITAL LETTER ET
0539	Թ	ARMENIAN CAPITAL LETTER TO
053A	Ժ	ARMENIAN CAPITAL LETTER ZHE
053B	Ի	ARMENIAN CAPITAL LETTER INI
053C	Լ	ARMENIAN CAPITAL LETTER LIWN
053D	Խ	ARMENIAN CAPITAL LETTER XEH
053E	Ծ	ARMENIAN CAPITAL LETTER CA
053F	Կ	ARMENIAN CAPITAL LETTER KEN
0540	Հ	ARMENIAN CAPITAL LETTER HO
0541	Ձ	ARMENIAN CAPITAL LETTER JA
0542	Ղ	ARMENIAN CAPITAL LETTER LAD
0543	Ճ	ARMENIAN CAPITAL LETTER CHEH
0544	Մ	ARMENIAN CAPITAL LETTER MEN
0545	Յ	ARMENIAN CAPITAL LETTER YI
0546	Ն	ARMENIAN CAPITAL LETTER NOW
0547	Շ	ARMENIAN CAPITAL LETTER SHA
0548	Ո	ARMENIAN CAPITAL LETTER VO
0549	Չ	ARMENIAN CAPITAL LETTER CHA
054A	Պ	ARMENIAN CAPITAL LETTER PEH
054B	Ջ	ARMENIAN CAPITAL LETTER JHEH
054C	Ռ	ARMENIAN CAPITAL LETTER RA
054D	Ս	ARMENIAN CAPITAL LETTER SEH
054E	Վ	ARMENIAN CAPITAL LETTER VEW
054F	Տ	ARMENIAN CAPITAL LETTER TIWN
0550	Ր	ARMENIAN CAPITAL LETTER REH
0551	Ց	ARMENIAN CAPITAL LETTER CO
0552	Ւ	ARMENIAN CAPITAL LETTER YIWN
0553	Փ	ARMENIAN CAPITAL LETTER PIWR
0554	Ք	ARMENIAN CAPITAL LETTER KEH
0555	Օ	ARMENIAN CAPITAL LETTER OH
0556	Ֆ	ARMENIAN CAPITAL LETTER FEH
0557		
0558		

Modifier letters

0559 ＇ ARMENIAN MODIFIER LETTER LEFT HALF RING
× (modifier letter reversed comma → 02BD)
× (modifier letter left half ring → 02BF)
× (greek non-spacing dasia pneumata → 0371)

055A ＇ ARMENIAN MODIFIER LETTER RIGHT HALF RING
= ISO ARMENIAN APOSTROPHE
× (modifier letter apostrophe → 02BC)
× (modifier letter right half ring → 02BE)
× (greek non-spacing psili pneumata → 0372)

055B ´ ARMENIAN EMPHASIS MARK
= shesht
× (modifier letter acute → 02CA)

055C ˏ ARMENIAN EXCLAMATION MARK
= batsaganchakan nshan

055D ` ARMENIAN COMMA
= boot
× (modifier letter grave → 02CB)

055E ⸮ ARMENIAN QUESTION MARK
= hartsakan nshan

055F ⸍ ARMENIAN ABBREVIATION MARK
= patiw

Lowercase letters

0560		
0561	ա	ARMENIAN SMALL LETTER AYB
0562	բ	ARMENIAN SMALL LETTER BEN
0563	գ	ARMENIAN SMALL LETTER GIM
0564	դ	ARMENIAN SMALL LETTER DA
0565	ե	ARMENIAN SMALL LETTER ECH
0566	զ	ARMENIAN SMALL LETTER ZA
0567	է	ARMENIAN SMALL LETTER EH
0568	ը	ARMENIAN SMALL LETTER ET
0569	թ	ARMENIAN SMALL LETTER TO
056A	ժ	ARMENIAN SMALL LETTER ZHE
056B	ի	ARMENIAN SMALL LETTER INI
056C	լ	ARMENIAN SMALL LETTER LIWN
056D	խ	ARMENIAN SMALL LETTER XEH
056E	ծ	ARMENIAN SMALL LETTER CA
056F	կ	ARMENIAN SMALL LETTER KEN
0570	հ	ARMENIAN SMALL LETTER HO
0571	ձ	ARMENIAN SMALL LETTER JA
0572	ղ	ARMENIAN SMALL LETTER LAD
0573	ճ	ARMENIAN SMALL LETTER CHEH
0574	մ	ARMENIAN SMALL LETTER MEN

0575	յ	ARMENIAN SMALL LETTER YI
0576	ն	ARMENIAN SMALL LETTER NOW
0577	շ	ARMENIAN SMALL LETTER SHA
0578	ո	ARMENIAN SMALL LETTER VO
0579	չ	ARMENIAN SMALL LETTER CHA
057A	պ	ARMENIAN SMALL LETTER PEH
057B	ջ	ARMENIAN SMALL LETTER JHEH
057C	ռ	ARMENIAN SMALL LETTER RA
057D	ս	ARMENIAN SMALL LETTER SEH
057E	վ	ARMENIAN SMALL LETTER VEW
057F	տ	ARMENIAN SMALL LETTER TIWN
0580	ր	ARMENIAN SMALL LETTER REH
0581	ց	ARMENIAN SMALL LETTER CO
0582	ւ	ARMENIAN SMALL LETTER YIWN
0583	փ	ARMENIAN SMALL LETTER PIWR
0584	ք	ARMENIAN SMALL LETTER KEH
0585	o	ARMENIAN SMALL LETTER OH
0586	ֆ	ARMENIAN SMALL LETTER FEH
0587		
0588		

Punctuation

0589	:	ARMENIAN PERIOD
		= vertsaket
		= Georgian period
		may also be used for Georgian
		× (colon → 003A)

	059	05A	05B	05C	05D	05E	05F
0			◌ְ	׀	א	נ	װ
1			◌ֱ	◌ׁ	ב	ס	ױ
2			◌ֲ	◌ׂ	ג	ע	ײ
3			◌ֳ	׃	ד	ף	׳
4			◌ִ		ה	פ	״
5			◌ֵ		ו	ץ	◌̆
6			◌ֶ		ז	צ	
7			◌ַ		ח	ק	
8			◌ָ		ט	ר	
9			◌ֹ		י	ש	
A					ך	ת	
B			◌ֻ		כ		
C			◌ּ		ל		
D			◌ֽ		ם		
E			־		מ		
F			◌ֿ		ן		

Cantillation marks, accents (TBD)

0590	
0591	
0592	
0593	
0594	
0595	
0596	
0597	
0598	
0599	
059A	
059B	
059C	
059D	
059E	
059F	
05A0	
05A1	
05A2	
05A3	
05A4	
05A5	
05A6	
05A7	
05A8	
05A9	
05AA	
05AB	
05AC	
05AD	
05AE	
05AF	

Points and punctuation

05B0		HEBREW POINT SHEVA
05B1		HEBREW POINT HATAF SEGOL
05B2		HEBREW POINT HATAF PATAH
05B3		HEBREW POINT HATAF QAMATS
05B4		HEBREW POINT HIRIQ
05B5		HEBREW POINT TSERE
05B6		HEBREW POINT SEGOL
05B7		HEBREW POINT PATAH
		furtive Patah is not a distinct character
05B8		HEBREW POINT QAMATS
05B9		HEBREW POINT HOLAM

05BA		
05BB		HEBREW POINT QUBUTS
05BC		HEBREW POINT DAGESH
		= *shuruq*
		= *mapiq*
		falls within the base letter
05BD		HEBREW POINT METEG
		= *siluq*
05BE	-	HEBREW PUNCTUATION MAQAF
05BF		HEBREW POINT RAFE
05C0	|	HEBREW POINT PASEQ
		= *legarmeh*
		may be treated as spacing punctuation,
		not as a point
05C1		HEBREW POINT SHIN DOT
05C2		HEBREW POINT SIN DOT
05C3	:	HEBREW PUNCTUATION SOF PASUQ
05C4		
05C5		
05C6		
05C7		
05C8		
05C9		
05CA		
05CB		
05CC		
05CD		
05CE		
05CF		

Based on ISO 8859-8

05D0	א	HEBREW LETTER ALEF
		= *aleph*
		$\times$ (first transfinite cardinal → 2135)
05D1	ב	HEBREW LETTER BET
		$\times$ (second transfinite cardinal → 2136)
05D2	ג	HEBREW LETTER GIMEL
		$\times$ (third transfinite cardinal → 2137)
05D3	ד	HEBREW LETTER DALET
		$\times$ (fourth transfinite cardinal → 2138)
05D4	ה	HEBREW LETTER HE
05D5	ו	HEBREW LETTER VAV
05D6	ז	HEBREW LETTER ZAYIN
05D7	ח	HEBREW LETTER HET
05D8	ט	HEBREW LETTER TET
05D9	י	HEBREW LETTER YOD
05DA	ך	HEBREW LETTER FINAL KAF
		= *terminal kaf*
05DB	כ	HEBREW LETTER KAF

05DC	ל	HEBREW LETTER LAMED
05DD	ם	HEBREW LETTER FINAL MEM
		= *terminal mem*
05DE	מ	HEBREW LETTER MEM
05DF	ן	HEBREW LETTER FINAL NUN
		= *terminal nun*
05E0	נ	HEBREW LETTER NUN
05E1	ס	HEBREW LETTER SAMEKH
05E2	ע	HEBREW LETTER AYIN
05E3	ף	HEBREW LETTER FINAL PE
		= *terminal pe*
05E4	פ	HEBREW LETTER PE
05E5	ץ	HEBREW LETTER FINAL TSADI
		= *terminal zade*
05E6	צ	HEBREW LETTER TSADI
		= *zade*
05E7	ק	HEBREW LETTER QOF
05E8	ר	HEBREW LETTER RESH
05E9	ש	HEBREW LETTER SHIN
05EA	ת	HEBREW LETTER TAV
05EB		
05EC		
05ED		
05EE		
05EF		

Yiddish digraphs

05F0	וו	HEBREW LETTER DOUBLE VAV
		= *tsvey vovn*
05F1	וי	HEBREW LETTER VAV YOD
05F2	יי	HEBREW LETTER DOUBLE YOD
		= *tsvey yudn*

Additional punctuation

| 05F3 | ׳ | HEBREW PUNCTUATION GERESH |
| 05F4 | ״ | HEBREW PUNCTUATION GERSHAYIM |

Additional point

| 05F5 | ֹ | HEBREW POINT VARIKA |
| | | *Ladino/Judezmo* |

	060	061	062	063	064	065	066	067
0				ذ	ـ	◌ِ	٠	◌ٰ
1			ء	ر	ف	◌ّ	١	ٱ
2			آ	ز	ق	◌ْ	٢	ٲ
3			أ	س	ك		٣	ٳ
4			ؤ	ش	ل		٤	ٴ
5			إ	ص	م		٥	ٵ
6			ئ	ض	ن		٦	ٶ
7			ا	ط	ه		٧	ٷ
8			ب	ظ	و		٨	ٸ
9			ة	ع	ى		٩	ٹ
A			ت	غ	ي		٪	ٺ
B		؛	ث		◌ً		د	ٻ
C	،		ج		◌ٌ		؍	ټ
D			ح		◌ٍ			ٽ
E			خ		◌ً			پ
F		؟	د		◌ُ			ٿ

	068	069	06A	06B	06C	06D	06E	06F
0	ڀ	ڐ	ڠ	ڰ	ۀ	ۍ		۰
1	ځ	ڑ	ڡ	ڱ	ہ	ێ		۱
2	ڂ	ڒ	ڢ	ڲ	ۂ	ے		۲
3	ڃ	ړ	ڣ	ڳ	ۃ	ۓ		۳
4	ڄ	ڔ	ڤ	ڴ	ۄ	‐		۴
5	څ	ڕ	ڥ	ڵ	ۅ	ە		۵
6	چ	ږ	ڦ	ڶ	ۆ			۶
7	ڇ	ڗ	ڧ	ڷ	ۇ			۷
8	ڈ	ژ	ڨ		ۈ			۸
9	ډ	ڙ	ک		ۉ			۹
A	ڊ	ښ	ڪ	ں	ۊ			
B	ڋ	ڛ	ګ	ڻ	ۋ			
C	ڌ	ڜ	ڬ	ڼ	ی			
D	ڍ	ڝ	ڭ	ڽ	ۍ			
E	ڎ	ڞ	ڮ	ھ	ێ			
F	ڏ	ڟ	گ					

Based on ISO 8859-6

0600		× (non-breaking space → 00A0)
0601		
0602		
0603		
0604		× (currency sign → 00A4)
0605		
0606		
0607		
0608		
0609		
060A		
060B		
060C	،	ARABIC COMMA
		× (comma → 002C)
060D		× (soft hyphen → 00AD)
060E		
060F		
0610		
0611		
0612		
0613		
0614		
0615		
0616		
0617		
0618		
0619		
061A		
061B	؛	ARABIC SEMICOLON
		× (semicolon → 003B)
061C		
061D		
061E		
061F	؟	ARABIC QUESTION MARK
		× (question mark → 003F)
0620		
0621	ء	ARABIC LETTER HAMZAH
		× (modifier letter right half ring → 02BE)
0622	آ	ARABIC LETTER MADDAH ON ALEF
0623	أ	ARABIC LETTER HAMZAH ON ALEF
0624	ؤ	ARABIC LETTER HAMZAH ON WAW
0625	إ	ARABIC LETTER HAMZAH UNDER ALEF
0626	ئ	ARABIC LETTER HAMZAH ON YA
0627	ا	ARABIC LETTER ALEF
0628	ب	ARABIC LETTER BAA

0629	ة	ARABIC LETTER TAA MARBUTAH
062A	ت	ARABIC LETTER TAA
062B	ث	ARABIC LETTER THAA
062C	ج	ARABIC LETTER JEEM
062D	ح	ARABIC LETTER HAA
062E	خ	ARABIC LETTER KHAA
062F	د	ARABIC LETTER DAL
0630	ذ	ARABIC LETTER THAL
0631	ر	ARABIC LETTER RA
0632	ز	ARABIC LETTER ZAIN
0633	س	ARABIC LETTER SEEN
0634	ش	ARABIC LETTER SHEEN
0635	ص	ARABIC LETTER SAD
0636	ض	ARABIC LETTER DAD
0637	ط	ARABIC LETTER TAH
0638	ظ	ARABIC LETTER DHAH
0639	ع	ARABIC LETTER AIN
		× (latin small letter reversed yogh → 01B9)
		× (modifier letter left half ring → 02BF)
063A	غ	ARABIC LETTER GHAIN
063B		
063C		
063D		
063E		
063F		
0640	ـ	ARABIC TATWEEL
		= kashida
		inserted to stretch characters
0641	ف	ARABIC LETTER FA
0642	ق	ARABIC LETTER QAF
0643	ك	ARABIC LETTER CAF
0644	ل	ARABIC LETTER LAM
0645	م	ARABIC LETTER MEEM
0646	ن	ARABIC LETTER NOON
0647	ه	ARABIC LETTER HA
0648	و	ARABIC LETTER WAW
0649	ى	ARABIC LETTER ALEF MAQSURAH
064A	ي	ARABIC LETTER YA

Points from ISO 8859-6

064B	ً	ARABIC FATHATAN
064C	ٌ	ARABIC DAMMATAN
064D	ٍ	ARABIC KASRATAN
064E	َ	ARABIC FATHAH
064F	ُ	ARABIC DAMMAH
0650	ِ	ARABIC KASRAH

0651	◌ّ	**ARABIC SHADDAH**
0652	◌ْ	**ARABIC SUKUN**
0653		
0654		
0655		
0656		
0657		
0658		
0659		
065A		
065B		
065C		
065D		
065E		
065F		

Arabic-Indic digits

0660	٠	ARABIC-INDIC DIGIT ZERO
0661	١	ARABIC-INDIC DIGIT ONE
0662	٢	ARABIC-INDIC DIGIT TWO
0663	٣	ARABIC-INDIC DIGIT THREE
0664	٤	ARABIC-INDIC DIGIT FOUR
0665	٥	ARABIC-INDIC DIGIT FIVE
0666	٦	ARABIC-INDIC DIGIT SIX
0667	٧	ARABIC-INDIC DIGIT SEVEN
0668	٨	ARABIC-INDIC DIGIT EIGHT
0669	٩	ARABIC-INDIC DIGIT NINE
066A	٪	ARABIC PERCENT SIGN
		× (percent sign → 0025)
066B	٫	ARABIC DECIMAL SEPARATOR
066C	٬	ARABIC THOUSANDS SEPARATOR
066D		
066E		
066F		

Point

0670	◌ٰ	ARABIC ALEF ABOVE

Extended Arabic letters

0671	ٱ	ARABIC LETTER HAMZAT WASL ON ALEF
		Arabic
0672	ٲ	ARABIC LETTER WAVY HAMZAH ON ALEF
		Baluchi, Kashmiri
0673	ٳ	ARABIC LETTER WAVY HAMZAH UNDER ALEF
		Baluchi, Kashmiri

0674	ٴ	ARABIC LETTER HIGH HAMZAH
		Kazakh
		forms digraphs
0675	ٵ	ARABIC LETTER HIGH HAMZAH ALEF
		Kazakh
0676	ٶ	ARABIC LETTER HIGH HAMZAH WAW
		Kazakh
0677	ٷ	ARABIC LETTER HIGH HAMZAH WAW WITH DAMMAH
		Kazakh
0678	ٸ	ARABIC LETTER HIGH HAMZAH YA
		Kazakh
0679	ٹ	ARABIC LETTER TAA WITH SMALL TAH
		Urdu
067A	ٺ	ARABIC LETTER TAA WITH TWO DOTS VERTICAL ABOVE
		Sindhi
067B	ٻ	ARABIC LETTER BAA WITH TWO DOTS VERTICAL BELOW
		Sindhi
067C	ټ	ARABIC LETTER TAA WITH RING
		Pashto
067D	ٽ	ARABIC LETTER TAA WITH THREE DOTS ABOVE DOWNWARD
		Sindhi
067E	پ	ARABIC LETTER TAA WITH THREE DOTS BELOW
		= peh
		Persian, Urdu, ...
067F	ٿ	ARABIC LETTER TAA WITH FOUR DOTS ABOVE
		Sindhi
0680	ڀ	ARABIC LETTER BAA WITH FOUR DOTS BELOW
		Sindhi
0681	ځ	ARABIC LETTER HAMZAH ON HAA
		Pashto
0682	ڂ	ARABIC LETTER HAA WITH TWO DOTS VERTICAL ABOVE
		Pashto
0683	ڃ	ARABIC LETTER HAA WITH MIDDLE TWO DOTS
		Sindhi
0684	ڄ	ARABIC LETTER HAA WITH MIDDLE TWO DOTS VERTICAL
		Sindhi
0685	څ	ARABIC LETTER HAA WITH THREE DOTS ABOVE
		Pashto
0686	چ	ARABIC LETTER HAA WITH MIDDLE THREE DOTS DOWNWARD
		= tcheh
		Persian, Urdu, ...
0687	ڇ	ARABIC LETTER HAA WITH MIDDLE FOUR DOTS
		Sindhi

0688	ڈ	ARABIC LETTER DAL WITH SMALL TAH *Urdu*
0689	ډ	ARABIC LETTER DAL WITH RING *Pashto*
068A	ڊ	ARABIC LETTER DAL WITH DOT BELOW *Sindhi*
068B	ڋ	ARABIC LETTER DAL WITH DOT BELOW AND SMALL TAH *Lahnda*
068C	ڌ	ARABIC LETTER DAL WITH TWO DOTS ABOVE *Sindhi*
068D	ڍ	ARABIC LETTER DAL WITH TWO DOTS BELOW *Sindhi*
068E	ڎ	ARABIC LETTER DAL WITH THREE DOTS ABOVE *Sindhi*
068F	ڏ	ARABIC LETTER DAL WITH THREE DOTS ABOVE DOWNWARD *Sindhi*
0690	ڐ	ARABIC LETTER DAL WITH FOUR DOTS ABOVE *Urdu*
0691	ڑ	ARABIC LETTER RA WITH SMALL TAH *Urdu*
0692	ڒ	ARABIC LETTER RA WITH SMALL V *Kurdish*
0693	ړ	ARABIC LETTER RA WITH RING *Pashto*
0694	ڔ	ARABIC LETTER RA WITH DOT BELOW *Kurdish*
0695	ڕ	ARABIC LETTER RA WITH SMALL V BELOW *Kurdish*
0696	ږ	ARABIC LETTER RA WITH DOT BELOW AND DOT ABOVE *Pashto*
0697	ڗ	ARABIC LETTER RA WITH TWO DOTS ABOVE *Dargwa*
0698	ژ	ARABIC LETTER RA WITH THREE DOTS ABOVE = jeh *Persian, Urdu, ...*
0699	ڙ	ARABIC LETTER RA WITH FOUR DOTS ABOVE *Sindhi*
069A	ښ	ARABIC LETTER SEEN WITH DOT BELOW AND DOT ABOVE *Pashto*
069B	ڛ	ARABIC LETTER SEEN WITH THREE DOTS BELOW *Uighur*
069C	ڜ	ARABIC LETTER SEEN WITH THREE DOTS BELOW AND THREE DOTS ABOVE *Moroccan Arabic*
069D	ڝ	ARABIC LETTER SAD WITH TWO DOTS BELOW *Turkic*
069E	ڞ	ARABIC LETTER SAD WITH THREE DOTS ABOVE *Berber*
069F	ڟ	ARABIC LETTER TAH WITH THREE DOTS ABOVE *old Hausa*
06A0	ڠ	ARABIC LETTER AIN WITH THREE DOTS ABOVE *old Malay*
06A1	ڡ	ARABIC LETTER DOTLESS FA *Adighe*
06A2	ڢ	ARABIC LETTER FA WITH DOT MOVED BELOW *Maghrib Arabic*
06A3	ڣ	ARABIC LETTER FA WITH DOT BELOW *Ingush*
06A4	ڤ	ARABIC LETTER FA WITH THREE DOTS ABOVE = veh *Arabic for foreign words*
06A5	ڥ	ARABIC LETTER FA WITH THREE DOTS BELOW *Arabic for foreign words*
06A6	ڦ	ARABIC LETTER FA WITH FOUR DOTS ABOVE *Sindhi*
06A7	ڧ	ARABIC LETTER QAF WITH DOT ABOVE *Maghrib Arabic*
06A8	ڨ	ARABIC LETTER QAF WITH THREE DOTS ABOVE *Tunisian Arabic*
06A9	ک	ARABIC LETTER OPEN CAF *Persian, Urdu, ...*
06AA	ڪ	ARABIC LETTER SWASH CAF *(various)*
06AB	ګ	ARABIC LETTER CAF WITH RING *Pashto*
06AC	ڬ	ARABIC LETTER CAF WITH DOT ABOVE *old Malay*
06AD	ڭ	ARABIC LETTER CAF WITH THREE DOTS ABOVE *Uighur, Kazakh, old Malay, ...*
06AE	ڮ	ARABIC LETTER CAF WITH THREE DOTS BELOW *Berber*
06AF	گ	ARABIC LETTER GAF *Persian, Urdu, ...*
06B0	ڰ	ARABIC LETTER GAF WITH RING *Lahnda*
06B1	ڱ	ARABIC LETTER GAF WITH TWO DOTS ABOVE *Sindhi*

06B2	گ	ARABIC LETTER GAF WITH TWO DOTS BELOW *Sindhi*
06B3	گ	ARABIC LETTER GAF WITH TWO DOTS VERTICAL BELOW *Sindhi*
06B4	گ	ARABIC LETTER GAF WITH THREE DOTS ABOVE *Sindhi*
06B5	ڵ	ARABIC LETTER LAM WITH SMALL V *Kurdish*
06B6	ڶ	ARABIC LETTER LAM WITH DOT ABOVE *Kurdish*
06B7	ڷ	ARABIC LETTER LAM WITH THREE DOTS ABOVE *Kurdish*
06B8		
06B9		
06BA	ں	ARABIC LETTER DOTLESS NOON *Urdu*
06BB	ڻ	ARABIC LETTER DOTLESS NOON WITH SMALL TAH *Sindhi*
06BC	ڼ	ARABIC LETTER NOON WITH RING *Pashto*
06BD	ڽ	ARABIC LETTER NOON WITH THREE DOTS ABOVE *old Malay*
06BE	ھ	ARABIC LETTER KNOTTED HA *Urdu* forms aspirate digraphs
06BF		
06C0	ۀ	ARABIC LETTER HAMZAH ON HA *Persian*
06C1	ہ	ARABIC LETTER HA GOAL *Urdu*
06C2	ۂ	ARABIC LETTER HAMZAH ON HA GOAL *Urdu*
06C3	ۃ	ARABIC LETTER TAA MARBUTAH GOAL *Urdu*
06C4	ۄ	ARABIC LETTER WAW WITH RING *Kashmiri*
06C5	ۅ	ARABIC LETTER WAW WITH BAR *Kirghiz*
06C6	ۆ	ARABIC LETTER WAW WITH SMALL V *Uighur, Kurdish, Kazah*
06C7	ۇ	ARABIC LETTER WAW WITH DAMMAH *Kirghiz*
06C8	ۈ	ARABIC LETTER WAW WITH ALEF ABOVE *Uighur*
06C9	ۉ	ARABIC LETTER WAW WITH INVERTED SMALL V *Kazakh, Kirghiz*

06CA	ۊ	ARABIC LETTER WAW WITH TWO DOTS ABOVE *Kurdish*
06CB	ۋ	ARABIC LETTER WAW WITH THREE DOTS ABOVE *Uighur, Kazakh*
06CC	ی	ARABIC LETTER DOTLESS YA *Arabic, Persian, Urdu, ...*
06CD	ۍ	ARABIC LETTER YA WITH TAIL *Pashto, Sindhi*
06CE	ێ	ARABIC LETTER YA WITH SMALL V *Kurdish*
06CF		
06D0	ې	ARABIC LETTER YA WITH TWO DOTS VERTICAL BELOW *Pashto, Uighur*
06D1	ۑ	ARABIC LETTER YA WITH THREE DOTS BELOW *old Malay*
06D2	ے	ARABIC LETTER YA BARREE *Urdu*
06D3	ۓ	ARABIC LETTER HAMZAH ON YA BARREE *Urdu*
06D4	۔	ARABIC PERIOD *Urdu*
06D5	ە	ARABIC LETTER AE *Uighur, Kazakh, Kirghiz*
06D6		
06D7		
06D8		
06D9		
06DA		
06DB		
06DC		
06DD		
06DE		
06DF		
06E0		
06E1		
06E2		
06E3		
06E4		
06E5		
06E6		
06E7		
06E8		
06E9		
06EA		
06EB		
06EC		

06ED
06EE
06EF

**Eastern Arabic-Indic digits
(Persian and Urdu)**

06F0	•	EASTERN ARABIC-INDIC DIGIT ZERO
06F1	١	EASTERN ARABIC-INDIC DIGIT ONE
06F2	٢	EASTERN ARABIC-INDIC DIGIT TWO
06F3	٣	EASTERN ARABIC-INDIC DIGIT THREE
06F4	۴|٢	EASTERN ARABIC-INDIC DIGIT FOUR
		different glyphs in Persian and Urdu
06F5	۵	EASTERN ARABIC-INDIC DIGIT FIVE
		Persian and Urdu share glyph different from Arabic
06F6	۶|٦	EASTERN ARABIC-INDIC DIGIT SIX
		Persian glyph different from Arabic
06F7	٧|۷	EASTERN ARABIC-INDIC DIGIT SEVEN
		Urdu glyph different from Arabic
06F8	٨	EASTERN ARABIC-INDIC DIGIT EIGHT
06F9	٩	EASTERN ARABIC-INDIC DIGIT NINE

	090	091	092	093	094	095	096	097
0		ऐ	ठ	र	ी	ॐ	ॠ	॰
1	◌ँ	ऑ	ड	ऱ	◌ु	◌॑	ॡ	
2	◌ं	ऒ	ढ	ल	◌ू	◌॒	◌ॢ	
3	◌ः	ओ	ण	ळ	◌ृ	◌॓	◌ॣ	
4		औ	त	ऴ	◌ॄ	◌॔	।	
5	अ	क	थ	व	◌ॅ		॥	
6	आ	ख	द	श	◌ॆ		०	
7	इ	ग	ध	ष	◌े		१	
8	ई	घ	न	स	◌ै	क़	२	
9	उ	ङ	ऩ	ह	ॉ	ख़	३	
A	ऊ	च	प		ॊ	ग़	४	
B	ऋ	छ	फ		ो	ज़	५	
C	ऌ	ज	ब	◌़	ौ	ड़	६	
D	ऍ	झ	भ	ऽ	◌्	ढ़	७	
E	ऎ	ञ	म	ा		फ़	८	
F	ए	ट	य	ि◌		य़	९	

Based on ISCII 1988

Various signs

0900		
0901	◌ँ	DEVANAGARI SIGN CANDRABINDU
		= anunasika
		✕ (non-spacing candrabindu → 0310)
0902	◌ं	DEVANAGARI SIGN ANUSVARA
		= bindu
0903	ः	DEVANAGARI SIGN VISARGA
0904		

Independent vowels

0905	अ	DEVANAGARI LETTER A
0906	आ	DEVANAGARI LETTER AA
0907	इ	DEVANAGARI LETTER I
0908	ई	DEVANAGARI LETTER II
0909	उ	DEVANAGARI LETTER U
090A	ऊ	DEVANAGARI LETTER UU
090B	ऋ	DEVANAGARI LETTER VOCALIC R
		= ISO DEVANAGARI LETTER RI
090C	ऌ	DEVANAGARI LETTER VOCALIC L
		= ISO DEVANAGARI LETTER LRI
090D	ऍ	DEVANAGARI LETTER CANDRA E
090E	ऎ	DEVANAGARI LETTER SHORT E
		for transcribing Dravidian short e
090F	ए	DEVANAGARI LETTER E
0910	ऐ	DEVANAGARI LETTER AI
0911	ऑ	DEVANAGARI LETTER CANDRA O
0912	ऒ	DEVANAGARI LETTER SHORT O
		for transcribing Dravidian short o
0913	ओ	DEVANAGARI LETTER O
0914	औ	DEVANAGARI LETTER AU

Consonants

0915	क	DEVANAGARI LETTER KA
0916	ख	DEVANAGARI LETTER KHA
0917	ग	DEVANAGARI LETTER GA
0918	घ	DEVANAGARI LETTER GHA
0919	ङ	DEVANAGARI LETTER NGA
091A	च	DEVANAGARI LETTER CA
091B	छ	DEVANAGARI LETTER CHA
091C	ज	DEVANAGARI LETTER JA
091D	झ	DEVANAGARI LETTER JHA
091E	ञ	DEVANAGARI LETTER NYA
091F	ट	DEVANAGARI LETTER TTA
0920	ठ	DEVANAGARI LETTER TTHA
0921	ड	DEVANAGARI LETTER DDA
0922	ढ	DEVANAGARI LETTER DDHA

0923	ण	DEVANAGARI LETTER NNA
		= ISO DEVANAGARI LETTER NDA
0924	त	DEVANAGARI LETTER TA
0925	थ	DEVANAGARI LETTER THA
0926	द	DEVANAGARI LETTER DA
0927	ध	DEVANAGARI LETTER DHA
0928	न	DEVANAGARI LETTER NA
0929	ऩ	DEVANAGARI LETTER NNNA
		= ISO DEVANAGARI LETTER NNA
		for transcribing Tamil alveolar n
092A	प	DEVANAGARI LETTER PA
092B	फ	DEVANAGARI LETTER PHA
092C	ब	DEVANAGARI LETTER BA
092D	भ	DEVANAGARI LETTER BHA
092E	म	DEVANAGARI LETTER MA
092F	य	DEVANAGARI LETTER YA
0930	र	DEVANAGARI LETTER RA
0931	ऱ	DEVANAGARI LETTER RRA
		for transcribing Tamil alveolar r
0932	ल	DEVANAGARI LETTER LA
0933	ळ	DEVANAGARI LETTER LLA
		= ISO DEVANAGARI LETTER LDA
0934	ऴ	DEVANAGARI LETTER LLLA
		= ISO DEVANAGARI LETTER LLA
		for transcribing Tamil l
0935	व	DEVANAGARI LETTER VA
0936	श	DEVANAGARI LETTER SHA
0937	ष	DEVANAGARI LETTER SSA
0938	स	DEVANAGARI LETTER SA
0939	ह	DEVANAGARI LETTER HA

Various signs

093A		
093B		✕ (zero width non-joiner → 200C)
093C	◌़	DEVANAGARI SIGN NUKTA
		for extending the alphabet to new letters
093D	ऽ	DEVANAGARI SIGN AVAGRAHA

Dependent vowel signs

093E	ा	DEVANAGARI VOWEL SIGN AA
093F	ि	DEVANAGARI VOWEL SIGN I
		stands to the left of the consonant
0940	ी	DEVANAGARI VOWEL SIGN II
0941	ु	DEVANAGARI VOWEL SIGN U
0942	ू	DEVANAGARI VOWEL SIGN UU
0943	ृ	DEVANAGARI VOWEL SIGN VOCALIC R
		= ISO DEVANAGARI VOWEL SIGN RI

0944	ृ	DEVANAGARI VOWEL SIGN VOCALIC RR
		= *ISO DEVANAGARI VOWEL SIGN RII*
0945	ॅ	DEVANAGARI VOWEL SIGN CANDRA E
		= *candra*
0946	ॆ	DEVANAGARI VOWEL SIGN SHORT E
		for transcribing Dravidian vowels
0947	े	DEVANAGARI VOWEL SIGN E
0948	ै	DEVANAGARI VOWEL SIGN AI
0949	ॉ	DEVANAGARI VOWEL SIGN CANDRA O
094A	ॊ	DEVANAGARI VOWEL SIGN SHORT O
		for transcribing Dravidian vowels
094B	ो	DEVANAGARI VOWEL SIGN O
094C	ौ	DEVANAGARI VOWEL SIGN AU

Various signs

094D	्	DEVANAGARI SIGN VIRAMA
		= *halant*
		suppresses inherent vowel
094E		
094F		
0950	ॐ	DEVANAGARI OM
0951	॑	DEVANAGARI STRESS SIGN UDATTA
0952	॒	DEVANAGARI STRESS SIGN ANUDATTA
0953	॓	DEVANAGARI GRAVE ACCENT
0954	॔	DEVANAGARI ACUTE ACCENT
0955		
0956		
0957		

Additional consonants

0958	क़	DEVANAGARI LETTER QA
0959	ख़	DEVANAGARI LETTER KHHA
095A	ग़	DEVANAGARI LETTER GHHA
095B	ज़	DEVANAGARI LETTER ZA
095C	ड़	DEVANAGARI LETTER DDDHA
095D	ढ़	DEVANAGARI LETTER RHA
095E	फ़	DEVANAGARI LETTER FA
095F	य़	DEVANAGARI LETTER YYA

Generic additions

0960	ॠ	DEVANAGARI LETTER VOCALIC RR
0961	ॡ	DEVANAGARI LETTER VOCALIC LL
0962	ॢ	DEVANAGARI VOWEL SIGN VOCALIC L
0963	ॣ	DEVANAGARI VOWEL SIGN VOCALIC LL
0964	।	DEVANAGARI DANDA
		= *phrase separator*
		× *(tibetan shad → 1034)*

0965	॥	DEVANAGARI DOUBLE DANDA
		× *(tibetan double shad → 104A)*
0966	०	DEVANAGARI DIGIT ZERO
0967	१	DEVANAGARI DIGIT ONE
0968	२	DEVANAGARI DIGIT TWO
0969	३	DEVANAGARI DIGIT THREE
096A	४	DEVANAGARI DIGIT FOUR
096B	५	DEVANAGARI DIGIT FIVE
096C	६	DEVANAGARI DIGIT SIX
096D	७	DEVANAGARI DIGIT SEVEN
096E	८	DEVANAGARI DIGIT EIGHT
096F	९	DEVANAGARI DIGIT NINE

Devanagari-specific additions

| 0970 | ॰ | DEVANAGARI ABBREVIATION SIGN |

	098	099	09A	09B	09C	09D	09E	09F
0		ঐ	ঠ	র	ৗ		ক্ষ	ৰ
1	ঁ		ড		ু		ৡ	ৱ
2	ং		ঢ	ল	ো		ৢ	৲
3	ঃ	ও	ণ		ৣ		ৣ	৳
4		ঔ	ত		ৄ			৴
5	অ	ক	থ					৵
6	আ	খ	দ	শ			০	৶
7	ই	গ	ধ	ষ	ে	ৗ	১	৷
8	ঈ	ঘ	ন	স	ৈ		২	৸
9	উ	ঙ		হ			৩	৹
A	ঊ	চ	প				৪	৺
B	ঋ	ছ	ফ		ো		৫	
C	ৌ	জ	ব	ঃ	ৌ	ড়	৬	
D		ঝ	ভ		ৢ	ঢ়	৭	
E		ঞ	ম	া			৮	
F	এ	ট	য	ি		য়	৯	

Based on ISCII 1988

Various signs

0980		
0981	ঁ	BENGALI SIGN CANDRABINDU
0982	ং	BENGALI SIGN ANUSVARA
0983	ঃ	BENGALI SIGN VISARGA
0984		

Independent vowels

0985	অ	BENGALI LETTER A
0986	আ	BENGALI LETTER AA
0987	ই	BENGALI LETTER I
0988	ঈ	BENGALI LETTER II
0989	উ	BENGALI LETTER U
098A	ঊ	BENGALI LETTER UU
098B	ঋ	BENGALI LETTER VOCALIC R
098C	ঌ	BENGALI LETTER VOCALIC L
098D		
098E		
098F	এ	BENGALI LETTER E
0990	ঐ	BENGALI LETTER AI
0991		
0992		
0993	ও	BENGALI LETTER O
0994	ঔ	BENGALI LETTER AU

Consonants

0995	ক	BENGALI LETTER KA
0996	খ	BENGALI LETTER KHA
0997	গ	BENGALI LETTER GA
0998	ঘ	BENGALI LETTER GHA
0999	ঙ	BENGALI LETTER NGA
099A	চ	BENGALI LETTER CA
099B	ছ	BENGALI LETTER CHA
099C	জ	BENGALI LETTER JA
099D	ঝ	BENGALI LETTER JHA
099E	ঞ	BENGALI LETTER NYA
099F	ট	BENGALI LETTER TTA
09A0	ঠ	BENGALI LETTER TTHA
09A1	ড	BENGALI LETTER DDA
09A2	ঢ	BENGALI LETTER DDHA
09A3	ণ	BENGALI LETTER NNA
09A4	ত	BENGALI LETTER TA
09A5	থ	BENGALI LETTER THA
09A6	দ	BENGALI LETTER DA
09A7	ধ	BENGALI LETTER DHA

09A8	ন	BENGALI LETTER NA
09A9		
09AA	প	BENGALI LETTER PA
09AB	ফ	BENGALI LETTER PHA
09AC	ব	BENGALI LETTER BA
		= Bengali va, wa
09AD	ভ	BENGALI LETTER BHA
09AE	ম	BENGALI LETTER MA
09AF	য	BENGALI LETTER YA
09B0	র	BENGALI LETTER RA
09B1		
09B2	ল	BENGALI LETTER LA
09B3		
09B4		
09B5		
09B6	শ	BENGALI LETTER SHA
09B7	ষ	BENGALI LETTER SSA
09B8	স	BENGALI LETTER SA
09B9	হ	BENGALI LETTER HA

Various signs

09BA		
09BB		
09BC	়	BENGALI SIGN NUKTA
		for extending the alphabet to new letters
09BD		

Dependent vowel signs

09BE	া	BENGALI VOWEL SIGN AA
09BF	ি	BENGALI VOWEL SIGN I
		stands to the left of the consonant
09C0	ী	BENGALI VOWEL SIGN II
09C1	ু	BENGALI VOWEL SIGN U
09C2	ূ	BENGALI VOWEL SIGN UU
09C3	ৃ	BENGALI VOWEL SIGN VOCALIC R
09C4	ৄ	BENGALI VOWEL SIGN VOCALIC RR
09C5		
09C6		
09C7	ে	BENGALI VOWEL SIGN E
		stands to the left of the consonant
09C8	ৈ	BENGALI VOWEL SIGN AI
		stands to the left of the consonant
09C9		
09CA		
09CB	ো	BENGALI VOWEL SIGN O
		pieces on both sides of the consonant
09CC	ৌ	BENGALI VOWEL SIGN AU
		pieces on both sides of the consonant

Various signs

09CD	্	BENGALI SIGN VIRAMA
		= halant
09CE		
09CF		
09D0		
09D1		
09D2		
09D3		
09D4		
09D5		
09D6		
09D7	ৗ	BENGALI AU LENGTH MARK

Additional consonants

09D8		
09D9		
09DA		
09DB		
09DC	ড়	BENGALI LETTER RRA
09DD	ঢ়	BENGALI LETTER RHA
09DE		
09DF	য়	BENGALI LETTER YYA

Generic additions

09E0	ৠ	BENGALI LETTER VOCALIC RR
09E1	ৡ	BENGALI LETTER VOCALIC LL
09E2	ৢ	BENGALI VOWEL SIGN VOCALIC L
09E3	ৣ	BENGALI VOWEL SIGN VOCALIC LL
09E4		
09E5		
09E6	০	BENGALI DIGIT ZERO
09E7	১	BENGALI DIGIT ONE
09E8	২	BENGALI DIGIT TWO
09E9	৩	BENGALI DIGIT THREE
09EA	৪	BENGALI DIGIT FOUR
09EB	৫	BENGALI DIGIT FIVE
09EC	৬	BENGALI DIGIT SIX
09ED	৭	BENGALI DIGIT SEVEN
09EE	৮	BENGALI DIGIT EIGHT
09EF	৯	BENGALI DIGIT NINE

Bengali-specific additions

| 09F0 | ৰ | BENGALI LETTER RA WITH MIDDLE DIAGONAL |
| | | Assamese |

09F1	ৱ	BENGALI LETTER VA WITH LOWER DIAGONAL
		Assamese
09F2	৲	BENGALI RUPEE MARK
09F3	৳	BENGALI RUPEE SIGN
09F4	৴	BENGALI CURRENCY NUMERATOR ONE
09F5	৵	BENGALI CURRENCY NUMERATOR TWO
09F6	৶	BENGALI CURRENCY NUMERATOR THREE
09F7	৷	BENGALI CURRENCY NUMERATOR FOUR
09F8	৸	BENGALI CURRENCY NUMERATOR ONE LESS THAN THE DENOMINATOR
09F9	৹	BENGALI CURRENCY DENOMINATOR SIXTEEN
09FA	৺	BENGALI ISSHAR

	0A0	0A1	0A2	0A3	0A4	0A5	0A6	0A7
0		ਐ	ਠ	ਰ	ੀ			ਁ
1			ਡ		ਿ			ਂ
2	ਂ		ਦ	ਲ	ੁ			ੲ
3		ੳ	ਣ	ਲ਼				ੳ
4		ਔ	ਤ					ੴ
5	ਅ	ਕ	ਥ	ਵ				
6	ਆ	ਖ	ਦ	ਸ਼			੦	
7	ਇ	ਗ	ਧ		ੇ		੧	
8	ਈ	ਘ	ਨ	ਸ	ੈ		੨	
9	ਉ	ਙ		ਹ		ਖ਼	੩	
A	ਊ	ਚ	ਪ			ਗ਼	੪	
B		ਛ	ਫ		ੋ	ਜ਼	੫	
C		ਜ	ਬ	ਂ	ੌ	ੜ	੬	
D		ਝ	ਭ				੭	
E		ਞ	ਮ	ਾ		ਫ਼	੮	
F	ਏ	ਟ	ਯ	ਿ			੯	

The Unicode Standard • Version 1.0

Based on ISCII 1988

Various signs

0A00		
0A01		
0A02	ੰ	GURMUKHI SIGN BINDI
0A03		
0A04		

Independent vowels

0A05	ਅ	GURMUKHI LETTER A
0A06	ਆ	GURMUKHI LETTER AA
0A07	ਇ	GURMUKHI LETTER I
0A08	ਈ	GURMUKHI LETTER II
0A09	ਉ	GURMUKHI LETTER U
0A0A	ਊ	GURMUKHI LETTER UU
0A0B		
0A0C		
0A0D		
0A0E		
0A0F	ਏ	GURMUKHI LETTER EE
0A10	ਐ	GURMUKHI LETTER AI
0A11		
0A12		
0A13	ਓ	GURMUKHI LETTER OO
0A14	ਔ	GURMUKHI LETTER AU

Consonants

0A15	ਕ	GURMUKHI LETTER KA
0A16	ਖ	GURMUKHI LETTER KHA
0A17	ਗ	GURMUKHI LETTER GA
0A18	ਘ	GURMUKHI LETTER GHA
0A19	ਙ	GURMUKHI LETTER NGA
0A1A	ਚ	GURMUKHI LETTER CA
0A1B	ਛ	GURMUKHI LETTER CHA
0A1C	ਜ	GURMUKHI LETTER JA
0A1D	ਝ	GURMUKHI LETTER JHA
0A1E	ਞ	GURMUKHI LETTER NYA
0A1F	ਟ	GURMUKHI LETTER TTA
0A20	ਠ	GURMUKHI LETTER TTHA
0A21	ਡ	GURMUKHI LETTER DDA
0A22	ਢ	GURMUKHI LETTER DDHA
0A23	ਣ	GURMUKHI LETTER NNA
0A24	ਤ	GURMUKHI LETTER TA
0A25	ਥ	GURMUKHI LETTER THA
0A26	ਦ	GURMUKHI LETTER DA
0A27	ਧ	GURMUKHI LETTER DHA

0A28	ਨ	GURMUKHI LETTER NA
0A29		
0A2A	ਪ	GURMUKHI LETTER PA
0A2B	ਫ	GURMUKHI LETTER PHA
0A2C	ਬ	GURMUKHI LETTER BA
0A2D	ਭ	GURMUKHI LETTER BHA
0A2E	ਮ	GURMUKHI LETTER MA
0A2F	ਯ	GURMUKHI LETTER YA
0A30	ਰ	GURMUKHI LETTER RA
0A31		
0A32	ਲ	GURMUKHI LETTER LA
0A33	ਲ਼	GURMUKHI LETTER LLA
0A34		
0A35	ਵ	GURMUKHI LETTER VA
0A36	ਸ਼	GURMUKHI LETTER SHA
0A37		
0A38	ਸ	GURMUKHI LETTER SA
0A39	ਹ	GURMUKHI LETTER HA

Various signs

0A3A		
0A3B		
0A3C	਼	GURMUKHI SIGN NUKTA
		for extending the alphabet to new letters
0A3D		GURMUKHI SIGN AVAGRAHA

Dependent vowel signs

0A3E	ਾ	GURMUKHI VOWEL SIGN AA
0A3F	ਿ	GURMUKHI VOWEL SIGN I
		stands to the left of the consonant
0A40	ੀ	GURMUKHI VOWEL SIGN II
0A41	ੁ	GURMUKHI VOWEL SIGN U
0A42	ੂ	GURMUKHI VOWEL SIGN UU
0A43		
0A44		
0A45		
0A46		
0A47	ੇ	GURMUKHI VOWEL SIGN EE
0A48	ੈ	GURMUKHI VOWEL SIGN AI
0A49		
0A4A		
0A4B	ੋ	GURMUKHI VOWEL SIGN OO
0A4C	ੌ	GURMUKHI VOWEL SIGN AU
0A4D		
0A4E		
0A4F		

0A74	𐨀	**GURMUKHI EK ONKAR**
		God is One

0A50
0A51
0A52
0A53
0A54
0A55
0A56
0A57

Additional consonants

0A58		
0A59	ਖ	GURMUKHI LETTER KHHA
0A5A	ਗ਼	GURMUKHI LETTER GHHA
0A5B	ਜ਼	GURMUKHI LETTER ZA
0A5C	ੜ	GURMUKHI LETTER RRA
0A5D		
0A5E	ਫ਼	GURMUKHI LETTER FA
0A5F		

Generic additions

0A60		
0A61		
0A62		
0A63		
0A64		
0A65		
0A66	੦	GURMUKHI DIGIT ZERO
0A67	੧	GURMUKHI DIGIT ONE
0A68	੨	GURMUKHI DIGIT TWO
0A69	੩	GURMUKHI DIGIT THREE
0A6A	੪	GURMUKHI DIGIT FOUR
0A6B	੫	GURMUKHI DIGIT FIVE
0A6C	੬	GURMUKHI DIGIT SIX
0A6D	੭	GURMUKHI DIGIT SEVEN
0A6E	੮	GURMUKHI DIGIT EIGHT
0A6F	੯	GURMUKHI DIGIT NINE

Gurmukhi-specific additions

0A70	ੰ	GURMUKHI TIPPI
		nasalization
0A71	ੱ	GURMUKHI ADDAK
		doubles following consonant
0A72	ੲ	GURMUKHI IRI
		base for vowels
0A73	ੳ	GURMUKHI URA
		base for vowels

The Unicode Standard • Version 1.0

	0A8	0A9	0AA	0AB	0AC	0AD	0AE	0AF
0		ઐ	ઠ	ર	ૉ	ૐ	ૠ	
1	ઁ		ડ		ૉ			
2	ં		ઢ	લ	ૂ			
3	ઃ	ઓ	ણ	ળ	ૃ			
4		ઔ	ત		ૄ			
5	અ	ક	થ	વ	ૅ			
6	આ	ખ	દ	શ			૦	
7	ઇ	ગ	ધ	ષ	ે		૧	
8	ઈ	ઘ	ન	સ	ૈ		૨	
9	ઉ	ઙ		હ			૩	
A	ઊ	ચ	પ				૪	
B	ઋ	છ	ફ		ૉ		૫	
C		જ	બ	઼	ૉ		૬	
D		ઝ	ભ	૨	ૌ		૭	
E		ઞ	મ	ૅ			૮	
F	ઍ	ટ	ય	િ			૯	

The Unicode Standard • Version 1.0

Based on ISCII 1988
Various signs

0A80		
0A81	ૐ	GUJARATI SIGN CANDRABINDU
0A82	ં	GUJARATI SIGN ANUSVARA
0A83	ઃ	GUJARATI SIGN VISARGA
0A84		

Independent vowels

0A85	અ	GUJARATI LETTER A
0A86	આ	GUJARATI LETTER AA
0A87	ઇ	GUJARATI LETTER I
0A88	ઈ	GUJARATI LETTER II
0A89	ઉ	GUJARATI LETTER U
0A8A	ઊ	GUJARATI LETTER UU
0A8B	ઋ	GUJARATI LETTER VOCALIC R
0A8C		
0A8D		
0A8E		
0A8F	એ	GUJARATI LETTER E
0A90	ઐ	GUJARATI LETTER AI
0A91		
0A92		
0A93	ઓ	GUJARATI LETTER O
0A94	ઔ	GUJARATI LETTER AU

Consonants

0A95	ક	GUJARATI LETTER KA
0A96	ખ	GUJARATI LETTER KHA
0A97	ગ	GUJARATI LETTER GA
0A98	ઘ	GUJARATI LETTER GHA
0A99	ઙ	GUJARATI LETTER NGA
0A9A	ચ	GUJARATI LETTER CA
0A9B	છ	GUJARATI LETTER CHA
0A9C	જ	GUJARATI LETTER JA
0A9D	ઝ	GUJARATI LETTER JHA
0A9E	ઞ	GUJARATI LETTER NYA
0A9F	ટ	GUJARATI LETTER TTA
0AA0	ઠ	GUJARATI LETTER TTHA
0AA1	ડ	GUJARATI LETTER DDA
0AA2	ઢ	GUJARATI LETTER DDHA
0AA3	ણ	GUJARATI LETTER NNA
0AA4	ત	GUJARATI LETTER TA
0AA5	થ	GUJARATI LETTER THA
0AA6	દ	GUJARATI LETTER DA
0AA7	ધ	GUJARATI LETTER DHA

0AA8	ન	GUJARATI LETTER NA
0AA9		
0AAA	પ	GUJARATI LETTER PA
0AAB	ફ	GUJARATI LETTER PHA
0AAC	બ	GUJARATI LETTER BA
0AAD	ભ	GUJARATI LETTER BHA
0AAE	મ	GUJARATI LETTER MA
0AAF	ય	GUJARATI LETTER YA
0AB0	ર	GUJARATI LETTER RA
0AB1		
0AB2	લ	GUJARATI LETTER LA
0AB3	ળ	GUJARATI LETTER LLA
0AB4		
0AB5	વ	GUJARATI LETTER VA
0AB6	શ	GUJARATI LETTER SHA
0AB7	ષ	GUJARATI LETTER SSA
0AB8	સ	GUJARATI LETTER SA
0AB9	હ	GUJARATI LETTER HA

Various signs

0ABA		
0ABB		
0ABC	઼	GUJARATI SIGN NUKTA
		for extending the alphabet to new letters
0ABD	ઽ	GUJARATI SIGN AVAGRAHA

Dependent vowel signs

0ABE	ા	GUJARATI VOWEL SIGN AA
0ABF	િ	GUJARATI VOWEL SIGN I
		stands to the left of the consonant
0AC0	ી	GUJARATI VOWEL SIGN II
0AC1	ુ	GUJARATI VOWEL SIGN U
0AC2	ૂ	GUJARATI VOWEL SIGN UU
0AC3	ૃ	GUJARATI VOWEL SIGN VOCALIC R
0AC4	ૄ	GUJARATI VOWEL SIGN VOCALIC RR
0AC5	ૅ	GUJARATI VOWEL SIGN CANDRA E
0AC6		
0AC7	ે	GUJARATI VOWEL SIGN E
0AC8	ૈ	GUJARATI VOWEL SIGN AI
0AC9		
0ACA		
0ACB	ો	GUJARATI VOWEL SIGN O
0ACC	ૌ	GUJARATI VOWEL SIGN AU

Various signs

0ACD	્	GUJARATI SIGN VIRAMA

0ACE		
0ACF		
0AD0	ૐ	GUJARATI OM
0AD1		
0AD2		
0AD3		
0AD4		
0AD5		
0AD6		
0AD7		
0AD8		
0AD9		
0ADA		
0ADB		
0ADC		
0ADD		
0ADE		
0ADF		

Generic additions

0AE0	ૠ	GUJARATI LETTER VOCALIC RR
0AE1		
0AE2		
0AE3		
0AE4		
0AE5		
0AE6	૦	GUJARATI DIGIT ZERO
0AE7	૧	GUJARATI DIGIT ONE
0AE8	૨	GUJARATI DIGIT TWO
0AE9	૩	GUJARATI DIGIT THREE
0AEA	૪	GUJARATI DIGIT FOUR
0AEB	૫	GUJARATI DIGIT FIVE
0AEC	૬	GUJARATI DIGIT SIX
0AED	૭	GUJARATI DIGIT SEVEN
0AEE	૮	GUJARATI DIGIT EIGHT
0AEF	૯	GUJARATI DIGIT NINE

Oriya

	0B0	0B1	0B2	0B3	0B4	0B5	0B6	0B7
0		ଐ	ଠ	ର	1		ର	✓
1	ଁ		ଡ		ୁ		୬	
2	ଂ		ଢ	ଳ	ୂ			
3	ଃ	ଓ	ଣ	ଲ	ୃ			
4		ଔ	ତ					
5	ଅ	କ	ଥ					
6	ଆ	ଖ	ଦ	ଶ			୦	
7	ଇ	ଗ	ଧ	ଷ	େ	ୀ	୧	
8	ଈ	ଘ	ନ	ସ	ୈ		୨	
9	ଉ	ଙ		ହ			୩	
A	ଊ	ଚ	ପ				୪	
B	ଋ	ଛ	ଫ		ୋ		୫	
C	ଌ	ଜ	ବ	଼	ୌ	ଡ଼	୭	
D		ଝ	ଭ	ଽ	୍	ଢ଼	୭	
E		ଞ	ମ	ା			୳	
F	ଏ	ଟ	ଯ	ଂ		ୟ	୯	

Based on ISCII 1988
Various signs

0B00		
0B01	ঁ	ORIYA SIGN CANDRABINDU
0B02	୦	ORIYA SIGN ANUSVARA
0B03	ଃ	ORIYA SIGN VISARGA
0B04		

Independent vowels

0B05	ଅ	ORIYA LETTER A
0B06	ଆ	ORIYA LETTER AA
0B07	ଇ	ORIYA LETTER I
0B08	ଈ	ORIYA LETTER II
0B09	ଉ	ORIYA LETTER U
0B0A	ଊ	ORIYA LETTER UU
0B0B	ଋ	ORIYA LETTER VOCALIC R
0B0C	ଌ	ORIYA LETTER VOCALIC L
0B0D		
0B0E		
0B0F	ଏ	ORIYA LETTER E
0B10	ଐ	ORIYA LETTER AI
0B11		
0B12		
0B13	ଓ	ORIYA LETTER O
0B14	ଔ	ORIYA LETTER AU

Consonants

0B15	କ	ORIYA LETTER KA
0B16	ଖ	ORIYA LETTER KHA
0B17	ଗ	ORIYA LETTER GA
0B18	ଘ	ORIYA LETTER GHA
0B19	ଙ	ORIYA LETTER NGA
0B1A	ଚ	ORIYA LETTER CA
0B1B	ଛ	ORIYA LETTER CHA
0B1C	ଜ	ORIYA LETTER JA
0B1D	ଝ	ORIYA LETTER JHA
0B1E	ଞ	ORIYA LETTER NYA
0B1F	ଟ	ORIYA LETTER TTA
0B20	ଠ	ORIYA LETTER TTHA
0B21	ଡ	ORIYA LETTER DDA
0B22	ଢ	ORIYA LETTER DDHA
0B23	ଣ	ORIYA LETTER NNA
0B24	ତ	ORIYA LETTER TA
0B25	ଥ	ORIYA LETTER THA
0B26	ଦ	ORIYA LETTER DA
0B27	ଧ	ORIYA LETTER DHA

0B28	ନ	ORIYA LETTER NA
0B29		
0B2A	ପ	ORIYA LETTER PA
0B2B	ଫ	ORIYA LETTER PHA
0B2C	ବ	ORIYA LETTER BA
		= Oriya va, wa
0B2D	ଭ	ORIYA LETTER BHA
0B2E	ମ	ORIYA LETTER MA
0B2F	ଯ	ORIYA LETTER YA
0B30	ର	ORIYA LETTER RA
0B31		
0B32	ଲ	ORIYA LETTER LA
0B33	ଳ	ORIYA LETTER LLA
0B34		
0B35	✕	(oriya letter ba → 0B2C)
0B36	ଶ	ORIYA LETTER SHA
0B37	ଷ	ORIYA LETTER SSA
0B38	ସ	ORIYA LETTER SA
0B39	ହ	ORIYA LETTER HA

Various signs

0B3A		
0B3B		
0B3C	଼	ORIYA SIGN NUKTA
		for extending the alphabet to new letters
0B3D	ଽ	ORIYA SIGN AVAGRAHA

Dependent vowel signs

0B3E	ା	ORIYA VOWEL SIGN AA
0B3F	ି	ORIYA VOWEL SIGN I
0B40	ୀ	ORIYA VOWEL SIGN II
0B41	ୁ	ORIYA VOWEL SIGN U
0B42	ୂ	ORIYA VOWEL SIGN UU
0B43	ୃ	ORIYA VOWEL SIGN VOCALIC R
0B44		
0B45		
0B46		
0B47	େ	ORIYA VOWEL SIGN E
		stands to the left of the consonant
0B48	ୈ	ORIYA VOWEL SIGN AI
		pieces left of and above the consonant
0B49		
0B4A		
0B4B	ୋ	ORIYA VOWEL SIGN O
		pieces on both sides of the consonant
0B4C	ୌ	ORIYA VOWEL SIGN AU
		pieces on both sides of the consonant

Various signs

0B4D	◌੍	ORIYA SIGN VIRAMA
0B4E		
0B4F		
0B50		
0B51		
0B52		
0B53		
0B54		
0B55		
0B56		
0B57	ꟾ	ORIYA AU LENGTH MARK

Additional consonants

0B58		
0B59		
0B5A		
0B5B		
0B5C	ଡ଼	ORIYA LETTER RRA
0B5D	ଢ଼	ORIYA LETTER RHA
0B5E		
0B5F	ୟ	ORIYA LETTER YYA

Generic additions

0B60	ୠ	ORIYA LETTER VOCALIC RR
0B61	ୡ	ORIYA LETTER VOCALIC LL
0B62		
0B63		
0B64		
0B65		
0B66	୦	ORIYA DIGIT ZERO
0B67	୧	ORIYA DIGIT ONE
0B68	୨	ORIYA DIGIT TWO
0B69	୩	ORIYA DIGIT THREE
0B6A	୪	ORIYA DIGIT FOUR
0B6B	୫	ORIYA DIGIT FIVE
0B6C	୬	ORIYA DIGIT SIX
0B6D	୭	ORIYA DIGIT SEVEN
0B6E	୮	ORIYA DIGIT EIGHT
0B6F	୯	ORIYA DIGIT NINE

Oriya-specific addition

0B70	୰	ORIYA ISSHAR

	0B8	0B9	0BA	0BB	0BC	0BD	0BE	0BF
0		ஐ		ரா	ொ			ம
1				ற	ௗ			மா
2	்	ஒ		ல	௮			த்த
3	்்	ஓ	ண	ள				
4		ஔ	த	ழ				
5	அ	க		வ				
6	ஆ			ெ				
7	இ			ஷ	ே	ௗ	க	
8	ஈ		ந	ஸ	ை			உ
9	உ	ங	ன	ஹ				ந
A	ௌ	ச	ப	ொ				சு
B				ோ				ரு
C		ஐ		ௌ				சூ
D				்்				எ
E	எ	ரு	ம	ா				அ
F	ஏ	ட	ய	்				கூ

Based on ISCII 1988

Various signs

0B80		
0B81		
0B82	°	TAMIL SIGN ANUSVARA
0B83	ஃ	TAMIL SIGN VISARGA
0B84		

Independent vowels

0B85	அ	TAMIL LETTER A
0B86	ஆ	TAMIL LETTER AA
0B87	இ	TAMIL LETTER I
0B88	ஈ	TAMIL LETTER II
0B89	உ	TAMIL LETTER U
0B8A	ஊ	TAMIL LETTER UU
0B8B		
0B8C		
0B8D		
0B8E	எ	TAMIL LETTER E
0B8F	ஏ	TAMIL LETTER EE
0B90	ஐ	TAMIL LETTER AI
0B91		
0B92	ஒ	TAMIL LETTER O
0B93	ஓ	TAMIL LETTER OO
0B94	ஔ	TAMIL LETTER AU

Consonants

0B95	க	TAMIL LETTER KA
0B96		
0B97		
0B98		
0B99	ங	TAMIL LETTER NGA
0B9A	ச	TAMIL LETTER CA
0B9B		
0B9C	ஜ	TAMIL LETTER JA
0B9D		
0B9E	ஞ	TAMIL LETTER NYA
0B9F	ட	TAMIL LETTER TTA
0BA0		
0BA1		
0BA2		
0BA3	ண	TAMIL LETTER NNA
0BA4	த	TAMIL LETTER TA
0BA5		
0BA6		
0BA7		

0BA8	ந	TAMIL LETTER NA
0BA9	ன	TAMIL LETTER NNNA
0BAA	ப	TAMIL LETTER PA
0BAB		
0BAC		
0BAD		
0BAE	ம	TAMIL LETTER MA
0BAF	ய	TAMIL LETTER YA
0BB0	ர	TAMIL LETTER RA
0BB1	ற	TAMIL LETTER RRA
0BB2	ல	TAMIL LETTER LA
0BB3	ள	TAMIL LETTER LLA
0BB4	ழ	TAMIL LETTER LLLA
0BB5	வ	TAMIL LETTER VA
0BB6		
0BB7	ஷ	TAMIL LETTER SSA
0BB8	ஸ	TAMIL LETTER SA
0BB9	ஹ	TAMIL LETTER HA
0BBA		
0BBB		
0BBC		
0BBD		

Dependent vowel signs

0BBE	ா	TAMIL VOWEL SIGN AA
0BBF	ி	TAMIL VOWEL SIGN I
0BC0	ீ	TAMIL VOWEL SIGN II
0BC1	ு	TAMIL VOWEL SIGN U
0BC2	ூ	TAMIL VOWEL SIGN UU
0BC3		
0BC4		
0BC5		
0BC6	ெ	TAMIL VOWEL SIGN E
		stands to the left of the consonant
0BC7	ே	TAMIL VOWEL SIGN EE
		stands to the left of the consonant
0BC8	ை	TAMIL VOWEL SIGN AI
		stands to the left of the consonant
0BC9		
0BCA	ொ	TAMIL VOWEL SIGN O
		pieces on both sides of the consonant
0BCB	ோ	TAMIL VOWEL SIGN OO
		pieces on both sides of the consonant
0BCC	ௌ	TAMIL VOWEL SIGN AU
		pieces on both sides of the consonant

Various signs

0BCD	◌	TAMIL SIGN VIRAMA
0BCE		
0BCF		
0BD0		
0BD1		
0BD2		
0BD3		
0BD4		
0BD5		
0BD6		
0BD7	ௗ	TAMIL AU LENGTH MARK
0BD8		
0BD9		
0BDA		
0BDB		
0BDC		
0BDD		
0BDE		
0BDF		

Generic additions

0BE0		
0BE1		
0BE2		
0BE3		
0BE4		
0BE5		
0BE6	✕	*(digit zero → 0030)*
0BE7	க	TAMIL DIGIT ONE
0BE8	உ	TAMIL DIGIT TWO
0BE9	௩	TAMIL DIGIT THREE
0BEA	௪	TAMIL DIGIT FOUR
0BEB	௫	TAMIL DIGIT FIVE
0BEC	௬	TAMIL DIGIT SIX
0BED	எ	TAMIL DIGIT SEVEN
0BEE	அ	TAMIL DIGIT EIGHT
0BEF	௯	TAMIL DIGIT NINE

Tamil-specific additions

0BF0	௰	TAMIL NUMBER TEN
0BF1	௱	TAMIL NUMBER ONE HUNDRED
0BF2	௲	TAMIL NUMBER ONE THOUSAND

	0C0	0C1	0C2	0C3	0C4	0C5	0C6	0C7
0		ఐ	థ	ర	‌ా		బూ	
1	ఁ		డ	ఆ	‌ి		ఞా	
2	ం	ఒ	ఢ	ల	‌ీ			
3	ః	ఓ	ణ	ఴ	‌ు			
4		ఔ	త		‌ూ			
5	అ	క	థ	వ		‌ృ		
6	ఆ	ఖ	ద	శ	‌ె	‌ౄ	౦	
7	ఇ	గ	ధ	ష	‌ే		౧	
8	ఈ	ఘ	న	స	‌ై		౨	
9	ఉ	జ		హ			౩	
A	ఊ	చ	ప	‌ొ			౪	
B	ఋ	ఛ	ఫ	‌ో			౫	
C	ఌ	జ	బ	‌ౌ			౬	
D		ఝ	భ	‌్			౭	
E	ఎ	ఞ	మ	‌ో			౮	
F	ఏ	ట	య	‌ం			౯	

Based on ISCII 1988

Various signs

0C00		
0C01	ఁ	TELUGU SIGN CANDRABINDU
0C02	ం	TELUGU SIGN ANUSVARA
0C03	ః	TELUGU SIGN VISARGA
0C04		

Independent vowels

0C05	అ	TELUGU LETTER A
0C06	ఆ	TELUGU LETTER AA
0C07	ఇ	TELUGU LETTER I
0C08	ఈ	TELUGU LETTER II
0C09	ఉ	TELUGU LETTER U
0C0A	ఊ	TELUGU LETTER UU
0C0B	ఋ	TELUGU LETTER VOCALIC R
0C0C	ఌ	TELUGU LETTER VOCALIC L
0C0D		
0C0E	ఎ	TELUGU LETTER E
0C0F	ఏ	TELUGU LETTER EE
0C10	ఐ	TELUGU LETTER AI
0C11		
0C12	ఒ	TELUGU LETTER O
0C13	ఓ	TELUGU LETTER OO
0C14	ఔ	TELUGU LETTER AU

Consonants

0C15	క	TELUGU LETTER KA
0C16	ఖ	TELUGU LETTER KHA
0C17	గ	TELUGU LETTER GA
0C18	ఘ	TELUGU LETTER GHA
0C19	ఙ	TELUGU LETTER NGA
0C1A	చ	TELUGU LETTER CA
0C1B	ఛ	TELUGU LETTER CHA
0C1C	జ	TELUGU LETTER JA
0C1D	ఝ	TELUGU LETTER JHA
0C1E	ఞ	TELUGU LETTER NYA
0C1F	ట	TELUGU LETTER TTA
0C20	ఠ	TELUGU LETTER TTHA
0C21	డ	TELUGU LETTER DDA
0C22	ఢ	TELUGU LETTER DDHA
0C23	ణ	TELUGU LETTER NNA
0C24	త	TELUGU LETTER TA
0C25	థ	TELUGU LETTER THA
0C26	ద	TELUGU LETTER DA
0C27	ధ	TELUGU LETTER DHA

0C28	న	TELUGU LETTER NA
0C29		
0C2A	ప	TELUGU LETTER PA
0C2B	ఫ	TELUGU LETTER PHA
0C2C	బ	TELUGU LETTER BA
0C2D	భ	TELUGU LETTER BHA
0C2E	మ	TELUGU LETTER MA
0C2F	య	TELUGU LETTER YA
0C30	ర	TELUGU LETTER RA
0C31	ఱ	TELUGU LETTER RRA
0C32	ల	TELUGU LETTER LA
0C33	ళ	TELUGU LETTER LLA
0C34		
0C35	వ	TELUGU LETTER VA
0C36	శ	TELUGU LETTER SHA
0C37	ష	TELUGU LETTER SSA
0C38	స	TELUGU LETTER SA
0C39	హ	TELUGU LETTER HA
0C3A		
0C3B		
0C3C		
0C3D		

Dependent vowel signs

0C3E	ా	TELUGU VOWEL SIGN AA
0C3F	ి	TELUGU VOWEL SIGN I
0C40	ీ	TELUGU VOWEL SIGN II
0C41	ు	TELUGU VOWEL SIGN U
0C42	ూ	TELUGU VOWEL SIGN UU
0C43	ృ	TELUGU VOWEL SIGN VOCALIC R
0C44	ౄ	TELUGU VOWEL SIGN VOCALIC RR
0C45		
0C46	ె	TELUGU VOWEL SIGN E
0C47	ే	TELUGU VOWEL SIGN EE
0C48	ై	TELUGU VOWEL SIGN AI
0C49		
0C4A	ొ	TELUGU VOWEL SIGN O
0C4B	ో	TELUGU VOWEL SIGN OO
0C4C	ౌ	TELUGU VOWEL SIGN AU

Various signs

0C4D	్	TELUGU SIGN VIRAMA
0C4E		
0C4F		
0C50		
0C51		

0C52		
0C53		
0C54		
0C55	ः	TELUGU LENGTH MARK
0C56	॒	TELUGU AI LENGTH MARK
0C57		
0C58		
0C59		
0C5A		
0C5B		
0C5C		
0C5D		
0C5E		
0C5F		

Generic additions

0C60	ఋ	TELUGU LETTER VOCALIC RR
0C61	ౡ	TELUGU LETTER VOCALIC LL
0C62		
0C63		
0C64		
0C65		
0C66	౦	TELUGU DIGIT ZERO
0C67	౧	TELUGU DIGIT ONE
0C68	౨	TELUGU DIGIT TWO
0C69	౩	TELUGU DIGIT THREE
0C6A	౪	TELUGU DIGIT FOUR
0C6B	౫	TELUGU DIGIT FIVE
0C6C	౬	TELUGU DIGIT SIX
0C6D	౭	TELUGU DIGIT SEVEN
0C6E	౮	TELUGU DIGIT EIGHT
0C6F	౯	TELUGU DIGIT NINE

	0C8	0C9	0CA	0CB	0CC	0CD	0CE	0CF
0		ಐ	ಠ	ರ	◌ೀ		ೠ	
1			ಡ	ಱ	ು		ೡ	
2	ಂ	ಒ	ಢ	ಲ	ೂ			
3	ಃ	ಓ	ಣ	ಳ	ೃ			
4		ಔ	ತ		ೄ			
5	ಅ	ಕ	ಥ	ವ		ೕ		
6	ಆ	ಖ	ದ	ಶ	◌ೆ	ೖ	೦	
7	ಇ	ಗ	ಧ	ಷ	◌ೇ		೧	
8	ಈ	ಘ	ನ	ಸ	◌ೈ		೨	
9	ಉ	ಙ		ಹ			೩	
A	ಊ	ಚ	ಪ		◌ೊ		೪	
B	ಋ	ಛ	ಫ		◌ೋ		೫	
C	ಌ	ಜ	ಬ		◌ೌ		೬	
D		ಝ	ಭ		◌್		೭	
E	ಎ	ಞ	ಮ	ಾ		ೞ	೮	
F	ಏ	ಟ	ಯ	◌ಿ			೯	

Based on ISCII 1988

Various signs

0C80		
0C81		
0C82	ಂ	KANNADA SIGN ANUSVARA
0C83	ಃ	KANNADA SIGN VISARGA
0C84		

Independent vowels

0C85	ಅ	KANNADA LETTER A
0C86	ಆ	KANNADA LETTER AA
0C87	ಇ	KANNADA LETTER I
0C88	ಈ	KANNADA LETTER II
0C89	ಉ	KANNADA LETTER U
0C8A	ಊ	KANNADA LETTER UU
0C8B	ಋ	KANNADA LETTER VOCALIC R
0C8C	ಌ	KANNADA LETTER VOCALIC L
0C8D		
0C8E	ಎ	KANNADA LETTER E
0C8F	ಏ	KANNADA LETTER EE
0C90	ಐ	KANNADA LETTER AI
0C91		
0C92	ಒ	KANNADA LETTER O
0C93	ಓ	KANNADA LETTER OO
0C94	ಔ	KANNADA LETTER AU

Consonants

0C95	ಕ	KANNADA LETTER KA
0C96	ಖ	KANNADA LETTER KHA
0C97	ಗ	KANNADA LETTER GA
0C98	ಘ	KANNADA LETTER GHA
0C99	ಙ	KANNADA LETTER NGA
0C9A	ಚ	KANNADA LETTER CA
0C9B	ಛ	KANNADA LETTER CHA
0C9C	ಜ	KANNADA LETTER JA
0C9D	ಝ	KANNADA LETTER JHA
0C9E	ಞ	KANNADA LETTER NYA
0C9F	ಟ	KANNADA LETTER TTA
0CA0	ಠ	KANNADA LETTER TTHA
0CA1	ಡ	KANNADA LETTER DDA
0CA2	ಢ	KANNADA LETTER DDHA
0CA3	ಣ	KANNADA LETTER NNA
0CA4	ತ	KANNADA LETTER TA
0CA5	ಥ	KANNADA LETTER THA
0CA6	ದ	KANNADA LETTER DA
0CA7	ಧ	KANNADA LETTER DHA

0CA8	ನ	KANNADA LETTER NA
0CA9		
0CAA	ಪ	KANNADA LETTER PA
0CAB	ಫ	KANNADA LETTER PHA
0CAC	ಬ	KANNADA LETTER BA
0CAD	ಭ	KANNADA LETTER BHA
0CAE	ಮ	KANNADA LETTER MA
0CAF	ಯ	KANNADA LETTER YA
0CB0	ರ	KANNADA LETTER RA
0CB1	ಱ	KANNADA LETTER RRA
0CB2	ಲ	KANNADA LETTER LA
0CB3	ಳ	KANNADA LETTER LLA
0CB4		
0CB5	ವ	KANNADA LETTER VA
0CB6	ಶ	KANNADA LETTER SHA
0CB7	ಷ	KANNADA LETTER SSA
0CB8	ಸ	KANNADA LETTER SA
0CB9	ಹ	KANNADA LETTER HA
0CBA		
0CBB		
0CBC		
0CBD		

Dependent vowel signs

0CBE	ಾ	KANNADA VOWEL SIGN AA
0CBF	ಿ	KANNADA VOWEL SIGN I
0CC0	ೀ	KANNADA VOWEL SIGN II
0CC1	ು	KANNADA VOWEL SIGN U
0CC2	ೂ	KANNADA VOWEL SIGN UU
0CC3	ೃ	KANNADA VOWEL SIGN VOCALIC R
0CC4	ೄ	KANNADA VOWEL SIGN VOCALIC RR
0CC5		
0CC6	ೆ	KANNADA VOWEL SIGN E
0CC7	ೇ	KANNADA VOWEL SIGN EE
0CC8	ೈ	KANNADA VOWEL SIGN AI
0CC9		
0CCA	ೊ	KANNADA VOWEL SIGN O
0CCB	ೋ	KANNADA VOWEL SIGN OO
0CCC	ೌ	KANNADA VOWEL SIGN AU

Various signs

0CCD	್	KANNADA SIGN VIRAMA
0CCE		
0CCF		
0CD0		
0CD1		

0CD2		
0CD3		
0CD4		
0CD5	ೕ	KANNADA LENGTH MARK
0CD6	ೖ	KANNADA AI LENGTH MARK
0CD7		

Additional consonants

0CD8		
0CD9		
0CDA		
0CDB		
0CDC		
0CDD		
0CDE	ೞ	KANNADA LETTER FA
0CDF		

Generic additions

0CE0	ೠ	KANNADA LETTER VOCALIC RR
0CE1	ೡ	KANNADA LETTER VOCALIC LL
0CE2		
0CE3		
0CE4		
0CE5		
0CE6	೦	KANNADA DIGIT ZERO
0CE7	೧	KANNADA DIGIT ONE
0CE8	೨	KANNADA DIGIT TWO
0CE9	೩	KANNADA DIGIT THREE
0CEA	೪	KANNADA DIGIT FOUR
0CEB	೫	KANNADA DIGIT FIVE
0CEC	೬	KANNADA DIGIT SIX
0CED	೭	KANNADA DIGIT SEVEN
0CEE	೮	KANNADA DIGIT EIGHT
0CEF	೯	KANNADA DIGIT NINE

	0D0	0D1	0D2	0D3	0D4	0D5	0D6	0D7
0		ഐ	ഠ	ര	ീ		ൠ	
1			ഡ	റ	◌ു		ൡ	
2	ം	ഒ	ഢ	ല	◌ൂ			
3	ഃ	ഓ	ണ	ള	◌ൃ			
4		ഔ	ത	ഴ				
5	അ	ക	ഥ	വ				
6	ആ	ഖ	ദ	ശ	െ◌		൦	
7	ഇ	ഗ	ധ	ഷ	േ◌	ൗ	൧	
8	ഈ	ഘ	ന	സ	ൈ◌		൨	
9	ഉ	ങ		ഹ			൩	
A	ഊ	ച	പ		◌ൊ		൪	
B	ഋ	ഛ	ഫ		◌ോ		൫	
C	ഌ	ജ	ബ		◌ൌ		൬	
D		ഝ	ഭ		◌്		൭	
E	എ	ഞ	മ	ാ			൮	
F	ഏ	ട	യ	ി			൯	

Based on ISCII 1988

Various signs

0D00		
0D01		
0D02	ം	MALAYALAM SIGN ANUSVARA
0D03	ഃ	MALAYALAM SIGN VISARGA
0D04		

Independent vowels

0D05	അ	MALAYALAM LETTER A
0D06	ആ	MALAYALAM LETTER AA
0D07	ഇ	MALAYALAM LETTER I
0D08	ഈ	MALAYALAM LETTER II
0D09	ഉ	MALAYALAM LETTER U
0D0A	ഊ	MALAYALAM LETTER UU
0D0B	ഋ	MALAYALAM LETTER VOCALIC R
0D0C	ഌ	MALAYALAM LETTER VOCALIC L
0D0D		
0D0E	എ	MALAYALAM LETTER E
0D0F	ഏ	MALAYALAM LETTER EE
0D10	ഐ	MALAYALAM LETTER AI
0D11		
0D12	ഒ	MALAYALAM LETTER O
0D13	ഓ	MALAYALAM LETTER OO
0D14	ഔ	MALAYALAM LETTER AU

Consonants

0D15	ക	MALAYALAM LETTER KA
0D16	ഖ	MALAYALAM LETTER KHA
0D17	ഗ	MALAYALAM LETTER GA
0D18	ഘ	MALAYALAM LETTER GHA
0D19	ങ	MALAYALAM LETTER NGA
0D1A	ച	MALAYALAM LETTER CA
0D1B	ഛ	MALAYALAM LETTER CHA
0D1C	ജ	MALAYALAM LETTER JA
0D1D	ഝ	MALAYALAM LETTER JHA
0D1E	ഞ	MALAYALAM LETTER NYA
0D1F	ട	MALAYALAM LETTER TTA
0D20	ഠ	MALAYALAM LETTER TTHA
0D21	ഡ	MALAYALAM LETTER DDA
0D22	ഢ	MALAYALAM LETTER DDHA
0D23	ണ	MALAYALAM LETTER NNA
0D24	ത	MALAYALAM LETTER TA
0D25	ഥ	MALAYALAM LETTER THA
0D26	ദ	MALAYALAM LETTER DA
0D27	ധ	MALAYALAM LETTER DHA

0D28	ന	MALAYALAM LETTER NA
0D29		
0D2A	പ	MALAYALAM LETTER PA
0D2B	ഫ	MALAYALAM LETTER PHA
0D2C	ബ	MALAYALAM LETTER BA
0D2D	ഭ	MALAYALAM LETTER BHA
0D2E	മ	MALAYALAM LETTER MA
0D2F	യ	MALAYALAM LETTER YA
0D30	ര	MALAYALAM LETTER RA
0D31	റ	MALAYALAM LETTER RRA
0D32	ല	MALAYALAM LETTER LA
0D33	ള	MALAYALAM LETTER LLA
0D34	ഴ	MALAYALAM LETTER LLLA
0D35	വ	MALAYALAM LETTER VA
0D36	ശ	MALAYALAM LETTER SHA
0D37	ഷ	MALAYALAM LETTER SSA
0D38	സ	MALAYALAM LETTER SA
0D39	ഹ	MALAYALAM LETTER HA
0D3A		
0D3B		
0D3C		
0D3D		

Dependent vowel signs

0D3E	ാ	MALAYALAM VOWEL SIGN AA
0D3F	ി	MALAYALAM VOWEL SIGN I
0D40	ീ	MALAYALAM VOWEL SIGN II
0D41	ു	MALAYALAM VOWEL SIGN U
0D42	ൂ	MALAYALAM VOWEL SIGN UU
0D43	ൃ	MALAYALAM VOWEL SIGN VOCALIC R
0D44		
0D45		
0D46	െ	MALAYALAM VOWEL SIGN E *stands to the left of the consonant*
0D47	േ	MALAYALAM VOWEL SIGN EE *stands to the left of the consonant*
0D48	ൈ	MALAYALAM VOWEL SIGN AI *stands to the left of the consonant*
0D49		
0D4A	ൊ	MALAYALAM VOWEL SIGN O *pieces on both sides of the consonant*
0D4B	ോ	MALAYALAM VOWEL SIGN OO *pieces on both sides of the consonant*
0D4C	ൌ	MALAYALAM VOWEL SIGN AU *pieces on both sides of the consonant*

Various signs

0D4D	$\dot{\bigcirc}^{\upsilon}$	MALAYALAM SIGN VIRAMA
		= *vowel half-u*
0D4E		
0D4F		
0D50		
0D51		
0D52		
0D53		
0D54		
0D55		
0D56		
0D57	ൗ	MALAYALAM AU LENGTH MARK
0D58		
0D59		
0D5A		
0D5B		
0D5C		
0D5D		
0D5E		
0D5F		

Generic additions

0D60	ൠ	MALAYALAM LETTER VOCALIC RR
0D61	ൡ	MALAYALAM LETTER VOCALIC LL
0D62		
0D63		
0D64		
0D65		
0D66	൦	MALAYALAM DIGIT ZERO
0D67	൧	MALAYALAM DIGIT ONE
0D68	൨	MALAYALAM DIGIT TWO
0D69	൩	MALAYALAM DIGIT THREE
0D6A	൪	MALAYALAM DIGIT FOUR
0D6B	൫	MALAYALAM DIGIT FIVE
0D6C	൬	MALAYALAM DIGIT SIX
0D6D	൭	MALAYALAM DIGIT SEVEN
0D6E	൮	MALAYALAM DIGIT EIGHT
0D6F	൯	MALAYALAM DIGIT NINE

Based on TIS 620-2529

Consonants

0E00		
0E01	ก	THAI LETTER KO KAI
0E02	ข	THAI LETTER KHO KHAI
0E03	ฃ	THAI LETTER KHO KHUAT
0E04	ค	THAI LETTER KHO KHWAI
0E05	ฅ	THAI LETTER KHO KHON
0E06	ฆ	THAI LETTER KHO RAKHANG
0E07	ง	THAI LETTER NGO NGU
0E08	จ	THAI LETTER CHO CHAN
0E09	ฉ	THAI LETTER CHO CHING
0E0A	ช	THAI LETTER CHO CHANG
0E0B	ซ	THAI LETTER SO SO
0E0C	ฌ	THAI LETTER CHO CHOE
0E0D	ญ	THAI LETTER YO YING
0E0E	ฎ	THAI LETTER DO CHADA
0E0F	ฏ	THAI LETTER TO PATAK
0E10	ฐ	THAI LETTER THO THAN
0E11	ฑ	THAI LETTER THO NANGMONTHO
0E12	ฒ	THAI LETTER THO PHUTHAO
0E13	ณ	THAI LETTER NO NEN
0E14	ด	THAI LETTER DO DEK
0E15	ต	THAI LETTER TO TAO
0E16	ถ	THAI LETTER THO THUNG
0E17	ท	THAI LETTER THO THAHAN
0E18	ธ	THAI LETTER THO THONG
0E19	น	THAI LETTER NO NU
0E1A	บ	THAI LETTER BO BAIMAI
0E1B	ป	THAI LETTER PO PLA
0E1C	ผ	THAI LETTER PHO PHUNG
0E1D	ฝ	THAI LETTER FO FA
0E1E	พ	THAI LETTER PHO PHAN
0E1F	ฟ	THAI LETTER FO FAN
0E20	ภ	THAI LETTER PHO SAMPHAO
0E21	ม	THAI LETTER MO MA
0E22	ย	THAI LETTER YO YAK
0E23	ร	THAI LETTER RO RUA
0E24	ฤ	THAI LETTER RU

     independent vowel letter used to write Pali

0E25	ล	THAI LETTER LO LING
0E26	ฦ	THAI LETTER LU

     independent vowel letter used to write Pali

0E27	ว	THAI LETTER WO WAEN
0E28	ศ	THAI LETTER SO SALA
0E29	ษ	THAI LETTER SO RUSI
0E2A	ส	THAI LETTER SO SUA
0E2B	ห	THAI LETTER HO HIP
0E2C	ฬ	THAI LETTER LO CHULA
0E2D	อ	THAI LETTER O ANG
0E2E	ฮ	THAI LETTER HO NOK HUK

Sign

0E2F	ๆ	THAI PAI YAN NOI

     ellipsis, abbreviation

Vowels

0E30	ะ	THAI VOWEL SIGN SARA A
0E31	ั	THAI VOWEL SIGN MAI HAN-AKAT
0E32	า	THAI VOWEL SIGN SARA AA
0E33	ำ	THAI VOWEL SIGN SARA AM
0E34	ิ	THAI VOWEL SIGN SARA I
0E35	ี	THAI VOWEL SIGN SARA II
0E36	ึ	THAI VOWEL SIGN SARA UE
0E37	ื	THAI VOWEL SIGN SARA UEE
0E38	ุ	THAI VOWEL SIGN SARA U
0E39	ู	THAI VOWEL SIGN SARA UU
0E3A	ฺ	THAI VOWEL SIGN PHINTHU

     Pali virama

0E3B	
0E3C	
0E3D	
0E3E	

Currency symbol

0E3F	฿	THAI BAHT SIGN

Vowels

0E40	เ	THAI VOWEL SIGN SARA E
0E41	แ	THAI VOWEL SIGN SARA AE
0E42	โ	THAI VOWEL SIGN SARA O
0E43	ใ	THAI VOWEL SIGN SARA MAI MUAN
0E44	ไ	THAI VOWEL SIGN SARA MAI MALAI

Signs

0E45	ๅ	THAI LAK KHANG YAO
0E46	ๆ	THAI MAI YAMOK

     repetition

Vowel

0E47	็	THAI VOWEL SIGN MAI TAI KHU

Tone marks

0E48	่	THAI TONE MAI EK
0E49	้	THAI TONE MAI THO
0E4A	๊	THAI TONE MAI TRI
0E4B	๋	THAI TONE MAI CHATTAWA

Signs

0E4C	์	THAI THANTHAKHAT
		cancellation mark
0E4D	ํ	THAI NIKKHAHIT
		final nasal
0E4E	๎	THAI YAMAKKAN
0E4F	๏	THAI FONGMAN

Digits

0E50	๐	THAI DIGIT ZERO
0E51	๑	THAI DIGIT ONE
0E52	๒	THAI DIGIT TWO
0E53	๓	THAI DIGIT THREE
0E54	๔	THAI DIGIT FOUR
0E55	๕	THAI DIGIT FIVE
0E56	๖	THAI DIGIT SIX
0E57	๗	THAI DIGIT SEVEN
0E58	๘	THAI DIGIT EIGHT
0E59	๙	THAI DIGIT NINE

Signs

0E5A	๚	THAI ANGKHANKHU
0E5B	๛	THAI KHOMUT
0E5C		
0E5D		
0E5E		
0E5F		
0E60		
0E61		
0E62		
0E63		
0E64		
0E65		
0E66		
0E67		
0E68		
0E69		
0E6A		
0E6B		
0E6C		

0E6D		
0E6E		
0E6F		

Phonetic order clones of left side vowel signs

0E70	เ◌	THAI PHONETIC ORDER VOWEL SIGN SARA E
0E71	แ◌	THAI PHONETIC ORDER VOWEL SIGN SARA AE
0E72	โ◌	THAI PHONETIC ORDER VOWEL SIGN SARA O
0E73	ใ◌	THAI PHONETIC ORDER VOWEL SIGN SARA MAI MUAN
0E74	ไ◌	THAI PHONETIC ORDER VOWEL SIGN SARA MAI MALAI

	0E8	0E9	0EA	0EB	0EC	0ED	0EE	0EF
0				ະ	ເ	໐		ເ◌
1	ກ		ມ	◌ັ	ແ	໑		ແ◌
2	ຂ		ຢ	າ	ໂ	໒		ໂ◌
3			ຣ	ຳ	ໃ	໓		ໃ◌
4	ຄ	ດ		◌ິ	ໄ	໔		ໄ◌
5		ຕ	ລ	◌ີ		໕		
6		ຖ		◌ຶ	ໆ	໖		
7	ງ	ທ	ວ	◌ື		໗		
8	ຈ			◌ຸ	◌່	໘		
9		ນ		◌ູ	◌້	໙		
A	ຊ	ບ	ສ		◌໊			
B		ປ	ຫ	◌ົ	◌໋			
C		ຜ		◌ຼ	◌໌	ໜ		
D	ຍ	ຝ	ອ	ຽ	◌ໍ	ໝ		
E		ພ	ຮ					
F		ຟ	ຯ					

Based on TIS 620-2529
Consonants

0E80		
0E81	ກ	LAO LETTER KO
0E82	ຂ	LAO LETTER KHO SUNG
0E83		
0E84	ຄ	LAO LETTER KHO TAM
0E85		
0E86		
0E87	ງ	LAO LETTER NGO
0E88	ຈ	LAO LETTER CO
0E89		
0E8A	ຊ	LAO LETTER SO TAM
0E8B		
0E8C		
0E8D	ຍ	LAO LETTER NYO
0E8E		
0E8F		
0E90		
0E91		
0E92		
0E93		
0E94	ດ	LAO LETTER DO
0E95	ຕ	LAO LETTER TO
0E96	ຖ	LAO LETTER THO SUNG
0E97	ທ	LAO LETTER THO TAM
0E98		
0E99	ນ	LAO LETTER NO
0E9A	ບ	LAO LETTER BO
0E9B	ປ	LAO LETTER PO
0E9C	ຜ	LAO LETTER PHO SUNG
0E9D	ຝ	LAO LETTER FO TAM
0E9E	ພ	LAO LETTER PHO TAM
0E9F	ຟ	LAO LETTER FO SUNG
0EA0		
0EA1	ມ	LAO LETTER MO
0EA2	ຢ	LAO LETTER YO
0EA3	ຣ	LAO LETTER LO LING
0EA4		
0EA5	ລ	LAO LETTER LO LOOT
0EA6		
0EA7	ວ	LAO LETTER WO
0EA8		
0EA9		
0EAA	ສ	LAO LETTER SO SUNG
0EAB	ຫ	LAO LETTER HO SUNG

0EAC		
0EAD	ອ	LAO LETTER O
0EAE	ຮ	LAO LETTER HO TAM

Sign

0EAF	ຯ	LAO ELLIPSIS

Vowels

0EB0	◌ະ	LAO VOWEL SIGN A
0EB1	◌ັ	LAO VOWEL SIGN MAI KAN *vowel shortener*
0EB2	າ	LAO VOWEL SIGN AA
0EB3	◌ຳ	LAO VOWEL SIGN AM
0EB4	◌ິ	LAO VOWEL SIGN I
0EB5	◌ີ	LAO VOWEL SIGN II
0EB6	◌ຶ	LAO VOWEL SIGN Y
0EB7	◌ື	LAO VOWEL SIGN YY
0EB8	◌ຸ	LAO VOWEL SIGN U
0EB9	◌ູ	LAO VOWEL SIGN UU
0EBA		

Vowel

0EBB	◌ົ	LAO VOWEL SIGN MAI KON

Signs

0EBC	◌ຼ	LAO SEMIVOWEL SIGN LO
0EBD	ຽ	LAO SEMIVOWEL SIGN NYO
0EBE		
0EBF		

Vowels

0EC0	ເ	LAO VOWEL SIGN E
0EC1	ແ	LAO VOWEL SIGN EI
0EC2	ໂ	LAO VOWEL SIGN O
0EC3	ໃ	LAO VOWEL SIGN AY
0EC4	ໄ	LAO VOWEL SIGN AI
0EC5		

Sign

0EC6	ໆ	LAO KO LA *repetition*
0EC7		

Tone marks

0EC8	◌່	LAO TONE MAI EK
0EC9	◌້	LAO TONE MAI THO

0ECA	◌	LAO TONE MAI TI
0ECB	◌	LAO TONE MAI CATAWA

Signs

0ECC	◌	LAO CANCELLATION MARK
0ECD	◌	LAO NIGGAHITA
		final nasal

0ECE

0ECF

Digits

0ED0	໐	LAO DIGIT ZERO
0ED1	໑	LAO DIGIT ONE
0ED2	໒	LAO DIGIT TWO
0ED3	໓	LAO DIGIT THREE
0ED4	໔	LAO DIGIT FOUR
0ED5	໕	LAO DIGIT FIVE
0ED6	໖	LAO DIGIT SIX
0ED7	໗	LAO DIGIT SEVEN
0ED8	໘	LAO DIGIT EIGHT
0ED9	໙	LAO DIGIT NINE

0EDA

0EDB

Digraphs

0EDC	ຫນ	LAO HO NO
0EDD	ຫມ	LAO HO MO

0EDE

0EDF

0EE0

0EE1

0EE2

0EE3

0EE4

0EE5

0EE6

0EE7

0EE8

0EE9

0EEA

0EEB

0EEC

0EED

0EEE

0EEF

Phonetic order clones of left side vowel signs

0EF0	ເ◌	LAO PHONETIC ORDER VOWEL SIGN E
0EF1	ແ◌	LAO PHONETIC ORDER VOWEL SIGN EI
0EF2	ໂ◌	LAO PHONETIC ORDER VOWEL SIGN O
0EF3	ໃ◌	LAO PHONETIC ORDER VOWEL SIGN AY
0EF4	ໄ◌	LAO PHONETIC ORDER VOWEL SIGN AI

	100	101	102	103	104	105
0	ཀ	པ	ས	༷	༠	
1	ཁ	ཕ	ཧ	༒	༡	
2	ག	བ	ཨ		༢	
3	ང	མ		༄	༣	
4	ཅ	ཙ		།	༤	
5	ཆ	ཚ		་	༥	
6	ཇ	ཛ	ི	ྃ	༦	
7	ཉ	ཝ	ྀ	ྂ	༧	
8	ཊ	ཞ	ུ	༔	༨	
9	ཋ	ཟ	ེ	༏	༩	
A	ཌ	འ	ཻ	༈	༎	
B	ཎ	ཡ	[illegible]	༵	྄	
C	ཏ	ར	ཿ	༺	༹	
D	ཐ	ལ		[illegible]		
E	ད	ཤ	ཾ	[illegible]		
F	ན	ཥ	༻			

Consonants

1000	ཀ	TIBETAN LETTER KA
1001	ཁ	TIBETAN LETTER KHA
1002	ག	TIBETAN LETTER GA
1003	ང	TIBETAN LETTER NGA
1004	ཙ	TIBETAN LETTER CA
1005	ཚ	TIBETAN LETTER CHA
1006	ཇ	TIBETAN LETTER JA
1007	ཉ	TIBETAN LETTER NYA
1008	ཊ	TIBETAN LETTER REVERSED TA
		= Sanskrit retroflex ta
1009	ཋ	TIBETAN LETTER REVERSED THA
		= Sanskrit retroflex tha
100A	ཌ	TIBETAN LETTER REVERSED DA
		= Sanskrit retroflex da
100B	ཎ	TIBETAN LETTER REVERSED NA
		= Sanskrit retroflex na
100C	ཏ	TIBETAN LETTER TA
100D	ཐ	TIBETAN LETTER THA
100E	ད	TIBETAN LETTER DA
100F	ན	TIBETAN LETTER NA
1010	པ	TIBETAN LETTER PA
1011	ཕ	TIBETAN LETTER PHA
1012	བ	TIBETAN LETTER BA
1013	མ	TIBETAN LETTER MA
1014	ཙ	TIBETAN LETTER TSA
1015	ཚ	TIBETAN LETTER TSHA
1016	ཛ	TIBETAN LETTER DZA
1017	ཝ	TIBETAN LETTER WA
1018	ཞ	TIBETAN LETTER ZHA
1019	ཟ	TIBETAN LETTER ZA
101A	འ	TIBETAN LETTER AA
101B	ཡ	TIBETAN LETTER YA
101C	ར	TIBETAN LETTER RA
101D	ལ	TIBETAN LETTER LA
101E	ཤ	TIBETAN LETTER SHA
101F	ཥ	TIBETAN LETTER REVERSED SHA
		= Sanskrit retroflex sha
1020	ས	TIBETAN LETTER SA
1021	ཧ	TIBETAN LETTER HA
1022	ཨ	TIBETAN LETTER A
		base for dependent vowels
1023		
1024		
1025		

Dependent vowel signs

1026	ི	TIBETAN VOWEL SIGN I
		= gigu
1027	ྀ	TIBETAN VOWEL SIGN SHORT I
		= reversed gigu
1028	ུ	TIBETAN VOWEL SIGN U
		= zhabskyu (shapkyu)
1029	ེ	TIBETAN VOWEL SIGN E
		= hgrengbu (drengpo)
102A	ོ	TIBETAN VOWEL SIGN O
		= snaro (naro)

Various

102B	ྂ	TIBETAN CHUCHENYIGE
102C	ༀ	TIBETAN VISARGA
		= mambcad (namchey)
102D		

Dependent vowel sign

102E	ཾ	TIBETAN ANUSVARA
		= ngaro

Punctuation

102F	༡	TIBETAN RIGHT BRACE
		× (tibetan left brace → 103C)
1030	༂	TIBETAN UNDER RING
		= rtags (tak)
		emphasis
1031	X	TIBETAN DITTO
		= duyik
1032		
1033	༄	TIBETAN SINGLE ORNAMENT
		= nyizla
		honorific; marks beginning of texts
1034	།	TIBETAN SHAD
		= shey
		phrase delimiter
		× (devanagari danda → 0964)
1035	་	TIBETAN TSEG
		= tsek
		syllable delimiter

Dependent vowel signs

1036	ྃ	TIBETAN CANDRABINDU
		= kladkor (lehkor)
1037	྄	TIBETAN CANDRABINDU WITH ORNAMENT
		= datsekthikley

Punctuation

1038	᠅	TIBETAN COMMA = *tertsek* *also used as TIBETAN VISARGA*
1039		TIBETAN RINCHANPHUNGSHAD = *rinchenpungshey*
103A		TIBETAN RGYANSHAD = *druishey*
103B		TIBETAN HONORIFIC UNDER RING
103C		TIBETAN LEFT BRACE ✕ *(tibetan right brace → 102F)*

Dependent vowel signs

103D		TIBETAN VOWEL SIGN AI
103E		TIBETAN VOWEL SIGN AU
103F		

Digits

1040	๐	TIBETAN DIGIT ZERO
1041	໑	TIBETAN DIGIT ONE
1042	໒	TIBETAN DIGIT TWO
1043	໓	TIBETAN DIGIT THREE
1044	໔	TIBETAN DIGIT FOUR
1045	໕	TIBETAN DIGIT FIVE
1046	໖	TIBETAN DIGIT SIX
1047	໗	TIBETAN DIGIT SEVEN
1048	໘	TIBETAN DIGIT EIGHT
1049	໙	TIBETAN DIGIT NINE
104A	‖	TIBETAN DOUBLE SHAD ✕ *(devanagari double danda → 0965)*

Various

104B		TIBETAN VIRAMA = *srog med*
104C		TIBETAN LENITION MARK

	10A	10B	10C	10D	10E	10F
0	Ⴀ	Ⴐ	Ⴠ	ა	ო	ჳ
1	Ⴁ	Ⴑ	Ⴡ	ბ	ს	ჴ
2	Ⴂ	Ⴒ	Ⴢ	გ	ტ	ჵ
3	Ⴃ	Ⴓ	Ⴣ	დ	უ	ჶ
4	Ⴄ	Ⴔ	Ⴤ	ე	ჟ	ჷ
5	Ⴅ	Ⴕ	Ⴥ	ვ	ფ	ჸ
6	Ⴆ	Ⴖ		ზ	ქ	ჶ
7	Ⴇ	Ⴗ		თ	ყ	
8	Ⴈ	Ⴘ		ი	შ	
9	Ⴉ	Ⴙ		კ	ჩ	
A	Ⴊ	Ⴚ		ლ	ც	
B	Ⴋ	Ⴛ		მ	ძ	჻
C	Ⴌ	Ⴜ		ნ	წ	
D	Ⴍ	Ⴝ		ო	ჭ	
E	Ⴎ	Ⴞ		პ	ხ	
F	Ⴏ	Ⴟ		ჟ	ჯ	

Archaic uppercase alphabet

10A0	Ⴀ	GEORGIAN CAPITAL LETTER AN
10A1	Ⴁ	GEORGIAN CAPITAL LETTER BAN
10A2	Ⴂ	GEORGIAN CAPITAL LETTER GAN
10A3	Ⴃ	GEORGIAN CAPITAL LETTER DON
10A4	Ⴄ	GEORGIAN CAPITAL LETTER EN
10A5	Ⴅ	GEORGIAN CAPITAL LETTER VIN
10A6	Ⴆ	GEORGIAN CAPITAL LETTER ZEN
10A7	Ⴇ	GEORGIAN CAPITAL LETTER TAN
10A8	Ⴈ	GEORGIAN CAPITAL LETTER IN
10A9	Ⴉ	GEORGIAN CAPITAL LETTER KAN
10AA	Ⴊ	GEORGIAN CAPITAL LETTER LAS
10AB	Ⴋ	GEORGIAN CAPITAL LETTER MAN
10AC	Ⴌ	GEORGIAN CAPITAL LETTER NAR
10AD	Ⴍ	GEORGIAN CAPITAL LETTER ON
10AE	Ⴎ	GEORGIAN CAPITAL LETTER PAR
10AF	Ⴏ	GEORGIAN CAPITAL LETTER ZHAR
10B0	Ⴐ	GEORGIAN CAPITAL LETTER RAE
10B1	Ⴑ	GEORGIAN CAPITAL LETTER SAN
10B2	Ⴒ	GEORGIAN CAPITAL LETTER TAR
10B3	Ⴓ	GEORGIAN CAPITAL LETTER UN
10B4	Ⴔ	GEORGIAN CAPITAL LETTER PHAR
10B5	Ⴕ	GEORGIAN CAPITAL LETTER KHAR
10B6	Ⴖ	GEORGIAN CAPITAL LETTER GHAN
10B7	Ⴗ	GEORGIAN CAPITAL LETTER QAR
10B8	Ⴘ	GEORGIAN CAPITAL LETTER SHIN
10B9	Ⴙ	GEORGIAN CAPITAL LETTER CHIN
10BA	Ⴚ	GEORGIAN CAPITAL LETTER CAN
10BB	Ⴛ	GEORGIAN CAPITAL LETTER JIL
10BC	Ⴜ	GEORGIAN CAPITAL LETTER CIL
10BD	Ⴝ	GEORGIAN CAPITAL LETTER CHAR
10BE	Ⴞ	GEORGIAN CAPITAL LETTER XAN
10BF	Ⴟ	GEORGIAN CAPITAL LETTER JHAN
10C0	Ⴠ	GEORGIAN CAPITAL LETTER HAE
10C1	Ⴡ	GEORGIAN CAPITAL LETTER HE
10C2	Ⴢ	GEORGIAN CAPITAL LETTER HIE
10C3	Ⴣ	GEORGIAN CAPITAL LETTER WE
10C4	Ⴤ	GEORGIAN CAPITAL LETTER HAR
10C5	Ⴥ	GEORGIAN CAPITAL LETTER HOE
10C6		
10C7		
10C8		
10C9		
10CA		
10CB		
10CC		

10CD		
10CE		
10CF		

Modern alphabet
= Archaic lowercase alphabet

10D0	ა	GEORGIAN SMALL LETTER AN
10D1	ბ	GEORGIAN SMALL LETTER BAN
10D2	გ	GEORGIAN SMALL LETTER GAN
10D3	დ	GEORGIAN SMALL LETTER DON
10D4	ე	GEORGIAN SMALL LETTER EN
10D5	ვ	GEORGIAN SMALL LETTER VIN
10D6	ზ	GEORGIAN SMALL LETTER ZEN
10D7	თ	GEORGIAN SMALL LETTER TAN
10D8	ი	GEORGIAN SMALL LETTER IN
10D9	კ	GEORGIAN SMALL LETTER KAN
10DA	ლ	GEORGIAN SMALL LETTER LAS
10DB	მ	GEORGIAN SMALL LETTER MAN
10DC	ნ	GEORGIAN SMALL LETTER NAR
10DD	ო	GEORGIAN SMALL LETTER ON
10DE	პ	GEORGIAN SMALL LETTER PAR
10DF	ჟ	GEORGIAN SMALL LETTER ZHAR
10E0	რ	GEORGIAN SMALL LETTER RAE
10E1	ს	GEORGIAN SMALL LETTER SAN
10E2	ტ	GEORGIAN SMALL LETTER TAR
10E3	უ	GEORGIAN SMALL LETTER UN
10E4	ფ	GEORGIAN SMALL LETTER PHAR
10E5	ქ	GEORGIAN SMALL LETTER KHAR
10E6	ღ	GEORGIAN SMALL LETTER GHAN
10E7	ყ	GEORGIAN SMALL LETTER QAR
10E8	შ	GEORGIAN SMALL LETTER SHIN
10E9	ჩ	GEORGIAN SMALL LETTER CHIN
10EA	ც	GEORGIAN SMALL LETTER CAN
10EB	ძ	GEORGIAN SMALL LETTER JIL
10EC	წ	GEORGIAN SMALL LETTER CIL
10ED	ჭ	GEORGIAN SMALL LETTER CHAR
10EE	ხ	GEORGIAN SMALL LETTER XAN
10EF	ჯ	GEORGIAN SMALL LETTER JHAN
10F0	ჰ	GEORGIAN SMALL LETTER HAE

Archaic letters

10F1	ჱ	GEORGIAN SMALL LETTER HE
10F2	ჲ	GEORGIAN SMALL LETTER HIE
10F3	ჳ	GEORGIAN SMALL LETTER WE
10F4	ჴ	GEORGIAN SMALL LETTER HAR
10F5	ჵ	GEORGIAN SMALL LETTER HOE

10F6   ф   GEORGIAN SMALL LETTER FI
10F7
10F8
10F9
10FA

Punctuation

10FB   ∶   GEORGIAN PARAGRAPH SEPARATOR

	200	201	202	203	204	205	206
0	En Quad	Hyphen —	†	‰	⌒		
1	Em Quad	NB	‡	‰o	⅄		
2	En SP	Figure	●	′	✱✱		
3	Em SP	—	▶	″	▬		
4	3 Em SP	—	·	‴	╱		
5	4 Em SP	—	· ·	‵			
6	6 Em SP	‖	· · ·	‶			
7	Fig SP	═	· HyphenPt	‷			
8	PunctSP	'	Line Sepr	∧			
9	Thin SP	'	Para Sepr	‹			
A	Hair SP	‚	LRE	›			
B	ZW SP	‛	RLE	⁂			
C	Non-Joiner	"	PDF	‼			
D	Joiner	"	LRO	⁇			
E	L-R Mark	„	RLO	▬			
F	R-L Mark	‟					

General punctuation

2000	En Quad	EN QUAD
2001	Em Quad	EM QUAD
2002	En SP	EN SPACE
2003	Em SP	EM SPACE
2004	3 Em SP	THREE-PER-EM SPACE
2005	4 Em SP	FOUR-PER-EM SPACE
2006	6 Em SP	SIX-PER-EM SPACE
2007	Fig SP	FIGURE SPACE
2008	PunctSP	PUNCTUATION SPACE
2009	Thin SP	THIN SPACE
200A	Hair SP	HAIR SPACE
200B	ZW SP	ZERO WIDTH SPACE

2000C · ZERO WIDTH NON-JOINER
= ZWNJ ("zwinj")

200D · ZERO WIDTH JOINER
= ZWJ ("zawj")

200E · LEFT-TO-RIGHT MARK
= LRM

200F · RIGHT-TO-LEFT MARK
= RLM

2010 · HYPHEN
× (hyphen-minus → 002D)

2011 · NON-BREAKING HYPHEN
× (hyphen-minus → 002D)

2012 · FIGURE DASH

2013 — EN DASH

2014 — EM DASH
× (katakana-hiragana prolonged sound mark → 30FC)

2015 — QUOTATION DASH
= HORIZONTAL BAR
long dash introducing quoted text

2016 ‖ DOUBLE VERTICAL BAR
used in pairs to indicate norm of a matrix
× (parallel to → 2225)

2017 ‗ SPACING DOUBLE UNDERSCORE
this is a spacing character
× (spacing underscore → 005F)
× (non-spacing double underscore → 0333)

2018 ' SINGLE TURNED COMMA QUOTATION MARK
this is the preferred character for opening single quotation mark
× (apostrophe-quote → 0027)
× (modifier letter turned comma → 02BB)
× (heavy single turned comma quotation mark ornament → 275B)

2019 ' SINGLE COMMA QUOTATION MARK
this is the preferred character for closing single quotation mark
× (apostrophe-quote → 0027)
× (modifier letter apostrophe → 02BC)
× (heavy single comma quotation mark ornament → 275C)

201A ‚ LOW SINGLE COMMA QUOTATION MARK
usually opening, sometimes closing, in European usage

201B ‛ SINGLE REVERSED COMMA QUOTATION MARK
glyph variant of 2018
× (modifier letter reversed comma → 02BD)

201C " DOUBLE TURNED COMMA QUOTATION MARK
this is the preferred character for opening quotation mark
× (quotation mark → 0022)
× (heavy double turned comma quotation mark ornament → 275D)
× (reversed double prime quotation mark → 301D)

201D " DOUBLE COMMA QUOTATION MARK
this is the preferred character for closing quotation mark
× (quotation mark → 0022)
× (double prime → 2033)
× (heavy double comma quotation mark ornament → 275E)
× (double prime quotation mark → 301E)

201E „ LOW DOUBLE COMMA QUOTATION MARK
usually opening, sometimes closing, in European usage
× (low double prime quotation mark → 301F)

201F ‟ DOUBLE REVERSED COMMA QUOTATION MARK
glyph variant of 201C

2020 † DAGGER

2021 ‡ DOUBLE DAGGER

2022 • BULLET
= BLACK SMALL CIRCLE
× (middle dot → 00B7)
× (one dot leader → 2024)
× (bullet operator → 2219)
× (inverse bullet → 25D8)
× (white bullet → 25E6)

2023 ▶ TRIANGULAR BULLET
× (end of proof → 220E)
× (black right pointing small triangle → 25B8)

2024 · ONE DOT LEADER
× (middle dot → 00B7)
× (bullet → 2022)
× (bullet operator → 2219)

2025 ·· TWO DOT LEADER

2026	⋯	**HORIZONTAL ELLIPSIS**
		= *three dot leader*
		✕ *(vertical ellipsis → 22EE)*
2027	·	**HYPHENATION POINT**
2028	[Line Sepr]	**LINE SEPARATOR**
		may be used to represent this semantic unambiguously
2029	[Para Sepr]	**PARAGRAPH SEPARATOR**
		may be used to represent this semantic unambiguously
202A	[LRE]	**LEFT-TO-RIGHT EMBEDDING**
		= *LRE*
202B	[RLE]	**RIGHT-TO-LEFT EMBEDDING**
		= *RLE*
202C	[PDF]	**POP DIRECTIONAL FORMATTING**
		= *PDF*
202D	[LRO]	**LEFT-TO-RIGHT OVERRIDE**
		= *LRO*
202E	[RLO]	**RIGHT-TO-LEFT OVERRIDE**
		= *RLO*
202F		
2030	‰	**PER MILLE SIGN**
		✕ *(percent sign → 0025)*
2031	‱	**PER TEN THOUSAND SIGN**
		✕ *(percent sign → 0025)*
2032	′	**PRIME**
		= *minutes*
		= *feet*
		✕ *(apostrophe-quote → 0027)*
		✕ *(spacing acute → 00B4)*
		✕ *(modifier letter prime → 02B9)*
2033	″	**DOUBLE PRIME**
		= *seconds*
		= *inches*
		✕ *(quotation mark → 0022)*
		✕ *(modifier letter double prime → 02BA)*
		✕ *(double comma quotation mark → 201D)*
		✕ *(ditto mark → 3003)*
		✕ *(double prime quotation mark → 301E)*
2034	‴	**TRIPLE PRIME**
2035	‵	**REVERSED PRIME**
		✕ *(spacing grave → 0060)*
2036	‶	**REVERSED DOUBLE PRIME**
		✕ *(reversed double prime quotation mark → 301D)*
2037	‷	**REVERSED TRIPLE PRIME**
2038	^	**CARET**

2039	‹	**LEFT POINTING SINGLE GUILLEMET**
		= *ISO SINGLE LEFT-POINTING ANGLE QUOTATION MARK*
		usually opening, sometimes closing
		✕ *(less-than sign → 003C)*
		✕ *(bra → 2329)*
		✕ *(opening angle bracket → 3008)*
203A	›	**RIGHT POINTING SINGLE GUILLEMET**
		= *ISO SINGLE RIGHT-POINTING ANGLE QUOTATION MARK*
		usually closing, sometimes opening
		✕ *(greater-than sign → 003E)*
		✕ *(ket → 232A)*
		✕ *(closing angle bracket → 3009)*
203B	※	**REFERENCE MARK**
		= *Japanese kome*
		= *Urdu paragraph separator*
203C	‼	**DOUBLE EXCLAMATION MARK**
		✕ *(exclamation mark → 0021)*
203D	‽	**INTERROBANG**
		✕ *(question mark → 003F)*
203E	—	**SPACING OVERSCORE**
		= *ISO OVERLINE*
203F		
2040	⁀	**CHARACTER TIE**
2041	⁁	**CARET INSERTION POINT**
		proofreader's mark: insert here
		✕ *(right semidirect product → 22CC)*
2042	⁂	**ASTERISM**
2043	⁃	**HYPHEN BULLET**
2044	⁄	**FRACTION SLASH**
		for composing arbitrary fractions
		✕ *(slash → 002F)*
		✕ *(division slash → 2215)*

	207	208	209
0	0	0	
1		1	
2		2	
3		3	
4	4	4	
5	5	5	
6	6	6	
7	7	7	
8	8	8	
9	9	9	
A	+	+	
B	–	–	
C	=	=	
D	(	(	
E	)	)	
F	n		

Superscripts and subscripts

2070	^{0}	SUPERSCRIPT DIGIT ZERO
2071		✕ *(superscript digit one → 00B9)*
2072		✕ *(superscript digit two → 00B2)*
2073		✕ *(superscript digit three → 00B3)*
2074	^{4}	SUPERSCRIPT DIGIT FOUR
2075	^{5}	SUPERSCRIPT DIGIT FIVE
2076	^{6}	SUPERSCRIPT DIGIT SIX
2077	^{7}	SUPERSCRIPT DIGIT SEVEN
2078	^{8}	SUPERSCRIPT DIGIT EIGHT
2079	^{9}	SUPERSCRIPT DIGIT NINE
207A	$^+$	SUPERSCRIPT PLUS SIGN
207B	$^-$	SUPERSCRIPT HYPHEN-MINUS
207C	$^=$	SUPERSCRIPT EQUALS SIGN
207D	$^($	SUPERSCRIPT OPENING PARENTHESIS
207E	$^)$	SUPERSCRIPT CLOSING PARENTHESIS
207F	^{n}	SUPERSCRIPT LATIN SMALL LETTER N
2080	$_0$	SUBSCRIPT DIGIT ZERO
2081	$_1$	SUBSCRIPT DIGIT ONE
2082	$_2$	SUBSCRIPT DIGIT TWO
2083	$_3$	SUBSCRIPT DIGIT THREE
2084	$_4$	SUBSCRIPT DIGIT FOUR
2085	$_5$	SUBSCRIPT DIGIT FIVE
2086	$_6$	SUBSCRIPT DIGIT SIX
2087	$_7$	SUBSCRIPT DIGIT SEVEN
2088	$_8$	SUBSCRIPT DIGIT EIGHT
2089	$_9$	SUBSCRIPT DIGIT NINE
208A	$_+$	SUBSCRIPT PLUS SIGN
208B	$_-$	SUBSCRIPT HYPHEN-MINUS
208C	$_=$	SUBSCRIPT EQUALS SIGN
208D	$_($	SUBSCRIPT OPENING PARENTHESIS
208E	$_)$	SUBSCRIPT CLOSING PARENTHESIS

Currency Symbols

	20A	20B	20C
0	₠		
1	₡		
2	₢		
3	₣		
4	₤		
5	₥		
6	₦		
7	₧		
8	₨		
9	₩		
A	₪		
B			
C			
D			
E			
F			

Currency symbols

× *(dollar sign → 0024)*
× *(cent sign → 00A2)*
× *(pound sign → 00A3)*
× *(currency sign → 00A4)*
× *(yen sign → 00A5)*
× *(bengali rupee mark → 09F2)*
× *(bengali rupee sign → 09F3)*
× *(thai baht sign → 0E3F)*

20A0	₠	EURO-CURRENCY SIGN
20A1	₡	COLON SIGN
		Costa Rica, El Salvador
20A2	₢	CRUZEIRO SIGN
		Brazil
20A3	₣	FRENCH FRANC SIGN
		France
20A4	₤	LIRA SIGN
		Italy, Turkey
		× *(pound sign → 00A3)*
20A5	₥	MILL SIGN
		USA (1/10 cent)
20A6	₦	NAIRA SIGN
		Nigeria
20A7	₧	PESETA SIGN
		Spain
20A8	₨	RUPEE SIGN
		India
20A9	₩	WON SIGN
		Korea
20AA	₪	NEW SHEQEL SIGN
		Israel

	20D	20E	20F
0			
1			
2			
3			
4			
5			
6			
7			
8			
9			
A			
B			
C			
D			
E			
F			

Diacritical marks for symbols

20D0	̼	NON-SPACING LEFT HARPOON ABOVE
20D1	̼	NON-SPACING RIGHT HARPOON ABOVE
		vector
20D2	⃒	NON-SPACING LONG VERTICAL BAR OVERLAY
20D3	⃓	NON-SPACING SHORT VERTICAL BAR OVERLAY
		negation
20D4	↶	NON-SPACING ANTICLOCKWISE ARROW ABOVE
20D5	↷	NON-SPACING CLOCKWISE ARROW ABOVE
		rotation
20D6	←	NON-SPACING LEFT ARROW ABOVE
20D7	→	NON-SPACING RIGHT ARROW ABOVE
		vector
20D8	⃘	NON-SPACING RING OVERLAY
20D9	⃙	NON-SPACING CLOCKWISE RING OVERLAY
20DA	⃚	NON-SPACING ANTICLOCKWISE RING OVERLAY
20DB	⃛	NON-SPACING THREE DOTS ABOVE
		= *third derivative*
20DC	⃜	NON-SPACING FOUR DOTS ABOVE
		= *fourth derivative*

Enclosing diacritics

20DD	◯	ENCLOSING CIRCLE
		= *JIS composition circle*
		× *(white circle → 25CB)*
		× *(ideographic number zero → 3007)*
20DE	▢	ENCLOSING SQUARE
20DF	◇	ENCLOSING DIAMOND
20E0	⃠	ENCLOSING CIRCLE SLASH
		prohibition

Additional diacritics

20E1	↔	NON-SPACING LEFT RIGHT ARROW ABOVE
		tensor

	210	211	212	213	214
0	a/c	ℐ	SM	ℰ	
1	a/s	ℑ	TEL	ℱ	
2	ℂ	ℒ	™	Ⅎ	
3	℃	ℓ	℣	ℳ	
4	℄	℔	ℤ	ℴ	
5	℅	N	℥	ℵ	
6	℆	№	Ω	ℶ	
7	ℇ	℗	℧	ℷ	
8	℈	℘	ℨ	ℸ	
9	℉	ℙ	℩		
A	ℊ	ℚ	K		
B	ℋ	ℛ	Å		
C	ℌ	ℜ	ℬ		
D	ℍ	ℝ	ℭ		
E	ℎ	℞	℮		
F	ℏℏ	℟	ℯ		

Letterlike symbols

2100	ᵃ/c	ACCOUNT OF
2101	ᵃ/s	ADDRESSED TO THE SUBJECT
2102	ℂ	DOUBLE-STRUCK C
		= *the set of complex numbers*
		× *(latin capital letter c → 0043)*
2103	°C	DEGREES CENTIGRADE
2104	₵	C L SYMBOL
		= *centerline*
		= *clone*
2105	°/₀	CARE OF
2106	°/ᵤ	CADA UNA
2107	Ɛ	EULERS
		× *(latin capital letter e → 0045)*
		× *(latin capital letter epsilon → 0190)*
2108	℈	SCRUPLE
2109	°F	DEGREES FAHRENHEIT
210A	ℊ	SCRIPT SMALL G
		= *real number symbol*
		× *(latin small letter g → 0067)*
210B	ℋ	SCRIPT H
		= *Hamiltonian function*
		× *(latin capital letter h → 0048)*
210C	ℌ	BLACK-LETTER H
		× *(latin capital letter h → 0048)*
210D	ℍ	DOUBLE-STRUCK H
		× *(latin capital letter h → 0048)*
210E	h	PLANCK CONSTANT
		× *(latin small letter h → 0068)*
210F	ℏ\ℏ	PLANCK CONSTANT OVER 2 PI
		× *(latin small letter h bar → 0127)*
		× *(cyrillic small letter tshe → 045B)*
2110	ℐ	SCRIPT I
		× *(latin capital letter i → 0049)*
2111	ℑ	BLACK-LETTER I
		= *ISO IMAGINARY PART SYMBOL*
		× *(latin capital letter i → 0049)*
2112	ℒ	SCRIPT L
		= *Laplace symbol*
		× *(latin capital letter l → 004C)*
2113	ℓ	*SCRIPT SMALL L*
		= *liter*
		× *(latin small letter l → 006C)*
2114	℔	L B BAR SYMBOL
		= *pounds*
2115	ℕ	DOUBLE-STRUCK N
		= *natural number*
		× *(latin capital letter n → 004E)*
2116	№	NUMERO
2117	℗	SOUND RECORDING COPYRIGHT
		= *published*
		× *(copyright sign → 00A9)*
2118	℘	SCRIPT P
		= *per*
		= *power set*
		= *Weierstrass elliptic function*
		× *(latin capital letter p → 0050)*
2119	ℙ	DOUBLE-STRUCK P
		× *(latin capital letter p → 0050)*
211A	ℚ	DOUBLE-STRUCK Q
		= *the set of rational numbers*
		× *(latin capital letter q → 0051)*
211B	ℛ	SCRIPT R
		= *Riemann Integral*
		× *(latin capital letter r → 0052)*
211C	ℜ	BLACK-LETTER R
		= *ISO REAL PART SYMBOL*
		× *(latin capital letter r → 0052)*
211D	ℝ	DOUBLE-STRUCK R
		= *the set of real numbers*
		× *(latin capital letter r → 0052)*
211E	℞	PRESCRIPTION TAKE
		= *recipe*
		= *cross ratio*
211F	℟	RESPONSE
2120	℠	SERVICE MARK
2121	℡	T E L SYMBOL
2122	™	TRADEMARK
2123	℣	VERSICLE
2124	ℤ	DOUBLE-STRUCK Z
		= *the set of integers*
		× *(latin capital letter z → 005A)*
2125	℥	OUNCE
		× *(latin small letter yogh → 0292)*
2126	Ω	OHM
		= *resistance*
		× *(greek capital letter omega → 03A9)*
2127	℧	MHO
		= *conductance*
		typographically a turned greek capital letter omega
		× *(latin capital letter upsilon → 01B1)*
		× *(greek capital letter omega → 03A9)*
2128	ℨ	BLACK-LETTER Z
		× *(latin capital letter z → 005A)*
2129	℩	TURNED GREEK SMALL LETTER IOTA
		unique element fulfilling a description (logic)
		× *(greek small letter iota → 03B9)*
212A	K	DEGREES KELVIN
		× *(latin capital letter k → 004B)*
212B	Å	ANGSTROM UNIT
		× *(latin capital letter a ring → 00C5)*
212C	ℬ	SCRIPT B
		= *Bernoulli function*
		× *(latin capital letter b → 0042)*

212D	𝕮	**BLACK-LETTER C**
		✕ *(latin capital letter c → 0043)*
212E	**e**	**ESTIMATED SYMBOL**
		used in European packaging
		✕ *(latin small letter e → 0065)*
212F	*e*	**SCRIPT SMALL E**
		= *error*
		✕ *(latin small letter e → 0065)*
2130	*ℰ*	**SCRIPT E**
		= *EMF (Electro-Magnetic Force)*
		✕ *(latin capital letter e → 0045)*
2131	*ℱ*	**SCRIPT F**
		= *Fourier transform*
		✕ *(latin capital letter f → 0046)*
2132	Ⅎ	**TURNED F**
		✕ *(latin capital letter f → 0046)*
2133	*ℳ*	**SCRIPT M**
		= *M-matrix (physics)*
		✕ *(latin capital letter m → 004D)*
2134	*o*	**SCRIPT SMALL O**
		= *order; of inferior order to*
		✕ *(latin small letter o → 006F)*
2135	א	**FIRST TRANSFINITE CARDINAL**
		= *cardinal of the set of integers*
		✕ *(hebrew letter alef → 05D0)*
2136	ב	**SECOND TRANSFINITE CARDINAL**
		= *cardinal of the continuum*
		✕ *(hebrew letter bet → 05D1)*
2137	ג	**THIRD TRANSFINITE CARDINAL**
		= *cardinal of functions of a real variable*
		✕ *(hebrew letter gimel → 05D2)*
2138	ד	**FOURTH TRANSFINITE CARDINAL**
		✕ *(hebrew letter dalet → 05D3)*

	215	216	217	218
0		I	i	ⅭⅮ
1		II	ii	Ⅾ
2		III	iii	ⅭⅭ
3	$\frac{1}{3}$	IV	iv	
4	$\frac{2}{3}$	V	v	
5	$\frac{1}{5}$	VI	vi	
6	$\frac{2}{5}$	VII	vii	
7	$\frac{3}{5}$	VIII	viii	
8	$\frac{4}{5}$	IX	ix	
9	$\frac{1}{6}$	X	x	
A	$\frac{5}{6}$	XI	xi	
B	$\frac{1}{8}$	XII	xii	
C	$\frac{3}{8}$	L	l	
D	$\frac{5}{8}$	C	c	
E	$\frac{7}{8}$	D	d	
F	$\frac{1}{}$	M	m	

Number forms

2150	×	*(fraction one quarter → 00BC)*
2151	×	*(fraction one half → 00BD)*
2152	×	*(fraction three quarters → 00BE)*
2153	$\frac{1}{3}$	FRACTION ONE THIRD
2154	$\frac{2}{3}$	FRACTION TWO THIRDS
2155	$\frac{1}{5}$	FRACTION ONE FIFTH
2156	$\frac{2}{5}$	FRACTION TWO FIFTHS
2157	$\frac{3}{5}$	FRACTION THREE FIFTHS
2158	$\frac{4}{5}$	FRACTION FOUR FIFTHS
2159	$\frac{1}{6}$	FRACTION ONE SIXTH
215A	$\frac{5}{6}$	FRACTION FIVE SIXTHS
215B	$\frac{1}{8}$	FRACTION ONE EIGHTH
215C	$\frac{3}{8}$	FRACTION THREE EIGHTHS
215D	$\frac{5}{8}$	FRACTION FIVE EIGHTHS
215E	$\frac{7}{8}$	FRACTION SEVEN EIGHTHS
215F	$\frac{1}{}$	FRACTION NUMERATOR ONE
2160	I	ROMAN NUMERAL ONE
2161	II	ROMAN NUMERAL TWO
2162	III	ROMAN NUMERAL THREE
2163	IV	ROMAN NUMERAL FOUR
2164	V	ROMAN NUMERAL FIVE
2165	VI	ROMAN NUMERAL SIX
2166	VII	ROMAN NUMERAL SEVEN
2167	VIII	ROMAN NUMERAL EIGHT
2168	IX	ROMAN NUMERAL NINE
2169	X	ROMAN NUMERAL TEN
216A	XI	ROMAN NUMERAL ELEVEN
216B	XII	ROMAN NUMERAL TWELVE
216C	L	ROMAN NUMERAL FIFTY
216D	C	ROMAN NUMERAL ONE HUNDRED
216E	D	ROMAN NUMERAL FIVE HUNDRED
216F	M	ROMAN NUMERAL ONE THOUSAND
2170	i	SMALL ROMAN NUMERAL ONE
2171	ii	SMALL ROMAN NUMERAL TWO
2172	iii	SMALL ROMAN NUMERAL THREE
2173	iv	SMALL ROMAN NUMERAL FOUR
2174	v	SMALL ROMAN NUMERAL FIVE
2175	vi	SMALL ROMAN NUMERAL SIX
2176	vii	SMALL ROMAN NUMERAL SEVEN
2177	viii	SMALL ROMAN NUMERAL EIGHT
2178	ix	SMALL ROMAN NUMERAL NINE
2179	x	SMALL ROMAN NUMERAL TEN
217A	xi	SMALL ROMAN NUMERAL ELEVEN
217B	xii	SMALL ROMAN NUMERAL TWELVE
217C	l	SMALL ROMAN NUMERAL FIFTY
217D	c	SMALL ROMAN NUMERAL ONE HUNDRED
217E	d	SMALL ROMAN NUMERAL FIVE HUNDRED
217F	m	SMALL ROMAN NUMERAL ONE THOUSAND
2180	ⅭⅮ	ROMAN NUMERAL ONE THOUSAND C D
2181	Ⅾ	ROMAN NUMERAL FIVE THOUSAND
2182	ⅭⅭ	ROMAN NUMERAL TEN THOUSAND

	219	21A	21B	21C	21D	21E	21F
0	←	→→	↰	→	⇐	⇠	
1	↑	↓↓	↱	⇀	⇑	⇡	
2	→	↢	↲	⇂	⇒	⇢	
3	↓	↣	↳	↓	⇓	⇣	
4	↔	↤	↴	⇄	⇔	↤	
5	↕	↥	↵	⇅	⇕	↦	
6	↖	↦	↶	⇆	⇖	⇦	
7	↗	↧	↷	⇇	⇗	⇧	
8	↘	↨	↸	⇈	⇘	⇨	
9	↙	↩	↹	⇉	⇙	⇩	
A	↚	↪	↺	⇊	⇚	⇪	
B	↛	↫	↻	⇋	⇛		
C	↜	↬	↼	⇌	⇜		
D	↝	↭	↽	⇍	⇝		
E	↞	↮	↾	⇎	⇞		
F	↟	↯	↿	⇏	⇟		

The Unicode Standard • Version 1.0

Arrows

2190	←	LEFT ARROW
2191	↑	UP ARROW
2192	→	RIGHT ARROW
2193	↓	DOWN ARROW
2194	↔	LEFT RIGHT ARROW
2195	↕	UP DOWN ARROW
2196	↖	UPPER LEFT ARROW
2197	↗	UPPER RIGHT ARROW
2198	↘	LOWER RIGHT ARROW
2199	↙	LOWER LEFT ARROW
219A	↚	LEFT ARROW WITH STROKE
219B	↛	RIGHT ARROW WITH STROKE
219C	↜	LEFT WAVE ARROW
219D	↝	RIGHT WAVE ARROW
219E	↞	LEFT TWO HEADED ARROW
219F	↟	UP TWO HEADED ARROW
21A0	↠	RIGHT TWO HEADED ARROW
21A1	↡	DOWN TWO HEADED ARROW
		= form feed
21A2	↢	LEFT ARROW WITH TAIL
21A3	↣	RIGHT ARROW WITH TAIL
21A4	↤	LEFT ARROW FROM BAR
21A5	↥	UP ARROW FROM BAR
21A6	↦	RIGHT ARROW FROM BAR
21A7	↧	DOWN ARROW FROM BAR
		= depth symbol
21A8	↨	UP DOWN ARROW WITH BASE
21A9	↩	LEFT ARROW WITH HOOK
21AA	↪	RIGHT ARROW WITH HOOK
21AB	↫	LEFT ARROW WITH LOOP
21AC	↬	RIGHT ARROW WITH LOOP
21AD	↭	LEFT RIGHT WAVE ARROW
21AE	↮	LEFT RIGHT ARROW WITH STROKE
21AF	↯	DOWN ZIGZAG ARROW
		= electrolysis
21B0	↰	UP ARROW WITH TIP LEFT
21B1	↱	UP ARROW WITH TIP RIGHT
21B2	↲	DOWN ARROW WITH TIP LEFT
21B3	↳	DOWN ARROW WITH TIP RIGHT
21B4	↴	RIGHT ARROW WITH CORNER DOWN
		= line feed
21B5	↵	DOWN ARROW WITH CORNER LEFT
		= carriage return
		= new line
21B6	↶	ANTICLOCKWISE TOP SEMICIRCLE ARROW
21B7	↷	CLOCKWISE TOP SEMICIRCLE ARROW

21B8	↸	UPPER LEFT ARROW TO LONG BAR
		= home
21B9	↹	LEFT ARROW TO BAR OVER RIGHT ARROW TO BAR
		= tab with shift tab
21BA	↺	ANTICLOCKWISE OPEN CIRCLE ARROW
21BB	↻	CLOCKWISE OPEN CIRCLE ARROW
21BC	↼	LEFT HARPOON WITH BARB UP
21BD	↽	LEFT HARPOON WITH BARB DOWN
21BE	↾	UP HARPOON WITH BARB RIGHT
21BF	↿	UP HARPOON WITH BARB LEFT
21C0	⇀	RIGHT HARPOON WITH BARB UP
21C1	⇁	RIGHT HARPOON WITH BARB DOWN
21C2	⇂	DOWN HARPOON WITH BARB RIGHT
21C3	⇃	DOWN HARPOON WITH BARB LEFT
21C4	⇄	RIGHT ARROW OVER LEFT ARROW
21C5	⇅	UP ARROW LEFT OF DOWN ARROW
21C6	⇆	LEFT ARROW OVER RIGHT ARROW
21C7	⇇	LEFT PAIRED ARROWS
21C8	⇈	UP PAIRED ARROWS
21C9	⇉	RIGHT PAIRED ARROWS
21CA	⇊	DOWN PAIRED ARROWS
21CB	⇋	LEFT HARPOON OVER RIGHT HARPOON
21CC	⇌	RIGHT HARPOON OVER LEFT HARPOON
21CD	⇍	LEFT DOUBLE ARROW WITH STROKE
21CE	⇎	LEFT RIGHT DOUBLE ARROW WITH STROKE
21CF	⇏	RIGHT DOUBLE ARROW WITH STROKE
21D0	⇐	LEFT DOUBLE ARROW
21D1	⇑	UP DOUBLE ARROW
21D2	⇒	RIGHT DOUBLE ARROW
21D3	⇓	DOWN DOUBLE ARROW
21D4	⇔	LEFT RIGHT DOUBLE ARROW
21D5	⇕	UP DOWN DOUBLE ARROW
21D6	⇖	UPPER LEFT DOUBLE ARROW
21D7	⇗	UPPER RIGHT DOUBLE ARROW
21D8	⇘	LOWER RIGHT DOUBLE ARROW
21D9	⇙	LOWER LEFT DOUBLE ARROW
21DA	⇚	LEFT TRIPLE ARROW
21DB	⇛	RIGHT TRIPLE ARROW
21DC	⇜	LEFT SQUIGGLE ARROW
21DD	⇝	RIGHT SQUIGGLE ARROW
21DE	⇞	UP ARROW WITH DOUBLE STROKE
		= page up
21DF	⇟	DOWN ARROW WITH DOUBLE STROKE
		= page down
21E0	⇠	LEFT DASHED ARROW
21E1	⇡	UP DASHED ARROW

21E2	⇢	RIGHT DASHED ARROW
21E3	⇣	DOWN DASHED ARROW
21E4	⇤	LEFT ARROW TO BAR
		= *leftward tab*
21E5	⇥	RIGHT ARROW TO BAR
		= *rightward tab*
21E6	⇦	WHITE LEFT ARROW
21E7	⇧	WHITE UP ARROW
		= *shift*
21E8	⇨	WHITE RIGHT ARROW
21E9	⇩	WHITE DOWN ARROW
21EA	⇪	WHITE UP ARROW FROM BAR
		= *caps lock*

	220	221	222	223	224	225	226	227
0	∀	∐	∠	∰	≀	≐	≠	≮
1	∁	∑	∡	∱	≁	∻	≡	≯
2	∂	−	∢	∲	≂	≒	≢	≰
3	∃	∓	∣	∳	≃	≓	≣	≱
4	∄	∔	∤	∴	≄	≔	≤	≲
5	∅	∕	∥	∵	≅	≕	≥	≳
6	∆	∖	∦	∶	≆	≖	≦	≴
7	∇	∗	∧	∷	≇	≗	≧	≵
8	∈	∘	∨	∸	≈	≘	≨	≶
9	∉	∙	∩	∹	≉	≙	≩	≷
A	∊	√	∪	∺	≊	≚	≪	≸
B	∋	∛	∫	∻	≋	≛	≫	≹
C	∌	∜	∬	∼	≌	≜	◊	≺
D	∍	∝	∭	∽	≍	≝	≭	≻
E	∎	∞	∮	∾	≎	≞	≮	≼
F	∏	∟	∯	∿	≏	≟	≯	≽

	228	229	22A	22B	22C	22D	22E	22F
0	⊀	⊐	⊠	⋋	⋀	⋐	⋠	⋰
1	⊁	⊑	⊡	⋌	⋁	⋑	⋡	⋱
2	⊂	⊒	⊢	⊲	⋂	⋒	⋢	
3	⊃	⊓	⊣	⊳	⋃	⋓	⋣	
4	⊄	⊔	⊤	⊴	⋄	⋔	⋤	
5	⊅	⊕	⊥	⊵	⋅	⋕	⋥	
6	⊆	⊖	⊦	⊶	⋆	⋖	⋦	
7	⊇	⊗	⊧	⊷	⋇	⋗	⋧	
8	⊈	⊘	⊨	⊸	⋈	⋘	⋨	
9	⊉	⊙	⊩	⊹	⋉	⋙	⋩	
A	⊊	⊚	⊪	⊺	⋊	⋚	⋪	
B	⊋	⊛	⊫	⊻	⋋	⋛	⋫	
C	⊌	⊜	⊬	⊼	⋌	⋜	⋬	
D	⊍	⊝	⊭	⊽	⋍	⋝	⋭	
E	⊎	⊞	⊮	⊾	⋎	⋞	⋮	
F	⊏	⊟	⊯	⊿	⋏	⋟	⋯	

Mathematical operators

2200	∀	FOR ALL
2201	∁	COMPLEMENT
		× (latin letter stretched c → 0297)
2202	∂	PARTIAL DIFFERENTIAL
2203	∃	THERE EXISTS
2204	∄	THERE DOES NOT EXIST
2205	∅	EMPTY SET
		= null set
		= diameter symbol
		× (latin capital letter o slash → 00D8)
2206	Δ	INCREMENT
		= Laplace operator
		= forward difference
		× (greek capital letter delta → 0394)
		× (white up pointing triangle → 25B3)
2207	∇	NABLA
		= Laplace operator (written with superscript 2)
		= backward difference
		= del
		× (white down pointing triangle → 25BD)
2208	∈	ELEMENT OF
2209	∉	NOT AN ELEMENT OF
220A	∊	SMALL ELEMENT OF
220B	∋	CONTAINS AS MEMBER
		= such that
220C	∌	DOES NOT CONTAIN AS MEMBER
220D	∍	SMALL CONTAINS AS MEMBER
220E	∎	END OF PROOF
		= qed
		× (triangular bullet → 2023)
220F	∏	N-ARY PRODUCT
		= product sign
		× (greek capital letter pi → 03A0)
2210	∐	N-ARY COPRODUCT
		= coproduct sign
2211	∑	N-ARY SUMMATION
		= summation sign
		× (greek capital letter sigma → 03A3)
2212	−	MINUS SIGN
		× (hyphen-minus → 002D)
2213	∓	MINUS-OR-PLUS SIGN
		× (plus-or-minus sign → 00B1)
2214	∔	DOT PLUS
2215	∕	DIVISION SLASH
		generic division operator
		× (slash → 002F)
		× (fraction slash → 2044)
2216	∖	SET MINUS
		= ISO SHORT BACKWARD DIAGONAL
		× (backslash → 005C)

2217	∗	ASTERISK OPERATOR
		× (asterisk → 002A)
2218	∘	RING OPERATOR
		= composite function
		= APL jot
		× (degree sign → 00B0)
		× (white bullet → 25E6)
2219	∙	BULLET OPERATOR
		× (middle dot → 00B7)
		× (bullet → 2022)
		× (one dot leader → 2024)
221A	√	SQUARE ROOT
		= radical sign
		× (check mark → 2713)
221B	∛	CUBE ROOT
221C	∜	FOURTH ROOT
221D	∝	PROPORTIONAL TO
		× (greek small letter alpha → 03B1)
221E	∞	INFINITY
221F	∟	RIGHT ANGLE
2220	∠	ANGLE
2221	∡	MEASURED ANGLE
2222	∢	SPHERICAL ANGLE
		= angle arc
2223	∣	DIVIDES
		= such that
		= APL stile
		× (vertical bar → 007C)
		× (latin letter pipe → 01C0)
2224	∤	DOES NOT DIVIDE
2225	∥	PARALLEL TO
		× (latin letter double pipe → 01C1)
		× (double vertical bar → 2016)
2226	∦	NOT PARALLEL TO
2227	∧	LOGICAL AND
		= wedge
2228	∨	LOGICAL OR
		= vee
2229	∩	INTERSECTION
		= cap
222A	∪	UNION
		= cup
222B	∫	INTEGRAL
		× (latin small letter esh → 0283)
222C	∬	DOUBLE INTEGRAL
222D	∭	TRIPLE INTEGRAL
222E	∮	CONTOUR INTEGRAL
222F	∯	SURFACE INTEGRAL
2230	∰	VOLUME INTEGRAL
2231	∱	CLOCKWISE INTEGRAL
2232	∲	CLOCKWISE CONTOUR INTEGRAL
2233	∳	ANTICLOCKWISE CONTOUR INTEGRAL

2234	∴	THEREFORE
2235	∵	BECAUSE
2236	:	RATIO
		✕ *(colon → 003A)*
2237	∷	PROPORTION
2238	∸	DOT MINUS
		= *symmetric difference*
2239	-:	EXCESS
223A	∺	GEOMETRIC PROPORTION
223B	∻	HOMOTHETIC
223C	∼	TILDE OPERATOR
		= *varies with (proportional to)*
		= *difference between*
		= *similar to*
		= *APL tilde*
		= *cycle*
		= *not*
		✕ *(tilde → 007E)*
		✕ *(spacing tilde → 02DC)*
223D	∽	REVERSED TILDE
		= *lazy S*
		reversed tilde and lazy S are glyph variants
223E	∾	INVERTED LAZY S
		= *most positive*
223F	∿	SINE WAVE
		= *alternating current*
2240	≀	WREATH PRODUCT
2241	≁	NOT TILDE
2242	≂	MINUS TILDE
2243	≃	ASYMPTOTICALLY EQUAL TO
2244	≄	NOT ASYMPTOTICALLY EQUAL TO
2245	≅	APPROXIMATELY EQUAL TO
2246	≆	APPROXIMATELY BUT NOT ACTUALLY EQUAL TO
2247	≇	NEITHER APPROXIMATELY NOR ACTUALLY EQUAL TO
2248	≈	ALMOST EQUAL TO
		= *asymptotic to*
2249	≉	NOT ALMOST EQUAL TO
224A	≊	ALMOST EQUAL OR EQUAL TO
224B	≋	TRIPLE TILDE
224C	≌	ALL EQUAL TO
		reversed tilde and lazy S are glyph variants
224D	≍	EQUIVALENT TO
224E	≎	GEOMETRICALLY EQUIVALENT TO
224F	≏	DIFFERENCE BETWEEN
2250	≐	APPROACHES THE LIMIT
2251	≑	GEOMETRICALLY EQUAL TO

2252	≒	APPROXIMATELY EQUAL TO OR THE IMAGE OF
		= *nearly equals*
2253	≓	IMAGE OF OR APPROXIMATELY EQUAL TO
2254	≔	COLON EQUAL
2255	≕	EQUAL COLON
2256	≖	RING IN EQUAL TO
2257	≗	RING EQUAL TO
		= *approximately equal to*
2258	≘	CORRESPONDS TO
2259	≙	ESTIMATES
		= *corresponds to*
225A	≚	EQUIANGULAR TO
225B	≛	STAR EQUALS
225C	≜	DELTA EQUAL TO
		= *equiangular*
		= *equal to by definition*
225D	≝	EQUAL TO BY DEFINITION
225E	≞	MEASURED BY
225F	≟	QUESTIONED EQUAL TO
2260	≠	NOT EQUAL TO
		✕ *(equals sign → 003D)*
		✕ *(latin letter pipe double bar → 01C2)*
2261	≡	IDENTICAL TO
2262	≢	NOT IDENTICAL TO
2263	≣	STRICTLY EQUIVALENT TO
2264	≤	LESS THAN OR EQUAL TO
2265	≥	GREATER THAN OR EQUAL TO
2266	≦	LESS THAN OVER EQUAL TO
2267	≧	GREATER THAN OVER EQUAL TO
2268	≨	LESS THAN BUT NOT EQUAL TO
2269	≩	GREATER THAN BUT NOT EQUAL TO
226A	≪	MUCH LESS THAN
		✕ *(left pointing guillemet → 00AB)*
226B	≫	MUCH GREATER THAN
		✕ *(right pointing guillemet → 00BB)*
226C	≬	BETWEEN
		= *plaintiff*
		= *quantic*
226D	≭	NOT EQUIVALENT TO
226E	≮	NOT LESS THAN
226F	≯	NOT GREATER THAN
2270	≰	NEITHER LESS THAN NOR EQUAL TO
2271	≱	NEITHER GREATER THAN NOR EQUAL TO
2272	≲	LESS THAN OR EQUIVALENT TO
2273	≳	GREATER THAN OR EQUIVALENT TO
2274	≴	NEITHER LESS THAN NOR EQUIVALENT TO
2275	≵	NEITHER GREATER THAN NOR EQUIVALENT TO

2276	≶	LESS THAN OR GREATER THAN
2277	≷	GREATER THAN OR LESS THAN
2278	≸	NEITHER LESS THAN NOR GREATER THAN
2279	≹	NEITHER GREATER THAN NOR LESS THAN
227A	≺	PRECEDES
		= *lower rank than*
		× *(precedes under relation → 22B0)*
227B	≻	SUCCEEDS
		= *higher rank than*
		× *(succeeds under relation → 22B1)*
227C	≼	PRECEDES OR EQUAL TO
227D	≽	SUCCEEDS OR EQUAL TO
227E	≾	PRECEDES OR EQUIVALENT TO
227F	≿	SUCCEEDS OR EQUIVALENT TO
2280	⊀	DOES NOT PRECEDE
2281	⊁	DOES NOT SUCCEED
2282	⊂	SUBSET OF
2283	⊃	SUPERSET OF
2284	⊄	NOT A SUBSET OF
2285	⊅	NOT A SUPERSET OF
2286	⊆	SUBSET OF OR EQUAL TO
2287	⊇	SUPERSET OF OR EQUAL TO
2288	⊈	NEITHER A SUBSET OF NOR EQUAL TO
2289	⊉	NEITHER A SUPERSET OF NOR EQUAL TO
228A	⊊	SUBSET OF OR NOT EQUAL TO
228B	⊋	SUPERSET OF OR NOT EQUAL TO
228C	⊌	MULTISET
228D	⊍	MULTISET MULTIPLICATION
228E	⊎	MULTISET UNION
228F	⊏	SQUARE IMAGE OF
2290	⊐	SQUARE ORIGINAL OF
2291	⊑	SQUARE IMAGE OF OR EQUAL TO
2292	⊒	SQUARE ORIGINAL OF OR EQUAL TO
2293	⊓	SQUARE CAP
2294	⊔	SQUARE CUP
2295	⊕	CIRCLED PLUS
		= *direct sum*
		= *vector pointing into page*
		× *(earth → 2641)*
2296	⊖	CIRCLED MINUS
		= *symmetric difference*
2297	⊗	CIRCLED TIMES
		= *tensor product*
		= *vector pointing into page*
2298	⊘	CIRCLED DIVISION SLASH
2299	⊙	CIRCLED DOT OPERATOR
		= *direct product*
		= *vector pointing out of page*
		× *(latin letter bullseye → 0298)*
		× *(sun → 2609)*

229A	⊚	CIRCLED RING OPERATOR
		× *(bullseye → 25CE)*
229B	⊛	CIRCLED ASTERISK OPERATOR
229C	⊜	CIRCLED EQUALS
229D	⊝	CIRCLED DASH
229E	⊞	SQUARED PLUS
229F	⊟	SQUARED MINUS
22A0	⊠	SQUARED TIMES
		× *(ballot box with x → 2612)*
22A1	⊡	SQUARED DOT OPERATOR
22A2	⊢	RIGHT TACK
		= *turnstile*
		= *proves, implies, yields*
		= *reducible*
22A3	⊣	LEFT TACK
		= *reverse turnstile*
		= *non-theorem, does not yield*
22A4	⊤	DOWN TACK
22A5	⊥	UP TACK
		= *orthogonal to*
		= *perpendicular*
		APL and other uses
22A6	⊦	ASSERTION
		= *reduces to*
22A7	⊧	MODELS
22A8	⊨	TRUE
		= *statement is true, valid*
		= *is a tautology*
		= *satisfies*
		= *results in*
22A9	⊩	FORCES
22AA	⊪	TRIPLE VERTICAL BAR RIGHT TURNSTILE
22AB	⊫	DOUBLE VERTICAL BAR DOUBLE RIGHT TURNSTILE
22AC	⊬	DOES NOT PROVE
22AD	⊭	NOT TRUE
22AE	⊮	DOES NOT FORCE
22AF	⊯	NEGATED DOUBLE VERTICAL BAR DOUBLE RIGHT TURNSTILE
22B0	⊰	PRECEDES UNDER RELATION
		× *(precedes → 227A)*
22B1	⊱	SUCCEEDS UNDER RELATION
		× *(succeeds → 227B)*
22B2	⊲	NORMAL SUBGROUP OF
22B3	⊳	CONTAINS AS NORMAL SUBGROUP
22B4	⊴	NORMAL SUBGROUP OF OR EQUAL TO
22B5	⊵	CONTAINS AS NORMAL SUBGROUP OR EQUAL TO
22B6	⊶	ORIGINAL OF
22B7	⊷	IMAGE OF
22B8	⊸	MULTIMAP

22B9	⊹	HERMITIAN CONJUGATE MATRIX
22BA	⊺	INTERCALATE
22BB	⊻	XOR
22BC	⊼	NAND
22BD	⊽	NOR
22BE	⊾	RIGHT ANGLE WITH ARC
22BF	⊿	RIGHT TRIANGLE
22C0	⋀	N-ARY LOGICAL AND
22C1	⋁	N-ARY LOGICAL OR
22C2	⋂	N-ARY INTERSECTION
22C3	⋃	N-ARY UNION
22C4	⋄	DIAMOND OPERATOR

× (*white diamond* → 25C7)

22C5	⋅	DOT OPERATOR

× (*middle dot* → 00B7)

22C6	⋆	STAR OPERATOR

     APL
     × (*black star* → 2605)

22C7	⋇	DIVISION TIMES
22C8	⋈	BOWTIE

× (*ocr bow tie* → 2445)

22C9	⋉	LEFT NORMAL FACTOR SEMIDIRECT PRODUCT
22CA	⋊	RIGHT NORMAL FACTOR SEMIDIRECT PRODUCT
22CB	⋋	LEFT SEMIDIRECT PRODUCT
22CC	⋌	RIGHT SEMIDIRECT PRODUCT

× (*caret insertion point* → 2041)

22CD	⋍	REVERSED TILDE EQUALS
22CE	⋎	CURLY LOGICAL OR
22CF	⋏	CURLY LOGICAL AND
22D0	⋐	DOUBLE SUBSET
22D1	⋑	DOUBLE SUPERSET
22D2	⋒	DOUBLE INTERSECTION
22D3	⋓	DOUBLE UNION
22D4	⋔	PITCHFORK

     = *proper intersection*

22D5	⋕	EQUAL AND PARALLEL TO

× (*viewdata square* → 2317)

22D6	⋖	LESS THAN WITH DOT
22D7	⋗	GREATER THAN WITH DOT
22D8	⋘	VERY MUCH LESS THAN
22D9	⋙	VERY MUCH GREATER THAN
22DA	⋚	LESS THAN EQUAL TO OR GREATER THAN
22DB	⋛	GREATER THAN EQUAL TO OR LESS THAN
22DC	⋜	EQUAL TO OR LESS THAN
22DD	⋝	EQUAL TO OR GREATER THAN
22DE	⋞	EQUAL TO OR PRECEDES
22DF	⋟	EQUAL TO OR SUCCEEDS

22E0	⋠	DOES NOT PRECEDE OR EQUAL
22E1	⋡	DOES NOT SUCCEED OR EQUAL
22E2	⋢	NOT SQUARE IMAGE OF OR EQUAL TO
22E3	⋣	NOT SQUARE ORIGINAL OF OR EQUAL TO
22E4	⋤	SQUARE IMAGE OF OR NOT EQUAL TO
22E5	⋥	SQUARE ORIGINAL OF OR NOT EQUAL TO
22E6	⋦	LESS THAN BUT NOT EQUIVALENT TO
22E7	⋧	GREATER THAN BUT NOT EQUIVALENT TO
22E8	⋨	PRECEDES BUT NOT EQUIVALENT TO
22E9	⋩	SUCCEEDS BUT NOT EQUIVALENT TO
22EA	⋪	NOT NORMAL SUBGROUP OF
22EB	⋫	DOES NOT CONTAIN AS NORMAL SUBGROUP
22EC	⋬	NOT NORMAL SUBGROUP OF OR EQUAL TO
22ED	⋭	DOES NOT CONTAIN AS NORMAL SUBGROUP OR EQUAL
22EE	⋮	VERTICAL ELLIPSIS

     these four ellipses are used for matrix row/column ellision
     × (*horizontal ellipsis* → 2026)

22EF	⋯	MIDLINE HORIZONTAL ELLIPSIS
22F0	⋰	UP RIGHT DIAGONAL ELLIPSIS
22F1	⋱	DOWN RIGHT DIAGONAL ELLIPSIS

	230	231	232	233	234	235	236	237	238
0	APL COMPOSE	⌐	∫						
1	⑪	⌑	⌡						
2	⌂	⌒	⌢						
3	⌃	⌓	⌣						
4	⌄	⌔	⌤						
5	⌅	⌕	⌥						
6	⌆	⌖	⌦						
7	⌇	⌗	⌧						
8	⌈	⌘	⌨						
9	⌉	⌊	〈						
A	⌊	⌚	〉						
B	⌋	⌛	⌫						
C	⌐	⌌	⬡						
D	⌍	⌎							
E	⌎	⌏							
F	⌏	⌐							

Miscellaneous technical

2300	APL COMPOSE	APL COMPOSE OPERATOR
2301	𝕀𝕀	APL OUT
2302	⌂	HOUSE
2303	^	UP ARROWHEAD

    × (spacing circumflex → 005E)
    × (modifier letter up arrowhead → 02C4)

2304	∨	DOWN ARROWHEAD
2305	⊼	PROJECTIVE
2306	⊼̄	PERSPECTIVE
2307	∿	WAVY LINE

    × (wavy dash → 3030)

2308	⌈	LEFT CEILING

    = APL upstile

2309	⌉	RIGHT CEILING
230A	⌊	LEFT FLOOR

    = APL downstile

230B	⌋	RIGHT FLOOR
230C	⌐	BOTTOM RIGHT CROP

    set of four "crop" corners, arranged facing outward

230D	⌐	BOTTOM LEFT CROP
230E	∟	TOP RIGHT CROP
230F	⌐	TOP LEFT CROP
2310	⌐	REVERSED NOT SIGN

    = beginning of line
    × (not sign → 00AC)

2311	⌑	SQUARE LOZENGE
2312	⌒	ARC
2313	⌓	SEGMENT
2314	⌔	SECTOR
2315	⌕	TELEPHONE RECORDER
2316	⌖	POSITION INDICATOR
2317	⌗	VIEWDATA SQUARE

    × (equal and parallel to → 22D5)

2318	⌘	COMMAND KEY

    = point of interest

2319	⌙	TURNED NOT SIGN

    = line marker

231A	⌚	WATCH
231B	⌛	HOURGLASS
231C	⌜	TOP LEFT CORNER

    set of four "quine" corners, for quincuncial arrangement

231D	⌝	TOP RIGHT CORNER
231E	⌞	BOTTOM LEFT CORNER
231F	⌟	BOTTOM RIGHT CORNER
2320	⌠	TOP HALF INTEGRAL
2321	⌡	BOTTOM HALF INTEGRAL

2322	⌢	FROWN
2323	⌣	SMILE
2324	⌤	ENTER KEY
2325	⌥	OPTION KEY
2326	⌦	DELETE TO THE RIGHT KEY
2327	⌧	CLEAR KEY
2328	⌨	KEYBOARD
2329	〈	BRA

    = ISO LEFT-POINTING ANGLE BRACKET
    × (less-than sign → 003C)
    × (left pointing single guillemet → 2039)
    × (opening angle bracket → 3008)

232A	〉	KET

    = ISO RIGHT-POINTING ANGLE BRACKET
    × (greater-than sign → 003E)
    × (right pointing single guillemet → 203A)
    × (closing angle bracket → 3009)

232B	⌫	DELETE TO THE LEFT KEY
232C	⬡	BENZENE RING

	240	241	242	243
0	NUL	DLE	SP	
1	SOH	DC1	DEL	
2	STX	DC2	ƀ	
3	ETX	DC3	⌴	
4	EOT	DC4	NL	
5	ENQ	NAK		
6	ACK	SYN		
7	BEL	ETB		
8	BS	CAN		
9	HT	EM		
A	LF	SUB		
B	VT	ESC		
C	FF	FS		
D	CR	GS		
E	SO	RS		
F	SI	US		

Graphic pictures for control codes

2400	NUL	GRAPHIC FOR NULL
2401	SOH	GRAPHIC FOR START OF HEADING
2402	STX	GRAPHIC FOR START OF TEXT
2403	ETX	GRAPHIC FOR END OF TEXT
2404	EOT	GRAPHIC FOR END OF TRANSMISSION
2405	ENQ	GRAPHIC FOR ENQUIRY
2406	ACK	GRAPHIC FOR ACKNOWLEDGE
2407	BEL	GRAPHIC FOR BELL
2408	BS	GRAPHIC FOR BACKSPACE
2409	HT	GRAPHIC FOR HORIZONTAL TABULATION
240A	LF	GRAPHIC FOR LINE FEED
240B	VT	GRAPHIC FOR VERTICAL TABULATION
240C	FF	GRAPHIC FOR FORM FEED
240D	CR	GRAPHIC FOR CARRIAGE RETURN
240E	SO	GRAPHIC FOR SHIFT OUT
240F	SI	GRAPHIC FOR SHIFT IN
2410	DLE	GRAPHIC FOR DATA LINK ESCAPE
2411	DC1	GRAPHIC FOR DEVICE CONTROL ONE
2412	DC2	GRAPHIC FOR DEVICE CONTROL TWO
2413	DC3	GRAPHIC FOR DEVICE CONTROL THREE
2414	DC4	GRAPHIC FOR DEVICE CONTROL FOUR
2415	NAK	GRAPHIC FOR NEGATIVE ACKNOWLEDGE
2416	SYN	GRAPHIC FOR SYNCHRONOUS IDLE
2417	ETB	GRAPHIC FOR END OF TRANSMISSION BLOCK
2418	CAN	GRAPHIC FOR CANCEL
2419	EM	GRAPHIC FOR END OF MEDIUM
241A	SUB	GRAPHIC FOR SUBSTITUTE
241B	ESC	GRAPHIC FOR ESCAPE
241C	FS	GRAPHIC FOR FILE SEPARATOR
241D	GS	GRAPHIC FOR GROUP SEPARATOR
241E	RS	GRAPHIC FOR RECORD SEPARATOR
241F	US	GRAPHIC FOR UNIT SEPARATOR
2420	SP	GRAPHIC FOR SPACE
2421	DEL	GRAPHIC FOR DELETE
2422	ƀ	BLANK

         graphic for space
         × *(latin small letter b bar → 0180)*

2423	␣	OPEN BOX

         graphic for space

2424	NL	GRAPHIC FOR NEWLINE

	244	245
0	⌐⌐	
1	⊣⌐	
2	⊔	
3	⊓	
4	⊔⊓	
5	⋈	
6	⁞	
7	⁞	
8	⁞	
9	⦀	
A	╱╱	
B		
C		
D		
E		
F		

OCR

2440	⌡	OCR HOOK
2441	⌐|	OCR CHAIR
2442	Ч	OCR FORK
2443	⌐⌐	OCR INVERTED FORK
2444	⊥⊤	OCR BELT BUCKLE
2445	⋈	OCR BOW TIE

　　　　× (bowtie → 22C8)

2446	ⵏ	OCR BRANCH BANK IDENTIFICATION

　　　　= transit

2447	ı⸍	OCR AMOUNT OF CHECK
2448	ıı⸍	OCR DASH

　　　　= on us

2449	ııı	OCR CUSTOMER ACCOUNT NUMBER

　　　　= dash

244A	⧵⧵	OCR DOUBLE BACKSLASH

	246	247	248	249	24A	24B	24C	24D	24E	24F
0	①	⑰	⒀	9.	(e)	(u)	Ⓚ	ⓐ	ⓠ	
1	②	⑱	⒁	10.	(f)	(v)	Ⓛ	ⓑ	ⓡ	
2	③	⑲	⒂	11.	(g)	(w)	Ⓜ	ⓒ	ⓢ	
3	④	⑳	⒃	12.	(h)	(x)	Ⓝ	ⓓ	ⓣ	
4	⑤	(1)	⒄	13.	(i)	(y)	Ⓞ	ⓔ	ⓤ	
5	⑥	(2)	⒅	14.	(j)	(z)	Ⓟ	ⓕ	ⓥ	
6	⑦	(3)	⒆	15.	(k)	Ⓐ	Ⓠ	ⓖ	ⓦ	
7	⑧	(4)	⒇	16.	(l)	Ⓑ	Ⓡ	ⓗ	ⓧ	
8	⑨	(5)	1.	17.	(m)	Ⓒ	Ⓢ	ⓘ	ⓨ	
9	⑩	(6)	2.	18.	(n)	Ⓓ	Ⓣ	ⓙ	ⓩ	
A	⑪	(7)	3.	19.	(o)	Ⓔ	Ⓤ	ⓚ	⓪	
B	⑫	(8)	4.	20.	(p)	Ⓕ	Ⓥ	ⓛ		
C	⑬	(9)	5.	(a)	(q)	Ⓖ	Ⓦ	ⓜ		
D	⑭	(10)	6.	(b)	(r)	Ⓗ	Ⓧ	ⓝ		
E	⑮	(11)	7.	(c)	(s)	Ⓘ	Ⓨ	ⓞ		
F	⑯	(12)	8.	(d)	(t)	Ⓙ	Ⓩ	ⓟ		

Circled numbers

2460	①	CIRCLED DIGIT ONE
2461	②	CIRCLED DIGIT TWO
2462	③	CIRCLED DIGIT THREE
2463	④	CIRCLED DIGIT FOUR
2464	⑤	CIRCLED DIGIT FIVE
2465	⑥	CIRCLED DIGIT SIX
2466	⑦	CIRCLED DIGIT SEVEN
2467	⑧	CIRCLED DIGIT EIGHT
2468	⑨	CIRCLED DIGIT NINE
2469	⑩	CIRCLED NUMBER TEN
246A	⑪	CIRCLED NUMBER ELEVEN
246B	⑫	CIRCLED NUMBER TWELVE
246C	⑬	CIRCLED NUMBER THIRTEEN
246D	⑭	CIRCLED NUMBER FOURTEEN
246E	⑮	CIRCLED NUMBER FIFTEEN
246F	⑯	CIRCLED NUMBER SIXTEEN
2470	⑰	CIRCLED NUMBER SEVENTEEN
2471	⑱	CIRCLED NUMBER EIGHTEEN
2472	⑲	CIRCLED NUMBER NINETEEN
2473	⑳	CIRCLED NUMBER TWENTY

Parenthesized numbers

2474	(1)	PARENTHESIZED DIGIT ONE
2475	(2)	PARENTHESIZED DIGIT TWO
2476	(3)	PARENTHESIZED DIGIT THREE
2477	(4)	PARENTHESIZED DIGIT FOUR
2478	(5)	PARENTHESIZED DIGIT FIVE
2479	(6)	PARENTHESIZED DIGIT SIX
247A	(7)	PARENTHESIZED DIGIT SEVEN
247B	(8)	PARENTHESIZED DIGIT EIGHT
247C	(9)	PARENTHESIZED DIGIT NINE
247D	(10)	PARENTHESIZED NUMBER TEN
247E	(11)	PARENTHESIZED NUMBER ELEVEN
247F	(12)	PARENTHESIZED NUMBER TWELVE
2480	(13)	PARENTHESIZED NUMBER THIRTEEN
2481	(14)	PARENTHESIZED NUMBER FOURTEEN
2482	(15)	PARENTHESIZED NUMBER FIFTEEN
2483	(16)	PARENTHESIZED NUMBER SIXTEEN
2484	(17)	PARENTHESIZED NUMBER SEVENTEEN
2485	(18)	PARENTHESIZED NUMBER EIGHTEEN
2486	(19)	PARENTHESIZED NUMBER NINETEEN
2487	(20)	PARENTHESIZED NUMBER TWENTY

Numbers period

2488	1.	DIGIT ONE PERIOD
2489	2.	DIGIT TWO PERIOD
248A	3.	DIGIT THREE PERIOD
248B	4.	DIGIT FOUR PERIOD
248C	5.	DIGIT FIVE PERIOD
248D	6.	DIGIT SIX PERIOD
248E	7.	DIGIT SEVEN PERIOD
248F	8.	DIGIT EIGHT PERIOD
2490	9.	DIGIT NINE PERIOD
2491	10.	NUMBER TEN PERIOD
2492	11.	NUMBER ELEVEN PERIOD
2493	12.	NUMBER TWELVE PERIOD
2494	13.	NUMBER THIRTEEN PERIOD
2495	14.	NUMBER FOURTEEN PERIOD
2496	15.	NUMBER FIFTEEN PERIOD
2497	16.	NUMBER SIXTEEN PERIOD
2498	17.	NUMBER SEVENTEEN PERIOD
2499	18.	NUMBER EIGHTEEN PERIOD
249A	19.	NUMBER NINETEEN PERIOD
249B	20.	NUMBER TWENTY PERIOD

Parenthesized Latin letters

249C	(a)	PARENTHESIZED LATIN SMALL LETTER A
249D	(b)	PARENTHESIZED LATIN SMALL LETTER B
249E	(c)	PARENTHESIZED LATIN SMALL LETTER C
249F	(d)	PARENTHESIZED LATIN SMALL LETTER D
24A0	(e)	PARENTHESIZED LATIN SMALL LETTER E
24A1	(f)	PARENTHESIZED LATIN SMALL LETTER F
24A2	(g)	PARENTHESIZED LATIN SMALL LETTER G
24A3	(h)	PARENTHESIZED LATIN SMALL LETTER H
24A4	(i)	PARENTHESIZED LATIN SMALL LETTER I
24A5	(j)	PARENTHESIZED LATIN SMALL LETTER J
24A6	(k)	PARENTHESIZED LATIN SMALL LETTER K
24A7	(l)	PARENTHESIZED LATIN SMALL LETTER L
24A8	(m)	PARENTHESIZED LATIN SMALL LETTER M
24A9	(n)	PARENTHESIZED LATIN SMALL LETTER N
24AA	(o)	PARENTHESIZED LATIN SMALL LETTER O
24AB	(p)	PARENTHESIZED LATIN SMALL LETTER P
24AC	(q)	PARENTHESIZED LATIN SMALL LETTER Q
24AD	(r)	PARENTHESIZED LATIN SMALL LETTER R
24AE	(s)	PARENTHESIZED LATIN SMALL LETTER S
24AF	(t)	PARENTHESIZED LATIN SMALL LETTER T
24B0	(u)	PARENTHESIZED LATIN SMALL LETTER U
24B1	(v)	PARENTHESIZED LATIN SMALL LETTER V
24B2	(w)	PARENTHESIZED LATIN SMALL LETTER W

24B3 (x) PARENTHESIZED LATIN SMALL LETTER X
24B4 (y) PARENTHESIZED LATIN SMALL LETTER Y
24B5 (z) PARENTHESIZED LATIN SMALL LETTER Z

Circled Latin letters

24B6 Ⓐ CIRCLED LATIN CAPITAL LETTER A
24B7 Ⓑ CIRCLED LATIN CAPITAL LETTER B
24B8 Ⓒ CIRCLED LATIN CAPITAL LETTER C
24B9 Ⓓ CIRCLED LATIN CAPITAL LETTER D
24BA Ⓔ CIRCLED LATIN CAPITAL LETTER E
24BB Ⓕ CIRCLED LATIN CAPITAL LETTER F
24BC Ⓖ CIRCLED LATIN CAPITAL LETTER G
24BD Ⓗ CIRCLED LATIN CAPITAL LETTER H
24BE Ⓘ CIRCLED LATIN CAPITAL LETTER I
24BF Ⓙ CIRCLED LATIN CAPITAL LETTER J
24C0 Ⓚ CIRCLED LATIN CAPITAL LETTER K
24C1 Ⓛ CIRCLED LATIN CAPITAL LETTER L
24C2 Ⓜ CIRCLED LATIN CAPITAL LETTER M
24C3 Ⓝ CIRCLED LATIN CAPITAL LETTER N
24C4 Ⓞ CIRCLED LATIN CAPITAL LETTER O
24C5 Ⓟ CIRCLED LATIN CAPITAL LETTER P
24C6 Ⓠ CIRCLED LATIN CAPITAL LETTER Q
24C7 Ⓡ CIRCLED LATIN CAPITAL LETTER R
24C8 Ⓢ CIRCLED LATIN CAPITAL LETTER S
24C9 Ⓣ CIRCLED LATIN CAPITAL LETTER T
24CA Ⓤ CIRCLED LATIN CAPITAL LETTER U
24CB Ⓥ CIRCLED LATIN CAPITAL LETTER V
24CC Ⓦ CIRCLED LATIN CAPITAL LETTER W
24CD Ⓧ CIRCLED LATIN CAPITAL LETTER X
24CE Ⓨ CIRCLED LATIN CAPITAL LETTER Y
24CF Ⓩ CIRCLED LATIN CAPITAL LETTER Z
24D0 ⓐ CIRCLED LATIN SMALL LETTER A
24D1 ⓑ CIRCLED LATIN SMALL LETTER B
24D2 ⓒ CIRCLED LATIN SMALL LETTER C
24D3 ⓓ CIRCLED LATIN SMALL LETTER D
24D4 ⓔ CIRCLED LATIN SMALL LETTER E
24D5 ⓕ CIRCLED LATIN SMALL LETTER F
24D6 ⓖ CIRCLED LATIN SMALL LETTER G
24D7 ⓗ CIRCLED LATIN SMALL LETTER H
24D8 ⓘ CIRCLED LATIN SMALL LETTER I
24D9 ⓙ CIRCLED LATIN SMALL LETTER J
24DA ⓚ CIRCLED LATIN SMALL LETTER K
24DB ⓛ CIRCLED LATIN SMALL LETTER L
24DC ⓜ CIRCLED LATIN SMALL LETTER M
24DD ⓝ CIRCLED LATIN SMALL LETTER N
24DE ⓞ CIRCLED LATIN SMALL LETTER O

24DF ⓟ CIRCLED LATIN SMALL LETTER P
24E0 ⓠ CIRCLED LATIN SMALL LETTER Q
24E1 ⓡ CIRCLED LATIN SMALL LETTER R
24E2 ⓢ CIRCLED LATIN SMALL LETTER S
24E3 ⓣ CIRCLED LATIN SMALL LETTER T
24E4 ⓤ CIRCLED LATIN SMALL LETTER U
24E5 ⓥ CIRCLED LATIN SMALL LETTER V
24E6 ⓦ CIRCLED LATIN SMALL LETTER W
24E7 ⓧ CIRCLED LATIN SMALL LETTER X
24E8 ⓨ CIRCLED LATIN SMALL LETTER Y
24E9 ⓩ CIRCLED LATIN SMALL LETTER Z

Additional circled numbers

24EA ⓪ CIRCLED DIGIT ZERO

	250	251	252	253	254	255	256	257
0	─	┐	┠	┰	┼	═	╊	╰
1	━	┑	┡	┱	┿	║	╋	╱
2	│	┒	┢	┲	╀	╒	╌	╲
3	┃	┓	┣	┳	╁	╓	╍	╳
4	┄	└	┤	┴	╂	╔	╤	╴
5	┅	┕	┥	┵	╃	╕	╥	╵
6	┆	┖	┦	┶	╄	╖	╦	╶
7	┇	┗	┧	┷	╅	╗	╧	╷
8	┈	┘	┨	┸	╆	╘	╨	╸
9	┉	┙	┩	┹	╇	╙	╩	╹
A	┊	┚	┪	┺	╈	╚	╪	╺
B	┋	┛	┫	┻	╉	╛	╫	╻
C	┌	├	┬	┼	╌	╜	╬	╼
D	┍	┝	┭	┽	╍	╝	╭	╽
E	┎	┞	┮	┾	╎	╞	╮	╾
F	┏	┠	┯	┿	╏	╟	╯	╿

Form and chart components

2500	—	FORMS LIGHT HORIZONTAL = *Videotex Mosaic DG 15*
2501	━	FORMS HEAVY HORIZONTAL
2502	│	FORMS LIGHT VERTICAL = *Videotex Mosaic DG 14*
2503	┃	FORMS HEAVY VERTICAL
2504	---	FORMS LIGHT TRIPLE DASH HORIZONTAL
2505	•••	FORMS HEAVY TRIPLE DASH HORIZONTAL
2506	┆	FORMS LIGHT TRIPLE DASH VERTICAL
2507	┇	FORMS HEAVY TRIPLE DASH VERTICAL
2508	····	FORMS LIGHT QUADRUPLE DASH HORIZONTAL
2509	····	FORMS HEAVY QUADRUPLE DASH HORIZONTAL
250A	┊	FORMS LIGHT QUADRUPLE DASH VERTICAL
250B	┋	FORMS HEAVY QUADRUPLE DASH VERTICAL
250C	┌	FORMS LIGHT DOWN AND RIGHT = *Videotex Mosaic DG 16*
250D	┍	FORMS DOWN LIGHT AND RIGHT HEAVY
250E	┎	FORMS DOWN HEAVY AND RIGHT LIGHT
250F	┏	FORMS HEAVY DOWN AND RIGHT
2510	┐	FORMS LIGHT DOWN AND LEFT = *Videotex Mosaic DG 17*
2511	┑	FORMS DOWN LIGHT AND LEFT HEAVY
2512	┒	FORMS DOWN HEAVY AND LEFT LIGHT
2513	┓	FORMS HEAVY DOWN AND LEFT
2514	└	FORMS LIGHT UP AND RIGHT = *Videotex Mosaic DG 18*
2515	┕	FORMS UP LIGHT AND RIGHT HEAVY
2516	┖	FORMS UP HEAVY AND RIGHT LIGHT
2517	┗	FORMS HEAVY UP AND RIGHT
2518	┘	FORMS LIGHT UP AND LEFT = *Videotex Mosaic DG 19*
2519	┙	FORMS UP LIGHT AND LEFT HEAVY
251A	┚	FORMS UP HEAVY AND LEFT LIGHT
251B	┛	FORMS HEAVY UP AND LEFT
251C	├	FORMS LIGHT VERTICAL AND RIGHT = *Videotex Mosaic DG 20*
251D	┝	FORMS VERTICAL LIGHT AND RIGHT HEAVY = *Videotex Mosaic DG 03*
251E	┞	FORMS UP HEAVY AND RIGHT DOWN LIGHT
251F	┟	FORMS DOWN HEAVY AND RIGHT UP LIGHT
2520	┠	FORMS VERTICAL HEAVY AND RIGHT LIGHT
2521	┡	FORMS DOWN LIGHT AND RIGHT UP HEAVY
2522	┢	FORMS UP LIGHT AND RIGHT DOWN HEAVY
2523	┣	FORMS HEAVY VERTICAL AND RIGHT
2524	┤	FORMS LIGHT VERTICAL AND LEFT = *Videotex Mosaic DG 21*
2525	┥	FORMS VERTICAL LIGHT AND LEFT HEAVY = *Videotex Mosaic DG 04*
2526	┦	FORMS UP HEAVY AND LEFT DOWN LIGHT
2527	┧	FORMS DOWN HEAVY AND LEFT UP LIGHT
2528	┨	FORMS VERTICAL HEAVY AND LEFT LIGHT
2529	┩	FORMS DOWN LIGHT AND LEFT UP HEAVY
252A	┪	FORMS UP LIGHT AND LEFT DOWN HEAVY
252B	┫	FORMS HEAVY VERTICAL AND LEFT
252C	┬	FORMS LIGHT DOWN AND HORIZONTAL = *Videotex Mosaic DG 22*
252D	┭	FORMS LEFT HEAVY AND RIGHT DOWN LIGHT
252E	┮	FORMS RIGHT HEAVY AND LEFT DOWN LIGHT
252F	┯	FORMS DOWN LIGHT AND HORIZONTAL HEAVY = *Videotex Mosaic DG 02*
2530	┰	FORMS DOWN HEAVY AND HORIZONTAL LIGHT
2531	┱	FORMS RIGHT LIGHT AND LEFT DOWN HEAVY
2532	┲	FORMS LEFT LIGHT AND RIGHT DOWN HEAVY
2533	┳	FORMS HEAVY DOWN AND HORIZONTAL
2534	┴	FORMS LIGHT UP AND HORIZONTAL = *Videotex Mosaic DG 23*
2535	┵	FORMS LEFT HEAVY AND RIGHT UP LIGHT
2536	┶	FORMS RIGHT HEAVY AND LEFT UP LIGHT
2537	┷	FORMS UP LIGHT AND HORIZONTAL HEAVY = *Videotex Mosaic DG 01*
2538	┸	FORMS UP HEAVY AND HORIZONTAL LIGHT
2539	┹	FORMS RIGHT LIGHT AND LEFT UP HEAVY
253A	┺	FORMS LEFT LIGHT AND RIGHT UP HEAVY
253B	┻	FORMS HEAVY UP AND HORIZONTAL
253C	┼	FORMS LIGHT VERTICAL AND HORIZONTAL = *Videotex Mosaic DG 24*
253D	┽	FORMS LEFT HEAVY AND RIGHT VERTICAL LIGHT
253E	┾	FORMS RIGHT HEAVY AND LEFT VERTICAL LIGHT
253F	┿	FORMS VERTICAL LIGHT AND HORIZONTAL HEAVY = *Videotex Mosaic DG 13*

2540	┿	FORMS UP HEAVY AND DOWN HORIZONTAL LIGHT
2541	┿	FORMS DOWN HEAVY AND UP HORIZONTAL LIGHT
2542	┿	FORMS VERTICAL HEAVY AND HORIZONTAL LIGHT
2543	┿	FORMS LEFT UP HEAVY AND RIGHT DOWN LIGHT
2544	┿	FORMS RIGHT UP HEAVY AND LEFT DOWN LIGHT
2545	┿	FORMS LEFT DOWN HEAVY AND RIGHT UP LIGHT
2546	┿	FORMS RIGHT DOWN HEAVY AND LEFT UP LIGHT
2547	┿	FORMS DOWN LIGHT AND UP HORIZONTAL HEAVY
2548	┿	FORMS UP LIGHT AND DOWN HORIZONTAL HEAVY
2549	┿	FORMS RIGHT LIGHT AND LEFT VERTICAL HEAVY
254A	┿	FORMS LEFT LIGHT AND RIGHT VERTICAL HEAVY
254B	╋	FORMS HEAVY VERTICAL AND HORIZONTAL
254C	╌	FORMS LIGHT DOUBLE DASH HORIZONTAL
254D	╍	FORMS HEAVY DOUBLE DASH HORIZONTAL
254E	╎	FORMS LIGHT DOUBLE DASH VERTICAL
254F	╏	FORMS HEAVY DOUBLE DASH VERTICAL
2550	═	FORMS DOUBLE HORIZONTAL
2551	║	FORMS DOUBLE VERTICAL
2552	╒	FORMS DOWN SINGLE AND RIGHT DOUBLE
2553	╓	FORMS DOWN DOUBLE AND RIGHT SINGLE
2554	╔	FORMS DOUBLE DOWN AND RIGHT
2555	╕	FORMS DOWN SINGLE AND LEFT DOUBLE
2556	╖	FORMS DOWN DOUBLE AND LEFT SINGLE
2557	╗	FORMS DOUBLE DOWN AND LEFT
2558	╘	FORMS UP SINGLE AND RIGHT DOUBLE
2559	╙	FORMS UP DOUBLE AND RIGHT SINGLE
255A	╚	FORMS DOUBLE UP AND RIGHT
255B	╛	FORMS UP SINGLE AND LEFT DOUBLE
255C	╜	FORMS UP DOUBLE AND LEFT SINGLE
255D	╝	FORMS DOUBLE UP AND LEFT
255E	╞	FORMS VERTICAL SINGLE AND RIGHT DOUBLE
255F	╟	FORMS VERTICAL DOUBLE AND RIGHT SINGLE
2560	╠	FORMS DOUBLE VERTICAL AND RIGHT
2561	╡	FORMS VERTICAL SINGLE AND LEFT DOUBLE
2562	╢	FORMS VERTICAL DOUBLE AND LEFT SINGLE
2563	╣	FORMS DOUBLE VERTICAL AND LEFT
2564	╤	FORMS DOWN SINGLE AND HORIZONTAL DOUBLE
2565	╥	FORMS DOWN DOUBLE AND HORIZONTAL SINGLE
2566	╦	FORMS DOUBLE DOWN AND HORIZONTAL
2567	╧	FORMS UP SINGLE AND HORIZONTAL DOUBLE
2568	╨	FORMS UP DOUBLE AND HORIZONTAL SINGLE
2569	╩	FORMS DOUBLE UP AND HORIZONTAL
256A	╪	FORMS VERTICAL SINGLE AND HORIZONTAL DOUBLE
256B	╫	FORMS VERTICAL DOUBLE AND HORIZONTAL SINGLE
256C	╬	FORMS DOUBLE VERTICAL AND HORIZONTAL
256D	╭	FORMS LIGHT ARC DOWN AND RIGHT
256E	╮	FORMS LIGHT ARC DOWN AND LEFT
256F	╯	FORMS LIGHT ARC UP AND LEFT
2570	╰	FORMS LIGHT ARC UP AND RIGHT
2571	╱	FORMS LIGHT DIAGONAL UPPER RIGHT TO LOWER LEFT = *ISO FORWARD DIAGONAL*
2572	╲	FORMS LIGHT DIAGONAL UPPER LEFT TO LOWER RIGHT = *ISO BACKWARD DIAGONAL*
2573	╳	FORMS LIGHT DIAGONAL CROSS
2574	╴	FORMS LIGHT LEFT
2575	╵	FORMS LIGHT UP
2576	╶	FORMS LIGHT RIGHT
2577	╷	FORMS LIGHT DOWN
2578	╸	FORMS HEAVY LEFT
2579	╹	FORMS HEAVY UP
257A	╺	FORMS HEAVY RIGHT
257B	╻	FORMS HEAVY DOWN
257C	╼	FORMS LIGHT LEFT AND HEAVY RIGHT
257D	╽	FORMS LIGHT UP AND HEAVY DOWN
257E	╾	FORMS HEAVY LEFT AND LIGHT RIGHT
257F	╿	FORMS HEAVY UP AND LIGHT DOWN

The Unicode Standard • Version 1.0

Blocks

2580	▄	UPPER HALF BLOCK
2581	▁	LOWER ONE EIGHTH BLOCK
2582	▂	LOWER ONE QUARTER BLOCK
2583	▃	LOWER THREE EIGHTHS BLOCK
2584	▄	LOWER HALF BLOCK
2585	▅	LOWER FIVE EIGHTHS BLOCK
2586	▆	LOWER THREE QUARTER BLOCK
2587	▇	LOWER SEVEN EIGHTHS BLOCK
2588	█	FULL BLOCK
		= solid
2589	▉	LEFT SEVEN EIGHTHS BLOCK
258A	▊	LEFT THREE QUARTER BLOCK
258B	▋	LEFT FIVE EIGHTHS BLOCK
258C	▌	LEFT HALF BLOCK
258D	▍	LEFT THREE EIGHTHS BLOCK
258E	▎	LEFT ONE QUARTER BLOCK
258F	▏	LEFT ONE EIGHTH BLOCK
2590	▐	RIGHT HALF BLOCK
2591	░	LIGHT SHADE
		25%
2592	▒	MEDIUM SHADE
		50%
2593	▓	DARK SHADE
		75%
2594	▔	UPPER ONE EIGHTH BLOCK
2595	▕	RIGHT ONE EIGHTH BLOCK

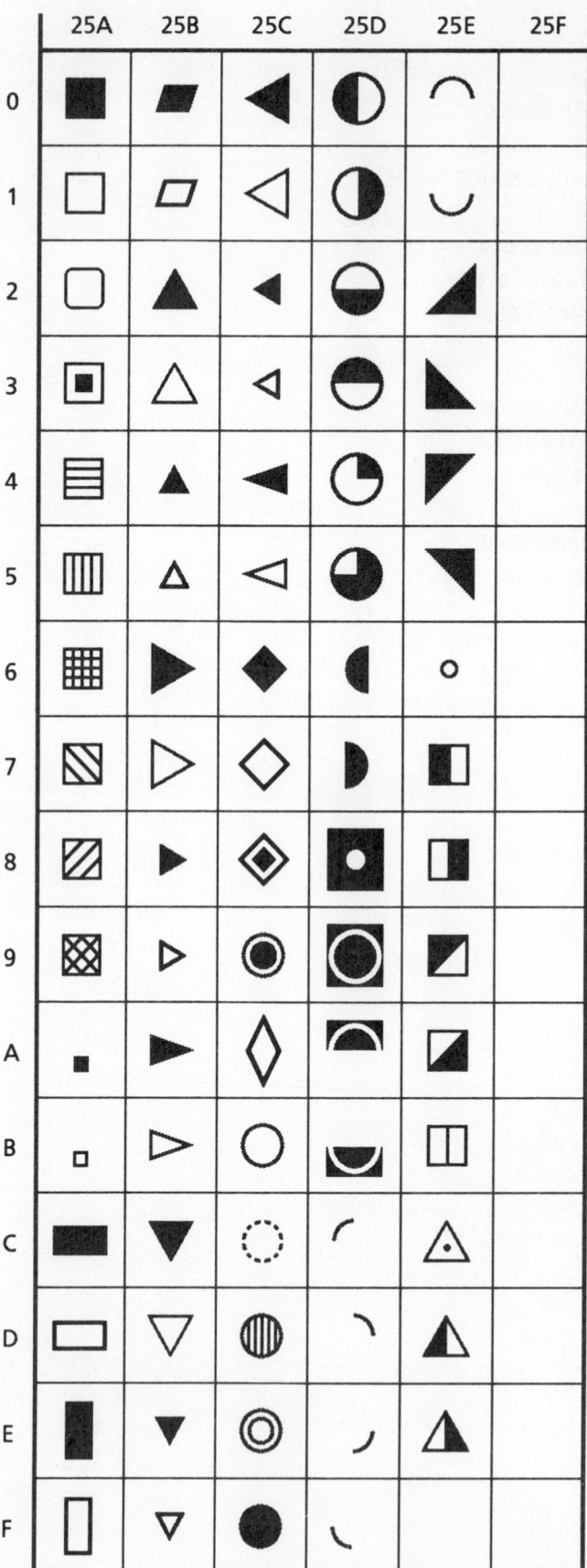

Geometric shapes

25A0	■	BLACK SQUARE
25A1	□	WHITE SQUARE
		= quadrature
		× (ballot box → 2610)
25A2	▢	WHITE SQUARE WITH ROUNDED CORNERS
25A3	▣	WHITE SQUARE CONTAINING BLACK SMALL SQUARE
25A4	▤	SQUARE WITH HORIZONTAL FILL
25A5	▥	SQUARE WITH VERTICAL FILL
25A6	▦	SQUARE WITH ORTHOGONAL CROSSHATCH FILL
25A7	▧	SQUARE WITH UPPER LEFT TO LOWER RIGHT FILL
25A8	▨	SQUARE WITH UPPER RIGHT TO LOWER LEFT FILL
25A9	▩	SQUARE WITH DIAGONAL CROSSHATCH FILL
25AA	▪	BLACK SMALL SQUARE
25AB	▫	WHITE SMALL SQUARE
25AC	▬	BLACK RECTANGLE
25AD	▭	WHITE RECTANGLE
25AE	▮	BLACK VERTICAL RECTANGLE
		= histogram marker
25AF	▯	WHITE VERTICAL RECTANGLE
		= APL quad
25B0	▰	BLACK PARALLELOGRAM
25B1	▱	WHITE PARALLELOGRAM
25B2	▲	BLACK UP POINTING TRIANGLE
25B3	△	WHITE UP POINTING TRIANGLE
		= trine
		× (increment → 2206)
25B4	▴	BLACK UP POINTING SMALL TRIANGLE
25B5	▵	WHITE UP POINTING SMALL TRIANGLE
25B6	▶	BLACK RIGHT POINTING TRIANGLE
25B7	▷	WHITE RIGHT POINTING TRIANGLE
25B8	▸	BLACK RIGHT POINTING SMALL TRIANGLE
		× (triangular bullet → 2023)
25B9	▹	WHITE RIGHT POINTING SMALL TRIANGLE
25BA	►	BLACK RIGHT POINTING POINTER
25BB	▻	WHITE RIGHT POINTING POINTER
		= forward arrow indicator
25BC	▼	BLACK DOWN POINTING TRIANGLE
25BD	▽	WHITE DOWN POINTING TRIANGLE
		× (nabla → 2207)
25BE	▾	BLACK DOWN POINTING SMALL TRIANGLE
25BF	▿	WHITE DOWN POINTING SMALL TRIANGLE
25C0	◀	BLACK LEFT POINTING TRIANGLE
25C1	◁	WHITE LEFT POINTING TRIANGLE
25C2	◂	BLACK LEFT POINTING SMALL TRIANGLE

25C3	◃	WHITE LEFT POINTING SMALL TRIANGLE
25C4	◄	BLACK LEFT POINTING POINTER
25C5	◅	WHITE LEFT POINTING POINTER
		= backward arrow indicator
25C6	◆	BLACK DIAMOND
		× (black diamond suit → 2666)
25C7	◇	WHITE DIAMOND
		× (diamond operator → 22C4)
		× (white diamond suit → 2662)
25C8	◈	WHITE DIAMOND CONTAINING BLACK SMALL DIAMOND
25C9	◉	FISHEYE
		= tainome (Japanese, a kind of bullet)
25CA	◊	LOZENGE
		× (white diamond suit → 2662)
25CB	○	WHITE CIRCLE
		× (enclosing circle → 20DD)
		× (ideographic number zero → 3007)
25CC	◌	DOTTED CIRCLE
25CD	◍	CIRCLE WITH VERTICAL FILL
25CE	◎	BULLSEYE
		× (circled ring operator → 229A)
25CF	●	BLACK CIRCLE
25D0	◐	CIRCLE WITH LEFT HALF BLACK
25D1	◑	CIRCLE WITH RIGHT HALF BLACK
25D2	◒	CIRCLE WITH LOWER HALF BLACK
25D3	◓	CIRCLE WITH UPPER HALF BLACK
25D4	◔	CIRCLE WITH UPPER RIGHT QUADRANT BLACK
25D5	◕	CIRCLE WITH ALL BUT UPPER LEFT QUADRANT BLACK
25D6	◖	LEFT HALF BLACK CIRCLE
25D7	◗	RIGHT HALF BLACK CIRCLE
25D8	◘	INVERSE BULLET
		× (bullet → 2022)
		× (white bullet → 25E6)
25D9	◙	INVERSE WHITE CIRCLE
25DA	◚	UPPER HALF INVERSE WHITE CIRCLE
25DB	◛	LOWER HALF INVERSE WHITE CIRCLE
25DC	◜	UPPER LEFT QUADRANT CIRCULAR ARC
25DD	◝	UPPER RIGHT QUADRANT CIRCULAR ARC
25DE	◞	LOWER RIGHT QUADRANT CIRCULAR ARC
25DF	◟	LOWER LEFT QUADRANT CIRCULAR ARC
25E0	◠	UPPER HALF CIRCLE
25E1	◡	LOWER HALF CIRCLE
25E2	◢	BLACK LOWER RIGHT TRIANGLE
25E3	◣	BLACK LOWER LEFT TRIANGLE
25E4	◤	BLACK UPPER LEFT TRIANGLE
25E5	◥	BLACK UPPER RIGHT TRIANGLE

25E6   ∘   WHITE BULLET
       ✕ *(bullet → 2022)*
       ✕ *(ring operator → 2218)*
       ✕ *(inverse bullet → 25D8)*

25E7   ◧   SQUARE WITH LEFT HALF BLACK

25E8   ◨   SQUARE WITH RIGHT HALF BLACK

25E9   ◩   SQUARE WITH UPPER LEFT DIAGONAL HALF BLACK

25EA   ◪   SQUARE WITH LOWER RIGHT DIAGONAL HALF BLACK

25EB   ▥   WHITE SQUARE WITH VERTICAL BISECTING LINE

25EC   △   WHITE UP POINTING TRIANGLE WITH DOT

25ED   ◮   UP POINTING TRIANGLE WITH LEFT HALF BLACK

25EE   ◭   UP POINTING TRIANGLE WITH RIGHT HALF BLACK

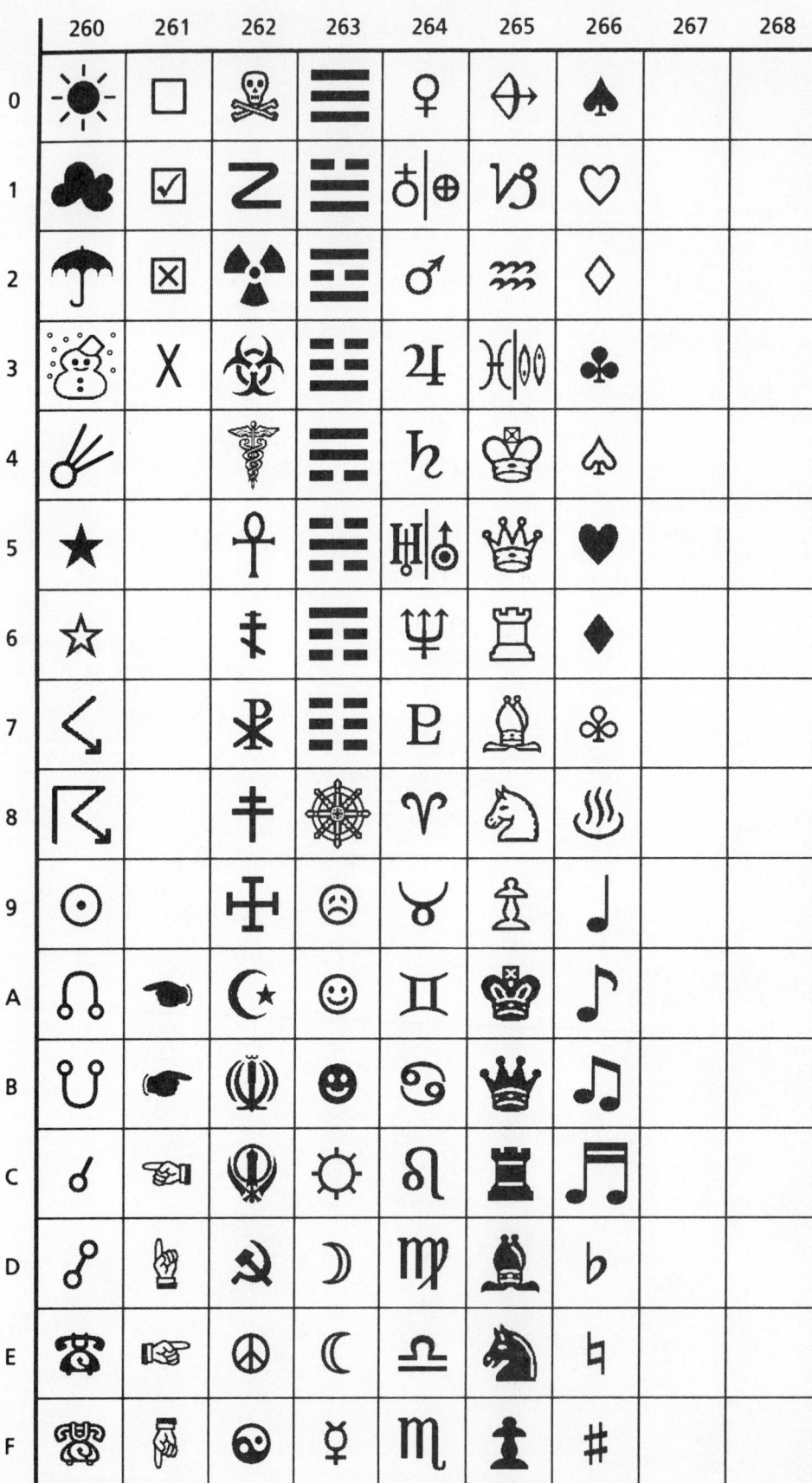

Miscellaneous dingbats

2600 ☀ BLACK SUN WITH RAYS
  = *clear weather*
  × *(sun → 2609)*

2601 ☁ CLOUD
  = *cloudy weather*

2602 ☂ UMBRELLA
  = *rainy weather*

2603 ☃ SNOWMAN
  = *snowy weather*

2604 ☄ COMET

2605 ★ BLACK STAR
  × *(star operator → 22C6)*

2606 ☆ WHITE STAR
  × *(stress outlined white star → 2729)*

2607 ☇ LIGHTNING

2608 ☈ THUNDERSTORM

2609 ☉ SUN
  × *(circled dot operator → 2299)*
  × *(black sun with rays → 2600)*
  × *(white sun with rays → 263C)*

260A ☊ ASCENDING NODE

260B ☋ DESCENDING NODE

260C ☌ CONJUNCTION

260D ☍ OPPOSITION

260E ☎ BLACK TELEPHONE

260F ☏ WHITE TELEPHONE

2610 ☐ BALLOT BOX
  × *(white square → 25A1)*

2611 ☑ BALLOT BOX WITH CHECK

2612 ☒ BALLOT BOX WITH X
  × *(squared times → 22A0)*

2613 ☓ SALTIRE
  = *St. Andrew's Cross*
  × *(ballot x → 2717)*

2614

2615

2616

2617

2618

2619

261A ☚ BLACK LEFT POINTING INDEX

261B ☛ BLACK RIGHT POINTING INDEX

261C ☜ WHITE LEFT POINTING INDEX

261D ☝ WHITE UP POINTING INDEX

261E ☞ WHITE RIGHT POINTING INDEX

261F ☟ WHITE DOWN POINTING INDEX

2620 ☠ SKULL AND CROSSBONES
  = *poison*

2621 ☡ CAUTION SIGN

2622 ☢ RADIOACTIVE SIGN

2623 ☣ BIOHAZARD SIGN

2624 ☤ CADUCEUS

2625 ☥ ANKH

2626 ☦ ORTHODOX CROSS

2627 ☧ CHI RHO

2628 ☨ CROSS OF LORRAINE

2629 ☩ CROSS OF JERUSALEM

262A ☪ STAR AND CRESCENT

262B ☫ SYMBOL OF IRAN

262C ☬ ADI SHAKTI

262D ☭ HAMMER AND SICKLE

262E ☮ PEACE SYMBOL

262F ☯ YIN YANG

2630 ☰ TRIGRAM FOR HEAVEN
  = *qian2*

2631 ☱ TRIGRAM FOR LAKE
  = *dui4*

2632 ☲ TRIGRAM FOR FIRE
  = *li2*

2633 ☳ TRIGRAM FOR THUNDER
  = *zhen4*

2634 ☴ TRIGRAM FOR WIND
  = *xun4*

2635 ☵ TRIGRAM FOR WATER
  = *kan3*

2636 ☶ TRIGRAM FOR MOUNTAIN
  = *gen4*

2637 ☷ TRIGRAM FOR EARTH
  = *kun1*

2638 ☸ WHEEL OF DHARMA

2639 ☹ WHITE FROWNING FACE

263A ☺ WHITE SMILING FACE
  = *have a nice day!*

263B ☻ BLACK SMILING FACE

263C ☼ WHITE SUN WITH RAYS
  = *compass*
  × *(sun → 2609)*

263D ☽ FIRST QUARTER MOON

263E ☾ LAST QUARTER MOON

263F ☿ MERCURY

2640 ♀ FEMALE SIGN
  = *Venus*

2641 ♁|⊕ EARTH
  × *(circled plus → 2295)*

2642 ♂ MALE SIGN
  = *Mars*

2643 ♃ JUPITER

2644 ♄ SATURN

2645 ♅ URANUS

2646	Ψ	NEPTUNE
2647	♇	PLUTO
2648	♈	ARIES
2649	♉	TAURUS
264A	♊	GEMINI
264B	♋	CANCER
264C	♌	LEO
264D	♍	VIRGO

= minim (alternate glyph)

264E	♎	LIBRA
264F	♏	SCORPIUS

= minim, drop

2650	♐	SAGITTARIUS
2651	♑	CAPRICORN
2652	♒	AQUARIUS
2653	♓	PISCES
2654	♔	WHITE CHESS KING
2655	♕	WHITE CHESS QUEEN
2656	♖	WHITE CHESS ROOK
2657	♗	WHITE CHESS BISHOP
2658	♘	WHITE CHESS KNIGHT
2659	♙	WHITE CHESS PAWN
265A	♚	BLACK CHESS KING
265B	♛	BLACK CHESS QUEEN
265C	♜	BLACK CHESS ROOK
265D	♝	BLACK CHESS BISHOP
265E	♞	BLACK CHESS KNIGHT
265F	♟	BLACK CHESS PAWN
2660	♠	BLACK SPADE SUIT
2661	♡	WHITE HEART SUIT
2662	◇	WHITE DIAMOND SUIT

× (white diamond → 25C7)
× (lozenge → 25CA)

2663	♣	BLACK CLUB SUIT

= shamrock

2664	♤	WHITE SPADE SUIT
2665	♥	BLACK HEART SUIT

= valentine
× (heavy black heart → 2764)

2666	♦	BLACK DIAMOND SUIT

× (black diamond → 25C6)

2667	♧	WHITE CLUB SUIT
2668	♨	HOT SPRINGS
2669	♩	QUARTER NOTE
266A	♪	EIGHTH NOTE
266B	♫	BARRED EIGHTH NOTES
266C	♬	BARRED SIXTEENTH NOTES
266D	♭	FLAT
266E	♮	NATURAL
266F	♯	SHARP

	270	271	272	273	274	275	276	277	278	279	27A	27B
0		✏	✠	✰	✿	❐			①	❼	➠	➡
1	✁	✑	✡	✱	❀	❑	❡		②	❽	➡	⇨
2	✂	✒	✢	✲	❁	❒	❢		③	❾	➢	➲
3	✃	✓	✣	✳	❂		❣		④	❿	➣	➳
4	✄	✔	✤	✴	❄		❤		⑤	➍	➤	➴
5		✕	✥	✵	❅		❥		⑥		➥	➵
6	✆	✖	✦	✶	❆	❖	❦	❶	⑦		➦	➶
7	✇	✗	✧	✷	❇		❧	❷	⑧		➧	➷
8	✈	✘		✸	❈	❘		❸	⑨	➘	➨	➸
9	✉	✙	✩	✹	❉	❙		❹	❿	➙	⇒	➹
A		✚	✪	✺	❊	❚		❺	➊	➚	⇨	➺
B		✛	✫	✻	❋	◗		❻	➋	➛	➭	➻
C	✌	✜	✬	✼		❜		❼	➌	➜	⇨	➼
D	✍	✝	✭	✽	◯	❝		❽	➍	➝	➭	➽
E	✎	✞	✮	✾		❞		❾	➎	➞	➭	⇛
F	✏	✟	✯	❃	❏				➏	➟	➠	⇨

Zapf dingbats

2700		
2701	✁	UPPER BLADE SCISSORS
2702	✂	BLACK SCISSORS
2703	✃	LOWER BLADE SCISSORS
2704	✄	WHITE SCISSORS
2705		✕ (black telephone → 260E)
2706	✆	TELEPHONE LOCATION SIGN
2707	✇	TAPE DRIVE
2708	✈	AIRPLANE
2709	✉	ENVELOPE
270A		✕ (black right pointing index → 261B)
270B		✕ (white right pointing index → 261E)
270C	✌	VICTORY HAND
270D	✍	WRITING HAND
270E	✎	LOWER RIGHT PENCIL
270F	✏	PENCIL
2710	✐	UPPER RIGHT PENCIL
2711	✑	WHITE NIB
2712	✒	BLACK NIB
2713	✓	CHECK MARK
		✕ (square root → 221A)
2714	✔	HEAVY CHECK MARK
2715	✕	MULTIPLICATION X
2716	✖	HEAVY MULTIPLICATION X
2717	✗	BALLOT X
		✕ (saltire → 2613)
2718	✘	HEAVY BALLOT X
2719	✙	OUTLINED GREEK CROSS
271A	✚	HEAVY GREEK CROSS
271B	✛	OPEN CENTER CROSS
271C	✜	HEAVY OPEN CENTER CROSS
271D	✝	LATIN CROSS
271E	✞	SHADOWED WHITE LATIN CROSS
271F	✟	OUTLINED LATIN CROSS
2720	✠	MALTESE CROSS
2721	✡	STAR OF DAVID
2722	✢	FOUR TEARDROP-SPOKED ASTERISK
2723	✣	FOUR BALLOON-SPOKED ASTERISK
2724	✤	HEAVY FOUR BALLOON-SPOKED ASTERISK
2725	✥	FOUR CLUB-SPOKED ASTERISK
2726	✦	BLACK FOUR POINTED STAR
2727	✧	WHITE FOUR POINTED STAR
2728		✕ (black star → 2605)
2729	✩	STRESS OUTLINED WHITE STAR
		✕ (white star → 2606)
272A	✪	CIRCLED WHITE STAR

272B	✫	OPEN CENTER BLACK STAR
272C	✬	BLACK CENTER WHITE STAR
272D	✭	OUTLINED BLACK STAR
272E	✮	HEAVY OUTLINED BLACK STAR
272F	✯	PINWHEEL STAR
2730	✰	SHADOWED WHITE STAR
2731	✱	HEAVY ASTERISK
		✕ (asterisk → 002A)
2732	✲	OPEN CENTER ASTERISK
2733	✳	EIGHT SPOKED ASTERISK
2734	✴	EIGHT POINTED BLACK STAR
2735	✵	EIGHT POINTED PINWHEEL STAR
2736	✶	SIX POINTED BLACK STAR
		= sextile
2737	✷	EIGHT POINTED RECTILINEAR BLACK STAR
2738	✸	HEAVY EIGHT POINTED RECTILINEAR BLACK STAR
2739	✹	TWELVE POINTED BLACK STAR
273A	✺	SIXTEEN POINTED ASTERISK
		= starburst
273B	✻	TEARDROP-SPOKED ASTERISK
273C	✼	OPEN CENTER TEARDROP-SPOKED ASTERISK
273D	✽	HEAVY TEARDROP-SPOKED ASTERISK
273E	✾	SIX PETALLED BLACK AND WHITE FLORETTE
273F	✿	BLACK FLORETTE
2740	❀	WHITE FLORETTE
2741	❁	EIGHT PETALLED OUTLINED BLACK FLORETTE
2742	❂	CIRCLED OPEN CENTER EIGHT POINTED STAR
2743	❃	HEAVY TEARDROP-SPOKED PINWHEEL ASTERISK
2744	❄	SNOWFLAKE
2745	❅	TIGHT TRIFOLIATE SNOWFLAKE
2746	❆	HEAVY CHEVRON SNOWFLAKE
2747	❇	SPARKLE
2748	❈	HEAVY SPARKLE
2749	❉	BALLOON-SPOKED ASTERISK
		= jack
274A	❊	EIGHT TEARDROP-SPOKED PROPELLER ASTERISK
274B	❋	HEAVY EIGHT TEARDROP-SPOKED PROPELLER ASTERISK
		= turbofan
274C		✕ (black circle → 25CF)
274D	◌	SHADOWED WHITE CIRCLE
274E		✕ (black square → 25A0)

274F	☐	LOWER RIGHT DROP-SHADOWED WHITE SQUARE
2750	☐	UPPER RIGHT DROP-SHADOWED WHITE SQUARE
2751	☐	LOWER RIGHT SHADOWED WHITE SQUARE
2752	☐	UPPER RIGHT SHADOWED WHITE SQUARE
2753		× (black up pointing triangle → 25B2)
2754		× (black down pointing triangle → 25BC)
2755		× (black diamond → 25C6)
2756	❖	BLACK DIAMOND MINUS WHITE X
2757		× (right half black circle → 25D7)
2758	|	LIGHT VERTICAL BAR
		× (vertical bar → 007C)
2759	❙	MEDIUM VERTICAL BAR
275A	❚	HEAVY VERTICAL BAR
275B	❛	HEAVY SINGLE TURNED COMMA QUOTATION MARK ORNAMENT
		× (single turned comma quotation mark → 2018)
275C	❜	HEAVY SINGLE COMMA QUOTATION MARK ORNAMENT
		× (single comma quotation mark → 2019)
275D	❝	HEAVY DOUBLE TURNED COMMA QUOTATION MARK ORNAMENT
		× (double turned comma quotation mark → 201C)
275E	❞	HEAVY DOUBLE COMMA QUOTATION MARK ORNAMENT
		× (double comma quotation mark → 201D)
275F		
2760		
2761	❡	CURVED STEM PARAGRAPH SIGN ORNAMENT
		× (paragraph sign → 00B6)
2762	❢	HEAVY EXCLAMATION MARK ORNAMENT
		× (exclamation mark → 0021)
2763	❣	HEAVY HEART EXCLAMATION MARK ORNAMENT
2764	❤	HEAVY BLACK HEART
		× (black heart suit → 2665)
2765	❥	ROTATED HEAVY BLACK HEART BULLET
2766	❦	FLORAL HEART
2767	❧	ROTATED FLORAL HEART BULLET
2768		× (black club suit → 2663)
2769		× (black diamond suit → 2666)
276A		× (black heart suit → 2665)
276B		× (black spade suit → 2660)
276C		× (circled digit one → 2460)
276D		× (circled digit two → 2461)
276E		× (circled digit three → 2462)
276F		× (circled digit four → 2463)
2770		× (circled digit five → 2464)
2771		× (circled digit six → 2465)
2772		× (circled digit seven → 2466)
2773		× (circled digit eight → 2467)
2774		× (circled digit nine → 2468)
2775		× (circled number ten → 2469)
2776	❶	INVERSE CIRCLED DIGIT ONE
2777	❷	INVERSE CIRCLED DIGIT TWO
2778	❸	INVERSE CIRCLED DIGIT THREE
2779	❹	INVERSE CIRCLED DIGIT FOUR
277A	❺	INVERSE CIRCLED DIGIT FIVE
277B	❻	INVERSE CIRCLED DIGIT SIX
277C	❼	INVERSE CIRCLED DIGIT SEVEN
277D	❽	INVERSE CIRCLED DIGIT EIGHT
277E	❾	INVERSE CIRCLED DIGIT NINE
277F	❿	INVERSE CIRCLED NUMBER TEN
2780	➀	CIRCLED SANS-SERIF DIGIT ONE
2781	➁	CIRCLED SANS-SERIF DIGIT TWO
2782	➂	CIRCLED SANS-SERIF DIGIT THREE
2783	➃	CIRCLED SANS-SERIF DIGIT FOUR
2784	➄	CIRCLED SANS-SERIF DIGIT FIVE
2785	➅	CIRCLED SANS-SERIF DIGIT SIX
2786	➆	CIRCLED SANS-SERIF DIGIT SEVEN
2787	➇	CIRCLED SANS-SERIF DIGIT EIGHT
2788	➈	CIRCLED SANS-SERIF DIGIT NINE
2789	➉	CIRCLED SANS-SERIF NUMBER TEN
278A	➊	INVERSE CIRCLED SANS-SERIF DIGIT ONE
278B	➋	INVERSE CIRCLED SANS-SERIF DIGIT TWO
278C	➌	INVERSE CIRCLED SANS-SERIF DIGIT THREE
278D	➍	INVERSE CIRCLED SANS-SERIF DIGIT FOUR
278E	➎	INVERSE CIRCLED SANS-SERIF DIGIT FIVE
278F	➏	INVERSE CIRCLED SANS-SERIF DIGIT SIX
2790	➐	INVERSE CIRCLED SANS-SERIF DIGIT SEVEN
2791	➑	INVERSE CIRCLED SANS-SERIF DIGIT EIGHT
2792	➒	INVERSE CIRCLED SANS-SERIF DIGIT NINE
2793	➓	INVERSE CIRCLED SANS-SERIF NUMBER TEN
2794	→	HEAVY WIDE-HEADED RIGHT ARROW
2795		× (right arrow → 2192)
2796		× (left right arrow → 2194)
2797		× (up down arrow → 2195)
2798	➘	HEAVY LOWER RIGHT ARROW
2799	➙	HEAVY RIGHT ARROW
279A	➚	HEAVY UPPER RIGHT ARROW
279B	➛	DRAFTING POINT RIGHT ARROW

279C	→	HEAVY ROUND-TIPPED RIGHT ARROW
279D	→	TRIANGLE-HEADED RIGHT ARROW
279E	→	HEAVY TRIANGLE-HEADED RIGHT ARROW
279F	⇢	DASHED TRIANGLE-HEADED RIGHT ARROW
27A0	⇢	HEAVY DASHED TRIANGLE-HEADED RIGHT ARROW
27A1	➡	BLACK RIGHT ARROW
27A2	➢	THREE-D TOP-LIGHTED RIGHT ARROWHEAD
27A3	➣	THREE-D BOTTOM-LIGHTED RIGHT ARROWHEAD
27A4	➤	BLACK RIGHT ARROWHEAD
27A5	➥	HEAVY BLACK CURVED DOWN AND RIGHT ARROW
27A6	➦	HEAVY BLACK CURVED UP AND RIGHT ARROW
27A7	➧	SQUAT BLACK RIGHT ARROW
27A8	➨	HEAVY CONCAVE-POINTED BLACK RIGHT ARROW
27A9	➩	RIGHT-SHADED WHITE RIGHT ARROW
27AA	➪	LEFT-SHADED WHITE RIGHT ARROW
27AB	➫	BACK-TILTED SHADOWED WHITE RIGHT ARROW
27AC	➬	FRONT-TILTED SHADOWED WHITE RIGHT ARROW
27AD	➭	HEAVY LOWER RIGHT-SHADOWED WHITE RIGHT ARROW
27AE	➮	HEAVY UPPER RIGHT-SHADOWED WHITE RIGHT ARROW
27AF	➯	NOTCHED LOWER RIGHT-SHADOWED WHITE RIGHT ARROW
27B0		
27B1	➱	NOTCHED UPPER RIGHT-SHADOWED WHITE RIGHT ARROW
27B2	➲	CIRCLED HEAVY WHITE RIGHT ARROW
27B3	➳	WHITE-FEATHERED RIGHT ARROW
27B4	➴	BLACK-FEATHERED LOWER RIGHT ARROW
27B5	➵	BLACK-FEATHERED RIGHT ARROW
27B6	➶	BLACK-FEATHERED UPPER RIGHT ARROW
27B7	➷	HEAVY BLACK-FEATHERED LOWER RIGHT ARROW
27B8	➸	HEAVY BLACK-FEATHERED RIGHT ARROW
27B9	➹	HEAVY BLACK-FEATHERED UPPER RIGHT ARROW
27BA	➺	TEARDROP-BARBED RIGHT ARROW
27BB	➻	HEAVY TEARDROP-SHANKED RIGHT ARROW
27BC	➼	WEDGE-TAILED RIGHT ARROW
27BD	➽	HEAVY WEDGE-TAILED RIGHT ARROW

27BE	⇒	OPEN-OUTLINED RIGHT ARROW

	300	301	302	303
0	Ideo SP	【	〒	〰
1	、	】	│	〱
2	。	〒	‖	〲
3	〃	▬	‖	〳
4	仝	〔	╳	〴
5	々	〕	〆	〵
6	〆	〖	上	㉠
7	〇	〗	中	
8	〈	〘	下	
9	〉	〙	甲	
A	《	〚	⦿	
B	》	〛	⦾	
C	「	⌐	◌	
D	」	"	◌	
E	『	"	◌	
F	』	„	◌	⊠

The Unicode Standard • Version 1.0

CJK symbols and punctuation

3000	⿰	IDEOGRAPHIC SPACE
		× (space → 0020)
3001	、	IDEOGRAPHIC COMMA
		× (comma → 002C)
3002	。	IDEOGRAPHIC PERIOD
		= ISO IDEOGRAPHIC FULL STOP
		× (period → 002E)
3003	〃	DITTO MARK
		× (double prime → 2033)
3004	仝	IDEOGRAPHIC DITTO MARK
3005	々	IDEOGRAPHIC ITERATION MARK
3006	〆	IDEOGRAPHIC CLOSING MARK
3007	〇	IDEOGRAPHIC NUMBER ZERO
		× (enclosing circle → 20DD)
		× (white circle → 25CB)
3008	〈	OPENING ANGLE BRACKET
		× (less-than sign → 003C)
		× (left pointing single guillemet → 2039)
		× (bra → 2329)
3009	〉	CLOSING ANGLE BRACKET
		× (greater-than sign → 003E)
		× (right pointing single guillemet → 203A)
		× (ket → 232A)
300A	《	OPENING DOUBLE ANGLE BRACKET
		= ISO LEFT-POINTING DOUBLE ANGLE BRACKET
		× (left pointing guillemet → 00AB)
300B	》	CLOSING DOUBLE ANGLE BRACKET
		= ISO RIGHT-POINTING DOUBLE ANGLE BRACKET
		× (right pointing guillemet → 00BB)
300C	「	OPENING CORNER BRACKET
		= ISO IDEOGRAPHIC LEFT BRACKET
300D	」	CLOSING CORNER BRACKET
		= ISO IDEOGRAPHIC RIGHT BRACKET
		used as quotation marks
300E	『	OPENING WHITE CORNER BRACKET
		= ISO IDEOGRAPHIC LEFT DOUBLE BRACKET
300F	』	CLOSING WHITE CORNER BRACKET
		= ISO IDEOGRAPHIC RIGHT DOUBLE BRACKET
		used as quotation marks
3010	【	OPENING BLACK LENTICULAR BRACKET
		= ISO LEFT BOLDFACE SQUARE BRACKET
3011	】	CLOSING BLACK LENTICULAR BRACKET
		= ISO RIGHT BOLDFACE SQUARE BRACKET
3012	〒	POSTAL MARK
3013	▬	GETA MARK
		substitute for ideograph not in font
3014	〔	OPENING TORTOISE SHELL BRACKET
		= ISO LEFT TORTOISE-SHELL BRACKET
3015	〕	CLOSING TORTOISE SHELL BRACKET
		= ISO RIGHT TORTOISE-SHELL BRACKET
3016	〖	OPENING WHITE LENTICULAR BRACKET
3017	〗	CLOSING WHITE LENTICULAR BRACKET
3018	〘	OPENING WHITE TORTOISE SHELL BRACKET
		= ISO LEFT EMPTY ANGULAR BRACKET SIGN
3019	〙	CLOSING WHITE TORTOISE SHELL BRACKET
		= ISO RIGHT EMPTY ANGULAR BRACKET SIGN
301A	〚	OPENING WHITE SQUARE BRACKET
		= ISO LEFT EMPTY BRACKET
301B	〛	CLOSING WHITE SQUARE BRACKET
		= ISO RIGHT EMPTY BRACKET
301C	〜	WAVE DASH
		JIS punctuation
		× (wavy dash → 3030)
301D	〝	REVERSED DOUBLE PRIME QUOTATION MARK
		× (double turned comma quotation mark → 201C)
		× (reversed double prime → 2036)
301E	〞	DOUBLE PRIME QUOTATION MARK
		× (double comma quotation mark → 201D)
		× (double prime → 2033)
301F	〟	LOW DOUBLE PRIME QUOTATION MARK
		× (low double comma quotation mark → 201E)
3020	〠	POSTAL MARK FACE

Hangzhou-style numerals

3021	〡	HANGZHOU NUMERAL ONE
3022	〢	HANGZHOU NUMERAL TWO
3023	〣	HANGZHOU NUMERAL THREE
3024	〤	HANGZHOU NUMERAL FOUR
3025	〥	HANGZHOU NUMERAL FIVE
3026	〦	HANGZHOU NUMERAL SIX
3027	〧	HANGZHOU NUMERAL SEVEN
3028	〨	HANGZHOU NUMERAL EIGHT
3029	〩	HANGZHOU NUMERAL NINE

Diacritics

302A	◌〪	IDEOGRAPHIC LEVEL TONE MARK
302B	◌〫	IDEOGRAPHIC RISING TONE MARK
302C	◌〬	IDEOGRAPHIC DEPARTING TONE MARK
302D	◌〭	IDEOGRAPHIC ENTERING TONE MARK

302E ⊙ HANGUL SINGLE DOT TONE MARK
302F ⊙ HANGUL DOUBLE DOT TONE MARK

Other CJK symbols

3030 ∿ WAVY DASH
    ✕ *(wavy line → 2307)*
    ✕ *(wave dash → 301C)*

3031 〱 VERTICAL KANA REPEAT MARK

3032 〲 VERTICAL KANA REPEAT WITH VOICED
    SOUND MARK
        the preceding two semantic characters
        are preferred to the following three
        glyphic forms

3033 〳 VERTICAL KANA REPEAT MARK UPPER
    HALF

3034 〴 VERTICAL KANA REPEAT WITH VOICED
    SOUND MARK UPPER HALF
        the preceding two are glyphs used in
        conjunction with the following glyph

3035 〵 VERTICAL KANA REPEAT MARK LOWER
    HALF

3036 ⊖ CIRCLED POSTAL MARK

3037

3038

3039

303A

303B

303C

303D

303E

303F ▨ IDEOGRAPHIC HALF FILL SPACE

	304	305	306	307	308	309
0		ぐ	だ	ば	む	ゐ
1	ぁ	け	ち	ぱ	め	ゑ
2	あ	げ	ぢ	ひ	も	を
3	ぃ	こ	っ	び	ゃ	ん
4	い	ご	つ	ぴ	や	ゔ
5	ぅ	さ	づ	ふ	ゅ	
6	う	ざ	て	ぶ	ゆ	
7	ぇ	し	で	ぷ	ょ	
8	え	じ	と	へ	よ	
9	ぉ	す	ど	べ	ら	゙
A	お	ず	な	ぺ	り	゚
B	か	せ	に	ほ	る	゛
C	が	ぜ	ぬ	ぼ	れ	゜
D	き	そ	ね	ぽ	ろ	ゝ
E	ぎ	ぞ	の	ま	わ	ゞ
F	く	た	は	み	ゎ	

Based on JIS X 0208

3040		
3041	あ	HIRAGANA LETTER SMALL A
3042	あ	HIRAGANA LETTER A
3043	い	HIRAGANA LETTER SMALL I
3044	い	HIRAGANA LETTER I
3045	う	HIRAGANA LETTER SMALL U
3046	う	HIRAGANA LETTER U
3047	え	HIRAGANA LETTER SMALL E
3048	え	HIRAGANA LETTER E
3049	お	HIRAGANA LETTER SMALL O
304A	お	HIRAGANA LETTER O
304B	か	HIRAGANA LETTER KA
304C	が	HIRAGANA LETTER GA
304D	き	HIRAGANA LETTER KI
304E	ぎ	HIRAGANA LETTER GI
304F	く	HIRAGANA LETTER KU
3050	ぐ	HIRAGANA LETTER GU
3051	け	HIRAGANA LETTER KE
3052	げ	HIRAGANA LETTER GE
3053	こ	HIRAGANA LETTER KO
3054	ご	HIRAGANA LETTER GO
3055	さ	HIRAGANA LETTER SA
3056	ざ	HIRAGANA LETTER ZA
3057	し	HIRAGANA LETTER SI = SHI
3058	じ	HIRAGANA LETTER ZI = JI (not unique)
3059	す	HIRAGANA LETTER SU
305A	ず	HIRAGANA LETTER ZU
305B	せ	HIRAGANA LETTER SE
305C	ぜ	HIRAGANA LETTER ZE
305D	そ	HIRAGANA LETTER SO
305E	ぞ	HIRAGANA LETTER ZO
305F	た	HIRAGANA LETTER TA
3060	だ	HIRAGANA LETTER DA
3061	ち	HIRAGANA LETTER TI = CHI
3062	ぢ	HIRAGANA LETTER DI = JI (not unique)
3063	っ	HIRAGANA LETTER SMALL TU = SMALL TSU
3064	つ	HIRAGANA LETTER TU = TSU
3065	づ	HIRAGANA LETTER DU = ZU (not unique)
3066	て	HIRAGANA LETTER TE
3067	で	HIRAGANA LETTER DE
3068	と	HIRAGANA LETTER TO
3069	ど	HIRAGANA LETTER DO
306A	な	HIRAGANA LETTER NA
306B	に	HIRAGANA LETTER NI
306C	ぬ	HIRAGANA LETTER NU
306D	ね	HIRAGANA LETTER NE
306E	の	HIRAGANA LETTER NO
306F	は	HIRAGANA LETTER HA
3070	ば	HIRAGANA LETTER BA
3071	ぱ	HIRAGANA LETTER PA
3072	ひ	HIRAGANA LETTER HI
3073	び	HIRAGANA LETTER BI
3074	ぴ	HIRAGANA LETTER PI
3075	ふ	HIRAGANA LETTER HU = FU
3076	ぶ	HIRAGANA LETTER BU
3077	ぷ	HIRAGANA LETTER PU
3078	へ	HIRAGANA LETTER HE
3079	べ	HIRAGANA LETTER BE
307A	ぺ	HIRAGANA LETTER PE
307B	ほ	HIRAGANA LETTER HO
307C	ぼ	HIRAGANA LETTER BO
307D	ぽ	HIRAGANA LETTER PO
307E	ま	HIRAGANA LETTER MA
307F	み	HIRAGANA LETTER MI
3080	む	HIRAGANA LETTER MU
3081	め	HIRAGANA LETTER ME
3082	も	HIRAGANA LETTER MO
3083	ゃ	HIRAGANA LETTER SMALL YA
3084	や	HIRAGANA LETTER YA
3085	ゅ	HIRAGANA LETTER SMALL YU
3086	ゆ	HIRAGANA LETTER YU
3087	ょ	HIRAGANA LETTER SMALL YO
3088	よ	HIRAGANA LETTER YO
3089	ら	HIRAGANA LETTER RA
308A	り	HIRAGANA LETTER RI
308B	る	HIRAGANA LETTER RU
308C	れ	HIRAGANA LETTER RE
308D	ろ	HIRAGANA LETTER RO
308E	ゎ	HIRAGANA LETTER SMALL WA
308F	わ	HIRAGANA LETTER WA
3090	ゐ	HIRAGANA LETTER WI
3091	ゑ	HIRAGANA LETTER WE
3092	を	HIRAGANA LETTER WO
3093	ん	HIRAGANA LETTER N
3094	ゔ	HIRAGANA LETTER VU

3095

3096

3097

3098

3099 ⦾̀ NON-SPACING KATAKANA-HIRAGANA
VOICED SOUND MARK

309A ⦾̊ NON-SPACING KATAKANA-HIRAGANA
SEMI-VOICED SOUND MARK

309B ˋ KATAKANA-HIRAGANA VOICED SOUND
MARK

309C ° KATAKANA-HIRAGANA SEMI-VOICED
SOUND MARK

309D ゝ HIRAGANA ITERATION MARK

309E ゞ HIRAGANA VOICED ITERATION MARK

	30A	30B	30C	30D	30E	30F
0		グ	ダ	バ	ム	ヰ
1	ア	ケ	チ	パ	メ	ヱ
2	ァ	ゲ	ヂ	ヒ	モ	ヲ
3	イ	コ	ッ	ビ	ャ	ン
4	ィ	ゴ	ツ	ピ	ヤ	ヴ
5	ウ	サ	ヅ	フ	ュ	ヵ
6	ゥ	ザ	テ	ブ	ユ	ヶ
7	エ	シ	デ	プ	ョ	
8	ェ	ジ	ト	ヘ	ヨ	
9	オ	ス	ド	ベ	ラ	
A	ォ	ズ	ナ	ペ	リ	
B	カ	セ	ニ	ホ	ル	・
C	ガ	ゼ	ヌ	ボ	レ	ー
D	キ	ソ	ネ	ポ	ロ	ヽ
E	ギ	ゾ	ノ	マ	ワ	ヾ
F	ク	タ	ハ	ミ	ヮ	

Based on JIS X 0208

30A0		
30A1	ア	KATAKANA LETTER SMALL A
30A2	ア	KATAKANA LETTER A
30A3	イ	KATAKANA LETTER SMALL I
30A4	イ	KATAKANA LETTER I
30A5	ウ	KATAKANA LETTER SMALL U
30A6	ウ	KATAKANA LETTER U
30A7	エ	KATAKANA LETTER SMALL E
30A8	エ	KATAKANA LETTER E
30A9	オ	KATAKANA LETTER SMALL O
30AA	オ	KATAKANA LETTER O
30AB	カ	KATAKANA LETTER KA
30AC	ガ	KATAKANA LETTER GA
30AD	キ	KATAKANA LETTER KI
30AE	ギ	KATAKANA LETTER GI
30AF	ク	KATAKANA LETTER KU
30B0	グ	KATAKANA LETTER GU
30B1	ケ	KATAKANA LETTER KE
30B2	ゲ	KATAKANA LETTER GE
30B3	コ	KATAKANA LETTER KO
30B4	ゴ	KATAKANA LETTER GO
30B5	サ	KATAKANA LETTER SA
30B6	ザ	KATAKANA LETTER ZA
30B7	シ	KATAKANA LETTER SI = SHI
30B8	ジ	KATAKANA LETTER ZI = JI (not unique)
30B9	ス	KATAKANA LETTER SU
30BA	ズ	KATAKANA LETTER ZU
30BB	セ	KATAKANA LETTER SE
30BC	ゼ	KATAKANA LETTER ZE
30BD	ソ	KATAKANA LETTER SO
30BE	ゾ	KATAKANA LETTER ZO
30BF	タ	KATAKANA LETTER TA
30C0	ダ	KATAKANA LETTER DA
30C1	チ	KATAKANA LETTER TI = CHI
30C2	ヂ	KATAKANA LETTER DI = JI (not unique)
30C3	ッ	KATAKANA LETTER SMALL TU = SMALL TSU
30C4	ツ	KATAKANA LETTER TU = TSU
30C5	ヅ	KATAKANA LETTER DU = ZU (not unique)
30C6	テ	KATAKANA LETTER TE
30C7	デ	KATAKANA LETTER DE
30C8	ト	KATAKANA LETTER TO
30C9	ド	KATAKANA LETTER DO
30CA	ナ	KATAKANA LETTER NA
30CB	ニ	KATAKANA LETTER NI
30CC	ヌ	KATAKANA LETTER NU
30CD	ネ	KATAKANA LETTER NE
30CE	ノ	KATAKANA LETTER NO
30CF	ハ	KATAKANA LETTER HA
30D0	バ	KATAKANA LETTER BA
30D1	パ	KATAKANA LETTER PA
30D2	ヒ	KATAKANA LETTER HI
30D3	ビ	KATAKANA LETTER BI
30D4	ピ	KATAKANA LETTER PI
30D5	フ	KATAKANA LETTER HU = FU
30D6	ブ	KATAKANA LETTER BU
30D7	プ	KATAKANA LETTER PU
30D8	ヘ	KATAKANA LETTER HE
30D9	ベ	KATAKANA LETTER BE
30DA	ペ	KATAKANA LETTER PE
30DB	ホ	KATAKANA LETTER HO
30DC	ボ	KATAKANA LETTER BO
30DD	ポ	KATAKANA LETTER PO
30DE	マ	KATAKANA LETTER MA
30DF	ミ	KATAKANA LETTER MI
30E0	ム	KATAKANA LETTER MU
30E1	メ	KATAKANA LETTER ME
30E2	モ	KATAKANA LETTER MO
30E3	ャ	KATAKANA LETTER SMALL YA
30E4	ヤ	KATAKANA LETTER YA
30E5	ュ	KATAKANA LETTER SMALL YU
30E6	ユ	KATAKANA LETTER YU
30E7	ョ	KATAKANA LETTER SMALL YO
30E8	ヨ	KATAKANA LETTER YO
30E9	ラ	KATAKANA LETTER RA
30EA	リ	KATAKANA LETTER RI
30EB	ル	KATAKANA LETTER RU
30EC	レ	KATAKANA LETTER RE
30ED	ロ	KATAKANA LETTER RO
30EE	ワ	KATAKANA LETTER SMALL WA
30EF	ワ	KATAKANA LETTER WA
30F0	ヰ	KATAKANA LETTER WI
30F1	ヱ	KATAKANA LETTER WE
30F2	ヲ	KATAKANA LETTER WO
30F3	ン	KATAKANA LETTER N
30F4	ヴ	KATAKANA LETTER VU

30F5	ヵ	KATAKANA LETTER SMALL KA
30F6	ヶ	KATAKANA LETTER SMALL KE
30F7		
30F8		
30F9		
30FA		
30FB	・	KATAKANA MIDDLE DOT

      × *(middle dot → 00B7)*

30FC	ー	KATAKANA-HIRAGANA PROLONGED SOUND MARK

      × *(em dash → 2014)*

30FD	ヽ	KATAKANA ITERATION MARK
30FE	ヾ	KATAKANA VOICED ITERATION MARK

	310	311	312
0		ㄐ	ㄠ
1		ㄑ	ㄡ
2		ㄒ	ㄢ
3		ㄓ	ㄣ
4		ㄔ	ㄤ
5	ㄅ	ㄕ	ㄥ
6	ㄆ	ㄖ	ㄦ
7	ㄇ	ㄗ	ㄧ
8	ㄈ	ㄘ	ㄨ
9	ㄉ	ㄙ	ㄩ
A	ㄊ	ㄚ	ㄪ
B	ㄋ	ㄛ	ㄫ
C	ㄌ	ㄜ	ㄬ
D	ㄍ	ㄝ	
E	ㄎ	ㄞ	
F	ㄏ	ㄟ	

Based on GB 2312

× (modifier letter hacek → 02C7)
× (modifier letter macron → 02C9)
× (modifier letter acute → 02CA)
× (modifier letter grave → 02CB)
× (spacing dot above → 02D9)

3100		
3101		
3102		
3103		
3104		
3105	ㄅ	BOPOMOFO LETTER B
3106	ㄆ	BOPOMOFO LETTER P
3107	ㄇ	BOPOMOFO LETTER M
3108	ㄈ	BOPOMOFO LETTER F
3109	ㄉ	BOPOMOFO LETTER D
310A	ㄊ	BOPOMOFO LETTER T
310B	ㄋ	BOPOMOFO LETTER N
310C	ㄌ	BOPOMOFO LETTER L
310D	ㄍ	BOPOMOFO LETTER G
310E	ㄎ	BOPOMOFO LETTER K
310F	ㄏ	BOPOMOFO LETTER H
3110	ㄐ	BOPOMOFO LETTER J
3111	ㄑ	BOPOMOFO LETTER Q
3112	ㄒ	BOPOMOFO LETTER X
3113	ㄓ	BOPOMOFO LETTER ZH
3114	ㄔ	BOPOMOFO LETTER CH
3115	ㄕ	BOPOMOFO LETTER SH
3116	ㄖ	BOPOMOFO LETTER R
3117	ㄗ	BOPOMOFO LETTER Z
3118	ㄘ	BOPOMOFO LETTER C
3119	ㄙ	BOPOMOFO LETTER S
311A	ㄚ	BOPOMOFO LETTER A
311B	ㄛ	BOPOMOFO LETTER O
311C	ㄜ	BOPOMOFO LETTER E
311D	ㄝ	BOPOMOFO LETTER EH
311E	ㄞ	BOPOMOFO LETTER AI
311F	ㄟ	BOPOMOFO LETTER EI
3120	ㄠ	BOPOMOFO LETTER AU
3121	ㄡ	BOPOMOFO LETTER OU
3122	ㄢ	BOPOMOFO LETTER AN
3123	ㄣ	BOPOMOFO LETTER EN
3124	ㄤ	BOPOMOFO LETTER ANG
3125	ㄥ	BOPOMOFO LETTER ENG
3126	ㄦ	BOPOMOFO LETTER ER
3127	ㄧ	BOPOMOFO LETTER I
3128	ㄨ	BOPOMOFO LETTER U

3129	ㄩ	BOPOMOFO LETTER IU

Dialect (non-Mandarin) letters

312A	万	BOPOMOFO LETTER V
312B	兀	BOPOMOFO LETTER NG
312C	广	BOPOMOFO LETTER GN

	313	314	315	316	317	318
0		랓	ㅐ	ㅠ	ㅁㅿ	ㅇㅇ
1	ㄱ	ㅁ	ㅑ	ㅡ	뭉	ㆁ
2	ㄲ	ㅂ	ㅒ	ㅢ	ㅂㄱ	ㅸ
3	ㄳ	ㅃ	ㅓ	ㅣ	ㅳ	ㅿㅿ
4	ㄴ	ㅄ	ㅔ	(채움)	ㅄㄱ	퐁
5	ㄵ	ㅅ	ㅕ	ㄴㄴ	ㅄㄷ	ㆅ
6	ㄶ	ㅆ	ㅖ	ㄴㄷ	ㅄㅅ	ㆆ
7	ㄷ	ㅇ	ㅗ	ㄴㅅ	ㅂㅌ	ㅛㅑ
8	ㄸ	ㅈ	ㅘ	ㄴㅿ	봉	ㅛㅒ
9	ㄹ	ㅉ	ㅙ	ㄹㅅ	뵹	ㅛㅣ
A	ㄺ	ㅊ	ㅚ	ㄹㄷ	ㅅㄱ	ㅠㅓ
B	ㄻ	ㅋ	ㅛ	ㄹㅄ	ㅅㄴ	ㅠㅔ
C	ㄼ	ㅌ	ㅜ	ㄹㅿ	ㅅㄷ	ㅠㅣ
D	ㄽ	ㅍ	ㅝ	ㄹㆆ	ㅄ	·
E	ㄾ	ㅎ	ㅞ	ㅁㅂ	ㅆ	ᆢ
F	ㄿ	ㅏ	ㅟ	ㅁㅅ	ㅿ	

Based on KS C 5601
Modern letters

3130		
3131	ㄱ	HANGUL LETTER GIYEOG
3132	ㄲ	HANGUL LETTER SSANG GIYEOG
3133	ㄳ	HANGUL LETTER GIYEOG SIOS
3134	ㄴ	HANGUL LETTER NIEUN
3135	ㄵ	HANGUL LETTER NIEUN JIEUJ
3136	ㄶ	HANGUL LETTER NIEUN HIEUH
3137	ㄷ	HANGUL LETTER DIGEUD
3138	ㄸ	HANGUL LETTER SSANG DIGEUD
3139	ㄹ	HANGUL LETTER LIEUL
313A	ㄺ	HANGUL LETTER LIEUL GIYEOG
313B	ㄻ	HANGUL LETTER LIEUL MIEUM
313C	ㄼ	HANGUL LETTER LIEUL BIEUB
313D	ㄽ	HANGUL LETTER LIEUL SIOS
313E	ㄾ	HANGUL LETTER LIEUL TIEUT
313F	ㄿ	HANGUL LETTER LIEUL PIEUP
3140	ㅀ	HANGUL LETTER LIEUL HIEUH
3141	ㅁ	HANGUL LETTER MIEUM
3142	ㅂ	HANGUL LETTER BIEUB
3143	ㅃ	HANGUL LETTER SSANG BIEUB
3144	ㅄ	HANGUL LETTER BIEUB SIOS
3145	ㅅ	HANGUL LETTER SIOS
3146	ㅆ	HANGUL LETTER SSANG SIOS
3147	ㅇ	HANGUL LETTER IEUNG
3148	ㅈ	HANGUL LETTER JIEUJ
3149	ㅉ	HANGUL LETTER SSANG JIEUJ
314A	ㅊ	HANGUL LETTER CIEUC
314B	ㅋ	HANGUL LETTER KIYEOK
314C	ㅌ	HANGUL LETTER TIEUT
314D	ㅍ	HANGUL LETTER PIEUP
314E	ㅎ	HANGUL LETTER HIEUH
314F	ㅏ	HANGUL LETTER A
3150	ㅐ	HANGUL LETTER AE
3151	ㅑ	HANGUL LETTER YA
3152	ㅒ	HANGUL LETTER YAE
3153	ㅓ	HANGUL LETTER EO
3154	ㅔ	HANGUL LETTER E
3155	ㅕ	HANGUL LETTER YEO
3156	ㅖ	HANGUL LETTER YE
3157	ㅗ	HANGUL LETTER O
3158	ㅘ	HANGUL LETTER WA
3159	ㅙ	HANGUL LETTER WAE
315A	ㅚ	HANGUL LETTER OE
315B	ㅛ	HANGUL LETTER YO
315C	ㅜ	HANGUL LETTER U
315D	ㅝ	HANGUL LETTER WEO
315E	ㅞ	HANGUL LETTER WE
315F	ㅟ	HANGUL LETTER WI
3160	ㅠ	HANGUL LETTER YU
3161	ㅡ	HANGUL LETTER EU
3162	ㅢ	HANGUL LETTER YI
3163	ㅣ	HANGUL LETTER I

Special character

3164	ㅤ	HANGUL CAE OM
		= FILL

Archaic letters

3165	ㅥ	HANGUL LETTER SSANG NIEUN
3166	ㅦ	HANGUL LETTER NIEUN DIGEUD
3167	ㅧ	HANGUL LETTER NIEUN SIOS
3168	ㅨ	HANGUL LETTER NIEUN BAN CHI EUM
3169	ㅩ	HANGUL LETTER LIEUL GIYEOG SIOS
316A	ㅪ	HANGUL LETTER LIEUL DIGEUD
316B	ㅫ	HANGUL LETTER LIEUL BIEUB SIOS
316C	ㅬ	HANGUL LETTER LIEUL BAN CHI EUM
316D	ㅭ	HANGUL LETTER LIEUL YEOLIN HIEUH
316E	ㅮ	HANGUL LETTER MIEUM BIEUB
316F	ㅯ	HANGUL LETTER MIEUM SIOS
3170	ㅰ	HANGUL LETTER BIEUB BAN CHI EUM
3171	ㅱ	HANGUL LETTER MIEUM SUN GYEONG EUM
3172	ㅲ	HANGUL LETTER BIEUB GIYEOG
3173	ㅳ	HANGUL LETTER BIEUB DIGEUD
3174	ㅴ	HANGUL LETTER BIEUB SIOS GIYEOG
3175	ㅵ	HANGUL LETTER BIEUB SIOS DIGEUD
3176	ㅶ	HANGUL LETTER BIEUB JIEUJ
3177	ㅷ	HANGUL LETTER BIEUB TIEUT
3178	ㅸ	HANGUL LETTER BIEUB SUN GYEONG EUM
3179	ㅹ	HANGUL LETTER SSANG BIEUB SUN GYEONG EUM
317A	ㅺ	HANGUL LETTER SIOS GIYEOG
317B	ㅻ	HANGUL LETTER SIOS NIEUN
317C	ㅼ	HANGUL LETTER SIOS DIGEUD
317D	ㅽ	HANGUL LETTER SIOS BIEUB
317E	ㅾ	HANGUL LETTER SIOS JIEUJ
317F	ㅿ	HANGUL LETTER BAN CHI EUM
3180	ㆀ	HANGUL LETTER SSANG IEUNG
3181	ㆁ	HANGUL LETTER NGIEUNG
		archaic velar nasal
3182	ㆂ	HANGUL LETTER NGIEUNG SIOS

3183	ᅀᅀ	HANGUL LETTER NGIEUNG BAN CHI EUM
3184	ㅸ	HANGUL LETTER PIEUP SUN GYEONG EUM
3185	ㆅ	HANGUL LETTER SSANG HIEUH
3186	ㆆ	HANGUL LETTER YEOLIN HIEUH
		archaic glottal stop
3187	ㆇ	HANGUL LETTER YOYA
3188	ㆈ	HANGUL LETTER YOYAE
3189	ㆉ	HANGUL LETTER YOI
318A	ㆊ	HANGUL LETTER YUYEO
318B	ㆋ	HANGUL LETTER YUYE
318C	ㆌ	HANGUL LETTER YUI
318D	ㆍ	HANGUL LETTER ALAE A
318E	ㆎ	HANGUL LETTER ALAE AE

	319	31A	31B	31C	31D	31E	31F
0	丨						
1	レ						
2	一						
3	二						
4	三						
5	四						
6	上						
7	中						
8	下						
9	甲						
A	乙						
B	丙						
C	丁						
D	天						
E	地						
F	人						

Kanbun symbols

3190	〡	KANBUN TATETEN
3191	レ	KAERITEN RE
3192	一	KAERITEN ITI
3193	二	KAERITEN NI
3194	三	KAERITEN SAN
3195	四	KAERITEN SI
3196	上	KAERITEN ZYOU
3197	中	KAERITEN TYUU
3198	下	KAERITEN GE
3199	甲	KAERITEN KOU
319A	乙	KAERITEN OTU
319B	丙	KAERITEN HEI
319C	丁	KAERITEN TEI
319D	天	KAERITEN TEN
319E	地	KAERITEN TI
319F	人	KAERITEN ZIN

	320	321	322	323	324	325	326	327
0	(ㄱ)	(다)	(一)	(日)	祭		㉠	㉰
1	(ㄴ)	(라)	(二)	(株)	(休)		㉡	㉱
2	(ㄷ)	(마)	(三)	(有)	(自)		㉢	㉲
3	(ㄹ)	(바)	(四)	(社)	(至)		㉣	㉳
4	(ㅁ)	(시)	(五)	(名)			㉤	㉴
5	(ㅂ)	(아)	(六)	(特)			㉥	㉵
6	(ㅅ)	(자)	(七)	(財)			㉦	㉶
7	(ㅇ)	(차)	(八)	(祝)			㉧	㉷
8	(ㅈ)	(카)	(九)	(労)			㉨	㉸
9	(ㅊ)	(타)	(十)	(代)			㉩	㉹
A	(ㅋ)	(파)	(月)	(呼)			㉪	㉺
B	(ㅌ)	(하)	(火)	(学)			㉫	㉻
C	(ㅍ)	(주)	(水)	(監)			㉬	
D	(ㅎ)		(木)	(企)			㉭	
E	(가)		(金)	(資)			㉮	
F	(나)		(土)	(協)			㉯	㉿

	328	329	32A	32B	32C	32D	32E	32F
0	㊀	㊐	㊠	㊰		㋐	㋠	㋰
1	㊁	㊑	㊡			㋑	㋡	㋱
2	㊂	㊒	㊢			㋒	㋢	㋲
3	㊃	㊓	㊣			㋓	㋣	㋳
4	㊄	㊔	㊤			㋔	㋤	㋴
5	㊅	㊕	㊥			㋕	㋥	㋵
6	㊆	㊖	㊦			㋖	㋦	㋶
7	㊇	㊗	㊧			㋗	㋧	㋷
8	㊈	㊘	㊨			㋘	㋨	㋸
9	㊉	㊙	㊩			㋙	㋩	㋹
A	㊊	㊚	㊪			㋚	㋪	㋺
B	㊋	㊛	㊫			㋛	㋫	㋻
C	㊌	㊜	㊬			㋜	㋬	㋼
D	㊍	㊝	㊭			㋝	㋭	㋽
E	㊎	㊞	㊮			㋞	㋮	㋾
F	㊏	㊟	㊯			㋟	㋯	㋿

Parenthesized Hangul elements

3200	(ㄱ)	PARENTHESIZED HANGUL GIYEOG
3201	(ㄴ)	PARENTHESIZED HANGUL NIEUN
3202	(ㄷ)	PARENTHESIZED HANGUL DIGEUD
3203	(ㄹ)	PARENTHESIZED HANGUL LIEUL
3204	(ㅁ)	PARENTHESIZED HANGUL MIEUM
3205	(ㅂ)	PARENTHESIZED HANGUL BIEUB
3206	(ㅅ)	PARENTHESIZED HANGUL SIOS
3207	(ㅇ)	PARENTHESIZED HANGUL IEUNG
3208	(ㅈ)	PARENTHESIZED HANGUL JIEUJ
3209	(ㅊ)	PARENTHESIZED HANGUL CIEUC
320A	(ㅋ)	PARENTHESIZED HANGUL KIYEOK
320B	(ㅌ)	PARENTHESIZED HANGUL TIEUT
320C	(ㅍ)	PARENTHESIZED HANGUL PIEUP
320D	(ㅎ)	PARENTHESIZED HANGUL HIEUH

Parenthesized Hangul syllables

320E	(가)	PARENTHESIZED HANGUL GA
320F	(나)	PARENTHESIZED HANGUL NA
3210	(다)	PARENTHESIZED HANGUL DA
3211	(라)	PARENTHESIZED HANGUL LA
3212	(마)	PARENTHESIZED HANGUL MA
3213	(바)	PARENTHESIZED HANGUL BA
3214	(사)	PARENTHESIZED HANGUL SA
3215	(아)	PARENTHESIZED HANGUL A
3216	(자)	PARENTHESIZED HANGUL JA
3217	(차)	PARENTHESIZED HANGUL CA
3218	(카)	PARENTHESIZED HANGUL KA
3219	(타)	PARENTHESIZED HANGUL TA
321A	(파)	PARENTHESIZED HANGUL PA
321B	(하)	PARENTHESIZED HANGUL HA
321C	(주)	PARENTHESIZED HANGUL JU
321D		
321E		
321F		

Parenthesized ideographs

3220	(一)	PARENTHESIZED IDEOGRAPH ONE
3221	(二)	PARENTHESIZED IDEOGRAPH TWO
3222	(三)	PARENTHESIZED IDEOGRAPH THREE
3223	(四)	PARENTHESIZED IDEOGRAPH FOUR
3224	(五)	PARENTHESIZED IDEOGRAPH FIVE
3225	(六)	PARENTHESIZED IDEOGRAPH SIX
3226	(七)	PARENTHESIZED IDEOGRAPH SEVEN
3227	(八)	PARENTHESIZED IDEOGRAPH EIGHT
3228	(九)	PARENTHESIZED IDEOGRAPH NINE

3229	(十)	PARENTHESIZED IDEOGRAPH TEN
322A	(月)	PARENTHESIZED IDEOGRAPH MOON
		Monday
322B	(火)	PARENTHESIZED IDEOGRAPH FIRE
		Tuesday
322C	(水)	PARENTHESIZED IDEOGRAPH WATER
		Wednesday
322D	(木)	PARENTHESIZED IDEOGRAPH WOOD
		Thursday
322E	(金)	PARENTHESIZED IDEOGRAPH METAL
		Friday
322F	(土)	PARENTHESIZED IDEOGRAPH EARTH
		Saturday
3230	(日)	PARENTHESIZED IDEOGRAPH SUN
		Sunday
3231	(株)	PARENTHESIZED IDEOGRAPH STOCK
		incorporated
3232	(有)	PARENTHESIZED IDEOGRAPH HAVE
		limited
3233	(社)	PARENTHESIZED IDEOGRAPH SOCIETY
		company
3234	(名)	PARENTHESIZED IDEOGRAPH NAME
3235	(特)	PARENTHESIZED IDEOGRAPH SPECIAL
3236	(財)	PARENTHESIZED IDEOGRAPH FINANCIAL
3237	(祝)	PARENTHESIZED IDEOGRAPH CONGRATULATION
3238	(労)	PARENTHESIZED IDEOGRAPH LABOR
3239	(代)	PARENTHESIZED IDEOGRAPH REPRESENT
323A	(呼)	PARENTHESIZED IDEOGRAPH CALL
323B	(学)	PARENTHESIZED IDEOGRAPH STUDY
323C	(監)	PARENTHESIZED IDEOGRAPH SUPERVISE
323D	(企)	PARENTHESIZED IDEOGRAPH ENTERPRISE
323E	(資)	PARENTHESIZED IDEOGRAPH RESOURCE
323F	(協)	PARENTHESIZED IDEOGRAPH ALLIANCE
3240	(祭)	PARENTHESIZED IDEOGRAPH FESTIVAL
3241	(休)	PARENTHESIZED IDEOGRAPH REST
3242	(自)	PARENTHESIZED IDEOGRAPH SELF
		from
3243	(至)	PARENTHESIZED IDEOGRAPH REACH
		to
3244		
3245		
3246		
3247		
3248		
3249		
324A		
324B		
324C		

324D		
324E		
324F		
3250		
3251		
3252		
3253		
3254		
3255		
3256		
3257		
3258		
3259		
325A		
325B		
325C		
325D		
325E		
325F		

Circled Hangul elements

3260	㉠	CIRCLED HANGUL GIYEOG
3261	㉡	CIRCLED HANGUL NIEUN
3262	㉢	CIRCLED HANGUL DIGEUD
3263	㉣	CIRCLED HANGUL LIEUL
3264	㉤	CIRCLED HANGUL MIEUM
3265	㉥	CIRCLED HANGUL BIEUB
3266	㉦	CIRCLED HANGUL SIOS
3267	㉧	CIRCLED HANGUL IEUNG
3268	㉨	CIRCLED HANGUL JIEUJ
3269	㉩	CIRCLED HANGUL CIEUC
326A	㉪	CIRCLED HANGUL KIYEOK
326B	㉫	CIRCLED HANGUL TIEUT
326C	㉬	CIRCLED HANGUL PIEUP
326D	㉭	CIRCLED HANGUL HIEUH

Circled Hangul syllables

326E	㉮	CIRCLED HANGUL GA
326F	㉯	CIRCLED HANGUL NA
3270	㉰	CIRCLED HANGUL DA
3271	㉱	CIRCLED HANGUL LA
3272	㉲	CIRCLED HANGUL MA
3273	㉳	CIRCLED HANGUL BA
3274	㉴	CIRCLED HANGUL SA
3275	㉵	CIRCLED HANGUL A
3276	㉶	CIRCLED HANGUL JA

3277	㉷	CIRCLED HANGUL CA
3278	㉸	CIRCLED HANGUL KA
3279	㉹	CIRCLED HANGUL TA
327A	㉺	CIRCLED HANGUL PA
327B	㉻	CIRCLED HANGUL HA
327C		
327D		
327E		

Symbol

327F	㉿	KOREAN STANDARD SYMBOL

Circled ideographs

3280	㊀	CIRCLED IDEOGRAPH ONE
		= *maru-iti, symbol of unification*
3281	㊁	CIRCLED IDEOGRAPH TWO
3282	㊂	CIRCLED IDEOGRAPH THREE
3283	㊃	CIRCLED IDEOGRAPH FOUR
3284	㊄	CIRCLED IDEOGRAPH FIVE
3285	㊅	CIRCLED IDEOGRAPH SIX
3286	㊆	CIRCLED IDEOGRAPH SEVEN
3287	㊇	CIRCLED IDEOGRAPH EIGHT
3288	㊈	CIRCLED IDEOGRAPH NINE
3289	㊉	CIRCLED IDEOGRAPH TEN
328A	㊊	CIRCLED IDEOGRAPH MOON
		Monday
328B	㊋	CIRCLED IDEOGRAPH FIRE
		Tuesday
328C	㊌	CIRCLED IDEOGRAPH WATER
		Wednesday
328D	㊍	CIRCLED IDEOGRAPH WOOD
		Thursday
328E	㊎	CIRCLED IDEOGRAPH METAL
		Friday
328F	㊏	CIRCLED IDEOGRAPH EARTH
		Saturday
3290	㊐	CIRCLED IDEOGRAPH SUN
		Sunday
3291	㊑	CIRCLED IDEOGRAPH STOCK
		incorporated
3292	㊒	CIRCLED IDEOGRAPH HAVE
		limited
3293	㊓	CIRCLED IDEOGRAPH SOCIETY
		company
3294	㊔	CIRCLED IDEOGRAPH NAME
3295	㊕	CIRCLED IDEOGRAPH SPECIAL
3296	㊖	CIRCLED IDEOGRAPH FINANCIAL
3297	㊗	CIRCLED IDEOGRAPH CONGRATULATION
3298	㊘	CIRCLED IDEOGRAPH LABOR

3299	秘	CIRCLED IDEOGRAPH SECRET
329A	男	CIRCLED IDEOGRAPH MALE
329B	女	CIRCLED IDEOGRAPH FEMALE
329C	適	CIRCLED IDEOGRAPH SUITABLE
329D	優	CIRCLED IDEOGRAPH EXCELLENT
329E	印	CIRCLED IDEOGRAPH PRINT
		name seal
329F	注	CIRCLED IDEOGRAPH ATTENTION
32A0	項	CIRCLED IDEOGRAPH ITEM
32A1	休	CIRCLED IDEOGRAPH REST
		holiday
32A2	写	CIRCLED IDEOGRAPH COPY
32A3	正	CIRCLED IDEOGRAPH CORRECT
32A4	上	CIRCLED IDEOGRAPH HIGH
32A5	中	CIRCLED IDEOGRAPH CENTER
32A6	下	CIRCLED IDEOGRAPH LOW
32A7	左	CIRCLED IDEOGRAPH LEFT
32A8	右	CIRCLED IDEOGRAPH RIGHT
32A9	医	CIRCLED IDEOGRAPH MEDICINE
32AA	宗	CIRCLED IDEOGRAPH RELIGION
32AB	学	CIRCLED IDEOGRAPH STUDY
32AC	監	CIRCLED IDEOGRAPH SUPERVISE
32AD	企	CIRCLED IDEOGRAPH ENTERPRISE
32AE	資	CIRCLED IDEOGRAPH RESOURCE
32AF	協	CIRCLED IDEOGRAPH ALLIANCE
32B0	夜	CIRCLED IDEOGRAPH NIGHT
32B1		
32B2		
32B3		
32B4		
32B5		
32B6		
32B7		
32B8		
32B9		
32BA		
32BB		
32BC		
32BD		
32BE		
32BF		
32C0		
32C1		
32C2		
32C3		
32C4		

32C5		
32C6		
32C7		
32C8		
32C9		
32CA		
32CB		
32CC		
32CD		
32CE		
32CF		

Circled Katakana

32D0	イ	CIRCLED KATAKANA I
32D1	ロ	CIRCLED KATAKANA RO
32D2	ハ	CIRCLED KATAKANA HA
32D3	ニ	CIRCLED KATAKANA NI
32D4	ホ	CIRCLED KATAKANA HO
32D5	ヘ	CIRCLED KATAKANA HE
32D6	ト	CIRCLED KATAKANA TO
32D7	チ	CIRCLED KATAKANA TI
32D8	リ	CIRCLED KATAKANA RI
32D9	ヌ	CIRCLED KATAKANA NU
32DA	ル	CIRCLED KATAKANA RU
32DB	ヲ	CIRCLED KATAKANA WO
32DC	ワ	CIRCLED KATAKANA WA
32DD	カ	CIRCLED KATAKANA KA
32DE	ヨ	CIRCLED KATAKANA YO
32DF	タ	CIRCLED KATAKANA TA
32E0	レ	CIRCLED KATAKANA RE
32E1	ソ	CIRCLED KATAKANA SO
32E2	ツ	CIRCLED KATAKANA TU
32E3	ネ	CIRCLED KATAKANA NE
32E4	ナ	CIRCLED KATAKANA NA
32E5	ラ	CIRCLED KATAKANA RA
32E6	ム	CIRCLED KATAKANA MU
32E7	ウ	CIRCLED KATAKANA U
32E8	ヰ	CIRCLED KATAKANA WI
32E9	ノ	CIRCLED KATAKANA NO
32EA	オ	CIRCLED KATAKANA O
32EB	ク	CIRCLED KATAKANA KU
32EC	ヤ	CIRCLED KATAKANA YA
32ED	マ	CIRCLED KATAKANA MA
32EE	ケ	CIRCLED KATAKANA KE
32EF	フ	CIRCLED KATAKANA HU
32F0	コ	CIRCLED KATAKANA KO

32F1	㋱	CIRCLED KATAKANA WE
32F2	㋒	CIRCLED KATAKANA TE
32F3	㋐	CIRCLED KATAKANA A
32F4	㋚	CIRCLED KATAKANA SA
32F5	㋖	CIRCLED KATAKANA KI
32F6	㋴	CIRCLED KATAKANA YU
32F7	㋝	CIRCLED KATAKANA ME
32F8	㋜	CIRCLED KATAKANA MI
32F9	㋛	CIRCLED KATAKANA SI
32FA	㋓	CIRCLED KATAKANA E
32FB	㋪	CIRCLED KATAKANA HI
32FC	㋲	CIRCLED KATAKANA MO
32FD	㋥	CIRCLED KATAKANA SE
32FE	㋨	CIRCLED KATAKANA SU

Symbol

32FF	㍿	JAPANESE INDUSTRIAL STANDARD SYMBOL

	330	331	332	333	334	335	336	337
0	アパート	ギガ	サンチーム	ピコ	ポンド	ユアン		
1	アルフア	ギニー	シリング	ビル	ホール	リットル		
2	アンペア	キュリー	センチ	フアラッド	ホン	リラ		
3	アール	ギルダー	セント	フイート	マイクロ	ルピー		
4	イニング	キロ	ダース	ブッシェル	マイル	ルーブル		
5	インチ	キログラム	デシ	フラン	マッハ	レム		
6	ウオン	キロメートル	ドル	ヘクタール	マルク	レントゲン		
7	エスクード	キロワット	トン	ペソ	マンション	ワット		
8	エーカー	グラム	ナノ	ペニヒ	ミクロン			
9	オンス	グラムトン	ノット	ヘルツ	ミリ			
A	オーム	クルゼイロ	ハイツ	ペンス	ミリバール			
B	カイリ	クローネ	パーセント	ページ	メガ			平成
C	カラット	ケース	パーツ	ベータ	メガトン			昭和
D	カロリー	コルナ	バーレル	ポイント	メートル			大正
E	ガロン	コーポ	ピアストル	ボルト	ヤード			明治
F	ガンマ	サイクル	ピクル	ホン	ヤール			株式会社

Squared Katakana words

3300	アパ ート	**SQUARED APAATO** *apartment*
3301	アル ファ	**SQUARED ARUHUA** *alpha*
3302	アン ペア	**SQUARED ANPEA** *ampere*
3303	アー ル	**SQUARED AARU** *are (unit of area)*
3304	イニ ング	**SQUARED ININGU** *inning*
3305	イン チ	**SQUARED INTI** *inch*
3306	ウォ ン	**SQUARED UON** *won (Korean currency)*
3307	エス クード	**SQUARED ESUKUUDO** *escudo (Portuguese currency)*
3308	エー カー	**SQUARED EEKAA** *acre*
3309	オン ス	**SQUARED ONSU** *ounce*
330A	オー ム	**SQUARED OOMU** *ohm*
330B	カイ リ	**SQUARED KAIRI** *kai-ri: nautical mile*
330C	カラ ット	**SQUARED KARATTO** *carat*
330D	カロ リー	**SQUARED KARORII** *calorie*
330E	ガロ ン	**SQUARED GARON** *gallon*
330F	ガン マ	**SQUARED GANMA** *gamma*
3310	ギ ガ	**SQUARED GIGA** *giga-*
3311	ギニ ー	**SQUARED GINII** *guinea*
3312	キュ リー	**SQUARED KYURII** *curie*
3313	ギル ダー	**SQUARED GIRUDAA** *guilder*
3314	キ ロ	**SQUARED KIRO** *kilo-*
3315	キロ グラム	**SQUARED KIROGURAMU** *kilogram*
3316	キロメ ートル	**SQUARED KIROMEETORU** *kilometer*
3317	キロ ワット	**SQUARED KIROWATTO** *kilowatt*
3318	グラ ム	**SQUARED GURAMU** *gram*
3319	グラム トン	**SQUARED GURAMUTON** *gram ton*
331A	クル ゼイロ	**SQUARED KURUZEIRO** *cruzeiro (Brazilian currency)*
331B	クロ ーネ	**SQUARED KUROONE** *krone*
331C	ケー ス	**SQUARED KEESU** *case*
331D	コル ナ	**SQUARED KORUNA** *koruna (Czech currency)*
331E	コー ポ	**SQUARED KOOPO** *co-op*
331F	サイ クル	**SQUARED SAIKURU** *cycle*
3320	サン チーム	**SQUARED SANTIIMU** *centime*
3321	シリ ング	**SQUARED SIRINGU** *shilling*
3322	セン チ	**SQUARED SENTI** *centi-*
3323	セン ト	**SQUARED SENTO** *cent*
3324	ダー ス	**SQUARED DAASU** *dozen*
3325	デ シ	**SQUARED DESI** *deci-*
3326	ド ル	**SQUARED DORU** *dollar*
3327	ト ン	**SQUARED TON** *ton*
3328	ナ ノ	**SQUARED NANO** *nano-*
3329	ノッ ト	**SQUARED NOTTO** *knot, nautical mile*
332A	ハイ ツ	**SQUARED HAITU** *heights*
332B	バー セント	**SQUARED PAASENTO** *percent*
332C	バー ツ	**SQUARED PAATU** *parts*
332D	バー レル	**SQUARED BAARERU** *barrel*
332E	ピア ストル	**SQUARED PIASUTORU** *piaster*
332F	ピク ル	**SQUARED PIKURU** *picul (unit of weight)*
3330	ピ コ	**SQUARED PIKO** *pico-*
3331	ビ ル	**SQUARED BIRU** *building*
3332	フア ラッド	**SQUARED HUARADDO** *farad*
3333	フィ ート	**SQUARED HUIITO** *feet*

3334	ブッ シェル	SQUARED BUSSYERU *bushel*
3335	フラ ン	SQUARED HURAN *franc*
3336	ヘク タール	SQUARED HEKUTAARU *hectare*
3337	ペ ソ	SQUARED PESO *peso*
3338	ペニ ヒ	SQUARED PENIHI *pfennig*
3339	ヘル ツ	SQUARED HERUTU *hertz*
333A	ペン ス	SQUARED PENSU *pence*
333B	ペー ジ	SQUARED PEEZI *page*
333C	ベー タ	SQUARED BEETA *beta*
333D	ポイ ント	SQUARED POINTO *point*
333E	ボル ト	SQUARED BORUTO *volt, bolt*
333F	ホ ン	SQUARED HON *hon: volume*
3340	ポン ド	SQUARED PONDO *pound*
3341	ホー ル	SQUARED HOORU *hall*
3342	ホー ン	SQUARED HOON *horn*
3343	マイ クロ	SQUARED MAIKURO *micro-*
3344	マイ ル	SQUARED MAIRU *mile*
3345	マッ ハ	SQUARED MAHHA *mach*
3346	マル ク	SQUARED MARUKU *mark*
3347	マン ション	SQUARED MANSYON *mansion*
3348	ミク ロン	SQUARED MIKURON *micron*
3349	ミ リ	SQUARED MIRI *milli-*
334A	ミリ バール	SQUARED MIRIBAARU *millibar*
334B	メ ガ	SQUARED MEGA *mega-*
334C	メガ トン	SQUARED MEGATON *megaton*
334D	メー トル	SQUARED MEETORU *meter*

334E	ヤー ド	SQUARED YAADO *yard*
334F	ヤー ル	SQUARED YAARU *yard*
3350	ユア ン	SQUARED YUAN *yuan (Chinese currency)*
3351	リッ トル	SQUARED RITTORU *liter*
3352	リ ラ	SQUARED RIRA *lira*
3353	ルピ ー	SQUARED RUPII *rupee*
3354	ルー ブル	SQUARED RUUBURU *ruble*
3355	レ ム	SQUARED REMU *rem (unit of radiation)*
3356	レン トゲン	SQUARED RENTOGEN *roentgen*
3357	ワッ ト	SQUARED WATTO *watt*
3358		
3359		
335A		
335B		
335C		
335D		
335E		
335F		
3360		
3361		
3362		
3363		
3364		
3365		
3366		
3367		
3368		
3369		
336A		
336B		
336C		
336D		
336E		
336F		
3370		
3371		
3372		
3373		
3374		

3375

3376

3377

3378

3379

337A

Japanese era names

337B   平成   SQUARED TWO IDEOGRAPHS ERA NAME HEISEI

337C   昭和   SQUARED TWO IDEOGRAPHS ERA NAME SYOUWA

337D   大正   SQUARED TWO IDEOGRAPHS ERA NAME TAISYOU

337E   明治   SQUARED TWO IDEOGRAPHS ERA NAME MEIZI

Japanese corporation

337F   株式会社   SQUARED FOUR IDEOGRAPHS CORPORATION
       = *kabusiki-gaisya*
       incorporated

	338	339	33A	33B	33C	33D	33E	33F
0	pA	Hz	cm²	ps	kΩ	lm		
1	nA	kHz	m²	ns	MΩ	ln		
2	µA	MHz	km²	µs	a.m.	log		
3	mA	GHz	mm³	ms	Bq	lx		
4	kA	THz	c m³	pV	cc	mb		
5	KB	µℓ	m³	nV	cd	mil		
6	MB	mℓ	km³	µV	C/kg	mol		
7	GB	dℓ	m/s	mV	Co.	PH		
8	cal	kℓ	m/s²	kV	dB	p.m.		
9	kcal	fm	Pa	MV	Gy	PPM		
A	pF	nm	kPa	pW	ha	PR		
B	nF	µm	MPa	nW	HP	sr		
C	µF	mm	GPa	µW	in	Sv		
D	µg	cm	rad	mW	KK	Wb		
E	mg	km	rad/s	kW	KM			
F	kg	mm²	rad/s²	MW	kt			

Squared Latin abbreviations

3380	pA	SQUARED PA AMPS
3381	nA	SQUARED NA
3382	μA	SQUARED MU A
3383	mA	SQUARED MA
3384	kA	SQUARED KA
3385	KB	SQUARED KB
3386	MB	SQUARED MB
3387	GB	SQUARED GB
3388	cal	SQUARED CAL
3389	kcal	SQUARED KCAL
338A	pF	SQUARED PF
338B	nF	SQUARED NF
338C	μF	SQUARED MU F
338D	μg	SQUARED MU G
338E	mg	SQUARED MG
338F	kg	SQUARED KG
3390	Hz	SQUARED HZ
3391	kHz	SQUARED KHZ
3392	MHz	SQUARED MHZ
3393	GHz	SQUARED GHZ
3394	THz	SQUARED THZ
3395	μℓ	SQUARED MU L
3396	mℓ	SQUARED ML
3397	dℓ	SQUARED DL
3398	kℓ	SQUARED KL
3399	fm	SQUARED FM
339A	nm	SQUARED NM
339B	μm	SQUARED MU M
339C	mm	SQUARED MM
339D	cm	SQUARED CM
339E	km	SQUARED KM
339F	mm²	SQUARED MM SQUARED
33A0	cm²	SQUARED CM SQUARED
33A1	m²	SQUARED M SQUARED
33A2	km²	SQUARED KM SQUARED
33A3	mm³	SQUARED MM CUBED
33A4	cm³	SQUARED CM CUBED
33A5	m³	SQUARED M CUBED
33A6	km³	SQUARED KM CUBED
33A7	m/s	SQUARED M OVER S
33A8	m/s²	SQUARED M OVER S SQUARED
33A9	Pa	SQUARED PA
33AA	kPa	SQUARED KPA
33AB	MPa	SQUARED MPA
33AC	GPa	SQUARED GPA
33AD	rad	SQUARED RAD
33AE	rad/s	SQUARED RAD OVER S
33AF	rad/s²	SQUARED RAD OVER S SQUARED
33B0	ps	SQUARED PS
33B1	ns	SQUARED NS
33B2	μs	SQUARED MU S
33B3	ms	SQUARED MS
33B4	pV	SQUARED PV
33B5	nV	SQUARED NV
33B6	μV	SQUARED MU V
33B7	mV	SQUARED MV
33B8	kV	SQUARED KV
33B9	MV	SQUARED MV MEGA
33BA	pW	SQUARED PW
33BB	nW	SQUARED NW
33BC	μW	SQUARED MU W
33BD	mW	SQUARED MW
33BE	kW	SQUARED KW
33BF	MW	SQUARED MW MEGA
33C0	kΩ	SQUARED K OHM
33C1	MΩ	SQUARED M OHM
33C2	a.m.	SQUARED AM
33C3	Bq	SQUARED BQ
33C4	cc	SQUARED CC
33C5	cd	SQUARED CD
33C6	C/kg	SQUARED C OVER KG
33C7	Co.	SQUARED CO
33C8	dB	SQUARED DB
33C9	Gy	SQUARED GY
33CA	ha	SQUARED HA
33CB	HP	SQUARED HP
33CC	in	SQUARED IN
33CD	KK	SQUARED KK
33CE	KM	SQUARED KM CAPITAL
33CF	kt	SQUARED KT
33D0	lm	SQUARED LM
33D1	ln	SQUARED LN
33D2	log	SQUARED LOG
33D3	lx	SQUARED LX
33D4	mb	SQUARED MB SMALL
33D5	mil	SQUARED MIL
33D6	mol	SQUARED MOL
33D7	PH	SQUARED PH
33D8	p.m.	SQUARED PM
33D9	PPM	SQUARED PPM
33DA	PR	SQUARED PR

33DB	sr	SQUARED SR
33DC	Sv	SQUARED SV
33DD	Wb	SQUARED WB

This page intentionally left blank. The material is undergoing review. The revised version will appear in Volume 2.

This page intentionally left blank. The material is undergoing review. The revised version will appear in Volume 2.

This page intentionally left blank. The material is undergoing review. The revised version will appear in Volume 2.

This page intentionally left blank. The material is undergoing review. The revised version will appear in Volume 2.

This page intentionally left blank. The material is undergoing review.
The revised version will appear in Volume 2.

This page intentionally left blank. The material is undergoing review. The revised version will appear in Volume 2.

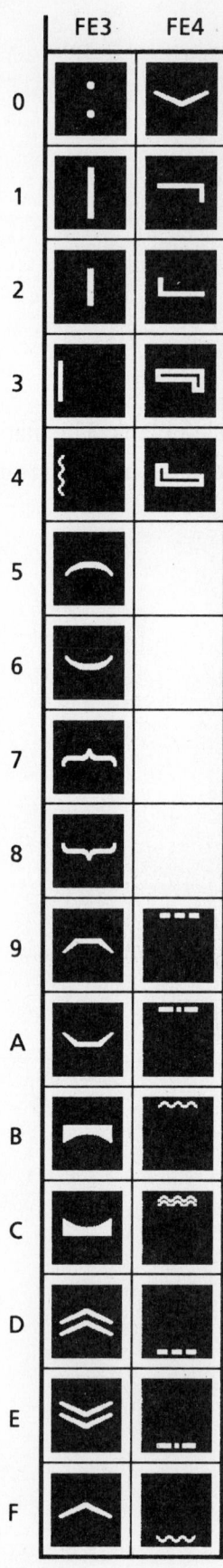

Glyphs for vertical variants

FE30	⦙	GLYPH FOR VERTICAL TWO DOT LEADER
FE31			GLYPH FOR VERTICAL EM DASH
FE32			GLYPH FOR VERTICAL EN DASH
FE33			GLYPH FOR VERTICAL SPACING UNDERSCORE
FE34	⦚	GLYPH FOR VERTICAL SPACING WAVY UNDERSCORE
FE35	⌢	GLYPH FOR VERTICAL OPENING PARENTHESIS
FE36	⌣	GLYPH FOR VERTICAL CLOSING PARENTHESIS
FE37		GLYPH FOR VERTICAL OPENING CURLY BRACKET
FE38		GLYPH FOR VERTICAL CLOSING CURLY BRACKET
FE39		GLYPH FOR VERTICAL OPENING TORTOISE SHELL BRACKET
FE3A		GLYPH FOR VERTICAL CLOSING TORTOISE SHELL BRACKET
FE3B		GLYPH FOR VERTICAL OPENING BLACK LENTICULAR BRACKET
FE3C		GLYPH FOR VERTICAL CLOSING BLACK LENTICULAR BRACKET
FE3D	⩵	GLYPH FOR VERTICAL OPENING DOUBLE ANGLE BRACKET
FE3E	⩶	GLYPH FOR VERTICAL CLOSING DOUBLE ANGLE BRACKET
FE3F		GLYPH FOR VERTICAL OPENING ANGLE BRACKET
FE40		GLYPH FOR VERTICAL CLOSING ANGLE BRACKET
FE41		GLYPH FOR VERTICAL OPENING CORNER BRACKET
FE42		GLYPH FOR VERTICAL CLOSING CORNER BRACKET
FE43		GLYPH FOR VERTICAL OPENING WHITE CORNER BRACKET
FE44		GLYPH FOR VERTICAL CLOSING WHITE CORNER BRACKET
FE45		
FE46		
FE47		
FE48		

Overscores and underscores

FE49		SPACING DASHED OVERSCORE
FE4A		SPACING CENTERLINE OVERSCORE
FE4B		SPACING WAVY OVERSCORE
FE4C		SPACING DOUBLE WAVY OVERSCORE
FE4D		SPACING DASHED UNDERSCORE
FE4E		SPACING CENTERLINE UNDERSCORE
FE4F		SPACING WAVY UNDERSCORE

Small Variants

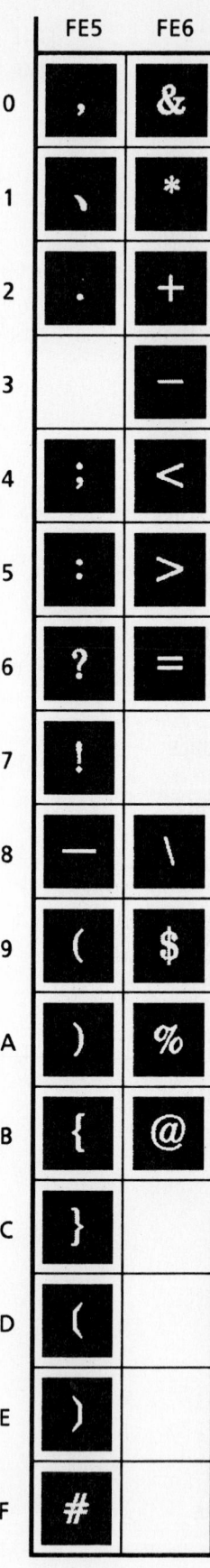

The Unicode Standard • Version 1.0

Small variants

FE50	,	SMALL COMMA
FE51	`	SMALL IDEOGRAPHIC COMMA
FE52	.	SMALL PERIOD
FE53		× (middle dot → 00B7)
FE54	;	SMALL SEMICOLON
FE55	:	SMALL COLON
FE56	?	SMALL QUESTION MARK
FE57	!	SMALL EXCLAMATION MARK
FE58	—	SMALL EM DASH
FE59	(	SMALL OPENING PARENTHESIS
FE5A	)	SMALL CLOSING PARENTHESIS
FE5B	{	SMALL OPENING CURLY BRACKET
FE5C	}	SMALL CLOSING CURLY BRACKET
FE5D	〔	SMALL OPENING TORTOISE SHELL BRACKET
FE5E	〕	SMALL CLOSING TORTOISE SHELL BRACKET
FE5F	#	SMALL NUMBER SIGN
FE60	&	SMALL AMPERSAND
FE61	*	SMALL ASTERISK
FE62	+	SMALL PLUS SIGN
FE63	–	SMALL HYPHEN-MINUS
FE64	<	SMALL LESS-THAN SIGN
FE65	>	SMALL GREATER-THAN SIGN
FE66	=	SMALL EQUALS SIGN
FE67		× (division slash → 2215)
FE68	\	SMALL BACKSLASH
FE69	$	SMALL DOLLAR SIGN
FE6A	%	SMALL PERCENT SIGN
FE6B	@	SMALL COMMERCIAL AT

Basic Glyphs for Arabic Language

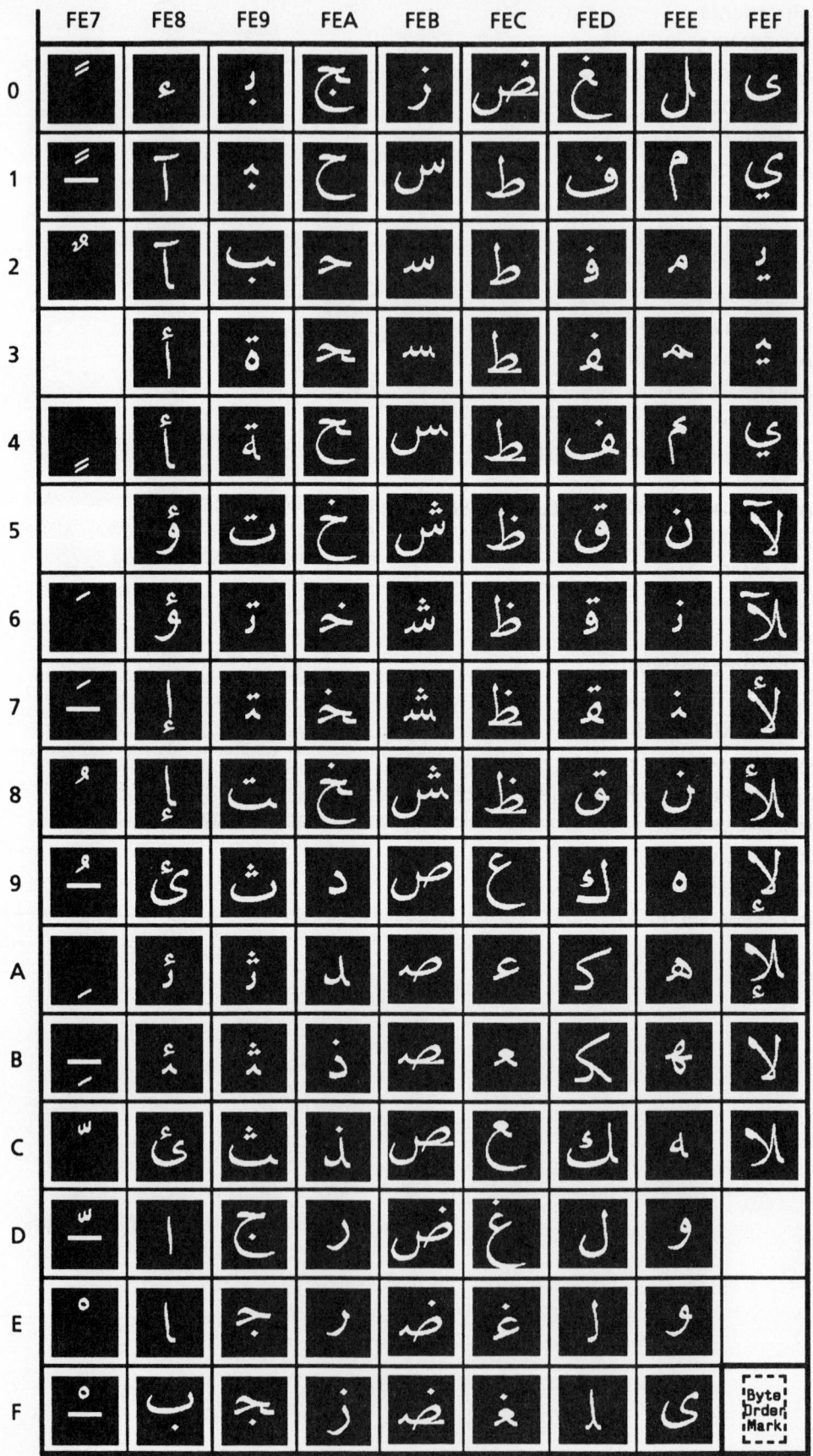

The Unicode Standard • Version 1.0

Glyphs for spacing forms of Arabic points

FE70		ARABIC SPACING FATHATAN
FE71		ARABIC FATHATAN ON TATWEEL
FE72		ARABIC SPACING DAMMATAN
FE73		
FE74		ARABIC SPACING KASRATAN
FE75		
FE76		ARABIC SPACING FATHAH
FE77		ARABIC FATHAH ON TATWEEL
FE78		ARABIC SPACING DAMMAH
FE79		ARABIC DAMMAH ON TATWEEL
FE7A		ARABIC SPACING KASRAH
FE7B		ARABIC KASRAH ON TATWEEL
FE7C		ARABIC SPACING SHADDAH
FE7D		ARABIC SHADDAH ON TATWEEL
FE7E		ARABIC SPACING SUKUN
FE7F		ARABIC SUKUN ON TATWEEL

Basic glyphs for Arabic language contextual forms

FE80		GLYPH FOR ISOLATE ARABIC HAMZAH
FE81		GLYPH FOR ISOLATE ARABIC MADDAH ON ALEF
FE82		GLYPH FOR FINAL ARABIC MADDAH ON ALEF
FE83		GLYPH FOR ISOLATE ARABIC HAMZAH ON ALEF
FE84		GLYPH FOR FINAL ARABIC HAMZAH ON ALEF
FE85		GLYPH FOR ISOLATE ARABIC HAMZAH ON WAW
FE86		GLYPH FOR FINAL ARABIC HAMZAH ON WAW
FE87		GLYPH FOR ISOLATE ARABIC HAMZAH UNDER ALEF
FE88		GLYPH FOR FINAL ARABIC HAMZAH UNDER ALEF
FE89		GLYPH FOR ISOLATE ARABIC HAMZAH ON YA
FE8A		GLYPH FOR INITIAL ARABIC HAMZAH ON YA
FE8B		GLYPH FOR MEDIAL ARABIC HAMZAH ON YA
FE8C		GLYPH FOR FINAL ARABIC HAMZAH ON YA
FE8D		GLYPH FOR ISOLATE ARABIC ALEF
FE8E		GLYPH FOR FINAL ARABIC ALEF
FE8F		GLYPH FOR ISOLATE ARABIC BAA
FE90		GLYPH FOR INITIAL ARABIC BAA
FE91		GLYPH FOR MEDIAL ARABIC BAA
FE92		GLYPH FOR FINAL ARABIC BAA
FE93		GLYPH FOR ISOLATE ARABIC TAA MARBUTAH
FE94		GLYPH FOR FINAL ARABIC TAA MARBUTAH
FE95		GLYPH FOR ISOLATE ARABIC TAA
FE96		GLYPH FOR INITIAL ARABIC TAA
FE97		GLYPH FOR MEDIAL ARABIC TAA
FE98		GLYPH FOR FINAL ARABIC TAA
FE99		GLYPH FOR ISOLATE ARABIC THAA
FE9A		GLYPH FOR INITIAL ARABIC THAA
FE9B		GLYPH FOR MEDIAL ARABIC THAA
FE9C		GLYPH FOR FINAL ARABIC THAA
FE9D		GLYPH FOR ISOLATE ARABIC JEEM
FE9E		GLYPH FOR INITIAL ARABIC JEEM
FE9F		GLYPH FOR MEDIAL ARABIC JEEM
FEA0		GLYPH FOR FINAL ARABIC JEEM
FEA1		GLYPH FOR ISOLATE ARABIC HAA
FEA2		GLYPH FOR INITIAL ARABIC HAA
FEA3		GLYPH FOR MEDIAL ARABIC HAA
FEA4		GLYPH FOR FINAL ARABIC HAA
FEA5		GLYPH FOR ISOLATE ARABIC KHAA
FEA6		GLYPH FOR INITIAL ARABIC KHAA
FEA7		GLYPH FOR MEDIAL ARABIC KHAA
FEA8		GLYPH FOR FINAL ARABIC KHAA
FEA9		GLYPH FOR ISOLATE ARABIC DAL
FEAA		GLYPH FOR FINAL ARABIC DAL
FEAB		GLYPH FOR ISOLATE ARABIC THAL
FEAC		GLYPH FOR FINAL ARABIC THAL
FEAD		GLYPH FOR ISOLATE ARABIC RA
FEAE		GLYPH FOR FINAL ARABIC RA
FEAF		GLYPH FOR ISOLATE ARABIC ZAIN
FEB0		GLYPH FOR FINAL ARABIC ZAIN
FEB1		GLYPH FOR ISOLATE ARABIC SEEN
FEB2		GLYPH FOR INITIAL ARABIC SEEN
FEB3		GLYPH FOR MEDIAL ARABIC SEEN
FEB4		GLYPH FOR FINAL ARABIC SEEN
FEB5		GLYPH FOR ISOLATE ARABIC SHEEN
FEB6		GLYPH FOR INITIAL ARABIC SHEEN
FEB7		GLYPH FOR MEDIAL ARABIC SHEEN
FEB8		GLYPH FOR FINAL ARABIC SHEEN
FEB9		GLYPH FOR ISOLATE ARABIC SAD
FEBA		GLYPH FOR INITIAL ARABIC SAD
FEBB		GLYPH FOR MEDIAL ARABIC SAD
FEBC		GLYPH FOR FINAL ARABIC SAD

FEBD	ض	GLYPH FOR ISOLATE ARABIC DAD
FEBE	ضـ	GLYPH FOR INITIAL ARABIC DAD
FEBF	ـضـ	GLYPH FOR MEDIAL ARABIC DAD
FEC0	ـض	GLYPH FOR FINAL ARABIC DAD
FEC1	ط	GLYPH FOR ISOLATE ARABIC TAH
FEC2	طـ	GLYPH FOR INITIAL ARABIC TAH
FEC3	ـطـ	GLYPH FOR MEDIAL ARABIC TAH
FEC4	ـط	GLYPH FOR FINAL ARABIC TAH
FEC5	ظ	GLYPH FOR ISOLATE ARABIC DHAH
FEC6	ظـ	GLYPH FOR INITIAL ARABIC DHAH
FEC7	ـظـ	GLYPH FOR MEDIAL ARABIC DHAH
FEC8	ـظ	GLYPH FOR FINAL ARABIC DHAH
FEC9	ع	GLYPH FOR ISOLATE ARABIC AIN
FECA	عـ	GLYPH FOR INITIAL ARABIC AIN
FECB	ـعـ	GLYPH FOR MEDIAL ARABIC AIN
FECC	ـع	GLYPH FOR FINAL ARABIC AIN
FECD	غ	GLYPH FOR ISOLATE ARABIC GHAIN
FECE	غـ	GLYPH FOR INITIAL ARABIC GHAIN
FECF	ـغـ	GLYPH FOR MEDIAL ARABIC GHAIN
FED0	ـغ	GLYPH FOR FINAL ARABIC GHAIN
FED1	ف	GLYPH FOR ISOLATE ARABIC FA
FED2	فـ	GLYPH FOR INITIAL ARABIC FA
FED3	ـفـ	GLYPH FOR MEDIAL ARABIC FA
FED4	ـف	GLYPH FOR FINAL ARABIC FA
FED5	ق	GLYPH FOR ISOLATE ARABIC QAF
FED6	قـ	GLYPH FOR INITIAL ARABIC QAF
FED7	ـقـ	GLYPH FOR MEDIAL ARABIC QAF
FED8	ـق	GLYPH FOR FINAL ARABIC QAF
FED9	ك	GLYPH FOR ISOLATE ARABIC CAF
FEDA	كـ	GLYPH FOR INITIAL ARABIC CAF
FEDB	ـكـ	GLYPH FOR MEDIAL ARABIC CAF
FEDC	ـك	GLYPH FOR FINAL ARABIC CAF
FEDD	ل	GLYPH FOR ISOLATE ARABIC LAM
FEDE	لـ	GLYPH FOR INITIAL ARABIC LAM
FEDF	ـلـ	GLYPH FOR MEDIAL ARABIC LAM
FEE0	ـل	GLYPH FOR FINAL ARABIC LAM
FEE1	م	GLYPH FOR ISOLATE ARABIC MEEM
FEE2	مـ	GLYPH FOR INITIAL ARABIC MEEM
FEE3	ـمـ	GLYPH FOR MEDIAL ARABIC MEEM
FEE4	ـم	GLYPH FOR FINAL ARABIC MEEM
FEE5	ن	GLYPH FOR ISOLATE ARABIC NOON
FEE6	نـ	GLYPH FOR INITIAL ARABIC NOON
FEE7	ـنـ	GLYPH FOR MEDIAL ARABIC NOON
FEE8	ـن	GLYPH FOR FINAL ARABIC NOON
FEE9	ه	GLYPH FOR ISOLATE ARABIC HA
FEEA	هـ	GLYPH FOR INITIAL ARABIC HA

FEEB	ـهـ	GLYPH FOR MEDIAL ARABIC HA
FEEC	ـه	GLYPH FOR FINAL ARABIC HA
FEED	و	GLYPH FOR ISOLATE ARABIC WAW
FEEE	ـو	GLYPH FOR FINAL ARABIC WAW
FEEF	ى	GLYPH FOR ISOLATE ARABIC ALEF MAQSURAH
FEF0	ـى	GLYPH FOR FINAL ARABIC ALEF MAQSURAH
FEF1	ي	GLYPH FOR ISOLATE ARABIC YA
FEF2	يـ	GLYPH FOR INITIAL ARABIC YA
FEF3	ـيـ	GLYPH FOR MEDIAL ARABIC YA
FEF4	ـي	GLYPH FOR FINAL ARABIC YA
FEF5	لآ	GLYPH FOR ISOLATE ARABIC MADDAH ON LIGATURE LAM ALEF
FEF6	ـلآ	GLYPH FOR FINAL ARABIC MADDAH ON LIGATURE LAM ALEF
FEF7	لأ	GLYPH FOR ISOLATE ARABIC HAMZAH ON LIGATURE LAM ALEF
FEF8	ـلأ	GLYPH FOR FINAL ARABIC HAMZAH ON LIGATURE LAM ALEF
FEF9	لإ	GLYPH FOR ISOLATE ARABIC HAMZAH UNDER LIGATURE LAM ALEF
FEFA	ـلإ	GLYPH FOR FINAL ARABIC HAMZAH UNDER LIGATURE LAM ALEF
FEFB	لا	GLYPH FOR ISOLATE ARABIC LIGATURE LAM ALEF
FEFC	ـلا	GLYPH FOR FINAL ARABIC LIGATURE LAM ALEF
FEFD		
FEFE		

Special

FEFF	[Byte Order Mark]	BYTE ORDER MARK = BOM *may be used to detect byte order by contrast with FFFE which is not a character* × (**not a character** → *FFFE*)

	FF0	FF1	FF2	FF3	FF4	FF5	FF6	FF7
0		0	@	P	`	p		一
1	!	1	A	Q	a	q	｡	ア
2	"	2	B	R	b	r	｢	イ
3	#	3	C	S	c	s	｣	ウ
4	$$	4	D	T	d	t	、	エ
5	%	5	E	U	e	u	・	オ
6	&	6	F	V	f	v	ヲ	カ
7	'	7	G	W	g	w	ァ	キ
8	(	8	H	X	h	x	ィ	ク
9	)	9	I	Y	i	y	ゥ	ケ
A	*	:	J	Z	j	z	エ	コ
B	+	;	K	[	k	{	オ	サ
C	,	<	L	\	l	|	ャ	シ
D	−	=	M	]	m	}	ユ	ス
E	.	>	N	^	n	~	ヨ	セ
F	/	?	O	_	o		ッ	ソ

The Unicode Standard • Version 1.0

Fullwidth ASCII variants

FF00			FF2D	M	FULLWIDTH LATIN CAPITAL LETTER M
FF01	!	FULLWIDTH EXCLAMATION MARK	FF2E	N	FULLWIDTH LATIN CAPITAL LETTER N
FF02	"	FULLWIDTH QUOTATION MARK	FF2F	O	FULLWIDTH LATIN CAPITAL LETTER O
FF03	#	FULLWIDTH NUMBER SIGN	FF30	P	FULLWIDTH LATIN CAPITAL LETTER P
FF04	$	FULLWIDTH DOLLAR SIGN	FF31	Q	FULLWIDTH LATIN CAPITAL LETTER Q
FF05	%	FULLWIDTH PERCENT SIGN	FF32	R	FULLWIDTH LATIN CAPITAL LETTER R
FF06	&	FULLWIDTH AMPERSAND	FF33	S	FULLWIDTH LATIN CAPITAL LETTER S
FF07	'	FULLWIDTH APOSTROPHE	FF34	T	FULLWIDTH LATIN CAPITAL LETTER T
FF08	(	FULLWIDTH OPENING PARENTHESIS	FF35	U	FULLWIDTH LATIN CAPITAL LETTER U
FF09	)	FULLWIDTH CLOSING PARENTHESIS	FF36	V	FULLWIDTH LATIN CAPITAL LETTER V
FF0A	*	FULLWIDTH ASTERISK	FF37	W	FULLWIDTH LATIN CAPITAL LETTER W
FF0B	+	FULLWIDTH PLUS SIGN	FF38	X	FULLWIDTH LATIN CAPITAL LETTER X
FF0C	,	FULLWIDTH COMMA	FF39	Y	FULLWIDTH LATIN CAPITAL LETTER Y
FF0D	−	FULLWIDTH HYPHEN-MINUS	FF3A	Z	FULLWIDTH LATIN CAPITAL LETTER Z
FF0E	.	FULLWIDTH PERIOD	FF3B	[	FULLWIDTH OPENING SQUARE BRACKET
FF0F	/	FULLWIDTH SLASH	FF3C	\	FULLWIDTH BACKSLASH
FF10	0	FULLWIDTH DIGIT ZERO	FF3D	]	FULLWIDTH CLOSING SQUARE BRACKET
FF11	1	FULLWIDTH DIGIT ONE	FF3E	^	FULLWIDTH SPACING CIRCUMFLEX
FF12	2	FULLWIDTH DIGIT TWO	FF3F	_	FULLWIDTH SPACING UNDERSCORE
FF13	3	FULLWIDTH DIGIT THREE	FF40	`	FULLWIDTH SPACING GRAVE
FF14	4	FULLWIDTH DIGIT FOUR	FF41	a	FULLWIDTH LATIN SMALL LETTER A
FF15	5	FULLWIDTH DIGIT FIVE	FF42	b	FULLWIDTH LATIN SMALL LETTER B
FF16	6	FULLWIDTH DIGIT SIX	FF43	c	FULLWIDTH LATIN SMALL LETTER C
FF17	7	FULLWIDTH DIGIT SEVEN	FF44	d	FULLWIDTH LATIN SMALL LETTER D
FF18	8	FULLWIDTH DIGIT EIGHT	FF45	e	FULLWIDTH LATIN SMALL LETTER E
FF19	9	FULLWIDTH DIGIT NINE	FF46	f	FULLWIDTH LATIN SMALL LETTER F
FF1A	:	FULLWIDTH COLON	FF47	g	FULLWIDTH LATIN SMALL LETTER G
FF1B	;	FULLWIDTH SEMICOLON	FF48	h	FULLWIDTH LATIN SMALL LETTER H
FF1C	<	FULLWIDTH LESS-THAN SIGN	FF49	i	FULLWIDTH LATIN SMALL LETTER I
FF1D	=	FULLWIDTH EQUALS SIGN	FF4A	j	FULLWIDTH LATIN SMALL LETTER J
FF1E	>	FULLWIDTH GREATER-THAN SIGN	FF4B	k	FULLWIDTH LATIN SMALL LETTER K
FF1F	?	FULLWIDTH QUESTION MARK	FF4C	l	FULLWIDTH LATIN SMALL LETTER L
FF20	@	FULLWIDTH COMMERCIAL AT	FF4D	m	FULLWIDTH LATIN SMALL LETTER M
FF21	A	FULLWIDTH LATIN CAPITAL LETTER A	FF4E	n	FULLWIDTH LATIN SMALL LETTER N
FF22	B	FULLWIDTH LATIN CAPITAL LETTER B	FF4F	o	FULLWIDTH LATIN SMALL LETTER O
FF23	C	FULLWIDTH LATIN CAPITAL LETTER C	FF50	p	FULLWIDTH LATIN SMALL LETTER P
FF24	D	FULLWIDTH LATIN CAPITAL LETTER D	FF51	q	FULLWIDTH LATIN SMALL LETTER Q
FF25	E	FULLWIDTH LATIN CAPITAL LETTER E	FF52	r	FULLWIDTH LATIN SMALL LETTER R
FF26	F	FULLWIDTH LATIN CAPITAL LETTER F	FF53	s	FULLWIDTH LATIN SMALL LETTER S
FF27	G	FULLWIDTH LATIN CAPITAL LETTER G	FF54	t	FULLWIDTH LATIN SMALL LETTER T
FF28	H	FULLWIDTH LATIN CAPITAL LETTER H	FF55	u	FULLWIDTH LATIN SMALL LETTER U
FF29	I	FULLWIDTH LATIN CAPITAL LETTER I	FF56	v	FULLWIDTH LATIN SMALL LETTER V
FF2A	J	FULLWIDTH LATIN CAPITAL LETTER J	FF57	w	FULLWIDTH LATIN SMALL LETTER W
FF2B	K	FULLWIDTH LATIN CAPITAL LETTER K	FF58	x	FULLWIDTH LATIN SMALL LETTER X
FF2C	L	FULLWIDTH LATIN CAPITAL LETTER L	FF59	y	FULLWIDTH LATIN SMALL LETTER Y
			FF5A	z	FULLWIDTH LATIN SMALL LETTER Z

FF5B	{	FULLWIDTH OPENING CURLY BRACKET
FF5C	|	FULLWIDTH VERTICAL BAR
FF5D	}	FULLWIDTH CLOSING CURLY BRACKET
FF5E	~	FULLWIDTH SPACING TILDE
FF5F		

Halfwidth Katakana variants

FF60		
FF61	｡	HALFWIDTH IDEOGRAPHIC PERIOD
FF62	｢	HALFWIDTH OPENING CORNER BRACKET
FF63	｣	HALFWIDTH CLOSING CORNER BRACKET
FF64	､	HALFWIDTH IDEOGRAPHIC COMMA
FF65	･	HALFWIDTH KATAKANA MIDDLE DOT
FF66	ｦ	HALFWIDTH KATAKANA LETTER WO
FF67	ｧ	HALFWIDTH KATAKANA LETTER SMALL A
FF68	ｨ	HALFWIDTH KATAKANA LETTER SMALL I
FF69	ｩ	HALFWIDTH KATAKANA LETTER SMALL U
FF6A	ｪ	HALFWIDTH KATAKANA LETTER SMALL E
FF6B	ｫ	HALFWIDTH KATAKANA LETTER SMALL O
FF6C	ｬ	HALFWIDTH KATAKANA LETTER SMALL YA
FF6D	ｭ	HALFWIDTH KATAKANA LETTER SMALL YU
FF6E	ｮ	HALFWIDTH KATAKANA LETTER SMALL YO
FF6F	ｯ	HALFWIDTH KATAKANA LETTER SMALL TU
FF70	ｰ	HALFWIDTH KATAKANA-HIRAGANA PROLONGED SOUND MARK
FF71	ｱ	HALFWIDTH KATAKANA LETTER A
FF72	ｲ	HALFWIDTH KATAKANA LETTER I
FF73	ｳ	HALFWIDTH KATAKANA LETTER U
FF74	ｴ	HALFWIDTH KATAKANA LETTER E
FF75	ｵ	HALFWIDTH KATAKANA LETTER O
FF76	ｶ	HALFWIDTH KATAKANA LETTER KA
FF77	ｷ	HALFWIDTH KATAKANA LETTER KI
FF78	ｸ	HALFWIDTH KATAKANA LETTER KU
FF79	ｹ	HALFWIDTH KATAKANA LETTER KE
FF7A	ｺ	HALFWIDTH KATAKANA LETTER KO
FF7B	ｻ	HALFWIDTH KATAKANA LETTER SA
FF7C	ｼ	HALFWIDTH KATAKANA LETTER SI
FF7D	ｽ	HALFWIDTH KATAKANA LETTER SU
FF7E	ｾ	HALFWIDTH KATAKANA LETTER SE
FF7F	ｿ	HALFWIDTH KATAKANA LETTER SO
FF80	ﾀ	HALFWIDTH KATAKANA LETTER TA
FF81	ﾁ	HALFWIDTH KATAKANA LETTER TI
FF82	ﾂ	HALFWIDTH KATAKANA LETTER TU
FF83	ﾃ	HALFWIDTH KATAKANA LETTER TE

FF84	ﾄ	HALFWIDTH KATAKANA LETTER TO
FF85	ﾅ	HALFWIDTH KATAKANA LETTER NA
FF86	ﾆ	HALFWIDTH KATAKANA LETTER NI
FF87	ﾇ	HALFWIDTH KATAKANA LETTER NU
FF88	ﾈ	HALFWIDTH KATAKANA LETTER NE
FF89	ﾉ	HALFWIDTH KATAKANA LETTER NO
FF8A	ﾊ	HALFWIDTH KATAKANA LETTER HA
FF8B	ﾋ	HALFWIDTH KATAKANA LETTER HI
FF8C	ﾌ	HALFWIDTH KATAKANA LETTER HU
FF8D	ﾍ	HALFWIDTH KATAKANA LETTER HE
FF8E	ﾎ	HALFWIDTH KATAKANA LETTER HO
FF8F	ﾏ	HALFWIDTH KATAKANA LETTER MA
FF90	ﾐ	HALFWIDTH KATAKANA LETTER MI
FF91	ﾑ	HALFWIDTH KATAKANA LETTER MU
FF92	ﾒ	HALFWIDTH KATAKANA LETTER ME
FF93	ﾓ	HALFWIDTH KATAKANA LETTER MO
FF94	ﾔ	HALFWIDTH KATAKANA LETTER YA
FF95	ﾕ	HALFWIDTH KATAKANA LETTER YU
FF96	ﾖ	HALFWIDTH KATAKANA LETTER YO
FF97	ﾗ	HALFWIDTH KATAKANA LETTER RA
FF98	ﾘ	HALFWIDTH KATAKANA LETTER RI
FF99	ﾙ	HALFWIDTH KATAKANA LETTER RU
FF9A	ﾚ	HALFWIDTH KATAKANA LETTER RE
FF9B	ﾛ	HALFWIDTH KATAKANA LETTER RO
FF9C	ﾜ	HALFWIDTH KATAKANA LETTER WA
FF9D	ﾝ	HALFWIDTH KATAKANA LETTER N
FF9E	ﾞ	HALFWIDTH KATAKANA VOICED SOUND MARK
FF9F	ﾟ	HALFWIDTH KATAKANA SEMI-VOICED SOUND MARK

Halfwidth Hangul variants

FFA0	(채움)	HALFWIDTH HANGUL CAE OM
FFA1	ㄱ	HALFWIDTH HANGUL LETTER GIYEOG
FFA2	ㄲ	HALFWIDTH HANGUL LETTER SSANG GIYEOG
FFA3	ㄳ	HALFWIDTH HANGUL LETTER GIYEOG SIOS
FFA4	ㄴ	HALFWIDTH HANGUL LETTER NIEUN
FFA5	ㄵ	HALFWIDTH HANGUL LETTER NIEUN JIEUJ
FFA6	ㄶ	HALFWIDTH HANGUL LETTER NIEUN HIEUH
FFA7	ㄷ	HALFWIDTH HANGUL LETTER DIGEUD
FFA8	ㄸ	HALFWIDTH HANGUL LETTER SSANG DIGEUD
FFA9	ㄹ	HALFWIDTH HANGUL LETTER LIEUL
FFAA	ㄺ	HALFWIDTH HANGUL LETTER LIEUL GIYEOG

FFAB	쾀	HALFWIDTH HANGUL LETTER LIEUL MIEUM
FFAC	쾁	HALFWIDTH HANGUL LETTER LIEUL BIEUB
FFAD	쾂	HALFWIDTH HANGUL LETTER LIEUL SIOS
FFAE	쾃	HALFWIDTH HANGUL LETTER LIEUL TIEUT
FFAF	쾄	HALFWIDTH HANGUL LETTER LIEUL PIEUP
FFB0	쾅	HALFWIDTH HANGUL LETTER LIEUL HIEUH
FFB1	ㅁ	HALFWIDTH HANGUL LETTER MIEUM
FFB2	ㅂ	HALFWIDTH HANGUL LETTER BIEUB
FFB3	ㅃ	HALFWIDTH HANGUL LETTER SSANG BIEUB
FFB4	ㅄ	HALFWIDTH HANGUL LETTER BIEUB SIOS
FFB5	ㅅ	HALFWIDTH HANGUL LETTER SIOS
FFB6	ㅆ	HALFWIDTH HANGUL LETTER SSANG SIOS
FFB7	ㅇ	HALFWIDTH HANGUL LETTER IEUNG
FFB8	ㅈ	HALFWIDTH HANGUL LETTER JIEUJ
FFB9	ㅉ	HALFWIDTH HANGUL LETTER SSANG JIEUJ
FFBA	ㅊ	HALFWIDTH HANGUL LETTER CIEUC
FFBB	ㅋ	HALFWIDTH HANGUL LETTER KIYEOK
FFBC	ㅌ	HALFWIDTH HANGUL LETTER TIEUT
FFBD	ㅍ	HALFWIDTH HANGUL LETTER PIEUP
FFBE	ㅎ	HALFWIDTH HANGUL LETTER HIEUH
FFBF		
FFC0		
FFC1		
FFC2	ㅏ	HALFWIDTH HANGUL LETTER A
FFC3	ㅐ	HALFWIDTH HANGUL LETTER AE
FFC4	ㅑ	HALFWIDTH HANGUL LETTER YA
FFC5	ㅒ	HALFWIDTH HANGUL LETTER YAE
FFC6	ㅓ	HALFWIDTH HANGUL LETTER EO
FFC7	ㅔ	HALFWIDTH HANGUL LETTER E
FFC8		
FFC9		
FFCA	ㅕ	HALFWIDTH HANGUL LETTER YEO
FFCB	ㅖ	HALFWIDTH HANGUL LETTER YE
FFCC	ㅗ	HALFWIDTH HANGUL LETTER O
FFCD	ㅘ	HALFWIDTH HANGUL LETTER WA
FFCE	ㅙ	HALFWIDTH HANGUL LETTER WAE
FFCF	ㅚ	HALFWIDTH HANGUL LETTER OE
FFD0		
FFD1		
FFD2	ㅛ	HALFWIDTH HANGUL LETTER YO
FFD3	ㅜ	HALFWIDTH HANGUL LETTER U
FFD4	ㅝ	HALFWIDTH HANGUL LETTER WEO
FFD5	ㅞ	HALFWIDTH HANGUL LETTER WE
FFD6	ㅟ	HALFWIDTH HANGUL LETTER WI

FFD7	ㅠ	HALFWIDTH HANGUL LETTER YU
FFD8		
FFD9		
FFDA	ㅡ	HALFWIDTH HANGUL LETTER EU
FFDB	ㅢ	HALFWIDTH HANGUL LETTER YI
FFDC	ㅣ	HALFWIDTH HANGUL LETTER I
FFDD		
FFDE		
FFDF		

Fullwidth symbol variants

FFE0	¢	FULLWIDTH CENT SIGN
FFE1	£	FULLWIDTH POUND SIGN
FFE2	¬	FULLWIDTH NOT SIGN
FFE3	￣	FULLWIDTH SPACING MACRON
FFE4	￤	FULLWIDTH BROKEN VERTICAL BAR
FFE5	¥	FULLWIDTH YEN SIGN
FFE6	₩	FULLWIDTH WON SIGN

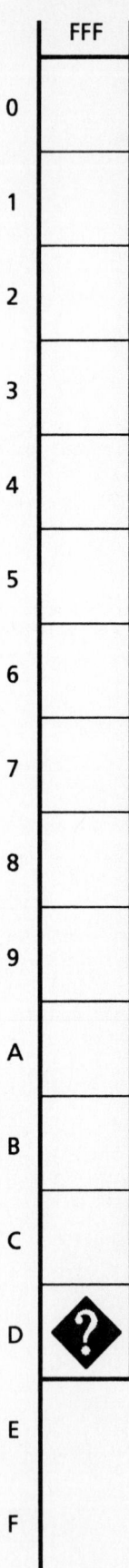

Special

FFF0

FFF1

FFF2

FFF3

FFF4

FFF5

FFF6

FFF7

FFF8

FFF9

FFFA

FFFB

FFFC

FFFD ◆❓ REPLACEMENT CHARACTER
used to replace incoming characters
whose values are unknown or
unrepresentable in Unicode
× *(substitute → 001A)*

<u>*Not character codes*</u>

FFFE **NOT A CHARACTER**
the value FFFE is guaranteed not to be
a Unicode character at all
may be used to detect byte order by
contrast with FEFF which is a character
× *(byte order mark → FEFF)*

FFFF **NOT A CHARACTER**
the value FFFF is guaranteed not to be
a Unicode character at all

4.0 *Character Properties*

The chapter on Character Properties discusses in detail the attributes of several character types and how they are dealt with in the Unicode encoding scheme.

Disclaimer

The content of all character property tables has been verified as far as possible by the Unicode Consortium. However, the Unicode Consortium does not guarantee that the tables are correct in every detail. The character property tables are provided for informational purposes only. The Unicode Consortium is not responsible for errors that may occur either in the character property tables or in software which implements those tables as they are printed in this volume.

4.1 Numeric

Numeric is a general classification of characters that represent numbers. This includes characters such as fractions, subscripts, superscripts, Roman numerals, currency numerators, encircled numbers, and script-specific digits. In many traditional numbering systems, letters are used with a numeric value. Examples include Greek and Hebrew letters, and Latin letters used in outlines (II.A.1.b). These are special cases, and are not included here as numeric.

Digits form a large subcategory of numerics consisting of those numerics which can combine in sequence to form numbers. This includes characters such as subscripts, superscripts, Roman numerals, and script-specific digits. Digits do not include characters such as encircled numbers or fractions.

Decimal digits form a large subcategory of digits consisting of those digits which can be used to form decimal-radix numbers. This includes characters such as subscripts, superscripts, and script-specific digits. Decimal digits do not include characters such as Roman numerals ($1 + 5 = 15 = $ fifteen, but $I + V = IV = $ four).

The Unicode standard assigns distinct codes to native forms of digits, specific to a given script or language. Examples are the digits used with the Arabic script, Chinese numbers or those of the Indic languages. (For naming conventions, see the introduction to the Arabic block.) An alternative would have been to provide codes only for the European digits (ASCII 0–9) and make the the other forms presentation variants only. The latter choice favors applications which focus on number parsing over word processing or display oriented applications. To help programs reduce the complexity of their parsers, the Unicode standard provides mapping tables which can be used to fold any of its digits into the ASCII range.

Decimal Digits

Decimal digits are digits which can be concatenated to build decimal numbers. This list is a proper subset of the *Digits* list.

UNIC	Unicode character name	Value
0030	DIGIT ZERO	0
0031	DIGIT ONE	1
0032	DIGIT TWO	2
0033	DIGIT THREE	3
0034	DIGIT FOUR	4
0035	DIGIT FIVE	5
0036	DIGIT SIX	6
0037	DIGIT SEVEN	7
0038	DIGIT EIGHT	8
0039	DIGIT NINE	9
00B2	SUPERSCRIPT DIGIT TWO	2
00B3	SUPERSCRIPT DIGIT THREE	3
00B9	SUPERSCRIPT DIGIT ONE	1
0660	ARABIC-INDIC DIGIT ZERO	0
0661	ARABIC-INDIC DIGIT ONE	1
0662	ARABIC-INDIC DIGIT TWO	2
0663	ARABIC-INDIC DIGIT THREE	3
0664	ARABIC-INDIC DIGIT FOUR	4
0665	ARABIC-INDIC DIGIT FIVE	5
0666	ARABIC-INDIC DIGIT SIX	6
0667	ARABIC-INDIC DIGIT SEVEN	7
0668	ARABIC-INDIC DIGIT EIGHT	8
0669	ARABIC-INDIC DIGIT NINE	9
06F0	EASTERN ARABIC-INDIC DIGIT ZERO	0
06F1	EASTERN ARABIC-INDIC DIGIT ONE	1
06F2	EASTERN ARABIC-INDIC DIGIT TWO	2
06F3	EASTERN ARABIC-INDIC DIGIT THREE	3
06F4	EASTERN ARABIC-INDIC DIGIT FOUR	4
06F5	EASTERN ARABIC-INDIC DIGIT FIVE	5
06F6	EASTERN ARABIC-INDIC DIGIT SIX	6
06F7	EASTERN ARABIC-INDIC DIGIT SEVEN	7
06F8	EASTERN ARABIC-INDIC DIGIT EIGHT	8
06F9	EASTERN ARABIC-INDIC DIGIT NINE	9
0966	DEVANAGARI DIGIT ZERO	0
0967	DEVANAGARI DIGIT ONE	1
0968	DEVANAGARI DIGIT TWO	2
0969	DEVANAGARI DIGIT THREE	3
096A	DEVANAGARI DIGIT FOUR	4
096B	DEVANAGARI DIGIT FIVE	5
096C	DEVANAGARI DIGIT SIX	6
096D	DEVANAGARI DIGIT SEVEN	7
096E	DEVANAGARI DIGIT EIGHT	8
096F	DEVANAGARI DIGIT NINE	9
09E6	BENGALI DIGIT ZERO	0
09E7	BENGALI DIGIT ONE	1
09E8	BENGALI DIGIT TWO	2
09E9	BENGALI DIGIT THREE	3
09EA	BENGALI DIGIT FOUR	4
09EB	BENGALI DIGIT FIVE	5
09EC	BENGALI DIGIT SIX	6

UNIC	Unicode character name	Value
09ED	BENGALI DIGIT SEVEN	7
09EE	BENGALI DIGIT EIGHT	8
09EF	BENGALI DIGIT NINE	9
0A66	GURMUKHI DIGIT ZERO	0
0A67	GURMUKHI DIGIT ONE	1
0A68	GURMUKHI DIGIT TWO	2
0A69	GURMUKHI DIGIT THREE	3
0A6A	GURMUKHI DIGIT FOUR	4
0A6B	GURMUKHI DIGIT FIVE	5
0A6C	GURMUKHI DIGIT SIX	6
0A6D	GURMUKHI DIGIT SEVEN	7
0A6E	GURMUKHI DIGIT EIGHT	8
0A6F	GURMUKHI DIGIT NINE	9
0AE6	GUJARATI DIGIT ZERO	0
0AE7	GUJARATI DIGIT ONE	1
0AE8	GUJARATI DIGIT TWO	2
0AE9	GUJARATI DIGIT THREE	3
0AEA	GUJARATI DIGIT FOUR	4
0AEB	GUJARATI DIGIT FIVE	5
0AEC	GUJARATI DIGIT SIX	6
0AED	GUJARATI DIGIT SEVEN	7
0AEE	GUJARATI DIGIT EIGHT	8
0AEF	GUJARATI DIGIT NINE	9
0B66	ORIYA DIGIT ZERO	0
0B67	ORIYA DIGIT ONE	1
0B68	ORIYA DIGIT TWO	2
0B69	ORIYA DIGIT THREE	3
0B6A	ORIYA DIGIT FOUR	4
0B6B	ORIYA DIGIT FIVE	5
0B6C	ORIYA DIGIT SIX	6
0B6D	ORIYA DIGIT SEVEN	7
0B6E	ORIYA DIGIT EIGHT	8
0B6F	ORIYA DIGIT NINE	9
0BE7	TAMIL DIGIT ONE	1
0BE8	TAMIL DIGIT TWO	2
0BE9	TAMIL DIGIT THREE	3
0BEA	TAMIL DIGIT FOUR	4
0BEB	TAMIL DIGIT FIVE	5
0BEC	TAMIL DIGIT SIX	6
0BED	TAMIL DIGIT SEVEN	7
0BEE	TAMIL DIGIT EIGHT	8
0BEF	TAMIL DIGIT NINE	9
0C66	TELUGU DIGIT ZERO	0
0C67	TELUGU DIGIT ONE	1
0C68	TELUGU DIGIT TWO	2
0C69	TELUGU DIGIT THREE	3
0C6A	TELUGU DIGIT FOUR	4
0C6B	TELUGU DIGIT FIVE	5
0C6C	TELUGU DIGIT SIX	6
0C6D	TELUGU DIGIT SEVEN	7
0C6E	TELUGU DIGIT EIGHT	8
0C6F	TELUGU DIGIT NINE	9
0CE6	KANNADA DIGIT ZERO	0
0CE7	KANNADA DIGIT ONE	1
0CE8	KANNADA DIGIT TWO	2
0CE9	KANNADA DIGIT THREE	3

UNIC	Unicode character name	Value
0CEA	KANNADA DIGIT FOUR	4
0CEB	KANNADA DIGIT FIVE	5
0CEC	KANNADA DIGIT SIX	6
0CED	KANNADA DIGIT SEVEN	7
0CEE	KANNADA DIGIT EIGHT	8
0CEF	KANNADA DIGIT NINE	9
0D66	MALAYALAM DIGIT ZERO	0
0D67	MALAYALAM DIGIT ONE	1
0D68	MALAYALAM DIGIT TWO	2
0D69	MALAYALAM DIGIT THREE	3
0D6A	MALAYALAM DIGIT FOUR	4
0D6B	MALAYALAM DIGIT FIVE	5
0D6C	MALAYALAM DIGIT SIX	6
0D6D	MALAYALAM DIGIT SEVEN	7
0D6E	MALAYALAM DIGIT EIGHT	8
0D6F	MALAYALAM DIGIT NINE	9
0E50	THAI DIGIT ZERO	0
0E51	THAI DIGIT ONE	1
0E52	THAI DIGIT TWO	2
0E53	THAI DIGIT THREE	3
0E54	THAI DIGIT FOUR	4
0E55	THAI DIGIT FIVE	5
0E56	THAI DIGIT SIX	6
0E57	THAI DIGIT SEVEN	7
0E58	THAI DIGIT EIGHT	8
0E59	THAI DIGIT NINE	9
0ED0	LAO DIGIT ZERO	0
0ED1	LAO DIGIT ONE	1
0ED2	LAO DIGIT TWO	2
0ED3	LAO DIGIT THREE	3
0ED4	LAO DIGIT FOUR	4
0ED5	LAO DIGIT FIVE	5
0ED6	LAO DIGIT SIX	6
0ED7	LAO DIGIT SEVEN	7
0ED8	LAO DIGIT EIGHT	8
0ED9	LAO DIGIT NINE	9
1040	TIBETAN DIGIT ZERO	0
1041	TIBETAN DIGIT ONE	1
1042	TIBETAN DIGIT TWO	2
1043	TIBETAN DIGIT THREE	3
1044	TIBETAN DIGIT FOUR	4
1045	TIBETAN DIGIT FIVE	5
1046	TIBETAN DIGIT SIX	6
1047	TIBETAN DIGIT SEVEN	7
1048	TIBETAN DIGIT EIGHT	8
1049	TIBETAN DIGIT NINE	9
2070	SUPERSCRIPT DIGIT ZERO	0
2074	SUPERSCRIPT DIGIT FOUR	4
2075	SUPERSCRIPT DIGIT FIVE	5
2076	SUPERSCRIPT DIGIT SIX	6
2077	SUPERSCRIPT DIGIT SEVEN	7
2078	SUPERSCRIPT DIGIT EIGHT	8
2079	SUPERSCRIPT DIGIT NINE	9
2080	SUBSCRIPT DIGIT ZERO	0
2081	SUBSCRIPT DIGIT ONE	1
2082	SUBSCRIPT DIGIT TWO	2

UNIC	Unicode character name	Value
2083	SUBSCRIPT DIGIT THREE	3
2084	SUBSCRIPT DIGIT FOUR	4
2085	SUBSCRIPT DIGIT FIVE	5
2086	SUBSCRIPT DIGIT SIX	6
2087	SUBSCRIPT DIGIT SEVEN	7
2088	SUBSCRIPT DIGIT EIGHT	8
2089	SUBSCRIPT DIGIT NINE	9

Digits

Digits include all of the characters labeled in the *Decimal Digits* list, plus the following characters, which cannot be concatenated to form decimal numbers. This list is a proper subset of the *Numbers* list.

UNIC	Unicode character name	Value
2460	CIRCLED DIGIT ONE	1
2461	CIRCLED DIGIT TWO	2
2462	CIRCLED DIGIT THREE	3
2463	CIRCLED DIGIT FOUR	4
2464	CIRCLED DIGIT FIVE	5
2465	CIRCLED DIGIT SIX	6
2466	CIRCLED DIGIT SEVEN	7
2467	CIRCLED DIGIT EIGHT	8
2468	CIRCLED DIGIT NINE	9
2474	PARENTHESIZED DIGIT ONE	1
2475	PARENTHESIZED DIGIT TWO	2
2476	PARENTHESIZED DIGIT THREE	3
2477	PARENTHESIZED DIGIT FOUR	4
2478	PARENTHESIZED DIGIT FIVE	5
2479	PARENTHESIZED DIGIT SIX	6
247A	PARENTHESIZED DIGIT SEVEN	7
247B	PARENTHESIZED DIGIT EIGHT	8
247C	PARENTHESIZED DIGIT NINE	9
2488	DIGIT ONE PERIOD	1
2489	DIGIT TWO PERIOD	2
248A	DIGIT THREE PERIOD	3
248B	DIGIT FOUR PERIOD	4
248C	DIGIT FIVE PERIOD	5
248D	DIGIT SIX PERIOD	6
248E	DIGIT SEVEN PERIOD	7
248F	DIGIT EIGHT PERIOD	8
2490	DIGIT NINE PERIOD	9
24EA	CIRCLED DIGIT ZERO	0
2776	INVERSE CIRCLED DIGIT ONE	1
2777	INVERSE CIRCLED DIGIT TWO	2
2778	INVERSE CIRCLED DIGIT THREE	3
2779	INVERSE CIRCLED DIGIT FOUR	4
277A	INVERSE CIRCLED DIGIT FIVE	5
277B	INVERSE CIRCLED DIGIT SIX	6
277C	INVERSE CIRCLED DIGIT SEVEN	7
277D	INVERSE CIRCLED DIGIT EIGHT	8
277E	INVERSE CIRCLED DIGIT NINE	9
2780	CIRCLED SANS-SERIF DIGIT ONE	1
2781	CIRCLED SANS-SERIF DIGIT TWO	2
2782	CIRCLED SANS-SERIF DIGIT THREE	3
2783	CIRCLED SANS-SERIF DIGIT FOUR	4
2784	CIRCLED SANS-SERIF DIGIT FIVE	5
2785	CIRCLED SANS-SERIF DIGIT SIX	6
2786	CIRCLED SANS-SERIF DIGIT SEVEN	7
2787	CIRCLED SANS-SERIF DIGIT EIGHT	8
2788	CIRCLED SANS-SERIF DIGIT NINE	9
278A	INVERSE CIRCLED SANS-SERIF DIGIT ONE	1
278B	INVERSE CIRCLED SANS-SERIF DIGIT TWO	2

UNIC	Unicode character name	Value
278C	INVERSE CIRCLED SANS-SERIF DIGIT THREE	3
278D	INVERSE CIRCLED SANS-SERIF DIGIT FOUR	4
278E	INVERSE CIRCLED SANS-SERIF DIGIT FIVE	5
278F	INVERSE CIRCLED SANS-SERIF DIGIT SIX	6
2790	INVERSE CIRCLED SANS-SERIF DIGIT SEVEN	7
2791	INVERSE CIRCLED SANS-SERIF DIGIT EIGHT	8
2792	INVERSE CIRCLED SANS-SERIF DIGIT NINE	9

Numbers

This list includes all of the *Digits* list, plus other characters which can be interpreted as having a numerical value associated with them. All of the Roman numerals are listed here, although some of them can be considered *Digits* within the Roman numeration scheme.

UNIC	Unicode character name	Value
00BC	FRACTION ONE QUARTER	1/4
00BD	FRACTION ONE HALF	1/2
00BE	FRACTION THREE QUARTERS	3/4
09F4	BENGALI CURRENCY NUMERATOR ONE	1
09F5	BENGALI CURRENCY NUMERATOR TWO	2
09F6	BENGALI CURRENCY NUMERATOR THREE	3
09F7	BENGALI CURRENCY NUMERATOR FOUR	4
09F8	BENGALI CURRENCY NUMERATOR ONE LESS THAN THE DENOMINATOR	—
09F9	BENGALI CURRENCY DENOMINATOR SIXTEEN	16
0BF0	TAMIL NUMBER TEN	10
0BF1	TAMIL NUMBER ONE HUNDRED	100
0BF2	TAMIL NUMBER ONE THOUSAND	1000
2153	FRACTION ONE THIRD	1/3
2154	FRACTION TWO THIRDS	2/3
2155	FRACTION ONE FIFTH	1/5
2156	FRACTION TWO FIFTHS	2/5
2157	FRACTION THREE FIFTHS	3/5
2158	FRACTION FOUR FIFTHS	4/5
2159	FRACTION ONE SIXTH	1/6
215A	FRACTION FIVE SIXTHS	5/6
215B	FRACTION ONE EIGHTH	1/8
215C	FRACTION THREE EIGHTHS	3/8
215D	FRACTION FIVE EIGHTHS	5/8
215E	FRACTION SEVEN EIGHTHS	7/8
215F	FRACTION NUMERATOR ONE	1
2160	ROMAN NUMERAL ONE	1
2161	ROMAN NUMERAL TWO	2
2162	ROMAN NUMERAL THREE	3
2163	ROMAN NUMERAL FOUR	4
2164	ROMAN NUMERAL FIVE	5
2165	ROMAN NUMERAL SIX	6
2166	ROMAN NUMERAL SEVEN	7
2167	ROMAN NUMERAL EIGHT	8
2168	ROMAN NUMERAL NINE	9
2169	ROMAN NUMERAL TEN	10
216A	ROMAN NUMERAL ELEVEN	11
216B	ROMAN NUMERAL TWELVE	12
216C	ROMAN NUMERAL FIFTY	50
216D	ROMAN NUMERAL ONE HUNDRED	100
216E	ROMAN NUMERAL FIVE HUNDRED	500
216F	ROMAN NUMERAL ONE THOUSAND	1000
2170	SMALL ROMAN NUMERAL ONE	1
2171	SMALL ROMAN NUMERAL TWO	2
2172	SMALL ROMAN NUMERAL THREE	3
2173	SMALL ROMAN NUMERAL FOUR	4
2174	SMALL ROMAN NUMERAL FIVE	5
2175	SMALL ROMAN NUMERAL SIX	6

UNIC	Unicode character name	Value
2176	SMALL ROMAN NUMERAL SEVEN	7
2177	SMALL ROMAN NUMERAL EIGHT	8
2178	SMALL ROMAN NUMERAL NINE	9
2179	SMALL ROMAN NUMERAL TEN	10
217A	SMALL ROMAN NUMERAL ELEVEN	11
217B	SMALL ROMAN NUMERAL TWELVE	12
217C	SMALL ROMAN NUMERAL FIFTY	50
217D	SMALL ROMAN NUMERAL ONE HUNDRED	100
217E	SMALL ROMAN NUMERAL FIVE HUNDRED	500
217F	SMALL ROMAN NUMERAL ONE THOUSAND	1000
2180	ROMAN NUMERAL ONE THOUSAND C D	1000
2181	ROMAN NUMERAL FIVE THOUSAND	5000
2182	ROMAN NUMERAL TEN THOUSAND	10000
2469	CIRCLED NUMBER TEN	10
246A	CIRCLED NUMBER ELEVEN	11
246B	CIRCLED NUMBER TWELVE	12
246C	CIRCLED NUMBER THIRTEEN	13
246D	CIRCLED NUMBER FOURTEEN	14
246E	CIRCLED NUMBER FIFTEEN	15
246F	CIRCLED NUMBER SIXTEEN	16
2470	CIRCLED NUMBER SEVENTEEN	17
2471	CIRCLED NUMBER EIGHTEEN	18
2472	CIRCLED NUMBER NINETEEN	19
2473	CIRCLED NUMBER TWENTY	20
247D	PARENTHESIZED NUMBER TEN	10
247E	PARENTHESIZED NUMBER ELEVEN	11
247F	PARENTHESIZED NUMBER TWELVE	12
2480	PARENTHESIZED NUMBER THIRTEEN	13
2481	PARENTHESIZED NUMBER FOURTEEN	14
2482	PARENTHESIZED NUMBER FIFTEEN	15
2483	PARENTHESIZED NUMBER SIXTEEN	16
2484	PARENTHESIZED NUMBER SEVENTEEN	17
2485	PARENTHESIZED NUMBER EIGHTEEN	18
2486	PARENTHESIZED NUMBER NINETEEN	19
2487	PARENTHESIZED NUMBER TWENTY	20
2491	NUMBER TEN PERIOD	10
2492	NUMBER ELEVEN PERIOD	11
2493	NUMBER TWELVE PERIOD	12
2494	NUMBER THIRTEEN PERIOD	13
2495	NUMBER FOURTEEN PERIOD	14
2496	NUMBER FIFTEEN PERIOD	15
2497	NUMBER SIXTEEN PERIOD	16
2498	NUMBER SEVENTEEN PERIOD	17
2499	NUMBER EIGHTEEN PERIOD	18
249A	NUMBER NINETEEN PERIOD	19
249B	NUMBER TWENTY PERIOD	20
277F	INVERSE CIRCLED NUMBER 10	10
2789	CIRCLED SANS-SERIF NUMBER 10	10
2793	INVERSE CIRCLED SANS-SERIF NUMBER 10	10
3007	IDEOGRAPHIC NUMBER ZERO	0
3021	HANGZHOU NUMERAL ONE	1
3022	HANGZHOU NUMERAL TWO	2
3023	HANGZHOU NUMERAL THREE	3
3024	HANGZHOU NUMERAL FOUR	4
3025	HANGZHOU NUMERAL FIVE	5
3026	HANGZHOU NUMERAL SIX	6

UNIC	Unicode character name	Value
3027	HANGZHOU NUMERAL SEVEN	7
3028	HANGZHOU NUMERAL EIGHT	8
3029	HANGZHOU NUMERAL NINE	9
3280	CIRCLED IDEOGRAPH ONE	1
3281	CIRCLED IDEOGRAPH TWO	2
3282	CIRCLED IDEOGRAPH THREE	3
3283	CIRCLED IDEOGRAPH FOUR	4
3284	CIRCLED IDEOGRAPH FIVE	5
3285	CIRCLED IDEOGRAPH SIX	6
3286	CIRCLED IDEOGRAPH SEVEN	7
3287	CIRCLED IDEOGRAPH EIGHT	8
3288	CIRCLED IDEOGRAPH NINE	9
3289	CIRCLED IDEOGRAPH TEN	10

4.2 Space Characters

Eight-bit character sets contain two space characters U+0020 SPACE and U+00A0 NON-BREAKING SPACE. The Unicode standard has several additional space characters which provide explicit control over their width (from zero-width or non-printing, on upward). U+2007 FIGURE SPACE is intended to be used as a thousands separator in those countries that use a space to separate groups of digits. It behaves like a numeric separator for the purposes of bidirectional layout (See Appendix A for a detailed discussion of bidirectional coding.)

Note that not all space characters have word- or line-breaking properties.

Space characters include:

U+0020	SPACE
U+00A0	NON-BREAKING SPACE
U+2000	EN QUAD
U+2001	EM QUAD
U+2002	EN SPACE
U+2003	EM SPACE
U+2004	THREE-PER-EM SPACE
U+2005	FOUR-PER-EM SPACE
U+2006	SIX-PER-EM SPACE
U+2007	FIGURE SPACE
U+2008	PUNCTUATION SPACE
U+2009	THIN SPACE
U+200A	HAIR SPACE
U+200B	ZERO WIDTH SPACE
U+3000	IDEOGRAPHIC SPACE

4.3 Dashes

In addition to spaces, the Unicode standard encodes several dashes. Here the semantics of the ASCII *hyphen-minus* (U+002D) is ambiguous. The Unicode standard provides two explicit codes, *hyphen* and *minus* for those applications that need to distinguish these two. Dashes of various length are provided as well. In a few cases, the Unicode standard makes a distinction purely on the basis of the intended semantics without a corresponding visual difference. For example, typographers typically use the *en-dash* to typeset the *minus*, but the Unicode character encoding has two different codes, so that it is possible to distinguish which one has the numeric quality.

Dash characters include

U+002D	HYPHEN-MINUS
U+2010	HYPHEN
U+2011	NON-BREAKING HYPHEN
U+2012	FIGURE DASH
U+2013	EN DASH
U+2014	EM DASH
U+2015	QUOTATION DASH
U+207B	SUPERSCRIPT HYPHEN-MINUS
U+208B	SUBSCRIPT HYPHEN-MINUS
U+2212	MINUS
U+301C	WAVE DASH
U+3030	WAVY DASH

4.4 Line Breaking

Rules of line breaking differ substantially from script to script and language to language. The rules for determining correct line break can be quite complex (especially when hyphenation is included) and are beyond the scope of the Unicode standard.

However, there are certain characters with distinguished semantics vis-a-vis line break. Certain characters are word delimiters, and always allow line break. These include all spaces except U+00A0 NON-BREAKING SPACE and U+2007 FIGURE SPACE.

Certain other characters generally disallow word-breaking on either side, including U+00A0 NON-BREAKING SPACE and U+2011 NON-BREAKING HYPHEN. These characters are included for compatibility (proper control of line break cannot be accomplished by simply cloning a small number of characters).

4.5 Non-spacing Marks

When rendered, the non-spacing marks are attached to the preceding base character in some manner, and do not to occupy a spacing position by themselves.

All of the characters in the range U+0300 → U+0348, U+20D0 → U+20E1, and U+302A → U+302F are non-spacing marks. In addition, the following characters are also non-spacing marks:

UNIC	Unicode character name
0370	GREEK NON-SPACING IOTA BELOW
0371	GREEK NON-SPACING DASIA PNEUMATA
0372	GREEK NON-SPACING PSILI PNEUMATA
0384	GREEK NON-SPACING TONOS
0385	GREEK NON-SPACING DIAERESIS TONOS
0483	CYRILLIC NON-SPACING TITLO
0484	CYRILLIC NON-SPACING PALATALIZATION
0485	CYRILLIC NON-SPACING DASIA PNEUMATA
0486	CYRILLIC NON-SPACING PSILI PNEUMATA
05B0	HEBREW POINT SHEVA
05B1	HEBREW POINT HATAF SEGOL
05B2	HEBREW POINT HATAF PATAH
05B3	HEBREW POINT HATAF QAMATS
05B4	HEBREW POINT HIRIQ
05B5	HEBREW POINT TSERE
05B6	HEBREW POINT SEGOL
05B7	HEBREW POINT PATAH
05B8	HEBREW POINT QAMATS
05B9	HEBREW POINT HOLAM
05BB	HEBREW POINT QUBUTS
05BC	HEBREW POINT DAGESH
05BD	HEBREW POINT METEG
05BF	HEBREW POINT RAFE
05C1	HEBREW POINT SHIN DOT
05C2	HEBREW POINT SIN DOT
05F5	HEBREW POINT VARIKA
064B	ARABIC FATHATAN
064C	ARABIC DAMMATAN
064D	ARABIC KASRATAN
064E	ARABIC FATHAH
064F	ARABIC DAMMAH
0650	ARABIC KASRAH
0651	ARABIC SHADDAH
0652	ARABIC SUKUN
0670	ARABIC ALEF ABOVE
0901	DEVANAGARI SIGN CANDRABINDU
0902	DEVANAGARI SIGN ANUSVARA
093C	DEVANAGARI SIGN NUKTA
0941	DEVANAGARI VOWEL SIGN U
0942	DEVANAGARI VOWEL SIGN UU
0943	DEVANAGARI VOWEL SIGN VOCALIC R

0944	DEVANAGARI VOWEL SIGN VOCALIC RR
0945	DEVANAGARI VOWEL SIGN CANDRA E
0946	DEVANAGARI VOWEL SIGN SHORT E
0947	DEVANAGARI VOWEL SIGN E
0948	DEVANAGARI VOWEL SIGN AI
094D	DEVANAGARI SIGN VIRAMA
0951	DEVANAGARI STRESS SIGN UDATTA
0952	DEVANAGARI STRESS SIGN ANUDATTA
0953	DEVANAGARI GRAVE ACCENT
0954	DEVANAGARI ACUTE ACCENT
0962	DEVANAGARI VOWEL SIGN VOCALIC L
0963	DEVANAGARI VOWEL SIGN VOCALIC LL
0981	BENGALI SIGN CANDRABINDU
09BC	BENGALI SIGN NUKTA
09C1	BENGALI VOWEL SIGN U
09C2	BENGALI VOWEL SIGN UU
09C3	BENGALI VOWEL SIGN VOCALIC R
09C4	BENGALI VOWEL SIGN VOCALIC RR
09CD	BENGALI SIGN VIRAMA
09E2	BENGALI VOWEL SIGN VOCALIC L
09E3	BENGALI VOWEL SIGN VOCALIC LL
0A02	GURMUKHI SIGN BINDI
0A3C	GURMUKHI SIGN NUKTA
0A41	GURMUKHI VOWEL SIGN U
0A42	GURMUKHI VOWEL SIGN UU
0A47	GURMUKHI VOWEL SIGN EE
0A48	GURMUKHI VOWEL SIGN AI
0A4B	GURMUKHI VOWEL SIGN OO
0A4C	GURMUKHI VOWEL SIGN AU
0A70	GURMUKHI TIPPI
0A71	GURMUKHI ADDAK
0A81	GUJARATI SIGN CANDRABINDU
0A82	GUJARATI SIGN ANUSVARA
0ABC	GUJARATI SIGN NUKTA
0AC1	GUJARATI VOWEL SIGN U
0AC2	GUJARATI VOWEL SIGN UU
0AC3	GUJARATI VOWEL SIGN VOCALIC R
0AC4	GUJARATI VOWEL SIGN VOCALIC RR
0AC5	GUJARATI VOWEL SIGN CANDRA E
0AC7	GUJARATI VOWEL SIGN E
0AC8	GUJARATI VOWEL SIGN AI
0ACD	GUJARATI SIGN VIRAMA
0B01	ORIYA SIGN CANDRABINDU
0B3C	ORIYA SIGN NUKTA
0B3F	ORIYA VOWEL SIGN I
0B41	ORIYA VOWEL SIGN U
0B42	ORIYA VOWEL SIGN UU
0B43	ORIYA VOWEL SIGN VOCALIC R
0B4D	ORIYA SIGN VIRAMA
0BC0	TAMIL VOWEL SIGN II
0BCD	TAMIL SIGN VIRAMA
0C3E	TELUGU VOWEL SIGN AA
0C3F	TELUGU VOWEL SIGN I
0C40	TELUGU VOWEL SIGN II
0C46	TELUGU VOWEL SIGN E
0C47	TELUGU VOWEL SIGN EE

UNIC	Unicode character name
0C48	TELUGU VOWEL SIGN AI
0C4A	TELUGU VOWEL SIGN O
0C4B	TELUGU VOWEL SIGN OO
0C4C	TELUGU VOWEL SIGN AU
0C4D	TELUGU SIGN VIRAMA
0C55	TELUGU LENGTH MARK
0C56	TELUGU AI LENGTH MARK
0CBF	KANNADA VOWEL SIGN I
0CC6	KANNADA VOWEL SIGN E
0CCC	KANNADA VOWEL SIGN AU
0CCD	KANNADA SIGN VIRAMA
0D41	MALAYALAM VOWEL SIGN U
0D42	MALAYALAM VOWEL SIGN UU
0D43	MALAYALAM VOWEL SIGN VOCALIC R
0D4D	MALAYALAM SIGN VIRAMA
0E31	THAI VOWEL SIGN MAI HAN-AKAT
0E34	THAI VOWEL SIGN SARA I
0E35	THAI VOWEL SIGN SARA II
0E36	THAI VOWEL SIGN SARA UE
0E37	THAI VOWEL SIGN SARA UEE
0E38	THAI VOWEL SIGN SARA U
0E39	THAI VOWEL SIGN SARA UU
0E3A	THAI VOWEL SIGN PHINTHU
0E47	THAI VOWEL SIGN MAI TAI KHU
0E48	THAI TONE MAI EK
0E49	THAI TONE MAI THO
0E4A	THAI TONE MAI TRI
0E4B	THAI TONE MAI CHATTAWA
0E4C	THAI THANTHAKHAT
0E4D	THAI NIKKHAHIT
0EB1	LAO VOWEL SIGN MAI KAN
0EB4	LAO VOWEL SIGN I
0EB5	LAO VOWEL SIGN II
0EB6	LAO VOWEL SIGN Y
0EB7	LAO VOWEL SIGN YY
0EB8	LAO VOWEL SIGN U
0EB9	LAO VOWEL SIGN UU
0EBB	LAO VOWEL SIGN MAI KON
0EBC	LAO SEMIVOWEL SIGN LO
0EC8	LAO TONE MAI EK
0EC9	LAO TONE MAI THO
0ECA	LAO TONE MAI TI
0ECB	LAO TONE MAI CATAWA
0ECC	LAO CANCELLATION MARK
0ECD	LAO NIGGAHITA
1026	TIBETAN VOWEL SIGN I
1027	TIBETAN VOWEL SIGN SHORT I
1028	TIBETAN VOWEL SIGN U
1029	TIBETAN VOWEL SIGN E
102A	TIBETAN VOWEL SIGN O
102E	TIBETAN ANUSVARA
1030	TIBETAN UNDER RING
1036	TIBETAN CANDRABINDU
1037	TIBETAN CANDRABINDU WITH ORNAMENT
103B	TIBETAN HONORIFIC UNDER RING
103D	TIBETAN VOWEL SIGN AI

UNIC	Unicode character name
103E	TIBETAN VOWEL SIGN AU
104B	TIBETAN VIRAMA
104C	TIBETAN LENITION MARK
3099	NON-SPACING KATAKANA-HIRAGANA VOICED SOUND MARK
309A	NON-SPACING KATAKANA-HIRAGANA SEMI-VOICED SOUND MARK

4.6 Directional Character Types

All Unicode characters without exception are directional. The directional types left-to-right and right-to-left are called *strong types*, and characters of those types are called strong directional characters. In addition, the Bidirecional Algorithm uses *weak types* and *neutrals*. The table below shows these types.

Strong Types

L	*Left-Right*	Left-to-right types include most alphabetic, syllabic, and Han ideographic characters.
Latin letters		U+0041 → U+005A, U+0061 → U+007A, U+00C0 → U+00D6, U+00D8 → U+00F6, U+00F8 → U+00FF
European Latin → Modifier Letters		U+0100 → U+02FF
General Diacriticals		U+0300 → U+036F
Greek → Armenian		U+0370 → U+058F
Devanagari → Georgian		U+0900 → U+10FF
Hiragana → Han		U+3040 → U+8BFF
Roman Numerals		U+2160 → U+2182
Left-Right Mark		U+200E
Symbol Diacritics		U+20D0 → U+20FF
Miscellaneous		U+0026, U+0040
R	*Right-Left*	Right-to-left types include Arabic, Hebrew, and punctuation specific to those scripts.
Arabic and Hebrew		U+0590 → U+065F, U+066D → U+06EF
Right-Left Mark		U+200F

Weak Types

EN	*European Number*	
European digits		U+0030 → U+0039
Eastern Arabic digits		U+06F0 → U+06F9
Super/Sub digits		U+2070, U+00B9, U+00B2 → U+00B3, U+2074 → U+2079, U+2080 → U+2089

ES   *European Number Separator*

Figure Space	U+2007
Period	U+002E
Slash	U+002F

ET   *European Number Terminator*

Plus sign	U+002B
Minus Sign	U+2212
Superscript plus and minus	U+207A, U+207B
Subscript plus and minus	U+208A, U+208B
Hyphen-Minus	U+002D
Plus-Minus	U+00B1
Minus-Plus	U+2213
Percents	U+0025, U+066A, U+2030, U+2031
Degree	U+00B0
Minute (Prime)	U+2032
Second (Double Prime)	U+2033
Currency symbols	U+00A2 → U+00A5, U+20A0 → U+20CF, U+0024
Number sign	U+0023

AN   *Arabic Number*

Arabic-based digits	U+0660 → U+0669
Arabic decimal & thousands separators	U+066B, U+066C

CS   *Common Number Separator*

Colon	U+003A
Comma	U+002C

Neutrals

B   *Block Separator*

Paragraph separator (PS)	U+2029
Line separator (LS)	U+2028

S   *Segment Separator*

(see below)

WS	Whitespace	
Space		U+0020
NBSP		U+00A0
General Punctuation Spaces		U+2000 → U+2006, U+2008 → U+200B, U+3000

ON	Other Neutrals	
All other characters		punctuation, symbols

As with other character properties, the Compatibility Zone characters have the same directional properties as their corresponding canonical characters. The directional type of all unassigned characters is not defined. This is also true of unassigned characters falling within the ranges used in the above tables; for brevity, not all unassigned characters in the ranges are called out separately where there are gaps. As unassigned characters are assigned in future versions of the Unicode standard, the new character properties will be documented.

Where unassigned characters are bidirectionally ordered for display (for example, as replacement glyphs), conformant processes are free to choose different directional properties. However, for best compatibility with future versions of the Unicode standard, it is recommended that unassigned characters be generally given the directional property *neutral* (N). The unassigned range U+0700 → U+08FF is reserved for use by future right-to-left scripts, however, so that a reasonable default in that case is the directional property *right-left* (R).

The definition of control code semantics is outside of the scope of the Unicode standard. Implementers should interpret the type of characters such as CR, LF, GS, and so on according the closest semantics to the types given here, such as interpreting CR (when used as paragraph separator) as being a block separator. *Horizontal tab* would generally be interpreted as a segment separator, which indicates that in a line containing tabs, the tab-delimited segments go in the base level direction (see the Bidirectional Algorithm, Appendix A).

Since horizontal Han ideographic characters are generally left-to-right, they have the *left-right* (L) directional character type. When they are written from right-to-left, their direction can overridden, as discussed in Bidirectional Algorithm, Appendix A.

5.0 Internal Mapping Tables

These mapping tables provide canonical mappings between precomposed characters and component character sequences and mappings from Compatibility Zone encodings to preferred Unicode values.

Disclaimer

The content of all mapping tables has been verified as far as possible by the Unicode Consortium. However, the Unicode Consortium does not guarantee that the tables are correct in every detail. The mapping tables are provided for informational purposes only. The Unicode Consortium is not responsible for errors that may occur either in the mapping tables or in software which implements those tables as they are printed in this volume.

5.1 Composite Character Mappings

The Unicode standard includes precomposed characters from existing standards. In the case of singly-accented characters, the precomposed form can be unambiguously decomposed into the sequence of baseform + non-spacing mark. Some letters, however, are multiply accented. In that case, the order of the non-spacing characters may be important. The following table of suggested decompositions for both of these cases identifies the precomposed form along with the base character and the non-spacing marks used to spell it, and their sequence.

This table can be used in two ways. It provides a standard spelling for those implementations that do not carry precomposed forms in their canonical representations of characters. It can also be used by implementers of rendering software to ensure that the composite sequence listed results in the intended visual output. Variations on the spellings in this table are not considered illegal, however, they may result in different visual output and software may interpret them differently. See Section 2.4, Alternate Spellings.

In the table, *Base* refers to the base character. *D1* and *D2* designate the first and second (if any) diacritic non-spacing mark. In some instances, a precomposed form can also be decomposed into another composite base character, designated *CB* in the table, plus a single diacritic non-spacing mark, also labeled *D1*.

Unicode Decomposition Mapping—Precomposed Letters

UNIC	Base	D1	D2	CB	D1	Unicode character name
00C0	0041	0300				LATIN CAPITAL LETTER A GRAVE
00C1	0041	0301				LATIN CAPITAL LETTER A ACUTE
00C2	0041	0302				LATIN CAPITAL LETTER A CIRCUMFLEX
00C3	0041	0303				LATIN CAPITAL LETTER A TILDE
00C4	0041	0308				LATIN CAPITAL LETTER A DIAERESIS
00C5	0041	030A				LATIN CAPITAL LETTER A RING
00C7	0043	0327				LATIN CAPITAL LETTER C CEDILLA
00C8	0045	0300				LATIN CAPITAL LETTER E GRAVE
00C9	0045	0301				LATIN CAPITAL LETTER E ACUTE
00CA	0045	0302				LATIN CAPITAL LETTER E CIRCUMFLEX
00CB	0045	0308				LATIN CAPITAL LETTER E DIAERESIS
00CC	0049	0300				LATIN CAPITAL LETTER I GRAVE
00CD	0049	0301				LATIN CAPITAL LETTER I ACUTE
00CE	0049	0302				LATIN CAPITAL LETTER I CIRCUMFLEX
00CF	0049	0308				LATIN CAPITAL LETTER I DIAERESIS
00D1	004E	0303				LATIN CAPITAL LETTER N TILDE
00D2	004F	0300				LATIN CAPITAL LETTER O GRAVE
00D3	004F	0301				LATIN CAPITAL LETTER O ACUTE
00D4	004F	0302				LATIN CAPITAL LETTER O CIRCUMFLEX
00D5	004F	0303				LATIN CAPITAL LETTER O TILDE
00D6	004F	0308				LATIN CAPITAL LETTER O DIAERESIS
00D8	004F	0338				LATIN CAPITAL LETTER O SLASH
00D9	0055	0300				LATIN CAPITAL LETTER U GRAVE
00DA	0055	0301				LATIN CAPITAL LETTER U ACUTE
00DB	0055	0302				LATIN CAPITAL LETTER U CIRCUMFLEX
00DC	0055	0308				LATIN CAPITAL LETTER U DIAERESIS
00DD	0059	0301				LATIN CAPITAL LETTER Y ACUTE
00E0	0061	0300				LATIN SMALL LETTER A GRAVE
00E1	0061	0301				LATIN SMALL LETTER A ACUTE
00E2	0061	0302				LATIN SMALL LETTER A CIRCUMFLEX
00E3	0061	0303				LATIN SMALL LETTER A TILDE
00E4	0061	0308				LATIN SMALL LETTER A DIAERESIS
00E5	0061	030A				LATIN SMALL LETTER A RING
00E7	0063	0327				LATIN SMALL LETTER C CEDILLA
00E8	0065	0300				LATIN SMALL LETTER E GRAVE
00E9	0065	0301				LATIN SMALL LETTER E ACUTE
00EA	0065	0302				LATIN SMALL LETTER E CIRCUMFLEX
00EB	0065	0308				LATIN SMALL LETTER E DIAERESIS
00EC	0069	0300				LATIN SMALL LETTER I GRAVE
00ED	0069	0301				LATIN SMALL LETTER I ACUTE
00EE	0069	0302				LATIN SMALL LETTER I CIRCUMFLEX
00EF	0069	0308				LATIN SMALL LETTER I DIAERESIS
00F1	006E	0303				LATIN SMALL LETTER N TILDE
00F2	006F	0300				LATIN SMALL LETTER O GRAVE
00F3	006F	0301				LATIN SMALL LETTER O ACUTE
00F4	006F	0302				LATIN SMALL LETTER O CIRCUMFLEX
00F5	006F	0303				LATIN SMALL LETTER O TILDE
00F6	006F	0308				LATIN SMALL LETTER O DIAERESIS
00F8	006F	0338				LATIN SMALL LETTER O SLASH
00F9	0075	0300				LATIN SMALL LETTER U GRAVE
00FA	0075	0301				LATIN SMALL LETTER U ACUTE
00FB	0075	0302				LATIN SMALL LETTER U CIRCUMFLEX
00FC	0075	0308				LATIN SMALL LETTER U DIAERESIS

UNIC	Base	D1	D2	CB	D1	Unicode character name
00FD	0079	0301				LATIN SMALL LETTER Y ACUTE
00FF	0079	0308				LATIN SMALL LETTER Y DIAERESIS
0100	0041	0304				LATIN CAPITAL LETTER A MACRON
0101	0061	0304				LATIN SMALL LETTER A MACRON
0102	0041	0306				LATIN CAPITAL LETTER A BREVE
0103	0061	0306				LATIN SMALL LETTER A BREVE
0104	0041	0328				LATIN CAPITAL LETTER A OGONEK
0105	0061	0328				LATIN SMALL LETTER A OGONEK
0106	0043	0301				LATIN CAPITAL LETTER C ACUTE
0107	0063	0301				LATIN SMALL LETTER C ACUTE
0108	0043	0302				LATIN CAPITAL LETTER C CIRCUMFLEX
0109	0063	0302				LATIN SMALL LETTER C CIRCUMFLEX
010A	0043	0307				LATIN CAPITAL LETTER C DOT
010B	0063	0307				LATIN SMALL LETTER C DOT
010C	0043	030C				LATIN CAPITAL LETTER C HACEK
010D	0063	030C				LATIN SMALL LETTER C HACEK
010E	0044	030C				LATIN CAPITAL LETTER D HACEK
010F	0064	030C				LATIN SMALL LETTER D HACEK
0110	0044	0335				LATIN CAPITAL LETTER D BAR
0111	0064	0335				LATIN SMALL LETTER D BAR
0112	0045	0304				LATIN CAPITAL LETTER E MACRON
0113	0065	0304				LATIN SMALL LETTER E MACRON
0114	0045	0306				LATIN CAPITAL LETTER E BREVE
0115	0065	0306				LATIN SMALL LETTER E BREVE
0116	0045	0307				LATIN CAPITAL LETTER E DOT
0117	0065	0307				LATIN SMALL LETTER E DOT
0118	0045	0328				LATIN CAPITAL LETTER E OGONEK
0119	0065	0328				LATIN SMALL LETTER E OGONEK
011A	0045	030C				LATIN CAPITAL LETTER E HACEK
011B	0065	030C				LATIN SMALL LETTER E HACEK
011C	0047	0302				LATIN CAPITAL LETTER G CIRCUMFLEX
011D	0067	0302				LATIN SMALL LETTER G CIRCUMFLEX
011E	0047	0306				LATIN CAPITAL LETTER G BREVE
011F	0067	0306				LATIN SMALL LETTER G BREVE
0120	0047	0307				LATIN CAPITAL LETTER G DOT
0121	0067	0307				LATIN SMALL LETTER G DOT
0122	0047	0327				LATIN CAPITAL LETTER G CEDILLA
0123	0067	0327				LATIN SMALL LETTER G CEDILLA
0124	0048	0302				LATIN CAPITAL LETTER H CIRCUMFLEX
0125	0068	0302				LATIN SMALL LETTER H CIRCUMFLEX
0126	0048	0335				LATIN CAPITAL LETTER H BAR
0127	0068	0335				LATIN SMALL LETTER H BAR
0128	0049	0303				LATIN CAPITAL LETTER I TILDE
0129	0069	0303				LATIN SMALL LETTER I TILDE
012A	0049	0304				LATIN CAPITAL LETTER I MACRON
012B	0069	0304				LATIN SMALL LETTER I MACRON
012C	0049	0306				LATIN CAPITAL LETTER I BREVE
012D	0069	0306				LATIN SMALL LETTER I BREVE
012E	0049	0328				LATIN CAPITAL LETTER I OGONEK
012F	0069	0328				LATIN SMALL LETTER I OGONEK
0130	0049	0307				LATIN CAPITAL LETTER I DOT
0134	004A	0302				LATIN CAPITAL LETTER J CIRCUMFLEX
0135	006A	0302				LATIN SMALL LETTER J CIRCUMFLEX
0136	004B	0327				LATIN CAPITAL LETTER K CEDILLA
0137	006B	0327				LATIN SMALL LETTER K CEDILLA
0139	004C	0301				LATIN CAPITAL LETTER L ACUTE

UNIC	Base	D1	D2	CB	D1	Unicode character name
013A	006C	0301				LATIN SMALL LETTER L ACUTE
013B	004C	0327				LATIN CAPITAL LETTER L CEDILLA
013C	006C	0327				LATIN SMALL LETTER L CEDILLA
013D	004C	030C				LATIN CAPITAL LETTER L HACEK
013E	006C	030C				LATIN SMALL LETTER L HACEK
0141	004C	0337				LATIN CAPITAL LETTER L SLASH
0142	006C	0337				LATIN SMALL LETTER L SLASH
0143	004E	0301				LATIN CAPITAL LETTER N ACUTE
0144	006E	0301				LATIN SMALL LETTER N ACUTE
0145	004E	0327				LATIN CAPITAL LETTER N CEDILLA
0146	006E	0327				LATIN SMALL LETTER N CEDILLA
0147	004E	030C				LATIN CAPITAL LETTER N HACEK
0148	006E	030C				LATIN SMALL LETTER N HACEK
014C	004F	0304				LATIN CAPITAL LETTER O MACRON
014D	006F	0304				LATIN SMALL LETTER O MACRON
014E	004F	0306				LATIN CAPITAL LETTER O BREVE
014F	006F	0306				LATIN SMALL LETTER O BREVE
0150	004F	030B				LATIN CAPITAL LETTER O DOUBLE ACUTE
0151	006F	030B				LATIN SMALL LETTER O DOUBLE ACUTE
0154	0052	0301				LATIN CAPITAL LETTER R ACUTE
0155	0072	0301				LATIN SMALL LETTER R ACUTE
0156	0052	0327				LATIN CAPITAL LETTER R CEDILLA
0157	0072	0327				LATIN SMALL LETTER R CEDILLA
0158	0052	030C				LATIN CAPITAL LETTER R HACEK
0159	0072	030C				LATIN SMALL LETTER R HACEK
015A	0053	0301				LATIN CAPITAL LETTER S ACUTE
015B	0073	0301				LATIN SMALL LETTER S ACUTE
015C	0053	0302				LATIN CAPITAL LETTER S CIRCUMFLEX
015D	0073	0302				LATIN SMALL LETTER S CIRCUMFLEX
015E	0053	0327				LATIN CAPITAL LETTER S CEDILLA
015F	0073	0327				LATIN SMALL LETTER S CEDILLA
0160	0053	030C				LATIN CAPITAL LETTER S HACEK
0161	0073	030C				LATIN SMALL LETTER S HACEK
0162	0054	0327				LATIN CAPITAL LETTER T CEDILLA
0163	0074	0327				LATIN SMALL LETTER T CEDILLA
0164	0054	030C				LATIN CAPITAL LETTER T HACEK
0165	0074	030C				LATIN SMALL LETTER T HACEK
0166	0054	0335				LATIN CAPITAL LETTER T BAR
0167	0074	0335				LATIN SMALL LETTER T BAR
0168	0055	0303				LATIN CAPITAL LETTER U TILDE
0169	0075	0303				LATIN SMALL LETTER U TILDE
016A	0055	0304				LATIN CAPITAL LETTER U MACRON
016B	0075	0304				LATIN SMALL LETTER U MACRON
016C	0055	0306				LATIN CAPITAL LETTER U BREVE
016D	0075	0306				LATIN SMALL LETTER U BREVE
016E	0055	030A				LATIN CAPITAL LETTER U RING
016F	0075	030A				LATIN SMALL LETTER U RING
0170	0055	030B				LATIN CAPITAL LETTER U DOUBLE ACUTE
0171	0075	030B				LATIN SMALL LETTER U DOUBLE ACUTE
0172	0055	0328				LATIN CAPITAL LETTER U OGONEK
0173	0075	0328				LATIN SMALL LETTER U OGONEK
0174	0057	0302				LATIN CAPITAL LETTER W CIRCUMFLEX
0175	0077	0302				LATIN SMALL LETTER W CIRCUMFLEX
0176	0059	0302				LATIN CAPITAL LETTER Y CIRCUMFLEX
0177	0079	0302				LATIN SMALL LETTER Y CIRCUMFLEX
0178	0059	0308				LATIN CAPITAL LETTER Y DIAERESIS

UNIC	Base	D1	D2	CB	D1	Unicode character name
0179	005A	0301				LATIN CAPITAL LETTER Z ACUTE
017A	007A	0301				LATIN SMALL LETTER Z ACUTE
017B	005A	0307				LATIN CAPITAL LETTER Z DOT
017C	007A	0307				LATIN SMALL LETTER Z DOT
017D	005A	030C				LATIN CAPITAL LETTER Z HACEK
017E	007A	030C				LATIN SMALL LETTER Z HACEK
0180	0062	0335				LATIN SMALL LETTER B BAR
0197	0049	0335				LATIN CAPITAL LETTER BARRED I
019A	006C	0335				LATIN SMALL LETTER BARRED L
019B	03BB	0335				LATIN SMALL LETTER BARRED LAMBDA
019F	004F	0335				LATIN CAPITAL LETTER BARRED O
01A0	004F	031B				LATIN CAPITAL LETTER O HORN
01A1	006F	031B				LATIN SMALL LETTER O HORN
01AB	0074	0321				LATIN SMALL LETTER T PALATAL HOOK
01AE	0054	0322				LATIN CAPITAL LETTER T RETROFLEX HOOK
01AF	0055	031B				LATIN CAPITAL LETTER U HORN
01B0	0075	031B				LATIN SMALL LETTER U HORN
01CD	0041	030C				LATIN CAPITAL LETTER A HACEK
01CE	0061	030C				LATIN SMALL LETTER A HACEK
01CF	0049	030C				LATIN CAPITAL LETTER I HACEK
01D0	0069	030C				LATIN SMALL LETTER I HACEK
01D1	004F	030C				LATIN CAPITAL LETTER O HACEK
01D2	006F	030C				LATIN SMALL LETTER O HACEK
01D3	0055	030C				LATIN CAPITAL LETTER U HACEK
01D4	0075	030C				LATIN SMALL LETTER U HACEK
01D5	0055	0308	0304	00DC	0304	LATIN CAPITAL LETTER U DIAERESIS MACRON
01D6	0075	0308	0304	00FC	0304	LATIN SMALL LETTER U DIAERESIS MACRON
01D7	0055	0308	0301	00DC	0301	LATIN CAPITAL LETTER U DIAERESIS ACUTE
01D8	0075	0308	0301	00FC	0301	LATIN SMALL LETTER U DIAERESIS ACUTE
01D9	0055	0308	030C	00DC	030C	LATIN CAPITAL LETTER U DIAERESIS HACEK
01DA	0075	0308	030C	00FC	030C	LATIN SMALL LETTER U DIAERESIS HACEK
01DB	0055	0308	0300	00DC	0300	LATIN CAPITAL LETTER U DIAERESIS GRAVE
01DC	0075	0308	0300	00FC	0300	LATIN SMALL LETTER U DIAERESIS GRAVE
01DE	0041	0308	0304	00C4	0304	LATIN CAPITAL LETTER A DIAERESIS MACRON
01DF	0061	0308	0304	00E4	0304	LATIN SMALL LETTER A DIAERESIS MACRON
01E0	0041	0307	0304			LATIN CAPITAL LETTER A DOT MACRON
01E1	0061	0307	0304			LATIN SMALL LETTER A DOT MACRON
01E2	00C6	0304				LATIN CAPITAL LETTER A E MACRON
01E3	00E6	0304				LATIN SMALL LETTER A E MACRON
01E4	0047	0335				LATIN CAPITAL LETTER G BAR
01E5	0067	0335				LATIN SMALL LETTER G BAR
01E6	0047	030C				LATIN CAPITAL LETTER G HACEK
01E7	0067	030C				LATIN SMALL LETTER G HACEK
01E8	004B	030C				LATIN CAPITAL LETTER K HACEK
01E9	006B	030C				LATIN SMALL LETTER K HACEK
01EA	004F	0328				LATIN CAPITAL LETTER O OGONEK
01EB	006F	0328				LATIN SMALL LETTER O OGONEK
01EC	004F	0328	0304	01EA	0304	LATIN CAPITAL LETTER O OGONEK MACRON
01ED	006F	0328	0304	01EB	0304	LATIN SMALL LETTER O OGONEK MACRON
01EE	01B7	030C				LATIN CAPITAL LETTER YOGH HACEK
01EF	0292	030C				LATIN SMALL LETTER YOGH HACEK
01F0	006A	030C				LATIN SMALL LETTER J HACEK
0386	0391	0384				GREEK CAPITAL LETTER ALPHA TONOS
0388	0395	0384				GREEK CAPITAL LETTER EPSILON TONOS
0389	0397	0384				GREEK CAPITAL LETTER ETA TONOS
038A	0399	0384				GREEK CAPITAL LETTER IOTA TONOS

UNIC	Base	D1	D2	CB	D1	Unicode character name
038C	039F	0384				GREEK CAPITAL LETTER OMICRON TONOS
038E	03A5	0384				GREEK CAPITAL LETTER UPSILON TONOS
038F	03A9	0384				GREEK CAPITAL LETTER OMEGA TONOS
0390	03B9	0385				GREEK SMALL LETTER IOTA DIAERESIS TONOS
03AA	0399	0308				GREEK CAPITAL LETTER IOTA DIAERESIS
03AB	03A5	0308				GREEK CAPITAL LETTER UPSILON DIAERESIS
03AC	03B1	0384				GREEK SMALL LETTER ALPHA TONOS
03AD	03B5	0384				GREEK SMALL LETTER EPSILON TONOS
03AE	03B7	0384				GREEK SMALL LETTER ETA TONOS
03AF	03B9	0384				GREEK SMALL LETTER IOTA TONOS
03B0	03C5	0385				GREEK SMALL LETTER UPSILON DIAERESIS TONOS
03CA	03B9	0308				GREEK SMALL LETTER IOTA DIAERESIS
03CB	03C5	0308				GREEK SMALL LETTER UPSILON DIAERESIS
03CC	03BF	0384				GREEK SMALL LETTER OMICRON TONOS
03CD	03C5	0384				GREEK SMALL LETTER UPSILON TONOS
03CE	03C9	0384				GREEK SMALL LETTER OMEGA TONOS
03D3	03D2	0384				GREEK CAPITAL LETTER UPSILON HOOK TONOS
03D4	03D2	0308				GREEK CAPITAL LETTER UPSILON HOOK DIAERESIS
0401	0415	0308				CYRILLIC CAPITAL LETTER IO
0403	0413	0301				CYRILLIC CAPITAL LETTER GJE
0407	0406	0308				CYRILLIC CAPITAL LETTER YI
040C	041A	0301				CYRILLIC CAPITAL LETTER KJE
040E	0423	0306				CYRILLIC CAPITAL LETTER SHORT U
0419	0418	0306				CYRILLIC CAPITAL LETTER SHORT II
0439	0438	0306				CYRILLIC SMALL LETTER SHORT II
0451	0435	0308				CYRILLIC SMALL LETTER IO
0453	0433	0301				CYRILLIC SMALL LETTER GJE
0457	0456	0308				CYRILLIC SMALL LETTER YI
045C	043A	0301				CYRILLIC SMALL LETTER KJE
045E	0443	0306				CYRILLIC SMALL LETTER SHORT U
0476	0474	030F				CYRILLIC CAPITAL LETTER IZHITSA DOUBLE GRAVE
0477	0475	030F				CYRILLIC SMALL LETTER IZHITSA DOUBLE GRAVE
0492	0413	0335				CYRILLIC CAPITAL LETTER GE BAR
0493	0433	0335				CYRILLIC SMALL LETTER GE BAR
0498	0417	0327				CYRILLIC CAPITAL LETTER ZE CEDILLA
0499	0437	0327				CYRILLIC SMALL LETTER ZE CEDILLA
04AA	0421	0327				CYRILLIC CAPITAL LETTER ES CEDILLA
04AB	0441	0327				CYRILLIC SMALL LETTER ES CEDILLA
04B0	04AE	0335				CYRILLIC CAPITAL LETTER STRAIGHT U BAR
04B1	04AF	0335				CYRILLIC SMALL LETTER STRAIGHT U BAR
04BE	04BC	0328				CYRILLIC CAPITAL LETTER IE HOOK OGONEK
04BF	04BD	0328				CYRILLIC SMALL LETTER IE HOOK OGONEK
04C1	0416	0306				CYRILLIC CAPITAL LETTER SHORT ZHE
04C2	0436	0306				CYRILLIC SMALL LETTER SHORT ZHE
04C5	041A	0328				CYRILLIC CAPITAL LETTER KA OGONEK
04C6	043A	0328				CYRILLIC SMALL LETTER KA OGONEK
04C9	0425	0328				CYRILLIC CAPITAL LETTER KHA OGONEK
04CA	0445	0328				CYRILLIC SMALL LETTER KHA OGONEK
0958	0915	093C				DEVANAGARI LETTER QA
0959	0916	093C				DEVANAGARI LETTER KHHA
095A	0917	093C				DEVANAGARI LETTER GHHA
095B	091C	093C				DEVANAGARI LETTER ZA
095C	0921	093C				DEVANAGARI LETTER DDDHA
095D	0922	093C				DEVANAGARI LETTER RHA
095E	092B	093C				DEVANAGARI LETTER FA
095F	092F	093C				DEVANAGARI LETTER YYA

UNIC	Base	D1	D2	CB	D1	Unicode character name
09DC	09A1	09BC				BENGALI LETTER RRA
09DD	09A2	09BC				BENGALI LETTER RHA
09DF	09AF	09BC				BENGALI LETTER YYA
0A59	0A16	0A3C				GURMUKHI LETTER KHHA
0A5A	0A17	0A3C				GURMUKHI LETTER GHHA
0A5B	0A1C	0A3C				GURMUKHI LETTER ZA
0A5C	0A21	0A3C				GURMUKHI LETTER RRA
0A5E	0A2B	0A3C				GURMUKHI LETTER FA
0B5C	0B21	0B3C				ORIYA LETTER RRA
0B5D	0B22	0B3C				ORIYA LETTER RHA
0B5F	0B2F	0B3C				ORIYA LETTER YYA
1014	1004	104C				TIBETAN LETTER TSA
1015	1005	104C				TIBETAN LETTER TSHA
1016	1006	104C				TIBETAN LETTER DZA

UNIC	Base	D1	D2	CB	D1	Unicode character name
00C6	0041	0045				LATIN CAPITAL LETTER A E
00E6	0061	0065				LATIN SMALL LETTER A E
0132	0049	004A				LATIN CAPITAL LETTER I J
0133	0069	006A				LATIN SMALL LETTER I J
013F	004C	00B7				LATIN CAPITAL LETTER L WITH MIDDLE DOT
0140	006C	00B7				LATIN SMALL LETTER L WITH MIDDLE DOT
0149	0027	006E				LATIN SMALL LETTER APOSTROPHE N
0152	004F	0045				LATIN CAPITAL LETTER O E
0153	006F	0065				LATIN SMALL LETTER O E
01C4	0044	005A	030C	0044	017D	LATIN CAPITAL LETTER D Z HACEK
01C5	0044	007A	030C	0044	017E	LATIN LETTER CAPITAL D SMALL Z HACEK
01C6	0064	007A	030C	0064	017E	LATIN SMALL LETTER D Z HACEK
01C7	004C	004A				LATIN CAPITAL LETTER L J
01C8	004C	006A				LATIN LETTER CAPITAL L SMALL J
01C9	006C	006A				LATIN SMALL LETTER L J
01CA	004E	004A				LATIN CAPITAL LETTER N J
01CB	004E	006A				LATIN LETTER CAPITAL N SMALL J
01CC	006E	006A				LATIN SMALL LETTER N J
02A3	0064	007A				LATIN SMALL LETTER D Z
02A4	0064	0292				LATIN SMALL LETTER D YOGH
02A5	0064	0291				LATIN SMALL LETTER D Z CURL
02A6	0074	0073				LATIN SMALL LETTER T S
02A7	0074	0283				LATIN SMALL LETTER T ESH
02A8	0074	0255				LATIN SMALL LETTER T C CURL
0409	041B	042C				CYRILLIC CAPITAL LETTER LJE
040A	041D	042C				CYRILLIC CAPITAL LETTER NJE
0459	043B	044C				CYRILLIC SMALL LETTER LJE
045A	043D	044C				CYRILLIC SMALL LETTER NJE
0EDC	0EAB	0E99				LAO HO NO
0EDD	0EAB	0EA1				LAO HO MO
203C	0021	0021				DOUBLE EXCLAMATION MARK
203D	003F	0021				INTERROBANG

5.2 Compatibility Mappings

Another form of multiple spellings is introduced in the Unicode standard by the Compatibility Zone. The Compatibility Zone contains duplicates of existing characters, but with additional attributes, such as directional ("vertical"), size ("small"), positional ("initial") and width ("half width"). This makes possible one-to-one conversion between the Unicode standard and widely-used standards which encode these properties in the character stream by duplicating characters. All characters in the compatiblilty zone can be replaced by regular Unicode characters, if perfect round-trip conversion is not a requirement, or where the software keeps track of these attributes outside of the character data stream itself.

Unicode Compatibility Zone Mapping

UNIC	Compatibility zone Unicode character name	UNIC	Maps to Unicode character name
FE30	GLYPH FOR VERTICAL TWO DOT LEADER	2025	TWO DOT LEADER
FE31	GLYPH FOR VERTICAL EM DASH	2014	EM DASH
FE32	GLYPH FOR VERTICAL EN DASH	2013	EN DASH
FE33	GLYPH FOR VERTICAL SPACING UNDERSCORE	005F	SPACING UNDERSCORE
FE34	GLYPH FOR VERTICAL SPACING WAVY UNDERSCORE	005F	SPACING UNDERSCORE
FE35	GLYPH FOR VERTICAL OPENING PARENTHESIS	0028	OPENING PARENTHESIS
FE36	GLYPH FOR VERTICAL CLOSING PARENTHESIS	0029	CLOSING PARENTHESIS
FE37	GLYPH FOR VERTICAL OPENING CURLY BRACKET	007B	OPENING CURLY BRACKET
FE38	GLYPH FOR VERTICAL CLOSING CURLY BRACKET	007D	CLOSING CURLY BRACKET
FE39	GLYPH FOR VERTICAL OPENING TORTOISE SHELL BRACKET	3014	OPENING TORTOISE SHELL BRACKET
FE3A	GLYPH FOR VERTICAL CLOSING TORTOISE SHELL BRACKET	3015	CLOSING TORTOISE SHELL BRACKET
FE3B	GLYPH FOR VERTICAL OPENING BLACK LENTICULAR BRACKET	3010	OPENING BLACK LENTICULAR BRACKET
FE3C	GLYPH FOR VERTICAL CLOSING BLACK LENTICULAR BRACKET	3011	CLOSING BLACK LENTICULAR BRACKET
FE3D	GLYPH FOR VERTICAL OPENING DOUBLE ANGLE BRACKET	300A	OPENING DOUBLE ANGLE BRACKET
FE3E	GLYPH FOR VERTICAL CLOSING DOUBLE ANGLE BRACKET	300B	CLOSING DOUBLE ANGLE BRACKET
FE3F	GLYPH FOR VERTICAL OPENING ANGLE BRACKET	3008	OPENING ANGLE BRACKET
FE40	GLYPH FOR VERTICAL CLOSING ANGLE BRACKET	3009	CLOSING ANGLE BRACKET
FE41	GLYPH FOR VERTICAL OPENING CORNER BRACKET	300C	OPENING CORNER BRACKET
FE42	GLYPH FOR VERTICAL CLOSING CORNER BRACKET	300D	CLOSING CORNER BRACKET
FE43	GLYPH FOR VERTICAL OPENING WHITE CORNER BRACKET	300E	OPENING WHITE CORNER BRACKET
FE44	GLYPH FOR VERTICAL CLOSING WHITE CORNER BRACKET	300F	CLOSING WHITE CORNER BRACKET
FE49	SPACING DASHED OVERSCORE	203E	SPACING OVERSCORE
FE4A	SPACING CENTERLINE OVERSCORE	203E	SPACING OVERSCORE
FE4B	SPACING WAVY OVERSCORE	203E	SPACING OVERSCORE
FE4C	SPACING DOUBLE WAVY OVERSCORE	203E	SPACING OVERSCORE
FE4D	SPACING DASHED UNDERSCORE	005F	SPACING UNDERSCORE
FE4E	SPACING CENTERLINE UNDERSCORE	005F	SPACING UNDERSCORE
FE4F	SPACING WAVY UNDERSCORE	005F	SPACING UNDERSCORE
FE50	SMALL COMMA	002C	COMMA
FE51	SMALL IDEOGRAPHIC COMMA	3001	IDEOGRAPHIC COMMA
FE52	SMALL PERIOD	002E	PERIOD
FE54	SMALL SEMICOLON	003B	SEMICOLON
FE55	SMALL COLON	003A	COLON
FE56	SMALL QUESTION MARK	003F	QUESTION MARK
FE57	SMALL EXCLAMATION MARK	0021	EXCLAMATION MARK
FE58	SMALL EM DASH	2014	EM DASH
FE59	SMALL OPENING PARENTHESIS	0028	OPENING PARENTHESIS

UNIC	Compatibility zone Unicode character name	UNIC	Maps to Unicode character name
FE5A	SMALL CLOSING PARENTHESIS	0029	CLOSING PARENTHESIS
FE5B	SMALL OPENING CURLY BRACKET	007B	OPENING CURLY BRACKET
FE5C	SMALL CLOSING CURLY BRACKET	007D	CLOSING CURLY BRACKET
FE5D	SMALL OPENING TORTOISE SHELL BRACKET	3014	OPENING TORTOISE SHELL BRACKET
FE5E	SMALL CLOSING TORTOISE SHELL BRACKET	3015	CLOSING TORTOISE SHELL BRACKET
FE5F	SMALL NUMBER SIGN	0023	NUMBER SIGN
FE60	SMALL AMPERSAND	0026	AMPERSAND
FE61	SMALL ASTERISK	002A	ASTERISK
FE62	SMALL PLUS SIGN	002B	PLUS SIGN
FE63	SMALL HYPHEN-MINUS	002D	HYPHEN-MINUS
FE64	SMALL LESS-THAN SIGN	003C	LESS-THAN SIGN
FE65	SMALL GREATER-THAN SIGN	003E	GREATER-THAN SIGN
FE66	SMALL EQUALS SIGN	003D	EQUALS SIGN
FE68	SMALL BACKSLASH	005C	BACKSLASH
FE69	SMALL DOLLAR SIGN	0024	DOLLAR SIGN
FE6A	SMALL PERCENT SIGN	0025	PERCENT SIGN
FE6B	SMALL COMMERCIAL AT	0040	COMMERCIAL AT
FE70	ARABIC SPACING FATHATAN	064B	ARABIC FATHATAN
FE71	ARABIC FATHATAN ON TATWEEL	064B	ARABIC FATHATAN
FE72	ARABIC SPACING DAMMATAN	064C	ARABIC DAMMATAN
FE74	ARABIC SPACING KASRATAN	064D	ARABIC KASRATAN
FE76	ARABIC SPACING FATHAH	064E	ARABIC FATHAH
FE77	ARABIC FATHAH ON TATWEEL	064E	ARABIC FATHAH
FE78	ARABIC SPACING DAMMAH	064F	ARABIC DAMMAH
FE79	ARABIC DAMMAH ON TATWEEL	064F	ARABIC DAMMAH
FE7A	ARABIC SPACING KASRAH	0650	ARABIC KASRAH
FE7B	ARABIC KASRAH ON TATWEEL	0650	ARABIC KASRAH
FE7C	ARABIC SPACING SHADDAH	0651	ARABIC SHADDAH
FE7D	ARABIC SHADDAH ON TATWEEL	0651	ARABIC SHADDAH
FE7E	ARABIC SPACING SUKUN	0652	ARABIC SUKUN
FE7F	ARABIC SUKUN ON TATWEEL	0652	ARABIC SUKUN
FE80	GLYPH FOR ISOLATE ARABIC HAMZAH	0621	ARABIC LETTER HAMZAH
FE81	GLYPH FOR ISOLATE ARABIC MADDAH ON ALEF	0622	ARABIC LETTER MADDAH ON ALEF
FE82	GLYPH FOR FINAL ARABIC MADDAH ON ALEF	0622	ARABIC LETTER MADDAH ON ALEF
FE83	GLYPH FOR ISOLATE ARABIC HAMZAH ON ALEF	0623	ARABIC LETTER HAMZAH ON ALEF
FE84	GLYPH FOR FINAL ARABIC HAMZAH ON ALEF	0623	ARABIC LETTER HAMZAH ON ALEF
FE85	GLYPH FOR ISOLATE ARABIC HAMZAH ON WAW	0624	ARABIC LETTER HAMZAH ON WAW
FE86	GLYPH FOR FINAL ARABIC HAMZAH ON WAW	0624	ARABIC LETTER HAMZAH ON WAW
FE87	GLYPH FOR ISOLATE ARABIC HAMZAH UNDER ALEF	0625	ARABIC LETTER HAMZAH UNDER ALEF

UNIC	Compatibility zone Unicode character name	UNIC	Maps to Unicode character name
FE88	GLYPH FOR FINAL ARABIC HAMZAH UNDER ALEF	0625	ARABIC LETTER HAMZAH UNDER ALEF
FE89	GLYPH FOR ISOLATE ARABIC HAMZAH ON YA	0626	ARABIC LETTER HAMZAH ON YA
FE8A	GLYPH FOR INITIAL ARABIC HAMZAH ON YA	0626	ARABIC LETTER HAMZAH ON YA
FE8B	GLYPH FOR MEDIAL ARABIC HAMZAH ON YA	0626	ARABIC LETTER HAMZAH ON YA
FE8C	GLYPH FOR FINAL ARABIC HAMZAH ON YA	0626	ARABIC LETTER HAMZAH ON YA
FE8D	GLYPH FOR ISOLATE ARABIC ALEF	0627	ARABIC LETTER ALEF
FE8E	GLYPH FOR FINAL ARABIC ALEF	0627	ARABIC LETTER ALEF
FE8F	GLYPH FOR ISOLATE ARABIC BAA	0628	ARABIC LETTER BAA
FE90	GLYPH FOR INITIAL ARABIC BAA	0628	ARABIC LETTER BAA
FE91	GLYPH FOR MEDIAL ARABIC BAA	0628	ARABIC LETTER BAA
FE92	GLYPH FOR FINAL ARABIC BAA	0628	ARABIC LETTER BAA
FE93	GLYPH FOR ISOLATE ARABIC TAA MARBUTAH	0629	ARABIC LETTER TAA MARBUTAH
FE94	GLYPH FOR FINAL ARABIC TAA MARBUTAH	0629	ARABIC LETTER TAA MARBUTAH
FE95	GLYPH FOR ISOLATE ARABIC TAA	062A	ARABIC LETTER TAA
FE96	GLYPH FOR INITIAL ARABIC TAA	062A	ARABIC LETTER TAA
FE97	GLYPH FOR MEDIAL ARABIC TAA	062A	ARABIC LETTER TAA
FE98	GLYPH FOR FINAL ARABIC TAA	062A	ARABIC LETTER TAA
FE99	GLYPH FOR ISOLATE ARABIC THAA	062B	ARABIC LETTER THAA
FE9A	GLYPH FOR INITIAL ARABIC THAA	062B	ARABIC LETTER THAA
FE9B	GLYPH FOR MEDIAL ARABIC THAA	062B	ARABIC LETTER THAA
FE9C	GLYPH FOR FINAL ARABIC THAA	062B	ARABIC LETTER THAA
FE9D	GLYPH FOR ISOLATE ARABIC JEEM	062C	ARABIC LETTER JEEM
FE9E	GLYPH FOR INITIAL ARABIC JEEM	062C	ARABIC LETTER JEEM
FE9F	GLYPH FOR MEDIAL ARABIC JEEM	062C	ARABIC LETTER JEEM
FEA0	GLYPH FOR FINAL ARABIC JEEM	062C	ARABIC LETTER JEEM
FEA1	GLYPH FOR ISOLATE ARABIC HAA	062D	ARABIC LETTER HAA
FEA2	GLYPH FOR INITIAL ARABIC HAA	062D	ARABIC LETTER HAA
FEA3	GLYPH FOR MEDIAL ARABIC HAA	062D	ARABIC LETTER HAA
FEA4	GLYPH FOR FINAL ARABIC HAA	062D	ARABIC LETTER HAA
FEA5	GLYPH FOR ISOLATE ARABIC KHAA	062E	ARABIC LETTER KHAA
FEA6	GLYPH FOR INITIAL ARABIC KHAA	062E	ARABIC LETTER KHAA
FEA7	GLYPH FOR MEDIAL ARABIC KHAA	062E	ARABIC LETTER KHAA
FEA8	GLYPH FOR FINAL ARABIC KHAA	062E	ARABIC LETTER KHAA
FEA9	GLYPH FOR ISOLATE ARABIC DAL	062F	ARABIC LETTER DAL
FEAA	GLYPH FOR FINAL ARABIC DAL	062F	ARABIC LETTER DAL
FEAB	GLYPH FOR ISOLATE ARABIC THAL	0630	ARABIC LETTER THAL
FEAC	GLYPH FOR FINAL ARABIC THAL	0630	ARABIC LETTER THAL
FEAD	GLYPH FOR ISOLATE ARABIC RA	0631	ARABIC LETTER RA
FEAE	GLYPH FOR FINAL ARABIC RA	0631	ARABIC LETTER RA

UNIC	Compatibility zone Unicode character name	UNIC	Maps to Unicode character name
FEAF	GLYPH FOR ISOLATE ARABIC ZAIN	0632	ARABIC LETTER ZAIN
FEB0	GLYPH FOR FINAL ARABIC ZAIN	0632	ARABIC LETTER ZAIN
FEB1	GLYPH FOR ISOLATE ARABIC SEEN	0633	ARABIC LETTER SEEN
FEB2	GLYPH FOR INITIAL ARABIC SEEN	0633	ARABIC LETTER SEEN
FEB3	GLYPH FOR MEDIAL ARABIC SEEN	0633	ARABIC LETTER SEEN
FEB4	GLYPH FOR FINAL ARABIC SEEN	0633	ARABIC LETTER SEEN
FEB5	GLYPH FOR ISOLATE ARABIC SHEEN	0634	ARABIC LETTER SHEEN
FEB6	GLYPH FOR INITIAL ARABIC SHEEN	0634	ARABIC LETTER SHEEN
FEB7	GLYPH FOR MEDIAL ARABIC SHEEN	0634	ARABIC LETTER SHEEN
FEB8	GLYPH FOR FINAL ARABIC SHEEN	0634	ARABIC LETTER SHEEN
FEB9	GLYPH FOR ISOLATE ARABIC SAD	0635	ARABIC LETTER SAD
FEBA	GLYPH FOR INITIAL ARABIC SAD	0635	ARABIC LETTER SAD
FEBB	GLYPH FOR MEDIAL ARABIC SAD	0635	ARABIC LETTER SAD
FEBC	GLYPH FOR FINAL ARABIC SAD	0635	ARABIC LETTER SAD
FEBD	GLYPH FOR ISOLATE ARABIC DAD	0636	ARABIC LETTER DAD
FEBE	GLYPH FOR INITIAL ARABIC DAD	0636	ARABIC LETTER DAD
FEBF	GLYPH FOR MEDIAL ARABIC DAD	0636	ARABIC LETTER DAD
FEC0	GLYPH FOR FINAL ARABIC DAD	0636	ARABIC LETTER DAD
FEC1	GLYPH FOR ISOLATE ARABIC TAH	0637	ARABIC LETTER TAH
FEC2	GLYPH FOR INITIAL ARABIC TAH	0637	ARABIC LETTER TAH
FEC3	GLYPH FOR MEDIAL ARABIC TAH	0637	ARABIC LETTER TAH
FEC4	GLYPH FOR FINAL ARABIC TAH	0637	ARABIC LETTER TAH
FEC5	GLYPH FOR ISOLATE ARABIC DHAH	0638	ARABIC LETTER DHAH
FEC6	GLYPH FOR INITIAL ARABIC DHAH	0638	ARABIC LETTER DHAH
FEC7	GLYPH FOR MEDIAL ARABIC DHAH	0638	ARABIC LETTER DHAH
FEC8	GLYPH FOR FINAL ARABIC DHAH	0638	ARABIC LETTER DHAH
FEC9	GLYPH FOR ISOLATE ARABIC AIN	0639	ARABIC LETTER AIN
FECA	GLYPH FOR INITIAL ARABIC AIN	0639	ARABIC LETTER AIN
FECB	GLYPH FOR MEDIAL ARABIC AIN	0639	ARABIC LETTER AIN
FECC	GLYPH FOR FINAL ARABIC AIN	0639	ARABIC LETTER AIN
FECD	GLYPH FOR ISOLATE ARABIC GHAIN	063A	ARABIC LETTER GHAIN
FECE	GLYPH FOR INITIAL ARABIC GHAIN	063A	ARABIC LETTER GHAIN
FECF	GLYPH FOR MEDIAL ARABIC GHAIN	063A	ARABIC LETTER GHAIN
FED0	GLYPH FOR FINAL ARABIC GHAIN	063A	ARABIC LETTER GHAIN
FED1	GLYPH FOR ISOLATE ARABIC FA	0641	ARABIC LETTER FA
FED2	GLYPH FOR INITIAL ARABIC FA	0641	ARABIC LETTER FA
FED3	GLYPH FOR MEDIAL ARABIC FA	0641	ARABIC LETTER FA
FED4	GLYPH FOR FINAL ARABIC FA	0641	ARABIC LETTER FA
FED5	GLYPH FOR ISOLATE ARABIC QAF	0642	ARABIC LETTER QAF

UNIC	Compatibility zone Unicode character name	UNIC	Maps to Unicode character name
FED6	GLYPH FOR INITIAL ARABIC QAF	0642	ARABIC LETTER QAF
FED7	GLYPH FOR MEDIAL ARABIC QAF	0642	ARABIC LETTER QAF
FED8	GLYPH FOR FINAL ARABIC QAF	0642	ARABIC LETTER QAF
FED9	GLYPH FOR ISOLATE ARABIC CAF	0643	ARABIC LETTER CAF
FEDA	GLYPH FOR INITIAL ARABIC CAF	0643	ARABIC LETTER CAF
FEDB	GLYPH FOR MEDIAL ARABIC CAF	0643	ARABIC LETTER CAF
FEDC	GLYPH FOR FINAL ARABIC CAF	0643	ARABIC LETTER CAF
FEDD	GLYPH FOR ISOLATE ARABIC LAM	0644	ARABIC LETTER LAM
FEDE	GLYPH FOR INITIAL ARABIC LAM	0644	ARABIC LETTER LAM
FEDF	GLYPH FOR MEDIAL ARABIC LAM	0644	ARABIC LETTER LAM
FEE0	GLYPH FOR FINAL ARABIC LAM	0644	ARABIC LETTER LAM
FEE1	GLYPH FOR ISOLATE ARABIC MEEM	0645	ARABIC LETTER MEEM
FEE2	GLYPH FOR INITIAL ARABIC MEEM	0645	ARABIC LETTER MEEM
FEE3	GLYPH FOR MEDIAL ARABIC MEEM	0645	ARABIC LETTER MEEM
FEE4	GLYPH FOR FINAL ARABIC MEEM	0645	ARABIC LETTER MEEM
FEE5	GLYPH FOR ISOLATE ARABIC NOON	0646	ARABIC LETTER NOON
FEE6	GLYPH FOR INITIAL ARABIC NOON	0646	ARABIC LETTER NOON
FEE7	GLYPH FOR MEDIAL ARABIC NOON	0646	ARABIC LETTER NOON
FEE8	GLYPH FOR FINAL ARABIC NOON	0646	ARABIC LETTER NOON
FEE9	GLYPH FOR ISOLATE ARABIC HA	0647	ARABIC LETTER HA
FEEA	GLYPH FOR INITIAL ARABIC HA	0647	ARABIC LETTER HA
FEEB	GLYPH FOR MEDIAL ARABIC HA	0647	ARABIC LETTER HA
FEEC	GLYPH FOR FINAL ARABIC HA	0647	ARABIC LETTER HA
FEED	GLYPH FOR ISOLATE ARABIC WAW	0648	ARABIC LETTER WAW
FEEE	GLYPH FOR FINAL ARABIC WAW	0648	ARABIC LETTER WAW
FEEF	GLYPH FOR ISOLATE ARABIC ALEF MAQSURAH	0649	ARABIC LETTER ALEF MAQSURAH
FEF0	GLYPH FOR FINAL ARABIC ALEF MAQSURAH	0649	ARABIC LETTER ALEF MAQSURAH
FEF1	GLYPH FOR ISOLATE ARABIC YA	064A	ARABIC LETTER YA
FEF2	GLYPH FOR INITIAL ARABIC YA	064A	ARABIC LETTER YA
FEF3	GLYPH FOR MEDIAL ARABIC YA	064A	ARABIC LETTER YA
FEF4	GLYPH FOR FINAL ARABIC YA	064A	ARABIC LETTER YA
FEF5	GLYPH FOR ISOLATE ARABIC MADDAH ON LIGATURE LAM ALEF (ligature)	0644	ARABIC LETTER LAM
		0622	ARABIC LETTER MADDAH ON ALEF
FEF6	GLYPH FOR FINAL ARABIC MADDAH ON LIGATURE LAM ALEF (ligature)	0644	ARABIC LETTER LAM
		0622	ARABIC LETTER MADDAH ON ALEF
FEF7	GLYPH FOR ISOLATE ARABIC HAMZAH ON LIGATURE LAM ALEF (ligature)	0644	ARABIC LETTER LAM
		0623	ARABIC LETTER HAMZAH ON ALEF
FEF8	GLYPH FOR FINAL ARABIC HAMZAH ON LIGATURE LAM ALEF (ligature)	0644	ARABIC LETTER LAM
		0623	ARABIC LETTER HAMZAH ON ALEF

UNIC	Compatibility zone Unicode character name
FEF9	GLYPH FOR ISOLATE ARABIC HAMZAH UNDER LIGATURE LAM ALEF (ligature)
FEFA	GLYPH FOR FINAL ARABIC HAMZAH UNDER LIGATURE LAM ALEF (ligature)
FEFB	GLYPH FOR ISOLATE ARABIC LIGATURE LAM ALEF (ligature)
FEFC	GLYPH FOR FINAL ARABIC LIGATURE LAM ALEF (ligature)
FF01	FULLWIDTH EXCLAMATION MARK
FF02	FULLWIDTH QUOTATION MARK
FF03	FULLWIDTH NUMBER SIGN
FF04	FULLWIDTH DOLLAR SIGN
FF05	FULLWIDTH PERCENT SIGN
FF06	FULLWIDTH AMPERSAND
FF07	FULLWIDTH APOSTROPHE
FF08	FULLWIDTH OPENING PARENTHESIS
FF09	FULLWIDTH CLOSING PARENTHESIS
FF0A	FULLWIDTH ASTERISK
FF0B	FULLWIDTH PLUS SIGN
FF0C	FULLWIDTH COMMA
FF0D	FULLWIDTH HYPHEN-MINUS
FF0E	FULLWIDTH PERIOD
FF0F	FULLWIDTH SLASH
FF10	FULLWIDTH DIGIT ZERO
FF11	FULLWIDTH DIGIT ONE
FF12	FULLWIDTH DIGIT TWO
FF13	FULLWIDTH DIGIT THREE
FF14	FULLWIDTH DIGIT FOUR
FF15	FULLWIDTH DIGIT FIVE
FF16	FULLWIDTH DIGIT SIX
FF17	FULLWIDTH DIGIT SEVEN
FF18	FULLWIDTH DIGIT EIGHT
FF19	FULLWIDTH DIGIT NINE
FF1A	FULLWIDTH COLON
FF1B	FULLWIDTH SEMICOLON
FF1C	FULLWIDTH LESS-THAN SIGN
FF1D	FULLWIDTH EQUALS SIGN
FF1E	FULLWIDTH GREATER-THAN SIGN
FF1F	FULLWIDTH QUESTION MARK

UNIC	Maps to Unicode character name
0644	ARABIC LETTER LAM
0625	ARABIC LETTER HAMZAH UNDER ALEF
0644	ARABIC LETTER LAM
0625	ARABIC LETTER HAMZAH UNDER ALEF
0644	ARABIC LETTER LAM
0627	ARABIC LETTER ALEF
0644	ARABIC LETTER LAM
0627	ARABIC LETTER ALEF
0021	EXCLAMATION MARK
0022	QUOTATION MARK
0023	NUMBER SIGN
0024	DOLLAR SIGN
0025	PERCENT SIGN
0026	AMPERSAND
0027	APOSTROPHE-QUOTE
0028	OPENING PARENTHESIS
0029	CLOSING PARENTHESIS
002A	ASTERISK
002B	PLUS SIGN
002C	COMMA
002D	HYPHEN-MINUS
002E	PERIOD
002F	SLASH
0030	DIGIT ZERO
0031	DIGIT ONE
0032	DIGIT TWO
0033	DIGIT THREE
0034	DIGIT FOUR
0035	DIGIT FIVE
0036	DIGIT SIX
0037	DIGIT SEVEN
0038	DIGIT EIGHT
0039	DIGIT NINE
003A	COLON
003B	SEMICOLON
003C	LESS-THAN SIGN
003D	EQUALS SIGN
003E	GREATER-THAN SIGN
003F	QUESTION MARK

UNIC	Compatibility zone Unicode character name		UNIC	Maps to Unicode character name
FF20	FULLWIDTH COMMERCIAL AT		0040	COMMERCIAL AT
FF21	FULLWIDTH LATIN CAPITAL LETTER A		0041	LATIN CAPITAL LETTER A
FF22	FULLWIDTH LATIN CAPITAL LETTER B		0042	LATIN CAPITAL LETTER B
FF23	FULLWIDTH LATIN CAPITAL LETTER C		0043	LATIN CAPITAL LETTER C
FF24	FULLWIDTH LATIN CAPITAL LETTER D		0044	LATIN CAPITAL LETTER D
FF25	FULLWIDTH LATIN CAPITAL LETTER E		0045	LATIN CAPITAL LETTER E
FF26	FULLWIDTH LATIN CAPITAL LETTER F		0046	LATIN CAPITAL LETTER F
FF27	FULLWIDTH LATIN CAPITAL LETTER G		0047	LATIN CAPITAL LETTER G
FF28	FULLWIDTH LATIN CAPITAL LETTER H		0048	LATIN CAPITAL LETTER H
FF29	FULLWIDTH LATIN CAPITAL LETTER I		0049	LATIN CAPITAL LETTER I
FF2A	FULLWIDTH LATIN CAPITAL LETTER J		004A	LATIN CAPITAL LETTER J
FF2B	FULLWIDTH LATIN CAPITAL LETTER K		004B	LATIN CAPITAL LETTER K
FF2C	FULLWIDTH LATIN CAPITAL LETTER L		004C	LATIN CAPITAL LETTER L
FF2D	FULLWIDTH LATIN CAPITAL LETTER M		004D	LATIN CAPITAL LETTER M
FF2E	FULLWIDTH LATIN CAPITAL LETTER N		004E	LATIN CAPITAL LETTER N
FF2F	FULLWIDTH LATIN CAPITAL LETTER O		004F	LATIN CAPITAL LETTER O
FF30	FULLWIDTH LATIN CAPITAL LETTER P		0050	LATIN CAPITAL LETTER P
FF31	FULLWIDTH LATIN CAPITAL LETTER Q		0051	LATIN CAPITAL LETTER Q
FF32	FULLWIDTH LATIN CAPITAL LETTER R		0052	LATIN CAPITAL LETTER R
FF33	FULLWIDTH LATIN CAPITAL LETTER S		0053	LATIN CAPITAL LETTER S
FF34	FULLWIDTH LATIN CAPITAL LETTER T		0054	LATIN CAPITAL LETTER T
FF35	FULLWIDTH LATIN CAPITAL LETTER U		0055	LATIN CAPITAL LETTER U
FF36	FULLWIDTH LATIN CAPITAL LETTER V		0056	LATIN CAPITAL LETTER V
FF37	FULLWIDTH LATIN CAPITAL LETTER W		0057	LATIN CAPITAL LETTER W
FF38	FULLWIDTH LATIN CAPITAL LETTER X		0058	LATIN CAPITAL LETTER X
FF39	FULLWIDTH LATIN CAPITAL LETTER Y		0059	LATIN CAPITAL LETTER Y
FF3A	FULLWIDTH LATIN CAPITAL LETTER Z		005A	LATIN CAPITAL LETTER Z
FF3B	FULLWIDTH OPENING SQUARE BRACKET		005B	OPENING SQUARE BRACKET
FF3C	FULLWIDTH BACKSLASH		005C	BACKSLASH
FF3D	FULLWIDTH CLOSING SQUARE BRACKET		005D	CLOSING SQUARE BRACKET
FF3E	FULLWIDTH SPACING CIRCUMFLEX		005E	SPACING CIRCUMFLEX
FF3F	FULLWIDTH SPACING UNDERSCORE		005F	SPACING UNDERSCORE
FF40	FULLWIDTH SPACING GRAVE		0060	SPACING GRAVE
FF41	FULLWIDTH LATIN SMALL LETTER A		0061	LATIN SMALL LETTER A
FF42	FULLWIDTH LATIN SMALL LETTER B		0062	LATIN SMALL LETTER B
FF43	FULLWIDTH LATIN SMALL LETTER C		0063	LATIN SMALL LETTER C
FF44	FULLWIDTH LATIN SMALL LETTER D		0064	LATIN SMALL LETTER D
FF45	FULLWIDTH LATIN SMALL LETTER E		0065	LATIN SMALL LETTER E
FF46	FULLWIDTH LATIN SMALL LETTER F		0066	LATIN SMALL LETTER F

UNIC	Compatibility zone Unicode character name	UNIC	Maps to Unicode character name
FF47	FULLWIDTH LATIN SMALL LETTER G	0067	LATIN SMALL LETTER G
FF48	FULLWIDTH LATIN SMALL LETTER H	0068	LATIN SMALL LETTER H
FF49	FULLWIDTH LATIN SMALL LETTER I	0069	LATIN SMALL LETTER I
FF4A	FULLWIDTH LATIN SMALL LETTER J	006A	LATIN SMALL LETTER J
FF4B	FULLWIDTH LATIN SMALL LETTER K	006B	LATIN SMALL LETTER K
FF4C	FULLWIDTH LATIN SMALL LETTER L	006C	LATIN SMALL LETTER L
FF4D	FULLWIDTH LATIN SMALL LETTER M	006D	LATIN SMALL LETTER M
FF4E	FULLWIDTH LATIN SMALL LETTER N	006E	LATIN SMALL LETTER N
FF4F	FULLWIDTH LATIN SMALL LETTER O	006F	LATIN SMALL LETTER O
FF50	FULLWIDTH LATIN SMALL LETTER P	0070	LATIN SMALL LETTER P
FF51	FULLWIDTH LATIN SMALL LETTER Q	0071	LATIN SMALL LETTER Q
FF52	FULLWIDTH LATIN SMALL LETTER R	0072	LATIN SMALL LETTER R
FF53	FULLWIDTH LATIN SMALL LETTER S	0073	LATIN SMALL LETTER S
FF54	FULLWIDTH LATIN SMALL LETTER T	0074	LATIN SMALL LETTER T
FF55	FULLWIDTH LATIN SMALL LETTER U	0075	LATIN SMALL LETTER U
FF56	FULLWIDTH LATIN SMALL LETTER V	0076	LATIN SMALL LETTER V
FF57	FULLWIDTH LATIN SMALL LETTER W	0077	LATIN SMALL LETTER W
FF58	FULLWIDTH LATIN SMALL LETTER X	0078	LATIN SMALL LETTER X
FF59	FULLWIDTH LATIN SMALL LETTER Y	0079	LATIN SMALL LETTER Y
FF5A	FULLWIDTH LATIN SMALL LETTER Z	007A	LATIN SMALL LETTER Z
FF5B	FULLWIDTH OPENING CURLY BRACKET	007B	OPENING CURLY BRACKET
FF5C	FULLWIDTH VERTICAL BAR	007C	VERTICAL BAR
FF5D	FULLWIDTH CLOSING CURLY BRACKET	007D	CLOSING CURLY BRACKET
FF5E	FULLWIDTH SPACING TILDE	007E	TILDE
FF61	HALFWIDTH IDEOGRAPHIC PERIOD	3002	IDEOGRAPHIC PERIOD
FF62	HALFWIDTH OPENING CORNER BRACKET	300C	OPENING CORNER BRACKET
FF63	HALFWIDTH CLOSING CORNER BRACKET	300D	CLOSING CORNER BRACKET
FF64	HALFWIDTH IDEOGRAPHIC COMMA	3001	IDEOGRAPHIC COMMA
FF65	HALFWIDTH KATAKANA MIDDLE DOT	30FB	KATAKANA MIDDLE DOT
FF66	HALFWIDTH KATAKANA LETTER WO	30F2	KATAKANA LETTER WO
FF67	HALFWIDTH KATAKANA LETTER SMALL A	30A1	KATAKANA LETTER SMALL A
FF68	HALFWIDTH KATAKANA LETTER SMALL I	30A3	KATAKANA LETTER SMALL I
FF69	HALFWIDTH KATAKANA LETTER SMALL U	30A5	KATAKANA LETTER SMALL U
FF6A	HALFWIDTH KATAKANA LETTER SMALL E	30A7	KATAKANA LETTER SMALL E
FF6B	HALFWIDTH KATAKANA LETTER SMALL O	30A9	KATAKANA LETTER SMALL O
FF6C	HALFWIDTH KATAKANA LETTER SMALL YA	30E3	KATAKANA LETTER SMALL YA
FF6D	HALFWIDTH KATAKANA LETTER SMALL YU	30E5	KATAKANA LETTER SMALL YU
FF6E	HALFWIDTH KATAKANA LETTER SMALL YO	30E7	KATAKANA LETTER SMALL YO
FF6F	HALFWIDTH KATAKANA LETTER SMALL TU	30C3	KATAKANA LETTER SMALL TU

UNIC	Compatibility zone Unicode character name	UNIC	Maps to Unicode character name
FF70	HALFWIDTH KATAKANA-HIRAGANA PROLONGED SOUND MARK	30FC	KATAKANA-HIRAGANA PROLONGED SOUND MARK
FF71	HALFWIDTH KATAKANA LETTER A	30A2	KATAKANA LETTER A
FF72	HALFWIDTH KATAKANA LETTER I	30A4	KATAKANA LETTER I
FF73	HALFWIDTH KATAKANA LETTER U	30A6	KATAKANA LETTER U
FF74	HALFWIDTH KATAKANA LETTER E	30A8	KATAKANA LETTER E
FF75	HALFWIDTH KATAKANA LETTER O	30AA	KATAKANA LETTER O
FF76	HALFWIDTH KATAKANA LETTER KA	30AB	KATAKANA LETTER KA
FF77	HALFWIDTH KATAKANA LETTER KI	30AD	KATAKANA LETTER KI
FF78	HALFWIDTH KATAKANA LETTER KU	30AF	KATAKANA LETTER KU
FF79	HALFWIDTH KATAKANA LETTER KE	30B1	KATAKANA LETTER KE
FF7A	HALFWIDTH KATAKANA LETTER KO	30B3	KATAKANA LETTER KO
FF7B	HALFWIDTH KATAKANA LETTER SA	30B5	KATAKANA LETTER SA
FF7C	HALFWIDTH KATAKANA LETTER SI	30B7	KATAKANA LETTER SI
FF7D	HALFWIDTH KATAKANA LETTER SU	30B9	KATAKANA LETTER SU
FF7E	HALFWIDTH KATAKANA LETTER SE	30BB	KATAKANA LETTER SE
FF7F	HALFWIDTH KATAKANA LETTER SO	30BD	KATAKANA LETTER SO
FF80	HALFWIDTH KATAKANA LETTER TA	30BF	KATAKANA LETTER TA
FF81	HALFWIDTH KATAKANA LETTER TI	30C1	KATAKANA LETTER TI
FF82	HALFWIDTH KATAKANA LETTER TU	30C4	KATAKANA LETTER TU
FF83	HALFWIDTH KATAKANA LETTER TE	30C6	KATAKANA LETTER TE
FF84	HALFWIDTH KATAKANA LETTER TO	30C8	KATAKANA LETTER TO
FF85	HALFWIDTH KATAKANA LETTER NA	30CA	KATAKANA LETTER NA
FF86	HALFWIDTH KATAKANA LETTER NI	30CB	KATAKANA LETTER NI
FF87	HALFWIDTH KATAKANA LETTER NU	30CC	KATAKANA LETTER NU
FF88	HALFWIDTH KATAKANA LETTER NE	30CD	KATAKANA LETTER NE
FF89	HALFWIDTH KATAKANA LETTER NO	30CE	KATAKANA LETTER NO
FF8A	HALFWIDTH KATAKANA LETTER HA	30CF	KATAKANA LETTER HA
FF8B	HALFWIDTH KATAKANA LETTER HI	30D2	KATAKANA LETTER HI
FF8C	HALFWIDTH KATAKANA LETTER HU	30D5	KATAKANA LETTER HU
FF8D	HALFWIDTH KATAKANA LETTER HE	30D8	KATAKANA LETTER HE
FF8E	HALFWIDTH KATAKANA LETTER HO	30DB	KATAKANA LETTER HO
FF8F	HALFWIDTH KATAKANA LETTER MA	30DE	KATAKANA LETTER MA
FF90	HALFWIDTH KATAKANA LETTER MI	30DF	KATAKANA LETTER MI
FF91	HALFWIDTH KATAKANA LETTER MU	30E0	KATAKANA LETTER MU
FF92	HALFWIDTH KATAKANA LETTER ME	30E1	KATAKANA LETTER ME
FF93	HALFWIDTH KATAKANA LETTER MO	30E2	KATAKANA LETTER MO
FF94	HALFWIDTH KATAKANA LETTER YA	30E4	KATAKANA LETTER YA
FF95	HALFWIDTH KATAKANA LETTER YU	30E6	KATAKANA LETTER YU
FF96	HALFWIDTH KATAKANA LETTER YO	30E8	KATAKANA LETTER YO

UNIC	Compatibility zone Unicode character name	UNIC	Maps to Unicode character name
FF97	HALFWIDTH KATAKANA LETTER RA	30E9	KATAKANA LETTER RA
FF98	HALFWIDTH KATAKANA LETTER RI	30EA	KATAKANA LETTER RI
FF99	HALFWIDTH KATAKANA LETTER RU	30EB	KATAKANA LETTER RU
FF9A	HALFWIDTH KATAKANA LETTER RE	30EC	KATAKANA LETTER RE
FF9B	HALFWIDTH KATAKANA LETTER RO	30ED	KATAKANA LETTER RO
FF9C	HALFWIDTH KATAKANA LETTER WA	30EF	KATAKANA LETTER WA
FF9D	HALFWIDTH KATAKANA LETTER N	30F3	KATAKANA LETTER N
FF9E	HALFWIDTH KATAKANA VOICED SOUND MARK	309B	KATAKANA-HIRAGANA VOICED SOUND MARK
FF9F	HALFWIDTH KATAKANA SEMI-VOICED SOUND MARK	309C	KATAKANA-HIRAGANA SEMI-VOICED SOUND MARK
FFA0	HALFWIDTH HANGUL CAE OM	3164	HANGUL CAE OM
FFA1	HALFWIDTH HANGUL LETTER GIYEOG	3131	HANGUL LETTER GIYEOG
FFA2	HALFWIDTH HANGUL LETTER SSANG GIYEOG	3132	HANGUL LETTER SSANG GIYEOG
FFA3	HALFWIDTH HANGUL LETTER GIYEOG SIOS	3133	HANGUL LETTER GIYEOG SIOS
FFA4	HALFWIDTH HANGUL LETTER NIEUN	3134	HANGUL LETTER NIEUN
FFA5	HALFWIDTH HANGUL LETTER NIEUN JIEUJ	3135	HANGUL LETTER NIEUN JIEUJ
FFA6	HALFWIDTH HANGUL LETTER NIEUN HIEUH	3136	HANGUL LETTER NIEUN HIEUH
FFA7	HALFWIDTH HANGUL LETTER DIGEUD	3137	HANGUL LETTER DIGEUD
FFA8	HALFWIDTH HANGUL LETTER SSANG DIGEUD	3138	HANGUL LETTER SSANG DIGEUD
FFA9	HALFWIDTH HANGUL LETTER LIEUL	3139	HANGUL LETTER LIEUL
FFAA	HALFWIDTH HANGUL LETTER LIEUL GIYEOG	313A	HANGUL LETTER LIEUL GIYEOG
FFAB	HALFWIDTH HANGUL LETTER LIEUL MIEUM	313B	HANGUL LETTER LIEUL MIEUM
FFAC	HALFWIDTH HANGUL LETTER LIEUL BIEUB	313C	HANGUL LETTER LIEUL BIEUB
FFAD	HALFWIDTH HANGUL LETTER LIEUL SIOS	313D	HANGUL LETTER LIEUL SIOS
FFAE	HALFWIDTH HANGUL LETTER LIEUL TIEUT	313E	HANGUL LETTER LIEUL TIEUT
FFAF	HALFWIDTH HANGUL LETTER LIEUL PIEUP	313F	HANGUL LETTER LIEUL PIEUP
FFB0	HALFWIDTH HANGUL LETTER LIEUL HIEUH	3140	HANGUL LETTER LIEUL HIEUH
FFB1	HALFWIDTH HANGUL LETTER MIEUM	3141	HANGUL LETTER MIEUM
FFB2	HALFWIDTH HANGUL LETTER BIEUB	3142	HANGUL LETTER BIEUB
FFB3	HALFWIDTH HANGUL LETTER SSANG BIEUB	3143	HANGUL LETTER SSANG BIEUB
FFB4	HALFWIDTH HANGUL LETTER BIEUB SIOS	3144	HANGUL LETTER BIEUB SIOS
FFB5	HALFWIDTH HANGUL LETTER SIOS	3145	HANGUL LETTER SIOS
FFB6	HALFWIDTH HANGUL LETTER SSANG SIOS	3146	HANGUL LETTER SSANG SIOS
FFB7	HALFWIDTH HANGUL LETTER IEUNG	3147	HANGUL LETTER IEUNG
FFB8	HALFWIDTH HANGUL LETTER JIEUJ	3148	HANGUL LETTER JIEUJ
FFB9	HALFWIDTH HANGUL LETTER SSANG JIEUJ	3149	HANGUL LETTER SSANG JIEUJ
FFBA	HALFWIDTH HANGUL LETTER CIEUC	314A	HANGUL LETTER CIEUC
FFBB	HALFWIDTH HANGUL LETTER KIYEOK	314B	HANGUL LETTER KIYEOK
FFBC	HALFWIDTH HANGUL LETTER TIEUT	314C	HANGUL LETTER TIEUT
FFBD	HALFWIDTH HANGUL LETTER PIEUP	314D	HANGUL LETTER PIEUP

UNIC	Compatibility zone Unicode character name	UNIC	Maps to Unicode character name
FFBE	HALFWIDTH HANGUL LETTER HIEUH	314E	HANGUL LETTER HIEUH
FFC2	HALFWIDTH HANGUL LETTER A	314F	HANGUL LETTER A
FFC3	HALFWIDTH HANGUL LETTER AE	3150	HANGUL LETTER AE
FFC4	HALFWIDTH HANGUL LETTER YA	3151	HANGUL LETTER YA
FFC5	HALFWIDTH HANGUL LETTER YAE	3152	HANGUL LETTER YAE
FFC6	HALFWIDTH HANGUL LETTER EO	3153	HANGUL LETTER EO
FFC7	HALFWIDTH HANGUL LETTER E	3154	HANGUL LETTER E
FFCA	HALFWIDTH HANGUL LETTER YEO	3155	HANGUL LETTER YEO
FFCB	HALFWIDTH HANGUL LETTER YE	3156	HANGUL LETTER YE
FFCC	HALFWIDTH HANGUL LETTER O	3157	HANGUL LETTER O
FFCD	HALFWIDTH HANGUL LETTER WA	3158	HANGUL LETTER WA
FFCE	HALFWIDTH HANGUL LETTER WAE	3159	HANGUL LETTER WAE
FFCF	HALFWIDTH HANGUL LETTER OE	315A	HANGUL LETTER OE
FFD2	HALFWIDTH HANGUL LETTER YO	315B	HANGUL LETTER YO
FFD3	HALFWIDTH HANGUL LETTER U	315C	HANGUL LETTER U
FFD4	HALFWIDTH HANGUL LETTER WEO	315D	HANGUL LETTER WEO
FFD5	HALFWIDTH HANGUL LETTER WE	315E	HANGUL LETTER WE
FFD6	HALFWIDTH HANGUL LETTER WI	315F	HANGUL LETTER WI
FFD7	HALFWIDTH HANGUL LETTER YU	3160	HANGUL LETTER YU
FFDA	HALFWIDTH HANGUL LETTER EU	3161	HANGUL LETTER EU
FFDB	HALFWIDTH HANGUL LETTER YI	3162	HANGUL LETTER YI
FFDC	HALFWIDTH HANGUL LETTER I	3163	HANGUL LETTER I
FFE0	FULLWIDTH CENT SIGN	00A2	CENT SIGN
FFE1	FULLWIDTH POUND SIGN	00A3	POUND SIGN
FFE2	FULLWIDTH NOT SIGN	00AC	NOT SIGN
FFE3	FULLWIDTH SPACING MACRON	00AF	SPACING MACRON
FFE4	FULLWIDTH BROKEN VERTICAL BAR	00A6	BROKEN VERTICAL BAR
FFE5	FULLWIDTH YEN SIGN	00A5	YEN SIGN
FFE6	FULLWIDTH WON SIGN	20A9	WON SIGN

5.3 Vietnamese Mappings

This table provides suggested spellings of existing letters of the Vietnamese alphabet for which the Unicode standard does *not* contain a precomposed form. Because of the special properties of the Vietnamese alphabet, an unambiguous spelling is suggested where the tone marks are non-spacing accents and are combined with precomposed vowels. Each row of the table can be interpreted as the decomposition for a single Vietnamese vowel with its tone mark.

The five Vietnamese tone marks are:

U+0341 NON-SPACING ACUTE TONE MARK
U+0340 NON-SPACING GRAVE TONE MARK
U+0309 NON-SPACING HOOK ABOVE
U+0303 NON-SPACING TILDE
U+0323 NON-SPACING DOT BELOW

The tilde (U+0303) and the dot below (U+0323) are generic, non-spacing characters; the other three are tone marks that are unique to Vietnamese.

Unicode Vietnamese Decomposition

UNIC	Unicode character name Base vowel (simple or composite)	UNIC	Unicode character name Non-spacing mark for tone
0041	LATIN CAPITAL LETTER A	0309	NON-SPACING HOOK ABOVE
0041	LATIN CAPITAL LETTER A	0323	NON-SPACING DOT BELOW
0041	LATIN CAPITAL LETTER A	0340	NON-SPACING GRAVE TONE MARK
0041	LATIN CAPITAL LETTER A	0341	NON-SPACING ACUTE TONE MARK
00C2	LATIN CAPITAL LETTER A CIRCUMFLEX	0303	NON-SPACING TILDE
00C2	LATIN CAPITAL LETTER A CIRCUMFLEX	0309	NON-SPACING HOOK ABOVE
00C2	LATIN CAPITAL LETTER A CIRCUMFLEX	0323	NON-SPACING DOT BELOW
00C2	LATIN CAPITAL LETTER A CIRCUMFLEX	0340	NON-SPACING GRAVE TONE MARK
00C2	LATIN CAPITAL LETTER A CIRCUMFLEX	0341	NON-SPACING ACUTE TONE MARK
0102	LATIN CAPITAL LETTER A BREVE	0303	NON-SPACING TILDE
0102	LATIN CAPITAL LETTER A BREVE	0309	NON-SPACING HOOK ABOVE
0102	LATIN CAPITAL LETTER A BREVE	0323	NON-SPACING DOT BELOW
0102	LATIN CAPITAL LETTER A BREVE	0340	NON-SPACING GRAVE TONE MARK
0102	LATIN CAPITAL LETTER A BREVE	0341	NON-SPACING ACUTE TONE MARK
0045	LATIN CAPITAL LETTER E	0303	NON-SPACING TILDE
0045	LATIN CAPITAL LETTER E	0309	NON-SPACING HOOK ABOVE
0045	LATIN CAPITAL LETTER E	0323	NON-SPACING DOT BELOW
0045	LATIN CAPITAL LETTER E	0340	NON-SPACING GRAVE TONE MARK
0045	LATIN CAPITAL LETTER E	0341	NON-SPACING ACUTE TONE MARK
00CA	LATIN CAPITAL LETTER E CIRCUMFLEX	0303	NON-SPACING TILDE
00CA	LATIN CAPITAL LETTER E CIRCUMFLEX	0309	NON-SPACING HOOK ABOVE
00CA	LATIN CAPITAL LETTER E CIRCUMFLEX	0323	NON-SPACING DOT BELOW
00CA	LATIN CAPITAL LETTER E CIRCUMFLEX	0340	NON-SPACING GRAVE TONE MARK
00CA	LATIN CAPITAL LETTER E CIRCUMFLEX	0341	NON-SPACING ACUTE TONE MARK
0049	LATIN CAPITAL LETTER I	0303	NON-SPACING TILDE
0049	LATIN CAPITAL LETTER I	0309	NON-SPACING HOOK ABOVE
0049	LATIN CAPITAL LETTER I	0323	NON-SPACING DOT BELOW
0049	LATIN CAPITAL LETTER I	0340	NON-SPACING GRAVE TONE MARK
0049	LATIN CAPITAL LETTER I	0341	NON-SPACING ACUTE TONE MARK
004F	LATIN CAPITAL LETTER O	0309	NON-SPACING HOOK ABOVE
004F	LATIN CAPITAL LETTER O	0323	NON-SPACING DOT BELOW
004F	LATIN CAPITAL LETTER O	0340	NON-SPACING GRAVE TONE MARK
004F	LATIN CAPITAL LETTER O	0341	NON-SPACING ACUTE TONE MARK
00D4	LATIN CAPITAL LETTER O CIRCUMFLEX	0303	NON-SPACING TILDE
00D4	LATIN CAPITAL LETTER O CIRCUMFLEX	0309	NON-SPACING HOOK ABOVE
00D4	LATIN CAPITAL LETTER O CIRCUMFLEX	0323	NON-SPACING DOT BELOW
00D4	LATIN CAPITAL LETTER O CIRCUMFLEX	0340	NON-SPACING GRAVE TONE MARK
00D4	LATIN CAPITAL LETTER O CIRCUMFLEX	0341	NON-SPACING ACUTE TONE MARK
01A0	LATIN CAPITAL LETTER O HORN	0303	NON-SPACING TILDE
01A0	LATIN CAPITAL LETTER O HORN	0309	NON-SPACING HOOK ABOVE
01A0	LATIN CAPITAL LETTER O HORN	0323	NON-SPACING DOT BELOW
01A0	LATIN CAPITAL LETTER O HORN	0340	NON-SPACING GRAVE TONE MARK
01A0	LATIN CAPITAL LETTER O HORN	0341	NON-SPACING ACUTE TONE MARK
0055	LATIN CAPITAL LETTER U	0303	NON-SPACING TILDE
0055	LATIN CAPITAL LETTER U	0309	NON-SPACING HOOK ABOVE
0055	LATIN CAPITAL LETTER U	0323	NON-SPACING DOT BELOW
0055	LATIN CAPITAL LETTER U	0340	NON-SPACING GRAVE TONE MARK
0055	LATIN CAPITAL LETTER U	0341	NON-SPACING ACUTE TONE MARK
01AF	LATIN CAPITAL LETTER U HORN	0303	NON-SPACING TILDE
01AF	LATIN CAPITAL LETTER U HORN	0309	NON-SPACING HOOK ABOVE
01AF	LATIN CAPITAL LETTER U HORN	0323	NON-SPACING DOT BELOW
01AF	LATIN CAPITAL LETTER U HORN	0340	NON-SPACING GRAVE TONE MARK
01AF	LATIN CAPITAL LETTER U HORN	0341	NON-SPACING ACUTE TONE MARK

UNIC	*Unicode character name* *Base vowel (simple or composite)*	UNIC	*Unicode character name* *Non-spacing mark for tone*
0059	LATIN CAPITAL LETTER Y	0303	NON-SPACING TILDE
0059	LATIN CAPITAL LETTER Y	0309	NON-SPACING HOOK ABOVE
0059	LATIN CAPITAL LETTER Y	0323	NON-SPACING DOT BELOW
0059	LATIN CAPITAL LETTER Y	0340	NON-SPACING GRAVE TONE MARK
0059	LATIN CAPITAL LETTER Y	0341	NON-SPACING ACUTE TONE MARK
0061	LATIN SMALL LETTER A	0309	NON-SPACING HOOK ABOVE
0061	LATIN SMALL LETTER A	0323	NON-SPACING DOT BELOW
0061	LATIN SMALL LETTER A	0340	NON-SPACING GRAVE TONE MARK
0061	LATIN SMALL LETTER A	0341	NON-SPACING ACUTE TONE MARK
00E2	LATIN SMALL LETTER A CIRCUMFLEX	0303	NON-SPACING TILDE
00E2	LATIN SMALL LETTER A CIRCUMFLEX	0309	NON-SPACING HOOK ABOVE
00E2	LATIN SMALL LETTER A CIRCUMFLEX	0323	NON-SPACING DOT BELOW
00E2	LATIN SMALL LETTER A CIRCUMFLEX	0340	NON-SPACING GRAVE TONE MARK
00E2	LATIN SMALL LETTER A CIRCUMFLEX	0341	NON-SPACING ACUTE TONE MARK
0103	LATIN SMALL LETTER A BREVE	0303	NON-SPACING TILDE
0103	LATIN SMALL LETTER A BREVE	0309	NON-SPACING HOOK ABOVE
0103	LATIN SMALL LETTER A BREVE	0323	NON-SPACING DOT BELOW
0103	LATIN SMALL LETTER A BREVE	0340	NON-SPACING GRAVE TONE MARK
0103	LATIN SMALL LETTER A BREVE	0341	NON-SPACING ACUTE TONE MARK
0065	LATIN SMALL LETTER E	0303	NON-SPACING TILDE
0065	LATIN SMALL LETTER E	0309	NON-SPACING HOOK ABOVE
0065	LATIN SMALL LETTER E	0323	NON-SPACING DOT BELOW
0065	LATIN SMALL LETTER E	0340	NON-SPACING GRAVE TONE MARK
0065	LATIN SMALL LETTER E	0341	NON-SPACING ACUTE TONE MARK
00EA	LATIN SMALL LETTER E CIRCUMFLEX	0303	NON-SPACING TILDE
00EA	LATIN SMALL LETTER E CIRCUMFLEX	0309	NON-SPACING HOOK ABOVE
00EA	LATIN SMALL LETTER E CIRCUMFLEX	0323	NON-SPACING DOT BELOW
00EA	LATIN SMALL LETTER E CIRCUMFLEX	0340	NON-SPACING GRAVE TONE MARK
00EA	LATIN SMALL LETTER E CIRCUMFLEX	0341	NON-SPACING ACUTE TONE MARK
0069	LATIN SMALL LETTER I	0309	NON-SPACING HOOK ABOVE
0069	LATIN SMALL LETTER I	0323	NON-SPACING DOT BELOW
0069	LATIN SMALL LETTER I	0340	NON-SPACING GRAVE TONE MARK
0069	LATIN SMALL LETTER I	0341	NON-SPACING ACUTE TONE MARK
006F	LATIN SMALL LETTER O	0309	NON-SPACING HOOK ABOVE
006F	LATIN SMALL LETTER O	0323	NON-SPACING DOT BELOW
006F	LATIN SMALL LETTER O	0340	NON-SPACING GRAVE TONE MARK
006F	LATIN SMALL LETTER O	0341	NON-SPACING ACUTE TONE MARK
00F4	LATIN SMALL LETTER O CIRCUMFLEX	0303	NON-SPACING TILDE
00F4	LATIN SMALL LETTER O CIRCUMFLEX	0309	NON-SPACING HOOK ABOVE
00F4	LATIN SMALL LETTER O CIRCUMFLEX	0323	NON-SPACING DOT BELOW
00F4	LATIN SMALL LETTER O CIRCUMFLEX	0340	NON-SPACING GRAVE TONE MARK
00F4	LATIN SMALL LETTER O CIRCUMFLEX	0341	NON-SPACING ACUTE TONE MARK
01A1	LATIN SMALL LETTER O HORN	0303	NON-SPACING TILDE
01A1	LATIN SMALL LETTER O HORN	0309	NON-SPACING HOOK ABOVE
01A1	LATIN SMALL LETTER O HORN	0323	NON-SPACING DOT BELOW
01A1	LATIN SMALL LETTER O HORN	0340	NON-SPACING GRAVE TONE MARK
01A1	LATIN SMALL LETTER O HORN	0341	NON-SPACING ACUTE TONE MARK
0075	LATIN SMALL LETTER U	0309	NON-SPACING HOOK ABOVE
0075	LATIN SMALL LETTER U	0323	NON-SPACING DOT BELOW
0075	LATIN SMALL LETTER U	0340	NON-SPACING GRAVE TONE MARK
0075	LATIN SMALL LETTER U	0341	NON-SPACING ACUTE TONE MARK
01B0	LATIN SMALL LETTER U HORN	0303	NON-SPACING TILDE
01B0	LATIN SMALL LETTER U HORN	0309	NON-SPACING HOOK ABOVE
01B0	LATIN SMALL LETTER U HORN	0323	NON-SPACING DOT BELOW
01B0	LATIN SMALL LETTER U HORN	0340	NON-SPACING GRAVE TONE MARK

UNIC	*Unicode character name* *Base vowel (simple or composite)*	UNIC	*Unicode character name* *Non-spacing mark for tone*
01B0	LATIN SMALL LETTER U HORN	0341	NON-SPACING ACUTE TONE MARK
0079	LATIN SMALL LETTER Y	0303	NON-SPACING TILDE
0079	LATIN SMALL LETTER Y	0309	NON-SPACING HOOK ABOVE
0079	LATIN SMALL LETTER Y	0323	NON-SPACING DOT BELOW
0079	LATIN SMALL LETTER Y	0340	NON-SPACING GRAVE TONE MARK
0079	LATIN SMALL LETTER Y	0341	NON-SPACING ACUTE TONE MARK

5.4 Polytonic Greek to Unicode Characters

This table provides suggested spellings of existing letters of Polytonic Greek for which the Unicode standard does not contain a pre-composed form.

Unicode Polytonic Greek Decomposition Mapping

Base	Diacritics			Polytonic Greek accented letter name
03B1	0300			LOWERCASE ALPHA GRAVE
03B1	0301			LOWERCASE ALPHA ACUTE
03B1	0302			LOWERCASE ALPHA CIRCUMFLEX
03B1	0370			LOWERCASE ALPHA IOTA
03B1	0370	0300		LOWERCASE ALPHA IOTA GRAVE
03B1	0370	0301		LOWERCASE ALPHA IOTA ACUTE
03B1	0370	0302		LOWERCASE ALPHA IOTA CIRCUMFLEX
03B1	0370	0371		LOWERCASE ALPHA IOTA DASIA
03B1	0370	0371	0300	LOWERCASE ALPHA IOTA DASIA GRAVE
03B1	0370	0371	0301	LOWERCASE ALPHA IOTA DASIA ACUTE
03B1	0370	0371	0302	LOWERCASE ALPHA IOTA DASIA CIRCUMFLEX
03B1	0370	0372		LOWERCASE ALPHA IOTA PSILI
03B1	0370	0372	0300	LOWERCASE ALPHA IOTA PSILI GRAVE
03B1	0370	0372	0301	LOWERCASE ALPHA IOTA PSILI ACUTE
03B1	0370	0372	0302	LOWERCASE ALPHA IOTA PSILI CIRCUMFLEX
03B1	0371			LOWERCASE DASIA ALPHA
03B1	0371	0300		LOWERCASE DASIA ALPHA GRAVE
03B1	0371	0301		LOWERCASE DASIA ALPHA ACUTE
03B1	0371	0302		LOWERCASE DASIA ALPHA CIRCUMFLEX
03B1	0372			LOWERCASE ALPHA PSILI
03B1	0372	0300		LOWERCASE ALPHA PSILI GRAVE
03B1	0372	0301		LOWERCASE ALPHA PSILI ACUTE
03B1	0372	0302		LOWERCASE ALPHA PSILI CIRCUMFLEX
03B5	0300			LOWERCASE EPSILON GRAVE
03B5	0301			LOWERCASE EPSILON ACUTE
03B5	0371			LOWERCASE EPSILON DASIA
03B5	0371	0300		LOWERCASE EPSILON DASIA GRAVE
03B5	0371	0301		LOWERCASE EPSILON DASIA ACUTE
03B5	0372			LOWERCASE EPSILON PSILI
03B5	0372	0300		LOWERCASE EPSILON PSILI GRAVE
03B5	0372	0301		LOWERCASE EPSILON PSILI ACUTE
03B7	0300			LOWERCASE ETA GRAVE
03B7	0301			LOWERCASE ETA ACUTE
03B7	0302			LOWERCASE ETA CIRCUMFLEX
03B7	0370			LOWERCASE ETA IOTA
03B7	0370	0300		LOWERCASE ETA IOTA GRAVE
03B7	0370	0301		LOWERCASE ETA IOTA ACUTE
03B7	0370	0302		LOWERCASE ETA IOTA CIRCUMFLEX
03B7	0370	0371		LOWERCASE ETA IOTA DASIA
03B7	0370	0371	0300	LOWERCASE ETA IOTA DASIA GRAVE
03B7	0370	0371	0301	LOWERCASE ETA IOTA DASIA ACUTE
03B7	0370	0371	0302	LOWERCASE ETA IOTA DASIA CIRCUMFLEX
03B7	0370	0372		LOWERCASE ETA IOTA PSILI
03B7	0370	0372	0300	LOWERCASE ETA IOTA PSILI GRAVE
03B7	0370	0372	0301	LOWERCASE ETA IOTA PSILI ACUTE
03B7	0370	0372	0302	LOWERCASE ETA IOTA PSILI CIRCUMFLEX
03B7	0371			LOWERCASE ETA DASIA
03B7	0371	0300		LOWERCASE ETA DASIA GRAVE
03B7	0371	0301		LOWERCASE ETA DASIA ACUTE
03B7	0371	0302		LOWERCASE ETA DASIA CIRCUMFLEX
03B7	0372			LOWERCASE ETA PSILI
03B7	0372	0300		LOWERCASE ETA PSILI GRAVE
03B7	0372	0301		LOWERCASE ETA PSILI ACUTE

Base	Diacritics			Polytonic Greek accented letter name
03B7	0372	0302		LOWERCASE ETA PSILI CIRCUMFLEX
03B9	0300			LOWERCASE IOTA GRAVE
03B9	0301			LOWERCASE IOTA ACUTE
03B9	0302			LOWERCASE IOTA CIRCUMFLEX
03B9	0308	0300		LOWERCASE IOTA DIAERESIS GRAVE
03B9	0308	0301		LOWERCASE IOTA DIAERESIS ACUTE
03B9	0308	0302		LOWERCASE IOTA DIAERESIS CIRCUMFLEX
03B9	0371			LOWERCASE IOTA DASIA
03B9	0371	0300		LOWERCASE IOTA DASIA GRAVE
03B9	0371	0301		LOWERCASE IOTA DASIA ACUTE
03B9	0371	0302		LOWERCASE IOTA DASIA CIRCUMFLEX
03B9	0372			LOWERCASE IOTA PSILI
03B9	0372	0300		LOWERCASE IOTA PSILI GRAVE
03B9	0372	0301		LOWERCASE IOTA PSILI ACUTE
03B9	0372	0302		LOWERCASE IOTA PSILI CIRCUMFLEX
03BF	0300			LOWERCASE OMICRON GRAVE
03BF	0301			LOWERCASE OMICRON ACUTE
03BF	0371			LOWERCASE OMICRON DASIA
03BF	0371	0300		LOWERCASE OMICRON DASIA GRAVE
03BF	0371	0301		LOWERCASE OMICRON DASIA ACUTE
03BF	0372			LOWERCASE OMICRON PSILI
03BF	0372	0300		LOWERCASE OMICRON PSILI GRAVE
03BF	0372	0301		LOWERCASE OMICRON PSILI ACUTE
03C1	0371			LOWERCASE RHO DASIA
03C1	0372			LOWERCASE RHO PSILI
03C5	0300			LOWERCASE UPSILON GRAVE
03C5	0301			LOWERCASE UPSILON ACUTE
03C5	0302			LOWERCASE UPSILON CIRCUMFLEX
03C5	0308	0300		LOWERCASE UPSILON DIAERESIS GRAVE
03C5	0308	0301		LOWERCASE UPSILON DIAERESIS ACUTE
03C5	0308	0302		LOWERCASE UPSILON DIAERESIS CIRCUMFLEX
03C5	0371			LOWERCASE UPSILON DASIA
03C5	0371	0300		LOWERCASE UPSILON DASIA GRAVE
03C5	0371	0301		LOWERCASE UPSILON DASIA ACUTE
03C5	0371	0302		LOWERCASE UPSILON DASIA CIRCUMFLEX
03C5	0372			LOWERCASE UPSILON PSILI
03C5	0372	0300		LOWERCASE UPSILON PSILI GRAVE
03C5	0372	0301		LOWERCASE UPSILON PSILI ACUTE
03C5	0372	0302		LOWERCASE UPSILON PSILI CIRCUMFLEX
03C9	0300			LOWERCASE OMEGA GRAVE
03C9	0301			LOWERCASE OMEGA ACUTE
03C9	0302			LOWERCASE OMEGA CIRCUMFLEX
03C9	0370			LOWERCASE OMEGA IOTA
03C9	0370	0300		LOWERCASE OMEGA IOTA GRAVE
03C9	0370	0301		LOWERCASE OMEGA IOTA ACUTE
03C9	0370	0302		LOWERCASE OMEGA IOTA CIRCUMFLEX
03C9	0370	0371		LOWERCASE OMEGA IOTA DASIA
03C9	0370	0371	0300	LOWERCASE OMEGA IOTA DASIA GRAVE
03C9	0370	0371	0301	LOWERCASE OMEGA IOTA DASIA ACUTE
03C9	0370	0371	0302	LOWERCASE OMEGA IOTA DASIA CIRCUMFLEX
03C9	0370	0372		LOWERCASE OMEGA IOTA PSILI
03C9	0370	0372	0300	LOWERCASE OMEGA IOTA PSILI GRAVE
03C9	0370	0372	0301	LOWERCASE OMEGA IOTA PSILI ACUTE
03C9	0370	0372	0302	LOWERCASE OMEGA IOTA PSILI CIRCUMFLEX
03C9	0371			LOWERCASE OMEGA DASIA
03C9	0371	0300		LOWERCASE OMEGA DASIA GRAVE

Base	Diacritics		Polytonic Greek accented letter name
03C9	0371	0301	LOWERCASE OMEGA DASIA ACUTE
03C9	0371	0302	LOWERCASE OMEGA DASIA CIRCUMFLEX
03C9	0372		LOWERCASE OMEGA PSILI
03C9	0372	0300	LOWERCASE OMEGA PSILI GRAVE
03C9	0372	0301	LOWERCASE OMEGA PSILI ACUTE
03C9	0372	0302	LOWERCASE OMEGA PSILI CIRCUMFLEX

5.5 Case Tables

In a few instances, upper- and lowercase mappings may differ from language to language. Examples include Turkish ("ı" LATIN SMALL DOTLESS LETTER I maps to "I" LATIN CAPITAL LETTER I)and French ("é" LATIN SMALL LETTER E WITH ACUTE may map to "E" LATIN CAPITAL LETTER E). However, in general the vast majority of case mappings are uniform across languages.

Two separate tables are provided for uppercasing and lowercasing. It is important to note that operations of uppercasing and lowercasing do not always provide a round trip mapping. Also, since many characters are really caseless (most of the IPA block, for example), uppercasing a string does not mean that it will no longer contain any lowercase letters.

The philosophy followed in these tables is to follow the path of greatest case uniformity where there is an ambiguity (for example, the lowercase of U+01CA LATIN CAPITAL LETTER N J is U+01CC LATIN SMALL LETTER N J and vice-versa. The lowercase of U+01C5 LATIN LETTER CAPITAL D SMALL Z HACEK is U+01C6 LATIN SMALL LETTER D Z HACEK but the uppercase of U+01C5 LATIN LETTER CAPITAL D SMALL Z HACEK is U+01C4 LATIN CAPITAL LETTER D Z HACEK.)

Because there are many more lowercase forms than there are upper, it is recommended that the lowercase be used for normalization rather than the uppercase, such as when strings are case-folded for loose comparison or indexing.

Case folding applications should perform in such a way that case correspondences are not always one-to-one: the result of case folding an operation may be a different character length than in the source string (for example, the LATIN SMALL LETTER SHARP S "ß" becomes "SS" in uppercase.) Unicode values which appear in neither of these tables are caseless.

"Case-less" code points (punctuation, non-spacing characters, digits, and uncased letters such as Hebrew or Katakana) are not included in the table.

Unicode Upper-Case to Lower-Case Character Mapping

UNIC	Upper-case Unicode character name	UNIC	Lower-case Unicode character name
0041	LATIN CAPITAL LETTER A	0061	LATIN SMALL LETTER A
0042	LATIN CAPITAL LETTER B	0062	LATIN SMALL LETTER B
0043	LATIN CAPITAL LETTER C	0063	LATIN SMALL LETTER C
0044	LATIN CAPITAL LETTER D	0064	LATIN SMALL LETTER D
0045	LATIN CAPITAL LETTER E	0065	LATIN SMALL LETTER E
0046	LATIN CAPITAL LETTER F	0066	LATIN SMALL LETTER F
0047	LATIN CAPITAL LETTER G	0067	LATIN SMALL LETTER G
0048	LATIN CAPITAL LETTER H	0068	LATIN SMALL LETTER H
0049	LATIN CAPITAL LETTER I	0069	LATIN SMALL LETTER I
004A	LATIN CAPITAL LETTER J	006A	LATIN SMALL LETTER J
004B	LATIN CAPITAL LETTER K	006B	LATIN SMALL LETTER K
004C	LATIN CAPITAL LETTER L	006C	LATIN SMALL LETTER L
004D	LATIN CAPITAL LETTER M	006D	LATIN SMALL LETTER M
004E	LATIN CAPITAL LETTER N	006E	LATIN SMALL LETTER N
004F	LATIN CAPITAL LETTER O	006F	LATIN SMALL LETTER O
0050	LATIN CAPITAL LETTER P	0070	LATIN SMALL LETTER P
0051	LATIN CAPITAL LETTER Q	0071	LATIN SMALL LETTER Q
0052	LATIN CAPITAL LETTER R	0072	LATIN SMALL LETTER R
0053	LATIN CAPITAL LETTER S	0073	LATIN SMALL LETTER S
0054	LATIN CAPITAL LETTER T	0074	LATIN SMALL LETTER T
0055	LATIN CAPITAL LETTER U	0075	LATIN SMALL LETTER U
0056	LATIN CAPITAL LETTER V	0076	LATIN SMALL LETTER V
0057	LATIN CAPITAL LETTER W	0077	LATIN SMALL LETTER W
0058	LATIN CAPITAL LETTER X	0078	LATIN SMALL LETTER X
0059	LATIN CAPITAL LETTER Y	0079	LATIN SMALL LETTER Y
005A	LATIN CAPITAL LETTER Z	007A	LATIN SMALL LETTER Z
00C0	LATIN CAPITAL LETTER A GRAVE	00E0	LATIN SMALL LETTER A GRAVE
00C1	LATIN CAPITAL LETTER A ACUTE	00E1	LATIN SMALL LETTER A ACUTE
00C2	LATIN CAPITAL LETTER A CIRCUMFLEX	00E2	LATIN SMALL LETTER A CIRCUMFLEX
00C3	LATIN CAPITAL LETTER A TILDE	00E3	LATIN SMALL LETTER A TILDE
00C4	LATIN CAPITAL LETTER A DIAERESIS	00E4	LATIN SMALL LETTER A DIAERESIS
00C5	LATIN CAPITAL LETTER A RING	00E5	LATIN SMALL LETTER A RING
00C6	LATIN CAPITAL LETTER A E	00E6	LATIN SMALL LETTER A E
00C7	LATIN CAPITAL LETTER C CEDILLA	00E7	LATIN SMALL LETTER C CEDILLA
00C8	LATIN CAPITAL LETTER E GRAVE	00E8	LATIN SMALL LETTER E GRAVE
00C9	LATIN CAPITAL LETTER E ACUTE	00E9	LATIN SMALL LETTER E ACUTE
00CA	LATIN CAPITAL LETTER E CIRCUMFLEX	00EA	LATIN SMALL LETTER E CIRCUMFLEX
00CB	LATIN CAPITAL LETTER E DIAERESIS	00EB	LATIN SMALL LETTER E DIAERESIS

UNIC	Upper-case Unicode character name	UNIC	Lower-case Unicode character name
00CC	LATIN CAPITAL LETTER I GRAVE	00EC	LATIN SMALL LETTER I GRAVE
00CD	LATIN CAPITAL LETTER I ACUTE	00ED	LATIN SMALL LETTER I ACUTE
00CE	LATIN CAPITAL LETTER I CIRCUMFLEX	00EE	LATIN SMALL LETTER I CIRCUMFLEX
00CF	LATIN CAPITAL LETTER I DIAERESIS	00EF	LATIN SMALL LETTER I DIAERESIS
00D0	LATIN CAPITAL LETTER ETH	00F0	LATIN SMALL LETTER ETH
00D1	LATIN CAPITAL LETTER N TILDE	00F1	LATIN SMALL LETTER N TILDE
00D2	LATIN CAPITAL LETTER O GRAVE	00F2	LATIN SMALL LETTER O GRAVE
00D3	LATIN CAPITAL LETTER O ACUTE	00F3	LATIN SMALL LETTER O ACUTE
00D4	LATIN CAPITAL LETTER O CIRCUMFLEX	00F4	LATIN SMALL LETTER O CIRCUMFLEX
00D5	LATIN CAPITAL LETTER O TILDE	00F5	LATIN SMALL LETTER O TILDE
00D6	LATIN CAPITAL LETTER O DIAERESIS	00F6	LATIN SMALL LETTER O DIAERESIS
00D8	LATIN CAPITAL LETTER O SLASH	00F8	LATIN SMALL LETTER O SLASH
00D9	LATIN CAPITAL LETTER U GRAVE	00F9	LATIN SMALL LETTER U GRAVE
00DA	LATIN CAPITAL LETTER U ACUTE	00FA	LATIN SMALL LETTER U ACUTE
00DB	LATIN CAPITAL LETTER U CIRCUMFLEX	00FB	LATIN SMALL LETTER U CIRCUMFLEX
00DC	LATIN CAPITAL LETTER U DIAERESIS	00FC	LATIN SMALL LETTER U DIAERESIS
00DD	LATIN CAPITAL LETTER Y ACUTE	00FD	LATIN SMALL LETTER Y ACUTE
00DE	LATIN CAPITAL LETTER THORN	00FE	LATIN SMALL LETTER THORN
0100	LATIN CAPITAL LETTER A MACRON	0101	LATIN SMALL LETTER A MACRON
0102	LATIN CAPITAL LETTER A BREVE	0103	LATIN SMALL LETTER A BREVE
0104	LATIN CAPITAL LETTER A OGONEK	0105	LATIN SMALL LETTER A OGONEK
0106	LATIN CAPITAL LETTER C ACUTE	0107	LATIN SMALL LETTER C ACUTE
0108	LATIN CAPITAL LETTER C CIRCUMFLEX	0109	LATIN SMALL LETTER C CIRCUMFLEX
010A	LATIN CAPITAL LETTER C DOT	010B	LATIN SMALL LETTER C DOT
010C	LATIN CAPITAL LETTER C HACEK	010D	LATIN SMALL LETTER C HACEK
010E	LATIN CAPITAL LETTER D HACEK	010F	LATIN SMALL LETTER D HACEK
0110	LATIN CAPITAL LETTER D BAR	0111	LATIN SMALL LETTER D BAR
0112	LATIN CAPITAL LETTER E MACRON	0113	LATIN SMALL LETTER E MACRON
0114	LATIN CAPITAL LETTER E BREVE	0115	LATIN SMALL LETTER E BREVE
0116	LATIN CAPITAL LETTER E DOT	0117	LATIN SMALL LETTER E DOT
0118	LATIN CAPITAL LETTER E OGONEK	0119	LATIN SMALL LETTER E OGONEK
011A	LATIN CAPITAL LETTER E HACEK	011B	LATIN SMALL LETTER E HACEK
011C	LATIN CAPITAL LETTER G CIRCUMFLEX	011D	LATIN SMALL LETTER G CIRCUMFLEX
011E	LATIN CAPITAL LETTER G BREVE	011F	LATIN SMALL LETTER G BREVE
0120	LATIN CAPITAL LETTER G DOT	0121	LATIN SMALL LETTER G DOT
0122	LATIN CAPITAL LETTER G CEDILLA	0123	LATIN SMALL LETTER G CEDILLA
0124	LATIN CAPITAL LETTER H CIRCUMFLEX	0125	LATIN SMALL LETTER H CIRCUMFLEX
0126	LATIN CAPITAL LETTER H BAR	0127	LATIN SMALL LETTER H BAR
0128	LATIN CAPITAL LETTER I TILDE	0129	LATIN SMALL LETTER I TILDE
012A	LATIN CAPITAL LETTER I MACRON	012B	LATIN SMALL LETTER I MACRON

UNIC	Upper-case Unicode character name
012C	LATIN CAPITAL LETTER I BREVE
012E	LATIN CAPITAL LETTER I OGONEK
0130	LATIN CAPITAL LETTER I DOT
0132	LATIN CAPITAL LETTER I J
0134	LATIN CAPITAL LETTER J CIRCUMFLEX
0136	LATIN CAPITAL LETTER K CEDILLA
0139	LATIN CAPITAL LETTER L ACUTE
013B	LATIN CAPITAL LETTER L CEDILLA
013D	LATIN CAPITAL LETTER L HACEK
013F	LATIN CAPITAL LETTER L WITH MIDDLE DOT
0141	LATIN CAPITAL LETTER L SLASH
0143	LATIN CAPITAL LETTER N ACUTE
0145	LATIN CAPITAL LETTER N CEDILLA
0147	LATIN CAPITAL LETTER N HACEK
014A	LATIN CAPITAL LETTER ENG
014C	LATIN CAPITAL LETTER O MACRON
014E	LATIN CAPITAL LETTER O BREVE
0150	LATIN CAPITAL LETTER O DOUBLE ACUTE
0152	LATIN CAPITAL LETTER O E
0154	LATIN CAPITAL LETTER R ACUTE
0156	LATIN CAPITAL LETTER R CEDILLA
0158	LATIN CAPITAL LETTER R HACEK
015A	LATIN CAPITAL LETTER S ACUTE
015C	LATIN CAPITAL LETTER S CIRCUMFLEX
015E	LATIN CAPITAL LETTER S CEDILLA
0160	LATIN CAPITAL LETTER S HACEK
0162	LATIN CAPITAL LETTER T CEDILLA
0164	LATIN CAPITAL LETTER T HACEK
0166	LATIN CAPITAL LETTER T BAR
0168	LATIN CAPITAL LETTER U TILDE
016A	LATIN CAPITAL LETTER U MACRON
016C	LATIN CAPITAL LETTER U BREVE
016E	LATIN CAPITAL LETTER U RING
0170	LATIN CAPITAL LETTER U DOUBLE ACUTE
0172	LATIN CAPITAL LETTER U OGONEK
0174	LATIN CAPITAL LETTER W CIRCUMFLEX
0176	LATIN CAPITAL LETTER Y CIRCUMFLEX
0178	LATIN CAPITAL LETTER Y DIAERESIS
0179	LATIN CAPITAL LETTER Z ACUTE
017B	LATIN CAPITAL LETTER Z DOT

UNIC	Lower-case Unicode character name
012D	LATIN SMALL LETTER I BREVE
012F	LATIN SMALL LETTER I OGONEK
0069	LATIN SMALL LETTER I
0133	LATIN SMALL LETTER I J
0135	LATIN SMALL LETTER J CIRCUMFLEX
0137	LATIN SMALL LETTER K CEDILLA
013A	LATIN SMALL LETTER L ACUTE
013C	LATIN SMALL LETTER L CEDILLA
013E	LATIN SMALL LETTER L HACEK
0140	LATIN SMALL LETTER L WITH MIDDLE DOT
0142	LATIN SMALL LETTER L SLASH
0144	LATIN SMALL LETTER N ACUTE
0146	LATIN SMALL LETTER N CEDILLA
0148	LATIN SMALL LETTER N HACEK
014B	LATIN SMALL LETTER ENG
014D	LATIN SMALL LETTER O MACRON
014F	LATIN SMALL LETTER O BREVE
0151	LATIN SMALL LETTER O DOUBLE ACUTE
0153	LATIN SMALL LETTER O E
0155	LATIN SMALL LETTER R ACUTE
0157	LATIN SMALL LETTER R CEDILLA
0159	LATIN SMALL LETTER R HACEK
015B	LATIN SMALL LETTER S ACUTE
015D	LATIN SMALL LETTER S CIRCUMFLEX
015F	LATIN SMALL LETTER S CEDILLA
0161	LATIN SMALL LETTER S HACEK
0163	LATIN SMALL LETTER T CEDILLA
0165	LATIN SMALL LETTER T HACEK
0167	LATIN SMALL LETTER T BAR
0169	LATIN SMALL LETTER U TILDE
016B	LATIN SMALL LETTER U MACRON
016D	LATIN SMALL LETTER U BREVE
016F	LATIN SMALL LETTER U RING
0171	LATIN SMALL LETTER U DOUBLE ACUTE
0173	LATIN SMALL LETTER U OGONEK
0175	LATIN SMALL LETTER W CIRCUMFLEX
0177	LATIN SMALL LETTER Y CIRCUMFLEX
00FF	LATIN SMALL LETTER Y DIAERESIS
017A	LATIN SMALL LETTER Z ACUTE
017C	LATIN SMALL LETTER Z DOT

UNIC	Upper-case Unicode character name	UNIC	Lower-case Unicode character name
017D	LATIN CAPITAL LETTER Z HACEK	017E	LATIN SMALL LETTER Z HACEK
0181	LATIN CAPITAL LETTER B HOOK	0253	LATIN SMALL LETTER B HOOK
0182	LATIN CAPITAL LETTER B TOPBAR	0183	LATIN SMALL LETTER B TOPBAR
0184	LATIN CAPITAL LETTER TONE SIX	0185	LATIN SMALL LETTER TONE SIX
0186	LATIN CAPITAL LETTER OPEN O	0254	LATIN SMALL LETTER OPEN O
0187	LATIN CAPITAL LETTER C HOOK	0188	LATIN SMALL LETTER C HOOK
0189	LATIN CAPITAL LETTER AFRICAN D	0256	LATIN SMALL LETTER D RETROFLEX HOOK
018A	LATIN CAPITAL LETTER D HOOK	0257	LATIN SMALL LETTER D HOOK
018B	LATIN CAPITAL LETTER D TOPBAR	018C	LATIN SMALL LETTER D TOPBAR
018E	LATIN CAPITAL LETTER TURNED E	01DD	LATIN SMALL LETTER TURNED E
018F	LATIN CAPITAL LETTER SCHWA	0259	LATIN SMALL LETTER SCHWA
0190	LATIN CAPITAL LETTER EPSILON	025B	LATIN SMALL LETTER EPSILON
0191	LATIN CAPITAL LETTER F HOOK	0192	LATIN SMALL LETTER SCRIPT F
0193	LATIN CAPITAL LETTER G HOOK	0260	LATIN SMALL LETTER G HOOK
0194	LATIN CAPITAL LETTER GAMMA	0263	LATIN SMALL LETTER GAMMA
0196	LATIN CAPITAL LETTER IOTA	0269	LATIN SMALL LETTER IOTA
0197	LATIN CAPITAL LETTER BARRED I	0268	LATIN SMALL LETTER BARRED I
0198	LATIN CAPITAL LETTER K HOOK	0199	LATIN SMALL LETTER K HOOK
019C	LATIN CAPITAL LETTER TURNED M	026f	LATIN SMALL LETTER TURNED M
019D	LATIN CAPITAL LETTER N HOOK	0272	LATIN SMALL LETTER N HOOK
019F	LATIN CAPITAL LETTER BARRED O	0275	LATIN SMALL LETTER BARRED O
01A0	LATIN CAPITAL LETTER O HORN	01A1	LATIN SMALL LETTER O HORN
01A2	LATIN CAPITAL LETTER O I	01A3	LATIN SMALL LETTER O I
01A4	LATIN CAPITAL LETTER P HOOK	01A5	LATIN SMALL LETTER P HOOK
01A7	LATIN CAPITAL LETTER TONE TWO	01A8	LATIN SMALL LETTER TONE TWO
01A9	LATIN CAPITAL LETTER ESH	0283	LATIN SMALL LETTER ESH
01AC	LATIN CAPITAL LETTER T HOOK	01AD	LATIN SMALL LETTER T HOOK
01AE	LATIN CAPITAL LETTER T RETROFLEX HOOK	0288	LATIN SMALL LETTER T RETROFLEX HOOK
01AF	LATIN CAPITAL LETTER U HORN	01B0	LATIN SMALL LETTER U HORN
01B1	LATIN CAPITAL LETTER UPSILON	028A	LATIN SMALL LETTER UPSILON
01B2	LATIN CAPITAL LETTER SCRIPT V	028B	LATIN SMALL LETTER SCRIPT V
01B3	LATIN CAPITAL LETTER Y HOOK	01B4	LATIN SMALL LETTER Y HOOK
01B5	LATIN CAPITAL LETTER Z BAR	01B6	LATIN SMALL LETTER Z BAR
01B7	LATIN CAPITAL LETTER YOGH	0292	LATIN SMALL LETTER YOGH
01B8	LATIN CAPITAL LETTER REVERSED YOGH	01B9	LATIN SMALL LETTER REVERSED YOGH
01BC	LATIN CAPITAL LETTER TONE FIVE	01BD	LATIN SMALL LETTER TONE FIVE
01C4	LATIN CAPITAL LETTER D Z HACEK	01C6	LATIN SMALL LETTER D Z HACEK
01C5	LATIN LETTER CAPITAL D SMALL Z HACEK	01C6	LATIN SMALL LETTER D Z HACEK
01C7	LATIN CAPITAL LETTER L J	01C9	LATIN SMALL LETTER L J
01C8	LATIN LETTER CAPITAL L SMALL J	01C9	LATIN SMALL LETTER L J

UNIC	Upper-case Unicode character name	UNIC	Lower-case Unicode character name
01CA	LATIN CAPITAL LETTER N J	01CC	LATIN SMALL LETTER N J
01CB	LATIN LETTER CAPITAL N SMALL J	01CC	LATIN SMALL LETTER N J
01CD	LATIN CAPITAL LETTER A HACEK	01CE	LATIN SMALL LETTER A HACEK
01CF	LATIN CAPITAL LETTER I HACEK	01D0	LATIN SMALL LETTER I HACEK
01D1	LATIN CAPITAL LETTER O HACEK	01D2	LATIN SMALL LETTER O HACEK
01D3	LATIN CAPITAL LETTER U HACEK	01D4	LATIN SMALL LETTER U HACEK
01D5	LATIN CAPITAL LETTER U DIAERESIS MACRON	01D6	LATIN SMALL LETTER U DIAERESIS MACRON
01D7	LATIN CAPITAL LETTER U DIAERESIS ACUTE	01D8	LATIN SMALL LETTER U DIAERESIS ACUTE
01D9	LATIN CAPITAL LETTER U DIAERESIS HACEK	01DA	LATIN SMALL LETTER U DIAERESIS HACEK
01DB	LATIN CAPITAL LETTER U DIAERESIS GRAVE	01DC	LATIN SMALL LETTER U DIAERESIS GRAVE
01DE	LATIN CAPITAL LETTER A DIAERESIS MACRON	01DF	LATIN SMALL LETTER A DIAERESIS MACRON
01E0	LATIN CAPITAL LETTER A DOT MACRON	01E1	LATIN SMALL LETTER A DOT MACRON
01E2	LATIN CAPITAL LETTER A E MACRON	01E3	LATIN SMALL LETTER A E MACRON
01E4	LATIN CAPITAL LETTER G BAR	01E5	LATIN SMALL LETTER G BAR
01E6	LATIN CAPITAL LETTER G HACEK	01E7	LATIN SMALL LETTER G HACEK
01E8	LATIN CAPITAL LETTER K HACEK	01E9	LATIN SMALL LETTER K HACEK
01EA	LATIN CAPITAL LETTER O OGONEK	01EB	LATIN SMALL LETTER O OGONEK
01EC	LATIN CAPITAL LETTER O OGONEK MACRON	01ED	LATIN SMALL LETTER O OGONEK MACRON
01EE	LATIN CAPITAL LETTER YOGH HACEK	01EF	LATIN SMALL LETTER YOGH HACEK
0386	GREEK CAPITAL LETTER ALPHA TONOS	03AC	GREEK SMALL LETTER ALPHA TONOS
0388	GREEK CAPITAL LETTER EPSILON TONOS	03AD	GREEK SMALL LETTER EPSILON TONOS
0389	GREEK CAPITAL LETTER ETA TONOS	03AE	GREEK SMALL LETTER ETA TONOS
038A	GREEK CAPITAL LETTER IOTA TONOS	03AF	GREEK SMALL LETTER IOTA TONOS
038C	GREEK CAPITAL LETTER OMICRON TONOS	03CC	GREEK SMALL LETTER OMICRON TONOS
038E	GREEK CAPITAL LETTER UPSILON TONOS	03CD	GREEK SMALL LETTER UPSILON TONOS
038F	GREEK CAPITAL LETTER OMEGA TONOS	03CE	GREEK SMALL LETTER OMEGA TONOS
0391	GREEK CAPITAL LETTER ALPHA	03B1	GREEK SMALL LETTER ALPHA
0392	GREEK CAPITAL LETTER BETA	03B2	GREEK SMALL LETTER BETA
0393	GREEK CAPITAL LETTER GAMMA	03B3	GREEK SMALL LETTER GAMMA
0394	GREEK CAPITAL LETTER DELTA	03B4	GREEK SMALL LETTER DELTA
0395	GREEK CAPITAL LETTER EPSILON	03B5	GREEK SMALL LETTER EPSILON
0396	GREEK CAPITAL LETTER ZETA	03B6	GREEK SMALL LETTER ZETA
0397	GREEK CAPITAL LETTER ETA	03B7	GREEK SMALL LETTER ETA
0398	GREEK CAPITAL LETTER THETA	03B8	GREEK SMALL LETTER THETA
0399	GREEK CAPITAL LETTER IOTA	03B9	GREEK SMALL LETTER IOTA
039A	GREEK CAPITAL LETTER KAPPA	03BA	GREEK SMALL LETTER KAPPA
039B	GREEK CAPITAL LETTER LAMBDA	03BB	GREEK SMALL LETTER LAMBDA
039C	GREEK CAPITAL LETTER MU	03BC	GREEK SMALL LETTER MU
039D	GREEK CAPITAL LETTER NU	03BD	GREEK SMALL LETTER NU
039E	GREEK CAPITAL LETTER XI	03BE	GREEK SMALL LETTER XI

UNIC	Upper-case Unicode character name	UNIC	Lower-case Unicode character name
039F	GREEK CAPITAL LETTER OMICRON	03BF	GREEK SMALL LETTER OMICRON
03A0	GREEK CAPITAL LETTER PI	03C0	GREEK SMALL LETTER PI
03A1	GREEK CAPITAL LETTER RHO	03C1	GREEK SMALL LETTER RHO
03A3	GREEK CAPITAL LETTER SIGMA	03C3	GREEK SMALL LETTER SIGMA
03A4	GREEK CAPITAL LETTER TAU	03C4	GREEK SMALL LETTER TAU
03A5	GREEK CAPITAL LETTER UPSILON	03C5	GREEK SMALL LETTER UPSILON
03A6	GREEK CAPITAL LETTER PHI	03C6	GREEK SMALL LETTER PHI
03A7	GREEK CAPITAL LETTER CHI	03C7	GREEK SMALL LETTER CHI
03A8	GREEK CAPITAL LETTER PSI	03C8	GREEK SMALL LETTER PSI
03A9	GREEK CAPITAL LETTER OMEGA	03C9	GREEK SMALL LETTER OMEGA
03AA	GREEK CAPITAL LETTER IOTA DIAERESIS	03CA	GREEK SMALL LETTER IOTA DIAERESIS
03AB	GREEK CAPITAL LETTER UPSILON DIAERESIS	03CB	GREEK SMALL LETTER UPSILON DIAERESIS
03D2	GREEK CAPITAL LETTER UPSILON HOOK	03C5	GREEK SMALL LETTER UPSILON
03D3	GREEK CAPITAL LETTER UPSILON HOOK TONOS	03CD	GREEK SMALL LETTER UPSILON TONOS
03D4	GREEK CAPITAL LETTER UPSILON HOOK DIAERESIS	03CB	GREEK SMALL LETTER UPSILON DIAERESIS
03DA	GREEK CAPITAL LETTER STIGMA	03DB	GREEK SMALL LETTER STIGMA
03DC	GREEK CAPITAL LETTER DIGAMMA	03DD	GREEK SMALL LETTER DIGAMMA
03DE	GREEK CAPITAL LETTER KOPPA	03DF	GREEK SMALL LETTER KOPPA
03E0	GREEK CAPITAL LETTER SAMPI	03E1	GREEK SMALL LETTER SAMPI
03E2	GREEK CAPITAL LETTER SHEI	03E3	GREEK SMALL LETTER SHEI
03E4	GREEK CAPITAL LETTER FEI	03E5	GREEK SMALL LETTER FEI
03E6	GREEK CAPITAL LETTER KHEI	03E7	GREEK SMALL LETTER KHEI
03E8	GREEK CAPITAL LETTER HORI	03E9	GREEK SMALL LETTER HORI
03EA	GREEK CAPITAL LETTER GANGIA	03EB	GREEK SMALL LETTER GANGIA
03EC	GREEK CAPITAL LETTER SHIMA	03ED	GREEK SMALL LETTER SHIMA
03EE	GREEK CAPITAL LETTER DEI	03EF	GREEK SMALL LETTER DEI
0401	CYRILLIC CAPITAL LETTER IO	0451	CYRILLIC SMALL LETTER IO
0402	CYRILLIC CAPITAL LETTER DJE	0452	CYRILLIC SMALL LETTER DJE
0403	CYRILLIC CAPITAL LETTER GJE	0453	CYRILLIC SMALL LETTER GJE
0404	CYRILLIC CAPITAL LETTER E	0454	CYRILLIC SMALL LETTER E
0405	CYRILLIC CAPITAL LETTER DZE	0455	CYRILLIC SMALL LETTER DZE
0406	CYRILLIC CAPITAL LETTER I	0456	CYRILLIC SMALL LETTER I
0407	CYRILLIC CAPITAL LETTER YI	0457	CYRILLIC SMALL LETTER YI
0408	CYRILLIC CAPITAL LETTER JE	0458	CYRILLIC SMALL LETTER JE
0409	CYRILLIC CAPITAL LETTER LJE	0459	CYRILLIC SMALL LETTER LJE
040A	CYRILLIC CAPITAL LETTER NJE	045A	CYRILLIC SMALL LETTER NJE
040B	CYRILLIC CAPITAL LETTER TSHE	045B	CYRILLIC SMALL LETTER TSHE
040C	CYRILLIC CAPITAL LETTER KJE	045C	CYRILLIC SMALL LETTER KJE
040E	CYRILLIC CAPITAL LETTER SHORT U	045E	CYRILLIC SMALL LETTER SHORT U
040F	CYRILLIC CAPITAL LETTER DZHE	045F	CYRILLIC SMALL LETTER DZHE

UNIC	Upper-case Unicode character name	UNIC	Lower-case Unicode character name
0410	CYRILLIC CAPITAL LETTER A	0430	CYRILLIC SMALL LETTER A
0411	CYRILLIC CAPITAL LETTER BE	0431	CYRILLIC SMALL LETTER BE
0412	CYRILLIC CAPITAL LETTER VE	0432	CYRILLIC SMALL LETTER VE
0413	CYRILLIC CAPITAL LETTER GE	0433	CYRILLIC SMALL LETTER GE
0414	CYRILLIC CAPITAL LETTER DE	0434	CYRILLIC SMALL LETTER DE
0415	CYRILLIC CAPITAL LETTER IE	0435	CYRILLIC SMALL LETTER IE
0416	CYRILLIC CAPITAL LETTER ZHE	0436	CYRILLIC SMALL LETTER ZHE
0417	CYRILLIC CAPITAL LETTER ZE	0437	CYRILLIC SMALL LETTER ZE
0418	CYRILLIC CAPITAL LETTER II	0438	CYRILLIC SMALL LETTER II
0419	CYRILLIC CAPITAL LETTER SHORT II	0439	CYRILLIC SMALL LETTER SHORT II
041A	CYRILLIC CAPITAL LETTER KA	043A	CYRILLIC SMALL LETTER KA
041B	CYRILLIC CAPITAL LETTER EL	043B	CYRILLIC SMALL LETTER EL
041C	CYRILLIC CAPITAL LETTER EM	043C	CYRILLIC SMALL LETTER EM
041D	CYRILLIC CAPITAL LETTER EN	043D	CYRILLIC SMALL LETTER EN
041E	CYRILLIC CAPITAL LETTER O	043E	CYRILLIC SMALL LETTER O
041F	CYRILLIC CAPITAL LETTER PE	043F	CYRILLIC SMALL LETTER PE
0420	CYRILLIC CAPITAL LETTER ER	0440	CYRILLIC SMALL LETTER ER
0421	CYRILLIC CAPITAL LETTER ES	0441	CYRILLIC SMALL LETTER ES
0422	CYRILLIC CAPITAL LETTER TE	0442	CYRILLIC SMALL LETTER TE
0423	CYRILLIC CAPITAL LETTER U	0443	CYRILLIC SMALL LETTER U
0424	CYRILLIC CAPITAL LETTER EF	0444	CYRILLIC SMALL LETTER EF
0425	CYRILLIC CAPITAL LETTER KHA	0445	CYRILLIC SMALL LETTER KHA
0426	CYRILLIC CAPITAL LETTER TSE	0446	CYRILLIC SMALL LETTER TSE
0427	CYRILLIC CAPITAL LETTER CHE	0447	CYRILLIC SMALL LETTER CHE
0428	CYRILLIC CAPITAL LETTER SHA	0448	CYRILLIC SMALL LETTER SHA
0429	CYRILLIC CAPITAL LETTER SHCHA	0449	CYRILLIC SMALL LETTER SHCHA
042A	CYRILLIC CAPITAL LETTER HARD SIGN	044A	CYRILLIC SMALL LETTER HARD SIGN
042B	CYRILLIC CAPITAL LETTER YERI	044B	CYRILLIC SMALL LETTER YERI
042C	CYRILLIC CAPITAL LETTER SOFT SIGN	044C	CYRILLIC SMALL LETTER SOFT SIGN
042D	CYRILLIC CAPITAL LETTER REVERSED E	044D	CYRILLIC SMALL LETTER REVERSED E
042E	CYRILLIC CAPITAL LETTER IU	044E	CYRILLIC SMALL LETTER IU
042F	CYRILLIC CAPITAL LETTER IA	044F	CYRILLIC SMALL LETTER IA
0460	CYRILLIC CAPITAL LETTER OMEGA	0461	CYRILLIC SMALL LETTER OMEGA
0462	CYRILLIC CAPITAL LETTER YAT	0463	CYRILLIC SMALL LETTER YAT
0464	CYRILLIC CAPITAL LETTER IOTIFIED E	0465	CYRILLIC SMALL LETTER IOTIFIED E
0466	CYRILLIC CAPITAL LETTER LITTLE YUS	0467	CYRILLIC SMALL LETTER LITTLE YUS
0468	CYRILLIC CAPITAL LETTER IOTIFIED LITTLE YUS	0469	CYRILLIC SMALL LETTER IOTIFIED LITTLE YUS
046A	CYRILLIC CAPITAL LETTER BIG YUS	046B	CYRILLIC SMALL LETTER BIG YUS
046C	CYRILLIC CAPITAL LETTER IOTIFIED BIG YUS	046D	CYRILLIC SMALL LETTER IOTIFIED BIG YUS
046E	CYRILLIC CAPITAL LETTER KSI	046F	CYRILLIC SMALL LETTER KSI

UNIC	Upper-case Unicode character name	UNIC	Lower-case Unicode character name
0470	CYRILLIC CAPITAL LETTER PSI	0471	CYRILLIC SMALL LETTER PSI
0472	CYRILLIC CAPITAL LETTER FITA	0473	CYRILLIC SMALL LETTER FITA
0474	CYRILLIC CAPITAL LETTER IZHITSA	0475	CYRILLIC SMALL LETTER IZHITSA
0476	CYRILLIC CAPITAL LETTER IZHITSA DOUBLE GRAVE	0477	CYRILLIC SMALL LETTER IZHITSA DOUBLE GRAVE
0478	CYRILLIC CAPITAL LETTER UK DIGRAPH	0479	CYRILLIC SMALL LETTER UK DIGRAPH
047A	CYRILLIC CAPITAL LETTER ROUND OMEGA	047B	CYRILLIC SMALL LETTER ROUND OMEGA
047C	CYRILLIC CAPITAL LETTER OMEGA TITLO	047D	CYRILLIC SMALL LETTER OMEGA TITLO
047E	CYRILLIC CAPITAL LETTER OT	047F	CYRILLIC SMALL LETTER OT
0480	CYRILLIC CAPITAL LETTER KOPPA	0481	CYRILLIC SMALL LETTER KOPPA
0490	CYRILLIC CAPITAL LETTER GE WITH UPTURN	0491	CYRILLIC SMALL LETTER GE WITH UPTURN
0492	CYRILLIC CAPITAL LETTER GE BAR	0493	CYRILLIC SMALL LETTER GE BAR
0494	CYRILLIC CAPITAL LETTER GE HOOK	0495	CYRILLIC SMALL LETTER GE HOOK
0496	CYRILLIC CAPITAL LETTER ZHE WITH RIGHT DESCENDER	0497	CYRILLIC SMALL LETTER ZHE WITH RIGHT DESCENDER
0498	CYRILLIC CAPITAL LETTER ZE CEDILLA	0499	CYRILLIC SMALL LETTER ZE CEDILLA
049A	CYRILLIC CAPITAL LETTER KA WITH RIGHT DESCENDER	049B	CYRILLIC SMALL LETTER KA WITH RIGHT DESCENDER
049C	CYRILLIC CAPITAL LETTER KA VERTICAL BAR	049D	CYRILLIC SMALL LETTER KA VERTICAL BAR
049E	CYRILLIC CAPITAL LETTER KA BAR	049F	CYRILLIC SMALL LETTER KA BAR
04A0	CYRILLIC CAPITAL LETTER REVERSED GE KA	04A1	CYRILLIC SMALL LETTER REVERSED GE KA
04A2	CYRILLIC CAPITAL LETTER EN WITH RIGHT DESCENDER	04A3	CYRILLIC SMALL LETTER EN WITH RIGHT DESCENDER
04A4	CYRILLIC CAPITAL LETTER EN GE	04A5	CYRILLIC SMALL LETTER EN GE
04A6	CYRILLIC CAPITAL LETTER PE HOOK	04A7	CYRILLIC SMALL LETTER PE HOOK
04A8	CYRILLIC CAPITAL LETTER O HOOK	04A9	CYRILLIC SMALL LETTER O HOOK
04AA	CYRILLIC CAPITAL LETTER ES CEDILLA	04AB	CYRILLIC SMALL LETTER ES CEDILLA
04AC	CYRILLIC CAPITAL LETTER TE WITH RIGHT DESCENDER	04AD	CYRILLIC SMALL LETTER TE WITH RIGHT DESCENDER
04AE	CYRILLIC CAPITAL LETTER STRAIGHT U	04AF	CYRILLIC SMALL LETTER STRAIGHT U
04B0	CYRILLIC CAPITAL LETTER STRAIGHT U BAR	04B1	CYRILLIC SMALL LETTER STRAIGHT U BAR
04B2	CYRILLIC CAPITAL LETTER KHA WITH RIGHT DESCENDER	04B3	CYRILLIC SMALL LETTER KHA WITH RIGHT DESCENDER
04B4	CYRILLIC CAPITAL LETTER TE TSE	04B5	CYRILLIC SMALL LETTER TE TSE
04B6	CYRILLIC CAPITAL LETTER CHE WITH RIGHT DESCENDER	04B7	CYRILLIC SMALL LETTER CHE WITH RIGHT DESCENDER
04B8	CYRILLIC CAPITAL LETTER CHE VERTICAL BAR	04B9	CYRILLIC SMALL LETTER CHE VERTICAL BAR
04BA	CYRILLIC CAPITAL LETTER H	04BB	CYRILLIC SMALL LETTER H
04BC	CYRILLIC CAPITAL LETTER IE HOOK	04BD	CYRILLIC SMALL LETTER IE HOOK
04BE	CYRILLIC CAPITAL LETTER IE HOOK OGONEK	04BF	CYRILLIC SMALL LETTER IE HOOK OGONEK
04C1	CYRILLIC CAPITAL LETTER SHORT ZHE	04C2	CYRILLIC SMALL LETTER SHORT ZHE
04C3	CYRILLIC CAPITAL LETTER KA HOOK	04C4	CYRILLIC SMALL LETTER KA HOOK
04C5	CYRILLIC CAPITAL LETTER KA OGONEK	04C6	CYRILLIC SMALL LETTER KA OGONEK
04C7	CYRILLIC CAPITAL LETTER EN HOOK	04C8	CYRILLIC SMALL LETTER EN HOOK
04C9	CYRILLIC CAPITAL LETTER KHA OGONEK	04CA	CYRILLIC SMALL LETTER KHA OGONEK
04CB	CYRILLIC CAPITAL LETTER CHE WITH LEFT DESCENDER	04CC	CYRILLIC SMALL LETTER CHE WITH LEFT DESCENDER
0531	ARMENIAN CAPITAL LETTER AYB	0561	ARMENIAN SMALL LETTER AYB

The Unicode Standard • Version 1.0

UNIC	Upper-case Unicode character name
0532	ARMENIAN CAPITAL LETTER BEN
0533	ARMENIAN CAPITAL LETTER GIM
0534	ARMENIAN CAPITAL LETTER DA
0535	ARMENIAN CAPITAL LETTER ECH
0536	ARMENIAN CAPITAL LETTER ZA
0537	ARMENIAN CAPITAL LETTER EH
0538	ARMENIAN CAPITAL LETTER ET
0539	ARMENIAN CAPITAL LETTER TO
053A	ARMENIAN CAPITAL LETTER ZHE
053B	ARMENIAN CAPITAL LETTER INI
053C	ARMENIAN CAPITAL LETTER LIWN
053D	ARMENIAN CAPITAL LETTER XEH
053E	ARMENIAN CAPITAL LETTER CA
053F	ARMENIAN CAPITAL LETTER KEN
0540	ARMENIAN CAPITAL LETTER HO
0541	ARMENIAN CAPITAL LETTER JA
0542	ARMENIAN CAPITAL LETTER LAD
0543	ARMENIAN CAPITAL LETTER CHEH
0544	ARMENIAN CAPITAL LETTER MEN
0545	ARMENIAN CAPITAL LETTER YI
0546	ARMENIAN CAPITAL LETTER NOW
0547	ARMENIAN CAPITAL LETTER SHA
0548	ARMENIAN CAPITAL LETTER VO
0549	ARMENIAN CAPITAL LETTER CHA
054A	ARMENIAN CAPITAL LETTER PEH
054B	ARMENIAN CAPITAL LETTER JHEH
054C	ARMENIAN CAPITAL LETTER RA
054D	ARMENIAN CAPITAL LETTER SEH
054E	ARMENIAN CAPITAL LETTER VEW
054F	ARMENIAN CAPITAL LETTER TIWN
0550	ARMENIAN CAPITAL LETTER REH
0551	ARMENIAN CAPITAL LETTER CO
0552	ARMENIAN CAPITAL LETTER YIWN
0553	ARMENIAN CAPITAL LETTER PIWR
0554	ARMENIAN CAPITAL LETTER KEH
0555	ARMENIAN CAPITAL LETTER OH
0556	ARMENIAN CAPITAL LETTER FEH
10A0	GEORGIAN CAPITAL LETTER AN
10A1	GEORGIAN CAPITAL LETTER BAN
10A2	GEORGIAN CAPITAL LETTER GAN

UNIC	Lower-case Unicode character name
0562	ARMENIAN SMALL LETTER BEN
0563	ARMENIAN SMALL LETTER GIM
0564	ARMENIAN SMALL LETTER DA
0565	ARMENIAN SMALL LETTER ECH
0566	ARMENIAN SMALL LETTER ZA
0567	ARMENIAN SMALL LETTER EH
0568	ARMENIAN SMALL LETTER ET
0569	ARMENIAN SMALL LETTER TO
056A	ARMENIAN SMALL LETTER ZHE
056B	ARMENIAN SMALL LETTER INI
056C	ARMENIAN SMALL LETTER LIWN
056D	ARMENIAN SMALL LETTER XEH
056E	ARMENIAN SMALL LETTER CA
056F	ARMENIAN SMALL LETTER KEN
0570	ARMENIAN SMALL LETTER HO
0571	ARMENIAN SMALL LETTER JA
0572	ARMENIAN SMALL LETTER LAD
0573	ARMENIAN SMALL LETTER CHEH
0574	ARMENIAN SMALL LETTER MEN
0575	ARMENIAN SMALL LETTER YI
0576	ARMENIAN SMALL LETTER NOW
0577	ARMENIAN SMALL LETTER SHA
0578	ARMENIAN SMALL LETTER VO
0579	ARMENIAN SMALL LETTER CHA
057A	ARMENIAN SMALL LETTER PEH
057B	ARMENIAN SMALL LETTER JHEH
057C	ARMENIAN SMALL LETTER RA
057D	ARMENIAN SMALL LETTER SEH
057E	ARMENIAN SMALL LETTER VEW
057F	ARMENIAN SMALL LETTER TIWN
0580	ARMENIAN SMALL LETTER REH
0581	ARMENIAN SMALL LETTER CO
0582	ARMENIAN SMALL LETTER YIWN
0583	ARMENIAN SMALL LETTER PIWR
0584	ARMENIAN SMALL LETTER KEH
0585	ARMENIAN SMALL LETTER OH
0586	ARMENIAN SMALL LETTER FEH
10D0	GEORGIAN SMALL LETTER AN
10D1	GEORGIAN SMALL LETTER BAN
10D2	GEORGIAN SMALL LETTER GAN

UNIC	Upper-case Unicode character name
10A3	GEORGIAN CAPITAL LETTER DON
10A4	GEORGIAN CAPITAL LETTER EN
10A5	GEORGIAN CAPITAL LETTER VIN
10A6	GEORGIAN CAPITAL LETTER ZEN
10A7	GEORGIAN CAPITAL LETTER TAN
10A8	GEORGIAN CAPITAL LETTER IN
10A9	GEORGIAN CAPITAL LETTER KAN
10AA	GEORGIAN CAPITAL LETTER LAS
10AB	GEORGIAN CAPITAL LETTER MAN
10AC	GEORGIAN CAPITAL LETTER NAR
10AD	GEORGIAN CAPITAL LETTER ON
10AE	GEORGIAN CAPITAL LETTER PAR
10AF	GEORGIAN CAPITAL LETTER ZHAR
10B0	GEORGIAN CAPITAL LETTER RAE
10B1	GEORGIAN CAPITAL LETTER SAN
10B2	GEORGIAN CAPITAL LETTER TAR
10B3	GEORGIAN CAPITAL LETTER UN
10B4	GEORGIAN CAPITAL LETTER PHAR
10B5	GEORGIAN CAPITAL LETTER KHAR
10B6	GEORGIAN CAPITAL LETTER GHAN
10B7	GEORGIAN CAPITAL LETTER QAR
10B8	GEORGIAN CAPITAL LETTER SHIN
10B9	GEORGIAN CAPITAL LETTER CHIN
10BA	GEORGIAN CAPITAL LETTER CAN
10BB	GEORGIAN CAPITAL LETTER JIL
10BC	GEORGIAN CAPITAL LETTER CIL
10BD	GEORGIAN CAPITAL LETTER CHAR
10BE	GEORGIAN CAPITAL LETTER XAN
10BF	GEORGIAN CAPITAL LETTER JHAN
10C0	GEORGIAN CAPITAL LETTER HAE
10C1	GEORGIAN CAPITAL LETTER HE
10C2	GEORGIAN CAPITAL LETTER HIE
10C3	GEORGIAN CAPITAL LETTER WE
10C4	GEORGIAN CAPITAL LETTER HAR
10C5	GEORGIAN CAPITAL LETTER HOE
24B6	CIRCLED LATIN CAPITAL LETTER A
24B7	CIRCLED LATIN CAPITAL LETTER B
24B8	CIRCLED LATIN CAPITAL LETTER C
24B9	CIRCLED LATIN CAPITAL LETTER D
24BA	CIRCLED LATIN CAPITAL LETTER E

UNIC	Lower-case Unicode character name
10D3	GEORGIAN SMALL LETTER DON
10D4	GEORGIAN SMALL LETTER EN
10D5	GEORGIAN SMALL LETTER VIN
10D6	GEORGIAN SMALL LETTER ZEN
10D7	GEORGIAN SMALL LETTER TAN
10D8	GEORGIAN SMALL LETTER IN
10D9	GEORGIAN SMALL LETTER KAN
10DA	GEORGIAN SMALL LETTER LAS
10DB	GEORGIAN SMALL LETTER MAN
10DC	GEORGIAN SMALL LETTER NAR
10DD	GEORGIAN SMALL LETTER ON
10DE	GEORGIAN SMALL LETTER PAR
10DF	GEORGIAN SMALL LETTER ZHAR
10E0	GEORGIAN SMALL LETTER RAE
10E1	GEORGIAN SMALL LETTER SAN
10E2	GEORGIAN SMALL LETTER TAR
10E3	GEORGIAN SMALL LETTER UN
10E4	GEORGIAN SMALL LETTER PHAR
10E5	GEORGIAN SMALL LETTER KHAR
10E6	GEORGIAN SMALL LETTER GHAN
10E7	GEORGIAN SMALL LETTER QAR
10E8	GEORGIAN SMALL LETTER SHIN
10E9	GEORGIAN SMALL LETTER CHIN
10EA	GEORGIAN SMALL LETTER CAN
10EB	GEORGIAN SMALL LETTER JIL
10EC	GEORGIAN SMALL LETTER CIL
10ED	GEORGIAN SMALL LETTER CHAR
10EE	GEORGIAN SMALL LETTER XAN
10EF	GEORGIAN SMALL LETTER JHAN
10F0	GEORGIAN SMALL LETTER HAE
10F1	GEORGIAN SMALL LETTER HE
10F2	GEORGIAN SMALL LETTER HIE
10F3	GEORGIAN SMALL LETTER WE
10F4	GEORGIAN SMALL LETTER HAR
10F5	GEORGIAN SMALL LETTER HOE
24D0	CIRCLED LATIN SMALL LETTER A
24D1	CIRCLED LATIN SMALL LETTER B
24D2	CIRCLED LATIN SMALL LETTER C
24D3	CIRCLED LATIN SMALL LETTER D
24D4	CIRCLED LATIN SMALL LETTER E

UNIC	Upper-case Unicode character name
24BB	CIRCLED LATIN CAPITAL LETTER F
24BC	CIRCLED LATIN CAPITAL LETTER G
24BD	CIRCLED LATIN CAPITAL LETTER H
24BE	CIRCLED LATIN CAPITAL LETTER I
24BF	CIRCLED LATIN CAPITAL LETTER J
24C0	CIRCLED LATIN CAPITAL LETTER K
24C1	CIRCLED LATIN CAPITAL LETTER L
24C2	CIRCLED LATIN CAPITAL LETTER M
24C3	CIRCLED LATIN CAPITAL LETTER N
24C4	CIRCLED LATIN CAPITAL LETTER O
24C5	CIRCLED LATIN CAPITAL LETTER P
24C6	CIRCLED LATIN CAPITAL LETTER Q
24C7	CIRCLED LATIN CAPITAL LETTER R
24C8	CIRCLED LATIN CAPITAL LETTER S
24C9	CIRCLED LATIN CAPITAL LETTER T
24CA	CIRCLED LATIN CAPITAL LETTER U
24CB	CIRCLED LATIN CAPITAL LETTER V
24CC	CIRCLED LATIN CAPITAL LETTER W
24CD	CIRCLED LATIN CAPITAL LETTER X
24CE	CIRCLED LATIN CAPITAL LETTER Y
24CF	CIRCLED LATIN CAPITAL LETTER Z
FF21	FULLWIDTH LATIN CAPITAL LETTER A
FF22	FULLWIDTH LATIN CAPITAL LETTER B
FF23	FULLWIDTH LATIN CAPITAL LETTER C
FF24	FULLWIDTH LATIN CAPITAL LETTER D
FF25	FULLWIDTH LATIN CAPITAL LETTER E
FF26	FULLWIDTH LATIN CAPITAL LETTER F
FF27	FULLWIDTH LATIN CAPITAL LETTER G
FF28	FULLWIDTH LATIN CAPITAL LETTER H
FF29	FULLWIDTH LATIN CAPITAL LETTER I
FF2A	FULLWIDTH LATIN CAPITAL LETTER J
FF2B	FULLWIDTH LATIN CAPITAL LETTER K
FF2C	FULLWIDTH LATIN CAPITAL LETTER L
FF2D	FULLWIDTH LATIN CAPITAL LETTER M
FF2E	FULLWIDTH LATIN CAPITAL LETTER N
FF2F	FULLWIDTH LATIN CAPITAL LETTER O
FF30	FULLWIDTH LATIN CAPITAL LETTER P
FF31	FULLWIDTH LATIN CAPITAL LETTER Q
FF32	FULLWIDTH LATIN CAPITAL LETTER R
FF33	FULLWIDTH LATIN CAPITAL LETTER S

UNIC	Lower-case Unicode character name
24D5	CIRCLED LATIN SMALL LETTER F
24D6	CIRCLED LATIN SMALL LETTER G
24D7	CIRCLED LATIN SMALL LETTER H
24D8	CIRCLED LATIN SMALL LETTER I
24D9	CIRCLED LATIN SMALL LETTER J
24DA	CIRCLED LATIN SMALL LETTER K
24DB	CIRCLED LATIN SMALL LETTER L
24DC	CIRCLED LATIN SMALL LETTER M
24DD	CIRCLED LATIN SMALL LETTER N
24DE	CIRCLED LATIN SMALL LETTER O
24DF	CIRCLED LATIN SMALL LETTER P
24E0	CIRCLED LATIN SMALL LETTER Q
24E1	CIRCLED LATIN SMALL LETTER R
24E2	CIRCLED LATIN SMALL LETTER S
24E3	CIRCLED LATIN SMALL LETTER T
24E4	CIRCLED LATIN SMALL LETTER U
24E5	CIRCLED LATIN SMALL LETTER V
24E6	CIRCLED LATIN SMALL LETTER W
24E7	CIRCLED LATIN SMALL LETTER X
24E8	CIRCLED LATIN SMALL LETTER Y
24E9	CIRCLED LATIN SMALL LETTER Z
FF41	FULLWIDTH LATIN SMALL LETTER A
FF42	FULLWIDTH LATIN SMALL LETTER B
FF43	FULLWIDTH LATIN SMALL LETTER C
FF44	FULLWIDTH LATIN SMALL LETTER D
FF45	FULLWIDTH LATIN SMALL LETTER E
FF46	FULLWIDTH LATIN SMALL LETTER F
FF47	FULLWIDTH LATIN SMALL LETTER G
FF48	FULLWIDTH LATIN SMALL LETTER H
FF49	FULLWIDTH LATIN SMALL LETTER I
FF4A	FULLWIDTH LATIN SMALL LETTER J
FF4B	FULLWIDTH LATIN SMALL LETTER K
FF4C	FULLWIDTH LATIN SMALL LETTER L
FF4D	FULLWIDTH LATIN SMALL LETTER M
FF4E	FULLWIDTH LATIN SMALL LETTER N
FF4F	FULLWIDTH LATIN SMALL LETTER O
FF50	FULLWIDTH LATIN SMALL LETTER P
FF51	FULLWIDTH LATIN SMALL LETTER Q
FF52	FULLWIDTH LATIN SMALL LETTER R
FF53	FULLWIDTH LATIN SMALL LETTER S

UNIC	Upper-case Unicode character name
FF34	FULLWIDTH LATIN CAPITAL LETTER T
FF35	FULLWIDTH LATIN CAPITAL LETTER U
FF36	FULLWIDTH LATIN CAPITAL LETTER V
FF37	FULLWIDTH LATIN CAPITAL LETTER W
FF38	FULLWIDTH LATIN CAPITAL LETTER X
FF39	FULLWIDTH LATIN CAPITAL LETTER Y
FF3A	FULLWIDTH LATIN CAPITAL LETTER Z

UNIC	Lower-case Unicode character name
FF54	FULLWIDTH LATIN SMALL LETTER T
FF55	FULLWIDTH LATIN SMALL LETTER U
FF56	FULLWIDTH LATIN SMALL LETTER V
FF57	FULLWIDTH LATIN SMALL LETTER W
FF58	FULLWIDTH LATIN SMALL LETTER X
FF59	FULLWIDTH LATIN SMALL LETTER Y
FF5A	FULLWIDTH LATIN SMALL LETTER Z

Unicode Lower-Case to Upper-Case Character Mapping

UNIC	Lower-case Unicode character name	UNIC	Upper-case Unicode character name
0061	LATIN SMALL LETTER A	0041	LATIN CAPITAL LETTER A
0062	LATIN SMALL LETTER B	0042	LATIN CAPITAL LETTER B
0063	LATIN SMALL LETTER C	0043	LATIN CAPITAL LETTER C
0064	LATIN SMALL LETTER D	0044	LATIN CAPITAL LETTER D
0065	LATIN SMALL LETTER E	0045	LATIN CAPITAL LETTER E
0066	LATIN SMALL LETTER F	0046	LATIN CAPITAL LETTER F
0067	LATIN SMALL LETTER G	0047	LATIN CAPITAL LETTER G
0068	LATIN SMALL LETTER H	0048	LATIN CAPITAL LETTER H
0069	LATIN SMALL LETTER I	0049	LATIN CAPITAL LETTER I
0069	LATIN SMALL LETTER I	0130	LATIN CAPITAL LETTER I DOT
006A	LATIN SMALL LETTER J	004A	LATIN CAPITAL LETTER J
006B	LATIN SMALL LETTER K	004B	LATIN CAPITAL LETTER K
006C	LATIN SMALL LETTER L	004C	LATIN CAPITAL LETTER L
006D	LATIN SMALL LETTER M	004D	LATIN CAPITAL LETTER M
006E	LATIN SMALL LETTER N	004E	LATIN CAPITAL LETTER N
006F	LATIN SMALL LETTER O	004F	LATIN CAPITAL LETTER O
0070	LATIN SMALL LETTER P	0050	LATIN CAPITAL LETTER P
0071	LATIN SMALL LETTER Q	0051	LATIN CAPITAL LETTER Q
0072	LATIN SMALL LETTER R	0052	LATIN CAPITAL LETTER R
0073	LATIN SMALL LETTER S	0053	LATIN CAPITAL LETTER S
0074	LATIN SMALL LETTER T	0054	LATIN CAPITAL LETTER T
0075	LATIN SMALL LETTER U	0055	LATIN CAPITAL LETTER U
0076	LATIN SMALL LETTER V	0056	LATIN CAPITAL LETTER V
0077	LATIN SMALL LETTER W	0057	LATIN CAPITAL LETTER W
0078	LATIN SMALL LETTER X	0058	LATIN CAPITAL LETTER X
0079	LATIN SMALL LETTER Y	0059	LATIN CAPITAL LETTER Y
007A	LATIN SMALL LETTER Z	005A	LATIN CAPITAL LETTER Z
00DF	LATIN SMALL LETTER SHARP S	0053 + 0053	LATIN CAPITAL LETTER S + LATIN CAPITAL LETTER S
00E0	LATIN SMALL LETTER A GRAVE	00C0	LATIN CAPITAL LETTER A GRAVE
00E1	LATIN SMALL LETTER A ACUTE	00C1	LATIN CAPITAL LETTER A ACUTE
00E2	LATIN SMALL LETTER A CIRCUMFLEX	00C2	LATIN CAPITAL LETTER A CIRCUMFLEX
00E3	LATIN SMALL LETTER A TILDE	00C3	LATIN CAPITAL LETTER A TILDE
00E4	LATIN SMALL LETTER A DIAERESIS	00C4	LATIN CAPITAL LETTER A DIAERESIS
00E5	LATIN SMALL LETTER A RING	00C5	LATIN CAPITAL LETTER A RING
00E6	LATIN SMALL LETTER A E	00C6	LATIN CAPITAL LETTER A E
00E7	LATIN SMALL LETTER C CEDILLA	00C7	LATIN CAPITAL LETTER C CEDILLA
00E8	LATIN SMALL LETTER E GRAVE	00C8	LATIN CAPITAL LETTER E GRAVE
00E9	LATIN SMALL LETTER E ACUTE	00C9	LATIN CAPITAL LETTER E ACUTE

UNIC	Upper-case Unicode character name
00CA	LATIN CAPITAL LETTER E CIRCUMFLEX
00CB	LATIN CAPITAL LETTER E DIAERESIS
00CC	LATIN CAPITAL LETTER I GRAVE
00CD	LATIN CAPITAL LETTER I ACUTE
00CE	LATIN CAPITAL LETTER I CIRCUMFLEX
00CF	LATIN CAPITAL LETTER I DIAERESIS
00D0	LATIN CAPITAL LETTER ETH
00D1	LATIN CAPITAL LETTER N TILDE
00D2	LATIN CAPITAL LETTER O GRAVE
00D3	LATIN CAPITAL LETTER O ACUTE
00D4	LATIN CAPITAL LETTER O CIRCUMFLEX
00D5	LATIN CAPITAL LETTER O TILDE
00D6	LATIN CAPITAL LETTER O DIAERESIS
00D8	LATIN CAPITAL LETTER O SLASH
00D9	LATIN CAPITAL LETTER U GRAVE
00DA	LATIN CAPITAL LETTER U ACUTE
00DB	LATIN CAPITAL LETTER U CIRCUMFLEX
00DC	LATIN CAPITAL LETTER U DIAERESIS
00DD	LATIN CAPITAL LETTER Y ACUTE
00DE	LATIN CAPITAL LETTER THORN
0178	LATIN CAPITAL LETTER Y DIAERESIS
0100	LATIN CAPITAL LETTER A MACRON
0102	LATIN CAPITAL LETTER A BREVE
0104	LATIN CAPITAL LETTER A OGONEK
0106	LATIN CAPITAL LETTER C ACUTE
0108	LATIN CAPITAL LETTER C CIRCUMFLEX
010A	LATIN CAPITAL LETTER C DOT
010C	LATIN CAPITAL LETTER C HACEK
010E	LATIN CAPITAL LETTER D HACEK
0110	LATIN CAPITAL LETTER D BAR
0112	LATIN CAPITAL LETTER E MACRON
0114	LATIN CAPITAL LETTER E BREVE
0116	LATIN CAPITAL LETTER E DOT
0118	LATIN CAPITAL LETTER E OGONEK
011A	LATIN CAPITAL LETTER E HACEK
011C	LATIN CAPITAL LETTER G CIRCUMFLEX
011E	LATIN CAPITAL LETTER G BREVE
0120	LATIN CAPITAL LETTER G DOT
0122	LATIN CAPITAL LETTER G CEDILLA
0124	LATIN CAPITAL LETTER H CIRCUMFLEX

UNIC	Lower-case Unicode character name
00EA	LATIN SMALL LETTER E CIRCUMFLEX
00EB	LATIN SMALL LETTER E DIAERESIS
00EC	LATIN SMALL LETTER I GRAVE
00ED	LATIN SMALL LETTER I ACUTE
00EE	LATIN SMALL LETTER I CIRCUMFLEX
00EF	LATIN SMALL LETTER I DIAERESIS
00F0	LATIN SMALL LETTER ETH
00F1	LATIN SMALL LETTER N TILDE
00F2	LATIN SMALL LETTER O GRAVE
00F3	LATIN SMALL LETTER O ACUTE
00F4	LATIN SMALL LETTER O CIRCUMFLEX
00F5	LATIN SMALL LETTER O TILDE
00F6	LATIN SMALL LETTER O DIAERESIS
00F8	LATIN SMALL LETTER O SLASH
00F9	LATIN SMALL LETTER U GRAVE
00FA	LATIN SMALL LETTER U ACUTE
00FB	LATIN SMALL LETTER U CIRCUMFLEX
00FC	LATIN SMALL LETTER U DIAERESIS
00FD	LATIN SMALL LETTER Y ACUTE
00FE	LATIN SMALL LETTER THORN
00FF	LATIN SMALL LETTER Y DIAERESIS
0101	LATIN SMALL LETTER A MACRON
0103	LATIN SMALL LETTER A BREVE
0105	LATIN SMALL LETTER A OGONEK
0107	LATIN SMALL LETTER C ACUTE
0109	LATIN SMALL LETTER C CIRCUMFLEX
010B	LATIN SMALL LETTER C DOT
010D	LATIN SMALL LETTER C HACEK
010F	LATIN SMALL LETTER D HACEK
0111	LATIN SMALL LETTER D BAR
0113	LATIN SMALL LETTER E MACRON
0115	LATIN SMALL LETTER E BREVE
0117	LATIN SMALL LETTER E DOT
0119	LATIN SMALL LETTER E OGONEK
011B	LATIN SMALL LETTER E HACEK
011D	LATIN SMALL LETTER G CIRCUMFLEX
011F	LATIN SMALL LETTER G BREVE
0121	LATIN SMALL LETTER G DOT
0123	LATIN SMALL LETTER G CEDILLA
0125	LATIN SMALL LETTER H CIRCUMFLEX

UNIC	Upper-case Unicode character name
0126	LATIN CAPITAL LETTER H BAR
0128	LATIN CAPITAL LETTER I TILDE
012A	LATIN CAPITAL LETTER I MACRON
012C	LATIN CAPITAL LETTER I BREVE
012E	LATIN CAPITAL LETTER I OGONEK
0049	LATIN CAPITAL LETTER I
0132	LATIN CAPITAL LETTER I J
0134	LATIN CAPITAL LETTER J CIRCUMFLEX
0136	LATIN CAPITAL LETTER K CEDILLA
0139	LATIN CAPITAL LETTER L ACUTE
013B	LATIN CAPITAL LETTER L CEDILLA
013D	LATIN CAPITAL LETTER L HACEK
013F	LATIN CAPITAL LETTER L WITH MIDDLE DOT
0141	LATIN CAPITAL LETTER L SLASH
0143	LATIN CAPITAL LETTER N ACUTE
0145	LATIN CAPITAL LETTER N CEDILLA
0147	LATIN CAPITAL LETTER N HACEK
014A	LATIN CAPITAL LETTER ENG
014C	LATIN CAPITAL LETTER O MACRON
014E	LATIN CAPITAL LETTER O BREVE
0150	LATIN CAPITAL LETTER O DOUBLE ACUTE
0152	LATIN CAPITAL LETTER O E
0154	LATIN CAPITAL LETTER R ACUTE
0156	LATIN CAPITAL LETTER R CEDILLA
0158	LATIN CAPITAL LETTER R HACEK
015A	LATIN CAPITAL LETTER S ACUTE
015C	LATIN CAPITAL LETTER S CIRCUMFLEX
015E	LATIN CAPITAL LETTER S CEDILLA
0160	LATIN CAPITAL LETTER S HACEK
0162	LATIN CAPITAL LETTER T CEDILLA
0164	LATIN CAPITAL LETTER T HACEK
0166	LATIN CAPITAL LETTER T BAR
0168	LATIN CAPITAL LETTER U TILDE
016A	LATIN CAPITAL LETTER U MACRON
016C	LATIN CAPITAL LETTER U BREVE
016E	LATIN CAPITAL LETTER U RING
0170	LATIN CAPITAL LETTER U DOUBLE ACUTE
0172	LATIN CAPITAL LETTER U OGONEK
0174	LATIN CAPITAL LETTER W CIRCUMFLEX
0176	LATIN CAPITAL LETTER Y CIRCUMFLEX

UNIC	Lower-case Unicode character name
0127	LATIN SMALL LETTER H BAR
0129	LATIN SMALL LETTER I TILDE
012B	LATIN SMALL LETTER I MACRON
012D	LATIN SMALL LETTER I BREVE
012F	LATIN SMALL LETTER I OGONEK
0131	LATIN SMALL LETTER DOTLESS I
0133	LATIN SMALL LETTER I J
0135	LATIN SMALL LETTER J CIRCUMFLEX
0137	LATIN SMALL LETTER K CEDILLA
013A	LATIN SMALL LETTER L ACUTE
013C	LATIN SMALL LETTER L CEDILLA
013E	LATIN SMALL LETTER L HACEK
0140	LATIN SMALL LETTER L WITH MIDDLE DOT
0142	LATIN SMALL LETTER L SLASH
0144	LATIN SMALL LETTER N ACUTE
0146	LATIN SMALL LETTER N CEDILLA
0148	LATIN SMALL LETTER N HACEK
014B	LATIN SMALL LETTER ENG
014D	LATIN SMALL LETTER O MACRON
014F	LATIN SMALL LETTER O BREVE
0151	LATIN SMALL LETTER O DOUBLE ACUTE
0153	LATIN SMALL LETTER O E
0155	LATIN SMALL LETTER R ACUTE
0157	LATIN SMALL LETTER R CEDILLA
0159	LATIN SMALL LETTER R HACEK
015B	LATIN SMALL LETTER S ACUTE
015D	LATIN SMALL LETTER S CIRCUMFLEX
015F	LATIN SMALL LETTER S CEDILLA
0161	LATIN SMALL LETTER S HACEK
0163	LATIN SMALL LETTER T CEDILLA
0165	LATIN SMALL LETTER T HACEK
0167	LATIN SMALL LETTER T BAR
0169	LATIN SMALL LETTER U TILDE
016B	LATIN SMALL LETTER U MACRON
016D	LATIN SMALL LETTER U BREVE
016F	LATIN SMALL LETTER U RING
0171	LATIN SMALL LETTER U DOUBLE ACUTE
0173	LATIN SMALL LETTER U OGONEK
0175	LATIN SMALL LETTER W CIRCUMFLEX
0177	LATIN SMALL LETTER Y CIRCUMFLEX

UNIC	Lower-case Unicode character name	UNIC	Upper-case Unicode character name
017A	LATIN SMALL LETTER Z ACUTE	0179	LATIN CAPITAL LETTER Z ACUTE
017C	LATIN SMALL LETTER Z DOT	017B	LATIN CAPITAL LETTER Z DOT
017E	LATIN SMALL LETTER Z HACEK	017D	LATIN CAPITAL LETTER Z HACEK
0183	LATIN SMALL LETTER B TOPBAR	0182	LATIN CAPITAL LETTER B TOPBAR
0185	LATIN SMALL LETTER TONE SIX	0184	LATIN CAPITAL LETTER TONE SIX
0188	LATIN SMALL LETTER C HOOK	0187	LATIN CAPITAL LETTER C HOOK
018C	LATIN SMALL LETTER D TOPBAR	018B	LATIN CAPITAL LETTER D TOPBAR
0192	LATIN SMALL LETTER SCRIPT F	0191	LATIN CAPITAL LETTER F HOOK
0199	LATIN SMALL LETTER K HOOK	0198	LATIN CAPITAL LETTER K HOOK
01A1	LATIN SMALL LETTER O HORN	01A0	LATIN CAPITAL LETTER O HORN
01A3	LATIN SMALL LETTER O I	01A2	LATIN CAPITAL LETTER O I
01A5	LATIN SMALL LETTER P HOOK	01A4	LATIN CAPITAL LETTER P HOOK
01A8	LATIN SMALL LETTER TONE TWO	01A7	LATIN CAPITAL LETTER TONE TWO
01AD	LATIN SMALL LETTER T HOOK	01AC	LATIN CAPITAL LETTER T HOOK
01B0	LATIN SMALL LETTER U HORN	01AF	LATIN CAPITAL LETTER U HORN
01B4	LATIN SMALL LETTER Y HOOK	01B3	LATIN CAPITAL LETTER Y HOOK
01B6	LATIN SMALL LETTER Z BAR	01B5	LATIN CAPITAL LETTER Z BAR
01B9	LATIN SMALL LETTER REVERSED YOGH	01B8	LATIN CAPITAL LETTER REVERSED YOGH
01BD	LATIN SMALL LETTER TONE FIVE	01BC	LATIN CAPITAL LETTER TONE FIVE
01C5	LATIN LETTER CAPITAL D SMALL Z HACEK	01C4	LATIN CAPITAL LETTER D Z HACEK
01C6	LATIN SMALL LETTER D Z HACEK	01C4	LATIN CAPITAL LETTER D Z HACEK
01C8	LATIN LETTER CAPITAL L SMALL J	01C7	LATIN CAPITAL LETTER L J
01C9	LATIN SMALL LETTER L J	01C7	LATIN CAPITAL LETTER L J
01CB	LATIN LETTER CAPITAL N SMALL J	01CA	LATIN CAPITAL LETTER N J
01CC	LATIN SMALL LETTER N J	01CA	LATIN CAPITAL LETTER N J
01CE	LATIN SMALL LETTER A HACEK	01CD	LATIN CAPITAL LETTER A HACEK
01D0	LATIN SMALL LETTER I HACEK	01CF	LATIN CAPITAL LETTER I HACEK
01D2	LATIN SMALL LETTER O HACEK	01D1	LATIN CAPITAL LETTER O HACEK
01D4	LATIN SMALL LETTER U HACEK	01D3	LATIN CAPITAL LETTER U HACEK
01D6	LATIN SMALL LETTER U DIAERESIS MACRON	01D5	LATIN CAPITAL LETTER U DIAERESIS MACRON
01D8	LATIN SMALL LETTER U DIAERESIS ACUTE	01D7	LATIN CAPITAL LETTER U DIAERESIS ACUTE
01DA	LATIN SMALL LETTER U DIAERESIS HACEK	01D9	LATIN CAPITAL LETTER U DIAERESIS HACEK
01DC	LATIN SMALL LETTER U DIAERESIS GRAVE	01DB	LATIN CAPITAL LETTER U DIAERESIS GRAVE
01DD	LATIN SMALL LETTER TURNED E	018E	LATIN CAPITAL LETTER TURNED E
01DF	LATIN SMALL LETTER A DIAERESIS MACRON	01DE	LATIN CAPITAL LETTER A DIAERESIS MACRON
01E1	LATIN SMALL LETTER A DOT MACRON	01E0	LATIN CAPITAL LETTER A DOT MACRON
01E3	LATIN SMALL LETTER A E MACRON	01E2	LATIN CAPITAL LETTER A E MACRON
01E5	LATIN SMALL LETTER G BAR	01E4	LATIN CAPITAL LETTER G BAR
01E7	LATIN SMALL LETTER G HACEK	01E6	LATIN CAPITAL LETTER G HACEK
01E9	LATIN SMALL LETTER K HACEK	01E8	LATIN CAPITAL LETTER K HACEK

UNIC	Upper-case Unicode character name
01EA	LATIN CAPITAL LETTER O OGONEK
01EC	LATIN CAPITAL LETTER O OGONEK MACRON
01EE	LATIN CAPITAL LETTER YOGH HACEK
0181	LATIN CAPITAL LETTER B HOOK
0186	LATIN CAPITAL LETTER OPEN O
0189	LATIN CAPITAL LETTER AFRICAN D
018A	LATIN CAPITAL LETTER D HOOK
018F	LATIN CAPITAL LETTER SCHWA
0190	LATIN CAPITAL LETTER EPSILON
0193	LATIN CAPITAL LETTER G HOOK
0194	LATIN CAPITAL LETTER GAMMA
0197	LATIN CAPITAL LETTER BARRED I
0196	LATIN CAPITAL LETTER IOTA
019C	LATIN CAPITAL LETTER TURNED M
019D	LATIN CAPITAL LETTER N HOOK
019F	LATIN CAPITAL LETTER BARRED O
01A9	LATIN CAPITAL LETTER ESH
01AE	LATIN CAPITAL LETTER T RETROFLEX HOOK
01B1	LATIN CAPITAL LETTER UPSILON
01B2	LATIN CAPITAL LETTER SCRIPT V
01B7	LATIN CAPITAL LETTER YOGH
0386	GREEK CAPITAL LETTER ALPHA TONOS
0388	GREEK CAPITAL LETTER EPSILON TONOS
0389	GREEK CAPITAL LETTER ETA TONOS
038A	GREEK CAPITAL LETTER IOTA TONOS
0391	GREEK CAPITAL LETTER ALPHA
0392	GREEK CAPITAL LETTER BETA
0393	GREEK CAPITAL LETTER GAMMA
0394	GREEK CAPITAL LETTER DELTA
0395	GREEK CAPITAL LETTER EPSILON
0396	GREEK CAPITAL LETTER ZETA
0397	GREEK CAPITAL LETTER ETA
0398	GREEK CAPITAL LETTER THETA
0399	GREEK CAPITAL LETTER IOTA
039A	GREEK CAPITAL LETTER KAPPA
039B	GREEK CAPITAL LETTER LAMBDA
039C	GREEK CAPITAL LETTER MU
039D	GREEK CAPITAL LETTER NU
039E	GREEK CAPITAL LETTER XI
039F	GREEK CAPITAL LETTER OMICRON

UNIC	Lower-case Unicode character name
01EB	LATIN SMALL LETTER O OGONEK
01ED	LATIN SMALL LETTER O OGONEK MACRON
01EF	LATIN SMALL LETTER YOGH HACEK
0253	LATIN SMALL LETTER B HOOK
0254	LATIN SMALL LETTER OPEN O
0256	LATIN SMALL LETTER D RETROFLEX HOOK
0257	LATIN SMALL LETTER D HOOK
0259	LATIN SMALL LETTER SCHWA
025B	LATIN SMALL LETTER EPSILON
0260	LATIN SMALL LETTER G HOOK
0263	LATIN SMALL LETTER GAMMA
0268	LATIN SMALL LETTER BARRED I
0269	LATIN SMALL LETTER IOTA
026F	LATIN SMALL LETTER TURNED M
0272	LATIN SMALL LETTER N HOOK
0275	LATIN SMALL LETTER BARRED O
0283	LATIN SMALL LETTER ESH
0288	LATIN SMALL LETTER T RETROFLEX HOOK
028A	LATIN SMALL LETTER UPSILON
028B	LATIN SMALL LETTER SCRIPT V
0292	LATIN SMALL LETTER YOGH
03AC	GREEK SMALL LETTER ALPHA TONOS
03AD	GREEK SMALL LETTER EPSILON TONOS
03AE	GREEK SMALL LETTER ETA TONOS
03AF	GREEK SMALL LETTER IOTA TONOS
03B1	GREEK SMALL LETTER ALPHA
03B2	GREEK SMALL LETTER BETA
03B3	GREEK SMALL LETTER GAMMA
03B4	GREEK SMALL LETTER DELTA
03B5	GREEK SMALL LETTER EPSILON
03B6	GREEK SMALL LETTER ZETA
03B7	GREEK SMALL LETTER ETA
03B8	GREEK SMALL LETTER THETA
03B9	GREEK SMALL LETTER IOTA
03BA	GREEK SMALL LETTER KAPPA
03BB	GREEK SMALL LETTER LAMBDA
03BC	GREEK SMALL LETTER MU
03BD	GREEK SMALL LETTER NU
03BE	GREEK SMALL LETTER XI
03BF	GREEK SMALL LETTER OMICRON

UNIC	Lower-case Unicode character name
03C0	GREEK SMALL LETTER PI
03C1	GREEK SMALL LETTER RHO
03C2	GREEK SMALL LETTER FINAL SIGMA
03C3	GREEK SMALL LETTER SIGMA
03C4	GREEK SMALL LETTER TAU
03C5	GREEK SMALL LETTER UPSILON
03C5	GREEK SMALL LETTER UPSILON
03C6	GREEK SMALL LETTER PHI
03C7	GREEK SMALL LETTER CHI
03C8	GREEK SMALL LETTER PSI
03C9	GREEK SMALL LETTER OMEGA
03CA	GREEK SMALL LETTER IOTA DIAERESIS
03CB	GREEK SMALL LETTER UPSILON DIAERESIS
03CC	GREEK SMALL LETTER OMICRON TONOS
03CD	GREEK SMALL LETTER UPSILON TONOS
03CE	GREEK SMALL LETTER OMEGA TONOS
03D0	GREEK SMALL LETTER CURLED BETA
03D1	GREEK SMALL LETTER SCRIPT THETA
03D5	GREEK SMALL LETTER SCRIPT PHI
03D6	GREEK SMALL LETTER OMEGA PI
03DB	GREEK SMALL LETTER STIGMA
03DD	GREEK SMALL LETTER DIGAMMA
03DF	GREEK SMALL LETTER KOPPA
03E1	GREEK SMALL LETTER SAMPI
03E3	GREEK SMALL LETTER SHEI
03E5	GREEK SMALL LETTER FEI
03E7	GREEK SMALL LETTER KHEI
03E9	GREEK SMALL LETTER HORI
03EB	GREEK SMALL LETTER GANGIA
03ED	GREEK SMALL LETTER SHIMA
03EF	GREEK SMALL LETTER DEI
03F0	GREEK SMALL LETTER SCRIPT KAPPA
03F1	GREEK SMALL LETTER TAILED RHO
03C2	GREEK SMALL LETTER LUNATE SIGMA
0430	CYRILLIC SMALL LETTER A
0431	CYRILLIC SMALL LETTER BE
0432	CYRILLIC SMALL LETTER VE
0433	CYRILLIC SMALL LETTER GE
0434	CYRILLIC SMALL LETTER DE
0435	CYRILLIC SMALL LETTER IE

UNIC	Upper-case Unicode character name
03A0	GREEK CAPITAL LETTER PI
03A1	GREEK CAPITAL LETTER RHO
03A3	GREEK CAPITAL LETTER SIGMA
03A3	GREEK CAPITAL LETTER SIGMA
03A4	GREEK CAPITAL LETTER TAU
03D2	GREEK CAPITAL LETTER UPSILON HOOK
03A5	GREEK CAPITAL LETTER UPSILON
03A6	GREEK CAPITAL LETTER PHI
03A7	GREEK CAPITAL LETTER CHI
03A8	GREEK CAPITAL LETTER PSI
03A9	GREEK CAPITAL LETTER OMEGA
03AA	GREEK CAPITAL LETTER IOTA DIAERESIS
03AB	GREEK CAPITAL LETTER UPSILON DIAERESIS
038C	GREEK CAPITAL LETTER OMICRON TONOS
038E	GREEK CAPITAL LETTER UPSILON TONOS
038F	GREEK CAPITAL LETTER OMEGA TONOS
0392	GREEK CAPITAL LETTER BETA
0398	GREEK CAPITAL LETTER THETA
03A6	GREEK CAPITAL LETTER PHI
03A0	GREEK CAPITAL LETTER PI
03DA	GREEK CAPITAL LETTER STIGMA
03DC	GREEK CAPITAL LETTER DIGAMMA
03DE	GREEK CAPITAL LETTER KOPPA
03E0	GREEK CAPITAL LETTER SAMPI
03E2	GREEK CAPITAL LETTER SHEI
03E4	GREEK CAPITAL LETTER FEI
03E6	GREEK CAPITAL LETTER KHEI
03E8	GREEK CAPITAL LETTER HORI
03EA	GREEK CAPITAL LETTER GANGIA
03EC	GREEK CAPITAL LETTER SHIMA
03EE	GREEK CAPITAL LETTER DEI
039A	GREEK CAPITAL LETTER KAPPA
03A1	GREEK CAPITAL LETTER RHO
03A3	GREEK CAPITAL LETTER SIGMA
0410	CYRILLIC CAPITAL LETTER A
0411	CYRILLIC CAPITAL LETTER BE
0412	CYRILLIC CAPITAL LETTER VE
0413	CYRILLIC CAPITAL LETTER GE
0414	CYRILLIC CAPITAL LETTER DE
0415	CYRILLIC CAPITAL LETTER IE

UNIC	Lower-case Unicode character name
0436	CYRILLIC SMALL LETTER ZHE
0437	CYRILLIC SMALL LETTER ZE
0438	CYRILLIC SMALL LETTER II
0439	CYRILLIC SMALL LETTER SHORT II
043A	CYRILLIC SMALL LETTER KA
043B	CYRILLIC SMALL LETTER EL
043C	CYRILLIC SMALL LETTER EM
043D	CYRILLIC SMALL LETTER EN
043E	CYRILLIC SMALL LETTER O
043F	CYRILLIC SMALL LETTER PE
0440	CYRILLIC SMALL LETTER ER
0441	CYRILLIC SMALL LETTER ES
0442	CYRILLIC SMALL LETTER TE
0443	CYRILLIC SMALL LETTER U
0444	CYRILLIC SMALL LETTER EF
0445	CYRILLIC SMALL LETTER KHA
0446	CYRILLIC SMALL LETTER TSE
0447	CYRILLIC SMALL LETTER CHE
0448	CYRILLIC SMALL LETTER SHA
0449	CYRILLIC SMALL LETTER SHCHA
044A	CYRILLIC SMALL LETTER HARD SIGN
044B	CYRILLIC SMALL LETTER YERI
044C	CYRILLIC SMALL LETTER SOFT SIGN
044D	CYRILLIC SMALL LETTER REVERSED E
044E	CYRILLIC SMALL LETTER IU
044F	CYRILLIC SMALL LETTER IA
0451	CYRILLIC SMALL LETTER IO
0452	CYRILLIC SMALL LETTER DJE
0453	CYRILLIC SMALL LETTER GJE
0454	CYRILLIC SMALL LETTER E
0455	CYRILLIC SMALL LETTER DZE
0456	CYRILLIC SMALL LETTER I
0457	CYRILLIC SMALL LETTER YI
0458	CYRILLIC SMALL LETTER JE
0459	CYRILLIC SMALL LETTER LJE
045A	CYRILLIC SMALL LETTER NJE
045B	CYRILLIC SMALL LETTER TSHE
045C	CYRILLIC SMALL LETTER KJE
045E	CYRILLIC SMALL LETTER SHORT U
045F	CYRILLIC SMALL LETTER DZHE

UNIC	Upper-case Unicode character name
0416	CYRILLIC CAPITAL LETTER ZHE
0417	CYRILLIC CAPITAL LETTER ZE
0418	CYRILLIC CAPITAL LETTER II
0419	CYRILLIC CAPITAL LETTER SHORT II
041A	CYRILLIC CAPITAL LETTER KA
041B	CYRILLIC CAPITAL LETTER EL
041C	CYRILLIC CAPITAL LETTER EM
041D	CYRILLIC CAPITAL LETTER EN
041E	CYRILLIC CAPITAL LETTER O
041F	CYRILLIC CAPITAL LETTER PE
0420	CYRILLIC CAPITAL LETTER ER
0421	CYRILLIC CAPITAL LETTER ES
0422	CYRILLIC CAPITAL LETTER TE
0423	CYRILLIC CAPITAL LETTER U
0424	CYRILLIC CAPITAL LETTER EF
0425	CYRILLIC CAPITAL LETTER KHA
0426	CYRILLIC CAPITAL LETTER TSE
0427	CYRILLIC CAPITAL LETTER CHE
0428	CYRILLIC CAPITAL LETTER SHA
0429	CYRILLIC CAPITAL LETTER SHCHA
042A	CYRILLIC CAPITAL LETTER HARD SIGN
042B	CYRILLIC CAPITAL LETTER YERI
042C	CYRILLIC CAPITAL LETTER SOFT SIGN
042D	CYRILLIC CAPITAL LETTER REVERSED E
042E	CYRILLIC CAPITAL LETTER IU
042F	CYRILLIC CAPITAL LETTER IA
0401	CYRILLIC CAPITAL LETTER IO
0402	CYRILLIC CAPITAL LETTER DJE
0403	CYRILLIC CAPITAL LETTER GJE
0404	CYRILLIC CAPITAL LETTER E
0405	CYRILLIC CAPITAL LETTER DZE
0406	CYRILLIC CAPITAL LETTER I
0407	CYRILLIC CAPITAL LETTER YI
0408	CYRILLIC CAPITAL LETTER JE
0409	CYRILLIC CAPITAL LETTER LJE
040A	CYRILLIC CAPITAL LETTER NJE
040B	CYRILLIC CAPITAL LETTER TSHE
040C	CYRILLIC CAPITAL LETTER KJE
040E	CYRILLIC CAPITAL LETTER SHORT U
040F	CYRILLIC CAPITAL LETTER DZHE

UNIC	Upper-case Unicode character name
0460	CYRILLIC CAPITAL LETTER OMEGA
0462	CYRILLIC CAPITAL LETTER YAT
0464	CYRILLIC CAPITAL LETTER IOTIFIED E
0466	CYRILLIC CAPITAL LETTER LITTLE YUS
0468	CYRILLIC CAPITAL LETTER IOTIFIED LITTLE YUS
046A	CYRILLIC CAPITAL LETTER BIG YUS
046C	CYRILLIC CAPITAL LETTER IOTIFIED BIG YUS
046E	CYRILLIC CAPITAL LETTER KSI
0470	CYRILLIC CAPITAL LETTER PSI
0472	CYRILLIC CAPITAL LETTER FITA
0474	CYRILLIC CAPITAL LETTER IZHITSA
0476	CYRILLIC CAPITAL LETTER IZHITSA DOUBLE GRAVE
0478	CYRILLIC CAPITAL LETTER UK DIGRAPH
047A	CYRILLIC CAPITAL LETTER ROUND OMEGA
047C	CYRILLIC CAPITAL LETTER OMEGA TITLO
047E	CYRILLIC CAPITAL LETTER OT
0480	CYRILLIC CAPITAL LETTER KOPPA
0490	CYRILLIC CAPITAL LETTER GE WITH UPTURN
0492	CYRILLIC CAPITAL LETTER GE BAR
0494	CYRILLIC CAPITAL LETTER GE HOOK
0496	CYRILLIC CAPITAL LETTER ZHE WITH RIGHT DESCENDER
0498	CYRILLIC CAPITAL LETTER ZE CEDILLA
049A	CYRILLIC CAPITAL LETTER KA WITH RIGHT DESCENDER
049C	CYRILLIC CAPITAL LETTER KA VERTICAL BAR
049E	CYRILLIC CAPITAL LETTER KA BAR
04A0	CYRILLIC CAPITAL LETTER REVERSED GE KA
04A2	CYRILLIC CAPITAL LETTER EN WITH RIGHT DESCENDER
04A4	CYRILLIC CAPITAL LETTER EN GE
04A6	CYRILLIC CAPITAL LETTER PE HOOK
04A8	CYRILLIC CAPITAL LETTER O HOOK
04AA	CYRILLIC CAPITAL LETTER ES CEDILLA
04AC	CYRILLIC CAPITAL LETTER TE WITH RIGHT DESCENDER
04AE	CYRILLIC CAPITAL LETTER STRAIGHT U
04B0	CYRILLIC CAPITAL LETTER STRAIGHT U BAR
04B2	CYRILLIC CAPITAL LETTER KHA WITH RIGHT DESCENDER
04B4	CYRILLIC CAPITAL LETTER TE TSE
04B6	CYRILLIC CAPITAL LETTER CHE WITH RIGHT DESCENDER
04B8	CYRILLIC CAPITAL LETTER CHE VERTICAL BAR
04BA	CYRILLIC CAPITAL LETTER H
04BC	CYRILLIC CAPITAL LETTER IE HOOK

UNIC	Lower-case Unicode character name
0461	CYRILLIC SMALL LETTER OMEGA
0463	CYRILLIC SMALL LETTER YAT
0465	CYRILLIC SMALL LETTER IOTIFIED E
0467	CYRILLIC SMALL LETTER LITTLE YUS
0469	CYRILLIC SMALL LETTER IOTIFIED LITTLE YUS
046B	CYRILLIC SMALL LETTER BIG YUS
046D	CYRILLIC SMALL LETTER IOTIFIED BIG YUS
046F	CYRILLIC SMALL LETTER KSI
0471	CYRILLIC SMALL LETTER PSI
0473	CYRILLIC SMALL LETTER FITA
0475	CYRILLIC SMALL LETTER IZHITSA
0477	CYRILLIC SMALL LETTER IZHITSA DOUBLE GRAVE
0479	CYRILLIC SMALL LETTER UK DIGRAPH
047B	CYRILLIC SMALL LETTER ROUND OMEGA
047D	CYRILLIC SMALL LETTER OMEGA TITLO
047F	CYRILLIC SMALL LETTER OT
0481	CYRILLIC SMALL LETTER KOPPA
0491	CYRILLIC SMALL LETTER GE WITH UPTURN
0493	CYRILLIC SMALL LETTER GE BAR
0495	CYRILLIC SMALL LETTER GE HOOK
0497	CYRILLIC SMALL LETTER ZHE WITH RIGHT DESCENDER
0499	CYRILLIC SMALL LETTER ZE CEDILLA
049B	CYRILLIC SMALL LETTER KA WITH RIGHT DESCENDER
049D	CYRILLIC SMALL LETTER KA VERTICAL BAR
049F	CYRILLIC SMALL LETTER KA BAR
04A1	CYRILLIC SMALL LETTER REVERSED GE KA
04A3	CYRILLIC SMALL LETTER EN WITH RIGHT DESCENDER
04A5	CYRILLIC SMALL LETTER EN GE
04A7	CYRILLIC SMALL LETTER PE HOOK
04A9	CYRILLIC SMALL LETTER O HOOK
04AB	CYRILLIC SMALL LETTER ES CEDILLA
04AD	CYRILLIC SMALL LETTER TE WITH RIGHT DESCENDER
04AF	CYRILLIC SMALL LETTER STRAIGHT U
04B1	CYRILLIC SMALL LETTER STRAIGHT U BAR
04B3	CYRILLIC SMALL LETTER KHA WITH RIGHT DESCENDER
04B5	CYRILLIC SMALL LETTER TE TSE
04B7	CYRILLIC SMALL LETTER CHE WITH RIGHT DESCENDER
04B9	CYRILLIC SMALL LETTER CHE VERTICAL BAR
04BB	CYRILLIC SMALL LETTER H
04BD	CYRILLIC SMALL LETTER IE HOOK

UNIC	Lower-case Unicode character name
04BF	CYRILLIC SMALL LETTER IE HOOK OGONEK
04C2	CYRILLIC SMALL LETTER SHORT ZHE
04C4	CYRILLIC SMALL LETTER KA HOOK
04C6	CYRILLIC SMALL LETTER KA OGONEK
04C8	CYRILLIC SMALL LETTER EN HOOK
04CA	CYRILLIC SMALL LETTER KHA OGONEK
04CC	CYRILLIC SMALL LETTER CHE WITH LEFT DESCENDER
0561	ARMENIAN SMALL LETTER AYB
0562	ARMENIAN SMALL LETTER BEN
0563	ARMENIAN SMALL LETTER GIM
0564	ARMENIAN SMALL LETTER DA
0565	ARMENIAN SMALL LETTER ECH
0566	ARMENIAN SMALL LETTER ZA
0567	ARMENIAN SMALL LETTER EH
0568	ARMENIAN SMALL LETTER ET
0569	ARMENIAN SMALL LETTER TO
056A	ARMENIAN SMALL LETTER ZHE
056B	ARMENIAN SMALL LETTER INI
056C	ARMENIAN SMALL LETTER LIWN
056D	ARMENIAN SMALL LETTER XEH
056E	ARMENIAN SMALL LETTER CA
056F	ARMENIAN SMALL LETTER KEN
0570	ARMENIAN SMALL LETTER HO
0571	ARMENIAN SMALL LETTER JA
0572	ARMENIAN SMALL LETTER LAD
0573	ARMENIAN SMALL LETTER CHEH
0574	ARMENIAN SMALL LETTER MEN
0575	ARMENIAN SMALL LETTER YI
0576	ARMENIAN SMALL LETTER NOW
0577	ARMENIAN SMALL LETTER SHA
0578	ARMENIAN SMALL LETTER VO
0579	ARMENIAN SMALL LETTER CHA
057A	ARMENIAN SMALL LETTER PEH
057B	ARMENIAN SMALL LETTER JHEH
057C	ARMENIAN SMALL LETTER RA
057D	ARMENIAN SMALL LETTER SEH
057E	ARMENIAN SMALL LETTER VEW
057F	ARMENIAN SMALL LETTER TIWN
0580	ARMENIAN SMALL LETTER REH
0581	ARMENIAN SMALL LETTER CO

UNIC	Upper-case Unicode character name
04BE	CYRILLIC CAPITAL LETTER IE HOOK OGONEK
04C1	CYRILLIC CAPITAL LETTER SHORT ZHE
04C3	CYRILLIC CAPITAL LETTER KA HOOK
04C5	CYRILLIC CAPITAL LETTER KA OGONEK
04C7	CYRILLIC CAPITAL LETTER EN HOOK
04C9	CYRILLIC CAPITAL LETTER KHA OGONEK
04CB	CYRILLIC CAPITAL LETTER CHE WITH LEFT DESCENDER
0531	ARMENIAN CAPITAL LETTER AYB
0532	ARMENIAN CAPITAL LETTER BEN
0533	ARMENIAN CAPITAL LETTER GIM
0534	ARMENIAN CAPITAL LETTER DA
0535	ARMENIAN CAPITAL LETTER ECH
0536	ARMENIAN CAPITAL LETTER ZA
0537	ARMENIAN CAPITAL LETTER EH
0538	ARMENIAN CAPITAL LETTER ET
0539	ARMENIAN CAPITAL LETTER TO
053A	ARMENIAN CAPITAL LETTER ZHE
053B	ARMENIAN CAPITAL LETTER INI
053C	ARMENIAN CAPITAL LETTER LIWN
053D	ARMENIAN CAPITAL LETTER XEH
053E	ARMENIAN CAPITAL LETTER CA
053F	ARMENIAN CAPITAL LETTER KEN
0540	ARMENIAN CAPITAL LETTER HO
0541	ARMENIAN CAPITAL LETTER JA
0542	ARMENIAN CAPITAL LETTER LAD
0543	ARMENIAN CAPITAL LETTER CHEH
0544	ARMENIAN CAPITAL LETTER MEN
0545	ARMENIAN CAPITAL LETTER YI
0546	ARMENIAN CAPITAL LETTER NOW
0547	ARMENIAN CAPITAL LETTER SHA
0548	ARMENIAN CAPITAL LETTER VO
0549	ARMENIAN CAPITAL LETTER CHA
054A	ARMENIAN CAPITAL LETTER PEH
054B	ARMENIAN CAPITAL LETTER JHEH
054C	ARMENIAN CAPITAL LETTER RA
054D	ARMENIAN CAPITAL LETTER SEH
054E	ARMENIAN CAPITAL LETTER VEW
054F	ARMENIAN CAPITAL LETTER TIWN
0550	ARMENIAN CAPITAL LETTER REH
0551	ARMENIAN CAPITAL LETTER CO

UNIC	Lower-case Unicode character name		UNIC	Upper-case Unicode character name
0582	ARMENIAN SMALL LETTER YIWN		0552	ARMENIAN CAPITAL LETTER YIWN
0583	ARMENIAN SMALL LETTER PIWR		0553	ARMENIAN CAPITAL LETTER PIWR
0584	ARMENIAN SMALL LETTER KEH		0554	ARMENIAN CAPITAL LETTER KEH
0585	ARMENIAN SMALL LETTER OH		0555	ARMENIAN CAPITAL LETTER OH
0586	ARMENIAN SMALL LETTER FEH		0556	ARMENIAN CAPITAL LETTER FEH

Note: *The modern Georgian alphabet is effectively caseless; Georgian SMALL LETTERs should not be upper-cased to CAPITAL LETTERs.*

UNIC	Lower-case Unicode character name		UNIC	Upper-case Unicode character name
24D0	CIRCLED LATIN SMALL LETTER A		24B6	CIRCLED LATIN CAPITAL LETTER A
24D1	CIRCLED LATIN SMALL LETTER B		24B7	CIRCLED LATIN CAPITAL LETTER B
24D2	CIRCLED LATIN SMALL LETTER C		24B8	CIRCLED LATIN CAPITAL LETTER C
24D3	CIRCLED LATIN SMALL LETTER D		24B9	CIRCLED LATIN CAPITAL LETTER D
24D4	CIRCLED LATIN SMALL LETTER E		24BA	CIRCLED LATIN CAPITAL LETTER E
24D5	CIRCLED LATIN SMALL LETTER F		24BB	CIRCLED LATIN CAPITAL LETTER F
24D6	CIRCLED LATIN SMALL LETTER G		24BC	CIRCLED LATIN CAPITAL LETTER G
24D7	CIRCLED LATIN SMALL LETTER H		24BD	CIRCLED LATIN CAPITAL LETTER H
24D8	CIRCLED LATIN SMALL LETTER I		24BE	CIRCLED LATIN CAPITAL LETTER I
24D9	CIRCLED LATIN SMALL LETTER J		24BF	CIRCLED LATIN CAPITAL LETTER J
24DA	CIRCLED LATIN SMALL LETTER K		24C0	CIRCLED LATIN CAPITAL LETTER K
24DB	CIRCLED LATIN SMALL LETTER L		24C1	CIRCLED LATIN CAPITAL LETTER L
24DC	CIRCLED LATIN SMALL LETTER M		24C2	CIRCLED LATIN CAPITAL LETTER M
24DD	CIRCLED LATIN SMALL LETTER N		24C3	CIRCLED LATIN CAPITAL LETTER N
24DE	CIRCLED LATIN SMALL LETTER O		24C4	CIRCLED LATIN CAPITAL LETTER O
24DF	CIRCLED LATIN SMALL LETTER P		24C5	CIRCLED LATIN CAPITAL LETTER P
24E0	CIRCLED LATIN SMALL LETTER Q		24C6	CIRCLED LATIN CAPITAL LETTER Q
24E1	CIRCLED LATIN SMALL LETTER R		24C7	CIRCLED LATIN CAPITAL LETTER R
24E2	CIRCLED LATIN SMALL LETTER S		24C8	CIRCLED LATIN CAPITAL LETTER S
24E3	CIRCLED LATIN SMALL LETTER T		24C9	CIRCLED LATIN CAPITAL LETTER T
24E4	CIRCLED LATIN SMALL LETTER U		24CA	CIRCLED LATIN CAPITAL LETTER U
24E5	CIRCLED LATIN SMALL LETTER V		24CB	CIRCLED LATIN CAPITAL LETTER V
24E6	CIRCLED LATIN SMALL LETTER W		24CC	CIRCLED LATIN CAPITAL LETTER W
24E7	CIRCLED LATIN SMALL LETTER X		24CD	CIRCLED LATIN CAPITAL LETTER X
24E8	CIRCLED LATIN SMALL LETTER Y		24CE	CIRCLED LATIN CAPITAL LETTER Y
24E9	CIRCLED LATIN SMALL LETTER Z		24CF	CIRCLED LATIN CAPITAL LETTER Z
FF41	FULLWIDTH LATIN SMALL LETTER A		FF21	FULLWIDTH LATIN CAPITAL LETTER A
FF42	FULLWIDTH LATIN SMALL LETTER B		FF22	FULLWIDTH LATIN CAPITAL LETTER B
FF43	FULLWIDTH LATIN SMALL LETTER C		FF23	FULLWIDTH LATIN CAPITAL LETTER C
FF44	FULLWIDTH LATIN SMALL LETTER D		FF24	FULLWIDTH LATIN CAPITAL LETTER D
FF45	FULLWIDTH LATIN SMALL LETTER E		FF25	FULLWIDTH LATIN CAPITAL LETTER E
FF46	FULLWIDTH LATIN SMALL LETTER F		FF26	FULLWIDTH LATIN CAPITAL LETTER F

UNIC	Upper-case Unicode character name
FF27	FULLWIDTH LATIN CAPITAL LETTER G
FF28	FULLWIDTH LATIN CAPITAL LETTER H
FF29	FULLWIDTH LATIN CAPITAL LETTER I
FF2A	FULLWIDTH LATIN CAPITAL LETTER J
FF2B	FULLWIDTH LATIN CAPITAL LETTER K
FF2C	FULLWIDTH LATIN CAPITAL LETTER L
FF2D	FULLWIDTH LATIN CAPITAL LETTER M
FF2E	FULLWIDTH LATIN CAPITAL LETTER N
FF2F	FULLWIDTH LATIN CAPITAL LETTER O
FF30	FULLWIDTH LATIN CAPITAL LETTER P
FF31	FULLWIDTH LATIN CAPITAL LETTER Q
FF32	FULLWIDTH LATIN CAPITAL LETTER R
FF33	FULLWIDTH LATIN CAPITAL LETTER S
FF34	FULLWIDTH LATIN CAPITAL LETTER T
FF35	FULLWIDTH LATIN CAPITAL LETTER U
FF36	FULLWIDTH LATIN CAPITAL LETTER V
FF37	FULLWIDTH LATIN CAPITAL LETTER W
FF38	FULLWIDTH LATIN CAPITAL LETTER X
FF39	FULLWIDTH LATIN CAPITAL LETTER Y
FF3A	FULLWIDTH LATIN CAPITAL LETTER Z

UNIC	Lower-case Unicode character name
FF47	FULLWIDTH LATIN SMALL LETTER G
FF48	FULLWIDTH LATIN SMALL LETTER H
FF49	FULLWIDTH LATIN SMALL LETTER I
FF4A	FULLWIDTH LATIN SMALL LETTER J
FF4B	FULLWIDTH LATIN SMALL LETTER K
FF4C	FULLWIDTH LATIN SMALL LETTER L
FF4D	FULLWIDTH LATIN SMALL LETTER M
FF4E	FULLWIDTH LATIN SMALL LETTER N
FF4F	FULLWIDTH LATIN SMALL LETTER O
FF50	FULLWIDTH LATIN SMALL LETTER P
FF51	FULLWIDTH LATIN SMALL LETTER Q
FF52	FULLWIDTH LATIN SMALL LETTER R
FF53	FULLWIDTH LATIN SMALL LETTER S
FF54	FULLWIDTH LATIN SMALL LETTER T
FF55	FULLWIDTH LATIN SMALL LETTER U
FF56	FULLWIDTH LATIN SMALL LETTER V
FF57	FULLWIDTH LATIN SMALL LETTER W
FF58	FULLWIDTH LATIN SMALL LETTER X
FF59	FULLWIDTH LATIN SMALL LETTER Y
FF5A	FULLWIDTH LATIN SMALL LETTER Z

6.0 *External Mapping Tables*

The Unicode standard exists in a world of other text and character encoding standards, some private, some national, some international. One of the major strengths of the Unicode standard is the number of other important standards that it covers. In many cases, decisions on whether to unify characters or not were influenced by distinctions made in established and widely-used standards.

Conversion of characters between standards is not always a straightforward proposition. There are many characters which have mixed semantics in one standard and may correspond to more than one character in another. Sometimes standards give duplicate encodings for one and the same character, at other times the interpretation of a whole set of characters may depend on the application. Finally, there are subtle differences in what a standard may consider a character.

To assist and guide implementers, *The Unicode Standard: Worldwide Character Encoding Version 1.0* provides a set of mapping tables to other standards. These tables consist of one-to-one mappings from the Unicode standard to another published character standard. They include occasional multiple mappings. Their primary function is to identify the characters in these standards in the context of the Unicode standard. In many cases, data conversion between the Unicode standard and other standards will be application-dependent or context-sensitive.

Disclaimer

The content of all mapping tables has been verified as far as possible by the Unicode Consortium. However, the Unicode Consortium does not guarantee that the tables are correct in every detail. The mapping tables are provided for informational purposes only. The Unicode Consortium is not responsible for errors that may occur either in the mapping tables or in software which implements those tables as they are printed in this volume. All implementers should check the relevant international, national, and vendor standards in cases where ambiguity of interpretation may occur.

6.1 ISO Mapping Tables

This section includes the following mapping tables:

- Unicode value to ISO 8859, which contains several 8-bit character sets covering the Latin, Greek, Cyrillic, Hebrew and Arabic scripts

- Unicode value to ISO 8879, which contains character mapping to SGML

- Unicode value to ISO DIS 6862.2, which contains a collection of mathematical symbols

Unicode Encoding to ISO 8859 Mappings

For Unicode U+0000 to U+007F all mappings are identities.

UNIC	2	3	4	5	6	7	8	9	Unicode character name
00A0	A0	A0	A0	A0	A0	A0	A0	A0	NON-BREAKING SPACE
00A1								A1	INVERTED EXCLAMATION MARK
00A2							A2	A2	CENT SIGN
00A3		A3				A3	A3	A3	POUND SIGN
00A4	A4	A4	A4		A4		A4	A4	CURRENCY SIGN
00A5							A5	A5	YEN SIGN
00A6						A6	A6	A6	BROKEN VERTICAL BAR
00A7	A7	A7	A7	FD		A7	A7	A7	SECTION SIGN
00A8	A8	A8	A8			A8	A8	A8	SPACING DIAERESIS
00A9						A9	A9	A9	COPYRIGHT SIGN
00AA								AA	FEMININE ORDINAL INDICATOR
00AB						AB	AB	AB	LEFT POINTING GUILLEMET
00AC						AC	AC	AC	NOT SIGN
00AD	AD	AD	AD	AD	AD	AD	AD	AD	SOFT HYPHEN
00AE							AE	AE	REGISTERED TRADE MARK SIGN
00AF			AF					AF	SPACING MACRON
00B0	B0	B0	B0			B0	B0	B0	DEGREE SIGN
00B1						B1	B1	B1	PLUS-OR-MINUS SIGN
00B2		B2				B2	B2	B2	SUPERSCRIPT DIGIT TWO
00B3		B3				B3	B3	B3	SUPERSCRIPT DIGIT THREE
00B4	B4	B4	B4				B4	B4	SPACING ACUTE
00B5		B5					B5	B5	MICRO SIGN
00B6							B6	B6	PARAGRAPH SIGN
00B7		B7				B7	B7	B7	MIDDLE DOT
00B8	B8	B8	B8				B8	B8	SPACING CEDILLA
00B9							B9	B9	SUPERSCRIPT DIGIT ONE
00BA								BA	MASCULINE ORDINAL INDICATOR
00BB						BB	BB	BB	RIGHT POINTING GUILLEMET
00BC							BC	BC	FRACTION ONE QUARTER
00BD		BD				BD	BD	BD	FRACTION ONE HALF
00BE							BE	BE	FRACTION THREE QUARTERS
00BF								BF	INVERTED QUESTION MARK
00C0		C0						C0	LATIN CAPITAL LETTER A GRAVE
00C1	C1	C1	C1					C1	LATIN CAPITAL LETTER A ACUTE
00C2	C2	C2	C2					C2	LATIN CAPITAL LETTER A CIRCUMFLEX
00C3			C3					C3	LATIN CAPITAL LETTER A TILDE
00C4	C4	C4	C4					C4	LATIN CAPITAL LETTER A DIAERESIS
00C5			C5					C5	LATIN CAPITAL LETTER A RING
00C6			C6					C6	LATIN CAPITAL LETTER A E
00C7	C7	C7						C7	LATIN CAPITAL LETTER C CEDILLA
00C8		C8						C8	LATIN CAPITAL LETTER E GRAVE
00C9	C9	C9	C9					C9	LATIN CAPITAL LETTER E ACUTE
00CA		CA						CA	LATIN CAPITAL LETTER E CIRCUMFLEX
00CB	CB	CB	CB					CB	LATIN CAPITAL LETTER E DIAERESIS
00CC		CC						CC	LATIN CAPITAL LETTER I GRAVE
00CD	CD	CD	CD					CD	LATIN CAPITAL LETTER I ACUTE
00CE	CE	CE	CE					CE	LATIN CAPITAL LETTER I CIRCUMFLEX
00CF		CF						CF	LATIN CAPITAL LETTER I DIAERESIS
00D1		D1						D1	LATIN CAPITAL LETTER N TILDE
00D2		D2						D2	LATIN CAPITAL LETTER O GRAVE
00D3	D3	D3						D3	LATIN CAPITAL LETTER O ACUTE

UNIC	2	3	4	5	6	7	8	9	Unicode character name
00D4	D4	D4	D4					D4	LATIN CAPITAL LETTER O CIRCUMFLEX
00D5			D5					D5	LATIN CAPITAL LETTER O TILDE
00D6	D6	D6	D6					D6	LATIN CAPITAL LETTER O DIAERESIS
00D7	D7	D7	D7				AA	D7	MULTIPLICATION SIGN
00D8			D8					D8	LATIN CAPITAL LETTER O SLASH
00D9		D9						D9	LATIN CAPITAL LETTER U GRAVE
00DA	DA	DA	DA					DA	LATIN CAPITAL LETTER U ACUTE
00DB		DB	DB					DB	LATIN CAPITAL LETTER U CIRCUMFLEX
00DC	DC	DC	DC					DC	LATIN CAPITAL LETTER U DIAERESIS
00DD	DD								LATIN CAPITAL LETTER Y ACUTE
00DF	DF	DF	DF					DF	LATIN SMALL LETTER SHARP S
00E0		E0						E0	LATIN SMALL LETTER A GRAVE
00E1	E1	E1	E1					E1	LATIN SMALL LETTER A ACUTE
00E2	E2	E2	E2					E2	LATIN SMALL LETTER A CIRCUMFLEX
00E3			E3					E3	LATIN SMALL LETTER A TILDE
00E4	E4	E4	E4					E4	LATIN SMALL LETTER A DIAERESIS
00E5			E5					E5	LATIN SMALL LETTER A RING
00E6			E6					E6	LATIN SMALL LETTER A E
00E7	E7	E7						E7	LATIN SMALL LETTER C CEDILLA
00E8		E8						E8	LATIN SMALL LETTER E GRAVE
00E9	E9	E9	E9					E9	LATIN SMALL LETTER E ACUTE
00EA		EA						EA	LATIN SMALL LETTER E CIRCUMFLEX
00EB	EB	EB	EB					EB	LATIN SMALL LETTER E DIAERESIS
00EC		EC						EC	LATIN SMALL LETTER I GRAVE
00ED	ED	ED	ED					ED	LATIN SMALL LETTER I ACUTE
00EE	EE	EE	EE					EE	LATIN SMALL LETTER I CIRCUMFLEX
00EF		EF						EF	LATIN SMALL LETTER I DIAERESIS
00F1		F1						F1	LATIN SMALL LETTER N TILDE
00F2		F2						F2	LATIN SMALL LETTER O GRAVE
00F3	F3	F3						F3	LATIN SMALL LETTER O ACUTE
00F4	F4	F4	F4					F4	LATIN SMALL LETTER O CIRCUMFLEX
00F5			F5					F5	LATIN SMALL LETTER O TILDE
00F6	F6	F6	F6					F6	LATIN SMALL LETTER O DIAERESIS
00F7	F7	F7	F7				BA	F7	DIVISION SIGN
00F8			F8					F8	LATIN SMALL LETTER O SLASH
00F9		F9						F9	LATIN SMALL LETTER U GRAVE
00FA	FA	FA	FA					FA	LATIN SMALL LETTER U ACUTE
00FB		FB	FB					FB	LATIN SMALL LETTER U CIRCUMFLEX
00FC	FC	FC	FC					FC	LATIN SMALL LETTER U DIAERESIS
00FD	FD								LATIN SMALL LETTER Y ACUTE
00FF								FF	LATIN SMALL LETTER Y DIAERESIS
0100			C0						LATIN CAPITAL LETTER A MACRON
0101			E0						LATIN SMALL LETTER A MACRON
0102	C3								LATIN CAPITAL LETTER A BREVE
0103	E3								LATIN SMALL LETTER A BREVE
0104	A1		A1						LATIN CAPITAL LETTER A OGONEK
0105	B1		B1						LATIN SMALL LETTER A OGONEK
0106	C6								LATIN CAPITAL LETTER C ACUTE
0107	E6								LATIN SMALL LETTER C ACUTE
0108		C6							LATIN CAPITAL LETTER C CIRCUMFLEX
0109		E6							LATIN SMALL LETTER C CIRCUMFLEX
010A		C5							LATIN CAPITAL LETTER C DOT
010B		E5							LATIN SMALL LETTER C DOT
010C	C8		C8						LATIN CAPITAL LETTER C HACEK
010D	E8		E8						LATIN SMALL LETTER C HACEK
010E	CF								LATIN CAPITAL LETTER D HACEK

The Unicode Standard · Version 1.0

UNIC	2	3	4	5	6	7	8	9	Unicode character name
010F	EF								LATIN SMALL LETTER D HACEK
0110	D0		D0						LATIN CAPITAL LETTER D BAR
0111	F0		F0						LATIN SMALL LETTER D BAR
0112			AA						LATIN CAPITAL LETTER E MACRON
0113			BA						LATIN SMALL LETTER E MACRON
0116			CC						LATIN CAPITAL LETTER E DOT
0117			EC						LATIN SMALL LETTER E DOT
0118	CA		CA						LATIN CAPITAL LETTER E OGONEK
0119	EA		EA						LATIN SMALL LETTER E OGONEK
011A	CC								LATIN CAPITAL LETTER E HACEK
011B	EC								LATIN SMALL LETTER E HACEK
011C		D8							LATIN CAPITAL LETTER G CIRCUMFLEX
011D		F8							LATIN SMALL LETTER G CIRCUMFLEX
011E		AB						D0	LATIN CAPITAL LETTER G BREVE
011F		BB						F0	LATIN SMALL LETTER G BREVE
0120		D5							LATIN CAPITAL LETTER G DOT
0121		F5							LATIN SMALL LETTER G DOT
0122			AB						LATIN CAPITAL LETTER G CEDILLA
0123			BB						LATIN SMALL LETTER G CEDILLA
0124		A6							LATIN CAPITAL LETTER H CIRCUMFLEX
0125		B6							LATIN SMALL LETTER H CIRCUMFLEX
0126		A1							LATIN CAPITAL LETTER H BAR
0127		B1							LATIN SMALL LETTER H BAR
0128			A5						LATIN CAPITAL LETTER I TILDE
0129			B5						LATIN SMALL LETTER I TILDE
012A			CF						LATIN CAPITAL LETTER I MACRON
012B			EF						LATIN SMALL LETTER I MACRON
012E			C7						LATIN CAPITAL LETTER I OGONEK
012F			E7						LATIN SMALL LETTER I OGONEK
0130		A9						DD	LATIN CAPITAL LETTER I DOT
0131		B9						FD	LATIN SMALL LETTER DOTLESS I
0134		AC							LATIN CAPITAL LETTER J CIRCUMFLEX
0135		BC							LATIN SMALL LETTER J CIRCUMFLEX
0136			D3						LATIN CAPITAL LETTER K CEDILLA
0137			F3						LATIN SMALL LETTER K CEDILLA
0138			A2						LATIN SMALL LETTER KRA
0139	C5								LATIN CAPITAL LETTER L ACUTE
013A	E5								LATIN SMALL LETTER L ACUTE
013B			A6						LATIN CAPITAL LETTER L CEDILLA
013C			B6						LATIN SMALL LETTER L CEDILLA
013D	A5								LATIN CAPITAL LETTER L HACEK
013E	B5								LATIN SMALL LETTER L HACEK
0141	A3								LATIN CAPITAL LETTER L SLASH
0142	B3								LATIN SMALL LETTER L SLASH
0143	D1								LATIN CAPITAL LETTER N ACUTE
0144	F1								LATIN SMALL LETTER N ACUTE
0145			D1						LATIN CAPITAL LETTER N CEDILLA
0146			F1						LATIN SMALL LETTER N CEDILLA
0147	D2								LATIN CAPITAL LETTER N HACEK
0148	F2								LATIN SMALL LETTER N HACEK
014A			BD						LATIN CAPITAL LETTER ENG
014B			BF						LATIN SMALL LETTER ENG
014C			D2						LATIN CAPITAL LETTER O MACRON
014D			F2						LATIN SMALL LETTER O MACRON
0150	D5								LATIN CAPITAL LETTER O DOUBLE ACUTE
0151	F5								LATIN SMALL LETTER O DOUBLE ACUTE

UNIC	2	3	4	5	6	7	8	9	Unicode character name
0154	C0								LATIN CAPITAL LETTER R ACUTE
0155	E0								LATIN SMALL LETTER R ACUTE
0156			A3						LATIN CAPITAL LETTER R CEDILLA
0157			B3						LATIN SMALL LETTER R CEDILLA
0158	D8								LATIN CAPITAL LETTER R HACEK
0159	F8								LATIN SMALL LETTER R HACEK
015A	A6								LATIN CAPITAL LETTER S ACUTE
015B	B6								LATIN SMALL LETTER S ACUTE
015C		DE							LATIN CAPITAL LETTER S CIRCUMFLEX
015D		FE							LATIN SMALL LETTER S CIRCUMFLEX
015E	AA	AA						DE	LATIN CAPITAL LETTER S CEDILLA
015F	BA	BA						FE	LATIN SMALL LETTER S CEDILLA
0160	A9		A9						LATIN CAPITAL LETTER S HACEK
0161	B9		B9						LATIN SMALL LETTER S HACEK
0162	DE								LATIN CAPITAL LETTER T CEDILLA
0163	FE								LATIN SMALL LETTER T CEDILLA
0164	AB								LATIN CAPITAL LETTER T HACEK
0165	BB								LATIN SMALL LETTER T HACEK
0166			AC						LATIN CAPITAL LETTER T BAR
0167			BC						LATIN SMALL LETTER T BAR
0168			DD						LATIN CAPITAL LETTER U TILDE
0169			FD						LATIN SMALL LETTER U TILDE
016A			DE						LATIN CAPITAL LETTER U MACRON
016B			FE						LATIN SMALL LETTER U MACRON
016C		DD							LATIN CAPITAL LETTER U BREVE
016D		FD							LATIN SMALL LETTER U BREVE
016E	D9								LATIN CAPITAL LETTER U RING
016F	F9								LATIN SMALL LETTER U RING
0170	DB								LATIN CAPITAL LETTER U DOUBLE ACUTE
0171	FB								LATIN SMALL LETTER U DOUBLE ACUTE
0172			D9						LATIN CAPITAL LETTER U OGONEK
0173			F9						LATIN SMALL LETTER U OGONEK
0179	AC								LATIN CAPITAL LETTER Z ACUTE
017A	BC								LATIN SMALL LETTER Z ACUTE
017B	AF	AF							LATIN CAPITAL LETTER Z DOT
017C	BF	BF							LATIN SMALL LETTER Z DOT
017D	AE		AE						LATIN CAPITAL LETTER Z HACEK
017E	BE		BE						LATIN SMALL LETTER Z HACEK
02C7	B7		B7						MODIFIER LETTER HACEK
02D8	A2	A2							SPACING BREVE
02D9	FF	FF	FF						SPACING DOT ABOVE
02DB	B2		B2						SPACING OGONEK
02DD	BD								SPACING DOUBLE ACUTE
0371						A1			GREEK NON-SPACING DASIA PNEUMATA
0372						A2			GREEK NON-SPACING PSILI PNEUMATA
0386						B6			GREEK CAPITAL LETTER ALPHA TONOS
0388						B8			GREEK CAPITAL LETTER EPSILON TONOS
0389						B9			GREEK CAPITAL LETTER ETA TONOS
038A						BA			GREEK CAPITAL LETTER IOTA TONOS
038C						BC			GREEK CAPITAL LETTER OMICRON TONOS
038E						BE			GREEK CAPITAL LETTER UPSILON TONOS
038F						BF			GREEK CAPITAL LETTER OMEGA TONOS
0390						C0			GREEK SMALL LETTER IOTA DIAERESIS TONOS
0391						C1			GREEK CAPITAL LETTER ALPHA
0392						C2			GREEK CAPITAL LETTER BETA

UNIC	2	3	4	5	6	7	8	9	Unicode character name
0393						C3			GREEK CAPITAL LETTER GAMMA
0394						C4			GREEK CAPITAL LETTER DELTA
0395						C5			GREEK CAPITAL LETTER EPSILON
0396						C6			GREEK CAPITAL LETTER ZETA
0397						C7			GREEK CAPITAL LETTER ETA
0398						C8			GREEK CAPITAL LETTER THETA
0399						C9			GREEK CAPITAL LETTER IOTA
039A						CA			GREEK CAPITAL LETTER KAPPA
039B						CB			GREEK CAPITAL LETTER LAMBDA
039C						CC			GREEK CAPITAL LETTER MU
039D						CD			GREEK CAPITAL LETTER NU
039E						CE			GREEK CAPITAL LETTER XI
039F						CF			GREEK CAPITAL LETTER OMICRON
03A0						D0			GREEK CAPITAL LETTER PI
03A1						D1			GREEK CAPITAL LETTER RHO
03A3						D3			GREEK CAPITAL LETTER SIGMA
03A4						D4			GREEK CAPITAL LETTER TAU
03A5						D5			GREEK CAPITAL LETTER UPSILON
03A6						D6			GREEK CAPITAL LETTER PHI
03A7						D7			GREEK CAPITAL LETTER CHI
03A8						D8			GREEK CAPITAL LETTER PSI
03A9						D9			GREEK CAPITAL LETTER OMEGA
03AA						DA			GREEK CAPITAL LETTER IOTA DIAERESIS
03AB						DB			GREEK CAPITAL LETTER UPSILON DIAERESIS
03AC						DC			GREEK SMALL LETTER ALPHA TONOS
03AD						DD			GREEK SMALL LETTER EPSILON TONOS
03AE						DE			GREEK SMALL LETTER ETA TONOS
03AF						DF			GREEK SMALL LETTER IOTA TONOS
03B0						E0			GREEK SMALL LETTER UPSILON DIAERESIS TONOS
03B1						E1			GREEK SMALL LETTER ALPHA
03B2						E2			GREEK SMALL LETTER BETA
03B3						E3			GREEK SMALL LETTER GAMMA
03B4						E4			GREEK SMALL LETTER DELTA
03B5						E5			GREEK SMALL LETTER EPSILON
03B6						E6			GREEK SMALL LETTER ZETA
03B7						E7			GREEK SMALL LETTER ETA
03B8						E8			GREEK SMALL LETTER THETA
03B9						E9			GREEK SMALL LETTER IOTA
03BA						EA			GREEK SMALL LETTER KAPPA
03BB						EB			GREEK SMALL LETTER LAMBDA
03BC						EC			GREEK SMALL LETTER MU
03BD						ED			GREEK SMALL LETTER NU
03BE						EE			GREEK SMALL LETTER XI
03BF						EF			GREEK SMALL LETTER OMICRON
03C0						F0			GREEK SMALL LETTER PI
03C1						F1			GREEK SMALL LETTER RHO
03C2						F2			GREEK SMALL LETTER FINAL SIGMA
03C3						F3			GREEK SMALL LETTER SIGMA
03C4						F4			GREEK SMALL LETTER TAU
03C5						F5			GREEK SMALL LETTER UPSILON
03C6						F6			GREEK SMALL LETTER PHI
03C7						F7			GREEK SMALL LETTER CHI
03C8						F8			GREEK SMALL LETTER PSI
03C9						F9			GREEK SMALL LETTER OMEGA

UNIC	2	3	4	5	6	7	8	9	Unicode character name
03CA						FA			GREEK SMALL LETTER IOTA DIAERESIS
03CB						FB			GREEK SMALL LETTER UPSILON DIAERESIS
03CC						FC			GREEK SMALL LETTER OMICRON TONOS
03CD						FD			GREEK SMALL LETTER UPSILON TONOS
03CE						FE			GREEK SMALL LETTER OMEGA TONOS
03F3						B4			GREEK SPACING TONOS
03F4						B5			GREEK SPACING DIAERESIS TONOS
0401				A1					CYRILLIC CAPITAL LETTER IO
0402				A2					CYRILLIC CAPITAL LETTER DJE
0403				A3					CYRILLIC CAPITAL LETTER GJE
0404				A4					CYRILLIC CAPITAL LETTER E
0405				A5					CYRILLIC CAPITAL LETTER DZE
0406				A6					CYRILLIC CAPITAL LETTER I
0407				A7					CYRILLIC CAPITAL LETTER YI
0408				A8					CYRILLIC CAPITAL LETTER JE
0409				A9					CYRILLIC CAPITAL LETTER LJE
040A				AA					CYRILLIC CAPITAL LETTER NJE
040B				AB					CYRILLIC CAPITAL LETTER TSHE
040C				AC					CYRILLIC CAPITAL LETTER KJE
040E				AE					CYRILLIC CAPITAL LETTER SHORT U
040F				AF					CYRILLIC CAPITAL LETTER DZHE
0410				B0					CYRILLIC CAPITAL LETTER A
0411				B1					CYRILLIC CAPITAL LETTER BE
0412				B2					CYRILLIC CAPITAL LETTER VE
0413				B3					CYRILLIC CAPITAL LETTER GE
0414				B4					CYRILLIC CAPITAL LETTER DE
0415				B5					CYRILLIC CAPITAL LETTER IE
0416				B6					CYRILLIC CAPITAL LETTER ZHE
0417				B7					CYRILLIC CAPITAL LETTER ZE
0418				B8					CYRILLIC CAPITAL LETTER II
0419				B9					CYRILLIC CAPITAL LETTER SHORT II
041A				BA					CYRILLIC CAPITAL LETTER KA
041B				BB					CYRILLIC CAPITAL LETTER EL
041C				BC					CYRILLIC CAPITAL LETTER EM
041D				BD					CYRILLIC CAPITAL LETTER EN
041E				BE					CYRILLIC CAPITAL LETTER O
041F				BF					CYRILLIC CAPITAL LETTER PE
0420				C0					CYRILLIC CAPITAL LETTER ER
0421				C1					CYRILLIC CAPITAL LETTER ES
0422				C2					CYRILLIC CAPITAL LETTER TE
0423				C3					CYRILLIC CAPITAL LETTER U
0424				C4					CYRILLIC CAPITAL LETTER EF
0425				C5					CYRILLIC CAPITAL LETTER KHA
0426				C6					CYRILLIC CAPITAL LETTER TSE
0427				C7					CYRILLIC CAPITAL LETTER CHE
0428				C8					CYRILLIC CAPITAL LETTER SHA
0429				C9					CYRILLIC CAPITAL LETTER SHCHA
042A				CA					CYRILLIC CAPITAL LETTER HARD SIGN
042B				CB					CYRILLIC CAPITAL LETTER YERI
042C				CC					CYRILLIC CAPITAL LETTER SOFT SIGN
042D				CD					CYRILLIC CAPITAL LETTER REVERSED E
042E				CE					CYRILLIC CAPITAL LETTER IU
042F				CF					CYRILLIC CAPITAL LETTER IA
0430				D0					CYRILLIC SMALL LETTER A
0431				D1					CYRILLIC SMALL LETTER BE
0432				D2					CYRILLIC SMALL LETTER VE

UNIC	2	3	4	5	6	7	8	9	Unicode character name
0433				D3					CYRILLIC SMALL LETTER GE
0434				D4					CYRILLIC SMALL LETTER DE
0435				D5					CYRILLIC SMALL LETTER IE
0436				D6					CYRILLIC SMALL LETTER ZHE
0437				D7					CYRILLIC SMALL LETTER ZE
0438				D8					CYRILLIC SMALL LETTER II
0439				D9					CYRILLIC SMALL LETTER SHORT II
043A				DA					CYRILLIC SMALL LETTER KA
043B				DB					CYRILLIC SMALL LETTER EL
043C				DC					CYRILLIC SMALL LETTER EM
043D				DD					CYRILLIC SMALL LETTER EN
043E				DE					CYRILLIC SMALL LETTER O
043F				DF					CYRILLIC SMALL LETTER PE
0440				E0					CYRILLIC SMALL LETTER ER
0441				E1					CYRILLIC SMALL LETTER ES
0442				E2					CYRILLIC SMALL LETTER TE
0443				E3					CYRILLIC SMALL LETTER U
0444				E4					CYRILLIC SMALL LETTER EF
0445				E5					CYRILLIC SMALL LETTER KHA
0446				E6					CYRILLIC SMALL LETTER TSE
0447				E7					CYRILLIC SMALL LETTER CHE
0448				E8					CYRILLIC SMALL LETTER SHA
0449				E9					CYRILLIC SMALL LETTER SHCHA
044A				EA					CYRILLIC SMALL LETTER HARD SIGN
044B				EB					CYRILLIC SMALL LETTER YERI
044C				EC					CYRILLIC SMALL LETTER SOFT SIGN
044D				ED					CYRILLIC SMALL LETTER REVERSED E
044E				EE					CYRILLIC SMALL LETTER IU
044F				EF					CYRILLIC SMALL LETTER IA
0451				F1					CYRILLIC SMALL LETTER IO
0452				F2					CYRILLIC SMALL LETTER DJE
0453				F3					CYRILLIC SMALL LETTER GJE
0454				F4					CYRILLIC SMALL LETTER E
0455				F5					CYRILLIC SMALL LETTER DZE
0456				F6					CYRILLIC SMALL LETTER I
0457				F7					CYRILLIC SMALL LETTER YI
0458				F8					CYRILLIC SMALL LETTER JE
0459				F9					CYRILLIC SMALL LETTER LJE
045A				FA					CYRILLIC SMALL LETTER NJE
045B				FB					CYRILLIC SMALL LETTER TSHE
045C				FC					CYRILLIC SMALL LETTER KJE
045E				FE					CYRILLIC SMALL LETTER SHORT U
045F				FF					CYRILLIC SMALL LETTER DZHE
05D0							E0		HEBREW LETTER ALEF
05D1							E1		HEBREW LETTER BET
05D2							E2		HEBREW LETTER GIMEL
05D3							E3		HEBREW LETTER DALET
05D4							E4		HEBREW LETTER HE
05D5							E5		HEBREW LETTER VAV
05D6							E6		HEBREW LETTER ZAYIN
05D7							E7		HEBREW LETTER HET
05D8							E8		HEBREW LETTER TET
05D9							E9		HEBREW LETTER YOD
05DA							EA		HEBREW LETTER FINAL KAF
05DB							EB		HEBREW LETTER KAF
05DC							EC		HEBREW LETTER LAMED

UNIC	2	3	4	5	6	7	8	9	Unicode character name
05DD							ED		HEBREW LETTER FINAL MEM
05DE							EE		HEBREW LETTER MEM
05DF							EF		HEBREW LETTER FINAL NUN
05E0							F0		HEBREW LETTER NUN
05E1							F1		HEBREW LETTER SAMEKH
05E2							F2		HEBREW LETTER AYIN
05E3							F3		HEBREW LETTER FINAL PE
05E4							F4		HEBREW LETTER PE
05E5							F5		HEBREW LETTER FINAL TSADI
05E6							F6		HEBREW LETTER TSADI
05E7							F7		HEBREW LETTER QOF
05E8							F8		HEBREW LETTER RESH
05E9							F9		HEBREW LETTER SHIN
05EA							FA		HEBREW LETTER TAV
060C					AC				ARABIC COMMA
061B					BB				ARABIC SEMICOLON
061F					BF				ARABIC QUESTION MARK
0621					C1				ARABIC LETTER HAMZAH
0622					C2				ARABIC LETTER MADDAH ON ALEF
0623					C3				ARABIC LETTER HAMZAH ON ALEF
0624					C4				ARABIC LETTER HAMZAH ON WAW
0625					C5				ARABIC LETTER HAMZAH UNDER ALEF
0626					C6				ARABIC LETTER HAMZAH ON YA
0627					C7				ARABIC LETTER ALEF
0628					C8				ARABIC LETTER BAA
0629					C9				ARABIC LETTER TAA MARBUTAH
062A					CA				ARABIC LETTER TAA
062B					CB				ARABIC LETTER THAA
062C					CC				ARABIC LETTER JEEM
062D					CD				ARABIC LETTER HAA
062E					CE				ARABIC LETTER KHAA
062F					CF				ARABIC LETTER DAL
0630					D0				ARABIC LETTER THAL
0631					D1				ARABIC LETTER RA
0632					D2				ARABIC LETTER ZAIN
0633					D3				ARABIC LETTER SEEN
0634					D4				ARABIC LETTER SHEEN
0635					D5				ARABIC LETTER SAD
0636					D6				ARABIC LETTER DAD
0637					D7				ARABIC LETTER TAH
0638					D8				ARABIC LETTER DHAH
0639					D9				ARABIC LETTER AIN
063A					DA				ARABIC LETTER GHAIN
0640					E0				ARABIC TATWEEL
0641					E1				ARABIC LETTER FA
0642					E2				ARABIC LETTER QAF
0643					E3				ARABIC LETTER CAF
0644					E4				ARABIC LETTER LAM
0645					E5				ARABIC LETTER MEEM
0646					E6				ARABIC LETTER NOON
0647					E7				ARABIC LETTER HA
0648					E8				ARABIC LETTER WAW
0649					E9				ARABIC LETTER ALEF MAQSURAH
064A					EA				ARABIC LETTER YA
064B					EB				ARABIC FATHATAN
064C					EC				ARABIC DAMMATAN

UNIC	2	3	4	5	6	7	8	9	Unicode character name
064D					ED				ARABIC KASRATAN
064E					EE				ARABIC FATHAH
064F					EF				ARABIC DAMMAH
0650					F0				ARABIC KASRAH
0651					F1				ARABIC SHADDAH
0652					F2				ARABIC SUKUN
0660					30				ARABIC-INDIC DIGIT ZERO
0661					31				ARABIC-INDIC DIGIT ONE
0662					32				ARABIC-INDIC DIGIT TWO
0663					33				ARABIC-INDIC DIGIT THREE
0664					34				ARABIC-INDIC DIGIT FOUR
0665					35				ARABIC-INDIC DIGIT FIVE
0666					36				ARABIC-INDIC DIGIT SIX
0667					37				ARABIC-INDIC DIGIT SEVEN
0668					38				ARABIC-INDIC DIGIT EIGHT
0669					39				ARABIC-INDIC DIGIT NINE
2015						AF			QUOTATION DASH
2017							DF		SPACING DOUBLE UNDERSCORE
203E							AF		SPACING OVERSCORE
2116				F0					NUMERO

Unicode Encoding to ISO 8879 (SGML) & ISO DIS 6862.2 Mappings

ISO 8879-1986 contains an ASCII-alphabetic encoding of a large number of "character entities" used as identifiers in SGML (Standard Graphic Markup Language). The following table maps Unicode character encodings to the entity reference names of those character entities which clearly constitute characters in the sense used by the Unicode standard. However, SGML also contains many identifiers for character entities which are glyph variants or stylistic variants which do not have one-to-one mappings with Unicode characters.

ISO/DIS 6862.2 contains two 7-bit character encodings of mathematical symbols of various types. The first encoding (set G0) is identified by numbers beginning with a digit 0 in the table below, for example, 07.13, while the second encoding (set G1) is identified by numbers beginning with a digit 1 in the table below, for example, 17.13. The other digits are to be interpreted as decimal values corresponding to regular ISO conventions for citing the position of characters in code tables; 17.13 can thus be interpreted as position 7/13 in the code table for set G1.

UNIC	6862.2	SGML	Unicode character name
0021		excl	EXCLAMATION MARK
0023		num	NUMBER SIGN
0024		dollar	DOLLAR SIGN
0025		percnt	PERCENT SIGN
0026		amp	AMPERSAND
0027		quot	APOSTROPHE-QUOTE
0028		lpar	OPENING PARENTHESIS
0029		rpar	CLOSING PARENTHESIS
002A		ast	ASTERISK
002B	05.00	plus	PLUS SIGN
002C		comma	COMMA
002D		hyphen	HYPHEN-MINUS
002E		period	PERIOD
002F		sol	SLASH
003A		colon	COLON
003B		semi	SEMICOLON
003C		lt	LESS-THAN SIGN
003D		equals	EQUALS SIGN
003E		gt	GREATER-THAN SIGN
003F		quest	QUESTION MARK
0040		commat	COMMERCIAL AT
005B		lsqb	OPENING SQUARE BRACKET
005C		bsol	BACKSLASH
005D		rsqb	CLOSING SQUARE BRACKET
005E		circ	SPACING CIRCUMFLEX
005F		lowbar	SPACING UNDERSCORE
0060		grave	SPACING GRAVE
007B		lcub	OPENING CURLY BRACKET
007C		verbar	VERTICAL BAR
007D		rcub	CLOSING CURLY BRACKET
007E		tilde	TILDE
00A0		nbsp	NON-BREAKING SPACE
00A1		iexcl	INVERTED EXCLAMATION MARK
00A2		cent	CENT SIGN
00A3		pound	POUND SIGN

UNIC	6862.2	SGML	Unicode character name
00A4		curren	CURRENCY SIGN
00A5		yen	YEN SIGN
00A6		brvbar	BROKEN VERTICAL BAR
00A7		sect	SECTION SIGN
00A8		die,Dot	SPACING DIAERESIS
00A8		uml	SPACING DIAERESIS
00A9		copy	COPYRIGHT SIGN
00AA		ordf	FEMININE ORDINAL INDICATOR
00AB		laquo	LEFT POINTING GUILLEMET
00AC	07.05	not	NOT SIGN
00AD		shy	SOFT HYPHEN
00AE		reg	REGISTERED TRADE MARK SIGN
00AF		macr	SPACING MACRON
00B0	03.12	deg	DEGREE SIGN
00B1	03.01	plusmn	PLUS-OR-MINUS SIGN
00B2		sup2	SUPERSCRIPT DIGIT TWO
00B3		sup3	SUPERSCRIPT DIGIT THREE
00B4		acute	SPACING ACUTE
00B5		micro	MICRO SIGN
00B6		para	PARAGRAPH SIGN
00B7		middot	MIDDLE DOT
00B8		cedil	SPACING CEDILLA
00B9		sup1	SUPERSCRIPT DIGIT ONE
00BA		ordm	MASCULINE ORDINAL INDICATOR
00BB		raquo	RIGHT POINTING GUILLEMET
00BC		frac14	FRACTION ONE QUARTER
00BD		frac12	FRACTION ONE HALF
00BE		frac34	FRACTION THREE QUARTERS
00BF		iquest	INVERTED QUESTION MARK
00C0		Agrave	LATIN CAPITAL LETTER A GRAVE
00C1		Aacute	LATIN CAPITAL LETTER A ACUTE
00C2		Acirc	LATIN CAPITAL LETTER A CIRCUMFLEX
00C3		Atilde	LATIN CAPITAL LETTER A TILDE
00C4		Auml	LATIN CAPITAL LETTER A DIAERESIS
00C5		Aring	LATIN CAPITAL LETTER A RING
00C6		AElig	LATIN CAPITAL LETTER A E
00C7		Ccedil	LATIN CAPITAL LETTER C CEDILLA
00C8		Egrave	LATIN CAPITAL LETTER E GRAVE
00C9		Eacute	LATIN CAPITAL LETTER E ACUTE
00CA		Ecirc	LATIN CAPITAL LETTER E CIRCUMFLEX
00CB		Euml	LATIN CAPITAL LETTER E DIAERESIS
00CC		Igrave	LATIN CAPITAL LETTER I GRAVE
00CD		Iacute	LATIN CAPITAL LETTER I ACUTE
00CE		Icirc	LATIN CAPITAL LETTER I CIRCUMFLEX
00CF		Iuml	LATIN CAPITAL LETTER I DIAERESIS
00D0		ETH	LATIN CAPITAL LETTER ETH
00D1		Ntilde	LATIN CAPITAL LETTER N TILDE
00D2		Ograve	LATIN CAPITAL LETTER O GRAVE
00D3		Oacute	LATIN CAPITAL LETTER O ACUTE
00D4		Oacute	LATIN CAPITAL LETTER O CIRCUMFLEX
00D5		Otilde	LATIN CAPITAL LETTER O TILDE
00D6		Ouml	LATIN CAPITAL LETTER O DIAERESIS
00D7	03.00	times	MULTIPLICATION SIGN
00D8		Oslash	LATIN CAPITAL LETTER O SLASH
00D9		Ugrave	LATIN CAPITAL LETTER U GRAVE
00DA		Uacute	LATIN CAPITAL LETTER U ACUTE

UNIC	6862.2	SGML	Unicode character name
00DB		Ucirc	LATIN CAPITAL LETTER U CIRCUMFLEX
00DC		Uuml	LATIN CAPITAL LETTER U DIAERESIS
00DD		Yacute	LATIN CAPITAL LETTER Y ACUTE
00DE		THORN	LATIN CAPITAL LETTER THORN
00DF		szlig	LATIN SMALL LETTER SHARP S
00E0		agrave	LATIN SMALL LETTER A GRAVE
00E1		aacute	LATIN SMALL LETTER A ACUTE
00E2		acirc	LATIN SMALL LETTER A CIRCUMFLEX
00E3		atilde	LATIN SMALL LETTER A TILDE
00E4		auml	LATIN SMALL LETTER A DIAERESIS
00E5		aring	LATIN SMALL LETTER A RING
00E6		aelig	LATIN SMALL LETTER A E
00E7		ccedil	LATIN SMALL LETTER C CEDILLA
00E8		egrave	LATIN SMALL LETTER E GRAVE
00E9		eacute	LATIN SMALL LETTER E ACUTE
00EA		ecirc	LATIN SMALL LETTER E CIRCUMFLEX
00EB		euml	LATIN SMALL LETTER E DIAERESIS
00EC		igrave	LATIN SMALL LETTER I GRAVE
00ED		iacute	LATIN SMALL LETTER I ACUTE
00EE		icirc	LATIN SMALL LETTER I CIRCUMFLEX
00EF		iuml	LATIN SMALL LETTER I DIAERESIS
00F0		eth	LATIN SMALL LETTER ETH
00F1		ntilde	LATIN SMALL LETTER N TILDE
00F2		ograve	LATIN SMALL LETTER O GRAVE
00F3		oacute	LATIN SMALL LETTER O ACUTE
00F4		ocirc	LATIN SMALL LETTER O CIRCUMFLEX
00F5		otilde	LATIN SMALL LETTER O TILDE
00F6		ouml	LATIN SMALL LETTER O DIAERESIS
00F7	04.00	divide	DIVISION SIGN
00F8		oslash	LATIN SMALL LETTER O SLASH
00F9		ugrave	LATIN SMALL LETTER U GRAVE
00FA		uacute	LATIN SMALL LETTER U ACUTE
00FB		ucirc	LATIN SMALL LETTER U CIRCUMFLEX
00FC		uuml	LATIN SMALL LETTER U DIAERESIS
00FD		yacute	LATIN SMALL LETTER Y ACUTE
00FE		thorn	LATIN SMALL LETTER THORN
00FF		yuml	LATIN SMALL LETTER Y DIAERESIS
0100		Amacr	LATIN CAPITAL LETTER A MACRON
0101		amacr	LATIN SMALL LETTER A MACRON
0102		Abreve	LATIN CAPITAL LETTER A BREVE
0103		abreve	LATIN SMALL LETTER A BREVE
0104		Aogon	LATIN CAPITAL LETTER A OGONEK
0105		aogon	LATIN SMALL LETTER A OGONEK
0106		Cacute	LATIN CAPITAL LETTER C ACUTE
0107		cacute	LATIN SMALL LETTER C ACUTE
0108		Ccirc	LATIN CAPITAL LETTER C CIRCUMFLEX
0109		ccirc	LATIN SMALL LETTER C CIRCUMFLEX
010A		Cdot	LATIN CAPITAL LETTER C DOT
010B		cdot	LATIN SMALL LETTER C DOT
010C		Ccaron	LATIN CAPITAL LETTER C HACEK
010D		ccaron	LATIN SMALL LETTER C HACEK
010E		Dcaron	LATIN CAPITAL LETTER D HACEK
010F		dcaron	LATIN SMALL LETTER D HACEK
0110		Dstrok	LATIN CAPITAL LETTER D BAR
0111		dstrok	LATIN SMALL LETTER D BAR
0112		Emacr	LATIN CAPITAL LETTER E MACRON

0113		emacr	LATIN SMALL LETTER E MACRON
0116		Edot	LATIN CAPITAL LETTER E DOT
0117		edot	LATIN SMALL LETTER E DOT
0118		Eogon	LATIN CAPITAL LETTER E OGONEK
0119		eogon	LATIN SMALL LETTER E OGONEK
011A		Ecaron	LATIN CAPITAL LETTER E HACEK
011B		ecaron	LATIN SMALL LETTER E HACEK
011C		Gcirc	LATIN CAPITAL LETTER G CIRCUMFLEX
011D		gcirc	LATIN SMALL LETTER G CIRCUMFLEX
011E		Gbreve	LATIN CAPITAL LETTER G BREVE
011F		gbreve	LATIN SMALL LETTER G BREVE
0120		Gdot	LATIN CAPITAL LETTER G DOT
0121		gdot	LATIN SMALL LETTER G DOT
0122		Gcedil	LATIN CAPITAL LETTER G CEDILLA
0123		gacute	LATIN SMALL LETTER G CEDILLA
0124		Hcirc	LATIN CAPITAL LETTER H CIRCUMFLEX
0125		hcirc	LATIN SMALL LETTER H CIRCUMFLEX
0126		Hstrok	LATIN CAPITAL LETTER H BAR
0127		hstrok	LATIN SMALL LETTER H BAR
0128		Itilde	LATIN CAPITAL LETTER I TILDE
0129		itilde	LATIN SMALL LETTER I TILDE
012A		Imacr	LATIN CAPITAL LETTER I MACRON
012B		imacr	LATIN SMALL LETTER I MACRON
012E		Iogon	LATIN CAPITAL LETTER I OGONEK
012F		iogon	LATIN SMALL LETTER I OGONEK
0130		Idot	LATIN CAPITAL LETTER I DOT
0131		inodot	LATIN SMALL LETTER DOTLESS I
0132		IJlig	LATIN CAPITAL LETTER I J
0133		ijlig	LATIN SMALL LETTER I J
0134		Jcirc	LATIN CAPITAL LETTER J CIRCUMFLEX
0135		jcirc	LATIN SMALL LETTER J CIRCUMFLEX
0136		Kcedil	LATIN CAPITAL LETTER K CEDILLA
0137		kcedil	LATIN SMALL LETTER K CEDILLA
0138		kgreen	LATIN SMALL LETTER KRA
0139		Lacute	LATIN CAPITAL LETTER L ACUTE
013A		lacute	LATIN SMALL LETTER L ACUTE
013B		Lcedil	LATIN CAPITAL LETTER L CEDILLA
013C		lcedil	LATIN SMALL LETTER L CEDILLA
013D		Lcaron	LATIN CAPITAL LETTER L HACEK
013E		lcaron	LATIN SMALL LETTER L HACEK
013F		Lmidot	LATIN CAPITAL LETTER L WITH MIDDLE DOT
0140		lmidot	LATIN SMALL LETTER L WITH MIDDLE DOT
0141		Lstrok	LATIN CAPITAL LETTER L SLASH
0142		lstrok	LATIN SMALL LETTER L SLASH
0143		Nacute	LATIN CAPITAL LETTER N ACUTE
0144		nacute	LATIN SMALL LETTER N ACUTE
0145		Ncedil	LATIN CAPITAL LETTER N CEDILLA
0146		ncedil	LATIN SMALL LETTER N CEDILLA
0147		Ncaron	LATIN CAPITAL LETTER N HACEK
0148		ncaron	LATIN SMALL LETTER N HACEK
0149		napos	LATIN SMALL LETTER APOSTROPHE N
014A		ENG	LATIN CAPITAL LETTER ENG
014B		eng	LATIN SMALL LETTER ENG
014C		Omacr	LATIN CAPITAL LETTER O MACRON
014D		omacr	LATIN SMALL LETTER O MACRON
0150		Odblac	LATIN CAPITAL LETTER O DOUBLE ACUTE

UNIC	6862.2	SGML	Unicode character name
0151		odblac	LATIN SMALL LETTER O DOUBLE ACUTE
0152		OElig	LATIN CAPITAL LETTER O E
0153		oelig	LATIN SMALL LETTER O E
0154		Racute	LATIN CAPITAL LETTER R ACUTE
0155		racute	LATIN SMALL LETTER R ACUTE
0156		Rcedil	LATIN CAPITAL LETTER R CEDILLA
0157		rcedil	LATIN SMALL LETTER R CEDILLA
0158		Rcaron	LATIN CAPITAL LETTER R HACEK
0159		rcaron	LATIN SMALL LETTER R HACEK
015A		Sacute	LATIN CAPITAL LETTER S ACUTE
015B		sacute	LATIN SMALL LETTER S ACUTE
015C		Scirc	LATIN CAPITAL LETTER S CIRCUMFLEX
015D		scirc	LATIN SMALL LETTER S CIRCUMFLEX
015E		Scedil	LATIN CAPITAL LETTER S CEDILLA
015F		scedil	LATIN SMALL LETTER S CEDILLA
0160		Scaron	LATIN CAPITAL LETTER S HACEK
0161		scaron	LATIN SMALL LETTER S HACEK
0162		Tcedil	LATIN CAPITAL LETTER T CEDILLA
0163		tcedil	LATIN SMALL LETTER T CEDILLA
0164		Tcaron	LATIN CAPITAL LETTER T HACEK
0165		tcaron	LATIN SMALL LETTER T HACEK
0166		Tstrok	LATIN CAPITAL LETTER T BAR
0167		tstrok	LATIN SMALL LETTER T BAR
0168		Utilde	LATIN CAPITAL LETTER U TILDE
0169		utilde	LATIN SMALL LETTER U TILDE
016A		Umacr	LATIN CAPITAL LETTER U MACRON
016B		umacr	LATIN SMALL LETTER U MACRON
016C		Ubreve	LATIN CAPITAL LETTER U BREVE
016D		ubreve	LATIN SMALL LETTER U BREVE
016E		Uring	LATIN CAPITAL LETTER U RING
016F		uring	LATIN SMALL LETTER U RING
0170		Udblac	LATIN CAPITAL LETTER U DOUBLE ACUTE
0171		udblac	LATIN SMALL LETTER U DOUBLE ACUTE
0172		Uogon	LATIN CAPITAL LETTER U OGONEK
0173		uogon	LATIN SMALL LETTER U OGONEK
0174		Wcirc	LATIN CAPITAL LETTER W CIRCUMFLEX
0175		wcirc	LATIN SMALL LETTER W CIRCUMFLEX
0176		Ycirc	LATIN CAPITAL LETTER Y CIRCUMFLEX
0177		ycirc	LATIN SMALL LETTER Y CIRCUMFLEX
0178		Yuml	LATIN CAPITAL LETTER Y DIAERESIS
0179		Zacute	LATIN CAPITAL LETTER Z ACUTE
017A		zacute	LATIN SMALL LETTER Z ACUTE
017B		Zdot	LATIN CAPITAL LETTER Z DOT
017C		zdot	LATIN SMALL LETTER Z DOT
017D		Zcaron	LATIN CAPITAL LETTER Z HACEK
017E		zcaron	LATIN SMALL LETTER Z HACEK
0192		fnof	LATIN SMALL LETTER SCRIPT F
02BC		apos	MODIFIER LETTER APOSTROPHE
02C7		caron	MODIFIER LETTER HACEK
02D8		breve	SPACING BREVE
02D9		dot	SPACING DOT ABOVE
02DA		ring	SPACING RING ABOVE
02DB		ogon	SPACING OGONEK
02DC		tilde	SPACING TILDE
02DD		dblac	SPACING DOUBLE ACUTE
0302	02.12		NON-SPACING CIRCUMFLEX

UNIC	6862.2	SGML	Unicode character name
0307	02.09		NON-SPACING DOT ABOVE
0308	02.10		NON-SPACING DIAERESIS
030C	02.13		NON-SPACING HACEK
0336	02.04		NON-SPACING LONG BAR OVERLAY
0338	02.01		NON-SPACING LONG SLASH OVERLAY
0386		Aacgr	GREEK CAPITAL LETTER ALPHA TONOS
0388		Eacgr	GREEK CAPITAL LETTER EPSILON TONOS
0389		EEacgr	GREEK CAPITAL LETTER ETA TONOS
038A		Iacgr	GREEK CAPITAL LETTER IOTA TONOS
038C		Oacgr	GREEK CAPITAL LETTER OMICRON TONOS
038E		Uacgr	GREEK CAPITAL LETTER UPSILON TONOS
038F		OHacgr	GREEK CAPITAL LETTER OMEGA TONOS
0390		idiagr	GREEK SMALL LETTER IOTA DIAERESIS TONOS
0391		Agr	GREEK CAPITAL LETTER ALPHA
0392		Bgr	GREEK CAPITAL LETTER BETA
0393		Ggr,Gamma	GREEK CAPITAL LETTER GAMMA
0394		Dgr,Delta	GREEK CAPITAL LETTER DELTA
0395		Egr	GREEK CAPITAL LETTER EPSILON
0396		Zgr	GREEK CAPITAL LETTER ZETA
0397		EEgr	GREEK CAPITAL LETTER ETA
0398		THgr,Theta	GREEK CAPITAL LETTER THETA
0399		Igr	GREEK CAPITAL LETTER IOTA
039A		Kgr	GREEK CAPITAL LETTER KAPPA
039B		Lgr,Lambda	GREEK CAPITAL LETTER LAMBDA
039C		Mgr	GREEK CAPITAL LETTER MU
039D		Ngr	GREEK CAPITAL LETTER NU
039E		Xgr,Xi	GREEK CAPITAL LETTER XI
039F		Ogr	GREEK CAPITAL LETTER OMICRON
03A0		Pgr,Pi	GREEK CAPITAL LETTER PI
03A1		Rgr	GREEK CAPITAL LETTER RHO
03A3		Sgr,Sigma	GREEK CAPITAL LETTER SIGMA
03A4		Tgr	GREEK CAPITAL LETTER TAU
03A5		Ugr,Upsi	GREEK CAPITAL LETTER UPSILON
03A6		PHgr,Phi	GREEK CAPITAL LETTER PHI
03A7		KHgr	GREEK CAPITAL LETTER CHI
03A8		PSgr,Psi	GREEK CAPITAL LETTER PSI
03A9		OHgr,Omega	GREEK CAPITAL LETTER OMEGA
03AA		Idigr	GREEK CAPITAL LETTER IOTA DIAERESIS
03AB		Udigr	GREEK CAPITAL LETTER UPSILON DIAERESIS
03AC		aacgr	GREEK SMALL LETTER ALPHA TONOS
03AD		eacgr	GREEK SMALL LETTER EPSILON TONOS
03AE		eeacgr	GREEK SMALL LETTER ETA TONOS
03AF		iacgr	GREEK SMALL LETTER IOTA TONOS
03B0		udiagr	GREEK SMALL LETTER UPSILON DIAERESIS TONOS
03B1		agr,alpha	GREEK SMALL LETTER ALPHA
03B2		bgr,beta	GREEK SMALL LETTER BETA
03B3		ggr,gamma	GREEK SMALL LETTER GAMMA
03B4		dgr,delta	GREEK SMALL LETTER DELTA
03B5		egr,epsi	GREEK SMALL LETTER EPSILON
03B6		zgr,zeta	GREEK SMALL LETTER ZETA
03B7		eegr,eta	GREEK SMALL LETTER ETA
03B8		thetas	GREEK SMALL LETTER THETA
03B8		thgr	GREEK SMALL LETTER THETA
03B9		igr,iota	GREEK SMALL LETTER IOTA
03BA		kgr,kappa	GREEK SMALL LETTER KAPPA
03BB		lgr,lambda	GREEK SMALL LETTER LAMBDA

UNIC	6862.2	SGML	Unicode character name
03BC		mgr,mu	GREEK SMALL LETTER MU
03BD		ngr,nu	GREEK SMALL LETTER NU
03BE		xgr,xi	GREEK SMALL LETTER XI
03BF		ogr	GREEK SMALL LETTER OMICRON
03C0		pgr,pi	GREEK SMALL LETTER PI
03C1		rgr,rho	GREEK SMALL LETTER RHO
03C2		sfgr,sigmav	GREEK SMALL LETTER FINAL SIGMA
03C3		sgr,sigma	GREEK SMALL LETTER SIGMA
03C4		tgr,tau	GREEK SMALL LETTER TAU
03C5		ugr,upsi	GREEK SMALL LETTER UPSILON
03C6		phgr,phis	GREEK SMALL LETTER PHI
03C7		khgr,chi	GREEK SMALL LETTER CHI
03C8		psgr,psi	GREEK SMALL LETTER PSI
03C9		ohgr,omega	GREEK SMALL LETTER OMEGA
03CA		idigr	GREEK SMALL LETTER IOTA DIAERESIS
03CB		udigr	GREEK SMALL LETTER UPSILON DIAERESIS
03CC		oacgr	GREEK SMALL LETTER OMICRON TONOS
03CD		uacgr	GREEK SMALL LETTER UPSILON TONOS
03CE		ohacgr	GREEK SMALL LETTER OMEGA TONOS
03D1		thetav	GREEK SMALL LETTER SCRIPT THETA
03D5		phiv	GREEK SMALL LETTER SCRIPT PHI
03D6		piv	GREEK SMALL LETTER OMEGA PI
03DD		gammad	GREEK SMALL LETTER DIGAMMA
03F0		kappav	GREEK SMALL LETTER SCRIPT KAPPA
03F1		rhov	GREEK SMALL LETTER TAILED RHO
0401		IOcy	CYRILLIC CAPITAL LETTER IO
0402		DJcy	CYRILLIC CAPITAL LETTER DJE
0403		GJcy	CYRILLIC CAPITAL LETTER GJE
0404		Jukcy	CYRILLIC CAPITAL LETTER E
0405		DScy	CYRILLIC CAPITAL LETTER DZE
0406		Iukcy	CYRILLIC CAPITAL LETTER I
0407		YIcy	CYRILLIC CAPITAL LETTER YI
0408		Jsercy	CYRILLIC CAPITAL LETTER JE
0409		LJcy	CYRILLIC CAPITAL LETTER LJE
040A		NJcy	CYRILLIC CAPITAL LETTER NJE
040B		TSHcy	CYRILLIC CAPITAL LETTER TSHE
040C		KJcy	CYRILLIC CAPITAL LETTER KJE
040E		Ubrcy	CYRILLIC CAPITAL LETTER SHORT U
040F		DZcy	CYRILLIC CAPITAL LETTER DZHE
0410		Acy	CYRILLIC CAPITAL LETTER A
0411		Bcy	CYRILLIC CAPITAL LETTER BE
0412		Vcy	CYRILLIC CAPITAL LETTER VE
0413		Gcy	CYRILLIC CAPITAL LETTER GE
0414		dcy	CYRILLIC CAPITAL LETTER DE
0415		IEcy	CYRILLIC CAPITAL LETTER IE
0416		ZHcy	CYRILLIC CAPITAL LETTER ZHE
0417		Zcy	CYRILLIC CAPITAL LETTER ZE
0418		Icy	CYRILLIC CAPITAL LETTER II
0419		Jcy	CYRILLIC CAPITAL LETTER SHORT II
041A		Kcy	CYRILLIC CAPITAL LETTER KA
041B		Lcy	CYRILLIC CAPITAL LETTER EL
041C		Mcy	CYRILLIC CAPITAL LETTER EM
041D		Ncy	CYRILLIC CAPITAL LETTER EN
041E		Ocy	CYRILLIC CAPITAL LETTER O
041F		Pcy	CYRILLIC CAPITAL LETTER PE
0420		Rcy	CYRILLIC CAPITAL LETTER ER

UNIC	6862.2	SGML	Unicode character name
0421		Scy	CYRILLIC CAPITAL LETTER ES
0422		Tcy	CYRILLIC CAPITAL LETTER TE
0423		Ucy	CYRILLIC CAPITAL LETTER U
0424		Fcy	CYRILLIC CAPITAL LETTER EF
0425		KHcy	CYRILLIC CAPITAL LETTER KHA
0426		TScy	CYRILLIC CAPITAL LETTER TSE
0427		CHcy	CYRILLIC CAPITAL LETTER CHE
0428		SHcy	CYRILLIC CAPITAL LETTER SHA
0429		SHCHcy	CYRILLIC CAPITAL LETTER SHCHA
042A		HARDcy	CYRILLIC CAPITAL LETTER HARD SIGN
042B		Ycy	CYRILLIC CAPITAL LETTER YERI
042C		SOFTcy	CYRILLIC CAPITAL LETTER SOFT SIGN
042D		Ecy	CYRILLIC CAPITAL LETTER REVERSED E
042E		YUcy	CYRILLIC CAPITAL LETTER IU
042F		YAcy	CYRILLIC CAPITAL LETTER IA
0430		acy	CYRILLIC SMALL LETTER A
0431		bcy	CYRILLIC SMALL LETTER BE
0432		vcy	CYRILLIC SMALL LETTER VE
0433		gcy	CYRILLIC SMALL LETTER GE
0434		dcy	CYRILLIC SMALL LETTER DE
0435		iecy	CYRILLIC SMALL LETTER IE
0436		zhcy	CYRILLIC SMALL LETTER ZHE
0437		zcy	CYRILLIC SMALL LETTER ZE
0438		icy	CYRILLIC SMALL LETTER II
0439		jcy	CYRILLIC SMALL LETTER SHORT II
043A		kcy	CYRILLIC SMALL LETTER KA
043B		lcy	CYRILLIC SMALL LETTER EL
043C		mcy	CYRILLIC SMALL LETTER EM
043D		ncy	CYRILLIC SMALL LETTER EN
043E		ocy	CYRILLIC SMALL LETTER O
043F		pcy	CYRILLIC SMALL LETTER PE
0440		rcy	CYRILLIC SMALL LETTER ER
0441		scy	CYRILLIC SMALL LETTER ES
0442		tcy	CYRILLIC SMALL LETTER TE
0443		ucy	CYRILLIC SMALL LETTER U
0444		fcy	CYRILLIC SMALL LETTER EF
0445		khcy	CYRILLIC SMALL LETTER KHA
0446		tscy	CYRILLIC SMALL LETTER TSE
0447		chcy	CYRILLIC SMALL LETTER CHE
0448		shcy	CYRILLIC SMALL LETTER SHA
0449		shchcy	CYRILLIC SMALL LETTER SHCHA
044A		hardcy	CYRILLIC SMALL LETTER HARD SIGN
044B		ycy	CYRILLIC SMALL LETTER YERI
044C		softcy	CYRILLIC SMALL LETTER SOFT SIGN
044D		ecy	CYRILLIC SMALL LETTER REVERSED E
044E		yucy	CYRILLIC SMALL LETTER IU
044F		yacy	CYRILLIC SMALL LETTER IA
0451		iocy	CYRILLIC SMALL LETTER IO
0452		djcy	CYRILLIC SMALL LETTER DJE
0453		gjcy	CYRILLIC SMALL LETTER GJE
0454		jukcy	CYRILLIC SMALL LETTER E
0455		dscy	CYRILLIC SMALL LETTER DZE
0456		iukcy	CYRILLIC SMALL LETTER I
0457		yicy	CYRILLIC SMALL LETTER YI
0458		jsercy	CYRILLIC SMALL LETTER JE
0459		ljcy	CYRILLIC SMALL LETTER LJE

UNIC	6862.2	SGML	Unicode character name
045A		njcy	CYRILLIC SMALL LETTER NJE
045B		tshcy	CYRILLIC SMALL LETTER TSHE
045C		kjcy	CYRILLIC SMALL LETTER KJE
045E		ubrcy	CYRILLIC SMALL LETTER SHORT U
045F		dzcy	CYRILLIC SMALL LETTER DZHE
2002		ensp	EN SPACE
2003		emsp	EM SPACE
2004		emsp13	THREE-PER-EM SPACE
2005		emsp14	FOUR-PER-EM SPACE
2007		numsp	FIGURE SPACE
2008		puncsp	PUNCTUATION SPACE
2009		thinsp	THIN SPACE
200A		hairsp	HAIR SPACE
2010		dash	HYPHEN
2013		ndash	EN DASH
2014		mdash	EM DASH
2015		horbar	QUOTATION DASH
2016	15.00	Verbar	DOUBLE VERTICAL BAR
2018		lsquo	SINGLE TURNED COMMA QUOTATION MARK
2018		rsquor	SINGLE TURNED COMMA QUOTATION MARK
2019		rsquo	SINGLE COMMA QUOTATION MARK
201A		lsquor	LOW SINGLE COMMA QUOTATION MARK
201C		ldquo	DOUBLE TURNED COMMA QUOTATION MARK
201C		rdquor	DOUBLE TURNED COMMA QUOTATION MARK
201D		rdquo	DOUBLE COMMA QUOTATION MARK
201E		ldquor	LOW DOUBLE COMMA QUOTATION MARK
2020		dagger	DAGGER
2021		Dagger	DOUBLE DAGGER
2022		bull	BULLET
2025		nldr	TWO DOT LEADER
2026		hellip	HORIZONTAL ELLIPSIS
2026		mldr	HORIZONTAL ELLIPSIS
2030	04.12	permil	PER MILLE SIGN
2032	07.00	prime	PRIME
2032		vprime	PRIME
2033	07.01	Prime	DOUBLE PRIME
2034	07.02	tprime	TRIPLE PRIME
2035		bprime	REVERSED PRIME
2041		caret	CARET INSERTION POINT
2043		hybull	HYPHEN BULLET
20D2	02.02		NON-SPACING LONG VERTICAL BAR OVERLAY
20D3	02.03		NON-SPACING SHORT VERTICAL BAR OVERLAY
20D4	02.08		NON-SPACING ANTICLOCKWISE ARROW ABOVE
20D5	02.15		NON-SPACING CLOCKWISE ARROW ABOVE
20D6	02.11		NON-SPACING LEFT ARROW ABOVE
20D7	02.14		NON-SPACING RIGHT ARROW ABOVE
20D8	02.05		NON-SPACING RING OVERLAY
20D9	02.07		NON-SPACING CLOCKWISE RING OVERLAY
20DA	02.06		NON-SPACING ANTICLOCKWISE RING OVERLAY
20DB		tdot	NON-SPACING THREE DOTS ABOVE
20DC		DotDot	NON-SPACING FOUR DOTS ABOVE
2105		incare	CARE OF
210B		hamilt	SCRIPT H
210E	07.06		PLANCK CONSTANT
210F	07.12	planck	PLANCK CONSTANT OVER 2 PI
2111		image	BLACK-LETTER I

UNIC	6862.2	SGML	Unicode character name
2112		lagran	SCRIPT L
2113		ell	SCRIPT SMALL L
2116		numero	NUMERO
2117		copysr	SOUND RECORDING COPYRIGHT
2118	17.13	weierp	SCRIPT P
211C		real	BLACK-LETTER R
211E	17.14	rx	PRESCRIPTION TAKE
2122		trade	TRADEMARK
2126		ohm	OHM
2129	17.12		TURNED GREEK SMALL LETTER IOTA
212B		angst	ANGSTROM UNIT
212C		bernou	SCRIPT B
2133		phmmat	SCRIPT M
2134		order	SCRIPT SMALL O
2135	07.13	aleph	FIRST TRANSFINITE CARDINAL
2136		beth	SECOND TRANSFINITE CARDINAL
2137		gimel	THIRD TRANSFINITE CARDINAL
2138		daleth	FOURTH TRANSFINITE CARDINAL
2153		frac13	FRACTION ONE THIRD
2154		frac23	FRACTION TWO THIRDS
2155		frac15	FRACTION ONE FIFTH
2156		frac25	FRACTION TWO FIFTHS
2157		frac35	FRACTION THREE FIFTHS
2158		frac45	FRACTION FOUR FIFTHS
2159		frac16	FRACTION ONE SIXTH
215A		frac56	FRACTION FIVE SIXTHS
215B		frac18	FRACTION ONE EIGHTH
215C		frac38	FRACTION THREE EIGHTHS
215D		frac58	FRACTION FIVE EIGHTHS
215E		frac78	FRACTION SEVEN EIGHTHS
2190		larr	LEFT ARROW
2191		uarr	UP ARROW
2192		rarr	RIGHT ARROW
2193		darr	DOWN ARROW
2194	05.10	harr	LEFT RIGHT ARROW
2195	06.10	varr	UP DOWN ARROW
2196	15.07	nwarr	UPPER LEFT ARROW
2197	16.07	nearr	UPPER RIGHT ARROW
2198	16.08	drarr	LOWER RIGHT ARROW
2199	15.08	dlarr	LOWER LEFT ARROW
219A	17.08	nlarr	LEFT ARROW WITH STROKE
219B	15.10	nrarr	RIGHT ARROW WITH STROKE
219D		rarrw	RIGHT WAVE ARROW
219E		Larr	LEFT TWO HEADED ARROW
21A0	16.10	Rarr	RIGHT TWO HEADED ARROW
21A2		larrtl	LEFT ARROW WITH TAIL
21A3		rarrtl	RIGHT ARROW WITH TAIL
21A6	05.12	map	RIGHT ARROW FROM BAR
21A9	16.11	larrhk	LEFT ARROW WITH HOOK
21AA	15.11	rarrhk	RIGHT ARROW WITH HOOK
21AB		larrlp	LEFT ARROW WITH LOOP
21AC		rarrlp	RIGHT ARROW WITH LOOP
21AD		harrw	LEFT RIGHT WAVE ARROW
21AE		nharr	LEFT RIGHT ARROW WITH STROKE
21B0		lsh	UP ARROW WITH TIP LEFT
21B1		rsh	UP ARROW WITH TIP RIGHT

UNIC	6862.2	SGML	Unicode character name
21B6	05.09	cularr	ANTICLOCKWISE TOP SEMICIRCLE ARROW
21B7	06.09	curarr	CLOCKWISE TOP SEMICIRCLE ARROW
21BA		olarr	ANTICLOCKWISE OPEN CIRCLE ARROW
21BB		orarr	CLOCKWISE OPEN CIRCLE ARROW
21BC		lharu	LEFT HARPOON WITH BARB UP
21BD		lhard	LEFT HARPOON WITH BARB DOWN
21BE	15.09	uharr	UP HARPOON WITH BARB RIGHT
21BF		uharl	UP HARPOON WITH BARB LEFT
21C0		rharu	RIGHT HARPOON WITH BARB UP
21C1		rhard	RIGHT HARPOON WITH BARB DOWN
21C2		dharr	DOWN HARPOON WITH BARB RIGHT
21C3		dharl	DOWN HARPOON WITH BARB LEFT
21C4	06.11	rlarr2	RIGHT ARROW OVER LEFT ARROW
21C5	06.12		UP ARROW LEFT OF DOWN ARROW
21C6	05.11	lrarr2	LEFT ARROW OVER RIGHT ARROW
21C7		larr2	LEFT PAIRED ARROWS
21C8		uarr2	UP PAIRED ARROWS
21C9		rarr2	RIGHT PAIRED ARROWS
21CA		darr2	DOWN PAIRED ARROWS
21CB		lrhar2	LEFT HARPOON OVER RIGHT HARPOON
21CC		rlhar2	RIGHT HARPOON OVER LEFT HARPOON
21CD		nlArr	LEFT DOUBLE ARROW WITH STROKE
21CE		nhArr	LEFT RIGHT DOUBLE ARROW WITH STROKE
21CF		nrArr	RIGHT DOUBLE ARROW WITH STROKE
21D0	05.14	lArr	LEFT DOUBLE ARROW
21D1	05.13	uArr	UP DOUBLE ARROW
21D2	06.14	rArr	RIGHT DOUBLE ARROW
21D3	06.13	dArr	DOWN DOUBLE ARROW
21D4	17.10	hArr,iff	LEFT RIGHT DOUBLE ARROW
21D5	17.11	vArr	UP DOWN DOUBLE ARROW
21DA		lAarr	LEFT TRIPLE ARROW
21DB		rAarr	RIGHT TRIPLE ARROW
21DC	17.09		LEFT SQUIGGLE ARROW
21DD	16.09	rarrw	RIGHT SQUIGGLE ARROW
2200	05.05	forall	FOR ALL
2201	05.06	comp	COMPLEMENT
2202	07.11	part	PARTIAL DIFFERENTIAL
2203	06.05	exist	THERE EXISTS
2204		nexist	THERE DOES NOT EXIST
2205	06.06	empty	EMPTY SET
2206	03.11		INCREMENT
2207	04.11	nabla	NABLA
2208	05.03	isin	ELEMENT OF
2209		notin	NOT AN ELEMENT OF
220A	15.06	epsis	SMALL ELEMENT OF
220B	06.03	ni	CONTAINS AS MEMBER
220D	16.06	bepsi	SMALL CONTAINS AS MEMBER
220E	16.13		END OF PROOF
220F	04.15	prod	N-ARY PRODUCT
2210		coprod	N-ARY COPRODUCT
2210		amalg	N-ARY COPRODUCT
2210		samalg	N-ARY COPRODUCT
2211	03.15	sum	N-ARY SUMMATION
2212	06.00	minus	MINUS SIGN
2213	04.01	mnplus	MINUS-OR-PLUS SIGN
2214	12.12	plusdo	DOT PLUS

UNIC	6862.2	SGML	Unicode character name
2216	16.02	setmn	SET MINUS
2218	07.14	compfn	RING OPERATOR
221A	06.15	radic	SQUARE ROOT
221D		vprop	PROPORTIONAL TO
221D	17.02	prop	PROPORTIONAL TO
221E	05.15	infin	INFINITY
221F	03.10	ang90	RIGHT ANGLE
2220	04.10	ang	ANGLE
2221		angmsd	MEASURED ANGLE
2222	16.15	angsph	SPHERICAL ANGLE
2223		mid	DIVIDES
2224	17.07	nmid	DOES NOT DIVIDE
2225	03.09	par	PARALLEL TO
2226	17.06	npar	NOT PARALLEL TO
2227	07.04	and	LOGICAL AND
2228	07.03	or	LOGICAL OR
2229	16.04	cap	INTERSECTION
222A	15.04	cup	UNION
222B	07.08	int	INTEGRAL
222C	07.09		DOUBLE INTEGRAL
222D	07.10		TRIPLE INTEGRAL
222E		conint	CONTOUR INTEGRAL
2234	12.05	there4	THEREFORE
2235	12.06	becaus	BECAUSE
2237	14.01		PROPORTION
2238	13.12		DOT MINUS
223A	17.01		GEOMETRIC PROPORTION
223B	12.14		HOMOTHETIC
223C		thksim	TILDE OPERATOR
223C	03.02	sim	TILDE OPERATOR
223D		bsim	REVERSED TILDE
223E	12.13		INVERTED LAZY S
2240		wreath	WREATH PRODUCT
2241		nsim	NOT TILDE
2243	04.02	sime	ASYMPTOTICALLY EQUAL TO
2244		nsime	NOT ASYMPTOTICALLY EQUAL TO
2245	04.03	cong	APPROXIMATELY EQUAL TO
2247		ncong	NEITHER APPROXIMATELY NOR ACTUALLY EQUAL TO
2248		thkap	ALMOST EQUAL TO
2248	03.03	ap	ALMOST EQUAL TO
2249		nap	NOT ALMOST EQUAL TO
224A	14.00	ape	ALMOST EQUAL OR EQUAL TO
224C		bcong	ALL EQUAL TO
224D		asymp	EQUIVALENT TO
224E	14.04	bump	GEOMETRICALLY EQUIVALENT TO
224F	04.04	bumpe	DIFFERENCE BETWEEN
2250	14.12	esdot	APPROACHES THE LIMIT
2251		eDot	GEOMETRICALLY EQUAL TO
2252	17.00	efDot	APPROXIMATELY EQUAL TO OR THE IMAGE OF
2253	13.01	erDot	IMAGE OF OR APPROXIMATELY EQUAL TO
2254		colone	COLON EQUAL
2255		ecolon	EQUAL COLON
2256		ecir	RING IN EQUAL TO
2257		cire	RING EQUAL TO
2259	13.13	wedgeq	ESTIMATES
225A	14.13		EQUIANGULAR TO

UNIC	6862.2	SGML	Unicode character name
225C		trie	DELTA EQUAL TO
2260	13.00	ne	NOT EQUAL TO
2261	03.04	equiv	IDENTICAL TO
2262		nequiv	NOT IDENTICAL TO
2264	03.05	le	LESS THAN OR EQUAL TO
2264		les	LESS THAN OR EQUAL TO
2265	04.05	ge	GREATER THAN OR EQUAL TO
2265		ges	GREATER THAN OR EQUAL TO
2266		lE	LESS THAN OVER EQUAL TO
2267		gE	GREATER THAN OVER EQUAL TO
2268		lnE	LESS THAN BUT NOT EQUAL TO
2268		lvnE	LESS THAN BUT NOT EQUAL TO
2269		gnE	GREATER THAN BUT NOT EQUAL TO
2269		gvnE	GREATER THAN BUT NOT EQUAL TO
226A		Lt	MUCH LESS THAN
226A	03.08		MUCH LESS THAN
226B		Gt	MUCH GREATER THAN
226B	04.08		MUCH GREATER THAN
226C		twixt	BETWEEN
226E		nlt	NOT LESS THAN
226F		ngt	NOT GREATER THAN
2270		nles	NEITHER LESS THAN NOR EQUAL TO
2270		nle	NEITHER LESS THAN NOR EQUAL TO
2271		nges	NEITHER GREATER THAN NOR EQUAL TO
2271		nge	NEITHER GREATER THAN NOR EQUAL TO
2272	03.07	lsim	LESS THAN OR EQUIVALENT TO
2273	04.07	gsim	GREATER THAN OR EQUIVALENT TO
2276	03.06	lg	LESS THAN OR GREATER THAN
2277	04.06	gl	GREATER THAN OR LESS THAN
227A	13.10	pr	PRECEDES
227B	14.10	sc	SUCCEEDS
227C	13.11	cupre	PRECEDES OR EQUAL TO
227D	14.11	sccue	SUCCEEDS OR EQUAL TO
227E	14.09	prsim	PRECEDES OR EQUIVALENT TO
227F	13.09	scsim	SUCCEEDS OR EQUIVALENT TO
2280		npr	DOES NOT PRECEDE
2281		nsc	DOES NOT SUCCEED
2282	05.01	sub	SUBSET OF
2282	15.05		SUBSET OF
2283	06.01	sup	SUPERSET OF
2283	16.05		SUPERSET OF
2284		nsub	NOT A SUBSET OF
2285		nsup	NOT A SUPERSET OF
2286	05.02	sube	SUBSET OF OR EQUAL TO
2287	06.02	supe	SUPERSET OF OR EQUAL TO
2288		nsube	NEITHER A SUBSET OF NOR EQUAL TO
2289		nsupe	NEITHER A SUPERSET OF NOR EQUAL TO
228A		subnE	SUBSET OF OR NOT EQUAL TO
228B		supnE	SUPERSET OF OR NOT EQUAL TO
228E		uplus	MULTISET UNION
228F	12.07	sqsub	SQUARE IMAGE OF
2290	12.08	sqsup	SQUARE ORIGINAL OF
2291		sqsube	SQUARE IMAGE OF OR EQUAL TO
2292		sqsupe	SQUARE ORIGINAL OF OR EQUAL TO
2293		sqcap	SQUARE CAP
2294		sqcup	SQUARE CUP

UNIC	6862.2	SGML	Unicode character name
2295	12.01	oplus	CIRCLED PLUS
2296	12.02	ominus	CIRCLED MINUS
2297	12.03	otimes	CIRCLED TIMES
2298		osol	CIRCLED DIVISION SLASH
2299	12.04	odot	CIRCLED DOT OPERATOR
229A		ocir	CIRCLED RING OPERATOR
229B		oast	CIRCLED ASTERISK OPERATOR
229D		odash	CIRCLED DASH
229E		plusb	SQUARED PLUS
229F		minusb	SQUARED MINUS
22A0		timesb	SQUARED TIMES
22A1		sdotb	SQUARED DOT OPERATOR
22A2	07.07	vdash	RIGHT TACK
22A3		dashv	LEFT TACK
22A4		top	DOWN TACK
22A5		bottom	UP TACK
22A5	04.09	perp	UP TACK
22A6	17.05		ASSERTION
22A7	17.04	models	MODELS
22A8		vDash	TRUE
22A9		Vdash	FORCES
22AA		Vvdash	TRIPLE VERTICAL BAR RIGHT TURNSTILE
22AC		nvdash	DOES NOT PROVE
22AD		nvDash	NOT TRUE
22AE		nVdash	DOES NOT FORCE
22AF		nVDash	NEGATED DOUBLE VERTICAL BAR DOUBLE RIGHT TURNSTILE
22B0	12.15		PRECEDES UNDER RELATION
22B2	13.08	vltri	NORMAL SUBGROUP OF
22B3		vrtri	CONTAINS AS NORMAL SUBGROUP
22B4	14.08	ltrie	NORMAL SUBGROUP OF OR EQUAL TO
22B5		rtrie	CONTAINS AS NORMAL SUBGROUP OR EQUAL TO
22B6	12.10		ORIGINAL OF
22B7	12.09		IMAGE OF
22B8		mumap	MULTIMAP
22B9	12.11		HERMITIAN CONJUGATE MATRIX
22BA		intcal	INTERCALATE
22BB		veebar	XOR
22BC		barwed	NAND
22C0	16.03		N-ARY LOGICAL AND
22C1	15.03		N-ARY LOGICAL OR
22C2	06.04		N-ARY INTERSECTION
22C3	05.04		N-ARY UNION
22C4		diam	DIAMOND OPERATOR
22C5		sdot	DOT OPERATOR
22C6		sstarf	STAR OPERATOR
22C7		divonx	DIVISION TIMES
22C8		bowtie	BOWTIE
22C9		ltimes	LEFT NORMAL FACTOR SEMIDIRECT PRODUCT
22CA		rtimes	RIGHT NORMAL FACTOR SEMIDIRECT PRODUCT
22CB		lthree	LEFT SEMIDIRECT PRODUCT
22CC		rthree	RIGHT SEMIDIRECT PRODUCT
22CD		bsime	REVERSED TILDE EQUALS
22CE		cuvee	CURLY LOGICAL OR
22CF		cuwed	CURLY LOGICAL AND
22D0		Sub	DOUBLE SUBSET
22D1		Sup	DOUBLE SUPERSET

UNIC	6862.2	SGML	Unicode character name
22D2		Cap	DOUBLE INTERSECTION
22D3		Cup	DOUBLE UNION
22D4		fork	PITCHFORK
22D6		ldot	LESS THAN WITH DOT
22D7		gsdot	GREATER THAN WITH DOT
22D8		Ll	VERY MUCH LESS THAN
22D9		Gg	VERY MUCH GREATER THAN
22DA		leg	LESS THAN EQUAL TO OR GREATER THAN
22DB		gel	GREATER THAN EQUAL TO OR LESS THAN
22DC		els	EQUAL TO OR LESS THAN
22DD		egs	EQUAL TO OR GREATER THAN
22DE		cuepr	EQUAL TO OR PRECEDES
22DF		cuesc	EQUAL TO OR SUCCEEDS
22E0		npre	DOES NOT PRECEDE OR EQUAL
22E1		nsce	DOES NOT SUCCEED OR EQUAL
22E6		lnsim	LESS THAN BUT NOT EQUIVALENT TO
22E7		gnsim	GREATER THAN BUT NOT EQUIVALENT TO
22E8		prnsim	PRECEDES BUT NOT EQUIVALENT TO
22E9		scnsim	SUCCEEDS BUT NOT EQUIVALENT TO
22EA		nltri	NOT NORMAL SUBGROUP OF
22EB		nrtri	DOES NOT CONTAIN AS NORMAL SUBGROUP
22EC		nltrie	NOT NORMAL SUBGROUP OF OR EQUAL TO
22ED		nrtrie	DOES NOT CONTAIN AS NORMAL SUBGROUP OR EQUAL
22EE	13.04	vellip	VERTICAL ELLIPSIS
2306		Barwed	PERSPECTIVE
2307	17.03		WAVY LINE
2308		lceil	LEFT CEILING
2309		rceil	RIGHT CEILING
230A		lfloor	LEFT FLOOR
230B		rfloor	RIGHT FLOOR
230C		drcrop	BOTTOM RIGHT CROP
230D		dlcrop	BOTTOM LEFT CROP
230E		urcrop	TOP RIGHT CROP
230F		ulcrop	TOP LEFT CROP
2315		telrec	TELEPHONE RECORDER
2316		target	POSITION INDICATOR
231C		ulcorn	TOP LEFT CORNER
231D		urcorn	TOP RIGHT CORNER
231E		dlcorn	BOTTOM LEFT CORNER
231F		drcorn	BOTTOM RIGHT CORNER
2322		frown	FROWN
2323		smile	SMILE
2329	03.13	lang	BRA
232A	04.13	rang	KET
2423		blank	OPEN BOX
24C8		oS	CIRCLED LATIN CAPITAL LETTER S
2500		boxh	FORMS LIGHT HORIZONTAL
2502		boxv	FORMS LIGHT VERTICAL
250C		boxdr	FORMS LIGHT DOWN AND RIGHT
2510		boxdl	FORMS LIGHT DOWN AND LEFT
2514		boxur	FORMS LIGHT UP AND RIGHT
2518		boxul	FORMS LIGHT UP AND LEFT
251C		boxvr	FORMS LIGHT VERTICAL AND RIGHT
2524		boxvl	FORMS LIGHT VERTICAL AND LEFT
252C		boxhd	FORMS LIGHT DOWN AND HORIZONTAL
2534		boxhu	FORMS LIGHT UP AND HORIZONTAL

UNIC	6862.2	SGML	Unicode character name
253C		boxvh	FORMS LIGHT VERTICAL AND HORIZONTAL
2550		boxH	FORMS DOUBLE HORIZONTAL
2551		boxV	FORMS DOUBLE VERTICAL
2552		boxdR	FORMS DOWN SINGLE AND RIGHT DOUBLE
2553		boxDr	FORMS DOWN DOUBLE AND RIGHT SINGLE
2554		boxDR	FORMS DOUBLE DOWN AND RIGHT
2555		boxdL	FORMS DOWN SINGLE AND LEFT DOUBLE
2556		boxDl	FORMS DOWN DOUBLE AND LEFT SINGLE
2557		boxDL	FORMS DOUBLE DOWN AND LEFT
2558		boxuR	FORMS UP SINGLE AND RIGHT DOUBLE
2559		boxUr	FORMS UP DOUBLE AND RIGHT SINGLE
255A		boxUR	FORMS DOUBLE UP AND RIGHT
255B		boxuL	FORMS UP SINGLE AND LEFT DOUBLE
255C		boxUl	FORMS UP DOUBLE AND LEFT SINGLE
255D		boxUL	FORMS DOUBLE UP AND LEFT
255E		boxvR	FORMS VERTICAL SINGLE AND RIGHT DOUBLE
255F		boxVr	FORMS VERTICAL DOUBLE AND RIGHT SINGLE
2560		boxVR	FORMS DOUBLE VERTICAL AND RIGHT
2561		boxvL	FORMS VERTICAL SINGLE AND LEFT DOUBLE
2562		boxVl	FORMS VERTICAL DOUBLE AND LEFT SINGLE
2563		boxVL	FORMS DOUBLE VERTICAL AND LEFT
2564		boxHd	FORMS DOWN SINGLE AND HORIZONTAL DOUBLE
2565		boxhD	FORMS DOWN DOUBLE AND HORIZONTAL SINGLE
2566		boxHD	FORMS DOUBLE DOWN AND HORIZONTAL
2567		boxHu	FORMS UP SINGLE AND HORIZONTAL DOUBLE
2568		boxhU	FORMS UP DOUBLE AND HORIZONTAL SINGLE
2569		boxHU	FORMS DOUBLE UP AND HORIZONTAL
256A		boxvH	FORMS VERTICAL SINGLE AND HORIZONTAL DOUBLE
256B		boxVh	FORMS VERTICAL DOUBLE AND HORIZONTAL SINGLE
256C		boxVH	FORMS DOUBLE VERTICAL AND HORIZONTAL
2571	15.01		FORMS LIGHT DIAGONAL UPPER RIGHT TO LOWER LEFT
2572	16.01		FORMS LIGHT DIAGONAL UPPER LEFT TO LOWER RIGHT
2580		uhblk	UPPER HALF BLOCK
2584		lhblk	LOWER HALF BLOCK
2588		block	FULL BLOCK
2591		blk14	LIGHT SHADE
2592		blk12	MEDIUM SHADE
2593		blk34	DARK SHADE
25A1	15.13	squ,square	WHITE SQUARE
25AA		squf	BLACK SMALL SQUARE
25AD	15.14	rect	WHITE RECTANGLE
25AE		marker	BLACK VERTICAL RECTANGLE
25B1	16.14		WHITE PARALLELOGRAM
25B3	13.15	xutri	WHITE UP POINTING TRIANGLE
25B4		utrif	BLACK UP POINTING SMALL TRIANGLE
25B5		utri	WHITE UP POINTING SMALL TRIANGLE
25B7	14.14		WHITE RIGHT POINTING TRIANGLE
25B8		rtrif	BLACK RIGHT POINTING SMALL TRIANGLE
25B9		rtri	WHITE RIGHT POINTING SMALL TRIANGLE
25BD	14.15	xdtri	WHITE DOWN POINTING TRIANGLE
25BE		dtrif	BLACK DOWN POINTING SMALL TRIANGLE
25BF		dtri	WHITE DOWN POINTING SMALL TRIANGLE
25C1	13.14		WHITE LEFT POINTING TRIANGLE
25C2		ltrif	BLACK LEFT POINTING SMALL TRIANGLE
25C3		ltri	WHITE LEFT POINTING SMALL TRIANGLE
25CA	15.15		LOZENGE

UNIC	6862.2	SGML	Unicode character name
25CB	15.12	cir	WHITE CIRCLE
25CB		xcirc	WHITE CIRCLE
25CF	16.12		BLACK CIRCLE
2605		starf	BLACK STAR
2606		star	WHITE STAR
260E		phone	BLACK TELEPHONE
2640		female	FEMALE SIGN
2642		male	MALE SIGN
2660		spades	BLACK SPADE SUIT
2661		hearts	WHITE HEART SUIT
2662		diams	WHITE DIAMOND SUIT
2663		clubs	BLACK CLUB SUIT
266A		sung	EIGHTH NOTE
266D		flat	FLAT
266E		natur	NATURAL
266F		sharp	SHARP
2713		check	CHECK MARK
2717		cross	BALLOT X
2720		malt	MALTESE CROSS
2726		lozf	BLACK FOUR POINTED STAR
2727		loz	WHITE FOUR POINTED STAR
2736		sextile	SIX POINTED BLACK STAR
3018	13.02		OPENING WHITE TORTOISE SHELL BRACKET
3019	14.02		CLOSING WHITE TORTOISE SHELL BRACKET
301A	03.14		OPENING WHITE SQUARE BRACKET
301B	04.14		CLOSING WHITE SQUARE BRACKET

SGML and ISO 6862.2 ligatures, glyphs, and glyph variants which are not encoded in Unicode:

		SGML
		fflig
		ffilig
		ffllig
		filig
		fllig
		fjlig
		jnodot
		spar
	16.00	smid
		nsmid
		nspar
		ssmile
		sfrown
		lap
		gap
		lnap
		gnap
		lEg
		gEl
		vsupne
		vsubne
		vsubnE
		vsupnE
		subne
		supne
		pre
		sce

prnE
scnE
prap
scap
prnap
scnap
xlArr
xrArr
xharr

6.2 Vendor Mapping Tables

This section includes mapping tables for character encoding schemes used by private vendors.

- Unicode value to Adobe Standard character encodings

- Unicode value to Apple Macintosh character sets

- Mappings for the Microsoft Windows code pages

- Unicode value to important IBM PC and EBCDIC code pages

The vendor mapping tables for DBCS code pages include the alphabetic sections of several Asian national standards: JIS X 0208, JIS X 0212, and the Korean standard KS C 5601.

Unicode Encoding to Adobe Standard Mappings

The following table is a mapping the Unicode encoding to four standard Adobe encoding vectors. An encoding vector is a PostScript® array object used to associate a character description (which might loosely be referred to as a glyph) in a PostScript font program with a character code. In other words, an encoding vector is a glyph encoding, not a character encoding. As a result, there are single Unicode values in this table mapped to more than one glyph (for example, U+00A9 COPYRIGHT SIGN), single glyphs encoded more than once in an encoding vector (for example, the glyph named *acute*), and several glyphs in StandardEncoding and Symbol which map to no corresponding Unicode value (for example, the glyphs named *fi* and *fl*).

The headings "StdEnc" and "ISOLatin1" refer to StandardEncoding and ISOLatin1Encoding, both of which are names associated with encoding vectors in systemdict, a dictionary object found in PostScript printers. Both StandardEncoding and ISOLatin1Encoding are documented in the *PostScript Language Reference Manual*, 2d edition, pp. 596–599 (the Red Book). "Symbol" and "ZapfDB" refer to encoding vectors in the Symbol and ITC Zapf Dingbats font programs found in PostScript printers. While Symbol is documented in the Red Book, pp. 604–606, ITC Zapf Dingbats is not. The table is ordered roughly per encoding vector; StdEnc first, ISOLatin1 second, etc.

UNIC	StdEnc	ISOLatin1	Symbol / ZapfDB	Adobe glyph name	Unicode character name
0020	20	20	20	space	SPACE
0021	21	21	21	exclam	EXCLAMATION MARK
0022	22	22		quotedbl	QUOTATION MARK
0023	23	23	23	numbersign	NUMBER SIGN
0024	24	24		dollar	DOLLAR SIGN
0025	25	25	25	percent	PERCENT SIGN
0026	26	26	26	ampersand	AMPERSAND
0027	A9			quotesingle	APOSTROPHE-QUOTE
0028	28	28	28	parenleft	OPENING PARENTHESIS
0029	29	29	29	parenright	CLOSING PARENTHESIS
002A	2A	2A		asterisk	ASTERISK
002B	2B	2B	2B	plus	PLUS SIGN
002C	2C	2C	2C	comma	COMMA
002D	2D	AD		hyphen	HYPHEN-MINUS
002D		2D		minus	HYPHEN-MINUS
002E	2E	2E	2E	period	PERIOD
002F	2F	2F	2F	slash	SLASH
0030	30	30	30	zero	DIGIT ZERO
0031	31	31	31	one	DIGIT ONE
0032	32	32	32	two	DIGIT TWO
0033	33	33	33	three	DIGIT THREE
0034	34	34	34	four	DIGIT FOUR
0035	35	35	35	five	DIGIT FIVE
0036	36	36	36	six	DIGIT SIX
0037	37	37	37	seven	DIGIT SEVEN
0038	38	38	38	eight	DIGIT EIGHT
0039	39	39	39	nine	DIGIT NINE
003A	3A	3A	3A	colon	COLON
003B	3B	3B	3B	semicolon	SEMICOLON

	ISOLatin1	ZapfDB			
UNIC	StdEnc		Symbol	Adobe glyph name	Unicode character name
003C	3C	3C	3C	less	LESS-THAN SIGN
003D	3D	3D	3D	equal	EQUALS SIGN
003E	3E	3E	3E	greater	GREATER-THAN SIGN
003F	3F	3F	3F	question	QUESTION MARK
0040	40	40		at	COMMERCIAL AT
0041	41	41		A	LATIN CAPITAL LETTER A
0042	42	42		B	LATIN CAPITAL LETTER B
0043	43	43		C	LATIN CAPITAL LETTER C
0044	44	44		D	LATIN CAPITAL LETTER D
0045	45	45		E	LATIN CAPITAL LETTER E
0046	46	46		F	LATIN CAPITAL LETTER F
0047	47	47		G	LATIN CAPITAL LETTER G
0048	48	48		H	LATIN CAPITAL LETTER H
0049	49	49		I	LATIN CAPITAL LETTER I
004A	4A	4A		J	LATIN CAPITAL LETTER J
004B	4B	4B		K	LATIN CAPITAL LETTER K
004C	4C	4C		L	LATIN CAPITAL LETTER L
004D	4D	4D		M	LATIN CAPITAL LETTER M
004E	4E	4E		N	LATIN CAPITAL LETTER N
004F	4F	4F		O	LATIN CAPITAL LETTER O
0050	50	50		P	LATIN CAPITAL LETTER P
0051	51	51		Q	LATIN CAPITAL LETTER Q
0052	52	52		R	LATIN CAPITAL LETTER R
0053	53	53		S	LATIN CAPITAL LETTER S
0054	54	54		T	LATIN CAPITAL LETTER T
0055	55	55		U	LATIN CAPITAL LETTER U
0056	56	56		V	LATIN CAPITAL LETTER V
0057	57	57		W	LATIN CAPITAL LETTER W
0058	58	58		X	LATIN CAPITAL LETTER X
0059	59	59		Y	LATIN CAPITAL LETTER Y
005A	5A	5A		Z	LATIN CAPITAL LETTER Z
005B	5B	5B	5B	bracketleft	OPENING SQUARE BRACKET
005C	5C	5C		backslash	BACKSLASH
005D	5D	5D	5D	bracketright	CLOSING SQUARE BRACKET
005E	5E	5E		asciicircum	SPACING CIRCUMFLEX
005F	5F	5F	5F	underscore	SPACING UNDERSCORE
0060	C1	91		grave	SPACING GRAVE
0061	61	61		a	LATIN SMALL LETTER A
0062	62	62		b	LATIN SMALL LETTER B
0063	63	63		c	LATIN SMALL LETTER C
0064	64	64		d	LATIN SMALL LETTER D
0065	65	65		e	LATIN SMALL LETTER E
0066	66	66		f	LATIN SMALL LETTER F
0067	67	67		g	LATIN SMALL LETTER G
0068	68	68		h	LATIN SMALL LETTER H
0069	69	69		i	LATIN SMALL LETTER I
006A	6A	6A		j	LATIN SMALL LETTER J
006B	6B	6B		k	LATIN SMALL LETTER K
006C	6C	6C		l	LATIN SMALL LETTER L
006D	6D	6D		m	LATIN SMALL LETTER M
006E	6E	6E		n	LATIN SMALL LETTER N
006F	6F	6F		o	LATIN SMALL LETTER O
0070	70	70		p	LATIN SMALL LETTER P
0071	71	71		q	LATIN SMALL LETTER Q
0072	72	72		r	LATIN SMALL LETTER R

UNIC	StdEnc	ZapfDB Symbol		Adobe glyph name	Unicode character name
0073	73	73		s	LATIN SMALL LETTER S
0074	74	74		t	LATIN SMALL LETTER T
0075	75	75		u	LATIN SMALL LETTER U
0076	76	76		v	LATIN SMALL LETTER V
0077	77	77		w	LATIN SMALL LETTER W
0078	78	78		x	LATIN SMALL LETTER X
0079	79	79		y	LATIN SMALL LETTER Y
007A	7A	7A		z	LATIN SMALL LETTER Z
007B	7B	7B	7B	braceleft	OPENING CURLY BRACKET
007C	7C	7C	7C	bar	VERTICAL BAR
007D	7D	7D	7D	braceright	CLOSING CURLY BRACKET
007E	7E	7E		asciitilde	TILDE
2019	27	27		quoteright	SINGLE COMMA QUOTATION MARK
2018	60	60		quoteleft	SINGLE TURNED COMMA QUOTATION MARK
00A1	A1	A1		exclamdown	INVERTED EXCLAMATION MARK
00A2	A2	A2		cent	CENT SIGN
00A3	A3	A3		sterling	POUND SIGN
2044	A4		A4	fraction	FRACTION SLASH
00A5	A5	A5		yen	YEN SIGN
0192	A6		A6	florin	LATIN SMALL LETTER SCRIPT F
00A7	A7	A7		section	SECTION SIGN
00A4	A8	A4		currency	CURRENCY SIGN
201C	AA			quotedblleft	DOUBLE TURNED COMMA QUOTATION MARK
00AB	AB	AB		guillemotleft	LEFT POINTING GUILLEMET
2039	AC			guilsinglleft	LEFT POINTING SINGLE GUILLEMET
203A	AD			guilsinglright	RIGHT POINTING SINGLE GUILLEMET
2013	B1			endash	EN DASH
2020	B2			dagger	DAGGER
2021	B3			daggerdbl	DOUBLE DAGGER
00B7	B4	B7		periodcentered	MIDDLE DOT
00B6	B6	B6		paragraph	PARAGRAPH SIGN
2022	B7		B7	bullet	BULLET
201A	B8			quotesinglbase	LOW SINGLE COMMA QUOTATION MARK
201E	B9			quotedblbase	LOW DOUBLE COMMA QUOTATION MARK
201D	BA			quotedblright	DOUBLE COMMA QUOTATION MARK
00BB	BB	BB		guillemotright	RIGHT POINTING GUILLEMET
2026	BC		BC	ellipsis	HORIZONTAL ELLIPSIS
2030	BD			perthousand	PER MILLE SIGN
00BF	BF	BF		questiondown	INVERTED QUESTION MARK
00B4	C2	92/B4		acute	SPACING ACUTE
02C6	C3	93		circumflex	MODIFIER LETTER CIRCUMFLEX
02DC	C4	94		tilde	SPACING TILDE
00AF	C5	95/AF		macron	SPACING MACRON
02D8	C6	96		breve	SPACING BREVE
02D9	C7	97		dotaccent	SPACING DOT ABOVE
00A8	C8	98/A8		dieresis	SPACING DIAERESIS
02DA	CA	9A		ring	SPACING RING ABOVE
00B8	CB	9B/B8		cedilla	SPACING CEDILLA
02DD	CD	9D		hungarumlaut	SPACING DOUBLE ACUTE
02DB	CE	9E		ogonek	SPACING OGONEK
02C7	CF	9F		caron	MODIFIER LETTER HACEK
2014	D0			emdash	EM DASH
00C6	E1	C6		AE	LATIN CAPITAL LETTER A E
00AA	E3	AA		ordfeminine	FEMININE ORDINAL INDICATOR
0141	E8			Lslash	LATIN CAPITAL LETTER L SLASH

		ISOLatin1	ZapfDB		
UNIC	StdEnc		Symbol	Adobe glyph name	Unicode character name
00D8	E9	D8		Oslash	LATIN CAPITAL LETTER O SLASH
0152	EA			OE	LATIN CAPITAL LETTER O E
00BA	EB	BA		ordmasculine	MASCULINE ORDINAL INDICATOR
00E6	F1	E6		ae	LATIN SMALL LETTER A E
0131	F5	90		dotlessi	LATIN SMALL LETTER DOTLESS I
0142	F8			lslash	LATIN SMALL LETTER L SLASH
00F8	F9	F8		oslash	LATIN SMALL LETTER O SLASH
0153	FA			oe	LATIN SMALL LETTER O E
00DF	FB	DF		germandbls	LATIN SMALL LETTER SHARP S
00A6		A6		brokenbar	BROKEN VERTICAL BAR
00A9		A9		copyright	COPYRIGHT SIGN
00A9			D3	copyrightserif	COPYRIGHT SIGN
00A9			E3	copyrightsans	COPYRIGHT SIGN
00AC		AC	D8	logicalnot	NOT SIGN
00AE		AE		registered	REGISTERED TRADE MARK SIGN
00AE			D2	registeredserif	REGISTERED TRADE MARK SIGN
00AE			E2	registeredsans	REGISTERED TRADE MARK SIGN
00B0		B0	B0	degree	DEGREE SIGN
00B1		B1	B1	plusminus	PLUS-OR-MINUS SIGN
00B2		B2		twosuperior	SUPERSCRIPT DIGIT TWO
00B3		B3		threesuperior	SUPERSCRIPT DIGIT THREE
00B5		B5		mu	MICRO SIGN
00B9		B9		onesuperior	SUPERSCRIPT DIGIT ONE
00BC		BC		onequarter	FRACTION ONE QUARTER
00BD		BD		onehalf	FRACTION ONE HALF
00BE		BE		threequarters	FRACTION THREE QUARTERS
00C0		C0		Agrave	LATIN CAPITAL LETTER A GRAVE
00C1		C1		Aacute	LATIN CAPITAL LETTER A ACUTE
00C2		C2		Acircumflex	LATIN CAPITAL LETTER A CIRCUMFLEX
00C3		C3		Atilde	LATIN CAPITAL LETTER A TILDE
00C4		C4		Adieresis	LATIN CAPITAL LETTER A DIAERESIS
00C5		C5		Aring	LATIN CAPITAL LETTER A RING
00C7		C7		Ccedilla	LATIN CAPITAL LETTER C CEDILLA
00C8		C8		Egrave	LATIN CAPITAL LETTER E GRAVE
00C9		C9		Eacute	LATIN CAPITAL LETTER E ACUTE
00CA		CA		Ecircumflex	LATIN CAPITAL LETTER E CIRCUMFLEX
00CB		CB		Edieresis	LATIN CAPITAL LETTER E DIAERESIS
00CC		CC		Igrave	LATIN CAPITAL LETTER I GRAVE
00CD		CD		Iacute	LATIN CAPITAL LETTER I ACUTE
00CE		CE		Icircumflex	LATIN CAPITAL LETTER I CIRCUMFLEX
00CF		CF		Idieresis	LATIN CAPITAL LETTER I DIAERESIS
00D0		D0		Eth	LATIN CAPITAL LETTER ETH
00D1		D1		Ntilde	LATIN CAPITAL LETTER N TILDE
00D2		D2		Ograve	LATIN CAPITAL LETTER O GRAVE
00D3		D3		Oacute	LATIN CAPITAL LETTER O ACUTE
00D4		D4		Ocircumflex	LATIN CAPITAL LETTER O CIRCUMFLEX
00D5		D5		Otilde	LATIN CAPITAL LETTER O TILDE
00D6		D6		Odieresis	LATIN CAPITAL LETTER O DIAERESIS
00D7		D7	B4	multiply	MULTIPLICATION SIGN
00D9		D9		Ugrave	LATIN CAPITAL LETTER U GRAVE
00DA		DA		Uacute	LATIN CAPITAL LETTER U ACUTE
00DB		DB		Ucircumflex	LATIN CAPITAL LETTER U CIRCUMFLEX
00DC		DC		Udieresis	LATIN CAPITAL LETTER U DIAERESIS
00DD		DD		Yacute	LATIN CAPITAL LETTER Y ACUTE
00DE		DE		Thorn	LATIN CAPITAL LETTER THORN

The Unicode Standard • Version 1.0

UNIC	ISOLatin1 StdEnc	ZapfDB Symbol	Adobe glyph name	Unicode character name
00E0	E0		agrave	LATIN SMALL LETTER A GRAVE
00E1	E1		aacute	LATIN SMALL LETTER A ACUTE
00E2	E2		acircumflex	LATIN SMALL LETTER A CIRCUMFLEX
00E3	E3		atilde	LATIN SMALL LETTER A TILDE
00E4	E4		adieresis	LATIN SMALL LETTER A DIAERESIS
00E5	E5		aring	LATIN SMALL LETTER A RING
00E7	E7		ccedilla	LATIN SMALL LETTER C CEDILLA
00E8	E8		egrave	LATIN SMALL LETTER E GRAVE
00E9	E9		eacute	LATIN SMALL LETTER E ACUTE
00EA	EA		ecircumflex	LATIN SMALL LETTER E CIRCUMFLEX
00EB	EB		edieresis	LATIN SMALL LETTER E DIAERESIS
00EC	EC		igrave	LATIN SMALL LETTER I GRAVE
00ED	ED		iacute	LATIN SMALL LETTER I ACUTE
00EE	EE		icircumflex	LATIN SMALL LETTER I CIRCUMFLEX
00EF	EF		idieresis	LATIN SMALL LETTER I DIAERESIS
00F0	F0		eth	LATIN SMALL LETTER ETH
00F1	F1		ntilde	LATIN SMALL LETTER N TILDE
00F2	F2		ograve	LATIN SMALL LETTER O GRAVE
00F3	F3		oacute	LATIN SMALL LETTER O ACUTE
00F4	F4		ocircumflex	LATIN SMALL LETTER O CIRCUMFLEX
00F5	F5		otilde	LATIN SMALL LETTER O TILDE
00F6	F6		odieresis	LATIN SMALL LETTER O DIAERESIS
00F7	F7	B8	divide	DIVISION SIGN
00F9	F9		ugrave	LATIN SMALL LETTER U GRAVE
00FA	FA		uacute	LATIN SMALL LETTER U ACUTE
00FB	FB		ucircumflex	LATIN SMALL LETTER U CIRCUMFLEX
00FC	FC		udieresis	LATIN SMALL LETTER U DIAERESIS
00FD	FD		yacute	LATIN SMALL LETTER Y ACUTE
00FE	FE		thorn	LATIN SMALL LETTER THORN
00FF	FF		ydieresis	LATIN SMALL LETTER Y DIAERESIS
2200		22	universal	FOR ALL
2203		24	existential	THERE EXISTS
220B		27	suchthat	CONTAINS AS MEMBER
2217		2A	asteriskmath	ASTERISK OPERATOR
2212		2D	minus	MINUS SIGN
2245		40	congruent	APPROXIMATELY EQUAL TO
2234		5C	therefore	THEREFORE
22A5		5E	perpendicular	UP TACK
203E		60	radicalex	SPACING OVERSCORE
223C		7E	similar	TILDE OPERATOR
0391		41	Alpha	GREEK CAPITAL LETTER ALPHA
0392		42	Beta	GREEK CAPITAL LETTER BETA
0393		47	Gamma	GREEK CAPITAL LETTER GAMMA
0394		44	Delta	GREEK CAPITAL LETTER DELTA
0395		45	Epsilon	GREEK CAPITAL LETTER EPSILON
0396		5A	Zeta	GREEK CAPITAL LETTER ZETA
0397		48	Eta	GREEK CAPITAL LETTER ETA
0398		51	Theta	GREEK CAPITAL LETTER THETA
0399		49	Iota	GREEK CAPITAL LETTER IOTA
039A		4B	Kappa	GREEK CAPITAL LETTER KAPPA
039B		4C	Lambda	GREEK CAPITAL LETTER LAMBDA
039C		4D	Mu	GREEK CAPITAL LETTER MU
039D		4E	Nu	GREEK CAPITAL LETTER NU
039E		58	Xi	GREEK CAPITAL LETTER XI
039F		4F	Omicron	GREEK CAPITAL LETTER OMICRON

	ISOLatin1	ZapfDB		
UNIC	StdEnc	Symbol	Adobe glyph name	Unicode character name
03A0	50		Pi	GREEK CAPITAL LETTER PI
03A1	52		Rho	GREEK CAPITAL LETTER RHO
03A3	53		SIgma	GREEK CAPITAL LETTER SIGMA
03A4	54		Tau	GREEK CAPITAL LETTER TAU
03A5	55		Upsilon	GREEK CAPITAL LETTER UPSILON
03A6	46		Phi	GREEK CAPITAL LETTER PHI
03A7	43		Chi	GREEK CAPITAL LETTER CHI
03A8	59		Psi	GREEK CAPITAL LETTER PSI
03A9	57		Omega	GREEK CAPITAL LETTER OMEGA
03B1	61		alpha	GREEK SMALL LETTER ALPHA
03B2	62		beta	GREEK SMALL LETTER BETA
03B3	67		gamma	GREEK SMALL LETTER GAMMA
03B4	64		delta	GREEK SMALL LETTER DELTA
03B5	65		epsilon	GREEK SMALL LETTER EPSILON
03B6	7A		zeta	GREEK SMALL LETTER ZETA
03B7	68		eta	GREEK SMALL LETTER ETA
03B8	71		theta	GREEK SMALL LETTER THETA
03B9	69		iota	GREEK SMALL LETTER IOTA
03BA	6B		kappa	GREEK SMALL LETTER KAPPA
03BB	6C		lambda	GREEK SMALL LETTER LAMBDA
03BC	6D		mu	GREEK SMALL LETTER MU
03BD	6E		nu	GREEK SMALL LETTER NU
03BE	78		xi	GREEK SMALL LETTER XI
03BF	6F		omicron	GREEK SMALL LETTER OMICRON
03C0	70		pi	GREEK SMALL LETTER PI
03C1	72		rho	GREEK SMALL LETTER RHO
03C2	56		sigma1	GREEK SMALL LETTER FINAL SIGMA
03C3	73		sigma	GREEK SMALL LETTER SIGMA
03C4	74		tau	GREEK SMALL LETTER TAU
03C5	75		upsilon	GREEK SMALL LETTER UPSILON
03C6	66		phi	GREEK SMALL LETTER PHI
03C7	63		chi	GREEK SMALL LETTER CHI
03C8	79		psi	GREEK SMALL LETTER PSI
03C9	77		omega	GREEK SMALL LETTER OMEGA
03D1	4A		theta1	GREEK SMALL LETTER SCRIPT THETA
03D2	A1		Upsilon1	GREEK CAPITAL LETTER UPSILON HOOK
03D5	6A		phi1	GREEK SMALL LETTER SCRIPT PHI
03D6	76		omega1	GREEK SMALL LETTER OMEGA PI
2032	A2		minute	PRIME
2033	B2		second	DOUBLE PRIME
2111	C1		Ifraktur	BLACK-LETTER I
2118	C3		weierstrass	SCRIPT P
211C	C2		Rfraktur	BLACK-LETTER R
2122	D4		trademarkserif	TRADEMARK
2122	E4		trademarksans	TRADEMARK
2126	57		Omega	OHM
2135	C0		aleph	FIRST TRANSFINITE CARDINAL
2190	AC		arrowleft	LEFT ARROW
2191	AD		arrowup	UP ARROW
2192	AE		arrowright	RIGHT ARROW
2192		D5	a161	RIGHT ARROW
2193	AF		arrowdown	DOWN ARROW
2194	AB		arrowboth	LEFT RIGHT ARROW
2194		D6	a163	LEFT RIGHT ARROW
2195		D7	a164	UP DOWN ARROW

UNIC	StdEnc	ISOLatin1 ZapfDB Symbol		Adobe glyph name	Unicode character name
21B5		BF		carriagereturn	DOWN ARROW WITH CORNER LEFT
21D0		DC		arrowdblleft	LEFT DOUBLE ARROW
21D1		DD		arrowdblup	UP DOUBLE ARROW
21D2		DE		arrowdblright	RIGHT DOUBLE ARROW
21D3		DF		arrowdbldown	DOWN DOUBLE ARROW
21D4		DB		arrowdblboth	LEFT RIGHT DOUBLE ARROW
2202		B6		partialdiff	PARTIAL DIFFERENTIAL
2205		C6		emptyset	EMPTY SET
2206		44		Delta	INCREMENT
2207		D1		gradient	NABLA
2208		CE		element	ELEMENT OF
2209		CF		notelement	NOT AN ELEMENT OF
220F		D5		product	N-ARY PRODUCT
2211		E5		summation	N-ARY SUMMATION
2215		A4		fraction	DIVISION SLASH
221A		D6		radical	SQUARE ROOT
221D		B5		proportional	PROPORTIONAL TO
221E		A5		infinity	INFINITY
2220		D0		angle	ANGLE
2227		D9		logicaland	LOGICAL AND
2228		DA		logicalor	LOGICAL OR
2229		C7		intersection	INTERSECTION
222A		C8		union	UNION
222B		F2		integral	INTEGRAL
2248		BB		approxequal	ALMOST EQUAL TO
2260		B9		notequal	NOT EQUAL TO
2261		BA		equivalence	IDENTICAL TO
2264		A3		lessequal	LESS THAN OR EQUAL TO
2265		B3		greaterequal	GREATER THAN OR EQUAL TO
2282		CC		propersubset	SUBSET OF
2283		C9		propersuperset	SUPERSET OF
2284		CB		notsubset	NOT A SUBSET OF
2286		CD		reflexsubset	SUBSET OF OR EQUAL TO
2287		CA		reflexsuperset	SUPERSET OF OR EQUAL TO
2295		C5		circleplus	CIRCLED PLUS
2297		C4		circlemultiply	CIRCLED TIMES
22C5		D7		dotmath	DOT OPERATOR
2320		F3		integraltp	TOP HALF INTEGRAL
2321		F5		integralbt	BOTTOM HALF INTEGRAL
2329		E1		angleleft	BRA
232A		F1		angleright	KET
25CA		E0		lozenge	LOZENGE
2660		AA		spade	BLACK SPADE SUIT
2663		A7		club	BLACK CLUB SUIT
2665		A9		heart	BLACK HEART SUIT
2666		A8		diamond	BLACK DIAMOND SUIT
2660			AB	a109	BLACK SPADE SUIT
2663			A8	a112	BLACK CLUB SUIT
2665			AA	a110	BLACK HEART SUIT
2666			A9	a111	BLACK DIAMOND SUIT
2460			AC	a120	CIRCLED DIGIT ONE
2461			AD	a121	CIRCLED DIGIT TWO
2462			AE	a122	CIRCLED DIGIT THREE
2463			AF	a123	CIRCLED DIGIT FOUR
2464			B0	a124	CIRCLED DIGIT FIVE

UNIC	ISOLatin1 StdEnc	ZapfDB Symbol	Adobe glyph name	Unicode character name
2465		B1	a125	CIRCLED DIGIT SIX
2466		B2	a126	CIRCLED DIGIT SEVEN
2467		B3	a127	CIRCLED DIGIT EIGHT
2468		B4	a128	CIRCLED DIGIT NINE
2469		B5	a129	CIRCLED NUMBER TEN
25A0		6E	a73	BLACK SQUARE
25B2		73	a76	BLACK UP POINTING TRIANGLE
25BC		74	a77	BLACK DOWN POINTING TRIANGLE
25C6		75	a78	BLACK DIAMOND
2605		48	a35	BLACK STAR
260E		25	a4	BLACK TELEPHONE
261B		2A	a11	BLACK RIGHT POINTING INDEX
261E		2B	a12	WHITE RIGHT POINTING INDEX
2701		21	a1	UPPER BLADE SCISSORS
2702		22	a2	BLACK SCISSORS
2703		23	a202	LOWER BLADE SCISSORS
2704		24	a3	WHITE SCISSORS
2706		26	a5	TELEPHONE LOCATION SIGN
2707		27	a119	TAPE DRIVE
2708		28	a118	AIRPLANE
2709		29	a117	ENVELOPE
270C		2C	a13	VICTORY HAND
270D		2D	a14	WRITING HAND
270E		2E	a15	LOWER RIGHT PENCIL
270F		2F	a16	PENCIL
2710		30	a105	UPPER RIGHT PENCIL
2711		31	a17	WHITE NIB
2712		32	a18	BLACK NIB
2713		33	a19	CHECK MARK
2714		34	a20	HEAVY CHECK MARK
2715		35	a21	MULTIPLICATION X
2716		36	a22	HEAVY MULTIPLICATION X
2717		37	a23	BALLOT X
2718		38	a24	HEAVY BALLOT X
2719		39	a25	OUTLINED GREEK CROSS
271A		3A	a26	HEAVY GREEK CROSS
271B		3B	a27	OPEN CENTER CROSS
271C		3C	a28	HEAVY OPEN CENTER CROSS
271D		3D	a6	LATIN CROSS
271E		3E	a7	SHADOWED WHITE LATIN CROSS
271F		3F	a8	OUTLINED LATIN CROSS
2720		40	a9	MALTESE CROSS
2721		41	a10	STAR OF DAVID
2722		42	a29	FOUR TEARDROP-SPOKED ASTERISK
2723		43	a30	FOUR BALLOON-SPOKED ASTERISK
2724		44	a31	HEAVY FOUR BALLOON-SPOKED ASTERISK
2725		45	a32	FOUR CLUB-SPOKED ASTERISK
2726		46	a33	BLACK FOUR POINTED STAR
2727		47	a34	WHITE FOUR POINTED STAR
2729		49	a36	STRESS OUTLINED WHITE STAR
272A		4A	a37	CIRCLED WHITE STAR
272B		4B	a38	OPEN CENTER BLACK STAR
272C		4C	a39	BLACK CENTER WHITE STAR
272D		4D	a40	OUTLINED BLACK STAR
272E		4E	a41	HEAVY OUTLINED BLACK STAR

The Unicode Standard • Version 1.0

UNIC	StdEnc	ISOLatin1 Symbol	ZapfDB	Adobe glyph name	Unicode character name
272F			4F	a42	PINWHEEL STAR
2730			50	a43	SHADOWED WHITE STAR
2731			51	a44	HEAVY ASTERISK
2732			52	a45	OPEN CENTER ASTERISK
2733			53	a46	EIGHT SPOKED ASTERISK
2734			54	a47	EIGHT POINTED BLACK STAR
2735			55	a48	EIGHT POINTED PINWHEEL STAR
2736			56	a49	SIX POINTED BLACK STAR
2737			57	a50	EIGHT POINTED RECTILINEAR BLACK STAR
2738			58	a51	HEAVY EIGHT POINTED RECTILINEAR BLACK STAR
2739			59	a52	TWELVE POINTED BLACK STAR
273A			5A	a53	SIXTEEN POINTED ASTERISK
273B			5B	a54	TEARDROP-SPOKED ASTERISK
273C			5C	a55	OPEN CENTER TEARDROP-SPOKED ASTERISK
273D			5D	a56	HEAVY TEARDROP-SPOKED ASTERISK
273E			5E	a57	SIX PETALLED BLACK AND WHITE FLORETTE
273F			5F	a58	BLACK FLORETTE
2740			60	a59	WHITE FLORETTE
2741			61	a60	EIGHT PETALLED OUTLINED BLACK FLORETTE
2742			62	a61	CIRCLED OPEN CENTER EIGHT POINTED STAR
2743			63	a62	HEAVY TEARDROP-SPOKED PINWHEEL ASTERISK
2744			64	a63	SNOWFLAKE
2745			65	a64	TIGHT TRIFOLIATE SNOWFLAKE
2746			66	a65	HEAVY CHEVRON SNOWFLAKE
2747			67	a66	SPARKLE
2748			68	a67	HEAVY SPARKLE
2749			69	a68	BALLOON-SPOKED ASTERISK
274A			6A	a69	EIGHT TEARDROP-SPOKED PROPELLER ASTERISK
274B			6B	a70	HEAVY EIGHT TEARDROP-SPOKED PROPELLER ASTERISK
274D			6D	a72	SHADOWED WHITE CIRCLE
274F			6F	a74	LOWER RIGHT DROP-SHADOWED WHITE SQUARE
2750			70	a203	UPPER RIGHT DROP-SHADOWED WHITE SQUARE
2751			71	a75	LOWER RIGHT SHADOWED WHITE SQUARE
2752			72	a204	UPPER RIGHT SHADOWED WHITE SQUARE
2756			76	a79	BLACK DIAMOND MINUS WHITE X
2758			78	a82	LIGHT VERTICAL BAR
2759			79	a83	MEDIUM VERTICAL BAR
275A			7A	a84	HEAVY VERTICAL BAR
275B			7B	a97	HEAVY SINGLE TURNED COMMA QUOTATION MARK ORNAMENT
275C			7C	a98	HEAVY SINGLE COMMA QUOTATION MARK ORNAMENT
275D			7D	a99	HEAVY DOUBLE TURNED COMMA QUOTATION MARK ORNAMENT
275E			7E	a100	HEAVY DOUBLE COMMA QUOTATION MARK ORNAMENT
2761			A1	a101	CURVED STEM PARAGRAPH SIGN ORNAMENT
2762			A2	a102	HEAVY EXCLAMATION MARK ORNAMENT

UNIC	StdEnc	*ISOLatin1* Symbol	*ZapfDB*	Adobe glyph name	Unicode character name
2763			A3	a103	HEAVY HEART EXCLAMATION MARK ORNAMENT
2764			A4	a104	HEAVY BLACK HEART
2765			A5	a105	ROTATED HEAVY BLACK HEART BULLET
2766			A6	a106	FLORAL HEART
2767			A7	a107	ROTATED FLORAL HEART BULLET
2776			B6	a130	INVERSE CIRCLED DIGIT ONE
2777			B7	a131	INVERSE CIRCLED DIGIT TWO
2778			B8	a132	INVERSE CIRCLED DIGIT THREE
2779			B9	a133	INVERSE CIRCLED DIGIT FOUR
277A			BA	a134	INVERSE CIRCLED DIGIT FIVE
277B			BB	a135	INVERSE CIRCLED DIGIT SIX
277C			BC	a136	INVERSE CIRCLED DIGIT SEVEN
277D			BD	a137	INVERSE CIRCLED DIGIT EIGHT
277E			BE	a138	INVERSE CIRCLED DIGIT NINE
277F			BF	a139	INVERSE CIRCLED NUMBER TEN
2780			C0	a140	CIRCLED SANS-SERIF DIGIT ONE
2781			C1	a141	CIRCLED SANS-SERIF DIGIT TWO
2782			C2	a142	CIRCLED SANS-SERIF DIGIT THREE
2783			C3	a143	CIRCLED SANS-SERIF DIGIT FOUR
2784			C4	a144	CIRCLED SANS-SERIF DIGIT FIVE
2785			C5	a145	CIRCLED SANS-SERIF DIGIT SIX
2786			C6	a146	CIRCLED SANS-SERIF DIGIT SEVEN
2787			C7	a147	CIRCLED SANS-SERIF DIGIT EIGHT
2788			C8	a148	CIRCLED SANS-SERIF DIGIT NINE
2789			C9	a149	CIRCLED SANS-SERIF NUMBER TEN
278A			CA	a150	INVERSE CIRCLED SANS-SERIF DIGIT ONE
278B			CB	a151	INVERSE CIRCLED SANS-SERIF DIGIT TWO
278C			CC	a152	INVERSE CIRCLED SANS-SERIF DIGIT THREE
278D			CD	a153	INVERSE CIRCLED SANS-SERIF DIGIT FOUR
278E			CE	a154	INVERSE CIRCLED SANS-SERIF DIGIT FIVE
278F			CF	a155	INVERSE CIRCLED SANS-SERIF DIGIT SIX
2790			D0	a156	INVERSE CIRCLED SANS-SERIF DIGIT SEVEN
2791			D1	a157	INVERSE CIRCLED SANS-SERIF DIGIT EIGHT
2792			D2	a158	INVERSE CIRCLED SANS-SERIF DIGIT NINE
2793			D3	a159	INVERSE CIRCLED SANS-SERIF NUMBER TEN
2794			D4	a160	HEAVY WIDE-HEADED RIGHT ARROW
2798			D8	a196	HEAVY LOWER RIGHT ARROW
2799			D9	a165	HEAVY RIGHT ARROW
279A			DA	a192	HEAVY UPPER RIGHT ARROW
279B			DB	a166	DRAFTING POINT RIGHT ARROW
279C			DC	a167	HEAVY ROUND-TIPPED RIGHT ARROW
279D			DD	a168	TRIANGLE-HEADED RIGHT ARROW
279E			DE	a169	HEAVY TRIANGLE-HEADED RIGHT ARROW
279F			DF	a170	DASHED TRIANGLE-HEADED RIGHT ARROW
27A0			E0	a171	HEAVY DASHED TRIANGLE-HEADED RIGHT ARROW
27A1			E1	a172	BLACK RIGHT ARROW
27A2			E2	a173	THREE-D TOP-LIGHTED RIGHT ARROWHEAD
27A3			E3	a162	THREE-D BOTTOM-LIGHTED RIGHT ARROWHEAD
27A4			E4	a174	BLACK RIGHT ARROWHEAD
27A5			E5	a175	HEAVY BLACK CURVED DOWN AND RIGHT ARROW
27A6			E6	a176	HEAVY BLACK CURVED UP AND RIGHT ARROW

UNIC	StdEnc	ISOLatin1 Symbol	ZapfDB	Adobe glyph name	Unicode character name
27A7			E7	a177	SQUAT BLACK RIGHT ARROW
27A8			E8	a178	HEAVY CONCAVE-POINTED BLACK RIGHT ARROW
27A9			E9	a179	RIGHT-SHADED WHITE RIGHT ARROW
27AA			EA	a193	LEFT-SHADED WHITE RIGHT ARROW
27AB			EB	a180	BACK-TILTED SHADOWED WHITE RIGHT ARROW
27AC			EC	a199	FRONT-TILTED SHADOWED WHITE RIGHT ARROW
27AD			ED	a181	HEAVY LOWER RIGHT-SHADOWED WHITE RIGHT ARROW
27AE			EE	a200	HEAVY UPPER RIGHT-SHADOWED WHITE RIGHT ARROW
27AF			EF	a182	NOTCHED LOWER RIGHT-SHADOWED WHITE RIGHT ARROW
27B1			F1	a201	NOTCHED UPPER RIGHT-SHADOWED WHITE RIGHT ARROW
27B2			F2	a183	CIRCLED HEAVY WHITE RIGHT ARROW
27B3			F3	a184	WHITE-FEATHERED RIGHT ARROW
27B4			F4	a197	BLACK-FEATHERED LOWER RIGHT ARROW
27B5			F5	a185	BLACK-FEATHERED RIGHT ARROW
27B6			F6	a194	BLACK-FEATHERED UPPER RIGHT ARROW
27B7			F7	a198	HEAVY BLACK-FEATHERED LOWER RIGHT ARROW
27B8			F8	a186	HEAVY BLACK-FEATHERED RIGHT ARROW
27B9			F9	a195	HEAVY BLACK-FEATHERED UPPER RIGHT ARROW
27BA			FA	a187	TEARDROP-BARBED RIGHT ARROW
27BB			FB	a188	HEAVY TEARDROP-SHANKED RIGHT ARROW
27BC			FC	a189	WEDGE-TAILED RIGHT ARROW
27BD			FD	a190	HEAVY WEDGE-TAILED RIGHT ARROW
27BE			FE	a191	OPEN-OUTLINED RIGHT ARROW

PostScript ligatures which are not encoded in Unicode:

AE		fi
AF		fl

PostScript glyph parts which are not encoded in Unicode:

BD	arrowvertex
BE	arrowhorizex
E6	parenlefttp
E7	parenleftex
E8	parenleftbt
E9	bracketlefttp
EA	bracketleftex
EB	bracketleftbt
EC	bracelefttp
ED	braceleftmid
EE	braceleftbt
EF	braceex
F4	integralex
F6	parenrighttp
F7	parenrightex

UNIC	StdEnc	ISOLatin1 ZapfDB Symbol	Adobe glyph name	Unicode character name
		F8	parenrightbt	
		F9	bracketrighttp	
		FA	bracketrightex	
		FB	bracketrightbt	
		FC	bracerighttp	
		FD	bracerightmid	
		FE	bracerightbt	

Unicode Encoding to Macintosh Character Mappings

The Macintosh associates one character set with each script system, including Roman, Greek, Hebrew, Arabic, Japanese, Chinese, Korean and Thai. The Roman script character set is an extension of ASCII. There are two special sets in the Roman range which are based on Adobe character sets: Symbol and Zapf Dingbats. The symbol character set is based on the Adobe Symbol set; the Zapf Dingbats set is identical to Adobe's.

For historical reasons, there are two Greek sets. The Greek script character set labeled GK2 below is an extension of the Apple II Greek character set while the other, labeled GRK, is identical in repertoire with ISO 8859-7. The Hebrew script set is an extension of ISO 8859-8, while the Arabic script character set is an extension of ISO 8859-6, and the Thai script character set is identical to TIS 620-2529.

The East Asian character sets are algorithmically derived from national character sets. The Macintosh Japanese script character set is based on JIS X0208. There are two Chinese scripts: Chinese and Traditional Chinese. The Chinese script character set is based on GB 2312, while the Traditional Chinese script character set is identical to Big 5. The Korean script character set is based on KS C 5601. The algorithms for converting between the Macintosh East Asian character sets and the national character sets are given by the following algorithms in C code:

```c
// given canonical JIS X0208 input of ku (row) and ten (cell)
// convert to Macintosh Shift-JIS

void RowCellToShiftJIS(char row, char cell, unsigned char* shiftJIS)
{
    char rowOffset = row < 63 ? 0x80: 0xC0;
    char cellOffset = ((row % 2) ? (0x3F + (cell > 63 ? 1 : 0)) : 0x9E);
    shiftJIS[0] = ((row+1) / 2 + rowOffset);
    shiftJIS[1] = (cell + cellOffset);
}

// given canonical KSC 5601 input of kwu (row) and cem (cell)
// convert to Macintosh Shift-KSC

void RowCellToShiftKS(char row, char cell, unsigned char* shiftKS)
{
    shiftKS[0] = row + 0xA0;
    shiftKS[1] = cell + 0xA0;
}

// given canonical GB 2312 input of qu (row) and wei (cell)
// convert to Macintosh Shift-GB

void RowCellToShiftGB(char row, char cell, unsigned char* shiftGB)
{
    shiftGB[0] = row + 0xA0;
    shiftGB[1] = cell + 0xA0;
}
```

Note that some Macintosh characters map to two Unicode characters. These are indicated by a plus sign between Unicode characters in the Unicode column in the table. The names shown in the names column in the table are italicized in this case, since these are not actual Unicode character names, but rather mnemonics for the Macintosh character.

There are also instances in which two Macintosh characters map to a single Unicode character. For example, there are right-to-left clones of ASCII for the Arabic and Hebrew script systems that, with the normal left-to-right ASCII, map to a single Unicode character. These two values are shown in the table separated by a slash.

UNIC	ROM	SYM	GRK	GK2	HEB	ARB	NAME
0020	20	20	20	20	20/A0	20/A0	SPACE
0021	21	21	21	21	21/A1	21/A1	EXCLAMATION MARK
0022	22		22	22	22/A2	22/A2	QUOTATION MARK
0023	23	23	23	23	23/A3	23/A3	NUMBER SIGN
0024	24		24	24	24/A4	24/A4	DOLLAR SIGN
0025	25	25	25	25	25/A5	25	PERCENT SIGN
0026	26	26	26	26	26	26/A6	AMPERSAND
0027	27		27	27	27/A7	27/A7	APOSTROPHE-QUOTE
0028	28	28	28	28	28/A8	28/A8	OPENING PARENTHESIS
0029	29	29	29	29	29/A9	29/A9	CLOSING PARENTHESIS
002A	2A		2A	2A	2A/AA	2A/AA	ASTERISK
002B	2B	2B	2B	2B	2B/AB	2B/AB	PLUS SIGN
002C	2C	2C	2C	2C	2C/AC	2C	COMMA
002D	2D		2D	2D	2D/AD	2D/AD	HYPHEN-MINUS
002E	2E	2E	2E	2E	2E/AE	2E/AE	PERIOD
002F	2F	2F	2F	2F	2F/AF	2F/AF	SLASH
0030	30	30	30	30	30/B0	30	DIGIT ZERO
0031	31	31	31	31	31/B1	31	DIGIT ONE
0032	32	32	32	32	32/B2	32	DIGIT TWO
0033	33	33	33	33	33/B3	33	DIGIT THREE
0034	34	34	34	34	34/B4	34	DIGIT FOUR
0035	35	35	35	35	35/B5	35	DIGIT FIVE
0036	36	36	36	36	36/B6	36	DIGIT SIX
0037	37	37	37	37	37/B7	37	DIGIT SEVEN
0038	38	38	38	38	38/B8	38	DIGIT EIGHT
0039	39	39	39	39	39/B9	39	DIGIT NINE
003A	3A	3A	3A	3A	3A/BA	3A/BA	COLON
003B	3B	3B	3B	3B	3B/BB	3B	SEMICOLON
003C	3C	3C	3C	3C	3C/BC	3C/BC	LESS-THAN SIGN
003D	3D	3D	3D	3D	3D/BD	3D/BD	EQUALS SIGN
003E	3E	3E	3E	3E	3E/BE	3E/BE	GREATER-THAN SIGN
003F	3F	3F	3F	3F	3F/BF	3F	QUESTION MARK
0040	40		40	40	40	40	COMMERCIAL AT
0041	41		41	41	41	41	LATIN CAPITAL LETTER A
0042	42		42	42	42	42	LATIN CAPITAL LETTER B
0043	43		43	43	43	43	LATIN CAPITAL LETTER C
0044	44		44	44	44	44	LATIN CAPITAL LETTER D
0045	45		45	45	45	45	LATIN CAPITAL LETTER E
0046	46		46	46	46	46	LATIN CAPITAL LETTER F
0047	47		47	47	47	47	LATIN CAPITAL LETTER G
0048	48		48	48	48	48	LATIN CAPITAL LETTER H
0049	49		49	49	49	49	LATIN CAPITAL LETTER I
004A	4A		4A	4A	4A	4A	LATIN CAPITAL LETTER J
004B	4B		4B	4B	4B	4B	LATIN CAPITAL LETTER K
004C	4C		4C	4C	4C	4C	LATIN CAPITAL LETTER L
004D	4D		4D	4D	4D	4D	LATIN CAPITAL LETTER M
004E	4E		4E	4E	4E	4E	LATIN CAPITAL LETTER N
004F	4F		4F	4F	4F	4F	LATIN CAPITAL LETTER O
0050	50		50	50	50	50	LATIN CAPITAL LETTER P
0051	51		51	51	51	51	LATIN CAPITAL LETTER Q
0052	52		52	52	52	52	LATIN CAPITAL LETTER R
0053	53		53	53	53	53	LATIN CAPITAL LETTER S
0054	54		54	54	54	54	LATIN CAPITAL LETTER T

UNIC	ROM	SYM	GRK	GK2	HEB	ARB	NAME
0055	55		55	55	55	55	LATIN CAPITAL LETTER U
0056	56		56	56	56	56	LATIN CAPITAL LETTER V
0057	57		57	57	57	57	LATIN CAPITAL LETTER W
0058	58		58	58	58	58	LATIN CAPITAL LETTER X
0059	59		59	59	59	59	LATIN CAPITAL LETTER Y
005A	5A		5A	5A	5A	5A	LATIN CAPITAL LETTER Z
005B	5B	5B	5B	5B	5B/FE	5B/DB	OPENING SQUARE BRACKET
005C	5C		5C	5C	5C	5C/DC	BACKSLASH
005D	5D	5D	5D	5D	5D/FC	5D/DD	CLOSING SQUARE BRACKET
005E	5E		5E	5E	5E	5E/DE	SPACING CIRCUMFLEX
005F	5F	5F	5F	5F	5F	5F/DF	SPACING UNDERSCORE
0060	60		60	60	60	60	SPACING GRAVE
0061	61		61	61	61	61	LATIN SMALL LETTER A
0062	62		62	62	62	62	LATIN SMALL LETTER B
0063	63		63	63	63	63	LATIN SMALL LETTER C
0064	64		64	64	64	64	LATIN SMALL LETTER D
0065	65		65	65	65	65	LATIN SMALL LETTER E
0066	66		66	66	66	66	LATIN SMALL LETTER F
0066+0069	DE						*LATIN SMALL LIGATURE FI*
0066+006C	DF						*LATIN SMALL LIGATURE FL*
0067	67		67	67	67	67	LATIN SMALL LETTER G
0068	68		68	68	68	68	LATIN SMALL LETTER H
0069	69		69	69	69	69	LATIN SMALL LETTER I
006A	6A		6A	6A	6A	6A	LATIN SMALL LETTER J
006B	6B		6B	6B	6B	6B	LATIN SMALL LETTER K
006C	6C		6C	6C	6C	6C	LATIN SMALL LETTER L
006D	6D		6D	6D	6D	6D	LATIN SMALL LETTER M
006E	6E		6E	6E	6E	6E	LATIN SMALL LETTER N
006F	6F		6F	6F	6F	6F	LATIN SMALL LETTER O
0070	70		70	70	70	70	LATIN SMALL LETTER P
0071	71		71	71	71	71	LATIN SMALL LETTER Q
0072	72		72	72	72	72	LATIN SMALL LETTER R
0073	73		73	73	73	73	LATIN SMALL LETTER S
0074	74		74	74	74	74	LATIN SMALL LETTER T
0075	75		75	75	75	75	LATIN SMALL LETTER U
0076	76		76	76	76	76	LATIN SMALL LETTER V
0077	77		77	77	77	77	LATIN SMALL LETTER W
0078	78		78	78	78	78	LATIN SMALL LETTER X
0079	79		79	79	79	79	LATIN SMALL LETTER Y
007A	7A		7A	7A	7A	7A	LATIN SMALL LETTER Z
007B	7B	7B	7B	7B	7B/FD	7B/FB	OPENING CURLY BRACKET
007C	7C	7C	7C	7C	7C/FF	7C/FC	VERTICAL BAR
007D	7D	7D	7D	7D	7D/FB	7D/FD	CLOSING CURLY BRACKET
007E	7E		7E	7E	7E	7E	TILDE
007F	7F		7F	7F	7F	7F	DELETE
00A0	CA			CA	CA	81	NON-BREAKING SPACE
00A1	C1						INVERTED EXCLAMATION MARK
00A2	A2						CENT SIGN
00A3	A3			92			POUND SIGN
00A4	DB						CURRENCY SIGN
00A5	B4						YEN SIGN
00A6				CB			BROKEN VERTICAL BAR
00A7	A4			AC			SECTION SIGN
00A8	AC			C5			SPACING DIAERESIS
00A9	A9	D3		A9			COPYRIGHT SIGN
00AA	BB						FEMININE ORDINAL INDICATOR

UNIC	ROM	SYM	GRK	GK2	HEB	ARB	NAME
00AB	C7			C7		8C	LEFT POINTING GUILLEMET
00AC	C2	D8		C2			NOT SIGN
00AE	A8	D2		A8			REGISTERED TRADE MARK SIGN
00AF	F8						SPACING MACRON
00B0	A1	B0		CF			DEGREE SIGN
00B1	B1	B1		B1			PLUS-OR-MINUS SIGN
00B2				C3			SUPERSCRIPT DIGIT TWO
00B3				C4			SUPERSCRIPT DIGIT THREE
00B4	AB						SPACING ACUTE
00B5	B5						MICRO SIGN
00B6	A6						PARAGRAPH SIGN
00B7	E1			AF			MIDDLE DOT
00B8	FC						SPACING CEDILLA
00B9				C1			SUPERSCRIPT DIGIT ONE
00BA	BC						MASCULINE ORDINAL INDICATOR
00BB	C8			C8		98	RIGHT POINTING GUILLEMET
00BD				CC			FRACTION ONE HALF
00BF	C0						INVERTED QUESTION MARK
00C0	CB						LATIN CAPITAL LETTER A GRAVE
00C1	E7						LATIN CAPITAL LETTER A ACUTE
00C2	E5						LATIN CAPITAL LETTER A CIRCUMFLEX
00C3	CC						LATIN CAPITAL LETTER A TILDE
00C4	80			80	80	80	LATIN CAPITAL LETTER A DIAERESIS
00C5	81						LATIN CAPITAL LETTER A RING
00C6	AE						LATIN CAPITAL LETTER A E
00C7	82				82	82	LATIN CAPITAL LETTER C CEDILLA
00C8	E9						LATIN CAPITAL LETTER E GRAVE
00C9	83				83	83	LATIN CAPITAL LETTER E ACUTE
00CA	E6						LATIN CAPITAL LETTER E CIRCUMFLEX
00CB	E8						LATIN CAPITAL LETTER E DIAERESIS
00CC	ED						LATIN CAPITAL LETTER I GRAVE
00CD	EA						LATIN CAPITAL LETTER I ACUTE
00CE	EB						LATIN CAPITAL LETTER I CIRCUMFLEX
00CF	EC						LATIN CAPITAL LETTER I DIAERESIS
00D1	84				84	84	LATIN CAPITAL LETTER N TILDE
00D2	F1						LATIN CAPITAL LETTER O GRAVE
00D3	EE						LATIN CAPITAL LETTER O ACUTE
00D4	EF						LATIN CAPITAL LETTER O CIRCUMFLEX
00D5	CD						LATIN CAPITAL LETTER O TILDE
00D6	85			85	85	85	LATIN CAPITAL LETTER O DIAERESIS
00D7		B4					MULTIPLICATION SIGN
00D8	AF						LATIN CAPITAL LETTER O SLASH
00D9	F4						LATIN CAPITAL LETTER U GRAVE
00DA	F2						LATIN CAPITAL LETTER U ACUTE
00DB	F3						LATIN CAPITAL LETTER U CIRCUMFLEX
00DC	86			86	86	86	LATIN CAPITAL LETTER U DIAERESIS
00DF	A7			A7			LATIN SMALL LETTER SHARP S
00E0	88			88	88	88	LATIN SMALL LETTER A GRAVE
00E1	87				87	87	LATIN SMALL LETTER A ACUTE
00E2	89			89	89	89	LATIN SMALL LETTER A CIRCUMFLEX
00E3	8B				8B		LATIN SMALL LETTER A TILDE
00E4	8A			8A	8A	8A	LATIN SMALL LETTER A DIAERESIS
00E5	8C				8C		LATIN SMALL LETTER A RING
00E6	BE						LATIN SMALL LETTER A E
00E7	8D			8D	8D	8D	LATIN SMALL LETTER C CEDILLA
00E8	8F			8F	8F	8F	LATIN SMALL LETTER E GRAVE

UNIC	ROM	SYM	GRK	GK2	HEB	ARB	NAME
00E9	8E			8E	8E	8E	LATIN SMALL LETTER E ACUTE
00EA	90			90	90	90	LATIN SMALL LETTER E CIRCUMFLEX
00EB	91			91	91	91	LATIN SMALL LETTER E DIAERESIS
00EC	93				93		LATIN SMALL LETTER I GRAVE
00ED	92				92	92	LATIN SMALL LETTER I ACUTE
00EE	94			94	94	94	LATIN SMALL LETTER I CIRCUMFLEX
00EF	95			95	95	95	LATIN SMALL LETTER I DIAERESIS
00F1	96				96	96	LATIN SMALL LETTER N TILDE
00F2	98				98		LATIN SMALL LETTER O GRAVE
00F3	97				97	97	LATIN SMALL LETTER O ACUTE
00F4	99			99	99	99	LATIN SMALL LETTER O CIRCUMFLEX
00F5	9B				9B		LATIN SMALL LETTER O TILDE
00F6	9A			9A	9A	9A	LATIN SMALL LETTER O DIAERESIS
00F7	D6	B8				9B	DIVISION SIGN
00F8	BF						LATIN SMALL LETTER O SLASH
00F9	9D			9D	9D	9D	LATIN SMALL LETTER U GRAVE
00FA	9C				9C	9C	LATIN SMALL LETTER U ACUTE
00FB	9E			9E	9E	9E	LATIN SMALL LETTER U CIRCUMFLEX
00FC	9F			9F	9F	9F	LATIN SMALL LETTER U DIAERESIS
00FF	D8						LATIN SMALL LETTER Y DIAERESIS
0131	F5						LATIN SMALL LETTER DOTLESS I
0152	CE						LATIN CAPITAL LETTER O E
0153	CF						LATIN SMALL LETTER O E
0178	D9						LATIN CAPITAL LETTER Y DIAERESIS
0192	C4	A6					LATIN SMALL LETTER SCRIPT F
02C6	F6						MODIFIER LETTER CIRCUMFLEX
02C7	FF						MODIFIER LETTER HACEK
02D8	F9						SPACING BREVE
02D9	FA						SPACING DOT ABOVE
02DA	FB						SPACING RING ABOVE
02DB	FE						SPACING OGONEK
02DC	F7						SPACING TILDE
02DD	FD						SPACING DOUBLE ACUTE
0386			B6	CD			GREEK CAPITAL LETTER ALPHA TONOS
0388			B8	CE			GREEK CAPITAL LETTER EPSILON TONOS
0389			B9	D7			GREEK CAPITAL LETTER ETA TONOS
038A			BA	D8			GREEK CAPITAL LETTER IOTA TONOS
038C			BC	D9			GREEK CAPITAL LETTER OMICRON TONOS
038E			BE	DA			GREEK CAPITAL LETTER UPSILON TONOS
038F			BF	DF			GREEK CAPITAL LETTER OMEGA TONOS
0390			C0	FD			GREEK SMALL LETTER IOTA DIAERESIS TONOS
0391		41	C1	81			GREEK CAPITAL LETTER ALPHA
0392		42	C2	82			GREEK CAPITAL LETTER BETA
0393		47	C3	83			GREEK CAPITAL LETTER GAMMA
0394		44	C4	84			GREEK CAPITAL LETTER DELTA
0395		45	C5	87			GREEK CAPITAL LETTER EPSILON
0396		5A	C6	8B			GREEK CAPITAL LETTER ZETA
0397		48	C7	8C			GREEK CAPITAL LETTER ETA
0398		51	C8	97			GREEK CAPITAL LETTER THETA
0399		49	C9	98			GREEK CAPITAL LETTER IOTA
039A		4B	CA	9C			GREEK CAPITAL LETTER KAPPA
039B		4C	CB	A0			GREEK CAPITAL LETTER LAMBDA
039C		4D	CC	AE			GREEK CAPITAL LETTER MU
039D		4E	CD	B0			GREEK CAPITAL LETTER NU
039E		58	CE	B4			GREEK CAPITAL LETTER XI
039F		4F	CF	B5			GREEK CAPITAL LETTER OMICRON

UNIC	ROM	SYM	GRK	GK2	HEB	ARB	NAME
03A0		50	D0	B6			GREEK CAPITAL LETTER PI
03A1		52	D1	B7			GREEK CAPITAL LETTER RHO
03A3		53	D3	B8			GREEK CAPITAL LETTER SIGMA
03A4		54	D4	B9			GREEK CAPITAL LETTER TAU
03A5		55	D5	BA			GREEK CAPITAL LETTER UPSILON
03A6		46	D6	BC			GREEK CAPITAL LETTER PHI
03A7		43	D7	BD			GREEK CAPITAL LETTER CHI
03A8		59	D8	BE			GREEK CAPITAL LETTER PSI
03A9		57	D9	BF			GREEK CAPITAL LETTER OMEGA
03AA			DA	AB			GREEK CAPITAL LETTER IOTA DIAERESIS
03AB			DB	BB			GREEK CAPITAL LETTER UPSILON DIAERESIS
03AC			DC	C0			GREEK SMALL LETTER ALPHA TONOS
03AD			DD	DB			GREEK SMALL LETTER EPSILON TONOS
03AE			DE	DC			GREEK SMALL LETTER ETA TONOS
03AF			DF	DD			GREEK SMALL LETTER IOTA TONOS
03B0			E0	FE			GREEK SMALL LETTER UPSILON DIAERESIS TONOS
03B1		61	E1	E1			GREEK SMALL LETTER ALPHA
03B2		62	E2	E2			GREEK SMALL LETTER BETA
03B3		67	E3	E7			GREEK SMALL LETTER GAMMA
03B4		64	E4	E4			GREEK SMALL LETTER DELTA
03B5		65	E5	E5			GREEK SMALL LETTER EPSILON
03B6		7A	E6	FA			GREEK SMALL LETTER ZETA
03B7		68	E7	E8			GREEK SMALL LETTER ETA
03B8		71	E8	F5			GREEK SMALL LETTER THETA
03B9		69	E9	E9			GREEK SMALL LETTER IOTA
03BA		6B	EA	EB			GREEK SMALL LETTER KAPPA
03BB		6C	EB	EC			GREEK SMALL LETTER LAMBDA
03BC		6D	EC	ED			GREEK SMALL LETTER MU
03BD		6E	ED	EE			GREEK SMALL LETTER NU
03BE		78	EE	EA			GREEK SMALL LETTER XI
03BF		6F	EF	EF			GREEK SMALL LETTER OMICRON
03C0	B9	70	F0	F0			GREEK SMALL LETTER PI
03C1		72	F1	F2			GREEK SMALL LETTER RHO
03C2		56	F2	F7			GREEK SMALL LETTER FINAL SIGMA
03C3		73	F3	F3			GREEK SMALL LETTER SIGMA
03C4		74	F4	F4			GREEK SMALL LETTER TAU
03C5		75	F5	F9			GREEK SMALL LETTER UPSILON
03C6		66	F6	E6			GREEK SMALL LETTER PHI
03C7		63	F7	F8			GREEK SMALL LETTER CHI
03C8		79	F8	E3			GREEK SMALL LETTER PSI
03C9		77	F9	F6			GREEK SMALL LETTER OMEGA
03CA			FA	FB			GREEK SMALL LETTER IOTA DIAERESIS
03CB			FB	FC			GREEK SMALL LETTER UPSILON DIAERESIS
03CC			FC	DE			GREEK SMALL LETTER OMICRON TONOS
03CD			FD	E0			GREEK SMALL LETTER UPSILON TONOS
03CE			FE	F1			GREEK SMALL LETTER OMEGA TONOS
03D1		4A					GREEK SMALL LETTER SCRIPT THETA
03D2		A1					GREEK CAPITAL LETTER UPSILON HOOK
03D5		6A					GREEK SMALL LETTER SCRIPT PHI
03D6		76					GREEK SMALL LETTER OMEGA PI
03F3			B4	D6			GREEK SPACING TONOS
03F4			B5	C6			GREEK SPACING DIAERESIS TONOS
05B0					D9		HEBREW POINT SHEVA
05B1					DB		HEBREW POINT HATAF SEGOL
05B2					DA		HEBREW POINT HATAF PATAH

UNIC	ROM	SYM	GRK	GK2	HEB	ARB	NAME
05B3					DF		HEBREW POINT HATAF QAMATS
05B4					CF		HEBREW POINT HIRIQ
05B5					CD		HEBREW POINT TSERE
05B6					CE		HEBREW POINT SEGOL
05B7					CC		HEBREW POINT PATAH
05B8					DE		HEBREW POINT QAMATS
05B8					CB		HEBREW POINT QAMATS
05B9					DD		HEBREW POINT HOLAM
05BB					DC		HEBREW POINT QUBUTS
05BE					D8		HEBREW PUNCTUATION MAQAF
05D0					E0		HEBREW LETTER ALEF
05D1					E1		HEBREW LETTER BET
05D1+05BC					C0		*HEBREW BET DAGESH*
05D2					E2		HEBREW LETTER GIMEL
05D2+05BC					C1		*HEBREW GIMEL DAGESH*
05D3					E3		HEBREW LETTER DALET
05D3+05BC					C2		*HEBREW DALET DAGESH*
05D4					E4		HEBREW LETTER HE
05D4+05BC					C3		*HEBREW HE DAGESH*
05D5					E5		HEBREW LETTER VAV
05D5+05BA					C7		*HEBREW VAV HOLEM LEFT*
05D5+05BC					C8		*HEBREW VAV DAGESH*
05D6					E6		HEBREW LETTER ZAYIN
05D7					E7		HEBREW LETTER HET
05D8					E8		HEBREW LETTER TET
05D9					E9		HEBREW LETTER YOD
05DA					EA		HEBREW LETTER FINAL KAF
05DB					EB		HEBREW LETTER KAF
05DB+05BC					C4		*HEBREW KAF DAGESH*
05DC					EC		HEBREW LETTER LAMED
05DD					ED		HEBREW LETTER FINAL MEM
05DE					EE		HEBREW LETTER MEM
05DF					EF		HEBREW LETTER FINAL NUN
05E0					F0		HEBREW LETTER NUN
05E1					F1		HEBREW LETTER SAMEKH
05E2					F2		HEBREW LETTER AYIN
05E3					F3		HEBREW LETTER FINAL PE
05E4					F4		HEBREW LETTER PE
05E4+05BC					C5		*HEBREW PE DAGESH*
05E5					F5		HEBREW LETTER FINAL TSADI
05E6					F6		HEBREW LETTER TSADI
05E7					F7		HEBREW LETTER QOF
05E8					F8		HEBREW LETTER RESH
05E9					F9		HEBREW LETTER SHIN
05E9+05C1					D6		*HEBREW SIN SHIN DOT*
05E9+05C2					D7		*HEBREW SIN SIN DOT*
05EA					FA		HEBREW LETTER TAV
05F2					81		HEBREW LETTER DOUBLE YOD
060C						AC	ARABIC COMMA
061B						BB	ARABIC SEMICOLON
061F						BF	ARABIC QUESTION MARK
0621						C1	ARABIC LETTER HAMZAH
0622						C2	ARABIC LETTER MADDAH ON ALEF
0623						C3	ARABIC LETTER HAMZAH ON ALEF
0624						C4	ARABIC LETTER HAMZAH ON WAW
0625						C5	ARABIC LETTER HAMZAH UNDER ALEF

The Unicode Standard • Version 1.0

UNIC	ROM	SYM	GRK	GK2	HEB	ARB	NAME
0626						C6	ARABIC LETTER HAMZAH ON YA
0627						C7	ARABIC LETTER ALEF
0628						C8	ARABIC LETTER BAA
0629						C9	ARABIC LETTER TAA MARBUTAH
062A						CA	ARABIC LETTER TAA
062B						CB	ARABIC LETTER THAA
062C						CC	ARABIC LETTER JEEM
062D						CD	ARABIC LETTER HAA
062E						CE	ARABIC LETTER KHAA
062F						CF	ARABIC LETTER DAL
0630						D0	ARABIC LETTER THAL
0631						D1	ARABIC LETTER RA
0632						D2	ARABIC LETTER ZAIN
0633						D3	ARABIC LETTER SEEN
0634						D4	ARABIC LETTER SHEEN
0635						D5	ARABIC LETTER SAD
0636						D6	ARABIC LETTER DAD
0637						D7	ARABIC LETTER TAH
0638						D8	ARABIC LETTER DHAH
0639						D9	ARABIC LETTER AIN
063A						DA	ARABIC LETTER GHAIN
0640						E0	ARABIC TATWEEL
0641						E1	ARABIC LETTER FA
0642						E2	ARABIC LETTER QAF
0643						E3	ARABIC LETTER CAF
0644						E4	ARABIC LETTER LAM
0645						E5	ARABIC LETTER MEEM
0646						E6	ARABIC LETTER NOON
0647						E7	ARABIC LETTER HA
0648						E8	ARABIC LETTER WAW
0649						E9	ARABIC LETTER ALEF MAQSURAH
064A						EA	ARABIC LETTER YA
064B						EB	ARABIC FATHATAN
064C						EC	ARABIC DAMMATAN
064D						ED	ARABIC KASRATAN
064E						EE	ARABIC FATHAH
064F						EF	ARABIC DAMMAH
0650						F0	ARABIC KASRAH
0651						F1	ARABIC SHADDAH
0652						F2	ARABIC SUKUN
0660						B0	ARABIC-INDIC DIGIT ZERO
0661						B1	ARABIC-INDIC DIGIT ONE
0662						B2	ARABIC-INDIC DIGIT TWO
0663						B3	ARABIC-INDIC DIGIT THREE
0664						B4	ARABIC-INDIC DIGIT FOUR
0665						B5	ARABIC-INDIC DIGIT FIVE
0666						B6	ARABIC-INDIC DIGIT SIX
0667						B7	ARABIC-INDIC DIGIT SEVEN
0668						B8	ARABIC-INDIC DIGIT EIGHT
0669						B9	ARABIC-INDIC DIGIT NINE
066A						A5	ARABIC PERCENT SIGN
0679						F4	ARABIC LETTER TAA WITH SMALL TAH
067E						F3	ARABIC LETTER TAA WITH THREE DOTS BELOW
0686						F5	ARABIC LETTER HAA WITH MIDDLE THREE DOTS DOWNWARD
0688						F9	ARABIC LETTER DAL WITH SMALL TAH

UNIC	ROM	SYM	GRK	GK2	HEB	ARB	NAME
0691						FA	ARABIC LETTER RA WITH SMALL TAH
0698						FE	ARABIC LETTER RA WITH THREE DOTS ABOVE
06A4						F7	ARABIC LETTER FA WITH THREE DOTS ABOVE
06AF						F8	ARABIC LETTER GAF
06BA						8B	ARABIC LETTER DOTLESS NOON
06D2						FF	ARABIC LETTER YA BARREE
06D5						F6	ARABIC LETTER AE
2010	D0						HYPHEN
2011	D0						NON-BREAKING HYPHEN
2012	D0						FIGURE DASH
2013	D0			D0	D0		EN DASH
2014	D1			D1	D1		EM DASH
2018	D4			D4	D4		SINGLE TURNED COMMA QUOTATION MARK
2019	D5			D5	D5		SINGLE COMMA QUOTATION MARK
201A	E2						LOW SINGLE COMMA QUOTATION MARK
201C	D2			D2	D2		DOUBLE TURNED COMMA QUOTATION MARK
201D	D3			D3	D3		DOUBLE COMMA QUOTATION MARK
201E	E3						LOW DOUBLE COMMA QUOTATION MARK
2020	A0						DAGGER
2021	E0						DOUBLE DAGGER
2022	A5	B7		96			BULLET
2026	C9	BC		C9	C9	93	HORIZONTAL ELLIPSIS
2028	0A	0A	0A	0A	0A	0A	LINE SEPARATOR
2029	0D	0D	0D	0D	0D	0D	PARAGRAPH SEPARATOR
2030	E4			FF			PER MILLE SIGN
2032		A2					PRIME
2033		B2					DOUBLE PRIME
2039	DC						LEFT POINTING SINGLE GUILLEMET
203A	DD						RIGHT POINTING SINGLE GUILLEMET
2044	DA						FRACTION SLASH
20AA					A6		NEW SHEQEL SIGN
2111		C1					BLACK-LETTER I
2118		C3					SCRIPT P
211C		C2					BLACK-LETTER R
2122	AA	D4		93			TRADEMARK
2126	BD						OHM
2135		C0					FIRST TRANSFINITE CARDINAL
2190		AC					LEFT ARROW
2191		AD					UP ARROW
2192		AE					RIGHT ARROW
2193		AF					DOWN ARROW
2194		AB					LEFT RIGHT ARROW
21B5		BF					DOWN ARROW WITH CORNER LEFT
21D0		DC					LEFT DOUBLE ARROW
21D1		DD					UP DOUBLE ARROW
21D2		DE					RIGHT DOUBLE ARROW
21D3		DF					DOWN DOUBLE ARROW
21D4		DB					LEFT RIGHT DOUBLE ARROW
2200		22					FOR ALL
2202	B6	B6					PARTIAL DIFFERENTIAL
2203		24					THERE EXISTS
2205		C6					EMPTY SET
2206	C6						INCREMENT
2207		D1					NABLA
2208		CE					ELEMENT OF
2209		CF					NOT AN ELEMENT OF

UNIC	ROM	SYM	GRK	GK2	HEB	ARB	NAME
220B		27					CONTAINS AS MEMBER
220F	B8	D5					N-ARY PRODUCT
2211	B7	E5					N-ARY SUMMATION
2212		2D					MINUS SIGN
2215		A4					DIVISION SLASH
2217		2A					ASTERISK OPERATOR
2219		D7					BULLET OPERATOR
221A	C3	D6					SQUARE ROOT
221D		B5					PROPORTIONAL TO
221E	B0	A5					INFINITY
2220		D0					ANGLE
2227		D9					LOGICAL AND
2228		DA					LOGICAL OR
2229		C7					INTERSECTION
222A		C8					UNION
222B	BA	F2					INTEGRAL
2234		5C					THEREFORE
2245		40					APPROXIMATELY EQUAL TO
2248	C5	BB					ALMOST EQUAL TO
2260	AD	B9		AD			NOT EQUAL TO
2261		BA					IDENTICAL TO
2264	B2	A3		B2			LESS THAN OR EQUAL TO
2265	B3	B3		B3			GREATER THAN OR EQUAL TO
2282		CC					SUBSET OF
2283		C9					SUPERSET OF
2284		CB					NOT A SUBSET OF
2286		CD					SUBSET OF OR EQUAL TO
2287		CA					SUPERSET OF OR EQUAL TO
2295		C5					CIRCLED PLUS
2297		C4					CIRCLED TIMES
22A5		5E					UP TACK
2318	11			11	11		COMMAND KEY
2329		E1					BRA
232A		F1					KET
25C6	13			13	13		BLACK DIAMOND
25CA	D7	E0					LOZENGE
2660		AA					BLACK SPADE SUIT
2663		A7					BLACK CLUB SUIT
2665		A9					BLACK HEART SUIT
2666		A8					BLACK DIAMOND SUIT
2713	12			12	12		CHECK MARK
FDFF	F0	F0					*APPLE LOGO*

Microsoft Windows Character Sets

The Microsoft Windows character sets are sorted here by the Windows values and grouped.by script or area of usage. EE refers to Eastern European. The numbers in the range 1250..1256 are code page identifiers for the Windows character sets. The terms UNDF or RSRV refer to undefined or reserved positions in a Windows character set. TBA stands for a GCGID value to be announced.

UNIC 1200	ANSI 1252	Turk 1254	EE 1250	Cyrl 1251	Greek 1253	Arab 1256	Hebr 1255	IBM GCGID	Unicode character name
ASCII									
0020	20	20	20	20	20	20	20	SP010000	SPACE
0021	21	21	21	21	21	21	21	SP020000	EXCLAMATION MARK
0022	22	22	22	22	22	22	22	SP040000	QUOTATION MARK
0023	23	23	23	23	23	23	23	SM010000	NUMBER SIGN
0024	24	24	24	24	24	24	24	SC030000	DOLLAR SIGN
0025	25	25	25	25	25	25	25	SM020000	PERCENT SIGN
0026	26	26	26	26	26	26	26	SM030000	AMPERSAND
0027	27	27	27	27	27	27	27	SP050000	APOSTROPHE-QUOTE
0028	28	28	28	28	28	28	28	SP060000	OPENING PARENTHESIS
0029	29	29	29	29	29	29	29	SP070000	CLOSING PARENTHESIS
002A	2A	2A	2A	2A	2A	2A	2A	SM040000	ASTERISK
002B	2B	2B	2B	2B	2B	2B	2B	SA010000	PLUS SIGN
002C	2C	2C	2C	2C	2C	2C	2C	SP080000	COMMA
002D	2D	2D	2D	2D	2D	2D	2D	SP100000	HYPHEN-MINUS
002E	2E	2E	2E	2E	2E	2E	2E	SP110000	PERIOD
002F	2F	2F	2F	2F	2F	2F	2F	SP120000	SLASH
0030	30	30	30	30	30	30	30	ND100000	DIGIT ZERO
0031	31	31	31	31	31	31	31	ND010000	DIGIT ONE
0032	32	32	32	32	32	32	32	ND020000	DIGIT TWO
0033	33	33	33	33	33	33	33	ND030000	DIGIT THREE
0034	34	34	34	34	34	34	34	ND040000	DIGIT FOUR
0035	35	35	35	35	35	35	35	ND050000	DIGIT FIVE
0036	36	36	36	36	36	36	36	ND060000	DIGIT SIX
0037	37	37	37	37	37	37	37	ND070000	DIGIT SEVEN
0038	38	38	38	38	38	38	38	ND080000	DIGIT EIGHT
0039	39	39	39	39	39	39	39	ND090000	DIGIT NINE
003A	3A	3A	3A	3A	3A	3A	3A	SP130000	COLON
003B	3B	3B	3B	3B	3B	3B	3B	SP140000	SEMICOLON
003C	3C	3C	3C	3C	3C	3C	3C	SA030000	LESS-THAN SIGN
003D	3D	3D	3D	3D	3D	3D	3D	SA040000	EQUALS SIGN
003E	3E	3E	3E	3E	3E	3E	3E	SA050000	GREATER-THAN SIGN
003F	3F	3F	3F	3F	3F	3F	3F	SP150000	QUESTION MARK
0040	40	40	40	40	40	40	40	SM050000	COMMERCIAL AT
0041	41	41	41	41	41	41	41	LA020000	LATIN CAPITAL LETTER A
0042	42	42	42	42	42	42	42	LB020000	LATIN CAPITAL LETTER B
0043	43	43	43	43	43	43	43	LC020000	LATIN CAPITAL LETTER C

UNIC 1200	ANSI 1252	Turk 1254	EE 1250	Cyrl 1251	Greek 1253	Arab 1256	Hebr 1255	IBM GCGID	Unicode character name
0044	44	44	44	44	44	44	44	LD020000	LATIN CAPITAL LETTER D
0045	45	45	45	45	45	45	45	LE020000	LATIN CAPITAL LETTER E
0046	46	46	46	46	46	46	46	LF020000	LATIN CAPITAL LETTER F
0047	47	47	47	47	47	47	47	LG020000	LATIN CAPITAL LETTER G
0048	48	48	48	48	48	48	48	LH020000	LATIN CAPITAL LETTER H
0049	49	49	49	49	49	49	49	LI020000	LATIN CAPITAL LETTER I
004A	4A	4A	4A	4A	4A	4A	4A	LJ020000	LATIN CAPITAL LETTER J
004B	4B	4B	4B	4B	4B	4B	4B	LK020000	LATIN CAPITAL LETTER K
004C	4C	4C	4C	4C	4C	4C	4C	LL020000	LATIN CAPITAL LETTER L
004D	4D	4D	4D	4D	4D	4D	4D	LM020000	LATIN CAPITAL LETTER M
004E	4E	4E	4E	4E	4E	4E	4E	LN020000	LATIN CAPITAL LETTER N
004F	4F	4F	4F	4F	4F	4F	4F	LO020000	LATIN CAPITAL LETTER O
0050	50	50	50	50	50	50	50	LP020000	LATIN CAPITAL LETTER P
0051	51	51	51	51	51	51	51	LQ020000	LATIN CAPITAL LETTER Q
0052	52	52	52	52	52	52	52	LR020000	LATIN CAPITAL LETTER R
0053	53	53	53	53	53	53	53	LS020000	LATIN CAPITAL LETTER S
0054	54	54	54	54	54	54	54	LT020000	LATIN CAPITAL LETTER T
0055	55	55	55	55	55	55	55	LU020000	LATIN CAPITAL LETTER U
0056	56	56	56	56	56	56	56	LV020000	LATIN CAPITAL LETTER V
0057	57	57	57	57	57	57	57	LW020000	LATIN CAPITAL LETTER W
0058	58	58	58	58	58	58	58	LX020000	LATIN CAPITAL LETTER X
0059	59	59	59	59	59	59	59	LY020000	LATIN CAPITAL LETTER Y
005A	5A	5A	5A	5A	5A	5A	5A	LZ020000	LATIN CAPITAL LETTER Z
005B	5B	5B	5B	5B	5B	5B	5B	SM060000	OPENING SQUARE BRACKET
005C	5C	5C	5C	5C	5C	5C	5C	SM070000	BACKSLASH
005D	5D	5D	5D	5D	5D	5D	5D	SM080000	CLOSING SQUARE BRACKET
005E	5E	5E	5E	5E	5E	5E	5E	SD150000	SPACING CIRCUMFLEX
005F	5F	5F	5F	5F	5F	5F	5F	SP090000	SPACING UNDERSCORE
0060	60	60	60	60	60	60	60	SD130000	SPACING GRAVE
0061	61	61	61	61	61	61	61	LA010000	LATIN SMALL LETTER A
0062	62	62	62	62	62	62	62	LB010000	LATIN SMALL LETTER B
0063	63	63	63	63	63	63	63	LC010000	LATIN SMALL LETTER C
0064	64	64	64	64	64	64	64	LD010000	LATIN SMALL LETTER D
0065	65	65	65	65	65	65	65	LE010000	LATIN SMALL LETTER E
0066	66	66	66	66	66	66	66	LF010000	LATIN SMALL LETTER F
0067	67	67	67	67	67	67	67	LG010000	LATIN SMALL LETTER G
0068	68	68	68	68	68	68	68	LH010000	LATIN SMALL LETTER H
0069	69	69	69	69	69	69	69	LI010000	LATIN SMALL LETTER I
006A	6A	6A	6A	6A	6A	6A	6A	LJ010000	LATIN SMALL LETTER J

UNIC 1200	ANSI 1252	Turk 1254	EE 1250	Cyrl 1251	Greek 1253	Arab 1256	Hebr 1255	IBM GCGID	Unicode character name
006B	6B	6B	6B	6B	6B	6B	6B	LK010000	LATIN SMALL LETTER K
006C	6C	6C	6C	6C	6C	6C	6C	LL010000	LATIN SMALL LETTER L
006D	6D	6D	6D	6D	6D	6D	6D	LM010000	LATIN SMALL LETTER M
006E	6E	6E	6E	6E	6E	6E	6E	LN010000	LATIN SMALL LETTER N
006F	6F	6F	6F	6F	6F	6F	6F	LO010000	LATIN SMALL LETTER O
0070	70	70	70	70	70	70	70	LP010000	LATIN SMALL LETTER P
0071	71	71	71	71	71	71	71	LQ010000	LATIN SMALL LETTER Q
0072	72	72	72	72	72	72	72	LR010000	LATIN SMALL LETTER R
0073	73	73	73	73	73	73	73	LS010000	LATIN SMALL LETTER S
0074	74	74	74	74	74	74	74	LT010000	LATIN SMALL LETTER T
0075	75	75	75	75	75	75	75	LU010000	LATIN SMALL LETTER U
0076	76	76	76	76	76	76	76	LV010000	LATIN SMALL LETTER V
0077	77	77	77	77	77	77	77	LW010000	LATIN SMALL LETTER W
0078	78	78	78	78	78	78	78	LX010000	LATIN SMALL LETTER X
0079	79	79	79	79	79	79	79	LY010000	LATIN SMALL LETTER Y
007A	7A	7A	7A	7A	7A	7A	7A	LZ010000	LATIN SMALL LETTER Z
007B	7B	7B	7B	7B	7B	7B	7B	SM110000	OPENING CURLY BRACKET
007C	7C	7C	7C	7C	7C	7C	7C	SM130000	VERTICAL BAR
007D	7D	7D	7D	7D	7D	7D	7D	SM140000	CLOSING CURLY BRACKET
007E	7E	7E	7E	7E	7E	7E	7E	SD190000	TILDE
007F	7F	7F	7F	7F	7F	7F	7F		DELETE

Common DTP Symbols (Plus Extended Latin1)

UNIC 1200	ANSI 1252	Turk 1254	EE 1250	Cyrl 1251	Greek 1253	Arab 1256	Hebr 1255	IBM GCGID	Unicode character name
UNDF	80	80	80		80		80		
UNDF	81	81	81		81		81		
201A	82	82	82	82	82	82	82	SP260000	LOW SINGLE COMMA QUOTATION MARK
0192	83	83			83		83	SC070000	LATIN SMALL LETTER SCRIPT F
201E	84	84	84	84	84	84	84	SP230000	LOW DOUBLE COMMA QUOTATION MARK
2026	85	85	85	85	85	85	85	SV520000	HORIZONTAL ELLIPSIS
2020	86	86	86	86	86	86	86	SM340000	DAGGER
2021	87	87	87	87	87	87	87	SM350000	DOUBLE DAGGER
02C6	88	88						SD150100	MODIFIER LETTER CIRCUMFLEX
2030	89	89	89	89	89		89	SM560000	PER MILLE SIGN
0160	8A	8A	8A					LS220000	LATIN CAPITAL LETTER S HACEK
2039	8B	8B	8B	8B	8B	8B	8B	SP270000	LEFT POINTING SINGLE GUILLEMET
0152	8C	8C						LO520000	LATIN CAPITAL LETTER O E
UNDF	8D	8D			8D		8D		
UNDF	8E	8E			8E		8E		

UNIC 1200	ANSI 1252	Turk 1254	EE 1250	Cyrl 1251	Greek 1253	Arab 1256	Hebr 1255	IBM GCGID	Unicode character name
UNDF	8F	8F			8F		8F		
UNDF	90	90	90		90		90		
2018	91	91	91	91	91	91	91	SP190000	SINGLE TURNED COMMA QUOTATION MARK
2019	92	92	92	92	92	92	92	SP200000	SINGLE COMMA QUOTATION MARK
201C	93	93	93	93	93	93	93	SP210000	DOUBLE TURNED COMMA QUOTATION MARK
201D	94	94	94	94	94	94	94	SP220000	DOUBLE COMMA QUOTATION MARK
2022	95	95	95	95	95	95	95	SM570000	BULLET
2013	96	96	96	96	96	96	96	SS680000	EN DASH
2014	97	97	97	97	97	97	97	SM900000	EM DASH
02DC	98	98						SD190100	SPACING TILDE
2122	99	99	99	99	99	99	99	SM540000	TRADEMARK
0161	9A	9A	9A					LS210000	LATIN SMALL LETTER S HACEK
203A	9B	9B	9B	9B	9B	9B	9B	SP280000	RIGHT POINTING SINGLE GUILLEMET
0153	9C	9C						LO510000	LATIN SMALL LETTER O E
UNDF	9D	9D			9D		9D		
UNDF	9E	9E			9E		9E		
0178	9F	9F				9F		LY180000	LATIN CAPITAL LETTER Y DIAERESIS
Latin1 (Including Common Symbols)									
00A0	A0	A0	A0	A0	A0	A0	A0	SP300000	NON-BREAKING SPACE
00A1	A1	A1						SP030000	INVERTED EXCLAMATION MARK
00A2	A2	A2					A2	SC040000	CENT SIGN
00A3	A3	A3			A3	A3	A3	SC020000	POUND SIGN
00A4	A4	A4	A4	A4	A4	A4	A4	SC010000	CURRENCY SIGN
00A5	A5	A5			A5		A5	SC050000	YEN SIGN
00A6	A6	A6	A6	A6	A6	A6	A6	SM650000	BROKEN VERTICAL BAR
00A7	A7	A7	A7	A7	A7	A7	A7	SM240000	SECTION SIGN
00A8	A8	A8	A8		A8		A8	SD170000	SPACING DIAERESIS
00A9	A9	A9	A9	A9	A9	A9	A9	SM520000	COPYRIGHT SIGN
00AA	AA	AA						SM210000	FEMININE ORDINAL INDICATOR
00AB	AB	AB	AB	AB	AB	AB	AB	SP170000	LEFT POINTING GUILLEMET
00AC	AC	AC	AC	AC	AC	AC	AC	SM660000	NOT SIGN
00AD	AD	AD	AD	AD	AD	AD	AD	SP320000	SOFT HYPHEN
00AE	AE	AE	AE	AE	AE	AE	AE	SM530000	REGISTERED TRADE MARK SIGN
00AF	AF	AF					AF	SM150000	SPACING MACRON
00B0	B0	B0	B0	B0	B0	B0	B0	SM190000	DEGREE SIGN
00B1	B1	B1	B1	B1	B1	B1	B1	SA020000	PLUS-OR-MINUS SIGN
00B2	B2	B2			B2		B2	ND021000	SUPERSCRIPT DIGIT TWO

UNIC 1200	ANSI 1252	Turk 1254	EE 1250	Cyrl 1251	Greek 1253	Arab 1256	Hebr 1255	IBM GCGID	Unicode character name
00B3	B3	B3					B3	ND031000	SUPERSCRIPT DIGIT THREE
00B4	B4	B4	B4		B3		B4	SD110000	SPACING ACUTE
00B5	B5	B5	B5	B5	B5	B5	B5	SM170000	MICRO SIGN
00B6	B6	B6	B6	B6	B6	B6	B6	SM250000	PARAGRAPH SIGN
00B7	B7	B7	B7	B7	B7	B7	B7	SD630000	MIDDLE DOT
00B8	B8	B8	B8				B8	SD410000	SPACING CEDILLA
00B9	B9	B9					B9	ND011000	SUPERSCRIPT DIGIT ONE
00BA	BA	BA						SM200000	MASCULINE ORDINAL INDICATOR
00BB	BB	BB	BB	BB	BB	BB	BB	SP180000	RIGHT POINTING GUILLEMET
00BC	BC	BC					BC	NF040000	FRACTION ONE QUARTER
00BD	BD	BD			BD		BD	NF010000	FRACTION ONE HALF
00BE	BE	BE					BE	NF050000	FRACTION THREE QUARTERS
00BF	BF	BF						SP160000	INVERTED QUESTION MARK
00C0	C0	C0				C0		LA140000	LATIN CAPITAL LETTER A GRAVE
00C1	C1	C1	C1					LA120000	LATIN CAPITAL LETTER A ACUTE
00C2	C2	C2	C2			C2		LA160000	LATIN CAPITAL LETTER A CIRCUMFLEX
00C3	C3	C3						LA200000	LATIN CAPITAL LETTER A TILDE
00C4	C4	C4	C4					LA180000	LATIN CAPITAL LETTER A DIAERESIS
00C5	C5	C5						LA280000	LATIN CAPITAL LETTER A RING
00C6	C6	C6						LA520000	LATIN CAPITAL LETTER A E
00C7	C7	C7	C7			C7		LC420000	LATIN CAPITAL LETTER C CEDILLA
00C8	C8	C8				C8		LE140000	LATIN CAPITAL LETTER E GRAVE
00C9	C9	C9	C9			C9		LE120000	LATIN CAPITAL LETTER E ACUTE
00CA	CA	CA				CA		LE160000	LATIN CAPITAL LETTER E CIRCUMFLEX
00CB	CB	CB	CB			CB		LE180000	LATIN CAPITAL LETTER E DIAERESIS
00CC	CC	CC						LI140000	LATIN CAPITAL LETTER I GRAVE
00CD	CD	CD	CD					LI120000	LATIN CAPITAL LETTER I ACUTE
00CE	CE	CE	CE			CE		LI160000	LATIN CAPITAL LETTER I CIRCUMFLEX
00CF	CF	CF				CF		LI180000	LATIN CAPITAL LETTER I DIAERESIS
00D0	D0							LD620000	LATIN CAPITAL LETTER ETH
00D1	D1	D1						LN200000	LATIN CAPITAL LETTER N TILDE
00D2	D2	D2						LO140000	LATIN CAPITAL LETTER O GRAVE
00D3	D3	D3	D3					LO120000	LATIN CAPITAL LETTER O ACUTE
00D4	D4	D4	D4			D4		LO160000	LATIN CAPITAL LETTER O CIRCUMFLEX
00D5	D5	D5						LO200000	LATIN CAPITAL LETTER O TILDE
00D6	D6	D6	D6					LO180000	LATIN CAPITAL LETTER O DIAERESIS
00D7	D7	D7	D7			D7	AA	SA070000	MULTIPLICATION SIGN
00D8	D8	D8						LO620000	LATIN CAPITAL LETTER O SLASH
00D9	D9	D9				D9		LU140000	LATIN CAPITAL LETTER U GRAVE

UNIC 1200	ANSI 1252	Turk 1254	EE 1250	Cyrl 1251	Greek 1253	Arab 1256	Hebr 1255	IBM GCGID	Unicode character name
00DA	DA	DA	DA					LU120000	LATIN CAPITAL LETTER U ACUTE
00DB	DB	DB				DB		LU160000	LATIN CAPITAL LETTER U CIRCUMFLEX
00DC	DC	DC	DC			DC		LU180000	LATIN CAPITAL LETTER U DIAERESIS
00DD	DD		DD					LY120000	LATIN CAPITAL LETTER Y ACUTE
00DE	DE							LT640000	LATIN CAPITAL LETTER THORN
00DF	DF	DF	DF					LS610000	LATIN SMALL LETTER SHARP S
00E0	E0	E0				E0		LA130000	LATIN SMALL LETTER A GRAVE
00E1	E1	E1	E1					LA110000	LATIN SMALL LETTER A ACUTE
00E2	E2	E2	E2			E2		LA150000	LATIN SMALL LETTER A CIRCUMFLEX
00E3	E3	E3						LA190000	LATIN SMALL LETTER A TILDE
00E4	E4	E4	E4					LA170000	LATIN SMALL LETTER A DIAERESIS
00E5	E5	E5						LA270000	LATIN SMALL LETTER A RING
00E6	E6	E6						LA510000	LATIN SMALL LETTER A E
00E7	E7	E7	E7			E7		LC410000	LATIN SMALL LETTER C CEDILLA
00E8	E8	E8				E8		LE130000	LATIN SMALL LETTER E GRAVE
00E9	E9	E9	E9			E9		LE110000	LATIN SMALL LETTER E ACUTE
00EA	EA	EA				EA		LE150000	LATIN SMALL LETTER E CIRCUMFLEX
00EB	EB	EB	EB			EB		LE170000	LATIN SMALL LETTER E DIAERESIS
00EC	EC	EC						LI130000	LATIN SMALL LETTER I GRAVE
00ED	ED	ED	ED					LI110000	LATIN SMALL LETTER I ACUTE
00EE	EE	EE	EE			EE		LI150000	LATIN SMALL LETTER I CIRCUMFLEX
00EF	EF	EF				EF		LI170000	LATIN SMALL LETTER I DIAERESIS
00F0	F0							LD630000	LATIN SMALL LETTER ETH
00F1	F1	F1						LN190000	LATIN SMALL LETTER N TILDE
00F2	F2	F2						LO130000	LATIN SMALL LETTER O GRAVE
00F3	F3	F3	F3					LO110000	LATIN SMALL LETTER O ACUTE
00F4	F4	F4	F4			F4		LO150000	LATIN SMALL LETTER O CIRCUMFLEX
00F5	F5	F5						LO190000	LATIN SMALL LETTER O TILDE
00F6	F6	F6	F6					LO170000	LATIN SMALL LETTER O DIAERESIS
00F7	F7	F7	F7			F7	BA	SA060000	DIVISION SIGN
00F8	F8	F8						LO610000	LATIN SMALL LETTER O SLASH
00F9	F9	F9				F9		LU130000	LATIN SMALL LETTER U GRAVE
00FA	FA	FA	FA					LU110000	LATIN SMALL LETTER U ACUTE
00FB	FB	FB				FB		LU150000	LATIN SMALL LETTER U CIRCUMFLEX
00FC	FC	FC	FC			FC		LU170000	LATIN SMALL LETTER U DIAERESIS
00FD	FD		FD					LY110000	LATIN SMALL LETTER Y ACUTE
00FE	FE							LT630000	LATIN SMALL LETTER THORN
00FF	FF	FF	FF			FF		LY170000	LATIN SMALL LETTER Y DIAERESIS

UNIC 1200	ANSI 1252	Turk 1254	EE 1250	Cyrl 1251	Greek 1253	Arab 1256	Hebr 1255	IBM GCGID	Unicode character name

Turkish

UNIC 1200	ANSI 1252	Turk 1254	EE 1250	Cyrl 1251	Greek 1253	Arab 1256	Hebr 1255	IBM GCGID	Unicode character name
011E		D0						LG240000	LATIN CAPITAL LETTER G BREVE
0130		DD						LI300000	LATIN CAPITAL LETTER I DOT
015E		DE						LS420000	LATIN CAPITAL LETTER S CEDILLA
011F		F0						LG230000	LATIN SMALL LETTER G BREVE
0131		FD						LI610000	LATIN SMALL LETTER DOTLESS I
015F		FE						LS410000	LATIN SMALL LETTER S CEDILLA

Eastern European (Latin2)

UNIC 1200	ANSI 1252	Turk 1254	EE 1250	Cyrl 1251	Greek 1253	Arab 1256	Hebr 1255	IBM GCGID	Unicode character name
UNDF			83						
UNDF			88						
015A			8C					LS120000	LATIN CAPITAL LETTER S ACUTE
0164			8D					LT220000	LATIN CAPITAL LETTER T HACEK
017D			8E					LZ220000	LATIN CAPITAL LETTER Z HACEK
0179			8F					LZ120000	LATIN CAPITAL LETTER Z ACUTE
UNDF			98						
015B			9C					LS110000	LATIN SMALL LETTER S ACUTE
0165			9D					LT210000	LATIN SMALL LETTER T HACEK
017E			9E					LZ210000	LATIN SMALL LETTER Z HACEK
017A			9F					LZ110000	LATIN SMALL LETTER Z ACUTE
02C7			A1					SD210000	MODIFIER LETTER HACEK
02D8			A2					SD230000	SPACING BREVE
0141			A3					LL620000	LATIN CAPITAL LETTER L SLASH
0104			A5					LA440000	LATIN CAPITAL LETTER A OGONEK
015E			AA					LS420000	LATIN CAPITAL LETTER S CEDILLA
017B			AF					LZ300000	LATIN CAPITAL LETTER Z DOT
02DB			B2					SD430000	SPACING OGONEK
0142			B3					LL610000	LATIN SMALL LETTER L SLASH
0105			B9					LA430000	LATIN SMALL LETTER A OGONEK
015F			BA					LS410000	LATIN SMALL LETTER S CEDILLA
013D			BC					LL220000	LATIN CAPITAL LETTER L HACEK
02DD			BD					SD250000	SPACING DOUBLE ACUTE
013E			BE					LL210000	LATIN SMALL LETTER L HACEK
017C			BF					LZ290000	LATIN SMALL LETTER Z DOT
0154			C0					LR120000	LATIN CAPITAL LETTER R ACUTE
0102			C3					LA240000	LATIN CAPITAL LETTER A BREVE

UNIC 1200	ANSI 1252	Turk 1254	EE 1250	Cyrl 1251	Greek 1253	Arab 1256	Hebr 1255	IBM GCGID	Unicode character name
0139			C5					LL120000	LATIN CAPITAL LETTER L ACUTE
0106			C6					LC120000	LATIN CAPITAL LETTER C ACUTE
010C			C8					LC220000	LATIN CAPITAL LETTER C HACEK
0118			CA					LE440000	LATIN CAPITAL LETTER E OGONEK
011A			CC					LE220000	LATIN CAPITAL LETTER E HACEK
010E			CF					LD220000	LATIN CAPITAL LETTER D HACEK
0110			D0					LD620000	LATIN CAPITAL LETTER D BAR
0143			D1					LN120000	LATIN CAPITAL LETTER N ACUTE
0147			D2					LN220000	LATIN CAPITAL LETTER N HACEK
0150			D5					LO260000	LATIN CAPITAL LETTER O DOUBLE ACUTE
0158			D8					LR220000	LATIN CAPITAL LETTER R HACEK
016E			D9					LU280000	LATIN CAPITAL LETTER U RING
0170			DB					LU260000	LATIN CAPITAL LETTER U DOUBLE ACUTE
0162			DE					LT420000	LATIN CAPITAL LETTER T CEDILLA
0155			E0					LR110000	LATIN SMALL LETTER R ACUTE
0103			E3					LA230000	LATIN SMALL LETTER A BREVE
013A			E5					LL110000	LATIN SMALL LETTER L ACUTE
0107			E6					LC110000	LATIN SMALL LETTER C ACUTE
010D			E8					LC210000	LATIN SMALL LETTER C HACEK
0119			EA					LE430000	LATIN SMALL LETTER E OGONEK
011B			EC					LE210000	LATIN SMALL LETTER E HACEK
010F			EF					LD210000	LATIN SMALL LETTER D HACEK
0111			F0					LD610000	LATIN SMALL LETTER D BAR
0144			F1					LN110000	LATIN SMALL LETTER N ACUTE
0148			F2					LN210000	LATIN SMALL LETTER N HACEK
0151			F5					LO250000	LATIN SMALL LETTER O DOUBLE ACUTE
0159			F8					LR210000	LATIN SMALL LETTER R HACEK
016F			F9					LU270000	LATIN SMALL LETTER U RING
0171			FB					LU250000	LATIN SMALL LETTER U DOUBLE ACUTE
0163			FE					LT410000	LATIN SMALL LETTER T CEDILLA
02D9			FF					SD290000	SPACING DOT ABOVE

Cyrillic

UNIC 1200	ANSI 1252	Turk 1254	EE 1250	Cyrl 1251	Greek 1253	Arab 1256	Hebr 1255	IBM GCGID	Unicode character name
0402				80				KD620000	CYRILLIC CAPITAL LETTER DJE
0403				81				KG120000	CYRILLIC CAPITAL LETTER GJE
0453				83				KG110000	CYRILLIC SMALL LETTER GJE
UNDF				88					
0409				8A				KL420000	CYRILLIC CAPITAL LETTER LJE

UNIC 1200	ANSI 1252	Turk 1254	EE 1250	Cyrl 1251	Greek 1253	Arab 1256	Hebr 1255	IBM GCGID	Unicode character name
040A				8C				KN120000	CYRILLIC CAPITAL LETTER NJE
040C				8D				KK120000	CYRILLIC CAPITAL LETTER KJE
040B				8E				KC120000	CYRILLIC CAPITAL LETTER TSHE
040F				8F				KG220000	CYRILLIC CAPITAL LETTER DZHE
0452				90				KD610000	CYRILLIC SMALL LETTER DJE
UNDF				98					
0459				9A				KL410000	CYRILLIC SMALL LETTER LJE
045A				9C				KN110000	CYRILLIC SMALL LETTER NJE
045C				9D				KK110000	CYRILLIC SMALL LETTER KJE
045B				9E				KC110000	CYRILLIC SMALL LETTER TSHE
045F				9F				KG210000	CYRILLIC SMALL LETTER DZHE
040E				A1				KU240000	CYRILLIC CAPITAL LETTER SHORT U
045E				A2				KU230000	CYRILLIC SMALL LETTER SHORT U
0408				A3				KJ020000	CYRILLIC CAPITAL LETTER JE
0490				A5				KG300000	CYRILLIC CAPITAL LETTER GE WITH UPTURN
0401				A8				KE180000	CYRILLIC CAPITAL LETTER IO
0404				AA				KE160000	CYRILLIC CAPITAL LETTER E
0407				AF				KI180000	CYRILLIC CAPITAL LETTER YI
0406				B2				KI120000	CYRILLIC CAPITAL LETTER I
0456				B3				KI110000	CYRILLIC SMALL LETTER I
0491				B4				KG290000	CYRILLIC SMALL LETTER GE WITH UPTURN
0451				B8				KE170000	CYRILLIC SMALL LETTER IO
2116				B9				SM000000	NUMERO
0454				BA				KE150000	CYRILLIC SMALL LETTER E
0458				BC				KJ010000	CYRILLIC SMALL LETTER JE
0405				BD				KZ160000	CYRILLIC CAPITAL LETTER DZE
0455				BE				KZ150000	CYRILLIC SMALL LETTER DZE
0457				BF				KI170000	CYRILLIC SMALL LETTER YI
0410				C0				KA020000	CYRILLIC CAPITAL LETTER A
0411				C1				KB020000	CYRILLIC CAPITAL LETTER BE
0412				C2				KV020000	CYRILLIC CAPITAL LETTER VE
0413				C3				KG020000	CYRILLIC CAPITAL LETTER GE
0414				C4				KD020000	CYRILLIC CAPITAL LETTER DE
0415				C5				KE020000	CYRILLIC CAPITAL LETTER IE
0416				C6				KZ220000	CYRILLIC CAPITAL LETTER ZHE
0417				C7				KZ020000	CYRILLIC CAPITAL LETTER ZE
0418				C8				KI020000	CYRILLIC CAPITAL LETTER II
0419				C9				KJ120000	CYRILLIC CAPITAL LETTER SHORT II
041A				CA				KK020000	CYRILLIC CAPITAL LETTER KA

UNIC 1200	ANSI 1252	Turk 1254	EE 1250	Cyrl 1251	Greek 1253	Arab 1256	Hebr 1255	IBM GCGID	Unicode character name
041B				CB				KL020000	CYRILLIC CAPITAL LETTER EL
041C				CC				KM020000	CYRILLIC CAPITAL LETTER EM
041D				CD				KN020000	CYRILLIC CAPITAL LETTER EN
041E				CE				KO020000	CYRILLIC CAPITAL LETTER O
041F				CF				KP020000	CYRILLIC CAPITAL LETTER PE
0420				D0				KR020000	CYRILLIC CAPITAL LETTER ER
0421				D1				KS020000	CYRILLIC CAPITAL LETTER ES
0422				D2				KT020000	CYRILLIC CAPITAL LETTER TE
0423				D3				KU020000	CYRILLIC CAPITAL LETTER U
0424				D4				KF020000	CYRILLIC CAPITAL LETTER EF
0425				D5				KH020000	CYRILLIC CAPITAL LETTER KHA
0426				D6				KC020000	CYRILLIC CAPITAL LETTER TSE
0427				D7				KC220000	CYRILLIC CAPITAL LETTER CHE
0428				D8				KS220000	CYRILLIC CAPITAL LETTER SHA
0429				D9				KS160000	CYRILLIC CAPITAL LETTER SHCHA
042A				DA				KU220000	CYRILLIC CAPITAL LETTER HARD SIGN
042B				DB				KY020000	CYRILLIC CAPITAL LETTER YERI
042C				DC				KX120000	CYRILLIC CAPITAL LETTER SOFT SIGN
042D				DD				KE140000	CYRILLIC CAPITAL LETTER REVERSED E
042E				DE				KU160000	CYRILLIC CAPITAL LETTER IU
042F				DF				KA160000	CYRILLIC CAPITAL LETTER IA
0430				E0				KA010000	CYRILLIC SMALL LETTER A
0431				E1				KB010000	CYRILLIC SMALL LETTER BE
0432				E2				KV010000	CYRILLIC SMALL LETTER VE
0433				E3				KG010000	CYRILLIC SMALL LETTER GE
0434				E4				KD010000	CYRILLIC SMALL LETTER DE
0435				E5				KE010000	CYRILLIC SMALL LETTER IE
0436				E6				KZ210000	CYRILLIC SMALL LETTER ZHE
0437				E7				KZ010000	CYRILLIC SMALL LETTER ZE
0438				E8				KI010000	CYRILLIC SMALL LETTER II
0439				E9				KJ110000	CYRILLIC SMALL LETTER SHORT II
043A				EA				KK010000	CYRILLIC SMALL LETTER KA
043B				EB				KL010000	CYRILLIC SMALL LETTER EL
043C				EC				KM010000	CYRILLIC SMALL LETTER EM
043D				ED				KN010000	CYRILLIC SMALL LETTER EN
043E				EE				KO010000	CYRILLIC SMALL LETTER O
043F				EF				KP010000	CYRILLIC SMALL LETTER PE
0440				F0				KR010000	CYRILLIC SMALL LETTER ER
0441				F1				KS010000	CYRILLIC SMALL LETTER ES

UNIC 1200	ANSI 1252	Turk 1254	EE 1250	Cyrl 1251	Greek 1253	Arab 1256	Hebr 1255	IBM GCGID	Unicode character name
0442				F2				KT010000	CYRILLIC SMALL LETTER TE
0443				F3				KU010000	CYRILLIC SMALL LETTER U
0444				F4				KF010000	CYRILLIC SMALL LETTER EF
0445				F5				KH010000	CYRILLIC SMALL LETTER KHA
0446				F6				KC010000	CYRILLIC SMALL LETTER TSE
0447				F7				KC210000	CYRILLIC SMALL LETTER CHE
0448				F8				KS210000	CYRILLIC SMALL LETTER SHA
0449				F9				KS150000	CYRILLIC SMALL LETTER SHCHA
044A				FA				KU210000	CYRILLIC SMALL LETTER HARD SIGN
044B				FB				KY010000	CYRILLIC SMALL LETTER YERI
044C				FC				KX110000	CYRILLIC SMALL LETTER SOFT SIGN
044D				FD				KE130000	CYRILLIC SMALL LETTER REVERSED E
044E				FE				KU150000	CYRILLIC SMALL LETTER IU
044F				FF				KA150000	CYRILLIC SMALL LETTER IA

Greek

UNIC 1200	ANSI 1252	Turk 1254	EE 1250	Cyrl 1251	Greek 1253	Arab 1256	Hebr 1255	IBM GCGID	Unicode character name
					88				
					98				
					8A				
					8C				
					9A				
					9C				
					9F				
UNDF					A1			SD730000	GREEK SPACING DIAERESIS TONOS
UNDF					A2			GA120000	GREEK CAPITAL LETTER ALPHA TONOS
2015					AF			SM120000	QUOTATION DASH
03F3					B4			SD110900	GREEK SPACING TONOS
0388					B8			GE120000	GREEK CAPITAL LETTER EPSILON TONOS
0389					B9			GE720000	GREEK CAPITAL LETTER ETA TONOS
038A					BA			GI120000	GREEK CAPITAL LETTER IOTA TONOS
038C					BC			GO120000	GREEK CAPITAL LETTER OMICRON TONOS
038E					BE			GU120000	GREEK CAPITAL LETTER UPSILON TONOS
038F					BF			GO720000	GREEK CAPITAL LETTER OMEGA TONOS
0390					C0			GI730000	GREEK SMALL LETTER IOTA DIAERESIS TONOS
0391					C1			GA020000	GREEK CAPITAL LETTER ALPHA
0392					C2			GB020000	GREEK CAPITAL LETTER BETA
0393					C3			GG020000	GREEK CAPITAL LETTER GAMMA
0394					C4			GD020000	GREEK CAPITAL LETTER DELTA

UNIC 1200	ANSI 1252	Turk 1254	EE 1250	Cyrl 1251	Greek 1253	Arab 1256	Hebr 1255	IBM GCGID	Unicode character name
0395					C5			GE020000	GREEK CAPITAL LETTER EPSILON
0396					C6			GZ020000	GREEK CAPITAL LETTER ZETA
0397					C7			GE320000	GREEK CAPITAL LETTER ETA
0398					C8			GT620000	GREEK CAPITAL LETTER THETA
0399					C9			GI020000	GREEK CAPITAL LETTER IOTA
039A					CA			GK020000	GREEK CAPITAL LETTER KAPPA
039B					CB			GL020000	GREEK CAPITAL LETTER LAMBDA
039C					CC			GM020000	GREEK CAPITAL LETTER MU
039D					CD			GN020000	GREEK CAPITAL LETTER NU
039E					CE			GX020000	GREEK CAPITAL LETTER XI
039F					CF			GO020000	GREEK CAPITAL LETTER OMICRON
03A0					D0			GP020000	GREEK CAPITAL LETTER PI
03A1					D1			GR020000	GREEK CAPITAL LETTER RHO
UNDF					D2				
03A3					D3			GS020000	GREEK CAPITAL LETTER SIGMA
03A4					D4			GT020000	GREEK CAPITAL LETTER TAU
03A5					D5			GU020000	GREEK CAPITAL LETTER UPSILON
03A6					D6			GF020000	GREEK CAPITAL LETTER PHI
03A7					D7			GH020000	GREEK CAPITAL LETTER CHI
03A8					D8			GP620000	GREEK CAPITAL LETTER PSI
03A9					D9			GO320000	GREEK CAPITAL LETTER OMEGA
03AA					DA			GI180000	GREEK CAPITAL LETTER IOTA DIAERESIS
03AB					DB			GU180000	GREEK CAPITAL LETTER UPSILON DIAERESIS
03AC					DC			GA110000	GREEK SMALL LETTER ALPHA TONOS
03AD					DD			GE110000	GREEK SMALL LETTER EPSILON TONOS
03AE					DE			GE710000	GREEK SMALL LETTER ETA TONOS
03AF					DF			GI110000	GREEK SMALL LETTER IOTA TONOS
03B0					E0			GU730000	GREEK SMALL LETTER UPSILON DIAERESIS TONOS
03B1					E1			GA010000	GREEK SMALL LETTER ALPHA
03B2					E2			GB010000	GREEK SMALL LETTER BETA
03B3					E3			GG010000	GREEK SMALL LETTER GAMMA
03B4					E4			GD010000	GREEK SMALL LETTER DELTA
03B5					E5			GE010000	GREEK SMALL LETTER EPSILON
03B6					E6			GZ010000	GREEK SMALL LETTER ZETA
03B7					E7			GE310000	GREEK SMALL LETTER ETA
03B8					E8			GT610002	GREEK SMALL LETTER THETA
03B9					E9			GI010000	GREEK SMALL LETTER IOTA
03BA					EA			GK010000	GREEK SMALL LETTER KAPPA
03BB					EB			GL010000	GREEK SMALL LETTER LAMBDA

UNIC 1200	ANSI 1252	Turk 1254	EE 1250	Cyrl 1251	Greek 1253	Arab 1256	Hebr 1255	IBM GCGID	Unicode character name
03BC					EC			GM010000	GREEK SMALL LETTER MU
03BD					ED			GN010000	GREEK SMALL LETTER NU
03BE					EE			GX010000	GREEK SMALL LETTER XI
03BF					EF			GO010000	GREEK SMALL LETTER OMICRON
03C0					F0			GP010000	GREEK SMALL LETTER PI
03C1					F1			GR010000	GREEK SMALL LETTER RHO
03C2					F2			GS610000	GREEK SMALL LETTER FINAL SIGMA
03C3					F3			GS010000	GREEK SMALL LETTER SIGMA
03C4					F4			GT010000	GREEK SMALL LETTER TAU
03C5					F5			GU010000	GREEK SMALL LETTER UPSILON
03C6					F6			GF010000	GREEK SMALL LETTER PHI
03C7					F7			GH010000	GREEK SMALL LETTER CHI
03C8					F8			GP610000	GREEK SMALL LETTER PSI
03C9					F9			GO310000	GREEK SMALL LETTER OMEGA
03CA					FA			GI170000	GREEK SMALL LETTER IOTA DIAERESIS
03CB					FB			GU170000	GREEK SMALL LETTER UPSILON DIAERESIS
03CC					FC			GO110000	GREEK SMALL LETTER OMICRON TONOS
03CD					FD			GU110000	GREEK SMALL LETTER UPSILON TONOS
03CE					FE			GO710000	GREEK SMALL LETTER OMEGA TONOS
UNDF					FF				

Bidi

UNIC	...	Arab 1256	Hebr 1255	IBM GCGID	Unicode character name
200E		FD	FD	<tba>	LEFT-TO-RIGHT MARK
200F		FE	FE	<tba>	RIGHT-TO-LEFT MARK

Hebrew

UNIC	Hebr 1255
UNDF	8A
UNDF	8C
UNDF	9A
UNDF	9C
UNDF	9F
UNDF	C0
UNDF	C1
UNDF	C2
UNDF	C3
UNDF	C4
UNDF	C5

UNIC 1200	ANSI 1252	Turk 1254	EE 1250	Cyrl 1251	Greek 1253	Arab 1256	Hebr 1255	IBM GCGID	Unicode character name
UNDF							C6		
UNDF							C7		
UNDF							C8		
UNDF							C9		
UNDF							CA		
UNDF							CB		
UNDF							CC		
UNDF							CD		
UNDF							CE		
UNDF							CF		
UNDF							D0		
UNDF							D1		
UNDF							D2		
UNDF							D3		
UNDF							D4		
UNDF							D5		
UNDF							D6		
UNDF							D7		
UNDF							D8		
UNDF							D9		
UNDF							DA		
UNDF							DB		
UNDF							DC		
UNDF							DD		
UNDF							DE		
2017							DF	SM100000	SPACING DOUBLE UNDERSCORE
05D0							E0	HX330000	HEBREW LETTER ALEF
05D1							E1	HB010000	HEBREW LETTER BET
05D2							E2	HG010000	HEBREW LETTER GIMEL
05D3							E3	HD010000	HEBREW LETTER DALET
05D4							E4	HH010000	HEBREW LETTER HE
05D5							E5	HW010000	HEBREW LETTER VAV
05D6							E6	HZ010000	HEBREW LETTER ZAYIN
05D7							E7	HH450000	HEBREW LETTER HET
05D8							E8	HT450000	HEBREW LETTER TET
05D9							E9	HY010000	HEBREW LETTER YOD
05DA							EA	HK610000	HEBREW LETTER FINAL KAF
05DB							EB	HK010000	HEBREW LETTER KAF
05DC							EC	HL010000	HEBREW LETTER LAMED

UNIC 1200	ANSI 1252	Turk 1254	EE 1250	Cyrl 1251	Greek 1253	Arab 1256	Hebr 1255	IBM GCGID	Unicode character name
05DD							ED	HM610000	HEBREW LETTER FINAL MEM
05DE							EE	HM010000	HEBREW LETTER MEM
05DF							EF	HN610000	HEBREW LETTER FINAL NUN
05E0							F0	HN010000	HEBREW LETTER NUN
05E1							F1	HS010000	HEBREW LETTER SAMEKH
05E2							F2	HX350000	HEBREW LETTER AYIN
05E3							F3	HP610000	HEBREW LETTER FINAL PE
05E4							F4	HP010000	HEBREW LETTER PE
05E5							F5	HS610000	HEBREW LETTER FINAL TSADI
05E6							F6	HS450000	HEBREW LETTER TSADI
05E7							F7	HQ010000	HEBREW LETTER QOF
05E8							F8	HR010000	HEBREW LETTER RESH
05E9							F9	HS210000	HEBREW LETTER SHIN
05EA							FA	HT010000	HEBREW LETTER TAV

Arabic

UNIC 1200	ANSI 1252	Turk 1254	EE 1250	Cyrl 1251	Greek 1253	Arab 1256	Hebr 1255	IBM GCGID	Unicode character name
060C						80		SP080007	ARABIC COMMA
061B						98		SP140007	ARABIC SEMICOLON
061F						9A		SP150007	ARABIC QUESTION MARK
0621						9C		AX300000	ARABIC LETTER HAMZAH
0622						9D		AA210000	ARABIC LETTER MADDAH ON ALEF
0623						9E		AA310000	ARABIC LETTER HAMZAH ON ALEF
0624						A1		AW310000	ARABIC LETTER HAMZAH ON WAW
0625						A2		AA310400	ARABIC LETTER HAMZAH UNDER ALEF
0626						A5		AY320000	ARABIC LETTER HAMZAH ON YA
0627						A8		AA010000	ARABIC LETTER ALEF
0628						AA		AB010000	ARABIC LETTER BAA
067E						AF		AP010000	ARABIC LETTER TAA WITH THREE DOTS BELOW
0629						B2		AT020000	ARABIC LETTER TAA MARBUTAH
062A						B3		AT010000	ARABIC LETTER TAA
062B						B4		AT470000	ARABIC LETTER THAA
062C						B8		AG230000	ARABIC LETTER JEEM
0686						B9		AC210000	ARABIC LETTER HAA WITH MIDDLE THREE DOTS DOWNWARD
062D						BA		AH450000	ARABIC LETTER HAA
062E						BC		AH470000	ARABIC LETTER KHAA
062F						BD		AD010000	ARABIC LETTER DAL
0630						BE		AD470000	ARABIC LETTER THAL
0631						BF		AR010000	ARABIC LETTER RA

UNIC 1200	ANSI 1252	Turk 1254	EE 1250	Cyrl 1251	Greek 1253	Arab 1256	Hebr 1255	IBM GCGID	Unicode character name
0632						C1		AZ010000	ARABIC LETTER ZAIN
0698						C3		AZ210000	ARABIC LETTER RA WITH THREE DOTS ABOVE
0633						C4		AS010006	ARABIC LETTER SEEN
0634						C5		AS230006	ARABIC LETTER SHEEN
0635						C6		AS450006	ARABIC LETTER SAD
0636						CC		AD450006	ARABIC LETTER DAD
0637						CD		AT450000	ARABIC LETTER TAH
0638						D0		AZ450000	ARABIC LETTER DHAH
0639						D1		AC470000	ARABIC LETTER AIN
063A						D2		AG310000	ARABIC LETTER GHAIN
0640						D3		SM860000	ARABIC TATWEEL
0641						D5		AF010000	ARABIC LETTER FA
0642						D6		AQ010000	ARABIC LETTER QAF
0643						D8		AK010000	ARABIC LETTER CAF
06AF						DA		AG010000	ARABIC LETTER GAF
0644						DD		AL010000	ARABIC LETTER LAM
0645						DE		AM010000	ARABIC LETTER MEEM
0646						DF		AN010000	ARABIC LETTER NOON
0647						E1		AH010000	ARABIC LETTER HA
06C0						E3		AH310000	ARABIC LETTER HAMZAH ON HA
0648						E4		AW010000	ARABIC LETTER WAW
0649						E5		AA020000	ARABIC LETTER ALEF MAQSURAH
064A						E6		AY010000	ARABIC LETTER YA
064B						EC		AA070000	ARABIC FATHATAN
064C						ED		AU070000	ARABIC DAMMATAN
064D						F0		AI070000	ARABIC KASRATAN
064E						F1		AA050000	ARABIC FATHAH
064F						F2		AU050000	ARABIC DAMMAH
0650						F3		AI050000	ARABIC KASRAH
0651						F5		AX100000	ARABIC SHADDAH
0652						F6		AE050000	ARABIC SUKUN
0660						81		ND100001	ARABIC-INDIC DIGIT ZERO
0661						83		ND010001	ARABIC-INDIC DIGIT ONE
0662						88		ND020001	ARABIC-INDIC DIGIT TWO
0663						89		ND030001	ARABIC-INDIC DIGIT THREE
0664						8A		ND040001	ARABIC-INDIC DIGIT FOUR
0665						8C		ND050001	ARABIC-INDIC DIGIT FIVE
0666						8D		ND060001	ARABIC-INDIC DIGIT SIX
0667						8E		ND070001	ARABIC-INDIC DIGIT SEVEN

UNIC 1200	ANSI 1252	Turk 1254	EE 1250	Cyrl 1251	Greek 1253	Arab 1256	Hebr 1255	IBM GCGID	Unicode character name
0668						8F		ND080001	ARABIC-INDIC DIGIT EIGHT
0669						90		ND090001	ARABIC-INDIC DIGIT NINE
RSRV						F8			
RSRV						FA			

UNIC	1004	M4	850	857	863	437	860	861	865	852	GCGID Unicode character name
0020	20	20	20	20	20	20	20	20	20	20	SP010000 SPACE
0021	21	21	21	21	21	21	21	21	21	21	SP020000 EXCLAMATION MARK
0022	22	22	22	22	22	22	22	22	22	22	SP040000 QUOTATION MARK
0023	23	23	23	23	23	23	23	23	23	23	SM010000 NUMBER SIGN
0024	24	24	24	24	24	24	24	24	24	24	SC030000 DOLLAR SIGN
0025	25	25	25	25	25	25	25	25	25	25	SM020000 PERCENT SIGN
0026	26	26	26	26	26	26	26	26	26	26	SM030000 AMPERSAND
0027	27	27	27	27	27	27	27	27	27	27	SP050000 APOSTROPHE-QUOTE
0028	28	28	28	28	28	28	28	28	28	28	SP060000 OPENING PARENTHESIS
0029	29	29	29	29	29	29	29	29	29	29	SP070000 CLOSING PARENTHESIS
002A	2A	2A	2A	2A	2A	2A	2A	2A	2A	2A	SM040000 ASTERISK
002B	2B	2B	2B	2B	2B	2B	2B	2B	2B	2B	SA010000 PLUS SIGN
002C	2C	2C	2C	2C	2C	2C	2C	2C	2C	2C	SP080000 COMMA
002D	2D	2D	2D	2D	2D	2D	2D	2D	2D	2D	SP100000 HYPHEN-MINUS
002E	2E	2E	2E	2E	2E	2E	2E	2E	2E	2E	SP110000 PERIOD
002F	2F	2F	2F	2F	2F	2F	2F	2F	2F	2F	SP120000 SLASH
0030	30	30	30	30	30	30	30	30	30	30	ND100000 DIGIT ZERO
0031	31	31	31	31	31	31	31	31	31	31	ND010000 DIGIT ONE
0032	32	32	32	32	32	32	32	32	32	32	ND020000 DIGIT TWO
0033	33	33	33	33	33	33	33	33	33	33	ND030000 DIGIT THREE
0034	34	34	34	34	34	34	34	34	34	34	ND040000 DIGIT FOUR
0035	35	35	35	35	35	35	35	35	35	35	ND050000 DIGIT FIVE
0036	36	36	36	36	36	36	36	36	36	36	ND060000 DIGIT SIX
0037	37	37	37	37	37	37	37	37	37	37	ND070000 DIGIT SEVEN
0038	38	38	38	38	38	38	38	38	38	38	ND080000 DIGIT EIGHT
0039	39	39	39	39	39	39	39	39	39	39	ND090000 DIGIT NINE
003A	3A	3A	3A	3A	3A	3A	3A	3A	3A	3A	SP130000 COLON
003B	3B	3B	3B	3B	3B	3B	3B	3B	3B	3B	SP140000 SEMICOLON
003C	3C	3C	3C	3C	3C	3C	3C	3C	3C	3C	SA030000 LESS-THAN SIGN
003D	3D	3D	3D	3D	3D	3D	3D	3D	3D	3D	SA040000 EQUALS SIGN
003E	3E	3E	3E	3E	3E	3E	3E	3E	3E	3E	SA050000 GREATER-THAN SIGN
003F	3F	3F	3F	3F	3F	3F	3F	3F	3F	3F	SP150000 QUESTION MARK
0040	40	40	40	40	40	40	40	40	40	40	SM050000 COMMERCIAL AT
0041	41	41	41	41	41	41	41	41	41	41	LA020000 LATIN CAPITAL LETTER A
0042	42	42	42	42	42	42	42	42	42	42	LB020000 LATIN CAPITAL LETTER B
0043	43	43	43	43	43	43	43	43	43	43	LC020000 LATIN CAPITAL LETTER C
0044	44	44	44	44	44	44	44	44	44	44	LD020000 LATIN CAPITAL LETTER D

UNIC	1004	M4	850	857	863	437	860	861	865	852	GCGID	Unicode character name
0045	45	45	45	45	45	45	45	45	45	45	LE020000	LATIN CAPITAL LETTER E
0046	46	46	46	46	46	46	46	46	46	46	LF020000	LATIN CAPITAL LETTER F
0047	47	47	47	47	47	47	47	47	47	47	LG020000	LATIN CAPITAL LETTER G
0048	48	48	48	48	48	48	48	48	48	48	LH020000	LATIN CAPITAL LETTER H
0049	49	49	49	49	49	49	49	49	49	49	LI020000	LATIN CAPITAL LETTER I
004A	4A	4A	4A	4A	4A	4A	4A	4A	4A	4A	LJ020000	LATIN CAPITAL LETTER J
004B	4B	4B	4B	4B	4B	4B	4B	4B	4B	4B	LK020000	LATIN CAPITAL LETTER K
004C	4C	4C	4C	4C	4C	4C	4C	4C	4C	4C	LL020000	LATIN CAPITAL LETTER L
004D	4D	4D	4D	4D	4D	4D	4D	4D	4D	4D	LM020000	LATIN CAPITAL LETTER M
004E	4E	4E	4E	4E	4E	4E	4E	4E	4E	4E	LN020000	LATIN CAPITAL LETTER N
004F	4F	4F	4F	4F	4F	4F	4F	4F	4F	4F	LO020000	LATIN CAPITAL LETTER O
0050	50	50	50	50	50	50	50	50	50	50	LP020000	LATIN CAPITAL LETTER P
0051	51	51	51	51	51	51	51	51	51	51	LQ020000	LATIN CAPITAL LETTER Q
0052	52	52	52	52	52	52	52	52	52	52	LR020000	LATIN CAPITAL LETTER R
0053	53	53	53	53	53	53	53	53	53	53	LS020000	LATIN CAPITAL LETTER S
0054	54	54	54	54	54	54	54	54	54	54	LT020000	LATIN CAPITAL LETTER T
0055	55	55	55	55	55	55	55	55	55	55	LU020000	LATIN CAPITAL LETTER U
0056	56	56	56	56	56	56	56	56	56	56	LV020000	LATIN CAPITAL LETTER V
0057	57	57	57	57	57	57	57	57	57	57	LW020000	LATIN CAPITAL LETTER W
0058	58	58	58	58	58	58	58	58	58	58	LX020000	LATIN CAPITAL LETTER X
0059	59	59	59	59	59	59	59	59	59	59	LY020000	LATIN CAPITAL LETTER Y
005A	5A	5A	5A	5A	5A	5A	5A	5A	5A	5A	LZ020000	LATIN CAPITAL LETTER Z
005B	5B	5B	5B	5B	5B	5B	5B	5B	5B	5B	SM060000	OPENING SQUARE BRACKET
005C	5C	5C	5C	5C	5C	5C	5C	5C	5C	5C	SM070000	BACKSLASH
005D	5D	5D	5D	5D	5D	5D	5D	5D	5D	5D	SM080000	CLOSING SQUARE BRACKET
005E	5E	5E	5E	5E	5E	5E	5E	5E	5E	5E	SD150000	SPACING CIRCUMFLEX
005F	5F	5F	5F	5F	5F	5F	5F	5F	5F	5F	SP090000	SPACING UNDERSCORE
0060	60	60	60	60	60	60	60	60	60	60	SD130000	SPACING GRAVE
0061	61	61	61	61	61	61	61	61	61	61	LA010000	LATIN SMALL LETTER A
0062	62	62	62	62	62	62	62	62	62	62	LB010000	LATIN SMALL LETTER B
0063	63	63	63	63	63	63	63	63	63	63	LC010000	LATIN SMALL LETTER C
0064	64	64	64	64	64	64	64	64	64	64	LD010000	LATIN SMALL LETTER D
0065	65	65	65	65	65	65	65	65	65	65	LE010000	LATIN SMALL LETTER E
0066	66	66	66	66	66	66	66	66	66	66	LF010000	LATIN SMALL LETTER F
0067	67	67	67	67	67	67	67	67	67	67	LG010000	LATIN SMALL LETTER G
0068	68	68	68	68	68	68	68	68	68	68	LH010000	LATIN SMALL LETTER H
0069	69	69	69	69	69	69	69	69	69	69	LI010000	LATIN SMALL LETTER I
006A	6A	6A	6A	6A	6A	6A	6A	6A	6A	6A	LJ010000	LATIN SMALL LETTER J
006B	6B	6B	6B	6B	6B	6B	6B	6B	6B	6B	LK010000	LATIN SMALL LETTER K
006C	6C	6C	6C	6C	6C	6C	6C	6C	6C	6C	LL010000	LATIN SMALL LETTER L

UNIC	1004	M4	850	857	863	437	860	861	865	852	GCGID	Unicode character name
006D	6D	6D	6D	6D	6D	6D	6D	6D	6D	6D	LM010000	LATIN SMALL LETTER M
006E	6E	6E	6E	6E	6E	6E	6E	6E	6E	6E	LN010000	LATIN SMALL LETTER N
006F	6F	6F	6F	6F	6F	6F	6F	6F	6F	6F	LO010000	LATIN SMALL LETTER O
0070	70	70	70	70	70	70	70	70	70	70	LP010000	LATIN SMALL LETTER P
0071	71	71	71	71	71	71	71	71	71	71	LQ010000	LATIN SMALL LETTER Q
0072	72	72	72	72	72	72	72	72	72	72	LR010000	LATIN SMALL LETTER R
0073	73	73	73	73	73	73	73	73	73	73	LS010000	LATIN SMALL LETTER S
0074	74	74	74	74	74	74	74	74	74	74	LT010000	LATIN SMALL LETTER T
0075	75	75	75	75	75	75	75	75	75	75	LU010000	LATIN SMALL LETTER U
0076	76	76	76	76	76	76	76	76	76	76	LV010000	LATIN SMALL LETTER V
0077	77	77	77	77	77	77	77	77	77	77	LW010000	LATIN SMALL LETTER W
0078	78	78	78	78	78	78	78	78	78	78	LX010000	LATIN SMALL LETTER X
0079	79	79	79	79	79	79	79	79	79	79	LY010000	LATIN SMALL LETTER Y
007A	7A	7A	7A	7A	7A	7A	7A	7A	7A	7A	LZ010000	LATIN SMALL LETTER Z
007B	7B	7B	7B	7B	7B	7B	7B	7B	7B	7B	SM110000	OPENING CURLY BRACKET
007C	7C	7C	7C	7C	7C	7C	7C	7C	7C	7C	SM130000	VERTICAL BAR
007D	7D	7D	7D	7D	7D	7D	7D	7D	7D	7D	SM140000	CLOSING CURLY BRACKET
007E	7E	7E	7E	7E	7E	7E	7E	7E	7E	7E	SD190000	TILDE
00A0	A0	20	FF	FF	FF	FF	FF	FF	FF	FF	SP300000	NON-BREAKING SPACE
00A1	A1	AD	AD	AD		AD	AD	AD	AD		SP030000	INVERTED EXCLAMATION MARK
00A2	A2	BD	BD	BD	9B	9B	9B				SC040000	CENT SIGN
00A3	A3	9C	9C	9C	9C	9C	9C	9C	9C		SC020000	POUND SIGN
00A4	A4	CF	CF	CF	98				AF	CF	SC010000	CURRENCY SIGN
00A5	A5	BE	BE	BE		9D					SC050000	YEN SIGN
00A6	A6	DD	DD	DD	A0						SM650000	BROKEN VERTICAL BAR
00A7	A7		15	15	15	15	15	15	15	15	SM240000	SECTION SIGN
		F5	F5	F5	8F					F5	SM240000	SECTION SIGN
00A8	A8	F9	F9	F9	A4					F9	SD170000	SPACING DIAERESIS
00A9	A9	B8	B8	B8							SM520000	COPYRIGHT SIGN
00AA	AA	A6	A6	A6		A6	A6	A6	A6		SM210000	FEMININE ORDINAL INDICATOR
00AB	AB	AE	AE	AE	AE	AE	AE	AE	AE	AE	SP170000	LEFT POINTING GUILLEMET
00AC	AC	AA	AA	AA	AA	AA	AA	AA	AA	AA	SM660000	NOT SIGN
00AD	AD	F0	F0	F0						F0	SP320000	SOFT HYPHEN
00AE	AE	A9	A9	A9							SM530000	REGISTERED TRADE MARK SIGN
00AF	AF	EE	EE	EE	A7						SM150000	SPACING MACRON
00B0	B0	F8	F8	F8	F8	F8	F8	F8	F8	F8	SM190000	DEGREE SIGN
00B1	B1	F1	F1	F1	F1	F1	F1	F1	F1		SA020000	PLUS-OR-MINUS SIGN
00B2	B2	FD	FD	FD		FD	FD	FD	FD		ND021000	SUPERSCRIPT DIGIT TWO
00B3	B3	FC	FC	FC	A6						ND031000	SUPERSCRIPT DIGIT THREE
00B4	B4	EF	EF	EF	A1					EF	SD110000	SPACING ACUTE

UNIC	1004	M4	850	857	863	437	860	861	865	852	GCGID	Unicode character name
00B5	B5	E6	E6	E6	E6	E6	E6	E6	E6		SM170000	MICRO SIGN
00B6	B6		14	14	14	14	14	14	14	14	SM250000	PARAGRAPH SIGN
00B6	B6	F4	F4	F4	86						SM250000	PARAGRAPH SIGN
00B7	B7	FA	FA	FA	FA	FA	FA	FA	FA		SD630000	MIDDLE DOT
00B8	B8	F7	F7	F7	A5					F7	SD410000	SPACING CEDILLA
00B9	B9	FB	FB	FB							ND011000	SUPERSCRIPT DIGIT ONE
00BA	BA	A7	A7	D0		A7	A7		A7		SM200000	MASCULINE ORDINAL INDICATOR
00BB	BB	AF	AF	AF	AF	AF	AF	AF		AF	SP180000	RIGHT POINTING GUILLEMET
00BC	BC	AC	AC	AC	AC	AC	AC	AC	AC		NF040000	FRACTION ONE QUARTER
00BD	BD	AB	AB	AB	AB	AB	AB	AB	AB		NF010000	FRACTION ONE HALF
00BE	BE	F3	F3	F3	AD						NF050000	FRACTION THREE QUARTERS
00BF	BF	A8	A8	A8		A8	A8	A8	A8		SP160000	INVERTED QUESTION MARK
00C0	C0	B7	B7	B7	8E		91				LA140000	LATIN CAPITAL LETTER A GRAVE
00C1	C1	B5	B5	B5			86	A4		B5	LA120000	LATIN CAPITAL LETTER A ACUTE
00C2	C2	B6	B6	B6	84		8F			B6	LA160000	LATIN CAPITAL LETTER A CIRCUMFLEX
00C3	C3	C7	C7	C7			8E				LA200000	LATIN CAPITAL LETTER A TILDE
00C4	C4	8E	8E	8E		8E		8E	8E	8E	LA180000	LATIN CAPITAL LETTER A DIAERESIS
00C5	C5	8F	8F	8F		8F		8F	8F		LA280000	LATIN CAPITAL LETTER A RING
00C6	C6	92	92	92		92		92	92		LA520000	LATIN CAPITAL LETTER A E
00C7	C7	80	80	80	80	80	80	80	80	80	LC420000	LATIN CAPITAL LETTER C CEDILLA
00C8	C8	D4	D4	D4	91		92				LE140000	LATIN CAPITAL LETTER E GRAVE
00C9	C9	90	90	90	90	90	90	90	90	90	LE120000	LATIN CAPITAL LETTER E ACUTE
00CA	CA	D2	D2	D2	92		89				LE160000	LATIN CAPITAL LETTER E CIRCUMFLEX
00CB	CB	D3	D3	D3	94					D3	LE180000	LATIN CAPITAL LETTER E DIAERESIS
00CC	CC	DE	DE	DE			98				LI140000	LATIN CAPITAL LETTER I GRAVE
00CD	CD	D6	D6	D6			8B	A5		D6	LI120000	LATIN CAPITAL LETTER I ACUTE
00CE	CE	D7	D7	D7	A8					D7	LI160000	LATIN CAPITAL LETTER I CIRCUMFLEX
00CF	CF	D8	D8	D8	95						LI180000	LATIN CAPITAL LETTER I DIAERESIS
00D0	D0	D1	D1					8B			LD620000	LATIN CAPITAL LETTER ETH
00D1	D1	A5	A5	A5		A5	A5		A5		LN200000	LATIN CAPITAL LETTER N TILDE
00D2	D2	E3	E3	E3			A9				LO140000	LATIN CAPITAL LETTER O GRAVE
00D3	D3	E0	E0	E0			9F	A6		E0	LO120000	LATIN CAPITAL LETTER O ACUTE
00D4	D4	E2	E2	E2	99		8C			E2	LO160000	LATIN CAPITAL LETTER O CIRCUMFLEX
00D5	D5	E5	E5	E5			99				LO200000	LATIN CAPITAL LETTER O TILDE
00D6	D6	99	99	99		99		99	99	99	LO180000	LATIN CAPITAL LETTER O DIAERESIS
00D7	D7	9E	9E	9E						9E	SA070000	MULTIPLICATION SIGN
00D8	D8	9D	9D	9D				9D	9D		LO620000	LATIN CAPITAL LETTER O SLASH
00D9	D9	EB	EB	EB	9D		9D				LU140000	LATIN CAPITAL LETTER U GRAVE
00DA	DA	E9	E9	E9			96	A7		E9	LU120000	LATIN CAPITAL LETTER U ACUTE
00DB	DB	EA	EA	EA	9E						LU160000	LATIN CAPITAL LETTER U CIRCUMFLEX

UNIC	1004	M4	850	857	863	437	860	861	865	852	GCGID	Unicode character name
00DC	DC	9A	9A	9A	9A	9A	9A	9A	9A	9A	LU180000	LATIN CAPITAL LETTER U DIAERESIS
00DD	DD	ED	ED					97		ED	LY120000	LATIN CAPITAL LETTER Y ACUTE
00DE	DE	E8	E8					8D			LT640000	LATIN CAPITAL LETTER THORN
00DF	DF	E1	E1	E1	E1	E1	E1	E1	E1	E1	LS610000	LATIN SMALL LETTER SHARP S
00E0	E0	85	85	85	85	85	85	85	85		LA130000	LATIN SMALL LETTER A GRAVE
00E1	E1	A0	A0	A0		A0	A0	A0	A0	A0	LA110000	LATIN SMALL LETTER A ACUTE
00E2	E2	83	83	83	83	83	83	83	83	83	LA150000	LATIN SMALL LETTER A CIRCUMFLEX
00E3	E3	C6	C6	C6			84				LA190000	LATIN SMALL LETTER A TILDE
00E4	E4	84	84	84		84		84	84	84	LA170000	LATIN SMALL LETTER A DIAERESIS
00E5	E5	86	86	86		86		86	86		LA270000	LATIN SMALL LETTER A RING
00E6	E6	91	91	91		91		91	91		LA510000	LATIN SMALL LETTER A E
00E7	E7	87	87	87	87	87	87	87	87	87	LC410000	LATIN SMALL LETTER C CEDILLA
00E8	E8	8A	8A	8A	8A	8A	8A	8A	8A		LE130000	LATIN SMALL LETTER E GRAVE
00E9	E9	82	82	82	82	82	82	82	82	82	LE110000	LATIN SMALL LETTER E ACUTE
00EA	EA	88	88	88	88	88	88	88	88		LE150000	LATIN SMALL LETTER E CIRCUMFLEX
00EB	EB	89	89	89	89	89		89	89	89	LE170000	LATIN SMALL LETTER E DIAERESIS
00EC	EC	8D	8D	EC		8D	8D		8D		LI130000	LATIN SMALL LETTER I GRAVE
00ED	ED	A1	A1	A1		A1	A1	A1	A1	A1	LI110000	LATIN SMALL LETTER I ACUTE
00EE	EE	8C	8C	8C	8C	8C			8C	8C	LI150000	LATIN SMALL LETTER I CIRCUMFLEX
00EF	EF	8B	8B	8B	8B	8B			8B		LI170000	LATIN SMALL LETTER I DIAERESIS
00F0	F0	D0	D0					8C			LD630000	LATIN SMALL LETTER ETH
00F1	F1	A4	A4	A4		A4	A4		A4		LN190000	LATIN SMALL LETTER N TILDE
00F2	F2	95	95	95		95	95		95		LO130000	LATIN SMALL LETTER O GRAVE
00F3	F3	A2	A2	A2	A2	A2	A2	A2	A2	A2	LO110000	LATIN SMALL LETTER O ACUTE
00F4	F4	93	93	93	93	93	93	93	93	93	LO150000	LATIN SMALL LETTER O CIRCUMFLEX
00F5	F5	E4	E4	E4			94				LO190000	LATIN SMALL LETTER O TILDE
00F6	F6	94	94	94		94		94	94	94	LO170000	LATIN SMALL LETTER O DIAERESIS
00F7	F7	F6	F6	F6	F6	F6	F6	F6	F6	F6	SA060000	DIVISION SIGN
00F8	F8	9B	9B	9B				9B	9B		LO610000	LATIN SMALL LETTER O SLASH
00F9	F9	97	97	97	97	97	97		97		LU130000	LATIN SMALL LETTER U GRAVE
00FA	FA	A3	A3	A3	A3	A3	A3	A3	A3	A3	LU110000	LATIN SMALL LETTER U ACUTE
00FB	FB	96	96	96	96	96		96	96		LU150000	LATIN SMALL LETTER U CIRCUMFLEX
00FC	FC	81	81	81	81	81	81	81	81	81	LU170000	LATIN SMALL LETTER U DIAERESIS
00FD	FD	EC	EC					98		EC	LY110000	LATIN SMALL LETTER Y ACUTE
00FE	FE	E7	E7					95			LT630000	LATIN SMALL LETTER THORN
00FF	FF	98	98	ED		98			98		LY170000	LATIN SMALL LETTER Y DIAERESIS
0102										C6	LA240000	LATIN CAPITAL LETTER A BREVE
0103										C7	LA230000	LATIN SMALL LETTER A BREVE
0104										A4	LA440000	LATIN CAPITAL LETTER A OGONEK
0105										A5	LA430000	LATIN SMALL LETTER A OGONEK

UNIC	1004	M4	850	857	863	437	860	861	865	852	GCGID	Unicode character name
0106										8F	LC120000	LATIN CAPITAL LETTER C ACUTE
0107										86	LC110000	LATIN SMALL LETTER C ACUTE
010C										AC	LC220000	LATIN CAPITAL LETTER C HACEK
010D										9F	LC210000	LATIN SMALL LETTER C HACEK
010E										D2	LD220000	LATIN CAPITAL LETTER D HACEK
010F										D4	LD210000	LATIN SMALL LETTER D HACEK
0110										D1	LD620000	LATIN CAPITAL LETTER D BAR
0111										D0	LD610000	LATIN SMALL LETTER D BAR
0118										A8	LE440000	LATIN CAPITAL LETTER E OGONEK
0119										A9	LE430000	LATIN SMALL LETTER E OGONEK
011A										B7	LE220000	LATIN CAPITAL LETTER E HACEK
011B										D8	LE210000	LATIN SMALL LETTER E HACEK
011E				A6							LG240000	LATIN CAPITAL LETTER G BREVE
011F				A7							LG230000	LATIN SMALL LETTER G BREVE
0130			D5	98							L1300000	LATIN CAPITAL LETTER I DOT
0131		D5		8D							L1610000	LATIN SMALL LETTER DOTLESS I
0139										91	LL120000	LATIN CAPITAL LETTER L ACUTE
013A										92	LL110000	LATIN SMALL LETTER L ACUTE
013D										95	LL220000	LATIN CAPITAL LETTER L HACEK
013E										96	LL210000	LATIN SMALL LETTER L HACEK
0141										9D	LL620000	LATIN CAPITAL LETTER L SLASH
0142										88	LL610000	LATIN SMALL LETTER L SLASH
0143										E3	LN120000	LATIN CAPITAL LETTER N ACUTE
0144										E4	LN110000	LATIN SMALL LETTER N ACUTE
0147										D5	LN220000	LATIN CAPITAL LETTER N HACEK
0148										E5	LN210000	LATIN SMALL LETTER N HACEK
0150										8A	LO260000	LATIN CAPITAL LETTER O DOUBLE ACUTE
0151										8B	LO250000	LATIN SMALL LETTER O DOUBLE ACUTE
0152	8C										LO520000	LATIN CAPITAL LETTER O E
0153	9C										LO510000	LATIN SMALL LETTER O E
0154										E8	LR120000	LATIN CAPITAL LETTER R ACUTE
0155										EA	LR110000	LATIN SMALL LETTER R ACUTE
0158										FC	LR220000	LATIN CAPITAL LETTER R HACEK
0159										FD	LR210000	LATIN SMALL LETTER R HACEK
015A										97	LS120000	LATIN CAPITAL LETTER S ACUTE
015B										98	LS110000	LATIN SMALL LETTER S ACUTE
015E				9E						B8	LS420000	LATIN CAPITAL LETTER S CEDILLA
015F				9F						AD	LS410000	LATIN SMALL LETTER S CEDILLA
0160	8A									E6	LS220000	LATIN CAPITAL LETTER S HACEK
0161	9A									E7	LS210000	LATIN SMALL LETTER S HACEK

UNIC	1004	M4	850	857	863	437	860	861	865	852	GCGID	Unicode character name
0162										DD	LT420000	LATIN CAPITAL LETTER T CEDILLA
0163										EE	LT410000	LATIN SMALL LETTER T CEDILLA
0164										9B	LT220000	LATIN CAPITAL LETTER T HACEK
0165										9C	LT210000	LATIN SMALL LETTER T HACEK
016E										DE	LU280000	LATIN CAPITAL LETTER U RING
016F										85	LU270000	LATIN SMALL LETTER U RING
0170										EB	LU260000	LATIN CAPITAL LETTER U DOUBLE ACUTE
0171										FB	LU250000	LATIN SMALL LETTER U DOUBLE ACUTE
0178	9F										LY180000	LATIN CAPITAL LETTER Y DIAERESIS
0179										8D	LZ120000	LATIN CAPITAL LETTER Z ACUTE
017A										AB	LZ110000	LATIN SMALL LETTER Z ACUTE
017B										BD	LZ300000	LATIN CAPITAL LETTER Z DOT
017C										BE	LZ290000	LATIN SMALL LETTER Z DOT
017D										A6	LZ220000	LATIN CAPITAL LETTER Z HACEK
017E										A7	LZ210000	LATIN SMALL LETTER Z HACEK
0192	9F	9F	9F		9F	9F		9F	9F		SC070000	LATIN SMALL LETTER SCRIPT F
02C6	88										SD150100	MODIFIER LETTER CIRCUMFLEX
02C7	0C										SD210000	MODIFIER LETTER HACEK
02C9	04										SD310000	MODIFIER LETTER MACRON
02D8	05										SD230000	SPACING BREVE
02D9	06										SD290000	SPACING DOT ABOVE
02DA	08										SD270000	SPACING RING ABOVE
02DB	0B										SD430000	SPACING OGONEK
02DC	98										SD190100	SPACING TILDE
02DD	0A										SD250000	SPACING DOUBLE ACUTE
0393					E2	E2	E2	E2	E2		GG020000	GREEK CAPITAL LETTER GAMMA
0398					E9	E9	E9	E9	E9		GT620000	GREEK CAPITAL LETTER THETA
03A3					E4	E4	E4	E4	E4		GS020000	GREEK CAPITAL LETTER SIGMA
03A6					E8	E8	E8	E8	E8		GF020000	GREEK CAPITAL LETTER PHI
03A9					EA	EA	EA	EA	EA		GO320000	GREEK CAPITAL LETTER OMEGA
03B1					E0	E0	E0	E0	E0		GA010000	GREEK SMALL LETTER ALPHA
03B4					EB	EB	EB	EB	EB		GD010000	GREEK SMALL LETTER DELTA
03B5					EE	EE	EE	EE	EE		GE010000	GREEK SMALL LETTER EPSILON
03C0					E3	E3	E3	E3	E3		GP010000	GREEK SMALL LETTER PI
03C3					E5	E5	E5	E5	E5		GS010000	GREEK SMALL LETTER SIGMA
03C4					E7	E7	E7	E7	E7		GT010000	GREEK SMALL LETTER TAU
03C6					ED	ED	ED	ED	ED		GF010000	GREEK SMALL LETTER PHI
2013	96										SS680000	EN DASH
2014	97	F2	F2								SM900000	EM DASH
2017					8D						SM100000	SPACING DOUBLE UNDERSCORE

UNIC	1004	M4	850	857	863	437	860	861	865	852	GCGID	Unicode character name
2018	91	60									SP190000	SINGLE TURNED COMMA QUOTATION MARK
2019	92	27									SP200000	SINGLE COMMA QUOTATION MARK
201A	82										SP260000	LOW SINGLE COMMA QUOTATION MARK
201C	93	1F									SP210000	DOUBLE TURNED COMMA QUOTATION MARK
201D	94	18									SP220000	DOUBLE COMMA QUOTATION MARK
201E	84										SP230000	LOW DOUBLE COMMA QUOTATION MARK
2020	86										SM340000	DAGGER
2021	87										SM350000	DOUBLE DAGGER
2022	95		07	07	07	07	07	07	07	07	SP570000	BULLET
2026	85										SV520000	HORIZONTAL ELLIPSIS
2030	89										SM560000	PER MILLE SIGN
2039	8B										SP270000	LEFT POINTING SINGLE GUILLEMET
203A	9B										SP280000	RIGHT POINTING SINGLE GUILLEMET
203C			13	13	13	13	13	13	13	13	SP330000	DOUBLE EXCLAMATION MARK
207F					FC	FC	FC	FC	FC		LN011000	SUPERSCRIPT LATIN SMALL LETTER N
20A7						9E	9E	9E	9E		SC060000	PESETA SIGN
2122	99										SM540000	TRADEMARK
2190			1B	1B	1B	1B	1B	1B	1B	1B	SM300000	LEFT ARROW
2191			18	18	18	18	18	18	18	18	SM320000	UP ARROW
2192			1A	1A	1A	1A	1A	1A	1A	1A	SM310000	RIGHT ARROW
2193			19	19	19	19	19	19	19	19	SM330000	DOWN ARROW
2194			1D	1D	1D	1D	1D	1D	1D	1D	SM780000	LEFT RIGHT ARROW
2195			12	12	12	12	12	12	12	12	SM760000	UP DOWN ARROW
21A8			17	17	17	17	17	17	17	17	SM770000	UP DOWN ARROW WITH BASE
2219					F9	F9	F9	F9	F9		SA790000	BULLET OPERATOR
221A					FB	FB	FB	FB	FB		SA800000	SQUARE ROOT
221E					EC	EC	EC	EC	EC		SA450000	INFINITY
221F			1C	1C	1C	1C	1C	1C	1C	1C	SA420000	RIGHT ANGLE
2229					EF	EF	EF	EF	EF		SA380000	INTERSECTION
2248					F7	F7	F7	F7	F7		SA700000	ALMOST EQUAL TO
2261					F0	F0	F0	F0	F0		SA480000	IDENTICAL TO
2264					F3	F3	F3	F3	F3		SA520000	LESS THAN OR EQUAL TO
2265					F2	F2	F2	F2	F2		SA530000	GREATER THAN OR EQUAL TO
2302			7F	7F	7F	7F	7F	7F	7F	7F	SM790000	HOUSE
2310					A9	A9		A9	A9		SM680000	REVERSED NOT SIGN
2320					F4	F4	F4	F4	F4		SS260000	TOP HALF INTEGRAL
2321					F5	F5	F5	F5	F5		SS270000	BOTTOM HALF INTEGRAL
2500			C4	C4	C4	C4	C4	C4	C4	C4	SF100000	FORMS LIGHT HORIZONTAL
2502		1C	B3	B3	B3	B3	B3	B3	B3	B3	SF110000	FORMS LIGHT VERTICAL
250C			DA	DA	DA	DA	DA	DA	DA	DA	SF010000	FORMS LIGHT DOWN AND RIGHT

UNIC	1004	M4	850	857	863	437	860	861	865	852	GCGID	Unicode character name
2510			BF	BF	BF	BF	BF	BF	BF	BF	SF030000	FORMS LIGHT DOWN AND LEFT
2514			C0	C0	C0	C0	C0	C0	C0	C0	SF020000	FORMS LIGHT UP AND RIGHT
2518			D9	D9	D9	D9	D9	D9	D9	D9	SF040000	FORMS LIGHT UP AND LEFT
251C			C3	C3	C3	C3	C3	C3	C3	C3	SF080000	FORMS LIGHT VERTICAL AND RIGHT
2524			B4	B4	B4	B4	B4	B4	B4	B4	SF090000	FORMS LIGHT VERTICAL AND LEFT
252C			C2	C2	C2	C2	C2	C2	C2	C2	SF060000	FORMS LIGHT DOWN AND HORIZONTAL
2534			C1	C1	C1	C1	C1	C1	C1	C1	SF070000	FORMS LIGHT UP AND HORIZONTAL
253C			C5	C5	C5	C5	C5	C5	C5	C5	SF050000	FORMS LIGHT VERTICAL AND HORIZONTAL
2550			CD	CD	CD	CD	CD	CD	CD	CD	SF430000	FORMS DOUBLE HORIZONTAL
2551			BA	BA	BA	BA	BA	BA	BA	BA	SF240000	FORMS DOUBLE VERTICAL
2552					D5	D5	D5	D5	D5		SF510000	FORMS DOWN SINGLE AND RIGHT DOUBLE
2553					D6	D6	D6	D6	D6		SF520000	FORMS DOWN DOUBLE AND RIGHT SINGLE
2554			C9	C9	C9	C9	C9	C9	C9	C9	SF390000	FORMS DOUBLE DOWN AND RIGHT
2555					B8	B8	B8	B8	B8		SF220000	FORMS DOWN SINGLE AND LEFT DOUBLE
2556					B7	B7	B7	B7	B7		SF210000	FORMS DOWN DOUBLE AND LEFT SINGLE
2557			BB	BB	BB	BB	BB	BB	BB	BB	SF250000	FORMS DOUBLE DOWN AND LEFT
2558					D4	D4	D4	D4	D4		SF500000	FORMS UP SINGLE AND RIGHT DOUBLE
2559					D3	D3	D3	D3	D3		SF490000	FORMS UP DOUBLE AND RIGHT SINGLE
255A			C8	C8	C8	C8	C8	C8	C8	C8	SF380000	FORMS DOUBLE UP AND RIGHT
255B					BE	BE	BE	BE	BE		SF280000	FORMS UP SINGLE AND LEFT DOUBLE
255C					BD	BD	BD	BD	BD		SF270000	FORMS UP DOUBLE AND LEFT SINGLE
255D			BC	BC	BC	BC	BC	BC	BC	BC	SF260000	FORMS DOUBLE UP AND LEFT
255E					C6	C6	C6	C6	C6		SF360000	FORMS VERTICAL SINGLE AND RIGHT DOUBLE
255F					C7	C7	C7	C7	C7		SF370000	FORMS VERTICAL DOUBLE AND RIGHT SINGLE
2560			CC	CC	CC	CC	CC	CC	CC	CC	SF420000	FORMS DOUBLE VERTICAL AND RIGHT
2561					B5	B5	B5	B5	B5		SF190000	FORMS VERTICAL SINGLE AND LEFT DOUBLE
2562					B6	B6	B6	B6	B6		SF200000	FORMS VERTICAL DOUBLE AND LEFT SINGLE
2563			B9	B9	B9	B9	B9	B9	B9	B9	SF230000	FORMS DOUBLE VERTICAL AND LEFT
2564					D1	D1	D1	D1	D1		SF470000	FORMS DOWN SINGLE AND HORIZONTAL DOUBLE
2565					D2	D2	D2	D2	D2		SF480000	FORMS DOWN DOUBLE AND HORIZONTAL SINGLE
2566			CB	CB	CB	CB	CB	CB	CB	CB	SF410000	FORMS DOUBLE DOWN AND HORIZONTAL
2567					CF	CF	CF	CF	CF		SF450000	FORMS UP SINGLE AND HORIZONTAL DOUBLE
2568					D0	D0	D0	D0	D0		SF460000	FORMS UP DOUBLE AND HORIZONTAL SINGLE
2569			CA	CA	CA	CA	CA	CA	CA	CA	SF400000	FORMS DOUBLE UP AND HORIZONTAL
256A					D8	D8	D8	D8	D8		SF540000	FORMS VERTICAL SINGLE AND HORIZONTAL DOUBLE
256B					D7	D7	D7	D7	D7		SF530000	FORMS VERTICAL DOUBLE AND HORIZONTAL SINGLE
256C			CE	CE	CE	CE	CE	CE	CE	CE	SF440000	FORMS DOUBLE VERTICAL AND HORIZONTAL
2580			DF	DF	DF	DF	DF	DF	DF	DF	SF600000	UPPER HALF BLOCK
2584			DC	DC	DC	DC	DC	DC	DC	DC	SF570000	LOWER HALF BLOCK
2588			DB	DB	DB	DB	DB	DB	DB	DB	SF610000	FULL BLOCK

The Unicode Standard • Version 1.0

UNIC	1004	M4	850	857	863	437	860	861	865	852	GCGID	Unicode character name
258C					DD	DD	DD	DD	DD		SF580000	LEFT HALF BLOCK
2590					DE	DE	DE	DE	DE		SF590000	RIGHT HALF BLOCK
2591			B0	B0	B0	B0	B0	B0	B0	B0	SF140000	LIGHT SHADE
2592			B1	B1	B1	B1	B1	B1	B1	B1	SF150000	MEDIUM SHADE
2593			B2	B2	B2	B2	B2	B2	B2	B2	SF160000	DARK SHADE
25A0			FE	FE	FE	FE	FE	FE	FE	FE	SM470000	BLACK SQUARE
25AC			16	16	16	16	16	16	16	16	SM700000	BLACK RECTANGLE
25B2			1E	1E	1E	1E	1E	1E	1E	1E	SM600000	BLACK UP POINTING TRIANGLE
25BA			10	10	10	10	10	10	10	10	SM590000	BLACK RIGHT POINTING POINTER
25BC			1F	1F	1F	1F	1F	1F	1F	1F	SV040000	BLACK DOWN POINTING TRIANGLE
25C4			11	11	11	11	11	11	11	11	SM630000	BLACK LEFT POINTING POINTER
25CB			09	09	09	09	09	09	09	09	SM750000	WHITE CIRCLE
25D8			08	08	08	08	08	08	08	08	SM570001	INVERSE BULLET
25D9			0A	0A	0A	0A	0A	0A	0A	0A	SM750002	INVERSE WHITE CIRCLE
263A			01	01	01	01	01	01	01	01	SS000000	WHITE SMILING FACE
263B			02	02	02	02	02	02	02	02	SS010000	BLACK SMILING FACE
263C			0F	0F	0F	0F	0F	0F	0F	0F	SM690000	WHITE SUN WITH RAYS
2640			0C	0C	0C	0C	0C	0C	0C	0C	SM290000	FEMALE SIGN
2642			0B	0B	0B	0B	0B	0B	0B	0B	SM280000	MALE SIGN
2660			06	06	06	06	06	06	06	06	SS050000	BLACK SPADE SUIT
2663			05	05	05	05	05	05	05	05	SS040000	BLACK CLUB SUIT
2665			03	03	03	03	03	03	03	03	SS020000	BLACK HEART SUIT
2666			04	04	04	04	04	04	04	04	SS030000	BLACK DIAMOND SUIT
266A			0D	0D	0D	0D	0D	0D	0D	0D	SM930000	EIGHTH NOTE
266B			0E	0E	0E	0E	0E	0E	0E	0E	SM910000	BARRED EIGHTH NOTES

Unicode Encoding to PC Code Page Mappings (Greek, Cyrillic, Arabic)

IBM code page 869 is for modern Greek. IBM code page 855 is for Cyrillic (primarily Russian). IBM code page 864 is for Arabic.

UNIC	869	855	864	GCGID	Unicode character name
0020	20	20	20	SP010000	SPACE
0021	21	21	21	SP020000	EXCLAMATION MARK
0022	22	22	22	SP040000	QUOTATION MARK
0023	23	23	23	SM010000	NUMBER SIGN
0024	24	24	24	SC030000	DOLLAR SIGN
0025	25	25		SM020000	PERCENT SIGN
0026	26	26	26	SM030000	AMPERSAND
0027	27	27	27	SP050000	APOSTROPHE-QUOTE
0028	28	28	28	SP060000	OPENING PARENTHESIS
0029	29	29	29	SP070000	CLOSING PARENTHESIS
002A	2A	2A	2A	SM040000	ASTERISK
002B	2B	2B	2B	SA010000	PLUS SIGN
002C	2C	2C	2C	SP080000	COMMA
002D	2D	2D	2D	SP100000	HYPHEN-MINUS
002E	2E	2E	2E	SP110000	PERIOD
002F	2F	2F	2F	SP120000	SLASH
0030	30	30	30	ND100000	DIGIT ZERO
0031	31	31	31	ND010000	DIGIT ONE
0032	32	32	32	ND020000	DIGIT TWO
0033	33	33	33	ND030000	DIGIT THREE
0034	34	34	34	ND040000	DIGIT FOUR
0035	35	35	35	ND050000	DIGIT FIVE
0036	36	36	36	ND060000	DIGIT SIX
0037	37	37	37	ND070000	DIGIT SEVEN
0038	38	38	38	ND080000	DIGIT EIGHT
0039	39	39	39	ND090000	DIGIT NINE
003A	3A	3A	3A	SP130000	COLON
003B	3B	3B	3B	SP140000	SEMICOLON
003C	3C	3C	3C	SA030000	LESS-THAN SIGN
003D	3D	3D	3D	SA040000	EQUALS SIGN
003E	3E	3E	3E	SA050000	GREATER-THAN SIGN
003F	3F	3F	3F	SP150000	QUESTION MARK
0040	40	40	40	SM050000	COMMERCIAL AT
0041	41	41	41	LA020000	LATIN CAPITAL LETTER A
0042	42	42	42	LB020000	LATIN CAPITAL LETTER B
0043	43	43	43	LC020000	LATIN CAPITAL LETTER C
0044	44	44	44	LD020000	LATIN CAPITAL LETTER D
0045	45	45	45	LE020000	LATIN CAPITAL LETTER E
0046	46	46	46	LF020000	LATIN CAPITAL LETTER F
0047	47	47	47	LG020000	LATIN CAPITAL LETTER G
0048	48	48	48	LH020000	LATIN CAPITAL LETTER H
0049	49	49	49	LI020000	LATIN CAPITAL LETTER I
004A	4A	4A	4A	LJ020000	LATIN CAPITAL LETTER J
004B	4B	4B	4B	LK020000	LATIN CAPITAL LETTER K
004C	4C	4C	4C	LL020000	LATIN CAPITAL LETTER L
004D	4D	4D	4D	LM020000	LATIN CAPITAL LETTER M
004E	4E	4E	4E	LN020000	LATIN CAPITAL LETTER N
004F	4F	4F	4F	LO020000	LATIN CAPITAL LETTER O
0050	50	50	50	LP020000	LATIN CAPITAL LETTER P
0051	51	51	51	LQ020000	LATIN CAPITAL LETTER Q

UNIC	869	855	864	GCGID	Unicode character name
0052	52	52	52	LR020000	LATIN CAPITAL LETTER R
0053	53	53	53	LS020000	LATIN CAPITAL LETTER S
0054	54	54	54	LT020000	LATIN CAPITAL LETTER T
0055	55	55	55	LU020000	LATIN CAPITAL LETTER U
0056	56	56	56	LV020000	LATIN CAPITAL LETTER V
0057	57	57	57	LW020000	LATIN CAPITAL LETTER W
0058	58	58	58	LX020000	LATIN CAPITAL LETTER X
0059	59	59	59	LY020000	LATIN CAPITAL LETTER Y
005A	5A	5A	5A	LZ020000	LATIN CAPITAL LETTER Z
005B	5B	5B	5B	SM060000	OPENING SQUARE BRACKET
005C	5C	5C	5C	SM070000	BACKSLASH
005D	5D	5D	5D	SM080000	CLOSING SQUARE BRACKET
005E	5E	5E	5E	SD150000	SPACING CIRCUMFLEX
005F	5F	5F	5F	SP090000	SPACING UNDERSCORE
0060	60	60	60	SD130000	SPACING GRAVE
0061	61	61	61	LA010000	LATIN SMALL LETTER A
0062	62	62	62	LB010000	LATIN SMALL LETTER B
0063	63	63	63	LC010000	LATIN SMALL LETTER C
0064	64	64	64	LD010000	LATIN SMALL LETTER D
0065	65	65	65	LE010000	LATIN SMALL LETTER E
0066	66	66	66	LF010000	LATIN SMALL LETTER F
0067	67	67	67	LG010000	LATIN SMALL LETTER G
0068	68	68	68	LH010000	LATIN SMALL LETTER H
0069	69	69	69	LI010000	LATIN SMALL LETTER I
006A	6A	6A	6A	LJ010000	LATIN SMALL LETTER J
006B	6B	6B	6B	LK010000	LATIN SMALL LETTER K
006C	6C	6C	6C	LL010000	LATIN SMALL LETTER L
006D	6D	6D	6D	LM010000	LATIN SMALL LETTER M
006E	6E	6E	6E	LN010000	LATIN SMALL LETTER N
006F	6F	6F	6F	LO010000	LATIN SMALL LETTER O
0070	70	70	70	LP010000	LATIN SMALL LETTER P
0071	71	71	71	LQ010000	LATIN SMALL LETTER Q
0072	72	72	72	LR010000	LATIN SMALL LETTER R
0073	73	73	73	LS010000	LATIN SMALL LETTER S
0074	74	74	74	LT010000	LATIN SMALL LETTER T
0075	75	75	75	LU010000	LATIN SMALL LETTER U
0076	76	76	76	LV010000	LATIN SMALL LETTER V
0077	77	77	77	LW010000	LATIN SMALL LETTER W
0078	78	78	78	LX010000	LATIN SMALL LETTER X
0079	79	79	79	LY010000	LATIN SMALL LETTER Y
007A	7A	7A	7A	LZ010000	LATIN SMALL LETTER Z
007B	7B	7B	7B	SM110000	OPENING CURLY BRACKET
007C	7C	7C	7C	SM130000	VERTICAL BAR
007D	7D	7D	7D	SM140000	CLOSING CURLY BRACKET
007E	7E	7E	7E	SD190000	TILDE
00A0	FF	FF	A0	SP300000	NON-BREAKING SPACE
00A2			C0	SC040000	CENT SIGN
00A3	9C		A3	SC020000	POUND SIGN
00A4		CF	A4	SC010000	CURRENCY SIGN
00A6	8A		DB	SM650000	BROKEN VERTICAL BAR
00A7	15			SM240000	SECTION SIGN
00A7	F5	15	15	SM240000	SECTION SIGN
00A8	F9			SD170000	SPACING DIAERESIS
00A9	97			SM520000	COPYRIGHT SIGN
00AB	AE	AE	97	SP170000	LEFT POINTING GUILLEMET
00AC	89		DC	SM660000	NOT SIGN

UNIC	869	855	864	GCGID	Unicode character name
00AD	F0	F0	A1	SP320000	SOFT HYPHEN
00B0	F8		80	SM190000	DEGREE SIGN
00B1	F1		93	SA020000	PLUS-OR-MINUS SIGN
00B2	99			ND021000	SUPERSCRIPT DIGIT TWO
00B3	9A			ND031000	SUPERSCRIPT DIGIT THREE
00B4	EF			SD110000	SPACING ACUTE
00B6	14			SM250000	PARAGRAPH SIGN
00B6		14	14	SM250000	PARAGRAPH SIGN
00B7	88		81	SD630000	MIDDLE DOT
00BB	AF	AF	98	SP180000	RIGHT POINTING GUILLEMET
00BC			95	NF040000	FRACTION ONE QUARTER
00BD	AB		94	NF010000	FRACTION ONE HALF
00D7			DE	SA070000	MULTIPLICATION SIGN
00F7			DD	SA060000	DIVISION SIGN
0386	86			GA120000	GREEK CAPITAL LETTER ALPHA TONOS
0388	8D			GE120000	GREEK CAPITAL LETTER EPSILON TONOS
0389	8F			GE720000	GREEK CAPITAL LETTER ETA TONOS
038A	90			GI120000	GREEK CAPITAL LETTER IOTA TONOS
038C	92			GO120000	GREEK CAPITAL LETTER OMICRON TONOS
038E	95			GU120000	GREEK CAPITAL LETTER UPSILON TONOS
038F	98			GO720000	GREEK CAPITAL LETTER OMEGA TONOS
0390	A1			GI730000	GREEK SMALL LETTER IOTA DIAERESIS TONOS
0391	A4			GA020000	GREEK CAPITAL LETTER ALPHA
0392	A5			GB020000	GREEK CAPITAL LETTER BETA
0393	A6			GG020000	GREEK CAPITAL LETTER GAMMA
0394	A7			GD020000	GREEK CAPITAL LETTER DELTA
0395	A8			GE020000	GREEK CAPITAL LETTER EPSILON
0396	A9			GZ020000	GREEK CAPITAL LETTER ZETA
0397	AA			GE320000	GREEK CAPITAL LETTER ETA
0398	AC			GT620000	GREEK CAPITAL LETTER THETA
0399	AD			GI020000	GREEK CAPITAL LETTER IOTA
039A	B5			GK020000	GREEK CAPITAL LETTER KAPPA
039B	B6			GL020000	GREEK CAPITAL LETTER LAMBDA
039C	B7			GM020000	GREEK CAPITAL LETTER MU
039D	B8			GN020000	GREEK CAPITAL LETTER NU
039E	BD			GX020000	GREEK CAPITAL LETTER XI
039F	BE			GO020000	GREEK CAPITAL LETTER OMICRON
03A0	C6			GP020000	GREEK CAPITAL LETTER PI
03A1	C7			GR020000	GREEK CAPITAL LETTER RHO
03A3	CF			GS020000	GREEK CAPITAL LETTER SIGMA
03A4	D0			GT020000	GREEK CAPITAL LETTER TAU
03A5	D1			GU020000	GREEK CAPITAL LETTER UPSILON
03A6	D2			GF020000	GREEK CAPITAL LETTER PHI
03A7	D3			GH020000	GREEK CAPITAL LETTER CHI
03A8	D4			GP620000	GREEK CAPITAL LETTER PSI
03A9	D5			GO320000	GREEK CAPITAL LETTER OMEGA
03AA	91			GI180000	GREEK CAPITAL LETTER IOTA DIAERESIS
03AB	96			GU180000	GREEK CAPITAL LETTER UPSILON DIAERESIS
03AC	9B			GA110000	GREEK SMALL LETTER ALPHA TONOS
03AD	9D			GE110000	GREEK SMALL LETTER EPSILON TONOS
03AE	9E			GE710000	GREEK SMALL LETTER ETA TONOS
03AF	9F			GI110000	GREEK SMALL LETTER IOTA TONOS
03B0	FC			GU730000	GREEK SMALL LETTER UPSILON DIAERESIS TONOS
03B1	D6			GA010000	GREEK SMALL LETTER ALPHA
03B2	D7		90	GB010000	GREEK SMALL LETTER BETA
03B3	D8			GG010000	GREEK SMALL LETTER GAMMA

UNIC	869	855	864	GCGID	Unicode character name
03B4	DD			GD010000	GREEK SMALL LETTER DELTA
03B5	DE			GE010000	GREEK SMALL LETTER EPSILON
03B6	E0			GZ010000	GREEK SMALL LETTER ZETA
03B7	E1			GE310000	GREEK SMALL LETTER ETA
03B8	E2			GT610000	GREEK SMALL LETTER THETA
03B9	E3			GI010000	GREEK SMALL LETTER IOTA
03BA	E4			GK010000	GREEK SMALL LETTER KAPPA
03BB	E5			GL010000	GREEK SMALL LETTER LAMBDA
03BC	E6			GM010000	GREEK SMALL LETTER MU
03BD	E7			GN010000	GREEK SMALL LETTER NU
03BE	E8			GX010000	GREEK SMALL LETTER XI
03BF	E9			GO010000	GREEK SMALL LETTER OMICRON
03C0	EA			GP010000	GREEK SMALL LETTER PI
03C1	EB			GR010000	GREEK SMALL LETTER RHO
03C2	ED			GS610000	GREEK SMALL LETTER FINAL SIGMA
03C3	EC			GS010000	GREEK SMALL LETTER SIGMA
03C4	EE			GT010000	GREEK SMALL LETTER TAU
03C5	F2			GU010000	GREEK SMALL LETTER UPSILON
03C6	F3		92	GF010000	GREEK SMALL LETTER PHI
03C7	F4			GH010000	GREEK SMALL LETTER CHI
03C8	F6			GP610000	GREEK SMALL LETTER PSI
03C9	FA			GO310000	GREEK SMALL LETTER OMEGA
03CA	A0			GI170000	GREEK SMALL LETTER IOTA DIAERESIS
03CB	FB			GU170000	GREEK SMALL LETTER UPSILON DIAERESIS
03CC	A2			GO110000	GREEK SMALL LETTER OMICRON TONOS
03CD	A3			GU110000	GREEK SMALL LETTER UPSILON TONOS
03CE	FD			GO710000	GREEK SMALL LETTER OMEGA TONOS
03F4	F7			SD730000	GREEK SPACING DIAERESIS TONOS
0401		85		KE180000	CYRILLIC CAPITAL LETTER IO
0402		81		KD620000	CYRILLIC CAPITAL LETTER DJE
0403		83		KG120000	CYRILLIC CAPITAL LETTER GJE
0404		87		KE160000	CYRILLIC CAPITAL LETTER E
0405		89		KZ160000	CYRILLIC CAPITAL LETTER DZE
0406		8B		KI120000	CYRILLIC CAPITAL LETTER I
0407		8D		KI180000	CYRILLIC CAPITAL LETTER YI
0408		8F		KJ020000	CYRILLIC CAPITAL LETTER JE
0409		91		KL420000	CYRILLIC CAPITAL LETTER LJE
040A		93		KN120000	CYRILLIC CAPITAL LETTER NJE
040B		95		KC120000	CYRILLIC CAPITAL LETTER TSHE
040C		97		KK120000	CYRILLIC CAPITAL LETTER KJE
040E		99		KU240000	CYRILLIC CAPITAL LETTER SHORT U
040F		9B		KG220000	CYRILLIC CAPITAL LETTER DZHE
0410		A1		KA020000	CYRILLIC CAPITAL LETTER A
0411		A3		KB020000	CYRILLIC CAPITAL LETTER BE
0412		EC		KV020000	CYRILLIC CAPITAL LETTER VE
0413		AD		KG020000	CYRILLIC CAPITAL LETTER GE
0414		A7		KD020000	CYRILLIC CAPITAL LETTER DE
0415		A9		KE020000	CYRILLIC CAPITAL LETTER IE
0416		EA		KZ220000	CYRILLIC CAPITAL LETTER ZHE
0417		F4		KZ020000	CYRILLIC CAPITAL LETTER ZE
0418		B8		KI020000	CYRILLIC CAPITAL LETTER II
0419		BE		KJ120000	CYRILLIC CAPITAL LETTER SHORT II
041A		C7		KK020000	CYRILLIC CAPITAL LETTER KA
041B		D1		KL020000	CYRILLIC CAPITAL LETTER EL
041C		D3		KM020000	CYRILLIC CAPITAL LETTER EM
041D		D5		KN020000	CYRILLIC CAPITAL LETTER EN

UNIC	869	855	864	GCGID	Unicode character name
041E		D7		KO020000	CYRILLIC CAPITAL LETTER O
041F		DD		KP020000	CYRILLIC CAPITAL LETTER PE
0420		E2		KR020000	CYRILLIC CAPITAL LETTER ER
0421		E4		KS020000	CYRILLIC CAPITAL LETTER ES
0422		E6		KT020000	CYRILLIC CAPITAL LETTER TE
0423		E8		KU020000	CYRILLIC CAPITAL LETTER U
0424		AB		KF020000	CYRILLIC CAPITAL LETTER EF
0425		B6		KH020000	CYRILLIC CAPITAL LETTER KHA
0426		A5		KC020000	CYRILLIC CAPITAL LETTER TSE
0427		FC		KC220000	CYRILLIC CAPITAL LETTER CHE
0428		F6		KS220000	CYRILLIC CAPITAL LETTER SHA
0429		FA		KS160000	CYRILLIC CAPITAL LETTER SHCHA
042A		9F		KU220000	CYRILLIC CAPITAL LETTER HARD SIGN
042B		F2		KY020000	CYRILLIC CAPITAL LETTER YERI
042C		EE		KX120000	CYRILLIC CAPITAL LETTER SOFT SIGN
042D		F8		KE140000	CYRILLIC CAPITAL LETTER REVERSED E
042E		9D		KU160000	CYRILLIC CAPITAL LETTER IU
042F		E0		KA160000	CYRILLIC CAPITAL LETTER IA
0430		A0		KA010000	CYRILLIC SMALL LETTER A
0431		A2		KB010000	CYRILLIC SMALL LETTER BE
0432		EB		KV010000	CYRILLIC SMALL LETTER VE
0433		AC		KG010000	CYRILLIC SMALL LETTER GE
0434		A6		KD010000	CYRILLIC SMALL LETTER DE
0435		A8		KE010000	CYRILLIC SMALL LETTER IE
0436		E9		KZ210000	CYRILLIC SMALL LETTER ZHE
0437		F3		KZ010000	CYRILLIC SMALL LETTER ZE
0438		B7		KI010000	CYRILLIC SMALL LETTER II
0439		BD		KJ110000	CYRILLIC SMALL LETTER SHORT II
043A		C6		KK010000	CYRILLIC SMALL LETTER KA
043B		D0		KL010000	CYRILLIC SMALL LETTER EL
043C		D2		KM010000	CYRILLIC SMALL LETTER EM
043D		D4		KN010000	CYRILLIC SMALL LETTER EN
043E		D6		KO010000	CYRILLIC SMALL LETTER O
043F		D8		KP010000	CYRILLIC SMALL LETTER PE
0440		E1		KR010000	CYRILLIC SMALL LETTER ER
0441		E3		KS010000	CYRILLIC SMALL LETTER ES
0442		E5		KT010000	CYRILLIC SMALL LETTER TE
0443		E7		KU010000	CYRILLIC SMALL LETTER U
0444		AA		KF010000	CYRILLIC SMALL LETTER EF
0445		B5		KH010000	CYRILLIC SMALL LETTER KHA
0446		A4		KC010000	CYRILLIC SMALL LETTER TSE
0447		FB		KC210000	CYRILLIC SMALL LETTER CHE
0448		F5		KS210000	CYRILLIC SMALL LETTER SHA
0449		F9		KS150000	CYRILLIC SMALL LETTER SHCHA
044A		9E		KU210000	CYRILLIC SMALL LETTER HARD SIGN
044B		F1		KY010000	CYRILLIC SMALL LETTER YERI
044C		ED		KX110000	CYRILLIC SMALL LETTER SOFT SIGN
044D		F7		KE130000	CYRILLIC SMALL LETTER REVERSED E
044E		9C		KU150000	CYRILLIC SMALL LETTER IU
044F		DE		KA150000	CYRILLIC SMALL LETTER IA
0451		84		KE170000	CYRILLIC SMALL LETTER IO
0452		80		KD610000	CYRILLIC SMALL LETTER DJE
0453		82		KG110000	CYRILLIC SMALL LETTER GJE
0454		86		KE150000	CYRILLIC SMALL LETTER E
0455		88		KZ150000	CYRILLIC SMALL LETTER DZE
0456		8A		KI110000	CYRILLIC SMALL LETTER I

UNIC	869	855	864	GCGID	Unicode character name
0457		8C		KI170000	CYRILLIC SMALL LETTER YI
0458		8E		KJ010000	CYRILLIC SMALL LETTER JE
0459		90		KL410000	CYRILLIC SMALL LETTER LJE
045A		92		KN110000	CYRILLIC SMALL LETTER NJE
045B		94		KC110000	CYRILLIC SMALL LETTER TSHE
045C		96		KK110000	CYRILLIC SMALL LETTER KJE
045E		98		KU230000	CYRILLIC SMALL LETTER SHORT U
045F		9A		KG210000	CYRILLIC SMALL LETTER DZHE
060C			AC	SP080007	ARABIC COMMA
061B			BB	SP140007	ARABIC SEMICOLON
061F			BF	SP150007	ARABIC QUESTION MARK
0640			E0	SM860000	ARABIC TATWEEL
0651			F1	AX100000	ARABIC SHADDAH
0660			B0	ND100001	ARABIC-INDIC DIGIT ZERO
0661			B1	ND010001	ARABIC-INDIC DIGIT ONE
0662			B2	ND020001	ARABIC-INDIC DIGIT TWO
0663			B3	ND030001	ARABIC-INDIC DIGIT THREE
0664			B4	ND040001	ARABIC-INDIC DIGIT FOUR
0665			B5	ND050001	ARABIC-INDIC DIGIT FIVE
0666			B6	ND060001	ARABIC-INDIC DIGIT SIX
0667			B7	ND070001	ARABIC-INDIC DIGIT SEVEN
0668			B8	ND080001	ARABIC-INDIC DIGIT EIGHT
0669			B9	ND090001	ARABIC-INDIC DIGIT NINE
066A			25	SM020007	ARABIC PERCENT SIGN
2015	8E			SM120000	QUOTATION DASH
2018	8B			SP190000	SINGLE TURNED COMMA QUOTATION MARK
2019	8C			SP200000	SINGLE COMMA QUOTATION MARK
2022	07	07		SM570000	BULLET
203C	13	13	13	SP330000	DOUBLE EXCLAMATION MARK
2116		EF		SM000000	NUMERO
2190	1B	1B	1B	SM300000	LEFT ARROW
2191	18	18	18	SM320000	UP ARROW
2192	1A	1A	1A	SM310000	RIGHT ARROW
2193	19	19	19	SM330000	DOWN ARROW
2194	1D	1D	1D	SM780000	LEFT RIGHT ARROW
2195	12	12	12	SM760000	UP DOWN ARROW
21A8	17	17	17	SM770000	UP DOWN ARROW WITH BASE
2219			82	SA790000	BULLET OPERATOR
221A			83	SA800000	SQUARE ROOT
221E			91	SA450000	INFINITY
221F	1C	1C	1C	SA420000	RIGHT ANGLE
2248			96	SA700000	ALMOST EQUAL TO
2302	7F	7F	7F	SM790000	HOUSE
2500	C4	C4	85	SF100000	FORMS LIGHT HORIZONTAL
2502	B3	B3	86	SF110000	FORMS LIGHT VERTICAL
250C	DA	DA	8D	SF010000	FORMS LIGHT DOWN AND RIGHT
2510	BF	BF	8C	SF030000	FORMS LIGHT DOWN AND LEFT
2514	C0	C0	8E	SF020000	FORMS LIGHT UP AND RIGHT
2518	D9	D9	8F	SF040000	FORMS LIGHT UP AND LEFT
251C	C3	C3	8A	SF080000	FORMS LIGHT VERTICAL AND RIGHT
2524	B4	B4	88	SF090000	FORMS LIGHT VERTICAL AND LEFT
252C	C2	C2	89	SF060000	FORMS LIGHT DOWN AND HORIZONTAL
2534	C1	C1	8B	SF070000	FORMS LIGHT UP AND HORIZONTAL
253C	C5	C5	87	SF050000	FORMS LIGHT VERTICAL AND HORIZONTAL
2550	CD	CD	05	SF430000	FORMS DOUBLE HORIZONTAL
2551	BA	BA	06	SF240000	FORMS DOUBLE VERTICAL

UNIC	869	855	864	GCGID	Unicode character name
2554	C9	C9	0D	SF390000	FORMS DOUBLE DOWN AND RIGHT
2557	BB	BB	0C	SF250000	FORMS DOUBLE DOWN AND LEFT
255A	C8	C8	0E	SF380000	FORMS DOUBLE UP AND RIGHT
255D	BC	BC	0F	SF260000	FORMS DOUBLE UP AND LEFT
2560	CC	CC	0A	SF420000	FORMS DOUBLE VERTICAL AND RIGHT
2563	B9	B9	08	SF230000	FORMS DOUBLE VERTICAL AND LEFT
2566	CB	CB	09	SF410000	FORMS DOUBLE DOWN AND HORIZONTAL
2569	CA	CA	0B	SF400000	FORMS DOUBLE UP AND HORIZONTAL
256C	CE	CE	07	SF440000	FORMS DOUBLE VERTICAL AND HORIZONTAL
2580	DF	DF		SF600000	UPPER HALF BLOCK
2584	DC	DC		SF570000	LOWER HALF BLOCK
2588	DB	DB		SF610000	FULL BLOCK
2591	B0	B0		SF140000	LIGHT SHADE
2592	B1	B1	84	SF150000	MEDIUM SHADE
2593	B2	B2		SF160000	DARK SHADE
25A0	FE	FE	FE	SM470000	BLACK SQUARE
25AC	16	16	16	SM700000	BLACK RECTANGLE
25B2	1E	1E	1E	SM600000	BLACK UP POINTING TRIANGLE
25BA	10	10	10	SM590000	BLACK RIGHT POINTING POINTER
25BC	1F	1F	1F	SV040000	BLACK DOWN POINTING TRIANGLE
25C4	11	11	11	SM630000	BLACK LEFT POINTING POINTER
25CB	09	09		SM750000	WHITE CIRCLE
25D8	08	08		SM570001	INVERSE BULLET
25D9	0A	0A		SM750002	INVERSE WHITE CIRCLE
263A	01	01	01	SS000000	WHITE SMILING FACE
263B	02	02		SS010000	BLACK SMILING FACE
263C	0F	0F	04	SM690000	WHITE SUN WITH RAYS
2640	0C	0C		SM290000	FEMALE SIGN
2642	0B	0B		SM280000	MALE SIGN
2660	06	06		SS050000	BLACK SPADE SUIT
2663	05	05		SS040000	BLACK CLUB SUIT
2665	03	03		SS020000	BLACK HEART SUIT
2666	04	04		SS030000	BLACK DIAMOND SUIT
266A	0D	0D	02	SM930000	EIGHTH NOTE
266B	0E	0E	03	SM910000	BARRED EIGHTH NOTES
FE7D			F0	AX100004	ARABIC SHADDAH ON TATWEEL
FE80			C1	AX300000	GLYPH FOR ISOLATE ARABIC HAMZAH
FE81			C2	AA210000	GLYPH FOR ISOLATE ARABIC MADDAH ON ALEF
FE82			A2	AA210002	GLYPH FOR FINAL ARABIC MADDAH ON ALEF
FE83			C3	AA310000	GLYPH FOR ISOLATE ARABIC HAMZAH ON ALEF
FE84			A5	AA310002	GLYPH FOR FINAL ARABIC HAMZAH ON ALEF
FE85			C4	AW310000	GLYPH FOR ISOLATE ARABIC HAMZAH ON WAW
FE8A			C6	AY310003	GLYPH FOR INITIAL ARABIC HAMZAH ON YA
FE8D			C7	AA010000	GLYPH FOR ISOLATE ARABIC ALEF
FE8E			A8	AA010002	GLYPH FOR FINAL ARABIC ALEF
FE8F			A9	AB010000	GLYPH FOR ISOLATE ARABIC BAA
FE90			C8	AB010003	GLYPH FOR INITIAL ARABIC BAA
FE93			C9	AT020000	GLYPH FOR ISOLATE ARABIC TAA MARBUTAH
FE95			AA	AT010000	GLYPH FOR ISOLATE ARABIC TAA
FE96			CA	AT010003	GLYPH FOR INITIAL ARABIC TAA
FE99			AB	AT470000	GLYPH FOR ISOLATE ARABIC THAA
FE9A			CB	AT470003	GLYPH FOR INITIAL ARABIC THAA
FE9D			AD	AG230000	GLYPH FOR ISOLATE ARABIC JEEM
FE9E			CC	AG230003	GLYPH FOR INITIAL ARABIC JEEM
FEA1			AE	AH450000	GLYPH FOR ISOLATE ARABIC HAA
FEA2			CD	AH450003	GLYPH FOR INITIAL ARABIC HAA

UNIC	869	855	864	GCGID	Unicode character name
FEA5			AF	AH470000	GLYPH FOR ISOLATE ARABIC KHAA
FEA6			CE	AH470003	GLYPH FOR INITIAL ARABIC KHAA
FEA9			CF	AD010000	GLYPH FOR ISOLATE ARABIC DAL
FEAB			D0	AD470000	GLYPH FOR ISOLATE ARABIC THAL
FEAD			D1	AR010000	GLYPH FOR ISOLATE ARABIC RA
FEAF			D2	AZ010000	GLYPH FOR ISOLATE ARABIC ZAIN
FEB1			BC	AS010000	GLYPH FOR ISOLATE ARABIC SEEN
FEB2			D3	AS010003	GLYPH FOR INITIAL ARABIC SEEN
FEB5			BD	AS230000	GLYPH FOR ISOLATE ARABIC SHEEN
FEB6			D4	AS230003	GLYPH FOR INITIAL ARABIC SHEEN
FEB9			BE	AS450000	GLYPH FOR ISOLATE ARABIC SAD
FEBA			D5	AS450003	GLYPH FOR INITIAL ARABIC SAD
FEBD			EB	AD450000	GLYPH FOR ISOLATE ARABIC DAD
FEBE			D6	AD450003	GLYPH FOR INITIAL ARABIC DAD
FEC1			D7	AT450000	GLYPH FOR ISOLATE ARABIC TAH
FEC5			D8	AZ450000	GLYPH FOR ISOLATE ARABIC DHAH
FEC9			DF	AC470000	GLYPH FOR ISOLATE ARABIC AIN
FECA			D9	AC470003	GLYPH FOR INITIAL ARABIC AIN
FECB			EC	AC470004	GLYPH FOR MEDIAL ARABIC AIN
FECC			C5	AC470002	GLYPH FOR FINAL ARABIC AIN
FECD			EE	AG310000	GLYPH FOR ISOLATE ARABIC GHAIN
FECE			DA	AG310003	GLYPH FOR INITIAL ARABIC GHAIN
FECF			F7	AG310004	GLYPH FOR MEDIAL ARABIC GHAIN
FED0			ED	AG310002	GLYPH FOR FINAL ARABIC GHAIN
FED1			BA	AF010000	GLYPH FOR ISOLATE ARABIC FA
FED2			E1	AF010003	GLYPH FOR INITIAL ARABIC FA
FED5			F8	AQ010000	GLYPH FOR ISOLATE ARABIC QAF
FED6			E2	AQ010003	GLYPH FOR INITIAL ARABIC QAF
FED9			FC	AK010000	GLYPH FOR ISOLATE ARABIC CAF
FEDA			E3	AK010003	GLYPH FOR INITIAL ARABIC CAF
FEDD			FB	AL010000	GLYPH FOR ISOLATE ARABIC LAM
FEDE			E4	AL010003	GLYPH FOR INITIAL ARABIC LAM
FEE1			EF	AM010000	GLYPH FOR ISOLATE ARABIC MEEM
FEE2			E5	AM010003	GLYPH FOR INITIAL ARABIC MEEM
FEE5			F2	AN010000	GLYPH FOR ISOLATE ARABIC NOON
FEE6			E6	AN010003	GLYPH FOR INITIAL ARABIC NOON
FEE9			F3	AH010000	GLYPH FOR ISOLATE ARABIC HA
FEEA			E7	AH010003	GLYPH FOR INITIAL ARABIC HA
FEEB			F4	AH010004	GLYPH FOR MEDIAL ARABIC HA
FEED			E8	AW010000	GLYPH FOR ISOLATE ARABIC WAW
FEEF			E9	AA020000	GLYPH FOR ISOLATE ARABIC ALEF MAQSURAH
FEF0			F5	AA020002	GLYPH FOR FINAL ARABIC ALEF MAQSURAH
FEF1			FD	AY010000	GLYPH FOR ISOLATE ARABIC YA
FEF2			EA	AY010003	GLYPH FOR INITIAL ARABIC YA
FEF4			F6	AY010002	GLYPH FOR FINAL ARABIC YA
FEF5			F9	AL220000	GLYPH FOR ISOLATE ARABIC MADDAH ON LIGATURE LAM ALEF
FEF6			FA	AL220003	GLYPH FOR FINAL ARABIC MADDAH ON LIGATURE LAM ALEF
FEF7			99	AL320000	GLYPH FOR ISOLATE ARABIC HAMZAH ON LIGATURE LAM ALEF

UNIC	869	855	864	GCGID	Unicode character name
FEF8			9A	AL320003	GLYPH FOR FINAL ARABIC HAMZAH ON LIGATURE LAM ALEF
FEFB			9D	AL020000	GLYPH FOR ISOLATE ARABIC LIGATURE LAM ALEF
FEFC			9E	AL020003	GLYPH FOR FINAL ARABIC LIGATURE LAM ALEF

The following code point does not have a one-to-one mapping against a Unicode character value:

| XXXX | | | 9F | SM870000 | *kasseh* |

UNIC	1040	1041	1043	Unicode character name
0020	20	20	20	SPACE
0021	21	21	21	EXCLAMATION MARK
0022	22	22	22	QUOTATION MARK
0023	23	23	23	NUMBER SIGN
0024	24	24	24	DOLLAR SIGN
0025	25	25	25	PERCENT SIGN
0026	26	26	26	AMPERSAND
0027	27	27	27	APOSTROPHE-QUOTE
0028	28	28	28	OPENING PARENTHESIS
0029	29	29	29	CLOSING PARENTHESIS
002A	2A	2A	2A	ASTERISK
002B	2B	2B	2B	PLUS SIGN
002C	2C	2C	2C	COMMA
002D	2D	2D	2D	HYPHEN-MINUS
002E	2E	2E	2E	PERIOD
002F	2F	2F	2F	SLASH
0030	30	30	30	DIGIT ZERO
0031	31	31	31	DIGIT ONE
0032	32	32	32	DIGIT TWO
0033	33	33	33	DIGIT THREE
0034	34	34	34	DIGIT FOUR
0035	35	35	35	DIGIT FIVE
0036	36	36	36	DIGIT SIX
0037	37	37	37	DIGIT SEVEN
0038	38	38	38	DIGIT EIGHT
0039	39	39	39	DIGIT NINE
003A	3A	3A	3A	COLON
003B	3B	3B	3B	SEMICOLON
003C	3C	3C	3C	LESS-THAN SIGN
003D	3D	3D	3D	EQUALS SIGN
003E	3E	3E	3E	GREATER-THAN SIGN
003F	3F	3F	3F	QUESTION MARK
0040	40	40	40	COMMERCIAL AT
0041	41	41	41	LATIN CAPITAL LETTER A
0042	42	42	42	LATIN CAPITAL LETTER B
0043	43	43	43	LATIN CAPITAL LETTER C
0044	44	44	44	LATIN CAPITAL LETTER D
0045	45	45	45	LATIN CAPITAL LETTER E
0046	46	46	46	LATIN CAPITAL LETTER F
0047	47	47	47	LATIN CAPITAL LETTER G
0048	48	48	48	LATIN CAPITAL LETTER H
0049	49	49	49	LATIN CAPITAL LETTER I
004A	4A	4A	4A	LATIN CAPITAL LETTER J
004B	4B	4B	4B	LATIN CAPITAL LETTER K
004C	4C	4C	4C	LATIN CAPITAL LETTER L
004D	4D	4D	4D	LATIN CAPITAL LETTER M
004E	4E	4E	4E	LATIN CAPITAL LETTER N
004F	4F	4F	4F	LATIN CAPITAL LETTER O
0050	50	50	50	LATIN CAPITAL LETTER P
0051	51	51	51	LATIN CAPITAL LETTER Q
0052	52	52	52	LATIN CAPITAL LETTER R
0053	53	53	53	LATIN CAPITAL LETTER S
0054	54	54	54	LATIN CAPITAL LETTER T

UNIC	1040	1041	1043	Unicode character name
0055	55	55	55	LATIN CAPITAL LETTER U
0056	56	56	56	LATIN CAPITAL LETTER V
0057	57	57	57	LATIN CAPITAL LETTER W
0058	58	58	58	LATIN CAPITAL LETTER X
0059	59	59	59	LATIN CAPITAL LETTER Y
005A	5A	5A	5A	LATIN CAPITAL LETTER Z
005B	5B	5B	5B	OPENING SQUARE BRACKET
005C	FE	FE	5C	BACKSLASH
005D	5D	5D	5D	CLOSING SQUARE BRACKET
005E	5E	5E	5E	SPACING CIRCUMFLEX
005F	5F	5F	5F	SPACING UNDERSCORE
0060	60	60	60	SPACING GRAVE
0061	61	61	61	LATIN SMALL LETTER A
0062	62	62	62	LATIN SMALL LETTER B
0063	63	63	63	LATIN SMALL LETTER C
0064	64	64	64	LATIN SMALL LETTER D
0065	65	65	65	LATIN SMALL LETTER E
0066	66	66	66	LATIN SMALL LETTER F
0067	67	67	67	LATIN SMALL LETTER G
0068	68	68	68	LATIN SMALL LETTER H
0069	69	69	69	LATIN SMALL LETTER I
006A	6A	6A	6A	LATIN SMALL LETTER J
006B	6B	6B	6B	LATIN SMALL LETTER K
006C	6C	6C	6C	LATIN SMALL LETTER L
006D	6D	6D	6D	LATIN SMALL LETTER M
006E	6E	6E	6E	LATIN SMALL LETTER N
006F	6F	6F	6F	LATIN SMALL LETTER O
0070	70	70	70	LATIN SMALL LETTER P
0071	71	71	71	LATIN SMALL LETTER Q
0072	72	72	72	LATIN SMALL LETTER R
0073	73	73	73	LATIN SMALL LETTER S
0074	74	74	74	LATIN SMALL LETTER T
0075	75	75	75	LATIN SMALL LETTER U
0076	76	76	76	LATIN SMALL LETTER V
0077	77	77	77	LATIN SMALL LETTER W
0078	78	78	78	LATIN SMALL LETTER X
0079	79	79	79	LATIN SMALL LETTER Y
007A	7A	7A	7A	LATIN SMALL LETTER Z
007B	7B	7B	7B	OPENING CURLY BRACKET
007C	7C	7C	7C	VERTICAL BAR
007D	7D	7D	7D	CLOSING CURLY BRACKET
007E	FF	FF	7E	TILDE
00A2	80	80	80	CENT SIGN
00A3		A0		POUND SIGN
00A5		5C		YEN SIGN
00A6	DF		FE	BROKEN VERTICAL BAR
00AC	FD	FD	FD	NOT SIGN
00AF	7E	7E		SPACING MACRON
20A9	5C			WON SIGN
2190	1F	1F	1F	LEFT ARROW
2191	1C	1C	1C	UP ARROW
2192	1E	1E	1E	RIGHT ARROW
2193	07	07	07	DOWN ARROW
2195	12	12	12	UP DOWN ARROW
21B5	1B	1B	1B	DOWN ARROW WITH CORNER LEFT
2502	1D	1D	1D	FORMS LIGHT VERTICAL

UNIC	1040	1041	1043	Unicode character name
2550	06	06	06	FORMS DOUBLE HORIZONTAL
2551	05	05	05	FORMS DOUBLE VERTICAL
2554	01	01	01	FORMS DOUBLE DOWN AND RIGHT
2557	02	02	02	FORMS DOUBLE DOWN AND LEFT
255A	03	03	03	FORMS DOUBLE UP AND RIGHT
255D	04	04	04	FORMS DOUBLE UP AND LEFT
2560	19	19	19	FORMS DOUBLE VERTICAL AND RIGHT
2563	17	17	17	FORMS DOUBLE VERTICAL AND LEFT
2566	16	16	16	FORMS DOUBLE DOWN AND HORIZONTAL
2569	15	15	15	FORMS DOUBLE UP AND HORIZONTAL
256C	10	10	10	FORMS DOUBLE VERTICAL AND HORIZONTAL
2591	1A	1A	1A	LIGHT SHADE
2593	14	14	14	DARK SHADE
25A0	0E	0E	0E	BLACK SQUARE
25CB	09	09	09	WHITE CIRCLE
263C	0F	0F	0F	WHITE SUN WITH RAYS
3001		A4		IDEOGRAPHIC COMMA
3002		A1		IDEOGRAPHIC PERIOD
300C		A2		OPENING CORNER BRACKET
300D		A3		CLOSING CORNER BRACKET
309B		DE		KATAKANA-HIRAGANA VOICED SOUND MARK
309C		DF		KATAKANA-HIRAGANA SEMI-VOICED SOUND MARK
30A1		A7		KATAKANA LETTER SMALL A
30A2		B1		KATAKANA LETTER A
30A3		A8		KATAKANA LETTER SMALL I
30A4		B2		KATAKANA LETTER I
30A5		A9		KATAKANA LETTER SMALL U
30A6		B3		KATAKANA LETTER U
30A7		AA		KATAKANA LETTER SMALL E
30A8		B4		KATAKANA LETTER E
30A9		AB		KATAKANA LETTER SMALL O
30AA		B5		KATAKANA LETTER O
30AB		B6		KATAKANA LETTER KA
30AD		B7		KATAKANA LETTER KI
30AF		B8		KATAKANA LETTER KU
30B1		B9		KATAKANA LETTER KE
30B3		BA		KATAKANA LETTER KO
30B5		BB		KATAKANA LETTER SA
30B7		BC		KATAKANA LETTER SI
30B9		BD		KATAKANA LETTER SU
30BB		BE		KATAKANA LETTER SE
30BD		BF		KATAKANA LETTER SO
30BF		C0		KATAKANA LETTER TA
30C1		C1		KATAKANA LETTER TI
30C3		AF		KATAKANA LETTER SMALL TU
30C4		C2		KATAKANA LETTER TU
30C6		C3		KATAKANA LETTER TE
30C8		C4		KATAKANA LETTER TO
30CA		C5		KATAKANA LETTER NA
30CB		C6		KATAKANA LETTER NI
30CC		C7		KATAKANA LETTER NU
30CD		C8		KATAKANA LETTER NE
30CE		C9		KATAKANA LETTER NO
30CF		CA		KATAKANA LETTER HA
30D2		CB		KATAKANA LETTER HI
30D5		CC		KATAKANA LETTER HU

UNIC	1040	1041	1043	Unicode character name
30D8		CD		KATAKANA LETTER HE
30DB		CE		KATAKANA LETTER HO
30DE		CF		KATAKANA LETTER MA
30DF		D0		KATAKANA LETTER MI
30E0		D1		KATAKANA LETTER MU
30E1		D2		KATAKANA LETTER ME
30E2		D3		KATAKANA LETTER MO
30E3		AC		KATAKANA LETTER SMALL YA
30E4		D4		KATAKANA LETTER YA
30E5		AD		KATAKANA LETTER SMALL YU
30E6		D5		KATAKANA LETTER YU
30E7		AE		KATAKANA LETTER SMALL YO
30E8		D6		KATAKANA LETTER YO
30E9		D7		KATAKANA LETTER RA
30EA		D8		KATAKANA LETTER RI
30EB		D9		KATAKANA LETTER RU
30EC		DA		KATAKANA LETTER RE
30ED		DB		KATAKANA LETTER RO
30EF		DC		KATAKANA LETTER WA
30F2		A6		KATAKANA LETTER WO
30F3		DD		KATAKANA LETTER N
30FC		B0		KATAKANA-HIRAGANA PROLONGED SOUND MARK
3131	C1			HANGUL LETTER GIYEOG
3132	C2			HANGUL LETTER SSANG GIYEOG
3133	C3			HANGUL LETTER GIYEOG SIOS
3134	C4			HANGUL LETTER NIEUN
3135	C5			HANGUL LETTER NIEUN JIEUJ
3136	C6			HANGUL LETTER NIEUN HIEUH
3137	C7			HANGUL LETTER DIGEUD
3138	C8			HANGUL LETTER SSANG DIGEUD
3139	C9			HANGUL LETTER LIEUL
313A	CA			HANGUL LETTER LIEUL GIYEOG
313B	CB			HANGUL LETTER LIEUL MIEUM
313C	CC			HANGUL LETTER LIEUL BIEUB
313D	CD			HANGUL LETTER LIEUL SIOS
313E	CE			HANGUL LETTER LIEUL TIEUT
313F	CF			HANGUL LETTER LIEUL PIEUP
3140	D0			HANGUL LETTER LIEUL HIEUH
3141	D1			HANGUL LETTER MIEUM
3142	D2			HANGUL LETTER BIEUB
3143	D3			HANGUL LETTER SSANG BIEUB
3144	D4			HANGUL LETTER BIEUB SIOS
3145	D5			HANGUL LETTER SIOS
3146	D6			HANGUL LETTER SSANG SIOS
3147	D7			HANGUL LETTER IEUNG
3148	D8			HANGUL LETTER JIEUJ
3149	D9			HANGUL LETTER SSANG JIEUJ
314A	DA			HANGUL LETTER CIEUC
314B	DB			HANGUL LETTER KIYEOK
314C	DC			HANGUL LETTER TIEUT
314D	DD			HANGUL LETTER PIEUP
314E	DE			HANGUL LETTER HIEUH
314F	E2			HANGUL LETTER A
3150	E3			HANGUL LETTER AE
3151	E4			HANGUL LETTER YA
3152	E5			HANGUL LETTER YAE

UNIC	1040	1041	1043	Unicode character name
3153	E6			HANGUL LETTER EO
3154	E7			HANGUL LETTER E
3155	EA			HANGUL LETTER YEO
3156	EB			HANGUL LETTER YE
3157	EC			HANGUL LETTER O
3158	ED			HANGUL LETTER WA
3159	EE			HANGUL LETTER WAE
315A	EF			HANGUL LETTER OE
315B	F2			HANGUL LETTER YO
315C	F3			HANGUL LETTER U
315D	F4			HANGUL LETTER WEO
315E	F5			HANGUL LETTER WE
315F	F6			HANGUL LETTER WI
3160	F7			HANGUL LETTER YU
3161	FA			HANGUL LETTER EU
3162	FB			HANGUL LETTER YI
3163	FC			HANGUL LETTER I
3164	C0			HANGUL CAE OM

Unicode Encoding to DBCS Code Page & Asian Standards Mappings

This table provides the cross-mapping between the Unicode encoding and major East Asian character encodings.

UGL refers to the Microsoft Universal Glyph Code, provided for reference.

948, 942, and 944 refer to IBM combined code page for DBCS languages. Code page 948 is a combined DBCS code page for Traditional Chinese. Code page 942 is a combined DBCS code page for Japanese. Code page 944 is a combined DBCS code page for Korean.

XJIS refers to a "Shift-JIS" encoding of JIS X 0208-1990, with a separable coding for JIS X 0212-1990 extensions (codes beginning with the digit 2). AX is another Shift-JIS type of encoding for Japanese. Shift-JIS encodings are considered to be vendor-specific implementations of the JIS standards, and should not be confused with the JIS standards themselves.

KSC refers to the KS C 5601 standard encoding for Korean.

The table also provides two columns of IBM GCGID identifiers. The second GCGID identifier is provided for cases in which a single Unicode value is mapped against two GCGID values from different combined DBCS code pages. The prefix to the second GCGID is provided here to identify which code page or pages the second GCGID should be associated with: K for the Korean combined DBCS code page; T for the Traditional Chinese combined DBCS code page; A for general applicability to any of the combined Asian code pages.

A few values from the Korean or Traditional Chinese combined DBCS code pages are left unmapped in this table due to unresolved issues of character identification on those code pages.

UNIC	UGL	948	XJIS	942	AX	KSC	944	GCGID	GCGID#2	Unicode character name
0020	032	0020	0020	0020	0020	0020	0020	SP010000		SPACE
0021	033	0021	0021	0021	0021	0021	0021	SP020000		EXCLAMATION MARK
0022	034	0022	0022	0022	0022	0022	0022	SP040000		QUOTATION MARK
0023	035	0023	0023	0023	0023	0023	0023	SM010000		NUMBER SIGN
0024	036	0024	0024	0024	0024	0024	0024	SC030000		DOLLAR SIGN
0025	037	0025	0025	0025	0025	0025	0025	SM020000		PERCENT SIGN
0026	038	0026	0026	0026	0026	0026	0026	SM030000		AMPERSAND
0027	039	0027	0027	0027	0027	0027	0027	SP050000		APOSTROPHE-QUOTE
0028	040	0028	0028	0028	0028	0028	0028	SP060000		OPENING PARENTHESIS
0029	041	0029	0029	0029	0029	0029	0029	SP070000		CLOSING PARENTHESIS
002A	042	002A	002A	002A	002A	002A	002A	SM040000		ASTERISK
002B	043	002B	002B	002B	002B	002B	002B	SA010000		PLUS SIGN
002C	044	002C	002C	002C	002C	002C	002C	SP080000		COMMA
002D	045	002D	002D	002D	002D	002D	002D	SP100000		HYPHEN-MINUS
002E	046	002E	002E	002E	002E	002E	002E	SP110000		PERIOD
002F	047	002F	002F	002F	002F	002F	002F	SP120000		SLASH
0030	048	0030	0030	0030	0030	0030	0030	ND100000		DIGIT ZERO
0031	049	0031	0031	0031	0031	0031	0031	ND010000		DIGIT ONE
0032	050	0032	0032	0032	0032	0032	0032	ND020000		DIGIT TWO
0033	051	0033	0033	0033	0033	0033	0033	ND030000		DIGIT THREE
0034	052	0034	0034	0034	0034	0034	0034	ND040000		DIGIT FOUR
0035	053	0035	0035	0035	0035	0035	0035	ND050000		DIGIT FIVE
0036	054	0036	0036	0036	0036	0036	0036	ND060000		DIGIT SIX
0037	055	0037	0037	0037	0037	0037	0037	ND070000		DIGIT SEVEN
0038	056	0038	0038	0038	0038	0038	0038	ND080000		DIGIT EIGHT
0039	057	0039	0039	0039	0039	0039	0039	ND090000		DIGIT NINE
003A	058	003A	003A	003A	003A	003A	003A	SP130000		COLON
003B	059	003B	003B	003B	003B	003B	003B	SP140000		SEMICOLON
003C	060	003C	003C	003C	003C	003C	003C	SA030000		LESS-THAN SIGN
003D	061	003D	003D	003D	003D	003D	003D	SA040000		EQUALS SIGN
003E	062	003E	003E	003E	003E	003E	003E	SA050000		GREATER-THAN SIGN
003F	063	003F	003F	003F	003F	003F	003F	SP150000		QUESTION MARK
0040	064	0040	0040	0040	0040	0040	0040	SM050000		COMMERCIAL AT
0041	065	0041	0041	0041	0041	0041	0041	LA020000		LATIN CAPITAL LETTER A
0042	066	0042	0042	0042	0042	0042	0042	LB020000		LATIN CAPITAL LETTER B
0043	067	0043	0043	0043	0043	0043	0043	LC020000		LATIN CAPITAL LETTER C
0044	068	0044	0044	0044	0044	0044	0044	LD020000		LATIN CAPITAL LETTER D
0045	069	0045	0045	0045	0045	0045	0045	LE020000		LATIN CAPITAL LETTER E
0046	070	0046	0046	0046	0046	0046	0046	LF020000		LATIN CAPITAL LETTER F
0047	071	0047	0047	0047	0047	0047	0047	LG020000		LATIN CAPITAL LETTER G

UNIC	UGL	948	XJIS	942	AX	KSC	944	GCGID	GCGID#2	Unicode character name
0048	072	0048	0048	0048	0048	0048	0048	LH020000		LATIN CAPITAL LETTER H
0049	073	0049	0049	0049	0049	0049	0049	LI020000		LATIN CAPITAL LETTER I
004A	074	004A	004A	004A	004A	004A	004A	LJ020000		LATIN CAPITAL LETTER J
004B	075	004B	004B	004B	004B	004B	004B	LK020000		LATIN CAPITAL LETTER K
004C	076	004C	004C	004C	004C	004C	004C	LL020000		LATIN CAPITAL LETTER L
004D	077	004D	004D	004D	004D	004D	004D	LM020000		LATIN CAPITAL LETTER M
004E	078	004E	004E	004E	004E	004E	004E	LN020000		LATIN CAPITAL LETTER N
004F	079	004F	004F	004F	004F	004F	004F	LO020000		LATIN CAPITAL LETTER O
0050	080	0050	0050	0050	0050	0050	0050	LP020000		LATIN CAPITAL LETTER P
0051	081	0051	0051	0051	0051	0051	0051	LQ020000		LATIN CAPITAL LETTER Q
0052	082	0052	0052	0052	0052	0052	0052	LR020000		LATIN CAPITAL LETTER R
0053	083	0053	0053	0053	0053	0053	0053	LS020000		LATIN CAPITAL LETTER S
0054	084	0054	0054	0054	0054	0054	0054	LT020000		LATIN CAPITAL LETTER T
0055	085	0055	0055	0055	0055	0055	0055	LU020000		LATIN CAPITAL LETTER U
0056	086	0056	0056	0056	0056	0056	0056	LV020000		LATIN CAPITAL LETTER V
0057	087	0057	0057	0057	0057	0057	0057	LW020000		LATIN CAPITAL LETTER W
0058	088	0058	0058	0058	0058	0058	0058	LX020000		LATIN CAPITAL LETTER X
0059	089	0059	0059	0059	0059	0059	0059	LY020000		LATIN CAPITAL LETTER Y
005A	090	005A	005A	005A	005A	005A	005A	LZ020000		LATIN CAPITAL LETTER Z
005B	091	005B	005B	005B	005B	005B	005B	SM060000		OPENING SQUARE BRACKET
005C	092	005C						SM070000		BACKSLASH
005D	093	005D	005D	005D	005D	005D	005D	SM080000		CLOSING SQUARE BRACKET
005E	094	005E	005E	005E	005E	005E	005E	SD150000		SPACING CIRCUMFLEX
005F	095	005F	005F	005F	005F	005F	005F	SP090000		SPACING UNDERSCORE
0060	096	0060	0060	0060	0060	0060	0060	SD130000		SPACING GRAVE
0061	097	0061	0061	0061	0061	0061	0061	LA010000		LATIN SMALL LETTER A
0062	098	0062	0062	0062	0062	0062	0062	LB010000		LATIN SMALL LETTER B
0063	099	0063	0063	0063	0063	0063	0063	LC010000		LATIN SMALL LETTER C
0064	100	0064	0064	0064	0064	0064	0064	LD010000		LATIN SMALL LETTER D
0065	101	0065	0065	0065	0065	0065	0065	LE010000		LATIN SMALL LETTER E
0066	102	0066	0066	0066	0066	0066	0066	LF010000		LATIN SMALL LETTER F
0067	103	0067	0067	0067	0067	0067	0067	LG010000		LATIN SMALL LETTER G
0068	104	0068	0068	0068	0068	0068	0068	LH010000		LATIN SMALL LETTER H
0069	105	0069	0069	0069	0069	0069	0069	LI010000		LATIN SMALL LETTER I
006A	106	006A	006A	006A	006A	006A	006A	LJ010000		LATIN SMALL LETTER J
006B	107	006B	006B	006B	006B	006B	006B	LK010000		LATIN SMALL LETTER K
006C	108	006C	006C	006C	006C	006C	006C	LL010000		LATIN SMALL LETTER L
006D	109	006D	006D	006D	006D	006D	006D	LM010000		LATIN SMALL LETTER M
006E	110	006E	006E	006E	006E	006E	006E	LN010000		LATIN SMALL LETTER N
006F	111	006F	006F	006F	006F	006F	006F	LO010000		LATIN SMALL LETTER O

UNIC	UGL	948	XJIS	942	AX	KSC	944	GCGID	GCGID#2	Unicode character name
0070	112	0070	0070	0070	0070	0070	0070	LP010000		LATIN SMALL LETTER P
0071	113	0071	0071	0071	0071	0071	0071	LQ010000		LATIN SMALL LETTER Q
0072	114	0072	0072	0072	0072	0072	0072	LR010000		LATIN SMALL LETTER R
0073	115	0073	0073	0073	0073	0073	0073	LS010000		LATIN SMALL LETTER S
0074	116	0074	0074	0074	0074	0074	0074	LT010000		LATIN SMALL LETTER T
0075	117	0075	0075	0075	0075	0075	0075	LU010000		LATIN SMALL LETTER U
0076	118	0076	0076	0076	0076	0076	0076	LV010000		LATIN SMALL LETTER V
0077	119	0077	0077	0077	0077	0077	0077	LW010000		LATIN SMALL LETTER W
0078	120	0078	0078	0078	0078	0078	0078	LX010000		LATIN SMALL LETTER X
0079	121	0079	0079	0079	0079	0079	0079	LY010000		LATIN SMALL LETTER Y
007A	122	007A	007A	007A	007A	007A	007A	LZ010000		LATIN SMALL LETTER Z
007B	123	007B	007B	007B	007B	007B	007B	SM110000		OPENING CURLY BRACKET
007C	124	007C	007C	007C	007C	007C	007C	SM130000		VERTICAL BAR
007D	125	007D	007D	007D	007D	007D	007D	SM140000		CLOSING CURLY BRACKET
007E	126	007E	007F	00FF	007F	007E	00FF	SD190000		TILDE
007F		007F	2242	007F	007F		007F			DELETE
00A1	173	00FE				A2AE	855B	SP030000		INVERTED EXCLAMATION MARK
00A2	189	0080		0080			0080	SC040000		CENT SIGN
00A3	156		2270	00A0				SC020000		POUND SIGN
00A4	207					A2B4	8561	SC010000		CURRENCY SIGN
00A5	190		005C	005C	005C			SC050000		YEN SIGN
00A6	221	00FE					00DF	SM650000		BROKEN VERTICAL BAR
00A7	245	8198	8198	8198	8198	A1D7	8176	SM240000		SECTION SIGN
00A8	249	814E	814E	814E	814E	A1A7	8146	SD170000		SPACING DIAERESIS
00A9	184		226D					SM520000		COPYRIGHT SIGN
00AA	166		226C			A8A3	AF42	SM210000		FEMININE ORDINAL INDICATOR
00AB	174				001E			SP170000		LEFT POINTING GUILLEMET
00AC	170	00FD		00FD			00FD	SM660000		NOT SIGN
00AD	240	815D	815D	815D	815D	A1A9	8148	SP320000		SOFT HYPHEN
00AE	169		226E					SM530000		REGISTERED TRADE MARK SIGN
00AF	238		007E	007E	007E		007E	SM150000		SPACING MACRON
00B0	248	818B	818B	818B	818B	A1C6	8165	SM190000		DEGREE SIGN
00B1	241	817D	817D	817D	817D	A1BE	815D	SA020000		PLUS-OR-MINUS SIGN
00B2	253					A9F7	AFF5	ND021000		SUPERSCRIPT DIGIT TWO
00B3	252	814C	814C	814C	814C	A9F8	AFF6	ND031000		SUPERSCRIPT DIGIT THREE
00B4	239	81F7	81F7	81F7	0001	A2A5	8552	SD110000		SPACING ACUTE
00B5	244	8AE4	2231		81F7	0014		SM250000		PARAGRAPH SIGN
00B6	250					A2D2	8580	SM250000		PARAGRAPH SIGN
00B7	247					A1A4	8143	SD630000		MIDDLE DOT
00B8						A2AC	8559	SD410000		SPACING CEDILLA

UNIC	UGL	948	XJIS	942	AX	KSC	944	GCGID	GCGID#2	Unicode character name
00B9	251					A9F6	AFF4	ND011000		SUPERSCRIPT DIGIT ONE
00BA	167					A8AC	AF4B	SM200000		MASCULINE ORDINAL INDICATOR
00BB	175		226B		001F			SP180000		RIGHT POINTING GUILLEMET
00BC	172					A8F9	AF99	NF040000		FRACTION ONE QUARTER
00BD	171					A8F6	AF96	NF010000		FRACTION ONE HALF
00BE	243					A8FA	AF9A	NF050000		FRACTION THREE QUARTERS
00BF	168		2244			A2AF	855C	SP160000		INVERTED QUESTION MARK
00C0	183		2A22					LA140000		LATIN CAPITAL LETTER A GRAVE
00C1	181		2A21					LA120000		LATIN CAPITAL LETTER A ACUTE
00C2	182		2A24					LA160000		LATIN CAPITAL LETTER A CIRCUMFLEX
00C3	199		2A2A					LA200000		LATIN CAPITAL LETTER A TILDE
00C4	142		2A23					LA180000		LATIN CAPITAL LETTER A DIAERESIS
00C5	143		2A29					LA280000		LATIN CAPITAL LETTER A RING
00C6	146		2921			A8A1	AF40	LA520000		LATIN CAPITAL LETTER A E
00C7	128		2A2E					LC420000		LATIN CAPITAL LETTER C CEDILLA
00C8	212		2A32					LE140000		LATIN CAPITAL LETTER E GRAVE
00C9	144		2A31					LE120000		LATIN CAPITAL LETTER E ACUTE
00CA	210		2A34					LE160000		LATIN CAPITAL LETTER E CIRCUMFLEX
00CB	211		2A33					LE180000		LATIN CAPITAL LETTER E DIAERESIS
00CC	222		2A40					LI140000		LATIN CAPITAL LETTER I GRAVE
00CD	214		2A3F					LI120000		LATIN CAPITAL LETTER I ACUTE
00CE	215		2A42					LI160000		LATIN CAPITAL LETTER I CIRCUMFLEX
00CF	216		2A41					LI180000		LATIN CAPITAL LETTER I DIAERESIS
00D0	209		2922			A8A2	AF41	LD620000		LATIN CAPITAL LETTER ETH
00D1	165		2A50					LN200000		LATIN CAPITAL LETTER N TILDE
00D2	227		2A52					LO140000		LATIN CAPITAL LETTER O GRAVE
00D3	224		2A51					LO120000		LATIN CAPITAL LETTER O ACUTE
00D4	226		2A54					LO160000		LATIN CAPITAL LETTER O CIRCUMFLEX
00D5	229		2A58					LO200000		LATIN CAPITAL LETTER O TILDE
00D6	153		2A53					LO180000		LATIN CAPITAL LETTER O DIAERESIS
00D7	158	817E	817E	817E	817E	A1BF	815E	SA070000		MULTIPLICATION SIGN
00D8	157		292C			A8AA	AF49	LO620000		LATIN CAPITAL LETTER O SLASH
00D9	235		2A63					LU140000		LATIN CAPITAL LETTER U GRAVE
00DA	233		2A62					LU120000		LATIN CAPITAL LETTER U ACUTE
00DB	234		2A65					LU160000		LATIN CAPITAL LETTER U CIRCUMFLEX
00DC	154		2A64					LU180000		LATIN CAPITAL LETTER U DIAERESIS
00DD	237		2A72			A8AD	AF4C	LY120000		LATIN CAPITAL LETTER Y ACUTE
00DE	232		2930					LT640000		LATIN CAPITAL LETTER THORN
00DF	225		294E			A9AC	AFAA	LS610000		LATIN SMALL LETTER SHARP S
00E0	133		2B22					LA130000		LATIN SMALL LETTER A GRAVE

UNIC	UGL	948	XJIS	942	AX	KSC	944	GCGID	GCGID#2	Unicode character name
00E1	160		2B21					LA110000		LATIN SMALL LETTER A ACUTE
00E2	131		2B24					LA150000		LATIN SMALL LETTER A CIRCUMFLEX
00E3	198		2B2A					LA190000		LATIN SMALL LETTER A TILDE
00E4	132		2B23					LA170000		LATIN SMALL LETTER A DIAERESIS
00E5	134		2B29					LA270000		LATIN SMALL LETTER A RING
00E6	145		2941			A9A1	AF9F	LA510000		LATIN SMALL LETTER A E
00E7	135		2B2E					LC410000		LATIN SMALL LETTER C CEDILLA
00E8	138		2B32					LE130000		LATIN SMALL LETTER E GRAVE
00E9	130		2B31					LE110000		LATIN SMALL LETTER E ACUTE
00EA	136		2B34					LE150000		LATIN SMALL LETTER E CIRCUMFLEX
00EB	137		2B33					LE170000		LATIN SMALL LETTER E DIAERESIS
00EC	141		2B40					LI130000		LATIN SMALL LETTER I GRAVE
00ED	161		2B3F					LI110000		LATIN SMALL LETTER I ACUTE
00EE	140		2B42					LI150000		LATIN SMALL LETTER I CIRCUMFLEX
00EF	139		2B41					LI170000		LATIN SMALL LETTER I DIAERESIS
00F0	208		2943			A9A3	AFA1	LD630000		LATIN SMALL LETTER ETH
00F1	164		2B50					LN190000		LATIN SMALL LETTER N TILDE
00F2	149		2B52					LO130000		LATIN SMALL LETTER O GRAVE
00F3	162		2B51					LO110000		LATIN SMALL LETTER O ACUTE
00F4	147		2B54					LO150000		LATIN SMALL LETTER O CIRCUMFLEX
00F5	228		2B58					LO190000		LATIN SMALL LETTER O TILDE
00F6	148		2B53					LO170000		LATIN SMALL LETTER O DIAERESIS
00F7	246	8180	8180	8180	8180	A1C0	815F	SA060000		DIVISION SIGN
00F8	155		294C			A9AA	AFA8	LO610000		LATIN SMALL LETTER O SLASH
00F9	151		2B63					LU130000		LATIN SMALL LETTER U GRAVE
00FA	163		2B62					LU110000		LATIN SMALL LETTER U ACUTE
00FB	150		2B65					LU150000		LATIN SMALL LETTER U CIRCUMFLEX
00FC	129		2B64					LU170000		LATIN SMALL LETTER U DIAERESIS
00FD	236		2B72					LY110000		LATIN SMALL LETTER Y ACUTE
00FE	231		2950			A9AD	AFAB	LT630000		LATIN SMALL LETTER THORN
00FF	152		2B73					LY170000		LATIN SMALL LETTER Y DIAERESIS
0100			2A27					LA320000		LATIN CAPITAL LETTER A MACRON
0101			2B27					LA310000		LATIN SMALL LETTER A MACRON
0102	338		2A25					LA240000		LATIN CAPITAL LETTER A BREVE
0103	337		2B25					LA230000		LATIN SMALL LETTER A BREVE
0104	340		2A28					LA440000		LATIN CAPITAL LETTER A OGONEK
0105	339		2B28					LA430000		LATIN SMALL LETTER A OGONEK
0106	342		2A2B					LC120000		LATIN CAPITAL LETTER C ACUTE
0107	341		2B2B					LC110000		LATIN SMALL LETTER C ACUTE
0108			2A2C					LC160000		LATIN CAPITAL LETTER C CIRCUMFLEX

UNIC	UGL	948	XJIS	942	AX	KSC	944	GCGID	GCGID#2	Unicode character name
0109			2B2C					LC150000		LATIN SMALL LETTER C CIRCUMFLEX
010A			2A2F					LC300000		LATIN CAPITAL LETTER C DOT
010B			2B2F					LC290000		LATIN SMALL LETTER C DOT
010C	344		2A2D					LC220000		LATIN CAPITAL LETTER C HACEK
010D	343		2B2D					LC210000		LATIN SMALL LETTER C HACEK
010E	346		2A30					LD220000		LATIN CAPITAL LETTER D HACEK
010F	345		2B30					LD210000		LATIN SMALL LETTER D HACEK
0111	347		2942			A9A2	AFA0	LD610000		LATIN SMALL LETTER D BAR
0112			2A37					LE320000		LATIN CAPITAL LETTER E MACRON
0113			2B37					LE310000		LATIN SMALL LETTER E MACRON
0116			2A36					LE300000		LATIN CAPITAL LETTER E DOT
0117			2B36					LE290000		LATIN SMALL LETTER E DOT
0118	351		2A38					LE440000		LATIN CAPITAL LETTER E OGONEK
0119	350		2B38					LE430000		LATIN SMALL LETTER E OGONEK
011A	349		2A35					LE220000		LATIN CAPITAL LETTER E HACEK
011B	348		2B35					LE210000		LATIN SMALL LETTER E HACEK
011C			2A3A					LG160000		LATIN CAPITAL LETTER G CIRCUMFLEX
011D			2B3A					LG150000		LATIN SMALL LETTER G CIRCUMFLEX
011E	333		2A3B					LG240000		LATIN CAPITAL LETTER G BREVE
011F	332		2B3B					LG230000		LATIN SMALL LETTER G BREVE
0120			2A3D					LG300000		LATIN CAPITAL LETTER G DOT
0121			2B3D					LG290000		LATIN SMALL LETTER G DOT
0122			2A3C					LG420000		LATIN CAPITAL LETTER G CEDILLA
0123			2B39					LG110000		LATIN SMALL LETTER G CEDILLA
0124			2A3E					LH160000		LATIN CAPITAL LETTER H CIRCUMFLEX
0125			2B3E					LH150000		LATIN SMALL LETTER H CIRCUMFLEX
0126			2924			A8A4	AF43	LH620000		LATIN CAPITAL LETTER H BAR
0127			2944			A9A4	AFA2	LH610000		LATIN SMALL LETTER H BAR
0128			2A47					LI200000		LATIN CAPITAL LETTER I TILDE
0129			2B47					LI190000		LATIN SMALL LETTER I TILDE
012A			2A45					LI320000		LATIN CAPITAL LETTER I MACRON
012B			2B45					LI310000		LATIN SMALL LETTER I MACRON
012E			2A46					LI440000		LATIN CAPITAL LETTER I OGONEK
012F			2B46					LI430000		LATIN SMALL LETTER I OGONEK
0130	334		2A44			A9A5	AFA3	LI300000		LATIN CAPITAL LETTER I DOT
0131	213		2945			A8A6	AF45	LI610000		LATIN SMALL LETTER DOTLESS I
0132			2926			A9A6	AFA4	LI520000		LATIN CAPITAL LETTER I J
0133			2946					LI510000		LATIN SMALL LETTER I J
0134			2A48					LJ160000		LATIN CAPITAL LETTER J CIRCUMFLEX
0135			2B48					LJ150000		LATIN SMALL LETTER J CIRCUMFLEX

The Unicode Standard • Version 1.0

UNIC	UGL	948	XJIS	942	AX	KSC	944	GCGID	GCGID#2	Unicode character name
0136			2A49					LK420000		LATIN CAPITAL LETTER K CEDILLA
0137			2B49					LK410000		LATIN SMALL LETTER K CEDILLA
0138			2947					LK610000	K:F1PI0000	LATIN SMALL LETTER KRA
0139	353		2A4A			A9A7	AFA5	LL120000		LATIN CAPITAL LETTER L ACUTE
013A	352		2B4A					LL110000		LATIN SMALL LETTER L ACUTE
013B			2A4C					LL420000		LATIN CAPITAL LETTER L CEDILLA
013C			2B4C					LL410000		LATIN SMALL LETTER L CEDILLA
013D	355		2A4B					LL220000		LATIN CAPITAL LETTER L HACEK
013E	354		2B4B					LL210000		LATIN SMALL LETTER L HACEK
013F			2929			A8A8	AF47	LL640000		LATIN CAPITAL LETTER L WITH MIDDLE DOT
0140			2949			A9A8	AFA6	LL630000		LATIN SMALL LETTER L WITH MIDDLE DOT
0141	357		2928			A8A9	AF48	LL620000		LATIN CAPITAL LETTER L SLASH
0142	356		2948			A9A9	AFA7	LL610000		LATIN SMALL LETTER L SLASH
0143	359		2A4D					LN120000		LATIN CAPITAL LETTER N ACUTE
0144	358		2B4D					LN110000		LATIN SMALL LETTER N ACUTE
0145			2A4F					LN420000		LATIN CAPITAL LETTER N CEDILLA
0146			2B4F					LN410000		LATIN SMALL LETTER N CEDILLA
0147	361		2A4E					LN220000		LATIN CAPITAL LETTER N HACEK
0148	360		2B4E					LN210000		LATIN SMALL LETTER N HACEK
0149			294A			A9B0	AFAE	LN630000	K:F1PR0000	LATIN SMALL LETTER APOSTROPHE N
014A			292B			A8AF	AF4E	LN620000		LATIN CAPITAL LETTER ENG
014B			294B			A9AF	AFAD	LN610000		LATIN SMALL LETTER ENG
014C			2A57					LO320000		LATIN CAPITAL LETTER O MACRON
014D			2B57					LO310000		LATIN SMALL LETTER O MACRON
0150	363		2A56					LO260000		LATIN CAPITAL LETTER O DOUBLE ACUTE
0151	362		2B56					LO250000		LATIN SMALL LETTER O DOUBLE ACUTE
0152	325		292D			A8AB	AF4A	LO520000		LATIN CAPITAL LETTER O E
0153	330		294D			A9AB	AFA9	LO510000		LATIN SMALL LETTER O E
0154	365		2A59					LR120000		LATIN CAPITAL LETTER R ACUTE
0155	364		2B59					LR110000		LATIN SMALL LETTER R ACUTE
0156			2A5B					LR420000		LATIN CAPITAL LETTER R CEDILLA
0157			2B5B					LR410000		LATIN SMALL LETTER R CEDILLA
0158	367		2A5A					LR220000		LATIN CAPITAL LETTER R HACEK
0159	366		2B5A					LR210000		LATIN SMALL LETTER R HACEK
015A	369		2A5C					LS120000		LATIN CAPITAL LETTER S ACUTE
015B	368		2B5C					LS110000		LATIN SMALL LETTER S ACUTE
015C			2A5D					LS160000		LATIN CAPITAL LETTER S CIRCUMFLEX
015D			2B5D					LS150000		LATIN SMALL LETTER S CIRCUMFLEX
015E	336		2A5F					LS420000		LATIN CAPITAL LETTER S CEDILLA
015F	335		2B5F					LS410000		LATIN SMALL LETTER S CEDILLA

UNIC	UGL	948	XJIS	942	AX	KSC	944	GCGID	GCGID#2	Unicode character name
0160	323		2A5E					LS220000		LATIN CAPITAL LETTER S HACEK
0161	328		2B5E					LS210000		LATIN SMALL LETTER S HACEK
0162	373		2A61					LT420000		LATIN CAPITAL LETTER T CEDILLA
0163	372		2B61					LT410000		LATIN SMALL LETTER T CEDILLA
0164	371		2A60					LT220000		LATIN CAPITAL LETTER T HACEK
0165	370		2B60					LT210000		LATIN SMALL LETTER T HACEK
0166			292F			A8AE	AF4D	LT620000		LATIN CAPITAL LETTER T BAR
0167			294F			A9AE	AFAC	LT610000		LATIN SMALL LETTER T BAR
0168			2A6C					LU200000		LATIN CAPITAL LETTER U TILDE
0169			2B6C					LU190000		LATIN SMALL LETTER U TILDE
016A			2A69					LU320000		LATIN CAPITAL LETTER U MACRON
016B			2B69					LU310000		LATIN SMALL LETTER U MACRON
016C			2A66					LU240000		LATIN CAPITAL LETTER U BREVE
016D			2B66					LU230000		LATIN SMALL LETTER U BREVE
016E	377		2A6B					LU280000		LATIN CAPITAL LETTER U RING
016F	376		2B6B					LU270000		LATIN SMALL LETTER U RING
0170	375		2A68					LU260000		LATIN CAPITAL LETTER U DOUBLE ACUTE
0171	374		2B68					LU250000		LATIN SMALL LETTER U DOUBLE ACUTE
0172			2A6A					LU440000		LATIN CAPITAL LETTER U OGONEK
0173			2B6A					LU430000		LATIN SMALL LETTER U OGONEK
0174			2A71					LW160000		LATIN CAPITAL LETTER W CIRCUMFLEX
0175			2B71					LW150000		LATIN SMALL LETTER W CIRCUMFLEX
0176			2A74					LY160000		LATIN CAPITAL LETTER Y CIRCUMFLEX
0177			2B74					LY150000		LATIN SMALL LETTER Y CIRCUMFLEX
0178	331		2A73					LY180000		LATIN CAPITAL LETTER Y DIAERESIS
0179	379		2A75					LZ120000		LATIN CAPITAL LETTER Z ACUTE
017A	378		2B75					LZ110000		LATIN SMALL LETTER Z ACUTE
017B	383		2A77					LZ300000		LATIN CAPITAL LETTER Z DOT
017C	382		2B77					LZ290000		LATIN SMALL LETTER Z DOT
017D	381		2A76					LZ220000		LATIN CAPITAL LETTER Z HACEK
017E	380		2B76					LZ210000		LATIN SMALL LETTER Z HACEK
01CD			2A26							LATIN CAPITAL LETTER A HACEK
01CE			2B26							LATIN SMALL LETTER A HACEK
01CF			2A43							LATIN CAPITAL LETTER I HACEK
01D0			2B43							LATIN SMALL LETTER I HACEK
01D1			2A55							LATIN CAPITAL LETTER O HACEK
01D2			2B55							LATIN SMALL LETTER O HACEK
01D3			2A67							LATIN CAPITAL LETTER U HACEK
01D4			2B67							LATIN SMALL LETTER U HACEK
01D5			2A70							LATIN CAPITAL LETTER U DIAERESIS MACRON

The Unicode Standard • Version 1.0

UNIC	UGL	948	XJIS	942	AX	KSC	944	GCGID	GCGID#2	Unicode character name
01D6			2B70							LATIN SMALL LETTER U DIAERESIS MACRON
01D7			2A6D							LATIN CAPITAL LETTER U DIAERESIS ACUTE
01D8			2B6D							LATIN SMALL LETTER U DIAERESIS ACUTE
01D9			2A6F							LATIN CAPITAL LETTER U DIAERESIS HACEK
01DA			2B6F							LATIN SMALL LETTER U DIAERESIS HACEK
01DB			2A6E							LATIN CAPITAL LETTER U DIAERESIS GRAVE
01DC			2B6E							LATIN SMALL LETTER U DIAERESIS GRAVE
02BA		8AB8					8594	SV090009	K:F1EC0000	MODIFIER LETTER DOUBLE PRIME
02C7	307	8952	2230			A2A7	8554	SD210000	T:SB390000	MODIFIER LETTER HACEK
02C9	301	8950	2234					SD310000	T:SB420000	MODIFIER LETTER MACRON
02CA		8951						SB380000		MODIFIER LETTER ACUTE
02CB		8953						SB400000		MODIFIER LETTER GRAVE
02D0						A2B0	855D	F1CU0000		MODIFIER LETTER TRIANGULAR COLON
02D8	302		222F			A2A8	8555	SD230000		SPACING BREVE
02D9	303	8954	2232			A2AB	8558	SD290000	T:SB410000	SPACING DOT ABOVE
02DA	304		2236			A2AA	8557	SD270000		SPACING RING ABOVE
02DB	306		2235			A2AD	855A	SD430000		SPACING OGONEK
02DC	326		2237					SD190100		SPACING TILDE
02DD	305		2233			A2A9	8556	SD250000		SPACING DOUBLE ACUTE
0386			2661					GA120000		GREEK CAPITAL LETTER ALPHA TONOS
0388			2662					GE120000		GREEK CAPITAL LETTER EPSILON TONOS
0389			2663					GE720000		GREEK CAPITAL LETTER ETA TONOS
038A			2664					GI120000		GREEK CAPITAL LETTER IOTA TONOS
038C			2667					GO120000		GREEK CAPITAL LETTER OMICRON TONOS
038E			2669					GU120000		GREEK CAPITAL LETTER UPSILON TONOS
038F			266C					GO720000		GREEK CAPITAL LETTER OMEGA TONOS
0390			2676					GI730000		GREEK SMALL LETTER IOTA DIAERESIS TONOS
0391		839F	839F	839F	839F	A5C1	83BF	GA020000		GREEK CAPITAL LETTER ALPHA
0392		83A0	83A0	83A0	83A0	A5C2	83C0	GB020000		GREEK CAPITAL LETTER BETA
0393	279	83A1	83A1	83A1	83A1	A5C3	83C1	GG020000		GREEK CAPITAL LETTER GAMMA
0394		83A2	83A2	83A2	83A2	A5C4	83C2	GD020000		GREEK CAPITAL LETTER DELTA
0395		83A3	83A3	83A3	83A3	A5C5	83C3	GE020000		GREEK CAPITAL LETTER EPSILON
0396		83A4	83A4	83A4	83A4	A5C6	83C4	GZ020000		GREEK CAPITAL LETTER ZETA
0397		83A5	83A5	83A5	83A5	A5C7	83C5	GE320000		GREEK CAPITAL LETTER ETA
0398	285	83A6	83A6	83A6	83A6	A5C8	83C6	GT620000		GREEK CAPITAL LETTER THETA
0399		83A7	83A7	83A7	83A7	A5C9	83C7	GI020000		GREEK CAPITAL LETTER IOTA
039A		83A8	83A8	83A8	83A8	A5CA	83C8	GK020000		GREEK CAPITAL LETTER KAPPA
039B		83A9	83A9	83A9	83A9	A5CB	83C9	GL020000		GREEK CAPITAL LETTER LAMBDA
039C		83AA	83AA	83AA	83AA	A5CC	83CA	GM020000		GREEK CAPITAL LETTER MU
039D		83AB	83AB	83AB	83AB	A5CD	83CB	GN020000		GREEK CAPITAL LETTER NU

UNIC	UGL	948	XJIS	942	AX	KSC	944	GCGID	GCGID#2	Unicode character name
039E		83AC	83AC	83AC	83AC	A5CE	83CC	GX020000		GREEK CAPITAL LETTER XI
039F		83AD	83AD	83AD	83AD	A5CF	83CD	GO020000		GREEK CAPITAL LETTER OMICRON
03A0		83AE	83AE	83AE	83AE	A5D0	83CE	GP020000		GREEK CAPITAL LETTER PI
03A1		83AF	83AF	83AF	83AF	A5D1	83CF	GR020000		GREEK CAPITAL LETTER RHO
03A3	281	83B0	83B0	83B0	83B0	A5D2	83D0	GS020000		GREEK CAPITAL LETTER SIGMA
03A4		83B1	83B1	83B1	83B1	A5D3	83D1	GT020000		GREEK CAPITAL LETTER TAU
03A5		83B2	83B2	83B2	83B2	A5D4	83D2	GU020000		GREEK CAPITAL LETTER UPSILON
03A6	284	83B3	83B3	83B3	83B3	A5D5	83D3	GF020000		GREEK CAPITAL LETTER PHI
03A7		83B4	83B4	83B4	83B4	A5D6	83D4	GH020000		GREEK CAPITAL LETTER CHI
03A8		83B5	83B5	83B5	83B5	A5D7	83D5	GP620000		GREEK CAPITAL LETTER PSI
03A9	286	83B6	83B6	83B6	83B6	A5D8	83D6	GO320000		GREEK CAPITAL LETTER OMEGA
03AA			2665					GI180000		GREEK CAPITAL LETTER IOTA DIAERESIS
03AB			266A					GU180000		GREEK CAPITAL LETTER UPSILON DIAERESIS
03AC			2671					GA110000		GREEK SMALL LETTER ALPHA TONOS
03AD			2672					GE110000		GREEK SMALL LETTER EPSILON TONOS
03AE			2673					GE710000		GREEK SMALL LETTER ETA TONOS
03AF			2674					GI110000		GREEK SMALL LETTER IOTA TONOS
03B0			267B					GU730000		GREEK SMALL LETTER UPSILON DIAERESIS TONOS
03B1	278	83BF	83BF	83BF	83BF	A5E1	83DF	GA010000		GREEK SMALL LETTER ALPHA
03B2		83C0	83C0	83C0	83C0	A5E2	83E0	GB010000		GREEK SMALL LETTER BETA
03B3		83C1	83C1	83C1	83C1	A5E3	83E1	GG010000		GREEK SMALL LETTER GAMMA
03B4	287	83C2	83C2	83C2	83C2	A5E4	83E2	GD010000		GREEK SMALL LETTER DELTA
03B5	290	83C3	83C3	83C3	83C3	A5E5	83E3	GE010000		GREEK SMALL LETTER EPSILON
03B6		83C4	83C4	83C4	83C4	A5E6	83E4	GZ010000		GREEK SMALL LETTER ZETA
03B7		83C5	83C5	83C5	83C5	A5E7	83E5	GE310000		GREEK SMALL LETTER ETA
03B8		83C6	83C6	83C6	83C6	A5E8	83E6	GT610002		GREEK SMALL LETTER THETA
03B9		83C7	83C7	83C7	83C7	A5E9	83E7	GI010000		GREEK SMALL LETTER IOTA
03BA		83C8	83C8	83C8	83C8	A5EA	83E8	GK010000		GREEK SMALL LETTER KAPPA
03BB		83C9	83C9	83C9	83C9	A5EB	83E9	GL010000		GREEK SMALL LETTER LAMBDA
03BC		83CA	83CA	83CA	83CA	A5EC	83EA	GM010000		GREEK SMALL LETTER MU
03BD		83CB	83CB	83CB	83CB	A5ED	83EB	GN010000		GREEK SMALL LETTER NU
03BE		83CC	83CC	83CC	83CC	A5EE	83EC	GX010000		GREEK SMALL LETTER XI
03BF	280	83CD	83CD	83CD	83CD	A5EF	83ED	GO010000		GREEK SMALL LETTER OMICRON
03C0		83CE	83CE	83CE	83CE	A5F0	83EE	GP010000		GREEK SMALL LETTER PI
03C1		83CF	83CF	83CF	83CF	A5F1	83EF	GR010000		GREEK SMALL LETTER RHO
03C2			2678					GS610000		GREEK SMALL LETTER FINAL SIGMA
03C3	282	83D0	83D0	83D0	83D0	A5F2	83F0	GS010000		GREEK SMALL LETTER SIGMA
03C4	283	83D1	83D1	83D1	83D1	A5F3	83F1	GT010000		GREEK SMALL LETTER TAU
03C5		83D2	83D2	83D2	83D2	A5F4	83F2	GU010000		GREEK SMALL LETTER UPSILON
03C6	289	83D3	83D3	83D3	83D3	A5F5	83F3	GF010000	A:GF010001	GREEK SMALL LETTER PHI

UNIC	UGL	948	XJIS	942	AX	KSC	944	GCGID	GCGID#2	Unicode character name
03C7		83D4	83D4	83D4	83D4	A5F6	83F4	GH010000		GREEK SMALL LETTER CHI
03C8		83D5	83D5	83D5	83D5	A5F7	83F5	GP610000		GREEK SMALL LETTER PSI
03C9		83D6	83D6	83D6	83D6	A5F8	83F6	GO310000		GREEK SMALL LETTER OMEGA
03CA			2675					GI170000		GREEK SMALL LETTER IOTA DIAERESIS
03CB			267A					GU170000		GREEK SMALL LETTER UPSILON DIAERESIS
03CC			2677					GO110000		GREEK SMALL LETTER OMICRON TONOS
03CD			2679					GU110000		GREEK SMALL LETTER UPSILON TONOS
03CE			267C					GO710000		GREEK SMALL LETTER OMEGA TONOS
03F3			2238					SD110900		GREEK SPACING TONOS
03F4			2239					SD730000		GREEK SPACING DIAERESIS TONOS
0401		8446	8446	8446	8446	ACA7	85A5	KE180000		CYRILLIC CAPITAL LETTER IO
0402			2742					KD620000		CYRILLIC CAPITAL LETTER DJE
0403			2743					KG120000		CYRILLIC CAPITAL LETTER GJE
0404			2744					KE160000		CYRILLIC CAPITAL LETTER E
0405			2745					KZ160000		CYRILLIC CAPITAL LETTER DZE
0406			2746					KI120000		CYRILLIC CAPITAL LETTER I
0407			2747					KI180000		CYRILLIC CAPITAL LETTER YI
0408			2748					KJ020000		CYRILLIC CAPITAL LETTER JE
0409			2749					KL420000		CYRILLIC CAPITAL LETTER LJE
040A			274A					KN120000		CYRILLIC CAPITAL LETTER NJE
040B			274B					KC120000		CYRILLIC CAPITAL LETTER TSHE
040C			274C					KK120000		CYRILLIC CAPITAL LETTER KJE
040D			274D					KU240000		CYRILLIC CAPITAL LETTER SHORT U
040E			274E					KG220000		CYRILLIC CAPITAL LETTER DZHE
040F		8440	8440	8440	8440	ACA1	859F	KA020000		CYRILLIC CAPITAL LETTER A
0410		8441	8441	8441	8441	ACA2	85A0	KB020000		CYRILLIC CAPITAL LETTER BE
0411		8442	8442	8442	8442	ACA3	85A1	KV020000		CYRILLIC CAPITAL LETTER VE
0412		8443	8443	8443	8443	ACA4	85A2	KG020000		CYRILLIC CAPITAL LETTER GE
0413		8444	8444	8444	8444	ACA5	85A3	KD020000		CYRILLIC CAPITAL LETTER DE
0414		8445	8445	8445	8445	ACA6	85A4	KE020000		CYRILLIC CAPITAL LETTER IE
0415		8446	8446	8446	8446	ACA8	85A6	KZ220000		CYRILLIC CAPITAL LETTER ZHE
0416		8447	8447	8447	8447	ACA9	85A7	KZ020000		CYRILLIC CAPITAL LETTER ZE
0417		8448	8448	8448	8448	ACAA	85A8	KI020000		CYRILLIC CAPITAL LETTER II
0418		8449	8449	8449	8449	ACAB	85A9	KJ120000		CYRILLIC CAPITAL LETTER SHORT II
0419		844A	844A	844A	844A	ACAC	85AA	KK020000		CYRILLIC CAPITAL LETTER KA
041A		844B	844B	844B	844B	ACAD	85AB	KL020000		CYRILLIC CAPITAL LETTER EL
041B		844C	844C	844C	844C	ACAE	85AC	KM020000		CYRILLIC CAPITAL LETTER EM
041C		844D	844D	844D	844D	ACAF	85AD	KN020000		CYRILLIC CAPITAL LETTER EN
041D		844E	844E	844E	844E	ACB0	85AE	KO020000		CYRILLIC CAPITAL LETTER O
041E		844F	844F	844F	844F	ACB1	85AF	KP020000		CYRILLIC CAPITAL LETTER PE
041F		8450	8450	8450	8450					

UNIC	UGL	948	XJIS	942	AX	KSC	944	GCGID	GCGID#2	Unicode character name
0420		8451	8451	8451	8451	ACB2	85B0	KR020000		CYRILLIC CAPITAL LETTER ER
0421		8452	8452	8452	8452	ACB3	85B1	KS020000		CYRILLIC CAPITAL LETTER ES
0422		8453	8453	8453	8453	ACB4	85B2	KT020000		CYRILLIC CAPITAL LETTER TE
0423		8454	8454	8454	8454	ACB5	85B3	KU020000		CYRILLIC CAPITAL LETTER U
0424		8455	8455	8455	8455	ACB6	85B4	KF020000		CYRILLIC CAPITAL LETTER EF
0425		8456	8456	8456	8456	ACB7	85B5	KH020000		CYRILLIC CAPITAL LETTER KHA
0426		8457	8457	8457	8457	ACB8	85B6	KC020000		CYRILLIC CAPITAL LETTER TSE
0427		8458	8458	8458	8458	ACB9	85B7	KC220000		CYRILLIC CAPITAL LETTER CHE
0428		8459	8459	8459	8459	ACBA	85B8	KS220000		CYRILLIC CAPITAL LETTER SHA
0429		845A	845A	845A	845A	ACBB	85B9	KS160000		CYRILLIC CAPITAL LETTER SHCHA
042A		845B	845B	845B	845B	ACBC	85BA	KU220000		CYRILLIC CAPITAL LETTER HARD SIGN
042B		845C	845C	845C	845C	ACBD	85BB	KY020000		CYRILLIC CAPITAL LETTER YERI
042C		845D	845D	845D	845D	ACBE	85BC	KX120000		CYRILLIC CAPITAL LETTER SOFT SIGN
042D		845E	845E	845E	845E	ACBF	85BD	KE140000		CYRILLIC CAPITAL LETTER REVERSED E
042E		845F	845F	845F	845F	ACC0	85BE	KU160000		CYRILLIC CAPITAL LETTER IU
042F		8460	8460	8460	8460	ACC1	85BF	KA160000		CYRILLIC CAPITAL LETTER IA
0430		8470	8470	8470	8470	ACD1	85C0	KA010000		CYRILLIC SMALL LETTER A
0431		8471	8471	8471	8471	ACD2	85C1	KB010000		CYRILLIC SMALL LETTER BE
0432		8472	8472	8472	8472	ACD3	85C2	KV010000		CYRILLIC SMALL LETTER VE
0433		8473	8473	8473	8473	ACD4	85C3	KG010000		CYRILLIC SMALL LETTER GE
0434		8474	8474	8474	8474	ACD5	85C4	KD010000		CYRILLIC SMALL LETTER DE
0435		8475	8475	8475	8475	ACD6	85C5	KE010000		CYRILLIC SMALL LETTER IE
0436		8477	8477	8477	8477	ACD8	85C7	KZ210000		CYRILLIC SMALL LETTER ZHE
0437		8478	8478	8478	8478	ACD9	85C8	KZ010000		CYRILLIC SMALL LETTER ZE
0438		8479	8479	8479	8479	ACDA	85C9	KI010000		CYRILLIC SMALL LETTER II
0439		847A	847A	847A	847A	ACDB	85CA	KJ110000		CYRILLIC SMALL LETTER SHORT II
043A		847B	847B	847B	847B	ACDC	85CB	KK010000		CYRILLIC SMALL LETTER KA
043B		847C	847C	847C	847C	ACDD	85CC	KL010000		CYRILLIC SMALL LETTER EL
043C		847D	847D	847D	847D	ACDE	85CD	KM010000		CYRILLIC SMALL LETTER EM
043D		847E	847E	847E	847E	ACDF	85CE	KN010000		CYRILLIC SMALL LETTER EN
043E		8480	8480	8480	8480	ACE0	85CF	KO010000		CYRILLIC SMALL LETTER O
043F		8481	8481	8481	8481	ACE1	85D0	KP010000		CYRILLIC SMALL LETTER PE
0440		8482	8482	8482	8482	ACE2	85D1	KR010000		CYRILLIC SMALL LETTER ER
0441		8483	8483	8483	8483	ACE3	85D2	KS010000		CYRILLIC SMALL LETTER ES
0442		8484	8484	8484	8484	ACE4	85D3	KT010000		CYRILLIC SMALL LETTER TE
0443		8485	8485	8485	8485	ACE5	85D4	KU010000		CYRILLIC SMALL LETTER U
0444		8486	8486	8486	8486	ACE6	85D5	KF010000		CYRILLIC SMALL LETTER EF
0445		8487	8487	8487	8487	ACE7	85D6	KH010000		CYRILLIC SMALL LETTER KHA
0446		8488	8488	8488	8488	ACE8	85D7	KC010000		CYRILLIC SMALL LETTER TSE
0447		8489	8489	8489	8489	ACE9	85D8	KC210000		CYRILLIC SMALL LETTER CHE

UNIC	UGL	948	XJIS	942	AX	KSC	944	GCGID	GCGID#2	Unicode character name
0448		848A	848A	848A	848A	ACEA	85D9	KS210000		CYRILLIC SMALL LETTER SHA
0449		848B	848B	848B	848B	ACEB	85DA	KS150000		CYRILLIC SMALL LETTER SHCHA
044A		848C	848C	848C	848C	ACEC	85DB	KU210000		CYRILLIC SMALL LETTER HARD SIGN
044B		848D	848D	848D	848D	ACED	85DC	KY010000		CYRILLIC SMALL LETTER YERI
044C		848E	848E	848E	848E	ACEE	85DD	KX110000		CYRILLIC SMALL LETTER SOFT SIGN
044D		848F	848F	848F	848F	ACEF	85DE	KE130000		CYRILLIC SMALL LETTER REVERSED E
044E		8490	8490	8490	8490	ACF0	85DF	KU150000		CYRILLIC SMALL LETTER IU
044F		8491	8491	8491	8491	ACF1	85E0	KA150000		CYRILLIC SMALL LETTER IA
0451		8476	8476	8476	8476	ACD7	85C6	KE170000		CYRILLIC SMALL LETTER IO
0452			2772					KD610000		CYRILLIC SMALL LETTER DJE
0453			2773					KG110000		CYRILLIC SMALL LETTER GJE
0454			2774					KE150000		CYRILLIC SMALL LETTER E
0455			2775					KZ150000		CYRILLIC SMALL LETTER DZE
0456			2776					KI110000		CYRILLIC SMALL LETTER I
0457			2777					KI170000		CYRILLIC SMALL LETTER YI
0458			2778					KJ010000		CYRILLIC SMALL LETTER JE
0459			2779					KL410000		CYRILLIC SMALL LETTER LJE
045A			277A					KN110000		CYRILLIC SMALL LETTER NJE
045B			277B					KC110000		CYRILLIC SMALL LETTER TSHE
045C			277C					KK110000		CYRILLIC SMALL LETTER KJE
045E			277D					KU230000		CYRILLIC SMALL LETTER SHORT U
045F			277E					KG210000		CYRILLIC SMALL LETTER DZHE
2015		815C	815C	815C	815C	A1AA	8149	SM120000		QUOTATION DASH
2018	308	8165	8165	8165	8165	A1AE	814D	SP190000		SINGLE TURNED COMMA QUOTATION MARK
2019	309	8166	8166	8166	8166	A1AF	814E	SP200000		SINGLE COMMA QUOTATION MARK
201C	310	8167	8167	8167	8167	A1B0	814F	SP210000		DOUBLE TURNED COMMA QUOTATION MARK
201D	311	8168	8168	8168	8168	A1B1	8150	SP220000		DOUBLE COMMA QUOTATION MARK
2020	319	81F5	81F5	81F5	81F5	A2D3	8581	SM340000	K:F1DT0000	DAGGER
2021	320	81F6	81F6	81F6	81F6	A2D4	8582	SM350000	K:F1DU0000	DOUBLE DAGGER
2022	007					0007		SM570000		BULLET
2025		8164	8164	8164	8164	A1A5	8144	SV430000		TWO DOT LEADER
2026	318	8163	8163	8163	8163	A1A6	8145	SV520000	A:SV440000	HORIZONTAL ELLIPSIS
2030	322	81F1	81F1	81F1	81F1	A2B6	8563	SM560000		PER MILLE SIGN
2032		818C	818C	818C	818C	A1C7	8166	SM500000		PRIME
2033		818D	818D	818D	818D	A1C8	8167	SM510000		DOUBLE PRIME
203B		81A6	81A6	81A6	81A6	A1D8	8177	SM040008		REFERENCE MARK
203C	019					0013		SP330000		DOUBLE EXCLAMATION MARK
203E		8650						SM620000	T:SM620001	SPACING OVERSCORE
2044		8AD9						SP120001		FRACTION SLASH
2074						A9F9	AFF7	ND041000		SUPERSCRIPT DIGIT FOUR

UNIC	UGL	948	XJIS	942	AX	KSC	944	GCGID	GCGID#2	Unicode character name
207F	300					A9FA	AFF8	LN011000		SUPERSCRIPT LATIN SMALL LETTER N
2081						A9FB	AFF9	ND012000		SUBSCRIPT DIGIT ONE
2082						A9FC	AFFA	ND022000		SUBSCRIPT DIGIT TWO
2083		81FC	81FC	81FC	81FC	A9FD	AFFB	ND032000		SUBSCRIPT DIGIT THREE
2084	947	818E	818E	818E	818E	A9FE	AFFC	ND042000		SUBSCRIPT DIGIT FOUR
20A9						·005C	005C	SC140000		WON SIGN
20DD						A1C9	8168	SV220000		ENCLOSING CIRCLE
2103								SM440000		DEGREES CENTIGRADE
2105		8ABA						SS640000		CARE OF
2109		8ADA				A2B5	8562	SM850000		DEGREES FAHRENHEIT
2113						A7A4	816F	SM160000		SCRIPT SMALL L
2116		8B60	2271	FA59	8782	A2E0	858E	SM000000	K:F1E60000	NUMERO
2121		8B61		FA5A	8784	A2E5	8593	SS710000		T E L SYMBOL
2122	327		226F			A2E2	8590	SM540000		TRADEMARK
2126						A7D9	84CE	SM180000		OHM
212A							8169	F06H0000		DEGREES KELVIN
212B		81F0	81F0	81F0	81F0	A1CA	8191	SM220000		ANGSTROM UNIT
2153						A8F7	AF97	F1P30000		FRACTION ONE THIRD
2154						A8F8	AF98	F1P40000		FRACTION TWO THIRDS
215B						A8FB	AF9B	NF180000		FRACTION ONE EIGHTH
215C						A8FC	AF9C	NF190000		FRACTION THREE EIGHTHS
215D						A8FD	AF9D	NF200000		FRACTION FIVE EIGHTHS
215E						A8FE	AF9E	NF210000		FRACTION SEVEN EIGHTHS
2160		8B41		FA4A	8754	A5B0	83AE	NR110000		ROMAN NUMERAL ONE
2161		8B42		FA4B	8755	A5B1	83AF	NR120000		ROMAN NUMERAL TWO
2162		8B43		FA4C	8756	A5B2	83B0	NR130000		ROMAN NUMERAL THREE
2163		8B44		FA4D	8757	A5B3	83B1	NR140000		ROMAN NUMERAL FOUR
2164		8B45		FA4E	8758	A5B4	83B2	NR150000		ROMAN NUMERAL FIVE
2165		8B46		FA4F	8759	A5B5	83B3	NR160000		ROMAN NUMERAL SIX
2166		8B47		FA50	875A	A5B6	83B4	NR170000		ROMAN NUMERAL SEVEN
2167		8B48		FA51	875B	A5B7	83B5	NR180000		ROMAN NUMERAL EIGHT
2168		8B49		FA52	875C	A5B8	83B6	NR190000		ROMAN NUMERAL NINE
2169		8B4A		FA53	875D	A5B9	83B7	NR200000		ROMAN NUMERAL TEN
2170		8B51		FA40		A5A1	839F	NR010000		SMALL ROMAN NUMERAL ONE
2171		8B52		FA41		A5A2	83A0	NR020000		SMALL ROMAN NUMERAL TWO
2172		8B53		FA42		A5A3	83A1	NR030000		SMALL ROMAN NUMERAL THREE
2173		8B54		FA43		A5A4	83A2	NR040000		SMALL ROMAN NUMERAL FOUR
2174		8B55		FA44		A5A5	83A3	NR050000		SMALL ROMAN NUMERAL FIVE
2175		8B56		FA45		A5A6	83A4	NR060000		SMALL ROMAN NUMERAL SIX
2176		8B57		FA46		A5A7	83A5	NR070000		SMALL ROMAN NUMERAL SEVEN

UNIC	UGL	948	XJIS	942	AX	KSC	944	GCGID	GCGID#2	Unicode character name
2177		8B58		FA47		A5A8	83A6	NR080000		SMALL ROMAN NUMERAL EIGHT
2178		8B59		FA48		A5A9	83A7	NR090000		SMALL ROMAN NUMERAL NINE
2179		8B5A		FA49		A5AA	83A8	NR100000		SMALL ROMAN NUMERAL TEN
2190		001F		001F	0007	001B	001F	SM300000		LEFT ARROW
2190	027	81A9	81A9	81A9	81A9	A1E7	8187	SM300000		LEFT ARROW
2191		001C		001C	0004	0018	001C	SM320000		UP ARROW
2191	024	81AA	81AA	81AA	81AA	A1E8	8188	SM320000		UP ARROW
2192		001E		001E	0006	001A	001E	SM310000		RIGHT ARROW
2192	026	81A8	81A8	81A8	81A8	A1E6	8186	SM310000		RIGHT ARROW
2193		0007		0007	0005	0007	0007	SM330000		DOWN ARROW
2193	025	81AB	81AB	81AB	81AB	A1E9	8189	SM330000		DOWN ARROW
2194					0003	001D		SM780000		LEFT RIGHT ARROW
2194	029					A1EA	818A	SM780000		LEFT RIGHT ARROW
2195		0012		0012	0002	0012	0012	SM760000		UP DOWN ARROW
2195	018					A2D5	8583	SM760000	K:F1DY0000	UP DOWN ARROW
2196		8AD3				A2D8	8586	SM970000		UPPER LEFT ARROW
2197		8AD4				A2D6	8584	SM950000		UPPER RIGHT ARROW
2198		8AD6				A2D9	8587	SM990000		LOWER RIGHT ARROW
2199		8AD5				A2D7	8585	SM980000	K:F1DX0000	LOWER LEFT ARROW
21B5	769	001B		001B			001B	SM720000		DOWN ARROW WITH CORNER LEFT
21B8		8AEE						SS070000		UPPER LEFT ARROW TO LONG BAR
21B9		8AEF						SS060000		LEFT ARROW TO BAR OVER RIGHT ARROW TO BAR
21D2		81CB	81CB	81CB	81CB	A2A1	854E	SM420000		RIGHT DOUBLE ARROW
21D4		81CC	81CC	81CC	81CC	A2A2	854F	SM410000		LEFT RIGHT DOUBLE ARROW
21E7		8AED						SM460000		WHITE UP ARROW
2200		81CD	81CD	81CD	81CD	A2A3	8550	SA210000		FOR ALL
2202		81DD	81DD	81DD	81DD	A1D3	8197	SA490000		PARTIAL DIFFERENTIAL
2203		81CE	81CE	81CE	81CE	A2A4	8551	SA230000		THERE EXISTS
2207		81DE	81DE	81DE	81DE	A1D4	8198	SL030000		NABLA
2208		81B8	81B8	81B8	81B8	A1F4	8544	SA670000		ELEMENT OF
220B		81B9	81B9	81B9	81B9	A1F5	8545	SA310000		CONTAINS AS MEMBER
220F						A2B3	8560	SA810000		N-ARY PRODUCT
2211						A2B2	855F	SS400000		N-ARY SUMMATION
221A					8794			SA800000		SQUARE ROOT
221A	299	8AC4	81E3	81E3	8795	A1EE	819D	SA800000		SQUARE ROOT
221D		81E5	81E5	81E5	81E5	A1F0	8540	SA470000		PROPORTIONAL TO
221E	288	8187	8187	8187	8187	A1C4	8187	SA450000		INFINITY
221F	028	8ACB			8798	001C		SA420000		RIGHT ANGLE
2220					8797			SA350008		ANGLE
2220		8ACA	81DA	81DA	81DA	A1D0	8194	SA350008		ANGLE

UNIC	UGL	948	XJIS	942	AX	KSC	944	GCGID	GCGID#2	Unicode character name
2225		8161	8161	8161	8161	A1AB	814A	SV370000	K:SA340000	PARALLEL TO
2227		81C8	81C8	81C8	81C8	A1FC	854C	SA330000		LOGICAL AND
2228		81C9	81C9	81C9	81C9	A1FD	854D	SA320000		LOGICAL OR
2229					879B			SA380000		INTERSECTION
2229	291	8AC7	81BF	81BF	81BF	A1FB	854B	SA380000		INTERSECTION
222A					879C			SA390000		UNION
222A		8AC8	81BE	81BE	81BE	A1FA	854A	SA390000		UNION
222B					8792			SA510000		INTEGRAL
222B		8ACF	81E7	81E7	81E7	A1F2	8542	SA510000		INTEGRAL
222C		81E8	81E8	81E8	81E8	A1F3	8543	SA840000		DOUBLE INTEGRAL
222E		8AD0			8793	A2B1	855E	SA720000		CONTOUR INTEGRAL
2234		8188	8188	8188	8188	A1C5	8164	SA370000		THEREFORE
2235					879A			SS540000		BECAUSE
2235		8AD7	81E6	FA5B	81E6	A1F1	8541	SS540000		BECAUSE
223C						A1AD	814C	SA160000		TILDE OPERATOR
223D		81E4	81E4	81E4	8790	A1EF	819E	SA830000		REVERSED TILDE
2252		8AC5	81E0	81E0	81E0	A1D6	819A	SA700001		APPROXIMATELY EQUAL TO OR OR THE IMAGE OF
2252						A1C1	818E	SA700001		APPROXIMATELY EQUAL TO OR THE IMAGE OF
2260								F07H0000		NOT EQUAL TO
2260		8182	8182	8182	8182	A1D5	8160	SA540000		NOT EQUAL TO
2261	292	8AC6			8791	A1C2	8199	SA480000		IDENTICAL TO
2261			81DF	81DF	81DF	A1C3	818F	SA480000		IDENTICAL TO
2264	294						8190	SA520000		LESS THAN OR EQUAL TO
2265	293							SA530000		GREATER THAN OR EQUAL TO
2266		8185	8185	8185	8185		8161	SA520002		LESS THAN OVER EQUAL TO
2267		8186	8186	8186	8186		8162	SA530002		GREATER THAN OVER EQUAL TO
226A		81E1	81E1	81E1	81E1	A1EC	819B	SA730000		MUCH LESS THAN
226B		81E2	81E2	81E2	81E2	A1ED	819C	SA740000		MUCH GREATER THAN
2282		81BC	81BC	81BC	81BC	A1F8	8548	SA400000		SUBSET OF
2283		81BD	81BD	81BD	81BD	A1F9	8549	SA410000		SUPERSET OF
2286		81BA	81BA	81BA	81BA	A1F6	8546	SA240000		SUBSET OF OR EQUAL TO
2287		81BB	81BB	81BB	81BB	A1F7	8547	SA270000		SUPERSET OF OR EQUAL TO
2295		8AD1			8796			SA550000		CIRCLED PLUS
2299		8AD2				A2C1	856E	SA590000	K:F1DB0000	CIRCLED DOT OPERATOR
22A5								SA780000		UP TACK
22A5		8AC9	81DB	81DB	81DB	A1D1	8195	SA780000		UP TACK
22BF		8ACC			8799			SA850000		RIGHT TRIANGLE
2302	127					007F		SM790000		HOUSE
2312		81DC	81DC	81DC	81DC	A1D2	8196	SV420000		ARC
2400		8680						SE010000		GRAPHIC FOR NULL

UNIC	UGL	948	XJIS	942	AX	KSC	944	GCGID	GCGID#2	Unicode character name
2401		8681						SE020000		GRAPHIC FOR START OF HEADING
2402		8682						SE030000		GRAPHIC FOR START OF TEXT
2403		8683						SE040000		GRAPHIC FOR END OF TEXT
2404		8684						SE050000		GRAPHIC FOR END OF TRANSMISSION
2405		8685						SE060000		GRAPHIC FOR ENQUIRY
2406		8686						SE070000		GRAPHIC FOR ACKNOWLEDGE
2407		8687						SE080000		GRAPHIC FOR BELL
2408		8688						SE090000		GRAPHIC FOR BACKSPACE
2409		8689						SE100000		GRAPHIC FOR HORIZONTAL TABULATION
240A		868A						SE110000		GRAPHIC FOR LINE FEED
240B		868B						SE120000		GRAPHIC FOR VERTICAL TABULATION
240C		868C						SE130000		GRAPHIC FOR FORM FEED
240D		868D						SE140000		GRAPHIC FOR CARRIAGE RETURN
240E		868E						SE150000		GRAPHIC FOR SHIFT OUT
240F		868F						SE160000		GRAPHIC FOR SHIFT IN
2410		8690						SE170000		GRAPHIC FOR DATA LINK ESCAPE
2411		8691						SE180000		GRAPHIC FOR DEVICE CONTROL ONE
2412		8692						SE190000		GRAPHIC FOR DEVICE CONTROL TWO
2413		8693						SE200000		GRAPHIC FOR DEVICE CONTROL THREE
2414		8694						SE210000		GRAPHIC FOR DEVICE CONTROL FOUR
2415		8695						SE220000		GRAPHIC FOR NEGATIVE ACKNOWLEDGE
2416		8696						SE230000		GRAPHIC FOR SYNCHRONOUS IDLE
2417		8697						SE240000		GRAPHIC FOR END OF TRANSMISSION BLOCK
2418		8698						SE250000		GRAPHIC FOR CANCEL
2419		8699						SE260000		GRAPHIC FOR END OF MEDIUM
241A		869A						SE270000		GRAPHIC FOR SUBSTITUTE
241B		869B						SE280000		GRAPHIC FOR ESCAPE
241C		869C						SE290000		GRAPHIC FOR FILE SEPARATOR
241D		869D						SE300000		GRAPHIC FOR GROUP SEPARATOR
241E		869E						SE310000		GRAPHIC FOR RECORD SEPARATOR
241F		869F						SE320000		GRAPHIC FOR UNIT SEPARATOR
2421		86A0						SE330000		GRAPHIC FOR DELETE
2460		8A40			8740	A8E7	AF87	NO010000		CIRCLED DIGIT ONE
2461		8A41			8741	A8E8	AF88	NO020000		CIRCLED DIGIT TWO
2462		8A42			8742	A8E9	AF89	NO030000		CIRCLED DIGIT THREE
2463		8A43			8743	A8EA	AF8A	NO040000		CIRCLED DIGIT FOUR
2464		8A44			8744	A8EB	AF8B	NO050000		CIRCLED DIGIT FIVE
2465		8A45			8745	A8EC	AF8C	NO060000		CIRCLED DIGIT SIX
2466		8A46			8746	A8ED	AF8D	NO070000		CIRCLED DIGIT SEVEN
2467		8A47			8747	A8EE	AF8E	NO080000		CIRCLED DIGIT EIGHT

UNIC	UGL	948	XJIS	942	AX	KSC	944	GCGID	GCGID#2	Unicode character name
2468		8A48			8748	A8EF	AF8F	NO090000		CIRCLED DIGIT NINE
2469		8A49			8749	A8F0	AF90	NO100000		CIRCLED NUMBER TEN
246A					874A	A8F1	AF91	F1OX0000		CIRCLED NUMBER ELEVEN
246B					874B	A8F2	AF92	F1OY0000		CIRCLED NUMBER TWELVE
246C					874C	A8F3	AF93	F1OZ0000		CIRCLED NUMBER THIRTEEN
246D					874D	A8F4	AF94	F1P00000		CIRCLED NUMBER FOURTEEN
246E					874E	A8F5	AF95	F1P10000		CIRCLED NUMBER FIFTEEN
246F					874F					CIRCLED NUMBER SIXTEEN
2470					8750					CIRCLED NUMBER SEVENTEEN
2471					8751					CIRCLED NUMBER EIGHTEEN
2472					8752					CIRCLED NUMBER NINETEEN
2473					8753					CIRCLED NUMBER TWENTY
2474		8A50				A9E7	AFE5	NO010001		PARENTHESIZED DIGIT ONE
2475		8A51				A9E8	AFE6	NO020001		PARENTHESIZED DIGIT TWO
2476		8A52				A9E9	AFE7	NO030001		PARENTHESIZED DIGIT THREE
2477		8A53				A9EA	AFE8	NO040001		PARENTHESIZED DIGIT FOUR
2478		8A54				A9EB	AFE9	NO050001		PARENTHESIZED DIGIT FIVE
2479		8A55				A9EC	AFEA	NO060001		PARENTHESIZED DIGIT SIX
247A		8A56				A9ED	AFEB	NO070001		PARENTHESIZED DIGIT SEVEN
247B		8A57				A9EE	AFEC	NO080001		PARENTHESIZED DIGIT EIGHT
247C		8A58				A9EF	AFED	NO090001		PARENTHESIZED DIGIT NINE
247D		8A59				A9F0	AFEE	NO100001		PARENTHESIZED NUMBER TEN
247E						A9F1	AFEF	F1RK0000		PARENTHESIZED NUMBER ELEVEN
247F						A9F2	AFF0	F1RL0000		PARENTHESIZED NUMBER TWELVE
2480						A9F3	AFF1	F1RM0000		PARENTHESIZED NUMBER THIRTEEN
2481						A9F4	AFF2	F1RN0000		PARENTHESIZED NUMBER FOURTEEN
2482						A9F5	AFF3	F1RO0000		PARENTHESIZED NUMBER FIFTEEN
249C						A9CD	AFCB	F1QK0000		PARENTHESIZED LATIN SMALL LETTER A
249D						A9CE	AFCC	F1QL0000		PARENTHESIZED LATIN SMALL LETTER B
249E						A9CF	AFCD	F1QM0000		PARENTHESIZED LATIN SMALL LETTER C
249F						A9D0	AFCE	F1QN0000		PARENTHESIZED LATIN SMALL LETTER D
24A0						A9D1	AFCF	F1QO0000		PARENTHESIZED LATIN SMALL LETTER E
24A1						A9D2	AFD0	F1QP0000		PARENTHESIZED LATIN SMALL LETTER F
24A2						A9D3	AFD1	F1QQ0000		PARENTHESIZED LATIN SMALL LETTER G
24A3						A9D4	AFD2	F1QR0000		PARENTHESIZED LATIN SMALL LETTER H
24A4						A9D5	AFD3	F1QS0000		PARENTHESIZED LATIN SMALL LETTER I
24A5						A9D6	AFD4	F1QT0000		PARENTHESIZED LATIN SMALL LETTER J
24A6						A9D7	AFD5	F1QU0000		PARENTHESIZED LATIN SMALL LETTER K
24A7						A9D8	AFD6	F1QV0000		PARENTHESIZED LATIN SMALL LETTER L
24A8						A9D9	AFD7	F1QW0000		PARENTHESIZED LATIN SMALL LETTER M

UNIC	UGL	948	XJIS	942	AX	KSC	944	GCGID	GCGID#2	Unicode character name
24A9						A9DA	AFD8	F1QX0000		PARENTHESIZED LATIN SMALL LETTER N
24AA						A9DB	AFD9	F1QY0000		PARENTHESIZED LATIN SMALL LETTER O
24AB						A9DC	AFDA	F1QZ0000		PARENTHESIZED LATIN SMALL LETTER P
24AC						A9DD	AFDB	F1R00000		PARENTHESIZED LATIN SMALL LETTER Q
24AD						A9DE	AFDC	F1R10000		PARENTHESIZED LATIN SMALL LETTER R
24AE						A9DF	AFDD	F1R20000		PARENTHESIZED LATIN SMALL LETTER S
24AF						A9E0	AFDE	F1R30000		PARENTHESIZED LATIN SMALL LETTER T
24B0						A9E1	AFDF	F1R40000		PARENTHESIZED LATIN SMALL LETTER U
24B1						A9E2	AFE0	F1R50000		PARENTHESIZED LATIN SMALL LETTER V
24B2						A9E3	AFE1	F1R60000		PARENTHESIZED LATIN SMALL LETTER W
24B3						A9E4	AFE2	F1R70000		PARENTHESIZED LATIN SMALL LETTER X
24B4						A9E5	AFE3	F1R80000		PARENTHESIZED LATIN SMALL LETTER Y
24B5						A9E6	AFE4	F1R90000		PARENTHESIZED LATIN SMALL LETTER Z
24D0						A8CD	AF6C	F1NX0000		CIRCLED LATIN SMALL LETTER A
24D1						A8CE	AF6D	F1NY0000		CIRCLED LATIN SMALL LETTER B
24D2						A8CF	AF6E	F1NZ0000		CIRCLED LATIN SMALL LETTER C
24D3						A8D0	AF6F	F1O00000		CIRCLED LATIN SMALL LETTER D
24D4						A8D1	AF70	F1O10000		CIRCLED LATIN SMALL LETTER E
24D5						A8D2	AF71	F1O20000		CIRCLED LATIN SMALL LETTER F
24D6						A8D3	AF72	F1O30000		CIRCLED LATIN SMALL LETTER G
24D7						A8D4	AF73	F1O40000		CIRCLED LATIN SMALL LETTER H
24D8						A8D5	AF74	F1O50000		CIRCLED LATIN SMALL LETTER I
24D9						A8D6	AF75	F1O60000		CIRCLED LATIN SMALL LETTER J
24DA						A8D7	AF76	F1O70000		CIRCLED LATIN SMALL LETTER K
24DB						A8D8	AF77	F1O80000		CIRCLED LATIN SMALL LETTER L
24DC						A8D9	AF78	F1O90000		CIRCLED LATIN SMALL LETTER M
24DD						A8DA	AF79	F1OA0000		CIRCLED LATIN SMALL LETTER N
24DE						A8DB	AF7A	F1OB0000		CIRCLED LATIN SMALL LETTER O
24DF						A8DC	AF7B	F1OC0000		CIRCLED LATIN SMALL LETTER P
24E0						A8DD	AF7C	F1OD0000		CIRCLED LATIN SMALL LETTER Q
24E1						A8DE	AF7D	F1OE0000		CIRCLED LATIN SMALL LETTER R
24E2						A8DF	AF7E	F1OF0000		CIRCLED LATIN SMALL LETTER S
24E3						A8E0	AF7F	F1OG0000		CIRCLED LATIN SMALL LETTER T
24E4						A8E1	AF80	F1OH0000		CIRCLED LATIN SMALL LETTER U
24E5						A8E2	AF81	F1OI0000		CIRCLED LATIN SMALL LETTER V
24E6						A8E3	AF82	F1OJ0000		CIRCLED LATIN SMALL LETTER W
24E7						A8E4	AF83	F1OK0000		CIRCLED LATIN SMALL LETTER X
24E8						A8E5	AF84	F1OL0000		CIRCLED LATIN SMALL LETTER Y
24E9						A8E6	AF86	F1OM0000		CIRCLED LATIN SMALL LETTER Z
2500	196	8A74	849F	849F	849F	A6A1	8440	SF100000		FORMS LIGHT HORIZONTAL

UNIC	UGL	948	XJIS	942	AX	KSC	944	GCGID	GCGID#2	Unicode character name
2501		84AA	84AA	84AA	84AA	A6AC	844B	SF100002		FORMS HEAVY HORIZONTAL
2502	179	8A75	84A0	84A0	84A0	A6A2	8441	SF110000		FORMS LIGHT VERTICAL
2502		001D	001D	001D	0014	001D	001D	SF110000		FORMS LIGHT VERTICAL
2503		84AB	84AB	84AB	84AB	A6AD	844C	SF110002		FORMS HEAVY VERTICAL
250C	218	8A77	84A1	84A1	84A1	A6A3	8442	SF010000		FORMS LIGHT DOWN AND RIGHT
250D						A6C8	8467	F12G0000		FORMS DOWN LIGHT AND RIGHT HEAVY
250E						A6C7	8466	F12F0000		FORMS DOWN HEAVY AND RIGHT LIGHT
250F		84AC	84AC	84AC	84AC	A6AE	844D	SF010002		FORMS HEAVY DOWN AND RIGHT
2510	191	8A78	84A2	84A2	84A2	A6A4	8443	SF030000		FORMS LIGHT DOWN AND LEFT
2511						A6C2	8461	F12A0000		FORMS DOWN LIGHT AND LEFT HEAVY
2512						A6C1	8460	F1290000		FORMS DOWN HEAVY AND LEFT LIGHT
2513		84AD	84AD	84AD	84AD	A6AF	844E	SF030002		FORMS HEAVY DOWN AND LEFT
2514	192	8A79	84A4	84A4	84A4	A6A6	8445	SF020000		FORMS LIGHT UP AND RIGHT
2515						A6C6	8465	F12E0000		FORMS UP LIGHT AND RIGHT HEAVY
2516						A6C5	8464	F12D0000		FORMS UP HEAVY AND RIGHT LIGHT
2517		84AF	84AF	84AF	84AF	A6B0	8450	SF020002		FORMS HEAVY UP AND RIGHT
2518	217	8A7A	84A3	84A3	84A3	A6A5	8444	SF040000		FORMS LIGHT UP AND LEFT
2519						A6C4	8463	F12C0000		FORMS UP LIGHT AND LEFT HEAVY
251A						A6C3	8462	F12B0000		FORMS UP HEAVY AND LEFT LIGHT
251B		84AE	84AE	84AE	84AE	A6B1	844F	SF040002		FORMS HEAVY UP AND LEFT
251C	195	8A72	84A5	84A5	84A5	A6A7	8446	SF080000		FORMS LIGHT VERTICAL AND RIGHT
251D		84BA	84BA	84BA		A6BC	845B	SF080004		FORMS VERTICAL LIGHT AND RIGHT HEAVY
251E						A6C9	8468	F12H0000		FORMS UP HEAVY AND RIGHT DOWN LIGHT
251F						A6CA	8469	F12I0000		FORMS DOWN HEAVY AND RIGHT UP LIGHT
2520		84B5	84B5	84B5	84B5	A6B7	8456	SF080003		FORMS VERTICAL HEAVY AND RIGHT LIGHT
2521						A6CB	846A	F12J0000		FORMS DOWN LIGHT AND RIGHT UP HEAVY
2522						A6CC	846B	F12K0000		FORMS UP LIGHT AND RIGHT DOWN HEAVY
2523		84B0	84B0	84B0	84B0	A6B2	8451	SF080002		FORMS HEAVY VERTICAL AND RIGHT
2524	180	8A71	84A7	84A7	84A7	A6A9	8448	SF090000		FORMS LIGHT VERTICAL AND LEFT
2525		84BC	84BC	84BC	84BC	A6BE	845D	SF090004		FORMS VERTICAL LIGHT AND LEFT HEAVY
2526						A6CD	846C	F12L0000		FORMS UP HEAVY AND LEFT DOWN LIGHT
2527						A6CE	846D	F12M0000		FORMS DOWN HEAVY AND LEFT UP LIGHT
2528		84B7	84B7	84B7	84B7	A6B9	8458	SF090003		FORMS VERTICAL HEAVY AND LEFT LIGHT
2529						A6CF	846E	F12N0000		FORMS DOWN LIGHT AND LEFT UP HEAVY
252A						A6D0	846F	F12O0000		FORMS UP LIGHT AND LEFT DOWN HEAVY
252B		84B2	84B2	84B2	84B2	A6B4	8453	SF090002		FORMS HEAVY VERTICAL AND LEFT
252C	194	8A70	84A6	84A6	84A6	A6A8	8447	SF060000		FORMS LIGHT DOWN AND HORIZONTAL
252D						A6D1	8470	F12P0000		FORMS LEFT HEAVY AND RIGHT DOWN LIGHT
252E						A6D2	8471	F12Q0000		FORMS RIGHT HEAVY AND LEFT DOWN LIGHT
252F		84B6	84B6	84B6	84B6	A6B8	8457	SF060003		FORMS DOWN LIGHT AND HORIZONTAL HEAVY

UNIC	UGL	948	XJIS	942	AX	KSC	944	GCGID	GCGID#2	Unicode character name
2530		84BB	84BB	84BB	84BB	A6BD	845C	SF060004		FORMS DOWN HEAVY AND HORIZONTAL LIGHT
2531						A6D3	8472	F12R0000		FORMS RIGHT LIGHT AND LEFT DOWN HEAVY
2532						A6D4	8473	F12S0000		FORMS LEFT LIGHT AND RIGHT DOWN HEAVY
2533		84B1	84B1	84B1	84B1	A6B3	8452	SF060002		FORMS HEAVY DOWN AND HORIZONTAL
2534	193	8A6F	84A8	84A8	84A8	A6AA	8449	SF070000		FORMS LIGHT UP AND HORIZONTAL
2535						A6D5	8474	F12T0000		FORMS LEFT HEAVY AND RIGHT UP LIGHT
2536						A6D6	8475	F12U0000		FORMS RIGHT HEAVY AND LEFT UP LIGHT
2537		84B8	84B8	84B8	84B8	A6BA	8459	SF070003		FORMS UP LIGHT AND HORIZONTAL HEAVY
2538		84BD	84BD	84BD	84BD	A6BF	845E	SF070004		FORMS UP HEAVY AND HORIZONTAL LIGHT
2539						A6D7	8476	F12V0000		FORMS RIGHT LIGHT AND LEFT UP HEAVY
253A						A6D8	8477	F12W0000		FORMS LEFT LIGHT AND RIGHT UP HEAVY
253B		84B3	84B3	84B3	84B3	A6B5	8454	SF070002		FORMS HEAVY UP AND HORIZONTAL
253C	197	8A6E	84A9	84A9	84A9	A6AB	844A	SF050000		FORMS LIGHT VERTICAL AND HORIZONTAL
253D						A6D9	8478	F12X0000		FORMS LEFT HEAVY AND RIGHT VERTICAL LIGHT
253E						A6DA	8479	F12Y0000		FORMS RIGHT HEAVY AND LEFT VERTICAL LIGHT
253F		84B9	84B9	84B9	84B9	A6BB	845A	SF050003		FORMS VERTICAL LIGHT AND HORIZONTAL HEAVY
2540						A6DB	847A	F12Z0000		FORMS UP HEAVY AND DOWN HORIZONTAL LIGHT
2541						A6DC	847B	F1300000		FORMS DOWN HEAVY AND UP HORIZONTAL LIGHT
2542		84BE	84BE	84BE	84BE	A6C0	845F	SF050004		FORMS VERTICAL HEAVY AND HORIZONTAL LIGHT
2543						A6DD	847C	F1310000		FORMS LEFT UP HEAVY AND RIGHT DOWN LIGHT
2544						A6DE	847D	F1320000		FORMS RIGHT UP HEAVY AND LEFT DOWN LIGHT
2545						A6DF	847E	F1330000		FORMS LEFT DOWN HEAVY AND RIGHT UP LIGHT
2546						A6E0	8480	F1340000		FORMS RIGHT DOWN HEAVY AND LEFT UP LIGHT
2547						A6E1	8481	F1350000		FORMS DOWN LIGHT AND UP HORIZONTAL HEAVY
2548						A6E2	8482	F1360000		FORMS UP LIGHT AND DOWN HORIZONTAL HEAVY
2549						A6E3	8483	F1370000		FORMS RIGHT LIGHT AND LEFT VERTICAL HEAVY
254A						A6E4	8484	F1380000		FORMS LEFT LIGHT AND RIGHT VERTICAL HEAVY
254B		84B4	84B4	84B4	84B4	A6B6	8455	SF050002		FORMS HEAVY VERTICAL AND HORIZONTAL
2550		0006	0006	0006	0008	0006	0006	SF430000		FORMS DOUBLE HORIZONTAL
2550	205	8A80			0013			SF430000		FORMS DOUBLE HORIZONTAL
2551	186	0005	0005	0005	0009	0005	0005	SF240000		FORMS DOUBLE VERTICAL
2554		0001	0001	0001	0015	0001	0001	SF390000		FORMS DOUBLE DOWN AND RIGHT
2554	201				000A			SF390000		FORMS DOUBLE DOWN AND RIGHT
2557		0002	0002	0002	0016	0002	0002	SF250000		FORMS DOUBLE DOWN AND LEFT
2557	187				000B			SF250000		FORMS DOUBLE DOWN AND LEFT
255A		0003	0003	0003	0018	0003	0003	SF380000		FORMS DOUBLE UP AND RIGHT
255A	200				000D			SF380000		FORMS DOUBLE UP AND RIGHT
255D		0004	0004	0004	0017	0004	0004	SF260000		FORMS DOUBLE UP AND LEFT
255D	188				000C			SF260000		FORMS DOUBLE UP AND LEFT
255E	264	8A81						SF360000		FORMS VERTICAL SINGLE AND RIGHT DOUBLE

UNIC	UGL	948	XJIS	942	AX	KSC	944	GCGID	GCGID#2	Unicode character name
2560					000E			SF420000		FORMS DOUBLE VERTICAL AND RIGHT
2560	204	0019		0019	0019	0019	0019	SF420000		FORMS DOUBLE VERTICAL AND RIGHT
2561	258	8A83						SF190000		FORMS VERTICAL SINGLE AND LEFT DOUBLE
2563					001B			SF230000		FORMS DOUBLE VERTICAL AND LEFT
2563	185	0017		0017	0010	0017	0017	SF230000		FORMS DOUBLE VERTICAL AND LEFT
2566					000F			SF410000		FORMS DOUBLE DOWN AND HORIZONTAL
2566	203	0016		0016	001A	0016	0016	SF410000		FORMS DOUBLE DOWN AND HORIZONTAL
2569					001C			SF400000		FORMS DOUBLE UP AND HORIZONTAL
2569	202	0015		0015	0011	0015	0015	SF400000		FORMS DOUBLE UP AND HORIZONTAL
256A	275	8A82						SF540000		FORMS VERTICAL SINGLE AND HORIZONTAL DOUBLE
256C					001D			SF440000		FORMS DOUBLE VERTICAL AND HORIZONTAL
256C	206	0010		0010	0012	0010	0010	SF440000		FORMS DOUBLE VERTICAL AND HORIZONTAL
256D		8A7B						SS160000		FORMS LIGHT ARC DOWN AND RIGHT
256E		8A7C						SS180000		FORMS LIGHT ARC DOWN AND LEFT
256F		8A7E						SS190000		FORMS LIGHT ARC UP AND LEFT
2570		8A7D						SS170000		FORMS LIGHT ARC UP AND RIGHT
2571		8A88						SH020000		FORMS LIGHT DIAGONAL UPPER RIGHT TO LOWER LEFT
2572		8A89						SH030000		FORMS LIGHT DIAGONAL UPPER LEFT TO LOWER RIGHT
2573		8A8A						SH040000		FORMS LIGHT DIAGONAL CROSS
2581		8A5F						SF700001		LOWER ONE EIGHTH BLOCK
2582		8A60						SF710001		LOWER ONE QUARTER BLOCK
2583		8A61						SF720001		LOWER THREE EIGHTHS BLOCK
2584	220	8A62						SF730001		LOWER HALF BLOCK
2585		8A63						SF740001		LOWER FIVE EIGHTHS BLOCK
2586		8A64						SF750001		LOWER THREE QUARTER BLOCK
2587		8A65						SF760001		LOWER SEVEN EIGHTHS BLOCK
2588	219	8A66						SF610000		FULL BLOCK
2589		8A6D						SF830001		LEFT SEVEN EIGHTHS BLOCK
258A		8A6C						SF820001		LEFT THREE QUARTER BLOCK
258B		8A6B						SF810001		LEFT FIVE EIGHTHS BLOCK
258C	276	8A6A						SF800001		LEFT HALF BLOCK
258D		8A69						SF790001		LEFT THREE EIGHTHS BLOCK
258E		8A68						SF780001		LEFT ONE QUARTER BLOCK
258F		8A67						SF770001		LEFT ONE EIGHTH BLOCK
2591	176	001A		001A		A2C6	001A	SF140000		LIGHT SHADE
2592	177					8573		SF150000	K:F1DG0000	MEDIUM SHADE
2593	178	0014		0014		0014		SF160000		DARK SHADE
2594		8A73						SF670000		UPPER ONE EIGHTH BLOCK
2595		8A76						SF650000		RIGHT ONE EIGHTH BLOCK
25A0		000E		000E			000E	SM470000		BLACK SQUARE

The Unicode Standard • Version 1.0

UNIC	UGL	948	XJIS	942	AX	KSC	944	GCGID	GCGID#2	Unicode character name
25A0	254	81A1	81A1	81A1	81A1	A1E1	8181	SM470000		BLACK SQUARE
25A1		81A0	81A0	81A0	81A0	A1E0	8180	SM450000		WHITE SQUARE
25A3						A2C3	8574	F1DD0000		WHITE SQUARE CONTAINING BLACK SMALL SQUARE
25A4						A2C7	8575	F1DH0000		SQUARE WITH HORIZONTAL FILL
25A5						A2C8	8575	F1DI0000		SQUARE WITH VERTICAL FILL
25A6						A2CB	8578	F1DL0000		SQUARE WITH ORTHOGONAL CROSSHATCH FILL
25A7						A2CA	8577	F1DK0000		SQUARE WITH UPPER LEFT TO LOWER RIGHT FILL
25A8						A2C9	8576	F1DJ0000		SQUARE WITH UPPER RIGHT TO LOWER LEFT FILL
25A9						A2CC	8579	F1DM0000		SQUARE WITH DIAGONAL CROSSHATCH FILL
25B2						001E		SM600000		BLACK UP POINTING TRIANGLE
25B2	030	81A3	81A3	81A3	81A3	A1E3	8183	SM600000		BLACK UP POINTING TRIANGLE
25B3		81A2	81A2	81A2	81A2	A1E2	8182	SM730000		WHITE UP POINTING TRIANGLE
25B6						A2BA	8567	SM600001		BLACK RIGHT POINTING TRIANGLE
25B7						A2B9	8566	SM600001		WHITE RIGHT POINTING TRIANGLE
25BC				0009		001F		SV040000		BLACK DOWN POINTING TRIANGLE
25BC	031	81A5	81A5	81A5	81A5	A1E5	8185	SV040000		BLACK DOWN POINTING TRIANGLE
25BD		81A4	81A4	81A4	81A4	A1E4	8184	SM740000		WHITE DOWN POINTING TRIANGLE
25C0						A2B8	8565	F1D20000		BLACK LEFT POINTING TRIANGLE
25C1						A2B7	8564	F1D10000		WHITE LEFT POINTING TRIANGLE
25C4	017					0011		SM630000		BLACK LEFT POINTING POINTER
25C6		819F	819F	819F	819F	A1DF	817E	SM610000		BLACK DIAMOND
25C7		819E	819E	819E	819E	A1DE	817D	SA660000		WHITE DIAMOND
25C8						A2C2	856F	F1DC0000		WHITE DIAMOND CONTAINING BLACK SMALL DIAMOND
25CB		819B	819B	819B	819B	A1DB	817A	SM750000		WHITE CIRCLE
25CB	009	0009		0009		0009	0009	SM750000		WHITE CIRCLE
25CE		819D	819D	819D	819D	A1DD	817C	SM810000		BULLSEYE
25CF		819C	819C	819C	819C	A1DC	817B	SM580000		BLACK CIRCLE
25D0						A2C4	8571	F1DE0000		CIRCLE WITH LEFT HALF BLACK
25D1						A2C5	8572	F1DF0000		CIRCLE WITH RIGHT HALF BLACK
25D8	008					0008		SM570001		INVERSE BULLET
25D9	010					000A		SM750002		INVERSE WHITE CIRCLE
25E2		8A84						SF840000		BLACK LOWER RIGHT TRIANGLE
25E3		8A85						SF850000		BLACK LOWER LEFT TRIANGLE
25E4		8A87						SF870000		BLACK UPPER LEFT TRIANGLE
25E5		8A86						SF860000		BLACK UPPER RIGHT TRIANGLE
2605		819A	819A	819A	819A	A1DA	8179	SS580000		BLACK STAR
2606		8199	8199	8199	8199	A1D9	8178	SS570000		WHITE STAR
260E						A2CF	857C	F1DP0000		BLACK TELEPHONE
260F						A2CE	857B	F1DO0000		WHITE TELEPHONE
261C						A2D0	857D	F1DQ0000		WHITE LEFT POINTING INDEX

UNIC	UGL	948	XJIS	942	AX	KSC	944	GCGID	GCGID#2	Unicode character name
261E						A2D1	857E	F1DR0000		WHITE RIGHT POINTING INDEX
263C	015	000F		000F		000F	000F	SM690000		WHITE SUN WITH RAYS
2640						000C		SM290000		FEMALE SIGN
2640	012	818A	818A	818A	818A	A1CF	8193	SM290000		FEMALE SIGN
2642						000B		SM280000		MALE SIGN
2642	011	8189	8189	8189	8189	A1CE	8192	SM280000		MALE SIGN
2660	006					A2BC	8569	SS050000		BLACK SPADE SUIT
2661						A2BD	856A	F1D70000		WHITE HEART SUIT
2663	005					A2C0	856D	SS040000		BLACK CLUB SUIT
2664						A2BB	8568	F1D50000		WHITE SPADE SUIT
2665	003					A2BE	856B	SS020000		BLACK HEART SUIT
2667						A2BF	856C	F1D90000		WHITE CLUB SUIT
2668						A2CD	857A	F1DN0000		HOT SPRINGS
2669						A2DB	8589	F1E10000		QUARTER NOTE
266A						000D		SM930000		EIGHTH NOTE
266A	013	81F4	81F4	81F4	81F4	A2DC	858A	SM930000		EIGHTH NOTE
266B	014					000E		SM910000		BARRED EIGHTH NOTES
266C						A2DD	858B	SM910000		BARRED SIXTEENTH NOTES
266D		81F3	81F3	81F3	81F3	A2DA	8588	SM890000		FLAT
266F		81F2	81F2	81F2	81F2			SM880000		SHARP
3000		8140	8140	8140	8140	A1A1	8140	SP010080		IDEOGRAPHIC SPACE
3001	773	8141	8141	8141	8141	A1A2	8141	JQ730080		IDEOGRAPHIC COMMA
3002	770	8142	8142	8142	8142	A1A3	8142	JQ700080		IDEOGRAPHIC PERIOD
3003		8156	8156	8156	8156	A1A8	8147	SV090001		DITTO MARK
3004		8157	8157	8157	8157			SS760000		IDEOGRAPHIC DITTO MARK
3005	891	8158	8158	8158	8158			SS770000		IDEOGRAPHIC ITERATION MARK
3006		8159	8159	8159	8159			SS720000		IDEOGRAPHIC CLOSING MARK
3007		815A	815A	815A	815A			ND100007		IDEOGRAPHIC NUMBER ZERO
3008		8171	8171	8171	8171	A1B4	8153	SP060002		OPENING ANGLE BRACKET
3009		8172	8172	8172	8172	A1B5	8154	SP070002		CLOSING ANGLE BRACKET
300A		8173	8173	8173	8173	A1B6	8155	SP060003		OPENING DOUBLE ANGLE BRACKET
300B		8174	8174	8174	8174	A1B7	8156	SP070003		CLOSING DOUBLE ANGLE BRACKET
300C	771	8175	8175	8175	8175	A1B8	8157	JQ710080		OPENING CORNER BRACKET
300D	772	8176	8176	8176	8176	A1B9	8158	JQ720080		CLOSING CORNER BRACKET
300E	888	8177	8177	8177	8177	A1BA	8159	JQ710001		OPENING WHITE CORNER BRACKET
300F	889	8178	8178	8178	8178	A1BB	815A	JQ720001		CLOSING WHITE CORNER BRACKET
3010		8179	8179	8179	8179	A1BC	815B	SP060004		OPENING BLACK LENTICULAR BRACKET
3011		817A	817A	817A	817A	A1BD	815C	SP070004		CLOSING BLACK LENTICULAR BRACKET
3012		81A7	81A7	81A7	81A7			SS730000		POSTAL MARK
3013		81AC	81AC	81AC	81AC	A1EB	818B	SS750000		GETA MARK

UNIC	UGL	948	XJIS	942	AX	KSC	944	GCGID	GCGID#2	Unicode character name
3014		816B	816B	816B	816B	A1B2	8151	SP060001		OPENING TORTOISE SHELL BRACKET
3015		816C	816C	816C	816C	A1B3	8152	SP070001		CLOSING TORTOISE SHELL BRACKET
301D		8AE8			8780			SP210001		REVERSED DOUBLE PRIME QUOTATION MARK
301E		8AE9						SP220001		DOUBLE PRIME QUOTATION MARK
301F					8781			SP230001		LOW DOUBLE PRIME QUOTATION MARK
3021		8940						NC010080		HANGZHOU NUMERAL ONE
3022		8941						NC020080		HANGZHOU NUMERAL TWO
3023		8942						NC030080		HANGZHOU NUMERAL THREE
3024		8943						NC040080		HANGZHOU NUMERAL FOUR
3025		8944						NC050080		HANGZHOU NUMERAL FIVE
3026		8945						NC060080		HANGZHOU NUMERAL SIX
3027		8946						NC070080		HANGZHOU NUMERAL SEVEN
3028		8947						NC080080		HANGZHOU NUMERAL EIGHT
3029		8948						NC090080		HANGZHOU NUMERAL NINE
303F	768	000B		000B			000B	SP500000		IDEOGRAPHIC HALF FILL SPACE
3041	833	829F	829F	829F	829F	AAA1	829F	RA010000		HIRAGANA LETTER SMALL A
3042	842	82A0	82A0	82A0	82A0	AAA2	82A0	RA000000		HIRAGANA LETTER A
3043	834	82A1	82A1	82A1	82A1	AAA3	82A1	RI010000		HIRAGANA LETTER SMALL I
3044	843	82A2	82A2	82A2	82A2	AAA4	82A2	RI000000		HIRAGANA LETTER I
3045	835	82A3	82A3	82A3	82A3	AAA5	82A3	RU010000		HIRAGANA LETTER SMALL U
3046	844	82A4	82A4	82A4	82A4	AAA6	82A4	RU000000		HIRAGANA LETTER U
3047	836	82A5	82A5	82A5	82A5	AAA7	82A5	RE010000		HIRAGANA LETTER SMALL E
3048	845	82A6	82A6	82A6	82A6	AAA8	82A6	RE000000		HIRAGANA LETTER E
3049	837	82A7	82A7	82A7	82A7	AAA9	82A7	RO010000		HIRAGANA LETTER SMALL O
304A	846	82A8	82A8	82A8	82A8	AAAA	82A8	RO000000		HIRAGANA LETTER O
304B	847	82A9	82A9	82A9	82A9	AAAB	82A9	RK100000		HIRAGANA LETTER KA
304C		82AA	82AA	82AA	82AA	AAAC	82AA	RG100000		HIRAGANA LETTER GA
304D	848	82AB	82AB	82AB	82AB	AAAD	82AB	RK200000		HIRAGANA LETTER KI
304E		82AC	82AC	82AC	82AC	AAAE	82AC	RG200000		HIRAGANA LETTER GI
304F	849	82AD	82AD	82AD	82AD	AAAF	82AD	RK300000		HIRAGANA LETTER KU
3050		82AE	82AE	82AE	82AE	AAB0	82AE	RG300000		HIRAGANA LETTER GU
3051	850	82AF	82AF	82AF	82AF	AAB1	82AF	RK400000		HIRAGANA LETTER KE
3052		82B0	82B0	82B0	82B0	AAB2	82B0	RG400000		HIRAGANA LETTER GE
3053	851	82B1	82B1	82B1	82B1	AAB3	82B1	RK500000		HIRAGANA LETTER KO
3054		82B2	82B2	82B2	82B2	AAB4	82B2	RG500000		HIRAGANA LETTER GO
3055	852	82B3	82B3	82B3	82B3	AAB5	82B3	RS100000		HIRAGANA LETTER SA
3056		82B4	82B4	82B4	82B4	AAB6	82B4	RZ100000		HIRAGANA LETTER ZA
3057	853	82B5	82B5	82B5	82B5	AAB7	82B5	RS200000		HIRAGANA LETTER SI
3058		82B6	82B6	82B6	82B6	AAB8	82B6	RZ200000		HIRAGANA LETTER ZI
3059	854	82B7	82B7	82B7	82B7	AAB9	82B7	RS300000		HIRAGANA LETTER SU

UNIC	UGL	948	XJIS	942	AX	KSC	944	GCGID	GCGID#2	Unicode character name
305A		82B8	82B8	82B8	82B8	AABA	82B8	RZ300000		HIRAGANA LETTER ZU
305B	855	82B9	82B9	82B9	82B9	AABB	82B9	RS400000		HIRAGANA LETTER SE
305C		82BA	82BA	82BA	82BA	AABC	82BA	RZ400000		HIRAGANA LETTER ZE
305D	856	82BB	82BB	82BB	82BB	AABD	82BB	RS500000		HIRAGANA LETTER SO
305E		82BC	82BC	82BC	82BC	AABE	82BC	RZ500000		HIRAGANA LETTER ZO
305F	857	82BD	82BD	82BD	82BD	AABF	82BD	RT100000		HIRAGANA LETTER TA
3060		82BE	82BE	82BE	82BE	AAC0	82BE	RD100000		HIRAGANA LETTER DA
3061	858	82BF	82BF	82BF	82BF	AAC1	82BF	RT200000		HIRAGANA LETTER TI
3062		82C0	82C0	82C0	82C0	AAC2	82C0	RD200000		HIRAGANA LETTER DI
3063	841	82C1	82C1	82C1	82C1	AAC3	82C1	RT310000		HIRAGANA LETTER SMALL TU
3064	859	82C2	82C2	82C2	82C2	AAC4	82C2	RT300000		HIRAGANA LETTER TU
3065		82C3	82C3	82C3	82C3	AAC5	82C3	RD300000		HIRAGANA LETTER DU
3066	860	82C4	82C4	82C4	82C4	AAC6	82C4	RT400000		HIRAGANA LETTER TE
3067		82C5	82C5	82C5	82C5	AAC7	82C5	RD400000		HIRAGANA LETTER DE
3068	861	82C6	82C6	82C6	82C6	AAC8	82C6	RT500000		HIRAGANA LETTER TO
3069		82C7	82C7	82C7	82C7	AAC9	82C7	RD500000		HIRAGANA LETTER DO
306A	862	82C8	82C8	82C8	82C8	AACA	82C8	RN100000		HIRAGANA LETTER NA
306B	863	82C9	82C9	82C9	82C9	AACB	82C9	RN200000		HIRAGANA LETTER NI
306C	864	82CA	82CA	82CA	82CA	AACC	82CA	RN300000		HIRAGANA LETTER NU
306D	865	82CB	82CB	82CB	82CB	AACD	82CB	RN400000		HIRAGANA LETTER NE
306E	866	82CC	82CC	82CC	82CC	AACE	82CC	RN500000		HIRAGANA LETTER NO
306F	867	82CD	82CD	82CD	82CD	AACF	82CD	RH100000		HIRAGANA LETTER HA
3070		82CE	82CE	82CE	82CE	AAD0	82CE	RB100000		HIRAGANA LETTER BA
3071		82CF	82CF	82CF	82CF	AAD1	82CF	RP100000		HIRAGANA LETTER PA
3072	868	82D0	82D0	82D0	82D0	AAD2	82D0	RH200000		HIRAGANA LETTER HI
3073		82D1	82D1	82D1	82D1	AAD3	82D1	RB200000		HIRAGANA LETTER BI
3074		82D2	82D2	82D2	82D2	AAD4	82D2	RP200000		HIRAGANA LETTER PI
3075	869	82D3	82D3	82D3	82D3	AAD5	82D3	RH300000		HIRAGANA LETTER HU
3076		82D4	82D4	82D4	82D4	AAD6	82D4	RB300000		HIRAGANA LETTER BU
3077		82D5	82D5	82D5	82D5	AAD7	82D5	RP300000		HIRAGANA LETTER PU
3078	870	82D6	82D6	82D6	82D6	AAD8	82D6	RH400000		HIRAGANA LETTER HE
3079		82D7	82D7	82D7	82D7	AAD9	82D7	RB400000		HIRAGANA LETTER BE
307A		82D8	82D8	82D8	82D8	AADA	82D8	RP400000		HIRAGANA LETTER PE
307B	871	82D9	82D9	82D9	82D9	AADB	82D9	RH500000		HIRAGANA LETTER HO
307C		82DA	82DA	82DA	82DA	AADC	82DA	RB500000		HIRAGANA LETTER BO
307D		82DB	82DB	82DB	82DB	AADD	82DB	RP500000		HIRAGANA LETTER PO
307E	872	82DC	82DC	82DC	82DC	AADE	82DC	RM100000		HIRAGANA LETTER MA
307F	873	82DD	82DD	82DD	82DD	AADF	82DD	RM200000		HIRAGANA LETTER MI
3080	874	82DE	82DE	82DE	82DE	AAE0	82DE	RM300000		HIRAGANA LETTER MU
3081	875	82DF	82DF	82DF	82DF	AAE1	82DF	RM400000		HIRAGANA LETTER ME

UNIC	UGL	948	XJIS	942	AX	KSC	944	GCGID	GCGID#2	Unicode character name
3082	876	82E0	82E0	82E0	82E0	AAE2	82E0	RM500000		HIRAGANA LETTER MO
3083	838	82E1	82E1	82E1	82E1	AAE3	82E1	RY110000		HIRAGANA LETTER SMALL YA
3084	877	82E2	82E2	82E2	82E2	AAE4	82E2	RY100000		HIRAGANA LETTER YA
3085	839	82E3	82E3	82E3	82E3	AAE5	82E3	RY310000		HIRAGANA LETTER SMALL YU
3086	878	82E4	82E4	82E4	82E4	AAE6	82E4	RY300000		HIRAGANA LETTER YU
3087	840	82E5	82E5	82E5	82E5	AAE7	82E5	RY510000		HIRAGANA LETTER SMALL YO
3088	879	82E6	82E6	82E6	82E6	AAE8	82E6	RY500000		HIRAGANA LETTER YO
3089	880	82E7	82E7	82E7	82E7	AAE9	82E7	RR100000		HIRAGANA LETTER RA
308A	881	82E8	82E8	82E8	82E8	AAEA	82E8	RR200000		HIRAGANA LETTER RI
308B	882	82E9	82E9	82E9	82E9	AAEB	82E9	RR300000		HIRAGANA LETTER RU
308C	883	82EA	82EA	82EA	82EA	AAEC	82EA	RR400000		HIRAGANA LETTER RE
308D	884	82EB	82EB	82EB	82EB	AAED	82EB	RR500000		HIRAGANA LETTER RO
308E		82EC	82EC	82EC	82EC	AAEE	82EC	RW110000		HIRAGANA LETTER SMALL WA
308F	885	82ED	82ED	82ED	82ED	AAEF	82ED	RW100000		HIRAGANA LETTER WA
3090		82EE	82EE	82EE	82EE	AAF0	82EE	RW200000		HIRAGANA LETTER WI
3091		82EF	82EF	82EF	82EF	AAF1	82EF	RW400000		HIRAGANA LETTER WE
3092	886	82F0	82F0	82F0	82F0	AAF2	82F0	RW500000		HIRAGANA LETTER WO
3093	887	82F1	82F1	82F1	82F1	AAF3	82F1	RN000000		HIRAGANA LETTER N
309B	831	814A	814A	814A	814A			JX710080		KATAKANA-HIRAGANA VOICED SOUND MARK
309C	832	814B	814B	814B	814B			JX720080		KATAKANA-HIRAGANA SEMI-VOICED SOUND MARK
309D		8154	8154	8154	8154			RQ750000		HIRAGANA ITERATION MARK
309E		8155	8155	8155	8155			RQ760000		HIRAGANA VOICED ITERATION MARK
30A1	776	8340	8340	8340	8340	ABA1	8340	JA010080		KATAKANA LETTER SMALL A
30A2	786	8341	8341	8341	8341	ABA2	8341	JA000080		KATAKANA LETTER A
30A3	777	8342	8342	8342	8342	ABA3	8342	JI010080		KATAKANA LETTER SMALL I
30A4	787	8343	8343	8343	8343	ABA4	8343	JI000080		KATAKANA LETTER I
30A5	778	8344	8344	8344	8344	ABA5	8344	JU010080		KATAKANA LETTER SMALL U
30A6	788	8345	8345	8345	8345	ABA6	8345	JU000080		KATAKANA LETTER U
30A7	779	8346	8346	8346	8346	ABA7	8346	JE010080		KATAKANA LETTER SMALL E
30A8	789	8347	8347	8347	8347	ABA8	8347	JE000080		KATAKANA LETTER E
30A9	780	8348	8348	8348	8348	ABA9	8348	JO010080		KATAKANA LETTER SMALL O
30AA	790	8349	8349	8349	8349	ABAA	8349	JO000080		KATAKANA LETTER O
30AB	791	834A	834A	834A	834A	ABAB	834A	JK100080		KATAKANA LETTER KA
30AC		834B	834B	834B	834B	ABAC	834B	JG100080		KATAKANA LETTER GA
30AD	792	834C	834C	834C	834C	ABAD	834C	JK200080		KATAKANA LETTER KI
30AE		834D	834D	834D	834D	ABAE	834D	JG200080		KATAKANA LETTER GI
30AF	793	834E	834E	834E	834E	ABAF	834E	JK300080		KATAKANA LETTER KU
30B0		834F	834F	834F	834F	ABB0	834F	JG300080		KATAKANA LETTER GU
30B1	794	8350	8350	8350	8350	ABB1	8350	JK400080		KATAKANA LETTER KE
30B2		8351	8351	8351	8351	ABB2	8351	JG400080		KATAKANA LETTER GE

UNIC	UGL	948	XJIS	942	AX	KSC	944	GCGID	GCGID#2	Unicode character name
30B3	795	8352	8352	8352	8352	ABB3	8352	JK500080		KATAKANA LETTER KO
30B4		8353	8353	8353	8353	ABB4	8353	JG500080		KATAKANA LETTER GO
30B5	796	8354	8354	8354	8354	ABB5	8354	JS100080		KATAKANA LETTER SA
30B6		8355	8355	8355	8355	ABB6	8355	JZ100080		KATAKANA LETTER ZA
30B7	797	8356	8356	8356	8356	ABB7	8356	JS200080		KATAKANA LETTER SI
30B8		8357	8357	8357	8357	ABB8	8357	JZ200080		KATAKANA LETTER ZI
30B9	798	8358	8358	8358	8358	ABB9	8358	JS300080		KATAKANA LETTER SU
30BA		8359	8359	8359	8359	ABBA	8359	JZ300080		KATAKANA LETTER ZU
30BB	799	835A	835A	835A	835A	ABBB	835A	JS400080		KATAKANA LETTER SE
30BC		835B	835B	835B	835B	ABBC	835B	JZ400080		KATAKANA LETTER ZE
30BD	800	835C	835C	835C	835C	ABBD	835C	JS500080		KATAKANA LETTER SO
30BE		835D	835D	835D	835D	ABBE	835D	JZ500080		KATAKANA LETTER ZO
30BF	801	835E	835E	835E	835E	ABBF	835E	JT100080		KATAKANA LETTER TA
30C0		835F	835F	835F	835F	ABC0	835F	JD100080		KATAKANA LETTER DA
30C1	802	8360	8360	8360	8360	ABC1	8360	JT200080		KATAKANA LETTER TI
30C2		8361	8361	8361	8361	ABC2	8361	JD200080		KATAKANA LETTER DI
30C3	784	8362	8362	8362	8362	ABC3	8362	JT310080		KATAKANA LETTER SMALL TU
30C4	803	8363	8363	8363	8363	ABC4	8363	JT300080		KATAKANA LETTER TU
30C5		8364	8364	8364	8364	ABC5	8364	JD300080		KATAKANA LETTER DU
30C6	804	8365	8365	8365	8365	ABC6	8365	JT400080		KATAKANA LETTER TE
30C7		8366	8366	8366	8366	ABC7	8366	JD400080		KATAKANA LETTER DE
30C8	805	8367	8367	8367	8367	ABC8	8367	JT500080		KATAKANA LETTER TO
30C9		8368	8368	8368	8368	ABC9	8368	JD500080		KATAKANA LETTER DO
30CA	806	8369	8369	8369	8369	ABCA	8369	JN100080		KATAKANA LETTER NA
30CB	807	836A	836A	836A	836A	ABCB	836A	JN200080		KATAKANA LETTER NI
30CC	808	836B	836B	836B	836B	ABCC	836B	JN300080		KATAKANA LETTER NU
30CD	809	836C	836C	836C	836C	ABCD	836C	JN400080		KATAKANA LETTER NE
30CE	810	836D	836D	836D	836D	ABCE	836D	JN500080		KATAKANA LETTER NO
30CF	811	836E	836E	836E	836E	ABCF	836E	JH100080		KATAKANA LETTER HA
30D0		836F	836F	836F	836F	ABD0	836F	JB100080		KATAKANA LETTER BA
30D1		8370	8370	8370	8370	ABD1	8370	JP100080		KATAKANA LETTER PA
30D2	812	8371	8371	8371	8371	ABD2	8371	JH200080		KATAKANA LETTER HI
30D3		8372	8372	8372	8372	ABD3	8372	JB200080		KATAKANA LETTER BI
30D4		8373	8373	8373	8373	ABD4	8373	JP200080		KATAKANA LETTER PI
30D5	813	8374	8374	8374	8374	ABD5	8374	JH300080		KATAKANA LETTER HU
30D6		8375	8375	8375	8375	ABD6	8375	JB300080		KATAKANA LETTER BU
30D7		8376	8376	8376	8376	ABD7	8376	JP300080		KATAKANA LETTER PU
30D8	814	8377	8377	8377	8377	ABD8	8377	JH400080		KATAKANA LETTER HE
30D9		8378	8378	8378	8378	ABD9	8378	JB400080		KATAKANA LETTER BE
30DA		8379	8379	8379	8379	ABDA	8379	JP400080		KATAKANA LETTER PE

UNIC	UGL	948	XJIS	942	AX	KSC	944	GCGID	GCGID#2	Unicode character name
30DB	815	837A	837A	837A	837A	ABDB	837A	JH500080		KATAKANA LETTER HO
30DC		837B	837B	837B	837B	ABDC	837B	JB500080		KATAKANA LETTER BO
30DD		837C	837C	837C	837C	ABDD	837C	JP500080		KATAKANA LETTER PO
30DE	816	837D	837D	837D	837D	ABDE	837D	JM100080		KATAKANA LETTER MA
30DF	817	837E	837E	837E	837E	ABDF	837E	JM200080		KATAKANA LETTER MI
30E0	818	8380	8380	8380	8380	ABE0	8380	JM300080		KATAKANA LETTER MU
30E1	819	8381	8381	8381	8381	ABE1	8381	JM400080		KATAKANA LETTER ME
30E2	820	8382	8382	8382	8382	ABE2	8382	JM500080		KATAKANA LETTER MO
30E3	781	8383	8383	8383	8383	ABE3	8383	JY110080		KATAKANA LETTER SMALL YA
30E4	821	8384	8384	8384	8384	ABE4	8384	JY100080		KATAKANA LETTER YA
30E5	782	8385	8385	8385	8385	ABE5	8385	JY310080		KATAKANA LETTER SMALL YU
30E6	822	8386	8386	8386	8386	ABE6	8386	JY300080		KATAKANA LETTER YU
30E7	783	8387	8387	8387	8387	ABE7	8387	JY510080		KATAKANA LETTER SMALL YO
30E8	823	8388	8388	8388	8388	ABE8	8388	JY500080		KATAKANA LETTER YO
30E9	824	8389	8389	8389	8389	ABE9	8389	JR100080		KATAKANA LETTER RA
30EA	825	838A	838A	838A	838A	ABEA	838A	JR200080		KATAKANA LETTER RI
30EB	826	838B	838B	838B	838B	ABEB	838B	JR300080		KATAKANA LETTER RU
30EC	827	838C	838C	838C	838C	ABEC	838C	JR400080		KATAKANA LETTER RE
30ED	828	838D	838D	838D	838D	ABED	838D	JR500080		KATAKANA LETTER RO
30EE		838E	838E	838E	838E	ABEE	838E	JW110080		KATAKANA LETTER SMALL WA
30EF	829	838F	838F	838F	838F	ABEF	838F	JW100080		KATAKANA LETTER WA
30F0		8390	8390	8390	8390	ABF0	8390	JW200000		KATAKANA LETTER WI
30F1		8391	8391	8391	8391	ABF1	8391	JW400000		KATAKANA LETTER WE
30F2	775	8392	8392	8392	8392	ABF2	8392	JW500080		KATAKANA LETTER WO
30F3	830	8393	8393	8393	8393	ABF3	8393	JN000080		KATAKANA LETTER N
30F4		8394	8394	8394	8394	ABF4	8394	JV000080		KATAKANA LETTER VU
30F5		8395	8395	8395	8395	ABF5	8395	JK110080		KATAKANA LETTER SMALL KA
30F6	890	8396	8396	8396	8396	ABF6	8396	JK410000		KATAKANA LETTER SMALL KE
30FB		8145	8145	8145	8145			JQ740080		KATAKANA MIDDLE DOT
30FC	785	815B	815B	815B	815B			JX700080		KATAKANA-HIRAGANA PROLONGED SOUND MARK
30FD		8152	8152	8152	8152			JQ750080		KATAKANA ITERATION MARK
30FE		8153	8153	8153	8153			JQ760080		KATAKANA VOICED ITERATION MARK
3105		8955						SB060000		BOPOMOFO LETTER B
3106		8956						SB290000		BOPOMOFO LETTER P
3107		8957						SB250000		BOPOMOFO LETTER M
3108		8958						SB160000		BOPOMOFO LETTER F
3109		8959						SB090000		BOPOMOFO LETTER D
310A		895A						SB340000		BOPOMOFO LETTER T
310B		895B						SB260000		BOPOMOFO LETTER N
310C		895C						SB240000		BOPOMOFO LETTER L

UNIC	UGL	948	XJIS	942	AX	KSC	944	GCGID	GCGID#2	Unicode character name
310D		895D						SB170000		BOPOMOFO LETTER G
310E		895E						SB230000		BOPOMOFO LETTER K
310F		895F						SB180000		BOPOMOFO LETTER H
3110		8960						SB220000		BOPOMOFO LETTER J
3111		8961						SB070000		BOPOMOFO LETTER Q
3112		8962						SB330000		BOPOMOFO LETTER X
3113		8963						SB210000		BOPOMOFO LETTER ZH
3114		8964						SB080000		BOPOMOFO LETTER CH
3115		8965						SB320000		BOPOMOFO LETTER SH
3116		8966						SB300000		BOPOMOFO LETTER R
3117		8967						SB350000		BOPOMOFO LETTER Z
3118		8968						SB360000		BOPOMOFO LETTER C
3119		8969						SB310000		BOPOMOFO LETTER S
311A		896A						SB010000		BOPOMOFO LETTER A
311B		896B						SB270000		BOPOMOFO LETTER O
311C		896C						SB100000		BOPOMOFO LETTER E
311D		896D						SB110000		BOPOMOFO LETTER EH
311E		896E						SB020000		BOPOMOFO LETTER AI
311F		896F						SB120000		BOPOMOFO LETTER EI
3120		8970						SB050000		BOPOMOFO LETTER AU
3121		8971						SB280000		BOPOMOFO LETTER OU
3122		8972						SB030000		BOPOMOFO LETTER AN
3123		8973						SB130000		BOPOMOFO LETTER EN
3124		8974						SB040000		BOPOMOFO LETTER ANG
3125		8975						SB140000		BOPOMOFO LETTER ENG
3126		8976						SB150000		BOPOMOFO LETTER ER
3127		8977						SB190000		BOPOMOFO LETTER I
3128		8978						SB370000		BOPOMOFO LETTER U
3129		8979						SB200000		BOPOMOFO LETTER IU
3131	896					A4A1	8260	OG000080		HANGUL LETTER GIYEOG
3132	897					A4A2	8261	OG100080		HANGUL LETTER SSANG GIYEOG
3133	898					A4A3	8262	OG200080		HANGUL LETTER GIYEOG SIOS
3134	899					A4A4	8263	ON000080		HANGUL LETTER NIEUN
3135	900					A4A5	8264	ON150080		HANGUL LETTER NIEUN JIEUJ
3136	901					A4A6	8265	ON100080		HANGUL LETTER NIEUN HIEUH
3137	902					A4A7	8266	OD000080		HANGUL LETTER DIGEUD
3138	903					A4A8	8267	OD100080		HANGUL LETTER SSANG DIGEUD
3139	904					A4A9	8268	OL000080		HANGUL LETTER LIEUL
313A	905					A4AA	8269	OL200080		HANGUL LETTER LIEUL GIYEOG
313B	906					A4AB	826A	OL400080		HANGUL LETTER LIEUL MIEUM

UNIC	UGL	948	XJIS	942	AX	KSC	944	GCGID	GCGID#2	Unicode character name
313C	907					A4AC	826B	OL100080		HANGUL LETTER LIEUL BIEUB
313D	908					A4AD	826C	OL600080		HANGUL LETTER LIEUL SIOS
313E	909					A4AE	826D	OL700080		HANGUL LETTER LIEUL TIEUT
313F	910					A4AF	826E	OL500080		HANGUL LETTER LIEUL PIEUP
3140	911					A4B0	826F	OL300080		HANGUL LETTER LIEUL HIEUH
3141	912					A4B1	8270	OM000080		HANGUL LETTER MIEUM
3142	913					A4B2	8271	OB000080		HANGUL LETTER BIEUB
3143	914					A4B3	8272	OB100080		HANGUL LETTER SSANG BIEUB
3144	915					A4B4	8273	OB200080		HANGUL LETTER BIEUB SIOS
3145	916					A4B5	8274	OS000080		HANGUL LETTER SIOS
3146	917					A4B6	8275	OS100080		HANGUL LETTER SSANG SIOS
3147	918					A4B7	8276	ON200080		HANGUL LETTER IEUNG
3148	919					A4B8	8277	OJ000080		HANGUL LETTER JIEUJ
3149	920					A4B9	8278	OJ100080		HANGUL LETTER SSANG JIEUJ
314A	921					A4BA	8279	OC200080		HANGUL LETTER CIEUC
314B	922					A4BB	827A	OK000080		HANGUL LETTER KIYEOK
314C	923					A4BC	827B	OT000080		HANGUL LETTER TIEUT
314D	924					A4BD	827C	OP000080		HANGUL LETTER PIEUP
314E	925					A4BE	827D	OH000080		HANGUL LETTER HIEUH
314F	926					A4BF	8282	OA000080		HANGUL LETTER A
3150	927					A4C0	8283	OA200080		HANGUL LETTER AE
3151	928					A4C1	8284	OY200080		HANGUL LETTER YA
3152	929					A4C2	8285	OY250080		HANGUL LETTER YAE
3153	930					A4C3	8286	OE200080		HANGUL LETTER EO
3154	931					A4C4	8287	OE000080		HANGUL LETTER E
3155	932					A4C5	828A	OY400080		HANGUL LETTER YEO
3156	933					A4C6	828B	OY300080		HANGUL LETTER YE
3157	934					A4C7	828C	OO000080		HANGUL LETTER O
3158	935					A4C8	828D	OO100080		HANGUL LETTER WA
3159	936					A4C9	828E	OO200080		HANGUL LETTER WAE
315A	937					A4CA	828F	OO300080		HANGUL LETTER OE
315B	938					A4CB	8292	OY500080		HANGUL LETTER YO
315C	939					A4CC	8293	OU000080		HANGUL LETTER U
315D	940					A4CD	8294	OU300080		HANGUL LETTER WEO
315E	941					A4CE	8295	OU200080		HANGUL LETTER WE
315F	942					A4CF	8296	OU400080		HANGUL LETTER WI
3160	943					A4D0	8297	OY600080		HANGUL LETTER YU
3161	944					A4D1	829A	OE300080		HANGUL LETTER EU
3162	945					A4D2	829B	OE400080		HANGUL LETTER YI
3163	946					A4D3	829C	OI000080		HANGUL LETTER I

UNIC	UGL	948	XJIS	942	AX	KSC	944	GCGID	GCGID#2	Unicode character name
3164	949					A4D4	825F	SP490080		HANGUL CAE OM
3165						A4D5	8240	F0G10000		HANGUL LETTER SSANG NIEUN
3166						A4D6	8241	F0G20000		HANGUL LETTER NIEUN DIGEUD
3167						A4D7	8242	F0G30000		HANGUL LETTER NIEUN SIOS
3168						A4D8	8243	F0G40000		HANGUL LETTER NIEUN BAN CHI EUM
3169						A4D9	8244	F0G50000		HANGUL LETTER LIEUL GIYEOG SIOS
316A						A4DA	8245	F0G60000		HANGUL LETTER LIEUL DIGEUD
316B						A4DB	8246	F0G70000		HANGUL LETTER LIEUL BIEUB SIOS
316C						A4DC	8247	F0G80000		HANGUL LETTER LIEUL BAN CHI EUM
316D						A4DD	8248	F0G90000		HANGUL LETTER LIEUL YEOLIN HIEUH
316E						A4DE	8249	F0GA0000		HANGUL LETTER MIEUM BIEUB
316F						A4DF	824A	F0GB0000		HANGUL LETTER MIEUM SIOS
3170						A4E0	824B	F0GC0000		HANGUL LETTER BIEUB BAN CHI EUM
3171						A4E1	824C	F0GD0000		HANGUL LETTER MIEUM SUN GYEONG EUM
3172						A4E2	824D	F0GE0000		HANGUL LETTER BIEUB GIYEOG
3173						A4E3	824E	F0GF0000		HANGUL LETTER BIEUB DIGEUD
3174						A4E4	824F	F0GG0000		HANGUL LETTER BIEUB SIOS GIYEOG
3175						A4E5	8250	F0GH0000		HANGUL LETTER BIEUB SIOS DIGEUD
3176						A4E6	8251	F0GI0000		HANGUL LETTER BIEUB JIEUJ
3177						A4E7	8252	F0GJ0000		HANGUL LETTER BIEUB TIEUT
3178						A4E8	8253	F0GK0000		HANGUL LETTER BIEUB SUN GYEONG EUM
3179						A4E9	8254	F0GL0000		HANGUL LETTER SSANG BIEUB SUN GYEONG EUM
317A						A4EA	8255	F0GM0000		HANGUL LETTER SIOS GIYEOG
317B						A4EB	8256	F0GN0000		HANGUL LETTER SIOS NIEUN
317C						A4EC	8257	F0GO0000		HANGUL LETTER SIOS DIGEUD
317D						A4ED	8258	F0GP0000		HANGUL LETTER SIOS BIEUB
317E						A4EE	8259	F0GQ0000		HANGUL LETTER SIOS JIEUJ
317F						A4EF	825A	F0GR0000		HANGUL LETTER BAN CHI EUM
3180						A4F0	825B	F0GS0000		HANGUL LETTER SSANG IEUNG
3181						A4F1	825C	F0GT0000		HANGUL LETTER NGIEUNG
3182						A4F2	825D	F0GU0000		HANGUL LETTER NGIEUNG SIOS
3183						A4F3	825E	F0GV0000		HANGUL LETTER NGIEUNG BAN CHI EUM
3184						A4F4	827E	F0GW0000		HANGUL LETTER PIEUP SUN GYEONG EUM
3185						A4F5	8280	F0GX0000		HANGUL LETTER SSANG HIEUH
3186						A4F6	8281	F0GY0000		HANGUL LETTER YEOLIN HIEUH
3187						A4F7	8288	F0GZ0000		HANGUL LETTER YOYA
3188						A4F8	8289	F0H00000		HANGUL LETTER YOYAE
3189						A4F9	8290	F0H10000		HANGUL LETTER YOI
318A						A4FA	8291	F0H20000		HANGUL LETTER YUYEO
318B						A4FB	8298	F0H30000		HANGUL LETTER YUYE

UNIC	UGL	948	XJIS	942	AX	KSC	944	GCGID	GCGID#2	Unicode character name
318C						A4FC	8299	F0H40000		HANGUL LETTER YUI
318D						A4FD	829D	F0H50000		HANGUL LETTER ALAE A
318E						A4FE	829E	F0H60000		HANGUL LETTER ALAE AE
3200						A9B1	AFAF	F1PS0000		PARENTHESIZED HANGUL GIYEOG
3201						A9B2	AFB0	F1PT0000		PARENTHESIZED HANGUL NIEUN
3202						A9B3	AFB1	F1PU0000		PARENTHESIZED HANGUL DIGEUD
3203						A9B4	AFB2	F1PV0000		PARENTHESIZED HANGUL LIEUL
3204						A9B5	AFB3	F1PW0000		PARENTHESIZED HANGUL MIEUM
3205						A9B6	AFB4	F1PX0000		PARENTHESIZED HANGUL BIEUB
3206						A9B7	AFB5	F1PY0000		PARENTHESIZED HANGUL SIOS
3207						A9B8	AFB6	F1PZ0000		PARENTHESIZED HANGUL IEUNG
3208						A9B9	AFB7	F1Q00000		PARENTHESIZED HANGUL JIEUJ
3209						A9BA	AFB8	F1Q10000		PARENTHESIZED HANGUL CIEUC
320A						A9BB	AFB9	F1Q20000		PARENTHESIZED HANGUL KIYEOK
320B						A9BC	AFBA	F1Q30000		PARENTHESIZED HANGUL TIEUT
320C						A9BD	AFBB	F1Q40000		PARENTHESIZED HANGUL PIEUP
320D						A9BE	AFBC	F1Q50000		PARENTHESIZED HANGUL HIEUH
320E						A9BF	AFBD	F1Q60000		PARENTHESIZED HANGUL GA
320F						A9C0	AFBE	F1Q70000		PARENTHESIZED HANGUL NA
3210						A9C1	AFBF	F1Q80000		PARENTHESIZED HANGUL DA
3211						A9C2	AFC0	F1Q90000		PARENTHESIZED HANGUL LA
3212						A9C3	AFC1	F1QA0000		PARENTHESIZED HANGUL MA
3213						A9C4	AFC2	F1QB0000		PARENTHESIZED HANGUL BA
3214						A9C5	AFC3	F1QC0000		PARENTHESIZED HANGUL SA
3215						A9C6	AFC4	F1QD0000		PARENTHESIZED HANGUL A
3216						A9C7	AFC5	F1QE0000		PARENTHESIZED HANGUL JA
3217						A9C8	AFC6	F1QF0000		PARENTHESIZED HANGUL CA
3218						A9C9	AFC7	F1QG0000		PARENTHESIZED HANGUL KA
3219						A9CA	AFC8	F1QH0000		PARENTHESIZED HANGUL TA
321A						A9CB	AFC9	F1QI0000		PARENTHESIZED HANGUL PA
321B						A9CC	AFCA	F1QJ0000		PARENTHESIZED HANGUL HA
321C						A2DF	858D	F1E50000		PARENTHESIZED HANGUL JU
3231		8B5F		FA58	878A			SS740000		PARENTHESIZED IDEOGRAPH STOCK
3232					878B					PARENTHESIZED IDEOGRAPH HAVE
3239					878C					PARENTHESIZED IDEOGRAPH REPRESENT
3260						A8B1	AF50	F1N50000		CIRCLED HANGUL GIYEOG
3261						A8B2	AF51	F1N60000		CIRCLED HANGUL NIEUN
3262						A8B3	AF52	F1N70000		CIRCLED HANGUL DIGEUD
3263						A8B4	AF53	F1N80000		CIRCLED HANGUL LIEUL
3264						A8B5	AF54	F1N90000		CIRCLED HANGUL MIEUM

UNIC	UGL	948	XJIS	942	AX	KSC	944	GCGID	GCGID#2	Unicode character name
3265						A8B6	AF55	F1NA0000		CIRCLED HANGUL BIEUB
3266						A8B7	AF56	F1NB0000		CIRCLED HANGUL SIOS
3267						A8B8	AF57	F1NC0000		CIRCLED HANGUL IEUNG
3268						A8B9	AF58	F1ND0000		CIRCLED HANGUL JIEUJ
3269						A8BA	AF59	F1NE0000		CIRCLED HANGUL CIEUC
326A						A8BB	AF5A	F1NF0000		CIRCLED HANGUL KIYEOK
326B						A8BC	AF5B	F1NG0000		CIRCLED HANGUL TIEUT
326C						A8BD	AF5C	F1NH0000		CIRCLED HANGUL PIEUP
326D						A8BE	AF5D	F1NI0000		CIRCLED HANGUL HIEUH
326E						A8BF	AF5E	F1NJ0000		CIRCLED HANGUL GA
326F						A8C0	AF5F	F1NK0000		CIRCLED HANGUL NA
3270						A8C1	AF60	F1NL0000		CIRCLED HANGUL DA
3271						A8C2	AF61	F1NM0000		CIRCLED HANGUL LA
3272						A8C3	AF62	F1NN0000		CIRCLED HANGUL MA
3273						A8C4	AF63	F1NO0000		CIRCLED HANGUL BA
3274						A8C5	AF64	F1NP0000		CIRCLED HANGUL SA
3275						A8C6	AF65	F1NQ0000		CIRCLED HANGUL A
3276						A8C7	AF66	F1NR0000		CIRCLED HANGUL JA
3277						A8C8	AF67	F1NS0000		CIRCLED HANGUL CA
3278						A8C9	AF68	F1NT0000		CIRCLED HANGUL KA
3279						A8CA	AF69	F1NU0000		CIRCLED HANGUL TA
327A						A8CB	AF6A	F1NV0000		CIRCLED HANGUL PA
327B						A8CC	AF6B	F1NW0000		CIRCLED HANGUL HA
327F						A2DE	858C	F1E40000		KOREAN STANDARD SYMBOL
32A3	8AB9							SS780000		CIRCLED IDEOGRAPH CORRECT
32A4					8785					CIRCLED IDEOGRAPH HIGH
32A5					8786					CIRCLED IDEOGRAPH CENTER
32A6					8787					CIRCLED IDEOGRAPH LOW
32A7					8788					CIRCLED IDEOGRAPH LEFT
32A8					8789					CIRCLED IDEOGRAPH RIGHT
3303					8765					SQUARED AARU
330D					8769					SQUARED KARORII
3314					8760					SQUARED KIRO
3318					8763					SQUARED GURAMU
3322					8761					SQUARED SENTI
3323					876B					SQUARED SENTO
3326					876A					SQUARED DORU
3327					8764					SQUARED TON
332B					876C					SQUARED PAASENTO
3336					8766					SQUARED HEKUTAARU

UNIC	UGL	948	XJIS	942	AX	KSC	944	GCGID	GCGID#2	Unicode character name
333B					876E					SQUARED PEEZI
3349					875F					SQUARED MIRI
334A					876D					SQUARED MIRIBAARU
334D					8762					SQUARED MEETORU
3351					8767					SQUARED RITTORU
3357					8768					SQUARED WATTO
337C					878F					SQUARED TWO IDEOGRAPHS ERA NAME SYOUWA
337D					878E					SQUARED TWO IDEOGRAPHS ERA NAME TAISYOU
337E					878D					SQUARED TWO IDEOGRAPHS ERA NAME MEIZI
3380						A7C9	84BE	F17K0000		SQUARED PA AMPS
3381						A7CA	84BF	F17L0000		SQUARED NA
3382						A7CB	84C0	F17M0000		SQUARED MU A
3383						A7CC	84C1	F17N0000		SQUARED MA
3384						A7CD	84C2	F17O0000		SQUARED KA
3388						A7BA	84AF	F1750000		SQUARED CAL
3389						A7BB	84B0	F1760000		SQUARED KCAL
338A						A7DC	84D1	F1830000		SQUARED PF
338B						A7DD	84D2	F1840000		SQUARED NF
338C						A7DE	84D3	F1850000		SQUARED MU F
338D						A7B6	84AD	F1730000		SQUARED MU G
338E		8AE1			8772	A7B7	8174	SS850000		SQUARED MG
338F		8AE2			8773	A7B8	8175	SS860000		SQUARED KG
3390						A7D4	84C9	F17V0000		SQUARED HZ
3391						A7D5	84CA	F17W0000		SQUARED KHZ
3392						A7D6	84CB	F17X0000		SQUARED MHZ
3393						A7D7	84CC	F17Y0000		SQUARED GHZ
3394						A7D8	84CD	F17Z0000		SQUARED THZ
3395						A7A1	849F	F16P0000		SQUARED MU L
3396						A7A2	816D	F06L0000		SQUARED ML
3397						A7A3	816E	F06M0000		SQUARED DL
3398						A7A5	84A0	F16Q0000		SQUARED KL
3399						A7AB	84A5	F16V0000		SQUARED FM
339A						A7AC	84A6	F16W0000		SQUARED NM
339B						A7AD	84A7	F16X0000		SQUARED MU M
339C		8ADC			876F	A7AE	8171	SS810000		SQUARED MM
339D		8ADD			8770	A7AF	8172	SS820000		SQUARED CM
339E		8ADE			8771	A7B0	8173	SS830000		SQUARED KM
339F						A7B1	84A8	F16Y0000		SQUARED MM SQUARED
33A0						A7B2	84A9	F16Z0000		SQUARED CM SQUARED
33A1		8AE0			8775	A7B3	84AA	SS840000		SQUARED M SQUARED

UNIC	UGL	948	XJIS	942	AX	KSC	944	GCGID	GCGID#2	Unicode character name
33A2						A7B4	84AB	F1710000		SQUARED KM SQUARED
33A3						A7A7	84A1	F16R0000		SQUARED MM CUBED
33A4						A7A8	84A2	F16S0000		SQUARED CM CUBED
33A5						A7A9	84A3	F16T0000		SQUARED M CUBED
33A6						A7AA	84A4	F16U0000		SQUARED KM CUBED
33A7						A7BD	84B2	F1780000		SQUARED M OVER S
33A8						A7BE	84B3	F1790000		SQUARED M OVER S SQUARED
33A9						A7E5	84DA	F18C0000		SQUARED PA
33AA						A7E6	84DB	F18D0000		SQUARED KPA
33AB						A7E7	84DC	F18E0000		SQUARED MPA
33AC						A7E8	84DD	F18F0000		SQUARED GPA
33AD						A7E1	84D6	F1880000		SQUARED RAD
33AE						A7E2	84D7	F1890000		SQUARED RAD OVER S
33AF						A7E3	84D8	F18A0000		SQUARED RAD OVER S SQUARED
33B0						A7BF	84B4	F17A0000		SQUARED PS
33B1						A7C0	84B5	F17B0000		SQUARED NS
33B2						A7C1	84B6	F17C0000		SQUARED MU S
33B3						A7C2	84B7	F17D0000		SQUARED MS
33B4						A7C3	84B8	F17E0000		SQUARED PV
33B5						A7C4	84B9	F17F0000		SQUARED NV
33B6						A7C5	84BA	F17G0000		SQUARED MU V
33B7						A7C6	84BB	F17H0000		SQUARED MV
33B8						A7C7	84BC	F17I0000		SQUARED KV
33B9						A7C8	84BD	F17J0000		SQUARED MV MEGA
33BA						A7CE	84C3	F17P0000		SQUARED PW
33BB						A7CF	84C4	F17Q0000		SQUARED NW
33BC						A7D0	84C5	F17R0000		SQUARED MU W
33BD						A7D1	84C6	F17S0000		SQUARED MW
33BE						A7D2	84C7	F17T0000		SQUARED KW
33BF						A7D3	84C8	F17U0000		SQUARED MW MEGA
33C0						A7DA	84CF	F1810000		SQUARED K OHM
33C1						A7DB	84D0	F1820000		SQUARED M OHM
33C2						A2E3	8591	F1E90000		SQUARED AM
33C3						A7EC	84E1	F18J0000		SQUARED BQ
33C4	8AE3				8774	A7A6	8170	SS870000		SQUARED CC
33C5						A7E0	84D5	F1870000		SQUARED CD
33C6						A7EF	84E4	F18M0000		SQUARED C OVER KG
33C7						A2E1	858F	F1E70000		SQUARED CO
33C8						A7BC	84B1	F1770000		SQUARED DB
33C9						A7ED	84E2	F18K0000		SQUARED GY

UNIC	UGL	948	XJIS	942	AX	KSC	944	GCGID	GCGID#2	Unicode character name
33CA						A7B5	84AC	F1720000		SQUARED HA
33CD					8783					SQUARED KK
33CE		8ADF						SS830001		SQUARED KM CAPITAL
33CF						A7B9	84AE	F1740000		SQUARED KT
33D0						A7EA	84DF	F18H0000		SQUARED LM
33D1		8ACE						SS890000		SQUARED LN
33D2		8ACD				A7EB	84E0	SS880000		SQUARED LOG
33D3								F18I0000		SQUARED LX
33D5		8ADB						SS800000		SQUARED MIL
33D6						A7DF	84D4	F1860000		SQUARED MOL
33D8						A2E4	8592	F1EA0000		SQUARED PM
33DB						A7E4	84D9	F18B0000		SQUARED SR
33DC						A7EE	84E3	F18L0000		SQUARED SV
33DD						A7E9	84DE	F18G0000		SQUARED WB
FE30		8640						SV550000		GLYPH FOR VERTICAL TWO DOT LEADER
FE31		8AA6						SV070000		GLYPH FOR VERTICAL EM DASH
FE32		8648						SM131000		GLYPH FOR VERTICAL EN DASH
FE33		8AA7						SV580000		GLYPH FOR VERTICAL SPACING UNDERSCORE
FE34		8AA9						SV560000		GLYPH FOR VERTICAL SPACING WAVY UNDERSCORE
FE35		8AAB						SP240000		GLYPH FOR VERTICAL OPENING PARENTHESIS
FE36		8AAC						SP250000		GLYPH FOR VERTICAL CLOSING PARENTHESIS
FE37		8AAD						SP340000		GLYPH FOR VERTICAL OPENING CURLY BRACKET
FE38		8AAE						SP350000		GLYPH FOR VERTICAL CLOSING CURLY BRACKET
FE39		8AAF						SP240001		GLYPH FOR VERTICAL OPENING TORTOISE SHELL BRACKET
FE3A		8AB0						SP250001		GLYPH FOR VERTICAL CLOSING TORTOISE SHELL BRACKET
FE3B		8AA3						SP240004		GLYPH FOR VERTICAL OPENING BLACK LENTICULAR BRACKET
FE3C		8AA4						SP250004		GLYPH FOR VERTICAL CLOSING BLACK LENTICULAR BRACKET
FE3D		8AB1						SP240003		GLYPH FOR VERTICAL OPENING DOUBLE ANGLE BRACKET
FE3E		8AB2						SP250003		GLYPH FOR VERTICAL CLOSING DOUBLE ANGLE BRACKET
FE3F		8AB3						SP240002		GLYPH FOR VERTICAL OPENING ANGLE BRACKET
FE40		8AB4						SP250002		GLYPH FOR VERTICAL CLOSING ANGLE BRACKET
FE41		8A9F						SP360000		GLYPH FOR VERTICAL OPENING CORNER BRACKET
FE42		8AA0						SP370000		GLYPH FOR VERTICAL CLOSING CORNER BRACKET
FE43		8AA1						SP360001		GLYPH FOR VERTICAL OPENING WHITE CORNER BRACKET
FE44		8AA2						SP370001		GLYPH FOR VERTICAL CLOSING WHITE CORNER BRACKET
FE49		8ABD						SV470000		SPACING DASHED OVERSCORE
FE4A		8ABE						SV490000		SPACING CENTERLINE OVERSCORE
FE4B		8AC1						SV500000		SPACING WAVY OVERSCORE

UNIC	UGL	948	XJIS	942	AX	KSC	944	GCGID	GCGID#2	Unicode character name
FE4C	8AC2							SV510000		SPACING DOUBLE WAVY OVERSCORE
FE4D	8ABF							SV120000		SPACING DASHED UNDERSCORE
FE4E	8AC0							SV480000		SPACING CENTERLINE UNDERSCORE
FE4F	8AAA							SV570000		SPACING WAVY UNDERSCORE
FE50	8641							SP081000		SMALL COMMA
FE51	8642							SP081004		SMALL IDEOGRAPHIC COMMA
FE52	8643							SP111000		SMALL PERIOD
FE54	8644							SP141000		SMALL SEMICOLON
FE55	8645							SP131000		SMALL COLON
FE56	8646							SP151000		SMALL QUESTION MARK
FE57	8647							SP021000		SMALL EXCLAMATION MARK
FE58	8649							SV251000		SMALL EM DASH
FE59	864A							SP061000		SMALL OPENING PARENTHESIS
FE5A	864B							SP071000		SMALL CLOSING PARENTHESIS
FE5B	864C							SM111000		SMALL OPENING CURLY BRACKET
FE5C	864D							SM141000		SMALL CLOSING CURLY BRACKET
FE5D	864E							SP061001		SMALL OPENING TORTOISE SHELL BRACKET
FE5E	864F							SP071001		SMALL CLOSING TORTOISE SHELL BRACKET
FE5F	8652							SM011000		SMALL NUMBER SIGN
FE60	8653							SM031000		SMALL AMPERSAND
FE61	8AC3							SM04008A		SMALL ASTERISK
FE62	8654							SA011000		SMALL PLUS SIGN
FE63	8655							SA001000		SMALL HYPHEN-MINUS
FE64	8656							SA031000		SMALL LESS-THAN SIGN
FE65	8657							SA051000		SMALL GREATER-THAN SIGN
FE66	8658							SA041000		SMALL EQUALS SIGN
FE68	8659							SM071000		SMALL BACKSLASH
FE69	865A							SC031000		SMALL DOLLAR SIGN
FE6A	865B							SM021000		SMALL PERCENT SIGN
FE6B	865C							SM051000		SMALL COMMERCIAL AT
FF01	8149		8149	8149	8149	A3A1	819F	SP020080		FULLWIDTH EXCLAMATION MARK
FF02	8B5E			FA57		A3A2	81A0	SP040080		FULLWIDTH QUOTATION MARK
FF03	8194		8194	8194	8194	A3A3	81A1	SM010080		FULLWIDTH NUMBER SIGN
FF04	8190		8190	8190	8190	A3A4	81A2	SC030080		FULLWIDTH DOLLAR SIGN
FF05	8193		8193	8193	8193	A3A5	81A3	SM020080		FULLWIDTH PERCENT SIGN
FF06	8195		8195	8195	8195	A3A6	81A4	SM030080		FULLWIDTH AMPERSAND
FF07	8B5D			FA56		A3A7	81A5	SP050080		FULLWIDTH APOSTROPHE
FF08	8169		8169	8169	8169	A3A8	81A6	SP060080		FULLWIDTH OPENING PARENTHESIS
FF09	816A		816A	816A	816A	A3A9	81A7	SP070080		FULLWIDTH CLOSING PARENTHESIS
FF0A	8AB7							SM040089		FULLWIDTH ASTERISK

UNIC	UGL	948	XJIS	942	AX	KSC	944	GCGID	GCGID#2	Unicode character name
FF0A		8196	8196	8196	8196	A3AA	81A8	SM040080		FULLWIDTH ASTERISK
FF0B		817B	817B	817B	817B	A3AB	81A9	SA010080		FULLWIDTH PLUS SIGN
FF0C		8143	8143	8143	8143	A3AC	81AA	SP080080		FULLWIDTH COMMA
FF0D		817C	817C	817C	817C	A3AD	81AB	SP100080		FULLWIDTH HYPHEN-MINUS
FF0E		8144	8144	8144	8144	A3AE	81AC	SP110080		FULLWIDTH PERIOD
FF0F		815E	815E	815E	815E	A3AF	81AD	SP120080		FULLWIDTH SLASH
FF10		824F	824F	824F	824F	A3B0	81AE	ND100080		FULLWIDTH DIGIT ZERO
FF11		8250	8250	8250	8250	A3B1	81AF	ND010080		FULLWIDTH DIGIT ONE
FF12		8251	8251	8251	8251	A3B2	81B0	ND020080		FULLWIDTH DIGIT TWO
FF13		8252	8252	8252	8252	A3B3	81B1	ND030080		FULLWIDTH DIGIT THREE
FF14		8253	8253	8253	8253	A3B4	81B2	ND040080		FULLWIDTH DIGIT FOUR
FF15		8254	8254	8254	8254	A3B5	81B3	ND050080		FULLWIDTH DIGIT FIVE
FF16		8255	8255	8255	8255	A3B6	81B4	ND060080		FULLWIDTH DIGIT SIX
FF17		8256	8256	8256	8256	A3B7	81B5	ND070080		FULLWIDTH DIGIT SEVEN
FF18		8257	8257	8257	8257	A3B8	81B6	ND080080		FULLWIDTH DIGIT EIGHT
FF19		8258	8258	8258	8258	A3B9	81B7	ND090080		FULLWIDTH DIGIT NINE
FF1A		8146	8146	8146	8146	A3BA	81B8	SP130080		FULLWIDTH COLON
FF1B		8147	8147	8147	8147	A3BB	81B9	SP140080		FULLWIDTH SEMICOLON
FF1C		8183	8183	8183	8183	A3BC	81BA	SA030080		FULLWIDTH LESS-THAN SIGN
FF1D		8181	8181	8181	8181	A3BD	81BB	SA040080		FULLWIDTH EQUALS SIGN
FF1E		8184	8184	8184	8184	A3BE	81BC	SA050080		FULLWIDTH GREATER-THAN SIGN
FF1F		8148	8148	8148	8148	A3BF	81BD	SP150080		FULLWIDTH QUESTION MARK
FF20		8197	8197	8197	8197	A3C0	81BE	SM050080		FULLWIDTH COMMERCIAL AT
FF21		8260	8260	8260	8260	A3C1	81BF	LA020080		FULLWIDTH LATIN CAPITAL LETTER A
FF22		8261	8261	8261	8261	A3C2	81C0	LB020080		FULLWIDTH LATIN CAPITAL LETTER B
FF23		8262	8262	8262	8262	A3C3	81C1	LC020080		FULLWIDTH LATIN CAPITAL LETTER C
FF24		8263	8263	8263	8263	A3C4	81C2	LD020080		FULLWIDTH LATIN CAPITAL LETTER D
FF25		8264	8264	8264	8264	A3C5	81C3	LE020080		FULLWIDTH LATIN CAPITAL LETTER E
FF26		8265	8265	8265	8265	A3C6	81C4	LF020080		FULLWIDTH LATIN CAPITAL LETTER F
FF27		8266	8266	8266	8266	A3C7	81C5	LG020080		FULLWIDTH LATIN CAPITAL LETTER G
FF28		8267	8267	8267	8267	A3C8	81C6	LH020080		FULLWIDTH LATIN CAPITAL LETTER H
FF29		8268	8268	8268	8268	A3C9	81C7	LI020080		FULLWIDTH LATIN CAPITAL LETTER I
FF2A		8269	8269	8269	8269	A3CA	81C8	LJ020080		FULLWIDTH LATIN CAPITAL LETTER J
FF2B		826A	826A	826A	826A	A3CB	81C9	LK020080		FULLWIDTH LATIN CAPITAL LETTER K
FF2C		826B	826B	826B	826B	A3CC	81CA	LL020080		FULLWIDTH LATIN CAPITAL LETTER L
FF2D		826C	826C	826C	826C	A3CD	81CB	LM020080		FULLWIDTH LATIN CAPITAL LETTER M
FF2E		826D	826D	826D	826D	A3CE	81CC	LN020080		FULLWIDTH LATIN CAPITAL LETTER N
FF2F		826E	826E	826E	826E	A3CF	81CD	LO020080		FULLWIDTH LATIN CAPITAL LETTER O
FF30		826F	826F	826F	826F	A3D0	81CE	LP020080		FULLWIDTH LATIN CAPITAL LETTER P
FF31		8270	8270	8270	8270	A3D1	81CF	LQ020080		FULLWIDTH LATIN CAPITAL LETTER Q

UNIC	UGL	948	XJIS	942	AX	KSC	944	GCGID	GCGID#2	Unicode character name
FF32		8271	8271	8271	8271	A3D2	81D0	LR020080		FULLWIDTH LATIN CAPITAL LETTER R
FF33		8272	8272	8272	8272	A3D3	81D1	LS020080		FULLWIDTH LATIN CAPITAL LETTER S
FF34		8273	8273	8273	8273	A3D4	81D2	LT020080		FULLWIDTH LATIN CAPITAL LETTER T
FF35		8274	8274	8274	8274	A3D5	81D3	LU020080		FULLWIDTH LATIN CAPITAL LETTER U
FF36		8275	8275	8275	8275	A3D6	81D4	LV020080		FULLWIDTH LATIN CAPITAL LETTER V
FF37		8276	8276	8276	8276	A3D7	81D5	LW020080		FULLWIDTH LATIN CAPITAL LETTER W
FF38		8277	8277	8277	8277	A3D8	81D6	LX020080		FULLWIDTH LATIN CAPITAL LETTER X
FF39		8278	8278	8278	8278	A3D9	81D7	LY020080		FULLWIDTH LATIN CAPITAL LETTER Y
FF3A		8279	8279	8279	8279	A3DA	81D8	LZ020080		FULLWIDTH LATIN CAPITAL LETTER Z
FF3B		816D	816D	816D	816D	A3DB	81D9	SM060080		FULLWIDTH OPENING SQUARE BRACKET
FF3C		815F	815F	815F	815F	A1AC	814B	SM070080		FULLWIDTH BACKSLASH
FF3D		816E	816E	816E	816E	A3DD	81DB	SM080080		FULLWIDTH CLOSING SQUARE BRACKET
FF3E		814F	814F	814F	814F	A3DE	81DC	SD150080		FULLWIDTH SPACING CIRCUMFLEX
FF3F		8151	8151	8151	8151	A3DF	81DD	SP090080		FULLWIDTH SPACING UNDERSCORE
FF40		814D	814D	814D	814D	A3E0	81DE	SD130080		FULLWIDTH SPACING GRAVE
FF41		8281	8281	8281	8281	A3E1	81DF	LA010080		FULLWIDTH LATIN SMALL LETTER A
FF42		8282	8282	8282	8282	A3E2	81E0	LB010080		FULLWIDTH LATIN SMALL LETTER B
FF43		8283	8283	8283	8283	A3E3	81E1	LC010080		FULLWIDTH LATIN SMALL LETTER C
FF44		8284	8284	8284	8284	A3E4	81E2	LD010080		FULLWIDTH LATIN SMALL LETTER D
FF45		8285	8285	8285	8285	A3E5	81E3	LE010080		FULLWIDTH LATIN SMALL LETTER E
FF46		8286	8286	8286	8286	A3E6	81E4	LF010080		FULLWIDTH LATIN SMALL LETTER F
FF47		8287	8287	8287	8287	A3E7	81E5	LG010080		FULLWIDTH LATIN SMALL LETTER G
FF48		8288	8288	8288	8288	A3E8	81E6	LH010080		FULLWIDTH LATIN SMALL LETTER H
FF49		8289	8289	8289	8289	A3E9	81E7	LI010080		FULLWIDTH LATIN SMALL LETTER I
FF4A		828A	828A	828A	828A	A3EA	81E8	LJ010080		FULLWIDTH LATIN SMALL LETTER J
FF4B		828B	828B	828B	828B	A3EB	81E9	LK010080		FULLWIDTH LATIN SMALL LETTER K
FF4C		828C	828C	828C	828C	A3EC	81EA	LL010080		FULLWIDTH LATIN SMALL LETTER L
FF4D		828D	828D	828D	828D	A3ED	81EB	LM010080		FULLWIDTH LATIN SMALL LETTER M
FF4E		828E	828E	828E	828E	A3EE	81EC	LN010080		FULLWIDTH LATIN SMALL LETTER N
FF4F		828F	828F	828F	828F	A3EF	81ED	LO010080		FULLWIDTH LATIN SMALL LETTER O
FF50		8290	8290	8290	8290	A3F0	81EE	LP010080		FULLWIDTH LATIN SMALL LETTER P
FF51		8291	8291	8291	8291	A3F1	81EF	LQ010080		FULLWIDTH LATIN SMALL LETTER Q
FF52		8292	8292	8292	8292	A3F2	81F0	LR010080		FULLWIDTH LATIN SMALL LETTER R
FF53		8293	8293	8293	8293	A3F3	81F1	LS010080		FULLWIDTH LATIN SMALL LETTER S
FF54		8294	8294	8294	8294	A3F4	81F2	LT010080		FULLWIDTH LATIN SMALL LETTER T
FF55		8295	8295	8295	8295	A3F5	81F3	LU010080		FULLWIDTH LATIN SMALL LETTER U
FF56		8296	8296	8296	8296	A3F6	81F4	LV010080		FULLWIDTH LATIN SMALL LETTER V
FF57		8297	8297	8297	8297	A3F7	81F5	LW010080		FULLWIDTH LATIN SMALL LETTER W
FF58		8298	8298	8298	8298	A3F8	81F6	LX010080		FULLWIDTH LATIN SMALL LETTER X
FF59		8299	8299	8299	8299	A3F9	81F7	LY010080		FULLWIDTH LATIN SMALL LETTER Y

UNIC	UGL	948	XJIS	942	AX	KSC	944	GCGID	GCGID#2	Unicode character name
FF5A		829A	829A	829A	829A	A3FA	81F8	LZ010080		FULLWIDTH LATIN SMALL LETTER Z
FF5B		816F	816F	816F	816F	A3FB	81F9	SM110080		FULLWIDTH OPENING CURLY BRACKET
FF5C		8162	8162	8162	8162	A3FC	81FA	SM130080		FULLWIDTH VERTICAL BAR
FF5D		8170	8170	8170	8170	A3FD	81FB	SM140080		FULLWIDTH CLOSING CURLY BRACKET
FF5E		8160	8160	8160	8160	A2A6	8553	SD190080		FULLWIDTH SPACING TILDE
FF61			00A1	00A1	00A1			JQ700000		HALFWIDTH IDEOGRAPHIC PERIOD
FF62			00A2	00A2	00A2			JQ710000		HALFWIDTH OPENING CORNER BRACKET
FF63			00A3	00A3	00A3			JQ720000		HALFWIDTH CLOSING CORNER BRACKET
FF64			00A4	00A4	00A4			JQ730000		HALFWIDTH IDEOGRAPHIC COMMA
FF65			00A5	00A5	00A5			JQ740000		HALFWIDTH KATAKANA MIDDLE DOT
FF66			00A6	00A6	00A6			JW500000		HALFWIDTH KATAKANA LETTER WO
FF67			00A7	00A7	00A7			JA010000		HALFWIDTH KATAKANA LETTER SMALL A
FF68			00A8	00A8	00A8			JI010000		HALFWIDTH KATAKANA LETTER SMALL I
FF69			00A9	00A9	00A9			JU010000		HALFWIDTH KATAKANA LETTER SMALL U
FF6A			00AA	00AA	00AA			JE010000		HALFWIDTH KATAKANA LETTER SMALL E
FF6B			00AB	00AB	00AB			JO010000		HALFWIDTH KATAKANA LETTER SMALL O
FF6C			00AC	00AC	00AC			JY110000		HALFWIDTH KATAKANA LETTER SMALL YA
FF6D			00AD	00AD	00AD			JY310000		HALFWIDTH KATAKANA LETTER SMALL YU
FF6E			00AE	00AE	00AE			JY510000		HALFWIDTH KATAKANA LETTER SMALL YO
FF6F			00AF	00AF	00AF			JT310000		HALFWIDTH KATAKANA LETTER SMALL TU
FF70			00B0	00B0	00B0			JX700000		HALFWIDTH KATAKANA-HIRAGANA PROLONGED SOUND MARK
FF71			00B1	00B1	00B1			JA000000		HALFWIDTH KATAKANA LETTER A
FF72			00B2	00B2	00B2			JI000000		HALFWIDTH KATAKANA LETTER I
FF73			00B3	00B3	00B3			JU000000		HALFWIDTH KATAKANA LETTER U
FF74			00B4	00B4	00B4			JE000000		HALFWIDTH KATAKANA LETTER E
FF75			00B5	00B5	00B5			JO000000		HALFWIDTH KATAKANA LETTER O
FF76			00B6	00B6	00B6			JK100000		HALFWIDTH KATAKANA LETTER KA
FF77			00B7	00B7	00B7			JK200000		HALFWIDTH KATAKANA LETTER KI
FF78			00B8	00B8	00B8			JK300000		HALFWIDTH KATAKANA LETTER KU
FF79			00B9	00B9	00B9			JK400000		HALFWIDTH KATAKANA LETTER KE
FF7A			00BA	00BA	00BA			JK500000		HALFWIDTH KATAKANA LETTER KO
FF7B			00BB	00BB	00BB			JS100000		HALFWIDTH KATAKANA LETTER SA
FF7C			00BC	00BC	00BC			JS200000		HALFWIDTH KATAKANA LETTER SI
FF7D			00BD	00BD	00BD			JS300000		HALFWIDTH KATAKANA LETTER SU
FF7E			00BE	00BE	00BE			JS400000		HALFWIDTH KATAKANA LETTER SE
FF7F			00BF	00BF	00BF			JS500000		HALFWIDTH KATAKANA LETTER SO
FF80			00C0	00C0	00C0			JT100000		HALFWIDTH KATAKANA LETTER TA
FF81			00C1	00C1	00C1			JT200000		HALFWIDTH KATAKANA LETTER TI
FF82			00C2	00C2	00C2			JT300000		HALFWIDTH KATAKANA LETTER TU

UNIC	UGL	948	XJIS	942	AX	KSC	944	GCGID	GCGID#2	Unicode character name
FF83			00C3	00C3	00C3			JT400000		HALFWIDTH KATAKANA LETTER TE
FF84			00C4	00C4	00C4			JT500000		HALFWIDTH KATAKANA LETTER TO
FF85			00C5	00C5	00C5			JN100000		HALFWIDTH KATAKANA LETTER NA
FF86			00C6	00C6	00C6			JN200000		HALFWIDTH KATAKANA LETTER NI
FF87			00C7	00C7	00C7			JN300000		HALFWIDTH KATAKANA LETTER NU
FF88			00C8	00C8	00C8			JN400000		HALFWIDTH KATAKANA LETTER NE
FF89			00C9	00C9	00C9			JN500000		HALFWIDTH KATAKANA LETTER NO
FF8A			00CA	00CA	00CA			JH100000		HALFWIDTH KATAKANA LETTER HA
FF8B			00CB	00CB	00CB			JH200000		HALFWIDTH KATAKANA LETTER HI
FF8C			00CC	00CC	00CC			JH300000		HALFWIDTH KATAKANA LETTER HU
FF8D			00CD	00CD	00CD			JH400000		HALFWIDTH KATAKANA LETTER HE
FF8E			00CE	00CE	00CE			JH500000		HALFWIDTH KATAKANA LETTER HO
FF8F			00CF	00CF	00CF			JM100000		HALFWIDTH KATAKANA LETTER MA
FF90			00D0	00D0	00D0			JM200000		HALFWIDTH KATAKANA LETTER MI
FF91			00D1	00D1	00D1			JM300000		HALFWIDTH KATAKANA LETTER MU
FF92			00D2	00D2	00D2			JM400000		HALFWIDTH KATAKANA LETTER ME
FF93			00D3	00D3	00D3			JM500000		HALFWIDTH KATAKANA LETTER MO
FF94			00D4	00D4	00D4			JY100000		HALFWIDTH KATAKANA LETTER YA
FF95			00D5	00D5	00D5			JY300000		HALFWIDTH KATAKANA LETTER YU
FF96			00D6	00D6	00D6			JY500000		HALFWIDTH KATAKANA LETTER YO
FF97			00D7	00D7	00D7			JR100000		HALFWIDTH KATAKANA LETTER RA
FF98			00D8	00D8	00D8			JR200000		HALFWIDTH KATAKANA LETTER RI
FF99			00D9	00D9	00D9			JR300000		HALFWIDTH KATAKANA LETTER RU
FF9A			00DA	00DA	00DA			JR400000		HALFWIDTH KATAKANA LETTER RE
FF9B			00DB	00DB	00DB			JR500000		HALFWIDTH KATAKANA LETTER RO
FF9C			00DC	00DC	00DC			JW100000		HALFWIDTH KATAKANA LETTER WA
FF9D			00DD	00DD	00DD			JN000000		HALFWIDTH KATAKANA LETTER N
FF9E			00DE	00DE	00DE			JX710000		HALFWIDTH KATAKANA VOICED SOUND MARK
FF9F			00DF	00DF	00DF			JX720000		HALFWIDTH KATAKANA SEMI-VOICED SOUND MARK
FFA0							00C0	SP490000		HALFWIDTH HANGUL CAE OM
FFA1							00C1	OG000000		HALFWIDTH HANGUL LETTER GIYEOG
FFA2							00C2	OG100000		HALFWIDTH HANGUL LETTER SSANG GIYEOG
FFA3							00C3	OG200000		HALFWIDTH HANGUL LETTER GIYEOG SIOS
FFA4							00C4	ON000000		HALFWIDTH HANGUL LETTER NIEUN
FFA5							00C5	ON150000		HALFWIDTH HANGUL LETTER NIEUN JIEUJ
FFA6							00C6	ON100000		HALFWIDTH HANGUL LETTER NIEUN HIEUH
FFA7							00C7	OD000000		HALFWIDTH HANGUL LETTER DIGEUD
FFA8							00C8	OD100000		HALFWIDTH HANGUL LETTER SSANG DIGEUD
FFA9							00C9	OL000000		HALFWIDTH HANGUL LETTER LIEUL
FFAA							00CA	OL200000		HALFWIDTH HANGUL LETTER LIEUL GIYEOG

UNIC	UGL	948	XJIS	942	AX	KSC	944	GCGID	GCGID#2	Unicode character name
FFAB							00CB	OL400000		HALFWIDTH HANGUL LETTER LIEUL MIEUM
FFAC							00CC	OL100000		HALFWIDTH HANGUL LETTER LIEUL BIEUB
FFAD							00CD	OL600000		HALFWIDTH HANGUL LETTER LIEUL SIOS
FFAE							00CE	OL700000		HALFWIDTH HANGUL LETTER LIEUL TIEUT
FFAF							00CF	OL500000		HALFWIDTH HANGUL LETTER LIEUL PIEUP
FFB0							00D0	OL300000		HALFWIDTH HANGUL LETTER LIEUL HIEUH
FFB1							00D1	OM000000		HALFWIDTH HANGUL LETTER MIEUM
FFB2							00D2	OB000000		HALFWIDTH HANGUL LETTER BIEUB
FFB3							00D3	OB100000		HALFWIDTH HANGUL LETTER SSANG BIEUB
FFB4							00D4	OB200000		HALFWIDTH HANGUL LETTER BIEUB SIOS
FFB5							00D5	OS000000		HALFWIDTH HANGUL LETTER SIOS
FFB6							00D6	OS100000		HALFWIDTH HANGUL LETTER SSANG SIOS
FFB7							00D7	ON200000		HALFWIDTH HANGUL LETTER IEUNG
FFB8							00D8	OJ000000		HALFWIDTH HANGUL LETTER JIEUJ
FFB9							00D9	OJ100000		HALFWIDTH HANGUL LETTER SSANG JIEUJ
FFBA							00DA	OC200000		HALFWIDTH HANGUL LETTER CIEUC
FFBB							00DB	OK000000		HALFWIDTH HANGUL LETTER KIYEOK
FFBC							00DC	OT000000		HALFWIDTH HANGUL LETTER TIEUT
FFBD							00DD	OP000000		HALFWIDTH HANGUL LETTER PIEUP
FFBE							00DE	OH000000		HALFWIDTH HANGUL LETTER HIEUH
FFC2							00E2	OA000000		HALFWIDTH HANGUL LETTER A
FFC3							00E3	OA200000		HALFWIDTH HANGUL LETTER AE
FFC4							00E4	OY200000		HALFWIDTH HANGUL LETTER YA
FFC5							00E5	OY250000		HALFWIDTH HANGUL LETTER YAE
FFC6							00E6	OE200000		HALFWIDTH HANGUL LETTER EO
FFC7							00E7	OE000000		HALFWIDTH HANGUL LETTER E
FFCA							00EA	OY400000		HALFWIDTH HANGUL LETTER YEO
FFCB							00EB	OY300000		HALFWIDTH HANGUL LETTER YE
FFCC							00EC	OO000000		HALFWIDTH HANGUL LETTER O
FFCD							00ED	OO100000		HALFWIDTH HANGUL LETTER WA
FFCE							00EE	OO200000		HALFWIDTH HANGUL LETTER WAE
FFCF							00EF	OO300000		HALFWIDTH HANGUL LETTER OE
FFD2							00F2	OY500000		HALFWIDTH HANGUL LETTER YO
FFD3							00F3	OU000000		HALFWIDTH HANGUL LETTER U
FFD4							00F4	OU300000		HALFWIDTH HANGUL LETTER WEO
FFD5							00F5	OU200000		HALFWIDTH HANGUL LETTER WE
FFD6							00F6	OU400000		HALFWIDTH HANGUL LETTER WI
FFD7							00F7	OY600000		HALFWIDTH HANGUL LETTER YU
FFDA							00FA	OE300000		HALFWIDTH HANGUL LETTER EU
FFDB							00FB	OE400000		HALFWIDTH HANGUL LETTER YI

UNIC	UGL	948	XJIS	942	AX	KSC	944	GCGID	GCGID#2	Unicode character name
FFDC							00FC	OI000000		HALFWIDTH HANGUL LETTER I
FFE0		8191	8191	8191	8191	A1CB	816A	SC040080		FULLWIDTH CENT SIGN
FFE1		8192	8192	8192	8192	A1CC	816B	SC020080		FULLWIDTH POUND SIGN
FFE2		8B5B	81CA	FA54	81CA	A1FE	818C	SM660080		FULLWIDTH NOT SIGN
FFE3		8150	8150	8150	8150	A3FE	81FC	SM150080		FULLWIDTH SPACING MACRON
FFE4		8B5C	2243	FA55			818D	SM650080		FULLWIDTH BROKEN VERTICAL BAR
FFE5		818F	818F	818F	818F	A1CD	816C	SC050080		FULLWIDTH YEN SIGN
FFE6						A3DC	81DA	SC140080		FULLWIDTH WON SIGN

UNIC	037	500V1	1026	875	GCGID	Unicode character name
0020	40	40	40	40	SP010000	SPACE
0021	5A	4F	4F	4F	SP020000	EXCLAMATION MARK
0022	7F	7F	FC	7F	SP040000	QUOTATION MARK
0023	7B	7B	EC	7B	SM010000	NUMBER SIGN
0024	5B	5B	AD	5B	SC030000	DOLLAR SIGN
0025	6C	6C	6C	6C	SM020000	PERCENT SIGN
0026	50	50	50	50	SM030000	AMPERSAND
0027	7D	7D	7D	7D	SP050000	APOSTROPHE-QUOTE
0028	4D	4D	4D	4D	SP060000	OPENING PARENTHESIS
0029	5D	5D	5D	5D	SP070000	CLOSING PARENTHESIS
002A	5C	5C	5C	5C	SM040000	ASTERISK
002B	4E	4E	4E	4E	SA010000	PLUS SIGN
002C	6B	6B	6B	6B	SP080000	COMMA
002D	60	60	60	60	SP100000	HYPHEN-MINUS
002E	4B	4B	4B	4B	SP110000	PERIOD
002F	61	61	61	61	SP120000	SLASH
0030	F0	F0	F0	F0	ND100000	DIGIT ZERO
0031	F1	F1	F1	F1	ND010000	DIGIT ONE
0032	F2	F2	F2	F2	ND020000	DIGIT TWO
0033	F3	F3	F3	F3	ND030000	DIGIT THREE
0034	F4	F4	F4	F4	ND040000	DIGIT FOUR
0035	F5	F5	F5	F5	ND050000	DIGIT FIVE
0036	F6	F6	F6	F6	ND060000	DIGIT SIX
0037	F7	F7	F7	F7	ND070000	DIGIT SEVEN
0038	F8	F8	F8	F8	ND080000	DIGIT EIGHT
0039	F9	F9	F9	F9	ND090000	DIGIT NINE
003A	7A	7A	7A	7A	SP130000	COLON
003B	5E	5E	5E	5E	SP140000	SEMICOLON
003C	4C	4C	4C	4C	SA030000	LESS-THAN SIGN
003D	7E	7E	7E	7E	SA040000	EQUALS SIGN
003E	6E	6E	6E	6E	SA050000	GREATER-THAN SIGN
003F	6F	6F	6F	6F	SP150000	QUESTION MARK
0040	7C	7C	AE	7C	SM050000	COMMERCIAL AT
0041	C1	C1	C1	C1	LA020000	LATIN CAPITAL LETTER A
0042	C2	C2	C2	C2	LB020000	LATIN CAPITAL LETTER B
0043	C3	C3	C3	C3	LC020000	LATIN CAPITAL LETTER C
0044	C4	C4	C4	C4	LD020000	LATIN CAPITAL LETTER D
0045	C5	C5	C5	C5	LE020000	LATIN CAPITAL LETTER E
0046	C6	C6	C6	C6	LF020000	LATIN CAPITAL LETTER F
0047	C7	C7	C7	C7	LG020000	LATIN CAPITAL LETTER G
0048	C8	C8	C8	C8	LH020000	LATIN CAPITAL LETTER H
0049	C9	C9	C9	C9	LI020000	LATIN CAPITAL LETTER I
004A	D1	D1	D1	D1	LJ020000	LATIN CAPITAL LETTER J
004B	D2	D2	D2	D2	LK020000	LATIN CAPITAL LETTER K
004C	D3	D3	D3	D3	LL020000	LATIN CAPITAL LETTER L
004D	D4	D4	D4	D4	LM020000	LATIN CAPITAL LETTER M
004E	D5	D5	D5	D5	LN020000	LATIN CAPITAL LETTER N
004F	D6	D6	D6	D6	LO020000	LATIN CAPITAL LETTER O
0050	D7	D7	D7	D7	LP020000	LATIN CAPITAL LETTER P
0051	D8	D8	D8	D8	LQ020000	LATIN CAPITAL LETTER Q
0052	D9	D9	D9	D9	LR020000	LATIN CAPITAL LETTER R
0053	E2	E2	E2	E2	LS020000	LATIN CAPITAL LETTER S
0054	E3	E3	E3	E3	LT020000	LATIN CAPITAL LETTER T

UNIC	037	500V1	1026	875	GCGID	Unicode character name
0055	E4	E4	E4	E4	LU020000	LATIN CAPITAL LETTER U
0056	E5	E5	E5	E5	LV020000	LATIN CAPITAL LETTER V
0057	E6	E6	E6	E6	LW020000	LATIN CAPITAL LETTER W
0058	E7	E7	E7	E7	LX020000	LATIN CAPITAL LETTER X
0059	E8	E8	E8	E8	LY020000	LATIN CAPITAL LETTER Y
005A	E9	E9	E9	E9	LZ020000	LATIN CAPITAL LETTER Z
005B	BA	4A	68	4A	SM060000	OPENING SQUARE BRACKET
005C	E0	E0	DC	E0	SM070000	BACKSLASH
005D	BB	5A	AC	5A	SM080000	CLOSING SQUARE BRACKET
005E	B0	5F	5F	5F	SD150000	SPACING CIRCUMFLEX
005F	6D	6D	6D	6D	SP090000	SPACING UNDERSCORE
0060	79	79	8D	79	SD130000	SPACING GRAVE
0061	81	81	81	81	LA010000	LATIN SMALL LETTER A
0062	82	82	82	82	LB010000	LATIN SMALL LETTER B
0063	83	83	83	83	LC010000	LATIN SMALL LETTER C
0064	84	84	84	84	LD010000	LATIN SMALL LETTER D
0065	85	85	85	85	LE010000	LATIN SMALL LETTER E
0066	86	86	86	86	LF010000	LATIN SMALL LETTER F
0067	87	87	87	87	LG010000	LATIN SMALL LETTER G
0068	88	88	88	88	LH010000	LATIN SMALL LETTER H
0069	89	89	89	89	LI010000	LATIN SMALL LETTER I
006A	91	91	91	91	LJ010000	LATIN SMALL LETTER J
006B	92	92	92	92	LK010000	LATIN SMALL LETTER K
006C	93	93	93	93	LL010000	LATIN SMALL LETTER L
006D	94	94	94	94	LM010000	LATIN SMALL LETTER M
006E	95	95	95	95	LN010000	LATIN SMALL LETTER N
006F	96	96	96	96	LO010000	LATIN SMALL LETTER O
0070	97	97	97	97	LP010000	LATIN SMALL LETTER P
0071	98	98	98	98	LQ010000	LATIN SMALL LETTER Q
0072	99	99	99	99	LR010000	LATIN SMALL LETTER R
0073	A2	A2	A2	A2	LS010000	LATIN SMALL LETTER S
0074	A3	A3	A3	A3	LT010000	LATIN SMALL LETTER T
0075	A4	A4	A4	A4	LU010000	LATIN SMALL LETTER U
0076	A5	A5	A5	A5	LV010000	LATIN SMALL LETTER V
0077	A6	A6	A6	A6	LW010000	LATIN SMALL LETTER W
0078	A7	A7	A7	A7	LX010000	LATIN SMALL LETTER X
0079	A8	A8	A8	A8	LY010000	LATIN SMALL LETTER Y
007A	A9	A9	A9	A9	LZ010000	LATIN SMALL LETTER Z
007B	C0	C0	48	C0	SM110000	OPENING CURLY BRACKET
007C	4F	BB	BB	6A	SM130000	VERTICAL BAR
007D	D0	D0	8C	D0	SM140000	CLOSING CURLY BRACKET
007E	A1	A1	CC	A1	SD190000	TILDE
00A0	41	41	41	74	SP300000	NON-BREAKING SPACE
00A1	AA	AA	AA		SP030000	INVERTED EXCLAMATION MARK
00A2	4A	B0	B0		SC040000	CENT SIGN
00A3	B1	B1	B1	B0	SC020000	POUND SIGN
00A4	9F	9F	9F		SC010000	CURRENCY SIGN
00A5	B2	B2	B2		SC050000	YEN SIGN
00A6	6A	6A	8E	DF	SM650000	BROKEN VERTICAL BAR
00A7	B5	B5	B5	EB	SM240000	SECTION SIGN
00A8	BD	BD	BD	70	SD170000	SPACING DIAERESIS
00A9	B4	B4	B4	FB	SM520000	COPYRIGHT SIGN
00AA	9A	9A	9A		SM210000	FEMININE ORDINAL INDICATOR
00AB	8A	8A	8A	EE	SP170000	LEFT POINTING GUILLEMET
00AC	5F	BA	BA	EF	SM660000	NOT SIGN
00AD	CA	CA	CA	CA	SP320000	SOFT HYPHEN

UNIC	037	500V1	1026	875	GCGID	Unicode character name
00AE	AF	AF	AF		SM530000	REGISTERED TRADE MARK SIGN
00AF	BC	BC	BC		SM150000	SPACING MACRON
00B0	90	90	90	90	SM190000	DEGREE SIGN
00B1	8F	8F	8F	DA	SA020000	PLUS-OR-MINUS SIGN
00B2	EA	EA	EA	EA	ND021000	SUPERSCRIPT DIGIT TWO
00B3	FA	FA	FA	FA	ND031000	SUPERSCRIPT DIGIT THREE
00B4	BE	BE	BE	A0	SD110000	SPACING ACUTE
00B5	A0	A0	A0		SM170000	MICRO SIGN
00B6	B6	B6	B6		SM250000	PARAGRAPH SIGN
00B7	B3	B3	B3	DD	SD630000	MIDDLE DOT
00B8	9D	9D	9D		SD410000	SPACING CEDILLA
00B9	DA	DA	DA		ND011000	SUPERSCRIPT DIGIT ONE
00BA	9B	9B	9B		SM200000	MASCULINE ORDINAL INDICATOR
00BB	8B	8B	8B	FE	SP180000	RIGHT POINTING GUILLEMET
00BC	B7	B7	B7		NF040000	FRACTION ONE QUARTER
00BD	B8	B8	B8	DB	NF010000	FRACTION ONE HALF
00BE	B9	B9	B9		NF050000	FRACTION THREE QUARTERS
00BF	AB	AB	AB		SP160000	INVERTED QUESTION MARK
00C0	64	64	64		LA140000	LATIN CAPITAL LETTER A GRAVE
00C1	65	65	65		LA120000	LATIN CAPITAL LETTER A ACUTE
00C2	62	62	62		LA160000	LATIN CAPITAL LETTER A CIRCUMFLEX
00C3	66	66	66		LA200000	LATIN CAPITAL LETTER A TILDE
00C4	63	63	63		LA180000	LATIN CAPITAL LETTER A DIAERESIS
00C5	67	67	67		LA280000	LATIN CAPITAL LETTER A RING
00C6	9E	9E	9E		LA520000	LATIN CAPITAL LETTER A E
00C7	68	68	4A		LC420000	LATIN CAPITAL LETTER C CEDILLA
00C8	74	74	74		LE140000	LATIN CAPITAL LETTER E GRAVE
00C9	71	71	71		LE120000	LATIN CAPITAL LETTER E ACUTE
00CA	72	72	72		LE160000	LATIN CAPITAL LETTER E CIRCUMFLEX
00CB	73	73	73		LE180000	LATIN CAPITAL LETTER E DIAERESIS
00CC	78	78	78		LI140000	LATIN CAPITAL LETTER I GRAVE
00CD	75	75	75		LI120000	LATIN CAPITAL LETTER I ACUTE
00CE	76	76	76		LI160000	LATIN CAPITAL LETTER I CIRCUMFLEX
00CF	77	77	77		LI180000	LATIN CAPITAL LETTER I DIAERESIS
00D0	AC	AC			LD620000	LATIN CAPITAL LETTER ETH
00D1	69	69	69		LN200000	LATIN CAPITAL LETTER N TILDE
00D2	ED	ED	ED		LO140000	LATIN CAPITAL LETTER O GRAVE
00D3	EE	EE	EE		LO120000	LATIN CAPITAL LETTER O ACUTE
00D4	EB	EB	EB		LO160000	LATIN CAPITAL LETTER O CIRCUMFLEX
00D5	EF	EF	EF		LO200000	LATIN CAPITAL LETTER O TILDE
00D6	EC	EC	7B		LO180000	LATIN CAPITAL LETTER O DIAERESIS
00D7	BF	BF	BF		SA070000	MULTIPLICATION SIGN
00D8	80	80	80		LO620000	LATIN CAPITAL LETTER O SLASH
00D9	FD	FD	FD		LU140000	LATIN CAPITAL LETTER U GRAVE
00DA	FE	FE	FE		LU120000	LATIN CAPITAL LETTER U ACUTE
00DB	FB	FB	FB		LU160000	LATIN CAPITAL LETTER U CIRCUMFLEX
00DC	FC	FC	7F		LU180000	LATIN CAPITAL LETTER U DIAERESIS
00DD	AD	AD			LY120000	LATIN CAPITAL LETTER Y ACUTE
00DE	AE	AE			LT640000	LATIN CAPITAL LETTER THORN
00DF	59	59	59		LS610000	LATIN SMALL LETTER SHARP S
00E0	44	44	44		LA130000	LATIN SMALL LETTER A GRAVE
00E1	45	45	45		LA110000	LATIN SMALL LETTER A ACUTE
00E2	42	42	42		LA150000	LATIN SMALL LETTER A CIRCUMFLEX
00E3	46	46	46		LA190000	LATIN SMALL LETTER A TILDE
00E4	43	43	43		LA170000	LATIN SMALL LETTER A DIAERESIS
00E5	47	47	47		LA270000	LATIN SMALL LETTER A RING

UNIC	037	500V1	1026	875	GCGID	Unicode character name
00E6	9C	9C	9C		LA510000	LATIN SMALL LETTER A E
00E7	48	48	C0		LC410000	LATIN SMALL LETTER C CEDILLA
00E8	54	54	54		LE130000	LATIN SMALL LETTER E GRAVE
00E9	51	51	51		LE110000	LATIN SMALL LETTER E ACUTE
00EA	52	52	52		LE150000	LATIN SMALL LETTER E CIRCUMFLEX
00EB	53	53	53		LE170000	LATIN SMALL LETTER E DIAERESIS
00EC	58	58	58		LI130000	LATIN SMALL LETTER I GRAVE
00ED	55	55	55		LI110000	LATIN SMALL LETTER I ACUTE
00EE	56	56	56		LI150000	LATIN SMALL LETTER I CIRCUMFLEX
00EF	57	57	57		LI170000	LATIN SMALL LETTER I DIAERESIS
00F0	8C	8C			LD630000	LATIN SMALL LETTER ETH
00F1	49	49	49		LN190000	LATIN SMALL LETTER N TILDE
00F2	CD	CD	CD		LO130000	LATIN SMALL LETTER O GRAVE
00F3	CE	CE	CE		LO110000	LATIN SMALL LETTER O ACUTE
00F4	CB	CB	CB		LO150000	LATIN SMALL LETTER O CIRCUMFLEX
00F5	CF	CF	CF		LO190000	LATIN SMALL LETTER O TILDE
00F6	CC	CC	A1		LO170000	LATIN SMALL LETTER O DIAERESIS
00F7	E1	E1	E1		SA060000	DIVISION SIGN
00F8	70	70	70		LO610000	LATIN SMALL LETTER O SLASH
00F9	DD	DD	DD		LU130000	LATIN SMALL LETTER U GRAVE
00FA	DE	DE	DE		LU110000	LATIN SMALL LETTER U ACUTE
00FB	DB	DB	DB		LU150000	LATIN SMALL LETTER U CIRCUMFLEX
00FC	DC	DC	E0		LU170000	LATIN SMALL LETTER U DIAERESIS
00FD	8D	8D			LY110000	LATIN SMALL LETTER Y ACUTE
00FE	8E	8E			LT630000	LATIN SMALL LETTER THORN
00FF	DF	DF	DF		LY170000	LATIN SMALL LETTER Y DIAERESIS
011E			5A		LG240000	LATIN CAPITAL LETTER G BREVE
011F			D0		LG230000	LATIN SMALL LETTER G BREVE
0130			5B		LI300000	LATIN CAPITAL LETTER I DOT
0131			79		LI610000	LATIN SMALL LETTER DOTLESS I
015E			7C		LS420000	LATIN CAPITAL LETTER S CEDILLA
015F			6A		LS410000	LATIN SMALL LETTER S CEDILLA
0386				71	GA120000	GREEK CAPITAL LETTER ALPHA TONOS
0388				72	GE120000	GREEK CAPITAL LETTER EPSILON TONOS
0389				73	GE720000	GREEK CAPITAL LETTER ETA TONOS
038A				75	GI120000	GREEK CAPITAL LETTER IOTA TONOS
038C				76	GO120000	GREEK CAPITAL LETTER OMICRON TONOS
038E				77	GU120000	GREEK CAPITAL LETTER UPSILON TONOS
038F				78	GO720000	GREEK CAPITAL LETTER OMEGA TONOS
0390				CC	GI730000	GREEK SMALL LETTER IOTA DIAERESIS TONOS
0391				41	GA020000	GREEK CAPITAL LETTER ALPHA
0392				42	GB020000	GREEK CAPITAL LETTER BETA
0393				43	GG020000	GREEK CAPITAL LETTER GAMMA
0394				44	GD020000	GREEK CAPITAL LETTER DELTA
0395				45	GE020000	GREEK CAPITAL LETTER EPSILON
0396				46	GZ020000	GREEK CAPITAL LETTER ZETA
0397				47	GE320000	GREEK CAPITAL LETTER ETA
0398				48	GT620000	GREEK CAPITAL LETTER THETA
0399				49	GI020000	GREEK CAPITAL LETTER IOTA
039A				51	GK020000	GREEK CAPITAL LETTER KAPPA
039B				52	GL020000	GREEK CAPITAL LETTER LAMBDA
039C				53	GM020000	GREEK CAPITAL LETTER MU
039D				54	GN020000	GREEK CAPITAL LETTER NU
039E				55	GX020000	GREEK CAPITAL LETTER XI
039F				56	GO020000	GREEK CAPITAL LETTER OMICRON
03A0				57	GP020000	GREEK CAPITAL LETTER PI

UNIC	037	500V1	1026	875	GCGID	Unicode character name
03A1				58	GR020000	GREEK CAPITAL LETTER RHO
03A3				59	GS020000	GREEK CAPITAL LETTER SIGMA
03A4				62	GT020000	GREEK CAPITAL LETTER TAU
03A5				63	GU020000	GREEK CAPITAL LETTER UPSILON
03A6				64	GF020000	GREEK CAPITAL LETTER PHI
03A7				65	GH020000	GREEK CAPITAL LETTER CHI
03A8				66	GP620000	GREEK CAPITAL LETTER PSI
03A9				67	GO320000	GREEK CAPITAL LETTER OMEGA
03AA				68	GI180000	GREEK CAPITAL LETTER IOTA DIAERESIS
03AB				69	GU180000	GREEK CAPITAL LETTER UPSILON DIAERESIS
03AC				B1	GA110000	GREEK SMALL LETTER ALPHA TONOS
03AD				B2	GE110000	GREEK SMALL LETTER EPSILON TONOS
03AE				B3	GE710000	GREEK SMALL LETTER ETA TONOS
03AF				B5	GI110000	GREEK SMALL LETTER IOTA TONOS
03B0				CD	GU730000	GREEK SMALL LETTER UPSILON DIAERESIS TONOS
03B1				8A	GA010000	GREEK SMALL LETTER ALPHA
03B2				8B	GB010000	GREEK SMALL LETTER BETA
03B3				8C	GG010000	GREEK SMALL LETTER GAMMA
03B4				8D	GD010000	GREEK SMALL LETTER DELTA
03B5				8E	GE010000	GREEK SMALL LETTER EPSILON
03B6				8F	GZ010000	GREEK SMALL LETTER ZETA
03B7				9A	GE310000	GREEK SMALL LETTER ETA
03B8				9B	GT610000	GREEK SMALL LETTER THETA
03B9				9C	GI010000	GREEK SMALL LETTER IOTA
03BA				9D	GK010000	GREEK SMALL LETTER KAPPA
03BB				9E	GL010000	GREEK SMALL LETTER LAMBDA
03BC				9F	GM010000	GREEK SMALL LETTER MU
03BD				AA	GN010000	GREEK SMALL LETTER NU
03BE				AB	GX010000	GREEK SMALL LETTER XI
03BF				AC	GO010000	GREEK SMALL LETTER OMICRON
03C0				AD	GP010000	GREEK SMALL LETTER PI
03C1				AE	GR010000	GREEK SMALL LETTER RHO
03C2				BA	GS610000	GREEK SMALL LETTER FINAL SIGMA
03C3				AF	GS010000	GREEK SMALL LETTER SIGMA
03C4				BB	GT010000	GREEK SMALL LETTER TAU
03C5				BC	GU010000	GREEK SMALL LETTER UPSILON
03C6				BD	GF010000	GREEK SMALL LETTER PHI
03C7				BE	GH010000	GREEK SMALL LETTER CHI
03C8				BF	GP610000	GREEK SMALL LETTER PSI
03C9				CB	GO310000	GREEK SMALL LETTER OMEGA
03CA				B4	GI170000	GREEK SMALL LETTER IOTA DIAERESIS
03CB				B8	GU170000	GREEK SMALL LETTER UPSILON DIAERESIS
03CC				B6	GO110000	GREEK SMALL LETTER OMICRON TONOS
03CD				B7	GU110000	GREEK SMALL LETTER UPSILON TONOS
03CE				B9	GO710000	GREEK SMALL LETTER OMEGA TONOS
03F4				80	SD730000	GREEK SPACING DIAERESIS TONOS
2015				CF	SM120000	QUOTATION DASH
2018				CE	SP190000	SINGLE TURNED COMMA QUOTATION MARK
2019				DE	SP200000	SINGLE COMMA QUOTATION MARK

Appendix A: Directionality

The Unicode standard always uses logical backing store order. When text is presented in horizontal lines, most scripts display characters from left to right. However, there are several scripts where the natural ordering of horizontal text is from right to left (such as Arabic or Hebrew). If all of the text has the same horizontal direction, then the ordering of the display text is unambiguous. However, when there is bidirectional text (a mixture of left-to-right and right-to-left horizontal text) there is a fundamental ambiguity in the ordering of the displayed characters.

The following describes the algorithm used to perform reordering for bidirectional Unicode text. It extends the implicit model currently in use on a number of computers, and combines it with explicit controls for special circumstances. In most cases, there is no need to include additional information with the text to get correct display ordering. However, additional information can be included in the text when necessary by means of a small set of directional formatting codes.

In principle, the Unicode standard does not supply formatting codes; formatting is left up to higher-level protocols. However, in the case of bidirectional text, there are certain circumstances where an implicit bidirectional ordering is not sufficient to produce comprehensible text. To deal with these cases, a minimal set of directional formatting codes are supplied to control the ordering of characters when rendered. This allows exact control of the display ordering for legible interchange, and also allows vendors who still want plain text for simple items like filenames or labels to ensure that that text can always be correctly ordered for display.

The directional formatting codes are *only* used to influence the display ordering of text. In all other respects they are ignored: they should have no effect on the comparison of text, nor on word breaks, parsing, or numeric analysis. In addition, these codes are to be completely ignored when text is presented in vertical lines. In that case, the default order is for all characters to proceed from top to bottom (except for non-spacing accents, which have the same position relative to the base character). The choice of whether text is to be presented horizontally or vertically is left up to higher-level protocols.

The ordering of bidirectional text depends upon the directional properties of the text. The Character Properties section following lists the ranges of characters that have each particular directional character type.

NOTE: The term European Digits is used to refer to decimal forms common in Europe and elsewhere, and Arabic-Indic digits to refer to the native Arabic forms. See the Arabic block description for more details on naming digits.

Directional Ordering Codes

There are two types of explicit codes that are used to modify the standard implicit Unicode bidirectional algorithm. In addition, there are implicit ordering codes, the *right-to-left* and *left-to-right* marks. All codes are limited to the current directional block; that is, their effects are terminated by a *block separator*. The directional types left-to-right and right-to-left are called *strong types*, and characters of those types are called strong directional characters. The directional types associated with numbers are called *weak types*, and characters of those types are called weak directional characters.

Explicit Directional Embedding

The following codes signal that a piece of text is to be treated as embedded. For example, an English quotation in the middle of an Arabic sentence could be marked as being embedded left-to-right text. If there were a Hebrew phrase in the middle of the English quotation, then that phrase could be marked as being embedded right-to-left. The following codes allow for nested embeddings.

```
LRE    Left-to-Right Embedding    Treat the following text as embedded
                                   left-to-right.

RLE    Right-to-Left Embedding    Treat the following text as embedded
                                   right-to-left.
```

The precise meaning of these codes will be made clear in the discussion of the algorithm. The effect of right-left line direction, for example, can be accomplished by simply embedding the text with RLE..PDF.

Explicit directional overrides

The following codes allow the character types to be overridden when required for special cases, such as for part numbers. The following codes allow for nested directional overrides.

```
RLO    Right-to-Left Override      Force following characters to be
                                   treated as strong right-to-left
                                   characters.

LRO    Left-to-Right Override      Force following characters to be
                                   treated as strong left-to-right
                                   characters.
```

The precise meaning of these codes will be made clear in the discussion of the algorithm. The right-to-left override, for example, can be used to force a part number made of mixed English, digits and Hebrew letters to be written from right to left.

Terminating Explicit Directional Code

The following code terminates the effects of the last explicit code (either embedding or override), and restores the bidirectional state to what it was before that code was encountered.

```
PDF    Pop Directional Format       Restore the bidirectional state to what
                                     it was before the last LRE, RLE, RLO,
                                     LRO.
```

Implicit Directional Marks

These characters are very light weight codes. They act exactly like right-to-left or left-to-right characters, except that they do not display (or have any other semantic effect). Their use is often more convenient than the explicit embeddings or overrides, since their scope is much more local (as will be made clear following).

```
RLM    Right-to-Left Mark           Right-to-left zero width character
LRM    Left-to-Right Mark           Left-to-right zero-width character
```

There is no special mention of the implicit directional marks in the following algorithm. That is because their effect on bidirectional ordering is exactly the same as a corresponding strong directional character; the only difference is that they do not appear in the display.

Basic Display Algorithm

This algorithm may be coded differently for speed, but logically speaking follows two phases. The input is a stream of text, up to a *block separator* (such as a paragraph separator), and the character types for each character.

Phase 1. Resolution of the embedding levels of the text. In this phase, the directional character types, plus the explicit controls, are used to produce resolved embedding levels.

Phase 2. Reordering the text on a line-by-line basis, using the resolved embedding levels.

Embedding levels are numbers that indicate the embedding level of text. ("Embedding levels" in this text are determined both by override controls and by embedding controls.) Odd levels are right-to-left, and even levels are left-to-right. The minimum embedding level of text is zero, and the maximum depth is level 15. (The reason for having a limitation is to provide a precise stack limit for implementations to guarantee the same results. Fifteen levels is far more than sufficient for ordering: the display becomes rather muddied with more than a small number of embeddings.)

For example, in a particular piece of text: Level 0 is plain English text, Level 1 is plain Arabic text, possibly embedded within English level 0 text. Level 2 is English text, possibly embedded within Arabic level 1 text and so on. Unless their direction is overridden, English text and numbers will always be an even level; Arabic text will always be an odd level. The exact meaning of the embedding level will become clear when the reordering algorithm is discussed, but the following provides an example of how the algorithm works.

Example. In the following examples, case is used to indicate different implicit character types for those unfamiliar with right-to-left letters. Uppercase letters stand for right-to-left characters (such as Arabic or Hebrew), while lowercase letters stand for left-to-right characters (such as English or Russian).

Backing store:	`foo is FOO BAR in arabic`
Character types:	`LLL-LL-RRR-RRR-LL-LLLLLL`
Resolved levels:	`000000001111110000000000`

Notice that the neutral character (space) between FOO and BAR gets the level of the surrounding characters. This is how the implicit directional marks have an effect; by inserting appropriate directional marks around neutral characters, the level of the neutral characters can be changed.

Resolving Embedding Levels

Combining character types and explicit codes to produce a list of resolved levels lies at the heart of the bidirectional algorithm. This process consists of seven steps: determining the base level; determining explicit embedding levels and directions; determining explicit overrides; determining embedding and override terminations; resolving numbers; resolving neutrals; and resolving implicit embedding levels.

The Base Level

First, determine the *base embedding level,* which determines the default horizontal orientation of the text in the current block.

B1.   *In the text, find the first strong directional character, RLO or LRO. (Because block separators delimit text in this algorithm, this will generally be the first strong character after a block separator or at the very beginning of the text.)*

B2.   *If the first strong directional character in the text is right-to-left or RLO, then set the base level to one, otherwise set it to zero.*

The direction of the base embedding level is called the *base direction* or *block direction.*

Explicit Levels & Directions

All explicit embedding levels are determined from the embedding and override codes. The directional level indicates how deeply the text is embedded, and the basic directional flow of the text. Each even level is a left-to-right embedding, and each odd level is a right-to-left embedding. Only levels from 0 to 15 are valid.

E1. Begin at the base embedding level. Set the directional override status to neutral.

E2. With each RLE, remember (push) the current embedding level and override status. Reset the current level to the least greater odd level (if it would be valid), and the override status to neutral.

For example, level 0 → 1; levels 1, 2 → 3; levels 3, 4 → 5;...13, 14 → 15; above 14, no change (don't change levels with LRE if the new level would be invalid).

E3. With each LRE, remember (push) the current level and override status. Reset the current level to the least greater even level (if it would be valid), and the override status to neutral.

For example, levels 0, 1 → 2; levels 2, 3 → 4; levels 4, 5 → 6; ...12, 13 → 14; above 13, no change (don't change levels with LRE if the new level would be invalid).

Explicit Overrides

A directional override changes all of the following characters within the current explicit embedding level to a given value, and sets the embedding level as with the embedding codes.

O1. With each RLO, remember (push) the current override status and embedding level. Reset the current override status to be right-to-left, and the current level to the least greater odd level (if it would be valid).

O2. With each LRO, remember (push) the current override status and embedding level. Reset the current override status to be left-to-right, and the current level to the least greater even level (if it would be valid.).

O3. Whenever the directional override status is not neutral, reset the current character type to the directional override status.

Resetting levels works as described for embeddings in the previous section.

For example, if the directional override status is neutral, then all intermediate characters retain their normal values: Arabic characters stay R, Latin characters stay L, neutrals stay N, etc.. If the directional override status is R, then all characters become R.

Terminating Embeddings & Overrides

There is a single code to terminate the scope of the current explicit code, whether an embedding or a directional override. All codes and pushed states are completely popped at block separators.

T4. With each PDF, restore (pop) the last remembered (pushed) bidirectional state (embedding level and directional override). If there is no pushed state, ignore PDF.

T5.   *All explicit directional embeddings and overrides are completely terminated at Block separators. Return to the state as of E1.*

All overrides and resolution of numbers and neutrals take effect within the bounds of an embedding. That is, nothing within an embedding or override will effect the character direction of codes outside of that embedding, and vice versa. The one exception is in resolving neutrals (see N5 below).

Resolving Numbers

The text is parsed for numbers. This parsing does *not* span explicit directional controls: LRO, RLO, LRE, RLE, PDF, RLM, LRM. This pass will change the directional types of the character types European Number Separator, European Number Terminator, and Common Number Separator to be European Number text, Arabic Number text, andOther Neutral text.

The text to be scanned may have already had its type altered by directional overrides. If so, then it will not parse as numeric. All parsing does not span explicit controls; that is, any explicit control such as an RLE will terminate a number parsing.

The table below lists the abbreviations used in the following examples.

ES	European Number Separator	AL	Arabic Letter
ET	European Number Terminator	LL	Latin Letter
CS	Common Number Separator	HL	Hebrew Letter
EN	European Number text	N	Neutral
AN	Arabic Number text	sot	start of text
ON	Other Neutral text	eot	end of text

P0.   *Search backwards from each instance of a European number until the first strong character (or block boundary) is found. If a character is found before a block boundary, and if that character belongs to the Arabic block, then change the type of the European number to Arabic number:*

```
AL,EN        =>     AL,AN
AL,N,EN      =>     AL,N,AN
sot,EN       =>     sot,EN
LL,EN        =>     LL,EN
HL,EN        =>     HL,EN
```

P1.   *Separators change to numbers when surrounded by appropriate numbers:*

```
EN,CS,EN     =>     EN,EN,EN
AN,CS,AN     =>     AN,AN,AN
```

P2.   *Terminators change to numbers when adjacent to an appropriate number:*

```
EN,ET        =>     EN,EN
ET,EN        =>     EN,EN
```

P3.   *Otherwise, terminators change to Other Neutral:*

```
L,ES,EN      =>    L,N,EN
EN,CS,AN     =>    EN,N,AN
. . .
```

Resolving Neutrals

The next phase resolves the direction of the neutrals. The results of this phase are that all neutrals become either R or L.

Generally, neutral characters take on the direction of the surrounding text. In case of a conflict, they take on the embedding level. End-of-text and start-of-text are treated as if there were a character of the embedding level at that position. In this phase, block separators, segment separators, whitespace and other neutrals act the same, and will be indicated by an "N" in the examples. "e" represents the text ordering type (either L or R) that matches the embedding level direction in the examples.

N1.   *A sequence of neutrals takes the direction of the surrounding strong text.*

```
R N R        =>    R R R
L N L        =>    L L L
```

N2.   *Where there is a conflict in adjacent strong directions, a sequence of neutrals takes the global direction.*

```
L N R        =>    L e R
R N L        =>    R e L
```

Since end-of-text and start-of-text are treated as if they were characters of the embedding level at that position, the following examples are covered by this rule:

```
L N eot      =>    L e eot
R N eot      =>    R e eot
sot N L      =>    sot e L
sot N R      =>    sot e R
```

N3.   *Otherwise, in any sequence of neutrals and numbers, the neutrals go by the surrounding characters, as in the following rules. The numbers (whether European or Arabic) remain numeric.*

```
R N EN N R   =>    R R EN R R
R N EN N L   =>    R R EN e L
L N EN N R   =>    L L EN e R
L N EN N L   =>    L L EN L L
R N AN N R   =>    R R AN R R
R N AN N L   =>    R R AN e L
L N AN N R   =>    L e AN R R
L N AN N L   =>    L L AN L L
```

N4. *When processing adjacent neutrals, any embedded text will be treated as if it were a single strong character of the appropriate direction. The following examples illustrate the effects on neutrals.*

```
R N [LRO <text> PDF] N L  =>  R R LRO <text> PDF L L
R N [RLE <text> PDF] N L  =>  R R RLE <text> PDF R L
```

Examples. A list of numbers separated by neutrals and embedded in a directional run will come out in the run's order.

Storage:	`he said "THE VALUES ARE 123, 456, 789, OK".`
Visual:	`he said "KO ,789 ,456 ,123 ERA SEULAV EHT".`

In this case, both the comma and the space between the numbers take on the direction of the surrounding text (uppercase = right-to-left), ignoring the numbers. The commas are not considered part of the number since they are not surrounded on both sides (see number parsing).

However, if there is an adjacent left-to-right sequence, then Western numbers will adopt that direction:

Storage:	`he said "IT IS A bmw 500, OK".`
Visual:	`he said "KO ,bmw 500 A SI TI".`

Resolving Implicit Levels

In the final phase, the embedding level of text may be increased, based upon the resolved character type. Right-to-left text will always have an odd level, and left-to-right and numeric text will always have an even level. In addition, numeric text will always have a higher level than the base level, except in one special case. This results in the following rules:

I1. *If the global direction is even (left-to-right) then the right-to-left text goes up one level. Numeric text (AN) goes up two levels. Numeric text (EN) goes up two levels unless preceeded by left-to-right text.*

I2. *If the global direction is odd (right-to-left) then the left-to-right text and numeric text (EN or AN) goes up one level.*

The following table summarizes the results of the implicit algorithm. The "L" indicates a preceding character type.

Embedding Level (EL)	Sequence Type	Result
Even	L	EL
	R	EL+1
	AN	EL+2
	EN	EL+2
	(L) EN	EL
Odd	R	EL
	L	EL+1
	AN	EL+1
	EN	EL+1

Reordering Resolved Levels

The following describes the logical process of finding the correct display order. As before, this logical process is *not necessarily* the actual implementation, which may diverge for efficiency. As opposed to resolution phases, the following algorithm acts on a per-line basis.

L1.   *Reset the embedding level of segment separators and trailing white space (including block separators) to be the base embedding level.*

In combination with the following, this means that trailing white space will appear at the visual end of the line (in the base direction). Tabulation will always have a consistant direction within a directional block.

L2.   *From the highest level found in the text to the lowest odd level on each line, reverse any sequence of characters that are at that level or higher.*

This reverses a progressively larger series of substrings. The four examples below illustrate this.

Backing store:	foo means FOO.
Resolved levels:	00000000001110
Reverse level 1:	foo means OOF.
Backing store:	foo MEANS FOO.
Resolved levels:	22211111111111
Reverse level 2:	oof MEANS FOO.
Reverse levels 1,2:	OOF SNAEM foo
Backing store:	he said "foo MEANS FOO."
Resolved levels:	00000000002221111111111100
Reverse level 2:	he said "oof MEANS FOO."
Reverse levels 1,2:	he said "OOF SNAEM foo."

Backing store:	`DID YOU SAY 'he said "foo MEANS FOO"'?`
Resolved levels:	`11111111111222222222244433333333333221`
Reverse level 4:	`DID YOU SAY 'he said "oof MEANS FOO"'?`
Reverse levels 3,4:	`DID YOU SAY 'he said "OOF SNAEM foo"'?`
Reverse levels 2-4:	`DID YOU SAY '"oof MEANS FOO" dias eh'?`
Reverse levels 1-4:	`?'he said "OOF SNAEM foo"' YAS UOY DID`

NOTE: The correct appearance should be used for OPEN and CLOSE characters depending on their level: for example, OPEN PARENTHESIS appears as "(" when its resolved level is even, and as ")"when its resolved level is odd.

Conformance

The bidirectional algorithm specifies part of the intrinsic semantics of right-to-left characters. In the absence of a higher level protocol, systems that encode these characters must make use of the implicit bidirectional algorithm.

Explicit Formatting Codes

As with any Unicode characters, systems do not have to make use of any particular explicit directional formatting code (although it is not generally useful to include a terminating code without including the initiator). Generally, systems will fall into three classes:

- No bidirectional formatting. No right-left characters are used.

- Implicit bidirectionality. The implicit bidirectional algorithm is present (including RLM and LRM).

- Full bidirectionality. Both the implicit bidirectional algorithm and the explicit directional formatting codes are included.

Examples of Higher-Level Protocols

The following are concrete examples of how systems may apply higher-level protocols to the ordering of bidirectional text.

- Override the basic level embedding (global direction). A higher-level protocol may provide for overriding the basic level embedding, either on a field, paragraph, document or system level.

- Override the number handling to provide for more (or less) sophisticated number parsing. For example, different types of numbers can be parsed differently; however, this requires additional information such as the language.

- Supplement or override the directional overrides or embedding codes by providing information via stylesheets about the embedding level or character direction.

The Unicode Standard • Version 1.0

- Remap the number shapes to match those of another set. For example, remap the Arabic number shapes to have the same appearance as the European numbers.

When text using a higher-level protocol is to be converted to Unicode plain text, formatting codes can be inserted to ensure that the order matches that of the higher-level protocol, or (as in the last example), the appropriate characters can be substituted.

Usage

Because of the implicit character types and the heuristics for resolving neutral and numeric directional behavior, the implicit bidirectional ordering will generally produce the correct display without any further work. However, bad cases may occur when a right-to-left paragraph begins with left-to-right characters, or there are nested segments of different-direction text, or there are weak characters on directional boundaries. In these cases, embeddings or directional marks may be required to get the right display. Part numbers may also require directional overrides.

The most common bad case is that of neutrals on the boundary of an embedded language. This can be addressed by setting the level of the embedded streak correctly. For example, with all the text at level 0 the following occurs:

| Backing store: | `he said "MEANS FOO!", and expired.` |
| Display result: | `he said "OOF SNAEM!", and expired.` |

If the exclamation mark is to be part of the Arabic quotation, then the user can select the text `MEANS FOO!` and explicitly mark it as embedded Arabic, which produces the following result:

| Display result: | `he said "!OOF SNAEM", and expired.` |

Another method of doing this is to place a right directional mark after the exclamation mark. Since the exclamation mark is now not on a directional boundary, this produces the correct result.

Appendix B: Implementation Guidelines

This section provides guidelines for implementing the Unicode character encoding scheme. It includes discussions of byte-ordering, special characters, compression, 7-bit transmission, sorting and searching, and conversion. The purpose of these guidelines is to promote good practice in Unicode implementations. As guidelines, they are *not* binding on the implementer and do not form part of the standard.

Byte Order Mark

Since Unicode plain text is a sequence of 16-bit codes, it is sensitive to the byte ordering which is used when writing text. Many processors place the least significant byte in the initial position, while others place the most significant byte in the initial position. Ideally, all Unicode would follow only one set of rules, but this would force one side to swap the byte order on reading and writing plain text files, even when the file never leaves the system on which it was created. To have an efficient way to indicate which byte order is used in a text, the Unicode standard has defined two values, U+FEFF BYTE ORDER MARK (BOM) and U+FFFE (not a character code), which are the byte-ordered mirror images of each other. The BYTE ORDER MARK is not a control character which selects the byte order of the text; rather its function is to insure recipients that they are looking at a correctly byte-ordered file. Furthermore, the sequence 0xFEFF is exceedingly rare at the outset of regular non-Unicode text files and may therefore easily serve as an implicit marker to identify a file as containing Unicode text. Strictly speaking, however, this constitutes a particular use of a Unicode character, and there is nothing in the standard itself that requires or endorses this usage. The BYTE ORDER MARK is completely ignored in all other text processing, including rendering, and can safely be removed from Unicode text without altering its interpretation. When it is used, the logical place for it is at the beginning of the text.

Special Character and Non-Character Values

U+FFFF and U+FFFE. These code points are *not* considered to be Unicode characters. They are therefore outside of any text which purports to be in Unicode encoding only. U+FFFF is reserved for private program use as a sentinel or other code. (U+FFFF is a short -1 in twos-complement notation.) Programs receiving this code, are not required to interpret it in any way. It is good practice, however, to recognize this code as an illegal condition and take appropriate error response action. U+FFFE is similar in all respects to U+FFFF, except that it is also the mirror image of U+FEFF BYTE ORDER MARK. (U+FFFE is a short -2 in twos-complement notation.) Therefore, its presence constitutes a strong hint that the text in question is byte-reversed. An appropriate error response could include trying to re-read the text after byte swapping it. Good practice would be to at least let the user know that the text contained this code with the information that the text may be byte swapped.

ASCII Control Characters. The first thirty-two 16-bit characters in the Unicode standard are intended for encoding of the thirty-two ASCII control characters. Programs that conform to the Unicode standard can treat these control codes in exactly the same way as they treat their equivalents in ASCII. When converting control codes from existing 8-bit text, they are merely zero extended.

Escape Characters. In converting text with escape sequences to the Unicode character encoding, text must be converted to its Unicode equivalent. Converting escape sequences into Unicode on a character basis, (for instance, ESC-A turns into U+001B ESCAPE, U+0041 LATIN CAPITAL LETTER A), will allow the reverse conversion to be performed without forcing the program to recognize the escape sequence as such. In general, escape sequence should be translated into the Unicode encoding character by character.

Line and Paragraph Separator. The Unicode standard has two special characters U+2028 LINE SEPARATOR and U+2029 PARAGRAPH SEPARATOR. A new line is begun after each LINE SEPARATOR. A new paragraph is begun after each PARAGRAPH SEPARATOR. Since these are separator codes, it is not necessary either to start the first line or paragraph or to end the last line or paragraph with them. Doing so would indicate that there was an empty paragraph or line following. The paragraph separator can be inserted between paragraphs of text. Its use allows plain text files to be created which can be laid out on a different line width at the receiving end. The line separator can be used to indicate unconditional end of line. These are considered the canonical form of Unicode plain text.

Interaction with CR/LF. The Unicode standard does not prescribe specific semantics for U+000D CARRIAGE RETURN and U+000A LINE FEED. These codes are provided to represent any CR or LF characters employed by a higher level protocol, or retained in text translated from other standards. It is left to each application to interpret these codes as well as to decide whether to require their use, and whether CR/LF pairs or single codes are needed.

The Unicode Encoding as ANSI C wchar_t

With the wchar_t wide character type, ANSI C provides for inclusion of fixed width, wide characters. ANSI leaves the semantics of the wide character set to the specific implementation, but requires that the characters from the C execution set correspond to their wide character equivalents by zero extension. The Unicode characters equivalent to ASCII are the values from U+0020 to U+007F, which satisfy these conditions for 16-bit implementations of wchar_t.

Compression

Under some circumstances, using Unicode character encoding will double the amount of storage or memory space dedicated to the text portion of files. Compressing Unicode files may therefore be an attractive option. There are commercially available compression algorithms, such as LZW, that will compress files to something near their theoretical minimum. That means, if a particular text in ASCII took a certain number of bytes to encode, the same text expressed in a Unicode encoding can be compressed to the size as if the compression had been applied to the ASCII file directly. Since Unicode text is composed from a 16-bit token set, algorithms such as LZW, which are sensitive to the width of the individual tokens, may stand to gain from being reimplemented based on 16-bit tokens.

The Unicode codespace is arranged such that characters within the same script are contiguous as much as possible. An efficient compression algorithm might run-length encode the most significant byte. However, compression employed at a level where it is visible to the text processing parts of the program reintroduces the kind of complexities found in multibyte or or other stateful encodings, which the Unicode character encoding was designed to avoid. Compression by definition does not conform to the Unicode standard; rather it constitutes a higher-level protocol.

Where compression is built into the underlying support layer, such as modem transmission protocols, it can be effective in eliminating the size overhead of a Unicode encoding without the cost of added complexity.

7-bit Transmission

Some transmission protocols use ASCII control codes for flow control. Others, including some UNIX mailers are notorious for their restrictions to 7-bit ASCII. In these cases, Unicode transmissions must be encapsulated. A number of encapsulation protocols exist today, such as UUENCODE and BTOA. These can be combined with compression in the same pass, reducing the transmission overhead.

Converting To and From Canonical Form

The Unicode standard contains explicit codes for the most frequently used accented characters. These characters can be composed from elements; in the case of accented letters, these are the base characters and non-spacing marks. The Unicode standard provides a table of suggested spellings (decompositions) of characters that can be composed of a base character plus a non-spacing mark. These tables can be used to unify spelling. As far as the Unicode standard is concerned, both canonical and composed spellings are equivalent, and there is certainly no need to retain a mixed mode spelling.

If the purpose of a program is essentially one of pass-through, it may not be advisable to use composed characters, especially since less ambitious programs may not be able to interpret non-spacing marks. However, the greatest generality may be obtained through use of composition, or by allowing both forms.

Characters Not Used in a Subset

The Unicode standard does not require that an application be capable of interpreting and rendering *all* of the Unicode characters in order to be conformant. Many systems will have fonts only for some scripts, but not for others; sorting and other text processing rules may be implemented only for a limited set of languages. There is therefore a subset of characters which an implementation is able to interpret.

In general, it is nonconformant to modify or remove any Unicode characters that are outside of the program's subset of implemented Unicode characters. This is especially true for data which is intended to be transmitted through to other applications.

The Unicode standard explicitly disallows coding such as the following:

```
char ch = getchar() & 0x7f;
```

Conformance to the Unicode standard *requires* that whenever characters are to be re-transmitted, that unreadable characters must not be removed. For a more detailed discussion of this issue, see Section 2.6 on Conformance.

Sorting

Only those aspects of sorting are discussed here that relate to the question of character encoding. Much of the information in this section is also applicable to searching, especially when the goal is not an exact match, but a case-insensitive or other near match.

Culturally-Expected Sorting

There is usually not one, but several possible types of sort order possibilities that vary from culture to culture. Rarely is there a one-to-one correspondence of character codes to sort methods.

As a result, it is neither possible to arrange characters in an encoding in the correct order, nor is it possible to provide single level sort weight tables. Therefore, character encoding details have only an indirect impact on culturally-expected sorting.

Sort order can be by word or sentence, case sensitive or insensitive, ignoring accents or not; it can also be phonetic or based on the identity of the character, such as ordering by stroke and radical for East Asian ideographs. Phonetic sorting of Han characters requires use of a look-up dictionary of words, or special programs to maintain a separate phonetic spelling for the words in the text.

Languages vary not only on which types of sorts to use (and in which order they are to be applied), but also in what constitutes a fundamental element for sorting. Swedish treats LATIN LETTER A DIAERESIS as an individual letter sorting after z in the alphabet, whereas German sorts it either like "æ" or like other accented forms of "ä" following a. Spanish sorts the digraph "ch" as if it were a letter between "c" and "d." Examples from other languages (and scripts) abound.

To address the complexities of culturally-expected sorting, a multi-pass sorting algorithm is typically employed.[1] In its first pass, several categories of weights are accumulated for each character in the sort string. Categories include alphabetic, case and diacritic weights, among others. At the end of the first pass, the sort key contains a string of alphabetic weights, followed by a string of case weights and so on. These substrings are then compared one by one, so that case and accent differences can be ignored, or applied only where needed to differentiate otherwise indentical sort strings. The first pass of this scheme looks very similar to the Unicode decomposition into base-form and accent. The fact that the Unicode standard allows multiple spellings (composed and composite) of the same accented letter, turns out not to matter at all. If anything, a completely decomposed text stream might simplify the first implementation of sorting.

Handling Non-spacing Marks

A fixed set of composed character sequences can be rendered effectively by means of fairly simple substitution. Wherever a sequence (of base character, non-spacing mark) occurs, a glyph representing the combined form can be substituted. In simple, fixed-width character rendering, a non-spacing mark has a zero advance width, and a composed character sequence will automatically have the same width as the base character. When truncating strings, it is easiest always to truncate starting from the end and working backwards. A trailing non-spacing mark will then not be separated from the preceeding base character.

More sophisticated text rendering systems may take further measures to account for those cases where the composed character sequence has a different advance width than the base character. Such systems can also supply more sophisticated truncation routines.

When rendering a sequence of more than one non-spacing mark, the non-spacing marks should be stacked outwards from the base character. That is, if two non-spacing marks appear over a base character, then the first non-spacing mark should appear on top of the base character, and the second non-spacing mark on top of the first. If two non-spacing marks appear under a base character, then the first non-spacing mark should appear beneath the base character, and the second non-spacing mark below the first. (See Section 2.5, "General Principles Governing Non-Spacing Marks.")

If there is an unknown composed character sequence which is outside of a fixed, renderable set, then there are several methods of dealing with it. One method indicates the inability to draw the sequence by first drawing the base character, and then rendering the non-spacing mark as floating on a dotted circle, as illustrated in the code charts. Another method is to use a default fixed positioning of the non-spacing mark, generally placed away from overlap with possible base characters. For example, the default positioning of a circumflex can be above the ascent, which will place it

---

1. A good example can be found in Denis Garneau, *Keys to Sort and Search for Culturally-Expected Results* (IBM document number GG24-3516, June 1, 1990), which addresses the problem for western European languages, Arabic and Hebrew.

above capitals. Even though this will not yield a particularly attractive result for letters such as *g-circumflex*, it should generally be recognizable. More sophisticated systems can provide better rendering for composed character sequences.

Correct multilingual comparison routines must already be able to compare a sequence of characters as one, or one character as if it were a sequence. Such routines can also handle composed character sequences when supplied the appropriate data. When searching strings, remember to check for additional non-spacing marks in the target string that may affect the interpretation of the last matching character. Line-break algorithms generally use state machines for determining word breaks. Such algorithms can also be adapted to prevent separation of non-spacing marks from base characters.

Appendix C: How to Deal with Unknown or Missing Characters

This section briefly discusses how users or implementers might deal with characters that are not understood or which though understood, are unavailable for legible rendering. Characters not currently included in the Unicode standard are discussed in Appendix E.

Unassigned or Private Use Characters

There are two classes of characters which even a "complete" Unicode implementation cannot necessarily interpret correctly:

- Characters in the Private Use Area where there is no private agreement specifying use of that area.

- Potentially legal characters which, in the version of the Unicode standard being implemented, are not assigned.

An implementation should treat such a character as an independent graphic entity. It is generally safe to assume that the character is a simple weak left-to-right non-letter and non-digit character about which nothing else is known, unless the code is in the range of Unicode values reserved for right-to-left scripts, U+0500 → U+08FF, in which case the suitable default would be a strong right-to-left character. Some options for rendering such unknown characters include printing four hexadecimal digits, printing a black or white box, using a glyph (for example, that shown at U+FFFD), or simply displaying nothing. In no case should an implementation *assume* anything else about the character's properties, nor should it blindly delete such characters. It should not unintentionally transform them into something else.

Conflicting Uses of Private Use Area

Multiple assignments for the Private Use area may exist, where different domains overlap.

In this case, one of the uses could be re-mapped to another, unused, part of the User Space. Some implementations might also wish to provide higher level protocols to switch between interpretations of the User Space. If such instances become common, it may be that the groups involved should reach a new mutual private agreement about use of User Space, or if they form a sizeable community, that they should request the formal inclusion of the characters, or scripts in question in a future version of the Unicode standard.

Known Character

An implementation may receive a character which is an assigned character in the Unicode character encoding, but be unable to render it with the appropriate semantics because it does not have a font for it, or is otherwise incapable of rendering it appropriately.

An implementation should treat such a character code as if it were a character in the Private Use Area of the Unicode standard. In this case, an implementation might be able to provide further limited feedback to the user's queries such as being able to sort the data properly, show what script (or language) it is, or display it in a manner which is documented to be used only for known legal characters which cannot be appropriately rendered. An implementation might, for instance, distinguish between unrenderable characters in assigned zones and a code value with no character assignment by printing one as a box and the other with hexadecimal digits, or by printing the known characters with a special glyph that gives some general indication of their type.

Handling Numbers

There are many sets of characters that represent decimal digits in different scripts. Systems that interpret those characters numerically should provide the correct numerical values. For example, the sequence *Devanagari digit two, Devanagari digit zero* are numerically interpreted as having the value twenty. When converting binary numerical values to a visual form, digits can be chosen from different scripts. The value twenty can either be represented by *digit two, digit zero*, or by *Devanagari digit two, Devanagari digit zero* or by *Arabic-Indic digit two, Arabic-Indic digit zero*. It is recommended that systems allow users to choose the format of the resulting digits, including the script. Some existing systems allow users to override the appearance of digits in plain text. For example, they provide controls that allow users to choose to see *digit zero* as if it were *Arabic-Indic digit zero*, and so on. Such a change can be interchanged in plain text by replacing the appropriate occurrence of *digit zero* with *Arabic-Indic digit zero*.

Glyphs and Fonts

Any implementation of a rendering process makes use of a collection of glyphs. A *font* is a collection of glyphs, all in the same stroke style, containing at most one glyph from each set of variants. The word *font* suffers from a considerable amount of abuse; what is important in the usage is the restriction to at most one glyph from each set of variants.

A font implementation must index glyphs within the font by unique ID's. A *glyphID* is a private code name or number used to index the glyphs within a font.

In general, a font and its associated rendering process define an abitrary mapping between glyphIDs and Unicode values. Some of the glyphs in a font may be independent forms for individual characters, while others may be rendering forms that do not directly correspond to any one character. For those glyphs that are independent forms, it may be convenient for the glyphID to have the same numerical value as the Unicode value, but this is not required.

Appendix D: How to Submit New Characters for Consideration

Unicode Inc. accepts proposals for inclusion of new characters or scripts in the Unicode standard. All proposals must be in writing, must include at least one picture of the proposed character (normally from a printed source), and must include documentation justifying the proposal. The identification of the sponsor(s) must be included, along with a postal or electronic mail address, and/or a phone number. Guidelines for the preparation of a proposal appear below.

The Unicode standard definition of character is stated in the Glossary. In particular, the distinction between the terms *character* and *glyph* should be noted. Because of this distinction, graphics such as ligatures, conjunct consonants, minor variant written forms, or abbreviations of longer forms are generally not acceptable as Unicode characters. Each proposal will be evaluated by the editorial subcommittee of the Unicode Technical Committee. The result of this evaluation will be communicated to the sponsor(s) of the proposal. All proposals (whether successful or not) will be retained by the Unicode Consortium. This archive will be indexed. The Unicode Consortium is also interested in obtaining information on known glyphs, minor variants, ligatures, conjunct consonants, and other such "non-characters," mainly for cataloging and research purposes.

Send proposals to:

Unicode Incorporated
c/o Metaphor Computer Systems
1965 Charleston Avenue
Mountain View, CA 94043
USA

E-mail contact:

Rick_McGowan@NeXT.COM
FAX: USA 415-780-3714

The sponsor proposing the addition of a new character to the Unicode standard should follow these guidelines:

1. Determine that the proposed addition is a character according to the definition given in the Unicode standard.

2. Determine that the proposed addition does not already exist in the Unicode standard. The sponsor must both take into account different names by which the character may be known and minor glyphic variation in the Unicode illustration, and ensure that documentation supporting

the proposal states whether any Unicode characters were examined as possible equivalents for the proposed character and, if so, why each was rejected.

3. Include at least one picture of the proposed character, showing it in a printed context. Photocopies are acceptable. The sponsor must cite the source of each picture. The requirement for an illustration from a printed source is waived in the case of historical characters that do not generally appear in printed contexts and characters in modern use by cultures that don't have or use printing.

4. List the proposed name or alternative name, in the Unicode name list style. The proposed name should be typed in upper case. Each alternative name should be preceded by an equal sign, and be entirely lower case.

5. List any known commercially available fonts that include the character. Give as much information as possible on where and how such fonts may be obtained.

6. Provide any additional information, including other sources of printed examples, and works about the character which discuss it or define it. Who uses (or did use) it? When? In what context? For what purpose? List any known information about the character and its place in current culture or historical perspective.

7. If the character is a Han (ideographic) character, strong evidence for its uniqueness, indispensability, and value to users must be submitted, including printed contexts where it is used. If it could be considered a variant of a character already included in the Unicode standard, the proposed character should be shown in a context that demonstrates why it must be distinguished as a separate character and not considered a variant of the character already included.

8. If the character is part of a dead language or obsolete/rare script, cite the most important modern sources of information on the script. Names (including academic affiliation) of researchers in the relevant field are welcomed.

9. Proposals to include entire scripts (Syriac and Egyptian hieroglyphics, for example) should also cite modern, definitive sources of information regarding such scripts. Sponsorship by the relevant academic bodies (such as *The International Association of Egyptologists*) may be helpful in determining the proper scope for encoding of characters in such cases.

In the meantime, there are ways for programmers and scholarly organizations to make use of Unicode character encoding, even if the script they want to use or transmit is not yet part of the Unicode standard.

The Private Use Area can always be used to store and transmit characters, with the understanding that the encoding should be changed to the standard one, if and when the character or script ends up being included in a future version. A few living scripts are very likely to be included in the near future, including Ethiopian, Mongolian, Sinhala, Burmese, Khmer and Cree/Inuktitut.

In the case where a rare script has been turned down, individual groups that make use of rare scripts can reach a private agreement about setting aside part of the Private Use Area to encode their private set of characters. This leaves open the question of what to do with character sets that are simply too big to fit into the Private Use Area; in that case, your group might consider an entire private encoding in which to exchange data. The Unicode Consortium is generally most predisposed toward early inclusion of scripts that are in modern use, however minor or rare (such as Maldivian); behind those rank the scripts which are clearly extinct, important as they may be (such as Demotic); behind those rank a number of scripts of more or less historical significance (such as Linear B); and behind those lie the multitude of other scripts that have been used at one historical locus (such as Rongo-Rongo). The fact that a script is turned down for inclusion is not necessarily indicative of its ultimate fate. Some important scripts may be set aside for later inclusion because of other more immediate needs. Some criteria in ranking items for potential inclusion may have to do with factors such as the documented level to which the script is already used with computers, or the overall size of its literature.

Appendix E: Proposed Scripts for Future Versions of the Unicode Standard

This informative appendix presents draft layouts for several scripts that are currently under study for future inclusion in the Unicode standard. These scripts are not included in the version 1.0 of the Unicode standard. Comments and suggestions regarding these scripts are invited by the Unicode consortium.

Ethiopian

The Ethiopian script is used for writing several languages of the sub-Saharan area, including Amharic, Tigre, and Oromo. The script, which is based on the writing of a dead language, Ge'ez, is graphically consistent. However, it is a syllabary rather than an alphabet, which has several encoding consequences discussed in the following section.

Array Structure. The basic Ge'ez syllabary is traditionally arranged as an array of thirty-three consonant initials crossed with seven vowel finals. Since most of the consonants also take a labialized final, this can be expanded to a 33 x 8 array, which is ideal for encoding. This orderly array forms the basis for the Unicode Ethiopian block; other characters are added afterward in a less systematic fashion.

Encoding Structure. The Unicode character block for the Ethiopian script is divided into two adjacent blocks Ethiopian and Extended Ethiopian.

Diacritical marks. The Ethiopian syllabic letterforms in most cases reveal their origin as composites of a consonant base character plus a vowel diacritical mark, with labialization represented by a further diacritical mark. In the Unicode encoding, the syllabic letters are represented as whole codes, rather than by composition, because the composites have truly become the units of the script (and besides, the compositional rules are very irregular). However, a syllabary is more difficult to extend than an alphabet, and there may be merit in accomplishing some extensions via the application of diacritical marks. The few marks in this range appear to be the most effective in producing extensions, and are provided in case there is a desire to use them this way.

Extended Ethiopian Letters. This group includes some extensions of the basic syllabary, plus a set of labialized series that is now part of the standard script (and which in some cases replicates syllables in the main array). The characters are arranged according to the same N x 8 scheme as the main array. The names given to the extended Ethiopian characters are somewhat artificial, intended mainly to create a unique identifier. The Ethiopian script has been extended for some relatively obscure languages which may have little tradition of printed typography, and obsolete alternative forms of some letters also exist. The available information on variant letter forms is often sporadic and inconsistent, so some of the codes may be regarded as unneeded (and/or invalid) for some applications. It is assumed that the encoding of various languages will make use of various different subsets of these extensions. Given the imperfection of information and the bulkiness of extensions to a syllabary, the currently unassigned range has been made larger for Ethiopian than for other scripts. (Enough singly-attested forms have already been collected to fill it).

Sinhala

The Sinhala script (also known as Sinhalese, the majority language of Sri Lanka) was removed from version 1.0 of the Unicode standard because new information about Sinhala encoding was received prior to publication of the Unicode standard. The Sri Lankan government is currently producing a standard encoding for Sinhala, and the proposed (draft) standard differs significantly from both the draft layout shown here and the Indian standard (ISCII) upon which the Unicode draft was based.

Mongolian

The proposed Unicode structure for encoding Mongolian includes no ideal forms for characters. The only forms for Mongolian are the contextual shapes. Nevertheless, the Unicode standard proposes an encoding which identifies a single form for each Mongolian letter for encoding; Mongolian thus requires contextual shaping rules for rendering, much as for Arabic.

Mongolian is traditionally rendered vertically.

Because the traditional Mongolian script is undergoing a revival in the Mongolian People's Republic, there may be standards-related activity in the near future which could significantly affect the encoding of the Mongolian script.

Burmese and Khmer are being investigated.

Appendix F: Glossary

Abstract character: A character as a semantic entity as opposed to a particular representation or shape of the character. *See also* character, 1.

Accent mark. A mark placed above, below or to the side of a character to alter its phonetic value. *See also* diacritic.

ANSI. (1) The American National Standards Institute. (2) the Microsoft Windows ANSI character set, essentially ISO 8859-1 plus two characters, so named because it was originally based on an ANSI draft standard.

Arabic digits. Forms of decimal digits used in most parts of the Arabic world (for instance, U+0660, U+0661, U+0662, U+0663 ‎٠١٢٣‎). Although European digits derive historically from these forms, they are visually distinct and coded separately. (Arabic digits are sometimes called Indic numerals; however, this leads to confusion with the digits currently used with the scripts of India.) Arabic digits are referred to as *Arabic-Indic digits* in the Unicode standard.

ASCII. Acronym for "American Standard Code for Information Interchange," a 7-bit code that is the US national variant of ISO 646. Formally, the U.S. standard ANSI X3.4-1986.

AX. Refers to a character encoding specified in the AX Technical Reference Guide, published by the AX Committee, based in Tokyo.

Backing store. Character storage in memory or on disk, as opposed to characters displayed or printed.

Base character. (1) A character which is neither non-spacing nor characterized by obligatory overlapping with adjacent characters, nor by dependence upon other characters—that is, one that stands on its own. (2) Any graphic character which is not a non-spacing character. Base characters are also known as "spacing" characters, because they generally have non-zero width (in horizontal contexts).

BIDI. Short for "bidirectional," in reference to mixed left-to-right and right-to-left text.

Big-endian. Referring to a computer architecture which stores multiple-byte numerical values with the most significant byte (MSB) values first.

Binary files. Files containing non-textual information.

Block. A convenient unit for grouping characters within the Unicode encoding space, based on a multiple of 16. A typical block may contain unencoded positions, which are reserved.

BOM. Acronym for "Byte Order Mark." The Unicode character (U+FEFF) used to indicate the byte order of a text. The BOM allows a receiver of Unicode text to distinguish between text arriving in big-endian order from text arriving in little-endian order *in the absence of a higher level protocol.* *See* Appendix B, Implementation Guidelines.

Canonical. Conforming to the general rules for encoding, that is, not compressed, compacted or in any other form specified by a higher protocol, and also not consisting of a Compatibility Zone encoding.

Character. (1) The smallest component of written language that has semantic value. Character refers to the abstract idea, rather than a specific shape (see also glyph), though in code tables some form of visual representation is essential for the reader's understanding. (2) The basic unit of encoding for the Unicode character encoding, 16 bits of information. (3) Synonym for "code element." (4) The English name for the ideographic written elements of Chinese origin.

Character encoding. Association of a unique number with each character in a set of characters. The distinction between characters and glyphs is not absolutely clear in all cases, and so most large character encodings also encode some set of glyphs.

CJK. Acronym for "Chinese, Japanese, and Korean."

Code element. The minimal bit combination that can represent a unit of encoded text for processing or exchange.

Code page. An ordered character set with a numerical index (*code point*) associated with each character.

Code point. A numerical index (or position) in an encoding table used for encoding characters.

Code set. A character encoding; this term is widely used by programmers.

Codespace. The range of numerical values available for encoding characters, given the set of principles for how numerical values are to be used for encoding.

Compatibility Zone. A section of the Unicode codespace, included for compatibility with pre-existing character encoding standards. The Compatibility Zone contains variant characters that can be mapped to Unicode canonical equivalents.

Composed character sequence. A sequence of characters consisting of a base character followed by one or more non-spacing marks.

Conjunct consonant. (1) The juxtaposition of two or more consonants in Indic scripts. "Conjunct" refers to the pronounciation of two consonants with no intervening vowel. (2) The term is also used to refer to the specific typographical forms themselves, where the consonants may be written together in a single typographical form (ligature) or may be written with a *virama* below one or more of the consonants.

The Unicode Standard • Version 1.0

DBCS. Double Byte Character Set. Any 2-byte form of Multi-Byte encoding. (*See* MBCS)

Decomposition. (1) The act of mapping a precomposed character into the corresponding composed character sequence. (2) The resulting composed character sequence.

Diacritic. Any character (spacing or non-spacing) used with the Latin script or related scripts such as IPA, typically indicating that a phonetic value is different from the unmarked state. This broad definition is intended to include accents. See also *non-spacing diacritic.*

Diaeresis. (plural -*eses*) Two horizontal dots over a letter, as in *naïve.* The same Unicode character is used to represent the *umlaut.* (*See* umlaut)

Digits. See *Arabic digits, European digits, Indic digits.*

Ductility. The ability of a cursive font to stretch or compress the connective baseline to effect text justification.

Encapsulated text. (1) Plain text surrounded by formatting information. (2) Text re-coded to pass through narrow transmission channels or to match communication protocols.

European digits. Forms of decimal digits used in Europe (for instance, 0, 1, 2, 3). Historically, these derive from the Arabic digits, but are visually distinct and coded separately. Many countries outside of Europe have also adopted these forms for decimal digits. (Although European digits are sometimes called "Arabic numerals," this leads to confusion with the real Arabic digits.)

Fancy text. A data or interchange format containing both plain text and additional formatting information such as font, style, margins, etc.

Floating (diacritic, accent, mark). *See* non-spacing mark.

Formatted text. *See* fancy text.

Formatting codes. Non-spacing characters that are inherently invisible but which have an effect on the surrounding characters. An example is the ZERO WIDTH NON-JOINER.

GCGID. Acronym for "Graphic Character Global Identifier." These are listed in the IBM document *Character Data Representation Architecture, Level 1, Registry SC09-1391.*

Glyph. (1) The actual shape (bit pattern, outline) of a character image. For example, an italic "*a*" and a roman "a" are two different glyphs representing the same underlying character. In this strict sense, any two images which differ in shape constitute different glyphs. In this usage, "glyph" is a synonym for "character image" or simply "image." (2) A kind of idealized surface form derived from some combination of underlying characters in some specific context, rather than an actual character image. In this broad usage, two images would constitute the same glyph whenever they have essentially the same topology (as in oblique "*a*" and roman "a"), but *different* glyphs when one is written with a hooked top and the other without (as in italic *a* and roman a). In this usage "glyph" is a synonym for "glyph type," where glyph is defined as in sense 1. (*See also* Text Processes, Section 2.1.)

Han. Generic adjective referring to ideographic characters of Chinese origin.

Han unification. Assignment of the same code point to characters from more than one of the East Asian ideographic character standards in which they may (or may not) be represented by slightly different glyphs (in either of the two senses of "glyph" defined previously). This process actually reunifies elements which are historically used as, or have been historically perceived as being, the same "character." *See also the block description for Han characters.*

Hangul. The Korean syllabic writing system.

Hanja. The Korean name for the ideographic characters of Chinese origin.

Hanzi (~Han tsu). The Chinese name for the ideographic characters of Chinese origin.

Ideographic character. A character that generally stands for a word or a morpheme, rather than a sound. In this context the term is applied to characters of the Chinese script used for writing various languages. The Chinese script can be more accurately described as "logographic," but the Unicode standard uses the more widely-known terminology. The term "ideographic" is often also applied to various hieroglyphic writing systems.

Indic digits. Forms of decimal digits used in various Indic scripts (for instance, Devanagari: U+0966, U+0967, U+0968, U+0969 ০ ৭ ২ ৩). Although Arabic digits (and, eventually, European digits) derive historically from these forms, they are visually distinct and coded separately.

ISCII. (1) Indian Standard Code for Information Interchange. (2) Iranian Standard Code for Information Interchange

Kanji. The Japanese name for the ideographic characters of Chinese origin.

Keyboard language. Synonym for "keyboard layout," when it refers to accepted national arrangements of characters.

Keyboard layout. The designation of which keys produce which characters (or scan-codes).

Letter. (1) Basic element of a script as understood by the end user. (2) A higher level of abstraction than "character." *See* text element.

Ligature. Two (or more) characters combined into a single typographical form. In the Latin script, there are only a few in modern use, such as the ligatures between "f" and "i" (= fi) or "f" and "l" (= fl). Other scripts make use of many ligatures, depending on the font and style. Some languages have mandatory ligatures; other languages have text elements that historically were derived from ligatures, but are now characters. Examples of the latter are the German *eszet* (the ligature of long and short "s") and the ampersand (&) which originated as a contracted form of the Latin word "et" (which derivation can still be discerned in many fonts).

Little-endian. Referring to a computer architecture which stores multiple-byte numerical values with the least significant byte (LSB) values first.

Locale. The national and/or cultural environment in which a system or program is running. Specifically, a software implementation of this environment. The locale determines sort order, language of messages, keyboard layout, date and time formatting conventions, etc. It is sometimes, but not necessarily, coincident with a language or country boundary. For example, French Swiss and German Swiss constitute different locales.

Localization. The process of adapting a program for a different international market. A program which requires only translation of the program's messages is said to be *locale independent;* the operating system provides the parameters for the program to reconfigure itself. The usual examples are different date and time formatting.

Logographic. See Ideographic Character. Chinese characters are more properly termed logographic than ideographic.

LSB. Acronym for *least significant byte.*

MBCS. Acronym for *multi byte character set.* This implies more than one byte per character and often, that the number of bytes may be different for different characters in the character set. Many large character sets have been defined as MBCS in order to keep strict compatibility with the ASCII subset and/or ISO 2022.

MSB. Acronym for *most significant byte.*

Multibyte. The term used for character encodings that employ more than one byte per character; some such encodings may have a variable number of bytes per character. These encodings typically follow the ISO 2022 model, avoiding use of byte values in the so-called control ranges to encode graphic characters. The essential factor which distinguishes the Unicode character encoding from a typical multibyte code set is that the Unicode encoding is *defined* not as a 2-byte standard, but as a 16-bit standard.

Multilingual. Referring to many languages. A multilingual program strives to handle data in a way that is not dependent on a particular language or writing system. Multilingual documents combine text which is written in different languages. Multilingual may refer to many languages which all use the same script (such as English, French, and German), or to many languages which use distinct scripts (such as German, Hebrew, and Korean). The latter case is also referred to as *multiscript.*

National convention. A convention which is specific to a particular nation or district, and which may refer to everything from the currency symbol to the names of the weekdays in any language or local dialect. Somewhat synonymous with "locale," but the emphasis is not on the computer representation.

Neutral character. A character which can be written either right-to-left or left-to-right, depending on context.

Non-spacing character. A character with character width (advance width) equal to zero. There are two types of non-spacing characters: formatting codes and non-spacing marks. *See* formatting codes and non-spacing marks.

Non-spacing diacritic. A diacritic which is a non-spacing mark.

Non-spacing mark. A non-spacing graphic character which is positioned with reference to a preceding base character.

Plain text. Computer encoded text which consists *only* of a sequence of code elements from a given standard, with no other formatting or structural information to indicate a specific interpretation. Plain text interchange is commonly used between computer systems which may have no other factors in common.

Points. The non-spacing vowels and other signs of written Hebrew.

Precomposed character. A single Unicode character which represents a composed character sequence, usually a combination of one or more diacritic marks with a base character.

Radical. Parts of Chinese characters used collectively as a method of indexing them. A character may contain more than one element which is recognized as being a Radical, but each contains only *one* element that is actually *used* as the indexing Radical for the character. Many radicals can exist as stand-alone Characters.

Rendering. The text process of displaying or printing a sequence of characters in a visible form.

Replacement character. Character used to substitute for an uninterpretable character from another encoding. The Unicode standard uses U+FFFD REPLACEMENT CHARACTER for this function.

Replacement glyph. (Synonym: missing glyph) A glyph used to render a character which cannot be rendered with the correct appearance in a particular font. It often is shown as an open box □ or as a black rectangle ▮.

SBCS. Acronym for *single byte character set.* Any 1-byte character encoding. This term is generally used in contrast with DBCS and/or MBCS.

Text Element. A minimal unit of text relative to some specific language and some specific process performed on the text.

Umlaut. Two horizontal dots over a letter, as in German *Köpfe.* The same Unicode character is used to represent the *diaeresis. See* diaeresis.

Unification. The folding together of elements that need not be distinguished, or the recognition that two things which are distinguished in some places should not, in general, be distinguished as encoded characters because their use is disjoint enough to be apparent from context. Two ends of the spectrum are "radical" unification, which might fold together the upper and lowercase forms of Greek A, Cyrillic A and Latin A into a single code point; and the more conservative unification of the Unicode standard, which maintains boundaries between scripts in the broadest sense and, for compatibility, preserves many distinctions made in other computer character encodings.

Vowel sign. In many scripts, a mark used to indicate a vowel or vowel quality. Typical vowel signs are either partially overlapping or non-spacing marks, but those are not necessary criteria. Vowel signs are characterized generally by *functional* dependence upon an adjacent or nearby consonant, the inherent vowel of which they typically modify.

wchar_t. The ANSI C defined *wide character* type, usually implemented as either 16 or 32 bits. ANSI specifies that wchar_t be an integral type and that the C language source character set be mappable by simple extension (zero- or sign-extension). A frequent assumption is that the source and target code sets are different, and that the size of the "char" data type is insufficiently "wide" to hold a character of the target code set.

Zero width. *See* non-spacing.

References

Citations for ANSI and ISO standards are modelled on entries in the catalog of each organization.

Citations for publications written in non-Roman scripts have been rendered into Latin letters by the person supplying the information. As a result, romanization is not consistent.

ANSI X3.4
American National Standards Institute. Coded character set — 7-bit American national standard code for information interchange. — New York, 1986. — (ANSI X3.4 - 1986)

ANSI X3.32
American National Standards Institute. American national standard graphic representation of the control characters of American national standard code for information interchange / secretariat, Computer and Business Equipment Manufacturers Association; approved July, 3, 1973, American National Standards Institute, Inc. — New York, N.Y. (1430 Broadway, New York 10018) : ANSI, c1973. — (ANSI X3.32-1973).

ANSI Y10.20
American National Standards Institute. Mathematic signs and symbols for use in physical sciences and technology. — New York, 1988. — (ANSI Y10.20 - 1975 (R1988))

ANSI Z39.47
American National Standards Institute. Extended Latin alphabet coded character set for bibliographic use. — New York, 1985. — (ANSI Z39.47 - 1985)

ANSI Z39.64
American National Standards Institute. East Asian character code for bibliographic use. — New Brunswick : Transaction, 1990. — (ANSI Z39.64 - 1989)

ASMO 449
Arab Organization for Standardization and Metrology. Data processing — 7-bit coded character set for information interchange. — [s.l.], 1983. — (Arab standard specifications ; 449-1982). Authorized English translation.

CCCII
Zhongwen Zixun Jiaohuanma (Chinese Character Code for Information Interchange). — Revised edition. — Taipei : Xingzhengyuan Wenhua Jianshe Xiaozu (Executive Yuan Committee for Cultural Construction), 1985.

CNS 11643

Tongyong hanzi biaozhun jiaohuanma (Han Character Standard Interchange Code for General Use). — Taibei : Xingzhengyuan (Executive Yuan), 1986.

ECMA Registry ... See ISO International Register ...

Esling, John. Computer coding of the IPA: supplementary report. Journal of the International Phonetic Association, 20:1 (1990), p. 22-26.

GB 2312

Code of Chinese Graphic Character Set for Information Interchange. — Beijing : Jishu Biaozhun Chubanshe (Technical Standards Publishing), 1981. — (GB 2312 - 1980)

ISCII

Indian standard code for information interchange. New Delhi : Department of Electronics, 1988.

ISO International Register of Character Sets

International Organization for Standardization. ISO international register of character sets to be used with escape sequences. [Geneva], 1990.

ISO 646

International Organization for Standardization. Information processing. — ISO 7-bit coded character set for information interchange. — 2d ed. — [Geneva], 1983. — (ISO 646:1983)

ISO 2047

International Organization for Standardization. Information processing — Graphical representations for the control characters of the 7-bit coded character set. — [Geneva], 1975. — (ISO 2047:1975).

ISO 2022

International Organization for Standardization. Information processing — ISO 7-bit and 8-bit coded character sets — Code extension techniques. — 3d ed. — [Geneva], 1986. — (ISO 2022:1986).

ISO 2033

International Organization for Standardization. Information processing — Coding of machine-readable characters (OCR and MICR) 2d ed. — [Geneva], 1983. — (ISO 2033:1983).

ISO 5426

International Organization for Standardization. Extension of the Latin alphabet coded character set for bibliographic information interchange. — 2d ed. — [Geneva], 1983. — (ISO 5426:1984).

ISO 5427

International Organization for Standardization. Extension of the Cyrillic alphabet coded character set for bibliographic information interchange. — [Geneva], 1984 — (ISO 5427:1984).

ISO 5428

International Organization for Standardization. Greek alphabet coded character set for bibliographic information interchange — [Geneva], 1984 — (ISO 5428-1984).

ISO 6438

International Organization for Standardization. Documentation — African coded character set for bibliographic information interchange — [Geneva], 1983 — (ISO 6438:1983).

ISO DIS 6861.2

International Organization for Standardization. Technical Committee 46. Subcommittee 4. Information and documentation — Cyrillic alphabet coded character sets for historic Slavonic languages and European non-Slavonic languages written in Cyrillic script, for bibliographic information interchange. — [Geneva], 1990. — (ISO DIS 6861.2, to be published as an International Standard).

ISO DIS 6862.2

International Organization for Standardization. Technical Committee 46. Subcommittee 4. Documentation — Mathematical coded character set for bibliographic information interchange. — [Geneva], 1990. — (ISO DIS 6862.2, to be published as an International Standard).

ISO 6937

International Organization for Standardization. Information processing — Coded character sets for text communication. — [Geneva], 1983-

> Contents: Part 1. General introduction (1983). — Part 2: Latin alphabetic and non-alphabetic graphic characters. — Part 7. Greek graphic characters (DIS 1987). — Part 8. Cyrillic graphic characters (DIS 1987).

ISO 8859

International Organization for Standardization. Information processing — 8-bit single-byte coded graphic character sets. [Geneva], 1987-

> Contents: Part 1. Latin alphabet No. 1 (1987). — Part 2. Latin alphabet No. 2 (1987). — Part 3. Latin alphabet No. 3 (1988). — Part 4. Latin alphabet No. 4 (1988). — Part 5. Latin/Cyrillic alphabet (1988) — Part 6. Latin/Arabic alphabet (1987) — Part 7. Latin/Greek alphabet (1987) — Part 8. Latin/Hebrew alphabet (1988?) — Part 9. Latin alphabet No. 5 (199?).

ISO 8879

International Organization for Standardization. Information processing — Text and office systems — Standard generalized markup language (SGML). — [Geneva], 1986. — (ISO 8879:1986)

ISO DP 8957

International Organization for Standardization. Technical Committee 46. Subcommittee 4. Hebrew alphabet character sets for bibliographic interchange. — Gathersburg, MD, 1987. (ISO/TC46/SC4 N 205).

ISO 9036

International Organization for Standardization. Information processing — Arabic 7-bit coded character set for information interchange. — [Geneva], 1987. — (ISO 9036:1983)

ISO/IEC DIS 10367

International Organization for Standardization. Joint Technical Committee 1. Subcommittee 2. Working Group 3. Information processing — Repertoire of standardized coded graphic character sets for use in 8-bit codes. — Geneva, 1990. — (ISO/IEC JTC1/SC2 N 2074)

ISO/IEC DIS 10646

International Organization for Standardization. Joint Technical Committee 1. Subcommittee 2. Information technology — Universal Coded Character Set (UCS). — [Geneva], 1990. — (ISO/IEC DIS 10646)

JIS X 0208

Japanese Standards Association. Jouhou koukan you kanji fugoukei (Code of the Japanese Graphic Character Set for Information Interchange). — Tokyo, 1990. — (JIS X 0208-1990) Revision of the 1983 edition.

JIS X 0212

Japanese Standards Association. [Jouhou koukan you kanji fugou-hojo kanji] (Code of the supplementary Japanese graphic character set for information interchange). — Tokyo, 1990. — (JIS X 0212-1990) 1990 extensions to JIS.

KS C 5601

Korea Industrial Standards Association. Cengpo kyohwan yong pwuho (hankul mich hanca). (Code for Information Interchange (Hangul and Hanja)). — Seoul, 1989. — (KS C 5601-1987)

Knuth, Donald E. The TeXbook. — 19th. printing, rev. — Reading, MA : Addison-Wesley, 1990.

Pullum, Geoffrey K. Phonetic symbol guide / Geoffrey K. Pullum and William A. Ladusaw. — Chicago : University of Chicago Press, 1986.

Pullum, Geoffrey K. Remarks on the 1989 revision of the International Phonetic Alphabet. Journal of the International Phonetic Association, 20:1 (1990), p. 33-40.

Selby, Samuel M. Standard mathematical tables. — 16th ed. — Cleveland, OH : Chemical Rubber Co., 1968.

Shepherd, Walter. Shepherd's glossary of graphic signs and symbols. \ Compiled and classified for ready reference by Walter Shepherd. — New York : Dover Publications, [1971]

Shinmura, Izuru, 1875-1967. Kojien / Shinmura Izuru hen. — Dai 3-han. — Tokyo : Iwanami Shoten, Showa 58 [1983]

TIS 620-2529
Thai Industrial Standards Institute, Ministry of Industry. Thai Industrial Standard for Thai Character Code for Computer. — Bangkok, 1986. — (TIS 620-2529 - 1986)

8859-1, ISO (Latin1)	00A0
8859-2, -3, -4, -9, ISO (European Latin)	0100
8859-5, ISO (Cyrillic)	0400
8859-6, ISO (Arabic)	0600
8859-7, ISO (Greek)	0370
8859-8, ISO (Hebrew)	05D0

A

A ACUTE, LATIN CAPITAL LETTER	00C1	Á
A ACUTE, LATIN SMALL LETTER	00E1	á
A BREVE, LATIN CAPITAL LETTER	0102	Ă
A BREVE, LATIN SMALL LETTER	0103	ă
A CIRCUMFLEX, LATIN CAPITAL LETTER	00C2	Â
A CIRCUMFLEX, LATIN SMALL LETTER	00E2	â
A DIAERESIS, LATIN CAPITAL LETTER	00C4	Ä
A DIAERESIS, LATIN SMALL LETTER	00E4	ä
A E, LATIN CAPITAL LETTER	00C6	Æ
A E, LATIN SMALL LETTER	00E6	æ
A GRAVE, LATIN CAPITAL LETTER	00C0	À
A GRAVE, LATIN SMALL LETTER	00E0	à
A HACEK, LATIN CAPITAL LETTER	01CD	Ǎ
A HACEK, LATIN SMALL LETTER	01CE	ǎ
A MACRON, LATIN CAPITAL LETTER	0100	Ā
A MACRON, LATIN SMALL LETTER	0101	ā
A OGONEK, LATIN CAPITAL LETTER	0104	Ą
A OGONEK, LATIN SMALL LETTER	0105	ą
A RING, LATIN CAPITAL LETTER	00C5	Å
A RING, LATIN SMALL LETTER	00E5	å
A TILDE, LATIN CAPITAL LETTER	00C3	Ã
A TILDE, LATIN SMALL LETTER	00E3	ã
A, LATIN SMALL LETTER, SCRIPT	0251	ɑ
A, LATIN SMALL LETTER, TURNED	0250	ɐ
A, LATIN SMALL LETTER, TURNED, SCRIPT	0252	ɒ
ACCOUNT NUMBER, OCR CUSTOMER	2449	⑈
ACCOUNT OF	2100	℀
ACKNOWLEDGE	0006	ACK
acute accent and diaeresis	0385	΅
ACUTE BELOW, NON-SPACING	0317	̗
ACUTE TONE MARK, NON-SPACING	0341	VIET
ACUTE, MODIFIER LETTER	02CA	ˊ
ACUTE, MODIFIER LETTER, LOW	02CF	ˏ

ACUTE, NON-SPACING	0301	́
ACUTE, SPACING	00B4	´
ADDRESSED TO THE SUBJECT	2101	℁
ADI SHAKTI	262C	☬
AIRPLANE	2708	✈
ALL EQUAL TO	224C	≌
ALL, FOR	2200	∀
ALMOST EQUAL OR EQUAL TO	224A	≊
ALMOST EQUAL TO	2248	≈
alternating current	223F	∿
AMOUNT OF CHECK, OCR	2447	⑇
AMPERSAND	0026	&
AND, LOGICAL	2227	∧
AND, N-ARY LOGICAL	22C0	⋀
ANGLE	2220	∠
ANGLE ABOVE, NON-SPACING, LEFT	031A	̚
angle arc	2222	∢
ANGLE BRACKET, CLOSING	3009	〉
ANGLE BRACKET, CLOSING DOUBLE	300B	》
ANGLE BRACKET, OPENING	3008	〈
ANGLE BRACKET, OPENING DOUBLE	300A	《
angle quotation mark, left-pointing double	00AB	«
angle quotation mark, right-pointing double	00BB	»
angle quotation mark, single left-pointing	2039	‹
angle quotation mark, single right-pointing	203A	›
ANGLE WITH ARC, RIGHT	22BE	⊾
ANGLE, MEASURED	2221	∡
ANGLE, RIGHT	221F	∟
ANGLE, SPHERICAL	2222	∢
ANGSTROM UNIT	212B	Å
ANKH	2625	☥
ANTICLOCKWISE ARROW ABOVE, NON-SPACING	20D4	⃔
ANTICLOCKWISE CONTOUR INTEGRAL	2233	∳
ANTICLOCKWISE RING OVERLAY, NON-SPACING	20DA	⃚
APL COMPOSE OPERATOR	2300	APL COMPOSE
apl downstile	230A	⌊
apl jot	2218	∘
APL OUT	2301	⌁
apl overbar	00AF	¯
apl quad	25AF	▯

The Unicode Standard • Version 1.0

BLACK-LETTER C	212D	𝕮
BLACK-LETTER H	210C	ℌ
BLACK-LETTER I	2111	ℑ
BLACK-LETTER R	211C	ℜ
BLACK-LETTER Z	2128	ℨ
BLANK	2422	␢
BLOCK, FULL	2588	█
Blocks	**2580**	
bom	FEFF	Byte Order Mark
Bopomofo, Chinese	**3100**	
BOW TIE, OCR	2445	⋈
BOWTIE	22C8	⋈
BOX, OPEN	2423	␣
BRA	2329	⟨
BRACKET, CLOSING ANGLE	3009	〉
BRACKET, CLOSING BLACK LENTICULAR	3011	】
BRACKET, CLOSING CORNER	300D	」
BRACKET, CLOSING CURLY	007D	}
BRACKET, CLOSING DOUBLE ANGLE	300B	》
BRACKET, CLOSING SQUARE	005D	]
BRACKET, CLOSING TORTOISE SHELL	3015	〕
BRACKET, CLOSING WHITE CORNER	300F	』
BRACKET, CLOSING WHITE LENTICULAR	3017	〗
BRACKET, CLOSING WHITE SQUARE	301B	〛
BRACKET, CLOSING WHITE TORTOISE SHELL	3019	〙
bracket, left-pointing angle	2329	⟨
bracket, left-pointing double angle	300A	《
BRACKET, OPENING ANGLE	3008	〈
BRACKET, OPENING BLACK, LENTICULAR	3010	【
BRACKET, OPENING CORNER	300C	「
BRACKET, OPENING CURLY	007B	{
BRACKET, OPENING DOUBLE ANGLE	300A	《
BRACKET, OPENING SQUARE	005B	[
BRACKET, OPENING TORTOISE SHELL	3014	〔
BRACKET, OPENING WHITE, CORNER	300E	『
BRACKET, OPENING WHITE, LENTICULAR	3016	〖
BRACKET, OPENING WHITE, SQUARE	301A	〚
BRACKET, OPENING WHITE, TORTOISE SHELL	3018	〘
bracket, right-pointing angle	232A	〉
bracket, right-pointing double angle	300B	》
BRANCH BANK IDENTIFICATION, OCR	2446	⑆
BREVE BELOW, NON-SPACING	032E	◌̮
BREVE BELOW, NON-SPACING, INVERTED	032F	◌̯

BREVE, NON-SPACING	0306	◌̆
BREVE, NON-SPACING, INVERTED	0311	◌̑
BREVE, SPACING	02D8	˘
BRIDGE BELOW, NON-SPACING	032A	◌̪
BRIDGE BELOW, NON-SPACING INVERTED	033A	◌̺
BROKEN VERTICAL BAR	00A6	¦
BULLET	2022	•
BULLET OPERATOR	2219	∙
BULLET, HYPHEN	2043	⁃
BULLET, INVERSE	25D8	◘
BULLET, TRIANGULAR	2023	‣
BULLET, WHITE	25E6	◦
BULLSEYE	25CE	◎
BULLSEYE, LATIN LETTER	0298	ʘ
BYTE ORDER MARK	FEFF	Byte Order Mark

C

C ACUTE, LATIN CAPITAL LETTER	0106	Ć
C ACUTE, LATIN SMALL LETTER	0107	ć
C CEDILLA, LATIN CAPITAL LETTER	00C7	Ç
C CEDILLA, LATIN SMALL LETTER	00E7	ç
C CIRCUMFLEX, LATIN CAPITAL LETTER	0108	Ĉ
C CIRCUMFLEX, LATIN SMALL LETTER	0109	ĉ
C CURL, LATIN SMALL LETTER	0255	ɕ
C DOT, LATIN CAPITAL LETTER	010A	Ċ
C DOT, LATIN SMALL LETTER	010B	ċ
C HACEK, LATIN CAPITAL LETTER	010C	Č
C HACEK, LATIN SMALL LETTER	010D	č
C HOOK, LATIN CAPITAL LETTER	0187	Ƈ
C HOOK, LATIN SMALL LETTER	0188	ƈ
C L SYMBOL	2104	℄
C, BLACK-LETTER	212D	𝕮
C, DOUBLE-STRUCK	2102	ℂ
C, LATIN LETTER, STRETCHED	0297	ʗ
C0 ASCII control codes	**0000**	
C1 control codes	**0080**	
CADA UNA	2106	℅
CADUCEUS	2624	☤
CANCEL	0018	CAN
CANCER	264B	♋
cap	2229	∩

CAP, SQUARE	2293	⊓	Circled numbers	2460	
CAPRICORN	2651	♑	Circled numbers, inverse	2776	
caps lock	21EA	⇪	Circled numbers, inverse sans-serif	278A	
Card suits	**2660**		Circled numbers, sans-serif	2780	
Cardinals, transfinite	**2135**		CIRCLED PLUS	2295	⊕
CARE OF	2105	℅	CIRCLED RING OPERATOR	229A	⊚
caret	028C	ʌ	CIRCLED TIMES	2297	⊗
CARET	2038	‸	**Circles**	**25CB**	
CARET INSERTION POINT	2041	⁁	CIRCUMFLEX BELOW, NON-SPACING	032D	
caron	030C		CIRCUMFLEX, MODIFIER LETTER	02C6	
carriage return	21B5	↵	CIRCUMFLEX, NON-SPACING	0302	
CARRIAGE RETURN	000D	CR	CIRCUMFLEX, SPACING	005E	^
CAUTION SIGN	2621	☡	**CJK letters and ideographs, enclosed**	**3200**	
cedilla above	0312		**CJK miscellaneous**	**3190**	
CEDILLA, NON-SPACING	0327		**CJK squared abbreviations**	**3380**	
CEDILLA, SPACING	00B8	¸	**CJK squared words**	**3300**	
CEILING, LEFT	2308	⌈	**CJK symbols and punctuation**	**3000**	
CEILING, RIGHT	2309	⌉	CLEAR KEY	2327	⌧
CENT SIGN	00A2	¢	CLOCKWISE ARROW ABOVE, NON-SPACING	20D5	
centerline	2104	℄	CLOCKWISE CONTOUR INTEGRAL	2232	∲
CENTIGRADE, DEGREES	2103	℃	CLOCKWISE INTEGRAL	2231	∱
CHAIR, OCR	2441		CLOCKWISE RING OVERLAY, NON-SPACING	20D9	
CANDRABINDU, NON-SPACING	0310		clone	2104	℄
Check mark dingbats	**2713**		CLOSED EPSILON, LATIN SMALL LETTER	029A	ɛ
CHECK, BALLOT BOX WITH	2611	☑	CLOSED OMEGA, LATIN SMALL LETTER	0277	ɷ
Chess pieces	**2654**		CLOSED REVERSED EPSILON, LATIN SMALL LETTER		
CHI RHO	2627	☧		025E	ɞ
Chinese Bopomofo	**3100**		CLOSING ANGLE BRACKET	3009	〉
CIRCLE SLASH, ENCLOSING	20E0		CLOSING BLACK LENTICULAR BRACKET	3011	】
CIRCLE, BLACK	25CF	●	CLOSING CORNER BRACKET	300D	」
CIRCLE, ENCLOSING	20DD		CLOSING CURLY BRACKET	007D	}
CIRCLE, WHITE	25CB	○	CLOSING DOUBLE ANGLE BRACKET	300B	》
CIRCLED ASTERISK OPERATOR	229B	⊛	CLOSING MARK, IDEOGRAPHIC	3006	〆
CIRCLED DASH	229D	⊝	CLOSING PARENTHESIS	0029	)
CIRCLED DIVISION SLASH	2298	⊘	CLOSING SQUARE BRACKET	005D	]
CIRCLED DOT OPERATOR	2299	⊙	CLOSING TORTOISE SHELL BRACKET	3015	〕
CIRCLED EQUALS	229C	⊜	CLOSING WHITE CORNER BRACKET	300F	』
Circled ideographs	**3280**		CLOSING WHITE LENTICULAR BRACKET	3017	〗
Circled Japanese Katakana	**32D0**		CLOSING WHITE SQUARE BRACKET	301B	〛
Circled Korean Hangul elements	**3260**		CLOSING WHITE TORTOISE SHELL BRACKET	3019	〙
Circled Korean Hangul syllables	**326E**		CLOUD	2601	☁
Circled Latin letters	**24B6**		CLUB SUIT, BLACK	2663	♣
CIRCLED MINUS	2296	⊖	**CNS 11643 compatibility**	**FE30**	

The Unicode Standard • Version 1.0

COLON	003A	:	CORNER BRACKET, CLOSING	300D	⌋
COLON EQUAL	2254	:=	CORNER BRACKET, CLOSING WHITE	300F	』
COLON SIGN	20A1	₡	CORNER BRACKET, OPENING	300C	⌈
COLON, MODIFIER LETTER, HALF TRIANGULAR			CORNER BRACKET, OPENING WHITE	300E	『
	02D1	·	CORNER, BOTTOM LEFT	231E	⌞
COLON, MODIFIER LETTER, TRIANGULAR	02D0	ː	CORNER, BOTTOM RIGHT	231F	⌟
COMET	2604	☄	CORNER, TOP LEFT	231C	⌜
COMMA	002C	,	CORNER, TOP RIGHT	231D	⌝
COMMA ABOVE RIGHT, NON-SPACING	0315	̕	CORRESPONDS TO	2258	≘
COMMA ABOVE, NON-SPACING	0313	̓	corresponds to	2259	≙
COMMA ABOVE, NON-SPACING, REVERSED	0314	̔	**Croatian digraphs matching Serbian Cyrillic letters**		
COMMA ABOVE, NON-SPACING, TURNED	0312	̒		01C4	
COMMA BELOW, NON-SPACING	0326	̦	CROP, BOTTOM LEFT	230D	⌍
COMMA, ARABIC	060C	،	CROP, BOTTOM RIGHT	230C	⌌
COMMA, ARMENIAN	055D	՝	CROP, TOP LEFT	230F	⌏
comma, georgian	00B7	·	CROP, TOP RIGHT	230E	⌎
COMMA, IDEOGRAPHIC	3001	、	**Cross dingbats**	**2719**	
COMMA, MODIFIER LETTER, REVERSED	02BD	̔	CROSS OF JERUSALEM	2629	☩
COMMA, MODIFIER LETTER, TURNED	02BB	ʻ	CROSS OF LORRAINE	2628	☨
COMMAND KEY	2318	⌘	cross ratio	211E	℞
COMMERCIAL AT	0040	@	CROSS, LATIN	271D	✝
compass	263C	☼	CROSS, MALTESE	2720	✠
Compatibility zone	**FE00**		CROSS, ORTHODOX	2626	☦
COMPLEMENT	2201	∁	cross, st. andrew's	2613	☓
complex numbers, the set of	2102	ℂ	CRUZEIRO SIGN	20A2	₢
COMPOSE OPERATOR, APL	2300	APL COMPOSE	CUBE ROOT	221B	∛
composite function	2218	∘	cubed	00B3	³
composition circle, jis	20DD	⃝	cup	222A	∪
conductance	2127	℧	CUP, SQUARE	2294	⊔
CONJUNCTION	260C	☌	CURLY BRACKET, CLOSING	007D	}
CONTAINS AS MEMBER	220B	∋	CURLY BRACKET, OPENING	007B	{
CONTAINS AS MEMBER, SMALL	220D	∍	CURRENCY SIGN	00A4	¤
CONTAINS AS NORMAL SUBGROUP	22B3	⊳	**Currency symbols**	**20A0**	
CONTOUR INTEGRAL	222E	∮	current, alternating	223F	∿
CONTOUR INTEGRAL, ANTICLOCKWISE	2233	∳	cycle	223C	∼
CONTOUR INTEGRAL, CLOCKWISE	2232	∲	**Cyrillic**	**0400**	
Control codes, C0 ASCII	**0000**		**Cyrillic, extended**	**0490**	
Control codes, C1	**0080**		CYRILLIC NON-SPACING DASIA PNEUMATA	0485	
Control codes, pictures for	**2400**		CYRILLIC NON-SPACING PALATALIZATION	0484	
COPRODUCT, N-ARY	2210	∐	CYRILLIC NON-SPACING PSILI PNEUMATA	0486	
Coptic-unique letters	**03E2**		CYRILLIC NON-SPACING TITLO	0483	
COPYRIGHT SIGN	00A9	©			
COPYRIGHT, SOUND RECORDING	2117	℗			

D

D BAR, LATIN CAPITAL LETTER	0110	Đ
D BAR, LATIN SMALL LETTER	0111	đ
D HACEK, LATIN CAPITAL LETTER	010E	Ď D'
D HACEK, LATIN SMALL LETTER	010F	ď d'
D HOOK, LATIN CAPITAL LETTER	018A	Ɗ
D HOOK, LATIN SMALL LETTER	0257	ɗ
D RETROFLEX HOOK, LATIN SMALL LETTER	0256	ɖ
D TOPBAR, LATIN CAPITAL LETTER	018B	Ƌ
D TOPBAR, LATIN SMALL LETTER	018C	ƌ
D YOGH, LATIN SMALL LETTER	02A4	ʤ
D Z CURL, LATIN SMALL LETTER	02A5	ʥ
D Z HACEK, LATIN CAPITAL LETTER	01C4	DŽ
D Z HACEK, LATIN SMALL LETTER	01C6	dž
D Z, LATIN SMALL LETTER	02A3	ʣ
DAGGER	2020	†
DAGGER, DOUBLE	2021	‡
DANDA, DEVANAGARI	0964	।
DARK SHADE	2593	▓
DASH, CIRCLED	229D	⊝
DASH, EM	2014	—
DASH, EN	2013	–
DASH, FIGURE	2012	‒
DASH, OCR	2448	⑈
DASH, QUOTATION	2015	―
DASH, WAVE	301C	〜
DASH, WAVY	3030	〰
DATA LINK ESCAPE	0010	DLE
DEGREE SIGN	00B0	°
DEGREES CENTIGRADE	2103	℃
DEGREES FAHRENHEIT	2109	℉
DEGREES KELVIN	212A	K
del	2207	∇
DELETE	007F	DEL
DELETE TO THE LEFT KEY	232B	⌫
DELETE TO THE RIGHT KEY	2326	⌦
DELTA EQUAL TO	225C	≜
DELTA, LATIN SMALL LETTER, TURNED	018D	ƍ
depth symbol	21A7	↧
derivative	0307	◌̇
derivative, double	0308	◌̈
derivative, third	20DB	◌⃛
derivative, fourth	20DC	◌⃜
DESCENDING NODE	260B	☋
Devanagari	**0900**	
DEVICE CONTROL ONE	0011	DC1
DEVICE CONTROL TWO	0012	DC2
DEVICE CONTROL THREE	0013	DC3
DEVICE CONTROL FOUR	0014	DC4
DHARMA, WHEEL OF	2638	☸
Diacritical marks, generic	**0300**	
Diacritical marks for symbols	**20D0**	
DIAERESIS TONOS, GREEK NON-SPACING	0385	◌̈́
DIAERESIS TONOS, GREEK SPACING	03F4	΅
diaeresis, acute accent and	0385	◌̈́
DIAERESIS, NON-SPACING	0308	◌̈
DIAERESIS, SPACING	00A8	¨
DIAGONAL ELLIPSIS, DOWN RIGHT	22F1	⋱
DIAGONAL ELLIPSIS, UP RIGHT	22F0	⋰
diagonal, backward	2572	╲
diagonal, forward	2571	╱
diagonal, short backward	2216	∖
diameter symbol	2205	∅
DIAMOND OPERATOR	22C4	⋄
DIAMOND SUIT, WHITE	2662	♢
DIAMOND, BLACK	25C6	◆
DIAMOND, ENCLOSING	20DF	◌⃟
DIAMOND, WHITE	25C7	◇
Diamonds	**25C6**	
DIFFERENCE BETWEEN	224F	≏
DIFFERENTIAL, PARTIAL	2202	∂
Digits, ASCII	**0030**	
Digits, Arabic-Indic	**0660**	
Digits, Bengali	**09E6**	
Digits, Devanagari	**0966**	
Digits, Eastern Arabic-Indic	**06F0**	
Digits, Gujarati	**0AE6**	
Digits, Gurmukhi	**0A66**	
Digits, Kannada	**0CE6**	
Digits, Lao	**0ED0**	
Digits, Malayalam	**0D66**	
Digits, Oriya	**0B66**	
Digits, Tamil	**0BE7**	
Digits, Telugu	**0C66**	
Digits, Thai	**0E50**	

Drop-shadowed dingbats   **274D**

E

E ACUTE, LATIN CAPITAL LETTER	00C9	É
E ACUTE, LATIN SMALL LETTER	00E9	é
E BREVE, LATIN CAPITAL LETTER	0114	Ĕ
E BREVE, LATIN SMALL LETTER	0115	ĕ
E CIRCUMFLEX, LATIN CAPITAL LETTER	00CA	Ê
E CIRCUMFLEX, LATIN SMALL LETTER	00EA	ê
E DIAERESIS, LATIN CAPITAL LETTER	00CB	Ë
E DIAERESIS, LATIN SMALL LETTER	00EB	ë
E DOT, LATIN CAPITAL LETTER	0116	Ė
E DOT, LATIN SMALL LETTER	0117	ė
E GRAVE, LATIN CAPITAL LETTER	00C8	È
E GRAVE, LATIN SMALL LETTER	00E8	è
E HACEK, LATIN CAPITAL LETTER	011A	Ě
E HACEK, LATIN SMALL LETTER	011B	ě
E MACRON, LATIN CAPITAL LETTER	0112	Ē
E MACRON, LATIN SMALL LETTER	0113	ē
E OGONEK, LATIN CAPITAL LETTER	0118	Ę
E OGONEK, LATIN SMALL LETTER	0119	ę
E, LATIN CAPITAL LETTER, TURNED	018E	Ǝ
E, LATIN SMALL LETTER, REVERSED	0258	ǝ
E, LATIN SMALL LETTER TURNED	01DD	ə
E, SCRIPT	2130	ℰ
E, SCRIPT SMALL	212F	ℯ
EARTH	2641	♁⊕
EARTH, TRIGRAM FOR	2637	☷
EK ONKAR, GURMUKHI	0A74	ੴ
electrolysis	21AF	↯
ELEMENT OF	2208	∈
ELEMENT OF, SMALL	220A	∊
ELLIPSIS, HORIZONTAL	2026	…
ELLIPSIS, MIDLINE HORIZONTAL	22EF	⋯
ELLIPSIS, VERTICAL	22EE	⋮
EM DASH	2014	—
EM QUAD	2001	⬚
EM SPACE	2003	⬚
emf (electro-magnetic force)	2130	ℰ
EMPTY SET	2205	∅
EN DASH	2013	–

EN QUAD	2000	⬚
EN SPACE	2002	⬚
Enclosed alphanumerics	**2460**	
Enclosed CJK letters and ideographs	**3200**	
ENCLOSING CIRCLE	20DD	◯
ENCLOSING CIRCLE SLASH	20E0	⃠
ENCLOSING DIAMOND	20DF	◇
ENCLOSING SQUARE	20DE	▢
END OF MEDIUM	0019	EM
END OF PROOF	220E	∎
END OF TEXT	0003	ETX
END OF TRANSMISSION	0004	EOT
END OF TRANSMISSION BLOCK	0017	ETB
ENG, LATIN CAPITAL LETTER	014A	Ŋ
ENG, LATIN SMALL LETTER	014B	ŋ
ENQUIRY	0005	ENQ
ENTER KEY	2324	⌤
ENVELOPE	2709	✉
EPSILON HOOK, LATIN SMALL LETTER, REVERSED	025D	ɝ
EPSILON, LATIN CAPITAL LETTER	0190	Ɛ
EPSILON, LATIN SMALL LETTER	025B	ɛ
EPSILON, LATIN SMALL LETTER, CLOSED	029A	ʚ
EPSILON, LATIN SMALL LETTER, CLOSED REVERSED	025E	ɞ
EPSILON, LATIN SMALL LETTER, REVERSED	025C	ɜ
EQUAL AND PARALLEL TO	22D5	⋕
EQUAL COLON	2255	≕
equal to by definition	225C	≜
EQUAL TO BY DEFINITION	225D	≝
EQUAL TO, QUESTIONED	225F	≟
EQUALS SIGN	003D	=
EQUALS, CIRCLED	229C	⊜
equiangular	225C	≜
EQUIANGULAR TO	225A	≚
EQUIVALENT TO	224D	≍
Era names, Japanese	**337B**	
error	212F	ℯ
ESCAPE	001B	ESC
escudo	0024	$
ESH CURL, LATIN SMALL LETTER	0286	ʆ
ESH LOOP, LATIN LETTER, REVERSED	01AA	ƪ
ESH, LATIN CAPITAL LETTER	01A9	Ʃ

ESH, LATIN SMALL LETTER	0283	ʃ
ESH, LATIN SMALL LETTER, SQUAT REVERSED		
	0285	ʅ
ess-zed	00DF	ß
ESTIMATED SYMBOL	212E	℮
ESTIMATES	2259	≙
ETH, LATIN CAPITAL LETTER	00D0	Ð
ETH, LATIN SMALL LETTER	00F0	ð
EULERS	2107	Ɛ
EURO-CURRENCY SIGN	20A0	₠
European Latin	**0100**	
EXCESS	2239	-:
EXCLAMATION MARK	0021	!
EXCLAMATION MARK ORNAMENT, HEAVY	2762	❢
EXCLAMATION MARK, DOUBLE	203C	‼
EXCLAMATION MARK, INVERTED	00A1	¡
EXCLAMATION MARK, LATIN LETTER	01C3	ǃ
EXISTS, THERE	2203	∃
Extended Arabic	**0670**	
Extended Cyrillic	**0490**	
Extended Latin	**0180**	

F

F HOOK, LATIN CAPITAL LETTER	0191	Ƒ
f with hook, small letter	0192	ƒ
F, LATIN SMALL LETTER, SCRIPT	0192	ƒ
F, SCRIPT	2131	ℱ
F, TURNED	2132	Ⅎ
FACE, BLACK SMILING	263B	☻
FACE, WHITE FROWNING	2639	☹
FACE, WHITE SMILING	263A	☺
factorial	0021	!
FAHRENHEIT, DEGREES	2109	°F
feet	2032	′
FEMALE SIGN	2640	♀
FEMININE ORDINAL INDICATOR	00AA	ª
FIGURE DASH	2012	Figure
FIGURE SPACE	2007	Fig SP
FILE SEPARATOR	001C	FS
FIRE, TRIGRAM FOR	2632	☲
FISHEYE	25C9	◉

FISHHOOK R, LATIN SMALL LETTER	027E	ɾ
FLAT	266D	♭
FLOOR, LEFT	230A	⌊
FLOOR, RIGHT	230B	⌋
FLORETTE, BLACK	273F	✿
FLORETTE, WHITE	2740	❀
florin currency symbol (dutch)	0192	ƒ
FOR ALL	2200	∀
FORCES	22A9	⊩
FORK, OCR	2442	⑂
FORK, OCR INVERTED	2443	⑃
form feed	21A1	↓
FORM FEED	000C	FF
Form and chart components	**2500**	
fourier transform	2131	ℱ
FOURTH ROOT	221C	∜
FRACTION ONE HALF	00BD	½ ½
FRACTION ONE THIRD	2153	⅓
FRACTION ONE QUARTER	00BC	¼ ¼
FRACTION THREE QUARTERS	00BE	¾ ¾
Fractions	**2153**	
FRENCH FRANC SIGN	20A3	₣
FROWN	2322	⌢
FROWNING FACE, WHITE	2639	☹
FULL BLOCK	2588	█
full stop	002E	.
Fullwidth ASCII variants	**FF00**	
Fullwidth symbol variants	**FFE0**	
function symbol	0192	ƒ

G

G BAR, LATIN CAPITAL LETTER	01E4	Ǥ
G BAR, LATIN SMALL LETTER	01E5	ǥ
G BREVE, LATIN CAPITAL LETTER	011E	Ğ
G BREVE, LATIN SMALL LETTER	011F	ğ
G CEDILLA, LATIN CAPITAL LETTER	0122	Ģ
G CEDILLA, LATIN SMALL LETTER	0123	ģ ǵ
G CIRCUMFLEX, LATIN CAPITAL LETTER	011C	Ĝ
G CIRCUMFLEX, LATIN SMALL LETTER	011D	ĝ
G DOT, LATIN CAPITAL LETTER	0120	Ġ
G DOT, LATIN SMALL LETTER	0121	ġ

G HOOK, LATIN CAPITAL LETTER	0193	Ɠ
G HOOK, LATIN LETTER, SMALL CAPITAL	029B	ɢ
G HOOK, LATIN SMALL LETTER	0260	ɠ
G, LATIN LETTER, SMALL CAPITAL	0262	ɢ
G, LATIN SMALL LETTER, SCRIPT	0261	ɡ
G, SCRIPT SMALL	210A	ℊ
gamma function	0393	Γ
GAMMA, LATIN CAPITAL LETTER	0194	Ɣ
GAMMA, LATIN SMALL LETTER	0263	ɣ
GAMMA, LATIN SMALL LETTER, BABY	0264	ɤ
GAMMA, MODIFIER LETTER, SMALL	02E0	ˠ
GEMINI	264A	♊
GEOMETRIC PROPORTION	223A	∺
Geometric shapes	**25A0**	
GEOMETRICALLY EQUAL TO	2251	≑
GEOMETRICALLY EQUIVALENT TO	224E	≎
Georgian	**10A0**	
Georgian alphabet, modern	**10D0**	
georgian comma	00B7	·
georgian period	0589	∶
GETA MARK	3013	▬
GLOTTAL STOP BAR, LATIN LETTER	02A1	ʡ
GLOTTAL STOP BAR, LATIN LETTER, INVERTED		
	01BE	ƾ
GLOTTAL STOP BAR, LATIN LETTER, REVERSED		
	02A2	ʢ
GLOTTAL STOP, LATIN LETTER	0294	ʔ
GLOTTAL STOP, LATIN LETTER, INVERTED	0296	ʖ
GLOTTAL STOP, LATIN LETTER, REVERSED	0295	ʕ
GLOTTAL STOP, MODIFIER LETTER	02C0	ˀ
GLOTTAL STOP, MODIFIER LETTER, REVERSED		
	02C1	ˁ
GLOTTAL STOP, MODIFIER LETTER, SMALL REVERSED		
	02E4	ˤ
Graphic pictures for control codes	**2400**	
GRAVE BELOW, NON-SPACING	0316	◌̖
GRAVE TONE MARK, NON-SPACING	0340	◌̀
GRAVE, MODIFIER LETTER	02CB	ˋ
GRAVE, MODIFIER LETTER, LOW	02CE	ˎ
GRAVE, NON-SPACING	0300	◌̀
GRAVE, SPACING	0060	`
GREATER THAN BUT NOT EQUAL TO	2269	≩
GREATER THAN OR EQUAL TO	2265	≥
GREATER THAN OR EQUIVALENT TO	2273	≳
GREATER THAN OR LESS THAN	2277	≷
GREATER THAN OVER EQUAL TO	2267	≧
GREATER-THAN SIGN	003E	>
Greek	**0370**	
greek middle dot	00B7	·
GREEK NON-SPACING DASIA PNEUMATA	0371	◌̔
GREEK NON-SPACING DIAERESIS TONOS	0385	◌̈́
GREEK NON-SPACING IOTA BELOW	0370	◌ͅ
GREEK NON-SPACING PSILI PNEUMATA	0372	◌̓
GREEK NON-SPACING TONOS	0384	◌́
GREEK SPACING DIAERESIS TONOS	03F4	
GREEK SPACING IOTA BELOW	03F5	
GREEK SPACING TONOS	03F3	΄
GREEK QUESTION MARK	03D7	;
GREEK SMALL LETTER IOTA, TURNED	2129	℩
GROUP SEPARATOR	001D	GS
GUILLEMET, LEFT POINTING	00AB	«
GUILLEMET, LEFT POINTING SINGLE	2039	‹
GUILLEMET, RIGHT POINTING	00BB	»
GUILLEMET, RIGHT POINTING SINGLE	203A	›
Gujarati	**0A80**	
Gurmukhi	**0A00**	

H

H BAR, LATIN CAPITAL LETTER	0126	Ħ
H BAR, LATIN SMALL LETTER	0127	ħ
H CIRCUMFLEX, LATIN CAPITAL LETTER	0124	Ĥ
H CIRCUMFLEX, LATIN SMALL LETTER	0125	ĥ
H HOOK, LATIN SMALL LETTER	0266	ɦ
H HOOK, MODIFIER LETTER, SMALL	02B1	ʱ
H V, LATIN SMALL LETTER	0195	ƕ
H, BLACK-LETTER	210C	ℌ
H, DOUBLE-STRUCK	210D	ℍ
H, LATIN LETTER, SMALL CAPITAL	029C	ʜ
H, LATIN SMALL LETTER, TURNED	0265	ɥ
H, MODIFIER LETTER, SMALL	02B0	ʰ
H, SCRIPT	210B	ℋ
HACEK BELOW, NON-SPACING	032C	◌̬
HACEK, MODIFIER LETTER	02C7	ˇ
HACEK, NON-SPACING	030C	◌̌

HALF FILL SPACE, IDEOGRAPHIC	303F	
HALF INTEGRAL, TOP	2320	
HALF INTEGRAL, BOTTOM	2321	
HALF RING BELOW, NON-SPACING, LEFT	031C	
HALF RING BELOW, NON-SPACING, RIGHT	0339	
HALF RING, ARMENIAN MODIFIER LETTER, LEFT		
	0559	
HALF RING, ARMENIAN MODIFIER LETTER, RIGHT		
	055A	
HALF RING, MODIFIER LETTER, CENTERED LEFT		
	02D3	
HALF RING, MODIFIER LETTER, CENTERED RIGHT		
	02D2	
HALF RING, MODIFIER LETTER, LEFT	02BF	
HALF RING, MODIFIER LETTER, RIGHT	02BE	
HALF TRIANGULAR COLON, MODIFIER LETTER		
	02D1	
HALF, FRACTION ONE	00BD	½
Halfwidth and fullwidth variants	**FF00**	
Halfwidth Japanese Katakana variants	**FF60**	
Halfwidth Korean Hangul variants	**FFA0**	
hamiltonian function	210B	$\mathcal{H}$
HAMMER AND SICKLE	262D	☭
HANGUL DOUBLE DOT TONE MARK	302F	
Hangul elements, circled Korean	**3260**	
Hangul elements, Korean	**3130**	
Hangul elements, parenthesized Korean	**3200**	
HANGUL SINGLE DOT TONE MARK	302E	
Hangul syllables, circled Korean	**326E**	
Hangul syllables, Korean	**3400**	
Hangul syllables, parenthesized Korean	**320E**	
Hangul variants, halfwidth Korean	**FFA0**	
Hangzhou-style numerals	**3021**	
HARPOON ABOVE, NON-SPACING, LEFT	20D0	
HARPOON ABOVE, NON-SPACING, RIGHT	20D1	
Harpoons	**2190**	
hat	0302	
have a nice day!	263A	☺
Hazard dingbats	**2620**	
Heart dingbats	**2763**	
HEART SUIT, WHITE	2661	♡
HEAVEN, TRIGRAM FOR	2630	☰
Hebrew	**0590**	

HENG HOOK, LATIN SMALL LETTER	0267	ɧ
HERMITIAN CONJUGATE MATRIX	22B9	
HIRAGANA ITERATION MARK	309D	
HIRAGANA VOICED ITERATION MARK	309E	
Hiragana, Japanese	**3040**	
histogram marker	25AE	▮
home	21B8	
HOMOTHETIC	223B	
HOOK ABOVE, NON-SPACING	0309	
HOOK BELOW, NON-SPACING, PALATALIZED		
	0321	
HOOK BELOW, NON-SPACING, RETROFLEX	0322	
HOOK, MODIFIER LETTER, RHOTIC	02DE	
HOOK, OCR	2440	
horizontal bar	2015	—
HORIZONTAL ELLIPSIS	2026	…
HORIZONTAL ELLIPSIS, MIDLINE	22EF	⋯
HORIZONTAL TABULATION	0009	HT
HORN, NON-SPACING	031B	
HOT SPRINGS	2668	♨
HOUSE	2302	⌂
HOURGLASS	231B	⌛
HYPHEN	2010	Hyphen
HYPHEN BULLET	2043	▬
HYPHEN, NON-BREAKING	2011	NB
HYPHEN, SOFT	00AD	—
HYPHEN-MINUS	002D	—
HYPHENATION POINT	2027	HyphenPt
hyphus	002D	—

I

I ACUTE, LATIN CAPITAL LETTER	00CD	Í
I ACUTE, LATIN SMALL LETTER	00ED	í
i bar	0197	Ɨ
i bar	0268	ɨ
I BREVE, LATIN CAPITAL LETTER	012C	Ĭ
I BREVE, LATIN SMALL LETTER	012D	ĭ
I CIRCUMFLEX, LATIN CAPITAL LETTER	00CE	Î
I CIRCUMFLEX, LATIN SMALL LETTER	00EE	î
I DIAERESIS, LATIN CAPITAL LETTER	00CF	Ï
I DIAERESIS, LATIN SMALL LETTER	00EF	ï

I DOT, LATIN CAPITAL LETTER	0130	İ
I GRAVE, LATIN CAPITAL LETTER	00CC	Ì
I GRAVE, LATIN SMALL LETTER	00EC	ì
I HACEK, LATIN CAPITAL LETTER	01CF	Ǐ
I HACEK, LATIN SMALL LETTER	01D0	ǐ
I J, LATIN CAPITAL LETTER	0132	IJ
I J, LATIN SMALL LETTER	0133	ij
I MACRON, LATIN CAPITAL LETTER	012A	Ī
I MACRON, LATIN SMALL LETTER	012B	ī
I OGONEK, LATIN CAPITAL LETTER	012E	Į
I OGONEK, LATIN SMALL LETTER	012F	į
I TILDE, LATIN CAPITAL LETTER	0128	Ĩ
I TILDE, LATIN SMALL LETTER	0129	ĩ
i with dot above, latin capital letter	0130	İ
i with no dot, latin small letter	0131	ı
I, BLACK-LETTER	2111	ℑ
I, LATIN CAPITAL LETTER, BARRED	0197	Ɨ
I, LATIN LETTER, SMALL CAPITAL	026A	ɪ
I, LATIN SMALL LETTER, BARRED	0268	ɨ
I, LATIN SMALL LETTER, DOTLESS	0131	ı
I, SCRIPT	2110	ℐ
IDENTICAL TO	2261	≡
IDEOGRAPHIC CLOSING MARK	3006	〆
IDEOGRAPHIC COMMA	3001	、
IDEOGRAPHIC DEPARTING TONE MARK	302C	
IDEOGRAPHIC DITTO MARK	3004	〄
IDEOGRAPHIC ENTERING TONE MARK	302D	
IDEOGRAPHIC HALF FILL SPACE	303F	〿
IDEOGRAPHIC ITERATION MARK	3005	々
ideographic left bracket	300C	「
ideographic left double bracket	300E	『
IDEOGRAPHIC LEVEL TONE MARK	302A	
IDEOGRAPHIC NUMBER ZERO	3007	〇
IDEOGRAPHIC PERIOD	3002	。
ideographic right bracket	300D	」
ideographic right double bracket	300F	』
IDEOGRAPHIC RISING TONE MARK	302B	
IDEOGRAPHIC SPACE	3000	⌴
Ideographs, circled	**3280**	
Ideographs, enclosed	**3200**	
Ideographs, KS C5601 Han compatibility	**3EF0**	
Ideographs, parenthesized	**3220**	
IMAGE OF	22B7	⊷

IMAGE OF OR APPROXIMATELY EQUAL TO	2253	≓
IMAGE OF OR EQUAL TO, SQUARE	2291	⊑
IMAGE OF, SQUARE	228F	⊏
imaginary part symbol	2111	ℑ
inches	2033	″
INCREMENT	2206	∆
Index finger dingbats	**261A**	
INFINITY	221E	∞
INSERTION POINT, CARET	2041	⁁
integers, the set of	2124	ℤ
INTEGRAL	222B	∫
INTEGRAL, ANTICLOCKWISE CONTOUR	2233	∳
INTEGRAL, BOTTOM HALF	2321	⌡
INTEGRAL, CLOCKWISE	2231	∱
INTEGRAL, CLOCKWISE CONTOUR	2232	∲
INTEGRAL, CONTOUR	222E	∮
INTEGRAL, DOUBLE	222C	∬
integral, riemann	211B	ℛ
INTEGRAL, SURFACE	222F	∯
INTEGRAL, TOP HALF	2320	⌠
INTEGRAL, TRIPLE	222D	∭
INTEGRAL, VOLUME	2230	∰
INTERCALATE	22BA	⊺
International Phonetic Alphabet	**0250**	
INTERROBANG	203D	‽
INTERSECTION	2229	∩
INTERSECTION, DOUBLE	22D2	⋒
INTERSECTION, N-ARY	22C2	⋂
intersection, proper	22D4	⋔
INVERSE BULLET	25D8	◘
INVERSE WHITE CIRCLE	25D9	◙
INVERTED BREVE BELOW, NON-SPACING	032F	
INVERTED BREVE, NON-SPACING	0311	
INVERTED DOUBLE ARCH BELOW, NON-SPACING		
	032B	
INVERTED EXCLAMATION MARK	00A1	¡
INVERTED FORK, OCR	2443	⑃
INVERTED GLOTTAL STOP BAR, LATIN LETTER		
	01BE	ƾ
INVERTED GLOTTAL STOP, LATIN LETTER	0296	ʖ
INVERTED LAZY S	223E	∾
INVERTED QUESTION MARK	00BF	¿
INVERTED R, LATIN LETTER, SMALL CAPITAL	0281	ʁ

INVERTED R, MODIFIER LETTER, SMALL CAPITAL	
	02B6 ʁ
IOTA, LATIN CAPITAL LETTER	0196 ɩ
IOTA, LATIN SMALL LETTER	0269 ɩ
IOTA, TURNED GREEK SMALL LETTER	2129 ℩
IPA	**0250**
IRAN, SYMBOL OF	262B ☫
ISCII 1988	**0900**
ISO 8859-1 (Latin1)	**00A0**
ISO 8859-2, -3, -4, -9 (European Latin)	**0100**
ISO 8859-5 (Cyrillic)	**0400**
ISO 8859-6 (Arabic)	**0600**
ISO 8859-7 (Greek)	**0370**
ISO 8859-8 (Hebrew)	**05D0**
ISSHAR, BENGALI	09FA ৺
ISSHAR, ORIYA	0B70 ୰
ITERATION MARK, HIRAGANA	309D ゝ
ITERATION MARK, HIRAGANA VOICED	309E ゞ
ITERATION MARK, IDEOGRAPHIC	3005 々
ITERATION MARK, KATAKANA	30FD ヽ
ITERATION MARK, KATAKANA VOICED	30FE ヾ

J

J BAR HOOK, LATIN SMALL LETTER, DOTLESS	0284 ʄ
J BAR, LATIN SMALL LETTER, DOTLESS	025F ɟ
J CIRCUMFLEX, LATIN CAPITAL LETTER	0134 Ĵ
J CIRCUMFLEX, LATIN SMALL LETTER	0135 ĵ
J HACEK, LATIN SMALL LETTER	01F0 ǰ
J, LATIN SMALL LETTER, CROSSED-TAIL	029D ʝ
J, MODIFIER LETTER, SMALL	02B2 ʲ
jack	2749 ✉
Japanese Hiragana	**3040**
JAPANESE INDUSTRIAL STANDARD SYMBOL	32FF ㋿
Japanese Katakana	**30A0**
Japanese Katakana variants, halfwidth	**FF60**
Japanese Katakana words, squared	**3300**
Japanese Katakana, circled	**32D0**
japanese kome	203B ※
JERUSALEM, CROSS OF	2629 ☩
JOINER, ZERO WIDTH	200D
jot, apl	2218 ∘

JUPITER	2643 ♃

K

K CEDILLA, LATIN CAPITAL LETTER	0136 Ķ
K CEDILLA, LATIN SMALL LETTER	0137 ķ
K HOOK, LATIN CAPITAL LETTER	0198 Ƙ
K HOOK, LATIN SMALL LETTER	0199 ƙ
K, LATIN SMALL LETTER, TURNED	029E ʞ
KANA REPEAT MARK, VERTICAL	3031 〱
KANA REPEAT WITH VOICED SOUND MARK, VERTICAL	3032 〲
KANA REPEAT MARK UPPER HALF, VERTICAL	
	3033 〳
KANA REPEAT WITH VOICED SOUND MARK UPPER HALF, VERTICAL	3034 〴
KANA REPEAT MARK LOWER HALF, VERTICAL	
	3035 〵
Kanbun symbols	**3190**
Kannada	**0C80**
KATAKANA ITERATION MARK	30FD ヽ
KATAKANA MIDDLE DOT	30FB ・
Katakana variants, halfwidth Japanese	**FF60**
Katakana words, squared Japanese	**3300**
KATAKANA VOICED ITERATION MARK	30FE ヾ
Katakana, circled Japanese	**32D0**
Katakana, Japanese	**30A0**
KATAKANA-HIRAGANA PROLONGED SOUND MARK	
	30FC ー
KATAKANA-HIRAGANA SEMI-VOICED SOUND MARK	309C ゜
KATAKANA-HIRAGANA SEMI-VOICED SOUND MARK, NON-SPACING	309A ゚
KATAKANA-HIRAGANA VOICED SOUND MARK	
	309B ゛
KATAKANA-HIRAGANA VOICED SOUND MARK, NON-SPACING	3099 ゙
KELVIN, DEGREES	212A K
KET	232A 〉
KEYBOARD	2328 ⌨
kome, japanese	203B ※
Korean Hangul elements	**3130**

Korean Hangul elements, circled	**3260**	
Korean Hangul elements, parenthesized	**3200**	
Korean Hangul syllables	**3400**	
Korean Hangul syllables, circled	**326E**	
Korean Hangul syllables, parenthesized	**320E**	
Korean Hangul variants, halfwidth	**FFA0**	
KOREAN STANDARD SYMBOL	327F	Ⓚ
KRA, LATIN SMALL LETTER	0138	ĸ
KS C5601 Han compatibility	**3EF0**	

L

L ACUTE, LATIN CAPITAL LETTER	0139	Ĺ
L ACUTE, LATIN SMALL LETTER	013A	ĺ
L B BAR SYMBOL	2114	℔
L BELT, LATIN SMALL LETTER	026C	ɬ
L CEDILLA, LATIN CAPITAL LETTER	013B	Ļ
L CEDILLA, LATIN SMALL LETTER	013C	ļ
L HACEK, LATIN CAPITAL LETTER	013D	ĽĽ
L HACEK, LATIN SMALL LETTER	013E	ľľ
L J, LATIN CAPITAL LETTER	01C7	LJ
L J, LATIN SMALL LETTER	01C9	lj
L RETROFLEX HOOK, LATIN SMALL LETTER	026D	ɭ
L SLASH, LATIN CAPITAL LETTER	0141	Ł
L SLASH, LATIN SMALL LETTER	0142	ł
L WITH MIDDLE DOT, LATIN CAPITAL LETTER	013F	Ŀ
L WITH MIDDLE DOT, LATIN SMALL LETTER	0140	ŀ
L WITH MIDDLE TILDE, LATIN SMALL LETTER	026B	ɫ
L YOGH, LATIN SMALL LETTER	026E	ɮ
L, LATIN LETTER, SMALL CAPITAL	029F	ʟ
L, LATIN SMALL LETTER, BARRED	019A	ƚ
L, MODIFIER LETTER, SMALL	02E1	ˡ
L, SCRIPT	2112	ℒ
l, script small	2113	ℓ
LAKE, TRIGRAM FOR	2631	☱
LAMBDA, LATIN SMALL LETTER, BARRED	019B	ƛ
Lao	**0E80**	
laplace operator	2206	∆
laplace symbol	2112	ℒ
Latin abbreviations, squared	**3380**	
Latin capital letters	**0041**	
LATIN CROSS	271D	✝

Latin letters, circled	**24B6**	
Latin letters, parenthesized	**249C**	
Latin small letters	**0061**	
Latin, European	**0100**	
Latin, extended	**0180**	
Latin1, ISO 8859/1	**00A0**	
lazy s	223D	∽
LAZY S, INVERTED	223E	∾
LEADER, ONE DOT	2024	․
LEADER, TWO DOT	2025	‥
leader, three dot	2026	…
left curly bracket	007B	{
left parenthesis	0028	(
LEFT POINTING GUILLEMET	00AB	«
LEFT POINTING SINGLE GUILLEMET	2039	‹
left square bracket	005B	[
left-pointing angle bracket	2329	〈
left-pointing angle quotation mark, single	2039	‹
left-pointing double angle bracket	300A	《
left-pointing double angle quotation mark	00AB	«
LEFT-TO-RIGHT EMBEDDING	202A	LRE
LEFT-TO-RIGHT MARK	200E	L-R Mark
LEFT-TO-RIGHT OVERRIDE	202D	LRO
leftward tab	21E4	⇤
LENTICULAR BRACKET, CLOSING BLACK	3011	】
LENTICULAR BRACKET, CLOSING WHITE	3017	〗
LENTICULAR BRACKET, OPENING BLACK	3010	【
LENTICULAR BRACKET, OPENING WHITE	3016	〖
LEO	264C	♌
LESS THAN BUT NOT EQUAL TO	2268	≨
LESS THAN OR EQUAL TO	2264	≤
LESS THAN OR EQUIVALENT TO	2272	≲
LESS THAN OR GREATER THAN	2276	≶
LESS THAN OVER EQUAL TO	2266	≦
LESS-THAN SIGN	003C	<
Letterlike symbols	**2100**	
LIBRA	264E	♎
LIGHT SHADE	2591	░
LIGHTNING	2607	☇
line feed	21B4	↴
LINE FEED	000A	LF
line marker	2319	⌙
LINE SEPARATOR	2028	Line Sep

line, beginning of	2310	⌐
LIRA SIGN	20A4	₤
liter	2113	ℓ
LOGICAL AND	2227	∧
LOGICAL AND, N-ARY	22C0	⋀
LOGICAL OR	2228	∨
LOGICAL OR, N-ARY	22C1	⋁
long	0304	◌̄
LONG BAR OVERLAY, NON-SPACING	0336	⊖
LONG SLASH OVERLAY, NON-SPACING	0338	⫽
LORRAINE, CROSS OF	2628	☨
LOW ACUTE, MODIFIER LETTER	02CF	ˏ
LOW DOUBLE COMMA QUOTATION MARK	201E	„
LOW DOUBLE PRIME QUOTATION MARK	301F	〟
LOW GRAVE, MODIFIER LETTER	02CE	ˎ
low line	005F	_
LOW MACRON, MODIFIER LETTER	02CD	ˍ
LOW SINGLE COMMA QUOTATION MARK	201A	‚
LOW VERTICAL LINE, MODIFIER LETTER	02CC	ˌ
LOZENGE	25CA	◊
LOZENGE, SQUARE	2311	⌑
lre	202A	LRE
lrm	200E	L-R Mark
lro	202D	LRO

M

M HOOK, LATIN SMALL LETTER	0271	ɱ
M WITH LONG LEG, LATIN SMALL LETTER, TURNED	0270	ɰ
M, LATIN CAPITAL LETTER, TURNED	019C	ⱳ
M, LATIN SMALL LETTER, TURNED	026F	ɯ
M, SCRIPT	2133	ℳ
MACRON BELOW, NON-SPACING	0331	◌̱
MACRON, MODIFIER LETTER	02C9	ˉ
MACRON, MODIFIER LETTER, LOW	02CD	ˍ
MACRON, NON-SPACING	0304	◌̄
MACRON, SPACING	00AF	
Malayalam	**0D00**	
MALE SIGN	2642	♂
MALTESE CROSS	2720	✠
mars	2642	♂

maru-iti, symbol of unification	3280	㊀
MASCULINE ORDINAL INDICATOR	00BA	º
Mathematical operators	**2200**	
MEASURED ANGLE	2221	∡
MEASURED BY	225E	≞
MEDIUM SHADE	2592	▒
MERCURY	263F	☿
MHO	2127	℧
MICRO SIGN	00B5	µ
MIDDLE DOT	00B7	·
middle dot, greek	00B7	·
MIDDLE DOT, KATAKANA	30FB	・
MILL SIGN	20A5	₥
milreis	0024	$\|$
minim, drop	264F	♏
minim (alternate glyph)	264D	♍
MINUS SIGN	2212	−
MINUS SIGN BELOW, NON-SPACING	0320	◌̠
MINUS SIGN, MODIFIER LETTER	02D7	˗
MINUS TILDE	2242	≂
MINUS, CIRCLED	2296	⊖
MINUS, HYPHEN-	002D	-
MINUS, SQUARED	229F	⊟
MINUS-OR-PLUS SIGN	2213	∓
minutes	2032	′
Modifier letters	**02B0**	
MOON, FIRST QUARTER	263D	☽
MOON, LAST QUARTER	263E	☾
most positive	223E	∾
MOUNTAIN, TRIGRAM FOR	2636	☶
MUCH GREATER THAN	226B	≫
MUCH LESS THAN	226A	≪
MULTIMAP	22B8	⊸
MULTIPLICATION SIGN	00D7	×
MULTISET	228C	⊌
MULTISET MULTIPLICATION	228D	⊍
MULTISET UNION	228E	⊎
Music symbol dingbats	**2669**	

N

N ACUTE, LATIN CAPITAL LETTER	0143	Ń

N ACUTE, LATIN SMALL LETTER	0144	ń
N CEDILLA, LATIN CAPITAL LETTER	0145	Ņ
N CEDILLA, LATIN SMALL LETTER	0146	ņ
N HACEK, LATIN CAPITAL LETTER	0147	Ň
N HACEK, LATIN SMALL LETTER	0148	ň
N HOOK, LATIN CAPITAL LETTER	019D	Ɲ
N HOOK, LATIN SMALL LETTER	0272	ɲ
N J, LATIN CAPITAL LETTER	01CA	NJ
N J, LATIN SMALL LETTER	01CC	nj
n preceded by apostrophe, latin small letter	0149	ŉ
N RETROFLEX HOOK, LATIN SMALL LETTER	0273	ɳ
N TILDE, LATIN CAPITAL LETTER	00D1	Ñ
N TILDE, LATIN SMALL LETTER	00F1	ñ
N WITH LONG RIGHT LEG, LATIN SMALL LETTER	019E	ŋ
N, DOUBLE-STRUCK	2115	ℕ
N, LATIN LETTER, SMALL CAPITAL	0274	ɴ
N-ARY COPRODUCT	2210	∐
N-ARY INTERSECTION	22C2	⋂
N-ARY LOGICAL AND	22C0	⋀
N-ARY LOGICAL OR	22C1	⋁
N-ARY PRODUCT	220F	∏
N-ARY SUMMATION	2211	∑
N-ARY UNION	22C3	⋃
NABLA	2207	∇
NAIRA SIGN	20A6	₦
NAND	22BC	⊼
NATURAL	266E	♮
natural number	2115	ℕ
nearly equals	2252	≒
negation, horizontal indicator of	0304	◌̄
negation, oblique indicator of	0338	◌̸
NEGATIVE ACKNOWLEDGE	0015	NAK
NEITHER A SUBSET OF NOR EQUAL TO	2288	⊈
NEITHER APPROXIMATELY NOR ACTUALLY EQUAL TO	2247	≇
NEITHER GREATER THAN NOR EQUAL TO	2271	≱
NEITHER GREATER THAN NOR EQUIVALENT TO	2275	≵
NEITHER GREATER THAN NOR LESS THAN	2279	≹
NEITHER LESS THAN NOR EQUAL TO	2270	≰
NEITHER LESS THAN NOR EQUIVALENT TO	2274	≴
NEITHER LESS THAN NOR GREATER THAN	2278	≸

NEPTUNE	2646	♆
new line, picture for	21B5	↵
NIB, BLACK	2712	✒
NIB, WHITE	2711	✑
NON-BREAKING HYPHEN	2011	NB
NON-BREAKING SPACE	00A0	NB SP
NON-JOINER, ZERO WIDTH	200C	Non-Joiner
NON-SPACING ACUTE	0301	◌́
NON-SPACING ACUTE BELOW	0317	◌̗
NON-SPACING ACUTE TONE MARK	0341	◌́
NON-SPACING ANTICLOCKWISE ARROW ABOVE	20D4	◌⃔
NON-SPACING ANTICLOCKWISE RING OVERLAY	20DA	◌⃚
NON-SPACING BREVE	0306	◌̆
NON-SPACING BREVE BELOW	032E	◌̮
NON-SPACING BRIDGE BELOW	032A	◌̪
NON-SPACING CEDILLA	0327	◌̧
NON-SPACING CANDRABINDU	0310	◌̐
NON-SPACING CIRCUMFLEX	0302	◌̂
NON-SPACING CIRCUMFLEX BELOW	032D	◌̭
Non-spacing CJK diacritics	**302A**	
NON-SPACING CLOCKWISE ARROW ABOVE	20D5	◌⃕
NON-SPACING CLOCKWISE RING OVERLAY	20D9	◌⃙
NON-SPACING COMMA ABOVE	0313	◌̓
NON-SPACING COMMA ABOVE RIGHT	0315	◌̕
NON-SPACING COMMA BELOW	0326	◌̦
NON-SPACING DASIA PNEUMATA, CYRILLIC	0485	◌҅
NON-SPACING DASIA PNEUMATA, GREEK	0371	◌
NON-SPACING DIAERESIS	0308	◌̈
NON-SPACING DIAERESIS TONOS, GREEK	0385	◌̈́
NON-SPACING DOT ABOVE	0307	◌̇
NON-SPACING DOT BELOW	0323	◌̣
NON-SPACING DOUBLE ACUTE	030B	◌̋
NON-SPACING DOUBLE DOT BELOW	0324	◌̤
NON-SPACING DOUBLE GRAVE	030F	◌̏
NON-SPACING DOUBLE OVERSCORE	033F	◌̿
NON-SPACING DOUBLE UNDERSCORE	0333	◌̳
NON-SPACING DOUBLE VERTICAL LINE ABOVE	030E	◌̎
NON-SPACING DOWN TACK BELOW	031E	◌̞
NON-SPACING FOUR DOTS ABOVE	20DC	◌⃜
NON-SPACING GRAVE	0300	◌̀

NON-SPACING GRAVE BELOW	0316	
NON-SPACING GRAVE TONE MARK	0340	
NON-SPACING HACEK	030C	
NON-SPACING HACEK BELOW	032C	
NON-SPACING HOOK ABOVE	0309	
NON-SPACING HORN	031B	
NON-SPACING INVERTED BREVE	0311	
NON-SPACING INVERTED BREVE BELOW	032F	
NON-SPACING INVERTED BRIDGE BELOW	033A	
NON-SPACING INVERTED DOUBLE ARCH BELOW		
	032B	
NON-SPACING IOTA BELOW, GREEK	0370	
NON-SPACING KATAKANA-HIRAGANA SEMI-VOICED SOUND MARK	309A	
NON-SPACING KATAKANA-HIRAGANA VOICED SOUND MARK	3099	
NON-SPACING LEFT ANGLE ABOVE	031A	
NON-SPACING LEFT ARROW ABOVE	20D6	←
NON-SPACING LEFT HALF RING BELOW	031C	
NON-SPACING LEFT HARPOON ABOVE	20D0	
NON-SPACING LEFT TACK BELOW	0318	
NON-SPACING LONG BAR OVERLAY	0336	
NON-SPACING LONG SLASH OVERLAY	0338	
NON-SPACING LONG VERTICAL BAR OVERLAY		
	20D2	
NON-SPACING MACRON	0304	
NON-SPACING MACRON BELOW	0331	
NON-SPACING MINUS SIGN BELOW	0320	
NON-SPACING OGONEK	0328	
NON-SPACING OVERSCORE	0305	
NON-SPACING PALATALIZATION, CYRILLIC	0484	
NON-SPACING PALATALIZED HOOK BELOW	0321	
NON-SPACING PLUS SIGN BELOW	031F	
NON-SPACING PSILI PNEUMATA, CYRILLIC	0486	
NON-SPACING PSILI PNEUMATA, GREEK	0372	
NON-SPACING RETROFLEX HOOK BELOW	0322	
NON-SPACING REVERSED COMMA ABOVE	0314	
NON-SPACING RIGHT ARROW ABOVE	20D7	→
NON-SPACING RIGHT HALF RING BELOW	0339	
NON-SPACING RIGHT HARPOON ABOVE	20D1	
NON-SPACING RIGHT TACK BELOW	0319	
NON-SPACING RING ABOVE	030A	
NON-SPACING RING BELOW	0325	
NON-SPACING RING OVERLAY	20D8	
NON-SPACING SEAGULL BELOW	033C	
NON-SPACING SHORT BAR OVERLAY	0335	
NON-SPACING SHORT SLASH OVERLAY	0337	
NON-SPACING SHORT VERTICAL BAR OVERLAY		
	20D3	
NON-SPACING SQUARE BELOW	033B	
NON-SPACING THREE DOTS ABOVE	20DB	
NON-SPACING TILDE	0303	
NON-SPACING TILDE BELOW	0330	
NON-SPACING TILDE OVERLAY	0334	
NON-SPACING TITLO, CYRILLIC	0483	
NON-SPACING TONOS, GREEK	0384	
NON-SPACING TURNED COMMA ABOVE	0312	
NON-SPACING UNDERSCORE	0332	
NON-SPACING UP TACK BELOW	031D	
NON-SPACING VERTICAL LINE ABOVE	030D	
NON-SPACING VERTICAL LINE BELOW	0329	
NON-SPACING VERTICAL TILDE	033E	
NON-SPACING X ABOVE	033D	
NOR	22BD	▽
NORMAL SUBGROUP OF	22B2	◁
not	223C	~
NOT A SUBSET OF	2284	⊄
NOT A SUPERSET OF	2285	⊅
NOT ALMOST EQUAL TO	2249	≉
NOT AN ELEMENT OF	2209	∉
NOT ASYMPTOTICALLY EQUAL TO	2244	≄
NOT EQUAL TO	2260	≠
NOT EQUIVALENT TO	226D	≭
NOT GREATER THAN	226F	≯
NOT IDENTICAL TO	2262	≢
NOT LESS THAN	226E	≮
NOT PARALLEL TO	2226	∦
NOT SIGN	00AC	¬
NOT SIGN, REVERSED	2310	⌐
NOT SIGN, TURNED	2319	⌙
NOT TILDE	2241	≁
NULL	0000	NUL
null set	2205	∅
Number forms	**2150**	
NUMBER SIGN	0023	#
Numbers period	**2488**	

Numbers, circled	**2460**	
Numbers, circled inverse	**2776**	
Numbers, circled inverse sans-serif	**278A**	
Numbers, circled sans-serif	**2780**	
Numbers, parenthesized	**2474**	
Numerals, Hangzhou-style	**3021**	
NUMERO	2116	№

O

O ACUTE, LATIN CAPITAL LETTER	00D3	Ó
O ACUTE, LATIN SMALL LETTER	00F3	ó
O BREVE, LATIN CAPITAL LETTER	014E	Ŏ
O BREVE, LATIN SMALL LETTER	014F	ŏ
O CIRCUMFLEX, LATIN CAPITAL LETTER	00D4	Ô
O CIRCUMFLEX, LATIN SMALL LETTER	00F4	ô
O DIAERESIS, LATIN CAPITAL LETTER	00D6	Ö
O DIAERESIS, LATIN SMALL LETTER	00F6	ö
O DOUBLE ACUTE, LATIN CAPITAL LETTER	0150	Ő
O DOUBLE ACUTE, LATIN SMALL LETTER	0151	ő
O E, LATIN CAPITAL LETTER	0152	Œ
O E, LATIN LETTER, SMALL CAPITAL	0276	Œ
O E, LATIN SMALL LETTER	0153	œ
O GRAVE, LATIN CAPITAL LETTER	00D2	Ò
O GRAVE, LATIN SMALL LETTER	00F2	ò
O HACEK, LATIN CAPITAL LETTER	01D1	Ǒ
O HACEK, LATIN SMALL LETTER	01D2	ǒ
O HORN, LATIN CAPITAL LETTER	01A0	Ơ
O HORN, LATIN SMALL LETTER	01A1	ơ
O I, LATIN CAPITAL LETTER	01A2	Ƣ
O I, LATIN SMALL LETTER	01A3	ƣ
O MACRON, LATIN CAPITAL LETTER	014C	Ō
O MACRON, LATIN SMALL LETTER	014D	ō
O SLASH, LATIN CAPITAL LETTER	00D8	Ø
O SLASH, LATIN SMALL LETTER	00F8	ø
O TILDE, LATIN CAPITAL LETTER	00D5	Õ
O TILDE, LATIN SMALL LETTER	00F5	õ
O, LATIN CAPITAL LETTER, BARRED	019F	Ɵ
O, LATIN CAPITAL LETTER, OPEN	0186	Ɔ
O, LATIN SMALL LETTER, BARRED	0275	ɵ
O, LATIN SMALL LETTER, OPEN	0254	ɔ
O, SCRIPT SMALL	2134	ℴ

OCR	**2440**	
OGONEK, NON-SPACING	0328	̨
OGONEK, SPACING	02DB	˛
OHM	2126	Ω
OM, DEVANAGARI	0950	ॐ
OM, GUJARATI	0AD0	ૐ
OMEGA, LATIN SMALL LETTER, CLOSED	0277	ɷ
on us	2448	⑈
ONE DOT LEADER	2024	․
OPEN BOX	2423	␣
OPEN O, LATIN CAPITAL LETTER	0186	Ɔ
OPEN O, LATIN SMALL LETTER	0254	ɔ
OPENING ANGLE BRACKET	3008	〈
OPENING BLACK LENTICULAR BRACKET	3010	【
OPENING CORNER BRACKET	300C	「
OPENING CURLY BRACKET	007B	{
OPENING DOUBLE ANGLE BRACKET	300A	《
OPENING PARENTHESIS	0028	(
OPENING SQUARE BRACKET	005B	[
OPENING TORTOISE SHELL BRACKET	3014	〔
OPENING WHITE CORNER BRACKET	300E	『
OPENING WHITE LENTICULAR BRACKET	3016	〖
OPENING WHITE SQUARE BRACKET	301A	〚
OPENING WHITE TORTOISE SHELL BRACKET	3018	〘
Operators, mathematical	**2200**	
OPPOSITION	260D	☍
Optical character recognition	**2440**	
OPTION KEY	2325	⌥
OR, LOGICAL	2228	∨
OR, N-ARY LOGICAL	22C1	⋁
order; of inferior order to	2134	ℴ
ORDINAL INDICATOR, FEMININE	00AA	ª
ORDINAL INDICATOR, MASCULINE	00BA	º
ORIGINAL OF	22B6	⊶
ORIGINAL OF OR EQUAL TO, SQUARE	2292	⊒
ORIGINAL OF, SQUARE	2290	⊐
Oriya	**0B00**	
ORTHODOX CROSS	2626	☦
orthogonal to	22A5	⊥
OUNCE	2125	℥
OUT, APL	2301	⌁
overbar, apl	00AF	¯
overline	0305	̅

overline	203E	
OVERSCORE, NON-SPACING	0305	
OVERSCORE, NON-SPACING DOUBLE	033F	
OVERSCORE, SPACING	203E	
Overstruck diacritics	**0334**	

P

P HOOK, LATIN CAPITAL LETTER	01A4	ℙ
P HOOK, LATIN SMALL LETTER	01A5	ꝑ ꝓ
P, DOUBLE-STRUCK	2119	ℙ
P, SCRIPT	2118	℘
page down	21DF	⇟
page up	21DE	⇞
PALATALIZED HOOK BELOW, NON-SPACING	0321	
PARAGRAPH SEPARATOR	2029	Para Sepr
paragraph separator, urdu	203B	※
PARAGRAPH SIGN	00B6	¶
PARAGRAPH SIGN ORNAMENT, CURVED STEM		
	2761	❡
PARALLEL TO	2225	∥
PARALLELOGRAM, BLACK	25B0	▰
PARALLELOGRAM, WHITE	25B1	▱
PARENTHESIS, CLOSING	0029	)
PARENTHESIS, OPENING	0028	(
Parenthesized ideographs	**3220**	
Parenthesized Korean Hangul elements	**3200**	
Parenthesized Korean Hangul syllables	**320E**	
Parenthesized Latin letters	**249C**	
Parenthesized numbers	**2474**	
PARTIAL DIFFERENTIAL	2202	∂
pdf	202C	PDF
PEACE SYMBOL	262E	☮
Pencil dingbats	**270E**	
per	2118	℘
PER MILLE SIGN	2030	‰
PER TEN THOUSAND SIGN	2031	‱
PERCENT SIGN	0025	%
PERCENT SIGN, ARABIC	066A	٪
PERIOD	002E	.
PERIOD, ARABIC	06D4	۔
PERIOD, ARMENIAN	0589	:

period, georgian	0589	:
PERIOD, IDEOGRAPHIC	3002	。
perpendicular	22A5	⊥
PERSPECTIVE	2306	⩑
PESETA SIGN	20A7	₧
PHI, LATIN SMALL LETTER	0278	ɸ
Phonetic modifiers derived from Latin letters		
		02B0
Phonetic, standard		**0250**
pilcrow sign	00B6	¶
PIPE DOUBLE BAR, LATIN LETTER	01C2	ǂ
PIPE, LATIN LETTER	01C0	ǀ
PIPE, LATIN LETTER, DOUBLE	01C1	ǁ
PISCES	2653	♓
PITCHFORK	22D4	⋔
plaintiff	226C	≬
PLANCK CONSTANT	210E	ℎ
PLANCK CONSTANT OVER 2 PI	210F	ℏ
Planet dingbats	**263F**	
PLUS SIGN	002B	+
PLUS SIGN BELOW, NON-SPACING	031F	
PLUS SIGN, MODIFIER LETTER	02D6	˖
PLUS, CIRCLED	2295	⊕
PLUS, SQUARED	229E	⊞
PLUS-OR-MINUS SIGN	00B1	±
PLUTO	2647	♇
point of interest	2318	⌘
Pointers	**25BA**	
Pointing finger dingbats	**261A**	
poison	2620	☠
POP DIRECTIONAL FORMATTING	202C	PDF
POSITION INDICATOR	2316	⌖
POSTAL MARK	3012	〒
POSTAL MARK FACE	3020	〠
POSTAL MARK, CIRCLED	3036	〶
pound sign	0023	#
POUND SIGN	00A3	£
pounds	2114	℔
power set	2118	℘
PRECEDES	227A	≺
PRECEDES OR EQUAL TO	227C	≼
PRECEDES OR EQUIVALENT TO	227E	≾
PRECEDES UNDER RELATION	22B0	⊰

PRESCRIPTION TAKE	211E	℞
PRIME	2032	′
PRIME QUOTATION MARK, DOUBLE	301E	″
PRIME QUOTATION MARK, LOW DOUBLE	301F	″
PRIME QUOTATION MARK, REVERSED DOUBLE		
	301D	‴
PRIME, DOUBLE	2033	″
PRIME, MODIFIER LETTER	02B9	′
PRIME, MODIFIER LETTER, DOUBLE	02BA	″
PRIME, REVERSED	2035	‵
PRIME, REVERSED DOUBLE	2036	‶
PRIME, REVERSED TRIPLE	2037	‷
PRIME, TRIPLE	2034	‴
PRODUCT, N-ARY	220F	∏
PROJECTIVE	2305	⌅
PROLONGED SOUND MARK, KATAKANA-HIRAGANA		
	30FC	―
PROPORTION	2237	∷
PROPORTION, GEOMETRIC	223A	∺
proportional to	223C	∼
PROPORTIONAL TO	221D	∝
published	2117	℗
Punctuation, general	**2000**	
Punctuation, CJK	**3000**	

Q

Q HOOK, LATIN SMALL LETTER	02A0	ɠ
Q, DOUBLE-STRUCK	211A	ℚ
qed	220E	∎
QUAD, APL	25AF	▯
QUAD, EM	2001	Em Quad
QUAD, EN	2000	En Quad
quadrature	25A1	□
quantic	226C	≬
QUARTER, FRACTION ONE	00BC	¼
QUARTERS, FRACTION THREE	00BE	¾
QUESTION MARK	003F	?
QUESTION MARK, ARABIC	061F	؟
QUESTION MARK, ARMENIAN	055E	՞
QUESTION MARK, GREEK	03D7	;
QUESTION MARK, INVERTED	00BF	¿

QUESTIONED EQUAL TO	225F	≟
QUOTATION DASH	2015	―
QUOTATION MARK	0022	"
Quotation mark dingbats	**275B**	
QUOTATION MARK, DOUBLE COMMA	201D	"
QUOTATION MARK, DOUBLE PRIME	301E	″
QUOTATION MARK, DOUBLE REVERSED COMMA		
	201F	‟
QUOTATION MARK, DOUBLE TURNED COMMA		
	201C	"
quotation mark, left-pointing double angle	00AB	«
QUOTATION MARK, LOW DOUBLE COMMA	201E	„
QUOTATION MARK, LOW DOUBLE PRIME	301F	″
QUOTATION MARK, LOW SINGLE COMMA	201A	‚
QUOTATION MARK, SINGLE COMMA	2019	'
QUOTATION MARK, SINGLE REVERSED COMMA		
	201B	‛
QUOTATION MARK, REVERSED DOUBLE PRIME		
	301D	‴
quotation mark, right-pointing double angle		
	00BB	»
quotation mark, single left-pointing angle	2039	‹
quotation mark, single right-pointing angle	203A	›
QUOTATION MARK, SINGLE TURNED COMMA		
	2018	'
quote, apl	0022	"
QUOTE, APOSTROPHE-	0027	'

R

R ACUTE, LATIN CAPITAL LETTER	0154	Ŕ
R ACUTE, LATIN SMALL LETTER	0155	ŕ
R CEDILLA, LATIN CAPITAL LETTER	0156	Ŗ
R CEDILLA, LATIN SMALL LETTER	0157	ŗ
R HACEK, LATIN CAPITAL LETTER	0158	Ř
R HACEK, LATIN SMALL LETTER	0159	ř
R HOOK, LATIN SMALL LETTER	027D	ɽ
R HOOK, LATIN SMALL LETTER, TURNED	027B	ɻ
R HOOK, MODIFIER LETTER, SMALL, TURNED	02B5	˵
R WITH LONG LEG, LATIN SMALL LETTER	027C	ɼ
R WITH LONG LEG, LATIN SMALL LETTER, TURNED		
	027A	ɺ

Unicode Name Index

R, BLACK-LETTER	211C	ℜ
R, DOUBLE-STRUCK	211D	ℝ
R, LATIN LETTER, SMALL CAPITAL	0280	ʀ
R, LATIN LETTER, SMALL CAPITAL INVERTED	0281	ʁ
R, LATIN SMALL LETTER, FISHHOOK	027E	ɾ
R, LATIN SMALL LETTER, REVERSED FISHHOOK	027F	ɿ
R, LATIN SMALL LETTER, TURNED	0279	ɹ
R, MODIFIER LETTER, SMALL	02B3	ʳ
R, MODIFIER LETTER, SMALL CAPITAL, INVERTED	02B6	ʶ
R, MODIFIER LETTER, SMALL, TURNED	02B4	ʴ
R, SCRIPT	211B	ℛ
radical sign	221A	√
RADIOACTIVE SIGN	2622	☢
RATIO	2236	∶
rational numbers, the set of	211A	ℚ
real number symbol	210A	ℊ
real numbers, the set of	211D	ℝ
real part symbol	211C	ℜ
recipe	211E	℞
RECORD SEPARATOR	001E	RS
RECORDING COPYRIGHT, SOUND	2117	℗
RECTANGLE, BLACK	25AC	▬
RECTANGLE, BLACK VERTICAL	25AE	▮
RECTANGLE, WHITE	25AD	▭
RECTANGLE, WHITE VERTICAL	25AF	▯
REFERENCE MARK	203B	※
REGISTERED TRADE MARK SIGN	00AE	®
Religious symbol dingbats	**2625**	
REPLACEMENT CHARACTER	FFFD	�
resistance	2126	Ω
RESPONSE	211F	℟
RETROFLEX HOOK BELOW, NON-SPACING	0322	◌̢
reverse solidus	005C	\
REVERSED COMMA ABOVE, NON-SPACING	0314	◌̔
REVERSED COMMA QUOTATION MARK, SINGLE	201B	‛
REVERSED COMMA, MODIFIER LETTER	02BD	ʽ
REVERSED DOUBLE PRIME	2036	‶
REVERSED DOUBLE PRIME QUOTATION MARK	301D	〝
REVERSED E, LATIN SMALL LETTER	0258	ɘ
REVERSED EPSILON HOOK, LATIN SMALL LETTER	025D	ɝ
REVERSED EPSILON, LATIN SMALL LETTER	025C	ɜ
REVERSED ESH LOOP, LATIN LETTER	01AA	ƪ
REVERSED FISHHOOK R, LATIN SMALL LETTER	027F	ɿ
REVERSED GLOTTAL STOP, LATIN LETTER	0295	ʕ
REVERSED GLOTTAL STOP, MODIFIER LETTER	02C1	ˁ
REVERSED GLOTTAL STOP, MODIFIER LETTER, SMALL	02E4	ˤ
REVERSED GLOTTAL STOP BAR, LATIN LETTER	02A2	ʢ
REVERSED NOT SIGN	2310	⌐
REVERSED PRIME	2035	‵
REVERSED TILDE	223D	∽
REVERSED TRIPLE PRIME	2037	‷
REVERSED YOGH, LATIN CAPITAL LETTER	01B8	Ƹ
REVERSED YOGH, LATIN SMALL LETTER	01B9	ƹ
RHOTIC HOOK, MODIFIER LETTER	02DE	˞
riemann integral	211B	ℛ
RIGHT ANGLE	221F	∟
RIGHT ANGLE WITH ARC	22BE	⊾
right curly bracket	007D	}
right parenthesis	0029	)
RIGHT POINTING GUILLEMET	00BB	»
RIGHT POINTING SINGLE GUILLEMET	203A	›
right square bracket	005D	]
RIGHT TRIANGLE	22BF	⊿
right-pointing angle bracket	232A	〉
right-pointing angle quotation mark, single	203A	›
right-pointing double angle bracket	300B	》
right-pointing double angle quotation mark	00BB	»
RIGHT-TO-LEFT EMBEDDING	202B	RLE
RIGHT-TO-LEFT MARK	200F	R-L Mark
RIGHT-TO-LEFT OVERRIDE	202E	RLO
rightward tab	21E5	⇥
RING ABOVE, NON-SPACING	030A	◌̊
RING ABOVE, SPACING	02DA	˚
RING BELOW, NON-SPACING	0325	◌̥
RING EQUAL TO	2257	≗
RING IN EQUAL TO	2256	≖
RING OPERATOR	2218	∘

RING OPERATOR, CIRCLED	229A	⊙
RING OVERLAY, NON-SPACING	20D8	◌
RING OVERLAY, NON-SPACING, ANTICLOCKWISE		
	20DA	◌
RING OVERLAY, NON-SPACING, CLOCKWISE	20D9	◌
rle	202B	RLE
rlm	200F	R-L Mark
rlo	202E	RLO
Roman numerals	**2160**	
RUPEE MARK, BENGAL	09F2	৲
RUPEE SIGN	20A8	Rs
RUPEE SIGN, BENGALI	09F3	৳
Russian alphabet, basic	**0410**	

S

S ACUTE, LATIN CAPITAL LETTER	015A	Ś
S ACUTE, LATIN SMALL LETTER	015B	ś
S CEDILLA, LATIN CAPITAL LETTER	015E	Ş|Ş
S CEDILLA, LATIN SMALL LETTER	015F	ş|ş
S CIRCUMFLEX, LATIN CAPITAL LETTER	015C	Ŝ
S CIRCUMFLEX, LATIN SMALL LETTER	015D	ŝ
S HACEK, LATIN CAPITAL LETTER	0160	Š
S HACEK, LATIN SMALL LETTER	0161	š
S HOOK, LATIN SMALL LETTER	0282	ʂ
S, INVERTED LAZY	223E	∾
s, lazy	223D	∽
S, MODIFIER LETTER, SMALL	02E2	ˢ
SAGITTARIUS	2650	♐
SALTIRE	2613	✕
SATURN	2644	♄
SCHWA HOOK, LATIN SMALL LETTER	025A	ɚ
SCHWA, LATIN CAPITAL LETTER	018F	Ə
SCHWA, LATIN SMALL LETTER	0259	ə
SCISSORS, BLACK	2702	✂
SCISSORS, LOWER BLADE	2703	✃
SCISSORS, UPPER BLADE	2701	✁
SCISSORS, WHITE	2704	✄
SCORPIUS	264F	♏
SCRIPT A, LATIN SMALL LETTER	0251	ɑ
SCRIPT A, LATIN SMALL LETTER, TURNED	0252	ɒ
SCRIPT B	212C	ℬ

SCRIPT E	2130	ℰ
SCRIPT F	2131	ℱ
SCRIPT F, LATIN SMALL LETTER	0192	ƒ
SCRIPT G, LATIN SMALL LETTER	0261	ɡ
SCRIPT H	210B	ℋ
SCRIPT I	2110	ℐ
SCRIPT L	2112	ℒ
SCRIPT M	2133	ℳ
SCRIPT P	2118	℘
SCRIPT R	211B	ℛ
SCRIPT SMALL E	212F	ℯ
SCRIPT SMALL G	210A	ℊ
SCRIPT SMALL L	2113	ℓ
SCRIPT SMALL O	2134	ℴ
SCRIPT V, LATIN CAPITAL LETTER	01B2	Ʋ
SCRIPT V, LATIN SMALL LETTER	028B	ʋ
SCRUPLE	2108	℈
SEAGULL BELOW, NON-SPACING	033C	◌
seconds	2033	″
SECTION SIGN	00A7	§
SECTOR	2314	⌔
SEGMENT	2313	⌓
SEMI-VOICED SOUND MARK, KATAKANA-HIRAGANA		
	309C	゜
SEMI-VOICED SOUND MARK, NON-SPACING		
KATAKANA-HIRAGANA	309A	◌
SEMICOLON	003B	;
SEMICOLON, ARABIC	061B	؛
SEPARATOR, LINE	2028	Line Sepr
SEPARATOR, PARAGRAPH	2029	Para Sepr
Serbian Cyrillic letters, Croatian digraphs matching		
	01C4	
SERVICE MARK	2120	℠
SET MINUS	2216	∖
sextile	2736	✶
shamrock	2663	♣
SHARP	266F	♯
SHARP S, LATIN SMALL LETTER	00DF	ß
SHEQEL SIGN, NEW	20AA	₪
shift	21E7	⇧
SHIFT IN	000F	SI
SHIFT OUT	000E	SO
shilling (british)	002F	/

short	0306	̆	SMALL W, MODIFIER LETTER	02B7	ʷ
SHORT BAR OVERLAY, NON-SPACING	0335	̵	SMALL X, MODIFIER LETTER	02E3	ˣ
SHORT SLASH OVERLAY, NON-SPACING	0337	̷	SMALL Y, MODIFIER LETTER	02B8	ʸ
similar to	223C	∼	SMILE	2323	‿
SINE WAVE	223F	∿	SMILING FACE, BLACK	263B	☻
SINGLE GUILLEMET, LEFT POINTING	2039	‹	SMILING FACE, WHITE	263A	☺
SINGLE GUILLEMET, RIGHT POINTING	203A	›	SNOWFLAKE	2744	❄
single left-pointing angle quotation mark	2039	‹	**Snowflake dingbats**	**2744**	
single right-pointing angle quotation mark	203A	›	SNOWMAN	2603	☃
SKULL AND CROSSBONES	2620	☠	SOFT HYPHEN	00AD	
SLASH	002F	/	solid	2588	█
slash overlay, long	0338	̸	solidus	002F	/
slash overlay, short	0337	̷	solidus, reverse	005C	\
SLASH, CIRCLED DIVISION	2298	⊘	SOUND RECORDING COPYRIGHT	2117	℗
SLASH, DIVISION	2215	∕	SPACE	0020	␣
SLASH, ENCLOSING CIRCLE	20E0	⃠	SPACE, IDEOGRAPHIC	3000	
SMALL CAPITAL B, LATIN LETTER	0299	ʙ	SPACE, NON-BREAKING	00A0	
SMALL CAPITAL G, LATIN LETTER	0262	ɢ	**Spaces**	**2000**	
SMALL CAPITAL G HOOK, LATIN LETTER	029B	ɢ	SPACING ACUTE	00B4	´
SMALL CAPITAL H, LATIN LETTER	029C	ʜ	SPACING BREVE	02D8	˘
SMALL CAPITAL I, LATIN LETTER	026A	ɪ	SPACING CEDILLA	00B8	¸
SMALL CAPITAL INVERTED R, LATIN LETTER	0281	ʁ	SPACING CIRCUMFLEX	005E	^
SMALL CAPITAL INVERTED R, MODIFIER LETTER			SPACING DIAERESIS	00A8	¨
	02B6	ʶ	SPACING DIAERESIS TONOS, GREEK	03F4	
SMALL CAPITAL L, LATIN LETTER	029F	ʟ	SPACING DOT ABOVE	02D9	˙
SMALL CAPITAL N, LATIN LETTER	0274	ɴ	SPACING DOUBLE ACUTE	02DD	˝
SMALL CAPITAL O E, LATIN LETTER	0276	ɶ	SPACING DOUBLE UNDERSCORE	2017	‗
SMALL CAPITAL R, LATIN LETTER	0280	ʀ	SPACING GRAVE	0060	`
SMALL CAPITAL Y, LATIN LETTER	028F	ʏ	SPACING IOTA BELOW, GREEK	03F5	ͺ
SMALL CONTAINS AS MEMBER	220D	∍	SPACING MACRON	00AF	¯
SMALL ELEMENT OF	220A	∊	SPACING OGONEK	02DB	˛
SMALL GAMMA, MODIFIER LETTER	02E0	ˠ	SPACING OVERSCORE	203E	‾
SMALL H HOOK, MODIFIER LETTER	02B1	ʱ	SPACING RING ABOVE	02DA	˚
SMALL H, MODIFIER LETTER	02B0	ʰ	SPACING TILDE	02DC	˜
SMALL J, MODIFIER LETTER	02B2	ʲ	SPACING TONOS, GREEK	03F3	΄
SMALL L, MODIFIER LETTER	02E1	ˡ	SPACING UNDERSCORE	005F	_
SMALL R, MODIFIER LETTER	02B3	ʳ	SPADE SUIT, BLACK	2660	♠
SMALL REVERSED GLOTTAL STOP, MODIFIER LETTER			SPHERICAL ANGLE	2222	∢
	02E4	ˤ	SQUARE BELOW, NON-SPACING	033B	̻
SMALL S, MODIFIER LETTER	02E2	ˢ	SQUARE BRACKET, CLOSING	005D	]
SMALL TURNED R HOOK, MODIFIER LETTER	02B5	˞	SQUARE BRACKET, CLOSING WHITE	301B	〛
SMALL TURNED R, MODIFIER LETTER	02B4	ɹ	SQUARE BRACKET, OPENING	005B	[
Small variants	**FE50**		SQUARE BRACKET, OPENING WHITE	301A	〚

SQUARE CAP	2293	⊓
SQUARE CUP	2294	⊔
SQUARE IMAGE OF	228F	⊏
SQUARE IMAGE OF OR EQUAL TO	2291	⊑
SQUARE LOZENGE	2311	⌑
SQUARE ORIGINAL OF	2290	⊐
SQUARE ORIGINAL OF OR EQUAL TO	2292	⊒
SQUARE ROOT	221A	√
SQUARE, BLACK	25A0	■
SQUARE, ENCLOSING	20DE	▢
SQUARE, WHITE	25A1	□
squared	00B2	²
Squared abbreviations, CJK	**3380**	
SQUARED DOT OPERATOR	22A1	⊡
SQUARED MINUS	229F	⊟
SQUARED PLUS	229E	⊞
Squared words, CJK	**3300**	
Squares	**25A0**	
SQUAT REVERSED ESH, LATIN SMALL LETTER	0285	ʅ
st. andrew's cross	2613	✗
STAR AND CRESCENT	262A	☪
Star dingbats	**2726**	
STAR OF DAVID	2721	✡
STAR OPERATOR	22C6	⋆
STAR, BLACK	2605	★
STAR, WHITE	2606	☆
START OF HEADING	0001	SOH
START OF TEXT	0002	STX
stile, apl	2223	∣
stress mark	0301	◌́
STRETCHED C, LATIN LETTER	0297	ʗ
STRICTLY EQUIVALENT TO	2263	≣
Subscripts	**2080**	
SUBSET OF	2282	⊂
SUBSET OF OR EQUAL TO	2286	⊆
SUBSET, DOUBLE	22D0	⋐
SUBSTITUTE	001A	SUB
SUCCEEDS	227B	≻
SUCCEEDS OR EQUAL TO	227D	≽
SUCCEEDS OR EQUIVALENT TO	227F	≿
SUCCEEDS UNDER RELATION	22B1	⋟
such that	220B	∋
such that	2223	∣

Suits of cards	**2660**	
SUMMATION, N-ARY	2211	Σ
SUN	2609	☉
SUN WITH RAYS, BLACK	2600	☀
SUN WITH RAYS, WHITE	263C	☼
SUPERSCRIPT DIGIT ZERO	2070	⁰
SUPERSCRIPT DIGIT ONE	00B9	¹
SUPERSCRIPT DIGIT TWO	00B2	²
SUPERSCRIPT DIGIT THREE	00B3	³
SUPERSCRIPT DIGIT FOUR	2074	⁴
Superscripts	**2070**	
SUPERSET OF	2283	⊃
SUPERSET OF OR EQUAL TO	2287	⊇
SUPERSET, DOUBLE	22D1	⋑
SURFACE INTEGRAL	222F	∯
symmetric difference	2238	∸
symmetric difference	2296	⊖
SYNCHRONOUS IDLE	0016	SYN

T

T BAR, LATIN CAPITAL LETTER	0166	Ŧ
T BAR, LATIN SMALL LETTER	0167	ŧ
T C CURL, LATIN SMALL LETTER	02A8	ʨ
T CEDILLA, LATIN CAPITAL LETTER	0162	Ţ
T CEDILLA, LATIN SMALL LETTER	0163	ţ
T E L SYMBOL	2121	TEL
T ESH, LATIN SMALL LETTER	02A7	ʧ
T HACEK, LATIN CAPITAL LETTER	0164	Ť
T HACEK, LATIN SMALL LETTER	0165	ť
T HOOK, LATIN CAPITAL LETTER	01AC	Ƭ
T HOOK, LATIN SMALL LETTER	01AD	ƭ
T PALATAL HOOK, LATIN SMALL LETTER	01AB	ƫ
T RETROFLEX HOOK, LATIN CAPITAL LETTER	01AE	Ʈ
T RETROFLEX HOOK, LATIN SMALL LETTER	0288	ʈ
T S, LATIN SMALL LETTER	02A6	ʦ
T, LATIN SMALL LETTER, TURNED	0287	ʇ
tab with shift tab	21B9	⇹
tab, leftward	21E4	⇤
tab, rightward	21E5	⇥
TABULATION, HORIZONTAL	0009	HT
TACK BELOW, NON-SPACING LEFT	0318	◌̘

TACK BELOW, NON-SPACING RIGHT	0319		**Tone letters**	**02E5**	
TACK, DOWN	22A4	⊤	TONE MARK, HANGUL DOUBLE DOT	302F	
TACK, LEFT	22A3	⊣	TONE MARK, HANGUL SINGLE DOT	302E	
TACK, RIGHT	22A2	⊢	TONE MARK, IDEOGRAPHIC DEPARTING	302C	
TACK, UP	22A5	⊥	TONE MARK, IDEOGRAPHIC ENTERING	302D	
tainome (japanese, a kind of bullet)	25C9	◉	TONE MARK, IDEOGRAPHIC LEVEL	302A	
Tamil	**0B80**		TONE MARK, IDEOGRAPHIC RISING	302B	
TAPE DRIVE	2707		TONE MARK, NON-SPACING ACUTE	0341	
TAURUS	2649	♉	TONE MARK, NON-SPACING GRAVE	0340	
Technical, miscellaneous	**2300**		TONE SIX, LATIN CAPITAL LETTER	0184	Ƅ
TELEPHONE LOCATION SIGN	2706	✆	TONE SIX, LATIN SMALL LETTER	0185	ƅ
TELEPHONE RECORDER	2315	⌕	TONE TWO, LATIN CAPITAL LETTER	01A7	Ƨ
TELEPHONE, BLACK	260E	☎	TONE TWO, LATIN SMALL LETTER	01A8	ƨ
TELEPHONE, WHITE	260F	☏	TORTOISE SHELL BRACKET, CLOSING	3015	〕
Telugu	**0C00**		TORTOISE SHELL BRACKET, CLOSING WHITE	3019	〗
tensor product	2297	⊗	TORTOISE SHELL BRACKET, OPENING	3014	〔
Thai	**0E00**		TORTOISE SHELL BRACKET, OPENING WHITE	3018	〖
THAI BAHT SIGN	0E3F	฿	TRADE MARK SIGN, REGISTERED	00AE	®
THERE DOES NOT EXIST	2204	∄	TRADEMARK	2122	™
THERE EXISTS	2203	∃	**Transfinite cardinals**	**2135**	
THEREFORE	2234	∴	transit	2446	
THIRD, FRACTION ONE	2153	⅓	TRIANGLE, BLACK UP POINTING	25B2	▲
THORN, LATIN CAPITAL LETTER	00DE	Þ	TRIANGLE, WHITE UP POINTING	25B3	△
THORN, LATIN SMALL LETTER	00FE	þ	**Triangles**	**25B2**	
THUNDER, TRIGRAM FOR	2633	☳	TRIANGULAR BULLET	2023	‣
THUNDERSTORM	2608	☈	TRIANGULAR COLON, MODIFIER LETTER	02D0	ː
Tibetan	**1000**		**Trigrams, Yi Jing**	**2630**	
TIE, CHARACTER	2040	⁀	trine	25B3	△
TILDE	007E	~	TRIPLE INTEGRAL	222D	∭
TILDE BELOW, NON-SPACING	0330		TRIPLE PRIME	2034	‴
TILDE OPERATOR	223C	∼	TRIPLE PRIME, REVERSED	2037	‷
TILDE OVERLAY, NON-SPACING	0334		TRIPLE TILDE	224B	≋
TILDE, NON-SPACING	0303		turbofan	274B	✻
TILDE, NON-SPACING, VERTICAL	033E		TURNED A, LATIN SMALL LETTER	0250	ɐ
TILDE, NOT	2241	≁	TURNED COMMA ABOVE, NON-SPACING	0312	
TILDE, REVERSED	223D	∽	TURNED COMMA, MODIFIER LETTER	02BB	ʻ
TILDE, SPACING	02DC	˜	TURNED DELTA, LATIN SMALL LETTER	018D	ƍ
TILDE, TRIPLE	224B	≋	TURNED E, LATIN CAPITAL LETTER	018E	Ǝ
TIMES, CIRCLED	2297	⊗	TURNED E, LATIN SMALL LETTER	01DD	ə
TIMES, DIVISION	22C7	⋇	TURNED F	2132	Ⅎ
TIS 620-2529	**0E00**		TURNED GREEK SMALL LETTER IOTA	2129	℩
TONE FIVE, LATIN CAPITAL LETTER	01BC	Ƽ	TURNED H, LATIN SMALL LETTER	0265	ɥ
TONE FIVE, LATIN SMALL LETTER	01BD	ƽ	TURNED K, LATIN SMALL LETTER	029E	ʞ

TURNED M WITH LONG LEG, LATIN SMALL LETTER		
	0270	barɰ
TURNED M, LATIN CAPITAL LETTER	019C	W
TURNED M, LATIN SMALL LETTER	026F	ɯ
TURNED NOT SIGN	2319	⌐
turned question mark	00BF	¿
TURNED R HOOK, LATIN SMALL LETTER	027B	ɻ
TURNED R HOOK, MODIFIER LETTER, SMALL	02B5	˵
TURNED R WITH LONG LEG, LATIN SMALL LETTER		
	027A	ɺ
TURNED R, LATIN SMALL LETTER	0279	ɹ
TURNED R, MODIFIER LETTER, SMALL	02B4	˴
TURNED SCRIPT A, LATIN SMALL LETTER	0252	ɒ
TURNED T, LATIN SMALL LETTER	0287	ʇ
TURNED V, LATIN SMALL LETTER	028C	ʌ
TURNED W, LATIN SMALL LETTER	028D	ʍ
TURNED Y, LATIN SMALL LETTER	028E	ʎ
Turnstiles	**22A2**	
TWO BAR, LATIN LETTER	01BB	ƻ
TWO DOT LEADER	2025	‥

U

U ACUTE, LATIN CAPITAL LETTER	00DA	Ú
U ACUTE, LATIN SMALL LETTER	00FA	ú
U BREVE, LATIN CAPITAL LETTER	016C	Ŭ
U BREVE, LATIN SMALL LETTER	016D	ŭ
U CIRCUMFLEX, LATIN CAPITAL LETTER	00DB	Û
U CIRCUMFLEX, LATIN SMALL LETTER	00FB	û
U DIAERESIS ACUTE, LATIN CAPITAL LETTER	01D7	Ǘ
U DIAERESIS ACUTE, LATIN SMALL LETTER	01D8	ǘ
U DIAERESIS GRAVE, LATIN CAPITAL LETTER	01DB	Ǜ
U DIAERESIS GRAVE, LATIN SMALL LETTER	01DC	ǜ
U DIAERESIS HACEK, LATIN CAPITAL LETTER	01D9	Ǔ
U DIAERESIS HACEK, LATIN SMALL LETTER	01DA	ǚ
U DIAERESIS MACRON, LATIN CAPITAL LETTER		
	01D5	Ǖ
U DIAERESIS MACRON, LATIN SMALL LETTER	01D6	ǖ
U DIAERESIS, LATIN CAPITAL LETTER	00DC	Ü
U DIAERESIS, LATIN SMALL LETTER	00FC	ü
U DOUBLE ACUTE, LATIN CAPITAL LETTER	0170	Ű
U DOUBLE ACUTE, LATIN SMALL LETTER	0171	ű

U GRAVE, LATIN CAPITAL LETTER	00D9	Ù
U GRAVE, LATIN SMALL LETTER	00F9	ù
U HACEK, LATIN CAPITAL LETTER	01D3	Ǔ
U HACEK, LATIN SMALL LETTER	01D4	ǔ
U HORN, LATIN CAPITAL LETTER	01AF	Ư
U HORN, LATIN SMALL LETTER	01B0	ư
U MACRON, LATIN CAPITAL LETTER	016A	Ū
U MACRON, LATIN SMALL LETTER	016B	ū
U OGONEK, LATIN CAPITAL LETTER	0172	Ų
U OGONEK, LATIN SMALL LETTER	0173	ų
U RING, LATIN CAPITAL LETTER	016E	Ů
U RING, LATIN SMALL LETTER	016F	ů
U TILDE, LATIN CAPITAL LETTER	0168	Ũ
U TILDE, LATIN SMALL LETTER	0169	ũ
UMBRELLA	2602	☂
umlaut	0308	̈
underline	0332	̲
underline, double	0333	̳
UNDERSCORE, NON-SPACING	0332	̲
UNDERSCORE, NON-SPACING DOUBLE	0333	̳
UNDERSCORE, SPACING	005F	_
UNDERSCORE, SPACING DOUBLE	2017	‗
unification, maru-iti symbol of	3280	㊀
UNION	222A	∪
UNION, DOUBLE	22D3	⋓
UNION, MULTISET	228E	⊎
UNION, N-ARY	22C3	⋃
UNIT SEPARATOR	001F	US
UP TACK	22A5	⊥
UP TACK BELOW, NON-SPACING	031D	̝
UP TACK, MODIFIER LETTER	02D4	˔
UPSILON, LATIN CAPITAL LETTER	01B1	Ʊ
UPSILON, LATIN SMALL LETTER	028A	ʊ
upstile, apl	2308	⌈
URANUS	2645	♅
urdu paragraph separator	203B	※

V

v above	030C	̌
v with hook, latin capital letter	01B2	Ʋ
V, LATIN CAPITAL LETTER, SCRIPT	01B2	Ʋ

V, LATIN SMALL LETTER, SCRIPT	028B	ʊ
V, LATIN SMALL LETTER, TURNED	028C	ʌ
valentine	2665	♥
varies with (proportional to)	223C	~
vector pointing into page	2295	⊕
vector pointing into page	2297	⊗
vector pointing out of page	2299	⊙
vee	2228	∨
venus	2640	♀
VERSICLE	2123	℣
VERTICAL BAR	007C	|
Vertical bar dingbats	**2758**	
VERTICAL BAR OVERLAY, NON-SPACING, LONG		
	20D2	⃒
VERTICAL BAR OVERLAY, NON-SPACING, SHORT		
	20D3	⃓
VERTICAL BAR, BROKEN	00A6	¦
VERTICAL BAR, DOUBLE	2016	‖
VERTICAL ELLIPSIS	22EE	⋮
VERTICAL KANA REPEAT MARK	3031	〱
VERTICAL KANA REPEAT WITH VOICED		
SOUND MARK	3032	〲
VERTICAL KANA REPEAT MARK UPPER HALF	3033	〳
VERTICAL KANA REPEAT WITH VOICED SOUND MARK		
UPPER HALF	3034	〴
VERTICAL KANA REPEAT MARK LOWER HALF		
	3035	〵
vertical line	007C	|
VERTICAL LINE ABOVE, NON-SPACING	030D	̍
VERTICAL LINE BELOW, NON-SPACING	0329	̩
VERTICAL LINE, MODIFIER LETTER	02C8	ˈ
VERTICAL LINE, MODIFIER LETTER, LOW	02CC	ˌ
VERTICAL TABULATION	000B	VT
VERTICAL TILDE, NON-SPACING	033E	̾
VERY MUCH GREATER THAN	22D9	⋙
VERY MUCH LESS THAN	22D8	⋘
VICTORY HAND	270C	✌
Vietnamese tone marks	**0340**	
VIEWDATA SQUARE	2317	⌗
VIRGO	264D	♍
virgule	002F	/
VOICED ITERATION MARK, HIRAGANA	309E	ゞ
VOICED ITERATION MARK, KATAKANA	30FE	ヾ

VOICED SOUND MARK, KATAKANA-HIRAGANA		
	309B	゛
VOICED SOUND MARK, NON-SPACING KATAKANA-HIRAGANA	3099	゙
VOLUME INTEGRAL	2230	∰

W

W CIRCUMFLEX, LATIN CAPITAL LETTER	0174	Ŵ
W CIRCUMFLEX, LATIN SMALL LETTER	0175	ŵ
W, LATIN SMALL LETTER, TURNED	028D	ʍ
W, MODIFIER LETTER, SMALL	02B7	ʷ
Warning dingbats	**2620**	
WATCH	231A	⌚
WATER, TRIGRAM FOR	2635	☵
WAVE DASH	301C	〜
WAVE, SINE	223F	∿
WAVY DASH	3030	〰
WAVY LINE	2307	⌇
Weather dingbats	**2600**	
wedge	028C	ʌ
wedge	2227	∧
weierstrass elliptic function	2118	℘
WHEEL OF DHARMA	2638	☸
Width variants	**FF00**	
WIND, TRIGRAM FOR	2634	☴
WON SIGN	20A9	₩
WREATH PRODUCT	2240	≀
WRITING HAND	270D	✍
WYNN, LATIN LETTER	01BF	ƿ

X

X ABOVE, NON-SPACING	033D	̽
X mark dingbats	**2715**	
X mark dingbats, ballot	**2612**	
X, MODIFIER LETTER, SMALL	02E3	ˣ
XOR	22BB	⊻

Y

Y ACUTE, LATIN CAPITAL LETTER	00DD	Ý
Y ACUTE, LATIN SMALL LETTER	00FD	ý
Y CIRCUMFLEX, LATIN CAPITAL LETTER	0176	Ŷ
Y CIRCUMFLEX, LATIN SMALL LETTER	0177	ŷ
Y DIAERESIS, LATIN CAPITAL LETTER	0178	Ÿ
Y DIAERESIS, LATIN SMALL LETTER	00FF	ÿ
Y HOOK, LATIN CAPITAL LETTER	01B3	Ƴ
Y HOOK, LATIN SMALL LETTER	01B4	ƴ
Y R, LATIN LETTER	01A6	Ɍ
Y, LATIN LETTER, SMALL CAPITAL	028F	ʏ
Y, LATIN SMALL LETTER, TURNED	028E	ʎ
Y, MODIFIER LETTER, SMALL	02B8	ʸ
YEN SIGN	00A5	¥|¥
Yi Jing trigrams	**2630**	
Yiddish digraphs	**05F0**	
YIN YANG	262F	☯
YOGH CURL, LATIN SMALL LETTER	0293	ʓ
YOGH WITH TAIL, LATIN SMALL LETTER	01BA	ƺ
YOGH, LATIN CAPITAL LETTER	01B7	Ʒ|Ʒ
YOGH, LATIN CAPITAL LETTER, REVERSED	01B8	Ƹ
YOGH, LATIN SMALL LETTER	0292	ʒ
YOGH, LATIN SMALL LETTER, REVERSED	01B9	ƹ
yuan sign	00A5	¥|¥

ZERO WIDTH JOINER	200D	Joiner
ZERO WIDTH NON-JOINER	200C	Non-Joiner
ZERO WIDTH SPACE	200B	ZW SP
ZERO, IDEOGRAPHIC NUMBER	3007	○
Zodiac dingbats	**2648**	
zwj ("zawj")	200D	Joiner
zwnj ("zwinj")	200C	Non-Joiner

Z

Z ACUTE, LATIN CAPITAL LETTER	0179	Ź
Z ACUTE, LATIN SMALL LETTER	017A	ź
Z BAR, LATIN CAPITAL LETTER	01B5	Ƶ
Z BAR, LATIN SMALL LETTER	01B6	ƶ
Z CURL, LATIN SMALL LETTER	0291	ʑ
Z DOT, LATIN CAPITAL LETTER	017B	Ż
Z DOT, LATIN SMALL LETTER	017C	ż
Z HACEK, LATIN CAPITAL LETTER	017D	Ž
Z HACEK, LATIN SMALL LETTER	017E	ž
Z RETROFLEX HOOK, LATIN SMALL LETTER	0290	ʐ
Z, BLACK-LETTER	2128	ℨ
Z, DOUBLE-STRUCK	2124	ℤ
Zapf dingbats	**2700**	
ZERO, CIRCLED DIGIT	24EA	⓪

General Index

The general index is a guide to the written text only. To find the range for a particular script, see the table on the end-papers. To find the code for a specific character, see the preceding Character Names Index. For the definition of specific terms, see the Glossary.

7-bit transmission 625

Adding characters 631–33

Alternate spellings 17–18, 625

ANSI C wide character type 624

Arabic glyphs 121–22

Architecture 7 ff.

Backing store 16–17

Bidirectionality 16–17, 77–78, 611–21

Braille 3

Burmese 636

Byte Order Mark (BOM) 23, 123, 623

Canonical forms and canonical mappings 411 ff., 625

Case pairs and case mapping 33, 34, 37, 440 ff.

Character order 16–21, 53–57

Character properties 15, 389–409

Character vs. Glyph 12–13

Characters, Unknown or Missing 629–30

Chinese/Japanese/Korean ideographs 110 ff.

   Ordering 116

   Selection 114–16

Chinese/Japanese/Korean phonetics and symbols 98 ff.

Compatibility blocks/zone 120–22

   Mapping to canonical forms 420 ff.

Codespace allocation 3, 13–14, 27–28, 74, 98, 110, 118, 120

Composite characters see Precomposed characters

Compression 624–25

Conformance 2, 21–25, 620–21

Consortium 5

Control characters 15–16, 29, 32, 88, 624

Conventions xv–xvii

Conversion to other codes 12, 465 ff.

Coptic 43

Coverage 2–3

Czech 33

Dashes 76, 401

Decimal digits 51, 391–94, 630

Decompositions 412 ff.

Diacritics 30, 32, 39, 81, 635; see also Non-spacing marks

Digits 51–52, 57, 395–96, 630

Digraphs

   Mapping to canonical forms 419

Directionality 9, 16–17, 407–9, 611–21, 629

East Asian see Chinese/Japanese/Korean

Ethiopian 635–36

Escape characters 624

Fancy text 9–10

Future development 4–5, 631–36

General scripts 28

Glagolitic 45

Glyphs 12–13, 121, 630

Indic scripts 53–59

Interchange (Conformance requirement) 21–23

International standards

   Mapping from Unicode characters 466 ff.

Interpretation (Conformance requirement) 23

Joiner 50, 77

Kanbun marks 104

Khmer 636

Ligatures

   Mapping to canonical forms 419

Line breaking 402

Line separator 16, 78, 624

Logical order 16–17

Mapping tables 411 ff.

Missing characters 629–30

Modification (Conformance requirement) 23

Mongolian 636

National standards

   Mapping from Unicode characters 560 ff.

New characters 631–33

Non-conformance 24–25

Non-Joiner 50, 55, 77

Non-spacing marks 18–21, 37, 40, 42, 47, 51, 56–57, 403–6, 627–28

Notations xv–xvii

Numbers 51, 390–99, 630

Paragraph separator 16, 78, 624

Pinyin 34

Plain text 9–10

Polytonic Greek 20, 42

   Mapping to canonical forms 436 ff.

Precomposed characters

   Mapping to canonical forms 412 ff.

Quick Guide to Unicode Character Blocks

Character Block Name	Unicode Range	Description	Chart
ASCII	U+0000 → U+007F	29	172
Latin1	U+0080 → U+00FF	32	176
European Latin	U+0100 → U+017F	33	180
Extended Latin	U+0180 → U+01FF	34	184
Standard Phonetic	U+0250 → U+02AF	36	188
Modifier Letters	U+02B0 → U+02FF	38	192
Generic Diacritical Marks	U+0300 → U+036F	40	196
Greek	U+0370 → U+03FF	42	200
Cyrillic	U+0400 → U+ 04FF	44	204
Armenian	U+0530 → U+058F	46	210
Hebrew	U+0590 → U+05FF	47	214
Arabic	U+0600 → U+ 06FF	49	218
Devanagari	U+0900 → U+097F	53	226
Bengali	U+0980 → U+09FF	60	230
Gurmukhi	U+0A00 → U+0A7F	61	234
Gujarati	U+0A80 → U+0AFF	62	238
Oriya	U+0B00 → U+0B7F	63	242
Tamil	U+0B80 → U+0BFF	64	246
Telugu	U+0C00 → U+0C7F	65	250
Kannada	U+0C80 → U+0CFF	66	254
Malayalam	U+0D00 → U+0D7F	67	258
Thai	U+0E00 → U+0E7F	68	262
Lao	U+0E80 → U+0EFF	70	266
Tibetan	U+1000 → U+105F	71	270
Georgian	U+10A0 → U+10FF	73	274
General Punctuation	U+2000 → U+206F	75	278
Superscripts and Subscripts	U+2070 → U+209F	79	282
Currency Symbols	U+20A0 → U+20CF	80	284
Diacritical Marks for Symbols	U+20D0 → U+20FF	81	286
Letterlike Symbols	U+2100 → U+214F	82	288
Number Forms	U+2150 → U+218F	83	292
Arrows	U+2190 → U+21FF	84	294
Mathematical Operators	U+2200 → U+22FF	85	298

Character Block Name	Unicode Range	Description	Chart
Miscellaneous Technical	U+2300 → U+23FF	87	304
Pictures for Control Codes	U+2400 → U+243F	88	306
Optical Character Recognition	U+2440 → U+245F	89	308
Enclosed Alphanumerics	U+2460 → U+24FF	90	310
Form and Chart Components	U+2500 → U+257F	91	314
Blocks	U+2580 → U+259F	92	318
Geometric Shapes	U+25A0 → U+25FF	93	320
Miscellaneous Dingbats	U+2600 → U+26FF	94	324
Zapf Dingbats	U+2700 → U+27BF	96	328
CJK Symbols and Punctuation	U+3000 → U+303F	99	332
Hiragana	U+3040 → U+309F	100	336
Katakana	U+30A0 → U+30FF	101	340
Bopomofo	U+3100 → U+312F	102	344
Hangul Elements	U+3130 → U+318F	103	346
CJK Miscellaneous	U+3190 → U+31FF	104	350
Enclosed CJK Letters and Ideographs	U+3200 → U+32FF	105	352
CJK Squared Words	U+3300 → U+337F	106	358
CJK Squared Abbreviations	U+3380 → U+33FF	107	362
Korean Hangul Syllables	U+3400 → U+3D2F	108	157
Chinese/Japanese/Korean Ideographs	U+4000 → U+8BFF	111	Vol. 2
Private Use Area	U+E800 → U+FDFF	119	—
Compatibility Zone	U+FE00 → U+FFEF	121	
CNS 11643 Compatibility	U+FE30 → U+FE4F	121	372
Small Variants	U+FE50 → U+FE6F	121	374
Basic Glyphs for Arabic Language	U+FE70 → U+FEFE	121	376
Halfwidth and Fullwidth Variants	U+FF00 → U+FFEF	121	380
Special	U+FFF0 → U+FFFD	123	386